Contemporary Literary Criticism

Contemporary Literary Criticism

Excerpts from Criticism of
the Works of Today's Novelists,
Poets, Playwrights, Short Story
Writers, Filmmakers, Screenwriters,
and Other Creative Writers

Sharon R. Gunton
Editor

Gerard J. Senick
Project Editor

Gale Research Company
Book Tower
Detroit, Michigan 48226

STAFF

Sharon R. Gunton, *Senior Editor*

Gerard J. Senick, *Project Editor*

Daniel G. Marowski, *Senior Assistant Editor*

Bridget Broderick, Jane C. Thacker, *Assistant Editors*

Phyllis Carmel Mendelson, *Contributing Editor*

Carolyn Bancroft, *Production Supervisor*
Lizbeth A. Purdy, *Production Coordinator*

Linda M. Pugliese, *Manuscript Coordinator*
Donna DiNello, Marie Lazzari, *Manuscript Assistants*

Robert J. Elster, *Research Coordinator*
Carol Angela Thomas, *Research Assistant*

Cherie D. Abbey, Earlene Alber, Frank J. Borovsky, Laura L. Britton, Ann Kathleen Crowley,
Lee Ferency, Jeanne A. Gough, Denise B. Grove, Serita Lanette Lockard, Brenda Marshall,
Marie M. Mazur, Francine M. Melotti-Bacon, Denise Michlewicz, Gloria A. Williams,
Robyn V. Young, *Editorial Assistants*

L. Elizabeth Hardin, *Permissions Supervisor*
Filomena Sgambati, *Assistant Permissions Coordinator*
Anna Maria DiNello, Janice M. Mach, Mary P. McGrane, Patricia A. Seefelt, *Permissions Assistants*

Copyright© 1982 by Gale Research Company

Library of Congress Catalog Card Number 76-38938
ISBN 0-8103-0117-2
ISSN 0091-3421

10 9 8 7 6

Contents

Preface 7

Authors Forthcoming in CLC 9

Appendix 481

Authors in this volume:

Cecil Bødker 1927- 11

Franklyn M. Branley 1915- 15

H. F. Brinsmead 1922- 25

Jackson Browne 1950- 34

Lenny Bruce 1925-1966 43

James Chambers
see Jimmy Cliff

Graham Chapman 1941(?)-
see Monty Python

John Cleese 1939-
see Monty Python

Jimmy Cliff 1948- 59

Elvis Costello 1955- 66

Gretchen Cryer 1936(?)- 77

Paula Danziger 1944- 83

Ray Davies 1944- 87

Vine Deloria, Jr. 1933- 108

Janis Fink
see Janis Ian

Louis Firbank
see Lou Reed

James D. Forman 1932- 115

Larry Gelbart 1923- 124

Terry Gilliam 1941(?)-
see Monty Python

Roderick L. Haig-Brown 1908-1976 133

Isabelle Holland 1920- 147

Mollie Hunter 1922- 155

Margaret O. Hyde 1917- 171

Janis Ian 1951- 182

Eric Idle
see Monty Python

Albert Innaurato 1948- 190

Waylon Jennings 1937- 200

Terry Jones 1942(?)-
see Monty Python

Robert Lipsyte 1938- 207

Maureen McIlwraith
see Mollie Hunter

Declan Patrick McManus
see Elvis Costello

Steven Millhauser 1943- 215

Monty Python 222

Van Morrison 1945- 231

Agnes Eckhardt Nixon 1927- 241

Flannery O'Connor 1925-1964 254

Michael Palin 1943-
see Monty Python

Philippa Pearce 1920- 280

Richard Peck 1934- 295

Lou Reed 1944- 302

Erich Paul Remark
see Erich Maria Remarque

Erich Maria Remarque 1898-1970 324

Tim Rice 1944-
see Andrew Lloyd Webber and Tim Rice

Trina Robbins 1938- 338

Smokey Robinson 1940- 342

William Robinson
   see Smokey Robinson

Leonard Schneider
   see Lenny Bruce

Joe Shuster   1914-
   see Jerome Siegel and Joe Shuster

Jerome Siegel   1914-
   see Jerome Siegel and Joe Shuster

Jerome Siegel and Joe Shuster 352

John Steinbeck   1902-1968 365

Noel Streatfeild   1897- 394

Mildred D. Taylor 418

Andrew Lloyd Webber   1948-
   see Andrew Lloyd Webber and Tim Rice

Andrew Lloyd Webber and Tim Rice........422

Richard Wright   1908-1960 434

Roger Zelazny   1937- 463

Preface

The last thirty years have brought about a type of literature which is directed specifically to a young adult audience. These works have recognized the uniqueness of young adult readers while preparing them for the subjects, styles, and emotional levels of adult literature. Much of this writing has also had a definite appeal for adult readers and a discernible influence on their literature. Because of the importance of this subject matter and its audience, *Contemporary Literary Criticism* devotes periodic volumes to writers whose work is directed to or appreciated by young adults. Until now, a collection of opinion has not existed which has centered on writers for the junior high to junior college age group. These special volumes of *CLC,* therefore, are meant to acknowledge this genre and its criticism as an important and serious part of recent literature.

In these special volumes we have broadened the definition of young adult literature to include not only writers who fit into the classic young adult mode, such as James D. Forman and Mollie Hunter, but also authors such as Flannery O'Connor and John Steinbeck, whose works are received enthusiastically by the young even though they were not originally the intended audience. In the latter category are writers whose works have such relevance for the YA sensibility that they have achieved mass appeal. A distinctive feature of these special volumes is the inclusion of criticism on writers whose work is not restricted to book form. Many songwriters, for instance, are recognized by young people as today's poets. Their lyrics have been critically analyzed and accepted as serious literary creations. Since young people look to film, television, and the theater to expand their knowledge and reflect their world view, the young adult volumes feature criticism on screenwriters, scriptwriters, and playwrights who appeal to the young, including Larry Gelbart, Gretchen Cryer, and Albert Innaurato in the present volume. Humorists and cartoonists such as Monty Python and Trina Robbins, whom young people look to for both social comment and entertainment, are also included.

Each periodic special volume on young adult literature is designed to complement other volumes of *CLC* and follows the same format with some slight variations. The list of authors treated is international in scope and, as in the other *CLC* volumes, includes creative writers who are living now or have died after January 1, 1960. Since this volume of *CLC* is intended to provide a definitive overview of the careers of the authors included, the editors have included approximately 40 writers (compared to 100 authors in the standard *CLC)* in order to devote more attention to each writer.

Criticism has been selected with the levels and interests of the young adult in mind. Many young adult authors have also written for younger children. Criticism on these works has been included when it is felt the works may be of interest to the young adult.

New Features

In the publishing history of *CLC,* numerous changes have been made in the coverage and format of the series, often at the suggestion of users. The editors are always glad to consider further suggestions. The following are some recent changes.

Beginning with Volume 10, *CLC* contains an appendix which lists the sources from which material has been printed in that volume. It does not, however, list books or periodicals merely consulted during the preparation of the volume. Also in Volume 10, for the first time, the critic's name is listed at the beginning of each selection.

Beginning with Volume 19, unsigned criticism is preceded by the title of the journal or book in which it appeared. Also beginning with Volume 19, in the text of each author entry, titles by that author are printed in boldface type. This allows the reader to ascertain without difficulty the works which are being discussed. In addition, the table of contents includes birth and, if applicable, death dates for each author.

Volume 21 includes a portrait or photograph of each author when available, a feature which will be continued in future volumes.

References and Notes

Page numbers appear after each fragment (unless the entire essay was contained on one page), and all credit lines include the complete essay title, volume, and issue number of all journal entries, inclusive pagination for all essays, and total pagination for all books. An asterisk following a credit line indicates that the essay or book contains information on more than one author.

Parenthetical material following most of the identification paragraphs includes references to biographical and critical reference books published by the Gale Research Company. These include past volumes of *CLC, Contemporary Authors, Something About the Author, Children's Literature Review,* and *Yesterday's Authors of Books for Children.*

Acknowledgments

The editors wish to thank the copyright holders of the excerpts included in this volume, the permission managers of many book and magazine publishing companies for assisting us in locating copyright holders, Fred S. Stein for his assistance with copyright research, and Louise Kertesz for her editorial assistance. We are also grateful to the staffs of the Wayne State University Library, the libraries of the University of Michigan, and the Detroit Public Library, especially Jean Church, Terence Gahman, Nancy Grylls, Agatha Pfeiffer Kalkanis, and Jeanne Salathiel.

Suggestions Are Welcome

If readers wish to suggest authors they are particularly anxious to have covered in upcoming volumes, or if they have other suggestions, they are cordially invited to write the editors.

Authors Forthcoming in *CLC*

With the publication of *Contemporary Literary Criticism,* Volume 12, the series expanded its scope to encompass songwriters, filmmakers, cartoonists, screenwriters, producers, and other creative writers whose work is often evaluated from a literary perspective. These writers take their place with the novelists, poets, dramatists, and short story writers who will continue to be the primary focus of *CLC.* Volumes 22 and 23 will include criticism on a number of authors not previously listed and will also feature criticism of newer works of authors included in earlier volumes.

To Be Included in Volume 22

Kōbō Abé (Japanese novelist, playwright, and short story writer)--His recently translated novel, *Secret Rendezvous,* has again focused critical attention on this Western-influenced oriental writer.

Vasily Aksenov (Russian author)--A recent immigrant to the United States, he writes about the contemporary scene in the Soviet Union.

Ben Belitt (American poet and translator)--His new volume, *The Double Witness,* is a selection from the poetry written during his forty-year career.

Anthony Burgess (English author)--His new novel, *Earthly Powers,* adds to his international reputation as a linguistically innovative writer.

Italo Calvino (Italian novelist and literary figure)--His collection of Italian folklore and his recent innovative novel, *If on a Winter's Night a Traveler,* confirm his position as Italy's most important living author.

Chien Chung-shu (Chinese author and literary historian)--His recently translated *Fortress Beseiged* is hailed as one of China's greatest contemporary novels.

E.M. Forster (English novelist)--*Arctic Summer and Other Fiction* is a posthumous collection of previously unpublished early writings.

William Gibson (American playwright)--He is the creator of the successful Broadway plays *The Miracle Worker* and *Two for the Seesaw.*

Günter Grass (German author)--His recent *The Meeting at Telgte* is a fictional account of a seventeenth-century conference of writers which parallels the 1947 formation of German literary figures in *Group of 47.*

Garson Kanin (American playwright and novelist)--He is well known for his play *Born Yesterday* and his novels of the movie industry.

Patrick Kavanagh (Irish poet and novelist)--He is best known for his long poem *The Great Hunger,* a bitter evocation of peasant life.

Robert Ludlum (American writer of spy thrillers)--His best-selling novels are characterized by espionage and international intrigue, exemplified by *The Bourne Identity, The Matarese Circle,* and *The Scarlatti Inheritance.*

Toni Morrison (Black American novelist)--Her recent *Tar Baby* is a symbolic novel set on a Caribbean island.

Philip Roth (American novelist and short story writer)--His recent *Zuckerman Unbound,* a sequel to *The Ghost Writer,* examines the meaning of fiction and the role of the writer.

Dave Smith (American poet and novelist)--He is a young poet who is gaining recognition for his direct experiential poetry.

D.M. Thomas (English novelist and poet)--His highly acclaimed novel, *The White Hotel,* is an imaginative blend of fiction, history, and psychoanalysis.

Jean Toomer (Black American author)--*The Wayward and the Seeking* is a posthumous collection of previously unpublished writings.

Monique Wittig (French novelist)--Her novels *Les Guerilleres* and *The Lesbian Body* attempt to establish a feminist mythology.

Rudolfo A. Anaya (Chicano author)--He is known for *Bless Me, Ultima, Heart of Aztlan,* and *Tortuga,* a trilogy about growing up in New Mexico.

Maya Angelou (Black American author)--*The Heart of a Woman* continues her autobiographical writings begun in *I Know Why the Caged Bird Sings.*

Donald Barthelme (American novelist and short story writer)--*Sixty Stories* affirms the innovative trend of his writing.

J.M. Coetzee (South African novelist)--He employs a variation of cinematic techniques in *In the Heart of the Country* to artfully blur reality and fantasy.

William Faulkner (American author)--The recent publication of his early poetry, *Helen: A Courtship and Mississippi Poems,* provides new insight for Faulkner scholars.

Ernest K. Gann (American novelist)--His novel *The Antagonist* was the basis for the television production *Masada.*

A.B. Guthrie (American novelist)--His novels, including *The Big Sky* and *The Way West,* reflect his love and fascination for the West.

Beth Henley (American playwright)--Her first play, *Crimes of the Heart,* won the 1981 Pulitzer Prize in drama.

Pavel Kohout (Czechoslovakian playwright and novelist)--His recent novel, *The Hangwoman,* fictionalizes the reinstitution of a Communist government in an Eastern European country.

Louis L'Amour (American novelist)--He is one of the most popular current writers of western novels.

Bette Bao Lord (Chinese-American novelist)--Her novel *Spring Moon* relates the story of a Chinese family from the last days of imperial rule through the Communist revolution.

Farley Mowat (Canadian author)--His books, including his most recent, *The Snow Walker,* reflect his admiration for nature and native North American peoples.

Ogden Nash (American poet)--His humorous and satirical poems find popular favor for their wit, outrageous rhyme, and ingenious word play.

Salman Rushdie (Indian novelist)--His recent novel, *Midnight's Children,* won the 1981 Booker Prize.

Ernesto Sábato (Argentinian author)--His recently translated *On Heroes and Tombs* is a major Latin American novel.

James Schuyler (American poet)--*The Morning of the Poem* won the 1981 Pulitzer Prize in poetry.

Robert Stone (American novelist)--In his new novel, *A Flag for Sunrise,* he continues his pessimistic examination of contemporary moral issues.

Miguel Torga (Portuguese poet)--He has been hailed as the outstanding Portuguese writer of his generation.

John Updike (American novelist)--*Rabbit Is Rich* probes the life and psyche of an older Harry "Rabbit" Angstrom introduced twenty years ago in *Rabbit Run.*

Gene Wolfe (American science fiction writer)--His major work is *The Fifth Head of Cerberus,* a series of novellas.

Cecil Bødker

1927-

Danish young adult and adult novelist, short story writer, and poet.

Bødker's importance as a writer for young people rests on the high literary quality of her adventure stories. Her works are both realistic and imaginative and are drawn from contemporary life and from the folktale tradition. She brings a keen sense of the grotesque to these latter works, reminiscent of such Eastern European writers as Franz Kafka and Jerzy Kosinski. Adult authority is largely absent from Bødker's works; when present, adults are usually untrustworthy and sometimes cruel. Bødker's landscapes are harsh and desolate, reflecting and influencing adult attitudes. Several of her books include a strong element of humor, however, often bordering on burlesque. She has been praised for her clear and poetic language, as well as for her crisp dialogue, and her books are characterized by their fast-paced action and effective use of suspense. Critics feel that both young people and adults enjoy these works because of Bødker's subtle weaving of social questions and character studies with exciting plots.

Bødker's series of *Silas* books are especially popular because of their engaging protagonist. Silas is particularly appealing for his independent, honest ways. Bødker, however, endows him with negative characteristics which are part of her method of survival, a technique which she uses consistently in her characterizations. This device is felt to enhance the realism of her portrayals. Most of Bødker's main characters are male; she feels this is a natural result of having spent her youth with four brothers, and several of her teenage years as a silversmith's apprentice, the only girl among fifty boys. In 1969 Bødker and her husband were invited to live in Ethiopia in order to write about the Ethiopian lifestyle for the country's children, since at that time they did not have a literature of their own. The first book Bødker published from this experience, *The Leopard,* was also her first to be published in the United States. Although some critics have commented that the novel's villain is too evil and the young protagonist improbable for having a large number of adventures in a short time, the reception of the novel was generally favorable, and Bødker was complimented for capturing the essence of Ethiopian life.

Very few of Bødker's works have been translated into English. Even her poetry, called visionary by Danish critics, has yet to appear. She has won numerous awards for her work, including the Drachmann Prize in 1973 for her poetry, prose, and children's books, the Hans Christian Andersen Medal in 1976, and the Mildred Batchelor Award in 1977. In 1967, *Silas and the Black Mare* received the only prize for children's literature ever awarded by The Danish Academy. (See also *Contemporary Authors,* Vols. 73-76, and *Something About the Author,* Vol. 14.)

BOOKBIRD

This fantastic adventure story [*Silas and the Black Mare*] is divided into eleven chapters in which everyday life changes into dreams, friendship into violence, and back again. Young

Nordisk Pressefoto

readers will sympathize with Silas, a clever, brave and insolent youth who masters every danger with elegance and dash. . . . The reader who attempts to outguess the outcome will be pleasantly surprised at the happy ending. (p. 44)

"Silas og den sorte hoppe (Silas and the Black Mare)," in Bookbird, *Vol. VIII, No. 2, June 15, 1970, pp. 44-5.*

MARGERY FISHER

For *The Leopard* [Bødker] has used a visitor's knowledge of Ethiopia, and her interest in the country and her sharp reactions to it are evident in the way she builds up the background of her story. It is clear, too, that in describing Tibeso's adventure she has gone far towards understanding the way such a boy might have felt and behaved. This book . . . relies on constant changes of scene and event to compel attention. It is a book I would not hesitate to recommend to English readers from twelve or so, for the story is well organised and swift and the atmosphere of mountain village, busy town and river-bank is definite and fascinating. . . . The author has used lightly idiomatic speech and has relied for excitement mainly on a swift alternation of moments of action with moments of doubt and speculation as the boy reviews each situation. (pp. 2362-63)

Margery Fisher, "The Face of Danger," in her Growing Point, Vol. 12, No. 9, April, 1974, pp. 2360-63.*

TAYE BROOKS

On one level, [*The Leopard*] is a gripping and suspenseful story about the occasionally exasperating adventures of a shepherd-boy, Tibeso, in a rural village in central Ethiopia. The underlying theme that gives the story its continuity is Tibeso's courageous fight for survival. . . . For older children, *The Leopard* is a book that anyone, even adults, would find very enjoyable and informative.

But the book has another dimension. It depicts graphically and, except for a few minor details, authentically, life in a small rural Ethiopian village. . . . The book offers a lot of relevant social commentary along the way. Among other things, Bodker succinctly describes the predominant economic and social role women play. Likewise, the male chauvinism prevalent in the rural society is tersely depicted. [The author] is to be commended for having captured so well the texture of life in that area.

The Leopard will be invaluable to all those wishing to know more about village life in Ethiopia. Bodker's style is clear and her handling of suspense surprisingly unobtrusive.

Taye Brooks, "The Bookshelf: 'The Leopard'," in Interracial Books for Children Bulletin (reprinted by permission of Interracial Books for Children Bulletin, 1841 Broadway, New York, N.Y. 10023), Vol. 6, No. 2, 1975, p. 3.

STAN BOCHTLER

There are two weaknesses in [*The Leopard*]. First of all the characters are rather unreal. Tibeso is almost too good, and the blacksmith is the epitome of evil. Secondly, it is hard to believe that one character could have so many adventures in such a short time.

However, despite these weaknesses, *The Leopard* is a thoroughly enjoyable book. There is constant action, with few lulls between episodes. Also, students will enjoy hating the blacksmith because he is so unmistakably wicked!

The Leopard is an excellent book for the turned-off reader . . . who thinks books are dull.

Stan Bochtler, "'The Leopard'" (copyright 1976 by the International Reading Association, Inc.; reprinted with permission of the International Reading Association and Stan Bochtler), in Journal of Reading, Vol. 19, No. 6, March, 1976, p. 513.

LUCIA BINDER

Even though Cecil Bødker turned to children's books relatively late in her writing career . . . this branch of literature has become the core of her creative work. . . .

Her popularity can be traced back to her subject matters as well as her style of presentation.

Research in reading has repeatedly shown that young readers between the ages of 12 and 14—the reading public addressed by Cecil Bødker's juvenile books—look first of all for suspense, action and atmosphere. . . . [In Cecil] Bødker's books they find all three of these elements. (p. 4)

The setting of her first book, *Silas and the Black Mare,* is the circus, but the story is far removed from the romantic stereotypes which so often characterize books about circus people. The life lead by Silas after his flight from the circus is also anything but romantic. The author depicts the light as well as the dark aspects of life. The boy Silas has to fight against hardships and financial need, but also against the injustice which is being done to him. That he thereby has to do things which are "not right", according to middle-class concepts, is a natural consequence.

It is a general characteristic of Cecil Bødker's human portrayals that there are no black-white depictions. Her narratives always remain grounded in reality and show how an unmerciful environment can produce unscrupulous people.

Besides the very lively action which can be found in most of Cecil Bødker's books, her unsparing candor and the unrestrained desire for freedom and independence of her characters have no doubt also contributed to their popularity among young readers. Her outstanding ability to understand young people, their behaviour and their problems comes from the fact that she had contact with a great many other young people in her childhood . . . and that she now has four teenage daughters.

Some critics have characterized her works—particularly the "Silas" books—as anti-authoritarian. This is not true, however. They merely dispense with the teaching of all lessons and morals and attempt to come to grips with the world in a very realistic way.

Even the early *Timmerlis,* which appeared in 1969, suggests the realism of Bødker's children's books. It contains a series of simple, realistic environmental stories of daily life, unsentimental, humorous in parts and very candid.

In spite of the excitement which arises out of her action-packed novels, Cecil Bødker also weaves atmospheric passages and nature descriptions into her works, which fascinate because of their unusualness and accuracy of aim. Such passages are particularly captivating in books such as *The Leopard*. . . . Cecil Bødker succeeds not only in painting vivid pictures with few words, but inserts these passages in such a way that the continuity of the plot is not impeded . . . , but help to carry it forward. They hint at coming developments, which the reader has already half-guessed, whereby the question, if what one has assumed will actually happen, even heightens the suspense. (pp. 4-5)

Lucia Binder, "Cecil Bødker," in Bookbird, Vol. XIII, No. 2, June 15, 1976, pp. 4-5.

THE JUNIOR BOOKSHELF

Cecil Bødker has lived in Ethiopia and she clearly has a strong affection for the people, a love which has in it no condescension or criticism.

Leopard is not . . . a book about animals in the wild. It is about village society. Tibeso, the appealing and by no means heroic hero, is a coward. . . . The discovery [that the Big One, thought to be a leopard, is in fact a man] is the beginning of a series of adventures in which Tibeso makes up in persistence what he lacks in courage. There is an exciting climax when the two Big Ones, feline and human, meet in combat.

Good as the story is, its effect is enhanced by the picture of Ethiopian rural society and the string of finely drawn characters. . . .

> *"For Children from Ten to Fourteen: 'Leopard',"*
> *in* The Junior Bookshelf, *Vol. 42, No. 3, June, 1978,*
> *p. 148.*

MARCUS CROUCH

The society [in **Silas and the Black Mare**] is that of peasants and the only representative of a wider world is the pedlar. Against these earth-bound, prejudiced, brutalized creatures born of poverty and ignorance shines Silas, . . . who owns nothing but his wits, an abundance of self-confidence, and a way with horses. Silas is much too big a creation to be squandered on one book. As he rides off, not into the sunset, at the close of this high-spirited frolic of a book, it is clear that more adventures lie ahead to be chronicled in the same blend of realism and lyricism. [Cecil Bødker] likes the byways of history and topography, but can sustain a major mainstream character, one who owes something to Tyl Eulenspiegel but who bids fair to win a small place among the immortals in his own right.

> *Marcus Crouch, "Rule of the Boy Kings," in* The
> Times Literary Supplement *(© Times Newspapers*
> *Ltd. (London) 1978; reproduced from* The Times
> Literary Supplement *by permission), No. 3979, July*
> *7, 1978, p. 767.**

KIRKUS REVIEWS

From the first-page moment when Silas drifts down the river into the horse trader's view [in **Silas and the Black Mare**], he commands a wary curiosity; and he continues to astound and to be astounded throughout his subsequent encounters. . . . The story ends with the full cast assembled for an auction of the mare on the one street of a mean, impoverished village; Bødker pulls off this climactic scene as adeptly as Silas does the recovery of his mount. The whole, highly original story is related with a degree of shrewd humor and an absence of moralizing interference that are still hard to come by in children's books.

> *"Younger Fiction: 'Silas and the Black Mare'," in*
> Kirkus Reviews *(copyright © 1978 The Kirkus Ser-*
> *vice, Inc.), Vol. XLIV, No. 14, July 15, 1978, p.*
> *749.*

THE JUNIOR BOOKSHELF

There are no blacks and whites [in **Silas and the Black Mare**]: one is . . . persuaded to see the viewpoint of and sympathise with even the nastiest characters. The tension and menace build up remarkably in this world of fear and suspicion. . . . At such a level of writing, one looks forward eagerly to the sequels. (p. 264)

> *"The New Books: 'Silas and the Black Mare'," in*
> The Junior Bookshelf, *Vol. 42, No. 5, October, 1978,*
> *pp. 263-64.*

WHITNEY ROGGE

Reminiscent of Heironymus Bosch paintings and the adult novels of Jerzy Kosinski, this almost surrealistic tale set in a timeless European landscape [**Silas and the Black Mare**] follows young Silas who runs away from his traveling circus family. . . . While the cruelty and avarice of the villagers Silas encounters are unremitting (almost all want to cheat him, beat him, or kidnap him), Silas himself is no bargain either. He survives only by putting his own needs first. . . . Bødker's writing, even in translation, is spare and clean, harshly appropriate to the country and people described. It is a bizarre and hostile story illuminated only rarely by glimmers of love or caring, but readers who felt an affinity with Julia Cunningham's *Dorp Dead* . . . will recognize and appreciate this novel's bleak power.

> *Whitney Rogge, "'Silas and the Black Mare'," in*
> School Library Journal *(reprinted from the Novem-*
> *ber, 1978 issue of* School Library Journal, *published*
> *by R. R. Bowker Co./A Xerox Corporation; copyright*
> *© 1978), Vol. 25, No. 3, November, 1978, p. 56.*

JOHN NAUGHTON

Silas and the Black Mare is [a grim] reminder that adult cruelty to children is perennial, and that, in earlier centuries, it was even more pervasive and brutal. Cecil Bødker [has] a reputation for Kafkaesque fiction which the present book does nothing to diminish. . . . Every encounter the child has with an adult is treacherous and problematic, and the boy's eventual survival is something of an improbable deliverance. (p. 626)

> *John Naughton, "Gangs and Fans" (© British*
> *Broadcasting Corp. 1978; reprinted by permission*
> *of John Naughton), in* The Listener, *Vol. 100, No.*
> *2585, November 9, 1978, pp. 625-26.**

DENISE M. WILMS

In **Silas and the Black Mare** . . . Bødker left her hero making a clean getaway with Ben-Godik after craftily retrieving his stolen mare from greedy villagers. Now, in two equally strong sequels, she follows his subsequent fortunes as a wanderer on the road with Ben-Godik in **Silas and Ben-Godik** and as an independent adventurer in **Silas and the Runaway Coach**. The harsh environment in the first book hasn't improved any in these two additions. Again poverty is rife and adults too often not to be trusted. . . . Bødker's characters, whether good or evil, are memorable, and Silas in particular continues to awe with his cool self-possession and wise-beyond-years abilities to deal with people—both these traits believable in light of his circus years described in the **Black Mare** book. More first-rate picaresque adventure.

> *Denise M. Wilms, "Children's Books: 'Silas and*
> *Ben-Godik' and 'Silas the the Runaway Coach'," in*
> Booklist *(reprinted by permission of the American*
> *Library Association; copyright © 1978 by the Amer-*
> *ican Library Association), Vol. 75, No. 6, November*
> *15, 1978, p. 542.*

KIRKUS REVIEWS

In **Silas and the Black Mare** . . . Bødker projected her resourceful young hero's memorable encounters with penetrating, uncompromising shrewdness; in **Silas and Ben-Godik** and **Silas and the Runaway Coach** she settles for merely *using* similar treacherous and bizarre figures to spice and propel Silas' adventures. Nevertheless, her strong, stinking, conniving Horse Crone . . . is a most imposing villain; and Silas' further adventures, particularly in the latter volume, are corking, invigorating ones. . . . This time Silas and the merchant's son are kidnapped by the horse crone; again, the mare is stolen, this time with one of the merchants'; and Silas' audacious, wily, and complicated maneuvers in recovering them keep the pages flying. By now the once-amoral Silas has developed a compassionate sense of humanity, and he is forever rescuing unsavory victims (even the Horse Crone, and a dancing bear more than once) from angry crowds and cohorts; but his kind deeds are undertaken with such dash and defiance of risk that there's no question of going soft. Silas continues to speak out refreshingly, to outwit opponents and readers, to maintain his wary independence and keen exuberance—well into a crackerjack series that shows no sign of lagging.

"Younger Fiction: 'Silas and Ben-Godik'," in Kirkus Reviews *(copyright © 1978 The Kirkus Service, Inc.), Vol. XLIV, No. 24, December 15, 1978, p. 130.*

MARY M. BURNS

The desolate setting against which the characters move [in *Silas and Ben-Godik*] is as evocative as an Ingmar Bergman landscape: It is at once a backdrop for the actors and an explanation for their deeds. The contrast between the provincial villagers and the quick-witted Silas not only heightens the suspense but also provides an earthy, humorous note. [Filled] with action, the book lends itself to reading aloud; however, the story can be better appreciated as a sequel to *Silas and the Black Mare* . . . than as a separate entity.

Mary M. Burns, "Stories for Intermediate Readers: 'Silas and Ben-Godik'," in The Horn Book Magazine *(copyright © 1979 by The Horn Book, Inc., Boston), Vol. LV, No. 1, February, 1979, p. 58.*

JAMES NORSWORTHY

Silas and Ben-Godik and *Silas and the Runaway Coach* can easily stand on their own as good literature, yet when one knows that they are part of a series, the reader will probably devour all of them and still want to read more. Through Silas, Bodker has created one of the most delightful boys in all of children's literature. He has such a zest and love of and for life! In addition to Silas is a complete cast of vividly memorable characters of all types. If for no other reason, Bodker's works should be read for her character portrayal. These two works are filled with the fast paced adventure, suspense and drama which young readers crave in their books. (pp. 447-48)

James Norsworthy, "Children's Books: 'Silas and Ben-Godik' and 'Silas and the Runaway Coach'," in Catholic Library World, *Vol. 50, No. 10, May/June, 1979, pp. 447-48.*

Franklyn M(ansfield) Branley

1915-

American nonfiction and fiction author and editor.

Branley is best known for the many science books he has written for young adults. He began writing in this genre when, as a young primary school teacher, he found few science books suitable for his young students. Branley also discovered that many instructors were not teaching science at all. Believing that young people are entitled to accurate and comprehensible scientific information about the natural world, Branley collaborated with an associate to produce a pamphlet that advised teachers on how to begin the teaching of science in the primary grades. He then began contributing articles to periodicals, and in 1947 published *Experiments with Science*, written with Nelson Frederick Beeler. Although Branley later taught college and served as the astronomer for the Hayden Planetarium in New York City, he continued to write science books specifically for a young adult audience.

Branley has been praised for respecting the young person's desire and ability to understand and apply complicated scientific concepts. Many of his early books, such as *Experiments with Electricity* and *Experiments with a Microscope*, both written with Beeler, are commended for their clarity and usefulness. These books let the young reader learn by active participation in and observation of cause-and-effect relationships. Many of his books, such as *The Earth: Planet Number Three*, present factual information and explore many scientific concepts while conveying a sense of wonder at the beauty and complexity of the subject. In books like *The Mystery of Stonehenge* and *The Christmas Sky*, Branley is able to combine scientific knowledge and legendary speculation and demonstrate that although science can answer many questions, it cannot answer them all.

Branley's books are considered by many critics to be well organized, precise, and comprehensible without being overly simplistic. His subject selection is almost unanimously praised. In spite of some criticism of occasional factual errors, Branley is generally acknowledged to be a thoughtful, conscientious scientist and a versatile, committed writer. (See also *Contemporary Authors*, Vols. 33-36, rev. ed., and *Something About the Author*, Vol. 4.)

Courtesy of Franklyn M. Branley

send to any teacher or parent faced with the problem of holding a pack at bay during a rainy afternoon.

> *Creighton Peet, "Books for Younger Readers: 'Experiments in Science'," in* The New York Times Book Review *(© 1947 by The New York Times Company; reprinted by permission), August 3, 1947, p. 18.*

CREIGHTON PEET

The mothers of America better get what rest and peace of mind they can right now, because after the boys of America get a good look at **"Experiments in Science,"** home isn't going to be the same any more. . . . [Here] are fifty simple experiments, which should be absolutely fascinating to any child, all in one book, and the urge to go right out to the kitchen and start messing around is irresistible.

The Messrs. Beeler and Branley are true scientists, and all on the children's side. They never flinch or turn away, although when making coke from coal they suggest, "you better hold your nose when you do this because the smell is awful." However, most experiments are innocent enough, and all are entertaining. **"Experiments in Science"** should prove a god-

THOMAS LASK

Teen-agers, summer counselors and just plain parents, who have to face long, irritating, wet days indoors, will welcome [Branley and Beeler's **"Experiments With Electricity"**]. For with a little patience and with material that is lying around the house or that can be easily and inexpensively bought, a host of ingenious contraptions can be rigged up and made to work. . . . A good deal of information is nicely blended in with the instructions. . . . A scientific-minded youngster will find this volume a cornucopia of knowledge and enjoyment.

> *Thomas Lask, "Among the New Books for Younger Readers: 'Experiments with Electricity'," in* The New York Times Book Review *(© 1949 by The New York*

15

Times Company; reprinted by permission), July 10, 1949, p. 18.

LOUISE S. BECHTEL

[Branley and Beeler call **"More Experiments in Science"**] a "doing book," not a reading book, one that proves again their motto, "Try it and see for yourself." Their former experiment books have been popular in homes and schools.

This time the thirty-seven experiments range all over the house and garden, kitchen and garage, for materials. Each has a list of things needed. . . . Some start you on collections, as the insect trap, the butterfly net, the wild-flower press. Some give you tricks to play, as the dancing moth-balls. Some offer useful things to make for your home, as the foam fire extinguisher, the telegraph set, the water-drop microscope. Most satisfy that ranging curiosity of the boy of twelve to fourteen, giving him answers about the corrosion of metals, colloids and molecules, erosion, water pressure and what makes the electric refrigerator work. Very interesting.

Louise S. Bechtel, "Books for Young People: 'More Experiments in Science'," in New York Herald Tribune Book Review, June 4, 1950, p. 10.

VIRGINIA KIRKUS' BOOKSHOP SERVICE

[*Experiments in Optical Illusions* is a] fascinating little book with lots of tantalizing "now you see it; now you don't" home experiments. Beginning with a discussion of the physiology of the eye, [Branley and Beeler] . . . investigate the phenomena of image reversal, focus, light and dark, space and line arising from the peculiar construction of the eye. Such famous diverting illusions such as the deceiving size of the rising moon, mirages, after-images, color tricks, and light "ghosts" are also explained in lucid, informal style. Pleasant supplementary material for science courses, for intrepid "experimenters" and fun for the whole family.

"Twelve to Fifteen: 'Experiments in Optical Illusions'," in Virginia Kirkus' Bookshop Service, Vol. XIX, No. 11, June 15, 1951, p. 298.

VIRGINIA KIRKUS' BOOKSHOP SERVICE

Beeler and Branley have had a fairly stable record of good information and safe experiments in their past books . . . though they have been occasionally weak in organization and explanation. [*Experiments with Atomics,*] as far as we can tell upholds that standard, though we'd advise checking with a science teacher or some other authority—as would doubtless be necessary due to the advanced nature of the material. Definitely it will need grounding and pre-established interest or a combination of both. Topics discussed—with simpler experiments and projects outlined to illustrate theory—include basics of atomic structure and electrical charges, the atomic family, discovery of radioactivity, natural and artificial radioactivity, particle acceleration for bombardment, separation of isotopes, fission, atomic reactors, plutonium and weapons—a pretty wide coverage of a big topic. The projects which are as simple as rubbing a fountain pen and as advanced as making a geiger counter, leave something to be desired *as per* instructions, and they'll also take time, space and money. But for the right person in the right setting, this is inspiration.

"Twelve to Sixteen: 'Experiments with Atomics'," in Virginia Kirkus' Bookshop Service, Vol. XXII, No. 5, March 1, 1954, p. 156.

JOHN PFEIFFER

[In **"Experiments with Atomics"**,] Messrs. Beeler and Branley present the facts needed to understand the basic elements of nuclear physics. They describe atomic weapons, atom-powered submarines, and recently developed atomic reactors, the precursors of the furnaces that will provide heat and power in the future. They indicate how "hot" radioactive materials are used to study the effectiveness of drugs and fertilizers, the operation of automobile engines, the quality of steel castings, and the blood circulation of patients selected for special surgery. These and other matters become clear with the aid of simple models and apparatus which can easily be assembled at home. Beeler and Branley are experts at imparting considerable information without calling on technical terms and mathematical equations.

John Pfeiffer, "Notes: 'Experiments with Atomics'," in The Saturday Review, New York (copyright © 1954 by Saturday Review; all rights reserved; reprinted by permission), Vol. XXXVII, No. 34, August 21, 1954, p. 20.

MARGARET SHERWOOD LIBBY

Another "experiment" book by Nelson Beeler and Franklyn Branley is welcome, especially one dealing with the use of the microscope. [**"Experiments with a Microscope"**] is useful for those fortunate young people who have a microscope and all who are beginning laboratory science. There are excellent chapters on the instrument itself, its construction and how it works. Then as "the world is yours for observing" many are the suggestions for things to look at, inanimate objects, plants, protozoa, yeasts, blood and bacteria. Wise advice is given on careful observation and the keeping of records as well as on ways of mounting specimens, staining colorless ones, and even on photo-micrography with a Brownie Hawkeye camera. . . . [This] is a fine new science book.

Margaret Sherwood Libby, "Books for Boys and Girls: 'Experiments with a Microscope'," in New York Herald Tribune Book Review (© I.H.T. Corporation; reprinted by permission), May 12, 1957, p. 12.

ALFRED D. BECK

[**"The Nine Planets"**] is a solidly packed reference book . . . which yields an exceptionally rich harvest of information per page.

Mr. Branley writes sincerely, accurately and with no attempt at glamorizing the facts. Any references he makes to things that are speculative are clearly identified with qualifying words. . . . Impressive also are the tables of statistics which have been included in the body of the text rather than in an appendix.

Near the end of the book the author has suggested nine titles for further reading. I wish he had listed twice as many because I believe he will stir in his readers a wider range of interest than is encompassed by these few titles.

Alfred D. Beck, "Orbs and Orbits," in The New York Times Book Review (© 1958 by The New York

Times Company; reprinted by permission), November 23, 1958, p. 48.

M. B. SAILSBURY

[*Experiments in Sky Watching*] can be recommended for young people from the upper elementary thru high school age and is worthwhile adult reading also. The proposed experiments are designed to lead to discovery instead of routine learning. . . . The material is presented in an unusually clear manner which suggests investigations and simple studies which one may make in order to comprehend the "stars," their positions, and motions.

> *M. B. Sailsbury, "Basic Knowledge for the Science Minded," in* Chicago Tribune *(© 1959 Chicago Tribune), November 1, 1959, p. 42.**

VIRGINIA KIRKUS' SERVICE

[In *The Moon: Earth's Natural Satellite*] Franklyn Branley, authority in the field, sorts out the various conventions and theories regarding the moon, separating fact from fancy, and, by his enthusiastic style, manages to render the factual study of the moon as exciting as any less rigorous analysis. In an atmosphere geared to the launching of man-made satellites, this account of earth's dazzling natural satellite is both revealing and profitable.

> *"Books for Younger Readers: 'The Moon: Earth's Natural Satellite'," in* Virginia Kirkus' Service, *Vol. XXVIII, No. 5, March 1, 1960, p. 186.*

WILLIAM J. WALLRICH

The daring program that is Project Mercury—its hardware, personnel, methods, and objectives—is vividly presented by Dr. Branley [in **"Exploring By Astronaut: The Story of Project Mercury"**]. . . . The program's goals and purposes, hazards and procedures, are all here in what is far and away one of the best of the recent spate of books produced on the subject.

> *William J. Wallrich, "Adventure of Space Travel in Fact and Fiction," in* Chicago Tribune *(© 1961 Chicago Tribune), November 12, 1961, p. 45.**

THE TIMES LITERARY SUPPLEMENT

Many books have been written about man's attempt to land on the moon, but, for once, this new book [*Exploration of the Moon*] is an agreeable surprise, for Dr. Branley . . . has a refreshingly easy style and a gift for clear explanation. The standard of the work is quite elementary and begins with an account of the nature of the moon, including a very fair description of the controversy over its origin. Methods of exploring the moon with unmanned and manned probes are then discussed (with results up to the end of 1964), and the third part describes some of the plans for the future establishment of permanent bases on the moon. This is popular science writing at its best.

> *"Books Received: 'Exploration of the Moon'," in* The Times Literary Supplement *(© Times Newspapers Ltd. (London) 1965; reproduced from* The Times Literary Supplement *by permission), No. 3312, August 19, 1965, p. 721.*

ELIZABETH F. GRAVE

[*The Earth: Planet Number Three* is a] stimulating account of man's present knowledge of planet Earth. The author considers three large topics: the atmosphere, sea, and land. He explores theories concerning the origin and age of the earth and tells how scientists study the motion, size, and shape of the planet, and how they probe the problems of gravity, geomagnetism, radiation belts, etc. At times the text is difficult, but the careful presentation of the subject matter, within historical perspective, brings to the reader a sense of excitement and wonder at man's endeavor to learn more about the universe. (pp. 160-61)

> *Elizabeth F. Grave, "Junior High Up: 'The Earth: Planet Number Three'," in* School Library Journal, *an appendix to* Library Journal *(reprinted from the May, 1966 issue of* School Library Journal, *published by R. R. Bowker Co./A Xerox Corporation; copyright © 1966), Vol. 12, No. 9, May, 1966, pp. 160-61.*

SCIENCE BOOKS

The composition of the earth and its atmosphere, its origins and age, its motions, shape, the force of gravity, and a discussion of geomagnetism are the major topics of this readable account that is packed with solid scientific data [*The Earth: Planet Number Three*]. An appendix, "Some facts about the earth," contains a summary of the mathematical data. In addition to its direct value as a source of factual information, it contains historical material and descriptions of the process of scientific inquiry. A reading list and an index are appended.

> *"Book Reviews: 'The Earth: Planet Number Three'," in* Science Books *(copyright 1966 by the American Association for the Advancement of Science), Vol. 2, No. 2 (September, 1966), p. 116.*

PHILIP MORRISON and PHYLIS MORRISON

[In **"The Christmas Sky"**, the] Star of Bethlehem is . . . sought by reason. Page by page in this clear and gentle book the possibilities are explored. It was not a meteor, because it endured; it was not a comet, because it was welcome; it was not a nova. The birth of Jesus is carefully and convincingly dated from the circumstances of history.

> *Philip Morrison and Phylis Morrison, "Books: 'The Christmas Sky'," in* Scientific American *(copyright © 1966 by Scientific American, Inc.; all rights reserved), Vol. 215, No. 6, December, 1966, p. 141.*

BENJAMIN W. BOVA

[*The Christmas Sky* is] a rather dry and conservative look at possible astronomical explanations for the "Star of Bethlehem". Personally, I find the astronomy too conservative in places, and the author makes argumentative statements without showing his evidence for them. In all, the book is a good example of what happens when you try to dissect a fairy tale.

> *Benjamin W. Bova, "'The Christmas Sky'," in* Appraisal: Science Books for Young People *(copyright © 1968 by the Children's Science Book Review Committee), Vol. 1, No. 2, Spring, 1968, p. 3.*

KIRKUS REVIEWS

Taking much-explored topics [in *The Milky Way: Galaxy No. 1*], Mr. Branley manages the usual range with ease: the known "facts" of our universe and galaxy; the historical dilemmas which have plagued sky watchers; the chronological history of great astronomers and their achievements relevant to galactic understanding. But he goes further: with the ease of a teacher, one very good at his trade, he leads the reader into the fascinating area of how we estimate some of our facts and in so doing presents more science than all of the "facts" taken together. The reader is introduced to the assumptions upon which total concepts are placed, often rather cautiously. He comes to realize that the great debates of science may arise from disputes about the validity of axioms rather than about the reliability of the data. Thus he will be able to appreciate such problems as the computation of stellar magnitudes, galactic distance, and the probable age of the milky way (including its likely future). (pp. 58-9)

> *"Older Non-Fiction: 'The Milky Way: Galaxy No. 1'," in* Kirkus Reviews *(copyright © 1969 The Kirkus Service, Inc.), Vol. XXXVII, No. 2, January 15, 1969, pp. 58-9.*

MARGARET F. O'CONNELL

We may sooner know the secrets of the moon than of Stonehenge. . . . Setting up ["**The Mystery of Stonehenge**"] as an informal inquiry, Franklyn Branley carefully sifts through archeological findings, scientific data and informed speculations, picking out the clues that shed a little light on Stonehenge's shadowed past. How did Stone Age men haul granite slabs, weighing 40 tons, without the wheel? And without metal tools, how did they cut and carve and then erect them vertically and horizontally? Was the site an ancient sun temple, or a sepulchral ground, or an astrological observatory? Mr. Branley doesn't come up with final answers to these centuries-old questions nor does he take a stand on present-day controversy. Still he has ably described the way primitive people may have achieved an engineering feat that in its time rivals today's space program.

> *Margaret F. O'Connell, "For Young Readers: 'The Mystery of Stonehenge'," in* The New York Times Book Review *(© 1969 by The New York Times Company; reprinted by permission), September 7, 1969, p. 34.*

PHILLIP W. ALLEY

[*The Milky Way: Galaxy Number One* is a] clear, logically ordered treatment covering historical progress in the understanding of the solar system, methods of determining astronomical distances, specific facts about the Milky Way, radio astronomy, and the evolution of galaxies. . . . Both advanced young readers and persons wanting to enlarge upon a casual acquaintanceship with astronomy can profit from this. . . .

> *Phillip W. Alley, "'The Milky Way: Galaxy Number One'," in* School Library Journal, *an appendix to* Library Journal *(reprinted from the October, 1969 issue of* School Library Journal, *published by R. R. Bowker Co./A Xerox Corporation; copyright © 1969), October, 1969, p. 147.*

MAY HILL ARBUTHNOT

All of [Branley's books are] remarkably informative. *A Book of the Milky Way Galaxy for You* gives a fascinating and understandable explanation of how vast distances are measured. *The Sun: Star Number One* and *The Earth: Planet Number Three* are fuller and more advanced than books on similar subjects by [Herbert] Zim, but the style . . . [makes] them comprehensible and fascinating. . . . The Branley books are well written and have made a brilliant contribution to children's science interests, especially in the field of astronomy. (p. 292)

> *May Hill Arbuthnot, "Informational Books," in her* Children's Reading in the Home *(copyright © 1969 by Scott, Foresman and Company; reprinted by permission), Scott, Foresman, 1969, pp. 279-308.**

CELESTE H. VINCENT

[*The Mystery of Stonehenge*] is a very readable account of this marvellous workmanship of mysterious origin. The author notes the efforts of many specialists including anthropologists, astronomers, engineers and others, using their knowledge and modern "know-how" even to the extent of computerizing this information, to try to bring forth some evidence as to the probable origin and methods of constructing this wonder and perhaps some reasons for its purpose of erection in the now lush area of Salisbury Plain in southwest England. Whether or not any authentic conclusions were found this slim book about Stonehenge is an intriguing piece of writing [and] a fascinating book for all ages.

> *Celeste H. Vincent, "'The Mystery of Stonehenge'," in* Appraisal: Science Books for Young People *(copyright © 1970 by the Children's Science Book Review Committee), Vol. 3, No. 2, Spring, 1970, p. 4.*

EDMUND R. MEŠKYS

[*A Book of Venus for You*] gives an excellent, extremely up-to-date survey of what is known about Venus. Every recent discovery about the planet by United States and Russian space probes and United States radar observations is included. The explanations are very clear and concise, and the book is quite readable. There is one quibble, however. Dr. Branley says a "day" on Venus is 247 days long, while a year is 225. "Day" is an ambiguous word in astronomy but most people would assume the author meant time from sunrise to sunrise. On Venus a Solar Day is only about 120 days long, while it is the "sidereal day" which is about 247 days long. Other than this little inaccuracy the book is flawless. (pp. 5-6)

> *Edmund R. Meškys, "'A Book of Venus for You'," in* Appraisal: Science Books for Young People *(copyright © 1970 by the Children's Science Book Review Committee), Vol. 3, No. 3, Fall, 1970, pp. 5-6.*

DAVID G. HOAG

[*The Milky Way: Galaxy No. 1*] could have been an excellent book. It is up-to-date, well-organized, . . . and for the most part is well written. Most of the technical explanation is clear and particularly good. However, the several places in the text having mathematical or geometrical descriptions are needlessly complex, confusing, not always relevant, and often wrong. The volume would be ever so much better over-all if these parts were removed. It would be excellent if a competent scientist helped the author make the needed repairs. In spite of these serious flaws, this is a worth-while science book about optical and radio astronomy explaining what we know and how we know about our galaxy: the Milky Way.

> *David G. Hoag, "'The Milky Way: Galaxy No. 1'," in* Appraisal: Science Books for Young People *(copyright © 1970 by the Children's Science Book Review Committee), Vol. 3, No. 3, Fall, 1970, p. 6.*

SATURDAY REVIEW

With just enough appreciative comment and historical background to keep [*Man in Space to the Moon*] from being arid, Franklyn Branley gives a detailed and accurate report of the Apollo 11 mission. There is some discussion of the importance of the data gathered, but the book is primarily devoted to what happened: the stages of flight and the manipulation of modules; how the three astronauts ate, slept, disposed of human waste; the mechanics of landing and communication with Mission Control; investigation of the moon, and the details of the return flight, re-entry, and recovery. One of the best books on the subject, it is dignified enough for slow older readers. . . .

> *"Children's Books: 'Man in Space to the Moon'," in* Saturday Review *(copyright © 1970 by Saturday Review; all rights reserved; reprinted by permission), Vol. LIII, No. 51, December 19, 1970, p. 32.*

EDMUND R. MEŠKYS

[*Man in Space to the Moon* is a] brief history of man's wonder and dreams of travel to the moon, space travel from Sputnik I to Apollo, and detailed description of the flight to the moon by Apollo 11. Much of the information is a straight repeat of what the fifth or sixth grader has already seen during TV coverage of the moon flights, but here and there the author makes some excellent points. . . . This book will give the child a good summary of what has happened—he should find the list of all manned space craft interesting—and should inspire the imagination of the curious. I believe every public and grade school library should have this. (pp. 7-8)

> *Edmund R. Meškys, "'Man in Space to the Moon'," in* Appraisal: Science Books for Young People *(copyright © 1971 by the Children's Science Book Review Committee), Vol. 4, No. 2, Spring, 1971, pp. 7-8.*

SCIENCE BOOKS

[*The Nine Planets*'s] strong advantages are its easy readability, coherent story design, and relative absence of ambiguity or equivocation. Its faults probably are not too important, but a few are worth mentioning. The explanation of mean value (p. 4) is wrong. An alternate symbol (p. 8) for Uranus is still used by some astronomers. The term "minor planets" (p. 11) is not correct as a substitute for "terrestrial planets." Once again, Isaac Newton's illustration of orbital and suborbital speed is reproduced (p. 18) without credit. The geometric utility of Venus transits (p. 39) is no longer relevant, because the same information is available to much higher accuracy by modern means. The mass of Pluto is now known to be much smaller than previously believed. Also, the myth that Pluto is sometimes nearer the sun than is Neptune is perpetuated. There is a list of sources of further information, and a useful index is appended.

> *"Solar System: 'The Nine Planets'," in* Science Books *(copyright 1971 by the American Association for the Advancement of Science), Vol. 7, No. 3 (December, 1971), p. 216.*

DAVID G. HOAG

Regretfully, this revised edition [of *Nine Planets*] did not benefit from a few corrections and clarifications which prevent the book from being rated far better. For instance, defining "mass" as "giving information about the relative number of molecules contained in a subject" leaves much unsaid and conveys little accurate information. Similarly, the author produces confusion in the concepts of force and motion and has difficulty with some of his geometric descriptions. But on balance, much is very good and some parts excellent in his concise, systematic historical and descriptive treatment of each of the planets in the solar system.

> *David G. Hoag, "'The Nine Planets'," in* Appraisal: Science Books for Young People *(copyright © 1972 by the Children's Science Book Review Committee), Vol. 5, No. 3, Fall, 1972, p. 11.*

JUDITH BOTSFORD

Youthful space scientists will be fascinated by Franklyn Branley's careful and often dramatic examination of the earth's newest "rock collection" brought back by the lunar astronauts of Apollo 11, 12 and 14. Early chapters [in *Pieces of Another World: The Story of Moon Rocks*] discuss the methods and tools used to collect moon rocks, the techniques used by scientists at the Lunar Receiving Laboratory in Houston to analyze them, and what they have discovered about the various rocks, dust, and crystals. A scant chapter is devoted to the few questions tentatively answered by moon rock findings, while subsequent chapters (over one-third of the book) explore the many questions these findings have raised about the moon's origins and geological structure. Dr. Branley's text is often marred by the lack of italics to emphasize technical terms and their definitions. No glossary alleviates this problem, and important concepts are often lost in a sea of text. . . . Dr. Branley's work . . . examines with clarity the careful scientific procedures and diverse theories resulting from this new and exciting lunar data. (pp. 8-9)

> *Judith Botsford, "'Pieces of Another World: The Story of Moon Rocks'," in* Appraisal: Science Books for Young People *(copyright © 1973 by the Children's Science Book Review Committee), Vol. 6, No. 3, Fall, 1973, pp. 8-9.*

DOUGLAS B. SANDS

Jules Verne himself would revel in [*Pieces of Another World: The Story of Moon Rocks,* a] fascinating account of the moon rocks. There is a sense of real discovery on every page. An absolute must for the young geologist, astronomer or space scientist, the book gives insight into the interplay of the most precise scientific work and the theories this work promotes.

> *Douglas B. Sands, "'Pieces of Another World: The Story of Moon Rocks'," in* Appraisal: Science Books for Young People *(copyright © 1973 by the Children's Science Book Review Committee), Vol. 6, No. 3, Fall, 1973, p. 9.*

HEDDIE KENT

First published in 1960, Franklyn Branley's *The Moon* has been revised to include the findings of recent lunar exploration: moon rocks, temperature, gasses, etc. The book cannot be handled by anyone younger than junior high. It is rather dry and quite scholarly, but crammed full of serious information, as well as the history, folklore and myths that have been connected with the moon for centuries. . . . This is a very comprehensive study, carefully documented. . . . (pp. 8-9)

> Heddie Kent, "'The Moon: Earth's Natural Satellite'," in Appraisal: Science Books for Young People (copyright © 1974 by the Children's Science Book Review Committee), Vol. 7, No. 1, Winter, 1974, pp. 8-9.

DAVID G. HOAG

The original copyright date for [*The Moon: Earth's Natural Satellite*] predates the adventures and discoveries of the manned lunar landings of Apollo. This edition has been updated with only a cursory and superficial acknowledgment of Apollo. This is not bad, however, since it leaves room for much of the fundamental coverage of lunar science and the earth moon system which would otherwise be displaced by material covered elsewhere in many new books about Apollo. However, although the organization is logical . . . , the text has many serious flaws. On page 24, the author identifies the intersection of the ecliptic with the horizon as being in the constellation Aries. It hasn't been there since ancient times. On page 25, he equates the ecliptic with the moon's orbit. They are 5 degrees different. . . . He confuses the convention for the east and west sides of the moon's face, both as seen directly and by inverting telescope. This, of course, disagrees with the correct convention shown later in a NASA lunar chart reproduction. These and other errors are too serious to ignore. Without them the book would be very good. As it is, I rank it only fair.

> David G. Hoag, "'The Moon: Earth's Natural Satellite'," in Appraisal: Science Books for Young People (copyright © 1974 by the Children's Science Book Review Committee), Vol. 7, No. 1, Winter, 1974, p. 9.

KIRKUS REVIEWS

[*Comets, Meteoroids, and Asteroids: Mavericks of the Solar System* is a] compact, up-to-date review of some intriguing astronomical odds and ends. Besides investigating the origin and makeup, paths and habits of the meteoroids, comets and asteroids of the title, Branley explores the possible genesis of the puzzling glasslike tektites which may or may not result from the impact of meteorites on the earth or moon, evaluates evidence of organic molecules in space, and discusses such recently studied phenomena as the "zodiacal light," solar wind (mostly hydrogen ions racing out from the sun), the Van Allen belts, and cosmic rays. Authoritative but properly tentative, and to the point.

> "Non-Fiction: 'Comets, Meteoroids, and Asteroids: Mavericks of the Solar System'," in Kirkus Reviews (copyright ©1974 The Kirkus Service, Inc.), Vol. XLII, No. 11, June 1, 1974, p. 588.

DAVID G. HOAG

How frustrating it is to review a book [*Comets, Meteoroids, and Asteroids*] so close to being excellent but damaged severely by carelessness. If only the author or publisher had insisted on a quick review by any careful engineer or scientist. For example, the statement on page 38 that all asteroids melted together would make a globe less than 500 miles diameter contradicts the table two pages earlier. On page 43 the book says very small tektites are "a millimeter or so across, and weigh only a few grams." By this, these strange objects found on earth would have a density 50 times that of uranium! And so on for at least several more outright errors. Yet, there is a lot of excellent material for a student in these pages albeit sometimes it's rather awkwardly organized.

> David G. Hoag, "'Comets, Meteoroids, and Asteroids'," in Appraisal: Science Books for Young People (copyright © 1975 by the Children's Science Book Review Committee), Vol. 8, No. 1, Winter, 1975, p. 8.

JOAN LEVINE

Lest we do ourselves in first with some nuclear holocaust there are any number of ways our planet can end—all perhaps as terrible, some more fascinating and beautiful to contemplate than others. . . . There is only one certainty: the world *will* end.

In order to understand why we can be so assured of an end, [in "**The End of the World**"] Franklyn Branley traces the evolution of the earth, sun and moon from their hypothetical births to the present and predicts possible futures, none of which are optimistic. [The text is controlled and clearly developed.] . . .

Branley consoles us with the knowledge that each of these potential catastrophes is billions of years away. Perhaps by then we will have colonies on other planets in other solar systems. . . . Meanwhile he helps us picture the incomprehensible, which is the strength of this book—providing the reader a solid precipice to stand on while surveying The End of the World.

> Joan Levine, "For Young Readers: 'The End of the World'," in The New York Times Book Review (© 1975 by The New York Times Company; reprinted by permission), March 2, 1975, p. 8.

HARRY C. STUBBS

[In his *The End of the World*,] Branley speculates on a number of possible ways in which the earth will eventually become uninhabitable. He has been only moderately successful in digesting a very complex subject. . . . He has not managed to avoid being dogmatic. He has also followed a couple of standard mistakes. It is about four million tons of mass, not of hydrogen, which the sun's fusion reaction consumes (the hydrogen loses only about a third of one percent of its mass in the reaction, so over a billion tons of hydrogen are used). The Roche limit value is that for a satellite of equal density with its primary; for a less dense body like our own moon the value would be larger. Granting that the distinction is beyond the grasp of the intended readers, why not mention only the correct figure? I am dubious about the statement that the early earth was covered by deep layers of ice, and I take strong objection to the claim that carbon dioxide would act as a "mirror" to reflect solar radiation back into space. It is generally credited with enhancing the greenhouse effect, keeping the heat in. The speculations themselves are interesting, but I would have been happier if their underlying reasons had been brought out more clearly. It seems to me that this might have provided more stimulation for readers to investigate the pertinent sciences more deeply.

Harry C. Stubbs, "'The End of the World'," in Appraisal: Science Books for Young People *(copyright © 1975 by the Children's Science Book Review Committee), Vol. 8, No. 2, Spring, 1975, p. 10.*

KIRKUS REVIEWS

Pointing out the alarming rate at which man's demand for energy has grown and will continue to grow, Branley examines possible methods for getting the most out of the fast dwindling fossil fuels which will nevertheless have to provide all our power for the next few years, then reviews the drawbacks, advantages and relative likelihood of nuclear fission and fusion, solar installations, and geothermal, wind, hydroelectric and tidal power [in *Energy for the Twenty-First Century*]. Considered too are problems and possibilities of storing energy, and Branley even mentions some intriguing though admittedly far out ideas such as laser-lithium fusion and using the gravitation of a black hole to generate electricity. The view throughout is calm, leaning toward optimism. One of many such surveys and no improvement over [Laurence A.] Pringle's *Energy* . . . , but you can rely on Branley for standable, technically reliable explanations.

"Younger Non-Fiction: 'Energy for the Twenty-First Century'," in Kirkus Reviews *(copyright © 1975 The Kirkus Service, Inc.), Vol. XLIII, No. 16, August 15, 1975, p. 921.*

ETHANNE SMITH

Without launching into arguments for the advisability of America's going metric, the author does state [in *Measure with Metric*] that most of the world uses the metric system. He then involves his readers in a series of simple projects to learn and absorb metric measures. . . . It is all so clear and practical, moving in such orderly sequence, that reluctant Americans of any age could profit from this introduction to the inevitable.

Ethanne Smith, "'Measure with Metric'," in Appraisal: Science Books for Young People *(copyright © 1976 by the Children's Science Book Review Committee), Vol. 9, No. 1, Winter, 1976, p. 11.*

HARRY C. STUBBS

[In *How Did We Find Out About Energy?*] Isaac Asimov gives us a history of the development of man's intellectual concept of energy; [in *Energy for the 21st Century*] Franklyn Branley confines his discussion of the basic concept to a brief first chapter and devotes most of the book to a consideration of practical energy sources. (p. 182)

Since Branley discusses the abstract concept of energy only in the first chapter, the idea does not come across too clearly. For example, the discussion of energy as work done against a force field (such as gravity) is rather weak; the distinction between recoverable and irrecoverable energy is missed. In the rest of the book, the history of man's increasing demand for

energy is especially well done; the quantitative examples are good. . . .

Some of his details are questionable. In the nuclear chapter he speaks of the heat wasted by atomic power plants and of the damage done to the environment; he fails to mention that a fossil fuel plant wastes at least as much heat in producing the same power. On page 30, he perpetuates the superstition that a nuclear power plant can explode like a nuclear bomb. All in all, Asimov is more optimistic about the energy situation than Branley. Whether anyone without an advanced degree in physics is qualified to choose between their viewpoints seems debatable. (p. 183)

Harry C. Stubbs, "Views on Science Books: 'Energy for the 21st Century'," in The Horn Book Magazine *(copyright © 1976 by the Horn Book, Inc., Boston), Vol. LII, No. 2, April, 1976, pp. 182-83.*

HARRY C. STUBBS

I like Branley's approach of describing the earth as it would be seen from another part of the universe [in *A Book of the Planet Earth for You*]. He contrasts what would be obvious to a distant observer with what would be obscure when one is too close—such things as the shape, the rotation, and the other motions of our planet. In the process, he does a good job of making clear how we actually did learn some of these facts.

There are some errors, mostly arithmetical, which even a young reader should be able to spot if he has been trained to read critically. On page 71, the figures given for Earth's distance from the sun suggest that there are 16 kilometers in a mile instead of 1.6; on page 78 the implication seems to be that there are only 0.16 kilometers per mile. However, on other pages, figures implying the correct ratio are provided. The inconsistency should be obvious to the careful reader; and if he cannot decide which pages to believe, he should at least be moved to check elsewhere.

Some of the statements are a bit dogmatic; I am not at all sure that "Earth is the only one of the nine planets that is teeming with life." In any case, the book should be fun for young readers. If they find the few inconsistencies, so much the better; it will help preserve them from growing up with the conviction that the written word is infallible.

Harry C. Stubbs, "Views on Science Books: 'A Book of the Planet Earth for You'," in The Horn Book Magazine *(copyright © 1976 by the Horn Book, Inc., Boston), Vol. LII, No. 2, April, 1976, p. 183.*

ROBERT D. GEHRZ

[In *Astronomy*, cowriters Franklyn M. Branley and Mark R. Chartrand, III and illustrator Helmut K. Wimmer] have taken a refreshing approach in their presentation of astronomy and astrophysics for the nonmathematically oriented undergraduate student. Traditionally, the beginning student is asked to suffer through a lengthy introduction that details the historical development of astronomy. . . .

Astronomy begins with the contents of the universe and the cosmological implications of recent important observations. The reader is thus able to approach the remainder of the text with a clear view of how the microscopic components, such as planets, stars, and galaxies, are related to the macroscopic structure of the universe. . . .

The authors have included many topics often omitted from introductory texts, such as experiments on the frontiers of astrophysical research. . . .

Chapter 19, "The Search for Life—Is Anybody There?" will be of particular interest to today's student, who belongs to a generation for which manned space travel and exploration may become commonplace. The section on extraterrestrial communication addresses a topic that attracts many students to introductory astronomy courses. The authors maintain credibility by describing recent scientific experiments in extraterrestrial communications, such as the searches for coherent radio signals and the inclusion of an identification plaque aboard Pioneer 10.

The book will also appeal to the beginning amateur astronomer, for whom Chapter 14 and the appendixes give a reasonable introduction to the locations of the constellations and brighter stars. A set of star charts would have been helpful. Also, the omission of southern hemisphere constellations is disappointing.

In general, the text is lucid and mathematical concepts are presented in a manner that should be easily understood by the student who lacks a strong technical background. In some instances, a more quantitative treatment would be helpful. For example, a formula for the resolving power of a telescope might emphasize the fact that this property depends strongly on the wavelength at which the instrument is used.

On the other hand, the sections on terrestrial and celestial coordinate systems are tactfully arranged. The authors keep the discussion concise and let the excellent conceptual diagrams speak for themselves. (p. 54)

Over all, *Astronomy* presents modern astrophysics in a very readable fashion, with the discussion structured to maintain the reader's interest. Amateurs and students alike should find this a valuable addition to the list of introductory texts. (p. 55)

Robert D. Gehrz, "Books and the Sky: 'Astronomy'," in Sky and Telescope (© 1976 Sky Publishing Corporation), Vol. 52, No. 1, July, 1976, pp. 54-5.

DAVID G. HOAG

The imaginative manner of presenting astronomy in [*A Book of Planet Earth For You*] is clever; but unfortunately, the execution of it is careless. A hypothetical astronomer on a fictitious planet "Omega," elsewhere in our galaxy, describes his observations of earth and our solar system. The astronomer observes that our earth "turns 365¼ times while it goes around its star." Actually he would see it turn 366¼ times (adding one extra turn to the number of days in our year for the one revolution about the sun). Perhaps the author could be excused for this somewhat subtle point. But, he cannot be excused for saying on page fifty-four that the Foucault pendulum would always "be lined up with the same stars." Not so—only at the North or South Pole would this happen. An even more serious error on page seventy-one, both on a figure and in the text, has the earth one billion, five hundred million kilometers from the sun. That is ten times too far. . . . In a bit of whimsey in the back, the author credits an imaginative consultant on Omega. He would have been better served by a real scientist or engineer on earth to proofread his work. Instead, a potentially very good book came out poorly. (pp. 11-12)

David G. Hoag, "'A Book of Planet Earth for You'," in Appraisal: Science Books for Young People (copy-

right © 1976 by the Children's Science Book Review Committee), Vol. 9, No. 3, Fall, 1976, pp. 11-12.

DAVID E. NEWTON

[*Energy for the 21st Century*] is about the most intelligent, most sophisticated, most clearly-written book for children about energy I have yet to see. The author does an outstanding job of describing just about every scientific and technological aspect of the present debate about energy use in this country (and, maybe, the world). My only concern is that no attention is given to the political, social, economic, and ethical issues involved in energy production and use. I can hardly criticize an author for a book he didn't intend to write, but anyone who takes such a sophisticated and intelligent approach to this topic perhaps might at least consider the enormous non-scientific factors involved in energy production and use. (pp. 12-13)

David E. Newton, "'Energy for the 21st Century'," in Appraisal: Science Books for Young People (copyright © 1976 by the Children's Science Book Review Committee), Vol. 9, No. 3, Fall, 1976, pp. 12-13.

KIRKUS REVIEWS

Though the subject is mind-boggling and still vastly unsettled, [in *Black Holes, White Dwarfs, and Superstars*] Branley comes through once again and gives us a splendidly clear, totally non-mathematical presentation of what is currently known about the life cycles of stars. . . . Whether the question is how we know T Tauri [stars] are young; why stars move as they do and some of the older ones pulsate; what makes novas explode; or how, in "neutron stars" and then black holes, atoms themselves can collapse until volume becomes zero and density reaches infinity—Branley is always on hand to explain the process of discovery, review rival theories, or, in the end, admit that neither "ordinary laws of science" nor "the special ones discovered by Einstein" seem to apply. Fuel for cosmic thoughts.

"Young Adult Non-Fiction: 'Black Holes, White Dwarfs, and Superstars'," in Kirkus Reviews (copyright © 1976 The Kirkus Service, Inc.), Vol. XLIV, No. 19, October 1, 1976, p. 1104.

DAPHNE ANN HAMILTON

Stars are not the steady, eternal beacons we short-lived groundlings once believed them to be. Our own sun, average yellow main-sequence star that it is, was once an RR Lyrae variable, will be a nova, a red giant, a white dwarf, and possibly end as a black hole—incredible changes which will take millions of years or a few seconds, depending on the stage in its life cycle. . . . [In *Black Holes, White Dwarfs, and Superstars*] Branley gives a clear and concise account of current *theories* (the word is continually stressed) on the nature and significance of these intriguing stellar objects and of stellar evolution in general. . . . This book requires some background, but for those interested in the newer horizons of astronomy it presents a good deal of material not generally available outside of texts. Whether it might be a little too simplified and orderly, I will leave to the experts, but it is a clear, understandable, and most interesting introduction to a complex subject, and should be of use in either adult or comprehensive juvenile collections. (pp. 9-10)

Daphne Ann Hamilton, "'Black Holes, White Dwarfs, and Superstars'," in Appraisal: Science Books for Young People (copyright © 1977 by the Children's Science Book Review Committee), Vol. 10, No. 3, Fall, 1977, pp. 9-10.

DAVID E. NEWTON

An author has to be really brave to write about this subject nowadays. Information about our solar system is arriving fast and furious, and it's fairly certain that anything in a book dated 1978 will be somewhat incomplete or out of date by the time it appears in print. That's the case with [*The Nine Planets,* the] latest revision of a book that first appeared twenty years ago. The author has obviously made an effort to incorporate the latest information on the planets, and has been successful to a limited extent. Still, information obtained in the last five years does not seem to have made its way into this revision to the extent that it might have. In the case that would have been of most interest—Mars—there is a striking failure to bring us up to date on the most recent information and theories. The text also suffers from the author's obsession to tell us a little bit about everything remotely connected with the planets. This concern means that many essentially irrelevant topics—thermocouples, ellipses, and Bode's Law for example—are treated so inadequately that they are not readily understandable. Most important of all, perhaps, is the deadliness of the text. It is, for the most part, a recital of unconnected and uninteresting facts. We are at the point now that someone could write a really fascinating story of the planets, making the tale an object lesson in the way scientists work. Here is a chance to show students what scientists do with conflicting and inadequate data. The last chapter of the text makes a beginning in this direction. Finally, the sexist use of "man" whenever "humans" is meant is especially striking in a field in which women have had so much to contribute! What we really should have had here is a totally new book on the planets, not another revision of a twenty-year old text.

David E. Newton, "'The Nine Planets'," in Appraisal: Science Books for Young People (copyright © 1979 by the Children's Science Book Review Committee), Vol. 12, No. 2, Spring, 1979, p. 10.

CONNIE TYRRELL

[In *The Electromagnetic Spectrum*] Branley brings his trademark of good scientific writing, clear, accurate and concise, to bear on a difficult albeit interesting subject: the spectrum of invisible radiation that abounds throughout the universe from radio waves, light waves, infrared and ultraviolet radiation to x-rays and gamma rays. . . . Hard-to-grasp concepts, such as the invisibility and speed of light, are defined in context. Equations and formulas are frequent and require effort to understand as well as some mathematical background. But Branley has succeeded in presenting a complex topic with clarity, while stimulating curiosity and encouraging experimentation and study. Little on the subject for any age group exists, and what is available is primarily found in scattered chapters of physics books.

Connie Tyrrell, "Junior High Up: 'The Electromagnetic Spectrum'," in School Library Journal (reprinted from the November, 1979 issue of School Library Journal, published by R. R. Bowker Co./ A Xerox Corporation; copyright © 1979), Vol. 26, No. 3, November, 1979, p. 84.

HARRY C. STUBBS

There have been several books on the space shuttle project lately. . . . Franklyn Branley's contribution [*Columbia and Beyond: The Story of the Space Shuttle*] is distinguished for going more deeply than most into the future missions in which the shuttle is expected to play a part. His descriptions of the shuttle itself and of the projects and operations are clear and generally accurate, though if the diameter of the space rescue ball is really 86.36 centimeters (34 inches), as he states, the human figure in the diagram is certainly a midget. The author gives many good reasons for taking some of our industries into space, though no very new ones.

Harry C. Stubbs, "Views on Science Books: 'Columbia and Beyond: The Story of the Space Shuttle'," in The Horn Book Magazine (copyright © 1979 by The Horn Book, Inc., Boston), Vol. LV, No. 6, December, 1979, p. 687).

HARRY C. STUBBS

[*The Electromagnetic Spectrum: Key to the Universe* is a] fine summary of the history of observation and reasoning which led to our present understanding of the phenomenon by which we see, communicate over long distances, and investigate both the largest and smallest parts of the universe. Mr. Branley nicely covers the connection between electricity and magnetism investigated by Faraday, the theoretical handling of that relationship worked out by James Clerk Maxwell, and even the rather difficult concept of radiation as being both wave and particle at the same time. The ways in which the behavior of radiation helped elucidate the structure of the atom is clearly explained, allowing for the nonmathematical treatment required by the intended audience and the consequent need to depend on analogy. Even the practical uses which follow from the properties and behavior of the various wavelengths of "light" are well covered.

Harry C. Stubbs, "Views on Science Books: 'The Electromagnetic Spectrum: Key to the Universe'," in The Horn Book Magazine (copyright © 1979 by The Horn Book, Inc., Boston), Vol. LV, No. 6, December, 1979, p. 689.

MARILYN KAYE

Beginning with a simple, cursory description of each of the 12 zodiac signs and their alleged characteristics, this coherent, if somewhat lifeless, discussion [*Age of aquarius: you and astrology*] offers an explanation as to how the belief in astrology developed and spread from ancient Babylonia through the Eastern world. There is a thorough account of various symbols and meanings that are involved in astrological forecasting, and detailed instructions are presented for readers who want to try their hand at casting their own horoscopes. Although Branley consistently treats the subject in an objective fashion, he dismisses belief in astrology at the end of the book by stating, "Astrology will continue to be popular as long as people allow themselves to believe in magic rather than in themselves." While it is certainly true that astrology has no credibility as a science, the sudden appearance of this skeptical line seems abrupt and rather curt. Despite this minor flaw, the book has value in its serious approach to a trendy topic. (pp. 553-54)

Marilyn Kaye, "Children's Books: 'Age of Aquarius: You and Astrology'," in Booklist (reprinted by permission of the American Library Association; copy-

right © 1979 by the American Library Association), Vol. 76, No. 7, December 1, 1979, pp. 553-54.

KIRKUS REVIEWS

This disappointingly slight offering from Branley [*Age of Aquarius: You and Astrology,*] is nevertheless an improvement on [Larry] Kettelkamp's *Astrology* (1973), which made over-much of "the scientific basis of astrology." After the usual profiles of Leos, Cancers, Scorpios, and so on, the usual survey of astrology in history from the Babylonians on, and the usual explanation of how horoscopes are cast using signs, rising signs, houses, planets, and aspects of planets, Branley does answer the question "Do objects in the sky really affect our lives" with a mild negative. The stars and planets are too far away to affect us, he says; ancients made up astrology because they didn't understand why the planets moved as they did; and "most scientists agree that astrology is . . . magic based upon the supposed connection between events which in truth are not connected." This certainly isn't the devastating analysis that [Roy A.] Gallant provided (along *with* more details on casting horoscopes) in his *Astrology* (1974). But for casual astrologers who can't be bothered with Gallant's depth, this is certainly harmless.

> *"Younger Non-Fiction: 'Age of Aquarius: You and Astrology',"* in Kirkus Reviews *(copyright © 1980 The Kirkus Service, Inc.), Vol. XLVIII, No. 3, February 1, 1980, p. 129.*

NORMAN METZGER

Although marred by an apocalyptic start, in which an alternative future of feast versus famine is limned, [*Feast or Famine? The Energy Future*] does a creditable job of presenting a melange of information on energy—its uses, sources and forms. The child reading this might wonder how that view fits with what is actually happening now: reduced oil consumption, vigorous energy conservation, in short, a future in which the manner of our lives is basically retained, albeit with energy thrift becoming a norm of transportation planning, housing design and industrial manufacturing. There are occasional gee whizzes ("within a few decades, people will not need to 'go shopping'") and some asides spurious to the intent of the book ("the race to produce the biggest bombs, the fastest planes, the most powerful tanks, the heaviest and fastest ships is nonsense"). These blemishes are, however, redeemed by the author's overall effect: accurate, reasonably fair, and for the most part, providing a careful description and assessment of various energy options. The part on nuclear fission power is particularly well done, one that might even satisfy both sides of that debate.

> *Norman Metzger, "Children's Reviews: 'Feast or Famine? The Energy Future',"* in Science Books & Films *(copyright 1981 by the American Association for the Advancement of Science), Vol. 16, No. 5 (May/June, 1981), p. 273.*

H(esba) F(ay) Brinsmead

1922-

Australian novelist for young adults and younger children.

Brinsmead is among the first Australian writers to write specifically for young adults. Her belief that their needs and feelings are important is reflected in her novels. With directness,
understanding, and relevance, she depicts realistic characters
learning to cope with themselves and their world. Brinsmead
began writing for a teenage audience when her own sons reached
adolescence and she discovered the lack of suitable, interesting
titles for them. She decided to write novels which would tell
the truth about life, doing so with hope and humor; her respected position among young adult readers suggests the
achievement of her goal.

Brinsmead is considered adept at portraying background and
characterization. She sets her books in both urban and rural
Australia, an unfamiliar landscape to most readers, but one
she describes evocatively; her stories reflect both the beauty
and the harshness of this land. She often writes both inside
and outside her characters, analyzing their emotions while
narrating their adventures. Usually concentrating on groups
rather than on individuals, she shows the growth and development of each member during the course of her stories. Brinsmead creates memorable adolescents and equally well-defined
adult characters.

Many of Brinsmead's books deal with social problems and the
tensions caused by racial and class prejudice. In her first novel,
Pastures of the Blue Crane, Ryl discovers she is part Aborigine;
in *Listen to the Wind* a black boy and white girl go into partnership to restore a trawler in a fishing community where
whites and blacks, both upper and lower class, live alongside
each other. *Beat of the City* is perhaps her most controversial
work. Brinsmead drops her usual role of detached narrator
to angrily expose the attitudes and actions of youth in the mid-
sixties. Although Brinsmead's overt authorial voice is often
considered moralistic and pretentious, critics recognize the
relevance of her subject and the accuracy of its depiction.
Brinsmead has drawn from her own childhood for *Longtime
Passing* and several of her recent books for younger readers.

Brinsmead's flaws, such as her lack of discipline, repetitiveness, and tendency to spoil the flow of her narratives with
tedious messages, are often felt to be compensated for by her
sincerity and exhilaration. Her genuine interest in young people and knowledge of human nature are perhaps the main
reasons for Brinsmead's universal appeal. Brinsmead received
the Australian Children's Book Council book of the year award
in 1965 for *Pastures of the Blue Crane* and in 1972 for *Longtime
Passing*. (See also *Contemporary Authors*, Vols. 21-24, rev. ed.)

H. F. Brinsmead-Hungerford

THE JUNIOR BOOKSHELF

[H. F. Brinsmead,] like Nan Chauncy and Patricia Wrightson,
writes within the narrow context of an Australian scene but
with an awareness of human values which is universal.

Pastures of the Blue Crane is a most appealing story of a young
girl's growth into womanhood. The theme is common enough,

though rarely carried out well; what gives an original slant to
this story is the honest treatment of an unfamiliar situation. . . .
[Ryl] grows, beautifully and convincingly, before our eyes
from a cold, priggish snob into a delightfully alive, unpredictable human being. It is a lovely study. The setting too is
vividly evoked.

There remains a doubt whether this is a book for children. It
is beyond question a sensitive and true picture of adolescence. . . . It is in fact a book for the odd child, and after all
we have plenty of books for the ordinary child.

> *"For the Intermediate Library: 'Pastures of the Blue
> Crane'," in* The Junior Bookshelf, *Vol. 28, No. 5,
> November, 1964, p. 327.*

THE TIMES LITERARY SUPPLEMENT

Pastures of the Blue Crane pretends to be a serious book, while
really being a romantic one. This is a pity, because if Mrs.
Brinsmead had been less ambitious, it would have been a good
romantic novel, about slightly older teenagers, which is just
what the younger ones like best. . . . It is quite a good story,
with some likeable characters, but Mrs. Brinsmead's intro-

duction of the race problem overwhelms it, and the discovery that the heroine is the half-caste boy's sister is too easy a solution of a difficult problem.

> *"Socio-Romantic: Novels for Older Girls," in* The Times Literary Supplement *(© Times Newspapers Ltd. (London) 1964; reproduced from* The Times Literary Supplement *by permission), No. 3274, November 26, 1964, p. 1074.**

THE TIMES LITERARY SUPPLEMENT

[*Season of the Briar* provides a] sense of real freshness. Here is a double story, converging in the end to make one: of a party of youngsters spending a summer with a weed-spraying unit, and another party who are bush-walking. The beginning has a tone of rather chummy facetiousness, but once the two parties arrive in a lost valley in Tasmania . . . , a fine sharpness sets in: beautiful natural descriptions, a great relish for oddity of character and for the irritations that arise among young people: and a final drama of truly breath-taking quality. . . . One of the virtues of this very distinguished story lies in the way it glances at the limitations of conventional heroism.

> *"A Wider World," in* The Times Literary Supplement *(© Times Newspapers Ltd. (London) 1965; reproduced from* The Times Literary Supplement *by permission), No. 3328, December 9, 1965, p. 1138.**

COLIN FIELD

[H. F. Brinsmead's] quality shows itself particularly in her characters' response to [the crisis in *Season of the Briar*]. There is Fred—apparently dull and phlegmatic—whose response is practical and realistic. And there is Matt, the philosophy student—lively, intelligent and idealistic—who overestimates his physical capacities, underestimates the powers of nature, and who becomes a liability to the rescue parties.

Season of the Briar also has the flavour of the best mountaineering and polar travel accounts, because the author is especially skilful and imaginative in recording the effects on her characters of the extremes of topography and of climate.

This book is not just another adventure story written for adolescents . . . for the action is the outcome of character. There is no manipulation of characters in order to give the reader a superficial thrill.

> *Colin Field, "Book Reviews: 'Season of the Briar'," in* The School Librarian and School Library Review, *Vol. 14, No. 1, March, 1966, p. 105.*

NANCY QUINT WEISS

The character stereotypes [in **"Pastures of the Blue Crane"**] and the busy plot strain the reader's credulity; and the race problem is so artificially imposed on the story one has the uncomfortable feeling that the author has used it solely to give her book tone and substance.

> *Nancy Quint Weiss, "For the Young Reader: 'Pastures of the Blue Crane'," in* The New York Times Book Review *(© 1966 by The New York Times Company; reprinted by permission), April 10, 1966, p. 20.*

ZENA SUTHERLAND

[*Pastures of the Blue Crane* is a] long junior novel, naive in one sense, sophisticated in another—and very good reading. [It has] a plot both romantic and provocatively different. . . . At the age of sixteen, [Amaryllis Merewether] is told by a lawyer that she has inherited half her father's fortune; the other half belongs to a man sitting across the room. This impoverished pensioner is her grandfather. The two go off to an inherited property and find the joys of family life, belonging, creative work, friendly neighbors, the beauty of nature, et cetera. The exotic quality of the topography and flora frequently described save the exposition from dullness, and the important message and theme woven through all this Utopia is race prejudice. Ryl's kindest friend is Perry, who is a quartercaste; Ryl is incensed at the occasional barbed remarks directed at Perry, but he takes such remarks very calmly. (In fact, he's almost too good to be true.) . . . The fact that Perry turns out to be Ryl's brother seems slightly contrived; the fact that Ryl is hardly shaken by her discovery seems a reaction unbelievably mature in a girl so young. However, the familial relationships, the peer group camaraderie, the high moral tone, and the message of the intrinsic worth of man all give the book strength. (pp. 143-44)

> *Zena Sutherland, "New Titles for Children and Young People: 'Pastures of the Blue Crane'," in* Bulletin of the Center for Children's Books *(reprinted by permission of The University of Chicago Press; copyright 1966 by the University of Chicago), Vol. 19, No. 9, May, 1966, pp. 143-44.*

GEOFFREY TREASE

In *Beat of the City* we have an outstanding illustration not only of the Australian efflorescence but of the revolution in themes, attitudes and vocabulary that has transformed children's fiction as a whole in the last decade or two. The particular city is Melbourne, but in a sense it could be any modern city. Here is the universal teenage world of puzzled parents and their sulky, sultry offspring—a world of transistors and motor-bikes, deception and delinquency, flick-knives and jazz groups and the juvenile courts, a world with an understandable fascination for countless boys and girls who never experience its seamier excitements for themselves.

I can hear the snorts of shocked grandfathers leafing through this book on Christmas afternoon. The way these four young characters talk—this appalling, mysterious, vivid Antipodean slang! (Isn't American bad enough?) And their truculent slogan: 'We are the only generation to be born superior to our parents!' And the things they *do*, and the things that (nearly) get done to them! Why, here on page 177 it's obvious that Raylene is about to be raped by Blade O'Reilley and his Death Riders—of course the author doesn't *say* so, or use any offensive expressions, but a child is sure to wonder why the boy hero told her so urgently: 'Get out, fast!' In the very next paragraph he gets someone's knee in the groin. That could never have happened to one of [G. A.] Henty's lads.

> *Geoffrey Trease, "Golden Age," in* New Statesman *(© 1966 The Statesman & Nation Publishing Co. Ltd.), Vol. 72, No. 1861, November 11, 1966, p. 708.**

THE TIMES LITERARY SUPPLEMENT

[*Beat of the City*] is a rich, honest, sometimes funny book. Unusually some of the real agonies—and ugliness—of the adolescent world come through. But there is also a tiresome tendency to hammer pretentiously poetic moral judgments and analyses, till they seem more or less facile.

> *"Groups and Gangs," in* The Times Literary Supplement *(© Times Newspapers Ltd. (London) 1966; reproduced from* The Times Literary Supplement *by permission), No. 3378, November 24, 1966, p. 1085.**

THE JUNIOR BOOKSHELF

[*Beat of the City*] is a mature book. . . . The author expounds the attitudes of the "beat generation" with sympathetic insight, at the same time showing she thinks them wrong-headed. The city of Melbourne is portrayed with the same critical affection. The principal characters are so alive that the reader develops a real concern for them.

> *"For the Intermediate Library: 'Beat of the City',"* in The Junior Bookshelf, *Vol. 31, No. 1, February, 1967, p. 65.*

ROBERT BELL

Modern youth is wont to complain that it is misunderstood; this author at least shows a deep understanding of the outlook, motives and values of contemporary adolescents, together with a rare sympathy and compassion. [*Beat of the City*] introduces the reader to a number of young people of wide diversity of character and circumstance whose lives touch each other, and tells of the effects this has on them. Adults play their part, too, and are just as vividly and sympathetically portrayed. Not the least dominant is the city [of Melbourne] itself, which virtually projects an identity of its own. The book has a sincere and genuine realism which will hold the attention and command the admiration of all teenage readers. . . .

> *Robert Bell, "Book Reviews: 'Beat of the City',"* in The School Librarian and School Library Review, *Vol. 15, No. 1, March, 1967, p. 87.*

DOROTHY M. BRODERICK

Season of the Briar . . . is not a good book by any standard. . . . There is foolish heroism (Matt) and studied cowardice (Douglas) and remorse by Bruce over his failure as a leader. . . .

The lack of a central character is not necessarily a defect, but the unfocused confusion of *Season of the Briar* is too much. Ivan Southall's *Ash Road* and *Hills End* are much better representatives of Australian books which depict the reaction of characters under stress.

> *Dorothy M. Broderick, "Children's Book World: 'Season of the Briar',"* in Book World—Chicago Tribune *(© 1967 Postrib Corp.; reprinted by permission of* Chicago Tribune *and* The Washington Post*), September 24, 1967, p. 22.*

MARGERY FISHER

In *A Sapphire for September* one character (the prospector Charlie Light) and one Blue Mountain township (the Old Vale) remind us of the past. In the ghost town one house is inhabited—the Huntsmans' home, built by an ancestor; the family stands for continuity, a factor dominant, though they hardly realise it, in the lives of the youths and girls whose talk is all of the present. They are on an expedition, these young people, to find uncut gem-stones, when they envelop the Huntsmans in their friendliness and, hearing the old house is threatened by speculators, work out a wild but surprisingly successful plot to rout them. . . . [Binny and Adam] gather the action round them but the author manages her narrative so skilfully that there is never a feeling of unbalance. She has already taken us into several odd pockets of Australian life. In this book the details of gem-hunting are enough to attract a reader but it is the way the various characters *see* sapphires and opals which will keep those readers till the last page. (p. 976)

> *Margery Fisher, "Under the Southern Cross," in her* Growing Point, *Vol. 6, No. 4, October, 1967, pp. 975-77.**

THE TIMES LITERARY SUPPLEMENT

At least half the anguish of adolescence is ecstatic clutching at the treasures of an opening world. Growing pains may come largely from indigestion, from too big and greedily gulped a helping of life.

So it is with H. F. Brinsmead's Binny Flambeau (in *A Sapphire for September*). . . . The author draws an irresistible picture of her absurd, adorable heroine in the pangs of first love. . . . After the absorbing, always convincing adventures, dramatic and comic, which form the action of the book, Binny has enjoyed—or suffered—many experiences, has visited worlds outside the crowded streets of Sydney, and is on the threshold of another discovery, of her self.

A Sapphire for September is one of those books into which the reader dips again and again and each time pulls out a different kind of gem: evocative descriptions of city and desert not grafted on to the narrative but growing out of it; portraits of colourful people, all individual, sometimes a shade larger than life but never exaggerated, all—even the nasty ones—drawn with an affectionate understanding; as much as anything a passionate concern for the beauty of stone and the technique of handling it.

Is it a quality of young countries to find serious things funny? Mrs. Brinsmead has in the richest measure this quality, which is to be found in so much of the vigorous literature of Australia.

> *"Overture, Beginners . . . ,"* in The Times Literary Supplement *(© Times Newspapers Ltd. (London) 1967; reproduced from* The Times Literary Supplement *by permission), No. 3431, November 30, 1967, p. 1155.**

THE JUNIOR BOOKSHELF

[*A Sapphire for September* is the] best Brinsmead yet—it will be interesting a few decades hence to know how many New Australians were inspired by reading her books in the '60s and '70s, though her main message is not "Come to Australia" but "Come to life". Her Binny Flambeau is lively enough, though somewhat rootless and aimless until dreamer and student Adam sweeps her into a group of rock-hounds in Sydney. She cannot understand Adam but adores him with a puppy-love whose waxing and waning is neatly conveyed as the group, a wildly assorted bunch, converges on a deserted township. . . . Full of young people and their talk, but with a memorable ballast of older people, like old Charley Light the gemspecker who sees that Binny might find gems but will never keep them and tells her to remember the mountain agate: "It's got a strong kind of beauty. Not much fire, but strong. And it's everywhere". Mrs. Brinsmead makes the reader feel people like that are everywhere, too. (pp. 385-86)

> *"For Children From Ten to Fourteen: 'A Sapphire for September'," in* The Junior Bookshelf, *Vol. 31, No. 6, December, 1967, pp. 385-86.*

JEAN C. THOMSON

Despite an uncommonly good writing style, the author's faintly ironical air [in *Beat of the City*] will seem to rebuke sensitive readers even before they've had a chance to get involved. Sounding like a parent all the way (calling a transistor radio a "perfect anesthetic," for example), the author remains an observer with an ax to grind—the reverse of S. E. Hinton's attitude in *The Outsiders*.

> *Jean C. Thomson, "Junior High Up: 'Beat of the City'," in* School Library Journal, *an appendix to* Library Journal *(reprinted from the January 15, 1968 issue of* School Library Journal, *published by R. R. Bowker Co./A Xerox Corporation; copyright © 1968), Vol. 93, No. 2, January 15, 1968, p. 80.*

E. N. BEWICK

[Brinsmead's] characterization is always strongly individual. Some of the people about whom she writes might well be termed eccentric, but all of them are lively and real. She is in particular sympathy with the needs of adolescents and her portrait of Binny [in *A Sapphire for September*], with her alternating moods of gaiety and despair, should have an instant appeal to adolescent readers.

> *E. N. Bewick, "Eleven to Fifteen: 'A Sapphire for September'," in* The School Librarian and School Library Review, *Vol. 16, No. 1, March, 1968, p. 88.*

SIDNEY OFFIT

Introducing ["**Beat of the City**"] her tale of youngsters in search of identity in an Australian metropolis, H. F. Brinsmead observes, "In Melbourne that year the way-outs were in." For Melbourne read New York or San Francisco and this teen-age shibboleth seems no less appropriate. . . .

[The] author describes her native land vividly and often lyrically. But the more reflective reader will find Mrs. Brinsmead's swiftly moving narrative rarely pauses to give a penetrating look into either teenagers themselves or the symbols of their aspirations.

> *Sidney Offit, "New Books for Young Readers: 'Beat of the City'," in* The New York Times Book Review *(© 1968 by The New York Times Company; reprinted by permission), March 31, 1968, p. 30.*

THE TIMES LITERARY SUPPLEMENT

[*Isle of the Sea Horse* contains] a perpetually interesting situation . . . —a group of people, isolated, fending for themselves, getting to know each other and themselves. The new book has a kinder view of human nature than [William Golding's] *Lord of the Flies*, for instance. The five learn to trust

and accept each other. . . . There is much of interest here but children need to recognize and identify. Ivan Southall's *To the Wild Sky* will mean much more to them. And it is disappointing that, in trying to produce something so very different, Mrs. Brinsmead has lost all the zest and pace of her last book, *A Sapphire for September*. (p. 1203)

> *"Half a World Away," in* The Times Literary Supplement *(© Times Newspapers Ltd. (London) 1969; reproduced from* The Times Literary Supplement *by permission), No. 3529, October 16, 1969, pp. 1202-03.**

MARGERY FISHER

This very ambitious Robinsonnade [*Isle of the Sea Horse*] does not entirely come off—partly perhaps because the author sets herself a task impossible to achieve even in an unusually long junior novel. Her castaways are as disparate as her groups of characters usually are. . . . Wrecked in a hurricane on an uninhabited island in the Great Barrier Reef, the group makes its shifting alignments while managing to sustain life and, more, to discover evidence of previous castaways, some very surprising. And there is the sea horse itself, symbol of freedom—symbol to the author, perhaps, of nature untamed by pushing civilisation. The book needs a harder, stiffer form to contain its many threads of feeling, of plot, of moral; but it is enlivened by the constant surprises—quirks of personal idiom, snatches of local colour—with which this author always delights her readers.

> *Margery Fisher, "Stories for the Teens: 'Isle of the Sea Horse'," in her* Growing Point, *Vol. 8, No. 5, November, 1969, p. 1426.*

MRS. G. V. BARTON

["**Isle of the Sea Horse**" contains plenty of emotional turmoil] which could, if over-exploited, become yet another agony-packed marathon, rather a feature of some current Australian fiction for young people.

However Mrs. Brinsmead handles her material with a restraint and lyricism reminiscent of her first and, in this reviewer's opinion, best book "**Pastures of the Blue Crane**". Emma is certainly her most sympathetic heroine to date, observed with a refreshing lack of that sense of condescension that has rather marred her last two books. Descriptions of desert island life are vivid, and there are some interesting sidelights on Australian history during the castaways' discoveries on the island.

> *Mrs. G. V. Barton, "Fiction: 'Isle of the Sea Horse'," in* Children's Book News *(copyright © 1969 by Baker Book Services Ltd.), Vol. 4, No. 6, November-December, 1969, p. 324.*

H. F. BRINSMEAD

I was painfully aware that, around the book shops, and especially around the most accessible ones—the shelves of paperbacks in the corner store, the stand in the railway station—there was not a great deal of material that catered to the teenager. So—thought I—"I'll do something about this!" I pictured myself turning out books that would *not* be so unsophisticated as to insult the young ego—*not* so trivial as to insult the young (and often deep) intelligence—yet not filled with adult experience far beyond their own, which I suspect leads to a distorted view of reality. I dreamed of a Utopia where any fourteen-year-old might walk up to a bookstall—any small bookstall near home—and pluck from the shelf a slice of good literature, suited to both his tastes and his development! . . .

Surely a young, growing person is entitled to hope, as well as truth! To glimpses of courage and fidelity, as well as cravenness and triumphant lust! And to a brand of humour that is not sick! I don't believe in telling lies—part of my writing programme was to tell the truth at all times—but surely a young person, growing up, is entitled to be armed, with moral and spiritual weapons, before being plunged head first into the battle!

So—feeling this way—I embarked on my first book for young people. . . . [What] I have to say can be said to them! Not that my characters are children. They are more like the young adults who are only a short step away from the age group of my readers. I have often noticed, with relish, how childish many adults are, and what good sense one sometimes sees in children. (p. 24)

And as to "how" do I write, for my chosen readers? Firstly, not so well as I'd like to, who does? The first essential, as I see it, is to discuss something that concerns them. I may be quite wrong, but (until recently, at least) I've felt that in this country they are interested in the present and the future, not the past. For this reason my books are set in the present; the writing of historical works I leave to others. Though my built-in barometer tells me that this may be changing. But even now, I have a feeling that it is perhaps only girls, in their wisdom, who like to escape into the past. I would like it if my books could be enjoyed by both boys and girls. I try to give them a "hard core". Now, in this day and age (as in any other) the most important problem facing adolescents is simply growing up. Now that I think of it, this seems to always be my theme.

Then again, a writer must always write to please himself. . . . I read once in a writer's magazine of a fox dancing, ". . . all alone in a clearing, waving his brush in the sun." So must the creative writer be. If his dance does not please himself, it is not a dance, but a pathetic travesty. So I write of things, people and places which please me, hoping that, as I am a microcosm of mankind, they will please others. And as I write, I play a sort of game with myself—a dance just for myself, that, if others see it, may please them, too; but if they don't, well never mind. This is a game of analogy. I propound to myself a theorem. In **"Season of the Briar"** it went something like this—"Life is like a mountain ahead of us all. There are people who are compulsive climbers; and other people who keep to a made pathway that finds a safe route over or around the mountain; and others who elect to live in a sheltered valley, at the foot of it." And so on. More recently, there was the idea behind **"Sapphire for September".**

It went somehow this-wise—"Life is a precious thing, it is a precious stone. Each of us has this gift. We can cut and polish it and make it into a jewel. We can buy things with it, or sell it or give it away; we can lose it and find it again—most likely in the ashes of past experience, perhaps changed, but indestructible. We might not know its true nature, but perhaps this does not matter; what matters is that, having been given the moonstone gift of life, we can go on to find the star stone of self-fulfilment; this way we may have a gem to lend and a gem to spend—finding ourselves, phoenix-like, when the dreams of childhood are nothing but ashes."

I think that this was the riddle that I set myself, behind the story of Binny Flambeau and her crazy friends. . . . Of course,

one can only write about people when one knows them very well. Because of this, I have to live with my people; their world has to be just as real to me as this other world, where I cook and shop and have my being. During the writing of the first draft of the book, one is still only making the acquaintance of one's characters. I write gropingly, mainly because at this time I can't be sure of their reactions. I have to feel my way. I could fall into the pit of setting the wrong tasks for the wrong people, so that they would be forced into doing things which they would not do, if left to themselves. The second time through, writing is easy, for, having worked out the correct circumstances, the characters will now take care of the rest.

When I set about writing **"Sapphire"**, my first step was to join a lapidary club. . . . All this time the characters were growing more and more clearcut, more irrepressible. But Binny Flambeau herself—I could not get close to her at first. "If only I could see her!" I thought. I took to watching out for her, among faces in crowds. One day I saw her. She was in a school uniform, hurrying to a train at peak hour, with another girl. The fleeting glimpse was enough. From the face of the unknown girl, Binny became tangible. From then on, she was as real to me as my own daughter would be, if I had one!

Now she's left home, of course, and gone out into the book shops. (Though not, unfortunately, to those railway station stalls!) But there are endless teenagers, fictitious amalgams of factual flesh and blood, with stories to be told—growing up has endless facets and connotations! No need to put the cover on the typewriter! (pp. 25-6)

> H. F. Brinsmead, *"How and Why I Write for Young People,"* in Bookbird, *Vol. VII, No. 4 (December 15, 1969), pp. 24-6.*

MARGERY FISHER

[In *Listen to the Wind*] there is a unique problem of class and colour. . . . H. F. Brinsmead explores the racial situation with understanding. . . . I am a little puzzled by the emotional content of the book. The actual given age of the two young people does not seem entirely borne out by their reaction to events nor by their attitude to each other, whether mildly romantic or comradely. . . . There is scope here for stronger and franker writing but it seems characteristic of this author that while she draws her backgrounds with a very mature force, her books leave the final impression of being rather longer versions of the good old "holiday adventure". (pp. 1580-81)

> *Margery Fisher, "Looking Inward," in her* Growing Point, *Vol. 9, No. 3, September, 1970, pp. 1578-81.**

THE TIMES LITERARY SUPPLEMENT

"Children's books"—what can be done with this awkward, misleading term? Readers here, of course, will know very well how nearly adult the novels can be that come within its scope. They may also have observed how increasingly fashionable is the fictional age-zone between 16 and 20 or so. . . . Has any one of our current leading dozen novelists yet resisted an experiment in this field? Probably not—and out of all of them, few can have attacked it with more personality and verve than H. F. Brinsmead, who has, in fact, preferred this "older" age-group from the start.

One has to remember that Brinsmead people are also Australian, in an Australian scene: suns burn brighter, spaces are vaster, landscapes wilder, humans more direct. Perhaps the Brinsmead approach might not match other settings; perhaps even here it imposes something of its own vigour. But in her novels the method does succeed; and *Listen to the Wind* is as characteristic a work as we may find.

How to describe this method? You take, as it were, a rich chunk of the Brinsmead life and landscape, then bring to the forefront a diverse set of characters, adult or younger (the young have the principal plotlines, but there are others). Running through also are one or two controversial ideas and some special expertise. In *Listen to the Wind,* idea, plotlines and expertise are fused through the friendship (in a small town on an island off the eastern Australian coast) of a white girl and a native (coloured) boy. . . .

A curious and exhilarating book, not all of it on the surface; not all of it to be absorbed at the first race through.

> *"Post-School Zone," in* The Times Literary Supplement *(© Times Newspapers Ltd. (London) 1970; reproduced from* The Times Literary Supplement *by permission), No. 3583, October 30, 1970, p. 1266.**

MRS. J. PATON WALSH

[*Listen to the Wind*] is basically a sentimental book; a love story in which everything comes all right in the end; it is also a very old-fashioned story, a long one, told with complete realism, describing a place and all its people faithfully until one knows it as well as anywhere: like a real place. The reader will also learn to sympathise both with the despised 'Islanders' and with Tam, who wants to get away from being one of them. Mrs. Brinsmead certainly justifies both her story and her way of telling it in this deeply satisfying, wise and tender book.

> *Mrs. J. Paton Walsh, "Fiction: 'Listen to the Wind'," in* Children's Book News *(copyright © 1970 by Baker Book Services Ltd.), Vol. 5, No. 6, November-December, 1970, p. 279.*

THE JUNIOR BOOKSHELF

Mrs. Brinsmead demonstrates once more her mastery of the social scene and her profound understanding of what makes humans tick [in *Listen to the Wind*]. Her demonstration is enlivened with wit and high humour; few writers today, whether they profess to write for children or for adults, have so keen and relevant a sense of fun.

The scene is O'Brian's Point. Places matter a great deal to this writer, and here she paints a beautiful picture of a broken-down settlement of blackfellers and poor whites. Here lives Bella Greenrush . . . , everybody's dream mum. One of her family is Tam who, alone of the Greenrushes, has ambition. He has, too, a white friend, the lovely teenage Loveday Smith. There are serious social problems implicit in the theme, and Mrs. Brinsmead shirks none of them; she explores them, however, with an understanding at once tender and realistic. The story, potentially tragic, is a comedy, occasionally—when Uncle Zac enters—even a farce.

Out of Australia, with its clash of contradictory cultures, comes yet another joyous, shrewd, devastatingly honest picture of ordinary folk tackling man-sized everyday problems. The setting is infinitely remote from our own and the problems very

different; it is difficult to believe, nevertheless, that . . . children will fail to recognise the truth and beauty of a fine story. (pp. 363-64)

> *"For Children from Ten to Fourteen: 'Listen to the Wind'," in* The Junior Bookshelf, *Vol. 34, No. 6, December, 1970, pp. 363-64.*

MARGERY FISHER

Who calls from afar? is built round a sturdy statement that we are all responsible for the future; is man capable of keeping the resolution recorded on the moon that he 'comes in peace'? The moral is well integrated in the story of a girl in her middle 'teens who leaves the urban rat race for back-of-beyond New South Wales and takes a job as secretary at an earth-station relaying messages via satellite to the United States. The flight of Apollo 11 provides the centrepiece for a story involving, as all H. F. Brinsmead's books do, a host of major and minor characters with their attendant prejudices and preoccupations. This could have been a first rate story but for two things—its excessive length and (both reason and result of this) its lack of consistency. In one sense this is a story with a message; from this point of view, the over-long preamble about Lyn Honeyfield and her new friend physicist Henry is in theory justified. In another sense it is the story of a journey—a hilarious, super-paced, brilliantly told saga. . . . Cut by a third, tightened up, this could have made a comic picaresque of a kind only too rare these days; as it is, it is a bit of a white elephant. (p. 1823)

> *Margery Fisher, "Travellers," in her* Growing Point, *Vol. 10, No. 5, November, 1971, pp. 1821-24.**

THE JUNIOR BOOKSHELF

There is much that is interesting in [*Who Calls From Afar?*], as, for instance, the description of the Earth Station with its complex instruments for telecommunication via "Fred" the satellite. There is humour and perhaps a message for young people too, for, as the Professor says, too many of our actions and thoughts are determined by "remote control", as are those of the cosmonauts, and it is essential that the pattern should be broken at times.

The author has a deep concern for young people and understands them, as is evident in this book as in her others, but the story is more superficial and not as absorbing as usual and the central characters are not as real as the four young people in *Beat of the City,* for instance, or Binny in *A Sapphire for September.*

> *"For Children from Ten to Fourteen: 'Who Calls from Afar?'" in* The Junior Bookshelf, *Vol. 35, No. 6, December, 1971, p. 393.*

FRANK EYRE

[H. F. Brinsmead writes] unusually varied stories of different aspects of Australian country and city life. Her first book, *Pastures of the Blue Crane,* dealt remarkably successfully and convincingly with the problems faced by a sixteen-year-old girl who . . . triumphs over a succession of setbacks, including the belated discovery that she is of part coloured blood. H. F. Brinsmead's books are all about adolescent girls and they are among the best examples of the newer type of children's book, which bridges the gap between the children's book proper and adult reading. *Beat of the City* dealt not altogether convincingly but courageously with under-privileged adolescents in Melbourne. Her later books are tending to become slightly 'fey', but she is the most promising of the new school of Australian writers. (pp. 166-67)

Frank Eyre, "Regional Writing," in his British Children's Books in the Twentieth Century *(copyright © 1971 by Frank Eyre; reprinted by permission of the publishers, E. P. Dutton & Co., Inc.; in Canada by Penguin Books Ltd.), Longman Books, 1971, Dutton, 1973, pp. 161-76.*

JOHN ROWE TOWNSEND

Mrs Brinsmead's novels are for teenagers and are mostly *about* teenagers. No pre-adolescent child has a significant part to play in any of them. The teenagers come and go, as teenagers will, in a crowd; they are always on the move. The books themselves are full of warmth and energy and tend to have large casts, plenty of incident, and unusual richness of background. Not only do things happen; people change and develop. All Mrs Brinsmead's books are concerned with what she herself calls 'the problem of how to cope with life'. They are also concerned with the stage which comes before coping: namely finding out who and what you are.

She is particularly good at drawing the teenager *as* teenager. Adolescent characters in novels by other contemporary writers (for instance Gwyn, Roger and Alison in Alan Garner's *The Owl Service;* Christina, Mark and Will in K. M. Peyton's *Flambards*) are shown as the people they essentially are and always will be. It is not difficult to imagine them at the ages of 25, 35 or 45. But Mrs Brinsmead's Syd and Sabie in *Beat of the City,* and Binny in *A Sapphire for September,* are specifically sixteen-year-olds, and their age is part of their character. Last year they were not as they are now; next year they will be different again; their self-discovery is still going on, and in discovering themselves they are still changing. (The difference here between Mrs Brinsmead and the other writers mentioned is not a matter of superiority or inferiority on either side; it lies partly in style of characterization, partly in the kind of person created.) And Mrs Brinsmead has an interesting way of moving into and out of her characters' minds, of seeing them now from inside, now from outside, in a way that gives perspective to her portraits. . . . If a generation gap exists— and in Mrs Brinsmead's books it exists in individual cases . . . , not as a general phenomenon—the author is on both sides of it.

A combination of sympathy and detachment in her treatment of teenagers is indeed one of Mrs Brinsmead's strengths. It is already apparent in her first book, *Pastures of the Blue Crane.* . . . Self-centred, stoical, snobby Ryl is one of those rare, infuriating heroines whom one doesn't much like but finds oneself caring about—presumably because the author, while seeing her clearly for the rather unlovable person she is, can also feel with her and perceive what she might become.

The four-dimensional character study of Ryl, over a period in which she changes greatly yet remains recognizably the same girl, is as fine in its way as anything Mrs Brinsmead has done. She has not again penetrated any individual to the same depth. Many of her young people are appealing, especially the girls: Gisela, the small person with the big voice and big boots in *Season of the Briar;* the cheerful urchin Binny in *A Sapphire for September;* sensitive Emma in *Isle of the Sea Horse.* But

they are more lightly sketched than Ryl, and the reader does not become involved with them in the same way. This is probably because of a tendency to put a group, rather than a single individual, at the centre of a story. Gisela, Binny and Emma can be considered as the heroines of the books in which they appear, but they do not dominate the scene. (pp. 39-41)

[*Beat of the City*] is not only a book about what happens to certain individuals; it is also a portrayal of a city and a composite study of the life of young people in it; it is an exploration, too, of certain values and relationships. It is a bold and forceful novel and, taken as a whole, is Mrs Brinsmead's most impressive book up to the time of writing. Where many authors have found it easier to concentrate on the enduring realities of human nature if they avoid those immediate surface details which are so hard to get right and so sure to fall out of date, *Beat of the City* is uncompromisingly contemporary. 'In Melbourne in 1965 the way-outs were in', it begins; and the Melbourne of 1965—no other time, no other place—is the setting of this story. And, paradoxically but deservedly, the sense of immediacy has so far proved lasting, for although it is no longer 1965 the feeling that everything is happening here and now remains fresh and strong.

The plot of *Beat of the City* is worked out in intricate detail: the characters are carefully balanced. (pp. 41-2)

Each character in turn moves into and out of the spotlight; but in spite of the lack of a continuous focus the story does not fall apart. What holds it together is the most impressive element of all, the city of Melbourne itself. Melbourne is alive on every page. . . . (p. 42)

The theme of the novel is the pursuit of happiness, as carried out by various people in various ways through the streets, homes and haunts of the city. Sabie's mother, expressing what it is safe to assume are the author's own views, contrasts true happiness—something to be built from your own inner resources—with an instant, ready-mixed substitute symbolized by the Tootle Bird, a mythical creature that 'probably nests in a box of empty Coke bottles' and has a call like the whirring noise of a fruit machine. This direct expression of view comes in a natural way at an appropriate moment, and does no harm to the story; but it is a pointer, I think, to the book's major flaw. One has a persistent sense that the characters and action have been designed to illustrate this very message.

The clash of values is direct and simple. Sabie and Raylene both look for 'kicks', and both come close to disaster. Mary and, increasingly, Syd create their own pleasures and are sensible and constructive. The good girl Mary, whose approach to life is the opposite of that summed up in the quest for the Tootle Bird, seems to me to be altogether too good to be true. Pains are taken to indicate that her activities, such as folksinging, dancing and playing the clarinet, are livelier and more with-it than canned amusements; yet the result is only to make her less convincing, less likeable. Like all excessively good fictional characters, she becomes a shade tiresome.

Emergence of the author's values is not in itself objectionable. In a story with a contemporary setting where the subject-matter, broadly, is what life is about, suppression would be difficult and in any case not praiseworthy. The point at which damage starts is when character or action is distorted, or the impression given that the story is only a vehicle for carrying a message. In *Beat of the City* the action, even if contrived, is strong, and the characters, except perhaps Mary, come alive as people. The damage is slight and the book can stand it. And it is possible that the author's strength of feeling about true and false happiness has provided the book's motive force, and is responsible for its power as well as its weakness.

Of Mrs Brinsmead's first five novels, the remaining three [*Season of the Briar, A Sapphire for September,* and *Isle of the Sea Horse*] are slighter than *Beat of the City* or *Pastures of the Blue Crane*. . . . These books are still concerned with 'the problem of how to cope with life', but they are less closely at grips and their situations are more specialized.

Mrs Brinsmead is a writer with several faults. The structure of her stories can be unsatisfactory: notably in *Pastures of the Blue Crane,* which falls away in the second half, and *Season of the Briar,* which lacks any clear focal point and never really pulls itself together at all. Her male characters are rarely memorable. She is apt to scatter minor figures around without taking enough pains to make them live for the reader, although it is plain that they live for *her,* and she even has an endearing habit in her novels of throwing parties for them. What is so attractive about her is her writing personality. There is a sense of the author's presence, of her sympathy with the people she is writing for and about. Her settings have ranged widely and are strongly realized. Her vitality compensates for a great many failings. The last thing one would wish on her, the negation of her true gift, would be a cool perfection. (pp. 43-4)

John Rowe Townsend, "H. F. Brinsmead," in his A Sense of Story: Essays on Contemporary Writers for Children *(copyright © 1971 by John Rowe Townsend; reprinted by permission of J. B. Lippincott, Publishers), Lippincott, 1971, pp. 39-47.*

THE TIMES LITERARY SUPPLEMENT

Longtime is the fictional name of a settlement in the Australian bluegum forest. Based on the author's own childhood, [*Longtime Passing*] is the story of the Truelance family who settled there in the years of the Depression. . . .

By turns funny and grim, this is an authentic narrative of a comparatively neglected, unheroic aspect of Australian development. Grown-ups and children are portrayed equally vividly: what they have in common is an essentially Australian blend of toughness and sentimentality which will appeal to readers. . . .

"Scratching a Living," in The Times Literary Supplement *(© Times Newspapers Ltd. (London) 1972; reproduced from* The Times Literary Supplement *by permission), No. 3661, April 28, 1972, p. 476.*

THE JUNIOR BOOKSHELF

Longtime Passing is a sincere and simple account of one family's experience in the Australian Outback. . . . The narrative . . . is vivid and exciting and honest. . . . [Four] children, of whom the author is the youngest, grow up in this wild, mysterious, majestic country and watch with secret horror "progress" take over their land.

There is little more for me to say. It is a very good book by any standards and will be enjoyed by readers of all ages. . . . [The] reader should have some experience of life to appreciate the heights and depths of the writing.

"For Children from Ten to Fourteen: 'Longtime Passing'," in The Junior Bookshelf, *Vol. 36, No. 4, August, 1972, p. 239.*

MARGO PETTS

Although the canvas [in *Longtime Passing*] is a small one, the many details are clearly defined, presenting us with a picture which is full of life and vitality, though what it depicts is now only a memory. . . .

A delightfully nostalgic piece of writing, full of domestic laughter and tears. . . .

Margo Petts, "Reviews: 'Longtime Passing'," in Children's Book Review *(© 1972 by Five Owls Press Ltd.; all rights reserved), Vol. II, No. 4, September, 1972, p. 112.*

DENNIS HAMLEY

To say that [*Longtime Passing*] is an example of a fairly common and by now fairly hackneyed type—the family saga—is in no way to devalue it. The story is partly autobiographical; the material is obviously very close to the author—and this comes out in the affectionate quality of the writing. There is a sensitive delineation of place and the effective, memorable drawing of character. However, probably because its plan is strictly chronological, the book lacks subtlety. (p. 251)

Nevertheless, the understanding shown in the chronicling of the unequal struggle between the old and the new, the sense of the passage of time and the relationships between the generations made me think—and the linking is not, I am sure, outlandish—of writers such as [Thomas] Hardy, Chinua Achebe and Raymond Williams. This book will probably appeal to girls rather than boys; however, any child between ten and fifteen will find the reading of it a rewarding experience—as will many adults. (pp. 251-52)

Dennis Hamley, "Book Reviews: 'Longtime Passing'," in The School Librarian, *Vol. 20, No. 3, September, 1972, pp. 251-52.*

MARCUS CROUCH

[H. F. Brinsmead's] interest and sympathy embrace the whole spectrum of Australia, urban and rural. Her first book, *Pastures of the Blue Crane* . . . , is mostly a country book, however, and one which shows the formative influence of landscape and a free life in the open upon an unhappy, neglected girl. (p. 159)

Mrs Brinsmead shows with exquisite sensibility how a girl who has had everything in life except affection grows in contact with real problems. . . .

No writer today knows more than Mrs Brinsmead about the workings of an adolescent girl's mind; certainly no one expounds her theme with greater affection, but it is an affection free of illusions. (p. 160)

[Race] is an important element in *Listen to the Wind.* . . . However deeply Mrs Brinsmead may feel about race she keeps her touch light, and *Listen to the Wind,* which has serious, indeed tragic, implications, is essentially a gay story. Bella Greenrush, who claims to be of royal blood—and who could doubt it?—is a person of heroic stature. . . . One of her tribe is Tam who works for, and loves, Loveday Smith. . . . Loveday is the meeting-point of black and white, and the working out of her relationship with Tam, inconclusive but quite satisfactory, makes the core of a rich and varied story. . . .

There is drama and exciting action in this story, more than is common in Mrs Brinsmead's books, but it is the tenderness and the gaiety which remains longest in the mind. Best of all is the joint action of God and Uncle Zac in providing a church for Bella's tribe. (p. 217)

There is bitterness alongside the fun in the story. Bella may be essentially a comic character, but she is serious about the integrity of her race. She does not want to be like the 'white-fellers' who took her people's land and now give them 'money and free food and send us the odd social worker.' The bitterness comes from the memories of the old. (p. 218)

Almost alone among creative writers H. F. Brinsmead is concerned to adjust the balance [between adults who never listen and adolescents with problems]. Although Mrs Brinsmead lets the reader know where her sympathies lie, she is normally a detached narrator. In *Beat of the City* . . . she abandons the role of observer. Her angry interpolations spoil the symmetry of the book, which by strict standards is her least satisfactory work. Mrs Brinsmead, however, has something to say about the beat generation, and she is worth hearing. (p. 226)

Mary is the touchstone of this story, a girl who walks in both worlds. . . . Mary would be too good to be true, but for her habit of collecting stray dogs, cats and delinquents.

It is Mary, with help from her uncle, policemen, probation officers and boredom, who lights candles in the eyes of these lost children. It is a long job and there is no final and complete success. What has been proved is that there is something after all behind the emptiness in the eyes of Syd, Sabie and Raylene. Not Blade. Blade O'Reilly, who rides down old women with his stolen bike, is beyond Mrs Brinsmead's compassion. The best she can do is to deflate Blade. (p. 228)

Beat of the City is no more tidy than back-street Melbourne. It is a messy hotch-potch of anger, violence, prejudice, love, confusion; in fact a picture of life. It breaks most of the traditional and formal rules of the novel, but it rises above them. . . . The flaws in *Beat of the City* are formal, however; in its passionate concern for human beings, its criticism of society, the serious and humorous truth of its characterization, its strong angry style, this is clearly an important novel of our time. In it the traditions of the children's novel, their roots reaching back strongly to their origins in E. Nesbit at the dawn of the century, are preserved and renewed. (pp. 228-29)

> *Marcus Crouch, in his* The Nesbit Tradition: The Children's Novel in England 1945-1970 *(© Marcus Crouch 1972), Ernest Benn, 1972, 239 p.**

MARGERY FISHER

Sandy Creek, a derelict mining settlement in Queensland, is the setting, harsh and compelling, for *The Ballad of Benny Perhaps*. Benny has dropped out of university and headed back to the shacks and shafts of his boyhood, where he is confronted with an old antagonist, Rozzer Bizley, just out of prison and looking for revenge for Benny's intervention in his trickery. . . . Raucous humour, rough sincerity and sentiment, characterise the noisy idiom and violent scenes of the book; worlds away from the deployment of young people in *Beat of the City,* this story has a harsh note in it that matches the setting. (p. 3364)

> *Margery Fisher, "An Experience of Conflict," in her* Growing Point, *Vol. 17, No. 2, July, 1978, pp. 3362-64.**

Jackson Browne

1950-

American songwriter, singer, and musician.

Browne's work is noted for poetic lyrics which express widely-felt moods and emotions. Although Browne's lyrics are intensely personal, his ability to universalize problems results in his wide appeal. Youthful uncertainty and the quest for spiritual identity, the central themes in Browne's work, are supported by recurring images of childhood and death.

Browne's songs were popularized by various artists before he gained a reputation as a singer/songwriter with his own recordings. His first album, *Jackson Browne*, was hailed by critics as brilliant and evocative, fulfilling the promise of his earlier writing. One song, "Jamaica Say You Will," is a straightforward narrative written in first-person singular, the style Browne uses for many of his most effective songs. The lyrics throughout the album are memorable for giving fresh meaning to overworked clichés. *The Pretender* is the story of Browne and his deceased wife, Phyllis. In a more general sense, the album concerns the individual in contemporary society. The songs analyze the human need to reconcile longing for love with the desire for material possessions. *The Pretender*, in its exploration of mortality and the inevitable passage of time, confirmed Browne's position as a major rock poet.

The lyrics on Browne's next releases lack the quality and polish of his previous efforts. *Running on Empty* is a live album which chronicles the life of a band on the road; the style of the songs is consciously documentary. Although all the material is new, the metaphor of the road, the album's controlling concept, appears throughout Browne's work. Some critics feel the lyrics are no more than commonplace, while other critics view the album as the compelling, mature product of an accomplished songwriter. *Hold Out* has received mostly unfavorable reviews. Even though the music makes advances in lightweight rock and roll, the lyrics are considered the weakest Browne has written for any album. The moral imagination, graceful style, and precision which characterize Browne's other albums are lacking here, giving the impression that Browne has nothing to say.

Browne's albums are an ongoing commentary on his own life, and each work, including the least successful, has its place within this framework. His following is still rather small when compared with other rock and roll stars, but his moving lyrics and accessible melodies assure an increasing audience.

BUD SCOPPA

It's not often that a single album is sufficient to place a new performer among the first rank of recording artists. Jackson Browne's long-awaited debut album chimes in its author with the resounding authority of [Van Morrison's] *Astral Weeks,* [Rod Stewart's] *Gasoline Alley,* or [Neil Young's] *After the Gold Rush.* Its awesome excellence causes one to wonder why, with Browne's reputation as an important songwriter established as far back as 1968, this album was so long in coming. . . . Whatever the reason, *Jackson Browne* . . . is more than worth the years it took to be hatched. . . .

Randee St. Nicholas/1980

The songs themselves reveal Browne as a classic romanticist; they're possessed of that same earnest intensity found in his voice, and their prevailing moods are so strong that singers as diverse as Tom Rush, Johnny Darrell, Nico, and Clarence White can sing them without significantly altering their tone or substance. Browne's songs, no matter who sings them, seem to have a life of their own. . . .

"Jamaica, Say You Will," the opening track, is an exquisite love song, and it perfectly embodies Browne's writing and performing approach. This narrative of the relationship between the singer and Jamaica, the daughter of a long-absent sailor, vividly confirms Richard Goldstein's 1968 perception that "Jackson writes with rocky seacoasts in his head." . . .

While the music sets the tone, Browne deftly tells the tale, his imagery charged with vivid suggestion. . . .

What's astounding about this record is that there are a half dozen tracks of **"Jamaica"** beauty (**"Song for Adam"** and **"From Silver Lake"** are especially affecting), and none of the ten songs is any less than brilliant *and* lovely. Each has the immediacy of a touch, due in part to Jackson's first-person approach.

The music is as direct and fluid as the lyrical content. . . .

Jackson Browne's sensibility is romantic in the best sense of the term: his songs are capable of generating a highly charged, compelling atmosphere throughout, and—just as important—of sustaining that pitch in the listener's mind long after they've ended.

> *Bud Scoppa, "Records: 'Jackson Browne'," in* Rolling Stone *(by Straight Arrow Publishers, Inc. © 1972; all rights reserved; reprinted by permission), Issue 103, March 2, 1972, p. 58.*

MICHAEL WATTS

["**Jackson Browne**" is Browne's] first album, and it's good; so good, in fact, that it establishes him not just as a versatile songwriter but as an artist of major stature. For a debut album Browne could not have wished to achieve a more profound impact. Broadly speaking, his songs are romantic, heart-in-the-mouth affairs, but structured with such subtlety, earnestness and intensity of feeling that their cumulative effect is rather like a return to innocence. . . . On an album which is uniformly gorgeous there are several stand-outs. "**Jamaica Say You Will**" opens the first side and also encapsulates the form of his writing. . . . The song embodies his compositional approach in that the emphasis is on writing a song through the first person singular and his fondness is for straightforward narration; he keeps his lines very uncluttered, eschewing obscurantist tendencies. Thus "**Song for Adam**" is about two friends who finally go their separate ways until one day the narrator learns that his boyhood buddy is dead. Again, the story-line is beautifully clear, the effect wistful and moving. . . . Altogether, "**Jackson Browne**" should do for Jackson Browne a whole lot more than "Neil Young" did for Neil Young. If it's not this album, it will be the next. But it should be this one.

> *Michael Watts, "Do Say Browne," in* Melody Maker *(© IPC Business Press Ltd.), March 25, 1972, p. 15.*

GEOFF BROWN

[Browne's] debut set I loved—"**Jamaica Say You Will**," "**Song For Adam**" and, especially, "**Doctor My Eyes**" and "**Rock Me On The Water**" were superb songs. The majority of those songs were the up-tempo part of the album—Jackson's rather mono-toned vocals became depressingly morbid on the slow songs. The same conditions prevail on his second album ["**For Everyman**"]. Both sides open with a fast 'un. The Eagles' hit "**Take It Easy**" (co-written by Browne and Glenn Frey) starts side one; the excellent "**Red Neck Friend**" gets side two rolling. . . . After the opener there's a rather tacky feeling to side one—a reliance on the slow-paced and the maudlin. On side two the pace varies more and the songs counterpoint each other the better for it. . . . Jackson takes "**Sing My Songs To Me**" back down to a minor mood . . . which segues into the stronger, title track which ends the side. As the two opening tracks on the first side had also been blended into one the effect is of placing quotation marks around the album. Between the quotes Jackson makes no astounding statements; just lays down his melodies and lyrics and leaves philosophising fairly well alone. A solid enough album but not as freshly appealing as his debut.

> *Geoff Brown, "Albums: 'For Everyman'," in* Melody Maker *(© IPC Business Press Ltd.), November 10, 1973, p. 28.*

JERRY LEICHTLING

For years, Jackson Browne wrote beautiful songs, other people sang them and Jackson took his own sweet time about recording an album. Two years ago his first record was released, so beautiful, ineffably sad and movingly perfect for gentle love on rainy nights. He was instantly revealed. And now ["**For Everyman**"].

Jackson is more than sweet, alive in dream ways and held childhood. He sings of childhood; the gap of retrograde motion, the life motion that causes us still to be so much of what we once were, reaching towards that more real past where experience held growth and the strings were tied together. Jackson's first record said it in "**I Am a Child in These Hills**" and "**Rock Me on the Water**."

Here, now, most directly in "**I Thought I Was a Child**." Where before "I am," now "I thought I *was*." Two years later and gone, grown. . . .

The songs are terrific, some tunes occasionally too similar in tone but nevertheless at the heart of many things. . . .

It's soft rock and Jackson's voice is thin and reedy. But it's a remarkably conceived and executed work, a testament, a manifest creation that moves logically, consistently and beautifully towards whatever's at the end of Jackson's road. To journey this way is a privilege.

> *Jerry Leichtling, "Records: 'For Everyman'," in* Crawdaddy *(copyright © 1974 by Crawdaddy Publishing Co., Inc.; all rights reserved; reprinted by permission), January, 1974, p. 78.*

HENRY EDWARDS

[On "**For Everyman**" Jackson Browne] presents a moody catalogue in which nothing is quite right: Life doesn't make too much sense; love and work don't quite work out; there is meaning, but not enough meaning, in the experience of being alive. Browne's melodies are not terribly fresh; his lyrics are not particularly original. But the tone of his work is perfectly suited to those overpowering and ambivalent adolescent moods that are so chic when one is of college age. While his work collapses under scrutiny, Browne—much like such novels as [J. D. Salinger's] *The Catcher in the Rye*—is an effective expression of the more romantic phases of the growing-up process.

> *Henry Edwards, "The Lighter Side: 'For Everyman'," in* High Fidelity *(copyright © by ABC Leisure Magazine, Inc.; all rights reserved; excerpted by permission), Vol. 24, No. 3, March, 1974, p. 108.*

STEPHEN HOLDEN

Like Browne's two previous albums, *Late for the Sky* contains no lyric sheet. The three or four hours required to make a full transcription will, however, be well worth the effort for anyone interested in discovering lyric genius. I can't think of another writer who merges with such natural grace and fluidity his private and public personas in a voice that is morally compelling yet noncoercive.

Late for the Sky, Jackson Browne's third . . . album, is his most mature, conceptually unified work to date. Its overriding theme: the exploration of romantic possibility in the shadow of apocalypse. No contemporary male singer/songwriter has dealt so honestly and deeply with the vulnerability of romantic idealism and the pain of adjustment from youthful narcissism to adult survival as Browne has in this album. *Late for the Sky* is the autobiography of his young manhood.

The album's eight loosely constructed narratives rely for much of their impact upon stunning sections of aphoristic verse, whose central images, the antinomies of water and sand, reality and dreams, sky and road, inextricably connect them. Browne's melodic style, though limited, serves his ideas brilliantly. He generally avoids the plaintive harmonies of southern California rock ballads for a starker, more eloquent musical diction derived from Protestant hymns. Likewise his open-ended poetry achieves power from the nearly religious intensity that accumulates around the central motifs. . . .

On side one, Browne tells bluntly about his personal conflict between fantasy and reality in erotic relationships, struggling with his quest for idyllic bliss. . . .

The second side of the album describes the precariousness of the journey, as Browne's sense of personal tragedy metamorphoses into a larger social apprehension. . . . **"For A Dancer"** . . . is one of the album's two masterpieces, a meditation on death that harks back to **"Song For Adam."** . . . But **"For A Dancer"** is not a lament; it calls for joyful procreation to combat metaphysical terror. Browne's graceful lyric, as fine as any he's written, finds its counterpart in the music. . . . **"Before The Deluge,"** the album's summary cut, brings together in a comprehensive social context the themes of the rest of the album. A march for three voices, . . . the song evokes the spiritual malaise following Woodstock. . . . (p. 61)

> Stephen Holden, "Manchild in the Promised Land," in Rolling Stone (by Straight Arrow Publishers, Inc. © 1974; all rights reserved; reprinted by permission), Issue 173, November 7, 1974, pp. 61-2.

DAVID SPIWACK

It's hard not to love Jackson Browne, even if you're not a teenage girl who can't believe how cute he is. Because the power of his songs extends beyond their compact, bittersweet appeal. They consistently express moods and emotions many of us have felt but couldn't conjure up the words to describe. Yet there is something about [*Late for the Sky*] that irks me. Something about what Jackson does and where he is going, or better, where he is not going, is beginning to show. (p. 74)

[This] recognizable persona comes across in the plaintive tone of his weighty statements that often border dangerously on the whine. And after a while, too much of this stuff is depressing. The combined effect of his straining, mournful voice, the resigned profundity of his lyrics, and the predictable sound of his musical style has begun to wear thin.

Unlike the gospel roots from which he derives much of his musical foundation (like the pounding "Amen" bass lines and hanging phrases which delay their eventual resolution), there seems little joy in Browne's performance. It is as though his commitment to being *heavy* is one which has been imposed upon him rather than being his own choice.

Like Joni Mitchell, most of Jackson's material is based in a type of introspective analysis which he describes in the title tune. . . . Not only does [the kind of image evoked here] lend itself to easy audience identification, but the tendency is for those without a developed consciousness of their own to embrace this vicarious experience and romanticize it preciously.

Indeed, at their best, Browne's songs do have enormous emotional impact. So clear are his insights into certain facets of personal relationships that the lines have that ring, "or perhaps it is an echo," as Norman Mailer says, "of that great bell which may toll whenever the literary miracle occurs and a writer sets down words to resonate with that sense of peace and proportion it is tempting to call truth."

"The Late Show" . . . is probably the album's strongest single track. The arrangement is coherent in the same way as the lyrics are. . . . (pp. 74-5)

Elsewhere, though, Jackson lapses into self-consciousness about the significance of his lyrics, and there are occasional instances where this shows up in a particularly awkward line. . . .

More importantly, he is beginning to paint himself into a corner musically. **"The Road And The Sky"** sounds like a deliberate attempt at a possible Top 40 hit, but its nagging resemblance to his previous **"Red Neck Friend"** betrays the limited scope of his uptempo conception. . . .

Browne has found some interesting ways to extend his songs thematically, to keep them from becoming too compact and predictable. Yet the elements—the musical lines and changes—never stray very far from his identifiable style. In this, Jackson has created a genre of his own, and established himself as perhaps its most skillful craftsman. But we've heard this song before, and it's time for something else. (p. 75)

> David Spiwack, "Records: 'Late for the Sky'," in Crawdaddy (copyright © 1975 by Crawdaddy Publishing Co., Inc.; all rights reserved; reprinted by permission), January, 1975, pp. 74-5.

JACK McDONOUGH

It seems safe [now], if somewhat brash, to make a claim: Jackson Browne is the most important American songwriter since Bob Dylan and is perhaps as true a voice of the 70's as we are going to hear.

The claim requires apologias on several fronts. The first is that Browne is nowhere near so loose, prolific or wide-ranging as Dylan, and we still have not seen all that much of his work yet. . . .

The second apologia is to recognize that "The 70's" is a vague and amorphous term. . . .

[This] decade does have its feel, defined, as all eras, by the overriding political and economic realities of the society. Much of the tone of the 70's is a result of the accommodation of people's minds to a geometrically expanding technology. (p. 242)

The songwriter has a special place in this scheme, for at his best he verbalizes the state of society, either directly by openly questioning or protesting things, or indirectly by depicting the private life and interior feelings of someone who moves within that society.

And what I detect the songwriters mirroring is a tone of mellow (but not capitulatory) resignation resulting from "our long national nightmare" that included not only Nixon and Watergate but Johnson, Vietnam, civil and racial strife, political assassinations, etc.

Early in the decade this feeling was represented most notably by James Taylor and Neil Young, both of whom touched the national nerve very deeply, Taylor so much that he was lionized on the cover of *Time.* Browne has continued on this road. (pp. 242-43)

Browne, like Dylan, has focused his light on the interior world of reflection and uncertainty that exists inside, under the skin of the young person alive and thinking in these times.

In addressing so directly the interior emotional life Browne has an inherent advantage, because the territory of the emotional imagination is much more vast than the territory of Long Island or New York City or Asbury Park or California. Browne, like all major artists, is able to speak simultaneously and at equal volume about himself and about society; consequently his appeal is instinctive and universal. I have not heard songs since Dylan's best of the mid-60's that work so magnificently on so many different levels as **"For Everyman"** or **"Before the Deluge"** or **"Rock Me on the Water"** or **"For a Dancer,"** nor lines that depict so chillingly the Nixonian death's head we've stared at for so long. We have seen the end coming down long enough (How long have I been sleeping, Jackson asks in another context) to know that we've heard the last warning—a warning sounded by the men who had learned to forge the earth's beauty into power. This at a time when we were watching the frightening ugliness of Bob Haldeman and John Erlichman on TV.

These are very insecure, violent and consequently sorrowful times, and Jackson has touched that nerve like no one else. Sing a joyful song, he says to his dancer, and sow some seeds of your own; and between the time you arrive and the time you go there just may lie a reason you were alive. But you'll never know.

Even Browne's love songs—wherein he is not addressing general problems—limn the doubts and psychological maneuvers of the lovers as surefootedly as Dylan's love songs. (p. 245)

[Browne, Dylan, and Neil Young] share another intriguingly similar central characteristic: their pose as a small boy hurt and vulnerable before a hard, cold and unyielding world. Childhood, a metaphor combining innocence, dream, primitive vitality and vision, seems natural to all three. (p. 246)

Browne's child images tend to be more universalized and less idiomatic than either Young's or Dylan's. He has two songs openly titled after the idea: **"I Am a Child in These Hills"** and **"I Thought I Was a Child."** He tells us how he has chosen to be gone from the house of his father, how he sits before his only candle that gives so little light to find his way. Help me find a way to fill these lifeless sails, he pleads. He asks, much as the boy from "Hard Rain" might have asked, if he was unwise to leave his eyes open for so long.

It might be noted that Browne and Young share a Los Angeles acculturation. . . . Both Browne and Young convey the feeling of having seen the sunny organic paradise, and a precious feeling of resignation and withdrawal at having experienced the highs and lows of that paradise, at having seen what the garden has been converted into. . . .

Aside from the child images, there are a few other parallels to draw between Browne and Dylan. One I've already suggested: the ability to enchant and evoke, and thereby to achieve multiple levels of meaning within a song. **"For Everyman,"** which calls forth a world spanning the medieval morality play *Ev-*

eryman to [Samuel] Beckett's *Waiting for Godot,* is a prime example.

These multiple levels are often provoked by the idea of death, about which both men write with precision and directness. (p. 248)

Like his child images, Browne's images of death are softer and more universalized than Dylan's. I can think of no other songwriter who has addressed himself so sensitively to the problem of death or who has intimated the afterlife so positively as does Browne in **"Song to Adam,"** **"For a Dancer"** and **"Rock Me on the Water."**

And Browne, like Dylan, has the perhaps unconscious ability to unify his *oeuvre* through consistent repetition of images. The use of the child image applies here. Browne's work is also suffused with a spiritually symbolic use of the element of water. **"From Silverlake,"** **"Rock Me on the Water,"** **"Our Lady of the Well,"** and **"Before the Deluge"** are some of his titles; "Who will show me the river?", "I'm looking for water, I'm looking for life" and "Our waters have run dry" are some of his lines. His work is a constant baptism. . . .

In **"Our Lady of the Well"** Browne plays Spanish lines on the guitar and addresses a girl named Maria. In **"Colors of the Sun"** he says goodbye to people named Joseph and Maria. The important thing about those names is that they follow immediately a touching and graphic verse about the California Jesus freaks. . . .

Here is perhaps the central theme of Browne's work, just as it was always the underlying core of all Dylan's work: the unrelenting and embarrassing search for The Answer, which ultimately each person must find for himself. (p. 249)

Browne, like Dylan, has the ability to state large and universal themes to a great many people at once, in a language they can understand. . . .

Browne is saying that these are not easy times and that one must find his own spiritual waters to drink if he wishes to see his way through. The Sisters of the Sun are there if you will seek them. In the naked dawn a few will survive; the buildings will keep our children dry, the music can keep our spirits high. . . .

His advice is (1) Find a place to make your stand . . . and (2) take it easy.

He is not talking about militancy. He is talking about making a stand the way Thoreau did at Walden Pond, where you can discover the ground of your soul and the water of salvation. Then you can take it easy.

If Browne himself continues, in that sense, to take it easy—if he takes his time, keeps his nerve, and allows himself room to grow within the potentially stultifying atmosphere of L.A.—then he may eventually wind up with a body of work as culturally important as Dylan's. (p. 250)

Jack McDonough, "Review Essay of Jackson Browne," in Popular Music & Society *(copyright © 1975 by R. Serge Denisoff), Vol. IV, No. 4, 1975, pp. 242-50.*

TIMOTHY WHITE

[Browne] writes and sings untiringly and without restraint about all the broken promises, the canceled appointments, the quintessential assumptions that have fallen through—all the pathetic kinks in the human condition.

It's been four albums and a lot of arid miles since the 28-year-old Browne first took a bow **"Under the Falling Sky"** on his debut *Jackson Browne* ''waterbag'' lp. More than ever, the leading songwriter of the '70s sounds like he could use a cool drink and some companionship—but is this the sort of person you'd want as a friend? Born in Germany and bruised in Greenwich Village circa '67, the brilliant balladeer is passing the last remnants of his 20s in Los Angeles, one of the richest, most class-, status- and *self*-conscious cities in the world. Also one of the most disposable. It is in this No Deposit/No Return atmosphere that he continues to rage against the creeping, crippling lethargy it breeds, simultaneously devouring and disdaining all the free time he apparently has to scrutinize emotions and exhaust ideas. . . .

Jackson Browne writes songs that are often incandescently poignant and offer bold, lucid insights into the reasons why people so frequently fail each other. But the songs always arrive in groups of ten or more; after a while, their thematic consistency raises the more depressing possibility that there's a carry-over into his day-to-day existence. If so, what we're getting in his records is a portrait-in-progress rather than a perspective.

The problem with Jackson Browne is that his messages are so personal and direct that they transcend their medium and must eventually be judged either friend or foe. I followed the man as far as *Late for the Sky* but *The Pretender,* both as an album and a (mythic?) individual, is no friend of mine. (p. 68)

After struggling through some fits of hopefulness, Browne has found new exhilaration in his fatalistic instincts, suggesting on *The Pretender*'s opening track that ''Whatever it is you might think you have, you have nothing to lose.'' The song eventually ends on an up note that mentions ''eternity'' but it comes out pat and unconvincing. This world, as we know it, is quite finite, and reverence for eternity leaves me cold. But life for Browne has become **"The Fuse,"** which is relentlessly ''burning, and the world is turning'' and the singer seems enamored of the possibility of impending explosion. This disturbing attitude provides most of the impetus for what could be Jackson's finest hour and, not coincidentally, his most self-destructive.

Dating as far back as his brief sojourn (in 1967) with the original Dark Lady, Nico, Browne has been lifting a magnifying glass to his own archeology the way that Gordon Liddy used to hold his palm over a candle flame—denying his own discomfort in order to maximize whatever responses his actions might elicit. But any caprice becomes a matter of conviction if you do it often enough. He's delved as deeply and with as much prosaic calculation as he could muster while making his own probing surgery. These rites, however imprudent, produced some of the most eloquently introspective songwriting of the last decade, but it's become harder to ignore all that nasty scar tissue. . . . Jackson has suffered considerably in the past few months and the cloak of resignation that covers this album could be a reaction to the recent apparent suicide of his wife, Phyllis—although Asylum says the album was for the most part completed prior to her death. This seems likely; nowhere on the album is there a song that could, obviously at least, be construed as a consideration of the tragedy and yet the overall tone is pessimistic enough to indicate that such matters [and] questions were on his mind.

Many of our best songwriters, Paul Simon in particular, complain that critics take an overly literal approach when reviewing their records. But to do otherwise in the case of Jackson Browne would be tantamount to ignoring him, since he seldom ventures out without wearing his battered soul on his sleeve—constantly consulting it as if it were a wristwatch. (pp. 68-9)

Still in all, this is Jackson Browne's most cogent statement, but the grandeur of his anguish makes me feel he's gone too far; the mournful picture he paints is so stark and unyielding that it saps most of the potential for enjoyment. Like Paul Simon's ''Peace Like a River,'' John Lennon's ''Mother,'' or Neil Young's ''Tonight's the Night,'' testimony this personal can turn on itself if its harrowing tone isn't tempered and defined by a humanistic ethos.

Unlike Simon, Lennon and Young, Browne fails to provide one. Rather, he seems to be saying that the only refuge for someone who lacks the power or the presence of mind to get out of his own way is something he ominously terms ''sleep's dark and silent gate.''

With his earlier efforts in mind, I began this record assuming that I'd be breaking bread with Jackson Browne, but halfway through it I got the feeling that I was chewing tinfoil. They say that nothing overflows that can continue to drip; I hope so. It's like a song I can hear, playing right in my ear, that I can't sing. But I can't help listening. (p. 69)

> *Timothy White, '''Pretender' Pleads Nolo Contendere,'' in* Crawdaddy *(copyright © 1977 by Crawdaddy Publishing Co., Inc.; all rights reserved; reprinted by permission), January, 1977, pp. 68-9.*

DAVE MARSH

Like most performers who transcend their genre, Jackson Browne often seems more a symbol than an artist. Singer/songwriter fans find in him the fulfillment of the style's promise: Browne's songs really do merge poetic vision and rock. But there are also those . . . who find the genre symptomatic of all of rock's current weaknesses. Browne is the epitome of everything they find disagreeable, both lyrically and musically.

It is odd that Browne is surrounded by such certainty of opinion, for ambivalence is the hallmark of his style. He has managed to make confusion an advantage, partly because he never hedges: he knows he doesn't know. *The Pretender,* the most complete development of his music, is bounded by contradiction. (p. 62)

The focus [of his work] is always lyrical. The arrangements and performances are successful precisely to the degree that they bring our full attention to the emotions and ideas he articulates.

And it is Browne the lyricist who is often taken as a symbol, and most often misunderstood. He has been condemned as a rampant sexist, and with good reason: cowriting the Eagles' chauvinistic anthem, **"Take It Easy,"** was inexcusable. But his romantic perspective is considerably more complicated. His affairs are never casual, not even when he's dismissive, as in **"Linda Paloma."** And in **"Here Come Those Tears Again,"** he uses his confusion to greatest advantage. The role of the singer isn't clear: is he anticipating the return of a lover who has jilted him, or is he imagining the reaction of a lover he's just jilted? Perhaps both. For this song, at least, his vision of love turns on something rare: friendship.

Browne may also be the apocalyptic visionary, the questing hero in search of the Big Bang of final romance that his hardcore cult sees him as. But as someone who's always has reservations about admiring him, I find that Jackson Browne touches me most deeply when he's most specific, least cosmic. Writing about mortality and parental roles, he is as mature as any writer in rock, and more cogent than most. The metaphysics are there, all right, but it is the characters and experiences on which they are based that make them compelling.

The most striking songs on *The Pretender* are concerned with death and parenthood, subjects not necessarily unrelated (see the earlier "For a Dancer"). Often, his apocalyptic imagery is merely a way of getting at his feelings of mortality—the crumbling towers of Babylon in "The Fuse" are as much about the inevitable erosion of time as anything else. And parenthood is seen as a symbol of the middle-class life he has experienced: it's both a joy and a trap. In "Daddy's Tune," he reaches out to his father, long ago alienated, in order to share with him the turmoil of advising his son in "The Only Child." In a way, this is his ultimate dilemma—to be a father, or to be a son. And his ultimate triumph is to realize and reconcile the parent and the child in each of us.

Such song-to-song concordances are not unusual. Lines and images overlap: the drum in "The Fuse" and "Daddy's Tune," and the opening lines of "Your Bright Baby Blues" and "Sleep's Dark and Silent Gate," which is about both the horror of a marriage gone bad and man at his most mortal. . . . And all of these cross-references come rushing to a climax in "The Pretender."

"The Pretender" is a breakthrough. Browne has always had traces of cynicism in his writing, but about romance he has remained firm. Love can make a difference, all of his songs say. But "The Pretender" is a song about why even that won't work, in the long run. In its most shattering moment, the hero imagines what he and his dream-lover will do, if ever they manage to meet. . . .

As a romantic ["The Pretender"] wants only love, but as a modern, middle-class southern Californian, he's unsure what to do with it. Clawing at the world, trying to make sense of something, one choice seems almost as good as another. The happy idiot who struggles for the legal tender is finally as free as the romantic fool who waits for love to change everything—and both are equally trapped. (p. 64)

What makes the song work, though, are its specifics, the way that even the junkman, pounding his fender, becomes a part of this cosmic cycle. The images are tied to a time and a place, as the best of any writer's work is—and the horror is in just such detail: the house beside the freeway, the packed lunch, the work, the endless evenings. Getting up and doing it again, seen this way, is not so very mystical, but simply the way each of us—even the artist—lives his life.

Repeating this inhumane cycle, which defines humanity, we are left with very little. . . . Jackson Browne's contradictions, his ambivalence, are not resolved, but they are reconciled. One might say that this is the end of the hero's quest. But there is no end to searches such as this. They repeat themselves from generation to generation, year to year, day to day. Just as all of our illusions last, until they shatter. (p. 65)

> Dave Marsh, "Stalking the Great Pretender," in
> Rolling Stone *(by Straight Arrow Publishers, Inc.* ©
> *1977; all rights reserved; reprinted by permission),*
> *Issue 231, January 27, 1977, pp. 62, 64-5.*

PETER KNOBLER

Jackson Browne is his own best chronicler. The profile has yet to be written which reveals him as incisively, or with as much

love for language, as Browne does himself. His struggles with love, mortality, innocence and the fall from grace have rung so true, and been described with such real yet elevated phrases, that he has become a man-child pioneer. The life and situations he has described have been close enough to a middle-class universal for both the sensitive and the banal to feel he knows their personal songs. He is his own subject and, to this point, his life has been sufficiently interesting to support a running, five-album autobiography. He has enjoyed the strength to show his vulnerability.

Running on Empty. I wish it were an ironic title. Browne's life, he says, is lived in large part on the road. It's a rock 'n roll cliche, but one looks to the smart people for new views of common ideas—and the classic road album has yet to be written. Browne hasn't got it here.

Jackson's four previous records were solitary affairs. He was exploring himself, with little or no outside help. He judged others by their effect on him. Now his life seems changed. He has found, or created, a family with which to travel and live. His touring company—the band, roadies, lighting and sound men, business people—serves as the nucleus and the audience as the invited relatives. Where his life alone was once all he needed for material, now he's got all these voices to consider. There's a conscious sense of consensus to the album. . . . And with this consensus comes a lowering of standards.

It seems as though Jackson Browne is trying to produce a true family album. Songs are recorded in rehearsal rooms, hotel rooms, on the bus. Getting everybody in the picture is fine in concept—all contribute to the scene from which Browne has traditionally written—but not everyone is a craftsman, and in his attempt to involve his group he loses touch with the brilliant language which made him so very special to begin with. His collaborations have little care for words, much attention to bathetic detail. . . . The scenes are real enough—in "Rosie" the drummer steals a backstage girl from a roadie; in "The Load-Out" the crew is packing it all in—but neither words nor music elevate them above the obvious. And that capacity is Jackson Browne's magic. . . .

Jackson's style is artful sentiments sung as if from a diary; *The Pretender* saw him bash his way out of that style for the first time. Despite the fact that he was admitting to his own "surrender," he opened an emotional channel which had been tightly closed before and seems to have been shut down again. It's a shame. Was he embarrassed, or unwilling to follow the [Bruce] Springsteen lead any further?

There are several fine songs on *Running on Empty*. . . . But even these songs could have been recorded more compellingly. What is worse, more than half the album is either throwaway material or filler. This is a *Jackson Browne* album we're talking about; even one dismissible song is unthinkable!

There is the sense that Jackson has hit a cold spell. Certainly he has supreme pride in his work; either he is pinioned by personality and unable to rescue his songs, or he has leaned too heavily on people who are not writers. Compadres may be counted on for perspective, for a parallel view of the road, but Browne should work out the language by himself.

Running on Empty is another installment in the Jackson Browne epic. He remains a fascinating, persuasive character. The album may well be an accurate recounting of what he's going through right now; unfortunately, it's not much fun to listen to.

Peter Knobler, "Jackson Browne: The Road Not Taken," in Crawdaddy (copyright © 1978 by Crawdaddy Publishing Co., Inc.; all rights reserved; reprinted by permission), March, 1978, p. 69.

PAUL NELSON

Whether or not he knows it, [Browne's] been writing about highways and their alternate routes since his beginnings, so the subject matter and thematic concerns of *Running on Empty* aren't all that different from those of his first four LPs. But the approach is. This time, Browne has consciously created a documentary, as brightly prosaic as it is darkly poetic, with a keen eye for the mundane as well as the magical. *Running on Empty* is a live album of new material about life on the road as conceived and recorded by a band of touring musicians in the places they spend most of their time (onstage, backstage, in hotel rooms, even on the bus). Since there are two separate concepts here, the audience gets an unprecedented double feature: ten songs they've never heard Browne sing, and a behind-the-scenes look at "the show they didn't see." Ostensibly, the Gawain of rock & roll has scaled down his heroic obsessions, re-covered the Round Table with Formica and invited us in for a cup of truck-stop coffee, thus proving a point we knew all along: that small gestures can be just as meaningful and revealing as large ones.

Ironically, when Browne tries for specifics, he achieves both facts and universals. But his inclination to ease up makes sense here because he's really running two different, very dangerous races: one positively mythopoeic (the Road and its metaphorical implications), the other presumably maudlin (musicians on the road). The first can barely be done justice to within the confines of a pop record, while the second has rarely risen above its inherent clichés. (p. 51)

For Browne, as for most of us, the question has always been whether to stay or to leave, the answer either or neither. We want commitment, but we're committed only to the quandary.

Of course, one apparent way around all this is to stay out on the road, simultaneously searching while sending constant letters home. But *Running on Empty*'s enormously moving **"Love Needs a Heart,"** cowritten with Lowell George and Valerie Carter, chillingly demonstrates what usually happens to men and women who attempt this. . . . **"Running on Empty"** (whose very title bristles with tenacious, win/lose duality) is an effective continuation of the songwriter's darkening **"Looking into You"/"Farther On"/"Your Bright Baby Blues"** cycle. Here, as with **"Love Needs a Heart"** and **"You Love the Thunder,"** Browne looks back on his life, revisits *The Pretender* and reaches similar conclusions. . . .

If love needs a heart, *Running on Empty* makes it clear that the road isn't a good place either to find or to hold one. But then, neither is a house in the shade of the freeway—**"The Pretender"** told us that. On the road, at least, there's that old gray magic, asphalt camaraderie and the special language of musicians who mark time by gigs and guitar cases. . . .

Best of all, there's a finale—a fusion of Jackson Browne's and Bryan Garofalo's **"The Load-Out"** and Maurice Williams and the Zodiacs' "Stay"—that's worthy of such earlier Browne anthems as **"For Everyman," "Before the Deluge"** and **"The Pretender."** **"The Load-Out"** is Jackson Browne's tribute to and summation of every aspect of live performance: the cheering audience out front, the band playing hard-nosed rock &

roll, the backstage crew loading up the trucks—and, always, the road to the next town. Packed to capacity with the data of first-rate reporting and with music so warm and soaring it belies the album's title, this song flows triumphantly into "Stay," where Browne tells us he doesn't ever want it to end. Taken together, **"The Load-Out"** and "Stay" are so accessible they're practically transparent. Maybe that's why they feel so good. . . .

It's simple enough to talk about lyrics, aims, structure and all the critical etceteras, but it's very difficult to pinpoint what it is that's actually moved you. It has to do with essences, I think, and all those corny virtues like truth, courage, conviction, kindness and the rest of them. In other words, as impressed as I am with Jackson Browne's art, I'm even more impressed with the humanity that shines through it. Maybe they're inseparable, but I doubt it. (p. 53)

Paul Nelson, "A Ticket to Ride," in Rolling Stone (by Straight Arrow Publishers, Inc. © 1978; all rights reserved; reprinted by permission), Issue 260, March 9, 1978, pp. 51, 53.

STEVE SIMELS

On the face of it, nothing would seem less likely right now than a gritty, unsentimental, insightful revitalization of one of rock's most played-out themes—the psychic travails of Life on the Road—by a singer/songwriter whose previous recorded Laments have verged perilously (to echo *Doonesbury* creator Garry Trudeau) on mere Whines. But clearly Jackson Browne, heretofore recognized as the Mellow Sound's Premier Metaphysical Pretty Face, is toughening up his act, and **"Running on Empty,"** his latest album for Asylum, has both the real rocker's raw-edged sensibility and a film maker's unflinching reportorial eye.

The film reference is not gratuitous. . . . [The] whole structure of the thing recalls *cinema verité* documentaries *à la* the Maysles Brothers. It was recorded live in a variety of settings, both in and out of concert halls, the apparent idea being to convey some sense of how a touring musician lives and how this life reflects upon the way he plays, to portray the alternately numbing (*Cocaine*, complete with somewhat updated lyrics) and inspiring (*The Load-Out*) effects of musical communication as a vocation. It's a concept fraught with the perils of mawkishness and self-pity, but it is brought off sensationally, even the potentially hokey stuff. . . . Truth to tell, his records have always had a superficial patina of "prettiness" that undercut what he seemed to want to get across. Here, however, his regular recording band works out with a vengeance, and the raw clatter adds a weight and an authority to his lyrics that the relative perfection of the sounds on his studio efforts never could.

In short, **"Running on Empty"** represents the work of an artist newly matured and unafraid to take risks, a breakthrough comparable to Neil Young's post-"Harvest" realization that the wonders of studio technology do not necessarily provide a path to Total Enlightenment. And, finally, it gives the most resonant and interesting answers to all the questions implicit in the Byrds' oversimplified *So You Wanna Be a Rock-and-Roll Star?* It's a marvelous, compelling piece of work that has converted this rather halfhearted admirer into a total, unabashed partisan. Phonorealism has never before sounded this good. (pp. 83-4)

Steve Simels, "Jackson Browne's 'Running on Empty': Mature, Chance-taking Phonorealism," in Stereo

*Review (copyright © 1978 by Ziff-Davis Publishing
Company), Vol. 40, No. 4, April, 1978, pp. 83-4.*

ANTHONY FAWCETT

["**The Road And The Sky**"] written by Jackson Browne over
four years ago, was the catalyst for an idea which evolved into
Running On Empty, a live album and conceptual statement
about the physical and psychic consequences of being on tour.
It is an unusual and powerful work. All the songs are new, all
of them except one are about life on the road, and they were
recorded in all the places where life on the road is lived—in
motel rooms, on buses, in backstage dressing rooms, as well
as on stage itself. The seamless fashion in which the motel
songs and the stage songs are fused together is part of the
magic.

The theme has been continued in each cycle of Jackson's development. . . . But it was his collection of songs on *The
Pretender* which established his position as both a major poet
and musician.

Jackson has captured in his songs the illusory nature of the
world, echoing the tradition of a long line of poets. Love and
death, birth and rebirth; symbols of futility are a strong part
of his imagery. . . . Browne's work offers the artistic re-creation of the individual's struggle in our times, a vision of life
within chaos. Its virtue lies in the perceptiveness of what it
offers.

For Jackson has used his songs as outlets for the pressures and
emotional conflicts that rage about inside him. In these songs
he often provides the raw material, how we interpret them will
depend on our presuppositions. He creates from an instinctive,
intuitive source. He has a unique way in which he describes
relationships and he is able to fuse conscious and unconscious,
emotion and the senses. Like other great poets, Browne transcends his period and confronts us with perennial facts of human nature. (p. 69)

Jackson's songwriting matured rapidly. His earliest songs were
concerned with a love of language, a poetic romanticism, but
by the age of eighteen he was writing in more universal terms;
the song "**Dancing Sam**" is a good example. (p. 75)

Browne's music can be seen as an evolving work, a perpetual
Bildungsroman, manifesting the always changing yet ever-the-
same awareness and celebration of the recovery of the divinity
of man. These are songs of transformations. "There is no
salvation," Henry Miller wrote, "only infinite realms of experience providing more and more tests, demanding more and
more faith." (p. 81)

> *Anthony Fawcett, "Jackson Browne—The Road and
> the Sky," in his* California Rock, California Sound:
> The Music of Los Angeles and Southern California
> *(copyright © 1978 APT Publishing AG), Reed Books,
> 1978, pp. 66-81.*

KIT RACHLIS

Everything that's right and everything that's wrong about *Hold
Out* . . . can be found in its climax: the spoken confession at
the end of the last cut, "**Hold On Hold Out.**" Eight minutes
long, "**Hold On Hold Out**" is the LP's anthem, its farewell
address and would-be summation. (p. 47)

It's a measure of both the grandiosity and simplicity of Browne's
intentions that this album comes down to his saying—without
the aid of melody or harmony—"I love you." And it's a
measure of *Hold Out*'s failure that these words sound flat,
forced, even selfish: a meaningful private act made embarrassing by its public expression. Also, the words are a letdown,
since they follow the funniest, most heartbreakingly romantic
line on the record. The singer is speaking directly to the woman
he's been falling in love with throughout the LP. You can sense
that he's awkwardly trying to breach the gulf between them.
And when he hitches up his pants and says, "See—I always
figured I was going to meet somebody here," you know that
Los Angeles' coolest, smartest urban cowboy is just as vulnerable and ridiculous as you and I. Browne, a romantic to the
end, makes such long-shot faith seem not only possible but
necessary.

Hold Out is a trade-off of such moments. Duff lines war with
taut ones, puffed-up commonplaces with perceptions. . . . Most
of the time, Browne loses. Lyrically, *Hold Out* is probably the
weakest record he's ever made—an album on which all of the
big decisions are carefully considered, but many of the small
ones backfire. What we have is a song cycle with scarcely a
single tune that has the moral imagination, pop grace or writerly
precision of Browne's best material. In the end, *Hold Out* is
simply a set of moods that don't quite catch.

On paper, the LP makes sense, and you can almost imagine
Browne's preproduction notes. A circle game, taking up where
The Pretender left off but reversing the order. From antiro-
mantic breakup to romantic renewal. Semiautobiographical.
About loss and fear, ties that bind and ties that bond. An
exploration of the pull of work, stardom and bittersweet expectations. Images that recur from composition to composition,
but songs that stand on their own. (pp. 47-8)

So what went wrong? Of all things, the writing. Jackson Browne
has never been as banal, sloppy, fake or pretentious as he is
here. *Hold Out* forces us to be editors and fill its margins with
questions. . . . [There's] the mock literariness ("Reaching into
the heart of the darkness"), the Dick-and-Jane sociology ("The
folks are home playing *Beat the Clock*"), the Hallmark card
from the Mount ("Hold a place for the human race"). Please
avoid.

With the exception of the title track, there's hardly a song on
Hold Out without one of these time bombs. And if more don't
go off, it's because the music represents a real advance: Browne's
concrete version of Los Angeles rock & roll. . . .

Despite its rock & roll accomplishments, however, what's
missing from *Hold Out* is much larger: humor, humility, detail,
lightness of touch. Browne has been Hollywood rock's moral
conscience and intellectual spokesman for so long—and has
performed his duties so completely—that it's probably taken
something out of him. *Hold Out* has the feel of someone desperately trying to break through, to make a Big Statement:
every line inflated with Meaning, each song Significant. When,
in "**Hold Out,**" the artist is offhand, it comes as such a surprise
that your heart flies. . . . (p. 48)

Still, I miss the Jackson Browne who felt free enough to say
"I don't know what happens when people die" in "**For a
Dancer,**" which is surely preferable to the piling up of polemic
sorrow in "**Of Missing Persons.**" I miss the singer who spoke
plainly in "**These Days.**" . . . And most of all, I miss the man
who could write a rock & roll number with the directness of
"**Running on Empty,**" and not weigh us down with the social

science fiction of **"Boulevard."** Unfortunately, the old Jackson Browne can rarely be found on *Hold Out.* So we'll have to give the new one a chance. (pp. 48-9)

Kit Rachlis, "Jackson Browne's 'Hold Out' Doesn't Quite Hold Up," in Rolling Stone *(by Straight Arrow Publishers, Inc. © 1980; all rights reserved; reprinted by permission), Issue 325, September 4, 1980, pp. 47-9.*

NOEL COPPAGE

Jackson Browne does not rock out; Jackson Browne meanders eloquently—sometimes to a big beat and loud guitars, but not so as to cover the words. Jackson Browne believes in words. That's one of the things I like about him. But in his new album, **"Hold Out,"** he seems determined to rock *harder* than he has before, and though the words still aren't covered with instruments, they're affected indirectly.

The desire to rock harder has led him to several decisions—mostly involving shortening his usually snaking, convoluted lines and opting for simplified melodies—that not only take the emphasis (pressure?) off the lyrics to some degree but contribute to an overall impression that he didn't have anything very large to say this time out anyway. . . . Coming from Browne, this album is more nearly a holding action than a case of holding out. To keep things in perspective, though, it does make some small, useful additions to a collection of his songs, and when you compare it with most *other* people's albums,

especially those that try to rock out, it would have to get a "Special Merit" tag.

This trying to rock too hard becomes annoying only once, really, in *That Girl Could Sing.* It is truly one of Browne's weakest songwriting efforts. . . . At the other extreme, there's *Of Missing Persons.* . . . Although it is nominally addressed to a girl child, it sounds to me as if the addressee might be Browne's son, whose mother committed suicide a few years ago. Browne is not maudlin or coy on the subject; in fact, I'd call this song graceful.

The rest certainly aren't weak songs, but they're all short on Browneness in subtle ways. *Disco Apocalypse,* the opener, is roughly about how it feels to be one of those characters in *Saturday Night Fever,* not exactly a ground-breaking theme. *Boulevard* works with it to book-end the first side with blue-collar/street-kid references (all oblique), sketchily describing a metaphorical turf where it's everyone for himself; it puts plenty of pictures in your head, but it doesn't find out the kind of thing a Browne song usually finds out. *Call It a Loan* is a nice song, but its ideas and ambition are small, and the title song gets its theme rehashed at unnecessary length in *Hold On Hold Out,* the last cut. Such overkill on the basically simple idea of holding out is probably the biggest mistake Browne makes here, since *both* songs tire you with their redundancy and make it appear that there's even more idea-stretching going on here than there actually is.

Noel Coppage, "Jackson Browne," in Stereo Review *(copyright © 1980 by Ziff-Davis Publishing Company), Vol. 45, No. 5, November, 1980, p. 112.*

Lenny Bruce

1925-1966

(Pseudonym of Leonard Schneider) American comedian, writer, and actor.

Bruce used comedy as a vehicle to shock audiences out of their complacent acceptance of the status quo in the late 1950s and early 1960s. Instead of the set routines favored by his contemporaries, he employed spontaneous monologues on the restrictions imposed by church and state on politics, sex, and religion. By lampooning outdated and bigoted American attitudes, Bruce wished to exorcise the narrowmindedness of his audience. Because of the vulgar, scatological language and iconoclastic satire integral to his act, Bruce was criticized during his lifetime as a "sick" comic and was eventually barred from performing in many establishments. Since his death, however, his comedy has been hailed as a forerunner of the political and social changes of the late 1960s.

Bruce's humor stemmed from his childhood disillusionment with movies, cartoons, and radio. He felt that through its popular culture, America instilled false hope of a perfect world. In response, Bruce introduced a style of humor that combined fantasy and reality to produce outrage by ridiculing such characters from the media as the Lone Ranger, and such leaders as Eisenhower, Hitler, and the Pope. By debunking them, Bruce felt that he would strip them of their mythical appeal and expose their essential ridiculousness. Bruce's pieces were often cinematic in scope—he produced a variety of characters and situations to dramatize society's foibles. In some of his most acclaimed pieces, including "Father Flotsky's Triumph" and "London Palladium," Bruce described characters and settings as if they were scenes from a movie.

Bruce used show business as a metaphor for life; his comedy is based on the assumption that all authority, whether political, social, or religious, was nothing but a racket run by petty hustlers and agents. Bruce regularly incurred the wrath of the outraged authorities he criticized. He made frequent appearances in court on obscenity and drug charges, and his humor became increasingly cynical and his act more unstructured. Bruce eventually dropped the routine format completely as his art and personal life merged. Bruce received support from his audience; in 1964 the courts of New York received a petition from over one hundred leaders in the arts, praising Bruce as a social satirist "in the tradition of Swift, Rabelais, and Twain." Bruce finally turned his performing talents to his own legal self-defense, and in his fight for the right to express himself onstage he lost interest in entertaining. Although his trials ended successfully, he felt his life had lost its challenge, and he died of a drug overdose which may have been intentional.

Bruce achieved his greatest fame posthumously. In the space of a few years, his reputation has reversed itself completely. He is currently considered a deeply moral pioneer of contemporary liberal thought, rather than a childish, perverted comedian, the opinion of most people during his lifetime. Young people are especially impressed by his courage and incisive wit. (See also *Contemporary Authors*, Vols. 89-92; obituary, Vols. 25-28, rev. ed.)

Courtesy of Fantasy Records

RALPH J. GLEASON

Lenny Bruce [is] a wildly insane comic whose material is beyond surrealism, farther out than Mort Sahl and devastating in its attacks on the pompous, the pious and the phony in American culture.

Although Bruce is heavily oriented with motion picture gags and inside jokes of the music business, there is enough of his searing commentary that can be grasped by the ordinary club audience. . . .

Bruce is a good bet for any jazz club in the country; his humor is right out of a roadband sideman's perspective and delivered in a heterogeneous mixture of underworld argot, hipster slang and show biz patter. A standup comic who takes off from the daily paper a la Sahl, Bruce occasionally strays into areas that will bug the sensitive but completely gas the rounders in the audience.

> Ralph J. Gleason, "Night Club Reviews: Ann's 440, S.F.," in Variety *(copyright 1958, by Variety, Inc.), April 9, 1958, p. 111.*

GILBERT MILLSTEIN

The newest and, in some ways, most scarifyingly funny proponent of significance, all social and some political, to be found in a night club these days is Lenny Bruce, a sort of abstract-expressionist stand-up comedian. . . .

[Bruce is] imbued with a fidgety sense of moral indignation. The latter is so highly developed that he is sometimes said to make Mort Sahl, a contemporary critic and friend, appear merely querulous. . . .

The reaction to Bruce is roughly comparable, although on a cerebral rather than a physical level, to that produced in chorus girls by Lou Holtz, who was once wont to prod them with a cane. Bruce's material, all of which he creates himself (some of it ad lib in a dank cranny of the subconscious) is delivered in nervous shards of hip talk accompanied by a series of impersonations made eerily abstruse by the fact. He sticks mainly to the American scene, for which he seems to cherish an affectionate replusion.

                Gilbert Millstein, *"Man, It's Like Satire," in* The New York Times Magazine (© *1959 by The New York Times Company; reprinted by permission), May 3, 1959, pp. 28, 30.*

NAT HENTOFF

Unlike Mort Sahl, whose heaviest ammunition is aimed at the Republicans, Lenny Bruce, the most controversial of the newer "intellectual" comedians, cuts beneath politics into the daily evasions of what he terms "first-plateau liberals." To my knowledge, no other comedian has ever talked scornfully in his performance on stage of "white Jews" who will not fight segregation or has explained in graphic detail how much "sicker" Philadelphia is than Little Rock. (p. 50)

In spite of his proselytizing, Bruce is much more professional as a straight comic when he wants to be than any of his colleagues who specialize in topical satire. Bruce has no equal in such set pieces as a re-creation of an old prison movie with Nat Pendleton and Barton MacLane or a devastatingly accurate odyssey of a Copacabana comic who wants to play a "class' house such as the Palladium in London, and "bombs" abysmally. Bruce knows show business so intimately that his rundown of a Palladium rehearsal is as precisely detailed as a [Theodore] Dreiser description of how a factory operates.

Bruce uses his considerable comic talent, he points out, "to say as much as I can get away with and still make the audience laugh." In his most coruscating monologues, one of his methods might be termed verbal sleight of hand. By stringing together enough Yiddish firecrackers, jazz jargon, advanced Broadwayese, and such bits as the dissection of old movies, he reaches his audiences with his more serious assaults before they are quite aware that they themselves are also included among his targets. (pp. 51-2)

The question now is how far Bruce will go in further exposing his most enthusiastic audiences—the very same "first plateau liberals" he denounces—to themselves. He has only begun to operate on the ways many of them delude themselves in nearly everything. . . . (p. 52)

                Nat Hentoff, *"Where Liberals Fear to Tread," in* The Reporter (© *1960 by The Reporter Magazine Co.), Vol. 22, No. 13, June 23, 1960, pp. 50-2.*

MARTIN WILLIAMS

Probably it is a symptom of our particular American education that nowadays when a man gets off a few good ones aimed at

City Hall or the local upper crust, our journalists will usually describe him as a "devastating social satirist" or something of the sort. Such pronouncements may become heavy burdens even for high comic artists to bear; they form an almost impossible billing for a promising night club comedian. Worse, they may encourage a comedian to look at his work in quite the wrong way.

Bruce did get off some very good ones. And he had the audacity not of a satirist but of a good low comedian, an audacity that popular American comedy has probably not seen since the heyday of pre-striptease burlesque. No attitude seemed too sacred for Bruce to lampoon, no word too improper for him to utter; he seemed perfectly willing to say absolutely anything. An intriguing airplane sketch on [**"The Sick Humor of Lenny Bruce"**], with Bruce as usual taking all the parts, offered a slovenly pilot who showed up for his flight after a couple of fortifying hours in the airport bar (he is afraid of heights, you see) and proceeded to expose every scurrilous suspicion one has ever secretly entertained about non-scheduled airlines. But Bruce followed this with a perfectly conventional bit about a kid who marked up the walls of the airplane with a crayon. Such irrelevance-for-a-laugh may be accepted low comedy, but it is hardly the sign of a true satirist.

Mostly Bruce saw everything as a part of the milieu of Lenny Bruce. There was a sketch about Hitler's discovery by a talent agency . . . , about Ike and Nixon . . . , about policy-making at the AMA . . . , about a conclave on integration by a group of revivalist preachers. All of these could be effectively lampooned so long as Bruce could pretend the people involved talk like booking agents, actors' managers, and hard-bitten publicity men.

Subsequently Bruce's work has taken a more pointedly superior, not to say self-righteous, position. Or to put it another way, Bruce seems to be losing his sense of comic fun. He had one lampoon [on **"Lenny Bruce: 'I Am Not a Nut, Elect Me'"**] about a rather pathetic, small-time comedian of innate bad taste, and his ambitions to play the London Palladium. It came very close to straight snobbery. On his recent **"Lenny Bruce, American"** . . . he comments on the problems of Bruce on tour and his bouts with small-town life. He suggests one might spend idle afternoons going through the local Woolworth's. Many of us would do just that, I think, and we laugh. But one gets the feeling that neither Bruce nor his audience is conceding that he would actually do anything so square, and the joke is really on those who would.

Bruce remains, nevertheless, a very talented man. (p. 60)

[Humor] is not, as some current commentators would have it, always a disguised hostility. Humor may even hold a kind of grudging respect. Try, for example, the famous burlesque encounter between a square disc jockey and a musician on **"The Interview"** [on **"Lenny Bruce's Interviews of Our Times"**]. It is painfully accurate, it is devastatingly skillful, it is hilarious, it is very nearly a work of low comic art. (p. 61)

                Martin Williams, *"The Comedy of Lenny Bruce," in* Saturday Review (copyright © *1962 by* Saturday Review; *all rights reserved; reprinted by permission,) Vol. XLV, No. 47, November 24, 1962, pp. 60-1.*

JONATHAN MILLER

Bruce is a beat magician, a Yiddish Ariel whose hesitant, mumbling, slipped-gear technique, full of breaks and riffs, untunes the ear of the conventional night-club audience who are used to getting their entertainment in a smooth flow of glossy chatter. He is not a public utility though. He mines his material from odd, irregular veins, surprising himself, as often as not, when he strikes a seam of original humor. . . . Following his act is like reading [James Joyce's] *Finnegan's Wake* over and over. (p. 150)

He has been called a sick comedian and yet I don't think the label could have been applied more inappropriately. He deals, it is true, with sex and disease, sometimes with unsettling frankness, but never with relish or just for kicks. He is a collagist, assembling the fragments of urban consciousness without much regard for conventions or taboo. He is almost a verbal Pop artist, pasting together the thousand sordid images of the urban American imagination. (pp. 150-51)

He is not just a snobbish satanist although many of his followers get a lot of satisfaction imagining themselves as members of a new Hellfire aristocracy. Bruce himself is too much of a naive, too innocent in a sense to get much of a social charge from his own ironies. He is really some sort of grubby simpleton whose very lack of sophistication lets him squint through the tissues of modern hypocrisy. He plays the bewildered rural innocent rather than the knowing urban cynic and his encounters with the absurdities of prejudice derive more force from this tone of untutored astonishment than they would from those glib ironies which come so easily out of initiated *Weltschmerz*. It is refreshing to enjoy this ignorant amazement as he draws up short in the face of color bars, prudishness, and all the other self-lacerating hypocrisies with which America is so unnecessarily tortured. He can exorcise, by astonishment alone, the black magic of four letter words. He simply goes on reciting them at his stunned audiences until the words are emptied of their meaning. Then in a mood of ecstatic re-appraisal he recharges them with joyful and entirely shameless significance. "You only want me for my body," he mincingly mimics some tendentious broad. "For what nicer thing *could* I want you," he snaps back with startling simplicity. This almost brash simplification often offends those who would otherwise be his most enthusiastic ally. But then he is not preaching to the converted. He rises to the occasion best of all in the conventional niteries where the bull-necked men from out of town are stung to uncontrollable fury by his gadfly innocence. "That's not very funny. Or perhaps I'm just too old to understand this sort of thing. Tell me, is it funny?" Bruce is really Peter Pan, who makes a therapeutic virtue of his failure to grow up, and one really doesn't have to be very new-fashioned to appreciate him. Nostalgic rather, like the romantic poets who out of their childhood suck up joy and a capacity for shocked amazement, surely the best prophylactic against callousness and bored indifference. (pp. 154-55)

Jonathan Miller, "The Sick White Negro," in Partisan Review *(copyright © 1963 by Partisan Review, Inc.), Vol. XXX, No. 1, Spring, 1963, pp. 149-55.*

ROBERT RUARK

[Lenny Bruce gives his] customers an hour of unleavened four-letter words plus gross assaults on motherhood, the Testaments Old and New, and vivid descriptions of the more basic physical and sexual processes. . . .

As high priest of the sick comedians, as the pinup boy of the hip set, Bruce puts on an act that would gag a goat. But when I caught him at the Village Vanguard, the cellar was packed and the customers hushed except for bursts of applause and loud laughter. I wasn't prepared for the unceasing stream of sewage which appeared to fascinate an audience devoted to Bruce.

Sick humor seems to have been a phenomenon of the '50's. If you will recall, the decade spawned a whole body of psychologically twisted humor. . . .

"Sick" became the catchword of the '50's. You never said anybody was nuts; you said: "Man, you're sick." The alleged humor built itself off that state of inverted mental sickness, and it was only natural that it would descend to the barnyard in its eventual amplification. It was aided considerably by "hip" talk, a sort of secret language known mostly to musicians and marijuana smokers, in which a whole lexicon of careless scatological terminology was added to the punctuation of ordinary conversation. Four-letter words displaced commas, and the profane attack on any established institution, from church to motherhood, became vital to the hipster's jargon. The end product is a man like Lenny Bruce. (p. 39)

Robert Ruark, "Let's Nix the Sickniks" (copyright © 1963 by Robert C. Ruark; reprinted by permission of the Harold Matson Company, Inc.), in The Saturday Evening Post, *Vol. 236, No. 25, June 29-July 6, 1963, pp. 38-9.*

ALBERT GOLDMAN

[What] explains Bruce's unique effect? Certainly, his impact cannot be attributed to his material alone. By now, so completely have the so-called "sick" comics caught on—and so quickly has the authentic radical satire of a few years ago been rendered innocuous by sheer acceptance and then imitation—that it no longer requires daring, originality, or courage to attack sacred cows like integration, Mother's Day, the Flag. Such things are done, albeit in diluted form, virtually on every network. Yet Bruce seems immune from that permissiveness that is in the end perhaps more subversive of true protest than censorship. Uniquely among members of his profession (and matched in others perhaps only among jazz musicians), Bruce continues to shock, to infuriate, to be the subject on the one hand of a passionate and almost unprecedented advocacy, and on the other of a constant surveillance amounting to persecution, so that today, at the height of his drawing power, it is doubtful whether a club in New York would dare to book him. (pp. 312-13)

Bruce's vision forbids the smallest hint of self-congratulation, allows no comfortable perch from which the audience can look complacently down on the thing satirized. Even his "conventional" routines take a bizarre and violent course which transforms them into something quite different from mere parody. There is one, for instance, in which an "ordinary white American" tries to put a Negro he has met at a party at ease. The predictable blunders with their underlying viciousness . . . are within the range of any gifted satirist with his heart in the right place; but Bruce gives the screw an added turn by making the protagonist, besotted with temporary virtue, a forthright and entirely ingenuous Jew-hater as well—sincerely making common cause with the Negro. This is closer to surrealism than to simple farce, a fantasy on the subject of bigotry far more startling than a merely perfect sociological rendition of the accents of race hatred would have been. And as the routine proceeds, the fantasy gets wilder and wilder, with the white man becoming more and more insinuatingly confidential in his friendliness . . . and the Negro becoming progressively stiffer and more bewildered. (p. 313)

Until a few years ago, this kind of humor had never been seen in a night club or theater. It appeared to be completely original, yet obviously it mined a rich, seemingly inexhaustible vein and was, moreover, enforced by a highly finished technique. Critics responded to Bruce at first as though he were *sui generis,* a self-created eccentric of genius without discernible origins. Yet nothing could be further from the truth. What Lenny Bruce is doing today in public had been done for years in private, not only by him, but by dozens of amateurs all over New York City—at private parties, on street corners, in candy stores. His originality consists in his having been the first to use the private urban language in public, and his genius lies in his ability to express the ethos out of which he comes in unadulterated form.

He is, in other words, a genuine folk artist who stands in a relation to the lower-middle-class adolescent Jewish life of New York not unlike that of [jazz musician] Charlie Parker to the Negroes of Harlem. And like Parker, he derives his strength from having totally available to himself—and then being able to articulate—attitudes, ideas, images, fragments of experience so endemic to a culture that they scarcely ever come to conscious awareness. Thus for many people the shock of watching Bruce perform is primarily the shock of recognition. (pp. 313-14)

[The] comic's sensitivity to imperfection and ugliness is heightened by a conviction of his own inadequacy, vulgarity, and hypocrisy, leading him to become doubly intolerant of these faults in others. They haunt him, they are demons which he seeks to exorcise by comic confrontation. The psychological source of such satire is, thus, a persistent, ineradicable hatred of the self, and this is particularly striking in the case of Bruce, whose sense of moral outrage is intimately connected with an awareness of his own corruption. . . . If the practitioner of this kind of comedy is in any way morally superior to his audience, it is only because he is *honest,* and willing to face himself, while they, the audience, are blind enough to think *they* are pure. (p. 314)

[The] novelty of [Mort] Sahl's act undoubtedly stimulated Bruce's own breakthrough and there was an audience ready to respond to Bruce's first original creation—a series of satirical bits based on a potent symbol evolved in the early "home-cooking" days—the shingle man.

A type of "con" man prevalent in the 40's, the shingle man spent much of his time on the road, usually traveling in groups, doing comic routines, smoking marijuana, taking time off now and then to talk gullible slum residents into buying new roofing. Though strictly a small-time operator, the ruthlessly manipulating shingle man came, in Bruce's universe, to represent any and all wielders of power and authority—up to and including the most grandiose. The great world, in short—all political, social, or religious activity—is nothing but a gigantic racket run by shingle men. (pp. 314-15)

Lavishly applying the metaphor of the shingle man to every social institution in the book, Bruce embarked upon a career whose underlying intention has remained constant, though his style has gone through many changes: to set up a remorselessly unqualified identification of power and respectability with corruption. (p. 315)

While he lacks the dramatic gifts of Elaine May, Sid Caesar, or Jonathan Winters—with their actors' techniques of mimicry,

foreign accents, and sound effects—Bruce is nevertheless at his best in personal narratives put across with just a suggestion of the dramatic. His work, in fact, is intensely personal and provides an obvious outlet for his private rage; nevertheless, there is a part of Bruce that is utterly disinterested. Like any satirist, he knows that the only effective way to attack corruption is to expose and destroy it symbolically; that the more elaborately and vividly this destruction is imagined, the greater will be his own satisfaction, and the more profound the cathartic effect on the audience. . . . [He] has taken on himself the role of exorcising the private fears and submerged fantasies of the public by articulating in comic form the rage and nihilistic savagery hidden beneath the lid of social inhibition. (p. 316)

[Bruce regards his audience] as an object of sadistic lust, he hates and loves it; it is the enticing enemy, and he attacks it repeatedly. In the past his aggression was masked, but now it is naked. He may pick up a chair and menace a patron; if the audience laughs, he will observe soberly that he might have killed the man and that if he had, everyone would have accepted the murder as part of the act. Here he demonstrates, almost in the manner of a classroom exercise, the repressed violence of modern society. By making the audience *laugh* at incipient murder, he has tricked them into exposing their own savage instincts. The implication is that given the slightest excuse for condoning a killing, even the absurd rationale of its being part of a nightclub act, society would join eagerly in the violence it so conscientiously deplores.

This public display of the ugly, the twisted, the perverse—offensive though it is at times—nevertheless serves a vital function, for it gives the audience a profound sense, not only of release, but of self-acceptance. Again and again, Bruce violates social taboos—and he does not die! Like the witch doctor or the analyst, he brings the unconscious to light, and thereby lightens the burden of shame and guilt. By its very nature his material cannot come out clear, decorous, and beautifully detached; it must be, and is, charged with self-pity, self-hatred, fear, horror, crudity, grotesquerie.

What is unsatisfactory in Bruce's work is his frequent failure to transmute his rage into real comedy. Sometimes he has nothing more to offer than an attitude ("Everything is rotten. Mother is rotten. The flag is rotten. God is rotten.") At other times, what starts with a promise of rounded development will flatten out into a direct and insulting statement. A sophisticated listener forgives the comic these lapses, understanding that the ad lib approach and the often intractable material are apt to betray the performer into mere obscenity; but people with no natural sympathy for this approach are shocked and offended—there has never been a lack of people in the audience to walk out during Bruce's act.

The reason for these occasional lapses into crudity is the almost total lack of "art" in Bruce's present act; he deliberately destroys the aesthetic distance which is a convention of the theater, established by tacit agreement between audience and performer that what is happening on the stage is an illusion of life, rather than life itself. Like other performers who deal in direct communication, Bruce has always tried to *reduce* the barrier between the stage and reality. He has never wanted to appear as an entertainer doing an act, but rather as himself, no different onstage from off, not really a performer, but a man who performs in order to share with others his most secret thoughts and imaginings. The desire, however, to eradicate the distinction between art and reality has at this stage almost completely destroyed the artistry with which Bruce formerly presented his material. Gone, now, are the metaphors of the shingle man and the show business manipulator; gone, too, are the story-telling devices of the personal narrative and the dramatic impersonations. All that remains are sketchy, often underdeveloped, sometimes incoherent, scraps of former routines. (pp. 316-17)

> *Albert Goldman, "The Comedy of Lenny Bruce"*
> *(reprinted by permission of The Sterling Lord Agency,*
> *Inc.; copyright © by Albert Goldman), in* Commen-
> tary, *Vol. 36, No. 4, October, 1963, pp. 312-17.*

NAT HENTOFF

Bruce has been exiled from the American way of laughter because of his unyielding insistence on excavating his material from our most cherished hypocrisies and most anxious self-images. His main trouble, and it's getting worse, has come from his attempts to make "dirty" words innocently naked again. He is engaged in showing what those words—and reactions to them—disclose of the sexual and other hang-ups of the *moyen* American. . . .

For the most part, *How to Talk Dirty and Influence People* is scoured of self-pity. Essentially it is a sometimes piercingly funny account of the odyssey of Leonard Alfred Schneider, battling through the myths endemic to a Jewish upbringing in New York, seeing other parts of the world from the outside as a Navy gunner and learning the slippery ropes of show business. There are incidents of farce and fraud (with Bruce not always the victim) and sudden illuminations (such as the Marseilles brothel which could have been the setting for Genet's *The Balcony*). And there are transient times of surcease from being a stubbornly provocative loner (as in his love affair with and marriage to a stripper). . . .

Bruce's book, like his monologues, is kaleidoscopic in structure, but it has an organic unity in that it keeps coming back to Bruce's unremitting attempts to break through shibboleths and credos-under-glass to find out what *is*—in himself and in this society. It is a dangerous game, even when you make your audiences laugh. . . . In a sense, deeper than Norman Mailer's fantasies at the time, Lenny Bruce was and still is The White Negro. (p. 10)

> *Nat Hentoff, "Only When It Hurts," in* Book Week—
> New York Herald Tribune *(© 1965, The Washington*
> Post*), November 7, 1965, pp. 8-10.**

KENNETH TYNAN

Constant, abrasive irritation produces the pearl: it is a disease of the oyster. Similarly—according to Gustave Flaubert—the artist is a disease of society. By the same token, Lenny Bruce is a disease of America. The very existence of comedy like his is evidence of unease in the body politic. Class chafes against class, ignorance against intelligence, puritanism against pleasure, majority against minority, easy hypocrisy against hard sincerity, white against black, jingoism against internationalism, price against value, sale against service, suspicion against trust, death against life—and out of all these collisions and contradictions there emerges the troubled voice of Lenny Bruce, a night-club Cassandra bringing news of impending chaos, a tightrope walker between morality and nihilism, a pearl miscast before swine. The message he bears is simple and basic: whatever releases people and brings them together is good, and whatever confines and separates them is bad. (p. vi)

[The] primary fact about Bruce . . . is that he is extremely funny. It is easy to leave that out when writing about him—to pass over the skill with which he plays his audience as an angler plays a big-game fish, and the magical timing, born of burlesque origins and jazz upbringing, that triggers off the sudden, startled yell of laughter. But he is seldom funny without an ulterior motive. You squirm as you smile. With Bruce a smile is not an end in itself, it is invariably a means. What begins as pure hilarity may end in self-accusation. (p. vii)

Bruce is the sharpest denter of taboos at present active in show business. Alone among those who work the clubs, he is a true iconoclast. Others josh, snipe and rib; only Bruce demolishes. He breaks through the barrier of laughter to the horizon beyond, where the truth has its sanctuary. People say he is shocking and they are quite correct. Part of his purpose is to force us to redefine what we mean by "being shocked." We all feel impersonally outraged by racialism; but when Bruce mimics a white liberal who meets a Negro at a party and instantly assumes that he must know a lot of people in show business, we feel a twinge of recognition and personal implication. Poverty and starvation, which afflict more than half of the human race, enrage us—if at all—only in a distant, generalized way; yet we are roused to a state of vengeful fury when Bruce makes public use of harmless, fruitful syllables like "come" (in the sense of orgasm) and "fuck." Where righteous indignation is concerned, we have clearly got our priorities mixed up. The point about Bruce is that he wants us to be shocked, *but by the right things;* not by four-letter words, which violate only convention, but by want and deprivation, which violate human dignity. This is not to deny that he has a disenchanted view of mankind as a whole. Even his least Swiftian bit, the monolog about a brash and incompetent American comic who tries to conquer the London Palladium, ends with the hero winning the cheers of the audience by urging them, in a burst of sadistic inspiration, to "screw the Irish." But the cynicism is just a facade. Bruce has the heart of an unfrocked evangelist. (pp. vii-viii)

> *Kenneth Tynan, in his foreword to* How to Talk Dirty
> and Influence People *by Lenny Bruce (copyright ©*
> *1963, 1964, 1965, 1966 by HMH Publishing Co.,*
> *Inc.; reprinted by permission of Kitty Bruce as ad-*
> *ministratrix of the Estate of Lenny Bruce), Playboy*
> *Press, 1965, pp. vi-xi.*

JOHN D. WEAVER

Two years after the death of Leonard Alfred Schneider . . . , the Lenny Bruce cult continues to flourish, especially among the young who never saw the prophet, never heard his voice or touched the hem of his garment. They know only his records and his writings, neither of which do justice to the man or his message.

At the peak of his powers, when he populated his pulpit with dozens of flawlessly articulated characters, . . . Lenny was incomparable, both as a comedian and as an evangelist. Toward the end of his ministry broke and beaten, his face puffy, his gaze uncertain, the man was something of a disaster area and his message had become a bit garbled. Both, however, have claimed the reverence of a generation whose own world is anything but tidy and rational. . . .

In student-union lounges where John Kennedy's thousand days have come to be regarded as Camelot on the Potomac, Lenny's final agony has become Calvary on the Pacific. In this hip version of the Passion Play, Lenny preached against the straighties, was crucified by the fuzz, and resurrected by the underground press. . . .

Long before the Flower Children began to flock to the holy land of Haight-Ashbury and the Sunset Strip, Lenny had worked the same wilderness, clearing the way for their sexual candor, their drug hangups, their freakouts. He had preached peace and pot, demanded an end to capital punishment, and called on organized religion to stop building new monuments to God's glory and start feeding His poor. . . .

To the young, Lenny is a groovy messiah who drove money-changing hypocrites from suburban temples where they had been salivating at the sight of a new and pretty leg in the choir loft. To their elders, he was a foul-mouthed drug addict who lived by the toilet and, fittingly enough, died by the toilet. . . .

A dark, slender, intense young man, he prowled the stage like a nervous cat, clutching a hand microphone. In those early days he punctuated his ramblings with set pieces (**Non Skeddo Flies Again, The Kid in the Well, Father Flotski's Triumph, Adolf Hitler and M.C.A.**). He used the jargon of the jazz scene, fortified by Yiddish expressions . . . and the public-rest-room prose that was to become his hallmark. The words at that time were a natural, inconsequential part of his act. In his latter years they *were* the act.

Lenny found nothing objectionable in the four-letter Anglo-Saxon words that served Britain's hardy islanders well until they learned 11th Century manners from Norman conquerors who taught them to say "fornicate" and "excrement." . . . He was simply trying to explain that the truly offensive words of the 20th Century have nothing to do with copulation or defecation. Today's dirty words, he contended, are those that put a human being down because of his race, his religion or his national origins. . . .

The ethnic words were intended to shock white Christians, to force them to face deeply buried feelings about black people, Jews and foreigners. The old Anglo-Saxon words made them even more uncomfortably aware of repressed guilt and shame and revulsion. Lenny was dragging his audiences into dark psychic byways they shrank from entering, then flicking on a light switch to show there was nothing to be afraid of.

Audiences squirmed and swallowed crooked, their uneasy laughter making it clear to everyone in the congregation, and especially to themselves, that of course *they* had never believed in the bogeyman. . . .

In one of his early bits, Lenny acted out a brief encounter with two anti-Semitic Texans who came into a Sunset Strip café one evening when he was having dinner. Taking offense at their remarks, Lenny sprang up, adjusted an imaginary cape, and introduced himself as "Superjew." One punch sufficed to send Superjew hurtling backward through the window, depositing him on the pavement in a puddle of blood and broken glass.

Such was the pattern of Lenny's life, the fantasy of the avenging thunderbolt from on high colliding with the reality of a frail *nebbish* pitting himself against the world's cruelty and violence. Onstage, Superjew's message confounded his elders in the temple, but once the man stepped outside, twenty-five dollars richer for the evening's work, he was simply a lonely *schlepper* shambling off to an all-night movie on Western Avenue. (p. 72)

Lenny Bruce and Mort Sahl were products of the Eisenhower years, when the land was awash with pieties and platitudes. Mort struck first, zeroing in on the era's political shortcomings. Lenny attacked its spiritual defects. They were often erroneously dismissed as beatniks, but neither of them had turned his back on society. Quite the contrary, they were calling it to repentance, trying to save it. (p. 74)

Lenny's combination of pacifism and pornography has turned on a peace-loving generation of young rebels at a time when their middle-aged parents have grown accustomed to watching war in living color during the cocktail hour. Small children are free to toddle in while young men are being blown to bits between cigarette commercials, but would be sent packing if they wandered in while a young woman was slipping out of her clothes. On the side of the generation gap where Lenny has come to be revered, the ultimate obscenity is war, not love. (p. 75)

John D. Weaver, "The Canonization of Lenny Bruce," in Holiday *(© 1968 Holiday Magazine Corporation; permission to reprint granted by Travel Magazine, Inc., Floral Park, N.Y. 10001), Vol. 44, No. 5, November, 1968, pp. 72-5.*

DOUGLAS WATT

Bruce's humor was savage as well as irreverent. A slight, intense figure, he would begin his turn, which lasted, I would guess, perhaps the better part of an hour, with a kind of warmup chat, and follow it with a couple of set routines. The chat [was] a somewhat disjointed "free-association" affair having to do with aspects of contemporary life that Bruce either admired or despised, and raddled with the obscenities that were to hobble him. . . . [He would then settle] into one or another of his memorable plotted efforts, such as the hilarious "**Comic at the Palladium**," in which his latent skill as an actor was at its most apparent, or "**Religions, Inc.**," that biting investigation of the executive level in organized religion. He lit up the night, there's no denying it, [with] his one-man war against cant and hypocrisy in high places. . . . The impression he gave was that of a cocky, half-educated young man bursting with opinions. (pp. 92, 95)

By the time of "**The Berkeley Concert**," which occupies about an hour and a half, the substantial routines of old had given way entirely to the small-talk approach that had once taken up just the first part of his act. It is, though, of course, no ordinary small talk; it is glittering, corrosive, and generally funny talk divided into various topics, one deftly flowing into another, and with occasional remarks that illuminate or summarize something discussed much earlier. There is probably too much preoccupation with sex, and there are certainly far too many scatological references, but it is, all the same, a performance of considerable virtuosity. The listener, very much aware of the sorry circumstances, is apt to feel, as I did, that Bruce can hardly wait to sting the police, who are unquestionably represented out there in the crowd. His quick and repeated employment of shock words and phrases, along with his blistering comments on the Catholic Church, is now almost surely directed as much at them as at his audience in general, and his little parable about a developing society that is obliged to sign on an enforcer (the man being hired is told confidentially that some people might think it takes "a certain kind of mentality to do that work") unmistakably is. . . .

Bruce was, at this time . . . fearful of losing the younger audience, to which, by then, racy language had become only mildly stimulating. At any rate, one becomes aware, without unduly exercising one's imagination, of a man practically rushing to an end that may have been propitiously, if unconsciously, timed to keep him from turning into a relic entertaining for handouts in café corners much as, say, Maxwell Bodenheim once peddled copies of his poems in Greenwich Village *boîtes*. The sad fact is, I suppose, that Lenny Bruce was really a wayward evangelist. Given a law degree and an interest in politics, he might have used them to brilliant purpose, possibly as a Naderlike but witty watchdog of the public interest. But then he wouldn't have been Lenny Bruce, an almost classic figure of the tragedian wearing the mask of comedy. (p. 95)

Douglas Watt, "Musical Events," in The New Yorker *(© 1969 by The New Yorker Magazine, Inc.), Vol. XLV, No. 17, June 14, 1969, pp. 92, 95.*

BENJAMIN DeMOTT

At one level [Bruce's] pitiable disasters amount only to another standard-form show biz fall—a chapter to be fitted between, say, James Dean and Janis Joplin. But at a different level the story moves out through the politics of obscenity to broad themes of responsibility—a range of unmet and largely unacknowledged moral and pedagogical obligations flowing from the intensified egalitarianism of the present age. Bruce's agonies, viewed in the latter perspective, cease to seem merely accidental or personal. And the reckoning made of them, by those who from year to year recover the performer to memory, emerges as a guide to conventional wisdom across the spectrum of contemporary cultural politics. (p. 88)

Lenny Bruce was unquestionably tormented by personal ambition, by resentment of the humiliations suffered by every "common" entertainer (celebrities inspire curiosity and judgmental scrutiny, not respect), and by awareness of the shabbiness, stupidity, and uncreativity of performers publicly regarded as his peers. But other forces drove him hard, and among these none seems to have matched the potency of the encouragement and tutelage of his educated audiences—hip reviewers, political and cultural liberals. The latter took up this comedian as a spokesman—at another level from theirs, naturally—a performer capable of translating the taunts at official morality hitherto contained in unread modern classics or small-circulation literary magazines into noise that might actually disturb the powerful.

No need for Lenny to become inward with the complicated quarrels of psychoanalytical theorists about the historical meaning and function of repression; exegesis of problems of cultural continuity was also, quite plainly, not on. To burden a comic with the familiar wearying ambiguities of men of mind would be to steal from his power to sting the complacent. He needed to know only enough to sneer. (p. 92)

Bruce was often praised for novelistic invention, the capacity to seize on the single detail that can spring an imagined person or situation into sight. For the present writer the major marvel was Bruce's way of erupting into voices—his sudden jagged furious casting off from himself into multiple personae. How many languages this man knew from inside! With what ferocity, agility, and swiftness he darted among them, snapping, searing, a wild mimetic wire—"early American demagogue," "hick," "old Jewish man," "impersonal commentator," "MCA shill," "senile moron," "delinquent kid," "toughie

gunman," "Britisher," "German agent," "religious leader," dozens more. Time and time over the laughter welled from an image of furious incomprehension—somebody stunned to blankness by accents that (in that day) hadn't been heard before. . . .

[Much of Bruce's] best comedy depended on a body of experience—show biz—that the bright-boy fans knew little about. Bruce's fiercest jokes were on his own world, not that of "organized religion" or organized repression. He was forever inviting his audiences to imagine the MCA shill as Universal Man—as Cardinal, as Pope, as President, as key Counselor to Youth: would this not be hell and are we out of it? The irony cut many ways, to be sure, and the comedian's control of it was uncertain, lacking in moral clarity (the comparison with Swift is waffle). But at many moments this "standup joker" has the harsh, aggressive abstractness of the show-biz-exploitative mind in exact focus. And in nailing its unreality he obliquely judged all whom show biz cons. (p. 94)

As goes without saying, Lenny Bruce's life story will sink beyond meaning in an instant if made to bear Symbolic Weight. It is, at the maximum, best seen as one more reminder of the poverty of interaction among the lettered, half-lettered, and unlettered in this avowedly democratizing society—a symptom, maybe, of the casualness with which obligations continue to be sloughed off. (p. 97)

Benjamin DeMott, "Lenny Bruce: Case Continued . . .," in Saturday Review *(copyright © 1972 by Saturday Review; all rights reserved; reprinted by permission), Vol. LV, No. 13, March 25, 1972, pp. 88, 90-2, 94, 97.*

GENE MARINE

[Why do] they love him, this over-40 veteran of the strip circuit and the sleazy clubs, who had become more or less famous without ever making it big?

What, in short, had—has—Lenny Bruce to do with [the] counter culture? . . . Lenny never, rigorously never, said "look away" or "look higher" or "deeper." Lenny always said "look squarely *at*." [J.R.R.] Tolkien, sure. [Hermann] Hesse, sure. [Robert] Heinlein, fascist implications and all, sure; you remember about *that,* too. But Lenny.

Was it because Lenny had had a drug bust? Identification? Hell, Robert Mitchum had a drug bust. Why not Bill Graham Presents In Concert GENE KRUPA? And anyway Lenny never talked about "the psychedelic experience," or any of the rest of that mid-'60s Learyesque Huxterism that made such good songs for *Hair*.

Was it some prophetic quality? Ralph J. Gleason has suggested that. But he is even older than Lenny Bruce, and for all his fame as a writer about the rock culture he was never as good (forgive me, Ralph) as when he was writing about jazz and *its* culture. Because that was Ralph's culture, too; he didn't *report* it, he *lived* in it. And so did Lenny, that was *his* culture (yes, and mine too). "I don't understand Chubby Checker," Lenny says in the 1961 performance on this record; but he tells a joke about Gene Ammons.

No, not a prophet, I think. . . .

[*Lenny Bruce Live at the Curran Theater*] is the absolute, complete, quintessential Lenny Bruce. It's all here and it's all you need. . . . If he is a legend for any reason beyond the kind of historical quirk that makes us remember, say, Will Kempe, then that reason is on this record.

Yes, but still, why now? Or why in that flower-entwined microworld of 1966, two months before Lenny died? Not for being "one of us," certainly. I am 45 and if Lenny were alive he would be two years older, which can be called damned near 50. . . . He was *my* brother; but how was he theirs?

There is politics. We have said "counter culture" and mentioned flowers and love, but we have not mentioned politics.

Well: Lenny was against The Establishment, I suppose. And he was a forerunner, a pioneer. I cannot imagine there having been a Dick Gregory ("having been" because he is not a comic any more) had Lenny Bruce not gone before. But there are a lot of pioneers. Finley Peter Dunne was a pioneer, and so— oh, yes!—was Bob Hope, once. . . .

No, you see (or, rather, you hear), Lenny Bruce was, in counter culture terms, politically naive. He was at best an outraged civil libertarian. He was to political humor what Aileen Hernandez is to radical feminism, what George McGovern is to the anti-war movement. Good, sometimes; sometimes *very* good; but not where it is.

Let us, then, in search, range backward. Possibly we can find a prophecy after all. For despite all these reservations, all these yes-buts, we feel somehow that Lenny is not, really, miscast in this hero's role, the armor fits, the incongruous lance manages to look right a-couch and ready.

1961, this recording is—after (right after) a phony drug bust in Philly and a ludicrous, though legally important, obscenity bust in San Francisco. Two acquittals, by the way. After the busts, it is, but before most of the harassment and general shit that turned his later performances into something more like secular sermons than comedy: fascinating or dull, important or inconsequential, but rarely, idolaters to the contrary, funny. This recording is *funny*.

So: 1961. Freedom riders, sit-ins—but no whites yet pouring into the South, not yet that part of the movement. No hippies. No hair. No Beatles. A brand new shining John F. Kennedy (no murders, no, not for a long generation, not at all in anyone's mind), and something strange in a weird place called Laos, but who knew about it? What was there, what that would later touch a flower child, a radical, a leftist European visitor, a disillusioned intellectual? (p. 58)

But, you see, it had begun; and when it began was just when . . . it became Lenny Bruce's world. Or, rather: The world that a startled and mid-thirtyish Lenny Bruce, stock Jewish comic coming up the dingy strip-joint ladder, had suddenly seen, had begun in excited outrage to talk about, became just suddenly, and independently, visible to a whole segment of society.

The Lie. That's what he calls it on the record: the whole thing, the whole plasticized formalized routinized *megillah* from the judge's robes to your mother's saying "ca-ca" when she means "shit". . . .

He says on the recording: "What I want to tell you is: The Lie." And he tells it, in hilarious detail. More than that. He says, suppose into this Lie, this massive institutional agreed-upon Lie, you insert your own private absurd lie for The Lie to deal with—what would happen? And he makes up, the private absurd lies (there is an almost unlistenably funny section in which he inserts into his own trial a pair of imaginary defense

attorneys), and sometimes describes the ensuing chaos and sometimes, because at what he does he is an artist, by dictionary and not show-biz definition, he simply leaves you to imagine your own result until you can't visualize any more for your own laughter.

But like all comedians he is serious. . . .

And so, perhaps, it is the simplest form of unity of all, this obvious unity of Lenny Bruce and whatever you want to call this "counter culture": the beloved mechanism of the socially conscious science fiction writers of Lenny's 1950s, the unity of the common enemy. In this case: hypocrisy. The Lie.

Surely the common focal point for The Movement at its beginning, despite a thousand differences to be hammered out and a hundred yet unresolved. . . . Surely the thing we all sense that somehow links the dropout apolitical do-your-thing hippie freak with the dedicated and communal revolutionary. Not pot. Not rock. Not a congruent mystic communion with Volkswagen buses. Recognition of, opposition to, hatred for, refusal to participate in The Lie.

And if that is a common altar, then it is also one at which some older folks, some of the Depression and World War II and pre-Bomb people, can worship, which explains some otherwise difficult Ginsbergs and Vonneguts and Pynchons and (yes) Woodrow Wilson Hermans.

Which is a good place to stop, except for one thing. Except that there is, I'm sorry, one sly, sneaky difference.

It is one thing to see hypocrisy, to perceive The Lie, and to point it out—or, if you are a comic artist, to point it out hilariously. But there is a touch more to the late Lenny than that. It's right on Side One of this set.

They used to give him a bad time for talking about his own experiences (his detractors called it "whining"), but he said, no, wait. It is only, he said, that I can't help it, I see all these things with an eye for the ludicrous, and I want to share that with you.

Ludicrous. The philosophical term, Albert, Jean-Paul, Henri, Simone, is "absurd." Yes.

It is important, it is in a whole generation an enormous breakthrough, to see angrily or wearily the hypocrisy of a cigarette-smoking, Scotch-drinking authority figure talking about marijuana, of a locker-room male world prosecuting dirty movies. It is another thing entirely, another step and one taken by very few, to perceive absurd-surdity. Because absurdity—ludicrousness, if you want, in exactly Lenny's sense—is no respecter of cultures.

It lurks, grinning and waiting, in the stack of rock records, in the open and honest collective confrontation, in the intensity of the revolutionary commune. The Lie is the culture in which we live; that fact makes Lenny Bruce a culture hero. There is no counter culture Lie, no single web of institutional hypocrisy simultaneously to anger and to tickle a 1972 Lenny Bruce. . . .

But there is enough *absurdity* to notice—oh, far more than enough. And Lenny looked always *at*—never at abstract meanings or at higher goals, but at what *is*. If you believe that you can tell a dirty toilet joke, then you must have a dirty toilet.

If Lenny Bruce had lived to see the culture, he would not be— could not have become—its hero. He could be the hero of no culture in which he lived. Posthumous sainthood, as [George Bernard] Shaw among others saw, comes only to those whom the living could not face; Lenny was, in fact, one of those rare humans too sane to be allowed freedom. (p. 60)

Gene Marine, "Lenny, You 'Meshugginah' You Can't Play the Hero!" in Ramparts *(copyright, 1972, by Noah's Ark, Inc. (for* Ramparts *Magazine); reprinted by permission), Vol. 10, No. 12, June, 1972, pp. 58-60.*

NAT HENTOFF

Before the Kuhs [the reference is to prosecuting attorney Richard Kuh] of his country wore him down, Lenny had become a prodigiously skillful juggler of images, fantasies, flashbacks, jump cuts—all fused into a constantly surprising stripping of personal and social history to the antic bones of the American way of life. Many American ways of life. By then, the mores of show business interested him much less than the opaque barriers behind which all manner of unmeltable ethnics and unbridgeable classes girded themselves for daily survival by making self-deception the only true national faith. . . .

Although everything he said inevitably, inextricably, related to his own pilgrim's progress into the quicksand, the man was protean. In his crackling kaleidoscopic way, Lenny was this age's stand-up equivalent of [Honore] Balzac and [Charles] Dickens. The novel may no longer have been bringing the news of how "the others" live, but Lenny was.

What exactly was he? Not an intellectual; certainly not an ideologue. Yes, he was a performer, but in a quite new dimension. "I'm not a comedian. I'm Lenny Bruce."

He was also not a writer. Just as writing down the notes of a [John] Coltrane solo takes all the overwhelming life out of it, so written transcripts of Bruce at his improvisatory work are as bleakly misleading as imitations of him. . . .

The only way to connect with the meaning of Lenny—at home or in "teaching" him to students—is through the few Lenny Bruce films and the growing number of newly discovered "live" recordings by him. Especially those albums which caught Lenny before his New York conviction started him on the slide to levels of despair that not even he could transmute into transiently liberating humor. . . .

So far, the best available ways of getting a sense of his life and work are *Lenny Bruce at Carnegie Hall* . . . and *Lenny Bruce Live at the Curran Theater*. . . . Though both are essential to the Bruce canon, the second, a San Francisco performance, is Lenny close to the highest stage of his development, beyond the need to depend on "bits" as security nets while he stretched his capacity for free association. He was getting to that high-risk point in the evening at Carnegie Hall; but by the end of the year, in San Francisco, he had the confidence to, as he put it, "just get out and wail . . . I just want to cook and free-form it all the way."

A number of the same themes are plumbed in both sets—his busts and court cases; homosexuals and straights; Las Vegas as a diorama of indigenous sexual rituals in the museum-without-walls of American natural history. But at the Curran Theater especially, Lenny was as I remember him night after night in the early 1960's at the Village Vanguard in New York. Lenny on a high wire, without a net, exhilarated at how he keeps surprising himself, drawing swift, intricate designs out of the air of his imagination, acutely open to all the simultaneous stimuli around and inside him.

At the Curran, as at the Vanguard, there are occasional stumbles, but he quickly regains his footing, and goes on wailing until the wire is somehow gone, too, and it's Lenny in space, a [Marc] Chagall spirit, borne on words and images. . . .

Nat Hentoff, "Lenny: Redeeming the Memory of a Heretic," in The New York Times, *Section 2 (© 1972 by The New York Times Company; reprinted by permission), July 2, 1972, p. 17.*

RICHARD LUCKETT

Bruce's acts depended to a great extent on a multitude of masks, as swiftly dropped as assumed, and each distinguished by a particular tone of voice and manner of delivery. Each act, moreover, would be lavishly decked out with a highly refined version of Victor Borge's "verbal punctuation," and continually interrupted by an exclamatory voice which must be taken to represent the reactions of Bruce the man to the statements of Bruce the comedian. The seriousness of his performances—and they were serious, though it is easy to overestimate just to what extent—depended on the multiple levels of implication that these devices suggested. . . . Bruce's shows were built around units, dramatic scenes, which he often repeated in future shows, but never in the same order and always with the addition of some novelty. The order and nature of the items was dictated by the need to build shows with a dramatic 'shape' to them, as well as by local considerations such as the threat of yet another prosecution or the mood of the audience. (p. 311)

Bruce's whole career depended on his ability to express his outrage at the world which he found himself in whilst simultaneously carrying his audience along with him. It would be false to say that the things which he said were in themselves outrageous, since the force of his act depended on his ability to keep the sympathetic attention of his audience and in order to do this he had to offer something more subtle than the merely insulting, and more interesting than the merely shocking. In fact when reading Mr. [John] Cohen's transcriptions [in *The Essential Lenny Bruce*] one realises that much of Bruce's technique was devoted to making his material seem more shocking than it actually was or to put it another way that he reached a point where he realised that he wanted to shock and found that in fact he was only amusing. (p. 311)

What he said was not so much peppered with four-letter words as oiled with them. The language which brought him into such trouble with the law fits naturally into the flow of his undistinguished sentences and actually generates some of that flow, along with his endless 'you know's and 'OK's. It was Bruce's natural idiom, and the only remarkable thing about his use of it was that he thought it good enough for his clientele and did not laboriously evolve an alternative diction for his acts. Though I understand that Vladimir Nabokov was one of his admirers it is futile to turn to Bruce in order to find instances of a telling use of language or of verbal dexterity. The startling thing about his use of language was his failure to bring it into line with the patter expected of comedians in the late 'fifties, just as the startling thing about what he said was not its substance but its context; it was not the kind of thing you expected to hear in a night-club or from a paid entertainer. As it happened, time caught up with Bruce, and the startling effect of hearing four-letter words used with such abandon wore off. . . . But Bruce was ahead of the game. By the time that the world had caught up with him so far as four-letter words were concerned he had embarked on a series of actions which were to prove, in fact as well as name, suicidal.

Presumably what impelled him onwards during his last years was the discovery that by going onto a night-club stage and delivering a monologue in a manner that was, for him, entirely natural, he could earn very substantial sums of money. The problem was, in the end, that his act was not an act, but was treated as one, nevertheless. Everyone thought that communication was taking place—except for Bruce, who knew it wasn't. Hence the extravagant behaviour of his last years, the deliberate courting of disaster, the drugs, and his eventual death. It was the only means left by which he could define himself.

For some reason this pattern of events is always supposed to be highly affecting. Certainly there is a sense in which it is tragic for no death of a talented individual can be ignored, and all suicides necessarily carry with them a sense of waste and failure that reflects on society at large. At the same time what happened to Bruce fell short of being the martyrdom that his disciples and admirers now peddle as the truth. He was a strange mixture, half Jewish comedian, and half Old Testament prophet. Take out the paradoxes and comic situations from some of the scripts and you come to reality: Isaiah translated by a team consisting of Damon Runyon (language levels and continuity), Ruth Draper (dialogue) and the Marx Brothers (banana skins). As for the four-letter words, on the rare occasions when they are used with specific intent they in fact stand for one consisting of five letters. Y*W*H. For Zion's sake he did not hold his peace, and for Jerusalem's sake he did not rest, hoping that the righteousness of it would go forth as brightness, and the salvation as a lamp that burneth.

If you want to be a prophet, even a minor one, night-clubs are likely to prove an inadequate forum. The world may, for a time, be delighted to be told what it knows already, and the proprietors will be pleased to discover the truth of Gilbert's hideous dictum: "small prophets, quick returns." But no amount of wit, artistry, or skilled delivery is likely to redeem the situation for long. (pp. 311-12)

He did not campaign for new freedoms; he chose instead to go out the grand romantic way, thus making the real issues of no greater or less importance than his personal existence. The book bears this out; he could not make anything that survived himself: the transcripts depend on a sense of their delivery, of a continuous, expletive-oiled, stream-of-consciousness present. The acts may have had artistry but the words do not, though they give us a sense of what that artistry might have been.

The Essential Lenny Bruce is a fascinating document, enormously promising in parts but always disappointing where more than a page is involved. No doubt the book will be a vital element of the cult, which will be with us for a long time. . . . It should kill once and for all the idea that Bruce ever managed to be genuinely obscene. On the other hand it makes something else clearer than it was before: Bruce thought the truth was show-biz. It was a fatal—though not uncommon—mistake. (p. 312)

Richard Luckett, "Richard Luckett on Lenny Bruce," in The Spectator *(© 1973 by The Spectator; reprinted by permission of* The Spectator*), Vol. 231, No. 7576, September 8, 1973, pp. 311-12.*

HAROLD CLURMAN

Bruce's life was disturbed and soiled by the physical, social and moral mess which city life on its lower levels often fosters. His attitude toward male sexuality, for instance, was distorted. He asserted with unconcealed pleasure that men are incapable of fidelity. But he was essentially intelligent, observant, extraordinarily receptive to a wide range of impressions. He was fundamentally honest and, for all that was coarse in him, he possessed an acute sensibility. He seems to have absorbed *everything* from his environment, so that while he was infested with its poisons, he was also sound enough to eject them in dismay, mockery and laughter. The result was ambiguous and, for those who are themselves balanced, largely salutary.

Bruce uncovered the sores of our urban life. He disclosed its filth and confusion without shame because he regarded them as the reality of contemporary existence. He thought them "funny" and was still keen enough to know that they were humanly destructive and that they had their source in the corruption of our society. His "art" was therefore partly a symptom of diseases of which we are victims and, in greater part, a curative. In this way it served a satiric function. If we do nothing but guffaw at its improprieties, we betray complicity with its negative aspects; if we also view it as evidence of what is noxious in the world about us, we must applaud it.

There are artistic as well as social reasons for doing so. Bruce's feeling for the vocabulary of our common speech is richly inventive. His language is a mishmash of gutter talk, the lingo of show business with all its clichés and the scrapings of sophistication such as a half-educated person of alert mind picks up. The mixture, through Bruce's natural volubility, becomes an amazing rhetoric, a poesy.

It would be worse than an exaggeration to call him the [Jean] Genet of the night clubs, because for one thing the Frenchman's language is thoroughly classic; but like Genet, Bruce in his own way created a radiance out of squalor.

Harold Clurman, "Theatre: 'The World of Lenny Bruce'," in The Nation *(copyright 1974 The Nation magazine, The Nation Associates, Inc.), Vol. 219, No. 4, August 17, 1974, pp. 122-23.*

MICHAEL MURRAY

Probably too much has been and will be made of Lenny Bruce. For all his passion for truth, his vision was one-dimensional and circumscribed by the world of strip-joints, jazz, narcotics and obsessive sex in which he lived. There is a primitive honesty in this world, perhaps, but he was mistaken to believe that it represents the "truth," a basic heritage that we are all afraid to face. In his last years, his satire, when it was not a tantrum of abuse, was often a self-righteous lecture. His defenders who compare him now to Swift are overstating the case considerably: granting that "Lenny was his own act," in Nat Hentoff's phrase, and that he cannot be fairly recaptured in transcripts, imitations or even recordings, his body of work, by any definition, was pathetically slim. (p. 214)

Michael Murray, "Media: Wilbur Mills and Lenny Bruce," in Commonweal *(copyright © 1974 Commonweal Publishing Co., Inc.; reprinted by permission of Commonweal Publishing Co., Inc.), Vol. CI, No. 8, November 29, 1974, pp. 213-14.**

ALBERT GOLDMAN

Nature had designed Lenny Bruce to be the kamikaze of the angry comics. He had an inexhaustible fountain of rage frothing up inside him. He also had the sort of spirit that exults in shaming people, and turning them bottomside up. (p. 184)

Lenny Bruce was a hipster. Lenny stood at the exact focal point of that great myth of the fifties: the Underground Man. In that age of universal conformity, it was believed, there lurked beneath the familiar surface of life an anachronistic underworld of ruthlessly appetitive and amoral beings who achieved heroic intensities through the violence of their rebellion against the middle-class norms. (p. 194)

Lenny aimed to be a real hipster. He hung out with the heavy cats—got right down with them. When he took off some okey-doke spook, he had the sound! He could get his voice up in that high falsetto jive range. Do those long, boxed-out pauses—those four-bar rests. Come up with the kind of words that you couldn't find in any *Hiptionary.* . . .

Actually, the ghetto idiom was far more than a badge of hipness to Lenny Bruce: it was a paradigm of his art. For what the language of the slums teaches a born talker is, first, the power of extreme linguistic compression, and second, the knack of reducing things to their vital essences in thought and image. (p. 195)

The vocal impression was not only the basic building block of Lenny's act; it became eventually his model for any sort of artistic statement. An instant shock of recognition, precipitating in a few highly charged seconds a whole wealth of accumulated associations and lending itself readily to dramatic manipulation in skits, bits and movie parodies. As Lenny ultimately saw, you could treat any subject the same way you did a movie star's accent. You could drop back, narrow your eyes, pick out the salient details and roll them up in a tight little verbal ball that would hit like a bullet. . . . [Eventually] everything became an impression.

When Lenny got into his hot creative period . . . , he parlayed all his monologist's tricks into a series of classic movie parodies that were direct descendants of Sid Caesar's movie takeoffs. These movie parodies, Lenny's true masterpieces, are really nothing more than large-scale impressions. Instead of doing one character or two characters in a famous scene from some current picture, he does a whole film. He takes off a whole cast of characters and does all the incidental sounds. . . . (p. 200)

What Lenny did achieve during his first fame . . . was a single comprehensive metaphor for human experience that grew out of his profound ambivalence toward show business and especially the character of the comedian. You find this basic metaphor in all his greatest work, which invariably poses the question: What if all the great people of this world—heroes of legend, leaders of nations, powers, potentates, principalities, the mighty God Himself—are simply the sort of crude, cynical shyster businessmen and degenerate hustlers that you find on Broadway, the New Jersey shingle business or out on the road pushing baby pictures, Swiss watches and fancy white leatherette Bibles? (pp. 202-03)

The first, and in some ways the greatest application of this new satiric metaphor is a famous routine called ***Religions, Inc.*** (p. 203)

In this most familiar of all Lenny Bruce bits, it's perfectly obvious that he has not only expanded the premise—"organized religion is big business"—to Rabelaisian proportions, but he has also rendered with extraordinary accuracy and insight the little worlds of the Bible salesman and the redneck preacher and the telephone-cradled-on-the-neck theatrical agent talking through the night to his "act" out there on the road. Even today—after the record has been played a hundred times and the routine is imprinted on the mind like an old Pepsi-Cola commercial—the exhilarating impiety, the comical obscenity of that last conversation fills the mind with silent laughter. What a way to address the Pope—"HEY, JOHNNY! WHAT'S SHAKIN', BABY!" (p. 204)

Lenny's greatest adventure in TV land—his biggest shot at the medium in a whole lifetime—took place [as a program in the series *One Night Stand,* which featured bright new entertainment personalities]. . . . *The World of Lenny Bruce* was planned as a hipster's vision of New York. It was to be a map of Lenny's sensibility: his favorite neighborhoods and entertainments, his private discoveries and special kicks. Above all, it was to be a dazzling demonstration of Lenny's *sophistication*—of his absolute and effortless command of all those mysteries that were being touted to the general public as the preoccupations of the essential heavyweights, beginning with jazz and ending with [French Impressionist painter Claude] Monet. (p. 231)

Poor Lenny! He was doomed from the first notes, and hadn't the wit to break off somewhere early on and turn the whole thing into a gag. . . .

Lenny's only proper medium was the small, dark, intimate nightclub, where he could take complete possession of the audience's mind, alternately seducing and antagonizing it, making it laugh and think, fascinating it with the rapid zigzag of his own mind and imprinting finally upon it an indelible impression of himself as the most brilliant, funny, charming, handsome and wise young man in the entertainment business. That was the impression Lenny achieved effortlessly in dozens of club settings all through his career. . . . (p. 233)

Lenny was most creative when he was most unhappy. During this triumphant era [his first engagement in New York at the Den in the Duane], he lacked the powerful motivation of tsuris, the etching acid that thrown on the soft shifty surface of his mind would burn away all the illusions and nonsense and reveal the stark outlines of his deepest emotions and convictions. Yet so compelling was the creative momentum that he had built up in the preceding two years that even at this moment of eccentric tinkering with TV and cabaret theater—and every-night dope-partying—he could still gather his wits together and fashion a masterpiece: the single most important composition of his entire career.

As anyone who knew Lenny back in those days will tell you, *The Palladium* was his favorite among all his bits. He regarded it as something apart from the general run of his work, and he treated it accordingly. (p. 235)

What makes *The Palladium* great is simply the fact that it is Lenny Bruce confronting his own essence. There was only one world that Lenny ever mastered and that was the smarmy little world of small-time show biz. Everything that Lenny achieved as a satirist depended on his ability to translate the great world into this little world. Having used the show-biz metaphor brilliantly to burlesque the high and mighty from the Vatican to the White House, Lenny finally turned the genius of his satire on his own metaphor, his own world and his own self in this climactic bit. (p. 236)

Impersonating [the] English conductor and the house booker, who enters the story later, he achieved a perfection of tone and attitude that is unmatched anywhere else in his bits. What these characters represented in Lenny Bruce's scheme of things was simply the coldest, most sharply crystallized ice of contempt for show business, with its mediocre talents and idiotic stage tricks. The characters were the mouthpieces of Lenny's own scorn. The fact that they're English and therefore—in Lenny's eyes—innately snobbish and condescending makes the irony of the comic's aspiration to "class" even keener. Indeed, the whole transposition of this story of comic hubris to England can be considered a device for intensifying the hate-charge to laserlike destructiveness. (p. 237)

Where the routine [ends] is not with a punch line but with a prophecy. Having made his ultimate statement about show biz—having castigated its desperate whoring after status, its preposterous smugness, its crybaby sentimentality and its secret contempt for the public it fawns upon—Lenny Bruce forecasts with the anarchic conclusion of this bit the future of his own art. Impelled by such a passion of moral disapproval, alienated on every level from the business in which he makes his money, heaping scorn and derision and contempt upon the whole idea of the stand-up comic, he obviously had to make a move that would dissociate himself completely from the despised self-image of the laff-grabber. How he would do this, what steps would lead him off the stage and into the arena of violent gladiatorial contention with the lions of law and order—all this must have been remote from his conscious mind when he created *The Palladium*. That it was not so remote from his imagination and his unconscious mind—much the same thing in his case—is proven by the bit. At the end, the message is perfectly clear. When the comic gets good and angry at the audience's failure to respond, he reaches for something heavier than a joke. He reaches for an emotional hand grenade and lobs it right into the house. Not surprisingly, it explodes—and the first person it kills is the comic! That was the prophecy implicit in the conclusion of Lenny Bruce's greatest routine. That he was talking about himself is clear from the booker's last speech, in which he mentions both Lenny's actual age at this time—thirty-four years old—and his addiction to narcotics: a stroke of characterization that would be utterly inappropriate to any Frank Dell type.

Lenny Bruce was talking about Lenny Bruce in *The Palladium*. He was castigating and casting out the ghost of his old self—the dumb putzy kid with his picture in the shoe-store window—and he was unconsciously predicting the course of his future career after the time when he had abandoned comedy for something far more desperate and earnest—*the reshaping of the theater*. For which you may read: American society, which more than any society since ancient Rome has taken show business as the symbol of its national values. (pp. 244-45)

The year 1960 marked a period of high professionalism in Lenny's development, and when he began to pick up flack, it wasn't so much because of what he said as because of the attitude with which he articulated these witticisms.

The hostility that had always lain in the back of Lenny's soul, the cruelty that sometimes emerged in his personal relations, the cold, radar-directed destructiveness that darted out in his deadly putdowns—these traits were now beginning to inform his nightclub act. Instead of superficially shocking the audience while subliminally wooing them, Lenny was now presenting an act that was authentically shocking because the nasty cracks appeared more and more to emerge from a nasty mind. Lenny

was getting cold and bitter on the stage; his act was becoming an act of provocation. Always the self-conscious craftsman, he knew exactly what he was doing—or, if you want to get tricky about it, he had furnished himself with a convincing rationalization for what he was prompted to do from the bottom of his heart. . . .

He was utterly sick of the long, carefully plotted bits on which he had based his fame. Doing *Religions, Inc.* and *The Palladium* hundreds of times from coast to coast had not only turned him against these once favorite pieces; it had turned him against the very idea of the bit as a miniature drama. Lenny had always seen himself as a jazzman, a cat who just walks out there and blows. Now he had the confidence and the technique to be a real jazzman and work free-form every night. That was exactly what he intended to do. (p. 278)

[In 1962 the] once handsome, animated, brilliant performer and commentator was now a fat, bent, shabby-looking street loafer, a horribly dissipated, baggy-eyed, numb-fleshed junkie, with a tragic darkness in his eyes. . . . [He] gave off almost palpable waves of alienation, a creepy, repellent aura, like a wounded animal or some deranged old bum who had wandered in from skid row. . . . There was something ominous about this new Lenny Bruce, something that began with the title of his show—*Let the Buyer Beware*—and extended through his beat, sinister appearance to emerge full-blown when he opened his mouth and began his hour-long Jeremiad. Talking in bursts, like the angry chatter of a Sten gun, riddling off his grimly phrased bits like excoriating be-bop solos, slamming headlong from one bit to another, with the air of a man restlessly groping for some combination of words that will adequately express his rage and pain and vindictive antagonism toward the world at large. . . . (p. 392)

What he had to say wasn't so much the issue anymore as the way he chose to say it. There were old bits like the Shelley Berman number and the Negro at the party. There were recent pieces like *We Killed Christ,* and the election of Norman Thomas. There were things that came out of that week's newspaper and out of his recent arrests in Los Angeles. What characterized all this material and held it together—in a unity that Lenny's act had never before possessed—was the mordant, biting tone with which every subject was seized and slashed and slapped in the audience's face. By pressing and compressing every bit until it achieved a harsh, strident musical line, by volleying these bits one after another into the audience's mind with no softening of tone or relenting of vigor, Lenny created a phantasmagoric nightscape, a wretched, suffering and embittered world. Like another Juvenal excoriating another Rome, Lenny lashed out at the hypocrisy, the cant, the self-deluding moralism of the police, the politicians, the liberals and the journalists. He also lashed himself in the guise of the Good Man, the man who says, "When I cheat, I always tell my wife." That was a new bit and its sour-mouthed irony encapsulated the mood of the whole show. . . . Men and women, husbands and wives, they make each other wretched and they drive their kids crazy, schlepping them back and forth in endless family quarrels.

So much for the family, that happy American home that Norman Rockwell and his ilk were always celebrating. . . . Now, we take the next step up the ladder of social organization to the body politic: our country, right or wrong. How right is our country, Lenny began to ask, when it stations its armies over half the earth, lets its troops rape Italian mothers for candy bars and burns up its enemies at long range with atom bombs?

Where is the right and wrong of war? "If the Japs had won, Jim, they would have strung up Truman by his balls!" (pp. 392-93)

That was the new Lenny Bruce. Not brilliant, imaginative or "inside." Not hilariously funny. You couldn't sing it in the back of the cab on the way home from the show. But it was true and it was *right*. . . . Like many a man before him, like that archetypal character—the old mad king out on the blasted heath—Lenny Bruce had been humanized through suffering. He had suddenly become a man. That was the meaning of it all—the obesity, the shabby clothes, the harsh tone, the *ad hominem* appeals to "Jim." Lenny Bruce, the Golden Boy of American comedy—the cute, the clever, the sick little, mean little, bright little master of the Funny-Funny-Funny pinball machine—had become a man! It had taken years. It would cost him his life. But he had finally found his fate and his theme. (p. 394)

Lenny worked at the Village Vanguard from January 3rd to February 10th. The terrible mental pressure of his fears and his angers continued to distend his act during this period, until finally something broke in his brain and he emerged as a startling new stage character—the shaman, exorciser of demons.

"In every primitive tribe," writes the Hungarian psychoanalyst Geza Roheim, "we find the shaman in the center of society, and it is easy to show that he is either a neurotic or psychotic: or at least that his art is based on the same mechanism as a neurosis or psychosis. The shaman makes both visible and public the systems of symbolic fantasy that are present in the psyche of every adult member of society. They are the leaders in an infantile game and the lightning conductors of common anxiety. They fight the demons so that others can hunt the prey and in general fight reality."

The shaman is not a priest, nor is he a medicine man. The closest thing to him in the Western world (shamanism is primarily a phenomenon of oriental civilizations, especially of the peoples who live along the line that descends from Siberia through Tibet to Indonesia) is the exorcist, the caster-out of demons and devils. The shaman, however, is also an artist—an artist who employs his art for the well-being of the tribe. What he offers the tribe is a performance, an act of intense make-believe. Gathering the people together in a lodge, he first puts himself into a trance. Then, through the use of drugs, drums, chants and other devices, he reaches a state of ecstasy. Eventually, he launches out on a spirit voyage. He travels in an imaginary boat or climbs an invisible tree. His destination is the other world. Along his path he encounters demons and gives battle. Every step of the way, every encounter and blow, he describes vividly to his audience, which sits around in fearful concentration. If the shaman reaches his goal in the spirit world and obtains the information or the powers which he is seeking on behalf of his people, his voyage is celebrated as a triumph for the whole tribe. If the shaman fails to reach the goal or loses control of the spirits, he must be killed.

Lenny's act was pure shamanism: the drugs, the lights, the chants and drumbeats. His spooky appearance and strange surrealistic visions. His symbolic acts, like climbing on chairs and throwing open stage doors. The threats of violence, the emoting, the deep primitive psychological fantasies. You could picture him perfectly in the setting described by the books. In the darkened, cavelike club, charged with tension, the audience sits hunched over, tense, breathless, their eyes fastened on the weird figure in the center of the magic circle. While the tribe looks on in fearful absorption, the shaman prepares himself with drugs in anticipation of the terrible struggle with the tribal demons. Then when the "unspeakable" has been shouted forth, there is mingled with the urgent applause a sigh of release. Purged of their demons by the shaman, the tribe has been freed for the moment, to "hunt the prey and . . . fight reality."

A wondrous achievement! But it entails a danger: losing control of the spirits! Some people want to be aroused and put through profound and shocking experiences. Others not only resist and resent such treatment but want to make it impossible for anyone else to undergo such a séance. As you pondered Bruce's amazing record of recent arrests, you could see that one of his troubles was simply the fact that he was turning everybody on. He had polarized the public: while one group was worshiping him, another was seeking to lock him up. If you followed the parallel of the shaman to its logical conclusion, it was clear that Lenny Bruce *was* letting the spirits get out of control. He was arousing more demons than he was defeating. If things got bad enough, Lenny might suffer the fate of the failed shaman. The tribe might turn around and kill him. (pp. 401-02)

Lenny was an alienated conservative, an exacerbated conservative, a typical satirist seeking revenge for outraged moral idealism through techniques of shock and obscenity as old as Aristophanes and Juvenal. All satirists are conservatives. It's an axiom of literary criticism: a lesson for sophomore-survey students. Turn Swift or Juvenal or Aristophanes inside out: insist upon the positive content of their beliefs—and what do you find? Something like the Houyhnhnms [in Jonathan Swift's *Gulliver's Travels*]: a cold, abstract, unreal universe of "reason" and "common sense" and "sanity" that is simply the pale moral reflex of unexamined moral prejudices.

Satirists are the last men in the world with whom the liberals and the avant-garde should consort. They are radical only in their choice of words. What they have to express is not a passion for change and improvement or a millennial vision of the earthly paradise but an endless reiteration of the follies and sins of humankind. Satirists are moralists, and the moralists of this world are precisely those people who are in the rear—not the vanguard of society.

Lenny Bruce was a man with an almost infantile attachment to everything that was sacred to the American lower-middle class. He believed in romantic love and lifelong marriage and sexual fidelity and absolute honesty and incorruptibility—all the preposterous absolutes of the unqualified moral conscience. He stood at the opposite extreme from the psychoanalyst or the social worker or the lower-court judge who, day in and day out, is compelled to examine humanity precisely as it is and come to terms with human imperfection. Lenny doted on human imperfection: sought it out and gloated over it—but only so he could use it as a *memento mori* for his ruthless moral conscience. So that he could sentimentalize and rhapsodize and carry on as if Eve had never bitten the apple. That was the essence of his moral being: that noting and emoting over human sin. A world where things were not conceived in the first instance in moral terms was unthinkable to him—as unthinkable as a world where sin did not instantly bring punishment down upon it. It's true, of course, that when Lenny got very defensive, he would grab sometimes for the clichés of the liberals and radicals: he would say that there was nothing dirty about the body or that "fuck" denoted "warmth" and "love" and that "the mores" were more important that the "the morals." That was Lenny "the philosopher" talking, generally for publication in a local newspaper. The man, the artist, the entertainer operated on different principles: he knew very well what dirty words were, how they struck a middle-class audience and what they denoted in terms of anger and ugliness. After all, in his day he had been "the sickest of the sick comics." The attempt to make Lenny superior to morality, to make him a hippie saint or a morally transcendental *artiste*, was tantamount to missing the whole point of his sermons, which were ferociously ethical in their thrust and firmly in touch with all the conventional values. (pp. 452-53)

Lenny Bruce was a fuckin' American hero, man. Fighting for the same shit that heroes always fought for in this country. If he was a martyr, it was only because the people of prejudice and limited education didn't understand what he was trying to do. (p. 507)

What Lenny knew at the end—and for many years prior to his death—was that he was in the grip of something much bigger than himself. He was the hero of a myth not of his own making. He was simply its latest embodiment. Just as there were many hanged gods before Christ, there were many brilliantly inspired and desperately self-destructive heroes in the cult of the American Underground. Once Lenny committed himself to the jazz life, to the jazz myth, he was destined to the doom that awaits all such cometlike figures flashing across the American night. He never withheld himself from his fate. Never sought to deflect his destiny. He knew he was doomed as well as he knew his name. (p. 544)

> *Albert Goldman, in his* Ladies and Gentlemen—Lenny Bruce!! *(copyright © 1974 by Alskog, Inc., and Albert Goldman; reprinted by permission of Random House, Inc.), Random House, 1974, 545 p.*

FRANK KOFSKY

[Bruce] arrived at an innovation that was, for its time, genuinely revolutionary: he would synthesize the vocation of night-club comedian with the point of view of a radical social critic. In this way, Lenny was able to reach far greater numbers—and, no less crucial, reach them at a visceral level where his words demanded to be taken seriously—than the intellectual radicals were ever able to do. This, alas, was probably the key to his undoing. Had he been content to write his satirical scenarios in, say, *Partisan Review* or the *New York Review*, he probably would be alive—and wholly obscure—today. (p. 24)

If it was Bruce's mass appeal that set him apart from other social critics, it was his radical stance that distinguished him from run-of-the-mill supper club comedians, however gifted. Unlike these performers, Lenny never restricted his wit to safe, socially accepted but essentially trivial topics. . . . Implicitly, his contention was that no proposition ought to be immune from such scrutiny, whether the case for immunity was made on the basis of sacred status or its secular equivalent, "national security."

It is possible, though probably not ascertainable, that Lenny's probing of society's leading institutions and ideologies became increasingly more radical than he had originally intended, as the pace of harassment by the police, the courts, and the other guardians of the status quo was stepped up. What is not at all open to question, however, is that his biting satire revealed a profoundly moral passion from the very outset. This was apparent in virtually every "bit." . . . (pp. 24-5)

If anybody deserves the spiritual credit for inspiring the slogan "Make Love Not War," it would have to be Lenny Bruce. Yet although Bruce . . . did devote considerable effort to undermining authoritarian ideologies that promoted sexual repression and irrational thinking generally, that was by no means the totality, or even the most important focus, of his work. Rather, Bruce turned his extremely fertile wit and incredibly quick and retentive mind to just about every form of socially sanctioned but logically untenable ideology. (p. 36)

For Lenny, human life loomed larger than ideology, and such slogans as "Better Dead than Red" comprised the *real* obscenity. (p. 37)

Perhaps the single greatest index of Lenny's independence of thought is manifested in the fact that, unlike virtually everyone else of his generation . . . , he never succumbed to the massive doses of cold war hysteria that were unleashed upon the U.S. public from above after World War II. Hence he was able to reject out of hand all forms of anticommunist intervention, whether military or ideological. . . . (p. 38)

Lenny also had the temerity to think the unthinkable, scoffing at the ultimate orthodoxy, that the cold war had resulted from a noble U.S. response to villainous Red aggression. . . . (p. 39)

[Bruce often displayed] his own considerable ability to *hab rachmones* (have compassion) for any group or person in need of it. (p. 42)

With typical Bruce perception, Lenny readily grasped the fact that all the crucial issues of domestic politics during the 1960s would be raised by the Black movement for human rights. Just as quickly, he noted that the liberal approach—integration—was fatally flawed by white condescension and paternalism, and was thus doomed to fail. He was too intimately involved with Black people—they comprised, he estimated at one point, about 30 percent of his audience—not to know that they would scarcely be grateful for tokenistic gestures on the part of white liberals. In short, Bruce was able to anticipate the rise of a Black Power movement that would not regard such would-be "friends of the Negro" with anything remotely resembling affection: "Liberal, schmiberal. Um, hm." (p. 43)

If one had to choose a single word to describe the effect that Lenny Bruce had on those who shared [his] moral concern . . .—keeping in mind that as early as the beginning of the 1960s Bruce was already dealing with the most controversial topics that he would ever touch, and in the most expressive language possible—that word would have to be "liberating." This was particularly true for that generation of young people. (p. 52)

Lenny increasingly served as a major prophet for young cultural and political enemies of the status quo—that is, for the two groups that were subsequently to crystallize as the counterculture on the one hand and the New Left on the other. (p. 53)

It was precisely because Bruce appeared to be such a potent rallying point for young political and cultural dissenters from the conventional wisdom that he was perceived as a threat by Those In Command. To be sure, by comparison with forms of dissent that would come later—ghetto rebellions, massive protest marches involving hundreds of thousands, explicitly radical and even revolutionary political activity, antiwar organizing within the military, and the like—Lenny's merely verbal onslaughts against the status quo may seem a trifle tame. But to judge Lenny by such a standard would be nothing more than an extended exercise in unhistorical thinking. At the time Lenny was at his peak—roughly from 1960 to 1964, a period that, probably not coincidentally, includes most of his nineteen or more arrests—few of these more massive protest activities had erupted through the surface. . . . Moreover, to a certain immeasurable but nonetheless very real extent, Lenny's work helped clear the decks for later waves of radical political opposition. The Berkeley Free Speech Movement, for instance . . . , the Yippies, and other militant left-wing groups were in all likelihood partially inspired by Lenny's own recurrent battles for free speech in the San Francisco Bay area. By the standards of the day, Bruce's work constituted a potentially dangerous attempt to undermine the established order, and as a result Bruce was persecuted for it. (pp. 55-6)

The aim of this campaign of Establishment harassment, in my opinion, was to throttle Bruce by preventing him from performing in public. And, regardless of the fact that Bruce ultimately won acquittal in all but one of the cases in which he stood trial (the Los Angeles "narcotics" arrest)—and continued to maintain his innocence even in that one—throttle him it did. (p. 58)

Lenny needed to work, we may hazard a guess, for more reasons than simply the financial ones. Performing inspired him in his most daring and creative thinking. Cut off from employment, he increasingly became obsessed with his legal defense, most likely in the hope that vindication by the courts would make it possible for him to appear in public once more. The details surrounding his death have never been clear. . . . Suffice it to say that his circumstances . . . would probably have resulted in the death of individuals whose physical stamina was far greater than frail Lenny's was. (p. 60)

That such a thing as Lenny Bruce the phenomenon did come into existence is a tribute both to his ideas and the skill and intelligence with which Lenny presented them. (p. 61)

His ideas were so explosive, his skill in presenting them so formidable, his ability to win followers so great, that he was marked out for destruction (at the very least, economic destruction through denial of the chance to perform) as a dangerous man. The more successful Bruce became at reaching and moving his audience, the closer he came to signing his own death warrant.

But the supreme contradiction is that the very act of snuffing out Bruce's life helped give posthumous currency to his words—and to his ideas. By compelling Bruce to become a martyr . . . his persecutors also helped make him a hero. . . . While his frontal assault on the leading repressive, authoritarian, and irrational ideologies of the status quo was hardly a complete success for Lenny personally, it unquestionably helped hasten the more overt challenges that were being launched even as he was being pushed prematurely into his grave. Many of the values for which he risked and ultimately sacrificed his own life have begun to triumph with the onset of a new generation— the generation that is causing the memory of Lenny Bruce to live on after the man himself is gone. In this way, Lenny starts to emerge victorious over his adversaries; and his victory can only become more secure with the passage of time.

The fact that Lenny is now being eulogized in front of the footlights testifies more vividly than anything else to the powerful effect he has had on the generation that came to maturity during the last decade. Not only are these comparatively young people resurrecting his life and his work but, by sheer weight of numbers, they have made the subject of Lenny Bruce a "respectable" one for their elders as well. Operating here is

a well-known principle of dialectics: with a change in quantity at a certain point comes a change in quality. When enough people subscribe to a heresy, it ceases to *be* heresy. In this way—as with the cold war, the U.S. in Vietnam, integration versus Black nationalism, marijuana, sexual relations without marriage, the status of women in society, the laws on abortion, and countless other topics—it has finally become possible to think the unthinkable about Lenny Bruce: that he was right after all, that the conventional wisdom is—bullshit. (pp. 61-2)

> *Frank Kofsky, in his* Lenny Bruce: The Comedian as Social Critic and Secular Moralist *(copyright © 1974 by Frank Kofsky), Monad Press, 1974, 128 p.*

ANDREW KOPKIND

Lenny Bruce's life was an event in the history of radical culture in America, as well as an episode in the development of comedy. From beginnings as a lousy Jewish "comic" whose jokes were soggier than the *knaidlach* at the Concord, he created a raucous and raunchy style that turned tastelessness into high humor. . . .

[By] the early Sixties he had gathered a reputation and a following that marked the breakout of beat art into mass culture. If you accept the validity of such milestones, the Underground began with Bruce. . . .

[Bruce's art] was perverse, radical, lower-class and unassimilatedly Jewish. . . .

Lenny Bruce was threatening to "square" America (at least to those square Americans who encountered him) precisely because of [these] qualities. . . . Bruce had his antecedents (Sahl, Shelley Berman), his contemporaries (Joseph Heller, Vonnegut) and his descendants (R. Crumb, Dick Gregory, the Fugs, the Firesign Theater). But he was not simply a point on the continuum of humor from Milton Berle (the "Sherman Hart" of the movie) to Monty Python. (p. 46)

Bruce both outstripped his times and fell behind them, in his own life no less than in his humor. There was no simple progression from ignorance to revelation; he always worked both sides of the contradictions.

Today we would call him a committed sexist. "Chicks are different," he told his audiences, and his wife and his girl friend felt him act out that belief. It is said . . . that he despised women: and it has been offered in argument that his wife, his mother, and his daughter—three women—were the only important people in his life. The argument does not necessarily contradict the proposition. Those women were immensely important to him—in their wifely, motherly, and daughterly roles. But they were still different, which made it "natural" for men to have casual sex and unattached lives, while women were "emotionally involved" and trapped in dependencies. He routinely (a bit *too* routinely) made "fag jokes" that only occasionally made the same points about the oppression of homosexuals that he made in every story, no matter how outrageous, about blacks, or Vietnamese, or just plain *schlemiels*. But the long (and tiresome) tirades about the injustices of the justice system went far ahead of the radical analyses of his day, and he saw clearly the banality of tolerance before [Herbert] Marcuse made the notion academically fashionable. . . .

Bruce was not so much a genius at comedy as a forceful actor— on stage and off. He was the first famous dropout of the Sixties:

a star who threw it all away not really to prove a point but to prove the pointlessness of it all. . . . "Words are my weapons," he said, but he was wrong. . . . His life was his weapon. Words are words.

It wasn't the dirty words that got Bruce into trouble, but his way of presenting himself *around* the words. What it came down to was a question of perspective: "a lot of shit with a little art in the middle, or a lot of art with a little shit in the middle." (p. 47)

Bruce put his body on the line for the great cultural revolution of the American Sixties, a political event of mixed blessings to be sure, but now a recognized historical development. I think that his greatest contribution was existential; that is, he dug it and did it when that was not only unpopular but unfamiliar: hence insane, "sick." But he also made important advance gifts of style and substance to what became known as the Underground.

For one example: he conveyed and to an extent translated jive talk and the cool mannerisms of black musicians into the square and straight white world. And to that he added usages of his own that became part of standard white "youth" vocabularies a decade after his death. (pp. 48-9)

Beyond that, he was one of the first comic stars to use the nostalgic heroes of popular culture as the butt of his humor. The Lone Ranger *shtick* (which can be seen as an animated short, *Thank You, Masked Man*), the Little Orphan Annie routine, and his characterization of movie stereotypes actually constituted a new style of satirical comedy. It's now commonplace, of course, to evoke nostalgic images for whatever trivial reasons. But 15 years ago that process broke through some of the mystification of standard middle-class culture and created a counter to it. Bruce's art was "pop" at its most bitter, and its best.

The last area of ground-breaking Bruce surveyed was sex. Not only did he "talk black" and make cruel jokes about Jackie Kennedy and Little Orphan Annie: he put all that in a sexual context. Burlesque comedians, of course, had been laying on smut for years (and Lenny was literally in that tradition). But they never talked about the First Lady's bosom or rambled on about intercourse with a chicken.

A lot of demolition and excavation work went on before the new foundations of a sexually liberated sensibility began building just a few years ago, and Bruce was there at the start with his own steel ball and dirty spade. The contradictions in his own sexual behavior—as well as within his routines—could not be resolved until the new structures were around for support. Bruce needed the women's and gay movements and the generalized sexual liberation consciousness to help him over his humps and hang-ups: not as therapy, of course, but to provide an alternative to ways of thinking that he had no external basis to question. For instance, his striking preoccupation with homosexuality and what he called "deviation" may or may not have sprung from anxiety or confusion about his own sexuality. . . . But until there were accepted ways for other people to talk about such matters, and understand them, Bruce had to make his own blind stabs in the dark. It is a sign of his remarkable intuition that so many of them were aimed at the right place.

Bruce had the anti-hero's typical dismal view of himself all along: the anti-egoist's own form of ego-tripping. "All my humor is based on destruction and despair," he said rather grandly. And not so grandly: "I'm a prisoner in a goddamn B movie." He was still, after all, a beatnik; in the absence of promising movements for change, it was every deviate for himself against an unyielding system. I usually recoil from the argument used in apologies for failed political leaders, like John Kennedy, that they would have been somehow "different" or better if they had lived to see the changes that came after their deaths. But it may just be true in Bruce's case. How he would have connected with the quite different world and changed heads just a few years after he died must be speculation, but not entirely the idle kind. Because now we can see him, hear him and read about him against the perspective of a decade he helped to inform. (p. 49)

Andrew Kopkind, "Resurrection of a Junkie Prophet," in Ramparts *(copyright, 1975, by Noah's Ark, Inc. (for* Ramparts *Magazine); reprinted by permission), Vol. 13, No. 6, March, 1975, pp. 45-9.*

Jimmy Cliff
1948-

(Born James Chambers) Jamaican songwriter, singer, and musician.

Cliff is credited with popularizing reggae, a combination of calypso music, African rhythms, and American rhythm-and-blues that began in the ghettos of Jamaica. His performance in the 1972 cult film *The Harder They Come* caused a critical and popular sensation, leading some people in the music industry to predict that reggae would become the essential music of the 1970s. This prediction was never fulfilled, and Cliff has had a difficult time pleasing critics since. He has, however, a group of loyal supporters who believe that he has opened many doors for reggae in England and America.

Cliff is known as an accessible reggae artist, a label that has both helped and hurt him. While it has made him popular with audiences unfamiliar with the form, it has been a source of contention between Cliff and reggae purists because Cliff has broken musical and lyrical reggae conventions. He produces music that sounds smoother and more polished than most reggae. His themes are universal and express vastly different concerns than those of other reggae artists. These differences, and the fact that his writing has its roots in Islam and not Rastafarianism, have made him a controversial figure in Jamaica. To this Cliff responds that reggae's greatest weakness has been its insistent isolation from the mainstream of western culture and the failure of its artists to write more original material. Cliff loyalists believe that he, like many artistic pioneers, has had to sacrifice the favor of critics to pursue his commitment to innovation.

Cliff's life bears considerable resemblance to that of Ivan, the hero of *The Harder They Come*. At the age of fourteen Cliff collected some of his songs, left his home in the small Jamaican village of Sommerton, and moved to Kingston, where he hoped to record successfully. Cliff faced the corruption and treachery of the Kingston recording network. He received little money for any of his work until he was twenty-one, despite the fact that he was considered a successful recording artist by the time he moved to England in 1965. Cliff's first years in England were traumatic. He confronted racism and bigotry and discovered that British audiences were not open to the reggae sound. It was at this point that he began to experiment, combining reggae and other musical forms in the hope of reaching a larger audience.

Cliff's work has focused on the racism and desolation he experienced in England and his faith in his ability to overcome their deadening psychological effects. "Hard Road to Travel" and "Many Rivers to Cross," both of which express this pain and faith, are considered his masterpieces. The acclaimed "Wonderful World, Beautiful People" is more optimistic and reveals Cliff's humanism and his holistic world view. While this song is credited with giving reggae international respectability, "Wonderful World, Beautiful People" also marked the beginning of Cliff's differences with reggae traditionalists. Some reggae supporters have interpreted the song's universal theme as Cliff's attempt to dilute the form. Other critics have stated that without "Wonderful World" reggae might still be struggling to gain a large audience.

In general, critics view Cliff's later work as disappointing. However, Cliff continues to move in a new direction lyrically and musically, and he remains a great influence on other reggae artists.

PAULINE KAEL

[The film "The Harder They Come"] is a mess, but the music is redeeming, and Jimmy Cliff's joy in music, along with the whole culture's, stays with you. (The title song goes on playing in your head.) (p. 121)

> Pauline Kael, "The Riddles of Pop," in The New Yorker (©1973 by The New Yorker Magazine, Inc.), Vol. XLIX, No. 1, February 24, 1973, pp. 119-22.*

LENNY KAYE

[The soundtrack from *The Harder They Come*] provides an introductory overview of the reggae world that is pretty much unequaled to date, at least in America, and thus highly recommended for any who wish to initially plumb the mysteries of this latter-day inheritor of the ska and rock steady tradition. . . .

[It] is essentially a greatest hits collection—leaning heavily on the work of the film's star, Jimmy Cliff—and one which appears to have been chosen as much for variety as for scenic relevance. It runs the gamut from the sleek and soul-influenced (most of Cliff's contribution falls in this vein) to voices deep within the reggae peer group. . . .

Fittingly, it's Cliff who sets the overtone for *The Harder They Come*, both in the movie's two themes and a matched set of jewel-like pieces that do much to describe the life-force that reggae attempts to deal with. In his hands, the songs are wailing allegories of triumphal hope, man working in the face of tremendous odds. . . .

> Lenny Kaye, ''Records: 'The Harder They Come','' in Rolling Stone *(by Straight Arrow Publishers, Inc. © 1973; all rights reserved; reprinted by permission), Issue 133, April 26, 1973, p. 55.*

ED WARD

Jimmy Cliff is the reggae-singing outlaw star of *The Harder They Come*, so naturally his music is featured in the soundtrack. . . . [The title song] deserves to be a hit. In fact, once the movie starts getting around . . . I don't see how anyone can stop it. The same goes for **"You Can Get It If You Really Want,"** . . . which Cliff does to perfection.

> Ed Ward, ''Records: 'The Harder They Come','' in Creem *(© copyright 1973 by Creem Magazine, Inc.), Vol. 5, No. 1, June, 1973, p. 63.*

CHARLIE GILLETT

Put the needle on Jimmy Cliff's *Unlimited* and the grooves writhe like a poised snake, the record grows hot with anger, and the air fills with the pungent smell of despair. . . .

The songs are almost all about exploitation, of Jamaica, its music and Jimmy himself. "You stole my history, destroyed my culture," he accuses in **"The Price of Peace,"** you "cut off my tongue so I can't communicate . . . hide my whole of life so myself I should hate." The slightly stilted language and the righteous indignation are reminiscent of Curtis Mayfield's songwriting style, although the music is less claustrophobic and mechanical than Mayfield's, more immediately accessible to an uncommitted listener. By the end of the second side the listener might accept Jimmy's arguments and feel contrite, but might also feel little inclination to play the record again: Too much condemnation is eventually intolerable, even when justified by strong evidence.

And there is plenty of justice to Jimmy's case. Jamaican music has been scandalously ignored by the American music business. . . . Since the mid-Sixties, a large proportion of the most *infectious* records have come from Jamaica, driven by rhythms which evolved and changed their forms and names while always compelling dance. . . . [Jamaican musicians] relied on subtlety and melody to weave their insidious way into their listeners. But not only were the musicians wonderful, so were the singers, who took advantage of the freedom a reggae rhythm offered by improvising melodies and lyrics. And Jimmy Cliff was one of the best, as the re-issued album, *Wonderful World, Beautiful People*, proves. . . .

Almost every track on that LP could have been a hit single, if there had been the appropriate push behind reggae at the time. But in 1969 reggae lacked the backing of people in positions of power. There was no one to cajole and convince the music business and its audience that this was *the* music. So these songs—**"Time Will Tell," "Hard Road to Travel"** and the startling **"Vietnam"**—got lost, leaving Jimmy to be judged by history for his sole hit **"Wonderful World, Beautiful People,"** whose lyrics hardly reflected his conclusions about life. . . .

Hence, *Unlimited,* with song titles like **"Commercialization"** and **"Rip Off."** But reggae seems incapable of infectiously conveying a down mood, the words sound harsh, even Jimmy's voice loses its charm. When he turns the ideas around, though, and sings with hope and promise, the magic is still there, and **"Born To Win"** and **"Oh Jamaica"** represent everything that reggae music in general and Jimmy Cliff in particular can do. But *Wonderful World* is the LP that everyone should have.

> Charlie Gillett, ''Records: 'Unlimited' and 'Wonderful World, Beautiful People','' in Rolling Stone *(by Straight Arrow Publishers, Inc. © 1973; all rights reserved; reprinted by permission), Issue 144, September 27, 1973, p. 98.*

ED WARD

Reggae is gonna make it. I know it. I know it with all the conviction of a religious convert, and I've been spreading the word. . . .

Unfortunately, the record which is going to change things so drastically is not Jimmy Cliff's new album. I say "unfortunately," because [*Unlimited*] is released on a major US label which is perfectly capable of doing a more than honorable job of promoting it, getting it into the stores, and keeping it in the public eye. But I'm afraid Jimmy Cliff, in his mid-20s, is already a has-been, at least as a singer. He was electrifying in the movie *The Harder They Come,* and both his acting and his songs held the picture together, but all those songs date from the same era which produced his LP masterpiece, *Wonderful World, Beautiful People*. . . . Since then, he's done a lot of work but little of it has been reggae. . . . And now, we're asked to believe that Jimmy has returned to his roots and cut *Unlimited.*

Well, it's not awful, I'll give it that. It could have been, especially given Jimmy's political proclivities these days, which make only slightly more sense than David Peel's. One song, **"On My Life,"** is even pretty decent. But on the whole, it's a very poor showing, with embarrassing lyrics on songs like **"Commercialization"** and **"Poor Slave."** . . . In fact, some of the songs aren't even reggae and sound more like low-budget soul music.

> Ed Ward, ''Records: 'Unlimited','' in Creem *(© copyright 1973 by Creem Magazine, Inc.), Vol. 5, No. 6, November, 1973, p. 70.*

JAMES ISAACS

[Jimmy Cliff] has for the past 10 years been the most commercially celebrated artist performing the highly stylized Jamaican pop musical idiom known as reggae. . . .

This metrical innovation from Jamaica is perhaps the ultimate "body music" and, with the possible exception of Bob Marley and The Wailers, nobody has it covered more completely than Jimmy Cliff. . . .

While [*Unlimited*] has several redeeming qualities, . . . the album is a far cry from his galvanic 1969 set, *Wonderful World, Beautiful People* . . . , which stands as a cornerstone of reggae.

Unlimited is a "concept album" whose theme is the oppression of black people, Jamaicans and the artist himself. Unfortunately Jimmy tends to wax a bit didactic, whereas his message was more universal and subtly rendered on *Wonderful World*. (p. 22)

Unlimited strives for righteous outrage but too often leaves us with self-righteous platitudes. (p. 23)

James Isaacs, "Record Reviews: "'Unlimited'," in down beat *(copyright 1973; reprinted with permission of* down beat*), Vol. 40, No. 19, November 22, 1973, pp. 22-3.*

SUSIN SHAPIRO

Jimmy Cliff is an artist to be watched. If you haven't seen *The Harder They Come*, starring Cliff in the first feature film made in and about Jamaica, do. Cliff wrote and sings five of the film's songs and they are stunners, embodying the kinky persona he projects in his role as a street singer who asks too many questions and wants the world to shake ass when he makes music. . . . [His] lyrics combine a touching sincerity with the arrogance of youth. He left me lost on the last notes of his persuasive lullabies, ready for more.

The soundtrack album . . . is a delight, offering a vivisection of Jamaican music by Cliff and other pop artists. . . . It's downright defiant, and only threatening if you got what you want. Yet, as in the movie, Cliff comes on strong and emerges as the music's man of most substance. His style was spawned from Jamaica's cradle and nourished by English and American pop until a cross-fertilization occurred to produce his singular sound. Reggae was his chief craft but, just as Marvin Gaye and Stevie Wonder were merely "soul" singers at first, Cliff's reggae thing keeps on growing and narrow definitions crumble.

This period of experimentation is far from over. It is in evidence on *Unlimited*. . . . The lp is hybrid; the departures from regular reggae are interesting even if they don't always work. (p. 81)

["**World of Peace**"] illustrates the excesses that mar this lp. It borders on the banal, lyrically; the message is larger than even the Mormon Tabernacle Choir could handle. The instruments sound great but they drown in the importance of the statement. Like Marley, Cliff spices the carefree easy beat with social conscience. Slavery and oppression are most often dealt with, the singers snickering at the wispy garments of pretension and dishonesty. But the power of such emotions, so well expressed in *The Harder They Come*, becomes pulverized too often here by a cloying earnestness. . . . This problem remains throughout, most notably on "**Commercialization**" and several cuts on side two, including the otherwise compelling "**Price of Peace.**" Where is the diamond in the rough of *Harder They Come*? Shimmering somewhere in the gold wristwatches and rings smothering the pluck of the funkiest rhythms on earth.

Still Cliff is by no means complacent; musically his mixing and matching of gospel, soul, reggae and pop can be exciting. . . . "**Oh Jamaica**" should be her national anthem. . . . Cliff opens the song with a jibe at all patriotic songs, then offers a more palatable alternative.

Wonderful World, Beautiful People, first released three years ago . . . , should not again go unnoticed. It contains Cliff's most moving personal testimony, "**Many Rivers to Cross.**" . . . Cliff is at his best when bemoaning all the shit he's had to swallow; the burdens he had to shoulder seem worthwhile when a song like this is the end product. "**Vietnam**" rocks okay and has something to say besides. . . . [You] can almost feel Cliff ready to spread his wings.

There can be no doubt of the expansion of energies from *Wonderful World* to the more eclectic *Unlimited*. Although *Harder They Come* stands apart on the strength of Cliff's inspiration and momentum from working on the film itself, *Unlimited* spans a wider stance and is a more adventurous effort. The passions of recklessness are giving way to a cooler professionalism. But because it lacks power, it doesn't deliver all the tempting promises that *Harder They Come* made. It's a substantial step up the stairs that lead where? with occasional slip-ups on the lyrical ladder. (pp. 81-2)

Susin Shapiro, "'Wonderful World, Beautiful People' and 'Unlimited'," in Crawdaddy *(copyright © 1974 by Crawdaddy Publishing Co., Inc.; all rights reserved; reprinted by permission), January, 1974, pp. 81-2.*

PETER REILLY

Of late there seems to be an awful lot of Jamaican reggae music, with its hypnotic, rock-influenced beat, around. Some of it is good, most of it bad, and so far I've heard only one recording in the well-mixed genre that I consider unique. It is Jimmy Cliff's even further hybridized new . . . release titled "**Unlimited.**" . . .

Track after track, it burns with the intense heat of a tropic afternoon as Cliff kneads and molds the basic reggae sound into a completely contemporary and individual new form. . . . [Though] Jamaican reggae is not an extempore art, it sometimes sounds that way, perhaps because of its heavily vernacular lyrics and the homely nature of its subject matter: Cliff's *Commercialization*, for example, is a rough-cut gem about street life and street people, and *Oh Jamaica* is a yearning and genuinely touching anthem of affection for his Caribbean homeland.

I was alternately stirred, delighted, moved, and enchanted by Jimmy Cliff's work here. He has taken a somewhat limited and restricting musical form, opened it up, and adapted it to the sensibilities of the Seventies. He has kept all the best of the flavorful original and added something personal and dramatic of his own. He's simply terrific, and so is this album.

Peter Reilly, "Jimmy Cliff's Individualized Reggae," in Stereo Review *(copyright © 1974 by Ziff-Davis Publishing Company), Vol. 32, No. 1, January, 1974, p. 86.*

DAVE MARSH

Jimmy Cliff's initial impact last year, based upon his starring role in the film, *The Harder They Come* and his work on its soundtrack LP, made it seem that he might come to be considered the best, or at least the most accessible to Americans, of the reggae singers. But the enormous expectations created by the movie have made his subsequent work—last year's *Unlimited* and this album—seem worse than it really is. Because Cliff is such a fine vocalist, even his worst efforts are listenable, but his initial promise has been marred by the uneven quality of much of the material he sings.

It was easy to see why **Unlimited** failed. Recorded for Warner Bros., it became trapped in the pitfall of that company's production mill, which has a pronounced tendency to reduce everything to a variant of Southern California pop. But hidden beneath the slickness were some good songs. . . . If the album lacked a song as powerful as **"You Can Get It if You Really Want"** or as deeply felt as **"Many Rivers to Cross,"** it gained impact through repeated exposure: The more you listened, the more you wanted to.

Struggling Man strays from reggae only once . . . but it still isn't the break-through recording Cliff needs to become a major artist. Part of the problem is generic—reggae is the most exciting form of American pop in years, but it has a disturbing tendency to become just a musical formula—and part of it is that the songs here aren't great ones. **"Let's Seize the Time,"** the worst, sounds like it was written by a Jesus freak trying to co-opt New Left rhetoric.

Interestingly, the songs Cliff wrote alone are the best. **"Going Back West"** is spiritual in the way that **"Many Rivers to Cross"** was, though its imagery is much more secular; **"Struggling Man"** has something of the life that made **"You Can Get It"** so great. . . . Cliff's instinct for melody and the alternately joyous and languid reggae beat still make this a most listenable album. When he sings like he means it . . . and when the material is worthwhile, this album proves that the promise is still there.

> Dave Marsh, ''Records: 'Struggling Man','' in Rolling Stone *(by Straight Arrow Publishers, Inc. © 1974; all rights reserved; reprinted by permission), Issue 168, August 29, 1974, p. 58.*

PETE WELDING

[**Struggling Man**] is a very pleasant reggae outing that is most effective as a program of low-keyed, easy dance music. While nicely crafted, the songs are not all that distinctive as pop fare. There's nothing wrong with them but, for all their unforced rythmic resilience and melodic infectiousness, there's nothing all that memorable about them either. Not one of them sticks in the mind, even after repeated playing. And if a pop song doesn't do that, what does it do?

The absence of striking song materials is a really serious deficiency and all of Cliff's virtues as singer and producer cannot compensate sufficiently for this lack. One cannot criticize or take exception to any of the songs. As I noted, there's nothing really ''wrong'' with them; melodically and textually they're quite attractive, very pleasant. . . . It's largely a matter of degree, I suppose. That is, in general outline the songs are consonant with the conventions of reggae music (they definitely have that sound and feel) but they never go any farther than that. None attains the singular, beautifully wrought, almost gemlike quality of the authentically successful pop song. There is, however, a knowing, consistent professionalism to the entire album and if your're a rabid reggae fan this will make for an engaging, though scarcely ear-opening, addition to your LP collection.

> Pete Welding, ''Record Reviews: 'Struggling Man','' in down beat *(copyright 1974; reprinted with permission of* down beat), *Vol. 41, No. 16, October 10, 1974, p. 22.*

ROBERT CHRISTGAU

Yes, I loved him in *The Harder They Come* even more the second time, and the soundtrack album is the bestest they come. It also contains only three Jimmy Cliff songs. All his other good ones are on **Wonderful World, Beautiful People**. . . . The hookless homiletics of [**Music Maker**], albeit better-realized than those of **Struggling Man** . . . , portend a non-star of the future—or a false one.

> Robert Christgau, ''The Christgau Consumer Guide: 'Music Maker','' in Creem *(© copyright 1975 by Creem Magazine, Inc.), Vol. 6, No. 9, February, 1975, p. 13.*

VERNON GIBBS

It has been three years since *The Harder They Come* lifted reggae from obscurity to culthood and raised hopes that Jimmy Cliff would begin a long reign as an arbiter of hip Caribbean liberalism. At the same time, people noticed Bob Marley, leader and political ideologist of The Wailers, who's managed to gain a level of notoriety that threatens to cast him in the mold of a minor league Dylan.

Thankfully, that kind of media hysteria passes, bolstered no doubt by the sobering reality of light sales. Both Marley and Cliff can now be examined in a more realistic light. In the last three years, Jamaican reggae bands have followed the political vision inspired by Cliff and The Wailers, rejecting ''commercialization''—an attempt at Jamaicanization of Black American pop by simply changing the beat. But materialism and commercialism are essential parts of Jamaican culture. Reggae is different not because Jamaicans wanted to create a different form of Western protest music, but because what they thought was an imitation of American music turned out to be their own.

Jimmy Cliff, long the most creative individual in the movement, has made the obvious surface changes by producing his latest albums in a style compatible with American tastes. . . . The romanticists who like their reggae served up in the primitive style (the Kingston studios have been turning it out for ten years) are quick to cry ''sell out,'' and claim that Cliff has lost the affection of the Jamaican people. They like to point to Marley as being representative of true reggae because his music hasn't been stained by slick production and his image hasn't been spoiled by a haircut.

What most of them don't realize is that Cliff represents Jamaica just as well as Marley ever will, because even if Cliff appears to be more of a member of the Jamaican ruling class, more Jamaicans aspire to be members of the ruling class than aspire to be rebels. . . .

In spite of what you might hear to the contrary, Cliff's brand of genteel respectability is genuinely Jamaican.

Whatever the limitations of music as an organizational rallying point (a lesson young Americans learned in the '60s), the ideology it represents is important. No one can deny that Dylan, the [Jefferson] Airplane and the political movements they embraced were crucial in abetting a new kind of attitude. The same cannot be said of reggae right now, even though both Cliff and Marley are intent on making strong political statements. . . .

Cliff and Marley are the leaders of a music that chronicles political oppression as one of its major precepts, but their effectiveness will be determined only when reggae as political music oversteps its boundaries of "minority suffering" music.

Even if that never happens, the reggae that has already been released in this country makes a good case for the reggae-as-political-protest romance. Particularly stunning are Jimmy Cliff's latest album, *Music Maker,* the soundtrack from the movie, *The Harder They Come* and The Wailers' *Burnin'* . . . .

The Harder They Come soundtrack is packed with protest. The title tune, with its wry play on both the cliche and the movie *The Harder They Fall* (Bogart), is Cliff at peak form and effectively delineates why it is he and not Marley who must be considered to be the Dylan of reggae. The song has an air of tightly controlled menace. . . .

The looming presence of Jimmy Cliff pervades the album and the other artists are essentially guests, but *The Harder They Come* is the cornerstone of the romance and cannot be overlooked. It sets the tone for Cliff's brilliant *Music Maker,* which has been ignored but nevertheless gives Cliff preeminence in the forum. . . .

Marley lacks the subtlety and innuendo that sometimes seems about to edge Cliff's lyrics upward into poetry; consequently Marley's songs seem more like ranting. . . .

Cliff's *Music Maker* is . . . to reggae what [Miles Davis's] *Bitches Brew* was to jazz or [Jimi Hendrix's] *Electric Ladyland* to acid rock—the ultimate definition of a major form of contemporary music. Originally called *House Of Exile,* it was changed to *Music Maker* because one song examines the Black struggle in political terms and the other examines it as a musical phenomenon. It is a prophecy of the decline of The West, and messages like **"Foolish Pride," "You Can't Be Wrong And Get Right," "No. 1 Rip-Off Man," "I've Been Dead 400 Years"** and **"Money Won't Save You"** are delivered with the restraint of knowledge that gives them the ring of inside information.

Jimmy Cliff speaks for The Third World too!

Vernon Gibbs, "A Reggae Politic" (revised by the author for this publication), in Crawdaddy *(copyright © 1975 by Crawdaddy Publishing Co., Inc.; all rights reserved; reprinted by permission), August, 1975, p. 71.**

STEPHEN DAVIS

Like rock and roll, reggae has both a light and a dark side. The light is perhaps personified by Jimmy Cliff. . . . Cliff's music, such as **"Many Rivers To Cross," "You Can Get It If You Really Want,"** and the title song of . . . **"The Harder They Come"** . . . reveals a proselytizing optimism that is a hallmark of light-hearted reggae.

Cliff also has a new album, **"Follow My Mind"** . . . , that is interesting because it shows how fragile reggae can be, and how difficult it is to export. The album's tracks recorded in Jamaica (**"Going Mad," "The News"**) bristle with the raw, assertive energy essential to authentic reggae. But the songs recorded in Los Angeles with the cream of that city's session musicians seem either ennervated or slick. It appears that the further reggae strays from its Trenchtown roots, the more likely its absorption into a more mainstream pop form. (p. D18)

Stephen Davis, "Reggae—Jamaica's Inside-Out Rock and Roll," in The New York Times *(© 1975 by The New York Times Company; reprinted by permission), November 30, 1975, pp. D1, D18.**

BRUCE MALAMUT

[*The Harder They Come*] catapulted Cliff to fame as a renegade culture hero. Too bad it's been downhill for Jimmy since—his own music has hardly attained the heroic status promised by his film role & the music he sang therein. His records since . . . tend to be more calypso/soul-slick than highlife/jass-raw. Sounds like a transmutation of Traffic and Freddie & the Dreamers with Richie Havens, closer to Vegas than God. Peace & carrots lyrics about how he loves his mom and how we should all get together. . . . With the right kinda band & a songwriting shakedown, Jimmy could do it. . . .

Bruce Malamut, "Royal Jamaican," in Crawdaddy *(copyright © 1976 by Crawdaddy Publishing Co., Inc.; all rights reserved; reprinted by permission), January, 1976, p. 73.**

JOHN MORTHLAND

Since he electrified audiences in *The Harder They Come,* Jimmy Cliff has been his own worst enemy. His songs in that film bristled with passion, energy and conviction. . . . They were also old songs, though, and by then he had already made his move towards soul and pop reggae, neither of which he performs with comparable commitment. [*Follow My Mind*] isn't much different. Considering its message, **"The News"** has none of the urgency of, say, **"Vietnam,"** and **"Remake the World"** comes off a rather desperate stab at duplicating the 1970 chart success of **"Wonderful World, Beautiful People."** He does manage to pull off the sentiment of **"Dear Mother."** . . . It may be one of his more listenable efforts in the genre, but it's still very soft-core fare and hard to get excited about.

John Morthland, "Records: 'Follow My Mind'," in Creem *(© copyright 1976 by Creem Magazine, Inc.), Vol. 7, No. 8, January, 1976, p. 65.*

JOEL VANCE

Such ambitious album titles as **"Follow My Mind"** usually signal mediocre content, and there is no exception here. I enjoy Jimmy Cliff as a singer and occasionally celebrate him as a writer, but the fellow has the most maddening habit of being good every *other* album. His selections in the soundtrack LP of *The Harder They Come* were excellent, and *Many Rivers to Cross* was particularly effective, but his next album, **"Struggling Man,"** was a collection of didactic, glum, corny songs about the peeeeople. **"Music Maker,"** in which he concentrated on making music, was fine. Now comes another snoozer, **"Follow My Mind,"** where the songs are melodically feeble and the subject matter sounds like a United Nations resolution. I vote no.

Joel Vance, "Popular Discs and Tapes: 'Follow My Mind'," in Stereo Review *(copyright © 1976 by Ziff-Davis Publishing Company), Vol. 36, No. 1, January, 1976, p. 79.*

KARL DALLAS

Jimmy Cliff's dilemma, more than amply illustrated by this well-planned double album [**"The Best Of"**], is that of the artist of ethnic origins who tries to break out of the confining boundaries of his background to become a citizen of the world. In the only partially successful search for wider acclaim with material like . . . his own, rather simplistically optimistic, **"Wonderful World, Beautiful People,"** he loses the chance to properly define himself. On the face of it, Cliff couldn't lose. On top of his undoubted talent he secured the lead role in one of the great cult movies of our time, "The Harder They Come," which more than anything was to be responsible for reggae breaking out of the lower-class ghetto to which the intellectual rock critics had consigned it till then. But by then, as Carl Gayle points out in his excellent notes to this compilation, Jimmy was onto "Another Cycle." He had abandoned his reggae roots . . . [and] finally eradicated [them] from his work after **"Struggling Man"** failed to make it as a hit single in 1972. A year later, Bob Marley's success with the first "proper" Wailers' album, "Catch A Fire," was to indicate how wrong he'd been to get off the train before it reached the station. . . . [He's] since been left watching the trains go by. So, to this album. In many ways, by including the obvious things like [Cat Stevens's] "Wide World," which were the closest Cliff was ever to get to chart success, the compilation unwittingly underlines the reasons for his lack of subsequent success. If it had been trimmed down to a single album, concentrating on things like **"Struggling Man," "Let Your Yeah Be Yeah,"** and the phenomenally exciting **"Keep Your Eyes On The Sparrow,"** it would have been more in accord with current taste. And less representative of Cliff's varied talents. You see the problem. Wrenched out of its place (Miami) and time (late psychedelia), a song like **"Synthetic World"** really has no lasting merit whatsoever, though it's easy to see how at the time it seemed like exactly the right thing to do. But pick up on this, which is rather better than most "Best of" sets, if the only Jimmy Cliff you've got is on the **"Harder They Come"** soundtrack album, because you'll be amazed at the breadth of his musicality.

> Karl Dallas, "Rolling Stones' Dance of Time: 'The Best Of','" in Melody Maker (© IPC Business Press Ltd.), April 24, 1976, p. 23.

STEVE SIMELS

There are two traditional critical lines on Jimmy Cliff, neither of which I buy. The first is that, like Toots Hibbert, Jimmy is an Otis Redding disciple, which strikes me as downright weird. . . . The second is that he hasn't written a decent song in years, which is unfair, but at least I can understand the basis for it. Although there are indeed some marvelous things scattered across the albums he's made since *The Harder They Come* made him a star, his early songs were just so good, and their impact on an American audience hearing them for the first time all at once was so overwhelming, that it's made it difficult for his admittedly less consistent recent stuff to get the fair hearing it deserves. (pp. 94-5)

The bottom line . . . is: get *The Harder They Come* soundtrack immediately if you don't already own a copy, hunt around for Jimmy's 1968 . . . album and wish him a lot better luck. . . . (p. 95)

> Steve Simels, "Popular Discs and Tapes: 'In Concert—The Best of Jimmy Cliff'," in Stereo Review (copyright © 1977 by Ziff-Davis Publishing Company), Vol. 38, No. 3, March, 1977, pp. 94-5.

LESTER BANGS

[Jimmy Cliff] leads off a collection of some of the very greatest examples of earlier reggae by several acknowledged masters [on **"The Harder They Come"**]. Some of the songs in this album—the Slickers' *Johnny Too Bad*, Cliff's own *You Can Get It If You Really Want* and *Many Rivers to Cross*, and the title tune—have already become standards. Certainly Cliff has never been as strong since this tour de force display of deceptively lilting Otis Redding vocal turns and street-tough lyrics. . . . **"The Harder They Come"** achieves total commercial accessibility without compromising its hardwon political principles or their religious base, nor does it teeter on the edge of the abyss of self-parody as so much subsequent topical reggae does. Convincing evidence in support of the argument that reggae is the soul music of the Seventies (American soul having been all but decimated by disco), this album will stand as a masterpiece for years and should be the cornerstone of any reggae collection, serious or otherwise. (pp. 66-7)

> Lester Bangs, "How to Learn to Love Reggae," in Stereo Review (copyright © 1977 by Ziff-Davis Publishing Company), Vol. 38, No. 4, April, 1977, pp. 65-70.*

VIVIEN GOLDMAN

An unusually passionate lament, [**"Many Rivers to Cross"**] brings into focus what you could see as Cliff's artistic problem: on record, he sounds so perky it's easy to overlook the agony of his lyrics. (p. 24)

The tension between rejection and Cliff's inherent optimism is the core of Cliff's music, its successes as well as its weaknesses. His adherence to Islam—though he now says simply, "My religion is God"—hasn't made his music any more overtly militant, though, perhaps because he's too intelligent to see the world as anything but a mass of contradictions, and that's why his bitter observations always sound so sweet. . . .

He is an immensely gifted, if flawed, musician; you are always aware of the potential for an explosion of talent from Jimmy Cliff. (p. 43)

> Vivien Goldman, "Jimmy Cliff: A Pioneer Returns," in Melody Maker (© IPC Business Press Ltd.), February 3, 1979, pp. 24, 43.

STEPHEN DAVIS

[Cliff's masterpiece is] **"Many Rivers to Cross,"** a profoundly emotional epic ballad about depression and getting started again after a bad time. The song was typical Cliff; wretchedness and desolation putting on a good face and trying to look to the future. . . .

[His] low-key but very forceful protest, **"Vietnam,"** was . . . much more rock and roll than reggae. A devastating antiwar polemic in the form of a letter to a mother telling of her son's death in Vietnam, the song was too honest and tough to be popular beyond the tiny Cliff cult. (p. 84)

Jimmy Cliff is the most misunderstood of the reggae masters. He has been vilified for abandoning his roots and the Jamaican styles that nourished him. His songs continually have described the hunger of a young man trying to assert himself in the face of prejudice and villainy. His stance is self-reliance and independence, and for those qualities he occasionally incurs the wrath of the crowd. In Jamaica, Cliff is respected as an artist who opened doors for reggae that might otherwise have remained shut. Others contend that Cliff moved to England so long ago he's lost contact. Critics point to the smoothness of some of his recent records, anathema to the fundamentally raw reggae sensibility. (p. 85)

> *Stephen Davis, "Three Reggae Masters," in his* Reggae Bloodlines: In Search of the Music and Culture of Jamaica *(copyright © 1977 by Stephen Davis; reprinted by permission of Doubleday & Company, Inc.), revised edition, Anchor Press, 1979, pp. 83-97.**

GARAUD MacTAGGART

How come when people think of reggae most people bow in the direction of Marley and the Wailers or some of the newer groups like Third World? While Cliff, who is definitely more accessible through his feel for the pop idiom, is relegated purely to the soundtrack of *The Harder They Come*. Jimmy Cliff has been responsible for some great songs. **"Many Rivers to Cross"** is probably one of the most obvious, but such classics as **"My Ancestors," "Struggling Man," "Viet Nam," "Sitting in Limbo"** and **"Universal Love"** also deserve more recognition from the masses. . . .

It took a while and some constant thought, but I think that this album has even replaced *Give Thankx* as my personal favorite Cliff album. . . .

[*I Am the Living*] has great songs, pop songs with lyric content that is far above the majority of material now heard. **"Gone Clear"** is an eloquent statement on nuclear power. . . . **"Morning Train"** moves out; **"All the Strength We Got"** and the title tune for the album could be legit singles.

This is a great record. I've heard it well over 50 times, and I can honestly say that I'm not tired of it. Given the durability of the majority of stuff out on the market, that has to mean something. My definite choice for reggae album of the year. . . .

> *Garaud MacTaggart, "Record Reviews: 'I Am the Living'," in* Detroit Metro Times *(copyright © 1980 Detroit Metro Times; reprinted by permission), Vol. 1, No. 6, December 24, 1980, p. 18.*

Elvis Costello

1955-

(Pseudonym of Declan Patrick McManus) British songwriter, singer, and musician.

Costello is the first artist emerging from the recent new wave of musicians to achieve commercial success. The movement, which began in 1976, was a social reaction to the repression and hopelessness of contemporary life and a musical reaction to the bland, overproduced product of holdover artists from the 1960s and uninspired groups of the mid-1970s. Costello presents an angry stance, both lyrically and in performance, and combines it with attention to content, song form, and melody, elements often lacking in the works of Costello's contemporaries. As a result, his songs are felt to be both reflective of the times and accessible to a wide range of listeners.

Costello has been called one of rock music's most literate songwriters. He uses puns, clever wordplay, and variations of grammar and syntax to relate his often cynical observations on politics, sex, the media and recording industries, and the ironies in the struggle for power in man/woman relationships. As an underlying theme, Costello writes that to live and to love are painful experiences, filled with dishonesty, betrayal, and denial; to trust, he feels, may be an invitation to suffer. Many of Costello's songs are self-evaluations in which he admits that his own vulnerability and guilt have caused some of his discomfort. However, his passion, romantic hopefulness, and sense of humor (often directed towards himself) keep Costello's compositions from total negativity.

One reason suggested for Costello's success is his alliance with classic pop songwriters such as Cole Porter and Rodgers and Hart. But his albums show a diversity of influences, such as country music, rhythm and blues, fifties rockabilly, reggae, the sixties sounds of the British Invasion, and prototype punk and garage bands. His appearance is reminiscent of Buddy Holly, and even his stage name suggests his affiliation with the rock tradition. Costello was initially compared to such songwriters as Bob Dylan, Bruce Springsteen, and Graham Parker, who had similar styles or concerns, but the variety of his songs and the originality of his approach keep him from being categorized.

Costello has been criticized for his obsessiveness, for the glibness of his language, for being overly serious, and for the depressing nature of many of his subjects and themes. It is also felt that his bitterness and eccentricity will keep him from achieving mass acceptance. However, young people respond to Costello's honest evaluations as a youthful perspective to which they can relate, and it is generally felt that his works have helped to raise the intellectual level and emotional intensity of popular songwriting.

ALLAN JONES

I'd like to see ["My Aim Is True"] on the chart within the week, please. In fact, "My Aim Is True" could, given the opportunity and exposure, rocket with ease to national prominence: the collection contains enough potential hit singles to stock a bloody juke-box, believe me.

© Neil Zlozower

Two of the cuts, **"Less Than Zero"** and **"Alison"**, . . . conveniently suggest the scope of Costello's writing and provide musical reference points for the uninitiated. Elvis . . . has a rare talent for seizing an image, an idea or a musical style and, however familiar its original shape, creating out of it something quite powerfully individual. . . .

"Less Than Zero" is a vivid reflection of Elvis' affection and empathy with Sixties' r&b; simultaneously, the song . . . introduces, through its colourful evocation of suburban perversions and wry cynicism, the mordant, Ortonesque humour that characterises several of the songs included here. **"Alison,"** by comparison, is a classically crafted pop song enhanced by stylish guitar inflections and Elvis' restrained vocal passion. The song also reflects Costello's other principal preoccupation as a writer: it's centered, like so many of the songs in this collection, around the termination of a relationship (a theme Elvis views with authentic insight, from a variety of perspectives).

Elsewhere, Elvis deals more explicitly with the emotional violence that attends the disintegration of love affairs, and with the frustrations and occasional humiliations of early adolescent love and sexual encounters. The fierce **"Miracle Man,"** for instance, has the song's protagonist admitting to his sexual inadequacy with an impassioned and convincing concern and painful authenticity.

The theme of rejection is examined on the irresistible "**(The Angels Wanna Wear My) Red Shoes**" (probably my favourite track on the album) but here the mood is more extrovert. . . . This song's effervescence is challenged only by the magnificent "**Mystery Dance**," a perfectly realised homage to Fifties rock and roll . . . which presents a concise account of a guy's first sexual adventure and its disastrous development.

"**My Aim Is True**" is already a personal favourite—I can think of only a few albums released this year that rival its general excellence—and I can only hope its delights will be universally recognised. Hell, you can dance to it, swoon to it, sing along with it, laugh and cry with it, smooch and romance to it. And, to paraphrase Elvis Costello's "**Welcome To The Working Week**" I think it might thrill you, I know it won't kill you. Buy-buy.

> *Allan Jones, "Deep Soul from Elvis," in* Melody Maker *(© IPC Business Press Ltd.), July 23, 1977, p. 17.*

DAVE SCHULPS

[*My Aim Is True* is] this year's most auspicious debut album. . . . [There's] an intangible quality about Elvis that . . . makes me think he's destined for great things in the near future. (pp. 42-3)

Perhaps it's the way he combines anger and vulnerability on "**I'm Not Angry**," "**Miracle Man**," or "**Alison**" to become every little guy who ever wanted to be something he wasn't; or maybe it's the way he just rocks away so hard, so loose and unselfconsciously that you're won over by the sheer guts of his performance. In a year that is beginning to look more and more like a landmark in rock 'n' roll history, Elvis Costello has produced a classic in his first try. Where he'll go from here should be exciting to watch. (p. 43)

> *Dave Schulps, "Records: 'My Aim Is True'," in* Trouser Press *(copyright © 1977 by Trans-Oceanic Trouser Press, Inc.), Vol. 4, No. 4, October, 1977, pp. 42-3.*

PAUL RAMBALI

We all know boys don't make passes at girls who wear glasses and vice versa, so bespectacled rockers should theoretically have an even harder time in the adulation stakes. Not so; Elvis Costello, the latest sensation to explode on these shores, proves you don't have to squint at an audience in order to get your message across. . . .

Costello's first appearance on vinyl was early this year with the single "**Less than Zero**." As abstract a record as could be, he gave few clues to his territory. . . . The lyrics were shrouded in a strange, twisted sarcasm and seemed to express contempt for the way everybody goes about living a lifestyle rather than simply living. I later discovered that the song has something to do with Oswald Mosley, a British fascist leader of the '30s, but it's still hard to make sense out of it. . . . [It] was intriguing . . . on a surreal basis—and catchy to boot. . . .

Some months later "**Alison**," Costello's second single, was released. In retrospect, "**Alison**" should have been the perfect summer hit, it has many qualities similar to 10cc's "I'm Not

in Love." A beautiful, tender and melancholy ballad that does for me what [Todd] Rundgren's *Something/Anything* used to do. But perhaps it was a little too close; the pain and hurt show too clearly. . . . Anyone whose heart doesn't tighten a little when they hear "**Alison**" must have been brought up in a steel cage. . . .

On the face of it *My Aim Is True* is nothing special. . . . [Costello's] tunes sound like [Graham] Parker tunes. He even has a similar knack with catchy little couplets. . . . So if we already have Parker, what, apart from the snappy image, do we need Costello for?

The trick is that Costello is real. . . .

Costello looks like a timid romantic but, as is supposed to be the fate of all romantics, he's really a cynical sod with shrewd perception. Since cynicism is the mood of the times Costello's success might seem unsurprising, but the truth is more complicated than that.

Costello's songs are about the pain and confusion of modern love and, to a lesser extent, modern life. He's honest, sometimes uncomfortably so, and cynicism is often the only recourse against emotional knocks. Few songwriters have tread so close to the pulse. . . .

Anyone who's been bitten can relate to Costello, who's more gratifying than the empty truisms peddled elsewhere.

> *Paul Rambali, "Elvis Costello: Specs Appeal," in* Trouser Press *(copyright © 1977 by Trans-Oceanic Trouser Press, Inc.), Vol. 4, No. 5, November, 1977, p. 32.*

SAM SUTHERLAND

Costello is the press agent's dream: a galvanic artist whose screwball appearance only heightens the force of his debut album, "**My Aim Is True**." If he appears to suffer from temporal dislocation, the visual symptoms only reinforce his music's rock classicism. . . .

His songs are ripe with a sense of history and a barbed wit, but he is neither a nostalgic impersonator nor a parodist. Visual and musical echoes of the '50s and '60s are undeniably there, but as a singer and writer, he appears to have absorbed his influences enough to obscure any singular models. . . .

Nor does Costello typify New Wave's assumed flamboyant primitivism. . . . [Both] playing and songwriting attest to a melodic sense forged directly from the best rock and pop sources. *Welcome to the Working Week,* which opens the album, may carry a scathing contempt for middle-class verities, but it rocks like crazy and even manages to kid Costello's own imminent celebrity. . . .

That tension between genuine rage and saving humor emerges as one of the album's, and the artist's, most convincing virtues. *Less than Zero* salts its blunt nihilism . . . with a quirky surrealism as pithy and truly funny as some of Dylan's more whimsical mid-'60s mindgames, yet the wordless refrain is at least as close to simple r&b workouts. Such intriguing fusions of musical and verbal sense recur throughout. *(The Angels Wanna Wear My) Red Shoes,* possibly the best cut, balances heartfelt lyricism . . . against a vaguely Faustian legend of eternal youth spiced with some wonderful, deadpanned jokes. *Mystery Dance* takes a classic rock metaphor for sex and enlightenment to equally bizarre extremes. . . . *No Dancing* turns its title phrase into a double-edged hook through a small-scale approximation of Phil Spector's syncopated ballads, enabling Costello to both mock romance and reaffirm it at the same time.

Yet he never settles for mere cleverness. His verbal playfulness and sneering delivery are augmented by a striking poetic sense and genuine passion, and on the album's one ballad, *Alison*, all of those qualities coexist: On the one hand, he offers absurd imagery (''Did you leave your pretty fingers lying in the wedding cake?'') with corny, garage-band guitar glissandos, yet his exasperation with his lover reveals a tenderness most rock males can only feign. . . .

[Costello has] forsaken the precision and virtuosity of '70s pop in order to rediscover the raw vitality of rock. Whether American listeners will embrace Costello's feisty intelligence . . . remains to be seen.

> Sam Sutherland, ''Elvis Costello: New Wave Rock Classicist,'' in High Fidelity (copyright © by ABC Leisure Magazine, Inc.; all rights reserved; excerpted by permission), Vol. 27, No. 12, December, 1977, p. 138.

SIMON FRITH

Costello is a craftsman. . . . [His songs] are, indeed, impressive. A master of ambiguity and cliche, pun and precision, Costello is an astonishingly adept writer. He has the confidence to defy conventions of rhyme and grammar and metre and imposes his own syntax on the world. If reviewing were the same thing as essay grading, I'd give him As for sheer cleverness. . . .

But, while I admire Costello's skills, I'm uneasy about what he does with them: There's something oppressive about his music. When I first heard his album [*My Aim Is True*] I thought my tetchy response was too subjective to make critical sense: Maybe I was just jealous that such an ambitious rock intellectual had made it. . . .

My immediate problem was with Costello's image. His name and pose suggest a joke: Here was this weed on stage, acting the star, calling himself Elvis. How ridiculous! But this was not how Costello saw himself. He took himself entirely seriously, bristled with self-righteousness. Faced with the person and not the image, my sense of the ridiculous faltered. Costello was grim; his frustrations—physical or otherwise—were no laughing matter.

Costello himself has always been explicit about the role of revenge in his work, but what I find disturbing in his songs is not their anger but their fatalism. [''Watching the Detectives''] makes his position clear.] . . . Costello coldly describes the come-uppance of a girl who was more stuck on TV heroes than on him. In his frustrated, vengeful imagination her absorption becomes literal: She vanishes through the screen, with real detectives looking for her! For Costello her fate is neither funny nor ironic: it is deserved. Yet at the same time it's not really a fate at all, because nothing has really happened—for her, the distinction between TV and reality has dissolved. ''She's filing her nails while they're dragging the lake''—trashy drama merges with trashy life, equally real, equally false.

''I was raised on romance,'' Costello begins on **''Pay It Back,''** and it's obviously true, because he's obsessed with the disil-

lusion that has resulted. Having based his hopes on the myths and fantasies of pop and been let down accordingly, he now trusts nothing and nobody. ''Everything means less than zero,'' he concludes in a song sparked off by the appearance of the old fascist Oswald Mosley on a TV talk show. Rather than being annoyed by the specific lies of fascists, Costello is taken with the insidious notion that nothing matters.

Throughout the album you can hear the consequences of this idea: doomed relationships, empty lives, futile emotions. . . . ''I used to be disgusted; now I try to be amused,'' he asserts and it's the credo of a pop obsessive, locked in his room with his facts and his fanzines, so upset that the world isn't like his record collection that he never bothers to take his headphones off at all. . . .

In any other year, Costello would have remained another clever, selfish, bitter singer/songwriter. But in 1977 musical power in Britain is drawn from collective energy, and Costello, whether he likes it or not, is part of a new rock'n'roll utopianism. He's going to have to start having some fun soon.

> Simon Frith, ''Elvis Costello's Not So Angry Anymore'' (reprinted by permission of The Village Voice and the author; copyright © The Village Voice, Inc., 1977), in The Village Voice, Vol. XXII, No. 52, December 26, 1977, p. 55.

ALLAN JONES

''This Year's Model''—and it's difficult to believe from the maturity of the writing and the performance that it's only The Man's *second* album!—is an achievement so comprehensive, so inspired, that it exhausts superlatives. It promotes its author to the foremost ranks of contemporary rock writers. Clear out of sight of most of his rivals and comparisons. . . .

Elvis Costello's prodigious talent, we can see in retrospect, was only superficially exposed on his first album.

While it is true that **''Aim's''** specific themes of revenge, jealousy, infidelity, deceit and betrayal are central to this album's most powerful songs—**''Lip Service,'' ''Lipstick Vogue''** and **''Living In Paradise''**—these obsessions are forced even more ruthlessly into the spotlight.

And, running parallel to these preoccupations, is the vague paranoia and unease of **''The Beat''** and **''Night Rally''** which hardens to vicious attack on **''(I Don't Want To Go To) Chelsea,''** a virulent indictment of the superficialities of style and fashion. . . .

The themes of infidelity and humiliation are pursued with relentless vigour and imagination. **''Hand In Hand''** . . . seems to propose love as a criminal conspiracy. . . .

The extraordinary **''Living In Paradise''** is set against a neurotic calypso backdrop, with Elvis phrasing his lyrics with a flippant, disquieting glee. The song unfolds as an epic of suspicion, jealousy and revenge, replete with the kind of dangerous images that elevated **''I'm Not Angry''** to such chilling peaks. . . .

Sex is again the central theme of **''This Year's Girl,''** a brilliant exposition of the hypocrisy that can be provoked by the exploitation of unattainable sex objects. . . .

The standard of the writing, where the penetration of the language matches the vaulting hysteria of the performance, is relaxed only twice—midway through side one—with **"Pump It Up"** and **"Little Triggers."**

The former is a routine rocker . . . ; while **"Triggers"** employs an overly familiar ballad scheme with a predictable melody, a fault that is not overcome by the rather intriguing lyrics.

Still, things are quickly whacked back into shape with **"You Belong To Me,"** which brings the side to a roaring conclusion, and by the complete magnificence of side two. . . .

Elvis and [producer Nick Lowe] . . . have left until last the album's most lethal broadside. **"Night Rally"** is a disturbing comment upon the popularity and potential menace of the National Front that achieves its resonance not from any sensational sloganeering but from the genuine apprehension conveyed by Lowe's discreet atmosphere of impending disaster and Elvis's desolate lyric. . . .

It is fitting that such an important song concludes such an impressive album. **"This Year's Model."** This Year's Masterpiece.

> Allan Jones, *"Elvis on Revenge,"* in Melody Maker (© IPC Business Press Ltd.), March 11, 1978, p. 23.

PATRICK GOLDSTEIN

First off, Elvis—no matter how vehemently he attacks his rock elders—is just as much a product of his influences as any other garage band veteran. He named himself after one rock idol and has capitalized on his striking resemblance to another. His lyrics borrow their venom from Pete Townshend and their resignation from Gram Parsons. And his band, the Attractions, with their Farfiso dominated mid-section, are direct Anglo descendents of Question Mark and the Mysterians.

And Elvis can strike his rock populist pose and rail against the music biz to his heart's content, but without CBS's awesome promotional muscle, our boy would be no more renowned in America than fellow Stiffers Wreckless Eric and Ian Dury. Hype may be a dirty word in the new wave lexicon, but most bands are going to live or die by its double-edged sword. (p. 65)

This is not to expose Elvis as some sort of fraud or charlatan, but to remind new wave sympathizers that bringing down the record industry's Jericho-like walls entails a bitter struggle. I merely advise Elvis to be on his guard. His gifts as an artist—whether he accepts the title or not—are assured. But his growth as a songwriter must survive the pressures of sudden notoriety and breast the fluctuating fortune of the new wave, whose rise has closely paralleled his own climb to prominence.

A more serious concern is whether Elvis will allow his recalcitrant public persona to corrupt his provocative songwriting talents.

His future depends on reconciling the tension between musical

aspirations and audience expectations. Despite his studied rejection of the trappings of rock artistry, an artist he remains. This gap between iconoclasm and idolatry was too much for the Sex Pistols, who formed a hit squad for aging rock heavyweights but made the fatal mistake of standing in a circle when they fired. Let's hope Elvis' aim is true. (p. 66)

> Patrick Goldstein, *"Can Elvis Costello Cure Acne?"* in Creem (© copyright 1978 by Creem Magazine, Inc.), Vol. 9, No. 12, May, 1978, pp. 36-7, 65-6.

ALLAN JONES

[Costello], clearly, was not the kind of talent that came every morning free with a packet of crackers. . . .

[The proposition that Elvis was reminiscent of Bob Dylan became clearer the more I thought about it.] It wasn't so much that Elvis was copping Dylanesque attitudes, lyrical stances or anything as specific as that (though it was clear that Dylan had left an emphatic mark on the boy). No; it was something a little deeper.

Later, I realised that this was something close to what it must have been like to have been drawn for the first time, in the Sixties, to Dylan's mesmerising universe. . . .

[Here] was someone who could potentially provoke similar associations, similar sympathies, a similar correspondence of emotions and perceptions. Someone who could sound as rabidly angry as a barracuda with a psychotic temperament and yet still not lose sight of an articulate perspective and an eloquent sensitivity. (p. 8)

From the moment, almost, that **"My Aim Is True"** hit the deck, I was more or less convinced that Elvis was The Man; one of the few possible contenders for all the rock'n'roll accolades on the shelf.

It wasn't that Elvis was, immediately and undeniably, presenting us with anything especially unique. The influences were there to be ticked off. Most commonly he was compared to Van Morrison, Graham Parker and Springsteen; and the ghost of Dylan hung ominously over the grooves.

But familiarity drove such tedious comparison straight under the bed. . . .

Elvis roared out of the suburban mess, expecting disaster, not glory. His bitterness and impatience allied his music to the new wave's violent indignation, and so they found him as acceptable as they had Graham Parker, whose songs, similarly, dealt with vicious frustrations and the repressive attitudes of the English class system.

But Elvis was advancing on a broader front than G.P. . . .

[It's] increasingly struck me that Parker virtually relishes the role of loud mouth but sensitive street urchin that he's adopted in perhaps several too many songs. He sounds as if he'd definitely be more comfortable on the block with the gang than

Elvis; and fair enough, that might be his chosen milieu, and he certainly has his creative finger securely on the beat of that particular pulse.

But Elvis wants nothing less than the keys to the kingdom (to paraphrase a line from his **"No Action"**); and he's perhaps more ruthlessly prepared to push himself to the necessary limits.

And Parker, too, is probably the more conventional of the pair; Parker, as I've just suggested, has been more prepared to (brilliantly) play the roughneck lover, deceived and betrayed but still violently arrogant. And Elvis overturned that whole cool, uncaring stance with **"Aim"**.

His songs about sex and love turned the whole rock'n'roll laconic, machismo vibe on its head. He came on grovelling and snarling; his guilt, his complicity in the failure of the various relationships he portrayed so clinically, a brazen fact, not a cruel excuse. (p. 9)

> Allan Jones, "The Man Who Would Be King," in Melody Maker (© IPC Business Press Ltd.), May 13, 1978, pp. 8-9.

JON PARELES

Somebody must have told Elvis Costello about "the Mystery Dance": sex. All about it. Told him, showed him—and burned him so badly that the idea of romance scares the living hell out of him, yet he can't get sex off his mind. . . . *This Year's Model* stays close to the thick of sexual warfare. Elvis vs. fear and lies, Elvis vs. anyone who gets close. . . .

This Year's Model shows none of the detachment of *My Aim Is True*. . . . [The] lyrics stay personal. No politics, very little philosophy (although **"Night Rally"** on the British version has a bit of both). Costello is still bugged by the same thing: "Knowing you're with him is driving me crazy"(**"No Action"**). This time, though, he won't "try to be amused" at rejection or infidelity. He cultivates his rage, to flash it at strangers, indiscriminately. Betrayed over and over again in the songs, Costello can barely contain himself.

Desire, fear, anger and guilt merge in these songs, and the mixture is volatile. Elvis equates lust with crime (**"The Beat"**) and terrorism (**"Lip Service"**); he shouldn't be surprised when his partners turn out to be duplicitous (**"Living in Paradise"**) or underage (**"You Belong to Me"**). No matter how many times Elvis sings "I don't wanna" on this lp, he can't escape his longing. "Sometimes I think that love is just a tumor," Costello blurts in **"Lipstick Vogue,"** but he has to "get to the slot machine" and "insert the token" anyway. His denials define his need. Even on the album's attempt at fairness, **"This Year's Girl"**—about a Farrah-type cover girl icon—Costello can't hold back lines like "You want her broken with her mouth wide open." . . .

[There's no way any] song on *This Year's Model* could sound as genial, superficially, as **"Alison"** or **"Waiting for the End of the World."** Costello is almost continuously savage. . . .

No doubt about it—*This Year's Model* rocks tough and committed. It is also so wrongheaded, so full of hatred, and so convinced of its moral superiority that it makes me uneasy. Costello's intelligence is evident in every lyric; it's easy to identify, for a little while, with his pained vindictiveness. I learned about love from pop songs, though, and these "don't tell me anything about it I don't know already." Costello distrusts his entire universe, particularly its female side, and I get the feeling negativity won't pull him through.

> Jon Pareles, "Below the Belt," in Crawdaddy (copyright © 1978 by Crawdaddy Publishing Co., Inc.; all rights reserved; reprinted by permission), June, 1978, p. 70.

KIT RACHLIS

Listening to Elvis Costello is like walking down a dark, empty street and hearing another set of heels. His music doesn't make you dance, it makes you jump. It doesn't matter that he's stalking his obsessions and not you, because nobody ought to be *this* sure of his obsessions. But Costello appears determined never to reach that age when, as Joan Didion once put it, "the wounds begin to heal whether one wants them to or not." *This Year's Model* . . . is Costello's attempt to make certain those wounds stay open.

Elvis Costello feeds off terror; sometimes it almost seems as if he deliberately conjures it up so he can finger its jagged grain and twist its neck. On last year's *My Aim Is True,* the fear centered on failure (**"Mystery Dance"**) and rejection (**"I'm Not Angry"**). On *This Year's Model,* it zeros in on success: Costello is afraid that fad and fashion will seduce and trample him. **"(I Don't Want to Go to) Chelsea"** is the title and refrain of his recent Top Twenty single in England, and he means those words to be taken literally. Chelsea represents Costello's nightmare world of success, where deceit is masked by propriety and last year's model is thrown out with yesterday's wash. (pp. 53-4)

Elvis Costello can describe Chelsea with such precision because he knows—or, at least, doesn't deny—its splendors. If the disdain in his voice appears a little too measured . . . , it's because it takes all of the singer's resolve to resist Chelsea's temptations. For all his surface cockiness, Costello is a man who's trembling underneath, a man so suspicious of the world that it doesn't matter whether you're bearing gifts or a blackjack, because *he's* not convinced it makes a difference. . . . I don't think there's been a rock & roller who's made fear so palpable or so attractive.

About the only thing wrong with the American version of *This Year's Model* is that it doesn't include **"(I Don't Want to Go to) Chelsea"** or **"Night Rally,"** the two additional songs on the import. While *This Year's Model* doesn't diminish the prodigal brilliance of *My Aim Is True,* the new record is musically and thematically more of a piece. . . .

From the beginning, Elvis Costello has insisted that he wants rock & roll success on his terms or not at all. In a way, this makes him a heroic figure, I guess, except that most of the time he refuses to accept even that. On *This Year's Model*, Costello is brutal toward everyone, but what saves him is that he's just as brutal toward himself. Which means that he can play Charles Bronson to his own Anthony Perkins, that stoic and stutterer become one. It also means that Costello, for all his anger and hostility, can express empathy for whomever he's going after. On **"Stranger in the House"** (the 45 that was included as a bonus with the initial English pressings of the LP), Costello coolly dissects both himself and the collapse of a relationship. He's so distant he takes on the woman's point of view: he's not a stranger just because he's been ostracized, but because he's become a zombie. The uninspired country instrumentation on **"Stranger in the House"** makes it the most musically conservative song the singer has ever recorded. But the song itself makes absolutely blatant the sexual warfare that lies at the heart of *This Year's Model*.

If he weren't his own harshest critic—if so many of the wounds weren't self-inflicted—perhaps Costello could be considered a rock & roll bounty hunter, ready to bag anyone if the money's right. But Elvis Costello never gets the girl. For all the immediacy of his emotions, all the romances on *This Year's Model* are either about to happen or are over, and he's caught between picking up the phone or slamming it down (**"No Action"**), between rejecting all compromises and trying to come to terms (**"Lipstick Vogue"**). "I don't want to be no goodie-goodie / I don't want just anybody / I don't want anybody sayin,' 'You belong to me,'" he sings at one point, blowing away years and years of pop tradition. But by song's end, he turns around and repeats "You belong to me" over and over again.

But there's something else here. If Costello's music is truly frightening, it's not devoid of joy—or, for that matter, humor. *This Year's Model* has the triumph of an adrenalin kick: **"The Beat"** or **"Pump It Up"** are not titles chosen randomly. There's bravado in the way Costello's machine-gun mouth sprays out each image, but like all obsessives, he has to get the details right, connect them through the sheer force of his will. So he's reeling and running, shooting from the hip but taking careful aim. He's ready to challenge all comers, it doesn't matter whether it's the rock & roll industry (**"Radio, Radio"**) or the National Front (**"Night Rally"**). "Don't you know I'm an animal," he sings on **"Hand in Hand."** But later, in **"Lipstick Vogue,"** he amends that: "Sometimes I almost feel just like a human being." Taken together, these are the words of a brutally honest optimist. Damon Runyon once suggested that life was basically a six-to-five proposition against. I suspect that Elvis Costello would consider those good odds. (p. 54)

Kit Rachlis, "Who's Afraid of Elvis Costello?" in Rolling Stone *(by Straight Arrow Publishers, Inc. © 1978; all rights reserved; reprinted by permission), Issue 268, June 29, 1978, pp. 53-4.*

TONY RAYNS

"Armed Forces" consolidates everything that Elvis Costello achieved with The Attractions on Last Year's Model. Some of the songs and arrangements here would have fitted on the last album [**"This Year's Model"**]; others seem designed to 'stretch' the band and demonstrate its flexibility. There's less gut attack, less overall aggression this time; instead a more relaxed display of energy and precision, of the kind that springs from unusual self-confidence. And the confidence is largely justified. Who else currently makes 12-cut albums without a single duff track? . . .

But it's still a sideways step. Costello has moved away from the put-down-by-numbers approach of his earlier songwriting towards—what? A 'concept'? . . .

Recent years have given everyone plenty of practice in ignoring overkill packaging and concentrating on the actual music, but in this case the conflicting implications of the (unsigned) artwork raise provocative questions about the songs inside. Neither the artwork nor the songs would stand as what the Surrealists called 'actes gratuites', things in and of themselves: both are riddled with far too many outside references for that. And yet any attempt to square them off with the things they refer to founders on their obliqueness or outright obscurity.

The album opens with Costello singing that he just doesn't know where to begin, as the preface to what sounds like a retraction of some sort: "You used to be a victim / Now you're not the only one / I don't wanna hear it / Because I know what I've done". The song is **"Accidents Will Happen"**. . . . And it closes with another autobiographical 'statement': "Two little Hitlers will fight it out until / one little Hitler does the other one's will / I will return / I will not burn . . ." (**"Two Little Hitlers"**). I have no idea what those lines might mean to their author, but if they have a 'public' meaning it must be that he is trying to transcend the motifs of recrimination and vindictiveness that have certainly dominated his work thus far.

Sure enough, most of the other songs here either use a fictionalised 'I' or look outwards at society or the world at large. It's a refreshing turn, and it would be even more refreshing if Costello grasped the courage of his convictions and came out with a coherent point of view. There's no rule that says a rock song has to be 'about' something, but if you start singing about being "in Palestine / Overrun by the Chinese line" then your consumers have a right to start asking questions. . . .

"Sunday's Best" uses a naggingly jaunty calliope-style backing for some quite credible English social commentary in the Ray Davies tradition until the lyric gets lost in melodrama about severed heads under the bed. It then hits the verse: "Listen to the decent people / Though you treat them just like sheep / Put them all in boots and khaki / Blame it all on the darkies . . ." What does that mean? Does it refer back to conscription? . . . Or is it supposed to invoke some threatening future? Either way, it's at best feeble and at worst offensive. . . .

Similarly, **"Oliver's Army"** is just fine when it starts out as the reverie of someone dreaming of a career in the army, but it becomes specious when the regular army blurs into a mercenary force, and it seems to me to lose all credibility when it refers to Hong Kong being up for grabs in one breath and to Mr. Churchill in the next. Political acumen that's not, and neither does it offer an interesting historical perspective. . . .

If there is a governing 'concept', it's probably the one signalled on the inner sleeve: 'emotional fascism'. It's a theme that Costello alternately evades and indulges, and the most promising thing about the album is undoubtedly the hint that he's beginning to get it into perspective. But his lyrics are still happiest when they move through genuinely random-sounding free-associations, at their best equal to anything by [Brian] Eno. There are many highly memorable formulations in the wordplay: "I'm in a grip-like vice" (**"Party Girl"**), "It's the death that's worse than fate" (**"Senior Service"**), "There's a shorthand typist taking seconds over minutes" (**"Green Shirt"**). . . .

Hell, whichever way it's moving, it's more excellent than not.

Tony Rayns, "Elvis: A Compulsive Confusion," in Melody Maker (© IPC Business Press Ltd.), December 30, 1978, p. 22.

KIT RACHLIS

"I'll do anything to confuse the enemy." If Elvis Costello had a business card, those words (from **"The Beat"**) would be on it, the equivalent of Paladin's "Have Gun Will Travel." Costello doesn't go on to tell us who the enemy is because he doesn't have to. He has made it clear from the first that he doesn't trust anyone entirely—the British government, the music industry, his fans, his lovers, least of all himself. These are the armed forces that the title of his new album is referring to. If Costello is not quite as belligerent on *Armed Forces* as he was on his previous two albums, the title announces that he still sees the world in terms of power. It's this fascination with power—more than his command of metaphor and image, more than his piercing moodiness—that makes the comparisons with Dylan apt for once. For Costello, everything is always personal, which means that while he is occasionally petty he is never cold-blooded, and that he's capable of identifying with his adversaries. On *Armed Forces* his use of "you" and "I" has become increasingly blurred, so much so that half the time it is impossible to figure out whether he's lashing himself or someone else. While this makes the album his most ambiguous, it also makes it his most generous. . . .

Costello has always been drawn to apocalyptic language and *Armed Forces* is no exception ("But you'll never get them to make a lamp shade out of me," he sings in **"Goon Squad"**). But what seems to frighten him in **"Accidents Will Happen"** is that his world doesn't explode but erodes away: "It's the damage that we do—and don't know / The words that we don't say that scare me so."

The mixed contexts that run through the rest of *Armed Forces* seem both to embody the danger Costello articulates here and to attempt to defeat it. The most overtly political songs (**"Senior Service," "Oliver's Army"**) speak with the abrasive intimacy of a lover's quarrel; the most explicit love songs are cast in political terms. . . . In the case of **"Green Shirt"** the lyrics are so open-ended that the song is either an elaborate sexual fantasy or a meditation on paranoia—or both. If Costello's language is rich with puns ("guilty party girl") and cliche-reversal ("You're mind is made up, but your mouth is undone"), it is also studded with non sequiturs and slurred phrases, a situation exacerbated by the numerous British references. But Costello has always understood that rock and roll language can be vague as long as its tone isn't. . . .

CBS would like to tell you that Costello has become more accessible. And even he admits in **"Big Boys"** that he's beginning to "function in the usual way." But don't let either one of them fool you. Whatever concessions Costello has made on *Armed Forces* are only to confuse the enemy.

Kit Rachlis, "Elvis Costello Presents Arms" (reprinted by permission of The Village Voice *and the author; copyright © The Village Voice, Inc., 1979), in The Village Voice, Vol. XXIV, No. 4, January 22, 1979, p. 61.*

JANET MASLIN

Costello writes songs that are elusive at times, bursting with bright phrases you can't always catch. . . . He sings about violence with a vibrant romanticism, and about love with murder in his heart. He writes short, blunt compositions that don't pretend to be artful, though they are, and don't demand to be taken seriously, even though they're more stunning and substantial than anything rock has produced in a good long while. He doubles back on himself at every turn, and you're forced to take it or leave it. . . .

There's only one way to listen to Elvis Costello's music: his way. The songs are so brief they barrel right by, leaving an impression of jubilant and spiteful energies at war with each other. Every now and then, words like "quisling" or "concertina" leap out of nowhere to add to the confusion. Images are etched hard and fast, then replaced by new ones even stronger. There's an overload of cleverness on [*Armed Forces*]— more smartly turned phrases than twelve songs ordinarily could bear. But the rapid pacing alleviates any hint of self-congratulation.

Costello's songs are dense the way Bob Dylan's used to be, driven by the singer's faith that if this line doesn't get you, the next one will, and compressed so tightly that they lend themselves to endless rediscovery. He has something like the younger Dylan's rashness, too, being hotheaded enough to oversimplify anything for the sake of a good line, and being a good enough writer to get away with it. His puns are so outrageous they're irresistible. . . .

Beneath all this gamesmanship lurks something like a grand passion. . . . The wise guy who can work Hitler into a song about competitive friendship [**"Two Little Hitlers"**] is also prey to authentic romantic agonies so exquisitely maddening they go hand in hand with danger. . . .

No Elvis Costello love song is without its ax to grind or its hatchet to bury, but at least the emotion, however strangled, comes through. Costello never sounds exactly willing to give himself over to sentiment, yet he works hard to make himself more than marginally accessible: a gangster with heart. Without that bit of humanizing, he'd be a specialty item. With it, he can be a star. . . .

Right now, Elvis Costello serves as a feisty and furiously talented middleman, halfway between rock's smoothest sellouts and the angriest fringes of its New Wave. He wants to be daring, but he also wants to dance. He'd like to seethe and sell records at the same time. He's mindful of—indeed, insistent upon—the form and its limitations: it's only rock & roll, after all. But he takes it to the limit just the same. (p. 60)

Janet Maslin, "Elvis Costello in Love and War," in Rolling Stone *(by Straight Arrow Publishers, Inc. © 1979; all rights reserved; reprinted by permission), Issue 287, March 22, 1979, pp. 59-60.*

IRA ROBBINS

When Bob Dylan broke up with his wife . . . a few years ago, the world was treated to the introspective and bitter *Blood on the Tracks*. Although Elvis's personal life is not quite as public (yet) as the Zim's, *Armed Forces* emerges from roughly the same emotional territory, although in Costello's case, since he was the dumper, not the dumpee, his venomous lyrics are a bit harder to comprehend. Of course, as the Sultan of Spite, Elvis has a reputation to protect, but you have to wonder about the emotional actions of someone who feeds on anger and frustration. Most of us wait for trouble to find us, but not

Elvis—he runs right out and creates his own. Interesting endothermic lifestyle. . . .

In Elvis's case, you can sense the specificness of his subject matter, but there aren't enough clues to jigsaw the puzzle together. The fact that the guy's got severe emotional and romantic disabilities is clear, but at whom or about what will probably remain a mystery for as long as he refuses to do interviews. . . .

After *This Year's Model* set stellar standards for future Elvis product, speculation about this third album grew and grew until its release started to loom anticlimactically. The double-edged danger of remaining stationary or veering off somewhere awful (like **"Stranger in the House"**) seemed to be a tricky tightrope to negotiate, but Elvis, in his infinite inscrutability, has, I'm relieved and pleased to report, done it in spades. *Armed Forces* exchanges musical violence for sophistication—in melodies, arrangements, performances—variety and subtlety. The lyrics suffer from an excessive penchant towards cheap puns and pseudo-Spoonerisms, which seem to be thrown in mechanically to insure that critics (?) will remark at what a clever dick Elvis is. . . .

There's a lyric at the end [of **"Party Girl"**] that illustrates the sometimes forced nature of his wit—"I'm in a grip-like vice"—raising horrible memories of the excesses of other lyrical smart alecks (Sparks, 10cc). It's difficult to be bitter and cute at the same time—sort of like sneezing and coughing simultaneously—and it doesn't wear all that well on Elvis. . . .

Armed Forces may not jump off the turntable with the same supercharged bile of Last Year's Model, but it certainly holds its own. Where it ultimately stacks up will take some time parked in front of speakers to discern, but that's a task I don't mind one bit.

> Ira Robbins, "Records: 'Armed Forces'," in Trouser Press *(copyright © 1979 by Trans-Oceanic Trouser Press, Inc.), Vol. 6, No. 3, April, 1979, p. 43.*

PETE SILVERTON

Right now, commenting on Costello or the Clash, you're not talking about just another artist, you're confronting rock'n'roll as a whole form as it stands now. They're both state-of-the-art, the living embodiments of more than a score of years and the linchpins of most probable futures. Who else is there? . . .

[The] Clash are real easy to write about. All that dynamite copy but genuine (if sometimes slightly forced) rude boy chic. Piece of cake.

But Costello, he's so, so tricky. . . .

[Like] most others, I can't help but be drawn like a voyeuristic moth to the panache of the Costello *Blut und Eisen* [*That's "blood and iron," folks—Ed.*] assault on the consciousness of the Western world. And the problem is that it's often difficult to pinpoint the precise reason for the success of that campaign—leaving aside, that is, the sheer hard work that's gone into it.

For starters, while everyone else around was heeding the rallying call of [the Sex Pistols's] "Anarchy in the UK," here was this four-eyed squirty gimp winging on about some lost love named Alison. . . .

[He] rarely struck me as anything more than a diffident performer. It's as though some innate traces of crippling shyness

surface every time he straps on his Jazzmaster and faces a braying crowd with only the microphone there to shelter his sense of inadequacy. So, operating on the reaction-action principle, he tries too hard to project an image of mean moodiness laced with the odd piece of blather which is sometimes fatuous. . . . (p. 25)

[He] seems to fall too easily into what's wanted rather than what's needed (there's a nice rehash of a Dylan/Costello paradox for you). Play the hits, keep the record company satisfied. And he plainly hates doing it. Sometimes, maybe, his brusque treatment of audiences has its roots in disgust at himself.

And while he started out with that whole bagful of exquisitely crafted songs, *My Aim Is True* still sounds like everything was made to suffer grievously at the hands of [backup band] Clover. (pp. 25-6)

And finally, the most telling chink in his armor is his habit of sometimes reaching for the first facile phrase, metaphor or paradox that comes his way. Balancing the terse precision of **"Pump It Up"** (the perfect phrase describing doing it all to death) there's the likes of the glib and inane "Your mouth is made up / But your mind is undone." And sometimes he ladles on the menace so deep and so thick, as on **"Hand in Hand,"** that it ends up sounding almost laughable. . . .

Really Elvis. You sound like a little boy threatening to bring in his dad 'cos he's bigger than the other kid's dad.

And yet, even taking all those Achilles tendons into account, Elvis is still one of those destined to carve out his name large in the history of rock'n'roll. He's a sly, sometimes deceptively casual, songwriter. He's got passion, guts, aggression, compassion, insight, all those things which on the printed page can look so much bullshit, but are in fact the lifeblood of any worthwhile artist, no matter whether it's paint he's daubing or strings he's plucking.

So far so good; but the same things could be said of quite a handful of rock'n'roll performers. What makes Elvis more compelling than the rest is the scope of his vision and the breadth of his ambition. Like the Clash, he's gonna use every last drop of his wit to ensure that his work is never treated as mere music.

And, at the moment, he's on a winning streak of almost awesome momentum. Like Dylan around the time of [*Highway 61 Revisited*], he's running before he's learned to walk and rubbing that uncomfortable fact in the face of anyone who dares to doubt. (p. 26)

Once upon an innocent time, I used to think that EC was satisfied with merely wishing he'd metamorphose one night—a rock'n'roll version of Kafka's creepy crawly—and wake up as [the Clash's] Joe Strummer. That way he'd have real credibility. Now I realize this kid Costello don't stop at no petty aims like that. He wants to go the whole way. Consumed by the romanticism of the Prometheus myth, he wants to plunge deep into the realms of the untalked-about and capture the fire singlehandedly for the rest of us less determined souls. . .before lunch, preferably. And all that in full knowledge that, on his return, he stands a good chance of having a load of messy birds passing the time of day by gobbling lumps out of his kidneys. Of course, like Dylan, who had similar visions, he'll probably be satisfied by a couple of years playing Faust, after which he'll settle down and write a book.

Still, world domination. Now there's a worthy concept. Personally, these days I don't trust anyone who isn't bent on their own trail of world domination. Since the Great American Novel dream started going down the pan the day [Jack] Kerouac got treated as a serious novelist, and finally gave up the ghost when it caught the Beatles on the Ed Sullivan Show, since the idea of making the perfect rock'n'roll album got lost soon after the twentieth tab of acid, what else is there for a poor boy to do?

In this Indian summer of a society, what hope of survival is there other than making sure you're the one that's calling the shots?

So Elvis has opted for bare-faced hubris, screaming at the gods to just dare to come and waste him. Which means, when all that's squeezed into song form, he's just as quotable as Dylan used to be when he was still patron saint to literate speedfreaks. What else is "bite the hand that feeds me" but the one true epigram for a generation that doesn't have the confidence or the misguided imagination to push "it doesn't take a weatherman to know which way the wind blows" to its ultimate conclusion?

And I'm sure that aura of overweening ambition is just what makes Costello so appealing to the wide wide world. Above all else, rock'n'roll is melodrama. The chants, the lights, the violent jerky moves, a good part of the whole rock'n'roll live experience is a late 20th century variant of the "died and never called my mother" school of art. (pp. 26-7)

With Costello, that melodrama shows itself in many ways. The surly but aggressive wit of his ad campaigns; the spindly fountains of white light that he used as a backdrop for his Dominion Theatre gigs in London; his hunched, tense postures at the mike; the Garbo-esque approach to interviews . . . ; the occasional step into pure hamminess like **"Hand in Hand"**; the global sweep of *Armed Forces* (from **"Goon Squad"** to **"Oliver's Army"** via the authoritative sounding **"Moods for Moderns"**—you can get a fair idea of where those songs are coming from without even listening to the music) and beyond all reasonable expectations, he's produced unsullied masterpieces like **"Watching the Detectives."**

The sheer eerie impotence of the lines "I don't know how much more of this I can take / She's filing her nails while they're dragging the lake" is positively suffocating in its harrowing evocation of domestic disharmony: wife watches *Starsky and Hutch,* husband squirms in his chair wishing he could be up there with the big boys, telling it all to the world from behind his guitar instead of being stuck here in his safe West London home in front of the box with wifey. . . .

[These] days even his private rage takes on an epic form. . . .

[The] suppleness of his melodies are invariably a decoy for the sharpness of the lyrics. **"Oliver's Army"** has been both his biggest British hit . . . and one of his most directly targeted lambasts of a power structure which recruits its killers in uniform from this year's tired poor wretched rabble. True subversion from a master of his past who's still fresh enough to be forcing himself to his own limits. (p. 27)

Pete Silverton, "Accidents Won't Happen," in Trouser Press (copyright © 1979 by Trans-Oceanic Trouser Press, Inc.), Vol. 6, No. 5, June, 1979, pp. 24-7.

IRA ROBBINS

The one factor that most strongly separates Elvis Costello from 99 per cent of the other artists that find their way onto this country's airwaves is his intensity. Some rockers wail convincingly; others write songs of depth and passion; a few play with real fire. But nobody (repeat: *nobody*) puts it all together with as much concerted power as Elvis and band. His second and third albums (the first suffers too much from imperfect execution) are ticking time bombs of flat-out fury. Even when he's not tapping his seemingly bottomless well-spring of venom, Costello delivers the goods with convulsive tension. No one else could charge even a love song with so much convincing anxiety.

[*Get Happy!!*] is different. Disregarding the title (Costello wouldn't dare use such an obvious ploy), the most noticeable change on *Get Happy!!* is the tempered sense of aggression. Some of the tunes work up a proper head of steam (and that doesn't refer specifically to volume, speed or angst), but the songs' overall effect is palpable inertia. Maybe Costello has worked all the vitriol out of his pained system; more plausibly, he has simply decided to try something different. Costello has taken a jaunty tack—with a decided slant towards '60s Motown—and plastered it all over 20 numbers that vary from ace to awful.

There is no pervasive theme as some have suggested; in no way is this Costello's "up" album. In fact, nothing about *Get Happy!!* seems thought out enough to indicate preconception or careful preparation towards a specific theme. . . . Haste, not forethought, is the strongest force here.

It's not a drastic change in musical direction that makes *Get Happy!!* difficult to accept; the overwhelming effect of so many songs, none of them sounding fully developed, defies comprehension (let alone absorption). . . . *Get Happy!!* takes some work.

If there had been only a dozen songs instead of 20, *Get Happy!!* could have been an incredible record. As it is, bad items detract from good ones. The album also suffers from a stupefying maze of verses, choruses and refrains. . . . Take out eight songs and *Get Happy!!* zips along in much more exciting fashion. Less is definitely more. . . .

Pick your own final cut and enjoy. But don't bother to get happy; I'm sure Costello wouldn't.

Ira Robbins, "Get Less Anxious," in Trouser Press (copyright © 1980 by Trans-Oceanic Trouser Press, Inc.), Vol. 7, No. 4, May, 1980, p. 34.

ALLAN JONES

The movie director Sam Fuller once famously defined the cinema as a battleground. That's exactly what rock 'n' roll becomes in Costello's raging hands. Wrestling with demons most of us have only vaguely imagined, Costello doesn't just write and perform songs that are among the most literate and penetrating in the entire repertoire of rock 'n' roll, he unleashes upon his audience the darkest possible realities. . . .

[You] never know how far he's capable of pushing himself. Every performance seems an attempt to achieve some kind of personal catharsis or an act of personal exorcism. It's compulsive and frightening, rarely entertaining in any conventional sense. He can make you feel as uncomfortable as he clearly feels. (p. 33)

*Allan Jones, "Nothing but Music and Fun," in Melody Maker (© IPC Business Press Ltd.), July 19, 1980, pp 24-5, 33.**

IRA ROBBINS

Costello maniacs will already own the bulk of this record [*Taking Liberties*]; for the rest, this is almost entirely first-run. . . .

If you've followed Costello, you pretty much know this album already. Suffice to say, this is prime stuff—as good as any of his preplanned albums, and certainly more consistent than *Get Happy!!*'s 20 maybes. Far from being basement tapes or a "History of," *Taking Liberties* provides further proof (if any were needed) of Costello's talent. Get it!

*Ira Robbins, "Album Reviews: 'Taking Liberties',"
in* Trouser Press *(copyright © 1980 by Trans-Oceanic Trouser Press, Inc.), Vol. 7, No. 10, November, 1980, p. 42.*

BILLY ALTMAN

Budding Costellogians are already filing away the chorus from **"Clean Money"** ("You won't take my love for tender") [on *Taking Liberties*] and, more importantly, the various references to currency—cash and/or plastic—abounding through such songs as **"Sunday's Best"** and **"Crawling To The U.S.A."** ("Attach me to your credit card and then you can undress me"). Shrewd devil that he is, Costello keeps everyone on their toes throughout most of his songs . . . and if you blink, you're apt to miss some of the cliche twisting and punning that are becoming his trademarks. For me, on this album, the most interesting things crop up where you'd least expect them, like Rodgers and Hart's "My Funny Valentine" (*Get Happy!!* is as much about the necessary precision work of lyrics and melody as it is about the history of Motown and Stax and the reading of this song neatly foreshadowed that increasing sense of care, about how compact you can make a song and still make it count; Costello just might be the only traditional young songwriter around right now). And the absolutely awesome **"Just A Memory"**, . . . [with] lyrics that wind around themselves tighter and tighter. . . .

There are stops along the road here that reveal much, from the lonesome resignation of **"Hoover Factory"** ("It's not a matter of life or death, what is? / It doesn't matter if I take another breath, who cares?") to the hypnotic landscapes of doom in **"Night Rally"** and **"Ghost Train"** and the abject rage of **"Tiny Steps"** ("She's your baby now, you can keep her"—when Costello gets ugly, he certainly gets ugly).

Elvis Costello still hasn't worked out all the kinks in his writing—I still cringe when I hear things like "you lack lust, you're so lacklustre" or the rhyming of Elsie with Chelsea in the Seeds-styled **"I Don't Want To Go To Chelsea,"** but there is so much crackling energy and unbridled talent running through most of Costello's recent work that one is at most times justifiably nonplussed. Realizing that a supposed "major talent" like Jackson Browne will take, at his present pace, five albums and 12 years to simply match the number of songs Costello's given us in less than 12 months, it makes you stop and think about who's fooling who in these days of diminished expectations. I guess Elvis Costello wasn't kidding when he said that he didn't intend to be around for his own artistic decline.

Billy Altman, "Costello's Inventory Closeout: B-Sides, 'A' Material," in Creem *(© copyright 1980 by Creem Magazine, Inc.), Vol. 12, No. 7, December, 1980, p. 52.*

ALLAN JONES

"Trust" arrives like a flurry of punches, pinning back your ears as it pins you to the ropes; ducking one punch, you walk into another.

Some of the individual blows might lack a decisive impact, but the final combination puts you down for the count. Time was when Elvis would've left you on your knees, bleeding into your tears. **"Trust"** holds out its hand, hauls you back on your feet. Costello's vision is as fierce as ever, but the malice has gone; he can still rage, but he no longer scolds. . . .

Having his albums around the house and playing them so often is still like having someone's abrasive conscience as a lodger though. No doubt, Elvis will remain too acerbic for comfortable popular consumption. . . .

This could explain the outrageous lack of notice suffered by **"Clubland"** (presently raging up the chart with an anvil around its neck). Taut contemporary lyricism set to an epic beat, **"Clubland"** is one of Costello's finest ever shots, and works effectively as a giddy introduction to **"Trust"**. . . .

"Clubland" is just too close to the bone; it has the muddy impetus of actuality. It's a perfect example of Costello panning across the social landscape and zooming in to expose the devious twists of our common lives, the duplicities, emotional conspiracies and petty humiliations that eventually provoke extreme reactions. Here, it's the flight into crime, looking for status, independence, recognition.

"Clubland" is also a brilliant *rock-noir* song (up there with **"Watching The Detectives"** and John Cale's "Gun"), its drama drawn from its atmosphere, its sinister shadows rather than any clear narrative progression. It bristles with marvellous images; **"Clubland"** has more quoteable lines than most albums have good songs.

And that points to another of Costello's problems as far as some confused spectators and innocent bystanders are concerned: he's so damned *prolific*. His songs are full of ideas, and there are so many *songs*; 20 on **"Get Happy!!"**, another 14 here: it makes people so suspicious. Someone *must* be getting duped somewhere along the line, surely?

The simple truth is that Costello does have a lot to say, and his talent is articulate enough to express every fleeting emotion, image or thought that attracts his attention, to turn them into songs that are often uncommonly memorable. . . . Elvis keeps his lip clipped, commits his energies to songwriting and gets away with murder.

A professional songwriter, heir to a tradition broader than most rock 'n' roll writers can accommodate, Costello writes well about virtually anything. His songs are rarely as confessional as they appear. Hence the versatility of his writing, the variety of musical settings and styles he deploys. He's an *investigative* songwriter, probably the best in rock. He owes allegiance only to his own vocation as a songwriter: that's maybe another reason he worries some people.

You have to advance towards his songs; they know where they stand, and they stay there. If you want to know more about them—and by implication *him*—it's your initiative, pal. Get inside them, do some work; start *thinking*. You don't even have to agree with what he's saying. Costello's songs seem to like nothing better than a good argument: they're meant to sting you into reacting.

It's this quality that convinces you that there's a *real* voice on the end of the line; someone who's put some real thought into the grooves; someone who treats his songs as a dialogue. His best songs are examples, perhaps, of what he describes on **"You'll Never Be A Man"** as "the physical art of conversation"....

You can believe that after finishing an album like **"Trust"**, Costello's got nothing left in his mouth but the sweat on his gums.

"Trust" is the work of someone who takes himself and his audience very seriously. He won't be looked up to, he won't talk down to you. There are familiar themes pursued on **"Trust"**, but increasingly his emotional concerns are placed in a broader social context.

Fortunately, we're spared the glib social ironies of **"Armed Forces"**, the flippant wisecracks and cheap shots of **"Senior Service"** and **"Goon Squad"**. The points here are harder won, the observations are more touching, tinged with a bruised humour, more *human*. It's the concerned commentary of, say, **"Opportunity"**, than the glossy tirades of **"Armed Forces"**; there's less of that album's disgust, more of the last record's compassion.

"You'll Never Be A Man" has steely tenderness that three years ago would've appeared as bitter rage. A study of someone Costello clearly thinks fails to stand up to the world, it . . . opens up to a glorious, tumbling chorus that's currently among my favourite moments in his music. . . .

"Watch Your Step" is another current favourite. Its premonition of universal conspiracies, in which families spy on each other, and are in turn watched over by a superior authority is familiar from **"Armed Forces"** (notably **"Green Shirt"**). Initially, Costello is wry, almost casual.

The mood, however, grows darker over the closing verses as he anticipates the mindlessly violent consequence of brutal intolerance. . . .

Invasion of privacy and the manipulation of the individual by outside agencies (one of Costello's greatest fears) has been approached earlier on **"Strict Time"**, a shuddering spasm of a track. . . . The lyric finds Costello effortlessly sharp. . . .

"Different Finger" is Elvis nodding toward country music. A direct descendant of **"Stranger In The House"** and a distant relative of **"Motel Matches"**, it's further evidence of his formidable range. [It is as] good as anything heard recently from Nashville. . . .

"New Lace Sleeves" is an immediate candidate for the higher echelons of Costello's repertoire. Built around a halting rhythm nudge, the song opens with a painfully accurate account of a soured love affair. . . .

Voice and writing reach a peak with this verse: "The salty lips of the socialite sisters / with their continental fingers / that have never seen working blisters / oh, I know they have their problems—I wish I was one of them."

Costello wriggles through the lines and rhymes, drawing out the greatest emphasis, the final line driven in with a slow twist; like a knife in the side, gleefully malevolent, savouring the careful ambiguity. . . .

Finally: **"Big Sister's Clothes"**, an ominous echo of **"Night Rally"**.

"Sheep to the slaughter," Elvis swoons over a light, jazz-inflected shuffle, popping bass and twanging guitar, "all your sons and daughters / in a stranglehold with a kid's glove . . ."". . . .

[The] song fades, a nightmare vision in a little over two minutes, a sombre conclusion.

If there are such dark days ahead, maybe only **"Trust"** will see you through.

Allan Jones, "The Physical Art of Conversation," in Melody Maker *(© IPC Business Press Ltd.), January 24, 1981, p. 18.*

Gretchen Cryer

1936(?)-

American playwright, lyricist, and actress.

Cryer writes unconventional musicals which reflect the particular concerns of the late 1960s and 1970s—the right to free speech, the growth of the media and its effect on interpersonal communication, and women striving for self-direction in a male-dominated society. It is generally felt that her work can be appreciated as both social commentary and entertainment and that she has helped female playwrights achieve equality and respect.

Cryer has collaborated most often with composer Nancy Ford; they are currently considered the most prominent female writing team in American theater. Their first major work, *Now Is the Time for All Good Men,* is a look at the generation gap and the disparity between liberal and conservative viewpoints. Their next play, *The Last Sweet Days of Isaac,* is an inventive, humorous musical divided into two related sketches about a dreamy young man who wants to make every moment "a perfect work of art," since he thinks every minute could be his last; he tape-records his life as a bequest to posterity. In the second sketch, a young Isaac is in jail for protesting the war. He communicates with the girl in the next cell through a television set, and possibly dies at the end of the act, choked to death by his camera strap. This "metaphor on McLuhanism," as Cryer called it, was recognized as the play's weak point, but *Isaac* was lauded by most critics, who praised the relevance and freshness of her concept and lyrics.

Cryer and Ford are perhaps best known for *I'm Getting My Act Together and Taking It On the Road,* a long-running musical with feminist considerations at its core. The play presents male chauvinism as something to be laughed at rather than challenged. The musical's message, that changes in relating to men are normal and common among women, touched responsive chords among audience members, many of whom felt it gave them a new perspective on their lives. Cryer was criticized for relying on feminist rhetoric and clichés too strongly and for not probing deeply enough into the situations women are facing. However, as with her other works, it is believed that Cryer has transferred personal concerns into universally entertaining theater.

CLIVE BARNES

[To] tell you the truth social significance is dear to my heart. But then so are songs, and I take the perhaps old-fashioned attitude that the first duty of a musical is to be musical. . . . I am writing about **"Now Is the Time for All Good Men."** . . . The news is not exactly good.

[The show] was terrible. . . .

[Perhaps] if the book had been stronger . . . the musical would have been more compelling. Oddly enough, the ideas behind the musical are good—this is where the social significance comes in. For a teacher, who has served jail for refusing to kill in Vietnam, comes to a high school in the wilds of Indiana and teaches the kids about Thoreau and civil disobedience. I

warmed to him, and to the young widow he wooed with hard words and high ideals.

Yet characters are not plays any more than kind words are speeches, and the situation with its melodramatic killing of the hero at the end ("West Side Story," what have you done to us down here?) is only superficially developed. It is all too much like "The Music Man" with angst, for comfort. As a result, with its conventional attitudes being paraded like toy soldiers, its sentiments crack into sentimentality.

Once in a while a line emerges to give the flavor of this Bloomdale, Indiana ("a town for the old in heart," as someone says), and when the line comes up the cast clings to it for dear life. I was glad, for instance, to hear about the "woman who saved all her life to go to Europe and there died of pneumonia." But such country-wise perceptions were almost totally obscured by the story's general drift and the music's general drizzle.

Clive Barnes, "Theater: Social Significance to Music," in The New York Times *(© 1967 by The New York Times Company; reprinted by permission), September 27, 1967, p. 42.*

EDITH OLIVER

["**Now Is the Time for All Good Men**"] rates quite high on what ordinarily matters most in a musical [the score, the staging, the acting, the direction]. . . . The trouble is the words. Now, banal words in a musical can often be dismissed, but these are not banal; in fact, a few of the scenes and lyrics are bright and refreshing. The rest of the book, though, is full of message—preachy, inspirational, and awfully intrusive. The idea of setting a musical in a small old-fashioned town in Indiana and then showing the nastiness and violence that lie beneath its nostalgic charm is defensible, but in this case the irony is too pat and heavily applied and too blunted by sentimentality and complacency. Nevertheless, Mrs. Cryer is young and talented and indignant, and young, talented people have much to be indignant about. (pp. 133-34)

> *Edith Oliver, "The Theatre," in* The New Yorker *(© 1967 by The New Yorker Magazine, Inc.), Vol. XLIII, No. 33, October 7, 1967, pp. 131-38.**

THEOPHILUS LEWIS

[In *Now Is the Time for All Good Men*] the leading character is a typical member of the New Left. That is to say, he attacks conservatism with ridicule, irreverence and civil disobedience and cries "foul" when the establishment fights back with nightsticks, tradition and the veterans' organizations.

Portrayed by playwright Gretchen Cryer in a sympathetic light, Mike Butler is a rather likable young man with an abundance of moral courage and, by normal standards, an unsavory past. . . . Measured by his own ethic and that of his New Left peers, he is a latter-day Thoreau. (pp. 421-22)

While Gretchen Cryer's story is obviously slanted toward the Left, it is a true reflection of life in numerous communities where "liberal" educators are confronting conservative school boards. And her play is really a play, rather than dramatic special pleading. (p. 422)

> *Theophilus Lewis, "Theatre: 'Now Is the Time for All Good Men',"* in *America (© America Press, 1967; all rights reserved), Vol. 117, No. 16, October 14, 1967, pp. 421-22.*

CLIVE BARNES

A number of letters have suggested, usually in gently reasonable terms, that I was unfair to the Gretchen Cryer and Nancy Ford musical . . . "**Now Is the Time for All Good Men**" [see excerpt above]. Perhaps more to the point, I was told that the entire musical had been tightened and the ending completely changed. And perhaps even more to the point still, I admired their courage in keeping going after a moderately unfavorable press. . . .

I thought that the new ending was a marked improvement. Instead of the Philadelphia schoolteacher, transplanted to an Indiana town, being murdered for his efforts at teaching Thoreau's concepts of civil disobedience, he is now merely run out of town. This, while perhaps not any more likely, happens to be less melodramatic (remember fiction must be less strange than truth) and therefore vastly more acceptable.

> *Clive Barnes, "Theater: Reappraisal," in* The New York Times *(© 1967 by The New York Times Company; reprinted by permission), October 27, 1967, p. 49.*

JAMES DAVIS

["**The Last Sweet Days of Isaac**"] isn't very entertaining. . . .

It did not seem an ideal wedding of book and music—perhaps, I think, because the book was so dull. . . .

If there had been less to say on the stage and more music from the background, the show perhaps would have been what it calls itself, "a 1970 musical." As it is, I found it pretty unexciting, like a nothing year.

> *James Davis, "'The Last Sweet Days' No Sweetheart of Show," in* Daily News *(© 1970, New York News Inc.; reprinted by permission), January 27, 1970 (and reprinted in* New York Theatre Critics' Reviews, *Vol. XXXI, No. 11, April 27, 1970, p. 292).*

CLIVE BARNES

With a well-groomed impudence and a cheerful antic wit, a new musical, "**The Last Sweet Days of Isaac**," arrived . . . last night for what should be a long stay. It is one of the most preposterous shows in New York and yet also one of the happiest.

I suspect that this very chic and up-to-the-second musical started out as a satire on the rock musical and the freaked-out generation. Yet in some strange way the approach seems to have been absorbed by the subject matter, and even if "**The Last Sweet Days of Isaac**" was intended as a kind of affectionate put-down, what has emerged is something very positive and extraordinarily attractive.

The book and lyrics by Gretchen Cryer and the music by Nancy Ford are easily among the best of the present Off Broadway crop. . . . The second half of the evening is marginally less entertaining than the first—but this is only a fleeting shadow on a fundamentally sunny night.

The first part of the show is set in an elevator. A stalled elevator—a frantic space, you might say, in stationary time. Occupying the space, trapped between life and death, are Isaac . . . and Ingrid. . . .

[Isaac]—in the 33d year of his life and convinced that he is about to die—believes that life is really intense only when it is recorded. With a tape recorder and a camera, he has made his life-style into a collage. He is collecting his life. And now he meets [Ingrid]. They very nearly fall in love—he undressing her while she sings into his tape recorder—but the moment passes and, for that matter, the elevator is repaired.

The writing here . . . is often gorgeously ridiculous. . . . But what gives the incident its special flavor is the insight Miss Cryer is showing into our all-recorded, all-documented society.

A generation to whom the camera and recorder have become extensions of the human senses is equally the subject matter of the second play. This is also about Isaac—but an Isaac this time only 19 years old. He is a professional protester. The only time his mother sees him is when he is on television. And now protesting he is inadvertently killed—or perhaps he has not been killed—strangled by the strap of his movie camera. Satisfyingly, his always-loyal camera recorded his own death.

A girl, also a professional protester, is taken to a police cell and existentially—if you will pardon the phrase—reaches Isaac. Isaac is once more concerned with the recording of an entire life, so that it could be put in a library as a surrogate for people whose lives would normally have been less interesting.

Miss Cryer has a strange, interesting mind [which has] convoluted and occasionally repetitive thought. . . .

I enjoyed the show . . .—I even liked its actual fumbling quality and absence of any focused viewpoint on youth and the camera.

> Clive Barnes, "Happy Musical: 'Sweet Days of Isaac' Has Cast of Three," in The New York Times (© 1970 by The New York Times Company; reprinted by permission), January 27, 1970, p. 49.

MARTIN GOTTFRIED

["**The Last Sweet Days of Isaac**"] is terribly intelligent and supermodern, very funny, pertinent and impertinent. . . . The problem is its problems—it ran into a great many of them, obviously tried to repair them, just as obviously couldn't, and decided to settle with what it had. I suggest you settle for that as well because it often succeeds at something nobody else has yet tried.

What Gretchen Cryer . . . tried to do was apply the ideas of Marshall McLuhan and the visual realities of primary artists to current American existence (television existence, sound tape existence, photographic existence) she kept her thoughts "linear" (as McLuhan would say), working in terms of dialogue and specific thoughts. This essential conflict—sort of trying to combine time with space—was never resolved, though you can sense that Miss Cryer thinks it could be and so do I: Finally, not knowing how to apply this unmixed mixture to the stage (itself still another dimension), she struggled.

The struggle was amazingly successful considering its novelty and if you haven't followed a word I've said, remember they're first steps for me too. This is a terribly new mode of sensation but I believe it is into the truth. . . .

"**The Last Sweet Days of Isaac**" is about personal contact, the first half set in the middle box (where a couple is trapped in an elevator in ultimate physical contact), the second half in the end boxes (the couple being connected only by television screens, perhaps the ultimate in some new kind of abstract contact). . . .

Though [the first] half is very funny, it is almost as often coy, alternately taking itself seriously and parodizing itself. The mood as well as that problem are very much like [Tom Jones and Harvey Schmidt's] "The Fantasticks." . . . Also, Miss Cryer has a problem common to many of us, being unable to commit herself to a set of beliefs because there is too much silliness in sets of beliefs. She wants to go with the radicals but she sees too much inconsistency, intolerance and naivete in their words and ways. In short, she is too bright to be a good soldier. . . .

The second act heads straight to the heart of electronic communication, the couple now separated in jail cells, having been arrested in a peace demonstration, one watching and the other being on television. Miss Cryer begins this act with a funny, affectionate parody of peace-marchers and their police oppressors, ending it in a confusion of electronic relationships. The act is noticeably the victim of cutting and ends the show quite abruptly, though its austere quality is extremely appropriate. . . .

Miss Cryer [possesses] an intelligence, a high-spiritedness and a questioning idealism. Between Miss Cryer's thinking and her cool, primary modernism, "**The Last Sweet Days of Isaac**" is an especially important theatre event.

> Martin Gottfried, "The Theatre: 'The Last Sweet Days of Isaac'," in Women's Wear Daily (copyright 1970, Fairchild Publications), January 27, 1970 (and reprinted in New York Theatre Critics' Reviews, Vol. XXXI, No. 11, April 27, 1970, p. 292).

WALTER KERR

"**The Last Sweet Days of Isaac**" is my favorite rock musical thus far for three reasons: (a) The songs end when they are over; (b) While a boy and girl are doing all that talking about coming alive, they *are* alive; and (c) Language at last is beginning to rise to the beat.

Take the last first. For the first time in my experience, someone—Gretchen Cryer, it turns out—has succeeded in writing a book that is not only as good as the music but walks right into the music without hemming and hawing about it. I say "book," although [it] is really (let's be honest) two enchanting one-acters. . . .

But the writing is actual writing—not pretentious writing, mind you, not self-conscious in its casual poetry, but not baby babble or mere latrine leftovers, either. (p. 1)

The evening is small (but that may be one reason why it comes so alive, there are persons to make contact with us instead of so many massed, and hence impersonal, bodies) and it is short (each half is over before you want it to be, a defect that is also a recommendation), . . . and I do hope you will go. (p. 5)

> Walter Kerr, "My Favorite Rock Musical Thus Far," in The New York Times, Section 2 (© 1970 by The New York Times Company; reprinted by permission), February 8, 1970, pp. 1, 5.*

HOWARD THOMPSON

What a novelty it would be, in a musical needling thick-skulled, set American traditions, to see the bad guys—the old reactionary ostriches—presented as something less than diehard dimwits. The good guys? They're altogether admirable. The other side—impossible, except to long for the simple life. That's their one attribute.

This nagging cliché gathers and hangs like a conventional cloud over "**Now Is the Time for All Good Men**." . . .

Let's get this on record fast, even while quibbling about the play's one flaw. . . .

The tone is quietly, sharply searching. . . .

The score is brightly jocular when spoofing the local yokels. It is an interesting score throughout, pleasantly fresh, with straightforward, almost conversational lyrics and some inventive, melodic turns.

But Misses Cryer and Ford are at their best minus the needling. . . .

The real Cryer-Ford knack also marks their best tunes, two ballads titled "**Tea in the Rain**" and "**Rain Your Love on Me**" (a lotta rain, granted) and "**Stuck-Up**", a sizzling barrelhouse. The most sophisticated number, "**See Everything New**," is original, intricate and beautiful. . . .

[The] show ends on a brilliant pin-point that says volumes. See for yourself. . . .

Howard Thompson, "Equity Revives a Musical," in
The New York Times (© 1971 by The New York
Times Company; reprinted by permission), May 2,
1971, p. 73.

DOUGLAS WATT

I don't expect you to believe any of this, but the hero of [Cryer
and Ford's] **"Shelter,"** an unnerving bit of musical whimsy
. . . , is a happily married fellow who lives apart from his
wife and their seven adopted children of as many races. He
lives in a set—kitchen, bedroom and bath—in a television
studio. And he is regularly visited by a young woman named
Wednesday November. . . .

From these sorry materials, which would be looked down upon
as childish by the Sesame Street audience, a gratingly mannered
and senseless book has been devised by Gretchen Cryer, who
is also responsible for the foolish lyrics. . . .

I didn't see ["**The Last Sweet Days of Isaac**"] but seem to
recall that the entire thing took place in an elevator. There's
an elevator in **"Shelter,"** too, and the ladies use it to depart,
one by one. I wish I'd thought of it first.

Douglas Watt, "A Whimsy-with-Music Called 'Shelter' Opens," in Daily News (© 1973, New York
News Inc.; reprinted by permission), February 7,
1973 (and reprinted in New York Theatre Critics'
Reviews, Vol. XXXIV, No. 3, February 3-10, 1973,
p. 370).

CLIVE BARNES

There is a lot of sweet music in the kooky musical, **"Shelter."**
. . . Whether this will prove enough remains to be seen. Certainly the show is very likable. . . .

It has been written by Gretchen Cryer and Nancy Ford, who
a few seasons back gave us the amiable eccentricities of **"The
Last Sweet Days of Isaac."** **"Shelter"** has something of that
same zany and disarming spirit to it. . . .

The show has a light heart and shows a certain insight into the
self-satisfied child-man, Michael, and the kind of women who
play house with him. Gretchen Cryer's book is too fantastic
in its story line—its central situation of a man living on a TV
set is unbelievable—which definitely detracts from the wry
humor of the writing. The lyrics are generally neat. . . .

People liking their Broadway musicals to be bold and brassy
will not take to **"Shelter."** But people appreciating more of a
chamber musical, intimate, even cozy, should find this a warmly
pleasant evening.

Clive Barnes, "'Shelter,' Musical, Arrives," in The
New York Times (© 1973 by The New York Times
Company; reprinted by permission), February 7, 1973,
p. 31.

WALTER KERR

Got the shock of my life. At **"Shelter,"** an intimate musical
surrounded by stereopticon slides, I found myself becoming
quite accustomed to the notion that all of the orchestration for
the tunes was being provided by a companionable computer
named Arthur, whose lights blinked in rhythm to the notes
being churned out. As one does at musicals, I found myself
turning my head in Arthur's direction each time an intro began,

accepting him (it?) as the source of all melody. Once, though,
I saw something other than Arthur. I saw two ghostly hands,
white, disembodied, waving frantically, like those of a drowning man making one last effort.

Then I realized what, or whose, they were. They belonged to
the conductor, the *real* conductor, hidden deep in the curtained
orchestra pit conducting his real hidden orchestra. Yes, there
was actual music being played here after all, just as there were
actual people playing it—though only the most flashing of
upbeats would bring those phantom fingers as high as the edge
of the stage. It was a spooky feeling, whether one read symbolism into it or not. Before my very eyes all things human
seemed to be going down, down, down.

That, by the way, is what **"Shelter"** is all about—or at least
what it starts out to be all about. . . . [Actress Marcia Rodd]
has a bit of a nervous breakdown while filming a commercial.
She can stand the ersatz no longer, "Words are corrupt!" she
cries, she announces that the ad men have already turned her
into a cardboard standup. . . .

TV writer Terry Kiser, skipping down an iron stairwell from
the control booth, has a cure-all for her highly unprofessional
hysteria. He has walked *into* the fake, lives there. He lives
right on the studio set, night and day, getting Arthur to program
his spring breezes, cockcrow sunrises, buttermilk skies. There
is a fake flowering plum tree under which love may easily
blossom. As Mr. Kiser points out, once you accept plastic
flowers, you have bypassed fraudulence: they're *real* plastic
flowers. The deception stops there. So why not adapt?

It's an amusing and possibly pertinent premise for a lightly
ironic entertainment, the only trouble being that the rest of the
entertainment doesn't have much to do with it. Mr. Kiser now
proceeds to get Miss Rodd into his bed precisely as any less
original man might, the brief idyll is interrupted by another of
Mr. Kiser's flames in just the way idylls are normally interrupted, a wife eventually turns up to clear the area for her man
as wives always have, plastic or no plastic. Even Arthur seems
to wilt, rather, as routine bedroom farce replaces what started
out as wryly inverted comment, and the loss of a slant is doubly
disappointing in that **"Shelter"** is the work of Gretchen Cryer
and Nancy Ford. . . . (p. 1)

Walter Kerr, "After an Amusing Premise, What?"
in The New York Times, Section 2 (© 1973 by The
New York Times Company; reprinted by permission),
February 18, 1973, pp. 1, 23.*

SUSAN DWORKIN

Gretchen Cryer and Nancy Ford have been composing fine
music and lyrics for the theater and for just plain singing for
a long time, and now, suddenly, people are beginning to listen
to them. They started too soon, before women's experience
was accepted as the stuff of hit songs, and so they had to wait.
And wait. But now the waiting may be over.

Their newest record, **"Cryer and Ford: You Know My Music"**
. . . has lyrics so timely (mostly by Cryer) and music so appealing (mostly by Ford) that it should make people look for
their earlier album, **"Cryer and Ford"** . . . ; between them,
they contain all the thematic music that American feminism
needs to keep it singing for a generation. . . .

Their music is made of the vast experience they have been
through: joblessness, love affairs, failure (their musical, *Shel-*

ter, which didn't stay long on the boards) and success (their musical, *The Last Sweet Days of Isaac,* which did), divorce, remarriage, children, joy. They stay as close as quarter notes, growing together, changing together. Their songs describe events we may have thought were uniquely ours; that is, in fact, how they create a bond with the audience which is uniquely theirs.

Sometimes they tell stories (**"Another Unhappy Love Song"**); sometimes they zing in a little bitterness (**"Last Day at the Job"**). . . . Gretchen Cryer's lyrics are not complicated ever; the perception that underlies them is accurate and has the force of the God's honest truth. (p. 64)

The main trouble with Cryer and Ford records is not the artists themselves, but just the way records are made today—overlays of violins that make it hard to concentrate on the lyrics, an otherworldly fade at the end of the otherwise excitingly real song.

Women looking for songs to sing on buses going to conventions should remember that Cryer and Ford have now made them available. **"Hang On to the Good Times"** is one, but it could also be belted out loudly around a piano. Same thing goes for their best song, **"Changing,"** which, like a lot of their music, echoes the church choirs in which they both sang.

Locked inside my headset, I tried it out: imagined I had just heard a rather inspiring sermon; okay, everybody rise, turn to page whatever; sing along with the women in the choir loft a song that is so true, it was familiar from the first time you heard it; sing it like an anthem that gets you out of the halls of worship and into the world, resensitized. (pp. 64-5)

> Susan Dworkin, *"Hang on to the Good Times,"* in Ms. (© 1977 Ms. Magazine Corp.), Vol. VI, No. 6, December, 1977, pp. 64-5.

RICHARD EDER

"I'm Getting My Act Together and Taking It on the Road" is a musical entertainment about a 39-year-old woman finding herself.

For once, the standard disclaimer must be reversed: The subject does not do justice to this summary description.

There is some freshness of aspiration but none of achievement in this collection of songs and skits about the troubles of a pop singer trying to find a new image for herself.

There is a touch of wit here and there. Gretchen Cryer . . . is trying to say something honest about aging and feminine identity. Her perception fails her, she falls into platitude after platitude and comes up with a show that is both insubstantial and very heavy. . . .

[Cryer and Ford] seem to be catching up with a number of theater conventions and ideas of the 70's, and arriving late. . . .

Self-celebration is the affliction of **"I'm Getting My Act."** Its songs and skits spell out the conflicts—the little girl who has to smile for her daddy; the wife who has to pick up her husband's socks and talk baby talk to him; the liberated women who find that men don't much like them—with little individual perception, imagination or rigor. The lyrics, and the music, are effortless and not in the best sense of the word.

There are exceptions. The skit about three overachieving women who conclude that men prefer incompetence, is charming. . . .

But **"I'm Getting My Act Together and Taking It on the Road"** is not so much a title as a pious hope.

> Richard Eder, *"'Getting Act Together'," in* The New York Times (© 1978 by The New York Times Company; reprinted by permission), June 15, 1978, p. C17.

EDITH OLIVER

[**"I'm Getting My Act Together and Taking It On the Road"**] was written by [Nancy Ford and Gretchen Cryer]. These are the two remarkable women whose **"The Last Sweet Days of Isaac"** was one of the glories of Off Broadway in 1970, which makes this show all the more disappointing. . . . **"I'm Getting My Act Together"** is a protest show, too, but it has a querulous undertone, and it is a lexicon of all those awful words and phrases (some of them used ironically, to be sure) that are the jargon of the nineteen-seventies—"relate," "relationship," "confrontation," "cleaning lady," "manipulating," "sick," and, worst of all, "celebrating me."

The show may indeed be disappointing, yet it is anything but a total loss. Miss Ford's buoyant music . . . and Mrs. Cryer's nimble lyrics, in a lot of the songs, belie that querulousness and all those grievances. (pp. 51, 54)

> Edith Oliver, *"Off Broadway: Lady Sings the Blues," in* The New Yorker (© 1978 by The New Yorker Magazine, Inc.), Vol. LIV, No. 19, June 26, 1978, pp. 51, 54.*

JULIUS NOVICK

Ms. Cryer sets forth the story of Heather Jones [in *I'm Getting My Act Together and Taking It on the Road*] in terms of feminist cliches. Heather tells us that she was "Daddy's smiling girl," and then she was her husband's smiling girl, because she was expected to be; but ninety-eight years after the first production of [Henrik Ibsen's] *A Doll's House,* this is not precisely a new insight. And I am sick and tired of the bit about the crass male who says approvingly of some bright woman that she has "brains like a man." Even if that one does persist in real life, can't we give it a rest in the theatre?

Ms. Cryer's show is not simply a performance of Heather's act; what we see is a rehearsal for the benefit of Joe, her manager, who is an insensitive oaf. He doesn't like her new, tough songs; they threaten him. Every few minutes, he interrupts with the most painfully obvious ojections, to which Heather replies with equally obvious feminist justifications. Joe can't see why Heather won't stick to her old stuff, especially his favorite, **"In a Simple Way I Love You"**: "I will listen while you sing your song, / While you do what you have to do. / I'll stand behind you rain or shine . . ." Reluctantly she sings it for him—and then breaks off and screams, "I can't keep doing this!" "It sounds great," he replies, "what's the matter?" Well, where the hell has he been for the last decade or so? Joe is Ms. Cryer's worst mistake: Not only is he implausibly—and maddeningly—obtuse in himself, but it weakens Heather to have no one to play against but this one-dimensional punching bag.

And yet Ms. Cryer has not written the feminist equivalent of a "get whitey" play. Fundamentally, she is looking not for revenge but for understanding, and here and there she even finds some. . . . [Actor] Don Scardino turns on some high-voltage, impish charm as a musician who is attracted to Heather though, or because, she is thirty-nine and he is twenty-four. He even sings her a few lines of **"In a Simple Way I Love You,"** but Heather ignores him. A pity: Their relationship might have been more interesting than anything Ms. Cryer has actually written. *I'm Getting My Act Together* is not a debacle, only a promising opportunity missed. Purged of the obnoxious Joe, who does not sing, it might have made—might still make—a record album with tides of feeling that men and women of good will might reasonably get off on.

Would *I'm Getting My Act Together* mean something special to a woman? You'll have to ask a woman. I spoke only to one, aged twenty-two, who said she was tired of thirty-nine-year-old women and their problems. Nobody ever asked *her* to smile and be a beauty queen and pick up men's socks. Was I, like Joe, threatened as a man by Heather the Strong Woman? Maybe, but I doubt it. Ms. Cryer's *Act* reminded me of a lot of platitudinous plays and musicals that had nothing to do with feminism. "To be a playwright is to see," said Ibsen. Ms. Cryer has just not been able to see deeply enough. (p. 80)

Julius Novick, "Heather and Wan" (reprinted by permission of The Village Voice *and the author; copyright © The Village Voice, Inc., 1978), in* The Village Voice, *Vol. 23, No. 26, June 26, 1978, pp. 79-80.*

WALTER KERR

As a natural male chauvinist who's simply never been able to get away with it . . . , I am endlessly fascinated by the varied cases the more ardent women's libbers make for themselves.

Gretchen Cryer, for instance, seems to me to be making the wrong one—or making it wrongly—in . . . **"I'm Getting My Act Together and Taking It On The Road."** Miss Cryer, of course, is the writer-singer-actress who collaborated so niftily with composer Nancy Ford on **"The Last Sweet Days of Isaac,"** and in the fretfully defiant challenge she's issuing now she does remind you—once or twice—how lyrically intelligent, how self-assertively bold she can be. She sings the phrase "Dear Tom, yes, I always fixed your suppers" with a liquid upward thrust that's enchanting, even as you quite understand that Dear Tom has been given the heave-ho sometime past.

But here's the thorn: Miss Cryer, in the entertainment, has firmly made her break with the image and the life-style imposed upon her by her daddy (daddy taught her to smile, smile, smile, so she'd look pretty enough to snare a man who'd take care of her the rest of her life), by her husband (she tried to be the "who" he wanted her to be but the charade was too dishonest to be endured), and by her manager (who is trying to adjust her outspoken nightclub act so that it will be more palatable to middle-brow, still macho, males).

Having "split" with everyone who's tried to impose an alien role or an alien look on her . . . , she is proud of her freedom. . . . Her career is quite enough . . . , she doesn't want to talk about success but about integrity . . . , she books no further argument. . . . Okay.

But. She's *still* miserable, burdened with a permanent frown, self-righteous and—much of the time—sorry for herself. . . . How are we to dredge up the sympathy we're supposed to feel? No one can feel sorry for the unliberated woman *and* the liberated woman at one and the same time. That's double jeopardy, or something. It *can't* be cricket.

Walter Kerr, "Two Women, Both Alone, Two Moods," in The New York Times, *Section 2 (© 1978 by The New York Times Company; reprinted by permission), July 9, 1978, p. 3.**

Paula Danziger

1944-

American young adult novelist.

Following the tradition of Judy Blume and Norma Klein, Danziger writes fiction for young adults which portrays contemporary adolescent life realistically. Since the publication of *The Cat Ate My Gymsuit* in 1974, Danziger has become one of the most popular writers among young adults. Her appeal can perhaps be attributed to the fact that she combines realism with humor and addresses some of the more difficult aspects of growing up with candor and empathy.

A junior high school reading instructor, Danziger has based much of her work on her own life and on the experiences of her students. *Cat,* for instance, stemmed from the stormy relationship she had with her father; like Marcy, she was a perpetual failure in gym and had a younger brother who stuffed his teddy bear with orange pits. Danziger's funny, somewhat self-effacing middle-class heroines face a variety of problems as they move between school, family, and friends. Her novels present dilemmas to which teenagers can relate, ranging from simple feelings of inadequacy to the trauma of divorced parents.

Critical reaction to her novels has been mixed. While it is acknowledged that her subjects are relevant, some critics feel that she explores such important issues as peer pressure, challenged sexual mores, and parental insensitivity without depth or fresh insight. While granting that Danziger does not romanticize her characters or their situations, some critics feel that she dilutes reality to the point where her books are valuable only as light reading. However, her use of wit and humor is universally applauded, as is her ability to create believable heroines. Despite critical reaction, the wide readership of young adults has affirmed their appreciation of Danziger's sensitive, accurate portrayals of their concerns and feelings.

Photograph by George Janoff; courtesy of Delacorte Press

CATHY S. COYLE

The issues of teacher independence and student protest [in *The Cat Ate My Gymsuit*] are topical, and Marcy, an intelligent and enjoyable adolescent, is an appealing heroine; however, the ending is anticlimactic and unsatisfying . . . and some of the characters like Marcy's bullying father are stereotypes.

Cathy S. Coyle, *"Junior High Up: 'The Cat Ate My Gymsuit',"* in School Library Journal, *an appendix to* Library Journal *(reprinted from the November, 1974 issue of* School Library Journal, *published by R. R. Bowker Co./A Xerox Corporation; copyright © 1974),* Vol. 21, No. 3, November, 1974, p. 62.

KIRKUS REVIEWS

At its worst, [*The Cat Ate My Gymsuit*] is a trite and trendy saga of how a junior high English class gets it together to fight for the job of Ms. Finney—a paragon of an innovative teacher who puts across dangling participles and sensitivity sessions with equal ease. The only relief from cliche is the relationship between lumpish, insecure Marcy and her father—a frustrated, angry, non-verbal man who can show his love only through providing food and shopping trips. The parent who can't communicate his love and concern is no doubt a more common problem than alcoholism or divorce, but he's seldom dealt with this forthrightly in contemporary stories, where parents, whatever their faults, are usually articulate. Marcy's tense family situation is really the subject here; the instant therapeutic effect of Ms. Finney, a sort of denim-skirted *deus ex machina*, is a cop-out.

"Young Adult Fiction: 'The Cat Ate My Gymsuit'," in Kirkus Reviews *(copyright © 1974 The Kirkus Service, Inc.),* Vol. XLII, No. 22, November 15, 1974, p. 1206.

VERONICA GENG

Barbara Finney is not exactly A. S. Neill, and **"The Cat Ate My Gymsuit"** stands in relation to literature as Judith Viorst's verses do to poetry. But it is funny and alive, and if it encourages readers to expect something more from teachers than they are getting, it is well worth [its price].

Veronica Geng, "'The Cat Ate My Gym Suit'," in The New York Times Book Review (© 1975 by The New York Times Company; reprinted by permission), January 5, 1975, p. 8.

JOURNAL OF READING

The Cat Ate My Gymsuit is such an unusual title that it is sure to arouse curiosity. If readers expect humor, they will get it, but it is well blended with worthwhile values and character development. (p. 333)

For all its marvelous humor, this book is still realistic. Marcy's sense of humor is a counterbalance to her father's negative influence and helps keep her going.

The Cat Ate My Gymsuit is a thoroughly enjoyable, tightly written, funny/sad tale of an unglamorous but plucky girl who is imaginative, believable, and worthy of emulation. (p. 335)

> *"Books for Young People: 'The Cat Ate My Gymsuit'" (copyright 1976 by the International Reading Association, Inc.; reprinted with permission of the International Reading Association), in* Journal of Reading, *Vol. 19, No. 4, January, 1976, pp. 333, 335.*

KIRKUS REVIEWS

Thirteen-year-old Cassie starts her first-person story [*The Pistachio Prescription*] with the assertion that "Pistachio nuts, the red ones, cure any problem," and she ends with "Twinkies, I bet, are the answer"—a fair enough indication of the level of growth that has transpired in between. And though Cassie does indeed have problems that neither pistachios nor twinkies can solve—chiefly, divorcing parents whose insensitivity brings on her frequent asthma attacks—her tone throughout is so glib and inauthentic that it's hard to believe in a real suffering child under all the predictably triggered hysterics. ("Sometimes I think my parents are wonderful, and sometimes I hate them" is a typical Danziger illustration of adolescent psychology.) . . . Not improbable, but shallow—a synthetic slice of "typical teenage" life.

> *"Young Adult Fiction: 'The Pistachio Prescription'," in* Kirkus Reviews *(copyright © 1978 The Kirkus Service, Inc.), Vol. XLVI, No. 7, April 1, 1978, p. 379.*

ZENA SUTHERLAND

The quotation from [Albert] Camus that precedes [*The Pistachio Prescription*] tells all: "In the midst of winter, I finally learned that there was in me an invincible summer." . . . Cassie begins to understand that the situation [between her parents] is irrevocable [and] that she can live through the years before she is able to leave home. . . . Not unusual in theme, this is unusually well done; the characterization and dialogue are strong, the relationships depicted with perception, and the writing style vigorous.

> *Zena Sutherland, "New Titles for Children and Young People: 'The Pistachio Prescription'," in* Bulletin of the Center for Children's Books *(reprinted by permission of The University of Chicago Press; © 1978 by the University of Chicago), Vol. 31, No. 9, May, 1978, p. 140.*

SELMA G. LANES

["The Pistachio Prescription"] is a novel no thoughtful 9- to 13-year-old should let parents see. They may not survive the instant ego deflation of viewing themselves through adolescent eyes. . . . On the other hand, Cassie's peers will surely identify with the ugly duckling heroine's inferiority complex, her hypochondria, her first love and her unexpected nomination for president of "the freshperson class" (my favorite phrase in the entire book). The work is really an extended monologue with lots of snappy one-liners, some good, some not. . . . And though her parents clearly seem headed for the divorce court by book's end, the heroine is beginning to make her own peace with them, and with the world as it is.

> *Selma G. Lanes, "Children's Books: 'The Pistachio Prescription'," in* The New York Times Book Review *(© 1979 by The New York Times Company; reprinted by permission), March 18, 1979, p. 26.*

CYRISSE JAFFE

Lively, believable and thoroughly readable, [*The Pistachio Prescription*] will have the same wide appeal as the author's previous book, *The Cat Ate My Gymsuit*. Cassie is beset with some typical teenage insecurities. . . . Cassie, who believes her only salvation lies in compulsive pistachio eating, is an energetic and likable heroine. Readers will identify with her troubles at home and at school, and enjoy the skillful rendering of Cassie's growth and maturing. Despite an occasionally superficial passage and a resolution that moves too swiftly to be satisfying, the juxtaposition of Cassie's personal triumphs . . . and her parents' impending divorce adds the necessary depth. . . .

> *Cyrisse Jaffe, "Fiction: 'The Pistachio Prescription'," in* Kliatt Young Adult Paperback Book Guide *(copyright © by Kliatt Paperback Book Guide), Vol. XIII, No. 3, Spring, 1979, p. 6.*

ZENA SUTHERLAND

[In *Can You Sue Your Parents for Malpractice?*, Lauren's parents] give her trouble, particularly her father, who is domineering; she's also troubled by her parents' fighting. Such general problems are the background for a wry and humorous story of Lauren's coping with the conformity her classmates and friends expect. . . . While Lauren is confronting the generation gap, establishing independence, giving adherence to standards of social behavior, and other universal problems of the adolescent, the book has enough humor and breezy dialogue to make it fun to read, and enough solidity in characters and relationships to make it thought-provoking. (pp. 172-73)

> *Zena Sutherland, "New Titles for Children and Young People: 'Can You Sue Your Parents for Malpractice?'" in* Bulletin of the Center for Children's Books *(reprinted by permission of The University of Chicago Press; © 1979 by the University of Chicago), Vol. 32, No. 10, June, 1979, pp. 172-73.*

KIRKUS REVIEWS

Ninth-grader Lauren [in *Can You Sue Your Parents for Malpractice?*] has a stereotypically impossible father (he rails against his wife going to work part-time; he disowns his college-age daughter for moving in with her boyfriend) and, like other Danziger heroines, she has "typical" concerns which are projected wholly from her shallow perspective. . . . Her ten-year-old sister Linda is dying for a training bra, so Lauren, remembering how important it was, gives her her old one—in a scene that makes Judy Blume's Margaret [in *Are You There, God? It's Me, Margaret*] seem complex. But Lauren's big problem is the flak she gets from other kids at junior high when she starts dating Zach, who is only in eighth grade and thus infra dig. When an older boy who had jilted her earlier returns complacently, Lauren realizes that she likes Zach and shouldn't worry about what the other kids say. In truth, Zach is a nice kid with some good lines, and Danziger writes fluently. Her superficial slices of suburbia have a facile appeal, but truly hip kids resent the generalized triviality.

> *"Older Fiction: 'Can You Sue Your Parents for Malpractice?'" in* Kirkus Reviews *(copyright © 1979 The Kirkus Service, Inc.), Vol. XLVII, No. 11, June 1, 1979, p. 641.*

JANE LANGTON

["**Can You Sue Your Parents for Malpractice?**"] takes place in the airless chamber of early adolescence.

The heavy problems of Lauren and Linda and Bonnie are: 1) Does it hurt to get your ears pierced? 2) Should ninth-grade girls go out with eighth-grade boys? 3) Should fifth-grade girls wear training bras?

The atmosphere is close and sweaty and mildly titillating, with cute boys on the telephone, copulating Ken and Barbie dolls, hair appearing or not appearing under the arm, and parents who are always fighting and deserve to be sued for malpractice. . . .

[The book] is clever and funny. The chapters rush by in a catapulting present tense. Adolescent and preadolescent girls, and even chubby children who might otherwise be reading "Winnie-the-Pooh," will giggle and pass it from hand to hand.

The author is a junior-high-school teacher, and she might say that the book is an honest picture and that she does, after all, wave some kind of flag for decency and general morals. But the flag is about the size of the Barbie doll's bikini. Case in point: As Zack and Lauren go upstairs to his room "to study," Zack's "nice" mother warns them kittenishly not to "study too hard." Oh, civilization! Oh, chastity! Oh, a hundred years of chaperones on Sunday afternoon park benches! Oh, the creak of the bedsprings as Lauren and Zack lie down! Six minutes later they sit up. What have they been doing? The world of early adolescence is certainly hot and perspiring and scruffy. Open the window, somebody.

> *Jane Langton, "Children's Books: 'Can You Sue Your Parents for Malpractice?'" in* The New York Times Book Review *(© 1979 by The New York Times Company; reprinted by permission), June 17, 1979, p. 25.*

FAITH McNULTY

[Paula Danziger is a writer like Judy Blume] who capitalizes on the sordid details of adolescence [and whose] "**Can You Sue Your Parents for Malpractice?**" . . . is ruefully and relentlessly funny, in a style reminiscent of Erma Bombeck's. Danziger's heroine is fourteen, and, it says on the jacket, "her life is the pits." . . . In the end, the heroine feels a lot better because, in a moment of revelation, she accepts her dreary

future. "My life's not going to drastically change," she muses. "It hardly ever does when you're a kid. My parents certainly aren't going to change that much. . . . What I am sure of is that I finally did something for myself, that I'm learning to do what I think is best for me." I took the last sentence to be the redeeming social message of the book. I also noticed that throughout this book and in many other "contemporary" novels an enormous amount of hostility and resentment is expressed by young heroes and heroines. In almost all these books, realism means not only a problem but a grievance. Is this a reason they are so popular? One has a disquieting impression of legions of angry kids out there fuming over the dishes, their parents' insensitivity, and many things far worse, who are eager to identify with similarly mistreated heroes and heroines. Often, the happy ending comes when the child casts off the adult yoke and becomes his or her "own person"—a boneless phrase that sets my teeth on edge. Trying to grasp its meaning is something like trying to grasp a jellyfish, but its elasticity makes it a convenient conclusion for any number of books. (pp. 196, 199)

> *Faith McNulty, "Children's Books for Christmas: 'Can You Sue Your Parents for Malpractice?'" in* The New Yorker *(© 1979 by The New Yorker Magazine, Inc.), Vol. LV, No. 42, December 3, 1979, pp. 196, 199.*

NATALIE BABBITT

Miss Danziger's popularity, like Mrs. [Judy] Blume's, is easily explained, but the reasons for it are quite different. In spite of its trendy title, "**Bunk Five**" is not a funny story any more than its predecessor was—notwithstanding the frequent one-liner zingers in both—and Marcy's family life continues to be miserable, her father a monster, the communication gap a chasm. Marcy begins, of course, to learn tolerance and understanding at camp, to become, presumably, more "adult." But in the world Miss Danziger presents, adults, with a couple of exceptions, are two-dimensional, egocentric and small-minded. If this is really the case, why try to be one? But Miss Danziger is playing pretty much flat out for the audience. You of the new generation, she seems to be saying, will be fine folk someday, unlike the poor saps from whom you sprang. That stance has increased her popularity, but it's pretty simplistic and questionable considering the complexity of the problem. (pp. 36-7)

Miss Danziger, . . . by romanticizing the distortions that complicate the healing of family rifts, may be perpetuating some of the very miseries for which she shows such sympathy. (p. 37)

> *Natalie Babbitt, "Children's Books: 'There's a Bat in Bunk Five'," in* The New York Times Book Review *(© 1980 by The New York Times Company; reprinted by permission), November 23, 1980, pp. 36-7.*

ZENA SUTHERLAND

In some ways [*There's A Bat in Bunk Five*] is the usual camping story of pranks, bunkmates, adjustment to separation from parents, etc. This doesn't, however, follow a formula plot; it has depth in the relationships and characterizations; and it's written with vigor and humor. Marcy learns not to expect too much from others, not to assume that all problems will—or can—be solved; she also learns not to expect too much from herself.

Zena Sutherland, "New Titles for Children and Young People: 'There's a Bat in Bunk Five'," in Bulletin of the Center for Children's Books (reprinted by permission of The University of Chicago Press; © 1980 by the University of Chicago), Vol. 34, No. 4, December, 1980, p. 68.

BARBARA ELLEMAN

Danziger's ability to create believable, funny dialogue and to capture the feelings and thoughts of a 14-year-old is highly evident [in *There's A Bat in Bunk Five*]. Episodes roll along without much tension or drama, unfortunately, and what is there is too quickly resolved; but readers will be captivated by the natural flow and breezy style.

Barbara Elleman, "Children's Books: 'There's a Bat in Bunk Five'," in Booklist (reprinted by permission of the American Library Association; copyright © 1980 by the American Library Association), Vol. 77, No. 8, December 15, 1980, p. 571.

HARRIET McCLAIN

[In *There's a Bat in Bunk Five* the] author has skillfully balanced her insight into the daily trauma of the young adult years with liberal doses of humor. The book is neither didactic nor reeking of bibliotherapeutic intentions; yet junior-high readers should feel reassured by it.

Harriet McClain, "Junior High Up: 'There's a Bat in Bunk Five'," in School Library Journal (reprinted from the January, 1981 issue of School Library Journal, published by R. R. Bowker Co./A Xerox Corporation; copyright © 1981), Vol. 27, No. 5, January, 1981, p. 68.

KIRKUS REVIEWS

From Barbara's exemplary surrogate-parenting to Marcy's continuing lack of communication with her father and her new fear of her feelings when kissing Ted, [*There's A Bat in Bunk Five*] gives us pop-psychology profiles instead of imagined characters and shallow with-it attitudes instead of sincere probing. Danziger's fans probably won't mind, but neither will they be stretched an inch.

"Older Fiction: 'There's a Bat in Bunk Five'," in Kirkus Reviews (copyright © 1981 The Kirkus Service, Inc.), Vol. XLIX, No. 1, January 1, 1981, p. 12.

Ray(mond Douglas) Davies
1944-

British songwriter, singer, musician, and actor.

Davies is a founding member and lead singer of the Kinks, a rock group which achieved success during pop music's "British Invasion" in 1964. Davies writes nearly all of the band's material, and his blend of catchy melodies and uniquely British subjects has established a cult following for the Kinks which continues to grow. Davies has gone through various stages in his songwriting career. He has written top 40-oriented pop songs, social satires, concept albums, vaudeville-type stage shows, and New Wave music with topical overtones. Through all of these changes, Davies has maintained the stance of a loner, and his songs most often reflect the alienation and unfulfilled aspirations of the lower middle class.

Davies first became involved in music while an art student in England. With his brother Dave, Peter Quaife, and Mick Avory, Davies began a rhythm-and-blues band called the Ravens. Soon after changing their name to the Kinks, the group signed a recording contract. After releasing two cover singles with little success, the Kinks recorded Davies's composition "You Really Got Me," which was highly successful worldwide. Davies continued to write popular hits through the mid-sixties, including "All Day and All of the Night," "Tired of Waiting for You," "Set Me Free," and "Till the End of the Day." These songs feature a basic beat embellished by distinctive guitar work and repetitive lyrics which reflect the experiences of young people. The Kinks's early albums were overshadowed by these singles, however, since Davies rarely surpassed the lyrical and musical limitations of his hits. Nevertheless, listeners were intrigued by Davies's quirky songs about aggressive women and passive men. The best example of this type of song is "Set Me Free," in which Davies, unlike other pop songwriters of the time, asks the girl to set *him* free. This sexual ambiguity is apparent both in Davies's soundtrack for the English television movie *Percy*, which concerns a homosexual, and in "Lola," a song about a person who "walked like a woman but talked like a man."

The release of the single "A Well Respected Man" in late 1965 saw a marked shift in Davies's song topics. This song centers on the themes of corruption and appearance-and-reality rather than love relationships. From this time on, Davies's work began to depict "serious" situations which are felt to be related from a specifically British viewpoint. These works include "Dedicated Follower of Fashion," "Sunny Afternoon," and "Deadend Street," and the albums *Something Else* and *The Kinks Are the Village Green Preservation Society. Village Green* is seen as a "concept album" with a surprising theme for a rock group: the preservation of traditional ideals and morals. The Kinks's next album, *Arthur (or the Decline and Fall of the British Empire)*, is considered the most successful of Davies's concept works. Written for an English television musical, *Arthur* shows the decline of English values through the life and views of one character. The Kinks's popularity in England reached its peak with *Arthur*, but the British nature of Davies's writing alienated American fans, and the Kinks were regarded in the United States as an eccentric cult band.

The Kinks had a hit single in 1971 with "Lola," a Davies song with a typically offbeat theme: transvestism. However, "Lola" is not representative of Davies's work in the early seventies. Davies continued to rely on specific themes for his albums, but his songs veered more toward music-hall vaudeville routines. Beginning with the album *Muswell Hillbillies*, Davies incorporated brass and a distinctly un-rocklike sound to many of the group's songs. The album was a popular success, but it proved to be the last one the Kinks would have for a few years. Davies's *Preservation* trilogy, *Soap Opera*, and *Schoolboys in Disgrace* are the most theatrical Kinks albums, and Davies took his ideas one step further by acting out his stories in elaborate stage shows. These shows were highly regarded by fans and critics, and were likened to Bertolt Brecht/Kurt Weill themes and productions. However, the albums are felt to be little more than soundtracks for the stage musicals and were not commercially successful. Also, there was dissatisfaction among other members of the band toward the direction Davies's music was taking; this resulted in some halfhearted performances and caused Davies to reevaluate his songwriting theories.

Sleepwalker, released in 1977, showed distinct changes in Davies's work. He was no longer writing theater pieces, opting instead for the *Something Else/Village Green* idea of individual songs working toward a collective theme. Critics heralded Davies's creative rebirth on *Sleepwalker* and the next Kinks album, *Misfits. Misfits* is considered to be one of Davies's most personal works, and the title song and "Rock 'n' Roll Fantasy" are felt to be among Davies's most beautiful and significant lyrics. The Kinks achieved commercial success with *Low Budget,* which was recorded while Davies was living in New York and contains lyrics which reflect American society much more than previous albums. The music on *Low Budget* has a harder edge to it, and Davies's topical themes and pessimistic viewpoint seems influenced by the songs of numerous new wave bands. Accordingly, the Kinks have attained a greater level of popularity in the United States than at any time since the years of their first albums, and they have become more popular in America than in England. This American resurgence proves that Davies still speaks to young people with his songs while working with the ideas and problems that have become his trademark.

RAY DAVIES

On the subject of songwriting, I try to put my own feelings in our records, apart from making them commercial. . . .

["**All Day and All of the Night**"]—despite what many critics say—is a sincere effort to convey the attitude of many people today. It seems that when a thing is "down-to-earth" and factual people always try to stamp it out, but eventually it becomes the established thing.

I could really call myself an apprentice songwriter at the moment and I hope eventually to become sufficiently capable of expressing people's everyday moods, thoughts and emotions in music.

Maybe we should be called the Francis Bacons of pop music!

> Ray Davies, "Kink Is Still a Naughty Word," in Melody Maker (© IPC Business Press Ltd.), November 28, 1964, p. 9.

PAUL WILLIAMS

If you are not a Kinks fan, you are either a) uninformed, or b) not a Kinks fan. If it's the latter, there's nothing you can do about it. The Kinks, rather like Johnny Hart's *B.C.* or the novels of Kurt Vonnegut, are absolutely indefensible (and unassailable). I can't tell you why they're great: there are no standards by which the Kinks can be judged. Ray Davies' music has nothing to do with almost anything else. It's in a category unto itself, and if you don't like it, well, there you are.

I would like to say that *Face to Face* is a tremendously funny lp. I'm uncomfortably aware, however, that there are those, even those I respect muchly and love warmly, who do not find *B.C.* at all funny. I hesitate, therefore, to urge upon them an album that starts with four rings of a telephone and a pristine male voice saying "Hello, who is that speaking please?", followed inexorably by a lead guitar and bass who sound like they've been perched for hours just waiting to play their little run and get into the song (a righteous complaint against whatever it is that interrupts phone conversations). The humor of the thing is indescribable: it's all in the timing, and I break down every time I hear it. But there are those who sit unmoved. It must have something to do with taste.

The Kinks are mostly—but not entirely—Ray Davies. Ray is . . . [the] motive force for the group, and it is his curious personality that comes through in every note the Kinks play. Some people think Ray is a genius (albeit a misguided one). I think it's more accurate to call him an amazingly articulate musician; his mood at any given time is reproduced impeccably in his songs, with no apparent effort on his part. Playing around with a familiar melody and an unusual break—"**Rosie Won't You Please Come Home?**"—he lets the words fall where they may. "And I'll bake a cake if you'll tell me you are on the first plane home." Sheer nonsense . . . but it all falls in place so perfectly, it's hard to imagine any other words could belong there. Ray's gift is his control of his music: whatever he does, it's right. (p. 36)

There's a lot of depth to this album. "**Rainy Day in June,**" for example: how can anything that starts with a thunderclap not be a pretty damn serious song? But it is, and it's a major work. The piano/bass thing rainy days all over you, while Ray's voice just stares out the window. The important part is "Everybody's got the rain," an unfinished line which is about as universal as they come. Wow. A work of beauty.

"**Rosie Won't You Please Come Home?**" is too unbearably funny. The nice thing is, he's not putting down anybody: he's just getting totally into the mother's part, with full sympathy but never a serious moment. "**Most Exclusive Residence For Sale**" is almost as good; Ray acts very straight and pseudo-tragic about the whole thing, but the ba-ba-ba-ba chorus that backs him up gives him away and completely gasses the listener.

"**Fancy**" is so lovely and so far-out musically that everyone should notice it and nobody will. Two years from now, when everyone's into this kind of thing, no one will remember that Ray Davies was into it first. They never do.

"**Little Miss Queen of Darkness**" is wonderfully well built. . . . If you can ignore the frenetic upstaging long enough to catch the words to the song, do; they're delightful. Davies is master of smiling pathos.

"**Sunny Afternoon**" is a song to end if not all other songs then at least several. It is a Davies tour de force; if "**Too Much On My Mind**" is his statement of policy, then "**Sunny Afternoon**"—following, as it does, a nervous breakdown—is Ray's State of the Union Address to the world. And it's beautiful. It starts off descending and just floats on down for another 3.5 minutes. It's a portrait of the artist as a happy, helpless himself, trapped on a sunshine carpet of psychosomatic flypaper . . .— and like every Davies portrait, it is razor-sharp but it draws absolutely no conclusions. Goods and bads do not enter into the picture. Ray is sympathetic to all things and all people, up to and including Ray Davies.

Face to Face is a fine lp; the Kinks have really never done a poor one. This is perhaps the best Kinks lp to meet them on; it hits hardest and fastest, it is the most sophisticated and in many ways the funniest and most musically inventive. . . . *Face* is not, however, the best Kinks album. That title would probably go to *Kink Kontroversy,* an early '66 album that had no single track as good or even as ambitious as "**Rainy Day in June**" or "**Sunny Afternoon.**" *Kontro* stands, however, as the best statement of the Ray Davies approach to music and/ or life. Its overall quality is much higher than *Face* partly because it doesn't fool around as much—as a result, it avoids the occasional self-consciousness of the new lp . . . and it doesn't display its low points as obviously ("**Holiday in Wai-**

kiki'' is a good example of a track that just doesn't fit on *Face*). *Face*, in many ways, is an overly arty lp; *Kontro* offers us Kinks in their natural habitat.

But Kinks, no matter where they are or what they're doing, are well worth your attention. Whether or not you enjoy them is surely a matter of taste. But if, like many, you've overlooked them, you're missing one of the finest groups we have. (p. 37)

Paul Williams, "'Face to Face': The Kinks," in Crawdaddy *(copyright © 1967 by Crawdaddy Publishing Co., Inc.; all rights reserved; reprinted by permission), March, 1967, pp. 36-7.*

SANDY PEARLMAN

[Ray Davies is not] the sort of hero to inspire faith. But he is pretty cynical. Thoroughly disenchanted. (p. 21)

On *Kinks Size* [the Kinks] do "Louie, Louie." This is highly significant because it seems that the Kingsmen and their "Louie, Louie" are the source for the Kinks' style. Recall that "Louie, Louie" was the big hit on the eve of the Beatles in late 1963. And realize that the Kinks loved it well enough to even do it again on *Kinks' Kinkdom* (a double cover). Played back-to-back . . . , **"You Really Got Me"** seems the plausible—if long awaited—sequel to "Louie, Louie." And "Louie, Louie" becomes archetypically astringent, an influential song in the tradition of "Can I Get A Witness," "Memphis," "Hang on Sloopy," "La Bamba" and "Tequila." *Kinks Size* also has the Kinks' second hit, **"All Day and All of The Night,"** a remake of **"You Really Got Me,"** in which (rare for a sequel) the internal tongue pressure remains enormous enough for grammatical structure to collapse as Ray Davies sings "Girl you and me last forever." **"So Tired of Waiting For You"** is, of course, beautiful beyond words, so sad and so weary. The first confluence of astringency and the big Kinks' theme of gentle and disappointed cynicism. Here it is that the Kinks first openly approach the abyss. . . . On [*Kinda Kinks*] the boys rounded out their methodology. Their tone of voice (and pronunciation) became disorienting. An apparently sincere song like **"Everybody's Gonna Be Happy"** was done questionably. . . . [It] got hard to say what the intention was. (p. 37)

Kinks Kinkdom was next. It had the unprecedented **"A Well Respected Man"** . . . , **"Who'll Be The Next In Line?"** and **"See My Friends."** And there were a lot of other great ones too. Obviously this record was an *ursus magnus*. It's the first Kinks' album to have noticeably fewer (absolutely and percentage-wise) repulsive cuts. **"A Well Respected Man"** spearheaded a then new—and currently dominant—trend toward brutal cynicism. They utilized the fragmentary enumeration of a few smutty or otherwise unsavory details as a method to discredit everything. ("He likes his fags the best . . . And his own sweat smells the best.") This was very economical and demonstrated a "flair for detail." Simultaneously the song sounded like Donovan. Impossible, you might think. . . . But the folksy melody and the cultural shock of hearing Ray Davies' voice thin, natural and alone, was actually enough to invoke the kind and flowery poet of the north. **"See My Friends"** proved atypically explicit and unambiguous. With **"So Tired Of Waiting For You"** the weltschmerz could have verged on horribly metaphysical despair. Could have. But these boys looked healthy and the ambiguity was easily resolvable in the direction of a superficial sad and weary cynicism. But what if Ray Davies had discovered the secret relationship between everybody's constant disappointment and the constancy of the

turning earth? . . . **"See My Friends"** makes all this clear. Here's real clarity, not given in a flash, but in the guise of, of all things, the Byrds.

First the words. They're chanted in recurring cycles. . . . The band plays Byrd-like categorical-magical patterns. Rhythmically constant percussion (both drums and metal), constant bass and guitar. Making the words and music mutually reinforcing. Atypically the interference effect has dropped out. And it's suddenly obvious that all that Kinks' cynicism was yet another compact rationalization in the face of the abyss. Logically the abyss renders all conclusions questionable. The only way to authentically (and descriptively) handle anything is to put it in constant question. Positioning is primary. (Stand them on their heads and other ways too.) Both being funny and the interference do that. Later the Kinks even got obviously funny— since the subtle humor of the interference effect wasn't subtle enough. But at this stage they settled for simplest subtlety. **"See My Friends"** is not only structurally (or formally) explicit. It's also that way cognitively. The song's words are the very ones at the core of the Kinks' cynicism. They're pretty art work about the abyss. In which case the Kinks have declined their old trick of making a statement inferring the abyss through— and by—the mere act of making that statement itself questionable.

Kinks Kontroversy is mainly a continuation of the radical decline of the repulsive and dialectically corresponding rise of the palatable move. But that implies much. At the same time it's a holding and perfection operation. An eclectic warehouse. (Starring hard rock, r&b, blues, Bizzaro blues and the wall of sound. Even a harmonica. And other things too.) And just the spot for the most cathedral and bell-like sounds in the history of the Kinks. Metaphysical cynicism—of the sad and weary variety—is one of the repetitious themes which are held and perfected. Even the titles are dead giveaways: **"The World Keeps Going Round," "Where Have All The Good Times Gone,"** "I Am Free" (by Dave Davies). Identifying futility as a characteristic of the universe and showing just how much the abyss has to do with impotence. Making these songs among the saddest of all things ever. (pp. 37-8)

The latest singles and albums complete the decline of the repulsive. Mainly because they lack repulsive cuts. However this question of the Kinks' repulsiveness—formerly preponderant enough to appear innate—is tough and knotty. Once repulsiveness, by itself, sufficed to make their sound unique. . . . But meanwhile you knew, deep down, that the currently familiar and ergo potentially palatable had once been immediately repulsive. Or at least until *The Kinks Greatest Hits!* Certainly one of the greatest of the greatest hits series, it proved uniformly palatable. Also charming. Familiarity (if only fleeting) with its numerous hits and hits-that-failed took out the possibilities for extraordinary repulsiveness. And nostalgia turned the formerly repulsive charming. (p. 38)

Face to Face came out of the boat, a vintage production, pretty well cured and aged by the "legal matters," just the Kinks' album to be found entirely (and right off the bat) palatable. All of the big Kinks' themes were there: from metaphysical despair (**"Fancy," "Rainy Day In June," "Sunny Afternoon," "Too Much On My Mind"**) to a new trend in the direction of an ever-increasingly brutal cynicism (**"Dandy"** . . . , **"Session Man," "House In The Country," "Little Miss Queen of Darkness"**) to simplest sarcasm (**"Party Line," "Rosy Won't You Please Come Home," "Holiday In Waikiki"**). Explicitly expanding (for the first time) the interference effect to album-wide dimensions. (Maybe *this* is the Kinks' high point.) Here everything is made questionable. And that does it for the Kinks. The Kinks have exchanged stable imaginative objects out of the bizarre . . . for disconcerting things put into motion via interference. Metaphysical desperation, cynicism and sarcasm are then all mutually out-of-phase (interfering) positions. (With cynicism the most inclusive position of them all.) Positions which make possible the exposure of all possible subjects in every which way. (Cynicism is motion and cynicism is exposure.) Absolute positioning has taken its place with bicycle riding and science as a way of life. Shimmering, cynically disjointed objects—themselves the isomorph of the abyss because they are just as unimaginably unstable as the very abyss—are the Kinks' meat.

Philosophically one can say only this: the Kinks are and have been very dynamic. (They breathe fire.) (pp. 38-9)

> *Sandy Pearlman, "Doors & Kinks," in* Crawdaddy *(copyright © 1968 by Crawdaddy Publishing Co., Inc.; all rights reserved; reprinted by permission), January, 1968, pp. 21, 25, 36-9.**

PAUL WILLIAMS

I certainly love the Kinks; it's been fifteen months since I've had a new Kinks album in my house, and though I've been listening to them I've missed that pleasure. . . . I've played [**The Village Green Preservation Society**] twice since it arrived here this afternoon, and already the songs are slipping into my mind, each new hearing is a combined joy of renewal and discovery. Such a joy, to make new friends! And each and every song Ray Davies has written is a different friend to me.

Ray makes statements, he says the sort of stuff that makes you delighted just to know that someone would say stuff like that. . . .

Now why is it Ray's songs always sound like something else, a different something else with each song and sometimes with each hearing? Sure, he's the world's master plagiarist, but it's more than that. It's more a feeling that it's all part of the same thing, it's all music and isn't it nice to run across this melody again? And it is, it's never a repetition, it's always some sort of opening. Ray Davies makes you realize how much there is all around us, waiting to be explored and explored again. Boredom? Every place you've been is a new frontier, now that you're someone different. . . .

I've bought their every album as it's been released, and that's four years now and ten albums, every one satisfactory and worth far more than double your money back. . . .

Each Kinks song [is] a friend. I really mean that. I can lie in my bed thinking about **"Love Me Till the Sun Shines,"** and I wonder when I'll hear it again, happy at the thought of its existence. Hearing **"Big Sky"** on this new album, I know we'll get along just fine. "I think of the big sky and nothing matters much to me." This is true, an experience I've shared. "Big sky's too big to sympathize; big sky's too occupied, though he would like to try." What a fine modification of Stephen Crane. And who but Ray Davies would share my interest in the theme of "The Open Boat"? . . .

[There may be] some sort of real bond between Kinks-lovers the world over. I mean it's not just some rock group. It's more like a taste for fine wines from a certain valley, a devotion to a particular breed of cocker spaniel. How many people are there who would feel good to know that **"Waterloo Sunset"**'s

Terry and Julie are Terence Stamp and Julie Christie—that is, they inspired the names, by appearing together in *Far from the Madding Crowd*? How many would understand not feeling afraid, as long as you gaze on that sunset? We're a select few, no doubt, so we may as well love each other and stick together.

This Kinks-love is, I think, something that can be consciously related to the sense of nostalgia, which in turn is something that has less to do with time and things past, and more to do with texture. Texture is sensuous; if style is how you do it, texture is the way you make it feel. Ray Davies' voice, with Dave Davies' guitar just behind it, not only feels a certain way regardless of what it's doing, it also establishes for you a certain relationship to things, which is maybe one reason why *deja vu* is such a large part of the Kinks listening experience. It's not that you heard this before, necessarily, but that you felt this way about something before, the common denominator is that the relationship between A and B is the same as the relationship, with which you're more familiar, between D and F. . . .

Nostalgia is the recapturing of a certain feeling you once had before. How else classify a feeling, save through personal past experience? Ray Davies' songs have a second-order relationship with the way people feel, not necessarily joy but the reaction to joy, if you follow me. Ray's vignettes are wry, ironic—and one suspects it's not just that he's capable of a certain detachment, but also that he can't escape that detachment, it's the way he's always known things are. . . .

And when texture is beautiful, . . . as of course it is in all (even despairing) Kinks-music, it's an affirmation in itself, just for things to feel this fine is enough for now. **"Sunny Afternoon"** is the song Ray wrote after or maybe during his famous breakdown. It may be one of the songs of the century. Doing nothing, feeling like nothing or worse, you still feel like this song . . . and it's one of the highest feelings man has yet recorded in art. Maybe just because it's so real. Or maybe something more than that. . . . It's so far down, and raises me so far up. . . . Surely, this is greatness.

I'm frustrated now. I was okay, trying to make you feel how good the Kinks make me feel, but I can't pass on greatness. I can't sit here and come up with phrases to argue genius, I can only shout, as modestly as possible, about how deeply I'm affected. I'm thinking, only genius could hit me so directly, destroy me and rebuild so completely, but that's ontology, proving has nothing to do with making you believe. I've never had much luck turning people on to the Kinks. I can only hope you're onto them already.

> *Paul Williams, "'The Kinks Are the Village Green Preservation Society'," in* Rolling Stone *(by Straight Arrow Publishers, Inc. © 1969; all rights reserved; reprinted by permission), Issue 35, June 14, 1969, p. 35.*

MIKE DALY

The Kinks' image is so strange, a group making it on the fact that they've never made it. The ultimate recording group—that's all they do, they just make records, you never see them but once a year they put out an album—a gift from themselves to their audience. The Kinks' last two albums, **Something Else** and **Village Green Preservation Society** sold a combined total, in America, of 25,000 copies—that ain't very many. I don't know whether people actually don't like their stuff or if they've just never heard it—whatever the reason, somebody's missing something, because the Kinks, since 1964, have been making some of the finest rock music this side of the Stones and the Beatles.

Things like **"You Really Got Me"**—really tough, grinding hardrock; and **"All Day and All of the Night"**—strange, stumbling, go-stop-go tempo; and **"So Tired of Waiting For You"**—repetition working, monotony makes it. . . .

The Kinks have always done it, one little gem after another, six years of treats: **"David Watts," "Waterloo Sunset,"** the *Face to Face* album . . . it's all there, folks, in the world of Ray Davies, the magical kingdom of the Kinks—the Disneyland of rock in its most beautiful form.

Arthur, the Kinks' new movie: such an incredible album. . . .

Arthur—The Decline and Fall of the British Empire: Ray's England with a brass section.

"Victoria"—the old queen, covered in pomp and circumstance, kicks it off in real shitkicker style—what an opening—a declaration of love for one's mother country. **"Victoria"** is a statement of fact in the nineteenth century, the Kinks' hymn to tradition—and with such fucking exuberance, man! . . . Being English with a vengeance. . . .

"Some Mother's Son"—you just cry; it's the whole story, from childhood to the battlefield to a grave, for no fucking reason at all; the waste, the absurd waste of a life—Ray's voice puts it across so movingly. The home fires are still burning, mom knows but she can't quite understand . . . "some mother's memory remains."

"Drivin'"—forget the hassles, for three minutes and fifteen seconds tragedy doesn't exist anymore—who's to say what's real. The Kinks take us on a picnic with them, skipping over the hills . . . , listening to the birds, watching the dogs run, falling out on the grass and just dreaming away, mmm. . . . . . .

"Shangri-la"—Paradise on earth. Starts off slowly, Ray speaking to an old man who's worked his ass off all his life, showing him all the little things he's earned, and then laying into the whole scheme of the man's life, coming back at the end to reassure the poor old guy: it's alright pops, it's OK—you *did* do your best.

"Mr. Churchill Says"—Ray reads Winston Churchill's speech and makes it work! The British people prepare to get together and repel the Nazi hordes, and the Blitz of Britain is on! "The War That Had To Be Fought"—the air raid sounds, it's real now, it's in the streets. . . .

"Young and Innocent Days"—Such a soft, beautiful hazy hymn to childhood and everything that went with it. . . . (p. 38)

"Nothing To Say"—Continued from the above; You Can't Go Home Again, Part Two. Such a great statement to rap to your parents . . . after all that time together you've just got nothing to say to each other . . . and finally—

"Arthur"—the poor dumb well-meaning guy, all he wants is just a bit of peace and quiet and a few little comforts; I mean, everybody's entitled to that, aren't they? The parade is just about over, but he really can't figure out what went wrong, why it didn't turn out as he had planned, as he'd hoped it would. Maybe those crazy ideas the young people have are worth something . . . (pp. 38-9)

That's *Arthur*—an Englishman's life and thoughts and hopes and dreams, stories that Ray Davies wrote and produced, little

scenes that the Kinks act out in playing and singing, an album that is a masterpiece on every level: Ray Davies' finest hour, the Kinks' supreme achievement. (p. 39)

JOHN MENDELSOHN

So, apparently having forgotten the Byrds' words of caution, you wanna be a rock and roll star, eh? Before you trade in your stereo components toward the price of an electric guitar, there's [*Lola vs. Powerman and the Moneygoround (Part One)*, a] rock and roll essay by Ray Davies and his boys that your ears just have to read. . . .

"The Contender"—*silly quasi-bluegrass yielding to some of the most energetic rock and roll noises the Kinks have made since their live-at-Kelvin-Hall LP.* Impatient to get out of the life you're presently leading . . . , you resolve to bust out by playing rock and roll. . . .

"Get Back In Line"—*the album's masterpiece: lovely musically, most poignant lyrically.* . . . It gets to the point where the union-man decides whether or not you eat, let alone bring your woman home some wine.

"Lola"—what praises remain to be sung for this perfectly magnificent piece? Let me mention only that, contrary to the belief of those who celebrated it in its single incarnation, Ray never comes out and tells us whether or not Lola is indeed a transvestite—the most he says is, "I know what I am and I'm glad I'm a man, and so is Lola." This fits in the essay contextually rather than thematically; that is, not because of its plot but because it was the hit record our attention is directed toward—

"Top of The Pops"—*the two most banal riffs Ray could remember, namely modified versions of those from "Louie Louie" and "Land of a Thousand Dances."* As your single makes its way up the chart you discover all manner of friends that were never around before, the press becomes interested in your politics and theories on religion, women scream at you in the street, and prominent queens invite you to dinner. As your record reaches No. One, which prompts your agent to suggest that here's your chance to make "some real money," celestial organs start to play.

But everyone thinks himself entitled to a cut of the profits from this song he's never heard, which puts you on **"The Moneygoround."** By the time you've had your solicitor serve the necessary writs, you're on the verge of a nervous breakdown, having wound up with "half of goodness knows what."

Given [such a] mixed-up, muddled-up, and shook-up world as this, it's no surprise that your fancy turns in the face of the horrors of the rock and roll life to simply escaping, the idea with which side two of the essay is most concerned.

Escaping to a blissfully-uncivilized existence is what the delightfully catchy follow-up to **"Lola," "Apeman,"** is all about. Herein Ray, affecting a West Indian accent, delivers such unforgettable lines as, "Come on and love me / Be my apeman girl." Light harmless stuff reminiscent of *Something Else*, but don't allow yourself to be lulled into a false sense of security, for these are, after all, the post-*Arthur* Kinks, and they paint pretty horrifying villains nowadays. . . .

What with all the rats and powermen about even the dubious freedom of hopelessness that is the theme of **"This Time Tomorrow"** seems inviting. What's crucial, they remind us in **"Got To Be Free,"** a knock-out finale in which Dave, the rocking kid brother, and Ray, who's older and more apt to take things philosophically, rebound off of one another's lines and music, is simply to get out of this life.

This just may be the best Kinks album yet. And, brother, that's saying one heaping mouthful.

> John Mendelsohn, "'Lola vs. Powerman and the
> Moneygoround (Part One)'," in Rolling Stone (by
> Straight Arrow Publishers, Inc. © 1971; all rights
> reserved; reprinted by permission), Issue 74, Janu-
> ary 7, 1971, p. 47.

ROY HOLLINGWORTH

Well, we all know what **"Percy"**'s about, don't we? Nudge, nudge, and a nod's as good as a wink.

Well this length from the film score, laid flat by Ray Davies, performed by the Kinks, hangs I'm afraid, limp, rather lank, cold—and lacking in guts.

But how can one really criticise a movie film score, how can one talk creatively about sets of music laid down to slip in, and fuse with a film? All tracks fail to rise, fail to reach any form of climax. . . . Possibly the best track is **"The Way Love Used To Be,"** a drifting ballad. . . . **"Whip Lady"** would I thought, have been a Kinky movement, but there's no naughtiness to get into. . . . Davies has undoubtedly been successful with the score—if you see the film with it—but it's a shame an album has to be released. It fails to rise to the occasion.

> Roy Hollingworth, "A Limp 'Percy' from the Kinks,"
> in Melody Maker (© IPC Business Press Ltd.), March
> 20, 1971, p. 17.

BOB PALMER

The Kinks are craftsmen in a musical genre that often relies on flash and force, literate chroniclers in a post-literate medium. They are also the most consistent band in rock and roll. Each of the Kinks' preceding twelve albums . . . is an absolutely integral piece of work. While other groups have dried up, broken down, spawned generations of side-man/superstar spinoffs, the Kinks roll on.

Ray Davies, the group's lead singer and songwriter, seems to be an inexhaustible source of pithy, self-contained songs. . . . All 12 songs on **"Muswell Hillbillies"** . . . are his, though the spirit of pub philosophy that dominates the album owes much to Dave's brand of tipsy populism.

But this is essentially a serious album. Ray used to paint pictures of well-respected men that were quaint and a little one-dimensional, and his descriptions of English working-class traditions occasionally verged on the lugubrious. **"Muswell Hillbillies"** deals with the kind of attitudes that rockers-in-rebellion and men who work with their hands can share over a pint of stout; it equates the Cockney's stubborn pride with the pride of the American "hillbilly," but Ray Davies is no drug store cowboy; and he doesn't care to record in Nashville. His idiom is still soaring hard rock, with side trips into the updated music hall idiom that has become a Kinks trademark.

The Kinks and their Muswell Hill cronies have a common enemy: the "people in grey." The album's first song delineates the nature of the enemy in Davies' typically plain English. . . . The rest of Side One empathizes with the citizen who's "too terrified to walk out of my own front door," whose holidays are uncomfortable outings to a seaside that has become "an open sewer," whose neighbors look like "skin and bone" or lose their positions of prominence to "old demon alcohol." Finally, there's a straightforward admonition: "Got to stand and face it, life is so complicated."

The conflict escalates on Side Two. The "people in grey" are clearing the slums, breaking up the old neighborhoods, trying to establish and enforce uniformity, and longhairs and shorthairs alike are menaced. The young suggest a militant answer: "a gun to keep the policemen away." But there's also Granny's answer: "For Christ's sake, have a cuppa tea. . . . An embattled Cockney fighting relocation gets the last word, and he shouts it loud and clear for every citizen whose liberty and personal value is compromised by the failed industrial "revolution," the rape of both privacy and sanity by the faceless hirelings of nameless bureaucracies: "They'll never make a zombie out of me." This last cut, the album's title tune, has the foot-stomping fervor of [Merle Haggard's] "Okie From Muskogee," but rather than aggravate existing conflicts, it stresses the unity of the disaffected young and society's older victims in the face of an interlocking power structure bent on the destruction of human dignity and, eventually, human life.

The Kinks' newest masterpiece is doubly welcome at a time when most rockers have abdicated their power to disseminate positive, constructive suggestions. Davies doesn't offer any easy solutions, but of course there aren't any. **"Muswell Hillbillies"** attempts to cut through idealistic rhetoric and sloganeering and deals objectively with the strengths, weaknesses, and possible lines of alliance between a stratified, fragmented citizenry and an equally disorganized subculture. A new urgency, a welcome emotional involvement, has replaced the Kinks' former dispassionate cynicism, and the result is great rock and roll.

> Bob Palmer, "The Kinks: Rockers in Rebellion," in
> The New York Times (© 1972 by The New York
> Times Company; reprinted by permission), January
> 23, 1972, p. 25.

MIKE SAUNDERS

Musically, the Kinks' roots in the British Music Hall tradition really show up strongly on *Muswell Hillbillies*. At least five songs could be described as this type, and when the country-ish material is added, the two styles account for almost the whole LP. . . . Most of the music-hall style songs come over pretty well, even if the genre is minor compared to things the Kinks have done in the past. **"Have A Cuppa Tea"** is reminiscent of previous Kinks quaintness, and **"Alcohol"** is particularly delightful—sort of a followup to Ray Davies' Maurice Chevalier tribute **"Just Friends"** on *Percy*.

The country stuff is another matter. A portion of it is fine, but some of the songs are so positively uninspired and unenergetic it drives me up the wall. Such as things like the Kinks nasally whining "I'm a Muswell hillbilly boy / But my heart lies in old West Virginia" or Ray singing the saga of **"Holloway Jail,"** a total doggerel of a song which would have been more at home on some forgotten Marty Robbins album ten years ago. The Kinks who roared out of Muswell Hill in 1964 . . .

weren't any shuffling hillbillies, they were grade-A urban *brats;* and they later matured in a way encompassing broadened scope and sensibilities that few rock bands have ever matched. And that's why it's such a drag to hear the routine 1971 country slide guitar rot turning up on a Kinks album, even if only in a couple spots. . . .

[In] several respects *Muswell Hillbillies* represents an uncertain crossroads for the Kinks' recording career. . . .

Overall, *Muswell Hillbillies* is a weird tangent for a group that've always been at their best when rocking their asses off . . . but the album succeeds, where it does, largely on its combination of cynicism, tenderness, and wit that the Kinks have long been known for.

As must be obvious by now to anyone who has ever encountered a true-blue rabid Kinks fan, each new Kinks album is an Officially Sanctioned major event, even in these post-*Village Green Preservation Society/Arthur* days. From an objective historical basis, there's a valid case for such devotion: the Kinks now have to their credit around 16 albums, and many Kinks fans would tell you that all but three or four of them are excellent. In fact, there are some crazed loons who would go so far as to claim that the Kinks are none other than the greatest rock and roll band of all time. The crazed loon writing this review couldn't agree more!

> Mike Saunders, "'Muswell Hillbillies'," in Rolling Stone *(by Straight Arrow Publishers, Inc. © 1972; all rights reserved; reprinted by permission), Issue 101, February 3, 1972, p. 43.*

MIKE SAUNDERS

The Kinks started out by being raunchier than any group in history. **"You Really Got Me," "All Day And All Of The Night," "I Need You,"** and **"Till The End Of The Day"** were truly the Kingsmen unleashed, and for my money more thrillingly raucous records have never been recorded.

After such successful rock and roll albums as *You Really Got Me, Kinda Kinks,* and particularly *The Kink Kontroversy,* not to mention *Well Respected Kinks,* Ray Davies decided it was time to explore some different alleys. This is precisely what the Kinks' work since *Kink Kontroversy* has been—a probe down one alley of expression, and once the genre has been satisfactorily mined, a move on to something else. . . .

Ray's effete, melodic side had been apparent all along, especially on . . . [*Kinda Kinks*]. So it is no surprise that the Kinks went into an extended introspective soft-rock period, recording *Face To Face, Something Else, Village Green, Arthur,* and *Lola Vs. Powerman.* It is this period that is the focus of *The Kink Kronikles.*

The Kink Kronikles opens with **"Victoria,"** the same song that had opened *Arthur* with the most overt rock and roll the Kinks had recorded in several years. *Arthur* was a culmination of all the themes from the three previous Kinks LPs: nostalgia, the little people in life, village greens, situations vacant, steam-powered trains, and Ray's intense dislike of photography. Tied together by the character of Arthur Morgan and the Kinks' bubbling, lopsidedly off-center wit, it all came together perfectly. . . .

No less important, *Arthur* also marked a culmination of Ray Davies' songwriting style. Some of the songs on *Arthur* are among the most intricate ever written to remain essentially

rock and roll. What makes the difference between **"Victoria"**'s being not just a good record but a classic one is the "Land of hope and gloria" bridge; it *expands* the song in such a way that when the Kinks come back into the original verse and chorus, their effect is overwhelmingly enhanced. **"Yes Sir, No Sir"** and **"Nothing to Say"** on *Arthur* are also similar in their structural makeup, and **"Shangri-La"** may stand forever as a masterpiece of rock songwriting.

From **"Victoria"** until the end of the second side, *The Kink Kronikles* doesn't let up for a minute. Previously unreleased, **"This Is Where I Belong"** serves as a magnificent theme song for Side One, which ends with **"Waterloo Sunset,"** the Kinks' all-time ballad and previous closing cut of both *Something Else* and their *Then Now And Inbetween* promo album.

"David Watts," previously the opening cut of *Something Else* and side two of *Then Now And Inbetween,* opens side two. What perfect planning! In addition to **"Shangri-La"** and the all-time-bourgeois-decadence-beer-drinking-and-singalong-anthem **"Sunny Afternoon,"** the side includes **"Dead End Street"** and **"Autumn Almanac,"** integral members of the Kinks' fantastic seven-single string of 1966-68: **"Sunny Afternoon," "Dead End Street," "Mr. Pleasant," "Waterloo Sunset," "Autumn Almanac," "Wonderboy,"** and **"Days."** You could take a complete course in rock melody—Ray Davies' knack throughout is superlative—just by listening to these seven singles, and they're all there on *Kink Kronikles.* . . .

[*The Kink Kronikles*] is more complicated an album than it might at first appear to be. Things start breaking down starting with side three, partly from incohesive programming (which is strange, because the structuring of the first two sides is superb), and partly because nothing ever catches fire.

The inclusion of previously unreleased tracks such as **"King Kong"** and **"Polly,"** to be sure, is alone justification for the existence of this last half of *Kink Kronikles* . . . but that doesn't change the fact that these last two sides don't work. I miss the absence of some good rock and roll—**"Johnny Thunder"** or **"Big Sky,"** say—that would shake things up a little. On the last two sides of *Kink Kronikles* the soft-rock Kinks simply sound too much like just another effete non-rocking English group, which is not at all what they were.

The Kink Kronikles is really not in any way representative of the Kinks' entire aura. An album without the Kinks' loud, chunky rock and roll is akin to an analysis of Van Morrison without any mention of Them. . . . What makes **"Waterloo Sunset"** so great is that these are the same guys who did **"You Really Got Me."** And they still play *both* of these songs on stage.

The first two sides of *Kink Kronikles* do, however, capture perfectly the Kinks' period when they were creating their own highly individual music, totally uninfluenced by current trends. Ultimately, the Kinks are one of the most underdog groups of all time. . . . That they've made some extraordinary music all along hardly hurts the case, and Ray Davies' sensibility as expressed in the Kinks' recordings is almost inseparable from the music in the final analysis.

> Mike Saunders, "'The Kink Kronikles'," in Rolling Stone *(by Straight Arrow Publishers, Inc. © 1972; all rights reserved; reprinted by permission), Issue 109, May 25, 1972, p. 64.*

BOB PALMER

Ray Davies continues to wear his English citizenship like a badge. The Kinks have often used American musical idioms

. . . but Ray has regularly used his considerable songwriting talents to anatomize situations of class and culture that are peculiarly English. . . . His nostalgia for the afternoon of the Empire, and his interest in the music hall/vaudeville traditions of his youth, continue unabated. His early efforts at the stand-up crooner idiom were often exquisite, especially **"Sunny Afternoon"** and **"End of the Season,"** and most recently he has shown ingenuity in adapting fashionable rock currents to his obsession. . . .

Everybody's in Showbiz, a double album containing a studio and a live record, is Ray's first extended look at America. The new songs deal for the most part with touring, and with the difference between Hollywood stereotypes and American reality: the live record comprises hard rock and vaudeville material from recent Kinks albums performed with juiced gusto, high spirits, and occasional rank sloppiness. But the tour sides hold together remarkably well, since most of the song situations deal with show business and its facade of tinsel and celluloid. . . . Some listeners may find parts of the album revoltingly reminiscent of the kind of entertainment favored by their mums and dads, but Davies isn't just trying to become the new Val Doonican; in fact, he seems to be magnifying and exaggerating the excesses of show business in order to call attention to its essentially grotesque character.

The album is not the homogeneously delightful sort of LP the Kinks were once known for; it has its ups and downs, its lapses and its masterpieces. The opener, **"Here Comes Yet Another Day,"** is a fashionably bored touring song . . . that rocks along nicely but has a curiously (and perhaps intentionally) unfinished quality. . . . **"Maximum Consumption"** describes the touring rocker as a "maximum consumption nonstop machine" and compares him to the inefficient, gas-gulping, often quickly discarded American automobile. . . . Beginning with images of abandoned and undifferentiated consumption and moving into more specifically unappealing comparisons, **"Maximum Consumption"** is the thematic meat of the album.

"Supersonic Rocket Ship" is quintessential Ray Davies. It invites the listener to travel the spaceways in a sort of flying Victorian music box that tinkles away with all the flavor of a period tintype. The words are quite explicit, and the following tune, **"Look a Little on the Sunny Side,"** is even more so. The rock business is show business; a rock group running through its hits, trying to please an essentially frivolous audience, isn't much different from a stand-up comic in Las Vegas or Rex Harrison doing Dr. Dolittle or *The Ed Sullivan Show.* Ray isn't likely to win a lot of new converts by emphasizing this truism, but he makes it perfectly clear that on *his* rocket ship "nobody has to be hip / nobody needs to be out of sight." This goes a long way toward explaining why the Kinks are so durable: no trippy giggles here, no heavy metal warlocks, just "a round, unvarnished tale" with plenty of belly laughs and solid rock & roll along the way.

"Celluloid Heroes" is the watershed of the album. It's a masterful, fully-realized six-minute cut with [several of Ray's] finest, quirkiest, most original lines. . . . The album could have ended here, but there are two more live sides. These sound at times like a juiced Jersey bar band with a semi-pro horn section chiming in. (p. 54)

Despite its faults and its unevenness, this is a delightfully varied, endlessly entertaining album; its best moments equal or surpass the best rock & roll of the last few years. And the indications are that Ray Davies is just beginning to loosen up. (p. 56)

Bob Palmer, "The Kinks: An Only Partially Mythical Freeway to Hollywood," in Rolling Stone *(by Straight Arrow Publishers, Inc. © 1972; all rights reserved; reprinted by permission), Issue 120, October 26, 1972, pp. 54, 56.*

NANCY ERLICH

The first question to be asked about a new Kinks album has to be: What is Ray Davies going to say about the world this time? . . . It is a fairly well-accepted opinion among people who listen to lyrics that Davies is a master songwriter, an unexcelled painter of people and scenes. In the course of 16 or so Kinks albums, he has created dozens—maybe hundreds—of incisive, bittersweet, funny-sad observations on the ways that people live. The British group's past several American tours have established an irreconcilable contrast between Ray Davies, the sensitive and intelligent songwriter, and the onstage buffoon of the same name.

"Everybody's In Show Biz" is about that contrast. . . .

The new material is desperately grim. On the one hand, Davies' lyrics with an unaccustomed lack of subtlety, come out and say how unpleasant the various aspects of the star's life are. On the other hand, that ambiguity of emotion, the understanding of several sides of a situation that usually characterizes Davies' songs, is here temporarily (I hope) suspended. The result is basically a series of musical complaints, literate, occasionally charming, at one point (**"Sunny Side"**) obnoxiously cynical, and consistently depressing. . . .

The two records were evidently not intended to be the Kinks' most enjoyable release. They can, however, be pretty instructive listening for all the young guitar players who would like to grow up to be pop stars.

Nancy Erlich, "Kinks' Contrast," in The New York Times, *Section 2 (© 1972 by The New York Times Company; reprinted by permission), November 12, 1972, p. D30.*

JIM MILLER

Ray Davies has enjoyed two periods of Kinky creativity, one marked by crude energy, raw nerve and powerful rock (**"All Day and All of the Night"**), the other by accomplished artiness, social commentary and wistful vignettes (**"Waterloo Sunset"**). *The Great Lost Kinks Album* . . . concentrates on this second period, which ran approximately from **"Sunny Afternoon"** to **"Lola";** together with last year's *Kink Kronikles,* it brings to light on album almost the complete Kinks works (although I do quibble with the exclusion of **"Sitting on My Sofa"**).

The world of the Kinks as it evolved after **"Sunny Afternoon"** evinced a characteristic blend of nostalgia for a quieter period of English history, coupled with an almost arrogant stance toward the status-seeking English bourgeois who would replace the green spaciousness of the past with an incessant and constricting rat race for fame and fortune. Into this world were introduced a panoply of Kinky characters, ranging from **"Dandy"** to **"Lola"** him/herself. The Kinks world created by Davies represented a charming oasis where the tradition of the music hall survived in a rock & roll incarnation.

Most of the *Lost* album's material is roughly contemporaneous with *Village Green Preservation Society.* At the time, Ray was particularly absorbed by antique strains of popular music as stylized vehicles for his lyrical concerns. Although the soft-shoe patina of songs like **"Pictures in the Sand"** and **"Mr. Songbird"** can sometimes sound a little soft-headed, Ray's antics, even at their cutest, are oddly engaging; he often seems appealingly inept, not unlike a homeless singing waif lost on the set of a Fred Astaire movie.

Davies' best compositions [such as **"Lavender Hill"** and **"Autumn Almanac"**] retain enough rock to provide his whimsies with a cutting edge. . . .

[Considering] that the record basically represents dregs, it contains a surprising number of undeservedly esoteric Kinks classics. I've always loved Ray's brooding persona on **"I'm Not Like Everybody Else,"** but my new-found favorite is **"Till Death Do Us Part,"** an archly banal plea for acceptance. . . .

Perhaps one day Ray Davies will return to the wry vision that animated a song like **"When I Turn Off the Living Room Light."** Until then, *The Great Lost Kinks Album* will sustain those archivists who, like myself, remain disappointed with Ray's recent Kinks recordings.

> Jim Miller, "Records: 'The Great Lost Kinks Album'," in Rolling Stone *(by Straight Arrow Publishers, Inc. ©1973; all rights reserved; reprinted by permission), Issue 131, March 29, 1973, p. 56.*

KEN EMERSON

[The songs on *The Great Lost Kinks Album*] marvelously cohere to make this a real album and not merely an assortment of unrelated curios. This of course says a lot for the organic consistency of The Kinks' work. File *TGLKA* between *Something Else* and *Village Green.*

Like most Kinks albums since 1966, this one is sad. Oh, some of the songs sound happy enough, but they're wistful thinking, pathetically evanescent fantasies. There's no getting away from pain, ugliness, and isolation, which a few tracks face squarely. **"Where Did the Spring Go?"** is an extremely upsetting song about an aging man who has gotten nothing from life but varicose veins. **"I'm Not Like Everybody Else"** is chilling. . . . I still feel in the vocal's grating, paranoiac edge the fear and the menace of a cornered dog. . . .

In his [liner notes John] Mendelsohn rather querulously argues that *The Great Lost Kinks Album* is the last great Kinks album, that since moving to RCA the group has sadly deteriorated. *Muswell Hillbillies* is "clumsily heavy-handed and obvious," and on *Everybody's in Showbiz* Ray is "bitchily egocentric." He is no longer "sensitizing us" with his "beautiful songs." But *MH* is surely no more heavy-handed and obvious than earlier numbers such as **"Powerman"** and **"Brainwashed"** (one of Mendelsohn's favorites), and Mendelsohn seems not to understand *MH*'s relation to *Village Green.* One a nostalgic reminiscence of an irrecoverable pastoral childhood, the other a depiction of an inescapable, squalid, urban adulthood, the two work together like [William] Blake's *Songs of Innocence and Experience.* As for the bitchy egocentricity of *Showbiz,* the charge pertains, if at all, to only four of the ten new songs on the album, and these songs possess varying degrees of grim irony, mordant accuracy, and sheer humorousness which more than make up for what ruins them for Mendelsohn. Moreover, *Showbiz*'s **"Sittin' in My Hotel"** is as beautiful and sensitive a song as one could wish for.

If The Kinks have fallen off somewhat, it is in the quality of their music—Ray's tunes and the band—not in the quality of Ray's lyrics and sensibility. Mendelsohn chooses the wrong line of attack. But why should one feel called upon to malign The Kinks today in order to enjoy them as they were? *TGLKA* is excellent, and the next Kinks album probably will be too.

> Ken Emerson, "'The Great Lost Kinks Album'," in Creem *(© copyright 1973 by Creem Magazine, Inc.), Vol. 4, No. 12, May, 1973, p. 59.*

STEVE SIMELS

[The odd thing about the Kinks] is that despite their frequent inability to remain vertical on stage, and despite the fact that they've been known to give performances in which they sounded like, in John Mendelsohn's phrase, "the first rehearsal of an inept teenage garage band," they've managed to create a body of recorded work that is quite clearly in the Beatles/Stones/Dylan class. Yet they've never really achieved the commensurate superstardom. . . .

Discussions of the Kinks have invariably centered around Ray Davies. . . . But in the beginning it was the Kinks as a *band* that knocked people out. And, strangely enough, they made their initial reputation as avant-gardists. But there really is no rock avant-garde anymore, John Lennon's protestations to the contrary, and the style of amphetamine raving pioneered on their early singles is by now—eight brief years later—totally absorbed into the mainstream. But avant-gardists they were, a totally electric rock-and-roll band that produced a cataclysmic wall of sound unlike anything that had ever been heard in rock before. (p. 96)

Somewhere along the line Ray began to write. At first his lyrics were the conventional boy-girl stuff of the period (though laced with a rather unambiguous sexuality that was perfectly mated to the sonic blitz the band was laying down), but he soon began to get itchy for something more serious. What he eventually came up with, *A Well Respected Man,* was Archie Rice with a backbeat. A clever merger of his r-&-b roots with his other major passion, the music-hall style, it was to serve as a model for an entire school of British rock. Lyrically, it was vaguely Dylanesque, but purely Davies' own were the song's wit and its particular kind of contempt for middle-class values.

From there Ray took off, turning out an uninterrupted series of brilliant singles and albums on subjects as diverse as steam-powered trains, session men, lower-class drug addiction, and the setting of the sun on the British Empire. He became a sort of rock-and-roll Damon Runyon, filling his songs with telling little character studies—as in *David Watts,* in which he neatly skewers both the eternal golden schoolboy and his own jealousy of him. And he couched it all in a verbal style of almost Gilbertian cleverness: "We are the Custard Pie Appreciation Consortium," he declares in one number. . . .

[This] lyric genius should by rights have served to put the Kinks up there with the major mythic figures of the past decade. No such luck, however. In fact, sometime around the middle of 1966, just as they were beginning to perfect the new approach, their work died an absolutely unheralded death in this country, and it stayed buried until late 1969. Granted, the American audience often has its head in the sand, but at least some of the fault is Ray's; he has obstinately refused to be fashionable—he claims, for instance, that he didn't even *listen* to [The Beatles's] "Sgt. Pepper" until two years after it came out, and I believe him.

This almost masochistic streak has run through much of his recent work, which has become increasingly autobiographical: the post-"**Arthur**" Kinks songs are more often than not as concerned with Ray's personal psychological problems as they are with the plight of the workingman. Ironically, as the Davies persona has emerged, the group has begun to sell records again. Perhaps time has simply caught up with them; these days, the sexual confusion of some of the songs (Lola, you recall, "walked like a woman and talked like a man") and Ray's on-stage antics are, thanks to Alice Cooper, not quite so problematical. Or perhaps, more disturbingly, it's the old Judy Garland fan syndrome: the perverse appeal of watching someone of immense talent and sensitivity fall apart before your eyes. After all, Ray has gone so far as to set his own suicide note to music, and the counter-culture has amply demonstrated a taste for such ghoulishness. Or, most likely, it's just that the music the band has made since Ray allowed himself the luxury of public self-analysis is in some ways more brilliant than ever. I find myself playing "**Muswell Hillbillies**" quite as often as "**Face to Face**" or "**Something Else**," which leads me to think that Ray as an individual is every bit as interesting as Wicked Annabella, or Dandy, or Pretty Polly, or any other creation of the Davies fancy. (p. 97)

> *Steve Simels, "The Kinks: What Comes Next?" in* Stereo Review *(copyright © 1973 by Ziff-Davis Publishing Company), Vol. 30, No. 5, May, 1973, pp. 96-7.*

IAN MASSEY

There are snatches of the Who in ["**Preservation Act 1**"], the first of a two-act musical by Ray Davies. In fact, insidious as most of them are, the influences of "**Tommy**" abound, and detract from this album.

That said, there are some Kinks gems, a pretty good, if somewhat hackneyed, storyline, and enough good music to swell the ranks of the Kinks Preservation Society.

At first listen "**Preservation Act 1**" is disappointing. It hasn't quite the impact of "**Muswell Hillbillies**" on the rock numbers, nor the lovability of "**Village Green Preservation Society**," which, for me, must be the definitive Kinks "musical." Ray Davies inevitably has his eyes on the past. Now he's looking to the future; to revolution and a new society. Stars of Act 1 are "the people," the tramp, Johnny Thunder, the vicar and Flash. As would be expected, Ray makes the tramp the hero and gives him the standout songs: "**Sitting In The Mid-day Sun**," "**Where Are They Now**" and "**Sweet Lady Genevieve**." All three are beauts; all three have Kinks stamped all over them; and all three look back into the past. There's no getting away from it, that's where Ray Davies is at. It's the faster, and in many ways too fast, tracks that owe a lot to, or rather bring back memories of, Pete Townshend's "Tommy": songs like "**There's A Change In The Weather**," "**One Of The Survivors**" . . . , and "**Here Comes Flash**." There's a lot of uneasiness in this album. . . . "**Muswell Hillbillies**" had "**20th Century Man**," "**Acute Schizophrenia Paranoia Blues**" and the Mike Cotton Sound brass, but that album came across in uncomplicated, even dry, Kinks style. Now we've got choir-like or soul-girl backings and some of the trappings of "Jesus Christ Superstar," "Tommy," and even a touch of "Grocer Jack." All that fails to knock Ray Davies from his pedestal.

His words remain supreme, his humour unsurpassed—the vicar's analogy between the game of cricket and the game of life, with that "demon bowler" bowling a maiden over. The story is of growing dissatisfaction with the status quo, the rise of a communist saviour, more disillusionment, and the saviour in the form of Flash and his men tearing down all and sundry to make way for their new world. Ray Davies and the Kinks . . . tell the story better than I could and I'm looking forward to Act II. Act I is not a great Kinks album, it's not the Kinks at their best, but it's well worth preserving.

> *Ian Massey, "Kinks: A Variety Act," in* Melody Maker *(© IPC Business Press Ltd.), November 17, 1973, p. 33.*

LORAINE ALTERMAN

"**Preservation Act 1**" is actually a full-length development of themes Davies began in 1968 on "**The Village Green Preservation Society**" album. The songs on this new album relate how greed in the guise of progress is swallowing up individuality and humanity as personified by the inhabitants of a small town. The concept may sound rather grandiose, but Davies . . . could never get swept up by pretension.

Sparked by his sardonic wit and keen sensitivity, Davies makes his point in very down-to-earth terms. The lyric sheet indicates that each song is to be sung by a different character in this musical so Davies, the songwriter and lead singer, gives us all sides of the story including the villain who gets rich knocking down the village's thatched cottages and the vicar who compares life to a game of cricket. . . .

By varying his music and arrangements to reflect the idea of his lyrics, Davies has created that rarity, a concept album (or "rock opera" if you must) that never gets dull. And though he is protesting the bulldozing of old values, Davies' wit saves him from the heaviness that lessens the impact of message songs.

The Kinks never got as much exposure in America as the Beatles or the Stones in the sixties so they have never had as much popular acclaim as they deserve. Yet there's no doubt that they continue to flourish as one of England's most original rock bands, anchored on the exceptional songwriting talents of Ray Davies. (p. D27)

> *Loraine Alterman, "What Happened to Swinging London?" in* The New York Times, *Section 2 (© 1973 by The New York Times Company; reprinted by permission), December 23, 1973, pp. D27-D28.**

STEVE LAKE

[If] the Kinks haven't taught us anything else, they've showed us that you can be real and make it. . . .

Who else but Ray Davies would sing about Waterloo Station and Muswell Hill and village greens?

It wasn't always that straightforward, though. . . .

[With "**You Really Got Me**"] The Kinks proved that they could execute a pretty mean boogie with two chords and a key change. . . .

Maybe it's the type of situation that occurs when a group achieves a measure of success before it's mature enough to handle it, but Ray Davies wrote a large number of variations on a theme of **"You Really Got Me,"** that filled up the bulk of the early albums and B-sides.

Still, it was a fine riff, and would bands like the Stooges have existed if folks like the Kinks hadn't shown what could be achieved with a modicum of instrumental ability? And think of the Velvet Underground's two-chord epic, "Sister Ray." (Sister Ray? Think about it.)

But how do you follow the success of such a hit record? Why, simple, you just doctor the riff, call it **"All Day And All Of The Night,"** and sing it out. . . .

I'd guess that the Kinks must have begun to get acute paranoia over what they were going to do when Ray ran out of variations. Clearly they were looking for a way out of the impasse, but weren't sure where they were supposed to look. . . .

"Tired Of Waiting For You" was again based on repetition, with limited verbal imagery, but it stressed that the Kinks had clearly created their own distinctive niche. . . .

In the period from 1965 into 1966, the Kinks had commercial success with a batch of singles that were mostly prototype heavy rockers. The two that weren't [**"See My Friends"** and **"Well Respected Man"**] were the most interesting. . . .

[In] terms of future development, it was **"Well Respected Man"** that was something of a milestone. Not only because Ray Davies contrived to rhyme "regatta" with "get at her," one of the truly inspired couplets in rock lyricism, but also because it underlined the arrival of the Kinks at Stage Two. . . .

It was satire, but mild satire, and delivered with a kind of bemused good humour that set the Kinks quite apart from the variety of "satirists" prone to appear on Bernard Braden TV shows, wielding guitars, upper lip curled in a perpetual sneer.

Another 1966 classic was **"Dedicated Follower Of Fashion,"** which poked gentle fun at the Carnaby Street Generation, of which the Kinks were assuredly a part themselves. . . .

"Sunny Afternoon" was tongue-in-cheek, the tale of a loser rocker, whose chart success leaves him his **"House In The Country"** . . . but whose chick deserts him, and his wealth is devoured by the taxman. . . .

In sharp contrast, **"Dead End Street"** was about a very real plight: the hopelessness of the lower working class situation. "What are we living for / two-roomed apartment on the second floor."

Perhaps the most beautiful of the Kinks hits was **"Waterloo Sunset,"** a vividly real little chapter depicting the meeting of two young lovers, Terry and Julie, on Waterloo Bridge. . . .

From **"Waterloo Sunset,"** Ray ventured towards his first concept album—**"The Kinks Are The Village Green Preservation Society,"** a kind of repentance for the foul ways of the Denmark Street pop scene, and a re-statement of the values of good old England surrounding us. . . .

"Village Green" was maybe less successful than the singles. There wasn't any one track, in fact, that would have stood up as a single, but the link connecting the songs on the album seemed a pretty tenuous one, and to date Davies hasn't really produced a totally satisfying concept album. He's a very acute writer, and can create delightful little cameos, character-sketches and pen portraits, but when it comes to an extended format, he tends to miss out.

Essentially, his style is a journalistic one. He writes great articles, but he doesn't appear to have the conceptual intelligence to write good novels.

But notwithstanding, **"Village Green"** had its moments. The title track, **"Animal Farm"** and **"Sitting By The Riverside"** were pro pastoral goodies. . . .

What with diminishing sales of singles, infrequent gigs and other disasters, it was hardly surprising that . . . **"Kinks Part One: Lola Versus Powerman And The Moneygoround"** was rather more vitriolic, packing far more punch than the usual fodder. It seems a bitter, disillusioned album, with Davies holding the business as a whole up to ridicule. Rightly so, I guess.

Indulgent? Egotistic? Well, perhaps, but it had to be said by somebody, and it's as well that it was said by someone with Ray Davies' gift for making a joke out of the blackest situation.

It was thus a little unfortunate that in this case the weight of the words proved almost too much for the slight melodies of the songs that, top heavy, are nothing like as catchy as the classic Kinks singles.

The exception of course being **"Lola"** itself, truly ranking with the greats. . . .

"Muswell Hillbillies" included a couple of numbers that rapidly became the core of stage performances, the highly theatrical **"Alcohol"** and **"Acute Schizophrenia Paranoia Blues"** with an authentic-sounding drunken New Orleans feel to it.

Finally, the Kinks had realised their potential as a stage act, after years of meandering and attempting to improve, they just gave in, and played it as casually and drunkenly as possible. From a band that at one time had difficulty in getting **"You Really Got Me"** together on stage, they gradually developed into a band that still had difficulty in getting **"You Really Got Me"** together on stage.

The difference was that they were no longer self-conscious about it. It was a joke. A shared joke. A party. . . .

Presumably conscious of their new-found appeal as on-stage looners and gooners, the next album, a double, featured one live and one studio record. **"Everybody's In Showbiz, Everybody's A Star."**

The album also contained **"Supersonic Rocket Ship,"** a chart hit single, fake calypso and lots of fun, and **"Celluloid Heroes"** which was probably the most eloquently expressed song that Ray has ever written.

"Celluloid heroes never feel any pain," which is why Ray does; he's not a movie star, he's just the guy that broods over his pint in the corner of the local boozer.

Most recently, there's **"Preservation Act I,"** yet another "concept album." And it's undoubtedly the best one yet, although without seeing the numbers performed live, it's difficult to imagine how the songs would translate into any kind of opera setting.

The album is a continuation of the themes implied by the **"Village Green"** record. Johnny Thunder re-appears roaring down the highway on his motorbike, with the strains of Dion and the Belmonts flowing through his brain.

It's coherent and concise, and doubtless one day in the distant future, scholars will write vast critiques of the poetry of Raymond Davies, analyse and categorise his style. Fair enough. He deserves that kind of attention. . . .

[What] the Kinks are about [is] the refusal to be manipulated, or turned into publicists' mouth-pieces, or to be caught up in musical trends, or indeed to take the whole circus too seriously.

Above all else, the Kinks stand as the victory of human character over the conveyor belt pop machine. They made it, and they made it on their own terms.

Steve Lake, *"The Kinks: Muswell's Hillbilly Satirists," in* Melody Maker *(© IPC Business Press Ltd.), January 26, 1974, p. 25.*

MICHAEL WATTS

To my mind the Kinks have always excelled at short, simple pop songs, the best of which—like **"Waterloo Sunset,"** **"Autumn Almanac"** and **"Days"**—have contained a warm, slightly old-fashioned sentimentality that cuts across any prejudices I have about the band's musicianship and general performance. . . .

[Ray Davies] has sharp ears and eyes for the ways of a world that seems to lap at his doorstep while eternally he gazes, hand on chin, behind the upstairs window; and of course, that world is specifically British. However, observer though he may be, satirist he is not. His eyes may be sharp, but his pen draws no blood, essentially because he's too kindly and loveable when he should be savage, cranky and eccentric instead of incisive. The two albums in his **"Preservation"** drama proffer Davies' view of the way in which his world is being dragged into the mud, a dirty struggle between the running dogs of Capitalism—represented in his dramatis personae by Mr Flash, a spiv and secondhand car salesman—and the odious forces of a puritanical Socialism—symbolised, appropriately, by Mr Black. Outside these ideological extremes, is The Tramp, a figure of tromaticism who would appear to speak for Davies himself, on the sidelines but deeply concerned. Surely there's something of Davies in the Tramp's cry of "Oh Where, Oh Where is Love?" The concurrence of time and political circumstance has given this vision of a downhill descent a very topical edge. It seems to me that the whole of this second act is informed by a sense of this country's current misfortunes, nowhere more pointedly than a song given to the Tramp called **"Nobody Gives,"** where Davies observes that "the workers told the unions who blamed it on the government, the politicians blamed it on the strikers and the militants." And he goes on, "everybody's guilty and everybody's innocent." In fact, this number, because it has something serious to say and offers no easy solutions, could have been the basis of a much better musical piece than **"Preservation"** has turned out to be. As an observation **"Preservation"** is fair; as a satire on moral and political ills, which is the form it takes, it falls down, because Davies' writing is ruled by his heart rather than his head and while we might agree with his sentiments, his simplistic constructions are too hard to swallow. Frequently the impression emerges that in working on this he's had Arturo Ui in mind, but Davies lacks the Brechtian irony and the genuine wit to render convincing his explanation of a corrupt capitalism overthrown by totalitarianism. It plays more like musical farce. . . . It ultimately becomes most notable for its references to the Davies pre-occupations: the horror of traditions being destroyed, the fascination with money (**"Money Talks"**), the fondness for English stereotypes (the spiv and the floosy) and the awareness of class distinction. Neither is it particularly auspicious in a

musical sense. As far as concept albums go, its libretto may be preferable to the ham-fisted stupidity of "Tommy"—what couldn't?—but there's little original music. These extended pieces don't really bring out the best in Davies, perhaps because he sacrifices the part to the whole, and there's not one song on this album that bears comparison with the singles he's released. His style is to go for pastiche. . . . And yet . . . **"Preservation"** is not dislikeable, riddled with holes though it be. It misses its marks, but it has a saving grace in its humour, that wry stuff so special to Davies. "Down with nudity, breasts that are bare and pubic hair," he mocks the unctuous Festival of Light in **"Shepherds Of The Nation."** And something it has even more special—ambition without pretentiousness. I hope that if and when Ray Davies stages his musical of the albums, I can offer criticism more favourable to him.

Michael Watts, *"Wry Davies," in* Melody Maker *(© IPC Business Press Ltd.), July 20, 1974, p. 38.*

FRED SCHRUERS

Some sweet irony has Ray Davies posted on [the cover of ***Preservation Act 2***] as a demagogic hustler when his refusal to merchandise himself has long impeded widespread recognition of the Kinks.

Because Ray, on this album, mingles his persona as a reluctant rock star and querulous love object with the characters of Flash, Mr. Black and the Tramp (with a bogglingly well-realized cameo as Flash's Special Floosie Belle), then marches these composite characters into a scenario that clicks (musically and narratively) with ***Preservation Act 1:*** because that scenario is informed by a superbly intuited moral sense of history, utterly germane to this year of deposed monarchies; and because the whole thing rocks, rolls and saunters its way across four sides, Ray cannot be denied his place as rock's ascendant genius.

Think about the congruence between Ray's morality play and the musical theatre of Bertolt Brecht and Kurt Weill, specifically their collaboration, *The Rise and Fall of the City of Mahagonny.* Germany was in upheaval when *Mahagonny* premiered in 1930. The production aimed for impact, with Weill drawing musical motifs from the cabarets and Brecht staging the performance to jar and alienate the audience, a principle of his politicized commitment. The whiteface make-up and repellent grin Ray sports on the cover are very much emblems of Brechtian theatre today; walking on Weill's side, Ray has always confessed his music-hall influences, and the scoring of the hand-picked female voices on ***Preservation*** is often reminiscent of the pallid cynicism with which Brecht coated his tawdry characters.

We could ask why Ray is in a cowboy hat, a mark of the amoral slickster since well before Brecht set *his* story on the American frontier. There's more: the "holocaust risin' over the horizon" in **"There's A Change In The Weather"** (*Preservation Act 1*) is a perfect analogue to a hurricane that threatens Mahagonny, but both storms disappear as the respective towns give themselves over to anarchic materialism. Flash is set upon by his soul as he sleeps, just as Moses descends on Mahagonny—Flash, facing Hell Fire, confesses. Brecht won't allow his city that eschatological dive. They kill Moses, figuring they're already in hell. Both stories end with the populace in factional riots.

So what? Just that a rock writer capable of the melting lyricism of **"Waterloo Sunset"** has had burgeoning within him a mordantly Marxist epic, and he has instinctively infused it with ideologues and social archetypes, and written compelling music for it, then driven the message home with a brilliant catalogue of his own vocal effects. It has the capacity of becoming the most effective populist 'musical' around for a long time, even as it arises out of a genre which has become the Saturday circus for a generation struck numb by television. (p. 69)

[Right] now we have from Ray a conception so prepossessing that it's milked a masterpiece six sides long from him. And he's giving us a very good idea just where all the good times have gone. (p. 70)

Fred Schruers, "Ray Rekindles Kinks," in Craw-daddy (copyright © 1974 by Crawdaddy Publishing Co., Inc.; all rights reserved; reprinted by permission), September, 1974, pp. 69-70.

JOHN SWENSON

British rock stagecraft has flirted with theatrical conceits for over a decade. What began as a performance dynamic in which movement was a direct function of the music itself (for example, the early Who and Stones) has evolved to the self-conscious spectacle of David Bowie's Cecil B. DeMille imitations and Jethro Tull's ridiculously cluttered, absurdist program pieces. . . .

What's missing from this Grand Opera approach to rock performance is the solid conceptualization which can only come from strong songwriting point-of-view. The clarity and simplicity of statement which has always been one of rock's most positive songwriting attributes is gone from the tangled web of solipsistic allusions which visual concerns seem to have necessitated. Only the most clever writer can overcome the immense problem posed by this artistic conflict of interest. It does not surprise me that the person to finally put it off is Ray Davies.

Davies is arguably the finest rock songwriter England has produced. Sure, Lennon-McCartney, Jagger-Richard and Townshend have written more standards than any of their peers, but only Ray Davies and Townshend have been able to completely articulate a unique point of view which evolves in direct relation to their on-going attempt to understand themselves and the world they live in. . . .

As their introspection led Davies and Townshend to song cycles, Townshend became mystical in the high Romantic tradition of [William] Wordsworth and [John] Keats, while Davies refined his cameos and determinedly became a social and political critic in the manner of the 19th century neo-Romantics, [George Bernard] Shaw and [Oscar] Wilde.

As a performer, however, Davies is strictly out of the English Music Hall-*cum*-vaudeville tradition, a stance which gives him ironic distance from his "Art" (which he may take seriously but would never admit to). For the last few years, Kinks shows have been drunken burlesques with equal parts rock and camp—the songs were great but Ray would always play the calculated onstage drunk, reaching for the automatic *good time* and fearful of the possible pretension involved in presenting his songs as they are. Thus, it was unexpected when the rambling socio-political dramatic treatise *Preservation* appeared as a full-blown stage production last year. In its staging, *Preservation* still had a Music Hall sensibility, but it was extremely well-disciplined for a rock show. . . .

It is not accidental that *Preservation,* Ray's modern epic, followed closely on the heels of Townshend's *Quadrophenia.* Both works were attempts at capsulizing the themes of a career into a coherent overview, and both failed onstage. *Quadrophenia* failed because the Who never felt confident that their American audience could relate to it, *Preservation* because there was too much to digest at one sitting for the average rock 'n roller who had come to hear **"Lola"** and **"You Really Got Me,"** so Ray streamlined his follow-up for maximum stage effectiveness. Where *Preservation* telescoped the three records worth of material down to a workable dramatic formula, *Soap Opera* serves as a blueprint for its much more elaborate stage treatment.

Indeed, *Soap Opera* is a confusing record until you've seen what the material becomes on stage. In this sense it is decidedly a soundtrack, as opposed to *Preservation*'s two-years-in-the-making proclivity for digression. *Soap Opera* is also . . . the perfect marriage of rock and theatre. It is light but not dumb (the essence of rock success), a restatement of various themes that have fascinated Ray in the past and are now given the sharpest edges they can possess. The message of *Soap Opera* is subliminal (as opposed to the conscious polemic of *Preservation*). The identity crisis which has plagued Ray's career and informed much of the pathos of his most moving songs in the past has never been dealt with more directly. (pp. 65-6)

[On **"Everybody's A Star"**] Ray, as the "Starmaker," has a particular point to make. In a subtle *Pygmalion*-esque allusion, Starmaker claims he can elevate the most ordinary life to stardom by exchanging places with one of the "Ordinary People" and writing about his mundane existence. The creator can re-shape the dross life of a mortal to be one of the god-like characters of gentility. This is not empty rhetoric on Ray's part. As simple as this story seems, it is also the cumulative expression of Davies' attempt to deal with the problems of the working man, a theme he first treated with contempt ten years ago in **"Well Respected Man"** but later with compassion in *Arthur* and *Muswell Hillbillies.* . . .

"You Make It All Worthwhile" is the central element of the soap opera. The Starmaker finds that he appreciates the security and simplicity of domestic life, and for a moment it appears that maudlin sentimentality will indeed triumph. The bubble bursts in **"Ducks On the Wall,"** a seeming throwaway to get things moving before the finale but actually a clever satire on bourgeois British taste. . . .

At this point, the album, which overall does manage to stand on its own because of the quality and vitality of the music, fails without the help of visuals. Starmaker has fooled himself—he no longer understands who he is. The confusion of roles makes him believe he is just **"(A) Face In the Crowd,"** and you really have to see Ray do this one on stage to understand its full impact. In the performance, Ray is left alone and sings directly about himself. . . .

"You Can't Stop the Music," which sounds like a reworked combination of **"One of the Survivors"** and **"Celluloid Heroes"** if taken by itself, is actually the epilogue of the stage production, as well as a statement about aging rock stars whose anthems outlive them, thus serving as another Davies introspection.

Just as it opened, *Soap Opera* closes with a vintage Kink chord sequence. After all, you can't stop the music. (p. 66)

John Swenson, "Ray Davies—Just an Ordinary Man?" in Crawdaddy (copyright © 1975 by Craw-

STEVE SIMELS

It's no secret that Ray Davies has, in comparison with his early work, dished out an awful lot of substandard dross of late. In this he is like most of the rest of the great songwriters of the Sixties rock explosion. . . .

The question of *why* Ray Davies' work has declined is a mite puzzling, however. Granted, he has tried of late to adapt his usual themes—the lives of little people, English traditions and their decline—to larger canvases than he's accustomed to. Even though his first attempt, the concept album ''Arthur,'' was a rousing success, I still maintain that he is primarily a short-story writer, if you will, rather than a novelist: into such songs as *Do You Remember Walter, Deadend Street,* and *Autumn Almanac,* for example, he was able to compress more detail, more nuance, than any other writer in the history of pop music. That's a strong statement, but it's true. Not one of his contemporaries, and that includes people like Harry Nilsson and Randy Newman, can touch him in terms of his ear for the essential *pathos* of everyday life. Why, then, was ''Arthur'' such a success, and his later attempt at broadening his scope, ''Preservation Act Two,'' such a boring failure?

I think the reason lies in the way the works were put together. Ray is essentially a miniaturist, but with ''Arthur'' the TV play the songs were written for never got beyond the stage of a broad plot outline; it was never produced, and thus his imagination was not constricted by specific scene requirements. The exact opposite was true with ''Preservation''; the project was conceived specifically in terms of staging, and while it worked (as anyone who saw the production can testify), it was still, if taken song-by-song on record, a tedious failure, obvious to the point of being insulting to the intelligence.

All of which leads us to the Kinks' latest album, ''Soap Opera.'' It's a tremendous advance in its handling of the traditions of a full-scale musical comedy (rock opera this ain't, thank the Lord), but it's still not a first-rate Kinks album, it still doesn't have more than a couple of first-rate Kinks *songs.* The reason is the same as it was with ''Preservation'': the demands of the story line intrude upon those of the songs themselves. Unlike ''Arthur,'' the TV show the songs were tailored for . . . *was* actually filmed and televised. But, though I have no doubt that it was marvelous on the tube, I can't help finding it forced as an album—frankly, it all sounds just too much like a sound-track. Without the visual element, Ray's new songs, witty as they are (and some of them, especially *Ordinary People,* are screamingly funny), just don't make it after repeated listenings. . . .

Don't get me wrong—I like the album. But it's not a classic. Even so, pester your local N.E.T. station to broadcast the BBC TV film all this comes from. . . . Then hope that Ray gets back to doing what he does best—creating poignant little two-and-a-half-minute vignettes. Fact is, these large-scale ''Soap Opera'' epics may merely be, as some critics have already pointed out, the result of Ray's trying to give people what he *thinks* they want. If that's the case, it's up to all of us to set him straight, and *toot sweet.*

Steve Simels, ''The Kinks' New 'Soap Opera','' in Stereo Review (copyright © 1975 by Ziff-Davis Publishing Company), Vol. 35, No. 1, July, 1975, p. 80.

ALLAN JONES

''Schoolboys in Disgrace'' is, without any doubt, the most impressive and enjoyable album that Ray Davies has written and produced since those halcyon days when the Kinks delivered that essential series of records which includes ''Face To Face,'' ''Something Else,'' ''Village Green'' and ''Arthur.''

Davies' recent work, particularly the ambitious ''Preservation'' trilogy, has not been entirely without its memorable moments, but all too often his vision has lacked that spectacular clarity which characterised many of his earlier compositions.

This album is a celebration of those qualities one admired so completely in Davies as a writer. He's not fully recovered his impressive facility for evocative, commercial melodies, but the majority of the songs contained in this collection have a similar, articulate, affectionate sense of nostalgia about them, which anyone at all familiar with that sequence of albums will immediately recognise. Davies has . . . rehabilitated himself as a writer. . . .

The essential concept of ''Schoolboys'' is an elaboration of a theme tentatively expressed as far back as ''David Watts''—the opening shot of ''Something Else.'' It examines the predicament of an adolescent confronting the pressures of an educational system which confuses rather than informs, and increases the pressures of living in a conformist society.

These are themes which Davies has explored more recently in the three acts of the ''Preservation'' saga, but here he has concentrated on a specific environment—the segregated, enclosed world of a boy's public school. The hero is a juvenile version of Flash, the villain of ''Preservation,'' who resists The System represented by his headmaster and is humiliated and punished for his rebellion. . . .

The bitterness and anger which runs through much of ''Schooldays'' is assuaged by the author's genuine concern and his ultimate lack of cynicism and misanthropy. Even a song like ''The First Time We Fall In Love,'' an overtly bitter composition, has its antithesis in ''I'm In Disgrace.'' ''Schoolboys In Disgrace'' is a beautifully sustained concept. When we've got writers like Ray Davies who really needs New York hoodlum poets and rock heroes who limp on and refuse to grow old gracefully. . . . Welcome back, Ray, we've really missed you.

Allan Jones, ''Kinks Is No Disgrace!'' in Melody Maker (© IPC Business Press Ltd.), January 3, 1976, p. 23.

LINDA J. FREDERICK

[Looking through my collection of the Kinks's] early Reprise albums, I was struck by how very many Kinks songs deal with the wish to be somewhere, sometime, someone, or even some*thing* else (*King Kong* is a good example). Long before it became fashionable in rock, Ray Davies was a master at creating a nostalgic mood. . . . And, now that it's once again out of vogue (for which mercy God be praised), Ray has returned to this genre [on ''Schoolboys in Disgrace''], if indeed he ever left it. Even given all that, the last thing in the world I expected now was an album full of yearnings for ''those happiest days of your life'' as a carefree student. I've always regarded Ray as, among other things, unalterably opposed to conformity, regimentation, intellectual repression, and all such dehumanizing horrors, which are the main things I remember from *my* school days. Yet, here we find him (well, technically it's Mr. Flash, arch-villain of the **"Preservation"** saga) claiming he'd gladly return to them "if only I could find a way." Things like that confuse me: have I totally misread the man? How disconcerting. . . .

"Schoolboys" seems intended as some sort of joke, and perhaps I've missed the punch line simply because I'm still more sympathetic to Chuck Berry's view of *Schooldays* as something one longs to escape, not re-experience. Like most recent Kinks material, all this probably makes a great stage vehicle for Ray and the crew, but the problem is that, just as many fine theatrical pieces make for tedious reading, so Davies' musical melodramas make emotionally flat, predictable records. The slapstick clowning and sight gags the Kinks use to such good advantage in their live shows can't be transferred to vinyl, and the plots and characters seem banal and lifeless when subjected to the careful scrutiny a record demands. **"Schoolboys,"** in particular, seems less a rock opera than a rock comic strip, which isn't altogether a bad idea when you think of it—at least we'd have to give up a few of our more ridiculous pretensions about what this music really is.

The trouble is, though, that this comic strip is not very *funny* (with the exception of one or two . . . er . . . "frames"), and that too is Ray Davies' responsibility, because the lyrics are unquestionably the album's greatest weakness. Everything else is just fine. . . . All this album needed were some credible lyrics, but for the most part they're not there.

In *Jack the Idiot Dunce* that doesn't matter, though. It's a dance number in the grand tradition of all such treasures, a real rocker, and it's hilarious despite its lyrical moralizing. Of course, it may only seem that good because the rest of side one is so dead, especially a seven-minute ditty called *Education* that sounds like a meeting between *Apeman* and Harry Nilsson on an off day for them both. Ray is so fond of it he feels compelled to bring it back for a last chorus to end the album—"even aborigines need education" indeed. . . .

Oddly enough, the best track here has a thoroughly contemporary, even trendy, arrangement, and it is titled *No More Looking Back*. The entire piece is played and sung to perfection and demonstrates once again with what ease Ray Davies could become one of our best schlock writers, cranking out hit singles at the drop of a hat. Perhaps he should. On the one hand, this is no **"Lola,"** and I suspect it will date very quickly, but then if Elton John is right, and music is or should be "disposable," that would be all to the good, wouldn't it? I devoutly hope not, but I'm beginning to wonder.

Linda J. Frederick, "The Kinks: Music as Disposable as the Komix," in Stereo Review *(copyright © 1976 by Ziff-Davis Publishing Company), Vol. 36, No. 3, March, 1976, p. 88.*

PETER REILLY

The Kinks and their mainspring, Raymond Douglas Davies, are presented [in **"The Kinks' Greatest Celluloid Heroes"**] in a ragtag collection of material dating as far back as 1972. Davies, who writes, produces, and arranges the group's material, seems to be making a lifelong career out of cheeky irreverence. Sometimes it works, as it does in *Muswell Hillbilly,* and sometimes it is woefully inappropriate, as it is in *Alcohol*—there's nothing really funny about that subject if you've read any of the new statistics on teenage (or any-age) alcoholism.

But most of the time, as in *Everybody's a Star* and *Celluloid Heroes,* it comes across as a creaky bore. Somehow the Seventies have made a lot of pop irreverence seem more like sour brattiness than healthy fun. (pp. 100, 104)

Peter Reilly, "Popular Discs and Tapes: 'The Kinks' Greatest Celluloid Heroes'," in Stereo Review *(copyright © 1976 by Ziff-Davis Publishing Company), Vol. 37, No. 5, November, 1976, pp. 100, 104.*

ALLAN JONES

[**"Sleepwalker"**] emphatically testifies to the dramatic artistic revival of Raymond Douglas Davies, whose supreme talents as a writer have been so distressingly overlooked during the first half of this decade.

Davies' restless imagination and determination to pursue, over the last six years, a unique musical course which paid no homage to prevailing fashions and ideas, undoubtedly cost the Kinks the praise of the popular audience they deserved and the commercial success that would have justified their leader's uncompromising idiosyncrasies in the face of often universal critical disdain and popular indifference.

But their achievements have been no less entertaining during this time, and those who persevered with Davies will argue that the Preservation trilogy, though flawed and inconsistent on record, provided the basis for one of the few successful fusions of rock and theatre when it was transferred to the stage.

Similarly, the Kinks' last album for RCA, **"Schoolboys in Disgrace"**, a retrospective scenario featuring the characters from the previous trilogy, was, in performance, a tour de force of lunatic drama.

Moreover, that album suggested that Davies was successfully returning to the precise writing style that had characterised his compositions of the mid-Sixties, when he produced such pop masterpieces as **"Dead End Street"**, **"Waterloo Sunset"** and **"Autumn Almanac"**.

Even his most ardent admirers (I count myself among them) would have to admit that there have been disappointments, when the cumbersome weight of the various concepts he explored on **"Preservation"** and **"Soap Opera"** unbalanced his writing.

"Sleepwalker", although its mood is unified by recurring themes of disillusion, defeat, the loss of innocence and a concern with the popular abdication of certain responsibilities, is restricted by no narrative design. The songs—nearly all of them potential 45s, I fancy—exist independently of any overall concept, and their melodic freshness and succinct lyrics recall the glorious days of **"Face To Face"** and **"Village Green Preservation Society"**, with occasional references to the elegiac tone of **"Arthur"**. It really is the group's strongest and most organised album in years.

"Life On The Road" opens; and finds the singer yearning, initially, for independence from his immediate family and seeking an escape to the City's neon excitements; and then, against a muscular Dave Davies guitar riff, catalogues the grief and disillusion that he encounters in the reality of city life, with its squalor and cynicism.

Raymond's lyrics are suffused with irony and a sense of humour that mitigates his bleak theme. Catch this, for instance: "Mama always told me that city ladies were bawdy and bold / So I searched night and day to catch a kiss from a lady / But all that I caught was a cold.''

A similar combination of infectious musical aggression and ironic lyrics characterises the irresistible **"Juke Box Music"**, a reckless piece about a lady and her addiction to a juke-box (really!), and **"Sleepless Night"**, on which Ray and Dave share the lead vocal, an anguished recollection about a past lover that contrasts her satisfaction with a new love to the isolation of the singer; such is the conviction and intimacy of the performance that one wonders just how personal the song is, in fact.

The more sedate and reflective **"Stormy Sky"**, with its cool electric piano and vulnerable vocal, is a particularly sombre piece in which Davies considers the futility of love as a defence against the bitter realities of the world.

The intensity of **"Sleepless Night"** recalls, as does **"Mr. Big Man"** even more, the surreal angst of Lou Reed's "Berlin". . . . The theme of the song—the inevitable corruption that attends success—has of course, been explored by Davies before, but never with such virulence.

The album's title track, and its companion piece, **"Full Moon"**, are, in comparison, quite irreverent pieces on the perils of somnambulism, which find Ray coming on like a burlesque midnight rambler. The subdued humour of these songs starkly contrasts with the bitter irony of **"Life Goes On"**, which closes the album on a note of defiance, and the tristesse of **"Brother"**, the record's most outstanding cut.

The former track, redolent of the weary cynicism and cutting absurdity of Loudon Wainwright, details the individual's unequal fight against life's imperatives and disasters: you have to surrender, Davies blackly suggests, to its absurdities and lunacies, and relish them while you can, "because you're a long time dead".

"Brother" is no less bleak, but its elegance and romance (it is enhanced by one of Davies' most evocative melodies) has no trace of sentimentality or pessimism.

"The world's going crazy and nobody gives a damn anymore / They're breaking off relationships and leaving on sailing ships for far and distant shores," the author sings over a drifting piano and acoustic guitar accompaniment. It's a song about people retreating from reality into fantasy, abdicating responsibilities and refusing to face the unpleasant truths of the world.

The climactic final sequence, where Davies repeats the opening verse over sweeping strings, framed by Dave Davies' stirring guitar, is quite overwhelming. . . . It really is magnificent.

And there you have it: an album as delightful, as moving and pertinent as the Kinks have ever produced. The Kinks, like life, go on. Thanks and amen for that.

Allan Jones, *"Have You Heard about the Midnight Rambler?: 'Sleepwalker',"* in Melody Maker *(© IPC Business Press Ltd.), February 26, 1977, p. 24.*

BILLY ALTMAN

Even as a staunch Kinks supporter, I was beginning to have my doubts. Although the band's following has grown steadily since they made it into the Seventies (by the skin of their teeth) with **"Lola,"** they seemed to have peaked with *Muswell Hillbillies*. Ray Davies seemed hopelessly stuck on a thematic dead-end street (perhaps he had started believing all those no-

tices about personifying the "voice of the little people"). But *Sleepwalker* . . . is a clear-cut triumph both for Davies and the band.

A few of these songs smack of the self-righteousness that's hindered Davies' recent writing; but the beautiful **"Stormy Sky,"** in which clouds become a symbol for romantic conflict, and **"Full Moon,"** a scary tune about madness and loss of self-recognition, are among his best efforts. The recurrent themes are fear, depression and failed utopianism; in **"Life Goes On,"** we are warned that "life'll hit you when you least expect it." Yet in the end, there always remains a faint glimmer of hope. . . . **"Juke Box Music,"** which seems strangely set apart from the rest, is the best song here, a rocker about a woman whose entire life is spent living inside the story lines of her favorite records. It should be a pathetic song, yet Davies has us tapping our feet, singing along.

Billy Altman, *"'Sleepwalker',"* in Rolling Stone *(by Straight Arrow Publishers, Inc. © 1977; all rights reserved; reprinted by permission), Issue 237, April 21, 1977, p. 95.*

ALLAN JONES

Raymond Douglas Davies is a metaphorical continent, removed from the archetypal macho-monster breathing blood and venom upon his audience as he carves a violent passage through their collective consciousness. Rather, he has the breezy bravado of a comic turn in an end-of-the-pier revue. . . .

Raymond Douglas Davies is unique. . . .

The Kinks' third single . . . was an event of some significance: the raw power and indefatigable exuberance of **"You Really Got Me"** . . . virtually introduced the genre of heavy metal in one devastating three-minute explosion of rabid sexual energy.

Ray Davies followed **"You Really Got Me"** with a further seven singles cast principally in the same basic fashion. These singles, as pertinently as any by the Beatles, provided an evocative soundtrack for mid-Sixties adolescents, tentatively exploiting their independence and investigating preliminary sexual activities. . . .

Ray Davies was, and this perhaps was the most immediate impression, no more extraordinary than any other confused and perplexed individual: he seemed to suffer the same mundane anxieties and expressed his concern with a casual honesty that refused to elevate the artist to the role of suffering martyr.

I remember the Kinks often performing on television in those days; decked out in their sublimely ridiculous red hunting jackets with frilled shirts, they seemed to gently parody the various uniforms of rock and roll. And there, stage centre, was Raymond Douglas Davies, gap-toothed and smiling like some sly old devil who knows intuitively that the whole deal is drenched in absurdity.

Indeed, it became increasingly clear that Ray Davies and the Kinks were slipping away from the rock mainstream and its predictable attitudes. In 1966, when every one of his contemporaries was caught up in the dizzy glamour of the London celebrity scene (y'know, "Swinging London" and all that phoney-baloney), Ray Davies stepped outside the frenzied circle.

From a detached and individual position he delivered the first in a sequence of pertinently satirical songs that deliberately questioned the whole dreadful schmear with a delightful irreverence. **"Well Respected Man,"** the first of these songs, simultaneously prefaced the sardonic disenchantment that would pervade both **"Face To Face"** (1966) and **"Something Else"** (as well as the intervening singles the Kinks released), and emphasised the increasing anglicisation of Davies' music.

The former allegiance to a raw form of R&B that had dominated the original Kinks' sound was almost entirely eradicated. Ray Davies eschewed the influences of American music and turned, instead, to the tradition of the English music hall for his inspiration. . . .

"Dedicated Follower Of Fashion," the second in the aforementioned sequence, was a perfectly realised burlesque, with Ray acting out the monologue with a theatrical verve that has since become a vivid characteristic of much of his work, further developed on the **"Face To Face"** and **"Something Else"** albums.

Ray Davies, it might be argued, was like an English provincial Lou Reed: New York's savage landscape, however, was substituted for an England fading into decay and dismay which Ray documented with clarity and humour and not a little regret for the loss of an idyllic innocence.

The melancholy that had attended much of his work reached a moving climax with **"Something Else,"** which contained the elegiac classic **"Waterloo Sunset"** . . . , as well as impressive miniatures of suburban dilemmas like **"Two Sisters,"** the sublime **"Afternoon Tea"** and the sardonic **"Situation Vacant"** (something of a post-script, this, to **"Dead End Street"**).

When Ray adopted various personae on these albums it wasn't (as was the case with Jagger and his penny-dreadful satanist projections) to nurture a popular image, but to create a specific environment and atmosphere for his observations; similarly, these roles were less ambitious than those that David Bowie, say, would later create for himself. Bowie is more concerned with the pursuit of abstract notions; Ray Davies is more closely concerned with a simple sense of humanity, by turns amused and appalled by the ironies of fate and life and those who live it.

He has assumed no epic or heroic roles in his career: he has been more comfortable assuming the identity of romantic dreamers (as on the wonderfully wistful, and often overlooked **"Days,"** and also the songs attributed to the tramp in **"Preservation Acts 1 and 2"** like **"Sitting In The Mid-Day Sun"** and **"Nobody Gives"**), cheapside hustlers and spivs (most notably as Flash in **"Preservation"**), the innocent who's finally corrupted (**"Lola," "Life On The Road"**).

Ray Davies embodies these various qualities just as he assumes, in the nostalgic and elegant tone of his writing, the mood of the times he reflects with **"Village Green Preservation Society"** and **"Arthur (Or The Decline And Fall Of The British Empire),"** which seek to evoke a past innocence. . . .

Ray Davies has never sacrificed his individuality for popularity, or relinquished his sense of humour and irony in a business that so often is intolerant of the kind of mischievous sense of the ridiculous that affects virtually everything connected with the Kinks.

> Allan Jones, "Davies: England's Glory Boy," in Melody Maker (© IPC Business Press Ltd.), April 30, 1977, p. 14.

JIM GREEN

The Brothers Davies—better known as the Kinks—have survived a decade and a half of the rock wars. As Ray puts it in **"A Rock and Roll Fantasy,"** "it's a miracle we're still here." Last year's *Sleepwalker* was the debut on their third label, Arista, and made the biggest impression in the charts of any Kinks LP yet. Considering the brilliance of their recorded output, it's about time [the Kinks had a commercial success].

On the evidence of *Misfits,* perhaps Ray Davies thinks so too, and decided to hasten the band's attainment of the commercial success they so richly deserve by doing what he could to homogenize the music for mass acceptance. Or maybe, after having worked on the album so long . . . , his judgement in selecting the best tracks was impaired. Whatever the reason (and don't tell me it's because they're old farts), *Misfits* is the first Kinks album I've found to be fairly bland, unexciting and, well, ordinary.

Not completely ordinary—how many hard-rockers do you find singing about **"Hay Fever"**? And there's also an embarrassing number called **"Black Messiah,"** about which the less said the better. But—and talk about embarrassing—who wants to say much about the Kinks' almost-disco track (**"Get Up"**)? And go figure **"Out of the Wardrobe,"** the touching story of a transvestite who reverses roles with his wife and they live happily ever after?

Yet the unique personal touch of Ray Davies, the thing that makes the Kinks truly special, is curiously muted or foregone in favor of obtaining a commercial sound, except for **"Rock and Roll Fantasy,"** which carries on another Kinks tradition, that of Ray stealing from himself—by borrowing from the theme of the excellent **"Jukebox Music"** (from *Sleepwalker*). Aside from some bright moments in some of the songs previously mentioned, there [is only one strikingly good Ray Davies track] . . . on the record—**"In a Foreign Land."** . . .

[The] promise held out by their brilliant Christmas single [**"Father Christmas"**/**"Prince of the Punks"**] has gone unfulfilled.

It hurts to have to say all this. After all, is this what we rabid Kinkophiles have been waiting for so long? I don't think so—it's hardly a Kinks album. God save the Kinks—from making another like this.

> Jim Green, "Album Reviews: 'Misfits'," in Trouser Press (copyright © 1978 by Trans-Oceanic Trouser Press, Inc.), Vol. 5, No. 6, July, 1978, p. 48.

KEN EMERSON

After twenty-odd albums, either you follow the Kinks or you don't. If you don't ("Gently pity those you can't persuade," as Jonathan Swift put it), it's unlikely you'll acquire the habit with *Misfits,* especially since none of the songs sounds like an immediate hit single. But if you do, this LP can make you cry. Not because *Misfits* is a bad record—on the contrary, it's the Kinks' best since, at the very least, 1974's underrated *Preservation Act 2.* No, what makes it heart-rending is its candor bordering on cruelty. And both the victim and the victor are Ray Davies.

It's as if the voice that has probably whispered for years inside Ray Davies' head, murmuring, "Come out, come out, wherever you are," has swollen into a scream that can no longer be stifled. No more hide-and-seek with the dramatis personae of the theatrical RCA albums or the metaphors of the last LP,

Sleepwalker. . . . No more peekaboo behind cute ambiguity (". . . I'm glad I'm a man / And so is Lola") or the disingenuous exhibitionism of drunkenness. Out of the closet, out of the Kinks even, and into the fire—not of damnation but, what's more excruciating, of irresolution. For sometimes, coming out isn't as difficult as it's cracked up to be: discovering where you are is often the hard part. That's why Davies, rather than answering the scream in kind, responds with a sigh that is desolating but that also speaks of a peace—a sadder but wiser awareness of his own ambivalence—that passeth all understanding.

Where, after all, does a misfit belong? To come out of the closet may be to leap into the void. Almost all of the songs on this record are about people who don't belong anywhere: a tax exile in a tropical land, a heterosexual transvestite, "the only honky living on an all black street" and most of all, Ray Davies himself. The title track, addressed to every performer whose time has come and gone, but especially to Davies, is a fitting introduction to the Kinks' most intimate album. . . . Apart from Johnny Rotten, the only other rock performers capable of such a brutal self-assessment are Pete Townshend and perhaps Neil Young. **"Misfits"** shows up a song like Jackson Browne's "Running on Empty" for the callow self-romanticization it really is.

"A Rock 'n' Roll Fantasy" is even more ruthless. It's a twofold fantasy: that of Davies, who'll "break up the band, start a new life, be a new man," and that of a diehard Kinks fan, Dan, who's wrapped up in their records. At its lovely beginning, the song suggests a breathy ballad by the Bee Gees, another veteran group but one that, unlike the Kinks, is now enjoying greater commercial success than ever before. As the lyrics describe Dan's rapt devotion, billowing harmonies deliberately evoke the Beach Boys, a band that seems to have soldiered on only for the sake of nostalgia. Then, as this description reaches its climax, the Kinks burst into an approximation of the sound of Boston's dense, swirling guitars. . . . **"A Rock 'n' Roll Fantasy"** ends with Davies insisting, "Don't want to spend my life, living in a rock 'n' roll fantasy / . . . Don't want to waste my life, hiding away anymore," but after nearly fifteen years as a rock & roller, it's clear that any alternative is every bit as much a fantasy. You can't teach an old dog new tricks.

Quoted in snatches, the lyrics of these two songs make them sound lacerating, but actually they're extraordinarily tender. Ray Davies sings them gently, almost conversationally, as if the last thing he wanted to do were to melodramatize his dilemma. Indeed, *Misfits* may be his best-sung—and most subtly sung—record yet. **"Misfits"** and **"A Rock 'n' Roll Fantasy"** are arranged as understated anthems; each begins on a delicate, confessional note and builds, layer upon layer, to a chaste grandeur that never topples over into pretentiousness. . . . This is rock & roll with a bittersweet restraint. (pp. 54-5)

Letting it all hang out as the brothers Davies do on *Misfits* has its limitations. The straightforward **"Out of the Wardrobe,"** a prosaic ode to transvestism, misses the dodgy wit of **"Lola."** Though **"Black Messiah"** rightly ridicules the naive enthusiasm of white audiences for the Rastafarianism of reggae . . . , the song raises without resolving the issue of Davies' own racism. And **"Get Up"** is saved from unseemly condescension ("Here's a message for the little guy") only by the excitement of its beat and because it becomes obvious that the exhortation is aimed, above all, at the singer himself.

Thanks to Ray Davies, *Misfits* is very nearly a masterpiece because it anatomizes rather than glorifies Davies' role as "**One of the Survivors,**" as the Kinks sang five years ago. After all, merely to have survived is nothing to crow about: Al Martino is hanging in there, too, and for all we know, Martin Bormann is alive and well and living in Argentina. For an artist (and anyone else, for that matter), the point is not only to survive, but to flourish. The Kinks aren't getting older—they're getting better. (p. 55)

Ken Emerson, "The Kinks: Victims and Victors," in Rolling Stone *(by Straight Arrow Publishers, Inc. © 1978; all rights reserved; reprinted by permission), Issue 269, July 13, 1978, pp. 54-5.*

JON PARELES

With the Era of Lowered Expectations upon us like a toxic thermal inversion, the Kinks are suddenly topical again. Ray Davies's pragmatic yet romantic pessimism—which he's maintained for 15 years—seems reasonable now, no longer a minority outlook. So when he names an album after the refrain "low budget," he doesn't sound petty or mundane; he sounds tough-minded, resonant, inspired. **"Low Budget"** (the song) lives up to its title; it's a monologue from a character who's forced to sacrifice quality for economy, a nigh-universal predicament. You don't have to be a Davies cultist or an expert on the English working class to know what he's singing about—and that shot of reality is exactly what the Kinks have needed.

They've been a cult band for too long. Because Davies has written so many brilliant songs since 1964—from **"You Really Got Me"** to **"Victoria"** to **"Lola"** to **"Ducks on the Wall,"** with lots of stops in between—he has a hardcore following that will sustain the Kinks through any folly as long as they can hear the oldies in concert. . . . But Davies's fans are so adoring they don't give him any clear sense of his strengths and weaknesses, encouraging filler-packed albums, sentimentality, and solipsism. In **"A Rock 'n' Roll Fantasy"** on 1978's *Misfits,* where Davies makes it seem that he's soldiering on unwillingly for the fan who "lives for our music," the bathos is overwhelming. If I never hear another Kinks song about stardom/showbiz/Hollywood (including **"Celluloid Heroes,"** a casualty of FM overkill), I'll still die happy; ditto for any song that says that "life is like" something. It's time these became private obsessions again. Like most storytellers, Davies is better dealing with specific characters and incidents than he is with generalities.

While Davies's lyrics grew preachy, his tunes were going slack. One reason was that Davies's mid-'70s experiments with rock theater (*Preservation, Soap Opera,* and *Schoolboys in Disgrace*) led him away from hard rock into music-hall and cabaret styles, and his production ignored guitars in favor of keyboards and horns. With stage action as diversion, Davies took less care in constructing each song; even when he gave up concert albums, Davies didn't enforce consistent standards on himself. Davies auterists egged him on—proud of his sadsack voice, they didn't mind hearing it in ever-more-vulnerable settings. And onwards to complacency, domesticity, mellowness. . . .

Side One of *Low Budget* makes an abrupt about-face: It rocks. For visceral impact, you'd have to go back to *Arthur* to match it. . . . Ray has for once lavished songwriting skills (smart lyrics, unstoppable riffs and hooks) and arranging savvy (build, build, build) on every track. . . .

Unfortunately, side two fizzles after the title cut. Although **"A Gallon of Gas"** is worth hearing for the way Ray turns "luxury'' into two syllables, the rest is negligible. Given the lowered expectations of Kinks fans, however, one good side is encouraging.

Jon Pareles, ''The Kinks Get Tough'' (reprinted by permission of The Village Voice *and the author; copyright © News Group Publications, Inc., 1979), in* The Village Voice, *Vol. XXIV, No. 32, August 6, 1979, p. 49.*

MARK FLEISCHMANN

[If you doubt that *Low Budget*'s] unifying idea is modern urban malaise à la Davies, you may have a bit of trouble accounting for the claustrophobic outlook of **"In a Space,"** the dancing whore and babbling street loon who meet Ray's compassionate eye in **"Little Bit of Emotion,"** his view of Captain America as a helpless giant in **"Catch Me Now I'm Falling,"** the disco arrangement of **"Superman,"** and the very existence of a song called **"Pressure"**—all on the same record. As the Kinks enter the '80s Ray's idealized village green is long gone, having been formally razed on *Preservation,* and perhaps even Arthur's suburban haunt may well have grown a little dirtier and more impersonal in the decade since 1969, as the world around it got a bit nastier year by year.

Not that the Kinks are ready to lay down and die. If **"Rock and Roll Fantasy"** and the title cut from *Misfits* limned Ray's internal struggle between intermittent self-doubt and self-affirmation, *Low Budget* shows the latter tendency winning out. In **"Attitude"** Raymond Douglas Davies the affirmer (or somebody) rebukes Raymond Douglas Davies the doubter for his defeatist attitude, perhaps with some prodding from the new wave, setting the stage for a record of tough—but in the Kinks tradition, almost invariably fun—rock and roll.

On the negative side, the choice of *Low Budget,* a so-so, sort of heavy-handed rocker, as title cut, is questionable....

Flaws aside, though, it's still a great album, certainly one of the year's best so far....

Mark Fleischmann, ''Album Reviews: 'Low Budget','' in Trouser Press *(copyright © 1979 by Trans-Oceanic Trouser Press, Inc.), Vol. 6, No. 9, October, 1979, p. 34.*

JANET MASLIN

At first I thought the biggest problem [in being stranded on a desert island with just one record] would be one of acoustics, but then I thought again. No friends. No enemies. No Christmas shoppers, but no Christmas presents, either. No way to start a stamp collection. No date at the movies. Hold the phone—no movies at all! Or books! Or talk shows! Or magazines (except for one yellowing copy of *People,* with Gregg and Cher and Baby Elijah on the cover)! Or records! *No records!*

Hah. *One* record, and—this being something of a trumped-up dilemma—all the time in the world to choose it. The final selection process didn't take me anywhere near that long: *Something Else by the Kinks,* and there's no second choice. If I couldn't pack that, I'd have to make other travel plans. (p. 100)

[There] are certain things about this situation that make it the Kinks' cup of tea. For one thing, they'd be invaluable tour guides, having made this same journey themselves any number of times. Yes, it may have started out as something of a joke—in **"I'm on an Island,"** on *The Kink Kontroversy,* Ray Davies

sang, to a beat midway between rock and cha-cha, of being literally left high and dry because he'd lost his girl. The trip had made him nothing if not cheerfully redundant: "I'm on an island / And I've got nowhere to run / Because I'm the only one / Who's on the island."

That was in 1965. By 1967, on *Face to Face,* the Kinks were ready for a more elaborate vacation, only to discover that a **"Holiday in Waikiki,"** spent beside billboards and high-priced souvenirs, in the company of hula dancers with New York accents, might not be the right choice. Since then, there have been the tropical exile on the *Lola* album, that flight in a **"Supersonic Rocket Ship"** from *Everybody's in Show Biz,* and a more ominous convalescence on *Muswell Hillbillies'* **"Holiday."** And those are only the literal trips. The Kinks are capable of making anything sound like a secluded retreat, whether it's a newly empty house (in **"Sunny Afternoon"**), or a room overlooking a busy train station (in **"Waterloo Sunset"**), or a café that's suddenly missing one's usual companion (in **"Afternoon Tea"**). In the Kinks' scheme of things, being alone is a given even when it isn't specified.

The trip on *Lola Versus Powerman and the Moneygoround* is the closest the Kinks may ever come to smooth sailing. On side one of the album, the adventures of a would-be rock star are detailed in the most beautifully melodic song Ray Davies has thus far written (**"Get Back in the Line"**) and one of the funniest (**"Moneyground"**). The singer is down on his luck, but then he writes a hit (**"Lola"**—Ray really *did* write a hit, his first in four years), tastes success (**"Top of the Pops"**) and has a devil of a time collecting his royalties. By side two, he's given up trying. On **"This Time Tomorrow,"** a serene song full of unexpectedly tranquil harmonies, the singer is on a plane musing about making his lonely getaway.

He looks down upon "fields full of houses" with the Kinks' particularly sharp awareness that everything has its price. The many Kinks songs that set up figures in opposition—like the two sisters in the song of the same name, one a housewife and one a glamorous bachelorette, or the competing politicians in *Preservation*—aim at a notion of seesawing destinies as well as at simple dramatic conflict. They suggest that one rival is happy only when the other is miserable, that cities are built at the expense of landscapes, that the cheerful rogue in **"Sunny Afternoon"** is only happy because someone, somewhere, has run off crying. And yet there's something benign about all this, something very much in keeping with Ray Davies's characteristic mixture of longing and revulsion. It's quite consistent with the idea, in so many of his songs, that life is at its most vivid when seen from a distance.

The *Lola* album's runaway has a dream of winding up in the jungle, in which he maintains that the only time he's happy is when he's swinging from the trees. "Oh what a life of luxury!" he cries. When Davies writes of "luxury" he's usually sending it up, as with that stately home and yacht in **"Sunny Afternoon."** But the mention here is more authentic. For one of Davies's super-civilized recluses, true luxury really would mean being able to run around in a loincloth without a second thought about whether it was well-tailored. And that's one freedom this music never even hints at, except in jest. That's what would make any Kinks album at home on a desert island; it would help you celebrate being away while still reminding you—keenly, keenly—of exactly what you were missing. (pp. 101-03)

Certainly *Something Else* is as exquisitely book-ended as a Kinks album could be, with **"David Watts"** for its beginning and **"Waterloo Sunset"** for a finale. There's a pure bitterness in **"David Watts"** that hasn't come through as bluntly in the Kinks' music before or since (although on the same album there's **"Harry Rag,"** sung with an uncharacteristic rudeness and in much the same spirit). David Watts is the schoolboy who has everything, the one whom everyone envies, a familiar figure who takes many forms (when I knew him, he was a little girl). There are later Kinks attacks on the same fellow— he's the **"Mr. Big Man"** of *Sleepwalker*—but none of them are brave enough to go after the little prig without using satire as a club. **"David Watts"** is plain, liberating malice, not co-incidentally one of the Kinks' toughest rock songs, and one of their most breathlessly economical performances. Even the first few seconds of introduction, with Ray instructing the band to make it "nice and smooth," contribute to the ferocity. They don't just begin this song; they tear its throat out.

When Ray goes machine-gunning his favorite middle-class squirrels, he's being every bit the bully that David Watts is. But **"Tin Soldier Man,"** setting its description of a pitifully regimented workaday Johnny to a military beat, is an unusually palatable example of Kinks Overkill. If any song is going to represent that genre, this might as well be the one. (pp. 103-04)

More interesting than either the prevailing fogginess of a song of such bizarre familiarity that the singer might just as easily be addressing his Uncle Phil, or the vaudeville phrasing at the end of each otherwise gloomy verse, are the abrupt swings between seemingly disjointed moods. There's a similar clash of tones on **"End of the Season,"** with its gray opening and then more vaudeville crooning, this time from someone who describes himself as covered with mud and dreaming of flowers. Even the painfully controlled romantic overtures the singer makes in **"Afternoon Tea"** are at odds with that song's jaunty, lighthearted sound, as the singer cheerfully encourages his date to "Take as long as you like / 'Cause I like you, girl." (By the end of the song, she has vanished; he wonders why.) In all of these songs, neither the overt attitude nor the trouble glimpsed behind it is as compelling as the play of these various elements, the way they intensify and undermine one another. The song is that much better for being an imperfect expression of the singer's state of mind.

Some of Ray Davies's most haunting work has been written and delivered in the spirit of inaccurate expression, of subdued turmoil. Perhaps what places **"Waterloo Sunset"** a cut above any other Kinks song is the way it takes a perfectly forthright route yet still arrives at the old ambiguity. Whatever that "dirty old river" suggests to the singer about himself, he's long since quietly resigned himself to it; whatever he means by saying someone is "in paradise," the phrase hangs just a tiny bit closer to weariness than to hope. He sits in a room at twilight, watching the crowds of tiny figures around a railway station; he singles out one couple and, with evident arbitrariness, imagines them to be singularly blessed. Ray was once an art student and, indeed, he might as easily have painted this as set it to music. That's another argument for choosing *Something Else,* for that bonus: an imaginary picture to hang on the imaginary lean-to wall. (pp. 104-05)

One grim liability of getting older is running the risk of meet-ing—even liking—people who aren't now and never have been rock fans. These people, I have begun to find, are likelier to take an interest in the Kinks than they are in hearing the entirety of one's Doors collection. And who would deny that having friends is nearly as important as having records?

So that's one extra selling point for *Something Else:* I'd want to have something to play for a new acquaintance, if the tides were to change and a likely-looking person swam by. After all, the wind might shift. Perhaps a shipwreck or a stray plane, or new neighbors on the atoll next door.

Desert island? I don't *need* a desert island. *Something Else by the Kinks* is with me anyway, wherever I go. (p. 106)

> *Janet Maslin, "'Something Else by the Kinks',"* in Stranded: Rock and Roll for a Desert Island, *edited by Greil Marcus (copyright © 1979 by Alfred A. Knopf, Inc.; reprinted by permission of Alfred A. Knopf, Inc.), Knopf, 1979, pp. 100-06.*

JOHN ROCKWELL

[The] Kinks have never really matched the top British groups in terms of mass success, and the reasons seem to be twofold. First, Ray Davies, the band leader, is too anarchic to conform to the rules and regulations of rock careerism. Rock may seem like an arena of wild men to outside observers. But it has its own rules, too, and for all their apparent eccentricity and icon-oclasm, stars like Mick Jagger and Pete Townshend obey those rules.

The other reason is that the distinction of the Kinks's songs has to do more with Mr. Davies's lyrics and his charisma than with any purely musical virtues. This makes him the darling of some rock writers, the kind that fastens first on the words instead of the music, and responds more to personality than to artistic abstraction. But a lack of consistently strong, memo-rable music has precluded the wider success that the Kinks might otherwise enjoy.

> *John Rockwell, "Is British Rock More Hip than American?"* in The New York Times *(© 1980 by The New York Times Company; reprinted by permission), July 18, 1980, p. 12.*

DAVE SCHULPS

What [the live album] *One for the Road* shows so well is how vital the Kinks are as we enter the '80s. After years on the fringe of mainstream rock, unwilling to compromise them-selves for the sake of trendiness, it's no accident that the Kinks are currently more popular than at any time since the mid-'60s. Rock has come back to the Kinks' way of thinking, and for the first time in a while the group is in a position to reap the benefits. If the Jam can have an English hit with **"David Watts,"** and the Pretenders score with **"Stop Your Sobbing"** why shouldn't the Kinks restore both to their set? Why shouldn't the Kinks, who fooled around with calypso in the early '70s (**"Apeman," "Supersonic Rocket Ship"**), concoct a sterling ska arrangement for the venerable **"'Til the End of the Day"**? The answer is simple: they should. And it's all here.

Maybe it's a sign of growth that the Kinks are able to reconcile past with present so neatly. When they were doing their the-atrical concept shows, the Kinks' run-through of old hits always seemed a bit uncomfortable and obligatory; now old meshes seamlessly with new, emphasized by the inclusion of six *Low Budget* songs (all of side three, the album's low-point).

Low Budget's simple approach has carried over to the band's stage show. They sound more youthful here than they have in years, especially on **"Pressure"** (which somehow suggests manic Buzzcocks more than Kinks). As comparatively straight as he plays it, Ray Davies is still a master of theatrics and man of a thousand voices. His gift for perfect inflections and phrasing is uncanny, his sense of timing that of a veteran entertainer.

Dave Schulps, "Livest Kinks: You've Heard the Record, Now Buy the Videotape," in Trouser Press *(copyright ©1980 by Trans-Oceanic Trouser Press, Inc.), Vol. 7, No. 7, August, 1980, p. 18.*

NICHOLAS SCHAFFNER

There's been a lot of talk about "dinosaurs" these past few years. It's gotten to the point where many longtime rock fans . . . might reluctantly vote in favor of banishing some of their aging heroes to a remote cave. (p. 63)

The Kinks, however, are one "Sixties" act that has never had to face the dilemma of living up to (or living down) an identity forged from teen anthems . . . Following several rewrites of his first youthful power-popper, **"You Really Got Me,"** Ray Davies grew up almost overnight. Most of the understated narratives he penned in the latter half of the Sixties are not only timeless but ageless. . . . Davies might well have soldiered on into the next century, writing and singing such wry and poignant ditties as **"Waterloo Sunset," "Autumn Almanac"** and **"Days,"** and nobody would have ever called him a dinosaur.

Yet now that he's actually approaching that age when people tend to grow partial to sweeping leaves into a sack, pasting snap shots in the family picture book or just sitting by the fire in their Shangri-La's, the songwriter who once immortalized these small pleasures has regressed into a second rock & roll childhood. (pp. 63-4)

Despite what he sings in one of his catchy new compositions, **"Predictable"** was always the last word anyone would have used to describe Ray Davies. His late-Seventies metamorphosis, however, was no mere kinky whim but, rather, a conscious determination to, uh, *Give the People What They Want.* After seventeen years and some twenty-odd albums, Davies feels entitled to sing at Madison Square Garden. And, as Big Sky knows, he deserves to.

But the real surprise here is that the Kinks are manifestly enjoying their reincarnation as reborn rock & roll superstars. On *Give the People What They Want* at least, they seldom sound tired and jaded, or even bored with their more hackneyed riffs. And their pleasure is passed on to the listener.

Not that the Kinks are entirely innocent of pandering: as a Davies character study, **"Killer's Eyes"** is dead obvious. **"Destroyer"** (wasn't that a title of a Kiss record?) is positively brontosauruslike in its heavy-handed appropriation, à la 1979's **"Catch Me Now I'm Falling,"** of a familiar mid-Sixties riff (this time though, Davies has had the taste to select the Kinks' **"All Day and All of the Night"**). And when it comes to nuances like rhyme and meter, this notable craftsman has grown notably careless. . . .

Then again, that in itself may be a deliberate stroke of Davies irony. Because, make no mistake, Ray Davies hasn't turned into enough of an idiot dunce to utilize a phrase like "give the people what they want" without a sly wink and a smile. . . . In any case, Davies' curse—and our blessing—is that he's too incurably quirky to qualify as a successful hack. Even when he does kowtow to mass taste, he just can't help being unique. . . .

Give the People What They Want concludes with a special treat for the long-suffering Kinks kultist. Musically and lyrically, **"Better Things"** is of a piece with 1968's **"Days,"** the important difference being that the better days are said to be ahead of us now, instead of irretrievably behind. . . .

Same to you, old friend. Some of *Give the People What They Want* may seem pedestrian back to back with *Face to Face,* et al., and the lyrics probably won't qualify as timeless literature and all that. But compared with most of the other yo-yo's heard around my dial lately, tunes like **"Around the Dial"** and **"Yo-Yo"** certainly provide an exhilarating noise delivered with a lightness of touch that hardly suggests the stamp of a dinosaur. They're funny and they're fun, and that, I'll venture, should be enough until Ray Davies gets around to writing *Preservation Act III.* (p. 64)

Nicholas Schaffner, "Kinks Klick," in Rolling Stone *(by Straight Arrow Publishers, Inc. © 1981; all rights reserved; reprinted by permission), Issue 356, November 12, 1981, pp. 63-4.*

Vine Deloria, Jr.

1933-

American Indian young adult and adult nonfiction writer and editor.

Deloria is representative of a new breed of American Indian: well-educated and concerned for the plight of the Indian forced to live in a white man's system. In his writings, Deloria argues for the return of sacred grounds and an isolationist policy that would enable his people to function as a separate nation within the United States. A Standing Rock Sioux born and raised on a reservation, Deloria is particularly qualified to enlighten the public on the Indian's present status in our society. Following in the footsteps of his father and grandfather, Deloria trained for a career as a minister. After receiving his degree in divinity from the Lutheran School of Theology, however, he realized a more effective means of serving the Indian's cause was through the legal system, and consequently earned a law degree from the University of Colorado. As executive director of the National Congress of American Indians in Washington, D.C., Deloria turned that nearly defunct organization into a forceful voice for the Indian tribes.

Deloria has stated that his exposure to Western culture has served to reaffirm his childhood commitment to the traditional Indian way of life. The main premise of his writings is the need for an Indian cultural nationalism, as opposed to the intellectual assimilation of minorities advocated by the white establishment. Deloria approaches the issues from a religious and legal standpoint. He believes that Christianity is no longer practical, with its promise of heaven so remote from everyday life in an industrial society, and that the naturalism of Indian religion is the only hope for Western civilization. Deloria also believes the government should honor the various treaties made with the Indians concerning their lands. Despite the seriousness of his subjects, Deloria's writing is informal and often wryly humorous, making it accessible to any reader interested in the modern Indian. Although many people do not agree with his ideas, Deloria is nevertheless respected for the sincerity and integrity of his works. (See also *Contemporary Authors*, Vols. 53-56.)

Used by Permission; Friendship Press, 1974

NANCY OESTREICH LURIE

[The differences in goals and methods of black militancy and red nationalism is a subject fraught with confusion and misunderstanding for the general public, both black and white.] Deloria's very equivocation as to any mutual relevance of the red and the black movements [in *Custer Died for Your Sins*] is characteristic of the thinking of many young Indians and thus informative. Another chapter—that on Indian humor—would have elucidated the Indian mood very well for the average, uninformed American and helped to explain what "Custer Died for Your Sins" implies. These chapters and those dealing with the central issue of treaties in Indian political ideology, the history of cross-purposes in Indian administration, the nature of Indian leadership, the interplay of cultural and social forces between country- and urban-based Indians, the range from assimilationists to traditionalists among Indians, and even Deloria's personal preferences as to policy and program reform justify the subtitle of his book as *An Indian Manifesto* rather than just *An Indian's Manifesto*. . . .

The book is certainly crotchety, and the three chapters dealing with anthropologists, missionaries, and the government are fully comprehensible only to an often infighting ingroup rather than to the general public for whom the book is intended. Nevertheless, whatever personal bias Deloria brings to his writing out of his more white than Siouan ancestry, a family history of three generations closely associated with Indian missionary endeavors, his own education for the ministry, and his present status as a law student, he must be considered a bona fide modern Indian and an experienced, informed activist in Indian organizational work. Deloria's is truly an Indian book. There are a few Indians who write professionally on Indian subjects as novelists or anthropologists, but Deloria represents a type of Indian, fairly often encountered, who threatens "to write a book" but never does. Deloria has. If nothing else, he should shake a patronizing public, self-righteous benefactors, and preciously scientific scholars into a realization that the day is past when we can talk or write as if Indians were either illiterate or extinct, no matter how benevolent or objective our intentions.

Whereas many Indians will disagree with Deloria on some of the specific points, broad generalizations, and recommendations, they can agree on the basic premise of the manifesto, whether they are vocal promulgators or supportive of it by simply being Indians: the tribals shall inherit the earth. (p. 80)

Perhaps all that Deloria is asking of the anthropologists, as well as of the missionaries, the government and other "friends" is that, if they cannot agree absolutely that the tribals actually will inherit the earth, they will agree to help Indians get a chance to try to inherit something either as a matter of humanitarian concern for their birthright or from the perspective that we are foolish to pass up anything that might be a good idea, things on earth being what they presently are. (p. 81)

> *Nancy Oestreich Lurie, "What the Red Man Wants in the Land That Was His," in* Saturday Review *(copyright © 1969 by* Saturday Review; *all rights reserved; reprinted by permission), Vol. LII, No. 40, October 4, 1969, pp. 39-41, 80-1.*

JAMES A. PHILLIPS

If ["**Custer Died for your Sins: an Indian Manifesto**"] is indicative of Deloria's methods, he's more interested in results than in being tactful.

Nauseated by the traditional Indian image, he asserts the worth if not the dignity of the redman and blasts the political, social, and religious forces that perpetuate the Little Big Horn and wigwam stereotyping of his people. Admittedly and intentionally he offends the people from whom help might come—Congress, anthropologists, and churches. When he's not specifically attacking these groups, he's vituperative about the general society that allows other groups to have predicaments, problems, or troubles, but insists that Indians have a "plight." . . . The threat of Indian insurrection is more latent than tacit, and understandably so if we can believe his lengthy discussion of how Indians have been neglected, cheated, and starved in a society so concerned with improving the lot of minority groups such as the Blacks. . . .

Although Deloria's subject is serious, he approaches it nonformally. In fact, he devotes a chapter to Indian humor in addition to generously sprinkling anecdotes and one-liners into his commentary. . . .

The plea of this book is retribalization of the people and recolonization of unsettled areas of the nation while Indians fearfully note the ever-present dangers of reservation entanglements and the black power movement. Indians must learn to employ unity as a weapon, something they have hitherto feared for minor, selfish reasons. If more voices as strong as Deloria's are heard, there may yet be a place in America for Indians. (p. 270)

> *James A. Phillips, "'Custer Died for Your Sins: An Indian Manifesto'," in* Best Sellers *(copyright 1969, by the University of Scranton), Vol. 29, No. 14, October 15, 1969, pp. 270-71.*

TYLER THOMPSON

If you are interested in savoring the emotional tone (as well as listening to some of the crucial ideas) of the emerging Indian protest movement, you will find [*Custer Died for Your Sins*] useful and important. Indian resentment toward white men and white society is set forth with memorable vividness. . . .

But this book is no mere negative diatribe. In it we find set forth the essence of a program for rehabilitating Indian society, perhaps even for saving white society in the bargain. . . .

The book is full of exaggeration—much of it quite deliberate. It contains many paradoxes, if not contradictions. Yet its message emerges with startling clarity. It is a message worth hearing.

> *Tyler Thompson, "Red, Brown Protest," in* The Christian Century *(copyright 1970 Christian Century Foundation; reprinted by permission from the February 18, 1970 issue of* The Christian Century), *Vol. 87, No. 7, February 18, 1970, p. 213.**

CECIL EBY

Deloria brings into focus the moods and habitat of the contemporary Indian as seen by a Standing Rock Sioux, not by a research anthropologist or a jobber in the basketry trades. He peels away layers of tinsel and feathers heaped upon the Indian by misinformed whites (beginning with Columbus), and he reveals an uncanny ability for impaling them on the fine points of their own illogic.

> *Cecil Eby, "Tonto Was an Uncle Tomahawk," in* Book World—The Washington Post *(© 1970 Postrib Corp.; reprinted by permission of* Chicago Tribune *and* The Washington Post), *October 4, 1970, p. 4.*

JOHN S. PHILLIPSON

[Mr. Deloria] is an Indian with an ironic sense of humor and an urgent message for the world today: to survive, it needs the flexibility of the tribe and the tribal viewpoint. (pp. 281-82)

In ["**We Talk, You Listen**" we have] a discussion interwoven of ecology, economics, politics, sociology, anthropology, history, and religion, all relating to man's sad plight today in which he faces fairly imminent extinction unless he drastically changes his way of life. Instead of the "liberal nonsense" he decries, Mr. Deloria gives us advice we should do well to heed. It makes sense. I found only Chapter 3 dull going, with a noticeable amount of social-scientific jargon, some faulty syntax ("a media") and tautology ("progressive motion forward") . . . . But elsewhere the book is a pleasure to read—assuming that one doesn't become too depressed by the revelation of the white man's folly—and it should be read. The Indians are talking, and we had better listen. (p. 282)

> *John S. Phillipson, "'We Talk, You Listen'," in* Best Sellers *(copyright 1970, by the University of Scranton), Vol. 30, No. 14, October 15, 1970, pp. 281-82.*

THE NEW YORKER

[*We Talk, You Listen: New Tribes, New Turf* is an] argumentative rather than informative book. . . . [The author] adopts a controversial style reminiscent of his forefathers' fighting style: avoid pitched battles, loose a shower of arrows, and dart off. The Parthians fought the Romans this way, the Turks the Crusaders; though it is not magnificent, it *is* war. Mr. Deloria's paleface readers are not persuaded or enlightened; they are simply attacked. Here and there, Mr. Deloria seems to be starting a conversation, but it always turns into a war whoop.

"Briefly Noted: 'We Talk, You Listen: New Tribes, New Turf'," in The New Yorker *(© 1970 by The New Yorker Magazine, Inc.), Vol. 46, No. 36, October 24, 1970, p. 76.*

W. ROGER BUFFALOHEAD

A number of American Indians have wanted to write a book like [*Custer Died For Your Sins*], or have threatened to. But while others dreamed, procrastinated, or found other outlets for their energies, Vine Deloria, Jr. . . . persevered and has produced a witty, provocative, and sometimes crotchety interpretation of the past and current state of affairs of American Indians.

Written for the general public, this is nevertheless an Indian book and, as such, contains much of significance for Indians and non-Indians alike. Many on both sides will find viewpoints designed to raise the blood pressure and force a reappraisal of Indian-white relations. (p. 553)

Unlike many younger Indians, Deloria opposes militant confrontation with white society. Rather, he argues, struggles in the "intellectual arena" will bring about the desired aims: self-determination in all phases of Indian life and a humane and personalized alternative to contemporary industrialized urban society. According to Deloria, Indians may realize their potential only by strengthening "tribalism" and integrating the desired fruits of Western culture into their way of life. At the same time, they must, by the difficult process of accretion, establish the legal, moral, and intellectual foundations which will enable Indians to save themselves and, perhaps, save America.

While this approach is commendable and has some validity, there is—to quote a man who knew Deloria very well—"a lot of bull"— on which much of the approach rests. Foremost and most obvious, not to mention crucial, is the underlying assumption that the powers-that-be in the nation are really interested in an alternative, humane and more personalized or otherwise. Certainly, little in current trends and moods of Americans suggests a withering away of the "status quo," or an increased tolerance for the kind of autonomy and differences which Deloria sees as essential for Indian people, if they are to rescue themselves from the consequences of past and current policies. As Deloria himself aptly demonstrates, nothing in the past—legal, moral, intellectual—prevented the exploitation of the Indian. Unfortunately, that awful truth is still truth, and, while an intellectual elite among Indian people may put up a grand battle, they will not win without powerful allies in the larger society. Deloria, as well as anyone, knows this to be true. Only he can truly say why the subject is soft-pedalled in his manifesto.

The traditional "allies" of Indians—missionaries, liberal or sympathetic politicians, and anthropologists—receive a drubbing, indeed are mauled, by Deloria. The "sins" of each group, as the author sees them are rolled out, page after page, in a deliberate bit of sheer overkill. The method, however, only seems like madness. The subtle psychology underlying the harsh indictments is to force Indians and their white "friends" into a meaningful dialogue—to stop being pawns in each other's games and get down to the important task of establishing mutual respect and understanding on sounder grounds than sentimentality, pity, guilt, and rationalizations for the furtherance of the science of mankind. Those on whom Deloria has "counted coup" will label the charges unfair, intemperate,

irrational, and, perhaps, even "racist." None, however, will be able to defend the activities of all of their comrades, and most will agree that "sins" or errors have been made, intentional or otherwise.

On the whole, *Custer Died For Your Sins* is a worthwhile and much-needed contribution to the literature on American Indians. Pardoning Deloria for excesses here and there and an exceptionally weak chapter on Indian-Black relations, the book must be judged the most thought-provoking and exciting study of American Indians in recent times. (p. 554)

W. Roger Buffalohead, "Reviews of Books: 'Custer Died for Your Sins: An Indian Manifesto'," in Pacific Historical Review *(© 1970, by the Pacific Coast Branch, American Historical Association), Vol. 39, No. 4, November, 1970, pp. 553-54.*

N. SCOTT MOMADAY

The title of Vine Deloria's new book, *We Talk, You Listen,* is significant in that it appears to express in itself a new and prevalent attitude among Indians, and young Indians in particular, a quality of anger and self-assertion that has been dormant for a long time, for generations indeed. The New Indian, as he has been called, talks of living standards and job opportunities, education and health programs—both on and off the reservations—and he talks as never before of political action and organization. (p. 39)

In two books to date, *Custer Died for Your Sins* and *We Talk, You Listen,* Vine Deloria, Jr., has written about the Indian world, traditional and contemporary, in terms that are congenial as well as authoritative. Deloria is . . . a man very much in tune with contemporary Indian affairs. But in presuming to speak for the Indian in all his diversity, he has been led more than once to generalize and sometimes to err. . . .

In *Custer Died for Your Sins,* Deloria is concerned primarily to advance a theory of "tribalism," but, regrettably, he fails to tell us precisely what he means by that term. . . .

In the more recent *We Talk, You Listen,* the notion of tribalism is amplified, extended by legal analysis. Deloria believes that the concept of individualism, as a tenet of the democratic faith, is outmoded. (p. 40)

Central to Deloria's thesis, again if I understand him rightly, is the idea that the basic common denominator of our legal system is, or ought to be, the group (i.e., tribe), presumably defined according to racial characteristics (as Indians, Blacks, Chicanos, etc.), and that legal protection of these groups ought to consist primarily in the guarantee of substantial rather than ideal value (material reparations, restitutions of monies and lands). Presumably, too, these considerations proceed logically from the nature and objectives of "tribalism." An Indian is, well, *tribalism.*

Deloria is a thoughtful man, and he is articulate as well; but his books are disappointing in one respect: they tell us very little about Indians, after all. In neither book is there any real evocation of that spirit and mentality which distinguishes the Indian as a man and as a race. . . .

This seems all the more regrettable in view of the fact that he really knows something about the subject by virtue of blood as well as experience. And yet he treats it very superficially, on the whole. The chapter on Indian humor in *Custer Died for Your Sins,* for example, is little more than a catalogue of ethnic jokes. In it we are told nothing whatever of the essential humor, of that profound gaiety of vision and delight in being which has marked most Indians I have known. Nor are we given any better to see the religious and philosophical aspects of the Indian world. In *We Talk, You Listen,* there is a plea for the return to nature, in the interest of "tribalism," of course, but it is made in the interest of an economic and not an ethical ideal; we are told nothing of what the landscape is or of how it functions as a vital entity in Indian tradition.

Much more explicitly, Deloria tells us what an Indian is not. He is particularly not a bureaucrat or an anthropologist. (The notion of an Indian writing about an anthropologist is somehow and at once sinister and just.) Deloria is very good on that score, full of righteousness and wit. He turns the tables, as it were. It is in his stereotype of the anthropologist that we see so clearly through the anthropologist's stereotype of the Indian. Indeed, in this curious combination of reflections we have almost a definition. (p. 41)

> *N. Scott Momaday, "Bringing on the Indians," in* The New York Review of Books *(reprinted with permission from* The New York Review of Books; *copyright © 1971 Nyrev, Inc.), Vol. XVI, No. 6, April 8, 1971, pp. 39-42.**

ALFONSO ORTIZ

[*Custer Died for Your Sins: An Indian Manifesto*] is the most ambitious and most successful overview of contemporary American Indian affairs and aspirations I have ever read, whether "contemporary" is defined as the 1950's, 1960's, or the beginning of the 1970's. . . . Neither the range of scholars who view the Indian from the confines of their own academic perspectives nor the areal specialists are likely to be satisfied with Deloria's coverage, but this is a danger inherent in any and every attempt at a general treatment of the Indian's current status in American life. The two chapters covering laws, treaties, and termination, for instance, are too programmatic, but the subjects have been well chronicled by others. Another chapter, entitled **"Indian Humor,"** is unrepresentative in that it is elitist; if most Indians could pierce through very complex if incongruous situations of the modern world and perceive the humor in them, as Deloria so obviously can, then we would not have quite the problems we do. Still another, entitled **"The Red and the Black,"** has had more than one commentator from among the latter up the wall for a variety of reasons. But, all in all, this is the most comprehensive treatment of the subject available in a readable format; every special interest group impinging on Indian communities today comes in for an unkind word at some time or other. (p. 953)

> *Alfonso Ortiz, "Other: 'Custer Died for Your Sins: An Indian Manifesto'," in* American Anthropologist *(copyright 1971 by the American Anthropological Association; reproduced by permission of the American Anthropological Association), Vol. 73, No. 4, 1971, pp. 953-55.*

PETER MAYER

[With **"God Is Red"** Deloria] has written yet another gripping account on the fate of the American Indian. Vine Deloria's interests range far and wide; the lore of his people is examined from an incredible number of different perspectives; various books of the Bible are introduced as history, and incredibly complex scientific (and other) data or explanations . . . are cited to give new twists to old beliefs. It is indeed a fascinating tale.

The discussion takes place on two levels. The first, and the one I can recommend to all readers, consists of a recital of selected injustices perpetrated upon the Red Man by the European settlers on this continent. The second, which is really the thesis of the book, I am far less sure about. Deloria seems to have concluded that in order to prove the Indians' way of life superior to that of the settlers', it was necessary to show that such superiority was no accident, but arose from the very basis of the two respective life styles.

The author finds the cause in the separate religious styles of the two peoples. Indian religion binds men to the soil, to their ancestry. The believer, his society, and the universe become one, and the religious experience is directly relevant to him. The message is cooperative, the life-style protective, and each member finds meaning and life itself in the very existence of his tribe. . . .

So far, so good. In this era of impending ecological disaster (of which we are from time to time reminded), any ecologically sound life-style commends itself. But Deloria deems it insufficient to demonstrate Indian cohesiveness. He attacks the Judean-Christian tradition, and especially its Churches, unmercifully. Some of the criticism is justified: various Crusades and aspects of Inquisitions constitute neither examples of Christian charity nor examples of love for one's fellow men; many of us choose our congregations not for their doctrine, but for the social standing membership connotes in the community; the list may be long, but that is to miss the point. Men are human, and do not necessarily follow in His footsteps.

Deloria could have made his point—that Indian religious practices are far more in accord with the necessities of contemporary life than are Christian—without dredging up the many failures of the sons of the Church upon earth. Few, I think, will disagree with his premise that Christianity is in search of its current identity. His thesis, that man himself is rooted in the soil, that removal from the ancestral home is achieved only at the price of self-alienation, and that religion therefore must be based upon territory, is a concept that merits our attention. But read the book; I found it hard to put down.

> *Peter Mayer, "Non-Fiction: 'God Is Red'," in* Best Sellers *(copyright 1973, by the University of Scranton), Vol. 33, No. 16, November 15, 1973, p. 363.*

ROBERT C. NELSON

Christ Jesus' guidelines have been judged impractical because difficult to obey. The falterings of his followers have been taken as proof enough that the Sermon on the Mount is too lofty to apply to real people.

But Christianity persists, in spite of its abusers. It survives all the perilous times. The Kingdom of God is not conquered, damaged, or displaced. It is always safely within—as Jesus said it would be—within consciousness centering more on God, less on self.

Thus Vine Deloria's indictments [in **"God is Red"**] are not new; his alternatives are. He finds American Christians bumbling and hypocritical; cruel, inane, and rootless. Rootless. That's his key. American Christians have no spiritual unity with the land on which their religion is practiced. American

Indians do. Their religions will lead the way out of empty Christian worship, he maintains. . . .

How this reformation of the Christian in America is to be accomplished is not spelled out. Perhaps that is because Mr. Deloria is not yet sure how—or whether—to blot out what he has learned of Christianity, so that what he feels as an Indian can dominate his being.

Thus this skilled writer, practicing lawyer, forceful spokesman for American Indian rights, speaks on two levels—one philosophical, one personal.

The insights into his country's Indian religious heritage are important reading. The barbs against Christianity are misdirected and flawed.

But we cannot afford, as a nation, to overlook our roots. Nor can those who are Christians afford to overlook their follies. This book nags on both scores—not as sensitively or tellingly as it might—but well enough just the same.

Robert C. Nelson, "Christianity Is Too White in American Indian's Eyes," in The Christian Science Monitor (reprinted by permission from The Christian Science Monitor; © 1974 The Christian Science Publishing Society; all rights reserved), January 2, 1974, p. F7.

GEORGE H. FREIN

[With *God Is Red* Deloria has written] a highly telling polemic against Christianity.

The core of *God Is Red* is a comparison of Christian and Indian beliefs about the nature of religion, creation, the meaning of history, the character of religious experience, death, human personality and community, and the role of religion in the contemporary world. The basic difference between the two religions is that one perceives the world in terms of time, the other in terms of space. (p. 186)

Many readers will find fault with the Christian writers Deloria relies upon to describe the Christian faith, but they serve well enough. Other writers more in keeping with one's own Christian bias would no doubt serve Deloria's criticism just as well. Most readers will wish that less space had been given to the defects of Christianity and more to the religion of the land and its native peoples. But, after reading *God Is Red* it will be impossible to be content with Indian history and romance. Deloria makes an irresistible case for reading *The Sacred Pipe*, *Black Elk Speaks*, *Lame Deer: Seeker of Visions*, and other sources of tribal religious wisdom as an aid to saving one's land and soul. (p. 187)

George H. Frein, "What Christians Do with History," in The Nation (copyright 1974 The Nation magazine, The Nation Associates, Inc.), Vol. 218, No. 6, February 9, 1974, pp. 186-87.

FRANCIS A. LALLEY

His native viewpoint is the unique strength of Deloria's writing. He can explain how the world appears to those who were here on this continent countless centuries before Europeans arrived. The world does not appear as an arena for struggle between humanity and nature, as the Christian creation story suggests. Death is not something evil that must be conquered, as the Christian resurrection may imply. Religion for the native peo-

ple has never been "other worldly" but intimately tied to the natural phenomena of this world. In these areas and others, Deloria discusses the differences of perception and feeling among Christian and native people with regard to this continent and its religious meaning.

[*God Is Red*] is not all serious theology. He writes with amusement about some extraordinary manifestations of contemporary Christianity. . . . There is both hope and despair in Deloria's book. He is hopeful about the survival of Indian religious experience when discussing the restoration of Blue Lake to the Taos Pueblo in New Mexico. He is more often despairing of any religious experience surviving in America, either Indian or Christian. . . .

Deloria is antagonistic toward much of Christian belief. In fairness, however, it must be noted that he has gone to our schools and learned our theology and is now urging us to do likewise—listen to his people and perhaps learn from them. Although his book will not be pleasant reading for most Christians, I think he has struck a fair bargain and perhaps one which will benefit both Christians and native Americans alike. (p. 200)

Francis A. Lalley, "'God Is Red'," in America (© America Press, 1974; all rights reserved), Vol. 130, No. 10, March 16, 1974, pp. 198, 200.

LEO E. OLIVA

[In *Behind the Trail of Broken Treaties*] Deloria argues effectively that the best solution to the "Indian problem," for Indians and the federal government alike, is to honor old treaties and to develop a new treaty relationship which gives tribes the status of quasi-international independence (with the U.S. acting as protector). The legal and moral arguments are set into historical developments; and the major objections to restoration of tribal sovereignty are countered with reason and with examples from around the world. . . . This well-written plea deserves the consideration of every American: Deloria is clearly a spokesman to be heard.

Leo E. Oliva, "The Contemporary Scene: 'Behind the Trail of Broken Treaties: An Indian Declaration of Independence'," in Library Journal (reprinted from Library Journal, August, 1974; published by R. R. Bowker Co. (a Xerox company); copyright © 1974 by Xerox Corporation), Vol. 99, No. 14, August, 1974, p. 1923.

DEE BROWN

Among his people Vine Deloria Jr. has achieved a status somewhat similar to that of Sitting Bull's leadership of the Sioux tribes a century ago. Deloria is not a warrior ("The time for playing cowboys and Indians is over," he said recently) but is more the strategist—the thinker and the planner. . . . What Deloria wants is affirmative action by the U.S. Congress to define Indian tribes as smaller nations to be left alone to run their own affairs. . . .

"**Behind the Trail of Broken Treaties**" is not only the best account yet written of events leading to Wounded Knee 1973, it is also a compelling argument for a reopening of the treaty-making procedure between Indian tribes and the U.S. Government; an action which the author is convinced would place this country in the forefront of civilized nations for its treatment of native peoples.

In presenting a historical background for events of the past decade, Deloria chides chroniclers of the Indian wars who believe that the first Wounded Knee (1890) marked the end of the Indian struggle to preserve national identity. The fighting has continued all these years, Deloria maintains, but without feathered war bonnets and slashing cavalry swords. . . .

Deloria also admonishes the New Left of the 1960's for regarding Indians as another domestic minority group. He says the Indians do not see themselves as such; they believe that their struggle is of historical significance, not a temporary domestic discontent. . . .

Deloria traces the rapid rise of the protest movement among Indians—from the Poor Peoples March of 1968 through the Red Power rallies and the birth of the American Indian Movement to the occupation of Alcatraz. . . . Expressing regret over the errors made there, he moves on to the dramatic Trail of Broken Treaties caravan that swept across America in 1972. . . .

["**Behind the Trail of Broken Treaties**" will] likely become a permanent source book for Indian historians. . . .

"**The Indian Affair,**" although in some parts a condensation of the longer "**Broken Treaties,**" is also an excellent historical account of legal devices used by the United States to deprive Indians of their lands and rights, with emphasis on the 20th century. Of special interest are the chapters on churches and social change and Indian education today—activities with which Deloria has been closely involved.

> *Dee Brown, "'Behind the Trail of Broken Treaties: An Indian Declaration of Independence' and 'The Indian Affair',"* in The New York Times Book Review *(© 1974 by The New York Times Company; reprinted by permission), November 24, 1974, p. 38.*

CHOICE

More than any other author, Indian or white, dealing with the topic of current Indian affairs, Vine Deloria has challenged and stimulated the general public and the academic community. The impact of his *Custer died for your sins* . . . , *We talk, you listen* . . . , and *God is red* . . . attests to that. [*Behind the trail of broken treaties*] is equally provocative. Deloria calls for government adoption of the "Twenty Points" of the caravan of Indians known as the Trail of Broken Treaties that occupied the Bureau of Indian Affairs in 1972. A major goal is to restore authority to make treaties with Indians and to restore Indian tribes to a status of quasi-international independence with the U.S. acting as their protector. Deloria evaluates arguments against this proposal and finds them wanting. He also provides a historical summary of federal treatment of Indians and explains the development of the current Indian protest movement. He is eloquent but occasionally eloquently unrealistic because of white attitudes.

> *"Social and Behavioral Sciences: 'Behind the Trail of Broken Treaties: An Indian Declaration of Independence',"* in Choice *(copyright © 1974 by American Library Association), Vol. 11, No. 10, December, 1974, p. 1508.*

JEAN K. BOEK

[*We Talk, You Listen: New Tribes, New Turf*] is another product of an era in which advocates are being heard for black power, women's lib, senior power, unionization of teachers, gay lib-

eration, consumer's rights, and unification of higher education. It is also observable that some of these advocates wish their audience simply to accept their version of the situation without being given the opportunity of examining it further. In common with these, Vine Deloria, Jr. gives the reader a view of Indian problems without providing independent means of assessing this information. Hence, as he hops from one topic to the next under the rubrics of the communications gap, stereotyping, black power, and the artificial universe, among others, he provides few clues as to the basics of who, when, where and what. Because of this, it is difficult to learn much from the examples cited, or, indeed, to be very certain of the accuracy of their reporting.

These difficulties are further compounded by his occasional use of sarcasm. . . . Moreover, his polarization and simplification of events becomes perhaps more entertaining than enlightening. . . .

Even when he discusses various programs aimed to ameliorate problems, one is not told his sources of information in order to follow up on these. . . .

If a person is not bothered by the feeling that he is being toyed with and largely left in the dark, he might be able to read to the end of Chapter 11 where he is told that,

> The ultimate conclusion of American society will be that even with respect to personal safety it was much safer and more humane when Indians controlled the whole continent. The only answer will be to adopt Indian ways to survive. For the white man even to exist, he must adopt a total Indian way of life. . . .

If taken seriously, one can begin by assaying the pre-Columbian commonalities between Aztecs and Athabaskans as well as of inhabitants of the palisaded villages that lay between.

> *Jean K. Boek, "Ethnology: 'We Talk, You Listen: New Tribes, New Turf',"* in American Anthropologist *(copyright 1975 by the American Anthropological Association; reproduced by permission of the American Anthropological Association), Vol. 77, No. 1, 1975, p. 109.*

CHOICE

[*The Indian Affair* is a] short, critical essay by a noted Indian author on the despoiling and exploiting of the American Indian by individuals, federal agencies, and corporations, all aided by Christian missionaries. Yet, churches are cited for educating the Indians when no one else would, and some leading government figures are credited because of their pro-Indian efforts. Due to its brevity the work offers little in the way of detail. It should serve, however, as a good general introduction to the topic for all those who like to read about Indians. It offers little, however, to the scholar or the researcher.

> *"Social and Behavioral Sciences: 'The Indian Affair',"* in Choice *(copyright © 1975 by American Library Association), Vol. 12, No. 2, April, 1975, p. 256.*

FRANCIS PAUL PRUCHA

In his *Behind the Trail of Broken Treaties: An Indian Declaration of Independence* . . . , Deloria draws together the arguments for autonomous status for the Indians. It is not an objective account, for Deloria is clearly promoting a cause. The book, too, has a good many factual errors, and it is frequently inconsistent in what it proposes. The author, moreover, has a hard time deciding just what status he is advocating for the Indians. Is it to be "international status," "quasi-protectorate status," "contractual sovereignty" or "a new treaty relationship"? Nor can he assert that he speaks for all the Indians. Yet the message that comes through despite these faults is an extremely important one. No one can read this book and continue to think complacently that the Indians' cries for justice and compensation are only a passing irritant for white America, which will soon quiet down and go away. Whoever is concerned about Indian affairs today must read books like this to get a feeling of what the agitation is all about. (p. 457)

> *Francis Paul Prucha, "The Land Was Theirs," in* America (© America Press, 1976; all rights reserved), Vol. 134, No. 20, May 22, 1976, pp. 456-57.*

FRANCES SVENSSON

[In *Behind the Trail of Broken Treaties* Deloria argues that] Indian tribes are, or should be under treaty law, semi-autonomous and self-determining communities. . . .

The usual claim of "pragmatists" in Indian policy today is that it is too late to redress the grievances of the past. Indians are too few, too politically and economically impotent, too little endowed with the capacity for self-improvement. Deloria chooses to counter these arguments with a comparative study of the political, economic, and educational profiles of various independent and semi-independent states recognized internationally. (p. 1306)

The argument, of course, is that "contract sovereignty" is akin to "protectorate" status, which has "a long history of acceptance in international diplomatic practice, even though at times the states in question have had difficulty maintaining their independence." . . . Such recognition would "clarify the status of Indian tribes and eliminate the inconsistencies that are presently found in the federal relationship with Indians." . . . Deloria ends the book by outlining steps to accomplish this reworking of the federal principle, based on negotiation between the tribes and the federal government.

The idealism in this idea," Deloria acknowledges, "is obvious." . . . So perhaps are some of the flaws. Legal arguments about Indian sovereignty are controversial; the international parallels shaky. The mysteries of independence and dependence often seem to defy rational analysis. Most serious is the absence of a thorough-going discussion of the dynamics of an American politics which would permit so drastic a re-structuring of political reality on behalf of Indians. Deloria raises far more

questions than he answers. But they are provocative questions, reaching beyond the Indian case. (p. 1307)

> *Frances Svensson, "Book Reviews and Essays: 'Behind the Trail of Broken Treaties'," in* The American Political Science Review (copyright, 1976, by The American Political Science Association), Vol. 70, No. 4, December, 1976, pp. 1306-07.

MARILY RICHARDS

[Deloria fills a gap with *Indians of the Pacific Northwest*] by describing the impact of rapid white settlement on the Puget Sound and Washington Coast tribes, which are often neglected in history books in favor of the potlatch and totem pole tribes farther north. The chapters which relate—in exhaustive detail—the long uphill battle waged to retain treaty-guaranteed fishing rights and maintain tribal identity may cause reader interest to lag. However, Deloria has a keen understanding of Indian rights and often enlivens his narrative with fascinating information such as the account of how the Lummis built an ultramodern aquaculture project capable of producing 100 million oysters a year in the traditional style of the cedar longhouse.

> *Marily Richards, "'Indians of the Pacific Northwest'," in* School Library Journal (reprinted from the April, 1977 issue of School Library Journal, published by R. R. Bowker Co./ A Xerox Corporation; copyright © 1977), Vol. 23, No. 8, April, 1977, p. 76.

LINDA MORGAN RUBENS

In what is essentially a legal and political history [*Indians of the Pacific Northwest: From the Coming of the White Man to the Present Day*], Deloria introduces the tribes of the Puget Sound region with an eye toward their historic and current victimization and their efforts at fighting back. He makes known the complex, fish-based economy that operated before the coming of the white man. . . . Deloria calls close attention to a series of treaties forged in the mid-19th century when Washington became a U.S. territory. These treaties have been pivotal in present-day battles over Indian fishing rights. The state of Washington and the U.S. Department of the Interior come in for heavy criticism; the author, who himself has worked on behalf of the tribes, pulls out statistics and arguments that soundly dispute sportsmen's and states' contentions that the Indians are ruining the region's fishing. . . . A feisty, forthright account; sympathetic, thorough, and never dull.

> *Linda Morgan Rubens, "Children's Books: 'Indians of the Pacific Northwest: From the Coming of the White Man to the Present Day'," in* Booklist (reprinted by permission of the American Library Association; copyright © 1977 by the American Library Association), Vol. 74, No. 1, September 1, 1977, p. 38.

James D(ouglas) Forman

1932-

American young adult novelist and nonfiction writer.

Forman is often concerned with social issues in his young adult fiction; racism, ecology, and war are among the subjects he has explored. Forman is considered one of the major war novelists writing today for his uncompromising presentation of the realities of war. Using present and past conflicts in Germany, Greece, Ireland, and the Middle East, he impresses upon his readers the futility of war. Forman's most successful works realistically examine the reactions of people caught up in the death and destruction of war, focusing especially on young adults who are forced into maturity by events beyond their control. Although his young heroes and heroines feel horror, disgust, and fear, they act with unfaltering strength and honor. Loyalty, courage, and the value of friendship and human life are important elements in Forman's studies of the stresses of war.

Forman's highly-acclaimed novel *Ceremony of Innocence* deals with the conflict between state and individual—whether or not to fight for one's convictions in opposition to government. Based on actual events, *Ceremony of Innocence* is the story of a brother and sister who are executed for distributing subversive pamphlets in World War II Germany. Praised as juvenile fiction at its best, the novel sensitively and honestly portrays the protagonists's dilemma. The question of human rights is considered in a different light in *Song of Jubilee*. Although this novel is similar in many respects to William Styron's *The Confessions of Nat Turner*, the differences are striking. Whereas Styron's hero is illiterate and rebellious, Forman's black protagonist is literate but seems afraid of freedom and decides to remain with his master. While some critics are disturbed by Forman's characterizations, others feel he successfully portrays the demoralizing effects of slavery on both blacks and whites.

Forman is also a practicing attorney and has written several books outlining the history and development of various political systems, including Nazism, anarchism, and communism. Forman concentrates on the relationship between government and the people, relating his material in easily understandable prose. These books are generally well received as excellent introductions for adolescent readers. Nonetheless, Forman's reputation as a writer rests on his young adult fiction and the values he stresses in these works. (See also *Contemporary Authors*, Vols. 9-12, rev. ed.)

MARGARET SHERWOOD LIBBY

One of the most vivid and moving of recent books, ["**The Skies of Crete**"] has as its theme the futility of war. . . .

Every element in the book rings true: the Cretans' picture of their long, heroic and colorful history; their passionate love of their island; the bravery, desperation and bewilderment they felt in the face of mechanized warfare and mass destruction, and the fumbling attempts of each individual to come to terms with the irrational evil that faced him.

Courtesy Charles Scribner's Sons

Margaret Sherwood Libby, "'The Skies of Crete'," in Book Week—New York Herald Tribune *(© 1963, The Washington Post), November 10, 1963, p. 5.*

MADELEINE L'ENGLE

In telling this story of Penelope Metaxas and the Nazi landing on Crete, James Forman has neither skimped nor evaded. War inevitably poses moral and ethical problems, and Penelope has to learn to face them squarely. . . .

Mr. Forman has given a fine blend of universal and particular [in "**The Skies of Crete**"]: the story is of 20th-century young people encountering Nazi brutality; it might well have been about young Minoans defending Crete against the Greeks. This sense of the past is always with us. . . . Penelope is every vital, flowering young girl, but the ancient customs and philosophy of Crete have fashioned her into the particular modern girl that she is. This is an unusually challenging and beautiful book. . . .

Madeleine L'Engle, "Teen-Age Fiction: 'The Skies of Crete'," in The New York Times Book Review

(© 1963 by The New York Times Company; reprinted by permission), November 10, 1963, p. 12.

EDMUND FULLER

"Ring the Judas Bell" is superior fiction. It has more depth, bite and stark realism than most of what is written for young readers. . . . Greatly different though the books are, it has something in common with Nikos Kazantzakis's "The Fratricides." Both works are about the anguish of civil war in Greece, following World War II. . . .

The plot is elaborately complex and suspenseful. . . .

It is a worthwhile tale of courage, faith and patriotism with the characters well drawn and the wild Greek terrain excellently evoked.

> *Edmund Fuller, "Books for Young Readers: 'Ring the Judas Bell',"* in The New York Times Book Review *(© 1965 by The New York Times Company; reprinted by permission), April 4, 1965, p. 22.*

SANDRA SCHMIDT

Primarily, [**The Shield of Achilles**] tells a solid, exciting, decidedly untrivial story. . . . [Its] picture of island life rings true. The young heroine caught between two friends whose feelings about Cyprus and themselves have placed them in opposition faces a real choice. This is undoubtedly a message book, but the message has nothing directly to do with growing up. It deals with more basic things: good and evil, courage, loyalty, the value of friendship and of human life, the effects of war. These are lessons that are the fabric of maturity, not just the pattern it is cut from—answers that are not adult-to-teen-ager clichés, but human truths.

> *Sandra Schmidt, "Object Lessons for Intrepid Girls,"* in The Christian Science Monitor *(reprinted by permission from* The Christian Science Monitor; *© 1966 The Christian Science Publishing Society; all rights reserved), May 5, 1966, p. 8B.**

PAUL HEINS

Although the plot [of **The Shield of Achilles**] is generally developed in a straightforward manner, with Eleni occupying the center of interest, many elements are richly woven into its texture: the constant presence of the sea and of fishermen, the sea as a symbol of beauty and freedom, and sympathetic portrayals of Turkish and British characters. For thoughtful older readers, the vivid strength of the style and the Biblical, classical, and historical allusions will evoke the rich background of the island. (p. 316)

> *Paul Heins, "Stories for the Older Boys and Girls: 'The Shield of Achilles',"* in The Horn Book Magazine *(copyright © 1966 by The Horn Book, Inc., Boston), Vol. XLII, No. 3, June, 1966, pp. 315-16.*

KIRKUS SERVICE

James Forman has dealt with the conflicts within a conflict, war, in earlier titles (**The Skies of Crete, The Shield of Achilles, Ring the Judas Bell**) and this time shifts to the German Gottedammerung, 1941-1945 [in **Horses of Anger**]. . . . Even though, as could be said of his earlier books, James Forman

does not quite manage to commit his readers emotionally to the story itself, and to some extent, to its participants, he has succeeded in presenting various aspects of [Adolf Hitler's] *Mein Kampf* with a range of ideological issues. He is an extremely good writer, although one suspects at times that he is writing beyond his audience. (pp. 278-79)

> *"Older Fiction: 'Horses of Anger',"* in Kirkus Service *(copyright © 1967 Virginia Kirkus' Service, Inc.), Vol. XXXV, No. 5, March 1, 1967, pp. 278-79.*

LORE SEGAL

["**Horses of Anger**"] is an extraordinary book to have been written for the young reader. It is uncompromising in the difficulty of its vocabulary, the integrity and complexity of its historical facts, and the gruesomeness of its detail.

The hero of **"Horses of Anger"** is a German boy, Hans Amann. Hans is inducted into that pathetic army of schoolboys whose task it was to fight a war the Third Reich had lost. . . .

The virtue of this book lies in its avoidance of oversimplification, false drama, heroics. Nazism is shown, not as the massive entity of total horror which it was possible to see from the outside at the time, and which it is impossible even for the Germans to miss now, looking back—but as it came piecemeal to the Amanns, as one aspect of their many-faceted lives. The members of the family are shown to have various and changing attitudes toward Hitler. (p. 2)

This is a well-researched, well-thought-out book. Why then, is it not a good book? The answer is simple and unkind: Mr. Forman doesn't write well.

Hans's re-education is not only imperceptible in the good sense, in the sense that our changes of mind and heart come upon us while we are not aware. It is, unfortunately, also imperceptible to the reader, because Mr. Forman has not sufficiently entered his young hero's mind with *his* imagination. I have praised the book for the avoidance of false drama and must now chastise it for the absence of any drama whatsoever. It is remarkable that I laid down a book in which a war has been lost, an Uncle Konrad maimed, a battalion of children destroyed, Hans's best friend burned up and Siegfried stabbed in the back, with a sense that nothing happened. Nothing *had* happened to my emotions.

Mr. Forman's scenes have a way of missing the point they are making. I do not mean that he frequently describes a large event out of the corner of the eye of the boy skiing down a mountain, taking a bath, kidding with friends. We know that it is just so that calamities do come upon us. It is rather that the descriptions of skiing, of bathing, of kidding miss the mark. . . .

I believe that Mr. Forman knows he is not writing his scenes from life. We feel him searching for the strong, live verb and coming up with the wrong one. The houses "vomit" out their insides. Mr. Forman wants to face us with violence and disgust—but the action of exploding, collapsing houses is not that of vomit, so that instead of drawing us into the scene, the false word stops us in doubt. . . .

A scene, a book that has not been written well has, in effect, remained unwritten. It has failed to happen.

And yet, I cannot leave **"Horses of Anger"** here. I ask myself if I would give this book to teenage children of my own and I answer with a definite, if unenthusiastic, yes.

We keep discovering, with unreasonable shock, that the growing generation is totally ignorant of the times that convulsed our own lives. Their education in recent history, if it happens at all, will be piecemeal and erratic, like Hans's re-education. They will gain insights from other books, will be moved, perhaps, by what they already know in their own imaginations. I recommend that they get the complex facts from Mr. Forman's honest account. (p. 46)

> *Lore Segal, "The Education of Hans," in* The New York Times Book Review *(© 1967 by The New York Times Company; reprinted by permission), May 7, 1967, pp. 2, 46.*

JEAN C. THOMSON

Forman delivers another passionate polemic against fascism [with **The Traitors**]. . . . More competent than most war novels which concern as well the maturing of a youthful protagonist, [it] is more truly about war than anything else, as the author underscores once again the horrors he seems to understand so well. The brute force of the message has more impact than the disparate elements of the story—which show developments in Germany from the mid-1930's to 1945 and include Paul's attempts to hide a Jewish friend, his father's defiance of the Nazis, and, finally, their desperate effort with the help of a few sympathizers to aid the advancing American army. Though strong audience identification with the leading characters is generally sought in juvenile fiction, Mr. Forman's relatively anonymous characterizations seem most appropriate to this somber study of what happens when war visits men.

> *Jean C. Thomson, "Junior High Up: 'The Traitors'," in* School Library Journal, *an appendix to* Library Journal *(reprinted from the December, 1968 issue of* School Library Journal, *published by R. R. Bowker Co./A Xerox Corporation; copyright © 1968), Vol. 15, No. 4, December, 1968, p. 53.*

JEAN C. THOMSON

There is no formal exposition or denouement for this moving story of an exodus of Jews [**My Enemy, My Brother**]. . . . After settling on a kibbutz, Dan becomes a shepherd, and forms a deep friendship with an Arab shepherd, Said, even saving his life during a flash flood. The novel abruptly comes to an end after the official independence of Israel is declared, with both Dan and Said preparing for war, in opposite camps. This jarring lack of resolution can only be a deliberate, stylistic gesture, a dramatization of the still unresolved, very live Arab/Israeli conflict. Like Forman's other more highly developed novels— [**Horses of Anger** and **Ring the Judas Bell**] . . .—this is powerful prose, replete with provocative metaphors, rich imagery, and an apparent but unobtrusive message on peace and the evils of war. The author's fans will understand and accept the unfinished coda to the novel; the uninitiated may feel cheated at the lack of neat plot resolution, but the mark James Forman's story-telling leaves on them is nevertheless likely to last.

> *Jean C. Thomson, "Junior High Up: 'My Enemy, My Brother'," in* School Library Journal, *an appendix to* Library Journal *(reprinted from the May, 1969 issue of* School Library Journal, *published by R. R.*

> *Bowker Co./A Xerox Corporation; copyright © 1969), Vol. 15, No. 9, May, 1969, p. 98.*

POLLY GOODWIN

James Forman has taken a large and important theme and produced an unforgettable epic novel [**My Enemy, My Brother**]. Sound in its historical background, uncompromising in its realism, [it] gives both sides of troubled questions. . . .

Many young people today, like the troubled Dan, are asking questions and seeking answers. Must there always be war and hatred? Does one war exist only to breed another? With its strong characterizations, compelling narrative style and high degree of objectivity, **My Enemy, My Brother** offers serious young readers not only an absorbing story but much that is timely for them to ponder.

> *Polly Goodwin, "Ages 12 to 16, 1st Prize: 'My Enemy, My Brother'," in* Book World—The Washington Post *(© 1969 Postrib Corp.; reprinted by permission of* Chicago Tribune *and* The Washington Post*), May 4, 1969, p. 3.*

MITCHEL LEVITAS

Taking history for his source and a lean narrative technique for his method, James Forman has written a convincing contemporary novel ["**My Enemy, My Brother**"] that probably will better inform many of today's 16-year-olds about a slice of the recent past than miles of microfilm on spools in the school library.

As in history, the cast of principal characters is small; and, if Dan's adventures often seem melodramatic, it may be because younger readers have no way of knowing that thousands of displaced persons followed the same path as the boy, from the suddenly open gates of the concentration camp to an exhausting and perilous trek through much of Europe to the shores of British-occupied Palestine. Like his hero, Forman is no propagandist for Israel. The place is simply a refuge, a haven to which Arabs (who occupied the land for thousands of years) have some claim. Dan's closest friend—before the 1948 war divides them—is Said, an Arab shepherd boy his own age. As the novel ends, Arab and Jew are preparing for the second round of battle in 1956. At this point, however, the plot seriously falters. The focus abruptly switches to Said, now a member of the Arab Legion. Dan Baratz is left in limbo, apparently having served the author's purpose—and history's.

> *Mitchel Levitas, "For Young Readers: 'My Enemy, My Brother'," in* The New York Times Book Review *(© 1969 by The New York Times Company; reprinted by permission), May 25, 1969, p. 32.*

JANE MANTHORNE

Daniel Baratz [in **My Enemy, My Brother**] is no mewling teenager with niggling concerns, but a boy coping with questions as broad as mankind. Caught up in the immediacy and personal implications of Dan's dilemma, the reader will be certain that Daniel is over there RIGHT NOW—in the Negev or Tel Aviv or Jerusalem—still probing his conscience, still asking questions about war and killing, about Nazism and brotherhood. (p. 328)

> *Jane Manthorne, "Outlook Tower," in* The Horn Book Magazine *(copyright © 1969 by The Horn Book,*

Inc., Boston), Vol. XLV, No. 3, June, 1969, pp. 326-28.*

CONSTANTINE GEORGIOU

Considered an epic of courage and a book of high principle in today's world to inspire teenagers, *Ring the Judas Bell* by James Forman is a deeply serious story reflecting the fury, destruction, and pathos of modern-day unrest.

Charged with electricity and tenderness, this book is compelling for its tension, power, and solid grasp of character. Unbearable conflicts and tragic episodes are handled with the stark realism that goes to the heart of the issues behind the times. . . .

In developing its dominant theme, "the power of the spirit to triumph even when it seems to fail most bitterly," the story traces the plans for escape that courageous Nicholos makes with the embittered children and his antagonistic sister. Sustained only by the memories of his idealistic father and the ideals for which the bell stood, the sturdy youth manfully leads the children past every imaginable hardship to their village home. (p. 327)

Although cruel and pitiful, the story is graced with truth and tenderness because it is written with integrity and from conviction. Stark, vivid realities fill in the framework of a historical structure that is sound and compelling. And without falsifying "history's fundamental record" of events during the dark years of Greek civil war, the book gives a poignant, dramatic account of ruthlessness and despair, yet not without pointing up the optimistic theme of man's power to triumph even in the midst of chaos and failure. . . .

[*Ring the Judas Bell*] tolls still another message: it reminds young readers and the world of war's grim and savage futility. (p. 328)

> *Constantine Georgiou, "History in Children's Literature," in his* Children and Their Literature *(© 1969 by Prentice-Hall, Inc.; reprinted by permission of Prentice-Hall, Inc., Englewood Cliffs, New Jersey), Prentice-Hall, 1969, pp. 303-58.**

KIRKUS REVIEWS

[In *Ceremony of Innocence*] Hans Scholl is in a Munich prison, caught with his sister Sophie distributing the anti-Nazi pamphlets that constituted the White Rose conspiracy: will he seize a chance to save himself, can he face death? The first is historical fact . . . , the second Mr. Forman's projection, as is an indeterminable portion of the memories that flood back upon Hans—in a chronological confusion that makes the propriety of putting a known person in an unknowable moral bind academic. The moral bind is however the chief thrust, and in the scrambled course of events from Hans' childhood attraction/repulsion to the Nazis through his medical service in France and Russia . . . to the final defiant daylight distribution, it is the sole thread: early on, the mutual commitment of Hans and Sophie and light-hearted Alex looms large, subsequently confrontation with Franz Bittner (the one fictional principal), a puny youngster puffed up as a Nazi officer, dominates the narrative. But one returns always to Hans and his dilemma (a side question: why does he confide it to his Nazi interrogators?), and, relatedly, to Mr. Forman's persistent weakness, characterization. Hans has no existence apart from his fateful choice so that his eventual triumphant "I Can!" is simply a

relief and a contribution to the world-pool of courage more than a personal victory.

> *"'Ceremony of Innocence'," in* Kirkus Reviews *(copyright © 1970 The Kirkus Service, Inc.), Vol. XXXVIII, No. 15, August 1, 1970, p. 805.*

ROBERT HOOD

Intricate and brooding, [**"Ceremony of Innocence"**] is a tragic profile of young martyrs: Sophia, fearless and foolhardy, a German Joan of Arc; Hans, intense and solemn, a fatalist with Socratic fortitude. . . . They knew their work would not change the world but, as Sophia says, "It's a way of keeping the world from changing you." Dramatizing the heroic Scholls, James Forman uses flashbacks to weave in powerful episodes, battle on the Western and Russian fronts, and cameo portraits. . . . But it is the Scholls who dominate the tapestry: Sophia and Hans, naive and childlike, but poignant and transcendent in their futile search for justice in an evil environment.

> *Robert Hood, "For Young Readers: 'Ceremony of Innocence'," in* The New York Times Book Review *(© 1971 by The New York Times Company; reprinted by permission), January 10, 1971, p. 26.*

JOHN W. CONNER

Resistance to militarism has become a relatively popular theme in books for adolescent readers. However, books about current social trends tend to be expeditiously written and often fail to achieve literary merit. In the midst of this current trend, James Forman's [*Ceremony of Innocence*] stands out because it presents an actual conflict between real people who denounced or supported Nazi activities in Germany during World War II in excellent prose which succeeds in portraying human elements of conflict despite the overriding presence of a national social conflict in which the characters lived. . . .

Ceremony of Innocence is a moving testimonial to the search for truth despite consequences. Adolescent readers will easily identify with the efforts of the pamphleteers, and the honesty with which the pamphleteers see their effects on the state. James Forman portrays the German people as patient, often humble human beings who are horrified at the extent to which the powerful Nazi force controls their lives but feel powerless to upset it. Hans, Sophie, and their friend have the temerity to speak against the state and the fortitude to lose their lives fighting for freedom of thought. *Ceremony of Innocence* concerns the epitome of personal and national conflict. It is an enormous tribute to the author that his words present that conflict in realistic terms. Forman's characters are believable, his plot is carefully structured to preserve the possibility of acquittal until the very end of the novel. Tension mounts as the web of events Hans narrates exposes the pamphleteers.

Ceremony of Innocence is possibly the best adolescent book about this theme ever written.

> *John W. Conner, "Book Marks: 'Ceremony of Innocence'," in* English Journal *(copyright © 1971 by the National Council of Teachers of English; reprinted by permission of the publisher and the author), Vol. 60, No. 5, May, 1971, p. 668.*

DOROTHY M. BRODERICK

[In **"Song of Jubilee"** Forman] seems to be saying that a literate slave can remain loyal to his masters, no matter the provocation. Jim Chase is the personification of Malcolm X's "house nigger" as described in his "Message to the Grass Roots" speech. He talks a good game; but the fact is that Jim Chase is plain scared of freedom and, even while the Civil War rages around his head, he remains faithful. His constant apologies and rationalizations for remaining loyal throughout the war are sickening.

"Song of Jubilee" can only add fuel to the argument that white men cannot, indeed should not, write about black people. James Forman, a usually compelling writer, has used turgid prose to present young readers with a pompous, self-righteous, often profane slave whose actions are not justified by the author-provided motivations.

> *Dorothy M. Broderick, "Teen-age Fiction: 'Song of Jubilee'," in* The New York Times Book Review *(© 1971 by The New York Times Company; reprinted by permission), May 2, 1971, p. 18.*

SHERYL B. ANDREWS

As a picture of the "awful insanity of it all," [*Song of Jubilee*] is a success and follows the standards set up by the author's previous works which deal with wartime situations. There is a wide range of characters; the background is richly detailed; and the story is smoothly and excitingly told. However, clichés seem to creep in whenever personalities versus events are being developed. For instance, Myles never goes beyond the author's original characterization of him that he "believed in God, white motherhood, and the Virginian way of life . . ."; Jim's father is pigeonholed glibly as having "a soft humble manner, mild, hesitant little smile; it comes from spending your life as a cuspidor"; while the very peculiar relationship between Sharon McAdam, Myles' twin sister, and Jim is suggestively skirted around but never artistically realized since Sharon as a character is never fully realized herself but remains a symbol for frustrated Southern womanhood. Yet, thematically the author manages to convey the debilitating influence which the institution of slavery had on white and black alike and, using material cankered by strong emotion, produces a balanced and solid adventure story.

> *Sheryl B. Andrews, "'Song of Jubilee'," in* The Horn Book Magazine *(copyright © 1971 by The Horn Book, Inc., Boston), Vol. XLVII, No. 4, August, 1971, p. 388.*

KIRKUS REVIEWS

As [Jonathan] Swift defined it "the law is a bottomless pit," and James Forman has taken upon himself the monumental task of exploring it [in *Law and Disorder*]. His discussion embraces the worldwide development of legal systems from their beginnings in a primitive state of Hobbesian disorder to present trends in the areas of negligence, civil liberties and international law with additional chapters on the nature of punishment and suggestions for court reform. The marshalling of so many complex topics into a readable, if not always orderly, narrative is something of an achievement, and the text is liberally sprinkled with case studies and historical comparisons which bespeak wide-ranging research. Most satisfying are the capsule discussions—of the pros and cons of the jury system, of evolving definitions of insanity, of capital punishment. But in tracing broad historical trends Forman is prone to generalizations. . . . Likewise, the trend of his arguments are not always clear. . . . Forman's unifying theme is respect for the law and sanguinity about its ultimate ability to change human society for the better, and despite the fact that he occasionally risks being overwhelmed by his subject, this tone of judicious optimism plus a wealth of intriguing specifics will reward the steadfast reader.

> *"Older Non-Fiction: 'Law and Disorder'," in* Kirkus Reviews *(copyright © 1972 The Kirkus Service, Inc.), Vol. XL, No. 1, January 1, 1972, p. 10.*

KIRKUS REVIEWS

[*People of the Dream* is the story of the] tragic retreat and surrender of the Nez Perce as seen through the eyes of Chief Joseph who emerges less as a hero than as a curiously alienated observer. . . . [He] is a pessimist from the first, and the novel is permeated by a single emotion—overwhelming sadness—expressed not only in his reaction to major defeats, but in small incidents such as the graphically described killing of a grizzly bear in which the wounded animal cries like a baby before its death. The novel's considerable strength lies in its adoption of the Indian point of view; however, in the midst of Joseph's extended sufferings the narrative thread does become a bit fuzzy. This one isn't intended to be read for the battles, but for the ambiguities of Joseph's character and the epic dignity of the Indians' defeat.

> *"Older Fiction: 'People of the Dream'," in* Kirkus Reviews *(copyright © 1972 The Kirkus Service, Inc.), Vol. XL, No. 10, May 15, 1972, p. 589.*

ELBRIDGE COLBY

It is difficult to characterize ["**Code Name Valkyrie**"]. We know of course how to distinguish between history and historical fiction; the latter adds to the bare bones of recorded fact certain imagined conversations in detail, certain interpretations of public trends as they may be assumed to affect individuals, and "purple passages" which may or may not be true. But what are you going to do with biography? . . . [Many] of the multitude of details are drawn not from records, not from facts, but from the biographer's attitude toward life and the biographer's vivid and consistent imagination of the times. What then do we call such a book?

This **"Code Name Valkyrie"** raises the question. It is, after all, a summary of the life of Count Claus von Stauffenberg. . . . It apparently is based upon an adequate and somewhat considerable bibliography on the subject. It names places, people, dates, and events sufficient to create an admirable verisimilitude.

The crippled colonel, the deus ex machina of the book, is represented in all of his hostile thoughts while lying in bed, and all his family thoughts in separation from the family. The language is decorated to distinction. . . . (p. 250)

If our reader today expects a former teacher of Freshman English to condemn this book as fine "writing" he is doomed to disappointment. It may not be necessary or true to say of living quarters in bombed Berlin that the "outside needed paint, the inside needed plaster, and glass blown from the windows crunched icily underfoot." But it does make for quickened reading. Let us make an end. Let us call it biographical fiction, and recommend it for exciting and suspenseful reading, even though "how it comes out" is already known. (pp. 250-51)

Elbridge Colby, "Nonfiction: 'Code Name Valkyrie'," in Best Sellers (copyright 1973, by the University of Scranton), Vol. 33, No. 11, September 1, 1973, pp. 250-51.

THE BOOKLIST

[*Code Name Valkyrie*] is given impact, immediacy, and sustained suspense through the author's effective novelistic style of writing. Opening with von Stauffenberg gaining consciousness after being severely wounded the narrative reviews his past, including his growing disillusionment with Hitler, through his reveries while recovering his strength and goes on to portray successfully his emotions and dedication to the necessity for Hitler's death during the conspiracy and actual assassination attempt. The treatment also gives a discerning portrayal of the ambivalent feelings of many Germans toward their Fuehrer and of a crumbling Reich under Allied attack.

"'Code Name Valkyrie'," in The Booklist (reprinted by permission of the American Library Association; copyright © 1973 by the American Library Association), Vol. 70, No. 5, November 1, 1973, p. 286.

KIRKUS REVIEWS

Forman merges two historical Yellow Birds [in *The Life and Death of Yellow Bird*]—one the son of Custer and a captive Indian princess, the other a medicine man follower of the Ghost Dance religion which precipitated the massacre at Wounded Knee. . . . Through Yellow Bird's eyes, the figures of Crazy Horse, Sitting Bull and others take on truly heroic proportions and his dreams invest the people's last stand with the grandeur of epic tragedy. This must be balanced against the novel's somewhat excessive self-importance, of which Yellow Bird's symbolic parentage is the best example: he is not just half white, but the son of General Custer himself; yet the significance of this remains ambiguous. Though more ambitious this is somehow less moving than Forman's more modest, gentle *People of the Dream*. While imposing on its own terms, *The Life and Death of Yellow Bird* is so starkly one-dimensional that one prefers to admire it from a distance.

"Young Adult Fiction: 'The Life and Death of Yellow Bird'," in Kirkus Reviews (copyright © 1973 The Kirkus Service, Inc.), Vol. XVI, No. 22, November 15, 1973, p. 1272.

KIRKUS REVIEWS

Forman's rigorous definition of fascism [in *Fascism: The Meaning and Experience of Reactionary Revolution*] requires the confluence of a number of factors—fear of communism, state dominated capitalism, mass support for a charismatic leader, and national chauvinism with ultimate extraterritorial goals—that occurred only in Nazi Germany and Mussolini's Italy. After a brief history of these two states, Forman compares them to other governments and to movements in America and elsewhere that share some fascist characteristics. The greatest shortcoming of this approach is that Forman advances his own definition without indicating where other theorists might disagree. But his comments, as well as a prefatory scenario for what a hypothetical fascist regime in the U.S. might be like,

will help students to sort out their own opinions on the differences between classical fascism and other forms of repressive or reactionary politics.

"Young Adult Non-Fiction: 'Fascism: The Meaning and Experience of Reactionary Revolution'," in Kirkus Reviews (copyright © 1974 The Kirkus Service, Inc.), Vol. XLII, No. 2, January 15, 1974, p. 63.

KIRKUS REVIEWS

Which of the following "represent" anarchism today: Ralph Nader, hippies, student activists, astrologists, Hell's Angels, citizen-action groups, Maoist youth, Black Panthers, feminists or Gay liberation groups? Well, according to Forman [in *Anarchism: Political Innocence or Social Violence*] they all do. And if you can accept that, this is an otherwise fairly serious and responsible roundup of anarchist thought and practice. Of course, Forman gives only a sketch of each notable anarchist thinker; there is only a pale reflection of Bakunin, and a tenuous analogy between existentialism and anarchism is finessed in a few short paragraphs. As a first outline of the subject, this serves some purpose by defining the perimeters of anarchist philosophy—including Tolstoy and the Christian anarchists—and relating it to the bomb-throwing activists who became the bogeymen of bourgeois society. But it might be worthwhile to read some of these works in the original before agreeing with Forman who seems to second [George Bernard] Shaw's opinion that "it (anarchism) would never do: we should get tired of it in no time." And why a basically intelligent commentator would shove the whole counterculture into the anarchist bag is simply a mystery.

"Young Adult Non-Fiction: 'Anarchism: Political Innocence or Social Violence'," in Kirkus Reviews (copyright © 1975 The Kirkus Service, Inc.), Vol. XLIII, No. 3, February 1, 1975, p. 129.

JANET G. POLACHECK

[*Anarchism*] is a competent, well-researched, and sympathetic treatment of the principles of anarchism espoused by [Jean Jacques] Rousseau, Georges Sorel, Herbert Spencer, [Leo] Tolstoi, [Henry David] Thoreau, etc. . . . A valuable historical analysis, this introduces the philosophies of numerous individuals who are not generally mentioned in books for young readers. (pp. 63-4)

Janet G. Polacheck, "'Anarchism'," in School Library Journal (reprinted from the May, 1975 issue of School Library Journal, published by R. R. Bowker Co./A Xerox Corporation; copyright © 1975), Vol. 21, No. 9, May, 1975, pp. 63-4.

KIRKUS REVIEWS

Fifteen years after Gandhi's death an international band of peace marchers follows the mystic Babu on a pilgrimage across India and eventually into the path of an advancing Chinese army in the Himalayan highlands. Two young marchers, Paul and Janaki, see the march and India's misery in terms of faith and reason respectively and Paul's persistence as he follows Babu right up to the saint's fiery self-sacrifice vindicates his belief in the need for some sort of spiritual purification just as his final decision to marry Janaki marks a creative merger of the two philosophies. With such an ambitious theme, Forman's characters carry a heavy burden, especially since India's problems are presented unsparingly. . . . Under the circumstances it's not surprising that Janaki's skeptical conclusion that India has "too many gods" should come off best. Paul on the other hand is supposed to be the son of a Nazi war criminal, but there's simply no outward indication of his German background—he reminds one, if anything, of a post-Vietnam American, and the dimensions of his inner life are similarly undefined. Purely as a first look at post-independence India *Follow the River* is of more than routine interest, and even as a novel of ideas this must rate as a good try—but more texture of place and language and richer characterization would have made Paul's unlikely quest less arid. (pp. 575-76)

> *"Young Adult Fiction: 'Follow the River','' in* Kirkus Reviews *(copyright © 1975 The Kirkus Service, Inc.), Vol. XLIII, No. 10, May 15, 1975, pp. 575-76.*

KIRKUS REVIEWS

Although Forman's tendency to let the sociologist in him eclipse the artist is more evident than ever [in *The Survivor*], the saga of the Ullman family and, especially, of David who survives Auschwitz where his twin brother dies, is grim and deeply affecting. . . . [The] psychological battle is really joined between David and Saul, as one twin's determination to live stiffens while the other becomes one of the walking dead camp inmates call Musselmen. Forman doesn't stint on the horrible details and perhaps, considering the intended audience, some narrative distancing and interpretation is essential. Nevertheless, the style of commentary . . . does work to make the Ullmans' experience more representative, and less immediate. Within the limitations of its intention—which is more to assimilate the impact of the Holocaust than to express any new insight—this is an impressive accomplishment indeed.

> *"Young Adult Fiction: 'The Survivor','' in* Kirkus Reviews *(copyright © 1976 The Kirkus Service, Inc.), Vol. XLIV, No. 8, April 15, 1976, p. 482.*

KIRKUS REVIEWS

The White Crow is no less than Adolf Hitler himself, and Forman asks us to travel inside that tortured mind from the traumatic deaths of Hitler's parents to its near breakdown in the wake of the unsuccessful beer hall coup. The characterization exerts a horrible fascination; one credits it from the outset with both psychological soundness and a ghastly particularity that goes beyond mere profile or case history. (The explanation of the origins of Hitler's anti-Semitism, largely drawn from [John] Toland's recent *Adolf Hitler,* might be debatable as fact but it fits here.) However, Forman never makes his demonic creation work for him to express any compelling viewpoint as one would expect from an adult writer of comparable talent. Indeed his terrible evocation of trench warfare—where Adolf sees gassed soldiers, "their faces swollen like bursting plums," and digs in a darkened trench through what he believes to be rotting tree roots only to find himself elbow deep in a putrid corpse—has both the intended effect of exposing the world's sickness and an unintended one of making us lose sight of Hitler's personal obsessions. Compared to the collage-like legend of *The Survivor* . . . the portrait is forcefully energized. But though the reader's curiosity may be sated, an element of irresolution (are we meant to see Hitler as an excrescence or as a fellow human being, however warped?) may also leave one vaguely confused and unsettled.

> *"Young Adult Fiction: 'The White Crow','' in* Kirkus Reviews *(copyright © 1976 The Kirkus Service, Inc.), Vol. XLIV, No. 23, December 1, 1976, p. 1268.*

MORRIS RABINOWITZ

[*The White Crow*] treats the early years of Hitler's life . . . in the swooning style of old romances, and is, like those romances, trash. Forman misses no opportunity to put in the mind of young Hitler thoughts Hitler might say later that he had when young. The insipid language needs no comment. . . . Books like these are dangerous, in that, purporting to offer a more balanced view, they succeed only in minimizing or trivializing evil. Difficult as it is to face such murderous power, these books offer an escape hatch for readers who are unwilling to face the suffering that is necessarily a part of fascist rule in general, and the Nazis in particular.

> *Morris Rabinowitz, "'The White Crow','' in* Young Adult Cooperative Book Review Group of Massachusetts, *Vol. 13, No. 4, April, 1977, p. 103.*

BOOKLIST

[*Nazism* is an] informative history of the Nazi party that demonstrates the inseparability of Hitler and the party he catapulted into power. Forman looks briefly at Hitler's early life and writings, as they influenced his later actions; examines the unique combination of social, political, and economic circumstances that spawned and perpetuated party activities until Germany's defeat in 1945; and sketches in Nazi war involvement. Although Forman is weak and sometimes contradictory in political analysis, fails to define the scope of his book and that of the Nazi party itself, and slights other party officials, he successfully captures an overall sense of the party's place in world history.

> *"Books for Young Adults: 'Nazism','' in* Booklist *(reprinted by permission of the American Library Association; copyright © 1978 by the American Library Association), Vol. 74, No. 11, February 1, 1978, p. 906.*

WALTER KRAUSE

Inflation is a short, easy-to-read book, spanning various pertinent aspects of the subject—the historical record, causes and cures, current prospects, etc. Authored by James D. Forman, who has to his credit several earlier topical books also written in highly readable style, this book seems particularly well-suited for readers wanting enlightened exposure relatively free of technical complexity. . . .

Overall, this reviewer sees some genuine strengths in this work. There is wide coverage of major subject matter, arranged in an orderly manner, and presented throughout in a clear and simple manner that should appeal especially to the non-professional reader. In the opinion of this reviewer, younger readers who haven't had formal economics courses, as well as others who may be interested but not necessarily formally trained in economics, should be able to garner considerable new understanding and insight from the experience of giving a few short hours to the reading of this timely volume.

> *Walter Krause, "Book Reviews: 'Inflation','' in* The Social Studies *(copyright © 1978 Helen Dwight Reid*

Educational Foundation), Vol. LXIX, No. 2, March-April, 1978, p. 85.

KIRKUS REVIEWS

Forman takes on the troubles in Belfast in this latest sober contemplation of collective suffering and wrong. [In *A Fine, Soft Day*] the protagonist, a young Catholic teenager named Brian O'Brien, watches helplessly as brother Conor becomes a hardened Revolutionary (or so it seems until the tragic end) and a much younger brother follows him feverishly into the streets. Grania, the strong older sister, is a flaming, marching pacifist; but Forman seems to conclude despairingly that her sort is ineffectual and the fighters hopeless madmen. Forman well conveys the terrors of living under siege. The tension in the house is of a piece with the action on the streets, and the appropriately oppressive atmosphere never lifts completely. . . . The inevitability of disaster is established at the start with a preview of the final scene, and kept in view through interspersed chapters tracing a machine gun's dirty progress around the world (from My Lai) to fulfill its "Irish destiny." The word "madness" is carved in the gun early on, and there are references elsewhere to Cain and Abel and to a legend of fairy blood, with two streams running red as both sides lose an epic battle. But all of this is a bit heavy, and though Forman's characters are varied and distinct, from the hand-wringing mother to the sinister, violently revolutionary uncle they are simplistically and sometimes insensitively typed. His argument is weakened by its one-sided deploring of Catholic violence: nowhere is the reader tempted or stirred by the patriots' passion. A grim, but distanced assessment.

> *"Older Fiction: 'A Fine, Soft Day'," in* Kirkus Reviews *(copyright © 1979 The Kirkus Service, Inc.), Vol. XLVII, No. 2, January 15, 1979, p. 70.*

PAULA TODISCO

The futility and tragedy of the conflict in Northern Ireland are eloquently expressed in this simple, direct, powerful story [*A Fine, Soft Day*]. . . . The adults that surround [Brian] are skillfully presented as a microcosm of the divergent forces that rend the city. . . . Grandfather Seamus reminisces about Ireland's past glories, and martyrs; Brian's father runs away; Mary, his mother, seeks solace in prayer. For the children life in Belfast presents fewer alternatives: Brian's older brother, influenced by Rory, becomes involved in terrorist activities while his younger brother, Kevin, wakes up in terror at night and can not remember what peace was like. Meanwhile, the reader follows the progress of a gun that will weave its way from Vietnam towards a fateful and fatal destination. The plot and subplot are joined convincingly to illustrate the uselessness of violence. Unlike many adult novels on this subject, the IRA is not romanticized, but neither is it blamed for all of Northern Ireland's troubles. Rather, a balanced treatment shows how many forces contribute to the hostile climate, and how nearly everyone loses in the wave of mindless terrorism that results. With vivid characterizations, convincing dialogue and a tightly controlled plot, this is a superior novel that should be assured a place in all young adult collections. (pp. 70-1)

> *Paula Todisco, "'A Fine, Soft Day'," in* Young Adult Cooperative Book Review Group of Massachusetts, *Vol. 5, No. 4, April, 1979, pp. 70-1.*

ROBERT UNSWORTH

Today's students will not know of Mickey Schwerner, James Chaney, and Andy Goodman, and Forman has done an especially fine job in resurrecting their memory [in *Freedom's Blood*]. (Schwerner takes on almost Gandhi-ish dimensions.) This is fiction based heavily on fact. Only the dialogue among the three young men and their murderers is fictionalized. We relive late spring in Mississippi where the only thing hotter than the weather was the hatred the KKKers felt for that "atheist," "goateed" "Jew" Schwerner and for those he represented. . . . It is believed that Chaney, a local Black youth, and Goodman, a New Yorker in Mississippi less than 24 hours, were killed simply because they were with Schwerner. There is a surprising suspense to the story though we know too well its ending. . . . Coming at a time when the fires of idealism have cooled considerably, Forman's moving recall of that summer's events commands our attention.

> *Robert Unsworth, "Book Reviews: 'Freedom's Blood'," in* School Library Journal *(reprinted from the September, 1979 issue of* School Library Journal, *published by R. R. Bowker Co./A Xerox Corporation; copyright © 1979), Vol. 26, No. 1, September, 1979, p. 156.*

BETTY S. REARDON

With a cast of cartoon characters the author insists [in *A Ballad for Hogskin Hill*] that here on the hill is love, security and music. The story moves swiftly from one contrived situation to the next. Working together to thwart the advance of strip mining, the Kentucky people moonshine, cheat on welfare, sing revival hymns and rejoice in repetitive unwed motherhood. Davey commits one large violent act against the coal company, slings his homemade banjo over his shoulder and heads for the highway. Not recommended . . . because its only strength, the humor, is achieved by stereotyped situations and characterizations. (pp. 29-30)

> *Betty S. Reardon, "Reviews: 'A Ballad for Hogskin Hill'," in* Young Adult Cooperative Book Review Group of Massachusetts, *Vol. 16, No. 2, December, 1979, pp. 29-30.*

KAREN MERGUERIAN

In recent literature, there have been many books of fiction dealing with the basic problem of a choice between traditional values and modern ways of life. There are also many books about a world of technology, sophistication, and complications of our society pushing out all that is traditional and part of a heritage.

A Ballad for Hogskin Hill is a fine addition to this category. The author, James Forman, has written many other books about crises of this century and ways of dealing with them. This particular story deals with a boy named David and his family, who are having their way of life threatened by the new strip-mining industry. The characterizations are excellent; they are enough to make the reader wish he were part of the story.

This is a good book for young adult collections because it offers a new setting and problem based on an old theme whose idea and question of traditional versus modern remains to be solved.

Karen Merguerian, "Review 2: 'A Ballad for Hog-skin Hill'," in Young Adult Cooperative Book Review Group of Massachusetts, *Vol. 16, No. 2, December, 1979, p. 30.*

LYLA HOFFMAN

[*Freedom Road,* previously titled *Freedom's Blood,*] is a "fictional reconstruction of the first weekend of that Freedom Summer" in 1964, during which three young civil rights workers were murdered by the Klan and its police allies. Because the occasion is still so vivid to anti-racists over thirty-five . . . , it is difficult to consider this as any sort of fiction. Michael Schwerner, the principal white character, is fleshed out by the author. James Chaney, the Black in the trio, is somewhat less clearly depicted. Andrew Goodman, the other white who arrived in the South one day before he was murdered, remains a shadowy, peripheral character. The story unfolds with chilling suspense—even for this reader who knew what was going to happen.

Children's books about the civil rights struggles of the sixties are indeed welcome and needed. Young people can benefit from understanding the kind of sustained efforts required to effect change. Therefore, this book is recommended, although a few points are troubling. (p. 21)

In this book, as in most others, the author's race is telegraphed without need of a jacket portrait. For instance, Forman's Introduction uses the word "Negro" interchangeably with "black," although "Negro" is not used by most Blacks today. Forman describes "Mobs, black and white . . . in a spectacle of racial violence which had been simmering for centuries." He then continues, "The black had good cause ever since he [sic] had been kidnapped from Africa and sold into bondage, the southern white since he had lost the Civil War." This equation of centuries of vicious oppression with the loss of a four-year war would hardly be a comparison offered by an Afro American writer.

At the end of this book Forman, writing about the changes which have occurred since 1964, says: "For the young of the television generation there are wider identifications. They do not want to be seen as rednecks in the space age." A Black author would not leave out the word "white" before "young," because the next sentence does not apply to Black youths. In addition, given today's headlines about the resurgence of the Klan in the South and its popularity with young whites in the North, Forman's conclusions seem unduly optimistic. (pp. 21-2)

Nevertheless, this is a good book, written to oppose racism. (p. 22)

Lyla Hoffman, "Bookshelf: 'Freedom Road'," in Interracial Books for Children Bulletin *(reprinted by permission of* Interracial Books for Children Bulletin, *1841 Broadway, New York, N.Y. 10023), Vol. 11, Nos. 3 & 4, 1980, pp. 21-2.*

KENNETH L. DONELSON and ALLEEN PACE NILSEN

Of all writers for young adults, James Forman stands out as the best war novelist. His books come closer than most to catching the misery and stink of war coupled with the pathos of real people caught up in events they cannot comprehend or manage. Perhaps most significant, Forman's novels give us heroes, believable ones, in the midst of war, acting as heroes might, unsure, frightened, bewildered, and horrified. Yet his characters have strength and nobility. They would probably deny the last adjective, but they would be wrong. *Ceremony of Innocence,* his best book, is based on an actual episode, but even had it not been factually documented, readers would have believed the events could have happened. We need to be able to think that people like Sophie and Hans Scholl, a sister and brother, had the courage in 1942 Germany to produce and disseminate leaflets attacking Nazism, no matter how sure their fate.

The Traitors takes place a few years earlier, but the story of Pastor Eichhorn and his two sons, Paul (a foster son), who is willing to fight Nazism, and Kurt, who is an ardent Nazi, is equally believable and almost as compelling. (p. 299)

Kenneth L. Donelson and Alleen Pace Nilsen, "Life Models: Of Heroes and Hopes," in their Literature for Today's Young Adults *(copyright © 1980 by Scott, Foresman and Company; reprinted by permission), Scott, Foresman, 1980, pp. 283-316.**

Larry Gelbart

1923-

American scriptwriter for radio, films, and television, playwright, producer, and director.

Gelbart is perhaps best known to a young adult audience as the creative force behind the television comedy series *M*A*S*H*, a program recognized as a classic of the medium. He is also well known for his plays, adaptations of period pieces restyled for contemporary audiences. These works are often considered more successful than the originals due to their relevance, humor, and twists of plot. Gelbart has also written scripts for such popular films as *The Wrong Box* and *Oh, God!*

Gelbart began his career at the age of sixteen as a gag writer for radio's *The Fanny Brice Show*. Turning to television, he wrote for such comedians as Bob Hope, Sid Caesar, and Art Carney; Gelbart won Emmy and Sylvania awards in 1960 for his writing on the Carney specials. His first theatrical comedy, *The Conquering Hero*, concerns a young man who is mistaken for a Marine celebrity. A slightly sarcastic look at Marine spirit, sentimentalized motherhood, and misguided war efforts, it was not critically well received. Gelbart's next play was *A Funny Thing Happened on the Way to the Forum*, which he coscripted with Burt Shrevelove. Critics hailed it as one of the most memorable musical comedies of recent years. The plot of this work is loosely based on the bawdy comedies of the ancient Roman, Plautus. *Forum* has been highly acclaimed for its entertaining combination of stock Roman characters and situations and the broad humor of American vaudeville; in 1963, Gelbart received an Antoinette Perry Award for the play. His play *Sly Fox* is adapted from Ben Jonson's Elizabethan classic *Volpone, or the Fox*. Gelbart's version is set in nineteenth-century San Francisco and deals, as Jonson's did, with the efforts of a confidence man to bilk the rich by appealing to their greed, but Gelbart emphasizes the farcical rather than the moral aspects of the situation. Although Gelbart has been attacked for dealing too lightly with the theme of the effects of lust for money, most critics feel the play's lively spirit is undeniable.

In 1971 Gelbart was asked to be chief writer for *M*A*S*H* (Mobile Army Surgical Hospital), a new television comedy about a group of surgeons behind the lines during the Korean War. Although the show got off to a slow start, it has established itself as one of television's most intelligent, humane, and innovative programs. The series attempts to show the destruction and futility of war through the responses of the members of M*A*S*H unit, many of whom try to alleviate their situation through irreverence. Popular with a wide range of viewers, *M*A*S*H* combines the assurance of strong values with dissatisfaction with outmoded American traditions, and is the first program to openly condemn war. Gelbart has been praised for the excellence of his scripts, which are felt to be both funny and affecting, and for the creativity of his technical work and direction. After five years, however, Gelbart left *M*A*S*H;* without his politically-oriented, strongly satirical scripts the show is felt to have lost some of its original edge. Gelbart was also responsible for *United States*, an experimental series which examined the subject of contemporary marriage. The program, characterized by sharp, witty dialogue and sexual

Courtesy of Larry Gelbart

frankness, was cancelled after less than one season. Despite an occasional failure, Gelbart is considered an influential figure in the entertainment industry, especially in television; his achievements here are felt to have provided enjoyable, thoughtful viewing that has brought the medium closer to reflecting real life. Gelbart received an Emmy Award in 1973 and the George Foster Peabody Award in 1975, both for *M*A*S*H*. (See also *Contemporary Authors*, Vols. 73-76.)

JOHN McCLAIN

["The Conquering Hero" is an] utterly charming, fast-moving and unpretentious musical—happily in the old tradition, and offering the rarity of a good, workable little book. . . .

Larry Gelbart has done a creditable job of adapting the story from a Preston Sturges movie. I believe it should persevere. . . .

"The Conquering Hero" is not a big one or a great one, but it gets a modest laurel wreath from this department.

*John McClain, "Poston Stars in Hit Musical," in
New York Journal-American (copyright 1961, Hearst*

Consolidated Publications, Inc.), January 17, 1961 (and reprinted in New York Theatre Critics' Reviews, *Vol. XXII, No. 2, January 23, 1961, p. 390).*

HOWARD TAUBMAN

The Preston Sturges movie, ''Hail the Conquering Hero,'' may have been fun, but the new musical based on it is a dud.

''The Conquering Hero'' . . . has the usual components of a routine assembly job. There are songs, dances, a few jokes and a lot of plot. . . .

Whatever the virtues of the Preston Sturges film script may have been, Larry Gelbart's book is weighed down with incident. It is handled conventionally. . . .

It is possible that an appealing musical could have been hammered out of the tale of the young fellow who comes home masquerading as a hero of Guadalcanal. It is even possible that something fresh and ingratiating could have been done with the business of his running for Mayor and his final public confession of fraud. But **''The Conquering Hero''** chose a heavy-handed approach most of the way—including the saccharine nobility at the end.

Howard Taubman, ''The Theatre: 'The Conquering Hero','' in The New York Times *(© 1961 by The New York Times Company; reprinted by permission), January 17, 1961 (and reprinted in* New York Theatre Critics' Reviews, *Vol. XXII, No. 2, January 23, 1961, p. 388).*

HOWARD TAUBMAN

Know what they found on the way to the forum? Burlesque, vaudeville and a cornucopia of mad, comic hokum.

The phrase for the title of the new musical comedy . . . might be, caveat emptor. **''A Funny Thing Happened on the Way to the Forum''** indeed! No one gets to the forum; no one even starts for it. And nothing really happens that isn't older than the forum, more ancient than the agora in Athens. But somehow you keep laughing as if the old sight and sound gags were as good as new.

Heed the Roman warning. Let the buyer beware if he knew burlesque and vaudeville and the old comic hokum and found nothing funny in it. For him the knockabout routines . . . will be noisy and dreary. . . .

For the rest of us who were young and risible in the days when comedians were hearty and comedy was rough and tumble and for the new generations who knew not the untamed gusto of this ancient and honorable style of fooling, it will be thumbs up for this uninhibited romp. . . .

[Burt Shevelove and Larry Gelbart's book] resorts to outrageous puns and to lines that ought to make you cringe. Like having a slave of slaves remark, ''I live to grovel.'' . . .

Say all the unkind and truthful things you wish about **''A Funny Thing.''** It's noisy, coarse, blue and obvious like the putty nose on a burlesque comedian. Resist these slickly paced old comic routines, if you can.

Howard Taubman, ''Theatre: 'A Funny Thing Happened . . .','' in The New York Times *(© 1962 by The New York Times Company; reprinted by permission), May 9, 1962 (and reprinted in* New York

Theatre Critics' Reviews, *Vol. XXIII, No. 12, May 14-21, 1962, p. 293).*

TIME

[**The Wrong Box** is a] slice of Victorian gingerbread. . . . Some of the gags crumble on impact, others are stretched out like taffy, but there is enough fun left over to leave most moviegoers happily wallowing in greed, sex, homicide, body snatching and other nefarious diversions. . . .

Larry Gelbart and Burt Shevelove . . . dress hip gags in a graceful English manner, and their wayward humor brightens train wrecks, horse-and-buggy chase scenes and a hearse-to-hearse search for missing bodies. . . . The vogue for sick screen comedy has obviously fallen into capable hands. Softened by the ruddy glow of the gaslight era, **Wrong Box** makes graveside humor a gas.

''Cinema: Grave Fun,'' in Time *(reprinted by permission from* Time, The Weekly Newsmagazine; *copyright Time Inc. 1966), Vol. 88, No. 7, August 12, 1966, p. 59.*

IVOR HOWARD

There's a lot wrong with **The Wrong Box,** and a lot that's right, too. . . .

The script by Larry Gelbart and Bert Shevelove (would that the former had labored alone) is much too smarty-pants. It begins with a wholesale bumping off, one by one, of British eccentrics, a la *Kind Hearts and Coronets,* but sans that fine film's wit. . . .

The film's climax is a chase involving horse-drawn hearses which ends with horseplay in a cemetery, which is not my idea of fun, a variety of sight gags, old and new, notwithstanding. Farce that wasn't always funny and never witty is the [film's] commodity. . . .

[Whether] the good acting in **The Wrong Box** will compensate for its unfunny farce or not depends on how magnanimous you're feeling when you see it.

Ivor Howard, ''Film Reviews: 'The Wrong Box','' in Films in Review *(copyright © 1966 by the National Board of Review in Motion Pictures, Inc.), Vol. XVII, No. 7, August-September, 1966, p. 450.*

TIME

The angle in [**Not With My Wife, You Don't!**], as it happens, is pretty obtuse: the Air Farce, according to the script [by Gelbart, Norman Panama, and Peter Barnes], is a gland-based gang of joy-stick jockeys who do almost nothing but make low-level attacks on garters of opportunity. As a result, the triangle in this picture is anything but acute. But it's cute, real cute. (p. 107)

[The film is an] airy nothing whooshing along so briskly that audiences may fail to notice how much of the ho ho is really just ho hum. (p. 108)

''Squaring the Triangle,'' in Time *(reprinted by permission from* Time, The Weekly Newsmagazine; *copyright Time Inc. 1966), Vol. 88, No. 20, November 11, 1966, pp. 107-08.*

RICHARD DAVIS

The ancient and hoary myth that the American Serviceman is somehow more virile than his Old-World counterparts: a myth which sustained Hollywood successfully during and immediately after the war years, when the implication was firmly rooted in the minds of the mass audiences that fighting with lethal weapons was rather a lark anyway, and that in any case it was only engaged in if there weren't any girls around to chase at that particular moment—this myth served to enhance the spurious glamour with which war subjects were treated. Nowadays, of course, this glamour has been replaced by cynical detachment. War is still a game, albeit a somewhat wry one. . . .

Not With My Wife You Don't . . . harks back to the 'glamour' school. (p. 31)

A reasonably good script helps the old chestnut along, and the double crosses and double-double crosses are diverting. . . . If present-day audiences tend to look for rather more cake in the cinema than of yore, bread and butter is still a staple diet. This story has been the cinema's bread and butter since Lumiere. (p. 32)

> *Richard Davis, "Reviews of New Films: 'Not with My Wife You Don't'" (© copyright Richard Davis 1967; reprinted with permission), in* Films and Filming, *Vol. 13, No. 5, February, 1967, pp. 31-2.*

CLIVE BARNES

Everyone ought to have a favorite Broadway musical. Personally my favorite for 10 years has been **"A Funny Thing Happened on the Way to the Forum."** . . .

Plautus was a disgusting old Roman playwright who specialized in writing dirty plays with an expertise that did his morals no possible credit. . . .

What the authors of **"A Funny Thing"** have done is to take a sampling of Plautus's kind of humor and link it with our contemporary sense of fun. The results are not merely hilarious, they are also immeasurably endearing.

Here in **"A Funny Thing"** the authors have caught so many of the classic comedy situations and yet given them a new freshness by making the prototype characters into song and dance men from American vaudeville. The blending works like a love potion.

> *Clive Barnes, "Stage: 'Funny Thing' Happens Again," in* The New York Times (© 1972 by The New York Times Company; reprinted by permission), *March 31, 1972, p. 13.*

JOHN J. O'CONNOR

From any angle, **"M*A*S*H"** is this season's most interesting new entry. Set in "Korea 1950, a hundred years ago," the series has been "developed for TV" by Larry Gelbart from the novel and the Robert Altman film of the same name. . . .

The series is likely to be no less controversial. On one side, some are going to note resemblances between Korea and Vietnam, and the charge will be made that the TV comedy trivializes a serious situation. On the other side, some are going to perceive that the military is portrayed as moronic, and the charge will be made that the series is subversive.

Using the premise, however, that black or absurd humor performs a legitimate function, in this case pushing personal existence to the limits of absurdity to cope with the absurdity of war, the real issue centers on the artistic persuasiveness and integrity of the TV series.

The first episode, written by Mr. Gelbart . . . , met the demands of this issue with surprising effectiveness. Brightly paced, it introduced its stable of wacky combat surgeons in a plot to raise money to send a Korean houseboy-martini mixer to medical school ("America has sent thousands of boys to Korea; the least we can do is send one Korean boy to America").

For television, the editing was refreshingly brisk and the humor unusually adult. Tomorrow evening, however, in the second episode . . . , the pacing and the comedy show distinct signs of slackening. Revolving around the routines of a Korean blackmarketeer, the story degenerates into standard situation-comedy skits.

"M*A*S*H" could be a major innovation for television. Or it could slip quietly into the category of "Hogan's Heroes."

> *John J. O'Connor, "TV: C.B.S. Still Serious about Serious Comedies," in* The New York Times (© 1972 by The New York Times Company; reprinted by permission), *September 23, 1972, p. 62.*

GERALD CLARKE

[*M*A*S*H*], which began as one of the most promising series of the new season, is now one of its biggest disappointments. . . . *M*A*S*H* started out as television's first black comedy. It is now as bleached out as *Hogan's Heroes*.

The creeping blandness was probably foreordained. Commercial television is simply not prepared to accept the savage satire of the movie original. Beyond that, no series could hope to recreate the film's peculiar tension between comedy and horror. The writers seem to have given up their initial efforts and now stand on their clichés.

> *Gerald Clarke, "Viewpoints: 'M*A*S*H'," in* Time (reprinted by permission from Time, The Weekly Newsmagazine; copyright Time Inc. 1972), *Vol. 100, No. 16, October 16, 1972, p. 95.*

CYCLOPS

"M*A*S*H" has become as necessary to my Sundays as strong coffee, strong drink and strong women. . . . [It] is a crutch for the hobbled human spirit.

There were those who predicted last fall after **"M*A*S*H"**'s television debut that the show couldn't last. How funny, after all, is wartime surgery? A onetime joke, isn't it? Perhaps in poor taste even the first time around: Korea with canned blood. And the endless hanky-panky with the nurses: now that sexism has become one of our critical categories, sex itself is suspect. Hotlips Hoolihan . . . was perceived by some of our gloomier ideologues to be an oppressed object.

Rubbish. Actually, Hotlips is one of the most sympathetic characters on the show, considerably more human, more multidimensional, than she was in the movie version of **"M*A*S*H."** She has a past and a present, and she seems to have enjoyed them both, and the writers have provided her with a fair share of one-liners, and if sex isn't healthy, let's hear it for disease. The joke—which wasn't a joke to begin with, anyway, but a manifest irony: doctors sent to a war to save lives, subversives in fatigues—has steadily gone deeper. Without ever moralizing, **"M*A*S*H"** is the most moral entertainment on commercial television. It proposes craft against butchery, humor against despair, wit as a defense mechanism against the senseless enormity of the situation. . . .

Hawkeye is to Trapper what Ping is to Pong, but we see them now no longer shadowless. They can be angry; their enthusiasms and their disgusts are fever charts. They embody the irony of the idea—to be pump hands and mechanics at a service station for human bodies—but they achieve dignity. What other defenses are there against death but pride of craft, sense of humor and healthy libido? You will reply: an enduring relationship. In war, such relationships are scarce: the closest we can come to it is fraternity. Hawkeye and Trapper exemplify fraternity. Stylized, joked-up, arbitrary as that relationship is, somehow it still works.

Two episodes of **"M*A*S*H"** seem to me particularly biting and appropriate. In one, a filmmaker visits the makeshift hospital to produce one of those strips of propagandistic uplift our armed services employ to congratulate themselves. It is the perfect combination of adman and war voyeur. Hawkeye would like the film to tell the truth and devises ways of bringing that truth into celluloid being; he should have known better. In another, the camp is invaded by an entertainment troupe—Bob Hope in drag, if that is possible—and we have the reality of the operating room rubbing against the packaged monologue, the dancing girls, the band of tootlers. Here is irony raised to its most abrasive; the mind is sore afterward. . . .

"M*A*S*H" is exceedingly funny. To be so consistently funny is the consequence of excellent acting, directing, writing.

> *Cyclops, ''Mashed Morality,'' in* Newsweek *(copyright 1973, by Newsweek, Inc.; all rights reserved; reprinted by permission), Vol. LXXXI, No. 17, April 23, 1973, p. 53.*

HORACE NEWCOMB

[One socially conscious comedy] has created a format and an attitude of its own, which moves farther along the direction pointed by the Bunkers [in "All in the Family"]. . . . [There is a family structure in **"M*A*S*H"**,] but] it is not a biological family. Rather, we have a set of characters forced into deep human relationships because they are serving in a field hospital, isolated from other groups. The central characters make their lives bearable by circumventing U.S. Army regulations. This, in itself, sets the tone of critical commentary. One of the characters portrays a pseudo-transvestite, hoping for a psychological discharge. Other characters openly engage in extramarital sex. Beneath the raucous humor lies the war in which they are directly involved, and some of the grimmest jokes take place in the operating room. . . .

[The] characters are often in anguish over their inability to heal the maimed soldiers who come into the hospital. But the war continues indefinitely. The cast of characters, then, has modified its values into an upside-down world, reminiscent of the novel *Catch-22* [by Joseph Heller]. Their humor is a means of retaining sanity in an insane world of war. The audience is caught between its laughter and its realization—gently prodded when things get too lighthearted—that the war provides the theater for the humor. Even so, the choice has been made to emphasize the comedy and to reduce the specific social com-

mentary. This show and "All in the Family" are strong indications that comedy is now the chief vehicle for social criticism on television. . . . (p. 226)

> *Horace Newcomb, in his* TV: The Most Popular Art *(copyright © 1974 by Horace Newcomb; reprinted by permission of Doubleday & Company, Inc.), Anchor Press, 1974, 272 p.**

CYCLOPS

They killed off Henry . . . the other Tuesday night on **"M*A*S*H."** . . . Henry was to have returned from Korea to the United States, to his wife and children. His plane crashed. There were no survivors. . . .

[The] end of Henry hurt. I can't recall another sit-com's solving a personnel problem in such a drastic fashion, especially when the character is dear in our affections. On the day-time detergents, to be sure, characters are always disappearing, plunging out of mind as though, stage-left, there were a revolving trapdoor; we will hear later that their subscriptions were cancelled by a car crash or encephalitis or terminal apathy, that they emigrated to Australia and were eaten by wombats.

But these are dramatized actuarial tables, not comedy programs. Nobody dies on a comedy program. And Henry was lovable. The gods with a karate chop dispatched him. Where is the soft rain, the bloody footprint on the snow, the dog on the grave, the mangy gull, June Allyson, "Little Brown Jug"? **"M*A*S*H"** resisted the sentimentalizing of Henry's demise. The sad fact was followed by snapshots of him in happier times, a koala bear in a fisherman's cap, his lures like charms on a bracelet or a halo. He was back the following week in the first of the reruns, but for a moment he was really gone. It *is* a war, we were reminded; not only strangers die in wars. And the premise of the program is reaffirmed—the mad cackling in the surgical unit is a kind of sweat to cool the absurdity, the insanity, of the situation. The situation persists. **"M*A*S*H"** is a sort of rectal thermometer applied to war. It is to "Hogan's Heroes" or "McHale's Navy" or "Mister Roberts" what Egon Schiele is to Walt Disney.

> *Cyclops, ''On Deep-sixing Sit-com Characters,'' in* The New York Times, *Section 2 (© 1975 by The New York Times Company; reprinted by permission), March 30, 1975, p. 25.**

CLIVE BARNES

Be warned. A man might die laughing at **"Sly Fox."** What Larry Gelbart once helped do for Plautus in **"A Funny Thing Happened on the Way to the Forum,"** he has now done for Ben Jonson in **"Sly Fox."** . . . Mr. Gelbart has resuscitated the great Elizabethan, modernized him, given him a new set of clothes and married him off to the old traditions of American vaudeville.

There is little point in comparing Mr. Jonson with Mr. Gelbart; the original play, "Volpone," is immeasurably the finer. But Broadway audiences will immeasurably prefer Mr. Gelbart. Also, in modern terms, Mr. Gelbart is the funnier. He is very funny, in a manner, interestingly, that is both cheap and subtle. The details of his humor are sometimes cheap and easy, but the craftsmanship of the play is subtle.

The present farce has been quite closely based on Jonson. The structure has been simplified and the ending changed and the characters have been broadened. But the theme of a confidence trickster feigning imminent death and persuading rich dupes who wish to inherit his wealth to give him opulent presents in the hope of being named his heir remains intact. So, more or less, do many of the characters. What a scheming, crafty, despicable, yet amusing crew they are! . . .

The writing has a certain ornate, deliberately distanced air, for the play is set, not all that seriously, in the San Francisco of the late 19th century. Mr. Gelbart specializes in quick puns, sharp double entendre, and unexpected inversions of clichés. Normally I do not quote a man's jokes but there are plenty enough, so let me give just as a sample of his technique—not his humor, for these have been deliberately taken as only average examples of his wit: the gallant naval officer "with decorations too many not to mention," or a gull lamenting in Fox "an attack of health."

Mr. Gelbart has set the stage, and, with a little help from his absent friend, filled it with a most astonishing collection of nearly-human frauds. Yet despite all his cleverness, even brilliance, he very much needed the assistance of his director and cast. Without them to flesh out his cartoon, some of its inherent flimsiness might be apparent. (p. 68)

We have not had many comedies on Broadway lately, and certainly few as stylish as this. Go and have a laugh; it will take your mind off whatever it needs to be taken off. (p. 69)

Clive Barnes, "Stage: 'Sly Fox', a Timeless Farce," in The New York Times *(© 1976 by The New York Times Company; reprinted by permission), December 15, 1976 (and reprinted in* New York Theatre Critics' Reviews, *Vol. XXXVII, No. 26, December 13-27, 1976, pp. 68-9).*

BRENDAN GILL

["**Sly Fox**"] is billed as an adaptation of Ben Jonson's "Volpone," but it is welcomely much more than that. The adapter, Larry Gelbart, is temperamentally closer to the Marx Brothers than he is to Jonson; his dialogue has the nervous quickness of early Groucho, with Groucho's unpredictable free-associational asides and his bent for the reasonable-outrageous. . . . Gelbart has caused the classical shapeliness of Jonson's plot to explode into harum-scarum twentieth-century show biz; anything goes. The stage becomes a minefield of gags, visual and oral, which detonate continuously and without warning. One is helpless not to laugh in the presence of so much sheer energy of tomfoolery. . . .

Brendan Gill, "The Triumph of Avarice," in The New Yorker *(© 1976 by The New Yorker Magazine, Inc.), Vol. LII, No. 45, December 27, 1976, p. 52.**

STANLEY KAUFFMANN

Some of Gelbart's dialogue [in *Sly Fox*] is good trapeze work, some of it is only moderately clever. . . .

[Most] of the time I just watched the patterns being made, pretty decently, and didn't laugh. Partly this is because Jonson's comic morality play has been thinned into farce. It just isn't a farce plot, it's the scaffolding for a savage indictment. More, farce has to be believable in its own landscape in order to be funny, and I just couldn't believe that these were the shenanigans of 19th-century San Franciscans. The whole thing smells of wrench and discomfort.

Stanley Kauffmann, "Version Territory" (reprinted by permission of Brandt & Brandt Literary Agents, Inc.; copyright © 1977 by Stanley Kauffmann), in The New Republic, *Vol. 176, No. 3, January 15, 1977, p. 24.**

RONALD GOETZ

[The] overall ambience of [*Oh, God!*] conveys a respect for God that hasn't been found in popular culture since Bill Cosby first began reporting on the construction of Noah's ark in his driveway ("Me and you, God, right?"). . . . [It is a film] that actually takes God seriously.

The film's premise is established early when Burns appears to an assistant supermarket manager, played by John Denver. The film's point of view is provided by Denver. The audience, which probably doesn't find much belief in God anywhere else—certainly not in a movie theater—is gradually invited to share with Denver his realization that God does exist. . . .

Gradually the audience is invited to consider God's basic message: love one another, and use what you already have to save the world.

The film is simplistic in the extreme, reminiscent of those movies of the 1930s that sent Mr. Deeds to town and Mr. Smith to Washington. And it concludes with a courtroom scene that could have been lifted from the trial of Santa Claus in *Miracle on 34th Street*. But in the context of a film comedy, simplicity is appropriate. The viewing experience leaves audiences with a positive feeling toward life, suggesting ("Of course it couldn't be true, but what if God did exist?") that there is a way to live above greed, avarice and cynicism.

Oh, God! is good. In fact, within its context, it's great. . . . Moviegoers will find *Oh, God!* a stimulus to ontological discussion—as well as fun.

Ronald Goetz, "'Oh, God!' Is Good," in The Christian Century *(copyright 1977 Christian Century Foundation; reprinted by permission from the November 23, 1977 issue of* The Christian Century), *Vol. XCIV, No. 38, November 23, 1977, p. 1085.*

RICHARD CORLISS

[The] dialogue in *Oh, God!* is already so low-sodium (its strongest obscenity is "crap") that it's just about the only current non-Disney film that could be shown, as is, on TV. Today's question: Why is it heading toward a $30-million domestic gross? Possible answer: Because, in some cases at least, people go to the movies to see exactly what they *can* get on TV—only more so. . . .

[The character of Jerry Landers suggests] nothing so much as the common-man hero of such Frank Capra social comedies as *Mr. Deeds Goes to Town* and *It's a Wonderful Life*. . . . *Oh, God!* is the very model of some modern minor Capracorn: from the seemingly random selection by fate (or, here, God) of an average Joe (here Jerry), to the hero's growing anger at his fellow Americans' apathy, to the ultimate, uplifting conversion of the infidels and the recognition that in each of us, no matter how laid-back or played-out, there is a capacity for Good.

Just describing this, I feel the way Dorothy Parker did about Shirley Temple: "She makes me want to fwow up." And it depresses me to think that *Oh, God!* is the work of men who were responsible for two of the funniest, and most influential, TV sit-coms: director Carl Reiner (*The Dick Van Dyke Show*) and screenwriter Larry Gelbart (*MASH*). . . . The problem with an inspirational comedy like *Oh, God!* is one inherent in any forthrightly ideological narrative: for the sake of making points, the story scores points off one-dimensional knaves and fools, instead of creating a comedy world like the Van Dyke household or the *MASH* army base in which (in Jean Renoir's famous phrase) everyone has his reasons. Granted, the ideological approach can work if the comedy is infused with the livid tinge of satire, in which case the villains often are more memorable than the passive, put-upon hero. But Reiner's and Gelbart's strength is the strength of the best liberal sit-coms: to describe, in comic terms, the passing triumphs and trials of your everyday, middle-class mensch. (p. 94)

Richard Corliss, *"Sit-Com: The Joke's on You"* (copyright © 1978 by New Times Publishing Company; reprinted by permission of the author), in New Times, Vol. 10, No. 1, January 9, 1978, pp. 94-5.*

ROGER L. HOFELDT

"**M*A*S*H**" provides excellent material for the study of television as a cultural force. . . . [No] other show has emerged to successfully imitate the "**M*A*S*H**" style. The formula combines the camaraderie of the acting company with an extremely talented team of writers, blending social comment with an inexhaustible supply of one-liners. . . . [The] formula has proven both flexible and durable. (p. 96)

[The] surface level antiwar theme may fuel the fire of those who claim that an antiestablishment tone is sweeping the airwaves. For example, inferences run through some scripts that the United States, not North Korea, is the real enemy in the war. Real, old-fashioned patriots are often portrayed as idiots. What's more, infidelity seems to run unchecked throughout the "**M*A*S*H**" unit. It would, indeed, appear that some basic principles of American citizenship are being ridiculed.

But there is a second level of conflict and commentary actively running through "**M*A*S*H**". The key to understanding this program lies in apprehending the significance of the characters. Their individual essences and interplay create the "**M*A*S*H**" message. Not surprisingly, the message comforts rather than threatens the audience.

Unquestionably, Colonel Sherman Potter is the elder statesman of the "**M*A*S*H**" unit. Surrounded by the artifacts of his long military career and prone to recollection, he is "tradition" personified. As chief arbiter of disputes and counselor for troubled souls, this surrogate father provides the moral leadership for all those around him. Justifiably proud of his accomplishments and worthy of the respect he commands, he is, nevertheless, sensitive to the "changing of the guard," and tips a sympathetic ear to the emerging generation's ideas. He is, in effect, what every American over the age of 50 is "supposed" to be.

Regarded by some to be the "hero" of "**M*A*S*H,**" "Hawkeye" Pierce takes over the counseling responsibilities when Colonel Potter isn't around. His brash, confident manner is an inspiration to the unit, but he cannot adjust to the surroundings. He is a bitter idealist, and his customary cynicism around the camp betrays his frustration. Although he realizes war is a human creation, he cannot turn his back on humanity. . . . [His] sense of duty and undying faith in the goodness of man

is really Hawkeye's outstanding trait, making him one of television's chief spokesmen for American optimism.

However, Hawkeye's idealism is quickly tempered by B. J. Hunnicut's realism. Although he too sees the insanity that surrounds them, B. J. maintains his equilibrium through roots in moral traditions. He is, for example, the devout young family man of the camp. . . . Together, B. J. and Hawkeye embody fraternity and teamwork in the face of adversity, as well as the moral conflicts suffered by all during periods of unrest and change. (pp. 96-7)

Trumpeting his family name and upper-class heritage as though they were keys to respect and special privilege, [Major Charles Emerson] Winchester is frequently rebuked by the others in the "**M*A*S*H**" unit, giving this character a historical significance. . . . America became the great "melting pot," where all men could shape their destinies, supposedly free from the shackles of a rigid social structure. As a member of America's inevitable wealthy stratum, Winchester is a victim of this ideology. Indeed, his first lesson from Colonel Potter, that "neatness don't count in meatball surgery," rings with the same conviction as the Founding Fathers' declaration that "all men are created equal." Although incongruous with the selfless aura surrounding the camp, Major Winchester is expected to contribute like all the others, and contribute he does.

In contrast to the moral and political character of the four surgeons, Radar O'Reilly personifies an institution of American society: Youth and its presumed innocence. Relying on his boyhood teddy bear for security, Radar admires the tradition and authority of Colonel Potter, while bashfully idolizing the irreverence of B. J. and Hawkeye. It's a role-model search common to all adolescents. In addition, his ability to "read minds" is a trait commonly ascribed to youth, as is his stammering shyness around women.

Another institution, religion, is embodied in Father Mulcahey. While some would criticize the "**M*A*S*H**" treatment of Mulcahey as a timid bumbler, made light of but always respected by the others, there are important reasons for such a characterization. On the one hand, religion and warfare present something of a contradiction. But on a larger level, Americans have always had a difficult time properly placing religion in their lives. . . . In trying to meet the rapidly changing needs of the population, most denominations have undergone radical secularization. Father Mulcahey's groping for a solid foothold around the hospital base reflects the real-life institution's search for a new identity.

Major Margaret Hoolihan is a natural representative for the American woman. Her struggle to balance haughty assertiveness with an unwillingness to sacrifice her femininity is a common crisis of decision facing modern women. Significantly, she is the "Chief Nurse" and *not* a surgeon. And while the doctors respect her for her expertise, *they* are still the ones who save lives. . . . The institution of American womanhood remains safe and secure.

Meanwhile, dressed in feminine splendor, Corporal Klinger assumes the role of another American tradition. This nation has long been proud of its reputation for providing a free and open forum for dissent. Klinger's perpetual transvestitism in his quest for a "section eight" discharge salutes the esprit de corps of America's historic crusaders. When organized, their "never-say-die" efforts have brought much progressive change to American society. Individually, however, as in the case of Klinger, they are rarely taken seriously. Instead, their views are simply acknowledged and they are accepted as part of the mainstream of American society—except, of course, by those outsiders who neither accept nor understand this American tradition. (pp. 97-8)

While there are those who might see Hawkeye's optimism disturbingly "liberal," it must be seen as only one aspect of the whole social structure presented by "M*A*S*H" and not as its chief element. The program does, indeed, offer a good dose of controversy, but its structure does not advocate change. Instead, the society portrayed mirrors America as it is today, or for that matter, America at any point in its history. . . .

[The **M*A*S*H** society relies] on traditional institutions and values. . . . Thus, the program suggests that its values and institutions are still viable, even in the face of ugly circumstances, wherever the "American mission" may lead. As such the show is a bulwark against change and social criticism. Although "M*A*S*H" may put America's traditions to severe test, in the end they ultimately survive. The emphasis is on stability. The tone is one of confidence.

This is certainly not to suggest that "M*A*S*H" was designed to be a propaganda vehicle, nor to recognize it as television par excellence. The dramatic sophistication of "M*A*S*H" may be applauded by those who scorn the current wave of pop comedy . . . , but the essence of the two styles is really one and the same. It is the single thread running through all continuing dramatic television series. Every series faces the task of audience reassurance by resolving issues or complications which in some way touch the lives of as many viewers as possible. These problems must be set in a framework familiar to the audience and resolved in a manner consistent with American cultural traditions. (p. 98)

By using the characters to create a replica of American society, the producers of "M*A*S*H" have discovered another format for examining issues which are relevant to a vast and highly differentiated audience. Indeed, the formula has proven to be even more flexible than the "family" structure. Where one conflict per program used to be the rule, most "M*A*S*H" episodes feature two or more storylines running simultaneously. What's more, the design virtually assures that each question will be resolved in a manner consistent with the audience's cultural heritage. With dissonance avoided, the program becomes very reassuring indeed. (p. 99)

*Roger L. Hofeldt, "Cultural Bias in 'M*A*S*H',"*
in Society *(copyright © July/August 1978 by Trans-*
action, Inc.), Vol. 15, No. 5, July-August, 1978, pp.
96-9.

PAULINE KAEL

Movie Movie is a dum-dum title for a pair of skillful parodies that were written by Larry Gelbart and Sheldon Keller under the provisional title *Double Feature*. The idea is to stir up our happy memories of early talkies—especially the Warners fight pictures and musicals, with their tenement-born heroes and heroines who conquered the big city. . . . The lines are stylized, cryptic: the dialogue of the thirties has been compacted into its essential clichés, which the characters innocently mismatch, so that the feelings they express go askew. And the way the characters say each other's names, as if to remind the person they're talking to of who he is, has a ritual quality. . . . (p. 501)

Movie Movie is almost terrific, but it's also a little flat. Some of the timing is off, and the second feature sags, but the problem goes deeper than these lapses. Watching the two linked features, we know that all our guesses about what's coming are going to be right—the authors aren't going to take the potentialities in the archetypal stories and throw a curve with them. They're going to stick to little jokes—and do exactly the same thing in both features. . . . The humor is almost all verbal, and though the fouled-up clichés are entertaining, you begin to wish that there had been a few additional gag writers brought in, to break the pattern of facetiousness and jump off from it. *Movie Movie* doesn't have the Dadaist mania that sometimes exploded in the movie satires Carol Burnett did on her show. . . . And *Movie Movie* could use some of that golden hysteria of taking the situations in old movies to a logical extreme, as Charles Ludlam does with the Ridiculous Theatrical Company, putting viewers' secret wild fantasies about the stars and the plot situations right into the story. Clearly, the moviemakers wanted to avoid sophistication, satire, and camp, and one can appreciate why. Their simple comedy-parody approach holds us for the length of *Dynamite Hands*. But *Baxter's Beauties of 1933* is so cautious that we don't feel the thirties excitement of shrill voices backstage telling the dancers to get out there faster, faster, and we don't have the elation of the final "hit," when the lovable unknowns stop the show. (p. 504)

Movie Movie is friendly and funny and enjoyable, but it also gives you a sense of the timidity of moviemaking now, and of how talented people who have been working in television, such as Larry Gelbart and Sheldon Keller, internalize the censorial pressures and restrictions. When they get a chance to work in movies, their own conventionality runs very deep. *Movie Movie* takes fewer chances than Gelbart's "M*A*S*H" series has taken. Movies were never really this tame: Burnett and Ludlam get closer to the true happy dirty madness. (p. 505)

Pauline Kael, "Taming the Movies" (originally pub-
lished in The New Yorker, *Vol. LIV, No. 42, De-*
cember 4, 1978), in her When the Lights Go Down
(copyright © 1975, 1976, 1977, 1978, 1979, 1980
by Pauline Kael; reprinted by permission of Holt,
Rinehart and Winston, Publishers), Holt, 1980, pp.
*501-06.**

ROBERT HATCH

It struck me, watching *Movie, Movie*, that a parody is rewarding roughly in proportion to the pleasure originally conveyed by the model. This film, as everyone must know by now, is a double feature such as you might have seen at any neighborhood house some forty-five years ago. The first movie, **"Dynamite Hands,"** is a sentimental prize-fight melodrama; the second, **"Baxter's Beauties of 1933,"** is a sentimental backstage musical romance. Both are only slight exaggerations of the type, the humor deriving, in part from naivete revisited, but more from a persistent resort to infelicities of dialogue that wear none too well. . . .

Larry Gelbart and Sheldon Keller wrote the screenplays. I'm sure they also laughed themselves silly as they roasted the chestnuts. I chuckled some, I confess, but it was a long two hours. Parody needs a substantial target—as, for example, Franklin Roosevelt was a sitting duck, but no one could draw a bead on Eisenhower. (p. 27)

Robert Hatch, "Films," in The Nation *(copyright*
1979 The Nation magazine, The Nation Associates,
*Inc.), Vol. 228, No. 1, January 6, 1979, pp. 27-8.**

HARRY F. WATERS

Attempting to categorize NBC's **"United States"** is like trying to imagine Ingmar Bergman's ''Scenes From a Marriage'' rewritten by Neil Simon and staged as a prime-time soap opera. Suffice it to say that this half-hour series . . . is unlike anything ever presented on TV. . . . **"United States"** sets out to examine contemporary wedlock—the state of being united—without resort to standard sitcom conventions. No audience attended the tapings, no laugh track was inserted to punch home the lines. The small screen becomes, in effect, a microscope slide on which Gelbart smears the psyches of his subjects. Their problems range from the dyslexia of a young son to a dinner party guest list, and not a single one of them gets solved in 23 minutes.

The Chapins of suburban Los Angeles are anything but a fun couple. Richard . . . is prone to windy soliloquies and, in moments of stress, a kind of paralysis by self-analysis. Libby . . . is a neurasthenic beauty with a talent for scathing [Edward] Albee-esque bitchery. Their twelve-year marriage seems like one long war of attrition. With time out for passionate sexual truces, they lacerate each other with an intensity approaching the sadistic. **"United States"** might best be described as a situation talkathon. Action is confined to her making the onion dip or his loading the dishwasher. The repartee, while uncommonly literate, drips with cloying aphorisms. (pp. 85-6)

And yet . . . Not since ''All in the Family'' has a weekly network series displayed the courage to take so many chances. Unlike the bubble-gum piffle that trivializes so much of prime time, the show deftly catches the spirit of a peculiarly upper-middle-class marital syndrome—hyperanalytical, overintellectualized and, at times, proudly neurotic. The Chapins are always refreshingly adult. Studded throughout every episode are glints of **"M*A*S*H"**-style wit. . . .

Even viewers who recognize some of themselves in the Chapins may be put off by the show's shrill, family-feud pitch and sexually frank tone. Larry Gelbart realizes all of that, but he also holds to a revolutionary conviction. ''Everyone keeps talking about the 12-year-old audience,'' he says. ''I believe there are a lot of 32- and 42-year-olds out there who are hungry for thinking and feeling, and who are willing to work with what they're watching.'' If only for the sake of encouraging experimental theater on TV, let's hope Gelbart is correct. **"United States"** may be flawed in execution, but its intentions are never less than honorable. (p. 86)

Harry F. Waters, ''The Fine Art of Connubial Blitz,'' in Newsweek *(copyright 1980, by Newsweek, Inc.; all rights reserved; reprinted by permission), Vol. XCV, No. 10, March 10, 1980, pp. 85-6.*

MARVIN KITMAN

[With] the premiere of [*United States*] . . . , it should be clear that a TV breakthrough has occurred worthy of heavy study. . . . Yet no one seems to be noticing.

On paper, it's a simple proposition. *United States* is about marriage. . . . Familiar as it may sound, though, Larry Gelbart has given us a show that violates all the rules of sitcom, a game as rigid as pinochle.

By American TV standards, Gelbart is a radical, a madman, a bomb-thrower. Instead of the usual frantic half-hour punch-punch of jokes, the scripts of *United States*, by Gelbart and Gary Markowitz, have an altogether different rhythm. The show is a comedy of observations and insights; it looks for involvement, identification *and* a laugh. There is a lot of dry material leavened by something that used to be called ''wit.'' Genuine wit coming off the screen today is like a foreign language. My ear needed tuning. *United States* is high octane stuff, very rich.

This is all the more surprising because the Gelbart name is associated with the frantic laughter of *M*A*S*H*. Yet in his new series Gelbart the *agent provocateur* has dared to turn off the laugh track. . . . Television trusts you to laugh at Laurel and Hardy, Marx Brothers or Burt Reynolds movies. But sitcoms in prime time are not allowed to go on without a running signal to inform the audience that something funny has been said. Even *M*A*S*H* has a laugh track; it always sounds as if hundreds of North Koreans have gathered in the bushes to giggle at Hawkeye and Corporal Klinger. Laugh tracks are hazardous to your health. . . .

United States obviously is trying to save lives. Still, it is unnerving to listen to a comedy without canned guffaws after being conditioned to expect such hollow heartiness. In this show you have to make up your own mind about what's funny. It's scary. . . .

Missing, too, are the trendy graphics and the introductory teases that tell you the whole story before it's acted out. Moreover, the show starts in the middle of a scene—a clever device that gives you the feeling of walking past an open window and overhearing your neighbors talking, forcing you to listen right away. (p. 21)

Most unnerving of all, however, is the fresh handling of the plot and the characters. *United States* does not have situations; there are no ''sits'' to go with the ''com.'' As a result, the dialogue is freed from serving the false master of a contrived story. The people speak their minds. Mr. and Mrs. Chapin are not silly and undignified TV folk. They're gutsy and sensitive; they don't disguise their feelings for each other. As with real people, we don't learn all about them at first glance by recognizing their type.

One of their two sons is named Dylan, not a TV name like Joey. The other has problems, and they evolve on screen. The parents do the things real parents do. The father doesn't just lather up, he actually shaves in the bathroom while the *Today* show drones along on the TV set. The couple even has sex—on one occasion before going to Uncle Charlie's funeral. It's a long way from the Bradys and the Partridges to the Chapins. Like *Mary Hartman, Mary Hartman* or the twin- or single-bed issue, *United States* will divide the nation into two camps.

Then there is the absurd title. What kind of curve ball is Gelbart throwing the American people with this double entendre on marriage? Mr. and Mrs. Nielsen won't get it, despite its brilliant subtitle, ''The State of Being United.'' They'll think it's a put-on or a documentary or, worse, a public TV show. (pp. 21-2)

Well, I love it. Of course, Kitman's law is: If a show pleases me, 99 per cent of the American people will hate it. Admittedly, *United States* is a difficult show for the usual TV audience. You know, the ''Mork and Shirley'' masses. But for people like us who are as excited by the Nielsen ratings in the papers on Wednesday as we are by the latest English soccer league scores, this is our cup of tea.

I'm not saying you will like the show right off. You may even wonder why it isn't funny. Remember this is not an average

American family; it is a California family. The alien nature of the characters is one of the show's few drawbacks. Perhaps, like the movie *10*, we have here another example of the complete breakdown in communication between New York and California.

Still, by normal TV standards *United States* is literature. (Now there's a selling word for you.) Pseudo-literature to be sure. On the other hand, could you find a comedy by [Maxim] Gorky, [Honoré de] Balzac or [Anthony] Trollope peppered with such fine slices of U.S. life as our commercials?

Any new show worth its salt must develop an audience. Offbeat comedy, especially, has to be given the opportunity to find its own voice—and viewers must be given a chance to appreciate it. Unlike movies or theater, TV shows have to grow on you, like hair on your face. Gelbart's *M*A*S*H* started out slowly, too. The audience had to adapt to its rather unlikely concept. A hospital unit with men dying from ghastly wounds as a source of situation comedy at first seemed about as funny as an open grave. But it caught on. Nowadays new and different shows are canceled before they get a chance to clear their throats.

If *United States* had been programed more daringly, it would have made more of an impact. On the opening night it should have been given an hour for two episodes, so that we could really get to know Gelbart's family. I would even have rerun the first episode as soon as it ended. Instant replay works in sports, why shouldn't it in comedy? The problem is people don't pay much attention to what's being said in comedy shows. They just monitor them while doing something else. Usually with good reason. I'm not the only viewer who has taken up crocheting and needlepoint, I assure you. . . .

If ever there was a show destined to find its audience the second time around in the summer, like *All in the Family*, it's *United States*. (p. 22)

Marvin Kitman, "'United States' Needs You," in The New Leader *(© 1980 by the American Labor Conference on International Affairs, Inc.), Vol. LXIII, No. 7, April 7, 1980, pp. 21-2.*

RICK MITZ

M*A*S*H was TV's first black sitcom. No, not like *Amos 'n' Andy* and *The Jeffersons* were black sitcoms. It was a sitcom about war. No, not like *Sergeant Bilko* and *Hogan's Heroes*. *M*A*S*H* was more than lovable lunks running around doing nutty things. This was comedy that showed war. Not like a John Wayne epic, but one of small-scale, more human dimensions. *M*A*S*H* showed the blood and violence of war without ever actually showing the blood and violence. It showed the inside and underside of battle. The loneliness, the fear, the emotional as well as physical casualties. It showed death.

And yet *M*A*S*H* was a lot of laughs.

Actually, *M*A*S*H*—maybe the most sophisticated sitcom of them all—was not a sitcom at all, but a minimovie with a laugh-track. (p. 297)

It was unusual in many ways. It took place in the early 1950s, during the Korean War—and it lasted four times as long as the Korean War. It had a daring sense of humor that took itself very seriously; and when it was serious, it always had a sense

of humor about it. And, like Silly-Putty, it could change its form. One week it was a strictly-for-laughs sitcom. The next week there was hardly any comedy at all, just the horror of trying to put back together the young men of war—and lamenting those who didn't make it to the operating room. Often, there'd be no situation at all, just vignettes (sometimes in the guise of a letter home).

Once, in a classic episode, the principals of *M*A*S*H* changed the principles of *M*A*S*H* when, "interviewed" by a US TV reporter, they talked about their fears, anger, and horror at the war (like a fifties newsreel, this episode was filmed in black and white; in fact *M*A*S*H*, which took place in the fifties, was the other side of *Happy Days*. *M*A*S*H* was Sad Days and Scary Nights). Another relic episode showed the *M*A*S*H* unit as seen—at bedside level—through the eyes of a wounded soldier whose mouth had been wired shut. Very often there would be no resolution at the end of an episode. Just as there would be no resolutions at the end of *our* episodes. And yet, no matter how it changed forms, *M*A*S*H* always managed to maintain its lightning humor, frightening reality, and enlightening insights. (pp. 297-98)

Futility and insanity were the passwords in *M*A*S*H*. A sense of humor was the survival kit. . . .

More than any other sitcom, the characters who peopled the show were people, not caricatures. . . . [They] were so real that they seemed interchangeable with the actors who portrayed them. Like its sitcom contemporaries—*Sanford and Son, Happy Days,* and [*Welcome Back*] *Kotter*—it had a proliferation of one-liners, but unlike the others, those jokes grew out of the characters' characters, and not just the networks' insistence on a laugh every twenty-eight seconds. (p. 298)

To understand the character of the show, you have to understand the characters. Alone, they were all interesting; together—interacting and reacting to one another—they were fascinating. (p. 299)

Reams, chapters, books could be written about *M*A*S*H*. But *M*A*S*H* deserves it—not because it was "the best" (others might be better), but because *M*A*S*H* helped change the way we think about America. In *M*A*S*H* the "good guys"—the superpatriots, the gung-ho war people—were often the bad guys. Even more so, no one in *M*A*S*H* was totally good or bad; it was the first sitcom to paint its characters in varying shades of grays. . . .

Most of all, though, *M*A*S*H* improved on the history of "service sitcoms," as they were called. Bilko told us that War Is Fun. Hogan went a little deeper and said that, perhaps, War Is Heck. *M*A*S*H* just came out and said it: War Is Hell.

Perhaps *M*A*S*H* melded so well because it was a contradiction of terms: war is supposed to take away lives. And here were these doctors in the middle of a deathly war—trying to save lives—which made them subversives. Which meant that we—the millions and millions of Americans tuning into *M*A*S*H* each week—were harboring war criminals in our living rooms. (p. 305)

Rick Mitz, "'M*A*S*H'," in his The Great TV Sitcom Book *(reprinted by permission of Richard Marek Publishers, a Division of the Putnam Publishing Group; copyright © 1980 by Rick Mitz), Richard Marek, 1980, pp. 297-306.*

Roderick L(angmere) Haig-Brown
1908-1976

British-born Canadian author of fiction and nonfiction for young adults and adults.

Like his father, who published a book on wildlife and fishing in 1913, Haig-Brown loved nature. It was a subject he knew thoroughly from his studies and experiences living and working in wilderness areas. At the age of seventeen, Haig-Brown emigrated from England to the Pacific Northwest, where he worked as a professional hunter, logger, trapper, and guide. In 1934 he settled at Campbell River, British Columbia and divided his time between hunting, fishing, observation of the land and its animal life, and writing. The nearly twenty-five works of fiction and nonfiction that Haig-Brown has written reflect his appreciation of the beauty of his adopted country. His nonfiction, particularly those works on angling, rivers, and fish, are considered his greatest achievements.

As a writer, Haig-Brown sought to share some of the great pleasures he had experienced in years of fishing, hunting, and observing wildlife. He was unquestionably successful; his *A River Never Sleeps* and *Return to the River* are classics of naturalist literature, unusual in their poetic descriptions. Like many of his other books, these describe nature with drama and authenticity and recreate the feelings and thoughts evoked by Haig-Brown's close contact with its beauty. While full of practical instruction and information for outdoorsmen, Haig-Brown's nonfiction is often read for its literate and inspired accounts of the calm and comfort to be found in nature.

Most of Haig-Brown's fictional heroes reflect his love and respect for the land. Themes of friendship, courage, trust, growth, integrity, and strength are explored against a wilderness setting. *Timber,* an acclaimed adult novel, is the story of the friendship of two young men who face great physical danger each day in their work as loggers. Considered sensitive and realistic, it is also a portrait of men reacting to the elemental beauties and dangers of their environment in the face of challenge and change. Haig-Brown's popular young adult novels *Starbuck Valley Winter* and *Saltwater Summer* pursue similar themes.

Haig-Brown sought to challenge his readers as well as to entertain them. His excellent critical reception is an indication that he was successful on both counts. He is acclaimed for the poetic dimension to naturalist writing and his well-constructed prose. (See also *Contemporary Authors,* Vols. 5-8, rev. ed.; obituary, Vols. 69-72, and *Something About the Author,* Vol. 12.)

THE TIMES LITERARY SUPPLEMENT

[*Pool and Rapid: The Story of a River*] is a nature-story of a decidedly original kind. By making a British Columbian river the central object of his narrative, Mr. Haig-Brown has ingeniously avoided one of the principal difficulties with which authors of this class of work have to contend. A story written round the life of an animal is almost compelled to falsify Nature to some extent by endowing the creature with a too human mentality. Personality conferred upon an inanimate object, on the other hand, is at once recognized as a harmless literary

Photograph by S. E. Read; courtesy of Valerie Haig-Brown

convention, which leaves the author free to adhere strictly to the truth in dealing with the living accessories to his picture. The story of the Tashish river begins, quite frankly, with a fascinating piece of Indian mythology to account for its creation, and the stream is everywhere treated as a human soul with a markedly feminine temperament. . . . This treatment, applied to an animal, would amount to an intolerable piece of "nature-faking," but here it is unobjectionable, since it cannot mislead. The life in the water and beside it, of the salmon, the bears, the beavers, the deers and the birds is left to be described with all the accuracy of a keen observer who knows what he is talking about and is under no temptation to distort his facts. Much of the charm of the book is due to such descriptions, though a large element of human interest is also contributed, through the introduction of the first settler and his family. These characters are perhaps somewhat idealized, but the account of their struggles is a true and vivid picture of the advance of civilization in such an environment.

On the question as to how far the interests of progress justify interference with the primitive amenities of the river and the livelihoods dependent on it the author has much to say; but he preserves so strict an impartiality that we hesitate to guess where his real sympathies lie—though he leaves the stream at least temporarily triumphant in its rebellion against control. Mr. Haig-Brown is, indeed, least successful when he abandons narrative for argument; his defence of trapping as contrasted with fur-farming will be found unconvincing even by those who are far from being extreme humanitarians. He is at his best as a descriptive writer; the culminating passage, telling of the great flood which thwarts the damming project, is particularly thrilling, but throughout the work the author contrives a happy blend of realistic observation and poetic fancy which cannot fail to have a wide appeal among the varied tastes of lovers of Nature.

> *"'Pool and Rapid'," in* The Times Literary Supplement *(© Times Newspapers Ltd. (London) 1932; reproduced from* The Times Literary Supplement *by permission), No. 1609, December 1, 1932, p. 915.*

THE TIMES LITERARY SUPPLEMENT

In his preface to **Panther** . . . Mr. Haig-Brown anticipates a possible criticism: "this story of a panther is too bloody, there is too much killing and cruelty in it." He answers that a panther is not "cruel": it kills for food or from sexual jealousy, because so to kill is the law of its being. And Mr. Haig-Brown's Ki-Yu is entirely a panther, not at all a four-legged philosopher. A more reasonable criticism is that the life story of an animal, when the author sternly resists the temptation to make the animal think and speak in human terms, is scarcely sufficient to fill a book. And a story written quite objectively can never be so enthralling as one which has in it a strong subjective element.

Perhaps, from the story-teller's point of view, it would have been wiser to establish a more definite human background. But the book undoubtedly has its fascination: it is a genuine piece of nature study based on long and accurate observation of the Vancouver Island panther (or cougar) and of its habits. . . .

Story-telling apart, Mr. Haig-Brown gives his readers much curious and interesting information about panthers' ways.

> *"Shorter Notices: 'Panther'," in* The Times Literary Supplement *(© Times Newspapers Ltd. (London) 1934; reproduced from* The Times Literary Supplement *by permission), No. 1709, November 15, 1934, p. 794.*

ELLEN LEWIS BUELL

["**Ki-Yu: A Story of Panthers,**" published in Britain as "**Panther,**"] is a superbly written biography . . . ; but it is also a story of the wild life of the northern forests told with the veracity of a man who has known this life for a long time, and who can translate the majesty as well as the cruelty of the eternal struggle for existence among animals into vivid, swinging prose. . . .

It is [the] long-drawn-out duel between man and beast which is the backbone of the narrative, and it is a fitting conclusion that neither wins. . . .

The conviction of the story is augumented by the author's objective treatment of his subject. With the woodsman's realism he wastes little space in conjecture on animal thought, but relies on his knowledge of habit and instinct to portray the panthers hunting, killing, playing or roaming in that apparently aimless wandering which has such sound instinct to guide it.

The book is, unfortunately, too long. It would have been more effective in condensed form, as much of the detail is repetitious, adding little to the original concept of the tale, so that the attention slackens at intervals. Nevertheless, it is, on the whole, a fine and vigorous story, which should appeal equally to sportsmen and older young people.

> *Ellen Lewis Buell, "The New Books for Boys and Girls: 'Ki-Yu: A Story of Panthers'," in* The New York Times Book Review *(© 1935 by The New York Times Company; reprinted by permission), February 24, 1935, p. 10.*

J. R. de la TORRE BUENO, JR.

There have been men before now who wrote of the Pacific salmon, especially of the chinooks and their amazing cycle of life. . . . R. L. Haig-Brown tells it again in "**Return to the River**"; and to this reviewer's knowledge not one of his predecessors has brought to the telling such a knowledge of the subject, so broad a vision, so fine a feeling for the mountains and waters of the Pacific Northwest, or prose of such magnificent simplicity and beauty. . . . [His] is a book practically perfect. If Henry Williamson's English counterpart, "Salar the Salmon," found its readers by thousands, Mr. Haig-Brown's audience should be counted by tens of thousands. No sportsman, no nature lover, no conservationist, no person sensitive to the grandeur and sweep of the process of living, can read this book without being profoundly moved.

It is, quite simply, the story of the life of one particular fish, a female chinook, whom the author identifies by naming her Spring. . . .

An ordinary enough story, to be sure. . . .

Yet, as Mr. Haig-Brown tells it, Spring's story is neither simple nor ordinary. There is not a single aspect of the fish's life with which he does not deal thoroughly, giving you all the details of how Spring feeds and grows and moves at each stage of her development, of the dangers she meets and how she is saved from them through a combination of luck and hair-trigger instinct; giving you a fine picture of the work of both state and Federal agencies to preserve the salmon runs. . . . Giving it to you straight and plain, using the ordinary word whenever he can, the technical word—without apology—whenever there is no substitute for it.

And beyond that, he gives you the men whose lives touch those of the fish, in a series of brief vignettes striking in their brevity, their sharpness, the fundamental justice and humanity of the author's outlook. . . . [These characters] are individuals who will command your understanding, your sympathy and your memory.

But chiefly it's the fish you will remember, and the magnificence of their struggle up the waterways to die—and, in dying, to give life to a new generation of their kind. "**Return to the River**" is, in its way, nothing less than a masterpiece; and R. L. Haig-Brown a trained ichthyologist who thinks as a scientist, feels as a humane and broad-minded man and writes like an angel.

> *J. R. de la Torre Bueno, Jr., "The Long Journey of a Chinook Salmon," in* New York Herald Tribune Books, *September 28, 1941, p. 1.*

RAYMOND R. CAMP

There is gallantry in sacrifice for an ideal. When such sacrifice is made by a reasoning human we term it heroism, but when performed by an unreasoning fish we pass it off lightly under the heading of instinct.

No one who reads Roderick L. Haig-Brown's **"Return to the River"** will deny the gallantry of the Chinook salmon. . . .

The book is much more than the mere tale of a salmon, for Mr. Haig-Brown has not neglected the dramatic values or the human equation. The contents are as far removed from scientific text as the Chinook is from the bullhead. It is enhanced by the author's ability to bring out what might well be termed the romance of the commonplace.

So pleasantly and easily does the story run, you are somewhat surprised at its conclusion to realize that you have learned quite a bit about Chinook salmon, the waters in which they live, and the men who seek them for recreation, profit or study.

There is, hidden in the story, a sharp knife for those who have gutted our natural resources for gain and who have had neither thought nor concern for the future. . . .

No one will classify as "dull" the story of Spring, the Chinook, for through the factual material there is a wide tracery of imagination. The birth, escapes, travels and ultimate death of Spring, all stressing the unity of purpose that enables the fish to return to the very pool in which it was spawned, form a narrative that is intensely interesting.

> *Raymond R. Camp, "The Gallant Life of the Chinook Salmon," in* The New York Times Book Review *(© 1941 by The New York Times Company; reprinted by permission), October 5, 1941, p. 11.*

JOSEPH HENRY JACKSON

To say that [**"Timber"**] is never dull is the sheerest understatement. **"Timber"** is as exciting as a shrewdly carpentered play. But it is much more, too. Here, set in a natural frame of overwhelming beauty, is a tale of natural men and how they react to natural stresses and strains. Mr. Haig-Brown doesn't go all Rousseau about what he is doing, no. He simply takes pains to discover the thoughts and emotions, the mechanics, so to put it, of the direct, simple man who works not merely with his hands but with all of himself, including his imagination. Having found out something of what makes such men tick, he lets them work out their own stories in a novel in which the physical setting of the forests is important to the author and the reader because it is the most important thing of all to the characters. . . .

Through the friendship of [Johnny and Slim] Mr. Haig-Brown gives his readers an extraordinarily vivid picture of the life of the logger, of how a logging camp is run, of the week-long sprees when the logger in town is expertly separated from six months' wages by men selling women and liquor, of the shifts in strain and emphasis when a logger marries, of the union organizings, the blacklist, the whole inner life of a trade about which the layman knows very little.

Along with this, Mr. Haig-Brown does something you might easily expect of him if you had read his **"Return to the River."** A naturalist of uncommon gifts for clear, strong and beautiful prose, he writes here of nature, of fishing, hunting, mountain-climbing and of a dozen associated matters, better than any one I can think of in that field today.

"Timber," however, is neither a nature novel nor a propaganda story about labor. Nor is it, in the ordinary sense, a romantic novel, though Johnny's and Julie's love story is no small part of its strength. Mr. Haig-Brown has made it all of these things and at the same time a novel of a trade so closely bound up with the earth that things happening within its scope partake of the earth's own violence and strength.

As for its regional significance, **"Timber"** has significance in this direction, too. In recent years the Pacific Northwest has been the setting for a dozen or two novels whose authors have taken pains to interpret its various aspects as well as they could and with varying success. Mr. Haig-Brown belongs high on any list of such interpreters, if not all the way at the top.

> *Joseph Henry Jackson, "Novel of the Logger's Hazardous Trade," in* New York Herald Tribune Books, *February 22, 1942, p. 2.*

MARGARET WALLACE

In part **"Timber"** is the simple, virile, roughly tender story of the friendship between . . . two young loggers—a friendship which survives, though narrowly, the strain of their attraction to the same girl . . . There is something not much short of Homeric in this chronicle of their hard and dangerous and zestful lives.

But beyond this, **"Timber"** will be remembered as a remarkable study of the logging industry, set down in full and loving detail as only a logger could have done it. One observes in this connection—and not by any means for the first time—how great an advantage it is to a novelist to know what he is talking about, and to know it from honest first-hand experience. . . .

This is what Roderick Haig-Brown does for the men who get out the giant logs from the steep forests of British Columbia. Like other writers who turn to fiction for the first time after notable success in the field of non-fiction, Mr. Haig-Brown is not at one bound so dexterous a story teller as he may well become. There are structural faults in **"Timber,"** moments when dramatic values are lost for lack of a few mechanical tricks. When it comes to description, however, he does not need to yield place to any one. His book has the veritable ring of axes and the smell of fir forests in it.

> *Margaret Wallace, "Western Loggers," in* The New York Times Book Review *(© 1942 by The New York Times Company; reprinted by permission), February 22, 1942, p. 22.*

J. R. de la TORRE BUENO, JR.

[**"A River Never Sleeps"**] is] a work of such excellence, such penetration and sureness and knowledge coupled with wisdom, that it stands very near the head of its class. Prediction may be unsafe, but it seems to me we are here dealing with a true classic, a book which will be read, and pondered over, and read again by generations of anglers to come, and always with appreciation and pleasure.

Like many books of substance, **"A River Never Sleeps"** does not fit easily into any clearly defined category. It is not a book of practical instruction, though it contains much fishing lore. It is not a series of entertaining and exciting fishing stories, though many of the incidents Mr. Haig-Brown treats have these qualities. It is not autobiography, though there is much personal history in it. It is not even a random collection of essays, though much of its content is of that character. It is something of all these, and it is something more besides—the probably unplanned self-revelation of a man who joins curiosity, keen observation and physical activity to a contemplative mind and a true, unsentimental love of nature. . . .

Each month of the year, each remembered scene and incident, suggests to him a phase in the great cycle of nature, and something, too, of the nature of man. These suggestions, rich, wide ranging, and expanded in English of precision and beauty, give **"A River Never Sleeps"** a broad and lasting worth beyond the range of all but the best anglers' writing.

Fishing, says Mr. Haig-Brown, can, if properly approached, become "the strong and sensitive pleasure of a civilized man." It is not the least virtue of this book that it demonstrates on every page the meaning and the truth of that statement.

> *J. R. de la Torre Bueno, Jr., "Angler's Year in Many Waters," in* New York Herald Tribune Weekly Book Review, *December 15, 1946, p. 4.*

ED ZERN

There is something in angling which provokes a host of its partisans and practitioners to write about it. Most of them write very badly indeed, with enthusiasm running lengths ahead of talent. Only rarely does marked literary skill combine with sound knowledge and rich experience to produce a really good angling book, but Roderick Haig-Brown's **"A River Never Sleeps"** is just that.

The author writes for his fellow-fishermen, and assumes the reader's sympathy for his piscatory approach to rivers, but there is much in this book to captivate those whose interest in nature is more sedentary. The spectacle of salmon migration, for example, loses none of its eternal and elemental excitement when seen through the eyes of a fisherman—especially when the fisherman is as competent a naturalist as Haig-Brown proved himself in his earlier book, **"Return to the River."**

Haig-Brown came to the Pacific Northwest after a youth well spent in the chalk-stream country of England, and is therefore able to juxtapose the placid, literature-laden waters of [Izaak] Walton, [Charles] Cotton & Co. and the relatively uncouth and unsung rivers of British Columbia and the Pacific Coast.

Geographically, then, this is a "sectional" book—but only in the sense that [Walton's] "The Compleat Angler" is sectional. For the author's feeling for rivers and the sport and fascination they afford is universally shared by fishermen—and if he dodges a direct grapple with the question of what makes fishermen fish, he goes far toward answering the same question obliquely, by a recital of many angling adventures—some briskly physical, some amiably contemplative, and all refreshingly free of the phony romanticism that mars so many angling volumes.

There are people in this book, as well as salmonoids and other lesser animals. But except for Major Greenhill . . . they are dim, sketchy people, chiefly useful in helping to keep their respective rivers in scale.

The author concludes with a tribute to his fellow-writers on fish and fishing in as concise and felicitous a summation of angling literature as you're ever likely to find.

> *Ed Zern, "Rivers—the Sport and Fascination They Afford," in* The New York Times Book Review *(© 1947 by The New York Times Company; reprinted by permission), February 9, 1947, p. 38.*

J. R. T. BUENO, JR.

["**The Western Angler: An Account of Pacific Salmon and Western Trout in British Columbia**"] is one of the few authentic classics of North American angling literature. . . .

Make no mistake, this is an outstanding book, worth the careful reading and prayerful consideration of every sportsman and conservationist—yes, and legislator too. . . .

Those chapters which deal with fishing techniques and methods are first-rate of their kind—succinct, informed, thoughtful and full of suggestion for the prospective angler in western waters, or indeed anywhere else. Other chapters cover the lives of these Northwestern fishes—their spawning, growth, feeding habits, and complex migratory patterns. This is natural history of the highest order, based on the author's own observations as well as the careful studies of many scientists, and set forth with luminous clarity and fascinating detail.

But perhaps the finest chapters of all are those in which Mr. Haig-Brown steps from the particular to the general, from the present to the future, to consider the ethics of fishing, its place in a workaday world, and the mutual obligation of the angler and the whole people. If sportsmen and everyone else would take these pages to heart, it would be a brighter world indeed.

> *J. R. T. Bueno, Jr., "Volumes for the Sportsman's Library: 'The Western Angler'," in* The New York Times Book Review *(© 1948 by The New York Times Company; reprinted by permission), February 8, 1948, p. 17.*

ANN SCHAKNE

Mr. Haig-Brown has written a moving and exciting novel about the majestic vastness of the Pacific Northwest and a man whose spirit was wholly given to it. . . .

["**On the Highest Hill**"] is written with resilience and strength. Mr. Haig-Brown knows and loves the mountains of Canada about which he writes and the way of a man among them, whose only need and only peace lie in their desert vastness. He details without emphasis, but with force, their wild, intrinsic beauty and the taxing skills required to cope with them. Colin is the contemporary Canadian equivalent of the mountain men whom A. B. Guthrie described so well in "The Big Sky." Like Boone Caudill he comprehends no satisfaction except in nature, and man-devised standards of behavior, emotion and conformity are beyond his understanding or achievement. . . .

Above all, he is an anachronism and when, inevitably, the world intrudes upon the mountain fastnesses he wants for himself, the end is as preordained as it is tragic. But this is tragedy in the classic sense, rising out of the very nature of the protagonist and not out of the petty, contrived strivings of our contemporary world. There is magnificence of spirit in a magnificent setting and for that spirit the reader feels pity, terror and awe, but never foolish regret.

> *Ann Schakne, "Between Two Worlds," in* The New York Times Book Review *(© 1949 by The New York Times Company; reprinted by permission), May 8, 1949, p. 5.*

BRADFORD SMITH

Colin Ensley [in **On the Highest Hill**] grew up in Canada's western lumbering country, hated conflict of any kind, was shy, withdrawn, and preferred the solitude of the mountains and forests to being with people. His teacher, young Mildred Hanson, thought him destined for greatness. . . . But all her encouragements and all Colin's travels including a trip to Europe made possible by the war failed to develop the greatness she had sensed. Colin remains shy and withdrawn, and when his beloved solitudes are destroyed by logging, he is destroyed too.

A few of the book's other folk—particularly Colin's father—come clearly into focus, but not enough to put springiness into a tale that Colin's own quietness seems to muffle.

Mr. Haig-Brown appears most inspired by the vast and un-peopled Canadian mountain country, which he evidently knows well. The reader who longs for forest solitudes, mountain climbing, and trap lines may find himself living vicariously through Colin Ensley. But Mr. Haig-Brown's skill as a story-teller is not sufficiently strong to arouse the enthusiasm of a reader, even a lover of nature, who expects more than the satisfying of such a special interest in his fiction.

The novel is competent on most counts but not exciting. Why not? I think because Mr. Haig-Brown has not clearly enough understood the central character on whom the whole book depends. We are led at the beginning to expect Colin to grow up to greatness, and we are disappointed. By the tests of our culture he fails because he fails to live with anyone or for anyone but himself. Mr. Haig-Brown seems to have notions of making Colin into a tragic character, but for tragedy one must have great aspirations, great struggles, in order that the ultimate failure may be full of meaning. Colin, despite his gentleness and his physical skill, never comes to grips with the world. His retreat is not even a retreat of one who has tasted the world's rewards and found them not worth striving for. The fixation on his mother is introduced too late and pursued too little to explain Colin and convince the reader.

It is possible that Colin's creator wanted to criticize a society in which such people as Colin must be judged failures. If so, he has failed to persuade, for Colin fails to contribute anything to society, and we have no other scale by which to measure a man's value.

Static rather than dramatic and lacking humor in either the wide or the narrow sense, **"On the Highest Hill"** is a book which will appeal primarily to readers who are already excited about lumbering, or western Canada, or living alone in virgin forest, or who find in Colin a spirit like their own.

> *Bradford Smith, "Quiet Chap," in* The Saturday Review of Literature *(copyright © 1949, copyright renewed © 1977, by* Saturday Review; *all rights reserved; reprinted by permission), Vol. XXXII, No. 22, May 28, 1949, p. 34.*

HAYDN PEARSON

By the time he has turned a dozen pages in this very pleasant and informative book [**"Fisherman's Spring"**], the reader appreciates that Roderick Haig-Brown is much more than an expert fisherman. This is a book for everyone who delights in the out-of-doors. If one happens to enjoy fishing, so much the better. . . .

"Fisherman's Spring" is rich in trout lore and fishing secrets. It is the distilled wisdom of a man who has learned to extract the essence of outdoor experiences. Mr. Haig-Brown knows the secrets of fishing and gladly shares them. Some of the chapters are minor classics: **Fishermen and Forestry, Recognizing Birds, A Boy and A Fish Pole, Northward Geese** and **Family Sortie** among others. . . .

This book is a little gem among fishing books; if there is a fisherman or nature lover in your family, this is a book for him and her. Mr. Haig-Brown writes about the fishing on the coast of British Columbia. Yet, his book is for all fishermen everywhere.

> *Haydn Pearson, "Every Day's for Fishing," in* The New York Times Book Review *(© 1951 by The New York Times Company; reprinted by permission), May 13, 1951, p. 12.*

J. R. de la TORRE BUENO

Thirty-three individual pieces make up [**"Fisherman's Spring"**], and every one of them is worth the full attention of any angler, conservationist, nature-lover, or appreciator of supple, clean writing. We find here what we have come to expect of Mr. Haig-Brown—great knowledge of angling, and of fishes; a common-sense approach to the "mysteries" of the sport; wise opinions modestly held; a deep realization of the importance of fishing to the fisherman himself, and to the whole people; and a sheaf of good stories out of his own broad experience, all built around fishing, but not all concerned with fish.

There are excellent pieces on wading, and on handling boats in fast water—how-to-do-it articles, really; a discussion of the qualities of double-taper and multiple-taper lines; an illuminating bit about the confusing multiplicity of fly patterns; articles on casting techniques, hook and leader sizes, waterside birds, the writings of Charles Cotton. . . . All through, there are incidents and anecdotes in profusion. . . . Perhaps more important than these, certainly more humanly valuable, are those essays in which Mr. Haig-Brown examines the sport of angling in relation to the nature of man, the physical world he inhabits, the society of which he is a part.

All told, this is a capital book for between-times reading; and that is exactly the purpose for which it is intended. "There is no sport better served by its literature than angling," says Mr. Haig-Brown in one of these essays. **"Fisherman's Spring"** furnishes abundant demonstration of that fact.

> *J. R. de la Torre Bueno, "Rainbow, Cutthroat, et al.," in* New York Herald Tribune Book Review, *May 20, 1951, p. 11.*

VIRGINIA KIRKUS' BOOKSHOP SERVICE

An invitation to fish the lakes and rivers of Chile and Argentina was a dream any fisherman would seize, and [in **Fisherman's Winter**] Haig-Brown converts the opportunity into a record that combines enchanting travel reading with a book on fishing that even a non-fisherman can enjoy. One gets a feel of the country and the people, particularly Chile. . . . [The] book is focussed on the fishing, and the factual data—which those who would follow in his footsteps need to know—is painlessly introduced along with personal experience. . . . While he is tactful in expressing his preference, one senses that Argentina, while it provided some superb fishing experiences, did not capture his heart as did Chile. An appendix supplies practical information on birds, trees, plants—and data on tackle—and on costs. Haig-Brown is my favorite writer on a subject on which I have no working knowledge.

'''Fisherman's Winter','' in Virginia Kirkus' Bookshop Service, Vol. XXII, No. 16, August 15, 1954, p. 568.

HAYDN S. PEARSON

["Fisherman's Winter"] is the account of a winter's fishing in Chile and Argentina and so far as I know there is no book like it. I recommend "Fisherman's Winter" without reservation to fishermen and to all readers who are interested in our neighbor countries to the south. The author does much more than describe fishing spots, equipment, hotels and travel conditions. He discusses the people, living conditions and the countryside. He evaluates social, cultural and economic conditions honestly and kindly. . . .

Mr. Haig-Brown is a true fisherman. He takes his big fish with commendable modesty and he is patiently philosophical when the big one gets away. He knows that fishing per se is just one part of the whole. . . . Only occasionally does a book of this sort come from a fisherman's pen.

> *Haydn S. Pearson, "A String of Fish," in* The New York Times Book Review *(© 1954 by The New York Times Company; reprinted by permission), October 24, 1954, p. 10.*

BILL KATZ

["Fisherman's Summer"] is the finest book of its kind to be published in many years. Fishermen, particularly devotees of the fly rod, recognize Haig-Brown as a 20th-century [Izaak] Walton—but this work proves he is more than a great authority on angling. His rich talk, quiet humor, and deep contentment, augmented by a fine literary style, deserve wider appreciation. The general reader will discover here one of the best analyses of how industry, tourism and dams change natural beauty; a chapter on Northwest explorers (many starved for lack of fishing knowledge) and much Indian lore. Practical tips on flies, rods and line for summer steelhead, cutthroats and salmon will drive any fisherman to the nearest stream. (pp. 2658-59)

> *Bill Katz, "'Fisherman's Summer'," in* Library Journal *(reprinted from* Library Journal, *September 15, 1959; published by R. R. Bowker Co. (a Xerox company); copyright © 1959 by Xerox Corporation), Vol. 84, No. 16, September 15, 1959, pp. 2658-59.*

HAYDN S. PEARSON

We land-locked lubbers should be forgiven our envious twinges when we read Roderick Haig-Brown's most recent book on fishing. As a nature writer, he is authentic; as a fisherman, he rates among the world's most capable. As a writer, his prose is lean, descriptive and always interesting. "Fisherman's Summer" will become a minor classic in its special field.

Best of all, from an ordinary fisherman's viewpoint, Roderick Haig-Brown has the faculty of talking man to man. He knows why fishing appeals to so many. . . . He has the sense of humor that a fisherman needs, for, indeed, a fisherman without it is a pitiful object. . . .

There is both a main course and dessert in "Fisherman's Summer." His arguments for better fishing, his recounting of results as dams have been built in his home river, his comments on fishing as a popular pastime, all have good meat. Dedicated

fishermen, nature lovers and conservationists will benefit from his thinking. . . .

The chapter on the Beaverskill that runs in the Catskills in New York is a classic in itself. Perhaps through this book this wonderful little river can be preserved for all time as a fisherman's paradise. Roderick Haig-Brown's gentle sermon on humor and his willingness to confer some credit on Lady Luck will be appreciated.

"Fisherman's Summer" is a book you will read and reread. . . . It is a book about fishing in the summer, but it is also the story of a man who knows that fishing is infinitely more than catching fish. And that is perhaps the only point on which all true fishermen will agree.

> *Haydn S. Pearson, "Angler's Delight," in* The New York Times Book Review *(© 1959 by The New York Times Company; reprinted by permission), September 27, 1959, p. 10.*

THE JUNIOR BOOKSHELF

[Captain of the Discovery is] a Canadian book [about] Captain George Vancouver, who discovered the coast which bears his name. It seems hard to say that this makes rather dull reading. It is certainly not the matter that is at fault, but there is some lack of spark in the telling. It may be because we never get any real picture of Vancouver himself. All the first chapters are about Captain Cook, with whom Vancouver sailed, and about Cook's voyages and tragic end. We really do not learn anything about Vancouver, who sailed as an Officer Cadet at the age of fifteen, and so far as he is concerned we are not particularly interested when he finally gets command of the "Discovery." This should be a great story and the book has many good points; it is simple and thorough . . . , the men are heroic in their endurance and enviable in their adventures, but the story comes out as a conscientious work but not as inspiring as might be expected.

> '''Captain of the Discovery','' in The Junior Bookshelf, Vol. 20, No. 4, October, 1959, p. 210.

THE JUNIOR BOOKSHELF

There is a wider tendency nowadays to take the romance out of more than one field of old-fashioned adventure. [In *The Whale People*] the author takes the old idea of fun and games among the Red Indians and transforms tradition into reality without gilding the pill in any way. Life for the Indian Peoples of the Northern Pacific coast appears as a hard business in which most of the pleasure comes from winning a living, an existence even, from the nature around them. The chief delight and ambition of Atlin, chief elect of the Hotsath tribe, is the killing, and capture of whales, and the way to success is hard and wearisome, spiritually as well as physically. One never feels really warm while reading this new book by the author of *Starbuck Valley Winter,* or really dry either. Nevertheless one thoroughly enjoys the rigours and vigour of the hunting and hardening incidents upon which the story revolves. There are many fine descriptions of fights with whales of various sizes and towards the end a human and even homely tinge to the story in the behaviour of Atlin over the wooing of a daughter of a rival chief. The total effect is at least heroic in tone if not quite epic, and a most successful study of a little known people in fictional guise.

"'The Whale People'," *in* The Junior Bookshelf, *Vol. 26, No. 5, November, 1962, p. 261.*

RUTH OSLER

In the beginning of *Silver,* his biography of an Atlantic salmon, Roderick Haig-Brown says of the Good Fisherman, "He loved salmon as some men love their wives or their books, and his whole heart was bound up in the delight of gaining knowledge of them." He might as well have been speaking of his own love of nature and the preoccupation with wild life that he has built into a literature on fishing and fishermen, life in the wilderness and wild animals. His books show by inference and direct telling the results of a long, deliberate and intelligent observation of the natural world and a deep respect for its laws and customs. Nor is this just a matter of contemplative enjoyment. He finds in the ways of wild life patterns and attitudes entirely worthy of adaptation to men, so that his books on wild life and men have a certain affinity, and in his masterpiece, *The Whale People,* the two are fused in a subject particularly sympathetic for the author, particularly compatible with his interests and beliefs.

For the subject matter of his work Haig-Brown has been able to draw often on the varied experiences of his own life. (p. 16)

From his interest in nature and his social interests have emerged six books of creative fiction for young people. . . . The books have in common the detailed development of a central character and exact and accurate background material. Themes which are the springboards of his adult novels: conservation, the encroachment of urban society on the wilderness appear only slightly, or by inference. He writes in a clear, polished prose which is often eloquent but seldom light or humorous. He is most successful where his plots develop from a natural background. It is frequently true that his peripheral characters and sub plots are below the standard of his central material. (pp. 16-17)

[His first book] is *Silver,* the biography of an Atlantic salmon from the time of its emergence from an egg until it is caught, a huge and glorious fish of sixty pounds. He interrupts the narrative from time to time to deliver small sermons on the fish and the art of fishing, and as a consequence it is far less intense than his later books. It has also a quality of light and freshness not often found in his work. . . .

Silver is an expression of Haig-Brown's intense delight in fishing. And this is a good deal more than the delight of catching a fish. It is the joy of observing the life cycle of the fish and learning his instincts and habits. This book is a detailed and sensitive reconstruction of the salmon's existence according to the laws of its kind and the exigencies of its natural surroundings. He expresses the honour and the respect of the fisherman for a formidable adversary which is later echoed and enlarged in the Indians' attitude to the whale in *The Whale People.*

In 1946 Haig-Brown produced another natural biography, *Panther,* but one of a vitally different style and character. Like *Silver* this is neither a tale of animal adventure nor an exercise in animal psychology. It is as true and accurate an account of the life cycle of a Vancouver Island panther as the author can state, and as such is a bloody, intense and disturbing *tour de force* of nature writing. . . .

The book offers a remarkable picture of life in the wilderness. More vivid than the physical descriptions are Haig-Brown's perceptions of the sensory world of the animals. And it is full of memorable scenes of wildlife. . . . (p. 17)

Principally [*Starbuck Valley Winter*] is a very full study of the development of a hardy, resourceful boy. It is also a satisfying story of action, boys learning and accomplishing. (p. 18)

The plot of [its sequel] *Saltwater Summer* is moved by a good deal of violent action. In *Mounted Police Patrol,* the most recent and most socially conscious of his adventure stories, this is also true. Its plot has elements of the stock mystery story: threats, robbery and murder. Basically, however, it is the story of the rehabilitation of a boy from a Toronto slum in a small prairie town. The results of crime both for the criminal and his victim are brought home to him through contact with the small community and he develops positive interests in the surrounding countryside. His change of outlook is influenced by a group of villains whose blackness of character almost puts them in the realm of fantasy.

It is a long stride from these books to the *Whale People,* the story of a young Indian chief's search for the whale spirit, his *tumanos.* . . . Haig-Brown has found in this material a theme to capture his imagination and fuse his interests, and he has produced a book noble in style and conception. (pp. 18-19)

The story is of the son of a great whaling chief who, when his father is killed must find his *tumanos* and lead his tribe. His training, physical and spiritual, his gradual maturing are told with a great economy of language more formal and rhythmic than Haig-Brown has used before. But then this is a book concerned with the spirit and has a theme that is at once more inspiring and more driving than those of his earlier books. Of all his material it is the most completely imagined work.

All Haig-Brown's books are the result of a thoroughness of thought and approach and a quality of imagination that is both creative and realistic. The strength of his writing is easy to underestimate. It often takes a second reading to grasp the breadth of skill, knowledge and understanding that has gone into them. (p. 19)

> *Ruth Osler, "Haig-Brown: Fisherman, Nature Lover, Author,"* in In Review: Canadian Books for Children, *Winter, 1967, pp. 16-19.*

CALLIE ISRAEL

Appearing as it did when the Canadian adventure story for boys was suffering birth-pangs [*Saltwater Summer*] was greeted enthusiastically by children and librarians. . . .

A re-reading brought a mixed reaction. The author's familiarity with the locale and his knowledge of fishing and fishermen are evident. The action is fast-paced and dramatic. However, the boys seem somewhat naive by to-day's standards. The use of such interjections as "gee" and "heck" somewhat dates the book. Some of the characters seem stereotyped and the ending is predictable. Teen-agers used to books that "tell it like it is" may find this too unreal.

> *Callie Israel, "'Saltwater Summer',"* in In Review: Canadian Books for Children, *Vol. 4, No. 2. Spring, 1970, p. 25.*

ADELE M. FASICK

Although [*Captain of the Discovery: The Story of Captain George Vancouver*] is a competent, straightforward biography which does not require significant revision, it is unfortunate that a few inexcusably patronising remarks about native peoples were not eliminated [in the revised edition]. To write as Haig-Brown does . . . , "Nearly all the natives they dealt with were natural—and highly skilful—thieves until checked," is to accept 18th century European standards without making allowance for cultural differences. And to say that a group of Indians "behaved well" because they were peaceful and traded willingly . . . is to imply that Indian behaviour can be judged by its convenience for Europeans.

Haig-Brown emphasises the careful, painstaking work of exploration which Vancouver did and the hardships he and his crew endured. Like most biographies for children, the book omits references to the less edifying aspects of Vancouver's life, notably the controversial Camelford Affair in which Vancouver was accused of having a midshipman flogged. . . .

Despite its flaws, this biography is an important one. . . .

Adele M. Fasick, "'Captain of the Discovery: The Story of Captain George Vancouver'," in In Review: Canadian Books for Children, *Vol. 8, No. 4, Autumn, 1974, p. 48.*

SHEILA EGOFF

One of the few examples in the series of the wholly unembellished biography is Roderick L. Haig-Brown's **Captain of the Discovery: The Story of Captain George Vancouver** (1956). Vancouver's voyages took him into the huts of the Hawaiian Islanders, the lodges of the West Coast Indians, and the galleys of Spanish men-of-war, and Haig-Brown takes full advantage of his opportunities for satisfying the child's natural interest in exotic settings, but never at the cost of distorting his subject. Vancouver was no swashbuckling explorer but a disciplined, skilled, conscientious navigator. Haig-Brown dares to show him as one, confident that solid achievement, however unspectacular in the accomplishment, is a theme that deserves and can hold an audience. (p. 51)

[Haig-Brown is the real heir of Ernest Thompson] Seton in the writing of the realistic animal story. . . . Completely authentic in its details of salmon life, [**Silver: The Life of an Atlantic Salmon**] is lightened by an intimate, at times almost lyrical style. Haig-Brown addresses his readers as if he were telling the story in person and is quite explicit when he is 'making things up', such as what Silver might have said or thought. Fishing skills, sportsmanship, and conservation are skilfully woven into a story. It takes a craftsman to make something as narrowly special as salmon interesting to the general reader, but Haig-Brown manages to do it.

Ki-Yu: A Story of Panthers is Seton and [Charles G.D.] Roberts brought to complete realism. Ki-Yu is by no means an attractive character. (Even the most predatory animals of the earlier writers are appealing.) The wilderness is presented in all its starkness and there is little to show 'the kindred of the wild'. Ki-Yu is perhaps more a documentary of wild-animal life than a sympathetic animal biography. Haig-Brown simply prefers to let the facts speak for themselves. The drama of the story appears in the deliberate stalking of Ki-Yu by a professional panther hunter; when his dogs are killed by the panther, the sympathy is with the dogs and the man rather than with the hunted animal. Although man plays no more important a role here than in Seton, we are made to feel much more the depredations of wild animals upon domestic animal life.

Haig-Brown, like Roberts and Seton, also shows the inevitableness of death in the wilderness. (pp. 118-19)

Ki-Yu is over-long and sometimes wearying, particularly in the description of the constant killing and feeding of the wild animals. Even so, all the details in the story are so realistically presented that they have a considerable holding power. Haig-Brown convinces by realism, not by invention. (p. 119)

Basically, Mr Haig-Brown does not care to engage our sympathies for Ki-Yu; he is concerned to present life in the wilderness—in this case Vancouver Island—and in carrying the realistic animal story to its logical conclusion he has perhaps gained in accuracy and restraint, but at the expense of dramatic emotion. (p. 120)

Starbuck Valley Winter (1943) and **Saltwater Summer** (1948) were obviously inspired by tremendous feeling for particular places—British Columbia's range lands and the seas that wash its coastline. However, there is more than feeling in these books. Haig-Brown has looked at what he describes and so feels with his hero not only a 'sudden pride' in his surroundings but also a 'sense of ownership through knowledge'. He invests his readers with this sense of ownership and can thus impart to them, without ever veering into pedagogy, many unfamiliar activities, like trolling, seining, skinning a buck, making a water-wheel, canoeing up a river, setting traps. He has a Homeric appreciation of the well-done task, the well-made artifact, and an observant eye that is never sentimental. He more than sees: he understands and feels as well. 'He looked at everything, trying to use it and make it his own'—this describes Haig-Brown as well as his hero. Such an intimacy between the hero and what he makes or creates enables Haig-Brown to escape the common pitfall of obtrusive information and explanation. . . . Haig-Brown is always sure-footed in traversing detail. **Starbuck Valley Winter** and **Saltwater Summer** are *real* stories as [Johannes Rhyss's] *Swiss Family Robinson* and [Robert Louis Stevenson's] *Kidnapped* are real.

Haig-Brown's honesty of description is reflected in his plots, which have drama but no impossible deeds. In **Starbuck Valley Winter,** Don's initial decision to save his friend's life is grandly heroic, but the actual journey he undertakes turns out to be almost devoid of sensational incident. The plots of both books are extremely simple but have implicit moral dimensions. In **Starbuck Valley Winter,** Don Morgan and his friend spend a winter trapping in the woods; in **Saltwater Summer** they spend the summer in commercial fishing. Both are basically chancy enterprises and it is the natural hazards, the inherent violence of outdoor life rather than artificial 'adventures', that give the tales their impact. The mistakes made, while adding to the suspense, are those that would plausibly be made by anyone of youth and inexperience.

Don Morgan's personality is as believable as his experiences. Haig-Brown presents him as a rather complex person, by no means as straightforwardly 'nice' as his great friend Tubby Miller. He is more moody, more ambitious, and impulsive enough to break the law on one occasion. His path to heroism is a process of development, not a melodramatic change of heart. Perhaps even more remarkably, Haig-Brown knows how to handle adults. In most Canadian children's books the world of youth is quite divorced from the world of adults. The latter are shadowy figures who are almost nameless: simply the Father, the Mother, the Boss, etc. Almost never do we find grownups as vivid and as memorable as [Stevenson's] Alan Breck or Long John Silver. Haig-Brown's adults do not catch the imagination as do Stevenson's great creations, but at least they exist. They have mixed motives, complexity, reality. We understand how they have come to live in isolation on range or coast and what their environment has done to them. (pp. 165-67)

Sheila Egoff, in her The Republic of Childhood: A Critical Guide to Canadian Children's Literature in English *(© Oxford University Press, Canadian Branch, 1975; reprinted by permission), second edition, Oxford University Press, Canadian Branch, 1975, 287 p.**

W. J. KEITH

Although I would not wish to imply that Haig-Brown is anything but Canadian in his mature writings, it is important to lay some emphasis on his connections with the essentially English rural tradition. . . .

One gets the impression when reading through Haig-Brown's work that he has been particularly conscious of a responsibility to justify his change of allegiance by a thorough mastery of all the historical, zoological and sociological aspects of the province in which he lives. (p. 9)

The image of exploration and discovery may be seen as a unifying thread that links his numerous writings. In his historical books for schoolchildren—*Captain of the Discovery* (1956), *The Farthest Shores* (1960) and *Fur and Gold* (1962)—he has brought to life the exploits of the men who first explored both the coast and the interior (Bering, the Spaniards, Vancouver, Mackenzie, Fraser, Thompson, etc.) and in the last-named the administrators and politicians (notably James Douglas) who consolidated the achievements of the explorers and initiated the subsequent development of British Columbia. In *Silver* and *Return to the River* (1941), at first sight books of a very different kind, a comparable interest is to be found, though this time the discovery is scientific; Haig-Brown is fascinated not only with the life-cycle of the salmon but with the efforts of dedicated human beings (the unnamed "Good Fisherman" in the first, Senator Evans and Don Gunner in the second) to discover and reveal the complex secrets of natural processes. In his juvenile adventure stories—especially *Starbuck Valley Winter* and *The Whale People* (1962)—the boy-heroes embark upon personal voyages of discovery, venturing into new places and proving themselves in new accomplishments. Haig-Brown's own role as fact-finder and sympathetic interpreter is less dramatic but no less real; he communicates to his readers a sense of intellectual discovery through painstaking research and a lifetime of practical experience.

His favourite subject is, of course, fishing, and he has written on virtually every aspect of it . . . ; he is at his best in the more personal mode, in such books as the four accounts of the fisherman's year divided according to the seasons, and books of essays on fishing subjects like *A River Never Sleeps*. . . . [The] seal on his intellectual ownership of his adopted province was set by his writing of *The Living Land* (1961)—a veritable anatomy of British Columbia. . . . (p. 10)

A detailed literary examination of Haig-Brown's writing soon reveals the existence of two marked—and, at first sight, opposed—attitudes recurring regularly in his work. The first, one of the features that probably derives from the English rural tradition, is an ever-riding concern for truth and accuracy. (p. 12)

Yet against this earnest preoccupation with unadorned fact is a balancing acknowledgement of the sense of elevating wonder to be derived from a knowledge of wild things. . . . Ultimately, however, these two attitudes are by no means incompatible. Haig-Brown is impressed by the realization that truth is itself wonderful. This is, indeed, one of the paradoxical (and pleasing) results of recent scientific discoveries in ichthyology. "In my own lifetime," he writes, "many questions about salmon have been answered, many mysteries have been revealed. But every answer, every revelation serves only to make these graceful forms lying over the gravels at the headwaters of a mountain stream a more affecting miracle." Haig-Brown finds the same principle at work in all branches of natural knowledge; it is not too much to say that the prime impulse in his work is to reveal this miracle of the living fact.

Fact and the interpretation of fact: these not only make up the content of Haig-Brown's writings but also define their form. . . . *Return to the River* is a narrative of natural history, a demonstration of ichthyological research, a conservationist tract and a celebration of the natural process all in one.

In an earlier book, *Pool and Rapid* (1932), Haig-Brown employs imaginative means to convey a comprehensive truth beyond the scope of statistics or prosaic description. . . . [It] is hardly fiction in the accepted sense. It is best described, I think, as imaginative history—history which recognizes myth as a legitimate part of the psychological, tradition-sanctioned truth of its subject, and admits created but representative figures . . . as elements within a contrived but essentially accurate account of an extended historical process. . . . [As] a whole the book well illustrates his attempt to reconcile the needlessly opposed perspectives of scientific fact and literary creation.

Haig-Brown seems to have been drawn towards fiction (though, under the circumstances, imaginative narrative might be a more suitable term) by the opportunity it provides for genuinely creative presentation. It is not altogether surprising, however, that his novels are most memorable for their informative, non-fiction qualities. This is as true, I believe, of his juvenile fiction as of his adult novels. Thus *Starbuck Valley Winter* derives its interest from the account of trapping in a remote valley, the dangers of such a life under tough conditions, the sheer struggle for survival; these are far more compelling than the rather perfunctory plot-mystery centred upon the sinister figure of a rival trapper. Similarly, in *Timber,* the recreation of life in the logging-camps, the techniques and even the terminology of logging (which Haig-Brown reproduces exactly, together with a useful glossary), hold the attention more readily than the inconclusive love-triangle or the excessively didactic (and now outmoded) discussion of trade-unionism. The background proves more absorbing than the events played out against it.

His most important novel is unquestionably *On the Highest Hill* (1949). Though it shares some of the weaknesses of *Timber*—a rather rambling narrative, an uneasy compound of elements that do not belong integrally together—its interest lies in its hero, Colin Ensley, whose compulsion towards a wilderness not yet discovered and spoiled by mankind provides the central focus of the book. It is a novel half-way towards allegory. (pp. 12-14)

On the Highest Hill records the withdrawal of a solitary; Colin's love of wilderness develops into acute misanthropy. . . . Ultimately, in a climax which offers an inadequate resolution of the tensions that have been building up in the plot, Colin turns to violence to defend his supposed right to isolation and dies a fugitive on the mountain to which he has retreated. . . .

In his neurotic escapism, Colin stands in marked contrast to Haig-Brown's own clear-sighted, balanced response to the often depressing tensions inherent in modern living. Part of the unease I detect in the novel stems from a difficulty in reconciling his apparently sympathetic presentation of his hero with the superiority of his own views as manifest in his writings as a whole. (p. 15)

Like so many writers on the natural world, [Haig-Brown] has effectively explored the indeterminate area between fiction and non-fiction. But his best work, I have no doubt, is to be found in his essays and discursive prose. Here he is most at his ease. An adequate structure is provided by the natural divisions of the seasons or, often enough, can be imposed by the terms of his own interests and personality. (One of the most satisfying of his books, *A River Never Sleeps,* combines unity of subject— fish-lore—with month-by-month seasonal presentation, and buttresses the artistic structure by juxtaposing biographical experiences in England with those in North America.) An open form allows him to combine practical advice with anecdotes, reminiscences, didactic argument, evocative description. As familiar essayist, he claims the right to roam as his fancy inclines, and although in *Measure of the Year,* properly considered among his best collections, he demonstrates his versatility by studiously avoiding any direct discussion of angling, for the most part we are rarely far from the river-bank.

Roderick Haig-Brown has strong claims to be considered the North American "Compleat Angler." This continent has, doubtless, produced more expert fishermen, but none who can rival him in his comprehensive grasp of all that makes up the experience of angling or can convey a quintessential impression of its manifold attractions. Fishing, we might say, is where he starts from. For him, as for Izaak Walton, it is a multi-faceted activity, and the satisfactions to be derived from it include appreciation of the beauty of his surroundings, recognition of the numerous species of wild life around him, sheer joy in a challenge that combines skill and judgment with strength and physical exertion, the warm companionship of friends, and (recalling Walton's definition, "the contemplative man's recreation") "the flowing ease of thought that comes upon me as I fish." . . . [The] words that tend to recur in his angling books are "pleasure," "beauty" and (especially) "observation." (pp. 15-16)

In *Fisherman's Summer* he makes an important distinction between "a parent stream" ("the river of growth, the scene of boyhood endeavors, successes and failures") and "a home river," to which the adult fisherman comes and brings experience and skill to be applied and tested. The former, for Haig-Brown, was the Dorset Frome, but his "home river" is the Campbell, and he shares with the reader a loving exploration of every inch of it. The child, in Wordsworthian phrase, is father of the man in a very real sense. The whole structure of *A River Never Sleeps* depends upon this relation. . . . (p. 17)

One might say that his prose shares its qualities with the rivers he loves—lucid, briskly and smoothly flowing, containing abundant life. (p. 18)

W. J. Keith, "Roderick Haig-Brown" (reprinted by permission of the author), in Canadian Literature, *No. 71, Winter, 1976, pp. 7-20.*

MARY KIRTON

It is difficult to imagine how anyone could possibly make the story of an Atlantic salmon as exciting and dramatic as the adventures of the great white shark so much in the news these days. Yet Roderick Haig-Brown in his [*Silver: The Life of an Atlantic Salmon*] does just that. . . . All the facts are presented with commendable accuracy and specificity. . . .

Haig-Brown has obviously observed the salmon in great detail, but *Silver* is far from a mere catalogue of facts. Rather, it is an intensely captivating drama of life and survival, brought alive by the author's own delight and interest in the salmon's saga. No text on the subject could offer such delightful vignettes as the month old fry ganging up on the water-boatman for sport, or Silver irritably snapping at two pesky birds on the shore. Purists might object to personalizing a fish, but this is handled with delicacy and fidelity. The fish are named, emotions suggested and communications recorded, but never in a way which distorts basic biological facts. For example Silver, while delighting in the presence of his first mate, feels no need to remain lovingly by her side as she sickens and dies. The use of quaint phrases such as "The Good Fisherman" and the "Great Feeding Grounds" does date the story, yet it never detracts from its overall appeal.

In his dedication of this book to a young friend, Haig-Brown indicates his apparently modest, yet nevertheless difficult goal. "I have tried to make it an interesting story and at the same time keep to the truth about salmon and their ways." Certainly he has been successful. The book will therefore appeal both to children looking for information about salmon and to those insatiable lovers of animal stories. Indeed, it would be difficult for even mere "fact-finders" to read *Silver* without experiencing some sense of awe at nature's wonders.

Mary Kirton, "Reviews in Retrospect: 'Silver: The Life Story of an Atlantic Salmon'," in In Review: Canadian Books for Children, *Vol. 10, No. 2, Spring, 1976, p. 25.*

ALEC LUCAS

[There] is no question that Haig-Brown aimed to make his animal biographies "authentic," to use his own term. He wished to be true to the facts and spirit of the natural world and to instill some appreciation of it in his readers. In this aim, his adult and children's books are one. He wanted "all people to see and understand more because there is both pleasure and fulfillment in seeing and understanding lives about them, whether they are the lives of trees and plants, or lives of animals or lives of fish." In such seeing and understanding lay, he believed, "the only hope of preserving the natural world." These aims motivated all Haig-Brown's animal stories, but *Silver* and *Return to the River* much more obviously than *Panther,* which works for the cause of conservation, if at all, almost wholly through the vivid presentation of a magnificent beast.

Haig-Brown is more at home in the animal biography than he ever was in the later boys' adventure stories and his fiction. In the first he avoids for the most part the difficulty he always had in creating living human characters. The Good Fisherman in *Silver* is largely peripheral to the story, however important he may be as a sensitive and reflective angler. Both he and the narrator of the story appear again, as it were, in *Return to the River* as Senator Evans and a biologist, Don Gunner. They enable Haig-Brown to drop the subjective first-person for the more objective (and "scientific") third person point of view and to present much of his natural history as dialogue rather than exposition. Yet they are essentially an animate frame of reference for the full-length biography of a magnificent Oregon salmon, Spring. The cougar hunter Milton in *Panther*, however, called for greater individuation than either Evans or Gunner. Milton shares the story and theme of the book with Ki-yu, representing man in nature's struggle to survive as civilization encroaches on the wilderness. Yet he fills his role simply by being a hunter; his struggle with nature is never psychological, and, as a flat character, he gives his creator much less trouble than the teenagers whom, in his boys' stories, Haig-Brown tries to depict dramatically and dialectically.

In *Silver*, Haig-Brown attempted to achieve three specific goals: to tell an interesting story, to keep to the truth about salmon and to instruct Master Dickie (to whom the narrator tells the story and Haig-Brown dedicates the book) in the ways of true sportsmanship. . . . To vitalize the facts of the life cycle of the salmon, he employs a variety of narrative techniques that children like and that range in this story from a short *in medias res* opening to a sharp climax and a brief and tranquil denouement, whose sadness reminds one of [Ernest Thompson] Seton's "Lobo" and "Redruff." He uses suspense effectively at times withholding or hinting, and at times providing curtain lines or curtain endings for his chapters. (pp. 21-2)

Here and there Haig-Brown dramatizes the action. . . . He creates little climaxes in which Silver is caught or nearly killed, working up to the great struggle . . . that concludes the book. Yet *Silver* is by no means an animal adventure story. The "conflict" of the plot centres largely on the annual cycle and life-death pattern in Silver's development. (p. 22)

As a result of [its] shifts and discrepancies, *Silver* comprises a strange melange of adults' and children's interests and attitudes. (p. 23)

With *Silver*, he perhaps simply wished to recreate a situation once his, when a devoted and learned father told him stories of fish and fishermen. [With it he] paid his last direct respects to his childhood and the humanized nature he had known then. After it he wrote under the influence of the new world wilderness. . . . [In *Silver* Haig-Brown] had tried to combine two views of nature—the English sentimental, romantic one and the Darwinian or realistic one (with a leavening of the old tradition of Walton and his followers)—and he seems to have thought it necessary to compensate for the latter by emphasizing the sentimental view, with the result that he axiomatically stressed the "cuteness" of his story.

As if again to compensate for the sentimentality of *Silver*, Haig-Brown with *Panther* came out firmly for the realistic animal story. In its objectivity it stands at the opposite pole to *Silver* and, in ways, even to *Return to the River*. It has none of the "cuteness" and anthropomorphism that he believed marred his first animal biography. That he did not write *Panther* "especially for children" is a fact significant not only in itself but also as an indication of his approach to his subject. He was free now to be "authentic," to let the facts speak for themselves. (pp. 23-4)

His research was that of naturalist and hunter rather than mammologist. Yet without the sophisticated methods of modern field work—tranquillizing bullets and electronic tracking—the book marks an important beginning in the study of the ecology and life history of the Pacific coast panther. (p. 24)

Panther is, however, more than matters of fact. As is also required of the animal biography, it is a work of fiction, and, in this example, one of considerable imaginative power. A living creature stalks through its pages. Haig-Brown is not trying to tell a story of heroic animal exploits, nor is he using animals as human archetypes. . . . The book is an animal biography, and Ki-yu is simply a great beast of instinct and primordial reason. . . . Typical of wild animal biographies, however, Ki-yu is the fittest of his kind, but not because . . . of human qualities, but because of his sheer animality. . . . As excessive anthropomorphism mars *Silver* as "science," so a marked anti-anthropomorphism mars *Panther*. The very realism of the protagonist tends to detract from his role. Purely animal, he consequently provides little with which the reader can identify. In trying to avoid humanizing Ki-yu, Haig-Brown has stripped him of much emotional impact.

Although *Panther* recounts Ki-yu's life history directly and chronologically, it is artistically patterned. Its setting balances farm and wilderness; its telling, narration and dramatic episodes; and its plot, hunted and hunter. It, however, avoids themes that are drawn from stories about people and that frequently characterize stories about people and animals. . . . He even concludes the biography as if to make an ironic comment on sentimental "fictional" plots of animal stories. (pp. 24-5)

On one hand the story is a simple one involving Ki-yu and Milton, a bounty hunter, worked out for the most part in terms of crises, hairbreadth yet plausible escapes and acts of derring-do. . . . Yet the sensationalism of these events is never sensationalism for its own sake, for *Panther* is more than an outdoors book of thrilling adventures. It has a theme of broad implications and tells a story rooted in the old conflict of man and nature.

If Ki-yu embodies the spirit of the animal world, Milton embodies that of man's, and the plot derives from Ki-yu's efforts to live between two worlds—one, nature's, red in tooth and claw, and the other, man's, forever encroaching on the wilderness. . . . Settler and cougar become involved automatically in the struggle to survive, and, in this way, Milton and Ki-yu are "kin." (p. 25)

Despite this central tension, *Panther* lacks overall dramatic effect. It tries to be two books in one, an animal biography and the life of a hunter. It lacks the focus that makes Seton's "Krag" so very effective. Despite the fact that hunting is an all-pervasive theme, the stories of Ki-yu and Milton often go their separate ways, except during the hunts and at the end when Ki-yu makes the settlement his stamping ground. In *Panther*, there are no heroes or villains, or perhaps better, the two protagonists are both heroes and villains caught up in a specific conflict that in the end neither wins. Haig-Brown's refusal to take sides, as he says, with either Ki-yu or Milton comes through almost as indifference. His emotions are scarcely ever involved. He never smiles or sheds a tear. Hence the emotions of the reader are scarcely ever involved. He is moved, however, by the deaths of Osa and her cubs, by the death of Ki-yu when his animal dignity rises to nobility, and by the faithful dogs who fight for their master's cause even unto death. In fact, the love Milton has for his dogs gives him a much-needed human touch and counteracts somewhat his callous killing of the mountain cougars. . . .

Nature for Haig-Brown may be amoral but it is not monstrous, and in *Panther* he presents it impartially in Darwinian terms and lets the "message" of the book stand at that. By refusing to express sympathy for the victims in the struggle for survival, he avoids the kind of adulterated Darwinism that Seton so frequently indulges in. (p. 26)

A story, a study of natural history and Darwinism, *Panther* is also an outdoors book about a hunter and, like most of the genre, incongruous as it may seem, about predator-control. Haig-Brown puts all his nature writing in human context so that here he is not simply following a literary pattern but also considering an extant problem of the time. Although he never reduces Ki-yu to vermin, he apparently speaks as one with the bounty hunter in the dramatized episodes of the story. At least he never speaks against bounty hunting and he obviously tries to make Milton into a kind of folk hero, the successful backwoods hunter. (pp. 26-7)

Panther combines the objectivity of science with the heartlessness, if not cruelty, of the hunter. It never questions the morality or benefits of bounty hunting. . . .

Criticized for all the cruelty and killing in *Panther*, Haig-Brown, despite a disclaimer against violence in children's books, justified his story on his usual grounds of authenticity. . . . Haig-Brown is dealing here, of course, with a problem common to many realistic stories of wild animals, but especially the animal biography and again especially when it is long and based on the life of a large predator.

Paradoxically some of this criticism derives from Haig-Brown's strengths as an author. The chapter on Milton's night alone with his dogs in the woods, a splendid vignette, clearly discloses his ability to write realistic description. . . . (p. 28)

When, however, Haig-Brown presents action in the same vivid manner, he catches it so dramatically that he seems consequently, as some critics argue, to emphasize violence. . . . There are no fewer than five fights [between animals] and seven hunting scenes described in detail in the book. As a result, some critics have attacked it for its repetitiveness as well as its violence. Yet in all the episodes involved (which one critic likes for their cumulative effect), Haig-Brown tries to solve the problem of repetition of scene, if not the sameness of violence. Ki-yu plays different tricks to elude his pursuers; he fights different adversaries for different reasons—a bear for food, a rival for a mate, a pack of wolves for life itself. Both flaws—if flaws—however, have a common source in the nature of the genre. *Panther*, even aside from the hunting scenes, again simply demonstrates the violence and repetition that must be part of a full-length realistic biography of a large predatory animal. (p. 29)

Unquestionably *Return to the River* was an off-shoot of his work on *The Western Angler*. It contains much the same natural history under the guise of fiction. In using this approach he had several aims. He wished to tell the story of a species in terms of an individual, the common aim of the animal biography, and so reduce his canvas to manageable size. He wished also "to straighten the records about salmon." Most of all, however, he wanted to create a general interest in salmon ichthyology and ecology, and to discuss the problem of electric power dams that were strangling the salmon rivers. . . .

[Whereas] *Panther* is admirable, *Return to the River* is both admirable and likeable. Moreover, with its vast setting, it provides an attraction lacking in *Panther*. The child, unconcerned with theories of migration and problems of fish management, can travel in imagination with Spring, the fishy "heroine," along great rivers, through forests and farmlands and cities to wander in the mysterious deeps of the ocean, led on by a story full of entertaining events.

For all the grandeur of the setting, however, Haig-Brown does not indulge in picturesque word-painting or the impressionism of the romantic. Neither is he Thoreauvian nor Wordsworthian.

He feels for his world without trying to draw it into a poetic vision. For one thing, he is not trying to drive his reader out into some vague abstract world but to make him stand in awe, specifically of Spring and her world, and Haig-Brown has the vision and skill to achieve this aim. The description of the river that opens the book skilfully moves from a dynamic prose to a more static form, a precise expository prose, to depict the spawning bed. Again, the almost rhythmical linking of verbs ending in "ing" and those in the past tense, in the description of Canyon Pool, which Spring will leave and to which she will return, catches superbly the life and death struggle there, and also reinforces the controlling image of the book.

Time, as the long ago, like the spaciousness of the setting, adds an important dimension to the book, for its historical perspective gives it depth and feeling. (p. 30)

In a neat contrast Haig-Brown brings the past into sharp focus in the present. Senator Evans, remembering his youth, speaks as Old America warning the New of the dangers to its natural resources if it continues to act on values that had effected "the rape of America." . . .

The nature of the material in *Return to the River* allowed Haig-Brown greater scope in one way than *Panther* had; yet it posed the old problems of the realistic animal biography, the sameness of chronological pattern, the similarity of event (escaping one predator being much like escaping another, climbing one fish ladder being much like climbing another), and writing fiction that would hold attention without falsifying natural history. With Spring he faced an even greater challenge than normal with the characteristic flatness of the protagonist's character. No salmon could have the "personality" of Ki-yu, nor could its story, since Haig-Brown refused to invent episodes, have the same dramatic possibilities as the cougar's with its terrestrial setting, its exciting scenes of violence, and its cast of hunters and farmers. Spring was an Everysalmon; Ki-yu was himself alone. *Return to the River* demanded of its author a different approach.

For one thing Haig-Brown emphasizes science more. He sets out the life history of the salmon (often in scientific terminology) in great detail. (p. 31)

If less openly didactic than *Silver*, *Return to the River* is far more subjective than *Panther*. Through Senator Evans, Haig-Brown adds an emotional element to his natural history, and he himself occasionally indulges openly in the pathetic fallacy, impressionistic biology, or anthropomorphism, call it what you will. . . . The humanizing of animal behaviour here strikes a happy balance between that of *Silver* and *Panther*. The author perhaps reads into Spring's behaviour more than is scientifically justified, but not more than what, lacking contradictory evidence, seems a valid interpretation and a sincere tribute to a vital and splendid creature. *Return to the River* combines something of the old sentimental tradition of his first book with the realistic tradition of *Panther* and so has a quite different tone and imaginative thrust from the latter book. *Return to the River* is of course more mellow anyway because the nature of its protagonist precludes ferocity and gore, and it is more mellow, too, since it concerns itself more with conservation, but it differs most from *Panther* in that it reveals that Haig-Brown has got the feel of the grandeur of North America and has combined it with attitudes rooted in the imaginative sympathies of his childhood and youth.

Return to the River is more unified than *Panther* with its introductory chapters on Blackstreak, Ki-yu's father, and its two protagonists and divided narrative. In *Return to the River*, the story centres on the salmon and has an overall "plot" in as much as Senator Evans, early in the book, marks the fingerling Spring and so sets up a book-length question—will she return and in view of the tremendous odds against a double recapture by the right people, will he recapture her? Moreover, if Senator Evans and Don Gunner are, like Milton in *Panther*, often absent from long stretches of the book, their absence is far less significant, for they are essentially observers, not participants, in the story. Even if Milton is seen as symbolizing the threat of civilization to the natural world, the divided narrative reduces greatly, if it does not deny altogether, his effectiveness as a unifying force in the story. Again, even though Haig-Brown, for the sake of variety, but mainly for the chance to discuss fish management in different areas, breaks the conclusion of *Return to the River* into accounts of Sachem, Chinook, the tagged salmon, and Spring, he does not harm the unity of the narrative in any serious way. All go through the same general experiences. All are salmon, and the reader does not identify so strongly with any one of them as to preclude the four fish, in large part, having a common identity.

Spring lives in two worlds. On one hand there are nets, dams, and pollution, as if all mankind, not one lone hunter, stood against her. Unlike Ki-yu, however, she does have protectors among these enemies, a fact that helps differentiate the tone of *Return to the River* from *Panther*. On the other hand there are nature's predators. . . . Each has a part in a drama governed largely by "the laws of hunger," which sets animal against animal and in which Spring is both hunted and huntress. Haig-Brown makes more of her in the former role, however, since it adds variety and some suspense to the story. (pp. 31-3)

For all of Spring's brushes with death in *Return to the River*, suspense does not become significant in itself, except perhaps in the remarkable descriptions of a heron fishing, an Indian boy waiting for Sachem, and one or two short episodes involving net or hook. The reader knows that Spring, for the sake of science and the story, bears a charmed life and will live out her days. . . .

[The] interludes involving Gunner and Evans seem text-bookish. Their opening discussion on migration reads like a debate, and only with the trollers, Red Gifkin and Charlie Wilson, does the conversation seem natural. They are not burdened with a mission. They are cut from the same cloth as Milton, the kind of men Haig-Brown met and liked when he was a hunter and fisherman. By contrast Evans . . . and Gunner never appear experiential or real; their *raison d'être* centres on the thematic and didactic.

Senator Evans looks much like an atonement for Milton (and the author of *Panther*). . . . Remembering the days of his youth when the salmon abounded, he introduces a feeling of nostalgia and remorse that gives the cause of salmon conservation an emotional basis. It fits the story and gives it emotional depth, too, that he, now an old man, at the conclusion should watch Spring in her spawning——on her life-giving death-bed—which he "felt in his heart" was the last natural spawning of the chinooks that belonged to his river. Like the salmon runs, his way of seeing nature faces the danger of being lost in a nation dedicated to industrial and commercial exploitation in the name of Progress, to science and to biologists like Don Gunner, Evans' foil. . . . (p. 33)

For Haig-Brown, these scientists are only half the problem. He has a place for the Senator Evanses, also, for he has Don

Gunner say to Evans when speaking of a salmon pool, "You may not be able to name all the whys and wherefores, but you understand without that. You feel it." . . . His central point, however, as regards the Evanses, is that they are the people who must motivate and direct the work on salmon. (p. 34)

Senator Evans and Don Gunner could fit easily into Haig-Brown's juvenile fiction. Kindly and wiser older men and resourceful young men are central to it. Evans and Gunner, like the protagonists of the boys' books, have little moral or psychological complexity. Their motivations and reactions are direct responses to things and circumstances rather than to matters of their own personalities. They are as much sounding boards and propagandists as they are human beings. Had they been otherwise, they might easily have drawn attention away from the true subject of the book.

Beyond all these characters is the river itself which, without being personified, is a living presence in the book. Haig-Brown loved rivers and had already written a story of one in *Pool and Rapid* . . . , and in *Return to the River* he has actually written another, for Spring is the embodiment of the spirit of the river. . . . [In] the end the river, in a magnificent gesture of defiance, rises like a champion and sweeps away the rack that keeps the salmon from their home waters. It would be easy to follow this line of thought too far and see it as a comment on nature's ultimate power over man and so on, or as a revelation of a wish fulfillment deriving from Haig-Brown's youthful attitudes to nature or from his fundamental dislike of the commercial world. Whatever its purpose or origin, however, it is more than a *deus ex machina* to supply the story with as happy an ending as possible, given the fact that Spring and all the others returning with her must die.

Return to the River does not . . . centre on Darwinism. . . . [The author's] concern over Spring is for a species in an environment that modern entrepreneurial man has refashioned, and not a concern over the killing of individual animals by hunter and fisherman. Haig-Brown's vision here has a different and broader orientation. (pp. 34-5)

Return to the River supposedly demonstrates the need to recognize, not fundamentally to deny, the view of Senator Evans. Without his way of seeing, there was the danger (as the Grand Coulee dam revealed) that technology would concern itself with fisheries *vis-a-vis* hydro-electric power development only if the value of the first allegedly surpassed the second. Like Senator Evans, Haig-Brown is caught in a dilemma. He, too, leans to the "sentimental" view of nature and yet believes that the one chance salmon have rests with science and engineering. So both author and Evans look with favour on the Bonneville dam. There is the suggestion also that they appreciate the whole programme of damming the rivers inasmuch as it made the "Fisheries guys" wise to all "them haywire" dams and ditches that do the "real harm." Certainly both are impressed by the ingenious way in which salmon are trapped and trucked to their spawning streams, for all these developments hold out hope for the future of the salmon runs. Yet though Evans (and the author) make little of the real difficulties of hydrologic coordination and fish management (the dangers of fish having the "bends" below the dams, of reservoir or so-called lake silting, and of temperature and chemical changes in the waters) the senator (and probably the author) is unsatisfied. The uncertainty enters to the detriment of the book because it superimposes the story of Senator Evans on the life history of Spring, for whatever the flood means as fiction, it takes almost all the emotional force of the argument for conservation away from science and technology, if it does not actually put them in a bad light. Haig-Brown's heart and head are not at one here. As *Panther* lacks focus since the author seems never quite decided whether his subject is Ki-yu or Milton, though the conflict between them is often direct and centre stage, so there is an ambivalence in *Return to the River*. Here Evans and Spring stand against a special manifestation of civilization so that according to the plot the balance favours nature and the old-time values of an old naturalist, though the gist and logic of the argument for conservation in the book would seem to tip it the other way. (pp. 35-6)

On [one] level *Return to the River* has not dated, for beyond all the matters of fiction, characters, and conservation, it treats with impressive sensitivity the miracle of migration, ''the far journey and faithful return,'' which constitutes the lives of salmon and in which Spring concretizes the dynamic force of nature. The story is more than a dramatized presentation of a natural wonder, however. Its roots are deep in the life of man, for it reflects aspects of his own world, the struggle for freedom against great odds, the questing spirit and the odyssean search for home. By juxtaposing the natural and the human, *Return to the River* puts each in a light that is common to both and that reveals the dangers of the alienation of man from nature.

Haig-Brown wants so much to be an affirmer. If all is ''cycles within cycles, freshness and decay,'' all is also, he writes, ''constant change, death and new life.'' In his animal biographies, this wish seems to put him on all sides at once: as hunter and nature lover, as scientist and sentimentalist, and as one who reveres the spirit of free enterprise, but laments what economic man has done and is doing to America. His ambivalence may derive from his English background. *Panther*, which is truly North American, seems in part to have been an experiment, since *Return to the River*, with its sentimentality and its interest in the rights of animals in a man-centred world,

turns back some distance to the English tradition. Here Haig-Brown differs from his peers [Charles G. D.] Roberts and Seton and gives the Canadian animal biography a new direction in that he openly makes his concern for the species and its environment integral to his theme and art. (pp. 36-7)

Alec Lucas, ''Haig-Brown's Animal Biographies,'' in Canadian Children's Literature: A Journal of Criticism and Review *(Box 335, Guelph, Ontario, Canada N1H6K5), No. 11, 1978, pp. 21-38.*

JANET ARNETT

[Roderick Haig-Brown left] a considerable quantity of unpublished short fiction and essays. Using this material, his daughter Valerie has planned a three-volume compilation, of which *Woods and River Tales* is the first. . . .

His empathy with the individualistic people who struggled in [the rugged environment of British Columbia] and his well-honed observational skills make these stories memorable.

Woods and River Tales contains 19 stories, many of them thought to be based on true experiences. All but four are published here for the first time.

The subjects Haig-Brown picked for his tales are typically wild and woolly west themes. . . . But far from being hackneyed, the stories are fresh and inviting saved by a skilled writer's touch with words and his ability to translate the world of nature into vivid descriptions on the printed page. Haig-Brown combines gentleness and humour with the swagger of the frontier, and the result is a book of tales that have literary beauty together with unwashed outdoorsman heroics, a most unusual combination.

Janet Arnett, ''Fiction: 'Woods and River Tales','' in Quill and Quire *(reprinted by permission of* Quill and Quire*), Vol. 46, No. 6, June, 1980, p. 34.*

Isabelle Holland

1920-

American young adult and adult novelist and short story writer.

Holland explores the lives of lonely, troubled adolescents and concentrates on issues important to contemporary young people. Her protagonists are sympathetically portrayed, triumphing over distressing family situations with ingenuity and good humor. Holland draws weak, ineffectual parents to illustrate that adolescent problems are caused by a lack of traditional authority figures. She also deals with the adult who becomes a guiding force in the young person's life, such as Justin McLeod in *The Man without a Face*. Holland's treatment of such themes as self-respect and the universal need for companionship has led critics to charge her with being didactic and imposing her conservative moral values on the reader. She has also been criticized for manipulating plot and action to lighten more disturbing episodes and for oversimplifying and distorting character and situation to make her points. It is generally agreed, however, that Holland's strengths lie in her convincing portrayals of and sensitivity to the needs of adolescents.

Because of their realism, several of her works are controversial, most prominently *The Man without a Face*, which includes a homosexual episode. Although it is generally felt that Holland handles the brief encounter between Charles and Justin tastefully, some critics see Justin's death in the end as Holland's way of avoiding a more natural resolution of the relationship; Holland has stated that the encounter is itself less important than Charles's resulting emotional maturity. *Of Love, Death, and Other Journeys* is considered one of Holland's most successful books. The reader follows Meg through difficulties, including the death of her mother, that lead her to a better understanding of herself and others. This book illustrates Holland's ability to capture adolescent qualities and is the first of her works to soften her earlier vision of the flighty, incompetent parent.

In the mid-1970s Holland began writing contemporary Gothic mysteries. These light, well-written novels are considered superior to most books of the genre. Like her novels for young people, these works are characterized by Holland's strong sense of humor. Her respect for the integrity of the young is especially evident in her books for them, and her popularity among this audience suggests a mutual admiration. (See also *Contemporary Authors*, Vols. 21-24, rev. ed., and *Something About the Author*, Vol. 8.)

EDITH C. HOWLEY

["**Cecily**"] is too slight to be a novel. The time span is short, the three dimensional characters few, the action limited, and little is finally resolved. What there is, however, is tightly knit and plausible, the characters of Tim, Elizabeth and Cecily clearly enough drawn so that Cecily's catalytic effect on an otherwise emotionally well-balanced Elizabeth is quite believable. It is well done, but slight.

Edith C. Howley, "Fiction: 'Cecily'," in Best Sellers *(copyright 1967, by the University of Scranton), Vol. 27, No. 1, April 1, 1967, p. 7.*

RUTH HILL VIGUERS

[*Cecily* is an] almost flawless novel. . . . Several of the mistresses of Langley School, the girls who play even small parts in Cecily's misery or reclamation, and certainly the main characters are so well understood, so alive, that they demand the reader's complete involvement. A beautifully polished gem of a novel . . . that will be a relief from tired stories written especially for teen-agers.

Ruth Hill Viguers, "'Cecily'," in The Horn Book Magazine *(copyright © 1967, by The Horn Book, Inc., Boston), Vol. XLIII, No. 3, June, 1967, p. 353.*

ALICE LOW

["**Amanda's Choice**"] is fragmented, veering between Amanda, the baffled adults who analyze and explain her strong language and delinquent behavior, and Manuel, a resentful Cuban teenage musician. . . . [In] a soap opera ending, Amanda, her father and his new wife relate with honesty, warmth and reason.

The author understands child-rearing, psychological nuances and social problems, but she uses her characters to carry messages rather than to tell their flesh and blood stories. She makes important points: among them that emotional deprivation scars more deeply than material deprivation, and that Spanish Harlem has a richer, more genuine life than Amanda's insulated island.

Alice Low, "For Young Readers: 'Amanda's Choice'," in The New York Times Book Review (© 1970 by The New York Times Company; reprinted by permission), May 3, 1970, p. 23.

ZENA SUTHERLAND

Like the author's *Cecily*, [*Amanda's Choice*] is a book with a young protagonist . . . but sensitive and sophisticated enough to appeal to older readers. . . . The ending is not as sharply etched as the rest of the book, but the whole is impressive. Memorable characterization, good style, and a note of poignancy in the harsh reality of the situation. . . . (pp. 9-10)

Zena Sutherland, "New Titles for Children and Young People: 'Amanda's Choice'," in Bulletin of the Center for Children's Books (reprinted by permission of The University of Chicago Press; © 1970 by the University of Chicago), Vol. 24, No. 1, September, 1970, pp. 9-10.

KIRKUS REVIEWS

[Chuck, in *The Man without a Face*, is a] teenage misogynist and compulsive underachiever. . . . Inevitably, he finds a mentor in the horribly scarred and romantic recluse Justin McLeod. . . . And inevitably again, this relationship between two emotional cripples leads to a once-only homosexual encounter (though the unsophisticated will have a tough time figuring out from the text just "what happened"). Chuck's bitterness is painfully real and the recognition of his sexual feelings commendably frank, but in return for this measure of honesty, the whole story is slanted to justify the "daring" subject matter—the psychological underpinnings are intrusive (talk of Oedipus complexes and sibling rivalry), the twin mysteries in the pasts of Chuck's dead father and Justin unlikely, the decadence and nastiness of Chuck's family overstressed (even Gloria's obnoxious boyfriend probably wouldn't kick the cat to death). For a hero *with* a face and a fully realized individuality, the bulkily packaged moral ("You can be free from everything but the consequences of what you do") just might not be too high a price to pay. (pp. 73-4)

"Older Fiction: 'The Man without a Face'," in Kirkus Reviews (copyright © 1972 The Kirkus Service, Inc.), Vol. XL, No. 2, January 15, 1972, pp. 73-4.

SHERYL B. ANDREWS

Without being mawkish or false, the author has delved into the joy and sorrow concomitant with love and growth [in *The Man Without a Face*]. . . . The author handles the homosexual experience with taste and discretion; the act of love between Justin and Charles is a necessary emotional catharsis for the boy within the context of his story, and is developed with perception and restraint. Justin McLeod is presented as neither a damned soul nor a fallen angel, but as a human being. . . . Over and over again, the reader is made aware of what maturity entails: *"You can be free from everything but the consequences of what you do."* . . . A highly moral book, powerfully and sensitively written; a book that never loses sight of the humor and pain inherent in the human condition. (pp. 375-76)

Sheryl B. Andrews, "'The Man without a Face'," in The Horn Book Magazine (copyright © 1972 by The Horn Book, Inc., Boston), Vol. XLVIII, No. 4, August, 1972, pp. 375-76.

ISABELLE HOLLAND

[I] didn't set out to write about homosexuality [in *The Man Without a Face*]. I started this book with only the idea of a fatherless boy who experiences with a man some of the forms of companionship and love that have been nonexistent in his life. Because the other side of Charles' dilemma or emotional history arises from his feeling of being both suffocated and rejected by the predominant female influence in his home—his four-times married mother and his older sister. His stepfathers have come and gone too fast for him to do anything but dislike them. Emotionally, Charles has lived his life as an armed camp, hanging onto a shadowy memory of his own father. Hence the revolutionary impact that Justin has on him.

I think I might diverge here and say something that has always interested me about the eternally fascinating subject of love: Into one person's love for another goes much of the love, either present or in default, that has gone, or should have gone, into other relationships. The title, *The Man Without a Face,* really has two meanings: It refers to the nickname by which Justin is called because of his facial disfigurement; but, on a deeper level, the man without a face is also Charles' father, whom he can barely remember. But Charles has wrapped his memory of his father around himself as a shield against a world that he finds, on the whole, hostile. Behind that shield, Charles is emotionally starved. When Justin steps into his life, he brings three qualities that mythologically as well as psychologically have always been the archetypes of fatherhood: Justin is masculine, he is authoritative, and he is undemonstratively kind. He steps into the vacuum of Charles' emotional life, and the result is cataclysmic.

Now, all of this interested me far more than the almost incidental fact that the book is about love between two people of the same sex. The story could have been about a boy whose deprivations and needs were the exact opposite from Charles'. Given another kind of boy, with another kind of emotional background, the instigator of his youthful love could have been female—as in [Herman Raucher's] *Summer of Forty-two.* And if that had been the case, how much of the love could have been that of the male child for the missing or inadequate female parent, and how much that of the male adolescent in his first sexual encounter with a female? As with Charles, I don't think it's either-or. I think it's both. (pp. 299-300)

Isabelle Holland, "Tilting at Taboos," in The Horn Book Magazine (copyright © 1973 by The Horn Book, Inc., Boston), Vol. XLIX, No. 3, June, 1973, pp. 299-305.

ETHEL L. HEINS

[*Heads You Win, Tails I Lose*] is capably written, full of clever, often bitter dialogue. But the author has not produced an important or powerful book—as she did with *The Man Without a Face.* Her new book lacks both the unity of theme and passionate focus of its predecessor. Perhaps she has pulled out too many stops and has diffused her creative energies in an attempt to cope with too many problems; for the life of almost every character has been touched by the wretchedness of drug addiction or alcoholism, divorce or estrangement, loneliness or isolation. (p. 57)

*Ethel L. Heins, "'Heads You Win, Tails I Lose',"
in* The Horn Book Magazine *(copyright © 1974 by
The Horn Book, Inc., Boston), Vol. L, No. 1, February, 1974, pp. 56-7.*

NORA E. TAYLOR

Isabelle Holland has moved into the field of the Gothic novel with somewhat gingerly tread. No screams of horror in ["**Kil-garen**"]; just muted moues of apprehension. For all of that, she has written a rippling story that unfolds skin after onionskin of the unexpected, until the core is reached. It is worth the peeling.

Miss Holland, as a novelist of considerable experience, is accustomed to fleshing out her characters until they become as real as relatives to the reader. And giving substance to her settings until they seem equally familiar.

She has done this with Barbara Kilgaren of Four Winds; with the West Indian island, Kilgaren itself; and to a lesser extent perhaps with Barbara's half-brother, Jonathan Kilgaren.

It all adds up to a tangled tale of torment.

Nora E. Taylor, "Escapism," in The Christian Science Monitor *(reprinted by permission from* The
Christian Science Monitor; © *1974 The Christian
Science Publishing Society; all rights reserved), June
12, 1974, p. F5.*

ZENA SUTHERLAND

A romantic story in the Gothic style [*Kilgaren*] comes, unexpectedly, from a writer who has excelled in contemporary realism. Isabelle Holland is too skilled a writer to portray characters who are not believable, and the style and dialogue are competently handled—but the plot is too intricate to be convincing, too dependent on Guilty Secrets Revealed. (p. 43)

*Zena Sutherland, "New Titles for Children and Young
People: 'Kilgaren'," in* Bulletin of the Center for
Children's Books *(reprinted by permission of The
University of Chicago Press; © 1974 by the Uni-
versity of Chicago), Vol. 28, No. 3, November, 1974,
pp. 43-4.*

DIANE A. PARENTE

"**Trelawny**" is a novel for a summer afternoon, a winter evening. In the modern Gothic style, complete with a haunted family mansion, it provides a temporary diversion from life's weightier problems.

The plot is relatively intricate and laced with enough surprises to maintain a high level of reader interest throughout despite a lack of any distinctive literary style or flair on the part of the author. A strong principal character, Kit Trelawny, provides the cohesive force in the story as she struggles to come to grips with the past through a weird and often frightening series of current events. (pp. 382-83)

[The] story line is as twisting and full of zigs and zags as the architecture of Trelawny's Fell, the well-described setting for the mystery.

An interesting cast of characters, each portrayed as a readily definable, knowable individual, adds much to the book's readability. While supplying us with no deep insights into human nature, they nonetheless admirably act out the roles for which they were created.

Those who still seek diversion in the printed page rather than the NBC Mystery Movie will find in these pages intrigue, suspense, and a literary work equal to and occasionally surpassing that of the novellas in the better women's magazines. (p. 383)

Diane A. Parente, "'Trelawny'," in Best Sellers
*(copyright 1974, by the University of Scranton), Vol.
34, No. 17, December 1, 1974, pp. 382-83.*

KIRKUS REVIEWS

[*Of Love and Death and Other Journeys*] begins on a deceptively supercilious note with an odd family assortment of emigres, calling themselves Flopsy, Mopsy, Peter and Cotton. . . . Mopsy discovers that her Mother (hitherto Flopsy) is dying of cancer and she (and we) begin to understand and admire this vulnerable eccentric. Much of what Mopsy learns is revealed by her father. . . . Holland is an aggressive writer and some of this—father's button-down sincerity as well as Mopsy's flip sophistication—seems manipulated. But Mother's character and Mopsy/Meg's sorrow at seeing her waste away in silence are genuinely moving, and though later Mopsy's grief is sublimated in a crush on Cotton and worked out through his rejection, one can respect the fact that a mother's death is not treated here as just another YA problem. Awkwardly developed at times, but there's some real emotion here that can't be ignored. (pp. 383-84)

*"Young Adult Fiction: 'Of Love and Death and Other
Journeys'," in* Kirkus Reviews *(copyright © 1975
The Kirkus Service, Inc.), Vol. XLIII, No. 7, April
1, 1975, pp. 383-84.*

ANNE MARIE STAMFORD

The plot itself [in *Of Love and Death and Other Journeys*] is interesting enough, but what makes the book really entertaining is Isabelle Holland's ability to capture all the precarious qualities of teenhood. Difficult as it must be to write through the eyes of a fifteen-year-old when one has passed that transient age, the author manages it with style and wit. The desperate throes of first love, the longing to be twenty-one, can be relived vicariously in these pages. The author's straightforward sense of humor when describing people and situations made me laugh out loud, a response rare indeed to novels these days.

*Anne Marie Stamford, "'Of Love and Death and
Other Journeys'," in* Best Sellers *(copyright © 1975
Helen Dwight Reid Educational Foundation), Vol.
35, No. 2, May, 1975, p. 33.*

PUBLISHERS WEEKLY

The tongue-in-cheek touch, the wry wit just beneath her heroine's frantic final plight, make Isabelle Holland's novels a great deal of fun for sophisticated readers. [In "**Moncrieff**"] the mysterious old house is in Brooklyn Heights (very aptly and authentically described), the damsel in distress knows damn well she is sometimes behaving foolishly, and she has a most engaging querulous small son, . . . able to take with a great deal of style his nervous mother's admission that her husband was not his father. . . . Ms. Holland does a neat job of putting it all together, and as always with that underlying sense of humor that distinguishes her work.

"Mystery and Suspense: 'Moncrieff'," in Publishers Weekly *(reprinted from the August 25, 1975, issue of* Publishers Weekly *by permission, published by R. R. Bowker Company, a Xerox company; copyright © 1975 by Xerox Corporation), Vol. 208, No. 8, August 25, 1975, p. 286.*

JOSEPH J. FEENEY

A pleasant entertainment though not a significant novel, **Moncrieff** offers the strange combination of a realistic domestic novel and a Gothic thriller. (p. 306)

This linking of the realistic and Gothic traditions is generally successful. As a Gothic novel **Moncrieff** offers chills and suspense, especially since it focuses much of the mystery on the old house of Antonia and her twelve-year-old son. It is carefully plotted, too, as a suspense novel requires. As a domestic novel **Moncrieff** tells about her failed marriage, about bringing up a bright son without his father, and about the motives of Antonia, her former husband, and the novelist. There are some problems, though, in combining the two sub-genres. The Gothic thriller suffers from needing the factual explanations demanded by realism; the realism suffers from overplotting and from having Dauntry, Antonia's former husband, act the Gothic villain from motives of pure self-interest and near-malignity.

Moncrieff is almost unfailingly interesting. Its exposition is smooth and natural; its first-person viewpoint, though sometimes bringing heavy-handed humor, adds immediacy both to the realism and to the fear. The style is sometimes awkward, but the novel reads smoothly. In a way it details a quest for father, son, husband, father, and love; in a way it is merely a mystery story. The fact that mystery and plot are the most striking aspects shows why **Moncrieff** stands as pleasant entertainment but not lasting fiction. (pp. 306-07)

Joseph J. Feeney, "'Moncrieff'," in Best Sellers *(copyright © 1976 Helen Dwight Reid Educational Foundation), Vol. 35, No. 10, January, 1976, pp. 306-07.*

FRANCES HANCKEL and JOHN CUNNINGHAM

Holland's novel [*The Man Without a Face*] contains one of the most destructive and fallacious stereotypes [in YA novels dealing with homosexuality and the homosexual lifestyle]—the homosexual as child molester. Justin, whose scarred face is noted by the title, is responsible for the death of a boy under unclarified circumstances. In light of such limited coverage of the gay experience in YA fiction, the possible identification of such a major character as a corrupter of children is grossly unfair. (p. 308)

Frances Hanckel and John Cunningham, "Can Young Gays Find Happiness in YA Books?" (copyright © 1976 by the H. W. Wilson Company; reprinted by permission of the authors and publisher), in Wilson Library Bulletin, Vol. 50, No. 7, March, 1976 (and reprinted in Young Adult Literature in the Seventies: A Selection of Readings, *edited by Jana Varlejs, The Scarecrow Press, Inc., 1978, pp. 302-09).**

JOSEPH A. CAWLEY, S.J.

["**Grenelle**" is bizarre]—until you recall happenings on college campuses in the '60s, the decade of uninhibited activities. Grenelle is both college and seminary of High Anglican persuasion. The clergy are both traditional and Now. And the troubles begin with the latter. That and an innocent relic. Well, the relic has been stolen and the campus hubbub begins. Much ado about nothing? So it seems—until disquieting phenomena transpire. . . . (p. 381)

The authoress wields a painter's brush in her delineation of the characters involved. Quite the master is she in rousing sympathy for or distrust of, admiration of or disgust for the actors as they come on sce, e, play their part, depart. The weaving of the plot is quite another matter. Levels of suspense build, as they ought, but the flashbacks and insights too frequently bisect the sequence. In the long run, I fear I lost my way . . . and read it a second time for clarification. (p. 382)

Joseph A. Cawley, S.J., "'Grenelle'," in Best Sellers *(copyright © 1977 Helen Dwight Reid Educational Foundation), Vol. 36, No. 12, March, 1977, pp. 381-82.*

KIRKUS REVIEWS

Sentimental as the basic situation is [in *Alan and the Animal Kingdom*], Alan's urban milieu and its population are drawn with reasonable verity, and his devotion to his kingdom is understandable, even to those who don't list keeping animals alive as a high priority value. For most kids, of course, Alan's is an eminently sympathetic cause, and the added interest of coping alone enhances his likely appeal.

"Younger Fiction: 'Alan and the Animal Kingdom'," in Kirkus Reviews *(copyright © 1977 The Kirkus Service, Inc.), Vol. XLV, No. 6, March 15, 1977, p. 285.*

FAITH McNULTY

Alan faces the world alone [in *Alan and the Animal Kingdom*]. This causes him no dismay. What does dismay him is the certain and terrible knowledge that if adults—any adults—take over his life they will destroy his animals. . . .

Isabelle Holland tells Alan's story the way fantasies are best told: with simplicity and convincing detail. Alan's problems are entirely credible. His journey, alas, is not a thrilling voyage on a raft. It is a trip into today's world. His crises and hair's breadth escapes involve ringing telephones, crime in the streets and above all money. How does a 12-year-old cash a check? How does he pay a vet when his cat is sick? Because of this urgent problem Alan meets a man as isolated and as proud as himself. Thereafter the story becomes both serious and touching.

As Alan's problems multiply it becomes inevitable that he will be cornered and his Kingdom will fall. Events force him to admit emotions he has long suppressed; rage, a longing for help and companionship, even a stirring of affection and hope. When at last Alan loses his long, brave battle to fend off the entire world he finds that surrender is not quite the defeat he feared. He learns it is possible to make peace with his own species and yet not betray his Kingdom. A story that began as a fantasy of escape ends by pointing out that emotional entanglements are inescapable—and not all bad. This is an "orphan story'' with an interesting twist. Alan tries his wings and crashes to earth, learning that in the real world no one flies alone.

Faith McNulty, "Flying Solo in Adult Skies," in Book World—The Washington Post *(© 1977, The Washington Post), June 12, 1977, p. E4.*

NORA E. TAYLOR

By art and artifice Isabelle Holland first establishes the pastoral ambience of life in a great English country house, then sends out chills of bewilderment and apprehension as that life is seen to be filled with the darkly unexpected [in **"The deMaury Papers."**] . . .

[This] is the stuff of suspense, of course, and Miss Holland makes the most of it.

As always, it is next to impossible to put down a Holland mystery until the last thread has been untangled. At that point one is likely to sigh, ''Of course, I should have guessed.'' But one never does.

Nora E. Taylor, "Isabelle Holland's Latest," in The Christian Science Monitor *(reprinted by permission from* The Christian Science Monitor; *© 1977 The Christian Science Publishing Society; all rights reserved), August 3, 1977, p. 23.*

JOE VINSON

[**The deMaury Papers**] is another of those logical suspense books which drop clues in just the right place to keep the reader interested. Unfortunately, there is almost nothing to keep the reader alert, and certainly no suspense. The few clues that are given turn out to be quite obvious. How about the plot? Unfortunately, that doesn't have any saving graces either. . . .

The most glaring deficiency of the book is the main character. She is simply a lousy person. She is always asking questions, making mountains out of molehills, and generally being insufferably nosey. She also turns out to be a terrible detective. In fact, the reader doesn't do very well either. The end of the story is both unexpected and ironic—ho hum.

Joe Vinson, "Sleuths and Spies: 'The deMaury Papers'," in Best Sellers *(copyright © 1977 Helen Dwight Reid Educational Foundation), Vol. 37, No. 6, September, 1977, p. 174.*

SHIRLEY WILTON

Angry with her father, 16-year-old Pud decides to hitchhike home from boarding school with her dog Ruff instead of taking a plane [in **Hitchhike**]. . . . As a result of her frightening experience [with four teenage boys who pick her up], she has to rethink her values and her judgments. The messages about the caring side of parental discipline and about learning responsibility come through, and Holland avoids the familiar teen novel trap of damning the older generation, but the relentlessly topical story is didactic and heavy-handed.

Shirley Wilton, "'Hitchhike'," in School Library Journal *(reprinted from the September, 1977 issue of* School Library Journal, *published by R. R. Bowker Co./A Xerox Corporation; copyright © 1977), Vol. 24, No. 1, September, 1977, p. 145.*

JOYCE MILTON

The suspense [in **"Hitchhike"**] gets bogged down in sour didacticism. Adults are always either lecturing Pud or reproaching themselves. In addition to the warning that girls who hitchhike invite rape, there are stern words on pot-smoking, people who mistreat animals, and watching one's weight. Perhaps it's the strain of handling potentially explicit material in a manner suitable to the age group, but Holland gives the impression of being out of sympathy with youth. (pp. 34, 36)

Joyce Milton, "Children's Books: 'Hitchhike'," in The New York Times Book Review *(© 1977 by The New York Times Company; reprinted by permission), October 30, 1977, pp. 34, 36.*

CORINNE HIRSCH

Deeply troubled youths struggle through the pages of Isabelle Holland's young adult novels. . . .

Holland uses [her] material successfully to explore her characters' loneliness and need for love, but she seems to mistrust her adolescent reader's ability to face the disturbing consequences of the situations she creates. To prevent her novels from becoming terribly distressing, she resorts both to shallow psychologizing and plot manipulation to ameliorate her characters' problems. (p. 25)

A further problem in Holland's fiction lies in her attempt to impose her moral values on her adolescent readers. Her eagerness to condemn what she sees as the loss of traditional authority in child rearing, education, and religion often leads her to oversimplification and distortion of character and situation. We can be sure that in a novel of Holland's, a permissive adult will be weak and foolish, while a stern, generally conservative disciplinarian will be presented sympathetically. . . . Holland's preference for conservative ideology, to the detriment of believable characterization, tilts the balance.

Nowhere are Holland's strengths and weaknesses more apparent than in **The Man Without a Face,** her most interesting novel to date. Resting on two conflicting sets of inner logic, it is a deeply affecting but nonetheless flawed novel. On the one hand, we have the cautionary tale of Charles, the fourteen-year-old product of a ludicrously permissive upbringing, who must experience the influence of traditional authority in order to develop a sense of responsibility and self-discipline. Character and plot are manipulated in order to illustrate the dangers of permissiveness and the value of discipline. Concurrently, we have the compelling development of a deep relationship between the lonely, fatherless Charles and his isolated, guilt-ridden, homosexual tutor. Holland movingly depicts their tentative groping toward one another and Charles' consequent emotional enrichment. It is only at the conclusion of their relationship, where the imposition of Holland's ideology is substituted for convincing human interaction, that belief falters.

The Man Without a Face makes a two-pronged attack on what Holland views as the obtuseness of those embracing liberal ideas either in child rearing or in politics. The chic inhabitants of the resort island where Charles spends his summers and the progressive New York private schools he has had the misfortune to attend are Holland's targets. Charles' mother is the prime example of those taken in by liberal doctrine. An exaggerated shallowness is the chief characteristic of her ideas, which change depending upon the latest fad or the identity of her latest husband. (pp. 26-7)

The progressive schools Charles attends are filled with teachers who lack any understanding of their students' individuality. Although they pay lip service to the goal of individual development, the teachers approve only of ideas that follow a liberal line. . . .

Holland's distortions of character and idea in the service of her conservative bias leave us unprepared for the delicacy of the Charles-McLeod relationship. But they certainly facilitate her positive characterization of McLeod, a traditional disciplinarian. She need only contrast his reactions to Charles' behavior with those of the other adults depicted. . . .

It is not so much in the fullness of characterization of Charles and McLeod that the novel's strength lies, but rather in the development of their intense emotional relationship and the corresponding enrichment of Charles' sensibilities. (p. 28)

Initially Charles and McLeod feel less than positive about one another. Charles is intimidated by and antagonistic toward McLeod's sternness and reserve, but it is, ironically, just those ostensibly negative qualities in McLeod that permit the withdrawn boy, fearful of suffocating relationships, to move toward him. His aloofness gives Charles the freedom to think about and become interested in him without threat to his emotional integrity. As the barriers between the two begin to break down, McLeod's evident capabilities, coupled with his masculine qualities and keen understanding, draw him into the center of Charles' fatherless universe. The undercurrent of physical attraction Charles feels for McLeod is realized through the romance and mystery of McLeod's characterization, the emphasis on his masculinity, and the constant tension of attraction and repulsion in the development of their emotional intimacy.

Charles' emergence from self-absorption to sensitivity and love for McLeod is movingly delineated. His interest in others' feelings has previously been nonexistent, except where his own selfish interests were immediately concerned. . . . Since he is not generally given to self-analysis, the early changes in Charles' feelings are appropriately divulged as a series of surprises to himself; then, as he becomes closer to McLeod, he develops a more conscious sensitivity to his tutor's feelings. (p. 29)

Holland uses Charles' dreams to express depths of feeling beyond the boy's ability to articulate or even to understand consciously. Immediately before his first dream, Charles arrives at McLeod's, and, finding his tutor out riding, goes into the stable and romps in the hay. His frolicking has a distinctly sensual quality. . . . He falls asleep and dreams of attempting to saddle McLeod's horse, which has grown to four times its actual size. The horse gets larger and larger and is about to kill him when the actual arrival of McLeod's frightened, rearing horse merges into the dream and wakes Charles.

The episode presages the undercurrent of physical desire and repulsion that runs through the novel. The coupling of the dream with Charles' sensual feelings as he plays in the barn underlines his desire, expressed in his wish to ride McLeod's frightened horse, to be both like McLeod and one with him. The disproportionate size of the horse and its terrifying attack emphasize Charles' sense that there is something fearfully wrong with his desire for identification and intimacy with McLeod.

Charles' need for McLeod as a substitute for the father he can barely remember is the ostensible subject of another dream, which occurs immediately after an upsetting incident. (p. 31)

Like the earlier dream, this one seems to deal with Charles' unacknowledged and uncontrollable sexual desires. His sub-conscious knowledge of the ambiguous nature of his feelings toward McLeod would explain both his apprehension that McLeod cannot satisfy his need for a father and his guilty horror at this realization.

Holland further develops the theme of sexual desire in scenes of physical activity between Charles and McLeod. (p. 32)

During the last weeks of Charles and McLeod's relationship, the two have become open, warm, and affectionate. Physical desire may be present, but it is expressed as companionable affection. Charles' mother and sisters have gone away for a while, so Charles has given the run of his cottage to a smelly stray cat he has befriended, whose presence in the house is forbidden. One evening, Charles returns home to find the cat kicked to death by Gloria's boyfriend for having soiled her bed. Gloria is having intercourse on Charles' bed. Distraught, he returns to McLeod for comfort, spends the night in his bed, and has a vaguely described sexual experience there.

This sudden onrush of melodramatic events is used to create a startling denouement which Holland proceeds to wrap up neatly and simply. We are led to believe that Charles deserves much of the blame for the cat's death because of his irresponsibility in allowing it into the house. . . . Evidently these disastrous incidents are further lessons in the responsibility and self-discipline that had been so lacking in Charles' permissive upbringing. Life is not all bad, however. McLeod conveniently dies of a heart attack, leaving a note forgiving Charles for rejecting him after their night together, and willing him all his belongings. Charles' mother marries her fifth husband, a good man who will make a good father (why he would want to marry her remains a mystery). Charles continues his education at boarding school, presumably a more responsible, self-disciplined person for his experiences.

The cautionary tale has taken over. It is unfortunate that Holland reverts to unconvincing plotting and rather questionable moralism to end her novel. Is a boy who allows an animal he loves into the house equally at fault with a young man who kicks it to death? Can a fourteen-year-old boy be held morally responsible for a sexual act with a grown man who knows himself to be a homosexual, no matter who actually initiated and most actively carried it through? Furthermore, as realistic fiction, *The Man Without a Face* owes its readers fidelity to human experience; it cannot sweep under the rug the problems it has been dealing with throughout. Having introduced themes rich with ambiguity, the exigencies of the novel demand that they be worked out more fully. How might Charles deal with the complicated emotional and sexual feelings he has developed? What would be a realistic outcome of his relationship with McLeod?

Adolescents, no less than adults, deserve a fully developed fictional experience. If Holland wishes to consider the difficult problems she does, she has a responsibility to explore their implications. Neither the desire to teach nor the wish to provide her readers with a positive ending is adequate reason for oversimplification. In *The Man Without A Face* more than anywhere else in her adolescent fiction, Holland perceptively raises and partially explores complex questions; but in the end she evades them by lapsing into didacticism and melodrama. (pp. 33-4)

Corinne Hirsch, "Isabelle Holland: Realism and Its Evasions in 'The Man Without a Face'," in Children's literature in education (© 1979, Agathon Press, Inc.; reprinted by permission of the publisher), Vol. 10, No. 1 (Spring), 1979, pp. 25-34.

ZENA SUTHERLAND

There have been other books about fat children, but few have explored causes and reactions with as much depth and perception as [*Dinah and the Green Fat Kingdom*]. . . . [The end of the novel brings] a clearing of the air that promises better future relations, but Holland never promises Dinah a rose garden; she's lost only five pounds, there's been no change in the behavior of her peers, and the new parental rapport is a hopeful sign but not an unrealistic capitulation. The writing style is smooth, with good dialogue and excellent characterization; it is, however, in insight into motivations and relationships that the author excels.

Zena Sutherland, "New Titles for Children and Young People: 'Dinah and the Green Fat Kingdom',' in Bulletin of the Center for Children's Books *(reprinted by permission of The University of Chicago Press; © 1979 by the University of Chicago), Vol. 32, No. 8, April, 1979, p. 138.*

EUGENIA E. SCHMITZ

This early-teenage novel [*Dinah and the Green Fat Kingdom*] is a thoroughly wholesome story. . . . (p. 111)

The book explores modern society's cruel treatment of people who are slightly different—the obese and the physically or mentally handicapped. It involves a perfectly normal family. Dinah learns that her parents really do love her, and that neither the pup nor the Green Fat Kingdom can compensate for her resentment of her rejection by society. She must decide to diet, not to please people or buy their good will but to please herself, or choose to stay fat and accept and respect herself that way.

A more artistic effect might have been created if the moral had been implied rather than completely defined by several characters. With the fiction market glutted with psychoanalyses of moral deviates, drug and alcohol addicts, children of divorced parents, and victims of persecution complexes, it is refreshing to find a well-written, humorous juvenile about normal people. The characters are three-dimensional, the plot simple, credible and fast moving. (pp. 111-12)

Eugenia E. Schmitz, "Young People's Books: 'Dinah and the Green Fat Kingdom',' in Best Sellers *(copyright © 1979 Helen Dwight Reid Educational Foundation), Vol. 39, No. 3, June, 1979, pp. 111-12.*

EMILY VINCENT

The buffetings of misfortune and bad judgment bring two unloving sisters together under their aunt's roof where with different approaches they become entangled in a mildly terrifying international plot. By the end [of *The Marchington Inheritance*] all the dangling teasers and red-herrings have been fully sorted out and there is only one victim who is so lightly mourned that he was apparently expendable. . . .

The suspense in this novel is on a par with the postman's anticipated daily delivery. A slight but not overpowering curiosity is evoked and held through the story. Most of the revelations at the end are telegraphed early in the book and depend on the inability or refusal of the characters to make connections. Avril, Ginevra, and Randy . . . are engaging and believable, but the rest of the characters come from the supernumerary stock at central casting. The atmosphere of old families going to seed is sketched with obsequious awe. There is little bite in this concoction although the juices from many sensational headlines have been squeezed into it.

Emily Vincent, "Fiction: 'The Marchington Inheritance',' in Best Sellers *(copyright © 1979 Helen Dwight Reid Educational Foundation), Vol. 39, No. 6, September, 1979, p. 198.*

KATE FINCKE

Holland seems to have a twofold purpose [in *The Man Without a Face*]. One is to speak some psychological truth on the matter of homosexuality; the other is to alleviate anxiety and to absolve guilt in the young adolescent reader about his own homosexual inclinations or acts. In order to do this and perhaps to take some of the fright out of homosexual longings, she presents a relationship between an older man and a young boy that facilitates growth. She locates the psychological motivation for the boy's love in his "lost" father. . . . Holland conveys what is missing in the family by what she includes in McLeod, the father surrogate. And this is, to my mind, a little alarming, for McLeod himself is an old patriarch—somewhat of a marine. It would seem that the moral of this story is the only way Charles can shore up his masculine identity in a family full of oppressive women and transient men is to love this masculine caricature.

McLeod is certainly a moral force to be reckoned with. The man speaks in aphorisms which feel condescending to the reader. We are suddenly in the presence of that nervous grown-up who is terribly anxious about getting his point across. We are forced to recollect our childhood irritation with adults who always knew better. Nonetheless, the point Holland is trying to make seems worthy: homosexual love can be helpful. But her point is interesting in this regard. For McLeod's greatest feat, and he is a man of prodigious feats, is to die—so that the homosexuality can be remembered by Charles as a wonderful but passing phase. The presentation of McLeod raises some important questions. Although he seems secure in his homosexual identity and is himself magnificent, he has been punished severely, that punishment including physical mutilation. McLeod is a tragic hero, an outlaw of sorts—his fate is not one you would wish on anybody. It may be romantic to love him but one would not want to be him. Thus, what Holland implies is that the transient adolescent homosexual is acceptable, but the mature homosexual is doomed.

This story is full of psychology—from the significance of the repressed memory to the intrusive mother whose love threatens Charles' masculinity. Charles' negativistic stance is carefully presented as a defense to his sister's aggressive sexuality. Psychology is most evident in the effect of the father's absence and in the collapsed father of his dramatically re-covered memory. Holland presents with noticeable oversimplification what is psychologically unsound about this family. What is needed then? A firm hand. Someone to set limits and to provide clear expectations. Someone who will not intrude. And a disciplinarian whose love must be won. An idealized man whose vulnerabilities in particular are more like tragic flaws than irritating habits. Indeed a romantic ideal. (pp. 87-9)

Kate Fincke, "The Breakdown of the Family: Fictional Case Studies in Contemporary Novels for Young People," in The Lion and the Unicorn *(copyright © 1980 The Lion and the Unicorn), Vol. 3, No. 2, Winter, 1979-80, pp. 86-95.**

MARILYN KAYE

While [*Now is not too late*] is a complex novel that revolves around an assortment of personalities and situations, it is to the author's credit that the complexity does not overwhelm the essential story or bury the main character in a sea of faces. Cathy comes across as a very real and substantial figure whose hopes and fears are as vivid to the reader as they are to herself. As usual, Holland writes with compassion and a sensitive understanding of human nature and its idiosyncrasies.

> *Marilyn Kaye, "Children's Books: 'Now Is Not Too Late'," in* Booklist *(reprinted by permission of the American Library Association; copyright © 1980 by the American Library Association), Vol. 76, No. 9, January 1, 1980, p. 667.*

ZENA SUTHERLAND

Holland builds clues into [*Now Is Not Too Late*], structuring it deftly so that Cathy's discovery that the artist [for whom she has been posing] is her mother . . . will come as no surprise to the reader. Because Holland writes with polish and perception, the crux of the story is not that the discovery is made but how Cathy will react, for her emotions and especially her feelings about those she loves have been explored deeply. Running throughout the book are some wonderfully intelligent conversations with Granny (a fine character) who helps Cathy see that it is possible to compromise with life and still maintain principles and dignity. . . .

> *Zena Sutherland, "New Titles for Children and Young People: 'Now Is Not Too Late'," in* Bulletin of the Center for Children's Books *(reprinted by permission of The University of Chicago Press; © 1980 by the University of Chicago), Vol. 33, No. 7, March, 1980, p. 135.*

MARY M. BURNS

The author has once again created a feisty character [in *Now Is Not Too Late*], bright and articulate, so that the narrative retains its conversational tone while remaining free of clichés. The elegantly crafted story offers palpable descriptions of setting and characters as well as wonderfully pungent and wise observations on the human condition.

> *Mary M. Burns, "'Now Is Not Too Late'," in* The Horn Book Magazine *(copyright © 1980, by The Horn Book, Inc., Boston), Vol. LVI, No. 3, June, 1980, p. 297.*

THE JUNIOR BOOKSHELF

Granted the initial subterfuge, the plot [of *Alan and the Animal Kingdom*] hangs together firmly, cemented by Alan's passionate concern for his animals. He commands our sympathy, however much we may disapprove of his actions; the clash of values for an orphan who has been badly let down by adults and scorns their trust is sharpened as practical demands overwhelm ideal-

istic devotion. The final resolution is neither sentimental nor engineered. . . . (pp. 143-44)

> *"The New Books: 'Alan and the Animal Kingdom'," in* The Junior Bookshelf, *Vol. 44, No. 3, June, 1980, pp. 143-44.*

PUBLISHERS WEEKLY

The youngsters [in **"Counterpoint"**], surly and rebellious, are completely believable, and as in all of Holland's damsel in distress suspense novels, there are some engaging animals. Less successful, however, is the plot, which finds Kate linking up with a bestselling author who possesses more than a touch of ESP to find out who is manipulating stepsister into near madness and causing things to go bump in the night. It isn't too difficult to figure out who the bad guys are, and once the clues begin to slip into place the suspense evaporates, which is too bad because there are some nice touches along the way involving Kate trying to win over the kids.

> *"Fiction: 'Counterpoint'," in* Publishers Weekly *(reprinted from the June 13, 1980, issue of* Publishers Weekly *by permission, published by R. R. Bowker Company, a Xerox company; copyright © 1980 by Xerox Corporation), Vol. 217, No. 23, June 13, 1980, p. 65.*

ISABELLE HOLLAND

My books have always dealt with the relationship between the child or adolescent and the adult or adults who live in and dominate the young person's portrait of self. In later years that child, become an adult, may be able to see that the first portrait was as much created by the prejudices, fears, anxieties and desires within the adult as within the child. But at the time the portrait was being painted—"You're lazy, you're stupid, you're untidy, you start well but you never finish, you're too . . ." (you can add anything to that)—they became the strong first strokes that created a self-image that the child will never wholly lose. He may use it intelligently, he may battle against it, he may suffer from self hatred, he may accept it and withdraw, he may reject it and fight the world—but it's there, like the monster over his shoulder, the shadow that follows him. And it is that struggle between the child and the adult in the creating of that self-portrait, that often preoccupies my writing. The lucky children are the ones who are taught to believe, as they go through life, that, whatever their faults may be, they themselves are lovable and estimable human beings. Most parents to not mean to convey a different message, but they often do. And if my books are about the wounds given in that message, they are also about the healing that can take place, given the right adult at the right time. And I suppose I will continue to write on this theme.

> *Isabelle Holland, "The People behind the Books: Isabelle Holland," in* Literature for Today's Young Adults *by Kenneth L. Donelson and Alleen Pace Nilsen (copyright © 1980 Scott, Foresman and Company; reprinted by permission), Scott, Foresman, 1980, p. 434.*

(Maureen) Mollie Hunter (McIlwraith)

1922-

Scottish novelist for young adults and younger children, playwright, and nonfiction writer.

Hunter is best known for her fantasies, historical novels, realistic fiction, thrillers, and mysteries. Her highly textured prose is often a synthesis of Scottish legend, Celtic myth, and realistic detail. A thoroughly Scottish literary voice, she has successfully captured the imagistic, poetic nature of the oral tradition of the Scottish Highlands. Hunter's knowledge of her country's history and folklore and a deep love for her native land are evident in much of her work. Her philosophy is humanistic, with a great faith in the potential and strength of individuals. The power of love and loyalty and the struggle of good against evil are among her major themes.

The Bodach, published in the United States as *The Walking Stones: A Story of Suspense,* is an example of Hunter's ability to combine myth and realism in her fiction. Here the author presents an ancient legend and the superstitions of an old man in conflict with modern technology. In addition to being an exciting story, it is a dramatic portrait of spiritual and moral conflict in the mind of its protagonist. *A Sound of Chariots* illustrates the versatility of Hunter's talent. Classified as modern realistic fiction, the novel explores the thoughts, feelings, and experiences of a young girl growing up in a colony of war veterans. Critics almost unanimously praised the book as a sensitive and powerful portrait of a young adult's coming of age under unusual circumstances. Hunter's views on writing for young adults can be found in *Talent Is Not Enough,* a collection of essays. Many critics and experts feel that these essays, like much of Hunter's other work, are astute, graceful, and thought-provoking.

Critical opinion of Hunter's work is overwhelmingly positive; she is at this time one of the most highly respected authors of books for young adults. While some of her work is considered too sophisticated for the average young reader, her popularity with diverse segments of this audience suggests that many young people enjoy the challenge, depth of insight, and feeling in Hunter's work. (See also *Contemporary Authors,* Vols. 29-32, rev. ed., and *Something About the Author,* Vol. 2.)

"For Children under Ten: 'The Kelpie's Pearls'," in The Junior Bookshelf, *Vol. 28, No. 5, November, 1964, p. 296.*

THE JUNIOR BOOKSHELF

As may be expected from [Mollie Hunter, *The Kelpie's Pearls*] is blended from the folk lore of the countryside, the common-sense of Morag—the old woman whose hill cottage at Abriachan forms a perfect setting for the story—and the loyalty of young Torquil, who had a great gift with animals, and who alone stood by Morag when the whole community would have hunted her as a witch.

The author's previous story [*Patrick Kentigern Keenan,* published in the United States as *The Smartest Man in Ireland,*] was centered in Ireland, but *The Kelpie's Pearls* shows that she writes with the same easy confidence in a Scottish setting. Her simple, economic dialogue forms a direct contrast to the fine prose of the descriptive passages which are embellished by a fitting use of imagery.

THE TIMES LITERARY SUPPLEMENT

Mollie Hunter's *The Kelpie's Pearls* is something of a triumph, for fantasy and magic are made to appear natural and inevitable in a modern context of reporters, buses and policemen. Its range is considerable, from humour to suspense and from pathos to something like primitive fear. Characters and landscape are realized with complete solidity, and what begins as a simple Highland story ends as a touching plea for the recognition of natural magic in the midst of mundane things.

"Breaking the Rules: Engagement and Extravaganza in Never-Never-Land," in The Times Literary Supplement *(©Times Newspapers Ltd. (London) 1964; reproduced from* The Times Literary Supplement *by permission), No. 3274, November 26, 1964, p. 1081.**

THE JUNIOR BOOKSHELF

[*The Spanish Letters*] is a good cloak-and-dagger, the plot moving at a fast pace, the characters reasonably well-developed for this type of book. There is plenty of suspense, although the usual kinds of trick are employed, the holding hostage of a beloved only daughter, and the boy hero's discovery of a secret passage to release her.

> *"For Children from Ten to Fourteen: 'The Spanish Letters',"* in The Junior Bookshelf, *Vol. 28, No. 6, December, 1964, p. 381.*

GORDON PARSONS

The 'Caddies', that strange band of beggars and guides that formed a distinctive feature of sixteenth-century Edinburgh, provide an exciting human flavouring to the vividly realized, physical setting of Mollie Hunter's story of murder, intrigue, treachery and political conspiracy [*The Spanish Letters*]. . . .

Mollie Hunter has portrayed an entirely credible society in which not all enemies are without honour. This story . . . will be seldom found on the library shelf.

> *Gordon Parsons, "Book Reviews: 'The Spanish Letters',"* in The School Librarian and School Library Review, *Vol. 13, No. 1, March, 1965, p. 95.*

ETHNA SHEEHAN

["**The Smartest Man in Ireland**" is an] exhilarating adventure-fantasy with real Irish flavor in the phrasing; and imagination, humor, gaiety and some underlying sadness in the fabric. Patrick and his neighbors have no doubts about the existence of the "Good People." Everyone who reads the book will know what to do when he encounters these not-so-admirable Celtic fairies.

> *Ethna Sheehan, "Books for Young Readers: 'The Smartest Man in Ireland',"* in The New York Times Book Review (© 1965 by The New York Times Company; reprinted by permission), *November 28, 1965, p. 46.*

THE TIMES LITERARY SUPPLEMENT

A Pistol in Greenyards confirms the view that, though Mollie Hunter falls short of the magic by which a [Rosemary] Sutcliff or a [Winifred] Bryher turns the raw stuff of history into imaginative gold, she is a fine story-teller, able to shape a plot without loss of historical integrity. . . . In the story of the short, doomed resistance of one township, and of a boy's fight against a vicious legal system that has his mother in its grip and is reaching out for his own life, the author has given the theme a spring and elation, a narrative excitement, that make this a book to recommend to two kinds of reader. It will thrill the young historian: and history will rub off from it on the reader who believes he is concerned only with being thrilled.

> *"Making the Most of Their Time,"* in The Times Literary Supplement (© Times Newspapers Ltd. (London) 1965; reproduced from The Times Literary Supplement *by permission), No. 3328, December 9, 1965, p. 1147.**

THE JUNIOR BOOKSHELF

[*A Pistol in Greenyards*] is a most vivid account of the tragedy of the Highland Clearances. . . .

This is a most gripping story, the dignity and bravery of the Highlanders in their doomed fight to save their homes makes one of the best historical tales I have read for some time—and it is a reminder that our national heritage has not always been a subject for pride.

> *"For the Intermediate Library: 'A Pistol in Greenyards',"* in The Junior Bookshelf, *Vol. 30, No. 1, February, 1966, p. 58.*

MARGERY FISHER

For Mollie Hunter, place is as important as people and causes. In *The Ghosts of Glencoe* she draws an almost unbearably vivid setting for the massacre of 1692—a brutal tale told in a forthright way. The Campbell's attack on the Macdonalds was for revenge, wrap it up in what political arguments they would; this is her interpretation of the facts, and she has gone back to contemporary documents, army papers among them, for support. . . . [Ensign Robert] Stewart is one of the heroes of the book and the very pivot of the plot: the old chief of the Glencoe Macdonalds dominates by his personality: but it is not fanciful, nor need it diminish the power of this excellent writer, to say that the spirit of old Scotland presides. (pp. 834-35)

> *Margery Fisher, "Conspiracy,"* in her Growing Point, *Vol. 5, No. 7, January, 1967, pp. 834-35.**

THE JUNIOR BOOKSHELF

Despite its inept title, [*The Ghosts of Glencoe*] is an excellent book, one of the best accounts of the famous massacre. Perhaps being a Scot without being a Campbell or a Macdonald gives the authoress insight without bias. Certainly she manages to convey the character of both Highlander and the Highlands very vividly. She also succeeds in the difficult exercise of presenting a piece of history as a novel that is convincing as a novel without distorting the facts.

> *"For Children from Ten to Fourteen: 'The Ghosts of Glencoe',"* in The Junior Bookshelf, *Vol. 31, No. 2, April, 1967, p. 123.*

THE TIMES LITERARY SUPPLEMENT

Mollie Hunter, in *The Ghosts of Glencoe,* gives fictional treatment to an historical event, and one of which every detail has already been closely studied. It would be exceedingly difficult to write an imaginative novel about Glencoe, and Miss Hunter has been content to let the tragedy speak for itself. She has chosen the device of an eye-witness who is not too strong a character to get in the way of the action, although in her concern to rescue him from the effects of his involvement with the Macdonalds she perhaps diverts too much attention from the central tragedy. This is no story for dispassionate treatment, and Miss Hunter rightly declares herself for the Macdonalds without reservation. Her portraits of the principals on both sides are brilliantly done. She is especially successful with the enigmatic Glenlyon who, by a combination of choice and fate, bears direct responsibility for the massacre. In a finely conceived epilogue the spokesman of the story meets Glenlyon behind the lines in Flanders and finds him seeking escape from the ghosts of his victims in the wine-dregs. This fine story deserves more readers than its austere format is likely to attract.

> *"Casualties of Change,"* in The Times Literary Supplement (© Times Newspapers Ltd. (London) 1967;

reproduced from The Times Literary Supplement *by permission), No. 3404, May 25, 1967, p. 447.**

THE TIMES LITERARY SUPPLEMENT

The perils of scoffing at the fairy world are . . . brought home hard to Thomas the blacksmith [in ***Thomas and the Warlock***]. A story in the true Gaelic manner, this book is more impressive in some startling individual vignettes—there is a wonderful description of Thomas, with the aid of all the village boys and their watering-cans, fixing a hot iron rim to the smouldering wooden wheel of the warlock's carriage—than in its sum. For will children really believe—and does the author want them to—that through Thomas's power over iron and his true love for his wife not only was the sinister warlock Henry Gifford overwhelmed, but also all the witches and wizards in the whole of Scotland?

> *"Over the Dream Wall," in* The Times Literary Supplement *(© Times Newspapers Ltd. (London) 1967; reproduced from* The Times Literary Supplement *by permission), No. 3404, May 25, 1967, p. 451.*

KIRKUS SERVICE

[***A Pistol in Greenyards*** is a] tale within a tale: the first an evocation of an 1854 estate eviction (Highland Scots), the second a frame for writing the experiences. . . . The duplicity of landlords, the cruelty of the law and its enforcers, the vitality of those who must defend a way of life—all enfolds in scene after scene of dramatic confrontation, and it is no mean achievement that the use of a gun for self-defense and protection of family is understood but discouraged. Whether a fifteen-year-old youngster in those circumstances could be so articulate (and literate) with only six months separating him from the events matters little; what emerges is a vivid recounting strengthened by personal reflection and subsequent distancing.

> *"Older Fiction: 'A Pistol in Greenyards'," in* Kirkus Service *(copyright © 1968 Virginia Kirkus' Service, Inc.), Vol. XXXVI, No. 1, January 1, 1968, p. 13.*

EDWARD FENTON

The point of view [of ***A Pistol in Greenyards***] is noble and humanitarian. Unfortunately, the style is so pedestrian, the dialogue so stilted and the characters so black-and-white that the story, which would be magnificent were it written with the subtle understanding of a Rebecca Caudill, ends up as melodrama.

> *Edward Fenton, "Children's Book World: 'A Pistol in Greenyards'," in* Book World—Chicago Tribune *(© 1968 Postrib Corp.; reprinted by permission of* Chicago Tribune *and* The Washington Post*), June 2, 1968, p. 20.*

DIANE G. STAVN

[***The Ferlie*** is an] overly long but nevertheless intriguing fantasy with authentic characters, setting and dialect. . . . The old question of the desirability of perfection is handled freshly here, and the story is sufficiently rooted in everyday happenings and concrete detail to hold the attention of young readers.

> *Diane G. Stavn, "Grades 3-6: 'The Ferlie'," in* School Library Journal, *an appendix to* Library Journal *(re-*

printed from the December, 1968 issue of School Library Journal, *published by R. R. Bowker Co./A Xerox Corporation; copyright © 1968), Vol. 15, No. 4, December, 1968, p. 45.*

THE TIMES LITERARY SUPPLEMENT

The detail [in ***The Ferlie***] is right, both human and traditional. The narrative moves in the proper traditional way. But ultimately the story lacks in the telling that proper grace and flow which a fairy tale really needs to make its full effect.

> *"Ordinary and Extraordinary Powers," in* The Times Literary Supplement *(© Times Newspapers Ltd. (London) 1968; reproduced from* The Times Literary Supplement *by permission), No. 3,484, December 5, 1968, p. 1376.**

JOHN SIGNORIELLO

[In ***The Lothian Run,*** sixteen]-year-old Sandy Maxwell, a bored and restless apprentice in a law office in Edinburgh, Scotland in the early 18th Century, is afforded an opportunity to escape the stifling confines of his employer's deed room when he is asked to help a customs agent track down a smuggler who managed to escape from captivity just seconds before he was scheduled to be hanged. . . . Lush with an abundance of gun-battles, escapes, murders and near-murders, this fast-paced story gathers momentum like a freight train and hurls readers into a climax involving no less than a full-scale riot in the streets of Edinburgh. The author's prose is consistently excellent, her characterizations vivid, and her familiarity with the Scottish landscape evident. This exciting, well-written novel will prove a welcome addition to any collection.

> *John Signoriello, "Junior High Up: 'The Lothian Run'," in* School Library Journal *(reprinted from the May, 1970 issue of* School Library Journal, *published by R. R. Bowker Co./A Xerox Corporation; copyright © 1970), Vol. 16, No. 9, May, 1970, p. 84.*

ZENA SUTHERLAND

[***The Lothian Run*** is a] romantic adventure story with an element of mystery and some meaty historical background. Few writers today are more skilled in this genre than is Mollie Hunter. . . . [The] story moves suspensefully through a series of intricate and dangerous adventures and counterploys. Gilmour is a glamorous Pimpernel, Sandy a diamond in the rough, and the villains are absolutely heinous. . . . [A] rousing tale. (pp. 69-70)

> *Zena Sutherland, "Children's Books for Spring: 'The Lothian Run'," in* Saturday Review *(copyright © 1970 by* Saturday Review; *all rights reserved; reprinted by permission), Vol. LIII, No. 19, May 9, 1970, pp. 69-70.*

KIRKUS REVIEWS

[***The Walking Stones*** is a] very light fantastic, deftly tripped story that seems to tell itself, to unfold] with no more of a prod than the turn of a page and the surest of elements. There's the old man by the Gaelic name of the Bodach who foresees the bringing of forest, lightning, and death to the glen by three men of the same name; his vision translates into hydroelectric power—first damming, then controlled flooding, then reforestation. . . . Donald Campbell [is] the Bodach's young friend and protege, awed by the old man's promise to forestall the flooding . . . and wondering why. But the how is a marvel: a wild now-you-see-him-now-you-don't dodge and chase with the Bodach positioning himself at the floodgates eluding capture, preventing the flip of the switch, impossibly yet unequivocally. . . . "It is known of old that this Copy, or Echo, or Living Picture, is under the command of the man of the Second Sight"; and then Donald discovers in Bocca, his private companion, his own Co-Walker—"You had only to imagine him and he was there beside you," the Bodach explains gently. "But this power fades . . . and it is only a man of the Second Sight who can keep it for the whole of his life." The ceremonious transmigration later of the dying Bodach's power into Donald's self rivals the vigorous this-wordly talk of dam-construction earlier for sheer entrancing boggling, but there's more . . . as Donald paces Bocca through the Bodach's race, now his, holding the waters back just long enough to let the stones that walk once every hundred years complete their rites. Then can the flood rush in, then can the Bodach "go to his herd"; and there will be other glens and stone-circles for Donald. . . . As graceful an unhurried talespin as ever you please or a silver-tongued Bodach could match.

> *"Younger Fiction: 'The Walking Stones',"* in Kirkus Reviews *(copyright © 1970 The Kirkus Service, Inc.), Vol. XXXVIII, No. 15, August 1, 1970, p. 800.*

THE TIMES LITERARY SUPPLEMENT

It takes a remarkable writer to push Mollie Hunter into second place. Here is that rarest of beings, the born story-teller. . . . *The Bodach* [British title of *The Walking Stones*] is a tale of the Highlands and could not belong anywhere else. Mollie Hunter paints a loving picture of her ancient hero, a "type" painting rather than a portrait, for the Bodach is a repository of traditional wisdom rather than a person. . . . The author sees no incongruity in the mingling of modern technology and ancient sorceries; nor does the reader, captive as he is to the power of her narrative. It is a charming and approachable story. . . .

> *"Modern Magic and Ancient Sorcery,"* in The Times Literary Supplement *(© Times Newspapers Ltd. (London) 1970; reproduced from The Times Literary Supplement by permission), No. 3,583, October 30, 1970, p. 1251.**

JANE YOLEN

Subtitled "a novel of suspense," *The Walking Stones* is not really a mystery tale. Rather, in a deeper sense, this story of the flooding of a Highland glen by the electric company is *about* a mystery—the deep mystery of Celtic magic. . . .

Unreal? Not in Mollie Hunter's crisply told tale. Readers, fantasy and fact lovers alike, will be caught up in the reality of unreality. As the Bodach says, "Magic is . . . something that happens when everything is right for it to happen." And in *The Walking Stones* the time, the prose, and the story are just right.

> *Jane Yolen, "Magic and Mystery: 'The Walking Stones',"* in Book World—The Washington Post *(© 1970 Postrib Corp.; reprinted by permission of Chicago Tribune and The Washington Post), November 10, 1970, p. 8.*

THE JUNIOR BOOKSHELF

The author has a strong feeling for fantasy and an ability for setting the atmosphere for magic and uncanny happenings. In all her books there is only a narrow frontier between the world of the supernatural and the everyday. . . .

The conflict between old and modern beliefs and values [in *The Bodach*] makes an absorbing story with an eerie atmosphere. The Bodach's mysterious powers will be accepted without question by most young readers because of the author's skill and ability to tell a story.

> *"For Children from Ten to Fourteen: 'The Bodach',"* in The Junior Bookshelf, *Vol. 35, No. 1, February, 1971, p. 62.*

GORDON PARSONS

It is only the high standard that Mollie Hunter's earlier novels has established that makes one express an edge of disappointment over her latest [*The Lothian Run*]. The author's native Scotland provides a setting for a fast-moving story . . . which, from many other pens, would be accepted with enthusiasm. The relatively thin characterization and mechanical manipulation of plot, however, both ring strangely from this writer. (p. 260)

> *Gordon Parsons, "Book Reviews: 'The Lothian Run',"* in The School Librarian, *Vol. 19, No. 3, September, 1971, pp. 260-61.*

SHERYL B. ANDREWS

Combining in [*The 13th Member: A Story of Suspense*] the feeling for history found in *The Lothian Run* . . . with the proven ability—as in *The Kelpie's Pearls* . . .—to create an atmosphere of the supernatural, the author has realized a new dimension in her storytelling. Witchcraft and a plot to destroy James the Sixth . . . mingle with the dawning romantic awareness of two young people to form a tale of intrigue and passion. . . . The writing is vivid—almost too realistic in certain of the "examination" scenes—while the personalities and motivations of the characters, both fictional and historical, ring true. The relationship between James and [the Earl of] Bothwell is particularly well drawn. . . . A controlled piece of writing—intense but not sensational—the book is a literary promise kept and a continuing artistic evolution implied. (pp. 489-90)

> *Sheryl B. Andrews, "Stories for Older Readers: 'The 13th Member: A Story of Suspense',"* in The Horn Book Magazine *(copyright © 1971 by The Horn Book, Inc., Boston), Vol. XLVII, No. 5, October, 1971, pp. 489-90.*

THE TIMES LITERARY SUPPLEMENT

The consummate ease with which the background of this unusual and powerful historical novel [*The Thirteenth Member*] is set masks the author's careful research into Scotland in the 1590s and the matter and manner of witchcraft. The characters are compelling. Adam, orphaned by a cruel law and now charity boy-of-all-work to Baillie Seton, is bitter towards the world until he unwillingly learns compassion for Gillie, the frail kitchen-maid who will never stand up for herself or resist circumstances. A born healer, Gillie was vowed as a baby by her mother to witchcraft, which she hates, yet is terrified of death if she betrays the coven.

The alchemist-recluse who has taught Adam book-learning is tortured also (perhaps a thought too melodramatically) by the burden of a terrible secret, but when witchcraft becomes allied to a plot to kill the king, he has to share his secret with these two innocents. . . .

The pace, always fast, increases further when the scene moves to the palace at Edinburgh, the witch trials and the final chase. The study of James VI, shortly to become king of England, the unexpected shrewdness and authority behind the slovenly exterior, and his relationship with his treacherous cousin Francis Bothwell, is masterly. James's curiosity in witches is well shown, and the contrast between Court schemers, simple fools and the three really dedicated witches. . . .

There is a matter-of-fact acceptance of the evil of witchcraft and horrors of torture which neither minimizes reality nor dwells unwholesomely on detail, but creates unforgettably the harsh, credulous atmosphere of the period.

> *"The Matter of Witchcraft," in* The Times Literary Supplement *(© Times Newspapers Ltd. (London) 1971; reproduced from* The Times Literary Supplement *by permission), No. 3640, December 3, 1971, p. 1509.*

ROBERT NYE

In Wales, you have the Tylwyth Teg, a strange and beautiful supernatural race, unfortunately much given to the stealing of children. In Scotland, a similar reputation attaches to what they call the Sidhe (pronounced "shee"). . . .

Mollie Hunter's **"The Haunted Mountain"** takes the Sidhe very seriously, as you would expect of an author who makes her home in a remote Highland cottage. The story is a powerful synthesis of legend and actuality. MacAllister, a young farmer living in the shadow of Ben MacDui (a haunted mountain) disobeys the taboo that leaves a field of every farm be unworked in case the Sidhe want it. He is stubborn and ambitious, driven partly by his love for his Peigi-Ann and partly by a deep feeling that it is up to him to make a stand for the land which is his life. He ploughs and sows the forbidden patch and reaps a whirlwind of trouble. (p. 5)

This is an uncommonly well-written tale of suspense with an unforced moral basis. Miss Hunter, while admirably matter-of-fact in the way she treats of wonders and perils, is more concerned at root to find significance in the *human* necessity of her hero's struggle to outwit dark forces. She achieves this by contrasting a sense of the vast and mysterious with a strict attention to what is small and close. (pp. 5, 24)

"There are rules to magic as there are rules to everything." Mollie Hunter keeps to them, and the result is an authentic spell-binder of a book, an allegory of modified good overcoming a sometimes pitiable evil. It is worth mentioning also that **"The Haunted Mountain"** is very much a told tale, full of the accent of burn and brae, its prose sweet with the speech-rhythms of the Scottish Highlands, elusive as the sting of peat-smoke on the wind. (p. 24)

> *Robert Nye, "Children's Books: 'The Haunted Mountain'," in* The New York Times Book Review *(© 1972 by The New York Times Company; reprinted by permission), May 7, 1972, pp. 5, 24.*

THE TIMES LITERARY SUPPLEMENT

The Haunted Mountain does not simply retell an old story, but reworks within the framework of a novel the story of Tam Lane, the man stolen by the fairies and released after seven years' bondage by the enduring power of human love. In constructing her framework Mollie Hunter uses many other familiar incidents and motifs from the fairy world. . . . The deft handling of plot, and the speed and fluency of the narrative, make this an easy read, but in its own fairly slight way it says some important things. About courage and suffering and something too about the dignity and responsibility of being only human?

> *"Celtic Revivals," in* The Times Literary Supplement *(© Times Newspapers Ltd. (London) 1972; reproduced from* The Times Literary Supplement *by permission), No. 3687, November 3, 1972, p. 1323.**

ELEANOR CAMERON

Mollie Hunter's two best books, to my way of thinking, are her second fantasy, **"The Kelpie's Pearls,"** and this, her first novel of realism, **"A Sound of Chariots."** What these two have in common is style, a fine fierce ability to share emotion. In **"Chariots,"** I find an increase in Miss Hunter's ability to go directly to the heart of a scene, to wring from it the final drop of meaning. I find an even more skillful interweaving of sights, sounds and feelings as these would be experienced by a child during a moment that will change that child's life forever.

There is a power at work in **"Chariots"** that I haven't met in Mollie Hunter's fantasies. And I cannot help but ask myself if this clarity of vision, that penetrates the smallest detail, may not have been the result of reliving a childhood of loss and turmoil. Whether it is a reliving or not, this is the most memorable of Miss Hunter's books, the distinguished account of a child's traumatic experiences and her struggle to gain the realization of selfhood.

> *Eleanor Cameron, "At Her Back She Always Heard," in* The New York Times Book Review, *Part II (© 1972 by The New York Times Company; reprinted by permission), November 5, 1972, p. 6.*

LILLIAN N. GERHARDT

The Child Study Association just gave [*A Sound of Chariots*] its annual award, but it is difficult to understand why: the pace is infinitesimally slow, the main character is a reactor rather than an initiator, the other characters pallid. . . . Bridie is described as on her way to becoming a writer, a form of creative introversion that lends no energy to this lifeless fiction.

> *Lillian N. Gerhardt, "Junior High Up: 'A Sound of Chariots'," in* School Library Journal, *an appendix to* Library Journal *(reprinted from the May, 1973 issue of* School Library Journal, *published by R. R. Bowker Co./A Xerox Corporation; copyright © 1973), Vol. 19, No. 9, May, 1973, p. 80.*

THE TIMES LITERARY SUPPLEMENT

Only a poet dares try to convey to the more earthbound of us the emotion he experiences when he sees a rainbow in the sky. A scientist, by reference to refraction, can explain all; but with the explanation the great mystery of artistic experience evaporates like a coastal haze.

Mollie Hunter is a poet, with a strong streak of the scientist in her, a streak which she handles with granite firmness while she uses it to explore the very nature of poetic imagination in her new novel, *A Sound of Chariots*. . . .

A Sound of Chariots is a tough yet tender, humorous yet tragic, sometimes horrific yet always gentle and compassionate autobiographical (surely?) novel. . . .

Though its theme is the growth and development of the poetic imagination, though its heroine is threatened and haunted through a tortured early adolescence, there is no time for self-pity here, no patience with mawkish concern over the psyche, no necessity for those esoteric intellectual fantasies so common in much of today's writing for the introspective young. This is real life, looked at through a sharply focused microscope and given artistic form.

Mollie Hunter, as admirers of her vivid folk stories and full-blooded historical novels would expect, has given us a brilliantly carpentered, no-nonsense novel of the old-fashioned kind: it has shape, plot, theme and heart. Any seasoned reader with a strong stomach, a social conscience, a sense of humour and an interest in the maturing craftsmanship of a writer will read *A Sound of Chariots* with delight—and remember it forever.

> *"The Gift of the Gab," in* The Times Literary Supplement *(© Times Newspapers Ltd. (London) 1973; reproduced from* The Times Literary Supplement *by permission), No. 3739, September 28, 1973, p. 1113.*

JILL PATON WALSH

There is a vast gulf, often remarked upon, between the childhoods of actual children, liable like all the rest of us to the fell grip of circumstance, to poverty, accident and death, and the image of childhood in children's books. Mollie Hunter's [*A Sound of Chariots*] tackles this gap head on by simply crossing it. . . . (p. 144)

This is a gripping book, though it has no plot to speak of, and whether it is or not, it reads like an autobiography rather than a 'story'. It has the sharp immediacy, the deep feeling of well-written autobiography. It will surely touch, grieve and interest adolescent readers, as it has your reviewer, but it is hardly a book for the younger child. Oddly, it takes a certain amount of maturity to cope with a childhood other than one's own. (p. 145)

> *Jill Paton Walsh, "Reviews: 'A Sound of Chariots'," in* Children's Book Review *(© 1973 Five Owls Press Ltd.; all rights reserved), Vol. III, No. 5, October, 1973, pp. 144-45.*

THE JUNIOR BOOKSHELF

[The reference to Andrew Marvell's poem "To His Coy Mistress" in the title of *A Sound of Chariots*] is apt, for two reasons. First, the themes of Marvell's poem run through the novel—joy in the body, the struggle involved in close relationships, the need for poetry and exaggeration, the inevitability of death and separation, all within a secure moral context. Second, the book is truly a part of the ongoing tradition of English Literature. . . .

The depths of grief and frustration are looked at head-on, without sentimentality, as well as achievement and joy. Mollie Hunter has told her story superbly, with power and grace.

> *"For Children from Ten to Fourteen: 'A Sound of Chariots'," in* The Junior Bookshelf, *Vol. 37, No. 6, December, 1973, p. 406.*

SUSAN COOPER

Mollie Hunter's **"The Stronghold"** takes an enormous leap back in time. . . .

The force of Druidical magic and the mercilessness of tribal ritual, are effectively shown without sadistic over-emphasis on detail. And the story of Coll's generation coming of age entwines neatly with the building of the first broch, and the rejection of an ambitious traitor. This . . . is a good book: well-written, original and convincing.

> *Susan Cooper, "Strains of Mark Twain," in* The Christian Science Monitor *(reprinted by permission from* The Christian Science Monitor; *© 1974 The Christian Science Publishing Society; all rights reserved), May 1, 1974, p. F5.*

ELEANOR CAMERON

[With **"The Stronghold"**] Mollie Hunter has given us a tumultuous yet clearly conceived and tautly constructed novel, narrated in one evoking scene after another in which there are always the swift, telling touches of detail regarding a movement, an expression, a change of mood, the precise shading of colors, the precise timbres of sounds. Too often in historical novels any lasting impression of individual characters is lost in the welter of events. But Coll, the girl Fand . . . , the fanatic Domnall, the traitor Taran, old Nectan and his wife Anu . . . , all are given tremendous vitality through the artistry of Mrs. Hunter's telling. An outstanding historical re-creation. (p. 10)

> *Eleanor Cameron, "History with Inventions: 'The Stronghold'," in* The New York Times Book Review *(© 1974 by The New York Times Company; reprinted by permission), July 21, 1974, pp. 8, 10.*

MARGERY FISHER

The Pictish broch, in spite of its likeness to the great Mycenean beehive tombs, is unique in its extraordinarily simple and effective defence-plan, and local enough to justify Mollie Hunter's attribution in *The Stronghold*. . . . In a long, entirely circumstantial novel, the author justifies her belief that the stone-built defensive tower "must . . . have been an idea before it was a fact; an idea springing from one single brilliant mind"; and in showing how Coll plans his tower, collects materials, stands firm against the opposition of the conservative Druids, she shows us also, most plausibly, what tensions and relationships must have existed in a world where superstition constituted as great a danger as the attacks of raiders or the jealousy of individuals. A close, detailed reconstruction of the past in practical terms—in descriptions of place, weather, buildings—helps to establish a brilliantly imagined picture of an ancient society which we can only know now through conjecture. (p. 2455)

> *Margery Fisher, "Power and Protection," in her* Growing Point, *Vol. 13, No. 3, September, 1974, pp. 2455-57.*

DAVID CHURCHILL

The brutal eviction of the tenant farmers of Greenyards, a valley in the Scottish Highlands, provides the core of this entirely absorbing novel [*A Pistol in Greenyards*]. The sufferings of the people are told through the eyes and experiences of one boy, who dares to draw a pistol in defence of his family, when the Sheriff-Officer comes to dispossess them so that the land can be sold for sheep grazing. . . .

The valley community is warmly evoked and the acts of simple heroism and affection are as effectively conveyed as the dreadful attack on the women and children which the Sheriff's men carry out. In all respects this is an outstanding book and must be strongly recommended. . . .

> David Churchill, "Eleven to Fifteen: 'A Pistol in Greenyards'," in The School Librarian, Vol. 23, No. 2, June, 1975, p. 147.

MOLLIE HUNTER

[It was] at the insistence of my two young sons that I wrote my first children's book, they being much charmed with two short stories I had written for them in a style which was then new to me.

There was an old, old device, however, at the heart of this style; the device on which I have since hung all the books my publishers call fantasies, and which I have borrowed from Celtic folk-lore.

A voice is implied, and as in folk-lore, the voice sounds as if recounting a familiar and accepted tale in which fact is seamlessly integrated with fancy. The modern story-teller, however, does not have an audience conditioned to accept and believe in all those incidents of the supernatural which give folk-lore its dramatic dimensions, and thus a further device is required to make such fantasies credible.

Quickly, on to the matter-of-fact opening scene, there must be brought characters with an equally matter-of-fact acknowledgment of certain superstitious beliefs and customs—and it makes no difference whether this acknowledgment is a scornful or a believing one. The seed has been sown. The reader has felt the touch of the Otherworld on his shoulder; and imperceptibly from this point, so imperceptibly that no-one notices the actual moment of lift-off, the story can soar into fantasy.

The stories I had already attempted on these lines concerned a foolish boastful Irishman called Patrick Kentigern Keenan. I liked Patrick. My sons persisted in wanting 'a proper book about Patrick', but my foolish hero by this time had discovered for me the pitfalls in trying to reproduce the authentic voice of folk-lore.

I will take the world for my pillow. Thus the hero of the Celtic tale speaks, traditionally, as he sets out on a journey which is also a quest through life. Thus the narrative of folk-lore flows in a style as spare and smooth as polished bone; and thus the high poetic insight of its verbal imagery. (p. 129)

I had given my Patrick the gift of laughter, a wife patiently enduring of his folly, and a young son dearly loved. Now I set him growing in stature as he pursued a running conflict in which he lost every battle, yet always learned a little wisdom in the process. And gained a small loser's prize too, for Patrick's opponents were fairies who always left some trace of their magic behind them. . . . (pp. 129-30)

These were the lordly and beautiful ones of the hollow hills; the skilful magicians of the Otherworld, the soul-less ones who were the ancient terror of men . . . I sensed the grue running up my children's backs as I read, the fascination of being within touching distance of that terror—yet always with the comfort of knowing there was Patrick's saving grace of laughter between it and them, always aware of the safe ground of human warmth to which they could retreat.

Until the moment finally came when it seemed there was no more room for laughter, or courage, or cunning; for this was the moment when Patrick's small son became a hostage in the conflict with the fairies, and Patrick was stripped of every weapon save his great love for the boy.

Yet still the hostage did not become the victim, for this—the love of one human for another—is the very thing the soul-less ones can never experience or understand, and over which they have therefore no power. . . . [In] basing its outcome on the triumph of human love over the dark powers of the soul-less ones, I had laid the cornerstone of my whole life's philosophy. (p. 130)

Jamie, the sixteenth-century street-boy, was also my challenge to the cosy tradition of middle-class heroes in historical novels for children; and with satisfaction, when I came to write [*The Spanish Letters*], I knew I was not addressing it to the privileged minority of readers for whom the tradition had been invented. I was writing it for all those in the shared state of being called childhood; and charging headlong with Jamie, I was going to demolish the barriers which prevented that sharing.

There were problems in all this, of course; the first being the one peculiar to Scottish writers in this field—how to set the scene in a country whose history is unknown to non-Scottish children. Secondly, I had to deal with an extension of the difficulty facing all writers attempting to convey the flavour of period dialogue without falling into the 'prithee' and 'sirrah' bog; for any dialogue in a Lowland Scots setting had also to give at least the impression of being conducted in the dialect proper to it. In narrative also, the Scot naturally uses dialect words which are infinitely richer in meaning than their nearest equivalent in standard English, and since I was determined to retain this native piquancy of expression, I had to find ways of making it self-explanatory in context.

The first 'historical' [*Hi, Johnny*] had been my 'prentice effort to cope with these problems. The second was my journeyman piece, and I emerged from it professional enough to know that this had been satisfactorily completed. (p. 131)

One other thing I knew was that a book altogether different from these two was growing in my mind, and that I had to write it.

Its scene was the Scottish Highlands. The time was the nineteenth century when thousands of poor crofting folk were 'cleared'—a euphemism for being driven with guns and dogs and whips from their native glens—to make way for sheep-farming. The incident which had gripped my imagination was that of a boy in the glen called Greenyards, unexpectedly pulling a pistol on a Sheriff Officer serving writs of evacuation there; and through this action, appearing briefly in history as the central figure in a short, doomed resistance to that particular clearance.

This boy haunted me. Looking at Ardgay Hill, from whence he and the other children of the glen had kept watch for the arrival of the Sheriff's forces, I found the thought of those other children also haunting me. (p. 132)

I knew much already of the Highlander's passionate, almost mystic attachment to his native land. Now I was reliving the despair of spirit which had filled them in the knowledge they were being driven from it, never to return. I was touching the edge of a sorrow so great that some of these people had literally died of it. But how to convey all this in a story for children? How to convey also the sense of kinship among these people, their respect for learning, their innate courtesy? Most of all, how to convey the courage of that pathetic little resistance?

I needed a new writing technique for this. I had my journeyman skill as a novelist. In the three fantasies I had written by this time, I had continued to refine the art of projecting verbal imagery. Now I needed to synthesize these separate skills into a first-person narrative spoken swiftly, bitterly, angrily, yet still with all the beauty of phrasing which comes naturally to the Highland tongue. And because children were an integral part of my story, it was the voice of a boy that was called for—the boy who had pulled the pistol on the Sheriff Officer in Greenyards.

I was unaware at the time of thinking this out, of course, that I was one with other iconoclasts then busily breaking all the rules previously observed in writing for children. (pp. 132-33)

Nor did it even occur to me that I was ripping away convention in allowing the voice of poetry to come through a boy's narrative; or by drawing this boy's character in depth so that, by showing all the linking strands of his emotions, I could also show the emotions of his people.

I had figured out a method of presenting the brutality of the attack on the women in a manner which would cause the young reader to rise in indignation rather than recoil in horror. I was eager to meet the challenge of language in my chosen medium. . . .

I felt a rage of pity for the innocent courage of these children. For they were real—they had lived through what I had to tell. And surely one child could cry out to another over any gap of years? Surely, surely, it was possible for other children to hear the courage in the cry? (p. 133)

I had already noted the compulsive force this book had exerted on the elder of my sons, although he was not by that time particularly interested in historical novels. Now the writer in me preened at this tribute—the one of all others which told me I had succeeded in what I had set out to do—and something dark which had been couching at the door of my mind began to diminish in size. But not to vanish entirely. That was not to happen until several books later, when I was walking alone in the hills around my home and thinking deeply of the fantasy then engaging me.

As always, on these occasions, I was keenly aware of the delight of manipulating language at its two extremes of exactitude and subtlety. The quiet of the glen held a sound beyond silence. The light on the hills had the gentle, ever-changing quality unique to the Highlands, necessary for the vision beyond sight; and as always, listening and watching like this, I became aware of my mind operating on two levels.

A blacksmith goes poaching. He finds evidence of a hare caught in one of his traps, but the trap has been destroyed by something infinitely more powerful than a hare. A boy makes a whistle. He plays on it some music remembered from a dream, and

finds he has discovered the secret of a call belonging to a dangerous and unnatural enemy. A young farmer ploughs land that has always before been left fallow, and finds that his action has also disturbed a dark and deadly magic.

This was the superficial level on which I had created *The Haunted Mountain,* and other fantasies; the level of the suspense story in which ordinary people suddenly encounter creatures from the Otherworld, and which a young reader could relish simply for the drama of events unfolded by the encounter. On the deeper level, however, I was continuing to pursue the philosophy which had led me to climax the first fantasy with the triumph of human love over the dark power of the soulless ones; and it was language used like a sharp tool which enabled me to penetrate to this depth, for here the suspense came from that duality of feeling which traditionally characterizes men's attitude to the Otherworld itself.

It was a world of perfection which held for them all the attraction of a golden age; a world without sickness, pain, or death, yet still a world without love in it, and thus hollow at the heart. For this was the world of the beautiful soul-less ones; and any man who entered it would be hopelessly in their thrall and became prisoner—as they were—of their desolate Eden.

And so, always between themselves and the temptation to enter this world, men interposed the barrier of this fearful knowledge. Always, for those who had been abducted to it, they clung to the redeeming promise in the power of human love. For this, men have always dimly known, is the essential of their lives. This is the thread in folk-lore that binds Greece to Connemara. That a man should retain the power to look up and see the face of his God—whatever face that god may wear. That a man should be able to stretch out a hand in the illimitable darkness of eternity, and always from somewhere in that darkness, feel the warmth and comforting touch of another human hand.

A one-to-one contact between man and God, and between man and man; this is all that ultimately matters.

This, too, is something known instinctively to the child young enough to be responding still to the pull of the wholly fantasy world of his very early years, yet still reluctant to lose the foothold he has just gained on the real world. In the half-remembered fantasy world, there are terrors lurking; in the real world, a certainty of safety. Thus, it seems to me, even the child reading the story at its superficial level will be touched by something of its underlying philosophy. As he feels the touch of the Otherworld in the prickle of his skin, so will he feel the emanation of this philosophy in a prickling of his mind. And even although the mind-prickling will be incomprehensible to him at the time, some day he may associate it with his own philosophic strivings; and remembering, will understand. (pp. 133-35)

A sixteen-year-old ordered to kill stealthily and in cold blood the people who have been his friends is no different in 1692 from a youngster of similar age in our own and other centuries. The horns of his dilemma are still the same—to obey the law, or to follow his conscience. So it was Robert Stewart's agony of conscience which became the theme of [*The Ghosts of Glencoe*]. And so it became a children's book, for Stewart's agony was the universal and timeless one which lies in wait for all young people compelled to take their first look at the distorted face of the adult world.

'History is people.' I have said this often enough to adults as well as to children, and this is the sum of all my research; this is the basis of everything I have learned about the historical novel. History is ordinary people shaped and shaken by the winds of their time, as we in our time are shaped and shaken by the wind of current events. And so, to write about the people of any time, one must know them so well that it would be possible to go back and live undetected among them.

Rather than writing from the outside looking in, then, one will write from the inside looking out. Then also, as when a raised window permits interior and exterior to merge in the air and sunlight flowing into a room, the past will merge with the present. The feelings of past and present will be shared. There will be engagement between reader and characters, irrespective of superficial differences in dress, speech, and habit; and in identifying with these characters, the reader will find his own identity.

A sense of identity. This is the key phrase in considering the desired impact of a historical novel. It was at this point in my thinking that the dark shape in my mind slipped away for good. I recognized it as it went, and knew it for that very mean emotion, self-pity. I felt an impulse to laugh at my own stupidity in having so long allowed it to linger with me; for surely, I argued, achieving a sense of one's own identity is the first step towards total identification with one's environment and one's kind? And surely, also, this total identification is only a more sophisticated term for the one-to-one contact which is all that ultimately matters?

I was back with the power of human love against the soul-less ones, but approaching it roundabout by analysis, instead of directly by intuition, as in my first fantasy. I was examining the component parts of this power—courage, compassion, humility, a passionate militancy in believing the importance of truth, justice, and honesty. I was taking a fresh look at my historical novels, and realizing why—apart from the joy of following my story-teller instinct—I had continued to write them for children.

The cloak and dagger of the first two had not obscured the fact that one had been essentially about a poor man's right to justice, and that the other had been concerned with integrity. I had followed this with a much deeper exploration into the themes of courage and conscience. Similarly, in every historical novel I had written since then, I had been concerned with some aspect of this power of human love; each of these being one that a child has to learn to recognize as a component part of the whole before it can grow from its first, intuitive reliance on this power to a reasoned alliance with it.

A caring alliance too, for loving implies caring. And caring, by its very nature, is something which stretches into the future as well as covering the present. Yet how can one care about the present unless one understands it; how understand the present without a sense of the past on which it is based? How, without a sense of the whole time-continuum of past, present, and future, achieve that contact which is all that ultimately matters?

Equally, with such a simple message to impart, how could I address my historical novels to those already lost in all the twists and guilts and deformations of the adult world? I had no interest in the crowns-and-cleavage school of writing, or in racy, sub-professorial sequences of bed-battle-bed. I could think of nothing more boring than presenting a painting-by-numbers panoramic view of a period, unless it was the repetition of a sure-to-sell formula as before.

I was interested only in trying to write well enough to tell a good story; in dipping into any period of history at will, and coming back from the experience having expressed something of my own philosophy of life. These were precisely what my historical novels for children had given me opportunity to do, and so what reason had *I* to feel sorry for myself?

We have in Scotland a saying which runs: *There's a providence looks after bairns, fools, and drunk men.* (pp. 136-38)

[If] it looks after the drunk, it surely has some pity for the mad also, for there was a time when I was—not clinically mad — but pressured beyond the brain's endurance by a book which had to be written.

I called it *A Sound of Chariots*. I wrote it one hot summer when the rest of my world was going about its business not realizing I was exploring into the great pain of my childhood which had been the beginning of my knowledge that I would be a writer. I finished it, put it in a drawer, and lived in peace at last, with my ghosts. (p. 138)

[Re-reading the manuscript after several years, I saw] for the first time how I had unconsciously demonstrated there what I had later waded through seas of reasoning to prove to myself— that I was first, last, and foremost a children's writer. For it was not an adult's remembered view of experience which came off the page, but a child's urgent view of living that experience.

With relief then, I realized how well the providence had looked after me, for although it was clearly a children's book, it was clearly also one which could never have been published as such unless there had been a revolution in children's writing during the years it lay hidden. But the revolution had taken place, and my other books had allowed me to take part in it! With shame also, however, as reviewers confirmed the editor's opinion, I recalled the foolish years; for the lesson had long been writ large in my mind by then, that self-pity, for a writer, is self-destruction.

There must be inward-lookingness, of course, but only in order to project outwards what one finds in one's inmost feelings; only for purposes of identifying in that projection with one's fellow human beings. And with that God—whatever face he wears—with whom we must all finally seek to identify, or be ever held in thrall to the soulless ones. (pp. 138-39)

Mollie Hunter, "The Last Lord of Redhouse Castle" (©1975 by Mollie Hunter; reprinted by permission of the author), in The Thorny Paradise: Writers on Writing for Children, *edited by Edward Blishen, Kestrel Books, 1975, pp. 128-39.*

ROBERT BELL

Mollie Hunter has already written successful junior novels set in the Orkneys and Shetlands. This latest one [*A Stranger Came Ashore*] is a product of her study of the Shetland lore and legend concerning the Selkie Folk, who are the seals that live in the waters round the islands. . . .

The author adapts her style in a remarkably effective way to convey the tension of the story and the impact of its climax. The language is direct, commanding and evocative, and she has a quite outstanding gift for conveying atmosphere. The book will certainly be voted a winner.

Robert Bell, "Eleven to Fifteen: 'A Stranger Came Ashore'," in The School Librarian, *Vol. 24, No. 1, March, 1976, p. 50.*

THE JUNIOR BOOKSHELF

[*A Stranger Came Ashore*] is not quite the work expected of a Carnegie winner, but it would make a lesser reputation. The hero is not young Robbie Henderson, who does some brave deeds, but Shetland. The scenery and the culture of the land, and the music of the surrounding sea, pervade the story, bringing an originality of colour to a rather conventional theme. . . . The writer sets the drama of the narrative effectively against the homeliness and simplicity of the island and its inhabitants, drawing the readers by degrees into a feeling of involvement in the beautifully primitive society. As an example of controlled development it could scarcely be bettered.

"'A Stranger Came Ashore',"" in The Junior Bookshelf, Vol. 40, No. 2, April, 1976, p. 105.

KIRKUS REVIEWS

[*Talent Is Not Enough* consists of five] essays based on a 1975 series of lectures in America and ranging from the moral obligations of a writer for children to the opportunities for language enrichment afforded a Scottish writer with access to English, Gaelic, and Doric dialects. Admirers of Hunter's fiction will be impressed by the depth of her research and by her thoughts on the sources of fairy lore; would-be practitioners of the junior fantasy or historical novel would do well to consider her technical analyses of these genres; and her thoughtful remarks on what is suitable and unsuitable in children's literature (she draws a tentative line between the normal and the aberrant)—though retaining some of the rhetoric of the platform—transcend the usual level of professional conference pleasantries. Mollie Hunter's talent has always been evident; so too, here, is her commitment.

"Young Adult Non-Fiction: 'Talent Is Not Enough'," in Kirkus Reviews (copyright © 1976 The Kirkus Service, Inc.), Vol. XLIV, No. 18, September 15, 1976, p. 1050.

MARY M. BURNS

[*Talent Is Not Enough: Mollie Hunter on Writing for Children*] emerges as a major study of the writer's craft, concerned with but certainly not limited to the art of writing for children. All too frequently, such books fall into one of two categories: the conventional "how-to" guide with emphasis on practicalities or a semi-autobiographical apologia for the writer's own productions. Rarely do such accounts, however interesting, transcend immediate concerns and deserve commendation as statements of sound critical principles. The publication of Mollie Hunter's observations and commentaries is one of these rare events. As a writer of fantasy, realistic novels, and historical fiction, she has the disciplined perspective and the knowledge to translate years of research and work into a definitive, yet personal, provocative, and warm presentation. The book, enhanced by the wit and felicitous style which is characteristic of her novels, should be required reading for all who would write or evaluate books for children—and for adults. (p. 637)

Mary M. Burns, "Of Interest to Adults: 'Talent Is Not Enough: Mollie Hunter on Writing for Children'," in The Horn Book Magazine (copyright © 1976 by the Horn Book, Inc., Boston), Vol. LII, No. 6, December, 1976, pp. 637-38.

PAUL HEINS

Mollie Hunter is best known for her historical narratives and fantasies for young people, but her present essays [collected in *Talent Is Not Enough: Mollie Hunter on Writing for Children*], originally delivered as lectures, pertain to the writing of any work of fiction, juvenile or adult. This gifted practitioner of the art of writing children's books assumes that there are natural and necessary connections linking the various areas of all good writing. She traces the filaments binding folklore to storytelling, storytelling to the experiences of an author, and an author's experiences to the sudden apprehensions often kindled by words in both writers and children.

In *A Sound of Chariots*, Mollie Hunter tells how Bridie McShane, overwhelmed by grief at the death of her father, became suddenly, instantly aware of her physical surroundings. . . . (p. ix)

From the various allusions to Mollie's own childhood experiences in **"Talent Is Not Enough,"** it becomes obvious that *A Sound of Chariots* is autobiographical. But more significant is Mollie Hunter's observation that "the range of a child's emotion has the same extent as that of an adult, and all the child lacks, by comparison, is the vocabulary to match his range." Bridie's emotions and experiences were obviously Mollie's own emotions and experiences, recollected—not necessarily in tranquillity, but certainly with intensity and with a hard-won power to convey that intensity in words. (p. x)

The whole collection of essays is an extraordinary combination of various patterns of thought and expression. . . . The general discussions of realistic and historical fiction, as well as of fantasy, are significant in their own right, but they are further enhanced by the author's feeling of responsibility toward children's literature. And her intuitive and poetic perceptions reveal her love of words and her constant desire to tell a story.

Although Mollie Hunter's stories are rooted in Scottish soil and history, the range of her fiction is wide-reaching in its sweep and universality; and, in a sense, her essays are confident assertions in another medium of what she does so well in storytelling. (pp. xi-xii)

Paul Heins, "Introduction" (copyright © 1976 by Paul Heins; reprinted by permission of the author), in Talent Is Not Enough: Mollie Hunter on Writing for Children by Mollie Hunter, Harper & Row, Publishers, Inc., 1976, pp. ix-xiii.

PETER HOLLINDALE

Mollie Hunter is by general consent Scotland's most distinguished modern children's writer. . . . [She] is read with pleasure not only in her own country or by the offspring of expatriate Scots, but by legions of young children whose prior knowledge of Celtic legend is nonexistent, and by older readers whose acquaintance with Scots history is at best rudimentary. (p. 109)

The fact is that one cannot talk about Mollie Hunter without talking about Scotland. If one finds her work parochial, one finds Scotland parochial. If one is surprised by the international interest shown in her work (given, of course, that it has the major intrinsic qualities that I for one believe it has) one is surprised that Scotland itself should be so interesting. The general idea that a confined setting means a confined range of interest was obviously laid to rest long ago. . . . But somehow the notion persists for some readers that Mollie Hunter subjects should by all the rules be indigenous, provincial, and abstruse, yet have somewhat eccentrically turned out not to be.

The opposite is true. . . . [She is a national] writer, and it is in her work that children can find the fullest recent expression of the legend and history which make Scots culture distinctive. On the other hand, she has achieved this without being at all eccentric, difficult, or insular. The chosen geographical bounds of her fiction are narrow, yet they reach to distant horizons. Her 'Scottishness' . . . is uncompromising, but it is not limiting: it is also open, hospitable and generous towards readers who are not Scottish, combining an imagination which is charged by the historic energy of a precise locale with a humane moral intelligence that seeks always to be accessible and understood.

The combination is admirable. It is also—if the impertinent generalisation can be pardoned—typically Scots. . . . Here the whole strength of Scots literary tradition is on her side, and without inferring direct 'influences,' it is not hard to see how it has aided her. First, the historical novel is one of its established forms and glories, not as in England a kind of sub-literature which has never fully severed the umbilical cord which binds it to 'escapist' romance. . . . [It enables] her to use the form with all the confidence and flexibility of a writer who knows that her national tradition fosters and respects it.

Second, and this is important for a writer who, like Mollie Hunter, is repeatedly concerned with witchcraft and the supernatural, Scots writing has a long history of concern with such phenomena. . . . A strong available tradition of this kind is clearly helpful to a modern writer like Mollie Hunter, whose historical novel *The Thirteenth Member* is also powerfully concerned with witchcraft and with bigotry, and whose 'fantasies' for younger readers touch constantly on the nearness and unsummoned energies of the supernatural.

Both technically and thematically, then, Mollie Hunter's work is assisted by a long and distinguished national tradition. She is helped, too, by its profound respect for the craft of storytelling. It is not uncommon for the storyteller to appear in some form, often very subtly, as a participant in his own stories. . . . At less-complicated levels of narrative procedure, the Scots novel is full of experiments in first-person storytelling and in identification of author and hero. For Mollie Hunter these have been particularly conscious problems—in achieving the special narrative 'voice' of the fantasies, and in judging the control of first-person narrative, or the correct 'distance' between author and protagonist, in the historical novels. *Pistols in Greenyards,* for instance, uses a 'double' first person narrative, through which the boy hero tells the story himself telling his story. The seeming oversubtlety of this method is justified both by the greater depth of insight we gain into the boy himself, and by the enhanced attention to some appalling events which is produced by our prior knowledge of their final outcome. This is the careful craftsmanship of a professional writer, but it is also the product of a tradition which regards stories highly as a means of transmitting simultaneous diversion and wisdom. That Mollie Hunter herself regards stories in this way is made clear through such characters, among others, as *The Bodach* in the story of that title, and Old Da' in *A Stranger Came Ashore.*

Linked closely to such respect for the storyteller's craft is the absence, in Scots literature, of a clearcut division between 'adult' and 'children's' literature such as exists elsewhere. . . . There is a professional certainty about her work which comes, I can only suppose, of writing in a secure tradition which respects children's literature, which acknowledges the adult reader's continuing need for tales, and which has produced a remarkable number of stories which belong to both children and adults alike and appeal exclusively to neither.

What, then, have her gifts and good fortune so far achieved? Her work falls broadly into three sections: the historical novels, the fantasies, and (so far unique in her work) the autobiographical novel *A Sound of Chariots.* (pp. 109-11)

The historical novels are diverse, both in subject and narrative tone; certain preoccupations tend to recur in them. . . . [Several] refer to the tension, not always hostile but always uneasy and ambivalent, in relations between Scotland and England. Again, they show a passionate concern for the poor, the neglected, the dispossessed, the underdogs. Both of these concerns are also present in *A Sound of Chariots,* and insofar as a coherent political mood is discernible in her writing, it perhaps has more to do with the fierce humanitarian socialism so ardently celebrated in that novel, rather than with anything specifically national.

In general, however, it is the diversity that needs to be stressed. The historical novels themselves fall into three groups. Three of them—*Hi Johnny, The Spanish Letters,* and *The Lothian Run*—I would term romances. They have serious themes, certainly, and they do not romanticise history, but the basic emphasis is on the vigorous development of stirring blood-and-thunder plots. Three others have a sharper historical focus and a more-searching investigation of human behaviour in crisis: they each involve, in Mollie Hunter's own words, 'a much deeper exploration into the themes of courage and conscience.' *The Thirteenth Member* is not affixed to any one notorious historical event, but in its depiction of innocent children trapped between the opposing cruelties of diabolism and superstitious repression—between the witch and witchfinder—it has much in common with *The Ghosts of Glencoe* and *Pistols in Greenyards.* Here too, in the recreated tragedies of the Glencoe Massacre and the Highland Clearances, young people are snared by forces more powerful than themselves, and must try against the odds to obey the dictates of conscience and keep their bravery alight.

Finally and most recently there is *The Stronghold.* In some respects this book has themes in common with the more 'serious' historical novels mentioned above: it deals with conflicting loyalties; it explores questions of belief and heresy; it presents the realities of power and the plight of the weak; it too isolates the young and tests their wits and courage to the utmost. In this way it develops basic preoccupations in Mollie Hunter's work. But this novel has a new historical dimension and a new, important theme. Its setting . . . is far more remote in time and place, far less documented, than anything Mollie Hunter has previously attempted, and places a different kind of demand on her historical imagination. And in its hypothesis concerning the origins of the 'brochs'—those extraordinary stone structures which are the 'strongholds' of the novel's title—the story explores the marvellous excitement of inaugural acts of imagination: those moments when history is altered by a single original mind. This is the novel's particular achievement—its utterly plausible and moving account of slow, meticulous, and brilliant innovation, a massive act of intellect and will. The historical depth of the novel is enormously enhanced by its reverence for this long-ago event. . . . Through Coll's vision past and present are united. Through the novel we reach out to make contact with our unnamed ancestors. In this way the book is a very impressive achievement.

In other respects, however, the book is perhaps rather less successful. It clearly prompts comparison with the work of Rosemary Sutcliff, not least because its hero, like so many of hers, is a cripple who wins his place in the sun under dreadful handicap. As a total atmospheric recreation of distant times it is less convincing than Rosemary Sutcliff's work usually is. It seems, too, incompletely imagined and structurally flawed, for reasons I should like to reapproach by way of the earlier historical novels. (pp. 111-13)

Each boy [in the 'romances' *The Spanish Letters* and *The Lothian Run*] is rewarded for loyalty and for that combination of virtues which Mollie Hunter so often links admiringly: 'courage and cunning.' Courage alone is never enough for her; without quick-wittedness and subtlety it is next to worthless. This delight in mental agility as well as physical daring is characteristic of all Mollie Hunter's work. It is refreshing and realistic, but it also raises problems.

In *The Spanish Letters* the problems are negligible. Any moral scruples for Jamie, as a Scottish boy, in serving an English master are resolved by the convenient fact that his own King James VI will shortly be king of both countries. But *The Lothian Run* is a more-complicated issue, and demands a more-complicated plot—a double plot, involving both Jacobite intrigue and smuggling. Here the rights and wrongs are less clearcut, and one cannot help feeling that the smuggling plot is adroitly used to divert attention from Jacobite and Hanoverian politics. The English master whom Sandy serves is, after all, a Customs Officer, and only by chance a political agent. (Attention is further diverted from the straight dynastic conflict by the fact that the chief Jacobite agent is not a committed Stuart loyalist but a cruel, unprincipled mercenary.) In this way contentious political matters, which Mollie Hunter is understandably reluctant to simplify, are instead evaded, and the unambiguous rights and wrongs of smuggling placed in their stead.

The trouble is that these rights and wrongs are *not* unambiguous except in law. Part of Sandy Maxwell's duties on 'secondment' to the Customs Service is to mingle with the fisherfolk of Prestonpans, helping them to repair their boats. In this way he can eavesdrop on their talk, and draw them into indiscretions. His first target is the fisherman Rob Grierson. This is all very well in the impersonal world of law enforcement. But Sandy's world is not impersonal. [These] are men whom Sandy has known from childhood, . . . men who, so far as their wariness allows, are his friends. . . . Later on, Sandy is directly responsible for Rob's capture and imprisonment.

We know that the exploitation of friendships is a time-honoured ruse of efficient law-enforcement. All the same, it is difficult not to feel distaste for Sandy's behaviour here, while also feeling that one is expected to admire its skill and daring. (pp. 113-114)

[Hunter's dialogue] is intensely dramatic—contentious, suspicious, watchful. Even so, the subtleties of Sandy Maxwell remain questionable, and with them there remains the possibility that Mollie Hunter, in celebrating certain intellectual and moral qualities with such impressive vigour and conviction, tends to overlook other aspects of behaviour, and hence to condone the unpardonable.

The same kind of tension between simple values and complex behaviour is also apparent in Mollie Hunter's love of double meanings. She is clearly fascinated by equivocation and ambiguity. This is another aspect of 'courage and cunning,' and it is the resource of good characters as well as bad. (p. 114)

To return to *The Stronghold*, here we have more double meanings. In the first part of the novel a power struggle takes place between the tribal chief, Nectan, and the Chief Druid, Domnall, and the reader's sympathies are clearly aligned with Nectan. In the aftermath of Domnall's uneasy victory comes his terrible counterstroke, the choice of Nectan's daughter Fand to be the virgin sacrifice at the sunrise festival of Beltane. Coll, whose brilliant mind conceived the brochs, is Fand's foster-brother and lover, and he conceives the further idea of saving her. To do this he need only disrupt the festival enough to delay Fand's death beyond the sacred moment of sunrise, and, having contrived disturbance of the ceremony by fostering doubts of Fand's virginity, he finally achieves his purpose with the superb ambiguous confession: 'I have spoiled the sacrifice.' This is cleverly and bravely done, for love.

However, a consequence of the Beltane festival . . . is the transformation of Domnall from enemy to ally. Aversion is abruptly converted to sympathy; religious tyrant becomes aged hero and sage. In itself the change is too sudden and extreme. But it also leaves unresolved the question of Domnall's choice of Fand as the Beltane sacrifice. Was this indeed a choice made by the gods themselves, and mediated through Domnall as their priest? Or was it Domnall's own vindictive revenge on Nectan and his tribe? Or was it a skilful manoeuvre to gain political power? All these are possibilities. . . . [The] whole distribution of sympathies in the novel, fundamental questions of faith and doubt which it has raised, the whole movement of the plot at the Beltane festival, are left unresolved in a cloud of devious ambiguity. For all its power, the novel thus lacks imaginative wholeness, and its fragile unity rests instead on mere verbal equivocation.

This points, I think, to a self-damaging conjunction of skills in Mollie Hunter's historical novels. They rest, in the end, on a few very simple, very profound values: courage, loyalty, initiative, truth, creative intelligence, and above all on love. Yet their superstructure depends on quite different terms of reference: on the realities of political intrigue and struggles for power, on expediency, on ruthless service to a cause, on ambition and opportunism, on equivocation and duplicity. I do not suggest that Mollie Hunter *approves* of all these things, only that she recognises their prevalence. The result is a certain imaginative discordancy and moral inconsistency. Two sets of values coexist in unreconciled confusion. Only *The Spanish Letters* and *The Thirteenth Member* (for differing reasons) are entirely cohesive. Of the other novels, *Pistols in Greenyards* and *The Stronghold* in particular are very impressive works in many ways, and all the stories have their merits. But Mollie Hunter has yet to write a historical novel which is fully commensurate with her gifts.

The fantasies are a different matter entirely.

In this group of stories, which take as their theme the relationship between humankind and the many supernatural beings of Celtic myth, we find a narrative form under immaculate, almost flawless control. The books have much in common. In all of them a child or an adolescent has a crucial role to play—'children see with the eyes of truth'—and even when the child is the hapless victim of adult folly . . . , he has moments of wisdom beyond the reach of his parents. Usually, however, the child has insights which are closed to adults, and with his understanding comes the need for a resolute courage in facing dangers which he alone knows to exist, or which he alone must undergo. In these stories it is a great happiness to be young, but it is also a solemn and momentous responsibility.

A conspiracy of vision commonly exists between the young and the old. . . . Death is not excluded from the compassionate humanism of these magical stories. . . . Natural rhythms of youthful strength and aged weakness, of growth and decay, coexist in the stories with the unearthly everlastingness of the nonhuman world.

Between young and old are the grown men and women, often deprived of the wisdom which belongs to elders and children. The parents, like Peter and Janet in *A Stranger Came Ashore* or the Campbells in *The Bodach,* are often good-natured and well-meaning, but unsuspicious of strangeness or danger. They are frequently more childlike than their children. This is especially true of those three reckless heroes of stories which resemble each other closely in theme, structure and feeling: Patrick in *Patrick Kentigern Keenan,* Thomas the blacksmith in *Thomas and the Warlock,* and MacAllister in *The Haunted Mountain.* All three are rash enough to challenge the malignant powers of magic; all three owe their final happiness to the reciprocal love between father and son; all three depend above all on their love of their wives, and the faithful, patient, and forgiving love they receive in return. Each of the three stories moves with relentless inevitability towards a climactic battle with the imprisoning forces of magic: these are titanic scenes, and in each of them the human victory is won by love, the redemptive emotion of mortals, which the timeless supernatural can neither feel nor understand. (pp. 115-16)

The matter of these stories accords completely with the manner of their telling. The narrative comes essentially from a *speaking* voice of distinctive quality. It is matter-of-fact and brisk, daring the reader (or listener) to find anything implausible in its strange tales; it is confidential and intimate; but it is also spare and economical, almost bardic in its adroit and dignified simplicity; and it is full of humour and full of music, not least the music of Gaelic idiom and sentence-forms. These diverse qualities merge, with remarkable consistency and control, to express a wide span of moods and emotions within a taut narrative structure. This style is an extraordinary achievement: one example of the effects it allows is the characteristic undulation of mood which occurs near the end of several of the stories. That is a smooth and delicate transition from sorrow and wistfulness to acceptance and joy. *The Kelpie's Pearls* has it to perfection; so do *The Haunted Mountain* and *The Bodach.* (p. 117)

Mollie Hunter's fantasies, and above all *The Haunted Mountain,* are in my judgement one of the outstanding and most-original achievements of contemporary children's fiction.

Last, and unique in her work, is *A Sound of Chariots.* It is an extraordinary novel, avowedly autobiographical, and of all her works the one least-sensibly labelled a 'children's book.' It is for children, certainly, if they are mature enough to cope with its relentless emotional honesty and the dark valley of childhood tragedy through which it passes. It is for adults equally: a far better, more accomplished, more demanding book than most novels of childhood published with an adult readership in view.

The patterning of the novel is an act of mature imagination. It opens with the central, cataclysmic event: the death in her mid-childhood of Bridie McShane's beloved father. The first half of the novel then reapproaches that moment of shattering bereavement; the second explores its aftermath. This structure invests many moments and episodes with searing irony, or haunting sadness, or almost unbearable pain. Through the shaping process of retrospect Mollie Hunter can also trace the pattern of Bridie's growth: her developing love and command of language, her fierce independence and stubbornness, the rebellious passion for justice that she inherits from her father. She can also highlight the crucial incidents which decide the wider pattern. It is this act of retrospective imagination which transforms the fiction of memory from mere reminiscence to art. And through it we can see the origins of those central themes and energies which inform her other work. (pp. 117-18)

It would be wrong to present *A Sound of Chariots* as a uniformly painful book. It is often very funny, and Bridie's turbulent, youthful spirit provides a counterpoint against the weight of loss and grief. All the same, its central subject is mortality, its central emotion Bridie's obsessive consciousness, having lost her father, with the passage of time and her own inevitable death. Within the mature patterning of the novel—and because of it—we are made vividly intimate with the youthful Bridie, and share with her the appalling clarity of initial experience. . . .

She goes forward from childhood, aware of so much life to be lived, so many words to be written, pursued by a sound of chariots. The novel which emerges from it is powerful, deeply felt, beautifully written, and starkly memorable.

To borrow another phrase from ["To His Coy Mistress" by Andrew Marvell], Scotland has given Mollie Hunter 'world enough, and time.' It is a sufficient canvas for her very distinguished work, and its historical and mythical depths have provided her with that deep time-perspective by which she has remained obsessed. There is an undertone of fateful sadness running through her novels, sadness with which the vibrant energies of youth and the spirit of human love must always find the courage to contend. (p. 118)

Peter Hollindale, "World Enough and Time: The Work of Mollie Hunter," in Children's literature in education (© *1977, Agathon Press, Inc.; reprinted by permission of the publisher), Vol. 8, No. 3 (Autumn), 1977, pp. 109-19.*

GORDON PARSONS

The Ghosts of Glencoe embodies most of the strengths that we associate with writing for children of a more confident day—pace, sustained excitement, clearly defined characters and a happy ending which is in no way marred by the moral questions raised by the subject, even though that subject may be the treachery and the gratuitous and bestial violence of the massacre of Glencoe.

Gordon Parsons, "Eleven to Fifteen: 'The Ghosts of Glencoe'," in The School Librarian, *Vol. 25, No. 4, December, 1977, p. 353.*

NORMAN CULPAN

[In *The Wicked One* action] is fast, events are credible and consistent given the magical premises, and a dry humour unobtrusively pervades the whole. . . . Tone and style I found most attractive: apparently casual but always economical; simple but neither patronising nor banal; sympathetic but never sentimental: a good story.

Norman Culpan, "Seven to Eleven: 'The Wicked One'," in The School Librarian, Vol. 26, No. 2, June, 1978, p. 42.

STANLEY COOK

It was providence that the book of Mollie Hunter's I read last was *A Sound of Chariots*. It is the author's answer to the questions that build up in covering the range of her works. She is a most compelling storyteller, yet sometimes one senses she is having a butterfly's troubles with its chrysalis in her use of the formulas of children's fiction. *A Sound of Chariots* is an emotional autobiography apparently and an apologia. . . .

The movement of Mollie Hunter's work is from the historical to the supernatural, to an Old Testament position where natural and supernatural rub shoulders in daily life. . . . The position is given in terms of the 'old religion' that Christianity superseded, but its exponents have the intensity of John Bunyan; the young men dream dreams and the old men see visions and the latter are in effect the Law and the Prophets. The penetration of ordinary life by the supernatural in earlier days requires, one can argue, this kind of presentation in order to provide an authentic picture. It is necessary even if we do not think it is literally true. . . . In practice, she writes too well not to achieve 'willing suspension of disbelief'. (p. 108)

Real powers of evil for witches and warlocks can be granted only on Christian terms: therefore with continued tact Mollie Hunter presents witchcraft mainly as fraud and delusion that are only too human. Compare her *The Thirteenth Member* and Shakespeare's *Macbeth,* which both use the account of the exposure of witchcraft in the sixteenth-century *Newes from Scotland,* to see how she explains as politics what Shakespeare suggests is supernatural. To her, witchcraft is to the old religion as pornography is to love stories; and as with pornography people are in it for gain. Thus witchcraft in Mollie Hunter's work is part of her *historical* fiction: her folk tales deal with the imaginative appeal of the supernatural; her stories of witchcraft with the social significance of a superstition. (pp. 108-09)

It is most obvious in the early *Hi Johnny,* where the kings of Scotland and the gypsies serve for Richard I home from the Crusades and Robin Hood respectively. It tends to write the story, though an exciting one, in *The Lothian Run,* for the hero's psychology is neglected so that he slips into becoming something of a secret police cadet who denounces the smuggler who delivers his mother's tea. *The Spanish Letters* seems to me a much happier version of *The Lothian Run.* . . .

It is unusual for a children's novel to put superstitions so much in historical perspective as does *The Thirteenth Member.* . . . Here and in *The Ghosts of Glencoe* there is, outside any formula, historical fact which has aroused Mollie Hunter's imagination. The choice of historical fact makes *The Ghosts of Glencoe* inevitably parallel to [Robert Louis Stevenson's] *Kidnapped,* a position it can sustain, for it is a moving story, better in my opinion than *The Stronghold,* which received a Carnegie Medal, and a near-classic. (p. 109)

[*The Stronghold*] proceeds with the dignity of a medal-winner, i.e. perhaps a shade too educationally. . . . Perhaps it is contemporary troubles that make me feel friction over nineteenth-century enclosures in *A Pistol in Greenyards* is rather journalistic. In both these books Mollie Hunter remains the born storyteller and they are successful realisations of interesting pe-

riods of history, but I think she does not make quite the clean lift of the story that one comes to expect from her.

Noteworthy achievement though her historical novels are, the form in which Mollie Hunter's Celtic powers move most sweetly and with an inevitability is the folk tale, about the old religion, the little people and, usually, the remoter parts of Scotland. She is the kind of traditional storyteller to whom she herself keeps referring. Above all she *sounds* like one.

I particularly admire *Patrick Kentigern Keenan* and *The Bodach*. . . . [Her] stories, linked to come to a climax through varied moods, of Patrick Kentigern Keenan, 'the smartest man in all Ireland', seem to me faultless. . . . In *The Kelpie's Pearls* the forceful man who tangles with supernature transfers from the role of hero to that of downright villain. The shift is plausible; there is a moving ending; it is another fine story.

The Bodach is a folk tale set against a hydro-electric scheme: a success and therefore something of a *tour de force*. To combine successfully two such apparently dissimilar elements as modern technology and Highland legend especially requires the charming *sound* I have referred to. . . . *The Bodach* is delivered direct to the reader. (pp. 109-10)

The Wicked One does extend the Mollie Hunter reader's knowledge of the old religion . . . but I felt that, while the story maintained a grip, it was not with as powerful magic as the folk tales I have criticised in my previous two paragraphs. I felt the same about *Thomas and the Warlock*. It ends with witchcraft, something I think Mollie Hunter does not believe in, and she does not make me believe in it either. On the other hand, while I was reading *A Stranger Came Ashore* I felt that its legend was history. This book resembles, but with a different balance, *The Stronghold:* in the latter the supernatural is part of daily life, but in *A Stranger Came Ashore* daily life is part of the supernatural. (p. 110)

Altogether I feel that while some of Mollie Hunter's books are especially memorable—*Patrick Kentigern Keenan, The Bodach* and *The Ghosts of Glencoe* for me—it is the mind behind them that is most compelling. The idea of her chosen landscape alive with people and itself alive is gospel to her. (p. 111)

Stanley Cook, "Children's Writers, 3: Mollie Hunter," in The School Librarian, Vol. 26, No. 2, June, 1978, pp. 108-11.

GERALDINE DeLUCA

A certain simplicity of explanation, an occasional withholding of details—what the heroine's father died of, for instance—identify [*A Sound of Chariots*] as a work for children. And Mollie Hunter is, of course, an accomplished writer of children's books. . . . [Her books] are heavily plotted and detailed, with a clear, unobtrusive style and a sure sense of storytelling. But *A Sound of Chariots* is a remarkable departure. It seems clearly to be her own story, and while she sustains the narrative at a level comprehensible to children, the writing is dense with lush language and startling, impressionistic passages of discovery and meditation. What's more . . . she writes a story that traces the gradual evolution of its heroine, Bridie McShane, from early childhood to young womanhood. And without ignoring the problems and the sense of alienation of adolescence, she places them in a framework of a life, of generations. Hunter offers her reader a sense that there are underlying structures to a life, and that adulthood can be something other than a descent into contemptible compromise, that it can bring with it a sense of competence, grace, and power.

Fortunately, even though the heroine plans to be a writer, the novel is not written in the first person. In the world of *A Sound of Chariots,* children would not make their voices heard that way. Moreover, Hunter is much too attached to the elegant and rhythmic use of language to limit herself by assuming a voice with less range and maturity than her own. For the progress of the novel is marked by intense, meditative moments of revelation, recorded in baroque swells of prose that describe Bridie's insights and her sometimes frightening epiphanies. When she gains a sudden awareness of the nature of death, for example, she feels the blood coursing through her with the passing of each second, and she understands how each second brings her closer to her own end. . . . (pp. 92-3)

This awareness grows from the central event in the novel, which is the death of Bridie's father, Patrick McShane. His death divides the book into its two parts. The first part opens with his funeral, flashes back to Bridie's life with him, and then closes again with the same scene—the limousine pulling up in front of the house and Bridie's mother getting out of the car. It is an effective structural device, because in the interim between the first scene and its repetition, the reader comes to know the father and to share Bridie's pain at her loss. The second part of the book records Bridie's response and adaptation over the next four years. (pp. 93-4)

The uniqueness and authenticity of *A Sound of Chariots* may stem from the fact that it is autobiographical. Absolutely uncontrived, it captures the mind of a young adolescent the way few adolescent novels do. (p. 96)

> *Geraldine DeLuca, "Unself-Conscious Voices: Larger Contexts for Adolescents," in* The Lion and the Unicorn *(copyright © 1978 The Lion and the Unicorn), Vol. 2, No. 2, Fall, 1978, pp. 89-108.**

JANET HICKMAN

Certainly it is hard to imagine how one could bring more of self to writing than [Mollie Hunter] does. Cultural heritage, life circumstances, love of language, passionate convictions—all the influences on the storyteller are in the stories. (p. 302)

If you cannot visit Scotland for yourself, Mollie Hunter's books are an agreeable substitute. . . . All of her writing demonstrates her deep feeling for the land where she was born. . . .

The settings of her books are not just faithfully represented, they are evoked. . . .

It is not only the author's ability to call up the sights of her country that makes Scotland so memorable in her books. She has long been interested in its history and folklore, and has expert knowledge in both fields. (p. 303)

All her books of fantasy are rooted in this intimate knowledge of folk culture. . . . In *The Kelpie's Pearls,* white witchcraft and a legendary water spirit in the guise of a horse are put in a modern context. The Selkie Folk and trows and *sidhe* of whom she writes are creatures of fantasy, but their origins are tied to the world we call real. . . .

Another significant part of Mollie Hunter's writing is historical fiction, a reflection of her interest in Scotland's past. . . . In her words, she carries "a fairly full and accurate picture of my own country's history in my mind." She brings that picture

to life in such books as *The Spanish Letters,* [*The Ghosts of Glencoe,* and *A Pistol in Greenyards*]. (pp. 303-05)

Her natural inclination to tell stories is as much a part of her work as is her passion for history or her knowledge of folklore. . . . She cares intensely about the right word. (p. 305)

Mollie Hunter is a self-made scholar whose lack of formal education has not kept her from learning, or from achieving. Her characters, too, are frequently unschooled; but they have native intelligence, a wisdom that cannot be taught, and an admirable eagerness to learn. One thinks of the brilliance of Coll's imagination in *The Stronghold,* of Torquil with his gift of King Solomon's Ring in *The Kelpie's Pearls,* and of Adam in *The 13th Member,* whom the alchemist calls "this most teachable of boys."

Again like Bridie [the protagonist of *A Sound of Chariots*], Mollie Hunter's characters are most often intense, strong-willed, passionate, outspoken. (pp. 305-06)

Passing on stories is the endeavor to which Mollie Hunter is most deeply committed. The strength of that commitment and her sense of responsibility to children are evident in her book of essays, *Talent Is Not Enough.* The title essay . . . paraphrases Emerson: "There must be a person behind the book." Mollie Hunter is the person behind all her books—a complex, caring, vividly alive person. She and her books are well worth knowing. (p. 306)

> *Janet Hickman, "The Person Behind the Book—Mollie Hunter" (copyright © 1979 by the National Council of Teachers of English; reprinted by permission of the publisher and the author), in* Language Arts, *Vol. 56, No. 3, March, 1979, pp. 302-03, 305-06.*

CHUCK SCHACHT

The usually reliable [Mollier Hunter's] latest [*The Third Eye*] can best be compared to haggis, a uniquely Scottish dish made primarily from sheep organs; it may be appreciated in its native land, but is unlikely to appeal to the appetites of young readers on this side of the ocean. What plot there is revolves around young Jinty Morrison, the youngest of three daughters in a poor but proud Scottish family during the Depression. Her *Third Eye* (psychic sensitivity) makes her especially aware of the troubles of people around her. . . . The tale is told as a series of flashbacks by Jinty, but precious little of interest occurs to her throughout and the various plot threads are neither well integrated nor especially riveting, although a number of the characters, especially Meg's oldest sister and the Earl, are portrayed with sympathy and insight.

> *Chuck Schacht, "Grades 3-6: 'The Third Eye'," in* School Library Journal *(reprinted from the April, 1979 issue of* School Library Journal, *published by R. R. Bowker Co./A Xerox Corporation; copyright © 1979), Vol. 25, No. 8, April, 1979, p. 57.*

THE JUNIOR BOOKSHELF

What a fine writer Mollie Hunter is! One might think that, with her preoccupation with the Scottish scene, her stories might slip into monotony, but not a bit; she is most resourceful in finding new themes, springing naturally from the conflicts generated between people and their environment.

The Third Eye is largely about a place, Ballinford in West Lothian. . . . The action is seen through the eyes of Jinty

Morrison, youngest of three girls, not the brightest but the most sensitive. Jinty is fey. Her love for her mother is mixed liberally with fear, and Mistress Morrison is certainly a difficult woman, and one with a past. I guessed the secret which made her so horrible to live with quite early in the story—and most readers will do so too—but this does not spoil the pleasure at all. This is not a mystery story but a complex study in character and a study of a community and a family.

Miss Hunter has adopted rather a difficult device for telling her story, mostly in extended flashbacks. Children are familiar with this, especially from their television viewing, and there should be no real problem. I find it impossible to believe that they will not pay the writer the compliment of total surrender to the powerful narrative and the quiet and persistent appeal of the young heroine. It is a strong drama, but there is plenty of fun to accompany the tragedy and to complete the picture of a whole community. How splendidly Miss Hunter rises to her big scenes, the anvil-wedding and the ice-party. A book to savour, to read slowly and then to read again noting how beautifully every episode is dovetailed into the main structure.

"The New Books: 'The Third Eye'," in The Junior Bookshelf, *Vol. 43, No. 4, August, 1979, p. 221.*

MARGARET MEEK

The grainy texture of the narrative and the evocation of doom (in the sense of judgement) are excellently done [in ***The Third Eye***].

The action takes place in 1932 when Jinty is made to recall a series of events leading to the death of the earl, in whose hands lies the fate of his retainers. . . . Despite the author's skill in keeping the resolution of the puzzle right to the end, the way in which Jinty unravels the threads of her awareness is too

predictable, too circumstantial. In short scenes, mother and daughter encounters, the book has power, but the fatal spell cast by the rich and authoritative detracts from the real heart of the matter, the simpler but more convincing annals of the poor.

Margaret Meek, "Eleven to Fifteen: 'The Third Eye'," in The School Librarian, *Vol. 27, No. 3, September, 1979, p. 273.*

MARGERY FISHER

The Third Eye [is] an extraordinarily vivid and impressive study of a family and a community in a Scottish town in the 1930's. Attention is held from that first sentence right up to the end of the book, by which time we have learned why Jinty had to be questioned and how her answers contributed to the explanation of a tragedy which affected the whole of Ballinford, the presumed suicide of the Earl. I said 'we have learned' but I think 'discovered' would be a truer word, for Mollie Hunter works out her plot so expertly and directs her narrative so firmly that we are drawn completely into the book, getting to know the characters in the slow, partial manner of real life. This is a book for an active and experienced reader. . . . Though this is not a first-person story, the revelations of a family secret and of the secret motives for the Earl's death are described as they might naturally have been received by a girl of fourteen for whom they bring a heavy responsibility. Unerring in its documentation, lucid and rhythmical in style, this is one of those rare novels which seems to have grown rather than to have been constructed, so that it satisfies as a unique piece of writing. (p. 3595)

Margery Fisher, "Generations," in her Growing Point, *Vol. 18, No. 4, November, 1979, pp. 3591-95.**

Margaret O(ldroyd) Hyde

1917-

American nonfiction writer for young adults and children, and editor.

Hyde is a noted writer of books dealing with scientific and social issues. She selects each subject for its importance to young people and approaches the material from a practical standpoint. Hyde thoroughly researches each of her topics and consults experts in order to provide the most recent information for her readers. Her writing style is clear and easy to follow, although some critics believe her books could be better organized. She has been praised for her talent of exploring the most fascinating questions in science and for rendering complex concepts, such as molecular structures, in understandable terms.

Hyde's books emphasize the day-to-day application of scientific information. *Atoms Today and Tomorrow* explains the properties of the atom and concentrates on the peaceful uses of atomic energy. In *Driving Today and Tomorrow* Hyde explains the mechanics of automobiles and offers suggestions on how to be a better driver. Other books on drugs, venereal disease, rape, and suicide objectively discuss relevant facts and implications and include references for further reading and counseling. Hyde has also written studies of such issues as pollution, overpopulation, and runaways. She has often been faulted for failing to present new facts on a subject, yet she offers her readers informative material and shows them ways to improve their lives and environment. (See also *Contemporary Authors*, Vols. 1-4, rev. ed., and *Something About the Author*, Vol. 1.)

VIRGINIA KIRKUS' BOOKSHOP SERVICE

[*Flight Today and Tomorrow* is a] satisfactory once-over-lightly on flight. . . . A personalized narrative puts the reader in the pilot's position and the flights he goes on rise from a monoplane to a moon-bound rocket. All possible essentials, for so short a book, are well presented, and its unique contribution is its over-all view instead of a particular aspect, of all flight.

> *"Eight to Eleven: 'Flight Today and Tomorrow',"* in Virginia Kirkus' Bookshop Service, *Vol. XXI, No. 16, August 15, 1953, p. 589.*

DOROTHY SCHUMACHER

[*Flight Today and Tomorrow* is an] elementary book on airplanes and the theory and technique of flight. . . . [Hyde writes in short], simple, declarative sentences. . . . Explanations are clear and examples, well chosen. . . . Since there is always need for more material on aviation, this book, with timely chapters on new war planes, rockets, and space travel will be useful. . . .

> *Dorothy Schumacher, "Older Boys and Girls: 'Flight Today and Tomorrow',"* in Library Journal *(reprinted from* Library Journal, *December 15, 1953; published by R. R. Bowker Co. (a Xerox company);*

copyright © 1953 by Xerox Corporation), Vol. 78, No. 22, December 15, 1953, p. 2226.

LOUISE S. BECHTEL

Mrs. Hyde writes for the teen-ager who soon will be a driver [in **"Driving Today and Tomorrow"**]. She opens cleverly with "personalities on the road," . . . then gives some excellent beginner's lessons. Special needs for special skills and dangers, highway rules, how to be an expert, all are most ably covered. An excellent book for schools, libraries and homes, this will be just as illuminating to adults as to teen-agers.

> *Louise S. Bechtel, "Books for Boys and Girls: 'Driving Today and Tomorrow',"* in New York Herald Tribune Book Review *(© I.H.T. Corporation; reprinted by permission), June 6, 1954, p. 11.*

LEARNED T. BULMAN

The combination of unskilled driver and car is one of man's most dangerous weapons. Too few drivers understand the simple scientific principles on which a car operates or have had

171

proper driving instruction. In **"Driving Today and Tomorrow"** Margaret O. Hyde . . . explains with admirable clarity the mechanics of the automobile, and its maintenance and discusses safe driving methods, the causes of accidents and ways to avoid them. This is a fine book for a beginning driver to read before he—or she—gets behind the wheel.

> Learned T. Bulman, "Driving and Riding," in The New York Times Book Review (© 1954 by The New York Times Company; reprinted by permission), June 6, 1954, p. 35.*

ALFRED D. BECK

Young people-and adults too-will find **"Atoms Today and Tomorrow"** informative, accurate and unexpectedly pleasant reading. Unlike so many books on atomic energy, this one does not foster fear and frustration. There are no pictures of menacing mushroom clouds, blasted buildings and pathetically maimed humans. [The text tells] an up-to-the-minute story of the many peacetime uses of atomic energy.

Mrs. Hyde discusses frankly the serious hazards of working with radioactive materials, but she stresses the elaborate safeguards provided to all workers. . . . An important contribution of this book may be the encouragement of young people to enter careers in atomic industries and professions.

> Alfred D. Beck, "For Younger Readers: 'Atoms Today and Tomorrow'," in The New York Times Book Review (© 1955 by The New York Times Company; reprinted by permission), August 28, 1955, p. 16.

VIRGINIA KIRKUS' SERVICE

Margaret Hyde's books on driving, flight and atoms have made her a name in the teen-age non-fiction field. [**Where Speed Is King,** written with Edwin Hyde,] covers a concept through activities that have come to denote all kinds of speed. The fields where speed is king include running; skiing; car, horse and boat racing; homing pigeons; cycling; flight and so forth. Incidents both typical and well known,—for example, a description of the Landy-Bannister race in Vancouver or of Col. Stapp's physical endurance tests for rocket travel experiments, are efficiently told. They are the direct manifestations of speed, but they also serve to illustrate the more indirect—how endurance must be achieved through years of training, how an engine must be precisely tuned and so forth. Interesting reading about a quality that must be reckoned with today.

> "Twelve to Sixteen: 'Where Speed Is King'," in Virginia Kirkus' Service, Vol. XXIII, No. 17, September 1, 1955, p. 658.

VIRGINIA KIRKUS' SERVICE

A creditable survey of the medical field and its various professions, [**Medicine in Action**] keeps up a record for good non-fiction and provides young interests with an efficient introduction to the world of doctoring and maintaining health. Chapter topics vary as widely as the field itself. There is a study of the teamwork necessary to perform an operation. Information about types of doctors and other medical jobs should help with career decisions. Military medicine, lab research, the miracle drugs, mental health, industrial hygiene, nursing, international health organizations—material on these and more illuminates the topic. . . . A valuable roundup.

> "Twelve to Sixteen: 'Medicine in Action'," in Virginia Kirkus' Service, Vol. XXIV, No. 17, September 1, 1956, p. 638.

FRANK G. SLAUGHTER

The major portion of this excellent book on the world of medicine ["**Medicine in Action**"] is devoted to discussing [medical] careers and how a young person may prepare for them. The author has devoted a chapter, in many cases, to each category and at the end of the book has summarized in a set of tables the many careers that do not require the long and arduous preparation necessary to become a surgeon or a medical specialist.

This is an extremely valuable and informative book for vocational guidance, as well as an instructive one for the general reader who wants to know more about the team of which the doctor is the captain.

> Frank G. Slaughter, "Science Books for Younger Readers: 'Medicine in Action'," in The New York Times Book Review (© 1957 by The New York Times Company; reprinted by permission), February 24, 1957, p. 31.

JOHN M. CONNOLE

The many ways in which modern science has revolutionized the art of warfare are graphically described in ["**From Submarines to Satellites: Science in Our Armed Forces**"]. . . . It is a safe bet that even those who have followed newspaper accounts of what has been happening recently in the field of weapon research and spatial experimentation will find material here that will be new.

Margaret O. Hyde writes about developments in all branches of the service. . . . She is especially good in explaining the complex mechanisms of our various missiles and satellites and the ways in which man is learning to cope with the high speeds, temperatures and weightless environment of outer space.

> John M. Connole, "Science in the Act of War," in The New York Times Book Review, Part II (© 1958 by The New York Times Company; reprinted by permission), November 2, 1958, p. 16.

VIRGINIA KIRKUS' SERVICE

[With **"Atoms Today and Tomorrow"** Margaret Hyde] writes an explicit and pertinent account of the atom, its dangers and potentials. Based on the hypothesis that man is now confronted with the choice of how and to what extent atomic energy should be used, this text presents a clear and informative exposition of what, so far, is being done and to what one may look in the future. An exceedingly difficult topic is handled here with admirable clarity and impartiality in this text which is as morally challenging as it is scientifically precise.

> "'Atoms Today and Tomorrow'," in Virginia Kirkus' Service, Vol. XXVI, No. 23, December 1, 1958, p. 873.

GEORGE A. WOODS

[**"Off Into Space! Science for Young Space Travelers"**] simulates an outward-bound venture. Mrs. Hyde concentrates more on scientific principles and offers experiments for the reader to conduct so that he might get some idea of the complexity of the problems space travelers will encounter. She keeps her text brisk and interesting throughout. This book . . . will encourage children to look forward to and be prepared for tomorrow's age of space.

> George A. Woods, "Outward-Bound," in The New York Times Book Review (© 1959 by The New York Times Company; reprinted by permission), August 2, 1959, p. 24.*

HERBERT DEUTSCH

[*Plants Today and Tomorrow* is a fascinating] exposition of the contributions of plants and plant products to the medical and economic advancement of mankind. Not as extensive as the recent Bertha S. Dodge's "Plants That Changed the World," but written in simpler wordage, thorough, interesting, and well-organized. Tells where plants grow, the different sizes, shapes, and varieties, photosynthesis, reproductive processes, plant breeding, and discoveries of such medicinal products as penicillin and streptomycin. Lengthy discussion about the important roles of plants in a space ship to supply oxygen and food and to get rid of carbon dioxide. Last section of the book suggests experiments in seed germination, cross-pollination, and creation of new species by use of chemicals. . . . Definitely recommended.

> Herbert Deutsch, "Junior High Up: 'Plants Today and Tomorrow'," in Library Journal (reprinted from Library Journal, June 15, 1960; published by R. R. Bowker Co. (a Xerox company); copyright © 1960 by Xerox Corporation), Vol. 85, No. 12, June 15, 1960, p. 2487.

VIRGINIA KIRKUS' SERVICE

The fascinating phenomenon of animal time telling and direction finding is described in [*Animal Clocks and Compasses*] which should interest even the most indifferent students of animal, fish, bird and insect behavior. How herons determine the changing of tides, how pigeons find their homes, how crabs tell time, these and many other examples of the keen intuitive mechanisms that govern non-human life are illustrated. Margaret Hyde provides the reader with the possibility of observing animal clocks and compasses himself, by providing him with suggestions of where to watch and how. [This] is an invitation to an intriguing and educational hobby.

> "Eleven to Thirteen: 'Animal Clocks and Compasses'," in Virginia Kirkus' Service, Vol. XXVIII, No. 13, July 1, 1960, p. 503.

NEW YORK HERALD TRIBUNE BOOK REVIEW

"Plants Today and Tomorrow" is so interesting for anyone over eleven that we hope it will not be read by budding scientists alone. It reports on the challenge to scientists in the mysteries of the plant world, on the effort to increase the nourishment that comes to man from the meadows of the sea, to find new and valuable crops in different parts of the world, to hasten mutations by radiation, to discover cures for diseases, effective hormones and the effects of a controlled climate on plants. The book ends with the most important question of the means to feed "tomorrow's hungry world," experimental space

gardens, a few sample experiments and reference to many useful books.

> "About Insects and Their Worlds: 'Plants Today and Tomorrow'," in New York Herald Tribune Book Review (© I.H.T. Corporation; reprinted by permission), November 13, 1960, p. 28.

VIRGINIA HAVILAND

[Miss Hyde compiles fascinating nature information in *Animal Clocks and Compasses, From Animal Migration to Space Travel,*] which combines much of what is given in Will Barker's *Wintersleeping Wild Life* . . . and Sigmund Lavine's *Strange Travelers* . . . , both excellent studies. Hers is equally authoritative and lively and goes beyond obvious facts of hibernation and migration to the *why* and *how* of living clocks—timing by tide, light, animal radar or echo-location—suggesting possible use of the principle of hibernation for man in spaceships, and outlining science projects based on observation of earthworms, frogs, flies, and birds. (pp. 65-6)

> Virginia Haviland, "Nature and Science: 'Animal Clocks and Compasses: From Migration to Space Travel'," in The Horn Book Magazine (copyright, 1961, by the Horn Book, Inc., Boston), Vol 38, No. 1, February, 1961, pp. 65-6.

VIRGINIA KIRKUS' SERVICE

A prolific "future directed" author well known for . . . lucid scientific books . . . focuses now on our own planet and its incredible population explosion, and how scientists are preparing to tap new channels in order to overcome the startling imbalance between people and resources [in *This Crowded Planet*]. We first "look to the earth", then the sea, and finally to the sky, and watch ingenious ideas take shape as all three areas are probed for the food, minerals and energy necessary for life. . . . Realistic, yet optimistic, this is a timely and worthwhile summary of man's struggle with his environment.

> "Thirteen to Fifteen: 'This Crowded Planet'," in Virginia Kirkus' Service, Vol. XXIX, No. 14, July 15, 1961, p. 622.

ALICE DALGLIESH

In [the closely packed but interesting pages of "This Crowded Planet"] young people will find the answer to the question "Why do we help to feed undernourished countries?" . . . One feels pushed off the earth by overcrowding while reading the first chapters; fortunately, a number of projected solutions follow, some of them seeming at the present time fantastic indeed. The author mentions birth control as only a partial answer and contrary to the religious beliefs of some.

In conclusion she challenges young people to accept responsibility for these problems; "there is no time to wait for tomorrow," she says. But, except for forming opinions, there seems little they can do but wait.

> Alice Dalgliesh, "Breaking Ice at SR: 'This Crowded Planet'," in Saturday Review (copyright © 1962 by Saturday Review; all rights reserved; reprinted by permission), Vol. 45, No. 7, February 17, 1962, p. 32.

ROBERT C. COWEN

With the help of explanatory sketches and diagrams, the author has undertaken to acquaint teenage readers with the molecular world [in **"Molecules Today and Tomorrow."**] She has succeeded well in making complicated phenomena and chemical manipulations understandable and interesting. This is a level at which matter is being harnessed in countless ways for the benefit of mankind. It is the level of fundamental action for many of the material phenomena that affect everyday living. The book covers the gamut of all these, including extensive exposition of molecular medicine, pathological viruses and the fast-growing knowledge of basic genetics. A chapter on simple illustrative experiments one can try out at home is a valuable feature of this well-executed volume.

> *Robert C. Cowen, "Nature and Natural Science, from Woodchucks to the Stars: Empire of the Sun," in* The Christian Science Monitor *(reprinted by permission from* The Christian Science Monitor; © 1963 *The Christian Science Publishing Society; all rights reserved), May 9, 1963, p. 7B.**

MARGARET SHERWOOD LIBBY

Margaret Hyde has the ability to discuss new developments in science simply and interestingly so that a little information is conveyed and also, what is more important, curiosity is aroused so that a brighter student will go on to more detailed study. . . .

[In **"Molecules Today and Tomorrow,"** the] introductory chapter defining molecules presumes rather too much knowledge on the reader's part, and we are afraid many will read the book thinking of molecules as somehow indistinguishable from microorganisms. However, after this, the exposition is more carefully developed, emphasizing the constant motion of molecules (with experiments to demonstrate this) and the amazing discoveries resulting from the slowing of their motion when the temperature nears absolute zero or when molecules exist at different energy levels (giving good comments on the new inventions of masers and lasers with their enormous amplifying powers).

> *Margaret Sherwood Libby, "The Building Blocks of Nature," in* Books (© I.H.T. Corporation; reprinted by permission), August 25, 1963, p. 9.*

ISADORA KUNITZ

While emphasizing the contribution of psychology to understanding human behavior and improving human relations, [Margaret O. Hyde and Edward S. Marks, the authors of *Psychology in Action,*] cover various therapeutic methods: testing, experimental psychology, perception and learning, and the psychological effects of the space age. Some of the clearest writing is about clinical psychologists and counselors. Examples of questions young people ask about themselves will strike a responsive chord in many adolescents, e.g. "How do you find your real self?" "Are you normal if you have not found yourself?" Social psychologists and their studies of both Negro and white attitudes toward each other are presented, and there is an attempt to distinguish between psychologists and psychiatrists. On the whole this is a useful and interesting book. (pp. 65-6)

> *Isadora Kunitz, "'Psychology in Action'," in* School Library Journal, *an appendix to* Library Journal *(reprinted from the May, 1967 issue of* School Library

Journal, *published by R. R. Bowker Co./ A Xerox Corporation; copyright © 1967), Vol. 13, No. 9, May, 1967, pp. 65-6.*

ROBERT W. O'CONNELL

Amateur psychology is a universal hobby if not an avocation in this day and age. Disagreeable acquaintances are now called "sick" or "paranoid" by those who would discredit an adversary and at the same time appear both charitable (condescending) and informed. **"Psychology in Action"** fills the obvious gap which exists between the frivolous use of this terminology and its actual meaning. More important, it describes the dimensions and functions of psychology and psychologists in layman's terms. It not only defines the popular but poorly understood terminology, but shows clearly the triumphs and limitations of this inexact science. . . .

Possibly too much space is allocated to testing and test interpretation—and an understandably chauvinistic tone prevails throughout. Nevertheless this book will give a teen-ager insight into a subject which, rightly or wrongly, will have a great effect on his future.

> *Robert W. O'Connell, "Teen-age, Science: 'Psychology in Action'," in* The New York Times Book Review, *Part II (© 1967 by The New York Times Company; reprinted by permission), May 7, 1967, p. 34.*

LOUIS LASAGNA

["**Mind Drugs"**] is an attempt to provide some facts for those interested in drug abuse. It is reasonably short, but not superficial. The style is "popular" (in the nonpejorative sense), but should not offend the sensibilities of the intelligent reader, young or old. Its facts are, so far as I can tell, generally correct.

The contributors are a mixed lot: four psychiatrists, two psychologists, and a young doctor who has been medical director of the hippie clinic in the Haight-Ashbury section of San Francisco. Mrs. Hyde (who doubles as editor and author of three of the chapters) is not only a professional writer but a teacher and a director of the Northeast Mental Health Clinic of Philadelphia.

The description of the various "mind drugs" is good—and, in some respects, exemplary. . . .

The book is primarily about young people—why they use drugs, what drugs do for and to them (good and bad), and some of the ways a person might be helped to kick his drug habit. It points out the semantic traps in defining "addiction," how complex the medico-legal ramifications are, how psychedelic "trips" can be pleasant or (unpredictably) catastrophic. It reminds us that it is not necessary for someone to suffer a psychotic break after the use of hallucinogens. It shows us how hard it is for LSD users to love even *one* other person, let alone "the world" or "humanity."

My major complaint about this useful volume is that it never gives in-depth reasons why youngsters take drugs; nor does it stress the alternative, non-drug challenges and satisfactions that might be provided by society. . . .

It is perhaps unfair to ask for definitive solutions from a book of this type, although some suggestions are offered. We must still ask ourselves why our children resort to drugs—and how we can change the world so they will no longer feel this need.

Louis Lasagna, *"The Grass Isn't Greener," in* The New York Times Book Review (© *1968 by The New York Times Company; reprinted by permission), November 3, 1968, p. 3.*

SCIENCE BOOKS

The intent of [*Atoms Today and Tomorrow*] is to give "young readers" . . . some familiarity with peacetime uses of atomic energy. The treatment is broad but superficial. Written in a familiar, colloquial style, the book is descriptive rather than explanatory. We are told, for example, that health physicists use instruments called "Cutie Pie" and "Pee Wee"—but not what they are used for nor how they work. On the credit side, [Margaret O. Hyde and Bruce G. Hyde] do cover a wide variety of applications and mention both sides of the controversies about the safety of nuclear power stations, and the effects of low dosage of radiation. There is virtually no mention of military applications—a fact that this reviewer counts as favorable. (pp. 255-56)

"Nuclear Engineering: 'Atoms Today and Tomorrow'," in Science Books (copyright 1970 by the *American Association for the Advancement of Science), Vol. 6, No. 3 (December, 1970), pp. 255-56.*

BEN IANZITO

[*Your Skin* is an] acceptable basic presentation of skin design, function and hygiene in 13 short chapters, interspersed with sound health advice on everything from athlete's foot to vitiligo. Unfortunately, this is not as well organized or comprehensive as Dr. Brauer's *Your Skin and Hair: a Basic Guide to Care and Beauty.* . . . The author has allotted only seven pages to acne, a minor disease of major concern to most of the young adolescents who will be attracted to this book. . . . [The] writing is clear and concise, without becoming clinical and dull.

Ben Ianzito, *"'Your Skin'," in* School Library Journal, *an appendix to* Library Journal (reprinted from the February, 1971 issue of School Library Journal, published by R. R. Bowker Co./A Xerox Corporation; copyright © 1971), Vol. 17, No. 6, February, 1971, p. 66.*

SCIENCE BOOKS

A far better text is still needed, but this short book [*Your Skin*] by an experienced science writer has mirrored adequately some conservative medical advice about common skin diseases and some of the science which underlies this advice. The book has an easy-reading quality, is brief, and the better chapters on skin language, burns, temperature control, sports, and beauty care make it just acceptable for high school readers. The flaws are many. The book offers far too much outdated medical opinion, and fails to indicate the new methods of research, new discoveries about the skin, and the emergence of many better medical practices. Chapter headings are well chosen, but the selection of further detail is blemished by trivial facts, misdirections, poorly interpreted information, much of it not related well to the main themes of the book. For critical readers, the discussions of acne, inflammation, venom, disability, disfiguration, allergy, and radiation are unsatisfactory in factual content, emphasis, and explanation. The book can be deemed "acceptable" only because it is a better book within a poor genre.

"'Your Skin'," in Science Books (copyright 1971 by *the American Association for the Advancement of Science), Vol. 6, No. 4 (March, 1971), p. 330.*

SCIENCE BOOKS

[*For Pollution Fighters Only*] is a fine primer for citizen action aimed at amelioration of environmental pollution. Mrs. Hyde has easily and coherently introduced the base concepts of spaceship earth—the interrelatedness of everything in a finite, essentially closed system. Her seven-page treatment of the life-support system of the biosphere is as good as this reviewer has seen for this audience. Subsequent chapters deal with individual pollution problems. . . . Final chapters treat examples of community efforts to fight pollution, suggestions for positive action by any individual or community group, and private and public sources of information and political response to articulated needs. Most impressive is a responsible, common sense chapter decrying emotionalism without facts, quick and easy solutions to complex problems, doomsdayers, overreaction by environmentalists, and the like. With but a few not too serious exceptions, the material is technically accurate, up-to-date and well-written. Recent examples of pollution problems from mercury in Lake St. Clair to the crown of thorns starfish infestation add to the book's interest.

"Conservation of Resources: 'For Pollution Fighters Only'," in Science Books (copyright 1971 by the *American Association for the Advancement of Science), Vol. 7, No. 3 (December, 1971), p. 191.*

RONALD J. KLEY

[*For Pollution Fighters Only*] is well written, well organized, and offers an excellent summary of today's outstanding problems in the area of environmental pollution: yet it leaves much to be desired in its approach to the solution of these problems. The text emphasizes the complexity of ecological relationships, and offers examples of well-intentioned "improvements" that have been far outweighed by their long-term negative effects; yet the book offers several rather simplistic suggestions for "pollution fighters" without attempting to evaluate their potential negative side effects. . . . Perhaps most unfortunate, in terms of the book's overall purpose and approach, is the fact that self-education is nowhere listed among the many actions that "pollution fighters" ought to take in order to improve their environment. For without some fundamental knowledge of chemistry, biology, economics, sociology, and other relevant disciplines it is difficult to imagine how young people can ever be integrated into the leadership of an effective "environmental revolution." This book seems to imply that the good intentions and dedicated activism of wide-eyed Aquarians are adequate to meet the challenge at hand. I doubt it. (pp. 20-1)

Ronald J. Kley, *"'For Pollution Fighters Only'," in* Appraisal: Science Books for Young People (copyright © 1972 by the Children's Science Book Review *Committee), Vol. 5, No. 1, Winter, 1972, pp. 20-1.*

RICHARD H. WELLER

[*Flight Today and Tomorrow*] is a broad and cursory whirlwind tour through aviation. . . . Crammed with facts and little anecdotes, apparently to keep the story moving, skims the tops of numerous waves but never seems to get its feet wet. [It] appears to be primarily a rewrite and a "brought-up-to-date-version of the original '53 edition." Although primarily accurate and broad in scope, it lacks verve, imagination, and "punch."

Richard H. Weller, "'Flight Today and Tomorrow'," in Appraisal: Science Books for Young People (copyright © 1972 by the Children's Science Book Review Committee), Vol. 5, No. 1, Winter, 1972, p. 20.

KIRKUS REVIEWS

The authors [of Mysteries of the Mind] clear up no mysteries in this slack, simplistic treatment of already overexploited topics. After an introductory chapter on neurons and synapses that establishes a tone of scientific respectability come discussions of sleep and dreams, witchcraft, hypnosis and ESP in which about all that we haven't heard many times over are either beside the psychic point (as are the examples of African witch doctors' cunning) or insufficiently documented (the intriguing attribution of the absence of violence among certain Malayan tribesmen to their application of Freudian-like dream interpretation). Worse however are the chapters on advertising and brainwashing: the former (entitled "Gentle Persuasion") treats the "eight basic propaganda techniques" with unincisive and platitudinous arguments. . . . The chapter on brainwashing uses the below-the-belt emotional methods it condemns in its second-person horror stories ("you arrive at the prison camp exhausted. . . . You have already collapsed a few times") about the psychic tortures to which "the communists" subject American prisoners. As the authors [Margaret O. Hyde, Edward S. Marks, and James B. Wells] themselves conclude, brainwashing is "basically a failure," "no magical technique" and a "meaningless term"—so why resurrect the cases of Cardinal Mindszenty and other lesser clergymen whose admittedly harrowing stories elicit here more outrage than understanding? Whether they are attacking bigots or communists Hyde and company indulge freely in sledge-hammer persuasion, never allowing their readers to make up their own minds or even acknowledging that they have minds to use.

"Older Non-Fiction: 'Mysteries of the Mind'," in Kirkus Reviews (copyright © 1972 The Kirkus Service, Inc.), Vol. XL, No. 17, September 1, 1972, p. 1038.

A. C. HAMAN

[Mysteries of the Mind is a] clear, scientific exploration of such psychic phenomena as sleep, persuasion, brainwashing, superstition, hypnotic states, extra sensory perception, stress and trances. The chapters on extra sensory perception and hypnosis are particularly well done. . . . [The] psychological aspects of the mind [are] treated here. This book will appeal to a wide audience of young readers interested in psychic phenomena, witchcraft, and mysticism.

A. C. Haman, "'Mysteries of the Mind'," in School Library Journal, an appendix to Library Journal (reprinted from the February, 1973 issue of School Library Journal, published by R. R. Bowker Co./A Xerox Corporation; copyright © 1973), Vol. 19, No. 6, February, 1973, p. 79.

PUBLISHERS WEEKLY

[The frightening statistics of venereal disease victims] make the reader wish that every young person would read ["VD: The Silent Epidemic"] and absorb its messages. The author proves that all kinds of social diseases are rampant despite comparative ease and availability of treatment. She tells how to avoid infection, how people are infected, how dangerous it is to neglect treatment and where cures can be had. . . . The book is encouraging. It proves that teenagers, doctors and public health officials are taking part in the fight against the silent menace.

"Children's Books: 'VD: The Silent Epidemic'," in Publishers Weekly (reprinted from the May 14, 1973, issue of Publishers Weekly by permission, published by R. R. Bowker Company, a Xerox company; copyright © 1973 by Xerox Corporation), Vol. 203, No. 20, May 14, 1973, p. 47.

SCIENCE BOOKS

Hyde's factual approach to venereal disease [in V.D.: The Silent Epidemic] avoids scare tactics and preaching and provides a very readable account for young people or even those who are older. The major venereal diseases, their symptoms and modes of spread are accurately described in a manner useful to one who fears he or she has contracted VD. . . . The information provided should also help readers avoid contracting VD. Brief summaries of control methods and research programs are presented. Intelligent parents should encourage their children to become familiar with the information in this book, and it is a good supplementary source for physical education and hygiene courses.

"'V.D.: The Silent Epidemic'," in Science Books (copyright © 1974 by the American Association for the Advancement of Science), Vol. IX, No. 4, March, 1974, p. 312.

SONIA BROTMAN

Poorly written, The New Genetics takes an inherently fascinating subject and makes it uninteresting and confusing. Genetic research from Gregor Mendel's peas to J. B. Gurdon's artificial cloning is traced and explained; unfortunately, the explanations are far from clear. Main ideas are lost in myriads of irrelevant facts; constant use of clichés (e.g., "ivory towers of science") and superlatives obfuscate the true impressiveness of genetic advances. . . . [The] writing is awkward and repetitive. An index, suggestions for further reading, and a list of organizations with special interest in the new genetics (e.g. American Diabetes Association) are perhaps the only worthwhile sections of this disappointing book.

Sonia Brotman, "'The New Genetics'," in Appraisal: Science Books for Young People (copyright © 1975 by the Children's Science Book Review Committee), Vol. 8, No. 2, Spring, 1975, p. 23.

ROBERT J. STEIN

The New Genetics is a book for advanced junior high or high school students. While the account is well written and complete in its survey of the recent advances in genetics, the material is inherently too complex for young readers. . . . The book includes interesting chapters on human genetic diseases and genetic testing techniques, the significance of tissue culture in diagnosis of genetic defects, and artificial insemination procedures. Throughout the book the author makes reference to the ethics involved in these research efforts and points to ways in which this work can help mankind. The attitude the author creates is one of thoughtful concern for the future of genetic engineering. There are only minor errors in grammar. . . . The absence of illustrations makes the book difficult to understand in some areas; however, the author's descriptions are very clear, and her use of analogies helpful. (pp. 23-4)

> *Robert J. Stein, "'The New Genetics'," in* Appraisal: Science Books for Young People *(copyright © 1975 by the Children's Science Book Review Committee), Vol. 8, No. 2, Spring, 1975, pp. 23-4.*

DOLORES KING

[*Hotline* is an] introduction to telephone hotlines, which serve as sources of information, solace, help with crises or long-term problems, or referral for more help. Hyde discusses the proliferation during the late '60's and early '70's of volunteer-run hotlines, often arising out of drug abuse or suicide prevention programs. She describes types of hotlines; how calls are handled; how hotline staffs are trained; and how to organize and fund a hotline. There is an extensive "National Directory of Hotline Services" arranged by state and city; however, hotlines are born and die so frequently that any list is always out of date. A good starting point for YA's working on hotlines as well as those who need to make calls.

> *Dolores King, "Non-Fiction: 'Hotline'," in* School Library Journal *(reprinted from the April, 1975 issue of* School Library Journal, *published by R. R. Bowker Co./ A Xerox Corporation; copyright © 1975), Vol. 21, No. 8, April, 1975, p. 76.*

SONIA BROTMAN

In attempting to discuss man's basic emotions and explain them for young people, [Margaret O. Hyde and Elizabeth Forsyth's] *Know Your Feelings* fails to be more than an unexceptional survey, a rather boring coverage of a potentially exciting subject. . . . Each [feeling] is defined insofar as it can be; scientific research into it is mentioned; and situations where it arises are discussed, unfortunately in an overly obvious, uninteresting way. Psychological terms are frequently used without sufficient explanation; clichés do nothing to add to the undistinguished writing style. One chapter devoted to changing awareness attempts to interest readers in meditation and biofeedback, but it, too, fails to explore the potential of its topic.

> *Sonia Brotman, "'Know Your Feelings'," in* Appraisal: Science Books for Young People *(copyright © 1975 by the Children's Science Book Review Committee), Vol. 8, No. 3, Fall, 1975, p. 17.*

ANNE E. MATTHEWS

Know Your Feelings is an excellent book that skillfully deals with the delicate subject of emotions. It should provide useful understanding for the young adolescent. Particularly valuable is the discussion of fear and anxiety: "sometimes used interchangeably, their meanings are different." This style of comparison and contrast used throughout the book is very effective in discussion. . . . It should hold the interest of students while guiding them in understanding their own feelings.

> *Anne E. Matthews, "'Know Your Feelings'," in* Appraisal: Science Books for Young People *(copyright © 1975 by the Children's Science Book Review Committee), Vol. 8, No. 3, Fall, 1975, p. 17.*

CYNTHIA JOHNSON

What Have You Been Eating? is an inappropriately specific title for such a general book. In fact, in addition to covering food composition and food additives, [Margaret O. Hyde and Elizabeth Held Forsyth] discuss the digestive system, food history, food customs, world food supply, and various plans for combating starvation now and in the future. The breadth of the subject and the brevity of the book impose a cursory and superficial coverage of each topic. A lack of structure makes it difficult to locate information without reading the entire book. The style is awkward and condescending. Students will already have covered much of the information in basic science and geography courses. Not recommended.

> *Cynthia Johnson, "Reviews: 'What Have You Been Eating? Do You Really Know?'" in* Young Adult Cooperative Book Review Group of Massachusetts, *Vol. 12, No. 1, October, 1975, p. 9.*

MONICA CAROLLO

Information on the food we eat is tightly packed into the eight chapters of this encompassing book [*What Have You Been Eating? Do You Really Know?*]. In clear prose, [Hyde and Forsyth] attempt to dispel myths and fallacies about food while bringing current scientific thought on the subject to light. Not only do the authors thus hope to answer questions but also to stimulate consumer awareness of food. To this end, there is also a discussion of food fads, food additives, obesity, digestion, organic foods, and alternative sources of food for a hungry world. Although the breadth of coverage is too wide to allow for in-depth treatment of each of these topics, this might well serve as a consciousness raiser.

> *Monica Carollo, "'What Have You Been Eating? Do You Really Know?'" in* School Library Journal *(reprinted from the November, 1975 issue of* School Library Journal, *published by R. R. Bowker Co./A Xerox Corporation; copyright © 1975), Vol. 22, No. 3, November, 1975, p. 91.*

KIRKUS REVIEWS

As usual Hyde has done a good deal of research and very little in the way of organization or analysis [for *Speak Out On Rape!*]. Conclusions are even scarcer, though that might be only prudent here where she repeatedly refers to the inconclusiveness of research to date. Feminist assertions that rape is an outgrowth of our sexist society and that much preventive advice restricts women's rightful freedom are mentioned without endorsement or rejection; and unlike [Susan] Brownmiller's more polemical *Against Our Will* (1975), which asserts that rapists are motivated by power needs and that victims should fight back, Hyde leaves both questions open and compiles no profile of the typical attacker, though she devotes chapters to indiscriminately reviewing different theories and viewpoints on both. (The one characteristic, she reports, which seems to ward off attack is an air of confidence.) Hyde does emphasize the severe emotional damage suffered by victims and the common ignorance or callousness toward such feelings on the part of medical and legal professionals. Here the NOW task force and other women's groups can be supportive, and Hyde lists a number which provided her with help and material. Her stated purpose is to alert young women to the prevalence of the problem and the sources of help; to that end, despite its shortcomings, *Speak Out On Rape!* must be counted a first step worth taking.

> *"Young Adult Non-Fiction: 'Speak Out on Rape!'"* in Kirkus Reviews *(copyright © 1976 The Kirkus Service, Inc.), Vol. XLIV, No. 4, February 15, 1976, p. 207.*

RHODA E. TAYLOR

Unlike some current feminist writers, Hyde does not treat rape as a political action or as class warfare between the sexes [in *Speak Out on Rape!*]; rather she treats it as a violent crime of assault assuming epidemic proportions and involving all of society. The author examines some of the myths concerning rapists and their victims (i.e., that women generally provoke rape), reasons why many rapes are never reported, medical and psychological needs of the victim and the antiquated but changing legal procedures wherein the victim often becomes the criminal defending her honor and rapist more often than not is set free. Many questions are raised but few are answered, primarily because so little is known—a point the author continually stresses. Some recent and current research efforts are described, but the book is seriously flawed by the lack of adequate references.

> *Rhoda E. Taylor, "Children's Books: 'Speak Out on Rape!'"* in Science Books & Films *(copyright 1976 by the American Association for the Advancement of Science), Vol. XII, No. 3 (December, 1976), p. 133.*

BOOKLIST

A prolific author of books for young people reviews the quality of American juvenile justice and its response to increasing youth crime [in *Juvenile Justice and Injustice*]. Punctuating her discussion with sample case studies, Hyde surveys the early history of the current system; describes punishment inconsistencies, some stemming from confusion about the meaning of the term delinquency itself; looks at the system's reaction to female delinquents and youth gangs; and paints a grim picture of problems juveniles face in courts overburdened by less serious, status offenders (runaways, truants, etc.) and plagued by insufficient staff and rising costs. A look at some current state and federal efforts to improve matters completes a thought-provoking, realistic, ultimately hopeful assessment.

> *"Books for Young Adults: 'Juvenile Justice and Injustice',"* in Booklist *(reprinted by permission of the American Library Association; copyright © 1977 by the American Library Association), Vol. 74, No. 4, October 15, 1977, p. 368.*

ZENA SUTHERLAND

[*Brainwashing and Other Forms of Mind Control*] is a serious discussion of various approaches to behavior shaping. . . . Hyde discusses religious cults, behavior modification in prisons, and legal precedents as well as theories of behavior shaping, hypnosis, therapy, meditation, and political brainwashing. The text is thoughtful and objective, the writing style straightforward, the topic one that should appeal to a large audience.

> *Zena Sutherland, "New Titles for Children and Young People: 'Brainwashing and Other Forms of Mind Control',"* in Bulletin of the Center for Children's Books *(reprinted by permission of The University of Chicago Press; © 1977 by the University of Chicago), Vol. 31, No. 3, November, 1977, p. 49.*

ZENA SUTHERLAND

In [her] detailed discussion of the laws and practices that apply to minors in the United States [*Juvenile Justice and Injustice*], Hyde is objective about inadequacies, critical in evaluating programs, and realistic in describing possible solutions. However, the material is not as well organized as it has been in her earlier books. . . . (pp. 96-7)

> *Zena Sutherland, "New Titles for Children and Young People: 'Juvenile Justice and Injustice',"* in Bulletin of the Center for Children's Books *(reprinted by permission of The University of Chicago Press; © 1978 by the University of Chicago), Vol. 31, No. 6, February, 1978, pp. 96-7.*

PAULA HOGAN

[*Brainwashing and Other Forms of Mind Control* is an] objective, well-researched account of the sociological effects of behavior modification which complements Elizabeth Hall's discussion of the psychological aspects of "be mod" in *From Pigeons to People: a Look at Behavior Shaping*. . . . Hyde discusses the benefits as well as the possible abuses of behavior control, psychosurgery, biofeedback, hypnosis, and commercial mind control courses. The motivation for membership in religious cults and the theory behind brainwashing techniques are explained. . . . [Over] all, this provides clear and timely information on an area of psychology that is of particular interest to teens.

> *Paula Hogan, "'Brainwashing and Other Forms of Mind Control',"* in School Library Journal *(reprinted from the March, 1978 issue of* School Library Journal, *published by R. R. Bowker Co./ A Xerox Corporation; copyright © 1978), Vol. 24, No. 7, March, 1978, p. 137.*

BOOKLIST

Taking a broad definition of addiction [in *Addictions: Gambling, Smoking, Cocaine Use, and Others*], Hyde presents a well-researched, across-the-board treatment that includes cigarettes, gambling, food (over- and underindulging), caffeine, cocaine and amphetamines, alcohol, barbiturates, and heroin. For each she provides up-to-date information on the characteristics of an addict, scientific research, and other aspects pertinent to the individual problem. She also explores the marijuana controversy, noting that addiction is apparently one of the less important issues and reporting on research into physical and psychological effects. She concludes with a look at positive addiction—jogging, cycling, and meditation used as mental strengthening. Concise, well-organized, and non-preachy.

> *"Books for Young Adults: 'Addictions: Gambling, Smoking, Cocaine Use, and Others',"* in Booklist *(reprinted by permission of the American Library Association; copyright © 1978 by the American Library Association), Vol. 75, No. 1, September 1, 1978, p. 39.*

BOOKLIST

[*Suicide: The Hidden Epidemic* is] a solid examination of one of the major causes of death in America—suicide. Emphasizing the complex, controversial nature of their subject, the collaborators [Margaret O. Hyde and Elizabeth Held Forsyth] (a reliable author of books for young people and a practicing child psychiatrist) discuss the misconceptions surrounding it, describe suicidal patterns, simplify principal causation theories, and explain some of the psychological factors that may motivate the act. Broader in scope than [Francine] Klagsbrun's *Too Young to Die: Youth and Suicide* . . . , Hyde and Forsyth's treatment still singles out teenage suicide for special attention in a separate chapter, while sections on suicide notes, interpretation of statistics, and clues for identifying a person who needs aid extend the coverage further. Although much information is given, occasional convoluted explanations and some oblique examples make this a demanding introduction.

> *"Books for Young Adults: 'Suicide: The Hidden Epidemic',"* in Booklist *(reprinted by permission of the American Library Association; copyright © 1978 by the American Library Association), Vol. 75, No. 4, October 15, 1978, p. 568.*

ZENA SUTHERLAND

More and more heavy drinkers are people under twenty; more and more accidents that are fatal and are caused by drinking have people under twenty as victims; the number of children who are drinking is increasing. Hyde does not preach [in *Know About Alcohol*]; she explains why people drink, why they are affected in different ways and at different rates. She describes the effects of alcohol on the body and suggests some ways in which alcoholics can be identified, and she gives information about organizations that help alcoholics. One chapter poses problems and gives multiple choice answers for questions of personal decision such as what to do if one is a baby sitter and a drunken parent offers a ride home, or if there is an alcoholic in the family and one wants to help. Straightforward in style, the book gives no unusual information, but it covers many aspects of the problem and it is written with clarity and objectivity.

> *Zena Sutherland, "New Titles for Children and Young People: 'Know about Alcohol',"* in Bulletin of the Center for Children's Books *(reprinted by permission of The University of Chicago Press; © 1979 by the University of Chicago), Vol. 32, No. 7, March, 1979, p. 119.*

KATHRYN WEISMAN

Alcohol's use, abuse and effects on the body are discussed in [*Know About Alcohol*]. . . . The author emphasizes her feeling that knowing the facts about alcohol (if they are presented in an unbiased manner) will help young people to make intelligent decisions; a section of hypothetical situations involving young people and alcohol is included, along with discussions of possible ways to handle them. . . . Hyde's book is . . . a good choice.

> *Kathryn Weisman, "'Know about Alcohol',"* in School Library Journal *(reprinted from the March, 1979 issue of* School Library Journal, *published by R. R. Bowker Co./A Xerox Corporation; copyright © 1979), Vol. 25, No. 7, March, 1979, p. 140.*

ROBERT J. STEIN

[*Suicide, the Hidden Epidemic* is a] thorough, well-written, well-organized, well-documented account of the theories about suicide, and the patterns of thought that characterize the suicidal person. It is made clear, at the outset, that reading or talking about suicide does not cause one to commit suicide. In fact, it is the premise of this detailed book, that understanding the suicidal mind may help to prevent attempted suicides. Ten chapters containing case history illustrations and diagnostic clues guide the reader to understand the psychological profiles of suicidal persons, the attitudes that promote suicidal behavior, statistics and research findings. An excellent selection of suggested readings is included, along with a comprehensive listing of State Suicide Prevention/Crisis Intervention Centers throughout the U.S. The book is as important for teachers to read as it may be to the adolescents needing such help.

> *Robert J. Stein, "'Suicide, the Hidden Epidemic',"* in Appraisal: Science Books for Young People *(copyright © 1979 by the Children's Science Book Review Committee), Vol. 12, No. 2, Spring, 1979, p. 28.*

PAUL LEUNG

Is addiction a matter of chemistry, social learning, or a basic human deficiency? This has been a question of concern and a matter of controversy for some time. While *Addictions* will not put the problem to rest, it is an excellent introduction to the concept of addictive behavior. Hyde's basic premise is that cigarette smoking, compulsive gambling, coffee drinking, food intake, and even jogging are similar, and that we should encourage positive addictions while discouraging undesirable ones. The weakness of the book is the inconsistent content, with some chapters more complete than others which are quite superficial. For example, alcohol, barbiturates, and tranquilizers are treated in one chapter. There is also a lack of documentation. Many resources, including interviews and research studies, are cited, but it would be impossible to locate them without any bibliographic material. The text is relatively short but the writing generally easy to follow. (pp. 11-12)

> *Paul Leung, "Children's Books: 'Addictions: Gambling, Smoking, Cocaine Use, and Others',"* in Science Books & Films *(copyright 1979 by the American Association for the Advancement of Science), Vol. XV, No. 1 (May, 1979), pp. 11-12.*

ROBIN SINER

The problem of nuclear wastes is the subject of much controversy today and tomorrow. In [*Everyone's Trash Problem: Nuclear Wastes*, Margaret O. Hyde and Bruce Hyde] present the reader with concise information that compels the learner to form an opinion of the nuclear analysis. The authors explain the specific chemical and physical process that must occur in order to release nuclear energy, and the controversy between the throwaway fuel cycle of the radioactive atoms and recycling spent fuel of nuclear wastes. The Hydes state the variety of radioactive wastes and then submit to the reader the diverse possibilities that nuclear researchers have considered to answer the nuclear waste problem. The information given in the book is explicit, and the terms and explanations are such that the reader comprehends the entire essence of the subject.

> *Robin Siner, "'Everyone's Trash Problem: Nuclear Wastes',"* in Young Adult Cooperative Book Review

Group of Massachusetts, *Vol. 16, No. 1, October, 1979, p. 12.*

DENISE M. WILMS

[*My Friend Wants to Run Away*] directs itself to runaways or their friends who want to help them. Hyde loosely follows several case histories representative of common runaway motivations—family problems, pregnancy, sexual abuse, alcoholism in the home, or simply being unwanted—with an aim to show that the street is not the place to be and that help is available through hotline systems that protect privacy and arrange for temporary shelter and counseling. The tone is young and the slant somewhat overly positive in that the case histories cited often end satisfactorily. Arnold Rubin's *The Youngest Outlaws* . . . offers more depth and reality; but for junior high-level students facing such situations, this offers a supportive, essentially nonjudgmental view of how to start dealing with the problem.

> *Denise M. Wilms, "'My Friend Wants to Run Away',"* in Booklist *(reprinted by permission of the American Library Association; copyright © 1979 by the American Library Association), Vol. 76, No. 3, October 1, 1979, p. 277.*

JANET B. WOJNAROSKI

The second edition of [Margaret O. Hyde and Bruce G. Hyde's] *Know About Drugs* revises and updates the original title (1972), containing much more material than was first presented. In clear detail, the authors examine drug use and abuse, paying attention to cocaine, heroin, and the current favorite, PCP. Without moralizing, they frequently use a story-telling technique to emphasize the psychological factors. The scope is broad but inclusive. . . .

> *Janet B. Wojnaroski, "'Know about Drugs',"* in School Library Journal *(reprinted from the March, 1980, issue of* School Library Journal, *published by R. R. Bowker Co./ A Xerox Corporation; copyright © 1980), Vol. 26, No. 7, March, 1980, p. 132.*

FLOYD D. JURY

Unfortunately, information about the disposal of radioactive wastes has been highly technical and difficult to evaluate. The authors [of *Everyone's Trash Problem: Nuclear Wastes*] have done an outstanding job of stripping away the mystery and technical jargon to explain the essence of the problem, why it exists and what can be done about it. Without trying to bias the reader either for or against nuclear power, the authors simply provide the basic education needed to intelligently discuss the issue so that readers can investigate further and make up their own minds. The book contains an excellent glossary that will help readers better understand the terminology used in the literature today. In addition, there is a comprehensive index, sources of further information and suggestions for additional reading. This book would make excellent collateral reading for any high school or adult education program dealing with current sociotechnological issues.

> *Floyd D. Jury, "Book Reviews: 'Everyone's Trash Problem: Nuclear Wastes',"* in Science Books & Films *(copyright 1980 by the American Association for the Advancement of Science), Vol. 15, No. 4 (March, 1980), p. 217.*

BOOKLIST

Hyde, the author of *Juvenile Justice and Injustice* . . . broadens her scope considerably [in *Crime and Justice in Our Time*] as she explores crime and the justice system in more general terms, touching on everything from prison reform, history, and common sense crime prevention tactics to gun control. Though her wide-ranging treatment yields a somewhat diluted view, Hyde still evidences a knack for culling significant information and presenting it in an accessible, thought-provoking manner. Her overview capably introduces current theories about criminal behavior (Is there a criminal type? Why do people commit crimes?), analyzes some of the principal controversies and inequities surrounding punishment, and follows the convoluted path of criminal proceedings from apprehension and trial to conviction and after. (p. 1419)

> *"Books for Young Adults: 'Crime and Justice in Our Time',"* in Booklist *(reprinted by permission of the American Library Association; copyright © 1980 by the American Library Association), Vol. 76, No. 19, June 1, 1980, pp. 1418-19.*

JOAN L. DOBSON

The vocabulary in Hyde's [*My Friend Wants to Run Away*] is aimed at the middle elementary grades but the examples of sexual abuse are more appropriate to an older age group. The chapter subheadings—"Cathy Ran in Fear," "Jennie: Alone and Pregnant," "Marci Had a Funny Uncle," and "Bob Ran Away to Have More Fun"—are suggestive of slick magazines. In most instances the solutions are too pat. Readers are introduced to Cathy, Marci and company in the first chapter and then must hunt for their stories in later chapters.

> *Joan L. Dobson, "'My Friend Wants to Run Away',"* in School Library Journal *(reprinted from the October, 1980 issue of* School Library Journal, *published by R. R. Bowker Co./ A Xerox Corporation; copyright © 1980), Vol. 27, No. 2, October, 1980, p. 156.*

PUBLISHERS WEEKLY

Hyde's clear, unsensationalized and documented report ["**Cry Softly! The Story of Child Abuse**"] on a terrible social problem really should be studied by every boy and girl as soon as he or she can read; it ought not be available just to teens and subteens. "Cry softly," warn adults who batter children, so that the neighbors won't hear, a command usually obeyed for fear of worse hurts. The author shows that the physical and mental mistreatment of minors (including babies) happens in families of all social strata and describes some of the causes. . . . This book can bring a shameful secret into the light where it can be dealt with.

> *"Children's Books: 'Cry Softly! The Story of Child Abuse',"* in Publishers Weekly *(reprinted from the December 5, 1980, issue of* Publishers Weekly *by permission, published by R. R. Bowker Company, a Xerox company; copyright © 1980 by Xerox Corporation), Vol. 218, No. 23, December 5, 1980, p. 15.*

ZENA SUTHERLAND

[In *Cry Softly! The Story of Child Abuse*] Hyde discusses the physical, emotional, and sexual abuse of children by adults, primarily by parents, and cites the statistics of known cases as evidence of the fact that child abuse is growing in the United States; she also gives historical material about child abuse, with separate chapters on abusive practices in England and the United States. While the material is not as carefully organized as in most of Hyde's books, the text gives a great deal of information, not only about child abuse practices, but also about how to recognize cases of it, what the reader can do to report such cases, what kinds of help can be given battered children and abusive parents, what organizations (including hotlines) can provide such help. The author is careful to point out that other situations can cause similar symptoms, and that therefore professional opinion should be sought before action is taken.

> *Zena Sutherland, "New Titles for Children and Young People: 'Cry Softly! The Story of Child Abuse'," in* Bulletin of the Center for Children's Books *(reprinted by permission of The University of Chicago Press; © 1981 by the University of Chicago), Vol. 34, No. 6, February, 1981, p. 112.*

Janis Ian

1951-

(Born Janis Fink) American songwriter, singer, and musician.

Ian is recognized as an important songwriter whose works are characterized by a deep feeling for humanity and a contempt for injustice. According to Ian, her pessimistic songs of teenage dilemmas reflect not her own circumstances but the confusion and rebellion felt by many teenagers during the mid-sixties. In a straightforward, concrete manner, Ian confronts such contemporary problems as prostitution, loneliness, interracial love, and religious corruption. Ian's lyrics are praised for their poetic quality, and her false rhyme scheme has been compared to that of Emily Dickinson. At the age of twenty, after four years of trying to cope with success in a world where the more experienced considered her a child, Ian dropped out of the music scene. Four years later, however, she began recording new material. Ian views her return not as a comeback, but as a separate life, for now she feels she is better able to handle the life of a pop star. The lyrics of these works convey Ian's matured outlook and satisfaction in her new role.

Ian's first hit single, "Society's Child," concerns a love affair between a white girl and a black boy. Ian not only attacks the adults who disapprove of the relationship, but also the girl, who relents under society's pressure and rejects her love. Banned by radio stations across the United States until Leonard Bernstein introduced Ian on a television special, the song eventually rose to number one on the charts. Ian's early albums were moderately successful, inspiring a small but strong following.

Ian's lyrics had mellowed somewhat by the time she recorded *Stars*, her first album after returning to the popular music business. The songs on *Stars* still discuss teenage problems, but the anger of her earlier work is conspicuously absent. Her next effort, *Between the Lines*, reestablished her reputation as an important songwriter. It has received mixed reviews, but there is at least one outstanding song, "At Seventeen," in which Ian explores the "ugly duckling" syndrome many teen-age girls face. Ian's subsequent albums have also received mixed reviews, and her confirmed followers remain comparatively small. However, her observations on contemporary issues and society present a stark and revealing message.

LIFE

[Janis Ian] is a national phenomenon, a composer and singer who makes bitter poetry of teen-age dilemmas. Her most successful record, entitled *Society's Child*, detailed the woes of interracial dating. . . . Her first album, [*Janis Ian*, touched] heavily on prostitution, corrupted religion and children. . . . The second album, [*For All the Seasons of Your Mind*], explores such subjects as suicide and loneliness. Her folk songs, tinged with funereal dissonances, tear up the old folks at home. Their lyrics are outbursts at squaredom, declarations of independence from contemporary U.S. society. Yet, despite the refractory content of her music, she is that society's child. (p. 53)

Parents who finesse their parental responsibilities rank high on Janis Ian's long list of things bad. . . .

Janis doesn't have much use for false gods either. . . .

© Neil Zlozower

Just what exactly has happened to this girl to provoke such [disillusioned] lines?

"I saw all the hypocrisy up front, and I devised ways of getting around it. Love is groovy." She pauses. "Hate is the ultimate insanity."

Not altogether clear perhaps, but it is talk which makes perfect sense to a generation weaned on Dylan, Donovan and the Beatles, a generation which pays as much attention to the words as the music. (p. 56)

"I Am Society's Child," in Life (courtesy of Life Magazine; © 1967 Time Inc.; reprinted with permission), Vol. 63, No. 17, October 27, 1967, pp. 53, 56.

VARIETY

The youth movement in the music biz was given a tremendous boost [recently] when Janis Ian made her concert bow to a near-capacity audience. Only 16 years old, Miss Ian stunned her peers and her elders with the power of the material. . . .

Miss Ian's celebrated number about an inter-racial love affair, **"Society's Child,"** was only a partial tipoff on the calibre of this girl's compositional talents. She can write blues, rock and folk on any topic, from prostitution, old age homes, masochism, suicide, self-pity to the Vietnam war. As remarkable as the material, even more striking was the absence of precocity or self-consciousness.

> *"Janis Ian, 16-Year-Old Folksinger, Whams House at Philharmonic Hall, N.Y.,"* in Variety *(copyright 1967, by Variety, Inc.) December 13, 1967, p. 45.*

HANK FOX

Sixteen-year-old Janis Ian has a message. But whether its content is reality or fantasy, one theme is predominant—disintegration of the mind, leading to mental destruction of society. . . .

[In a recent live performance, the] recording artist methodically and unemotionally spelled out her message in song. With her crisp voice, she soared to the heights while dousing her audience with her macabre incantations. Insanity, frustration and apathy, Vietnam, poverty and loneliness—she sang them all—each with the same pessimistic view towards destruction. She sang of love, yet the air was fraught with death. She laughed, but there was a morbid echo. . . .

[It] is hoped that she doesn't take all her lyrics to heart. She has the makings of one of this generation's greatest poets.

> *Hank Fox, "Janis Ian's Messages: How to Succeed by Being Grim,"* in Billboard *(© copyright 1967 by Billboard Publications, Inc.; reprinted by permission), Vol. 79, No. 51, December 23, 1967, p. 16.*

ALAN HEINEMAN

[Among contemporary lyricists, Janis Ian] is second as a poet only to John Lennon (certainly) and Dylan and the Airplane's Slick-Kantner-Balin combination (maybe). She does not indulge in the obscurantist, free-associational quasi-poetry that passes for profundity among many of her contemporaries—and elders. She has, instead, the rather quaint notion that words are designed for meaningful communication. Which does not mean that she is simplistic or obvious—merely that most of her songs mean something, and mean it in an original, striking, but understandable way.

Janis deals, in her songs, with real contemporary problems in a concrete manner: dishonesty, lack of communication, the suicidal impulse. And just when you think she's taking the facile, kids-under-25-against-the-world hard line, she turns on her own world (and herself) and deflates it: *Honey D'Ya Think* deals with the phonily hip, *Shady Acres* with the irresponsibility of kids toward parents, and *Society's Child*—the most famous instance—with not only the bigotry of the older generation but the sheeplike, albeit unwilling, imitation of that bigotry by the younger.

She is the first to admit that many—too many—of her first songs concern problems considered (sometimes wrongly) exclusively adolescent. (p. 16)

Yet her songs are a sensitive delineation of adolescence. . . .

I have referred to her poetry. Let me finish by citing some examples. The two albums are full of words and phrases that stick and resonate, as well as with a few forgettable pieces that

she will surely grow out of. Her close rhymes and false rhymes are daring in a way not unreminiscent of Emily Dickinson; she will give a metaphor an additional twist and add a level of meaning. For example, in *Son of Love*. . . , she rhymes "muse" with "music," "sin" with "medicine," and "scent" with "incense." . . .

I think my favorite of her songs, in terms of sheer poetry, is *Pro-Girl.* The whole song is a completely realized contemporary poem of considerable merit. . . .

If the Poetic Muse sees fit to keep this little chick creative and receptive and sane, she will surely be one of the foremost lyricists of our period. And if her composing and performing talents grow proportionately, one of the most influential musicians.

And even if none of this happens, she will have written, between the ages of 14 and 16, several superior songs. That is a gift few are granted. (p. 17)

> *Alan Heineman, "In Love with Janis Ian," in* down beat *(copyright 1968; reprinted with permission of* down beat*), Vol. 35, No. 7, April 4, 1968, pp. 16-17.*

ALAN HEINEMAN

[*The Secret Life of J. Eddy Fink* is] a real down. It's pretty awful, despite containing some interesting elements. There are only three truly good songs on it: *Friends, Misery* and *Son;* I include the latter on the basis of some rich, imagistic lyrics.

Friends is delightful, a loving parody of Dylan's c&w-tinged stuff, performed with exactly the right balance between mockery and conviction (except when Janis breaks up at one point). The words aren't parodic, for the most part, though they catch the flavor of Dylan in early songs like *Don't Think Twice* and *All I Really Wanna Do. And I Did, Ma,* on Janis' second album, was pure comedy, and can't be listened to very often; *Friends* invites rehearing.

Misery is one of the few hard rock things Janis has tried, and it works pretty well: good words. . . . (p. 19)

[*Psycho*] is really a shame: it's a bitter, heartfelt and much-needed indictment of the sordid side of the music business, but the words are clumsy (because too strongly felt?). Janis is beginning to labor images of self-prostitution, strong when she first employed them but now losing their impact. Similarly, the metaphor of a narrator (singer) needing a blind man to show him the way, which appears in *Psycho,* had worn thin eons ago. (pp. 19-20)

But for this record, if you can find copies of the lyrics, you'll get most of what there is to get. I think the next will be considerably more representative, and representative Janis is compulsory listening. (p. 20)

> *Alan Heineman, "Record Reviews: 'The Secret Life of J. Eddy Fink',"* in down beat *(copyright 1969; reprinted with permission of* down beat*), Vol. 36, No. 15, July 24, 1969, pp. 19-20.*

JACQUES VASSAL

The first thing that struck one about Janis Ian was her youth and the precocity of her talent. (p. 205)

It was in 1966, after her dramatic first appearances at Greenwich Village's Village Gate, that Janis made her first album for Verve-Forecast [*Janis Ian*]. Immediately the record earned the admiration of the educated public, but also the disapproval of the Establishment. This was due to the most noticed song on the album, "**Society's Child,**" which tackled the problem of racial discrimination in a new fashion and without mincing words: for a schoolgirl of fifteen, not a bad start.

Why so much hassle over a song? Making use of an episode in the life of one of society's children (one would like to think that it is Janis Ian herself, but she has definitely stated that it is not), she attacks, all at the same time, racial discrimination, familial authority, the reactionary antiquity of the educational system, the contempt for love, the alienation which is its result, through the fact that at least temporarily a young white girl resigns herself to accepting what she is told, to stop meeting the young black whom she loves. Lyrically and musically, the "schoolgirl" doesn't miss a trick.

Certainly, her education in song is established on a base that she herself has defined as "Baezo-Seegerian" [referring to folksingers Joan Baez and Pete Seeger] and, as she has often said, since she grew up with folk music, all her songs are capable of being sung to the sole accompaniment of the acoustic guitar. . . .

From *Janis Ian,* her first album, to *Stars,* her fifth, by way of *For All the Seasons of Your Mind, The Secret Life of J. Eddy Fink,* and *Who Really Cares?* there is no doubt that there has grown up a "Janis Ian sound": the way of combining the voice and the instruments, done with a great delicacy and possibly also a certain detachment, are extremely individualistic. . . . (p. 206)

Janis Ian's recordings have always been extremely well arranged. Unfortunately, in *Who Really Cares?* the themes of the songs are not in the most distinguished or individualistic vein. One hunts for the masterpiece but, unlike her earlier records, the hunt is in vain.

As far as we can see, the problem for her at the time of *Who Really Cares?* is very clear: the early works of Janis Ian were signified by her extreme precocity. Her preoccupations (racism, interracial love, education, the dilemmas of the young in the world of the old) testified to her rare maturity. Now that she has achieved physical maturity, it seems that she has difficulty in reaching her second wind; the songs on *Who Really Cares?* are attempts to find it. On two or three of the tracks there are moments of great beauty: in "Galveston," the very jazzy "Orphan of the Wind," and above all in "Month of May." But taken all together, *Who Really Cares?* hasn't the same cohesion as an album like *The Secret Life of J. Eddy Fink.*

Nevertheless it seems that the future holds great promise for Janis Ian as songwriter. . . . Her first four albums are now hard to get. . . : they have long ago been deleted. But with behind her the power of these years, she can hardly fail to make a lasting impact on the world of folkrock in particular and the world of pop music in general. Her more recent releases, especially *Between the Lines,* offer strong evidence of her increasingly mature and developing talent. (pp. 206-07)

> *Jacques Vassal, "Americans," in his* Electric Children: Roots and Branches of Modern Folkrock, *translated and adapted by Paul Barnett (translation copyright © 1976 by Paul Barnett; published by Taplinger Publishing Co., Inc., New York; reprinted by per-*

mission; originally published as Folksong: Une histoire de la musique populaire aux Etats-Unis, *Editions Albin Michel, 1971), Taplinger, 1976, pp. 187-221.**

NOEL COPPAGE

[I find Janis Ian interesting because she uses a] powerful cerebrum more to move people than to impress them. Sometimes she overdoes it and works for shock value alone. . . . In such cases, she's merely doing what worked so well before—*Society's Child,* written when Janis was a little kid, separated the liberal men from the liberal boys. But she is a prodigy growing up, and her later work deserves a larger audience. (p. 60)

> *Noel Coppage, "Troubadettes, Troubadoras, and Troubadines . . . or . . . What's a Nice Girl Like You Doing in a Business Like This?" in* Stereo Review *(copyright © 1972 by Ziff-Davis Publishing Company), Vol. 29, No. 3, September, 1972, pp. 58-61.**

PETER REILLY

Seven years after the success of *Society's Child,* a watershed topical song written when she was fifteen, Janis Ian is back, at the age of twenty-two, with songs composed during her own private season of hell. Always one of the most sensitive of composer/performers, often hypersensitive in live performance, she has at last stopped meandering artistically and [on "**Stars**" has] come to some positive conclusions: yes, the public will eat you alive if you let it, but she still wants to be a *Star;* yes, she was deeply in love with *Jesse,* and though he's gone she's still in love (*You've Got Me on a String*). However, she's still looking around (*Sweet Sympathy*) and has a pretty good idea of what kind of life she wants with any new love (*Page Nine*), and, what-the-hell, life goes on anyway (*Applause*). The old bitter rage is evident only once here, in *Dance with Me,* in which her fury over the contemporary American scene can send smoke spiraling out of your speakers. It's very strong, tough stuff, and it makes Lauro Nyro and some of the other female composers of protest songs sound like the bluestocking mumblers of bitchery that they often are (I loved it).

Unfortunately there still lingers an air of veiled contempt, a touch of the common scold, about Ian's performances which often contradicts the more positive sense of the lyrics. *I* don't mind it, but I know that others do and will be turned off by it. But this is an album definitely worth listening to nonetheless, most importantly as an opportunity to hear a real artist struggling to sort out and to communicate through a morass of negative and positive emotions. Ian is trying her damndest to mellow, and except for that one track here she seems to be succeeding. (pp. 84, 86)

> *Peter Reilly, "Popular Discs and Tapes: 'Stars'," in* Stereo Review *(copyright © 1974 by Ziff-Davis Publishing Company), Vol. 33, No. 2, August, 1974, pp. 84, 86.*

SUSIN SHAPIRO

In her soft-spoken way, Society's Child, Janis Ian, deserves mention for all her credible tunes on *Between the Lines.* Alternating between eerie nostalgia and low-key hysteria, her violin pathos is straight out of a Max Ophuls melodrama, and that's not half bad. Janis plays the ugly duckling, the hard-headed waif with the heart of gold. She plays with her pain, is a perfect candidate for Janov's primal scream therapy, but instead sublimates the hurt into mellow, melodic sighs. *Between the Lines* is a studiously earnest attempt at self-discovery and Ian asks only that you meet her somewhere in the middle of your life, and hers. (p. 69)

> Susin Shapiro, "Rock around the Crotch," in Craw-
> daddy *(copyright © 1975 by Crawdaddy Publishing
> Co., Inc.; all rights reserved; reprinted by permis-
> sion), May, 1975, pp. 68-9.**

KARL DALLAS

There's a song on ["**Between the Lines**"] about a spotty-faced 17-year-old who never gets the Valentines or dates, the lyrics of which work fairly well until we remember that it is hardly autobiographical. . . . [Janis Ian] was closer to the beauty queens in her song, who marry young and then retire, than to the abandoned and unrequited heroines of it. . . . I realised that, once again, Janis Ian was failing to say anything particularly noteworthy about one of her chosen subjects. She affects now to disown ["**Society's Child**"], but because of the historical and social context within which it appeared, her "shocking" song about a love affair that crossed the colour line was important at the time, no matter how naive and even offensive it may be in retrospect. In contrast, nothing she produced during her current come-back has that sort of relevance. The voice has matured, the tunes have that sort of instant acceptability and equally instant forgettability which fills up a remarkable number of albums still, even in these days of alleged austerity, the production is immaculate, and none of it matters a jot. Society's child in America today has different needs and problems than those she touches on but hardly illuminates in her lyrics. Which doesn't mean she should be writing more "political" songs, but a seemingly significant writer should surely be aware [that] what happens to a couple when they are between the sheets doesn't stop at the bedroom door. Sometimes, love songs can be the most political of all.

> Karl Dallas, "'Between the Lines'," in Melody Maker
> (© IPC Business Press Ltd.), May 10, 1975, p. 33.

PETER REILLY

Janis Ian was one of the authentic voices of the Sixties, one of the street kids who told it exactly as it was without any of the "poetic" trimmings. She directed her coruscating wit, gelid eye, and scolding fury as much at the opportunists of her own generation who were corrupting the dream as at the society that feared and brutally repressed anyone not stamped out by the cookie cutter. But Ian seems to have paid a high price for her own involvement and convictions. She came back about a year ago with a new album, and, aside from a lot of media palaver about her now being able to accept being a "star," it never really went anywhere beyond reminding her old fans that she was up and about again.

"**Between the Lines**" seems to be another water-treader, but it has one brilliant track: *At Seventeen,* not about Viet Nam but about an ugly duckling, is filled with the same pitiless observation and ice-hard anger as her earlier work. . . . A popular lyric that actually implies that someone has learned something, that things do sort themselves out, given enough time, that experience can result in wisdom. And there's not a touch of cosmic Melanie or Laura Nyro style. *At Seventeen* is

just a simple story about a girl-woman. But then so is [Gustave Flaubert's novel] *Madame Bovary.*

It would be too much to ask that the rest of the album measure up to that gem, but there *are* some other nice things here: the mordant *Watercolors; The Come-On,* a wry, funny appraisal of the difficulties of being promiscuous when your heart just ain't in it; *Light a Light,* a solemn little love song. Ian is now definitely back in the ascendant, and I hope she continues in the vein of exploring characters and personality types of our time rather than taking on overworked, overheated social issues. She is very fine, and eventually, I think, she will contribute some unique and lasting work. But she is like a fine diamond: a lot of hoopla and celebration upon initial discovery, the tense moment of the first cut (and in her case there was some regrettable splintering), and then the long period of polishing. One thing is sure. When she does make it, she'll be absolutely glittering.

> Peter Reilly, "Popular Discs and Tapes: 'Between
> the Lines'," in Stereo Review *(copyright © 1975 by
> Ziff-Davis Publishing Company), Vol. 35, No. 1,
> July, 1975, p. 78.*

JOHN LISSNER

["**Between the Lines**"] is one of those rarities—a best-seller that focuses on musicianship. Though not without its flaws, "**Between the Lines**" has substance and depth, qualities absent from Ian's adolescent career and her hit song of those years, "**Society's Child**," a bristling tirade against adult injustice. This precocious hit was followed by "**Janey's Blues**," "**Honey Do Ya Think?**" and "**New Christ Cardiac Hero**" which zeroed in on dishonesty, exploitation, lack of communication, even suicidal impulses. At 15-going-on-16 Ian became the urchin at large, pinpointing the hypocrisies of society, ever at the mercy of its mores, wounded by its snubs. . . .

Her songs of the late sixties, lacking even a ray of sunshine, began to sound vaguely familiar; moreover, her accompaniment, often awkward, could not support her often powerful verbal images. No wonder that her career seemed to terminate at age 20.

In 1974, Janis Ian's "comeback" was launched with the release of . . . "**Stars**," a collection which got mixed reviews, but much praise for its title song, a vivid and poignant self-portrait. "**Between the Lines**" . . . reveals "**Society's Child**" as a grown-up, worldly woman. Along with several forgettable tracks, there are four, possibly five outstanding productions.

"**Watercolors**," a moving portrait of a flawed lover and a fading love affair, is the finest song in the album. . . .

On "**Between the Lines**" Ian's lyrics are stamped with her old introspective brand of realism. With the exception of the mildly buoyant "**When the Party's Over**," Ian remains as serious as ever. Indeed, Ian is at her best when she creates personal scenarios centering on the social stresses and emotional crises, the sexual and romantic frustration experienced by many young women. . . .

Ian's talent is still developing, imperfect. . . . [The] lyrics of both "**In the Winter**" and "**Tea and Sympathy**" skirt the edge of soap opera. "**Lover's Lullaby**" and "**Light a Light**" are pretty maudlin. . . . The title track, "**Between the Lines**," veers toward pretentiousness with its 1920's neo-Brechtian voicings, and "**From Me To You**" seems to be a rather tense reworking of Dylan's "It's Alright Ma." As a total musical package, however, **"Between the Lines"** is a strong indication of Ian's increasing potential.

John Lissner, "Janis Ian—Society's Child Grows Up," in The New York Times, Section D (© 1975 by The New York Times Company; reprinted by permission), December 7, 1975, p. 19.

BOB SARLIN

Janis Ian has grown into a charming, mature singer-songwriter. There is surely some of the snotty kid in there somewhere, but what was once called uppityness is now called arrogance. . . .

Recently, with the re-release of her very first recordings, that pretentious teenager has come back to haunt Janis Ian. . . .

Listening now to **"Society's Child,"** **"Janey's Blues"** or even **"New Christ Cardiac Hero,"** all songs on that first album, one has to allow for the period of time during which they were made. It was a time of musical exploration, the emergence of folk-rock as a viable form; a time of great self-righteousness and pretension. What does shine through is the quality of both Janis' musical ideas and voice. She makes Tanya Tucker seem like some shallow upstart as she wails through strong lyrics with poise and emotional intensity. No wonder teenagers who prided themselves on their "sensitivity" went ga-ga over this album. . . . [The] album screams, "Beware: Sensitive Artist At Work."

Many of Janis Ian's recent songs, like **"Stars"** and **"At Seventeen,"** seem to refer to this period of her life. (p. 52)

Since the beginning of her career, Janis has made good, yet uneven albums. From the very first, she had a tendency to be wordy, perhaps in an attempt to do a Dylan. But Dylan has the rare ability to stuff a song with a hundred disparate images and still thread the whole thing into an emotionally meaningful whole. On Janis' new album, *Aftertones*, there's less in the way of wasted words. Her strongest point has always been her sheer musicality. She is a happy sponge, not unlike Paul Simon, able to integrate many elements into her work. For all the influences, the songs remain personal statements that could only come from Janis. . . .

[There] isn't one moment on this new album when you can rise up self-righteously and say, 'Ah hah, overpopulation.' It's a tasteful, understated album.

With a *salsa* song called **"I Would Like To Dance,"** Janis is the first pop artist to attempt to integrate this Latin form into her work. . . .

The song is a charmer, all about the singer's inability to dance, to get her feet to follow her head. . . .

There is an odd set of songs that finish up the album. **"This Must Be Wrong"** seems to be an S&M love song. . . . It's a funny tune, reminiscent of Randy Newman. . . .

The next song is called **"Don't Cry, Old Man"** and also shows the Newman influence. In fact, it could be an answer song to Randy's "Old Man," in which the narrator kisses off his father, coaxing him toward an easy death. In Janis' version, aided by a rather eerie arrangement, there's much more encouragement to live.

The most surprising cut on the album is called **"Hymn."** . . . [It is] a haunting song with great religious feeling, the loveliest moment in *Aftertones*.

The album is a strong continuation of an encouraging process. . . .

Janis Ian is growing and her records and live performances are expanding with her. Although still tinged with her early "tough girl" image, Janis has become a frank, creative artist. (p. 54)

Bob Sarlin, "Janis Ian at 24," in Crawdaddy (copyright © 1976 by Crawdaddy Publishing Co., Inc.; all rights reserved; reprinted by permission), February, 1976, pp. 52-4.

PAUL NELSON

Melancholic self-pity and petulant revenge would appear to be the two main colors in Janis Ian's rather precious, nearly monochromatic rainbow. At her infrequent best, this chronically forlorn artist is sometimes able to elevate the former hue into genuinely moving introspection and the latter into valid social criticism, but too often she seems strangely content to tell us how fashionably miserable she is and that it is all our fault. Ian does not lack talent—**"At Seventeen"** and **"Water Colors"** from *Between the Lines* are fine songs—but could sorely use an unfettered sense of humor and the ability to separate the posture of sensitivity from the perceptions of selectivity.

Listening to *Aftertones* is somewhat like hearing an Amy Vanderbilt treatise on the emotional etiquette of a Doomed Outsider who "measures out the time in coffee spoons" . . . , ad infinitum, ad nauseam. Exceptions are the Dylanesque **"Boy I Really Tied One On"** and the LP's best song, **"This Must Be Wrong."** . . . **"I Would Like to Dance"** is okay, too.

Janis Ian, Janis Ian, stop living your life like a soap opera. Cut the pettiness and the poetaster's crap, and maybe we'll love you for who you really are: Mickey Spillane trying to pass for Johnnie Ray at the high school prom. (pp. 66, 69)

Paul Nelson, "Records: 'Aftertones'," in Rolling Stone (by Straight Arrow Publishers, Inc. © 1976; all rights reserved; reprinted by permission), Issue 210, April 8, 1976, pp. 66, 69.

PETER REILLY

Janis Ian has arrived. The ugly duckling of *Society's Child* has, all these years later, become the most glittering and luminescent of swans. [**"Aftertones"**], her best album to date, is one of those joyous things that probably happen only once in an artist's lifetime: that particular moment when everything that has gone before finally coalesces into sustained, articulate, and controlled statement. The intelligence is remarkable, the craftsmanship superb and the attack dazzling throughout. Stay tuned, because there is going to be a great deal more said about this album—and I hope to add my own strong feelings to what has become the happiest success story in current popular music. Buy it, of course, and while you are listening remember that old bromide about the hare and the tortoise.

Peter Reilly, "Popular Discs and Tapes: 'Aftertones'," in Stereo Review (copyright © 1976 by Ziff-Davis Publishing Company), Vol. 36, No. 5, May, 1976, p. 84.

FRED De VAN

The elusive Janis Ian "Queen of the melodic bittersweet" has again emerged into the public eye as a major artist. Her introspective, self-evaluation type lyrics have finally found their time and audience. . . . [Her] images of love are both full-blown and cautiously sultry. Her images touch on areas that in one way or another exist in all of us. Her love songs are a full indication of this maturation.

The songs in **Between The Lines** are all strong, and total good taste is to be found in every note and word on the record. (p. 82)

In **Aftertones,** her music like her words, is the work of a serious musical artist, charged with the competence of a committed energetic artist. . . . The album is eloquent, she gets it all on.

Aftertones is her only album without a "supersong," yet it hangs together so well as to be enchanting from start to finish. *This Must Be Wrong, Aftertones, Belle Of The Blues, Don't Cry Old Man* and *Hymn* all have that look of whimsy, warmth and wisdom that has always been a part of this young woman. Each song on the album has its own special magic. Janis Ian has emerged from a puckish, arrogant kid to a real stand-up and take-notice artist. (pp. 82-3)

> *Fred De Van, "The Column: 'Between the Lines' and 'Aftertones',"* in Audio (© *1976, CBS Publications, The Consumer Publishing Division of CBS Inc.), Vol. 60, No. 6, June, 1976, pp. 82-3.*

STEPHEN HOLDEN

Most of Ian's new material [on **Miracle Row**] recycles old musical ideas, again evoking the hypocrisies of social rituals and romantic encounters. However, these miniatures are problematic due to the obsessiveness of Ian's craft: by combining melodramatic chords and claustrophobic rhymes, she reconstructs her psychological perceptions too literally.

Still, there are a couple of nice moments. **"I Want to Make You Love Me"** has a more relaxed melodiousness than one customarily associates with Ian, and the ambitious **"Miracle Row/Maria"** successfully evokes a complex relationship between two women. But nothing here can compare with **"At Seventeen"** and **"Water Colors,"** which are Ian's two finest songs because they blend her propensity for psychodrama into a broader narrative scheme. Maybe Ian should develop her ability to be expansive as well as clinical. (p. 79)

> *Stephen Holden, "Records: 'Miracle Row',"* in Rolling Stone (*by Straight Arrow Publishers, Inc.* © *1977; all rights reserved; reprinted by permission), Issue 234, March 10, 1977, pp. 78-9.*

STEPHEN HOLDEN

["**Miracle Row**"] is a disappointing production and contains no songs of the *At Seventeen/Watercolors* caliber found on Ian's best-selling **"Between the Lines"** album. (p. 144)

[Crucial] to the failure of **"Miracle Row"** is its dearth of strong material. Many of the new songs are inferior recyclings of old ideas. *Party Lights, Let Me Be Lonely, Slow Dance Romance, Will You Dance?* and *I'll Cry Tonight* in one way or another all touch on a theme that Ian has treated more directly in the past: the plight of the grownup wallflower who can't get over the traumas of teenage rejection, even as she recognizes the

hypocrisy and shallowness of the rituals that caused that trauma. Only in the ambitious diptych **Miracle Row/Maria,** a detailed psychological portrait of the relationship between two women, does Ian extend herself beyond the short-form still-life songs that seem increasingly like carbon copies of a single humorless and self-pitying idea. (pp. 144-45)

> *Stephen Holden, "Backbeat Records: 'Miracle Row',"* in High Fidelity (*copyright* © *by ABC Leisure Magazine, Inc.; all rights reserved; excerpted by permission), Vol. 27, No. 4, April, 1977, pp. 144-45.*

MICHAEL TEARSON

With **Miracle Row** Janis Ian is no longer the "poor, sad dear" her many fans perceived. . . .

Janis' writing has grown. . . . It is not so self-centered. The remaining traces of what has evidently been self-pity and self-righteousness are turning quickly into maturity. Songs such as **Take to the Sky** and the building **Candlelight** reflect this growth. The grand finale of the intertwined stories **Miracle Row/Maria** is as impressive a piece as she has ever put together.

> *Michael Tearson, "The Column: 'Miracle Row',"* in Audio (© *1977, CBS Publications, The Consumer Publishing Division of CBS Inc.), Vol. 61, No. 5, May, 1977, p. 89.*

PETER REILLY

Janis Ian is for the trendies one of the most exciting, red-hot writer/performers in pop at the moment; for the rest of us she's definitely here to stay. With **"Miracle Row,"** . . . she has seized for herself the title of Girl Most Likely to Get Pop off Its Moribund Ass in the Late Seventies.

Like the lady herself, **"Miracle Row"** exudes theatricality. It has equal amounts of the high romance of the low life and the jaded, dark-red-nail-polish lows that accompany the high life. Ian's theatricality, like that of another Great Proletarian, Bertolt Brecht, may not be immediately discernible, but it is there. She, too, chooses street argot as her lyric form, and the nonchalant gut punch seems to be her favorite device. But she is more than an artistic descendant of Brecht in her sardonic, toughly humorous acceptance of an existential world in which the cunning, the avaricious, and the brutal all too often float to the top while the *Lumpen* below devour each other in desperation—she is also Brecht's Pirate Jenny come to stinging, poignant, poetic life.

Like Brecht, Ian is an angry artist. In the years succeeding *Society's Child,* her first musical outburst at the age of sixteen, it was touch and go as to whether or not the anger would consume the artist. *At Seventeen,* that bitter little paean to the arid joys of "settling for" (from **"Between the Lines,"** her second "comeback" album) gave notice that the old fire could still scorch its subject despite its deceptively gentle melody. With **"Aftertones,"** however, the mature Ian emerged. She kept traces of the daydreaming, slightly murderous gamine—the Pirate Jenny—that she'd always been, but she was now in control of herself and her enormous talents. Instead of blindly flailing at the objects of her scorn and only sometimes hitting the mark, she projected a serene self-confidence. This sense of assurance came through not only in her angry moments such as the hilarious and raucous *Boy, I Really Tied One On* (probably the best song of its kind since *It Was Just One of Those*

Things), but also in her ability to be unabashedly and yearningly romantic as in *I Really Would Like to Dance.*

The songs in "Miracle Row" are chiaroscuro sketches in both words and music. Ian uses the technique masterfully in *Party Lights,* for instance. She sheds equal amounts of intense light . . . and the most chilling darkness . . . in telling the story of someone who has Made It, the guest of honor at one of those grotesque Marvelous Parties designed to show the world you've arrived. . . .

The most ambitious track here is *Miracle Row/Maria,* two related songs about summer in a ghetto and a girl with "eyes like a demon lover's child." It succeeds admirably on every professional level . . . , but it fails ultimately because it is theatrical in the wrong context—[Brecht's] *Mother Courage* playing Radio City Music Hall. Absolutely on target in every way, however, unique and securely in Brecht-Ian territory, is the bloodcurdling Spanish-flavored serenade *Will You Dance?* . . .

["Miracle Row"] is a lovely exercise in seriousness without a trace of grandiosity. It's an album by a real person about real things.

> Peter Reilly, "Janis Ian: The Girl Most Likely," in Stereo Review *(copyright © 1977 by Ziff-Davis Publishing Company), Vol. 38, No. 6, June, 1977, p. 100.*

PETER REILLY

[Janis Ian] has proved herself to be one of the most important writer-performers of the Seventies, and she looks at and into you from the cover photo with a veiled stare that can X-ray a situation, the people in it, and the probable outcome easily, knowingly, compassionately.

Janis Ian operates in the pop-music business, which perhaps denies her the instant credentials the fancier literary and artistic worlds might provide. But what she's been creating for the last several years is a body of work that, for awareness and insight into life as it's being lived (or played) in our time, stands creditably alongside the best in any field of contemporary creative expression. . . . ["Janis Ian"] finds Ian in a more subdued and contemplative mood than the flash and fireworks of her previous "Miracle Row." There isn't anything here that raises the emotional temperature in quite the same way as, for instance, *Party Lights,* or the grim Latin melodrama of *Will You Dance?* did. But, while most of the material here may be emotionally in a minor key, it is some of the most assured and elegant work of her career. In this group of eleven songs, literal meaning often gives way to less logical—but equally valid—color, mood, and texture. The key song seems to be the last one, *Hopper Painting.* It isn't about Edward Hopper, or even about one of his paintings. Instead, it is an ambiguous piece, either about Ian herself or about someone with whom she's once been close. . . . [By] the time she reached the second chorus I had long since ceased to care much about what the song *meant,* and much more about the way it was making me feel. I surrendered to the atmosphere Ian was creating, and it was an entrance into a very Hopper-like world indeed. This song, like several others here *The Bridge, Some People,* and *Streetlife Serenaders,* has the same cryptic beauty, the fascination with the everyday, and the moment-caught-forever feeling as Hopper's paintings.

Not that Ian isn't still her familiar, prematurely wise, sardonic self in such things as *Hotels and One-Night Stands,* a sad-funny description of life on the road equally applicable to a rock star or a Fuller brush salesman. Two songs, *Silly Habits* and *I Need to Live Alone Again* (which, for sheer sound, is the best thing on the album), are the kind of thing that Carly Simon has been trying to write for several years but that Ian knocks off the way Chrissie Evert serves. And then there is the still beauty of *My Mama's House.* It is a song about how very much a child loves her sexually promiscuous mother despite the community's frowning disapproval.

"Janis Ian" is not—and surely was not meant to be—an Important, Significant, or Milestone album. It is simply another addition to an established body of work. [Ian] is one of those ladies who Know Something. And one of the things she surely knows is that she doesn't have to count the critical handraises on her side to reassure herself of her unique talent. The ayes already have it.

> Peter Reilly, "Janis Ian," in Stereo Review *(copyright © 1978 by Ziff-Davis Publishing Company), Vol. 41, No. 6, December, 1978, p. 110.*

DON SHEWEY

As far as hype goes, it may have been all over for Janis Ian when she quit writing hit songs about being an ugly teenager with a hit song. But as her craft matures, Ian's lyrics get more distilled, her emotions more subtle, the brisk melodies more distinctive. And her best numbers have become the kind of adult love songs that make singers cry and other composers bite their lips. . . .

[Janis Ian] contains at least three tunes ("That Grand Illusion," "Tonight Will Last Forever," "Silly Habits") as fine and strong as her classic "Jesse." . . .

The LP has mistakes, but they are few: the solo-piano backing on "Hopper Painting" grows dull, and "The Bridge" presents an embarrassing string of corny metaphors about "the oceans of our lives." Otherwise, the new disc's delightful consistency makes it easy to empathize with the veiled bitterness of "Hotels & One-Night Stands." . . .

Despite their considerable virtues, *Janis Ian* and 1977's *Miracle Row* have gone practically unnoticed. Why the huge successes of "At Seventeen" and *Between the Lines* haven't carried over to Ian's subsequent work is a complete mystery to me.

> Don Shewey, "Records: 'Janis Ian'," in Rolling Stone *(by Straight Arrow Publishers, Inc. © 1979; all rights reserved; reprinted by permission), Issue 287, March 22, 1979, p. 64.*

AIDA PAVLETICH

[In the early 1960s, the genre of teen songs had "the boyfriend" as their central theme. The demons of teendom were the other girls. Parents] were another conflicting force. Her parents usually disapproved of Jimmy or Eddie or Johnny, and made vague but forceful class distinctions to keep the lovers apart. Their objections were met with either rebellion or death. Only Janis Ian capitulated in "Society's Child," breaking the mold. (p. 77)

Outside of a few songs written by Shirley Owens and the Shirelles, Shirley Ellis' dance numbers, and a few songs Lesley

Gore wrote after the teen vogue had subsided [in the late sixties], the majority of the teen singers were interpreters of other people's material. An adult, predominantly male sensibility codified the teen genre laws.

George [Shadow] Morton discovered and produced the one exception, Janis Ian, the prodigious teenaged singer-songwriter whose folk-based melodies and social concern went beyond the pale of teen sensibility.

Ian was part of a new generation. She identified more with Bob Dylan than with the Shangri-Las. Since she was sixteen years old at the time, she was the first and only authentic teen composer and writer who singly created her own songs.

"Society's Child," the song that flung her to the attention of a large audience, was a statement that blended the social concern of the folk movement with the teenaged feeling of helplessness. The parent's disapproval in this case is backed by the clout of an entire society. The boy is black. He comes to the girl's house, to her mother's consternation, and the mother forbids her to see him.

The song was rough. The writer did not simplify an adult perception into teen terms, she was already there. She had cut through the fluff to a real problem, one that might not be solved by growing up, even though she does hold out the hope for change. It was a brilliant coup by Janis Ian that revealed an innate talent that would have surfaced even if the song had not become a succès de scandale. (p. 90)

No other song had faced that racial issue, *what if your daughter married one?* A teenaged white girl! A black boy! Her mother closes the door to him; it was dynamite, even though the girl acquiesces. She obeys her mother, accepts her judgment, since she is, after all, only "society's child." . . .

It was a teenage lament. It was not written by the adults in the Brill building, the songwriters' factory . . . in New York. A real young girl had written it and she had the promise of a

brilliant writer. Because of the promise, more than the song's actual merit, Janis received an inordinate amount of attention. . . .

Janis Ian's songs at the time were bitter to the point that they could only have been developmental, the natural depression of the late teens. . . . [Producer Shadow Morton] brought out some of her adolescent strength, but she was too original an artist to go teen. Her songs were protest songs, concerned with a rapidly changing minority: teenagers. (p. 215)

[Janis Ian] did not take part in the change in popular music from the sixties to the seventies. She remained in the background while other songwriters, singing their own songs, asserted their personal vision and changed the hit formulas of popular music. (p. 216)

[With **"Jesse"**] Janis Ian was a commercial songwriter once more. She joined producer Brooks Arthur for a run of excellent albums: *Stars, Between the Lines,* and *Aftertones.* (p. 230)

Her songs were, by new standards, sentimental, regressive, and promoted attitudes that were against the better interests of women, so said the doctrinaire fringe of the women's movement who demanded adherence to its principles by every woman writing. Janis' **"You've Got Me on a String"** was singled out. . . .

If a theme persists throughout her work, it is the feeling of being an outsider. **"Jesse"** finds her urging a lover to come home; **"At Seventeen,"** she's the high school outcast; **"Stars"** is a view of the loneliness of fame; and **"In the Winter"** is a chance meeting with a former lover, a song that could have been sung by Edith Piaf, such is the mettle of the undaunted yet vulnerable heroine. (p. 231)

Aida Pavletich, "Teen Angels" and "Women of Heart and Mind," in her Rock-A-Bye, Baby *(copyright © 1980 by Aida Pavletich; reprinted by permission of Doubleday & Company, Inc.), Doubleday, 1980, pp. 73-96, 207-36.**

Albert Innaurato

1948-

American playwright, screenwriter, and director.

Innaurato's works blend naturalism and surrealism and center on the need of all individuals, no matter how unusual or eccentric, to be loved and understood. Many of his characters are grotesques, losers, and misfits, and his situations often border on farce. But Innaurato places serious themes at the core of his plays, despite the madness at their peripheries. He believes contemporary society judges people on the basis of appearance and sexuality, and forces them into competitive situations they are unable to handle. Innaurato feels, however, that people have an intrinsic strength and dignity that enables them to transcend background and environment. He explores the effects of society on emotional life by examining such subjects as sexual dilemmas, prejudice, the loss of the American heroic impulse, and the search for love. Because of his success in depicting these concerns, he is considered one of the most promising talents of the American theater.

Innaurato has said that all of his characters are reflections of himself. Raised in South Philadelphia, the setting of many of his plays, Innaurato was considered a backward child. Because of this experience, he became interested in the problems of those rejected by society. At the age of eight, he began composing opera librettos; several critics have noted the structural similarities between his plays and the opera. Innaurato began his career as a playwright while a teenager. His first major work, the black comedy *The Transfiguration of Benno Blimpie*, is based on recollections of parochial school brutality and on the Catholic fixation with suffering; Innaurato saw the play, fully formed, in a nightmare. Benno, a grossly overweight adolescent who literally eats himself to death, is Innaurato's Christlike symbol of the innocent victim of society. Innaurato was praised for his imaginative conception and for the excellence of the play's language; he has since been recognized as a leader in the new emphasis on language in the theater. His next play, *Gemini*, is a humorous look at sexual identity: Francis, a Harvard student, is unsure whether he is hetero- or homosexual. The appeal of Innaurato's principle and secondary characters, and the sensitivity with which he approaches the issue, won accolades from critics and audiences; however, some homosexual critics found the play inaccurate and offensive. *Gemini* moved from its initial off-off-Broadway location to off-Broadway to Broadway, where it has become a long-running classic.

None of Innaurato's subsequent plays have equalled the popularity of his earlier works. Though he is not considered an unqualified success, Innaurato is usually perceived as a highly original playwright with a vivid moral vision. Young people appreciate his representations of their doubts and concerns and his satiric stabs at contemporary society.

MEL GUSSOW

Visions of [Eugene] Ionesco, and especially of [Franz] Kafka, go through our minds as we watch this pitch-black comedy ["The Transfiguration of Benno Blimpie"]. In a sense, "Benno"

is Mr. Innaurato's "Metamorphosis"—man into bug; everyone is trying to squash Benno.

He is the butt of all insults. He tells—and is—the story. But what the play is really about is the decay of the American family. In comparison, Edward Albee's "The American Dream" and Bruce Jay Friedman's "A Mother's Kisses" seem almost wistful. "Benno" is a nightmare, dreamed by Lenny Bruce. . . .

[Benno] is treated as an object, a slave, forced to observe the defilement of civilization. He is in torment, teetering out of existence. He will explode. Life can not contain him.

Beneath the fat, he is a saintly spirit. The only real human on stage, he is treated inhumanely. The playwright is serious about the "transfiguration." What if Christ were fat and ugly?

Not everyone should see this play. Many will be offended, even insulted, but it has a dramatic and a comic power. . . . At times, Mr. Innaurato's humor is itself a blunt instrument, but this is not a play one will easily forget.

Mel Gussow, "Stage: 2 Perplexed Men," in The New York Times (© 1976 by The New York Times Company; reprinted by permission), May 8, 1976, p. 15.*

GAUTAM DASGUPTA

[*Gemini* is a] witty and exuberant new play. . . . It is a world of opposites, a melting pot of differing sensibilities energized by a series of perpetual inversions and transformations.

Appropriately enough, the play is titled after the third sign of the Zodiac, and significantly, in keeping with the twin symbolism of that sign, continually seizes on the nature of dualistic phenomena evidenced in human behavior. *Gemini* is built on a well-defined pattern that synthesizes opposing polarities. Homosexual and heterosexual longings are counterpoised with one another, while the slim and beautiful is contrasted with the overweight and grotesque. On a more important level, and one that is sensitively handled, there are the opposing forces of life and death, paradiso and inferno, the generational conflict, and the morphological changes in every human experience. . . .

Innaurato groups [his] strikingly eloquent characters in a variety of situations, hilarious in the tradition of many of the old situational comedies one finds on TV reruns. There are moments, luckily very brief, when the playwright refuses to let go of a joke and uses it past its comic purpose, but the willful use of lines and situations repeated twice throughout the play is a structurally relevant device that underscores the twin element of the Zodiac sign. . . .

An exhilarating evening in the theater, *Gemini* is intelligent, subversive in a humane sense, and ultimately, a sympathetic portrait of life.

> *Gautam Dasgupta, "Wheel of Transformation," in* The Soho Weekly News, *December 16, 1976, p. 28.*

CARLL TUCKER

Albert Innaurato may have too much talent for his own good.

Much as a playwright may try to resist or ignore it, his or her bones, like an arthritic's, are affected by weather: box-office weather. When an audience is laughing and applauding and leaving the theatre with suffused faces, it is tough to doubt that artistically as well as popularly the hit is palpable. Conversely, a less effervescent audience can't help but seem to imply a less excellent play. . . .

More than most, playwrights love to be loved, and being loved makes them assume they're doing right.

Innaurato has done very much right in *Gemini.* He has created a credible milieu—a South Philly tenement—and peopled it with brutal caricatures who evolve into brittle characters. With fine-tuned comic instincts, [he] brakes the farce at the brink of excess and dispels heartbreak with pratfalls. I laughed and laughed. And then began looking for the heart of the comedy, the issue. . . .

Sexual ambiguity is adolescent trauma. Drama begins when a person loves for reasons other than what does or doesn't dangle between another's legs. Francis craves Randy and shirks his sister, exclusively because of gender.

Though Innaurato tries to tie Francis's predicament to the human condition by stressing the importance of being who you are and the strangeness, when you come to think of it, of all love matches, he cannot disguise the fact that his theme is biological, not existential. The Innaurato play I want to see is the next one, after Francis has resolved his sexual doubts and gone on to the larger issue of how to live and love meaningfully in the world. I hope Innaurato will resist repeating this too-

easy success—it's easy to laugh at adolescents once you've overcome their confusions—and write a play about adults, for adults, that will make adults uneasy by attacking them where they live.

> *Carll Tucker, "Caricatures Evolve into Characters" (reprinted by permission of* The Village Voice *and the author; copyright © The Village Voice, Inc., 1976), in* The Village Voice, *Vol. XXI, No. 52, December 27, 1976, p. 74.*

ALAN RICH

Mr. Innaurato . . . is very young (28), and some of the problems with *Gemini* stem from a young man's tendency toward untidiness. His play is a romance of an attractively old-fashioned sort, with an overlay of sexual ambivalence that may or may not bring it up to date. His ending, as I saw it, was a cop-out. . . .

What is brilliant about the work—and it is quite astounding—is the author's immaculate control over the farcical setting into which his romance has been inserted. It all takes place in a two-family backyard in South Philadelphia, where domestic hell is obviously a way of life. If you think of old-time farce, in which climactic situations rise merely from people talking louder, your admiration then must grow for Mr. Innaurato's ability to orchestrate magnificent human tangles without any of this sacrifice of line and clarity. The man can write; his play . . . is clearly aimed at a far horizon.

> *Alan Rich, "Dramaturgy and Drama Turgid," in* New York *Magazine (copyright © 1977 by News Group Publications, Inc.; reprinted with the permission of* New York *Magazine), Vol. 10, No. 1, January 3, 1977, p. 95.**

MEL GUSSOW

[Comparing "*Gemini*" with opera] has a certain validity. The emotions, even occasionally the voice, are huge. At one point, a character expresses her distaste for opera: "All that screaming. It's not like real life." Actually it is like life in "**Gemini.**" Mr. Innaurato has a tendency toward overstatement, but to reprimand him for that is almost like scolding Kafka for writing about cockroaches. It comes with the territory. . . .

[The] play is a spiraling comedy—a cascade of human frailties, fealties and pretenses. There are mock fainting spells and threatened suicides—the many things that people do to gain attention—and there is uproarious laughter.

Mr. Innaurato . . . is already a master at surprising us with jarring juxtapositions and seeming contradictions (a violent argument interrupted by the sudden singing of "Happy Birthday") and at staging comic tableaux. . . .

"**Gemini**" is filled with . . . infectious moments. It springs with humor—and in the strangest places. Mr. Innaurato is a natural writer, who has a feeling for the precise word that makes a line both spontaneous and genuinely amusing. For example, an absurdly fat boy pleads, "If I promised to lose weight and get less weird, can't we be friends?" Scanning that sentence, we realize that the word "less" is what makes it so funny. . . .

"**Gemini**" is not as powerful as Mr. Innaurato's "**The Transfiguration of Benno Blimpie.**" . . . "**Benno Blimpie**" is a haunting nightmare. "**Gemini**" is lighter and more expansive.

The two plays share a sensibility, subject matter and theme. In each we see obsessive characters formed and entrapped by family, background and environment. The plays, opening within days of each other, are conclusive evidence that Mr. Innaurato is a playwright with his own extraordinary voice and the imaginative talent of a conjurer.

Mel Gussow, "Theater: 'Gemini' Is Exceptional," in The New York Times (© 1977 by The New York Times Company; reprinted by permission), March 14, 1977, p. 36.

MICHAEL FEINGOLD

The two plays that are being produced together under the collective title of *Monsters* have a common theme: the child as freak. But the difference between Albert Innaurato's *The Transfiguration of Benno Blimpie* and William Dews's *Side Show* is the difference between a real playwright's use of this theme and a wordsmith's clever juggling with it.

Benno Blimpie is a naturalistic family play transposed into the realm of the grotesque, like one of those Jack Levine or Ivan Albright paintings that, walked by casually in a museum, appears to be an innocent urban landscape; only on closer inspection does one see the bleakness of the landscape, the rotting flesh of the figures: The freak emerges naturally from a world that, looked at in a certain light, suddenly seems freakish itself. . . .

Benno Blimpie, though the picture it paints is of total squalor, deals with that squalor honestly. . . .

It is Innaurato's literary sensibility that rescues Benno's story from banal naturalism or Hubert Selbyish clinicality—a matter of stylistic heightening. The cheap squabbling of the parents and the sordid flirtations of the grandfather are turned, by a writer's combination of the overheard and the unexpected, into moments that carry compassion and contempt, pained objectivity and bitter comedy. The naturalistic elements are all in place, but beneath them is heard the violent scream of the grotesque, intensifying everything and making it harsher. Benno's grandiose monologues, similarly, are given their full value in grandeur—this is how he transcends the squalid world around him—without losing any of their pathetic comedy as the hysterical expressions of a badly frightened boy. (p. 81)

[What] emerges from Benno's squalor and freakishness can at least be called dignity, if not tragedy. (p. 83)

Michael Feingold, "The World Is Freakish, Too" (reprinted by permission of The Village Voice and the author; copyright © The Village Voice, Inc., 1977), in The Village Voice, Vol. XXII, No. 12, March 21, 1977, pp. 81, 83.

T. E. KALEM

The play of middling merit fills an evening; the play of lasting merit fills a void. Subtly, or drastically, high drama alters our perception of existence. In this decade, up to now, the most promising young dramatists all seem to fall within the confines of middling merit. What knits some recent playwrights together more excitingly than their works is a sense that they are stage animals prowling their natural and necessary habitat. One such prowling indigene is Albert Innaurato. . . .

In his full-length off-Broadway entry, *Gemini,* he seems most at ease behind the mask of comedy. . . . [It] is a zinging display of comic fireworks, most of which explode underfoot. . . .

Gemini is the kind of play the early William Saroyan might have enjoyed or, for that matter, written.

To see Albert Innaurato's sensibility operating from a totally different angle of vision, one needs to attend his one-acter *The Transfiguration of Benno Blimpie.* . . . In contrast to *Gemini, Blimpie* is as joyous as a bleeding welt. It is a lacerating look at adolescence. . . .

[Benno Blimpie] is no freak in spirit. In his desperate need for love, his touching vulnerability, and his wistful desire for the approval of other children, he is linked to every human being who ever has been or ever will be born.

T. E. Kalem, "Stage Animal on the Prowl," in Time (reprinted by permission from Time, The Weekly Newsmagazine; copyright Time Inc. 1977), Vol. 109, No. 13, March 28, 1977, p. 95.

CATHARINE HUGHES

It makes me just a bit nervous to see new playwrights hailed quite as lavishly as Albert Innaurato. . . . Even in the current American dramatic desert, it seems advisable to be somewhat careful in meting out excessive praise to talent that is still relatively untried. . . .

That said, there is no denying, and I have no desire to deny, that the 28-year-old Innaurato seems an exceptionally promising dramatist on the basis of two plays that recently opened off-Broadway ["Gemini" and "The Transfiguration of Benno Blimpie"]. He has an extraordinary ear for dialogue, an ability to create believable characters and a sympathy for those who seldom figure other than peripherally on our stages. . . . (p. 363)

Catharine Hughes, "New American Playwrights," in America (© America Press, 1977; all rights reserved), Vol. 136, No. 15, April 16, 1977, pp. 363-64.*

ROSS WETZSTEON

[We're witnessing,] especially in the theatre, a caricatured homosexuality, based on defensive pride and sneering hostility.

We have no word that stands in the same relation to homosexuality as "macho" stands to heterosexuality—or rather we have plenty of such words, but they're all so repellent I'd rather invent a neutral one: Let's call this attitude "gayist." . . .

[Innaurato] seems to me to best exemplify the new gayism. . . .

At first glance, his work seems pre- rather than post-camp—that is, *Gemini* in particular is conventionally naturalistic, with the gay "problem" dealt with on a straightforward plot level. . . .

What makes it seem pre-camp is the treatment of homosexuality as a subject rather than an attitude, as naturalistic "reality" rather than stylish posturing. But what actually makes it post-camp is that it takes the attitudes and posturing of camp and integrates them into a conventional theatrical structure. If this play had been written before camp, it probably would have been a propagandistic appeal for "tolerance"—"gays are people too." Instead, it assumes that gay is not merely okay, it's better than straight—an extension of camp's attitude that straight is not merely intolerant but often ridiculous.

Gemini is structured largely in pejorative polarities—not only gay and straight, but young and old, son and father, thin and fat, assimilated and ethnic, sensitive and vulgar—to such an extent that one feels Innaurato is less interested in creating credible characters than in utilizing stock characters who will allow him to express his disgust. The gay protagonist is virtually the only character untouched by contempt—he seems surrounded by a kind of nimbus—and the fact that this contempt is often disguised as affection makes it all the more disturbing. I think of the lusty neighborhood mama, for instance, who bounces around the stage as if the playwright were enraptured by her vulgar, fleshy, joie de vivre. Actually, with her crude sexual appetites, big boobs, and hysterical bitchiness, she's straight out of camp. I wouldn't be at all surprised if Innaurato were to say he warmly regarded her as "larger than life," but I'd be astonished to hear any woman say the mama's anything but hyperbolically gross. Camp's idealization of women is but a subtler form of contempt.

Even more distressing than Innaurato's apparent assumption that one form of sexuality is superior to another . . . is the death of feeling at the heart of his work. Unlike [Christopher] Durang, whose characters have no emotions whatsoever (only a certain obsessive, almost manic selfishness), Innaurato at least grants feelings to his homosexual protagonist. As for the rest, oh they may feel, but Innaurato feels nothing *for* them—nothing, that is, but scorn. That lusty mama, for instance, supposedly treated with humorous affection, is actually so monstrous she drives her son to attempt suicide (hah hah), and her own suicide attempt becomes a jovial comic turn (hah hah hah). And for a kicker—such is the playwright's love for his characters—we're treated to an epileptic fit as comic shtick: that one has the audience in the aisles.

But the characters in *Gemini* seem positively adorable when compared to the loathsome gallery in *Benno Blimpie*—with the exception of poor, sensitive Benno, of course, who's supposed to arouse our compassion for all the suffering victims of a vermin-infested world. Benno is fat, unloved, and eating himself to death, and who wouldn't, surrounded by a despicably nagging mother, a hatefully bullying father, a perverted grandfather, and an obnoxious teen-age bitch who'd cause any man to choose either celibacy or homosexuality (and all of whom, incidentally, are considered as laughable as they are monstrous).

That Benno is gang-raped isn't enough—the gang then stuffs dogshit in his mouth. Indeed, and this is the central point, it's clear that Benno actually wallows in every new degradation for the opportunity it allows him to feel sorry for himself. "Talent and sensitivity don't matter in this world," he moans, "only looks and sex." (It's revealing that Benno sees sensitivity and sex as opposites.) Poor Benno. Despicably ugly everyone else.

Yet the play is presented as Benno's interior monologue—an alternation between Benno's memories of his family life and his exposition to the audience—and I can see no reason for taking Benno's account at face value. On the contrary, he doesn't see the cruelty in people; he sees people cruelly—they're credible only as figments of his self-serving sado-masochistic fantasies. So the real monstrosity isn't in the characters who oppress Benno but in Benno himself—there's more inhumanity in his revenge than in those who ridicule and reject him.

I'm not arguing that ugliness is an unacceptable subject for art. Innaurato's vision of the ugliness of life seems to match

[Jonathan] Swift and [Louis-Ferdinand] Celine in scope (if not in depth), but the crucial difference is that Swift and Celine regarded themselves as sharing in the human condition, whereas Innaurato regards Benno as exceptional. One couldn't even count the plays that have portrayed family life, in particular, as hateful—it may well be—but that doesn't mean the plays themselves have to be hateful. Benno likes to draw, but "Benno wasn't interested in drawing people," he says of himself—"he knew what they looked like." If this is what Innaurato really thinks people look like, I can't help wishing he wouldn't be interested in drawing them either.

Ross Wetzsteon, "Gay Theatre after Camp: From Ridicule to Revenge" (reprinted by permission of The Village Voice *and the author; copyright © The Village Voice, Inc., 1977), in* The Village Voice, *Vol. XXII, No. 16, April 18, 1977, p. 87.*

MEL GUSSOW

["**Earth Worms**"] is a black comic version of a rapacious society consuming its young. . . .

"**Earth Worms,**" Mr. Innaurato's most ambitious effort, is the theatrical equivalent of a grand opera—and perhaps it would benefit from a score by a contemporary Puccini. The characters are larger than life, and the play is bigger than the stage at Playwrights Horizon. . . .

[The] play is a nightmare of grotesqueries. . . .

One of the prolems with this play is that too much attention is paid to the exotic background and not enough to the principal characters, an odd triangle composed of a young man in doubt about his sexual identity, his hillbilly bride [Mary] and a 70-year-old homosexual [Bernard] who strikes up a Pygmalion-Galatea relationship with the young wife.

The last two—opposites allied in lovelessness—are, by far, the most interesting people on stage. They are original creations, particularly the aged homosexual. . . .

[Mary] is an innocent with a forked tongue, a nervy country girl who easily rises to anger. Mr. Innaurato never seems to create placid characters; his people are the opposite of meek.

The pivot of the play is the young man . . . , torn between his wife and the transvestite. As written . . . , the character seems too indecisive and mercurial. He moves, but does not build to his climactic, guilt-ridden confession.

The flaws of the script [are] the wavering focus, the cluttered background. . . .

There are many moments, however, particularly between [Bernard and Mary] that are pure Innaurato. "**Earth Worms**" is both a weird love story and a disturbing look at man's indifference to man.

Mel Gussow, "Stage: 'Earth Worms,' Innaurato's Grand Opera," in The New York Times *(© 1977 by The New York Times Company; reprinted by permission), May 27, 1977, p. C3.*

ALAN RICH

Earth Worms is an important play. Set, like *Gemini* and *Benno Blimpie*, in Innaurato's own South Philadelphia Italian ghetto, it tells a disturbing story about a bride brought in from "outside" and abandoned by a weak husband who cannot outgrow his background. The story is surrounded by ritual, a venomous ballet about narrowminded parochial schools. The play is . . . imperfect, but so much power comes through that its eventual stature is easy to predict. . . .

Alan Rich, ''Sturm und Durang,'' in New York *Magazine (copyright © 1977 by News Group Publications, Inc.; reprinted with the permission of* New York *Magazine), Vol. 10, No. 23, June 6, 1977, pp. 66-7.**

MICHAEL FEINGOLD

[*Earth Worms*] is better thought of as a work-in-progress than as a fully realized creation. Set in what is now the familiar Innaurato stamping ground—the dingy row houses of South Philadelphia—it pulls a group of familiarly unhappy Innaurato people into fantastic shapes, like some horror-comic version of *Gemini* in which the people have melted down into hideous, viscous blobs that, one is shocked to find, have human feelings even so.

The relatively stable family patterns of *Gemini* and even *Benno Blimpie,* like the characters themselves, are here stretched into weirdness. The time is the Korean War. A soldier from South Philly, on duty in Virginia, meets and marries the daughter of a Baptist minister, and brings her home with him. But home is a madness: . . . his aunt [who raised him] is blind, her only pleasure crawling on the floor to kill roaches. The house has been taken over by a retired professor, an unbalanced secret transvestite. . . .

The wife, intelligent but uneducated, is annexed by the draggy professor, and what follows is what customarily follows in Innaurato: screams, fights, violence, and lonely inner pain—dirt level opera, in which the higher aspirations crawl like everyone and everything else, but still sing out ferociously.

Sometimes Innaurato's vision seems almost too narrow and gloomy; sometimes the will to degrade life appears to take over the pen, so that his writing loses control of the characters' lives and actions in its eagerness to make them swallow more dirt. The inevitability of *Earth Worms,* and its connection to us, are hard to infer immediately on seeing it. Rethought . . . , it will probably come clearer, be more valid as well as more moderate. . . .

The fact of *Gemini*'s having been written after *Earth Worms* suggests that Innaurato knows better than to fall into the trap of rehashing the same cheap tricks for the paying customers, that he is willing to earn his characters' existence the hard way, by imagining them fully. We're all waiting and hoping.

Michael Feingold, ''Worms-Eye View'' (revised by the author for this publication; reprinted by permission of The Village Voice *and the author; copyright © The Village Voice, Inc., 1977), in* The Village Voice, *Vol. XXII, No. 26, June 27, 1977, p. 91.*

RICHARD EDER

Shakespeare may have said that all the world was a stage—not one of his better lines, in fact—but it seems a mistake for Albert Innaurato to go on from there to say that all the world is a graduate school of drama.

It is the central metaphor for **"Ulysses in Traction".** . . . It also allows Mr. Innaurato, when he is not advancing the dra-

matic action, to get a lot of things off his chest about drama schools.

Some of these things are interesting and some are amusing, but the play is a mess. Mr. Innaurato has his assortment of theater students and teachers trapped in a rehearsal hall during a veritable Armageddon of a race riot. . . .

This entrapment under pressure—a sort of "Lifeboat" situation—allows the characters to conduct a rough and drastic session of self-revelation; group therapy by clawing striptease. Mr. Innaurato is a promising new playwright—his **"Transfiguration of Benno Blimpie"** was extraordinary—but here he is using an old melodramatic device and using it badly.

It begins nicely enough with a funny parody of a Vietnam War play being rehearsed at a drama school in Detroit. The soldier protagonist alternately throws himself about as if under fire, and engages in strenuous flashbacks with his hysterical parents, and his mad and homosexual commanding officer.

The parody is not merely of the play, although David Rabe and his army trilogy is clearly a target. Mainly it is of the players, of drama schools and dramatic theories, and even of the theater itself. . . .

"University theater has kept theater alive in Detroit," [drama school head Steve] trumpets, citing their [Harold] Pinter and [Jean] Anouilh and [Jean] Giraudoux. With black crowds screaming outside the steel door at one end of the stage, and the blasts and the shooting, this manages to be both fierce and funny.

So far so good, but unfortunately it is about as far as the good goes. The seven characters in the besieged building proceed through two acts of mutual laceration, but it is attitudes clashing, not people. Whip cuts whip; there is very little flesh in evidence. . . .

It is a dizzying compendium of contemporary brittlenesses and old-fashioned mush. The messages about tolerance and the unlikely spots where the human spirit catches fire and shines, are not the problem; the problem is that none of the figures are believable people.

And the situation in which they are caught is even less believable. The pandemonium outside can't subsist forever as a symbol. It is actually there and it goes on being there for the whole play; yet it quite turns its back on all reality. We never believe in this warfare outside; and it is a kind of crowning carelessness at the end, after all the bombs and shooting, to have the characters escape over the rooftops to alert the police. Presumably even the thickest police force would have known that something was going on. . . .

It is premature to say that Mr. Innaurato's promise is broken by **"Ulysses."** But it certainly is dispersed; no doubt temporarily.

Richard Eder, ''Drama: Innaurato Falters,'' in The New York Times *(© 1977 by The New York Times Company; reprinted by permission), December 9, 1977, p. C3.*

EDITH OLIVER

The characters [in **"Ulysses in Traction"**] scuffle and fight and reminisce and make advances—homo- and heterosexual—and generally allow Mr. Innaurato to get quite a lot off his chest on any number of matters. Needless to say of [this author], most of what is on his chest is original and scathing and humorous. Yet in the midst of the fun (much of it intramural theatre about theatre) we are never allowed to forget the unhappiness beneath—everyone except the cleaning woman is a failure and knows it—and the presence of a maimed young man in considerable agony of spirit.

It must be said, regretfully, that "Ulysses in Traction" never jells. Its principal weakness, I think, is that so much of what we learn about the characters has to be told in monologues—a not uncommon defect these days. With the exception of the assistant head's war recollections, which are stagy and unconvincing, the monologues are good, however, and a scalding eruption by the playwright on the curriculum at Yale is pretty wonderful. Mr. Innaurato, a born merciless satirist, moves in and out of the cabaret style with merry results.

> Edith Oliver, "Off Broadway: 'Ulysses in Traction'," in The New Yorker (© 1977 by The New Yorker Magazine, Inc.), Vol. 53, No. 44, December 19, 1977, p. 112.

DEAN VALENTINE

If allusions a play made, Albert Innaurato's *Ulysses in Traction* would be the hit of the off-Broadway season, instead of the puny and lifeless affair that it is. Along with the title's bow to Homer and James Joyce, there are references, verbal or visual, to Shakespeare's *A Midsummer Night's Dream* and *King Lear*, [Anton] Chekhov's *The Cherry Orchard*, [Luigi] Pirandello's *Six Characters in Search of an Author*, and Gunter Grass' *The Plebeians Rehearse the Uprising*. Doubtless there were others, but the tedious catch-the-writer-quoting game should be saved for English professors. The theatergoer deserves to be enlightened, or at least entertained, not quizzed. And by that test *Ulysses* fails miserably. When not busy climbing onto the backs of the literary giants, it is clubbing its audience with half-baked Big Ideas, vulgar melodrama and whopping clichés.

"Existence is strife" is the gist of Innaurato's message. (p. 28)

[His] hackneyed conception is matched by hackneyed characters. Actually, they are less characters than caricatures, problems or traumas incarnate. . . . Lest we think Innaurato's assessment of humanity is completely dour, he has given us a foil: Mae, the black cleaning woman. She is gritty and down to earth, as blacks are wont to be when whites create them, and to her belongs the uncertain distinction of describing the road out of the surrounding Sturm and Drang: "And between us—we'll find something to praise. . . . That's the music of every inch of our insides, praising this life!"

No, that's bathos of the rankest kind, rendered fouler for being uttered by a patently phoney character. Innaurato's earlier works, *The Transfiguration of Benno Blimpie* and *Gemini,* also had their false moments, but these were overwhelmed by a genuine power, plus the urgency of a voice that had a great deal to say. In *Ulysses* urgency and content have everywhere been replaced by pseudo-profundity. Take, for example, the opening scene—the play-within-a-play. This time-honored device invariably has been used, first, to rouse the audience from its stolid belief in a distinction between drama and life, dreaming and waking, madness and sanity, illusion and reality; and, second, to illuminate the larger action. Innaurato includes it hoping to whet our appetite for serious drama, or perhaps to prove he did not receive his MFA for nothing. Yet the device, once introduced,

is rapidly shorn of its purposes and degenerates into an extended—albeit funny—parody of David Rabe and Ron Cowen.

Innaurato is more loyal to the subject of homosexuality; indeed, he rarely misses a chance to drag it in. Hence, when insults are to be landed, the *coup de grâce* is delivered below the belt. The longest scene, moreover, pits the limp-wristed Lenny against the merely limp John. And *Ulysses'* sole functioning heterosexuals, Doris and Steve, are its sole truly unlikeable characters as well. Homosexuality is so important to Innaurato, in fact, that he has provided a discussion of whether American theater is dominated by "nihilistic faggots" who write because "they can't come." Despite this energy spent telling us that homosexuality is a crucial issue, the climax of the play incredibly insists that sexuality does not count; we are all brothers. Such willed bonhomie can possibly be explained as bid to get to Broadway, although even the Great White Way's patrons, willing to put up with anything if it is cloying enough, would be hard pressed to sit through *Ulysses.* (pp. 28-9)

> Dean Valentine, "Theater of the Inane," in The New Leader (© 1978 by the American Labor Conference on International Affairs, Inc.), Vol. LXI, No. 1, January 2, 1978, pp. 28-9.*

JENNIFER DUNNING

The credits for "**Verna: U.S.O. Girl**" . . . end with the assurance that any resemblance to individuals living or dead is coincidental. It is not likely any such resemblance will be noted. . . .

In an opening scene, the camera sweeps past a war-bonds poster, and we are told it is 1944, but the soldiers' faces lack the lean period flavor of that other generation. None of this would matter if, for more than an instant, the three hapless U.S.O. entertainers could carry us into some tangy private world, but they are stock characters, and that promised glimpse at life in the wings fails to materialize.

Verna Vane . . . is a stage-struck orphan signed on in last-minute desperation for a U.S.O. jeep tour of the front lines. She is talentless, a fact she doggedly refuses to admit in the ultimately moronic litany that runs through the show. . . .

The major problem . . . is the one-note play. Until the last half hour or so, we are treated to a string of realistically awful shows, broken occasionally by a love scene or a skillet meal wolfed down in a doorway.

But the most convincing moments are those registered in the faces of the soldiers, so much so that when the jeep carrying the performers careens down a road to avoid a German ambush, leaving behind it the bodies of soldiers shot by the enemy, one fleetingly regrets the death of the play's most interesting characters.

In its last moments, "**Verna: U.S.O. Girl**" suddenly promises to become black comedy. Killed instantly, though unblemished, by an enemy mine, Verna becomes the occasion for a state funeral in Paris. . . .

A white cross with her name a soldier's helmet draped over it, tastelessly fronts one of those endless green fields of anonymous burial crosses that remain the saddest of war memorials. Soldiers raise their guns for a salute. And we know the worst. The pulp romances that fed the Vernas of that era have come to life.

Jennifer Dunning, "TV: 'Verna,' Trouper for U.S.O.," in The New York Times (© 1978 by The New York Times Company; reprinted by permission), January 25, 1978, p. C18.

ROB BAKER

[Albert Innaurato is] the most interesting young playwright to emerge on the New York scene in the past ten years. . . .

No one is safe from his barbed wit [onstage]—no racial or ethnic group (including his own, which is Italian), no physical type, no sexual type. This is particularly true with his new work, *Ulysses in Traction.* . . .

The whole "sexuality question" was first raised by *Gemini.* . . . It centers on the sexual crisis of a young twenty-one-year old Harvard student who can't relate to his admittedly beautiful girlfriend because he thinks he has a crush on her younger brother. The crush remains platonic, though when the boy dares him to consummate the pent-up desire, our hero is more than willing to try, except that the brother chickens out at the moment of truth. Sister and brother then pack their tent and leave, and the hero, realizing that he can't live without them, rushes after them as the curtain falls and his father states, "I think they're going to make it." We still don't know who's going to make it, however; or, more specifically, whom/which the hero is going to make it with—which is the nicest touch of all. . . .

Innaurato's plays are all about outcasts—people with weight problems and pimples (either physical or psychic), people with missing limbs, people who simply don't fit into the "real" world of middle-class America. . . .

Maybe what it boils down to is that Innaurato writes about the little people, the losers, the loners—the kind of people we meet in Robert Altman films or see chasing flying saucers in [Steven Speilberg's] *Close Encounters of the Third Kind.* Us, maybe, and ninety percent of the people we know? And he doesn't glamorize them, doesn't protect them, doesn't pussyfoot around about their insecurities, their hatreds, their prejudices. . . .

There are three controversial subject areas in [*Ulysses in Traction*:] academic theater; . . . black militancy; and homosexuality. Again? Yes. And in this case the gay character is, in Innaurato's own words, "an unsympathetic character who is a militant homosexual." Militant may not be exactly the right term. He's a swish, a ninny, a classic self-hating gay who covers up his inadequacies, which have little to do with his sexuality, by camping and preening and delivering self-consciously "bitchy" putdowns. . . .

Not being able to come, or even get it up, for whatever internal or external reasons, is a continuing metaphor in Innaurato's plays, and it's particularly important here, where the hero . . . can't do either because of a chronic infection of the urinary tract. Ironically, his impotence gives him a kind of levelheadedness that makes him the most sane spokesman in the play on the three touchy questions, especially the one about homosexuality. When the aging fairy type (and once again I stress, this is a characterization that this type of person has *chosen* for himself—his escape, if you will—not a stigma that Innaurato or I have inflicted on him) talks about seducing him when the lights go out (as the race riot gets closer and closer), the blond says: "I don't suppose there is anything wrong with homosexuality in the abstract, but anything that breeds that level of inhumanity and superficiality is disgusting."

The racial questions raised by the play are even touchier. I can think of no subject more difficult to broach, even objectively, on a New York stage at the current time than this one of black terrorism—unless it would be Israeli aggression, expressed in anything other than the most hysterically vicious anti-Arab terms. No, the New York "liberal" press is hardly willing to see its platitudes undercut by realities, since the realities don't conform with the careful structure of those platitudes. This is why Albert Innaurato is a revolutionary, though I doubt he would ever define himself as such.

Rob Baker, "Innaurato in Traction" (© 1978 by Danad Publishing Company, Inc.; reprinted by permission of the author), in After Dark, Vol. 10, No. 11, March, 1978, pp. 70-3.

PETER JAMES VENTIMIGLIA

[*Gemini* provides proof] that contemporary playwrights often combine traditional material and a contemporary approach. In outline, *Gemini* has its origins in the "rites of passage" drama of which Eugene O'Neill's *Ah, Wilderness!* is an example. The contemporary twist given to this traditional comic situation, however, is to be found in Innaurato's addition of a complexity to the basic plot. His protagonist cannot be entirely certain whether his sexual preferences are heterosexual or homosexual. (p. 201)

From its inception, comedy has been concerned with the search for identity which often accompanies the rite of passage from youth to maturity. *Gemini* explores the dramatic consequences of this journey for a young man named Francis Geminiani. . . . The play takes place on the eve of his twenty-first birthday, the traditional date for decision-making about adult life. . . .

Innaurato's greatest strength is his gift for creating characters who transcend stereotype. For [Francis's father] Fran there is the shame that surrounds his wife's desertion and the nagging fear that his son is not a "regular guy." For Lucille Pompi, there is the shame of her relationship with Fran which is at odds with her loneliness as a widow. For Bunny, there is the external brashness that conceals an inner insecurity. In each of the older characters there is a large measure of acceptance and resignation. (p. 202)

Innaurato's portraits of the Italian-American characters are fully realized. Though such distinguished playwrights as Arthur Miller, Clifford Odets, and Tennessee Williams have attempted to create credible characters from this particular background, Innaurato succeeds where the others do not. Lucille Pompi, one of the most comic characters in the play, provides the best example of those representing the older generation. Lucille's loneliness and isolation are strong elements of her characterization. . . . Lucille behaves according to the old code which is an established part of the Italian-American tradition. She cooks and provides for Fran; he is the center of her world. At the same time she is torn between this sense of duty and the fulfillment it brings, and the restrictions which are placed upon her by this code. She admits to feeling like an old sheet—"clean, neat, but used." But she tells Judith that the most "important thing is to show respect to her man." To show respect is to acknowledge his importance—the traditional mode of behavior. To challenge that tradition, in Lucille's eyes, would result in her becoming too much like Bunny, a poor wife, a poor mother, and a promiscuous woman. In the spaghetti dinner scene, Lucille "just picks"; she is forced to feign indifference to the meal by the role she has adopted in an effort to compensate for her loneliness and frustration. Even at the dinner table, she must adhere to the traditional pattern of behavior for the Italian woman, who prepares the meal but whose enjoyment comes from watching others eat it.

Francis, who represents the younger generation of Italian-Americans, undergoes the same trial of conscience. Unlike Lucille, however, he is ready to break with tradition and accept the consequences for his actions. At the end of the play, Francis has chosen to return to Boston rather than remain in Philadelphia. In Philadelphia there is only lack of understanding and rejection; in Boston there is the hope of acceptance and friendship. As his name suggests, Francis is at the center of the ambiguity which he must face. In his eyes, Judith and Randy are sibling rivals for his attention. Innaurato has cleverly chosen this mirror device to support his theme. Francis' decisions are two-sided. Whether they affect his sexuality or his struggle with his ethnic background, there are always complexities which make these decisions more difficult and ultimately more meaningful. (pp. 202-03)

If Innaurato's play is about the frustration and loneliness which surround the growth to maturity, it is also about the sense of independence and an unwillingness to conform that have long characterized the American people. (p. 203)

> *Peter James Ventimiglia, "Recent Trends in American Drama: Michael Cristopher, David Mamet, and Albert Innaurato," in* Journal of American Culture *(copyright © 1978 by Ray B. Browne), Vol. 1, No. 1, Spring, 1978, pp. 195-204.**

MARTIN DUBERMAN

I am [not] sure about Albert Innaurato's potential, though most of the critics seem to feel it's unlimited. . . .

Gemini is the better of Innaurato's two works produced in New York this season. That doesn't say much, since the second, *Ulysses in Traction,* was semidroll trivia, and his teleplay, *Verna: USO Girl* . . . was such a mechanical stockpile of romantic clichés that I began to expect a cameo by, or at least a screen credit for, Barbara Cartland. (p. 83)

[*Gemini*'s] artistic merit seems to me dubious. . . .

What follows [Francis's announcement of his sexual dilemma] is a tangled merry-go-round whose outer mechanics Innaurato expertly controls but whose inner life rarely resonates above a guffaw.

Laughs are frequent enough to establish Innaurato as a genuinely gifted comic writer. Grotesquerie is his forte. The best example in *Gemini* is Herschel, a mountainous teen-ager next door who is "into" Transportation. Herschel is contrived and bizarre—yet believable; more so than most of Innaurato's other grotesques.

The play's exaggerated theatricality, its breathless (and nicely timed) antics and pratfalls, fail to conceal basic flaws in construction. Too often static monologues—awkwardly introduced, insufficiently motivated—are used to fill us in on information Innaurato has been unable to convey in any more integral way. He further interrupts the narrative flow by pausing for show-off turns—some overly cute or irrelevantly literary lines, sometimes an extended "bit" (like an argument between Judith and Francis over IQ testing).

These set pieces and asides do more than disrupt the play's momentum: they create distrust for the playwright's integrity.

He seems willing to rob his own characters of coherence in order to get off a quick gag, to risk knocking a scene off-center rather than forgo some circus byplay. The more Innaurato opts for secondary surface effects, the more we begin to wonder if he has any pressing primary purpose. The play's cheap ending confirms all earlier misgivings. (p. 84)

> *Martin Duberman, "The Great Gray Way," in* Harper's *(copyright © 1978 by Harper's Magazine; reprinted by permission of the author), Vol. 256, No. 1536, May, 1978, pp. 79-87.**

ALBERT INNAURATO

Francis [in "**Gemini**"] is a heterosexual; that is made quite clear from the beginning. What he is going through is a sexual crisis from a heterosexual view. He's having homosexual doubts, which is not unusual among sensitive heterosexuals. In the course of the play, the emphasis is on making *relationships* or not. In other words, the choice for Francis, in dealing with Judith and Randy, is not whether he is going to fuck one or another, but, how is he going to continue developing relationships despite problems. In both instances Francis' first instinct is to go into his room and put on Maria Callas. And, the choice he makes is not between being straight or gay—which I think is irrelevant . . . I'm way past the sexual liberation groups. I think there is nothing more boring than "straight or gay." The emphasis in "**Gemini**" is not on making children, or, anal intercourse . . . it is really on having a relationship. At the end he calls them back to make an attempt. That's all the play is saying about him. It's not anti or pro gay, or anti or pro hetero. . . . That stuff is irrelevant to the play . . . yes, and to the writer if you want to know. It has simply been used as an excuse for nonsense by people. . . . (p. 8)

All my plays deal with outcasts who try to succeed in a society that ostracizes them very readily and very easily. I think we live in a society almost totally geared to the cosmetic. Everything is appearance. A constant emphasis on uniformity in appearance. One of its effects is that people who are easily identifiable as being different are ostracized right away, regardless of their values as people. "**Benno Blimpie**" becomes the example of the outcast, freethinker, cripple, black, artist, etc. . . . "**Benno Blimpie**" is not about a fat person. The important thing is not that he could go on the Stillman Diet and lose 40 pounds in a week. The point is that he is an outsider and that is expressed physically. It is a sexually obsessed play, in some ways . . . so is "**Earthworms.**" . . . If I were asked about "**Benno**" and "**Earthworms**" six years from now, I would probably say they were anti-sexual plays. There is a horror at sexuality in both these plays. Especially the kind of sexuality very prevalent in this country. The "sex on parade" part of the cities. You can't escape it. (p. 9)

> *Albert Innaurato, "Albert Innaurato: An Interview," in an interview with Marc Katz, in* New York Arts Journal *(copyright © 1978 by Richard W. Burgin), No. 10, July-August, 1978, pp. 7-9.*

JOHN SIMON

Albert Innaurato is too young to be cannibalizing himself, even if eating and overeating are leitmotifs in his dramaturgy. In *Passione,* he is at it again. . . .

The seven characters passionately love, hate, or love *and* hate one another. The play is taken up with bouts of lovemaking, fisticuffs, and eating of every sort, from the most voracious to the barely nibbling. There is also conspicuous consumption of wine and coffee. Gutter philosophy and bed-sheet dialectics abound. Haters become lovers and vice versa; friends fall out vehemently and are vehemently reconciled. Everyone blames everyone else for having ruined his life. Or for having saved it. . . . It is all full of every kind of Italian, or Italo-American, or stage-Italo-American, passion—or *passione*—and the dialogue is racy, absurd, obscene, and sometimes quite funny.

In calmer moments, there is genuine wistfulness. And there are the obligatory reversals: The failures have their dignity and strength; the successes, their anxieties and grinding needs. Tenderness comes out violent; fights turn into acts of love. It's not exactly unpredictable, as it recapitulates previous Innaurato plays. If it does not nourish your soul, it does tickle your soles and clutch at your heart. Though often inordinately coarse, its vulgarity has a redeeming touch of originality, a twist of eccentricity, that lifts it above the morass. Frequently exasperating, *Passione* is nearly saved by its crazy gusto, by respect for the imaginative intemperance with which some people—Italians, Italo-Americans, or stage-Italo-Americans—operaticize the prosiness around, and even within, them. . . .

Passione hangs, in the words of a *canzone* by Tasso, *tra l'arte e la natura incerta*—between art and dubious nature—or even between dubious nature and uncertain art. One observes it with mixed wonder and weariness as it fluctuates between Verdi and Leoncavallo, between real people and stage Italo-Americans. (p. 58)

John Simon, "Aria da capo," in New York Magazine (copyright © 1980 by News Group Publications, Inc.; reprinted with the permission of New York Magazine), Vol. 13, No. 23, June 9, 1980, pp. 58-9.*

FRANK RICH

[Albert Innaurato] is one of the most brilliant iconoclasts of the American theater. In "Passione," as in "Gemini" and "The Transfiguration of Benno Blimpie," Mr. Innaurato pays lip service to kitchen-sink realism, but, for him, reality is merely an elastic means to a cockeyed end. This man is an artist, not a documentarian. He is driven—compulsively, breathlessly—to remake a familiar, even clichéd world into a new and often hilarious place of his own startling design.

"Passione" . . . is far from a total success, but its first act is vintage Innaurato. It is there that we find the playwright's feverish sensibility twisting a seemingly commonplace ethnic family into all sorts of bizarre shapes. . . .

When [the] extended family gets to eating and bickering in Act I, the surprises and funny lines come so fast that we quickly accept the psychological reality of the characters, however farfetched or grotesque they might otherwise seem. The playwright tries to get away with everything, and he often succeeds. One moment his antagonists draw knives and guns on each other; a little later they pair off and sway romantically to an old Tommy Dorsey record. Mr. Innaurato also thinks nothing of halting the action entirely for impassioned debates about such tangential subjects as women's liberation, television commercials and coffee percolators. These digressions are so passionately and wittily set forth that at times Mr. Innaurato could almost pass for South Philly's half-crazed, proletarian answer to [George Bernard] Shaw.

Still, for all his kamikaze humor, the playwright never condescends to his losers and misfits. He truly likes them, and his infectious compassion is what keeps his fantastic conceits on a human scale. Unfortunately, Mr. Innaurato's big heart is also the source of his greatest esthetic failing. When, in Act II, he tries to resolve the homely specifics of the family's dilemmas, he simply cannot find a way to assimilate such prosaic matters into his high-flying, operatic comic style. "Passione" soon devolves into an ordinary domestic drama—one that sits very uneasily on what has come before.

Disappointingly enough, much of Act II consists of heart-to-heart conversations in which the characters confront one another, rehash the past and make amends. Suddenly the relatively minor character of Little Tom is launching into dramatically unearned monologues about his suicide attempts. Suddenly Aggy and Berto are recapping their marital history in somber words that merely repeat information that had been conveyed comically earlier on. Sarah and Renzo's final confrontation works better because it springs from the play's farcical underpinnings: they consummate their relationship in a wild, if overextended, slapstick boxing match.

Mr. Innaurato had a parallel difficulty in "Gemini," whose serious love triangle was at odds with the play's more outrageous shenanigans, but he finessed it better there. The introspective interludes were more adeptly interwoven, and the central plot question was left unresolved. In "Passione," the playwright seems, if anything, overly possessed by his generous emotions. He is too eager to reconcile his play's family, no matter what the price in narrative credibility, and he is too quick to have his characters endorse his own credo of tolerance. When a mother's attitude toward her son changes from rage to affection in an instant, the patness of such a transformation saps its pathos. Some lines of dialogue—"When you love somebody, you got to let them be what they are"—state the play's theme rather than dramatize it. . . .

Fat Francine is the only character who successfully rides all of Mr. Innaurato's moods. In Act I, she erupts in one of the playwright's inimitable arias: a foul-mouthed defense of obesity that goes to the outer limits of farce without ever losing touch with genuine feeling. In Act II, her circumspect dissection of her marriage is the one quiet scene that works: she goes for our emotional jugular without ever forsaking her initial comic beat. From Francine, we can extrapolate that Innaurato play that is entirely faithful to its creator's remarkable vision. If "Passione" is not that play, it nonetheless keeps the promise alive.

Frank Rich, "Theater: 'Passione,' Innaurato Comedy," in The New York Times (© 1980 by The New York Times Company; reprinted by permission), September 24, 1980, p. C23.

JOHN SIMON

Let me hope that Albert Innaurato intends his *Passione* to be farce with some serious overtones rather than a significant statement about life couched in farcical terms. Taken as pure knockabout farce—with one character literally knocked all over the stage—*Passione* gives modest but fairly consistent delight, the wild swings made up for by riotous haymakers. But when it goes serious, it has serious problems.

The play covers familiar Innaurato territory topographically, emotionally, gastronomically. Once again we are in Italo-

American South Philadelphia; once again everything from love-making to making coffee is done with brio, bravura, pepperoni, or some other hot Italian ingredient; once again eating and drinking become a physical and metaphysical consummation, with the thinnest of lines between passionate consuming and consuming passions. . . .

Everyone then is slightly defective—missing fingers, excess fat . . . ; or a disappointment—the educated Tom, a clown, the inventive Berto, a failed cabbie; or laboring under a criminal past—Oreste's arson, Renzo's heists. And the southern ladies' superiority is revealed as bravado or funny truculence merely cloaking loneliness. But defects and shortcomings are the entrance tickets into the grand symbiosis of compassion that finally makes the walking wounded walk into the haven of one another's arms.

Unfortunately, the play does not really dramatize this charity that leads to love, this love that generates passion (or vice versa), even though we are told: "First you've got to let 'em find out what they are. Then you've got to let 'em be that. That's lovin'." I hear it, but I am not shown it. And we are shown even less in this new, streamlined Broadway production. . . . The [earlier,] longer, fuller version, despite some excesses, allowed these bizarre but human creatures to achieve their full, human density and believability. The cramped stage made the play, as it were, burst at the seams—an objective correlative for the explosive aspirations and frustrations that the characters are so powerless to contain.

On Broadway, the thinnesses become more apparent; the haste to wrap up everything turns, in the second act, frantic, and an uncomfortable, by-the-numbers quality sets in. The disorderly passions of Albert Innaurato cannot take so much tightening and tidying up: The nice thing about a stable (among other nice things) is that it is neither a production line nor a salon. (p. 75)

I suppose the best thing about *Passione* is that its characters are so palpably droll that they can make even their less funny lines beget laughs in context. Francine taunting Tom that he might have married "a nice blond girl who don't give you no lip—only she won't give you no head, neither," and Tom's reply, "This is the eighties—everybody gives head!" might not seem to be particularly amusing. But in that fat, sassy, juicily alive onstage ambience, it is, it is. (p. 76)

John Simon, "Food for a Little Thought," in New York *Magazine (copyright © 1980 by News Group Publications, Inc.; reprinted with permission of* New York *Magazine), Vol. 13, No. 39, October 6, 1980, pp. 75-6.**

JULIUS NOVICK

[*Passione*] is a jolly, cozy, sentimental, thoroughly Broadway comedy, and not a good one. . . .

There are signs that Innaurato meant the confrontation between Aggie and Berto to become a significant comic confrontation between two contrasting ways of life, but nothing much comes of it. Italian-American life as represented in *Passione* is such a welter of lusty, gusty, earthy, emotional, pasta-and-vino stereotypes that I'm surprised any Italian-American could have the face to write it. How, I wonder, did Innaurato manage to leave out an organ grinder and a monkey? On the other hand, Aggie and Sarah lack even a clear stereotype to sustain them; there is no consistent sense at all of where they might have come from, of what kind of life might have shaped them.

Passione is noisy and busy; dud jokes abound. . . . The attempts at tear-jerking are arbitrary and crass, and bringing down the first-act curtain on the sudden collapse of an old man is the cheapest trick in the book. (p. 387)

[The play is a] clumsy piece of hackwork. . . . (p. 388)

Julius Novick, "Theater: 'Passione'," in The Nation *(copyright 1980* The Nation *magazine, The Nation Associates, Inc.), Vol. 231, No. 12, October 18, 1980, pp. 387-88.*

Waylon Jennings

1937-

©Neil Zlozower

American songwriter, singer, and musician.

Jennings is well known for his efforts to revitalize country music and is considered one of the leading "outlaws" in the field because of his rebellion against the traditional, rigid sound of Nashville. Jennings combines the unpredictable, independent attitudes of such early country-and-western personalities as Hank Williams and Bob Wills with the country-rock sounds of Buddy Holly and Elvis Presley to create his own rugged, freewheeling style. However, it was not until he gained some control over the production of his albums that Jennings finally reached beyond a strictly country-and-western audience.

Jennings's massive appeal lies in his simple, honest approach to music and the sympathy his songs express for the people who, like himself, refuse to conform to "the way things are going." The warm-hearted rebel populates Jennings's songs, and he reinforces this image through his own sincere attitude and unkempt appearance. His unconventional style has been described as bridging the gap between old Southern-poverty folkways and modern stresses and doubts. Jennings encourages his listeners to go their own ways and attempts to convince them that it is all right to make mistakes and have feelings. In some of his more recent songs, Jennings has objected to the image of the romanticized outlaw with which he and others have been identified. In other songs, he questions the motivations and intentions of record producers and the lifestyles of country music stars. His work also explores the theme of growing old, particularly as it effects him as a performer.

Jennings's reputation as a popular singer rests largely on his ability to personalize almost any song he sings, whether it is written specifically for him or not. He is not a prolific song-writer, and his albums are mostly made up of material written by other artists. Critics agree that it is Jennings's distinctive baritone which sets him apart from other singers in the same field, but some critics feel that his albums are occasionally marred by selections that do not suit Jennings's rough, un-polished vocals. Jennings, however, has voiced his indifference to what the critics have to say, for as he claims, "My music is me. I have to feel which way I should go next. All music is good. There's good in all music and bad in all music too." The formula seems to work, because his popularity continues to grow beyond country-and-western boundaries.

ROBERT HILBURN

Funny how time slips away. It has been more than a dozen years now since a group of country boys, led by Elvis Presley, got together in some Tennessee recording studios and started a revolution in American music. With the help of such songs as "Blue Suede Shoes," "Bye, Bye Love" and "Heartbreak Hotel," they came up with a country-rock sound that helped reshape pop music.

Since that golden age of country-rock, hundreds of acts have been influenced by that early sound, but no one new has captured the essence of that emotional, driving music of the mid-1950's. No one, that is, until Waylon Jennings.

In recent months, Jennings has established himself as the most exciting new country singer in years. He features a hard, tough sound that has much of the same earthy appeal as the early country-rock numbers. In many ways, Jennings is a natural musical descendant of Presley, Buddy Holly, Roy Orbison and other country-rock pioneers. . . .

Though Jennings is a descendant of the early country-rock sound, it would be a mistake to think of him only in that light. He more truly represents the realization of the promise generated in those initial days of the new sound. His voice is stronger, his arrangements more polished and his themes generally are more meaningful.

While there is the strong beat of such early rock hits as "That'll Be the Day" in Jennings' version of **"Only Daddy That'll Walk the Line,"** there's a definite lyric and melodic maturity in such other Jennings offerings as **"Love of the Common People"** and **"Walk On Out of My Mind."** [He is a] man with modern propensities in song. . . .

Robert Hilburn, "Waylon Jennings," in BMI: The Many Worlds of Music *(© 1969 by Broadcast Music, Inc.), April, 1969, p. 16.*

J. R. YOUNG

RCA labeled [the early music of Waylon Jennings] "Country-Folk" at first, and then finally let it ride as straight country. It was a soft country sound, melodic and reminiscent of early Marty Robbins. Very tasty stuff. . . . [Around this same time, Jennings] also lined up a freak band and lit out after that rock country sound and incorporated the best of folk, rock, and country into his trip. . . .

The new Waylon Jennings seemed to fall into place for the first time with *Singer of Sad Songs*. . . . *Sad Songs* is a much fuller album than the others, steeped in a true rock/country context: the rhythm and drive of rock, the vitality of country, and, of course, the same monster voice of Waylon himself. An exquisite match. The album makes your head ring. The obvious highlight is the title song, . . . a neatly fashioned country ditty that literally sparkles. . . . It has all the spirit that the kids who think they do country music today lack. . . .

Nothing to excess. But then that's what the whole album's about.

The following album, *The Taker/Tulsa*, [is the same way]. . . . It's so good I don't even know what to say about it. Music ain't going to get any better than this. It really puts away that self-consciousness that gets in the way of the Poco/Flying Burritos ilk.

The newest album is *Cedartown, Georgia*. . . . Another devastator, but not as raw and rock & rolled. The pace is gentler but still *out there*. . . . It's this album that Waylon goes after everybody (even your mother) and intends to bring everybody over to his side. It's all *Dynamite stuff*, as they say at Tower Records. Word is that if Waylon Jennings isn't already a country superstar, he soon will be. And once that occurs, he'll even move beyond the country tag. . . .

[So] if your ears are tired, depressed, and generally down, let this dude get inside your mind and realign your senses. Listen to what a song can really be. You'll get more than you ever bargained for, and you, too, will wonder where in the hell you've been since '66, because Waylon's been over in the C&W rack all along.

> *J. R. Young, "The Monster Voice of Waylon Jennings," in* Rolling Stone *(by Straight Arrow Publishers, Inc. © 1971; all rights reserved; reprinted by permission), Issue 97, December 9, 1971, p. 58.*

CHET FLIPPO

[Jennings is] like a tough, savvy minstrel, a maverick wanderer who's still able to rejoice in life. Jennings is the kind of man who has the same wink whether he's getting thrown out of a bar or he's punching out some little wimp and taking his woman. It's all the same, he laughs, just life. You can count on one finger the number of singers in any field today who can communicate that kind of wicked, joyful irreverence. (p. 68)

[It's] hard to explain why *Ladies Love Outlaws* is a slight disappointment in comparison to Jennings' recent albums. The material is extremely uneven. . . . Two of the better cuts are Jennings' only compositions here: **"Sure Didn't Take Him Long"** is a wry comment on woman stealing and **"I Think It's Time She Learned"** addresses itself to the correction of an errant woman. . . . In sum, a good album but not a great one. (p. 70)

> *Chet Flippo, "Country Music's Perennials: Four of the Most Distinctive Voices," in* Rolling Stone *(by Straight Arrow Publishers, Inc. © 1972; all rights reserved; reprinted by permission), Issue 122, November 23, 1972, pp. 68, 70.**

MICHAEL WATTS

Waylon Jennings has found himself to be something of a star, not merely of the country circuits, but of the entire ball-game of popular music.

He is more equipped for this than anyone else who has set out from Nashville. . . .

Jennings is happening at a time when country has never been more acceptable in rock music; when the excursions of the Byrds, the [Grateful] Dead and others into C and W areas have prepared rock audiences for an artist like Jennings, who has always been iconoclastic enough to bring in many influences outside country. . . .

A maverick in other words, not only in his musical Catholicism, but in his attitude to Nashville's hierarchy, which can be scathing and contemptuous, and his manner of dress and appearance. . . .

His sense of rebellion, well-publicised, is an infectuous breeding ground in which the styles and tastes of pop and country may mate. But no one has ever questioned his artistic abilities, either. . . .

[The] mood and nature of the South seems an ever-fitting backcloth for a Greek tragedy; the harmonicas straining mournfully are the music, the chorus are those country voices, heavy with grief and resignation. The songs of the South, the white tradition, are dominated by a sense of loss mixed with an acceptance of it. It's as if they've never recovered from their failure in the Civil War.

Perhaps this is why Jennings is so compulsive. He invited our respect because he's the embodiment of peculiarly Southern virtues of manliness and honest emotions when all around is neurosis. Like all great artists his music is himself, and he stands for realness. In a time of sophistication he is simplicity. There but for fate would have gone Buddy Holly. (p. 24)

> *Michael Watts, "You Gotta Be a Man First, 'fore You Can Be Anything . . . ," in* Melody Maker *(© IPC Business Press Ltd.), August 11, 1973, pp. 24-5.*

DANIEL HARMON

Waylon Jennings is one of the few artists who sound (and look) knowledgeable when speaking of bad times and broken-down love affairs. Trouble is, there are too few songs available to match his authenticity. The title cut [of *Lonesome, On'ry & Mean*] and *San Francisco Mabel Joy* are earthy but too sensationalized. *Lay It Down*, though appealing, is a bit sophisticated. . . . Some good and meaningful music among the weaknesses.

> *Daniel Harmon, "The Journal Reviews: 'Lonesome, On'ry & Mean'," in* Music Journal *(copyright © 1973 by Sar-Les Music, Inc.), Vol. XXXI, No. 7, September, 1973, p. 44.*

ALLAN PARACHINI

Stylistically, Jennings certainly is a country artist. But his material is culled from a variety of sources, and the lyrics are a cut above most c-&-w tunes. . . . That he uses rock sources and has a rock audience is not really surprising, considering . . . that youthful association with Buddy Holly. . . .

He has actively sought to raise the level of the material he performs, and he has shown that he wants to reach as wide an audience as possible while retaining an authenticity and flavor that are beyond dispute.

He has often been compared with Kris Kristofferson, who, some say, cares more about his new rock audience than about the country crowd that gave him his start. But Jennings seems determined to remain a *country* artist, convinced that broad-based audiences will continue to seek him out. He thinks the people who really listen to what he does won't care who *else* likes to listen to him. Waylon Jennings is perhaps as good an indicator of the true appeal of country music as you can find, and he's been right so far. (p. 64)

> *Allan Parachini, "Waylon Jennings," in* Stereo Review *(copyright © 1974 by Ziff-Davis Publishing Company), Vol. 32, No. 2, February, 1974, pp. 63-4.*

NOEL COPPAGE

If you don't have any Waylon Jennings albums and ["**Honky Tonk Heroes**"] is the only one you can find, by all means get it and get to know that voice. If a sufficient number of people do that, maybe we can pressure him into putting some real thought into producing these things. Not to get over-serious about it, but Jennings is one of the contemporary performers most likely to get country music off the dime it's been on for close to forty years.

> *Noel Coppage, "Popular Discs and Tapes: 'Honky Tonk Heroes'," in* Stereo Review *(copyright © 1974 by Ziff-Davis Publishing Company), Vol. 32, No. 2, February, 1974, p. 90.*

MICHAEL WATTS

["**Honky Tonk Heroes**"] is distinguished by its celebration of The Last Round-up, its air of cowboys trying to reconcile the present with the past, which Waylon's big, weary voice, always at the heart of the arrangement, brilliantly conveys. "**Old Five And Dimers**" and "**Willie The Wandering Gypsy And Me**" (about Willie Nelson) are great, existentialist songs of boozy camaraderie, which unleash in the imagination huge vistas of prairies and an older America for the roaming and roving thereof. They're tough and sad and grizzled. In "**Willie**" Waylon sings, "well, I reckon we're gonna ramble till hell freezes over," and it's all there in that line, the conviction and authority, seem so appealing to ears usually assaulted by foppery and punkiness. If you want some good, matured stuff, I urge you to get this album. Do yourself a favour.

> *Michael Watts, "Albums: 'Honky Tonk Heroes'," in* Melody Maker *(© IPC Business Press Ltd.), May 4, 1974, p. 41.*

MICHAEL WATTS

Still mad about the boy, but ["**This Time**"] is pedestrian compared to "**Honky Tonk Heroes.**" . . . It works if you think of it as a relaxed mood piece, but Jennings might have to make up his mind to go much further along the way with rock, and that's dicing with commercial death as far as his C and W fans will be concerned. Not this time; maybe next.

> *Michael Watts, "Albums: 'This Time'," in* Melody Maker *(© IPC Business Press Ltd.), June 8, 1974, p. 43.*

TONY GLOVER

[If *Honky Tonk Heroes*] was a bar album, then *This Time* is an after-hours mellow-out partner.

As usual, the subject matter is basic: bar/drinking songs, songs about the West and outlaws and women. . . .

"**This Time**" is a Waylon composition (wish he'd write more) and it defines his macho image pretty aptly. . . . But Waylon can also get inside tenderness and sorrow. . . .

An album that grows on you, and a fine companion to *Heroes*—if not quite the one we've all been waiting for.

> *Tony Glover, "Records: 'This Time'," in* Rolling Stone *(by Straight Arrow Publishers, Inc. © 1974; all rights reserved; reprinted by permission), Issue 165, July 18, 1974, p. 64.*

NICHOLAS R. SPITZER

["**Bob Wills Is Still the King**" on the album *Dreaming My Dreams*] defies the categories of hard-core and progressive country. Based on record sales it fulfills both genres. The song is sung by Waylon Jennings, whose initial audience had been the fans of hard-core or "straight" country music. Admittedly, Waylon has always defied labels. . . .

Lyrically the song toughly espouses the virtues of Texas life in the nostalgic terms of cowboy self-reliance and chivalry. Further, it invokes an animistic fashion, a past regional hero as the basis for present day self-pride. (p. 192)

In relation to the function of popular culture artists and art forms in shaping an expanded sense of community and cultural contiguity, I should point out that Waylon Jennings, based on the lyrics of many of his songs is a symbolic, normative outlaw. Country and western music is rife with them as fantasy characters providing *honorable* ways to break the law. His power as a performer for Austin audiences is further amplified in his rebellion from Nashville. That is, he also iconically represents an outlaw of sorts. (p. 193)

> *Nicholas R. Spitzer, "'Bob Wills Is Still the King': Romantic Regionalism and Convergent Culture in Central Texas," in* JEMF Quarterly, *Vol. XI, No. 40, Winter, 1975, pp. 191-94.**

TONY GLOVER

The standouts [on *Dreaming My Dreams*] are "**Are You Sure Hank Done It This Way**," an autobiographical commentary about the state of Music City, and the bouncy "**Waymore's Blues**," a Jimmie Rodgers-like hobo song.

Most cuts are more reflective. In **"Let's All Help the Cowboys (Sing the Blues),"** Waylon continues his series of Western mythology; he speaks both for himself and a vanishing breed of sensitive studs. . . .

The last track, **"Bob Wills Is Still the King,"** is a live track from an Austin gig. A tribute to the King of Western Swing, it demonstrates how well Waylon knows and moves his fans. The fire and drive in this cut foreshadow an upcoming live album—and that ought to be the one to spread Waylon into *everybody*'s ears. (p. 72)

> *Tony Glover, "Records: 'Dreaming My Dreams'," in* Rolling Stone *(by Straight Arrow Publishers, Inc. © 1975; all rights reserved; reprinted by permission), Issue 194, August 28, 1975, pp. 70, 72.*

NOEL COPPAGE

Several of his previous albums have been hurt by erratic song selection, but in RCA's new **"Dreaming My Dreams"** Jennings has smoothed that out pretty well. . . . *Let's All Help the Cowboys* is a simple three-chord country song (C-F-G, if that saves *you* some time), but it has such charm that, well, I couldn't do anything else until I'd sat down with the guitar and *learned* that little sucker. The song that gives the album its title is clearly an outstanding one; you can hate country music and still love it. . . . *High Time (You Quit Your Low-Down Ways)*, whose country clichés are maybe a little too commonplace, *too* everyday, is the album's low point, but it isn't serious enough about being a bad country song to keep this album from being one of the year's better recordings.

> *Noel Coppage, "Waylon Jennings: Suddenly a Low-pitched Baritone Is the Voice to Have," in* Stereo Review *(copyright © 1975 by Ziff-Davis Publishing Company), Vol. 35, No. 4, October, 1975, p. 74.*

KEN TUCKER

Waylon's main problem has always been the unevenness of his material; while [*Are You Ready for the Country*] is better than his last few efforts, it still stumbles badly in a few places. Waylon is a sucker for the sort of romantic, hard-boiled poesy that people such as Billy Joe Shaver and Shel Silverstein turn out like poker hands. . . . Waylon's songwriting suffers from this approach as well, and three of his four compositions on *Are You Ready* are more or less disposable. But the fourth, **"I'll Go Back to Her,"** is one of the album's triumphs, just a good, lean love song.

Part of Jennings's attractiveness and value is his willingness to blend a couple of the rock culture's pleasures—fast, loud music and a reckless demeanor—with country's more precise discipline and tradition. But he has no instinct for rock music. . . .

Another matter is the persistence of the style from which Jennings, Willie Nelson, et al., are supposed to be rebelling. . . . [Their] subject matter and melodies are really no different from those of Ray Price and other progressive boys. This residue of sentimentality tends to draw them more to folk music forms than to the cynical, coarse rock they feign to embrace.

> *Ken Tucker, "'Are You Ready for the Country'," in* Rolling Stone *(by Straight Arrow Publishers, Inc. © 1976; all rights reserved; reprinted by permission), Issue 222, September 23, 1976, p. 115.*

NOEL COPPAGE

Lumping Jennings with, say, David Allen Coe or Asleep at the Wheel or Michael Murphey or any of the other ["redneck rock" or "progressive country"] "movement" entities is a mistake in the first place, as the whole idea with Jennings is going it *alone*. The way he, specifically, has elected to sound does not extend The Way Things Are Going (the old definition of "progress") but goes against it. (p. 104)

[The] pose Jennings strikes is symbolic, a truth-in-fiction device. He doesn't ask you to take him literally and go up against the computers with six-guns blazing. The point he's making visually is literary and relates to the point he's making musically: remember the poor cowboy, the romantic misfit; have a kind thought for those who can't or won't constantly adapt to The Way Things Are Going. . . .

Artistically, Jennings went on a winning streak with parts of **"Good Hearted Woman,"** **"Lonesome, On'ry and Mean"** and **"Ladies Love Outlaws"** and then hit his stride, leather flapping, turquoise flashing, with what is still the heart of his work so far: **"Honky Tonk Heroes"** . . . , **"This Time,"** **"The Ramblin' Man,"** and **"Dreaming My Dreams."** The archetypal Waylon Jennings album, I think, is **"This Time."** It carries the life-style thematics that translate so readily into the visual, but it is essentially about feelings—which is what the experience, the aging in that big, textured voice is about—and it eloquently asserts that it's all right for cowboys to have them. (p. 105)

The latest album, **"Are You Ready for the Country,"** is not a safe spot from which to launch guesses into Jennings' latest assessment of his role or how he's playing it. He seems to have cruised through it without concentrating as intently as he did during that string of really good ones. . . .

Yet the album has its own integrity, and some characteristic Jennings quirks. . . .

What seems crucial . . . is some sort of resonance with the experience you can hear in Jennings' voice and with the literary statement he is trying, with his whole life-style, to make. . . . But what really shapes his sound is the awareness he soaked up through experience and the memory he kept of how it felt. He makes it seem all right to be over thirty and have a few scars—and maybe that, too, helps explain his popularity just now; maybe there's a reaction against the youth-worshiping that sold like McDonald's hamburgers a few years back. He advocates, mostly in indirect ways, *finding out for yourself*, winning a few and losing a few in your own human and therefore fumbly way. Subtle things about a song convey whether it knows about this in its bones, the way he does.

His own writing, while he still isn't prolific, is increasingly a factor. It is simple, but when it works (as in *Waymore's Blues*, a two-chord song), it suggests something about a background of old Southern-poverty folkways careening around in the same head with modern doubts and stresses. And Jennings bridges those worlds, along with the generation gap and several other paradoxes. One thing I suspect he is wary of now is the idea of leading this "redneck rock" thing, for you can't go your *own* way leading a counter-establishment any more than you could by following the old one. . . .

"Nothing is relevant any more," Gore Vidal said. "What the individual has to do now is order his own survival." Waylon Jennings, in his own style, seems to have said that first. (p. 106)

Noel Coppage, "Crossing Over with Waylon Jennings," in Stereo Review *(copyright © 1976 by Ziff-Davis Publishing Company), Vol. 37, No. 4, October, 1976, pp. 104-06.*

MELODY MAKER

["**Are You Ready For The Country**" is an] horrendously lame, almost Vegas-style album that's extremely disappointing after "**Dreaming My Dreams**," possibly the best country album of 1975. . . . But camp-followers will enjoy the awful, elephantine "**MacArthur Park (Revisited)**", a big clanger, like the album, in the career of this most uneven and frustrating artist.

"Albums: 'Are You Ready for the Country'," in Melody Maker *(© IPC Business Press Ltd.), January 22, 1977, p. 23.*

JOHN MORTHLAND

It wasn't until late 1974 that the Waylon Jennings mystique took hold for me. This is partly because to my mind that's when his sound coalesced—resulting in the great *Dreaming My Dreams*—but more because that's when I first saw him live. . . .

Live has little to do with the prefab "progressive" country albums that seem to dominate the market today. It may bog down in a place or two, but if you only want one Waylon Jennings album, this is the essential one.

John Morthland, "Records: 'Waylon Live'," in Creem *(© copyright 1977 by Creem Magazine, Inc.), Vol. 8, No. 11, April, 1977, p. 60.*

ROBIN GRAYDEN

For several years or so Waylon Jennings has been spearheading the so-called Nashville "rebel" movement, and, along with such artists as Willie Nelson and Tompall Glaser, has kicked all the old country music traditions out of the back door and opted for a "new wave" stance, combining country music with rock.

But ol' Waylon is in danger of falling between two stools. Strictly speaking, ["**Ol' Waylon**"] is not an album by a country singer. It's aimed at the rock audience, and yet I can't really see it appealing to that market either. . . .

The album has a concept of sorts—the theme, as expressed by the ["**Luckenbach, Texas (Back to the Basics of Love)**"] track, is getting back to the basics, to the simple ways. Laudable sentiments, but the majority of tracks are not strong enough to retain attention for this message to be conveyed. Generally, the album lacks the impact of his earlier records like the superb "**Only the Greatest**" and "**The Taker/Tulsa**," which were full of good tunes.

And that's the crux of the matter. Jennings seems to have difficulty in coming up with enough strong songs to make one strong album. "**Ol' Waylon**" sags in too many places. . . .

He seems to have dried up, both as a song-penner and song-picker.

Waylon has got the fire, he just needs the right kind of coal. A disappointing album.

Robin Grayden, "Waning Waylon," in Melody Maker *(© IPC Business Press Ltd.), July 9, 1977, p. 23.*

NICK TOSCHES

There are problems [with *Ol' Waylon*]. *Luckenbach, Texas (Back to the Basics of Love)* is a bad song, a fan letter to Waylon and Willie Nelson from Waylon and Willie Nelson. If these guys don't stop cooing to each other, somebody's gonna think something's funny. But I guess that's what being an Outlaw is all about: making goo-goo eyes at yourself in the mirror. Pass the Lone Star, Red. . . .

Waylon's great, but the Outlaw silliness is waxing rotten. No more cuts like *Luckenbach, Texas (Back to the Basics of Love)*. Instead something like: *Beaumont, Texas (Back to the Basics of Sleaze)*.

Nick Tosches, "Records: 'Ol' Waylon'," in High Fidelity *(copyright © by ABC Leisure Magazine, Inc.; all rights reserved; excerpted by permission), Vol. 27, No. 8, August, 1977, p. 118.*

NOEL COPPAGE

Waylon's last album was hurt by having too many vaguely similar songs in it, and this one ["**Ol' Waylon**"] is quite a radical departure from that: here is what they used to call a mixed bag. Mostly it's a good one, much more interesting than "**Are You Ready for the Country**," and only a little too interesting in a negative way a few times. These have to do not with versatility . . . but with how he identifies with a particular song: *Luckenbach, Texas* and *If You See Me Getting Smaller* portray characters he can get into playing; *Lucille* (which first caught on for Kenny Rogers) and *Sweet Caroline* (a golden oldie by Neil Diamond) are supposed to come out of the heads of characters Waylon can't quite see himself being. . . . It's not a great Waylon album but it's a good Waylon album. (pp. 93-4)

Noel Coppage, "Popular Discs and Tapes: 'Ol' Waylon'," in Stereo Review *(copyright © 1977 by Ziff-Davis Publishing Company), Vol. 39, No. 2, August, 1977, pp. 93-4.*

ROBIN GRAYDEN

Apart from two gentle ballads, "**Girl I Can Tell**" and "Whistlers And Jugglers," which are both plaintive above-average standard country fare, the rest of ["**I've Always Been Crazy**"] finds Jennings living up to his image as a wandering, wild-living anti-Establishment hell-raiser, cocking two fingers at society. "**I've Always Been Crazy**" has the delicious second line, "but it's kept me from going insane". This and "**Don't You Think This Outlaw Bit's Done Got Out Of Hand**" . . . find him treating the whole outlaw image with tongue firmly in cheek.

By contrast, "**Billy**" is a sensitive dialogue with an old good-time buddy about getting too old for the outlaw life and settling down. Can't help feeling that there's an autobiographical slant to this and the two aforementioned songs. Is Waylon going soft? Will he be recording with strings again? The mind boggles. Possibly the answer lies in "**As The 'Billy World Turns**," the weirdest cut of the pack. It starts out simply enough, about writing a song, but then things, well, get a little fuzzy around the edges. . . . [Proceedings] gradually degenerate into something approaching a boozed-up impromptu session amid empty bottles of Jack Daniels in a border town bar room. Fascinating. Don't be put off by the cover, which finds The Man looking like an extra from Moby Dick, nor by the [Buddy] Holly medley; investigate for the rest of the content.

*Robin Grayden, "Albums: 'I've Always Been Crazy',"
in Melody Maker (© IPC Business Press Ltd.), January 13, 1979, p. 23.*

NOEL COPPAGE

Waylon Jennings seemed to be trying for more looseness, more spontaneity, in his last two or three albums, and now with **"I've Always Been Crazy"** . . . he's started to arrive at what he must have had in mind. The album has an open, unfussy sound and a natural, flowing feel about it. And Jennings himself is as unbuttoned as it's wise for anyone to get. . . .

"I've Always Been Crazy" is not perfect, of course; it goes out a little weak with Waylon's *Girl, I Can Tell* and Shel Silverstein's *Whistlers and Jugglers*. But generally it uses the throwaway, whether it be a single line or a whole song, the way a throwaway is supposed to be used, and it has that touch of wildness . . . one wants from Waylon and the Waylors. Last and far from least it has the voice of Waylon Jennings. And that's a lot.

Noel Coppage, "Waylon Jennings: About as Unbuttoned as It's Wise for Anyone to Get," in Stereo Review (copyright © 1979 by Ziff-Davis Publishing Company), Vol. 42, No. 2, February, 1979, p. 104.

NICK TOSCHES

[The] contents of Jennings' albums have often left much to be desired, especially by those of us who tire easily of anyone who apparently feels he must constantly remind us, through the use of literary devices learned from *Gunsmoke* reruns, of what a tough-ass he is. After a while, you got the eerie impression that this guy actually believed he was an outlaw. . . .

I've Always Been Crazy is a relief. There are still traces of the tough guy act, especially in a title track which finds the singer warning some purpling suffragette of "the chances you're takin' lovin' a free-livin' man" (exactly the sort of line that gets laughs in movie theaters), but I think Jennings has finally realized that at this point, only the Village People comprehend the true meaning of macho.

Of course, the thematic centerpiece is **"Don't You Think This Outlaw Bit's Done Got Out of Hand,"** which deals nicely with Texas chic, ill-perceived irony and Jennings' Nashville coke bust in the summer of 1977. Yahoo, indeed. . . .

I've Always Been Crazy even has its moment of, God help me, humor. **"As the 'Billy World Turns"** is a tune about good ole country music, with helpful instructions on how to write ("You get a pen and I'll get a paper./We're gonna steal ourselves a song"), how to speak ("*fantastic*") and how to cut a record ("seven-and-a-half-bar endin'").

Well done, Waylon.

Nick Tosches, "Waylon Jennings' Farewell to Outlawry," in Rolling Stone (by Straight Arrow Publishers, Inc. © 1979; all rights reserved; reprinted by permission), Issue 284, February 8, 1979, p. 57.

BRUCE PALEY

Whether lamenting over a girl, attempting to exorcise the whole "outlaw" schtick with a stinging, punchy diatribe, or breathing new life into tired C&W standards, Jennings goes straight for the gut [on *I've Always Been Crazy*]. . . .

This isn't quite the blockbuster Waylon is capable of delivering—I'd like to see him loosen up and rock out more—but it's close enough for now.

Bruce Paley, "'I've Always Been Crazy'," in Feature (copyright © 1979 Feature Publishing Co., Inc.; all rights reserved; reprinted by permission), No. 94, March, 1979, p. 76.

PETER GURALNICK

[Waylon Jennings] is part of the vanguard that is said to be revolutionizing country music. Or at least making inroads by reinjecting the maverick element into a music that was populated to begin with by such maverick, unpredictable, and slightly unsavory spirits as Jimmie Rodgers, Bob Wills, and Hank Williams.

His songs present a picture of the raffish hero in love with the essential seediness of twentieth-century America, the unregenerate rebel who looks back with a mixture of pride and regret on all the loves he's lost and all the hell-raising fun he's had. . . . His landmark album, **Honky Tonk Heroes,** reflected the same hell-raising image. The defiant stance suits Waylon Jennings. You get the feeling that in another life he might have been a buccaneer. And yet you sense somehow that this is oversimplification. If there were no more to the self-described 'lovable losers and no-account boozers and honky tonk heroes' who make up Nashville's new breed, then what can account for their remarkable staying power, the perseverance that's kept them knocking around Nashville all these years just looking for a hearing for their music? And in the case of Waylon Jennings—sensitive, articulate, warm, and sardonic by turns—you look for the intelligence, the dedication, and the vulnerability that lie beneath the hard-bitten facade. (pp. 206-07)

The first thing that strikes you about the music of Waylon Jennings is its sincerity. Drawn from a surprising diversity of sources—Dylan, the Beatles, Chuck Berry, and rockabilly, as well as flat-out country—its one unifying factor has been Jennings's patent integrity, and like the work of . . . Johnny Cash, it depends for its effect more on force of personality than on strictly musical considerations. (p. 209)

There remain . . . uncharacteristic traces of self-consciousness even on his best recorded work, a stiff grandiosity of purpose that is very much at odds with the straightforward, plain-spoken stance of his in-person performance. Here the music is looser, more ragged, but somehow more exuberant and more right. And I think that if Waylon Jennings never made another record, the personal message that he manages to convey to anyone who goes to see him perform would be record enough, a strikingly intimate and vivid memory of the occasion. . . .

[In live performances], the old songs don't come up that often; the emphasis is understandably on the more recent material. . . . Even so, there's room for many of the hits, from some of the earliest sides like **'The Only Daddy That'll Walk the Line'** through the Kris Kristofferson period of **'The Taker'** right up to the present day. It's a scrupulously careful winnowing of material. The songs exist side by side without quarrel or complaint, and presented in this way, each song reflecting a very personal vision from different stages of a lifetime, it is as if they are really just pieces of a larger work. (p. 213)

After a while the songs sound linked, not just thematically but melodically as well. . . . And each one is distinctively and recognizably Waylon Jennings; each song tells a different strand of a single story. A tale of pride and regret . . . , bitterness and nostalgia . . . , failure in love . . . , and beat resignation. . . . The songs look back with a weary kind of wisdom on a life that's still going on. . . . They're songs for aging cowboys. (pp. 213-14)

> *Peter Guralnick, "Waylon Jennings: The Pleasures of Life in a Hillbilly Band," in his* Lost Highway: Journeys & Arrivals of American Musicians *(copyright © 1979 by Peter Guralnick; reprinted by permission of David R. Godine, Publisher, Inc.), David R. Godine, 1979, pp. 204-16.*

BOB ALLEN

Over the years, Waylon has . . . developed into a songwriter of considerable scope and talent. Though his original songs lack the endurance or universality of many of the songs from the early Willie Nelson catalog, they have nonetheless supplied him with a number of hits, and they have been recorded by many other artists as well. While Willie has often written outside of the style of music in which he was most actively working (i.e. country music), Waylon, on the other hand, seems to use his writing talents to create songs that are perfectly tailored to his own unique personal style. They are often explicitly autobiographical. (p. 106)

To many, [*Dreamin' My Dreams*] marks a turning point for Waylon: the assimilation of his various musical influences into what is widely considered to be his best album ever. It features the haunting Jennings original, **"Are You Sure Hank Done It This Way,"** which is the closest thing that Waylon has to an anthem. Sweeping and powerful, this song sums up the frustration and desperation of Waylon's first decade in the music business. . . . It is as compelling and powerful a personal statement as almost any country or rock song that has ever been recorded. (p. 113)

> *Bob Allen, in his* Waylon & Willie: The Full Story in Words and Pictures of Waylon Jennings & Willie Nelson *(copyright © 1979 by Quick Fox), Quick Fox, 1979, 127 p.**

Robert Lipsyte

1938-

American young adult and adult novelist, nonfiction writer, and journalist.

Lipsyte's diverse works combine a creative sensibility with journalistic instincts and skills. As sports columnist for *The New York Times,* he distinguished himself by his thoughtfulness, insight, and commitment to truth. It is generally felt that these same qualities distinguish his novels and nonfiction works, many of which utilize sports as their subject or background. Lipsyte bases much of his work on the struggles of individuals to maintain and develop their sense of self-worth in the face of hostile and negative forces within society.

In Lipsyte's first novel for a young adult audience, *The Contender,* a young boy caught in a ring of sex, violence, and drugs in his Harlem neighborhood comes to a kind of spiritual transformation as he endures the rigors of training to become a champion boxer. Although Alfred does not become a champion he gains the self-confidence and vision he needs to transcend his situation. This is consistent with Lipsyte's belief that having the spiritual strength to meet a physical challenge is more important than having the physical strength to win. In *Sportsworld: An American Dreamland,* a retrospective collection of his thoughts about the world of athletics, Lipsyte mourns the fact that much of the joy of such activity has been lost, replaced by an intense emphasis on winning for winning's sake. His second novel for young adults, *One Fat Summer,* is another exploration of the value of challenge in the young person's search for self-confidence. In this work, the overweight, self-conscious protagonist comes to terms with himself and his peers through an arduous summer of cutting lawns. Lipsyte has also written several novels for adults, such as *Something Going,* a novel about horseracing which he cowrote with Steve Cady. He also collaborated with Dick Gregory on the latter's autobiography.

Critics have commended Lipsyte's efforts to portray real and fictional personalities with reverence for their depth and complexity. He has been criticized, however, for being overly moralistic and didactic when commenting on the evils of society, and for creating incomplete characterizations, especially in his adult works. Some critics find Lipsyte's fiction most successful; others feel that his nonfiction is superior. Critics from both groups, however, commend the freshness of his approach. Young people who are attracted to Lipsyte's books have discovered a writer who combines enthusiastic coverage of sports with perceptive awareness of social issues and human nature. (See also *Contemporary Authors,* Vols. 17-20, rev. ed., and *Something About the Author,* Vol. 5.)

EDWARD B. HUNGERFORD

In the manner of modern adult fiction, Lipsyte writes [in *The Contender*] from deeply within the boy's self and the life of the ghetto. The reader suffers with Alf's humiliations, is stirred by his strivings. Mechanics disappear, and between reader and struggling boy no obstacle stands. A fine book in which interest combines with compassion and enlightenment. (p. 43)

Edward B. Hungerford, "Ages 12—Up," in Book World—Chicago Tribune (© 1967 Postrib Corp.; reprinted by permission of Chicago Tribune and The Washington Post), November 5, 1967, pp. 38, 43.*

NAT HENTOFF

Far too many writers of fiction for the young seem to believe their primary function is to teach rather than to create textures of experience which are their own reasons for being. [In "The Contender," Robert Lipsyte] alternates between these two roles. . . .

On [a] homiletic level, the material is so neatly and obviously manipulated that virtue will have to be its own reward because "The Contender"—as a whole—fails as believable fiction. In several of its parts, however, didacticism recedes, and lo, there is life! In particular, whenever Lipsyte writes about boxing itself he indicates how intensely evocative he can be and he moves the reader beyond maxims into participation.

Lipsyte is most convincing in his unfolding of the inner transformation of a boy gone slack into a boxer gradually responding to different and compelling rhythms as he is driven by self-stretching imperatives, as emotional as they are physical. Within his factitious outer framework Lipsyte occasionally lets his main character become palpable.

It is when he leaves the gym and the ring that Lipsyte is too often content to map the road to salvation, rather than explore much more deeply the present ghetto terrain of his dropout. Can the lessons in more-than-survival that are learned in the ring be as easily applied as **"The Contender"** promises in neighborhoods where the rules of the game and the odds are set by distant outside societal forces? If the Horatio Alger approach is to be at all relevant in a work of fiction set in the ghetto, it needs to be considerably updated and treated with much less naiveté than here.

Nat Hentoff, "New Books for Young Readers: 'The Contender'," in The New York Times Book Review (© 1967 by The New York Times Company; reprinted by permission), November 12, 1967, p. 42.

SUSAN O'NEAL

Admirably, the author tries to portray Alfred's world [in *The Contender*] through the boy's own eyes, and like [Frank Bonham's] *Durango Street*, in his own language, but too often Mr. Lipsyte oversimplifies. For instance, white characters are paragons of interest and devotion; black nationalist ideas invariably come from the mouths of addicts and thugs, thus constituting a kind of guilt by association. Most important, only one way of responding to complicated problems is made to appear valid. Alfred's decision to compete by conventional methods is considered by the author to be the only proper action and is pitted against the attitude of Alfred's unsuccessful friends that, in any case, "Whitey" won't let you make it in his world. The implication whether intended or not, is that Alfred's friends are the chief cause of their own trouble. Such assignment of blame, however, makes the very real pressures that provoke these feelings in the ghetto teen-agers seem trivial. As a sports story, this is a superior, engrossing, insider's book; but as social commentary on problems in a Negro ghetto, it is a superficial, outsider's book which doesn't increase real understanding.

Susan O'Neal, "Junior High Up: 'The Contender'," in School Library Journal, an appendix to Library Journal (reprinted from the November 15, 1967 issue of School Library Journal, published by R. R. Bowker Co./A Xerox Corporation; copyright © 1967), Vol. 92, No. 20, November 15, 1967, p. 78.

MARY SILVA COSGRAVE

[Alfred's story in **The Contender**] is a grim and frightening one, but one that does hold out some hope for Negro teen-agers in a restless Harlem seething with hostility. There are warm relations with understanding adults and flashes of humor to relieve the agony. If it is honesty and realism that teen-agers want in their books, this is one for those who have not yet switched to books for adults.

Mary Silva Cosgrave, "Stories for Older Boys and Girls: 'The Contender'," in The Horn Book Magazine (copyright © 1967, by The Horn Book, Inc., Boston), Vol. XLIII, No. 6, December, 1967, p. 759.

KIRKUS REVIEWS

Not tips but performance [are covered in **Assignment: Sports**]. . . . The line-up is seasonal, with a little personal journal-ese by Lipsyte introducing each, from the Mets' first spring training . . . to, well, **"Winter Thoughts of a Bush-League Ballplayer"** who's ahead of the long-lost game except when "the air is faintly touched with the smell of the outfield grass." [Some] of Lipsyte's best pieces are illimitable, like the tale of Bozo Miller, the world's champion eater, and the 'no-sob-story' **"Athletes in Wheelchairs Compete for the Paralympic Team."** "I found in sports a very rich field for writing," observes once-great Russian weight-lifter Vlasov, and so has Lipsyte; countering the 'fun and games' aspersion, he notes that "politics, race, religion, money, the law—all play roles in sports." He's tackled all of them, and here he takes on **"The 1968 Olympics: The Reds and the Blacks and the Gold"** in a sequence of vivid vignettes. Stanley Woodward's *Sportswriter* tells more about the metier, and so, indirectly, does John Tunis' autobiography; but this is the best of the field—for example.

"Older Non-Fiction: 'Assignment: Sports'," in Kirkus Reviews (copyright © 1970 The Kirkus Service, Inc.), Vol. XXXVIII, No. 9, May 1, 1970, p. 520.

WALTER B. CHASKEL

[Robert Lipsyte] has collected in **Assignment: Sports** . . . a sampling of his articles and vignettes from the world of sports which transcend mere reportage to achieve a kind of literary quality rare in standard newspaper writing. He moves beyond line-ups, box scores, and statistics to reveal the essence of the people who have chosen sports as a way of life. His vision encompasses a vast panoply of human activity: from the individuality of boxing to the collective unity of collegiate rowing; from the adulation of a golf hero to the loneliness of the race track bettor. . . . Wise use of this outstanding addition to any collection could open a world of fine writing to sports fans addicted to statistics.

Walter B. Chaskel, "Special Journalism," in School Library Journal, an appendix to Library Journal (reprinted from the May 15, 1970 issue of School Library Journal, published by R. R. Bowker Co./A Xerox Corporation; copyright © 1970), Vol. 16, No. 9, May 15, 1970, p. 1967.

SAM ELKIN

In his detached style and writing rhythms, Lipsyte makes **"Assignment: Sports"** the unsentimental report about sports figures and sports. "The sweetness drained out of the afternoon," he writes in a long piece about Muhammad Ali. Not only does this image pungently rise off the printed page, it is the quintessence of what the book is about—the winners, the losers, the in-betweeners. . . . [The] book makes it because finally you realize that only the background is sports.

Which means you don't have to be a fan or even knowledgeable about sports to understand Lipsyte's own admission that "the crowd roared with a bloodlust that never fails to frighten me at prizefights." Or the Russian weight-lifter, his competitive years behind him, recalling "the salty pleasure of the white moment" when he won every world weight-lifting title in the Rome Olympics of 1960. Then, after attempting a comeback which fails, "the pleasure is gone forever and only the salt remains."

This is no-nonsense writing in a field too often drowned in bathos and outright dishonesty. Even Lipsyte's choice of subjects—a 15-year-old caddying in his first pro tournament, a world's champion eater, girl athletes in wheelchairs competing for the Paralympic Team—shows a writer concerned about characters, what they think and feel and how they act in human circumstances.

The "new journalism," this nonfiction style is called in our time. It is, in fact, an old technique, used by the best fiction writers since the genre was invented. Robert Lipsyte's public will need no reminder of his skills in this department. Readers meeting him for the first time, regardless of age-group, have a rare treat in store.

> *Sam Elkin, "For Young Readers: 'Assignment: Sports'," in* The New York Times Book Review *(© 1970 by The New York Times Company; reprinted by permission), May 31, 1970, p. 14.*

JOHN W. CONNER

Any adolescent who has enjoyed *The Contender* will need no introduction to Robert Lipsyte's new book [*Assignment: Sports*] or encouragement to read it. The same careful control of language, the same ability to develop a well-rounded character through conflict with a sport are evident. . . .

Robert Lipsyte never castigates, never ridicules, and rarely praises his characters. . . . As a reader completes each article, he senses Robert Lipsyte's insight on human frailty. The effect is devastating. Pretense is stripped away and the athlete is revealed as Lipsyte sees him. Lipsyte's ability to capsulize life effectively permeates *Assignment: Sports*. It is a rare skill and adds immeasurably to a reader's enjoyment.

> *John W. Conner, "Book Marks: 'Assignment: Sports'," in* English Journal *(copyright © 1971 by the National Council of Teachers of English; reprinted by permission of the publisher and the author), Vol. 60, No. 4, April, 1971, p. 529.*

JOHN S. SIMMONS

My admiration for and promotion of [*The Contender*] is because it adheres to certain established traditions for adolescent fiction . . . and yet also reflects some recent, significant trends in popular, well-written novels for young people. Lipsyte's ability to produce a picture of life which is credible for today's adolescents and at the same time stay within those constrictions which continue to be observed by hot-eyed censors of "school literary materials" is a tribute to his craftsmanship. . . . (p. 116)

There is a good bit of didacticism [in *The Contender*], but it is not out of proportion and Lipsyte on occasion places two adult pontificators, Spoon and Uncle Wilson, in slightly ironic postures. Spoon occasionally recognizes that he is preaching, and Uncle Wilson is the object of some ribbing by the boys to whom he is giving the good word. . . . Lipsyte has . . . handled the matter of taboos with restraint and imagination. Concern with drugs, sex, poverty, and violence are found throughout the novel, as well as some speculation on the value of religious belief, but none of these is dwelled on at length, and profanity and other objectionable language are avoided. Thus some no-no's are there but fit nicely into the total texture of the work. . . .

The content of the work, alienated young people searching for a place in a modern urban setting, is relevant as is Lipsyte's accurate reproduction of the idiom and syntax of the Harlem resident, both teenage and adult. The novel is presented with stylistic simplicity and brevity. . . . (p. 117)

[The theme of the search for self-identity] is clearly at the center of *The Contender*. . . . More tribute to the author lies in the fact that in his search for himself, Alfred has scaled no Matterhorn peaks at the novel's conclusion. . . . Instead we find the *process of becoming* the focus of the work. . . . Alfred hasn't really accomplished anything startling at the conclusion of the novel, and the lack of outer evidence that he has now "become somebody" is to Lipsyte's further credit. His (Alfred's) gains are modest and his successes frequently tainted with fear, reproach, and self-depreciation. His achievements are tentative, as is appropriate to the time, setting, and action of the work.

Another crucial theme, that of male adolescent friendship, is also well symbolized. Alfred has two such relationships during the novel, but it is the complex aspects of such friendship, doubt, suspicion, cynicism, despair, which are emphasized instead of the superficial and melodramatic comradeship found in many "books for boys." There is further no triumphal resolution to be found as the result of such friendship. Again the tentative nature of Alfred's relationships with his friends closely corresponds with what *is* among teenage boys. (pp. 117-18)

In both thematic and stylistic matters, Lipsyte's novel illustrates some of the more recent directions taken by junior novels written most recently.

The environment developed in the novel is not one customarily found in earlier ones. It is an urban one and focuses most specifically on filth and squalor of a black ghetto. Moreover, the plot produces no "emergence" from the setting; the main characters in the work will apparently remain in their present living situation. Attendant to this environment is found treatment of problems endured by those who must live there, especially the teenagers of a lower class minority group. Several contemporary concerns are evident: the plight and self-concept of the school dropout, the militancy of some blacks, the fearful espousal of an "Uncle Tom" status quo of others, the concerns of white merchants in a black community, all are found in *The Contender* and are clearly related to Alfred's continuing search for self. Most interesting of these is the continuing presence of white policemen in the black community, and what their presence means to the inhabitants of the ghetto. Once again, Lipsyte has neither extolled nor damned the police. He has merely included them as factors in the life of a boy such as Alfred Brooks. (p. 118)

In my opinion, Lipsyte has done a masterful job of reconciling "controversial" issues with the realities of censorship. Throughout the novel a good deal of brutality, cruelty, and violence is described. The characterization of Alfred's peer, Major, illustrates a young black who has pretty largely turned to violence as *his* answer. The use of drugs and alcohol is also an important factor. . . . Sexual involvement is also suggested. . . . But all of these inclusions are made both with great restraint and with direct relevance to Alfred's growth and change as a human being. They are there because they *belong* there and not for faddish or sensationalistic reasons.

In his inclusion of the generation gap as one of the thematic concerns of the novel, Lipsyte is simultaneously dealing with a concern of profound significance to young and old people of today, and venturing into an area of adolescent fiction which [is considered] one of its most glaring weaknesses: adult-adolescent relations. . . . In my opinion, Lipsyte has avoided many of the stereotypes found in earlier junior novels in his adult characterizations. They are not unmitigated bumblers, but they are not totally "with it" either. They are complex.

As significant as new thematic directions in this novel are the departures from the rigid stylistic conventions to be found in *The Contender*. There is little of the quasi-Victorian sentimentality of past adolescent works. The carefully drawn pictures of ghetto life accentuate its grimness and resultant dearth of hope. In his awareness of taboos, the author doesn't go all the way, but some of his Harlem descriptions are reminiscent of James Baldwin in *Go Tell It On The Mountain*. . . . The narrative is also made more complex and enjoyable by the mixing of relevant memories of the past and idealistic speculations of the future in Alfred's mind. Flashback is used frequently and effectively to give those reveries dramatic intensity. (pp. 118-19)

The Contender provides a couple of fairly obvious [symbols]. Comprehending the significance of the continued use of the cave and the stairs in the novel will not constitute an overly frustrating task for large numbers of early adolescent readers. Their placing in the novel and the care taken with their description make them relatively easy to place in clear symbolic perspective. . . .

[Let] me hasten to the claim that there are some weaknesses in the work. There is a good bit of moralizing about the virtues of an establishment-oriented good life here, especially in pronouncements by Spoon . . . , Donatelli . . . , and the already much-maligned Uncle Wilson. Lipsyte may also be called to question for presenting so many whites with good-guy images. Some balance is needed for the indulgent boss, the manager, the manager's dentist friend, and the "friendly cops" who applaud Alfred's morning run through the park. But many of the apparent weaknesses in the novel can be at least partially related to the limitations which continue to be inherent to the genre itself. I have tried to make it evident that I do not feel them to be overwhelming. (p. 119)

> *John S. Simmons, "Lipsyte's 'Contender': Another Look at the Junior Novel," in* Elementary English *(copyright © 1972 by the National Council of Teachers of English; reprinted by permission of the publisher and the author), Vol. XLIX, No. 1, January, 1972, pp. 116-19.*

PUBLISHERS WEEKLY

[Cady and Lipsyte] combine for a novel ["**Something Going**"] that horseracing devotees may take to but others are likely to find much ado about pretty little. There's hardly a live character in the lot. . . . The big shots apparently live happily ever after but just about everyone else either has been compromised or winds up a loser.

> *"'Something Going'," in* Publishers Weekly *(reprinted from the January 8, 1973, issue of* Publishers Weekly *by permission, published by R. R. Bowker Company, a Xerox company; copyright © 1973 by Xerox Corporation), Vol. 203, No. 2, January 8, 1973, p. 62.*

JON L. BREEN

Thoroughbred racing has become a popular subject for writers of fiction. In Joe McGinniss' *The Dream Team* . . . we had the bettor's viewpoint; Lipsyte and Cady give us the point of view of the horseman and the track executive [in *Something Going*]. Although this is not as fine a work as McGinniss' book, it is a fairly good example of a certain type of popular novel: one in which a specialized background is delineated authoritatively and in detail. It has a large cast of not-too-complex characters; many subplots; and carefully measured quotas of sex, violence, and other types of confrontation. There's "social significance," too, in the rather heavy-handed, ironic treatment of the heartless executives and their lack of concern for employees.

> *Jon L. Breen, "'Something Going'," in* Library Journal *(reprinted from* Library Journal, *March 1, 1973; published by R. R. Bowker Co. (a Xerox company); copyright © 1973 by Xerox Corporation), Vol. 98, No. 5, March 1, 1973, p. 764.*

PETE AXTHELM

["**Something Going**"] is about thoroughbred horse racing, but it is definitely not recommended to anyone who cherishes a belief in the romance of the turf. "**Something Going**" is a hard-edged, thoroughly unsentimental look at a precarious old-world society in the throes of an upheaval it can't even begin to comprehend. There are no heroes among the pompous aristocrats, struggling horsemen or exploited stablehands in this fast-moving book; there are only lost and frightened men, grasping desperately at crumbling pillars of tradition that can no longer support the structure of a world whose time is past. (p. 93)

[Lipsyte and Cady's] novel is loosely based on the horsemen's boycott that tore open New York racing in 1969, exposing ugly pockets of high-level bigotry and lower-level venality—and leaving scars on the sport's once-placid façade. The authors have channeled all the raw emotion of that boycott into a suspenseful narrative that should enthrall racetrack regulars, denizens of off-track betting parlors, and even readers who don't know what a morning line is. (pp. 93-4)

[All] the spoils prove illusory and, in the end, nobody wins that one big bet. Perhaps there is a glimmer of hope in one black groom's affirmation of his own manhood. . . . For the most part, however, Lipsyte and Cady have painted a dark fictional picture of big-time racing that may well be no darker than the truth. (p. 94)

> *Pete Axthelm, "Down the Stretch," in* Newsweek *(copyright 1973, by Newsweek, Inc.; all rights reserved; reprinted by permission), Vol. LXXXI, No. 14, April 2, 1973, pp. 93-4.*

JONATHAN YARDLEY

[Unfortunately "**Liberty Two**"] does not build with much suspense or persuasiveness—two essential ingredients of the political thriller. . . . [Lipsyte's] debut as a novelist is a distinct disappointment. Perhaps the greatest surprise to anyone who followed and admired his journalistic career is that the tough-mindedness of his sports writing is replaced here by easy sentimentality. . . .

[Lipsyte's people] are burdened with cliché: the misguided zealot, the rich and cold-blooded manipulator, the man caught in the middle, the girl who captures and frees his heart. They are stock characters in a political set-piece, capable perhaps of piquing the reader's mild curiosity but not of engaging his emotions.

This is not to say that Lipsyte fails to make his point. Manipulation—of one sort or another—is all too often the name of the game in contemporary politics. But it is one thing to say the right thing, quite another to make good fiction out of it. The latter Lipsyte has failed to do.

> *Jonathan Yardley, "Astronaut and Revolutionary," in* The New York Times Book Review *(© 1974 by The New York Times Company; reprinted by permission), April 28, 1974, p. 36.*

FRED ROTONDARO

[Robert Lipsyte] was one of the first, and I'm referring to the recent past, who wrote critically about the sports world; for he knew that sports figures had blemishes just like the rest of us. Lipsyte's column disappeared one day but I soon found out that he was turning to free lance writing. **"Liberty Two"** is the result. . . .

Unfortunately, Lipsyte's abilities have not carried over into this new venture. . . . The toughness that was once a staple of Lipsyte's columns is now gone. The narrative vivacity that was present even in short items is now mired in the description of people we don't care very much about because we've seen them all too often.

A novel should either tell an interesting tale so as to keep the reader moving forward or it should present characters of interest to the reader. Mr. Lipsyte's first novel does neither. But he has demonstrated both of these abilities in previous work, and I hope and believe his next venture will be more fruitful. (pp. 144-45)

> *Fred Rotondaro, "'Liberty Two'," in* Best Sellers *(copyright 1974, by the University of Scranton), Vol. 34, No. 6, June 15, 1974, pp. 144-45.*

JOHN R. COYNE, JR.

[*Liberty Two* has a good] plot, intriguing characters, superb visual qualities that will translate easily into a first rate film, authentic dialogue, a thoughtful and detailed picture of contemporary American society, and above all, with its Watergate analogies, timeliness. . . . [Central figure Charles] Rice is the quintessential fascist leader—charismatic, pure, single-minded, somehow managing to evoke both fear and adoration. Not an easy character for a novelist to draw. But Lipsyte handles the problem adeptly by telling Rice's story through a troubled and complex narrator, Cable, a figure much like Jack Burden in [Robert Penn Warren's] *All the King's Men*. A fascinating novel, especially if you believe that a large lumpenproletariat has developed in America, aching for some way to vent its frustrations; that a significant number of Americans have lost faith in their elected officials and in the political process itself; and that therefore the time is right for a man on horseback. If these things were true, and if that man were to appear, one suspects that he'd be much like Charles Rice.

> *John R. Coyne, Jr., "Books in Brief: 'Liberty Two'," in* National Review *(© National Review, Inc., 1975; 150 East 35th St., New York, NY 10016), Vol. XXVII, No. 1, January 17, 1975, p. 54.*

ROGER KAHN

No one reading **"SportsWorld"** will doze. Lipsyte's portraits of Muhammad Ali and Joe Namath ring beautifully. His political commentary proceeds from a decent respect for mankind. But in the end **"SportsWorld"** works as an entertainment, not as social commentary, which, indeed, may be true of sports itself.

"SportsWorld" is Lipsyte's newspeak for the hierarchy of owners, television executives and journalists who sell and propagandize spectator sports. He dislikes their collective view for its hyperbole, its cynicism and its preachment that watching games automatically ennobles the spirit. Then he asserts, "The 1972 Arab massacre of Israeli athletes was a hideously logical extension of SportsWorld philosophy." No. That was an extension of nationalism, which is part of the Olympics and nihilism, which is not. Hyperbole on one side is not well met with hyperbole from another.

He criticizes writers "who shed SportsWorld tears for the knees of Joe Namath and all our crippled heroes, playing through agony to teach us courage." He prefers to find bravery in "Jacqueline Susann and Cornelius Ryan writing through agony for us, dying of cancer." I am as anti-cancer as Mr. Lipsyte but if Miss Susann was writing that wretched book for me, she was not only suffering, but wasting her time. (pp. 4-5)

Sportswriters, Lipsyte asserts, have been the most harmful of newspapermen. Their puffery, their reluctance to ask unpleasant questions created the dreamland that so troubles him. I covered the Dodgers in 1952 and Barry Goldwater in 1964. Newspapermen traveling with the old Dodgers dug harder and, on the whole, wrote better, than political reporters assigned to the Goldwater debacle. . . .

Great athletes are performing artists. My spirits lift when I behold Luis Tiant pitch a shutout. They lift, in different arcs, when I hear Claudio Arrau play Opus 111. After reading **"SportsWorld"** twice I am not convinced that Mr. Lipsyte has ever thrilled to Tiant's triumphs.

I admired his column and I wanted to like his book. But **"SportsWorld"** lacks a sense of joy. Tell me about the hacks, the sadists and the misers, but let me hear as well the tunes of glory. (p. 5)

> *Roger Kahn, "No Tears for Namath: 'SportsWorld'," in* The New York Times Book Review *(© 1975 by The New York Times Company; reprinted by permission), November 9, 1975, pp. 4-5.*

PAUL D. ZIMMERMAN

For fourteen years, as the most original and elegant writer on the sports staff of The New York Times, Robert Lipsyte served as a high priest of that secular religion he now calls SportsWorld. He promoted its mythologies, helped enshrine its gods—but with a growing disaffection that has given birth to this persuasive volume of dissent. **"SportsWorld"** is more than Lipsyte's record of his own loss of innocence and growing apostasy. And it is more than a peppery chronicle of the changing sports ethos of the '60s and '70s, although the book sparkles with insightful portraits of figures ranging from the self-protectively spaced-out Kareem Abdul-Jabbar to Muhammad Ali, Lipsyte's premier subject throughout his journalistic career.

The book is a culmination of that gathering body of radical, wised-up sports writing that has tried to view sports as the principal disseminator of the American way. (pp. 120, 122)

Lipsyte's SportsWorld is a state of mind, a constellation of sentimental standards, a universe of invented heroes who are cast by the press to satisfy and act out our fantasies. "A sports-writer learns early," he writes, "that his readers are primarily interested in the affirmation of their faiths and their prejudices. . . ." So Sonny Liston plays the role of the Black Heavy. Mickey Mantle, in private often arrogant and abusive, is cast publicly as the Golden Boy. Yogi Berra, gratuitously rude to fans, succumbs to the cuddly-clown image invented for him by Joe Garagiola. And Vince Lombardi, because he wins, is cast as a saint. (p. 122)

Lipsyte's book, for all its keen theorizing, is not a tract, but a collection of essays with a common theme. Along the way, he leaves himself room to include a marvelously self-disparaging account of his narcissistic flirtation with tennis; a capsule history of sports writing with clearly drawn dynastic lines, and a wry obituary on pro basketball, which the national media have stopped promoting as the "Sport of the Seventies," he charges, because it is so dominated by blacks.

For all his disaffection, Lipsyte still loves sports. He only laments our transformation into a nation of sideline fantasists. . . . Read him, and you will never look at a sports event in quite the same way again. (p. 125)

Paul D. Zimmerman, "Cold Shower," in Newsweek *(copyright 1975, by Newsweek, Inc.; all rights reserved; reprinted by permission), Vol. LXXXVI, No. 21, November 24, 1975, pp. 120, 122, 125.*

BETSY HEARNE

[*One Fat Summer* is a] smoothly written, funny-sad story of growing up male and fat in the fifties. . . . [It] is satisfying to watch a more-than-200-pound self-loather get himself an exhausting job, stick to it, defy some rural Mean Street hecklers as well as the more insidious hold of his loving family, and reject his own diving champion role model. The author . . . builds sympathy, tension, and a nicely mixed—if not always subtle—feeling for each character.

Betsy Hearne, "Children's Books: 'One Fat Summer'," in Booklist *(reprinted by permission of the American Library Association; copyright © 1977 by the American Library Association), Vol. 73, No. 13, March 1, 1977, p. 1015.*

KIRKUS REVIEWS

In [*One Fat Summer,*] Robert Lipsyte's first novel since *The Contender*, Bobby Marks recalls much more than the weight lost cutting Dr. Kahn's "chlorophyll monster" of a lawn that summer of 1952. He remembers the deadly peanut butter strangles and ice cream headaches of overeating; the good, jittery fear that the lawnboy he replaced will pulverize him ("your ass is grass, faggot, and I'm the lawnmower"); the loss of his best friend Joanie, whose nose job makes her vain, no longer a fellow freak; the late summer confrontation with his crazy-drunk, rifle-toting nemesis. But Bobby can take it. Underneath all that fat he's a spunky city kid, occasionally escaping to Mittyesque daydream . . . , more often knifing back with a fast one-liner. . . . You're bound to like this fat boy right from the start. And throughout, the light touch, snappy patter, and on-target characterization make his summer very funny and fully alive.

"Young Adult Fiction: 'One Fat Summer'," in Kirkus Reviews *(copyright © 1977 The Kirkus Service, Inc.), Vol. XLV, No. 7, April 1, 1977, p. 359.*

STEPHEN KRENSKY

The time [of "**One Fat Summer**"] is 1952, and Lipsyte mingles the flavor of the era in his prose; the issues, tastes and expressions of the day echo through the narrative. . . .

[The] first-person narrative gives us an inner perspective of Bobby's thoughts and feelings. Refreshingly, he is neither precocious nor off-beat, in the manner of so many teen-age protagonists, but simply a normal boy in abnormal circumstances.

Bobby, however, is Lipsyte's only fully realized character; the supporting cast shifts in and out of the reader's focus, not only because of the plot, but also because our perception of them varies. For example, Bobby's father is alternately stiff, compassionate, machine-like and impulsive. His mother is sharp, sensitive, but sometimes blindly overprotective. In one way, these contrasting qualities reflect the changing ways in which Bobby sees them. In another way, they're confusing.

Nonetheless, the dramatic movement of Bobby's metamorphosis is effectively rendered. As the summer progresses, he sheds pounds and illusions in equal measure, and in the process, both his mind and body begin to shape up. His long struggle culminates in the realization that he has the independence to meet life on his terms—and that's a weighty enough idea for anyone.

Stephen Krensky, "Children's Books: 'One Fat Summer'," in The New York Times Book Review *(© 1977 by The New York Times Company; reprinted by permission), July 10, 1977, p. 20.*

ZENA SUTHERLAND

[*One Fat Summer*] is far superior to most of the summer-of-change stories: any change that takes place is logical and the protagonist learns by action and reaction to be both self-reliant and compassionate, understanding Pete's weakness as well as the bullying persecutor's motivation. The plot elements are nicely balanced and paced, the characterization is developed with insight, and the writing style is deft and polished.

Zena Sutherland, "New Titles for Children and Young People: 'One Fat Summer'," in Bulletin of the Center for Children's Books *(reprinted by permission of The University of Chicago Press; © 1977 by the University of Chicago), Vol. 30, No. 11, July-August, 1977, p. 177.*

KIRKUS REVIEWS

[*Free to Be Muhammad Ali*, a] forthright, fair-minded biography, nicely chronicles the champ's highly publicized career, circling in on the man's genuine talents and pointing out much of the "fakelore" as well—three versions of the Olympic medal story, for example. The approach requires a mature reader (Ali's "vanity has always bordered on narcissism"), able to comprehend the political climate of the Sixties, when the champ asserted his rights as an individual—to convert, to change his name, to refuse induction—and suffered undeserved recriminations from sportswriters, boxing associations, and the U.S. Army. Lipsyte doesn't dance away from the contradictions in his personality, and although he clearly acknowledges Ali's worldwide appeal and popularity, he doesn't muddle his account with the rhetoric of the literary heavyweights. No mention of the second Spinks fight, however, which limits this even before publication. A contender nonetheless.

*"Older Non-Fiction: 'Free to Be Muhammad Ali',"
in* Kirkus Reviews *(copyright © 1978 The Kirkus
Service, Inc.), Vol. XLVI, No. 22, November 15,
1978, p. 1256.*

MEL WATKINS

Of those sports journalists who have covered Muhammad Ali
throughout his turbulent career, Robert Lipsyte consistently
has provided the most lucid and perceptive accounts. Neither
siding with critics who castigated Ali during his exile from
boxing, nor accepting without reservation the bombast of Ali's
mythologizers, Mr. Lipsyte's portraits of the heavyweight
champion have been both revealing and temperate. Its brevity
notwithstanding, **"Free to Be Muhammad Ali"** adheres to those
standards. . . .

What one finally derives from this slim biography is a sense
not only of Ali's mercurial personality, but also of the affection
and respect the author feels for him as an athlete and as a man.
Without suppressing Ali's largesse and athletic ability or his
hucksterism, Mr. Lipsyte presents a thoughtful, complex portrait of one of America's greatest athletes. He does so with
taste and an honest resolve to delve beyond the usual level of
puffery and jock hype, which in his own field makes him almost
as unique as Ali.

*Mel Watkins, "Children's Books: 'Free to Be Mu-
hammad Ali',"* in The New York Times Book Review *(© 1979 by The New York Times Company;
reprinted by permission), March 4, 1979, p. 32.*

ROBERT LIPSYTE

I recently watched a sports program on television in which a
commentator was discussing a basketball coach who pounds
on his players—kicks them, calls them dirty names. And the
reporter said, "Well, I'm not sure I would want to be treated
like that. I would want to be treated like a human being. But
who can argue with this kind of treatment when the coach's
won/lost record is so good."

Across America, kids are sitting in front of their T.V. sets
taking that in. And too many of the sports books they read
reinforce that same ethic: *Winning is the only thing. When
things are tough, try harder. Success is up to you.*

Sports is, or should be, just one of the things people do—an
integral part of life, but only one aspect of it. Sports is a good
experience. It's fun. It ought to be inexpensive and accessible
to everybody. Kids should go out and play, test and extend
their bodies, feel good about what they can achieve on their
own or with a team. And children's books about sports should
encourage that approach.

Instead, adults try to make sports into a metaphor—a preparation for life. We endow sports with mystical qualities that
don't exist and raise unreal expectations about what it can do.
At the same time, by making sports into a metaphor, we devalue
it for itself. It's no wonder that the kids who read sports books
are confused by them. The things that happen to people in the
books bear very little relation to their own experiences and
anxieties in real life. So the kids read them and wonder, "What's
wrong with me?"

What the books don't say is that in our society, sports is a
negative experience for most boys and almost all girls. Soon
after they start school, at an age when they have no other

standards on which to judge themselves, we force children to
judge each other on their bodies, which is the thing that everyone's most scared about. They're required to define themselves
on the basis of competitive physical ability. (pp. 43-4)

I'd like to see sports books for children that would take away
some of the pressures they feel and defuse the sense of competition and rejection. To do this, I think the books must acknowledge children's real fears about sports.

The first, perhaps ultimate, fear is of being ridiculed—the fear
that everyone's going to laugh at you because you're not good.
(pp. 44-5)

A second fear is the fear of getting hurt. . . .

A third fear that kids have about sports is of disappointing their
parents. (p. 45)

Finally, there's the basic, overall fear of not measuring up in
sports—of not being man enough, or woman enough. This may
be the most meaningless definition of being a worthy person
in our society.

I don't think we have to make any rules for sports books for
children beyond asking that they present some sense of truth
about the role of sports in our lives. But most books perpetuate
the old myths. Even in the new, trendy sports stories, where
problems like pregnancy, dope, and so on are admitted, the
basic point that comes across to the reader is that if you're
willing to take orders, if you're determined to succeed, everything else will work itself out. Blacks and whites will get
together, the coach will be understanding, poor kids will get
rich, and the team will win the championship. Kids who read
these books wonder why such things don't seem to happen in
real life, to them or to people they know. Most of them, no
matter how hard they push themselves, will never make the
team, and of those who do, many will discover that the coach
is a tyrant who exploits his players and that the brotherhood
of sports they've read so much about doesn't exist. (pp. 45-6)

The myth that sports is a way out of the slums has been exploded. But as long as there's a Rocky image, as long as the
books lionize one or two real kids like Sugar Ray Leonard
who've made it, we're saying to all the others, "It's your
fault for staying poor. It's not society's fault. You didn't try
hard enough. You didn't listen to coach. You didn't play
hurt." . . .

Sports biographies for children, which perpetuate all these myths,
are really the junk food of publishing. They're all too easy to
produce. You get scissors and a paste pot, raid the newspapers
for false biographies of the hero of the moment—and sports
writers never were trustworthy in terms of biographical material—and make a book. . . . But the kids who get hooked
on them aren't going to be able to move on to books in which
every other adjective isn't "immortal" or "fabulous" and
every sentence doesn't end with an exclamation mark. Or in
which every hero's success isn't simply a matter of hard work
and determination. (p. 46)

Trying to reform sports books for children is discouraging, but
you've got to start somewhere. That's what we do as writers.
If we can reach one kid, affect some program somewhere,
wake up one teacher, it's probably worthwhile. We should be
trying to write books that acknowledge kids' fears about sports
and say that other people, even heroes, share them. Books in
which nice guys do finish last and it doesn't matter. In which
making the team doesn't end all the problems and the team

doesn't win all the games. Books that integrate sports into the rest of life. If we write more truthfully about sports, perhaps we can encourage kids to relax and have fun with each other—to challenge themselves for the pleasure of it, without self-doubt and without fear. (p. 47)

Robert Lipsyte, "Robert Lipsyte on Kids/Sports/ Books," in Children's literature in education *(© 1980, Agathon Press, Inc.; reprinted by permission of the publisher), Vol. 11, No. 1 (Spring), 1980, pp. 43-7.*

Steven Millhauser

1943-

American adult novelist.

Millhauser explores the pains and pleasures of growing up through the fascination children and teenagers have for violence and the unknown. Suicide and deadly games often play important roles in his books. The adult world has a peripheral existence in the author's fiction and is important only as an illumination of childhood. Millhauser relieves his unsentimental, sometimes harsh vision of childhood through a subtle playfulness of tone. Another major concern in Millhauser's writings is literature; his works parody specific genres and authors and abound in literary allusions.

Millhauser deeply impressed critics and readers with his fresh approach to childhood and adolescence in his first two books. *Edwin Mullhouse: The Life and Death of an American Writer, 1943-1954,* **by Jeffrey Cartwright satirizes literary biographies which too often concentrate on the trivialities of a writer's life. On the surface, a comprehensive study of the language and lore of middle-class childhood, the story also presents childhood genius and creativity cut short by the limitations imposed by adults. The tone and characterization of the book have been compared to both Vladimir Nabokov's** *Pale Fire* **and J. D. Salinger's stories about the Glass family. The admittedly beautiful prose has been criticized for lacking any real meaning, yet critics cite a maturity and originality not often found in a first novel.**

Portrait of a Romantic, **Millhauser's second book, continues the subjects of** *Edwin***—art, human relationships, and childhood—into their later, darker phases and deals mostly with the more disturbing and destructive forces of growing up. With** *Portrait,* **Millhauser has been accused of neglecting acne, guilt, paranoia, and other aspects of a normal adolescence, while drawing praise for his competent handling of the characters's sensibilities. Millhauser is considered an important new talent in contemporary literature for his unconventional attitudes toward childhood and for his outstanding talent at description.**

THE NEW REPUBLIC

Edwin Mullhouse was a Connecticut boy who wrote the novel *Cartoons* and who died under strange circumstances at age 11; Jeffrey Cartwright, his neighbor, classmate and friend, wrote this biography a year later. That's Steven Millhauser's *donnee,* as Henry James would say; that's what we readers must accept [in *Edwin Mullhouse: The Life and Death of an American Writer (1943-1954) by Jeffrey Cartwright*] with a willing suspension of our disbelief. Believe it or not, it's well worth accepting. This is no "Peanuts"; Jeffrey is no oleaginous and self-pitying Charlie Brown; the novel has no Christian Message. Jeffrey is a Nabokovian child: witty, literate, perceptive and disturbingly complex. Edwin is different, an artist of the Beckettian sort. Their acquaintances, their schooldays, their relationship—all is grist for Jeffrey's mill and for Millhauser's beautifully shaped and polished description of the pleasures, sorrows and evils of childhood, of art and of life. Don't be put off by the apparent whimsy of the title and the youth of the characters; this is a

mature, skillful, intelligent and often very funny novel—and the author's first. (p. 30)

[Childhood] is a life in itself, of course, with rather more variety to it than grownup life offers, and it is experienced with much more intensity than we jaded adults can generally manage. Millhauser's narrator conveys it marvelously, and he does equally well with the intricacies of that other Nabokovian theme, the relationship of the reader-critic to his author. On these topics and many others, the novel offers a steady stream of profits and pleasures. . . . (p. 31)

"A Few Novels: 'Edwin Mullhouse: The Life and Death of an American Writer (1943-1954) by Jeffrey Cartwright','" in The New Republic *(reprinted by permission of* The New Republic; © *1972 The New Republic, Inc.), Vol. 167, No. 10, September 16, 1972, pp. 30-1.*

WILLIAM HJORTSBERG

[**"Edwin Mullhouse: The Life and Death of an American Writer (1943-1954). By Jeffrey Cartwright"**], Steven Millhauser's deft first novel, . . . offers a substantial amount of truth disguised as elegant artifice. . . .

Stop for a moment and consider the child as artist. In a sense every child is an artist. Just as the intricately-contrived private lunacies of madmen are at heart one with the creative act, so too, the uninhibited crayon scrawls of an infant are the joyously self-indulgent motions of an artist. Art is a magic act. The Cro-Magnon of Lascaux knew that; Picasso knows it too. Children dwell in a world of magic. At will, any child can conjure up surroundings more desirable than the material world of his elders; he, too, is a magician, an artist.

Although Steven Millhauser knows this, his narrator, young Jeffrey Cartwright, does not. Disappointed by Edwin Mullhouse's answers to his queries into the meaning of "Cartoons," he writes: "Either he did not understand the nature and meaning of his book, and its relation to life, or else his mind grappled with these matters in so curious and personal a manner as to be unable to communicate its findings to intellects organized in a more commonplace way." Poor Jeffrey misses the point. Sadly, he is not alone.

But what of Steven Millhauser's novel, considered as a work of art? Certainly, it displays an enviable amount of craft, the harsh discipline that carves through the scar-tissue of personality painfully developed during a process known as "growing-up." Only by the slow acquisition of craft is it possible to return to the mad-child-artist who got lost somewhere in the shuffle. In spite of Jeffrey Cartwright's occasionally pedantic tone (the tedium of the device might be likened to the sting of the master's cane), **"Edwin Mullhouse"** evokes the world of children with delicacy and precision.

Millhauser's eye is trained to observe with a child's perceptions. He appreciates the mystic importance of trivial objects (baseball cards, homemade Valentines, comic books) and he sees the intensity of colors and textures in a world still new. His ear is attuned to the nuances of children's speech from the attempts of a preschooler to imitate his father quoting Chaucer . . . to the roundabout formalities of two second-graders discussing a class room romance. . . . Disbelief is successfully suspended. The author's world has become the reader's.

Along with its other virtues Steven Millhauser's playground of runny-nosed geniuses also serves as an excellent vehicle for satire. The 11-year-old biographer and his meticulous attention to trivia—Jeffrey is forever providing exact lists: of every title in Edwin's library at age 4, of the bubble-gum cards he collects at 9, of all the novelty-shop gifts he gives his second-grade love, Rose Dorn—recall Carlos Baker giving us the inside information on Hemingway by telling the number of trout caught in three days' fishing the Clark's Fork of the Yellowstone. . . . Yet no author is singled out; it is the genre of literary biography itself that is the target. If this seems a balloon easily punctured, it is to the book's credit that it succeeds as a story in spite of the satirical intention.

Steven Millhauser has written a rare and carefully evoked novel. He tells us quite a bit about the nature of children and supplies us with a few useful clues about art in the process. . . . If the story is sometimes slow, it is never uninteresting, and the high points soar with the breath-held clarity of true fiction.

*William Hjortsberg, "Fiction: 'Edwin Mullhouse',"
in* The New York Times Book Review *(© 1972 by The New York Times Company; reprinted by permission), September 17, 1972, p. 2.*

J. D. O'HARA

Let me make one thing perfectly clear: [**Edwin Mullhouse**] is a novel. . . .

Let me add one more thing. Steven Millhauser, who is the only begetter of Cartwright, Mullhouse, Cartwright's biography, and Millhauser's novel, is a dazzlingly successful writer. He is also a precocious imitator of Vladimir Nabokov, as he graciously acknowledges by characterizing Cartwright as a biographer who lives next to his subject; who, more or less accidentally, becomes involved in his subject's death; who admires his subject but also competes with him and is neglected by him; and who begins the book with a reference to an "invisible amusement park"—all signs of his literary father, Kinbote in Nabokov's *Pale Fire*. In evoking the tangled intellectual and emotional bonds between author and biographer, Millhauser is very nearly Nabokov's equal. And that's not all.

Millhauser seriously rivals his master in pellucid and witty descriptions. . . . Like Nabokov, he is quiveringly alert to metaphors: when he describes a girl "holding the spout of a watering can over the rim of a red plastic flowerpot from which a dark green plant overflowed," that last word is marvelously surprising, expected, and satisfying all at once. Like Nabokov, Millhauser surprises us with ironically structured actions as well as metaphors: "suddenly a shot rang out. It was only Edwin, chomping on a plump radish." Like Nabokov, Millhauser plays with allusions: "I also recall a little white cloud, very like a rubber whale I played with in the bathtub." Like Nabokov, he lets us see beyond the narrator, as you'll find by noticing clowns as you read. And, like Nabokov, Millhauser sees vividly the banal surface of ordinary life, but also the strangeness of it, and the strangeness in people's heads, and the constant availability of evil.

But Millhauser doesn't dog one man only. Novelist Edwin complains to Jeffrey about the difficulty of writing: "And you see, there are all these words, nothing but words, what are these words, and there they are, so that's what you're faced with, words, words. . . ." If Jeffrey is Nabokovian, Edwin is rooted in [Samuel] Beckett—an origin acknowledged in Edwin's predilection for radishes and carrots.

Millhauser, then, is a conscious and diligent imitator. But this is said descriptively; no putdown. Most imitators merely imitate, and when you've perceived the resemblance you've perceived everything. But Millhauser is also an author in his own right: intelligent, witty, sensitive, enormously skilled, and bubbling over with original comments on childhood, on art, on human relationships, on life. His characters, like [J. D.] Salinger's in one way (though quite different in most), are absurdly precocious children, but their story is for adults. That Edwin Mullhouse should have written a novel at the age of eleven is unlikely; that Jeffrey Cartwright should have become his biographer is even more so. But their perceptions of life are not weird, or cute, or adult; they are (we flatter ourselves) the perceptions we had back then, but that we had without their apperceptions and without their words, unfortunately. Now Millhauser has evoked our past potential childhood, with all its delight, its limitations, and its grimness. This is no platitudinous, stale and oily collection of *Peanuts;* as Jeffrey points out, an unrealistic viewpoint can be profitable: "We are shocked by distortion into the sudden perception of the forgotten strangeness of things." Millhauser renews and enhances our sense of that strangeness outside us and in. This is an extraordinarily good novel. And it's only his first.

J. D. O'Hara, "Novels; Nabokovian, Plangent, Simple, Sparse, Decorative, Decadent and Good: 'Edwin Mullhouse'," in Book World—The Washington Post *(copyright © 1972 The Washington Post Company), September 24, 1972, p. 8.*

JOSEPH KANON

Like great actors in mediocre plays, there are some writers whose talent seems larger than the vehicles they have chosen to contain it. A case in point is [**Edwin Mullhouse**], a remarkably well-written and sometimes funny account of the hitherto unrecognized genius Edwin Mullhouse. . . . [The] narrative takes us from Edwin's first gurgles to his creative Later Years and, as such, is a devilish satire on those exhaustive biographies that weigh down shelves with their bulky worthiness and unrelieved tedium. The tone is sly and articulate, as if written by one of Salinger's Glass children, and though the initial idea is admittedly small and even fey, Millhauser makes the most (if not too much) of it, detailing for us the most ordinary of childhoods through Jeffrey's pompous New Crit perspective. (The two boys react to each other like a sinister Holmes and Watson—Edwin makes fun of Jeffrey, whom he rightly sees as a drip, and Jeffrey's underlying resentment and disapproval occasionally come to the narrative surface with quiet hilarity.) (pp. 73, 78)

This kind of elaborate literary conceit, of course, is beloved by academics because it presupposes not only a familiarity with existing literature but a conscious limiting of scope to emphasize verbal dexterity (something Nabokov used to more comic effect in *Pale Fire*). Millhauser takes some sideswipes at this approach and has some fun dropping pseudopedantic clues. But given his own material, it is all pretty much a case of biting the hand that feeds. The danger in this kind of cerebral writing is an absence of emotion, and Millhauser, alas, runs the familiar gamut from A to B. Certainly he can't be faulted for his fluency and sense of prose style—he can write like a streak—but even the dazzling eventually wearies. Such a lot of cleverness! Detail after detail, send-up after send-up, are piled one on top of another, rococo style, until the structure becomes top-heavy and collapses—a 300-page game. What begins as a satire on exhaustive biographies becomes, itself, an exhausting satire.

The trouble is that such jokes (especially at this length) are self-defeating. To write about an uninteresting childhood in all its minutiae is to make the account itself uninteresting and boring. Beyond the initial joke, who could possibly *care* about these children? This novel has some of the most beautiful pointless prose in recent fiction. Moreover, the other level on which the book operates—that of a commentary on, and remembrance of, childhood—is licked before it starts by the distance a satirical style imposes. Millhauser plays his nostalgic cards well—scarcely a detail is left out, from root-beer barrels and Mary Janes to penny-filled plastic containers for the March of Dimes—but they hang there in decorative isolation, like a list of Golden Oldies, because there is nothing to pin them on, no internal life in the book to connect with. At times one gets the impression of Millhauser playing hide-and-seek with his own talent, trapped by cleverness and by irony that turns on itself endlessly. And it is all too bad because, despite is length and fundamental triviality, this is the work of a very gifted young writer. No doubt one's disappointment is partly the result of the inflated expectations these very gifts arouse. But it is disappointing all the same. Young Edwin Mullhouse ends his *Cartoons* with a Looney Tunes' "That's All, Folks!" But for a talent like Millhauser's, this cleverly executed number is not nearly enough. (p. 78)

> Joseph Kanon, *"Satire and Sensibility,"* in Saturday Review *(copyright © 1972 by* Saturday Review; *all rights reserved; reprinted by permission), Vol. LV, No. 40, September 30, 1972, pp. 73, 78.**

J. JUSTIN GUSTAINIS

Steven Millhauser, it seems to me, is attempting to do several things with his novel ["**Edwin Mullhouse**"]. First, and perhaps basically, he is writing a subtle satire on all of those biographies, which we occasionally find ourselves reading, that deal with the lives of people we never heard of when they were alive, and probably would not have cared much about if we did. You know the type. Ponderous details abound, regardless. . . . Unfortunately, there is such a thing as doing a job too well. Satirizing ponderousness is all very well, until it becomes ponderous.

Another facet of the book is, one suspects, designed to show the fabulous time that is childhood, with its constant discovery and continuing mysteries. Personally, I don't think childhood is that wonderful (at least mine wasn't, but perhaps I was deprived). Mr. Millhauser's favorite device for exhibiting the wonderfulness (to borrow a word from Bill Cosby) of being really young is a merciless, unremitting assault of visual images upon every sentence in the book. Description is fine, even necessary, but this kind of stuff is plain ridiculous: "He looked forward to these weekly shopping trips with an eagerness bordering on frenzy, and not simply for the sake of the peanut machines . . . : he looked forward to the trips also for the sake

of the numbers." . . . Three hundred pages of this is enough to give one dysentery.

I found this novel tedious, irritating, and just a little too cute to stomach.

> J. Justin Gustainis, *"Fiction: 'Edwin Mullhouse: The Life and Death of an American Writer',"* in Best Sellers *(copyright 1972, by the University of Scranton), Vol. 32, No. 14, October 15, 1972, p. 335.*

PEARL K. BELL

Little could James Joyce have foreseen the avalanche of cliché he was setting in motion when he began *A Portrait of the Artist as a Young Man* with [a] now legendary sentence. . . . In thousands of first novels since Joyce's revolutionary use of the baby artist's earliest lisping literacies half a century ago, a precocious horde of sensitive, rebellious, grimly ambitious children—every last one of them wise and gifted beyond his tender years—have marched to the same leitmotif: The child is father of the novelist, and the proper study of a young writer is Himself when young.

It has been left to the ingenious imagination of still another first novelist, a Brown University graduate student named Steven Millhauser, to stand the *Künstlerroman* genre on its swollen head in *Edwin Mullhouse: The Life and Death of an American Writer, 1943-1954, by Jeffrey Cartwright*. . . . Not in the least by chance, he has also produced a brilliant parody of Literary Biography (Semi-Worshipful). . . . Compared to Jeffrey's zealous sense of purpose, his industrious concentration on his subject's infinite variety and plenitude of sameness, James Boswell seems inattentive, Richard Ellmann's *Joyce* slipshod, Leon Edel's *James* cursory. (p. 15)

If the Graduate Student's Revenge were all that Steven Millhauser had in mind for his cunningly literate mockery, *Edwin Mullhouse* would still be an extraordinary achievement. But he is aiming at much more than parody. At the heart of the book, all kidding aside, is a metaphor of childhood as a state of genius.

Except for the tormented year that Edwin sweated over the writing of *Cartoons*, there was nothing in the least Mozartian about the boy novelist. . . . When Jeffrey's literary horizons were expanding into Dickens and Mark Twain, Edwin was still engrossed in *Walt Disney's Comics & Stories* and his kid sister's first-grade texts. . . .

What sets Edwin apart, the essence of his singularity, is his stubborn refusal to surrender the transient genius bestowed upon children, "the capacity to be obsessed," whether the obsession is with Bugs Bunny or Pick Up Sticks. . . . Edwin successfully defied life's cruel assault on a child's playful freedom, "the obscenity of maturity"—and if Jeffrey cannot resist patting himself on the back for this "memorable phrase," the little monster should be forgiven. A biographer's lot is not a happy one.

Even more than a remarkable tour de force of parody, equal in its way to the best of [Max] Beerbohm, *Edwin Mullhouse* is a portrait not so much of the artist as a young child as of the *ordinary* child as artist. At the age of 29, Millhauser seems to have forgotten nothing of the way children go about the business of being children, at once succored by the adult world and stymied by its elephantine misreading of what children need and want. With all its satiric exaggeration and absurdity,

Edwin Mullhouse is the most comprehensive account I've read of the language and lore of American middle-class children.

Of course the idea of childhood as a state of grace—in the psychological, not religious, sense—is a sacred liberal shibboleth of our time. From Paul Goodman's *Growing up Absurd,* through the radical educational theorists like John Holt, Ivan Illich, Edgar Friedenberg, *et al.,* we have been told that children possess a spontaneous creativity, a capacity for freedom of feeling and thought, that adult society inexorably stifles or deflects through such repressive institutions as school. It is the old Rousseauian idea of the natural child doomed by the harness of unnatural necessity. And Jeffrey Cartwright, that child of his time, knows all about the "obscenity of maturity." But Steven Millhauser knows something more—that the end of childhood is not necessarily a form of death, just as the violence of Mickey Mouse or Tom and Jerry cartoons doesn't really hurt. And parody is a higher form of comedy than slapstick. (p. 16)

Pearl K. Bell, "It's a Wise Child," in The New Leader (© 1972 by the American Labor Conference on International Affairs, Inc.), Vol. LV, No. 20, October 16, 1972, pp. 15-16.

J. D. O'HARA

Millhauser's first novel received wide critical attention and excellent reviews but few readers. (Although those readers tend to grapple him to their soul with hoops of steel.) If these facts mean anything, they probably mean not that Millhauser is a coterie writer but that he is less confusable with other writers. . . . We tend not to like new things; for this reason our first question about a novelty is likely to be "what's it like?" If it is like nothing we know, we shy away. In art this happens all the time. When we say that a first-rate writer must create his own audience, we mean little more than that he must bring out latent tastes in his audience since he has chosen not to appeal to those already developed. In *Edwin Mullhouse* and now in *Portrait of a Romantic* Millhauser deals with topics that Anglo-American life and art have worn down into clichés over the last two centuries: the child, growing up, school days, nature and nurture, the fall from innocence, sex, all that jazz. (p. 251)

But Millhauser has managed to put things differently; no wonder people backed off nervously. Although one reads *Edwin Mullhouse* with recurrent pops of amused recognition—that's it exactly! that's the way it was! I'd forgotten!—one also reads with a steadily deepening realization that Millhauser has much more on his mind than childhood games and games with childhood, and that his 13-year-old narrator Jeffrey has considerably more on his mind, and his conscience, than an affectionate biography of his late neighbor, good buddy, and budding writer Edwin. There are deep waters and dark passages, and curious discoveries about art, readers and human relationships. Like a movie about children from which children are banned by the movies' censorship code, *Edwin Mullhouse* is hardly a children's book, though definitely a book for former children.

Portrait of a Romantic carries many of the same topics into later and darker stages, though its relationship to the first novel is too complex to be stated briefly. Early on, [Leo] Tolstoy wrote a trilogy of novels, *Childhood, Boyhood* and *Youth.* Millhauser seems to have embarked upon a similar sequence, developing, with different characters, similar or related themes and settings and giving them a chronological basis. But there

the comparison ends; Millhauser's preoccupations are with the dark, disturbing and destructive forces of our growing up, and with the curious foreshadowings of maturity they reveal. If the Millhauser child is father of the man, [William] Wordsworth would be appalled.

There is no artist like Edwin in *Portrait,* and no work like Edwin's novel *Cartoons.* The artists of this novel, boys on their way into and through high school, are characteristic Romantics; they take themselves as their material and life as their *magnum opus* . . . and if that sounds pompous and overblown, think back to yourself as a teen-aged romantic; the tone is appropriate. (pp. 251-52)

As Millhauser brought unexpected significant issues into the bright Connecticut childhoods of *Edwin Mullhouse,* so into this one ("I was born in the shady corner of a sunny Connecticut town," Arthur says) he introduces love and death, with proper childhood comedy (the sex scenes are among the funniest ever written, surely) but also with traditional overblown romanticism. . . . All the adolescent withdrawals from life and affirmation, from hostile delinquents up against scrawled walls through the boredom and weariness and languor and indifference of exasperating adolescence, are reported, photographed and evoked here; but once again Millhauser refuses simply to *remind* us. Interlarded with the dull summers, classrooms and Ping-Pong games are grimmer matters, from the sick comedy of a preference for sickness over health . . . as far as the psychological sickness and even horror of blood-brother pacts, Russian roulette, suicide clubs, and violent death . . . to name only them.

The whole comic and frightening story is reported in Arthur Grumm's self-indulgent hothouse prose, but it is shaped also by Millhauser's cool artistic intelligence, recurrently reminding the reader to keep a safe distance. . . .

[Millhauser does not intrude] upon us with the tempting sincerity of a tastelessly direct statement . . . , [nor does he] insert résumés of [his] own philosophical and moral positions. . . . Millhauser lets Arthur tell his own artful tale, but [stays] the hell out of it, as [he] should, letting [his] selection and arrangement of characters and incidents speak for [him. Millhauser speaks] eloquently and memorably. (p. 252)

J. D. O'Hara, "Two Mandarin Stylists," in The Nation (copyright 1977 The Nation magazine, The Nation Associates, Inc.), Vol. 225, No. 8, September 17, 1977, pp. 250-52.*

SHELDON FRANK

There is something very disconcerting and peculiar about Steven Millhauser's fiction. It is written with the discipline of a man far beyond his thirty-four years. Millhauser is a novelist of decided yet disquieting talent, a prisoner of his own acute intelligence and self-consciousness. A young man who knows too much, Millhauser has to learn to relax when he writes. . . .

[*Edwin Mullhouse: The Life and Death of an American Writer, 1943-1954, by Jeffrey Cartwright*] was a debut of striking inventiveness written in dazzling visual prose, yet marred by a coy and self-congratulatory cleverness and an almost spooky self-control. His new novel, *Portrait of a Romantic,* picks up where *Mullhouse* left off and traces the adolescence of the romantic Arthur Grumm—an adolescence dense with elaborate daydreams and night dreams that fill pages of the book. As he did in his first novel, Millhauser pays acute attention to physical and psychological details and maintains the same disturbing distance and detachment.

Millhauser is blessed with spectacular descriptive gifts. He can capture in a sentence or two the smell of a summer day or the feel of a dusty old volume. Yet he also overwrites with a vengeance. If he writes something well once, he will write it twice, or three times, or maybe four; never is a noun permitted to wander unaccompanied by an adjective or a flood of adjectives. Both of his novels are stretched out beyond necessity, bloated with Millhauserian prose.

Portrait of a Romantic is a sad, witty, accurate chronicle of growing up strange and dreamy, but far too often it reads like the work of a man who spent so much of his youth in a library that his knowledge could not be brought to life by experience. Steven Millhauser has an enviable talent, but up to now he has only created two extremely impressive sarcophagi.

Sheldon Frank, "Books in Brief: 'Portrait of a Romantic'," in Saturday Review *(copyright © 1977 by Saturday Review; all rights reserved; reprinted by permission), Vol. 5, No. 1, October 1, 1977, p. 28.*

GEORGE STADE

Steven Millhauser's first novel, **"Edwin Mullhouse: The Life and Death of an American Writer, 1943-1954, by Jeffrey Cartwright,"** is probably the best Nabokovian novel not written by the master himself. . . . As it turns out, the back-and-forths through which the biographer invents his author and the author his biographer stir the mind and agitate the emotions as unexpectedly as do the ins and outs through which nature and art invent each other in Nabokov—through which, for example, the critic Kinbote and the poet John Shade invent each other in "Pale Fire." Millhauser's demonstration that the preadolescent imagination is a lost genius within us all provides the Nabokovian note of pathos. That the author's name is so close to his character's (Millhauser/Mullhouse) adds reflections for us to reflect upon. (p. 13)

"A work of fiction is a radical act of the imagination whose sole purpose is to supplant the world," says Arthur Grumm, the hero of ["**Portrait of a Romantic**"]; but he is a romantic. Millhauser's second novel, which reflects on his first, is in the form of an account by the 29-year-old Grumm of events that take place mostly during his 12th to 15th years, when genius lapses into adolescence, when myth succumbs to romantic agony. The mere thought of his childhood years bores Grumm. . . . What he seeks is "not the crude pleasure of sense but the subtle pleasure of transgression." His unsuccessful attempt to commit suicide and his successful attempt to put a finger into the fan are more like premonitions of what is to come.

What is to come, during four winters, is a deeper and deeper submersion into the alluring dangers of the romantic subreal. The first and last of these winters and the summertime recoveries of actuality in between are spent by Arthur Grumm with his "double," a wonderfully real boy named William Mainwaring. . . . He is one of the best realized boys in American literature since Huck Finn, whom in some respects he resembles. Realist Mainwaring, Grumm's quotidian parents, his commonplace aunt and uncle, his conventional cousin, the banal summer excursions they take together are all made uncommonly vivid and sympathetic by Millhauser, who finds poetry where his adolescent hero gets bored. This family life is the ordinary against which the extraordinary measures itself.

The extraordinary is exemplified in part by Grumm's companion during the second winter, his "triple," Philip Schoolcraft, whose main expression is a mocking smile; who dismisses Mainwaring as a "scientist" and "philistine"; who lives in a crumbling and gloomy old house with his dotty mother; who lies on the bed in his garret, smoking, staring at the ceiling, listening to a record of "Afternoon of a Faun," memorizing Poe, playing Russian roulette. It is he who reveals to Grumm the secret kinship between fiction and suicide. . . . The two boys solemnly seal a suicide pact with drops of blood.

During the next winter Arthur Grumm seals another suicide pact with the pale, doleful enchantress, the "Lady" Eleanor Schumann, age 13, who may be taken as the objectification of his Gothic longings. . . . What goes on between her and Arthur Grumm in the murky closets and haunted alcoves of her chamber is a set piece of deadpan comedy, of obsession turning round and round on itself until what lurks inside comes out.

During the fourth winter, Arthur Grumm and William Mainwaring solemnly seal a third suicide pact with drops of blood, and the battle for Grumm's soul—between his double and his triple, between his good and bad angels, between the romantic and the realist within him—is fought out. I won't say what happens, but if what happens were reducible to a proposition, it might be one like this: Reality is the source of all value, but it is ticklish, you can only grip it with fictions—which, however, destroy it, along with life. Romanticism turns out to be not so much suicidal as murderous.

But to say that is to say practically nothing about this remarkable book, which says much more in a rapt march of particulars that pull you irresistibly after them into dangerous moods. If your experience is anything like mine, you will want to risk those moods twice. For one thing, the book is very good, and in ways that clearly require a second go-around. For another, its aftershock is terrific. And it goes on rumbling through the mind, knocking things over. You will want to know how you were set up for it.

Once you reread the book the particulars begin to look different. The foreshadowings become luminous with afterglow. What first seemed merely realistic—an abandoned sneaker in a brook, a Raggedy Ann doll hung out to dry—becomes symbolic. What seemed mere fantasy—Grumm's transformation into a mechanical doll, the endless corridors of Eleanor's playroom—become the workings of an iron psychological necessity. You come to see how you were set up by an elegant design and an exacting intelligence. You come to recognize romanticism as an age, an era, a condition, a propensity within all of us to murder reality. Millhauser makes you feel both the cost and the pleasure of yielding to it. (pp. 13, 30)

George Stade, "Reality Gripped by Fictions," in The New York Times Book Review *(© 1977 by The New York Times Company; reprinted by permission), October 2, 1977, pp. 13, 30.*

WILLIAM KENNEDY

William Faulkner argued that the problems of children were not worth writing about. He wrote frequently about children himself, but he treated their lives as windows on the adult world, or as early parallels to mature venality, obsession, or tragedy. Similarly, he placed high value on [J. D. Salinger's] *The Catcher In The Rye*, mainly because the odyssey of Holden

Caulfield was such an earnest and telling rebuke to contemporary morality. . . .

[*Portrait of a Romantic*] is a rebuke to Faulkner's view of youth as trivial, for Millhauser successfully excavates childhood to reveal its hidden wonders and dismal dangers. His children are not paradigms of their own later existence, for they do not grow up; nor are they mirrors of the grownup world, which exists in the novel only insofar as it illuminates childhood.

His children—three boys and two girls in continuing crisis from ages six to fourteen—are special creatures, all in frenzied swarm around the incandescent dangers of the forbidden. If the children represent anything outside themselves, it is as metaphor for conditions common to men, women and children of any age—mournful friendship, seductive decadence, the recurring tides of boredom, and an enduring flirtation with easeful death.

In his story, Millhauser presents himself as a kind of [Marcel] Proust of pubescence and adolescence. His book, written in immaculate prose, is a prodigious feat of memory, with an enormous density of felt and observed life. His narrator writes at one point of his desire to be an artist: ". . . if only I could create a world superior to this world, which would annihilate and replace it." This is part of the romantic strain in the narrator, and the romantic strain in Millhauser as well, who achieves what his narrator yearns for. He creates a world that is exquisite in its tortures and terrors, a world which only the heightened consciousness of an artist or a dreamer could inhabit.

The children of this story would never be found in television commercials, family comedies, or on Little League teams. They live their lives in a solitude so inviolable that even companionship becomes only another agent for heightening isolation. They are constant readers with acute insights into literature and life. . . .

The story is narrated in first person by Arthur Grumm, whose opening paragraph echoes both [Walt] Whitman and the [Saul] Bellow of *Augie March*. . . .

But Arthur leaves Whitman and Bellow swiftly behind and moves into a comic depiction of everybody's climactic moment in prepubescence—the show party. "One, two, three," says Arthur's cousin Marjorie, age six. Up goes her dress and down come her panties, nonplusing Arthur. He will, in time, strip to his underpants; but alas, he will not get far beyond that barrier. He and Marjorie will be caught in bed, she naked, pulling at Arthur's knee-length drawers, while Arthur, the reluctant, anguished lover, is romping with Eeyore, friend of Pooh.

This is the most overtly sexual moment in the novel. As the children grow older, sex becomes sublimated, and the flirtations are all with mystery, romantic kisses and the dangerous edge of life. What lurks beneath the friendships of the boys is unspoken. (A word only—"traitor"—is the accusation to Arthur when he abandons his friendship with a boy he calls his double, William Mainwaring, in order to pursue his obsession with a girl who is chronically ill.) With both his double and his triple, Philip Schoolcraft, Arthur seals the ties with potions of blood and wine: fingers pricked and the blood dripped into the glass. And with both boys Arthur plays the deadliest of games—Russian roulette—introduced to it by Philip, passing its pleasures along to William.

But it is Eleanor Schumann—the sickly girl whose absences from school, whose empty desk, whose dreamy indolence when she does come to class, wholly captivate Arthur—who brings the book to its high point. Millhauser's writing here changes and becomes complex with repetitions and confusions of the real, the imagined, the remembered. . . . [It] is magically evocative of the secret, uncertain world that children hope to create with make-believe.

But Millhauser is not always as magical as this. His novel is too long, too anxious to reconstitute every detail, however insignificant. . . . A little of this goes a long way, and so does his repetition. Coming atop his anatomizing of the states and stages of youthful boredom, it often flattens us in the same way [Michaelangelo] Antonioni's most boring films about boredom did years ago. And, too, some of Arthur's adolescent epiphanies are too familiar, or too unremarkable, to be saved even by Millhauser's linguistic felicities.

Nevertheless, his overall achievement is of a high order. The novel moves with relentless, if snailishly slow, logic toward a dreadful climax. And what we come away with is childhood without treacle, childhood mythicized, a poetically gothic history of living and dying in miniature.

> William Kennedy, "Childhood without Treacle," in Book World—The Washington Post (© 1977, The Washington Post), October 9, 1977, p. E5.

JOHN CALVIN BATCHELOR

In Millhauser's *Portrait Of A Romantic*, 29-year-old Arthur Grumm sits down to reminisce about his youth. The story thus has a limitation placed upon it that is as provocative as it is claustrophobic. We can only suppose what has become of the mature Arthur by imagining the potential of his vision of himself as a pubescent in suburban New York.

This is not as irksome as it might seem, however, if it is recalled that Millhauser's well-received first novel, *Edwin Mullhouse* (1972), pretended to be the biography of a precocious 11-year-old suicide who is remembered, years later, by a childhood chum. Millhauser seems to be writing the seven ages of man, or, perhaps more scientifically, the breastlike curve our lives follow. His first novel broke off with the melodramatic suicide of the pre-pubescent Edwin, who, for many reasons too lengthy for this discussion, acted out his fantasy life.

Now, Millhauser picks up his oeuvre-to-be with four difficult years—12 to 15—endured by the equally precocious Arthur Grumm. One critic has suggested Nabokovian overtones to Millhauser's art, but I think more of Salinger, and of his defense of Seymour's suicide in relation to the rest of the self-critical Glass family.

Arthur Grumm sees himself as a sickly, bookish, easily bored boy. He is an only child. He tells us early on that "by some accident the children in my neighborhood were older than I and so excluded me from their dusty games." This is not only a powerful clue to his introverted soul but also the chief premise of the novel. Arthur is a lonely boy, and so invents companions out of his learned psyche. Real people, like his vague, chummy father, his vaguer mother, and his voluptuous, open-faced cousin, Marjorie, do not interest him. They can even revolt him. After he and Marjorie are discovered as grade-schoolers exposing themselves to each other, Arthur rejects all family games, such as mother love, incest, and rebellion. He enters his mind's closet.

Millhauser writes this cleverly, with sometimes a suffocating amount of sights and sound. It could be taken merely as a portrait of a young wimp. But this is not the case. Arthur invents—complete with houses, parents, seats on the bus—the membership list of his secret childhood club.

The first, and most involved, is William Mainwaring, Arthur's "scientific" (positivist) double. Mainwaring is polite, respectful, list-bound, and correspondingly well liked. He is not wholly different from Arthur, and is best held as Arthur's sense of his good self. Their relationship blossoms—Arthur's parents delight in the Mainwaring manifestation—until the day Arthur, in eighth grade, encounters his triple, Philip Schoolcraft, said to have been expelled from a private school. Schoolcraft quickly asserts himself as Arthur's bad self.

It is Schoolcraft who fascinates. Yet, for reasons that can only have come from some personality quirk in the 29-year-old Grumm (Millhauser?), Schoolcraft is slighted here. He is brought on to introduce Arthur to the romance of suicide, as in Robert Louis Stevenson's "The Suicide Club." Schoolcraft reintroduces the theme of suicide-equals-fiction (both slay fact) that was arrested in *Edwin Mullhouse* by Edwin's passing. Schoolcraft is then dismissed as Arthur investigates his sexual awakenings with the invention of Eleanor Schumann, a Poe-like female so weak and cloying that her fate was a matter of indifference to me.

But Schoolcraft—ah, here is the heroic consciousness of Arthur Grumm. Schoolcraft smokes cigarettes, calls his mother "the old lady," listens to sentimental foreign songs, and owns a pistol. Schoolcraft is the rude madness in young males—the daredevil, the defamer, the conqueror, the cad. Millhauser resolves his novel along other lines—suicide again, of course—but I can only hope he continues his work with the truest romantic in his art, Philip Schoolcraft. (pp. 70-2)

John Calvin Batchelor, "Destiny of Champions" (reprinted by permission of The Village Voice *and the author; copyright © The Village Voice, Inc., 1978), in* The Village Voice, *Vol. XXIII, No. 10, March 6, 1978, pp. 70-3.**

WILLIAM BOYD

Portrait of a Romantic is about 30,000 words too long, and most of them are adjectives; massed battalions of them, lovingly marshalled in pages of relentlessly detailed description for what is, at a second glance, a disarmingly slight tale.

The romantic in question is the prosaically named Arthur Grumm and the novel concerns itself with the first year or so of his adolescence and his relationships with three friends in an anonymous American suburb some time—I would guess—in the 1950s. The friends slot themselves easily into prototypical roles. . . . Such narrative drive as there is laboriously works its way around to dangerous games of Russian roulette with a loaded pistol that finally put paid to the pragmatic William who has, by the end of the novel, fatally caught the romantic malaise that so virulently infects the others.

This romanticism is of the most lush and hackneyed sort. Millhauser regularly breaks into flights of purplish descriptive fancy and makes lavish use of clichés which one might have thought long gone. . . .

For a while one hopes that this might be some elaborate ironic ploy, a sustained parody of a genre, but that can not be admitted in the end. Millhauser's endless reiteration of lyrical, moody description effectively blankets the novel beneath a fog of sub-Keatsian excess. His characters are damagingly one-sided too, as if seen through the soft-focus gaze of some benign Victorian cleric. He seems to have forgotten that only one lens of the adolescent's visionary spectacles is rose-tinted; the other is shaded muddy brown, and is frequently flawed or cracked to the detriment of the world upon which it unflinchingly peers.

The darker side of adolescence, the paranoia, the guilt, the grime, the unswerving pursuit of taboo subjects, the spots and pimples and everything else produced by the inevitable hormone-shake are absent, making the portrayal of these years curiously inert. For Millhauser's children the most innocuous covert acts—brief glimpses of nude adults, tremulous pubertal exhibitionism—merit no real curiosity or illicit glee, only swoonings and hot flushes and pages of intense pulse-taking analysis.

American writing of the past fifty years has dominated the field of the fictional presentation of adolescence and has honourably established a tradition of acute and wry observation. One thinks particularly of [Ernest] Hemingway's Nick Adams, [F. Scott] Fitzgerald's Basil Duke Lee and of course of [J. D.] Salinger's Holden Caulfield. And although it is possible to perceive—with some effort—that Steven Millhauser has a real affection for his adolescents and sometimes writes knowingly and poignantly about them, Arthur Grumm, on this showing, is some distance away from joining that select band.

William Boyd, "Adolescent Agonies," in The Times Literary Supplement *(© Times Newspapers Ltd. (London) 1978; reproduced from* The Times Literary Supplement *by permission), No. 3982, July 28, 1978, p. 872.*

Monty Python

Graham Chapman (1941?-)—British comedian, scriptwriter, author, songwriter, and actor.

John Cleese (1939-)—British comedian, scriptwriter, and actor.

Terry Gilliam (1941?-)—American animator, comedian, actor, and director.

Eric Idle—British comedian, scriptwriter, songwriter, and actor.

Terry Jones (1942?-)—Welsh comedian, scriptwriter, songwriter, author, actor, and director.

Michael Palin (1943-)—British comedian, scriptwriter, songwriter, and director.

Collectively known as Monty Python and Monty Python's Flying Circus, the group attacks foolishness in contemporary behavior with the combination of literate, sophisticated satire and crude burlesques, gags, and slapstick that forms its popular brand of surrealism. Monty Python is unique among comedy groups, as they have gained a large, appreciative audience outside the United Kingdom for their very British brand of political and social satire. The group was influenced by the British comedy classic *The Goon Show*, a madcap postwar radio broadcast, and the satirical undergraduate revue *Beyond the Fringe*. Using such sketches and bits as "Hell's Grannies," "The Lumberjack Song," "The Ministry of Silly Walks," "The Dead Parrot," and "Upper Class Twit of the Year," the Pythons satirize the ridiculous postures of which we are all capable. Most critics feel that the combined sensibilities of the six men have produced a body of work that is admirable for its innovation, insight, and comic effectiveness.

A British comedy consultant formed the group in 1969 to fill a late night opening on BBC television. Cleese, Idle, and Chapman, all Cambridge University graduates, had been writing for David Frost's comedy show *The Frost Report*. Palin and Jones, both graduates of Oxford University, had worked with Idle on the British humor series *Do Not Adjust Your Set*. Terry Gilliam was enlisted to do the group's visuals and animation. The resultant series, *Monty Python's Flying Circus*, ran for four seasons on the Public Broadcasting System and developed a cult following both in Britain and the United States. Comprised of fast-moving, seemingly unconnected sketches with subjects ranging from pointed parodies of British culture and burlesques of everyday living to satires on some of the strongholds of Western civilization, the show was hailed by most critics as hilarious and inventive.

The group's first feature film, *And Now for Something Completely Different,* consists mostly of sketches from their albums and television shows; critics unfamiliar with the group's material reacted to it with disdain. Their next film, *Monty Python and the Holy Grail,* was successful both critically and commercially. A satirical attack on the Arthurian legend, the movie employs many of the comic devices that had been perfected on the television series. Although some critics find the humor sophomoric and distasteful, others believe the film witty and imaginative. The group's albums, which had initially been ignored, also began to achieve success. In 1979 the group released its controversial film *Life of Brian,* about a man who was continually mistaken for the Messiah because he was born in the manger next to Christ's. Many religious leaders were offended by the film; Idle explained, "We're laughing at *man,* not *God.*" Most criticism has praised the film as being perhaps the best work the group has done.

Since *Life of Brian,* Python members have continued to come together for occasional live performances and for *The Contractual Obligation Album,* but have worked mainly on individual projects. In spite of the favorable critical response many of these projects received, most critics feel that the Python members are most successful as a team.

BLAINE ALLEN

It is difficult, one must admit, to write anything clever after viewing a film which includes such episodes as "Hell's Grannies," "Joke Warfare," the brand-new television game show, "Herbert Anchovy Presents BLACKMAIL," and, inevitably, "The Upper Class Twit of the Year Race." These and other sketches are the substance of [*And Now For Something Completely Different,*] one of the most hilarious and original movies to come along in a while. (p. 22)

As far as the cinema world is concerned, *And Now For Something Completely Different* is. One cannot enter the theatre expecting any kind of narrative. In fact, one cannot expect any kind of sanity or human reason at all. . . .

[Even] for those who have seen the sketches before, the material is still fresh and as funny as ever. (p. 23)

> *Blaine Allen, "'And Now for Something Completely Different'," in* Take One *(copyright © 1972 by Unicorn Publishing Corp.), Vol. 3, No. 5, May-June, 1971, pp. 22-3.*

JOE MEDJUCK

If you liked Auschwitz you'll love *And Now For Something Completely Different.* Virtually every joke is based on killing, maiming, destruction or sexism. This film exploits women, homosexuals and anyone who pays to see it. It ends with a skit about the "upper class twit of the year." My nomination goes to Monty Python's Flying Circus.

> *Joe Medjuck, "'And Now for Something Completely Different': Associate Editor Joe Medjuck Gets in His Two Cents," in* Take One *(copyright © 1972 by Unicorn Publishing Corp.), Vol. 3, No. 5, May-June, 1971, p. 23.*

E. S. TURNER

Nobody likes to intrude into a private joke. Seven pages of [*Monty Python's Big Red Book*] (there are only 64) are taken up with letters and telegrams expressing the supposed reactions of BBC and ITV notables to a supposed foreword by Reginald Bosanquet, the ITV newscaster. It's a fair enough jest, and should convulse all whose names are mentioned, but is it worth so much of the admission money? There are further references to Bosanquet sprinkled about the book.

'What's behind it all?' the suspicious reader may wonder. 'Am I missing out somewhere? Is there something terribly funny about Bosanquet I never noticed—something that everyone else knows about?' Moodily, this wary reader begins to study some of the other jokes, which include a mock advertisement, asking: 'Why not be different this Christmas? Why not send your friends a lump of cold sick?'; a full-page study of a hand about to descend on what looks like the embryo of a two-legged elephant with a human thumb thrusting out above the tusks; a Silly Party candidate called Tarquin Fintimlinbinwhimbinlin Bus Stop F'Tang F'Tang Olé Biscuit-Barrel; and a poem printed upside down because it is about Australia.

Ho, ho, says the now resentful reader, so this is what Monty Python consists of, when you snatch it from the screen and transfix it on the page. He may even begin to wonder why there is such an apparent obsession with swollen pink flesh, not to mention vomit and excrement. And why are these trendy mirthmen falling back on such traditional devices as cod advertisements and cod answers-to-correspondents, the staple of joke factories elsewhere?

Of course, the reader is now becoming far too captious. It is time he allowed that there is freshness as well as frenzy in these pages, ingenious nonsense as well as silliness, and a reasonable measure of that scatty insouciance which the entertainment had on the screen (where brisk animation, legerdemain and rapid turnover prevented us dwelling on failed jokes). . . . Easily the best item [in the book] is 'The Piranha Brothers', a skit on one of those now-it-can-be-told programmes about a criminal gang. . . .

> *E. S. Turner, "Busty Substances" (© British Broadcasting Corp. 1971; reprinted by permission of E. S. Turner), in* The Listener, *Vol. 86, No. 2226, November 25, 1971, p. 730.*

MATTHEW COADY

Not all the Python funnies work [in *Monty Python's Big Red Book*]. In print one is more aware of a sagging jest than on a screen which, in the next instant, is manically alive with Terry Gilliam's animations. . . . [A] deal of the material is no more than a reworking of gags which the addicted viewer has already tasted. Even so, the *Big Red Book* embodies that consistently savage view of the universe which characterises the programme at its devastating best. It depicts a world in which the Haves are for ever on the make, the Have-nots are ceaselessly gulled and a comic randiness informs almost every action. The ageing are left with a suspicion that many of their cherished values are being mocked, while the young are reminded that by joining the Army they can not only climb mountains in Cyprus and play football in Germany, but can have a decent military burial as well. (pp. 794-95)

> *Matthew Coady, "Pro Bono Pubico," in* New Statesman *(© 1971 The Statesman & Nation Publishing Co. Ltd.), Vol. 82, No. 2124, December 3, 1971, pp. 794-95.*

HENRY EDWARDS

[The members of Monty Python's Flying Circus are] precocious adolescents. **"Another Monty Python Record"** offers up a dash of cannibalism and a moment in which Pablo Casals plays Bach while plunging hundreds of feet into a bucket of hot fat. It is all very civilized lunacy, however. For example, on *World Forum,* none other than Lenin, Marx, Ché Guevara, and Mao Tse-tung engage in the typical inane games-show competition. During this disc the listener is constantly being reminded that he is listening to a phonograph record, an unusual use of a typical Brechtian device. . . . For all their seeming cleverness though, Monty Python's Flying Circus members are just another bunch of aging college cut-ups, creating the kind of material that is just far out enough to make the unknowing feel truly sophisticated. (p. 77)

> Henry Edwards, "Black Comedies," in High Fidelity (copyright © by ABC Leisure Magazine, Inc.; all rights reserved; excerpted by permission), Vol. 23, No. 1, January, 1973, pp. 76-7.*

GREG SHAW

Monty Python are hugely funny [on **Monty Python's Previous Album**] if you can get past their strange accents, and concerns, which are mostly veddy British, which is unfortunate. Safe to say that they are better than just about all the current satirists, but whether that has anything to do with wanting to listen to them is an interesting, unending question.

> Greg Shaw, "Rock-a-Rama: 'Monty Python's Previous Album'," in Creem (© copyright 1973 by Creem Magazine, Inc.), Vol. 5, No. 1, June, 1973, p. 70.

SHERWOOD L. WEINGARTEN

[**Monty Python's Previous Record**] points up the difference in senses of humor between those on this side of the pond and those in Britain. It just isn't funny, by American standards, despite moments of high hilarity. The "comedy" disc . . . is of interest more to scholars of the genre than to listeners.

> Sherwood L. Weingarten, "Weingarten of the Record: 'Monty Python's Previous Record'," in Audio (© 1973, CBS Publications, The Consumer Publishing Division of CBS Inc.), Vol. 57, No. 8, August, 1973, p. 52.

RICHARD A. BLAKE

Monty Python's Flying Circus is a disease, one of those mad maladies propagated by public television, the same people who hooked audiences on Julia Child's personality by promising them an educational cooking show, *The French Chef.* In fact, the *Flying Circus* has less to do with the three rings of Barnum and Bailey fame than does a boarding-house bathtub.

The success of the *Flying Circus* is an anomaly. It is so terribly, terribly British that the political and social satire soars archly over the heads of an American audience. . . .

Yet, despite its incorrigible and mysterious Britishness, *Monty Python's Flying Circus* threatens to become an authentic hit. . . . Cleese and his collaborators have . . . captured a sense of the television medium itself. To revert to a mildly quaint McLuhanism, they have exploited the medium so completely that the Albion-bound message is really reduced to an insignificant

position of importance. Who cares if I don't understand the joke? They tell it so damnably well.

Like its linear ancestor on American television, *Laugh In,* the *Flying Circus* has mastered the principle of television timing. It uses the commercial as the measure of the longest possible attention span of its audience. . . . Like commercials, the units are quick and discrete, in the Aristotelean sense, but far from discreet in the Victorian. A viewer can tune in at any point in the program and not miss any background, an editor can jumble the parts and rearrange them in any sequence and nothing would be lost. (p. 348)

Part of the fascination is wondering what the point of all this nonsense is, and then wondering what has been missed when no point emerges. It is a voyage into the absurd on a Humean raft. Experience means nothing, since all laws of logical sequence have been suspended. Does, for example, a music-hall song about transvestite lumberjacks really mock transvestites, lumberjacks or the bleary-minded viewer trying to make sense out of this Mad Hatter world?

With such pogo-stick pacing, **Monty Python's Flying Circus** moves too quickly to offend, to shock, to provoke or even to enrage. It merely bewilders. In a world of television, American or British, when every creator of electronic schlock feels he must make a point, the fictional Monty Python has again reasserted the primacy of the pointless. Not a bad commentary on television itself. (p. 349)

> Richard A. Blake, "Python, Python, Burning Bright," in America (© America Press, 1975; all rights reserved), Vol. 132, No. 17, May 3, 1975, pp. 348-49.

PENELOPE GILLIATT

["**Monty Python and the Holy Grail**"] is a cheerfully loused-up reworking of the legend of King Arthur's Grail hunt. This is the legend that has been such a nuisance to children and others. . . . [Almost everything] that has ever worried you about the Holy Grail, wimples, King Arthur, Malory, and the general mucking about of poets with the same old story is tackled head on. (p. 115)

In this version of the Grail-tale, King Arthur's knights are extremely cowardly, dirty, testy, and ill-starred. . . . The King himself, who hesitantly presents himself as Arthur, King of the Britons, to everyone he meets, has remarkably little effect on the lowly for a man of such high estate. . . . He seems exceptionally underprivileged as well as mentally underendowed. Perhaps this is because he is such an early king. He hasn't even got a horse. . . . [Many of the best debates in the film are yelled]. Musical geniuses have begged for centuries that arias in opera should advance the action; the creators of Monty Python now beg that rows in drama should have an equivalent right to drag the action to a standstill, and quite possibly send it packing.

If the film can be said to have a theme, it has three. These are swallows, mud, and the Grail. Swallows keep recurring. So does mud, and all manner of other dirt. (pp. 115-16)

The whole film, which is often recklessly funny and sometimes a matter of comic genius, is a triumph of errancy and muddle. Its mind strays like an eye, and it thrives on following false trails. The Monty Python people have won a peculiar right to be funny even when they make a mess of things, because their style accepts floundering as a condition of life. (p. 117)

Penelope Gilliatt, "The Current Cinema: Light-Years Ahead of the Cuckoo Clock," in The New Yorker *(© 1975 by The New Yorker Magazine, Inc.), Vol. LI, No. 11, May 5, 1975, pp. 111-17.**

STANLEY KAUFFMANN

Monty Python and the Holy Grail . . . is neither as sparkling as it is said to be nor as bad as it seems to be at the start. But it's pretty good—thus, as British phenomena go these days, exceptional. . . .

The previous Python film, *And Now for Something Completely Different* . . . had the hijinks ebullience of university humor, than which jinks there is none higher, and was a series of skits that hit or missed. *Holy Grail* is a series of skits on one general theme, so is disguised as an organic story. It too has hits and misses. When it hits, it makes some clear statements of national humor. . . .

Leg-pull is the British term, and the pleasant glow of the leg-pull, rather than the yok or boff, is the aim of *Holy Grail*. What's up for teasing here is the whole body of Arthurian legend, and the basic leg-pull is of the sanctity of that legend and of British sanctimoniousness toward it. Part of the leg-pull is through period realism. (Arthur identifies himself to two bedraggled caitiffs, and after he passes, one grimy serf says to the other, "He *must* be a king. He hasn't got shit all over him.") Part of it is just the reverse: anachronism. (A peasant launches a political tirade at Arthur in modern lingo.) Part of it is by digression into *non sequitur*. (Arthur hails a sentry at a castle, and in 10 seconds the formal military exchange has gone off into a long irrelevant discussion.) Part depends on obvious lunacy. (All the knights "ride" by hopping around as children do on their own two feet, while attendants behind them clomp coconut shells to sound like horses' hoofs.) Part depends on contemporary recognitions. (Arthur's upper-class accent is markedly different from that of almost everyone he meets, and seems to underscore his incomprehension of everything around him.)

I, with inverted snobbism, tend to resist the snobbism of this kind of comedy, the sort of film that heavily implies, "You and I are cultivated, just a wee bit jaded, and will get these superior jokes." (In another culture it's the Marcel Marceau syndrome.) And *Holy Grail* gets off to a particularly lame start in this vein by using fake Swedish subtitles under the credits, a gag that was not fresh when it was used, in reverse, in *The Dove* several years ago. But soon the picture reaches the good leg-pull level, mostly sustained and just moves along in a comic temperament without much actual laughter. I laughed aloud only once. Some wretch is hanging by his wrists from a castle wall in chains. A group of knights below do an anachronistic song and dance. When they finish, the chained wretch manages, above his head, to applaud wanly. (p. 20)

Stanley Kauffmann, "Stanley Kauffmann on Films" (reprinted by permission of Brandt & Brandt Literary Agents, Inc.; copyright © 1975 by Stanley Kauffmann), in The New Republic, *Vol. 172, No. 21, May 24, 1975, pp. 20, 33.**

TIME

At least 2 million Americans are now aware of the Ministry of Silly Walks. College students are finding new meanings for the word stupid, and old ladies may even be getting ideas about beating up kids. What is this pernicious influence, bordering on a cult, that is now sweeping the U.S.? The word is Monty Python. Five roopy young Englishmen, who methodically take the world apart each week in a series of sketches mysteriously called *Monty Python's Flying Circus*. . . .

Whether or not Americans actually do understand the Pythons' uniquely English nonsense is moot. Their comedy is crowded with jokes about British TV announcers and politicians; their best sketches are intimate parodies of the idiocies of British life. Moreover, their style is the opposite of hard-hitting American humor. The Pythons can hardly summon a wisecrack among them. . . .

They have done their best to remove themselves from boring reality and construct something far more pleasurable.

"Killer Joke Triumphs," in Time *(reprinted by permission from* Time, The Weekly Newsmagazine; *copyright Time Inc. 1975), Vol. 105, No. 22, May 26, 1975, pp. 58-9.*

ED NAHA

The legend of King Arthur gets a well deserved swipe in what may be the comedy film of the decade or at least the week. . . . [*Monty Python and the Holy Grail* is] a smorgasboard of sight gags, puns, black humor and satire that reduces Camelot to a madhouse. . . . The comedy pace is faster than the Marx Brothers ever dreamed of and the humor is cerebral enough to make Woody Allen wince. If you enjoy laughing, drooling or sticking your thumb up your nose and making strange noises, you owe it to yourself to see this film as opposed to listening to it which would be a fairly silly move on your part.

Ed Naha, "Short Takes: 'Monty Python and the Holy Grail'," in Creem *(© copyright 1975 by Creem Magazine, Inc.), Vol. 7, No. 5, October, 1975, p. 63.*

JOEL VANCE

The humor [on **"Monty Python's Matching Tie and Handkerchief"**] is quick-fire, literate, demonic, and cheerfully laced with English sadism. . . . It's not possible to describe their routines in detail without spoiling them, but there are several choice ones here: the Church police investigating the death of a halibut; a discussion of medieval open-field farming supposedly sung by reggae star Jimmy Cliff and rocker Gary Glitter; an interview with a surgeon who's aroused controversy by "grafting a pederast onto an Anglican bishop"; and a particularly treasurable and lunatic sketch about a man in a record shop listening to something called "World War One Noises." There are some weak moments in the album, as there are in all Python outings, but the best of the material and performances here are better than my former favorite of their LP skits . . .: a concert by the Royal Philharmonic topped off with Pablo Casals taking a solo while jumping four hundred feet into a jar of hot fat. Noble Python, for this relief, many thanks.

Joel Vance, "Spoken Word: 'The Monty Python Matching Tie and Handkerchief'," in Stereo Review *(copyright © 1975 by Ziff-Davis Publishing Company), Vol. 35, No. 4, October, 1975, p. 92.*

ROGER HUGHES

"You have just wasted over £2" proclaims the inner sleeve [of *The Album of the Soundtrack of the Trailer of the Film "Monty Python and the Holy Grail"*] as it emerges from the tatty, sticky-taped outer cover, and there may be more than a hint of truth in that. First of all, let no-one be misled into believing that this is the soundtrack from *Monty Python and the Holy Grail*. Of course it's not. Did we really expect it to be? For the Python team it is the concept behind the medium in which they are working that becomes the challenge. As with television, so with records. It is the concept of soundtrack albums that is being sent up in this record. After all, we are regularly reminded, the film is mainly visual. . . . [There is a] warning on the sleeve that "this record can only be played once". And that may well sum it up. For the Holy Grail soundtrack does not stand up to the repeated playings that were such a joy with earlier Python albums.

> Roger Hughes, "Monty Python: 'The Album of the Soundtrack of the Trailer of the Film "Monty Python and the Holy Grail'," in Gramophone (© Gramophone—1975), Vol. 53, No. 630, November, 1975, p. 921.

JON TIVEN

There's no doubt in my mind that the Monty Python group is not only very funny, but that they're very accessible to U.S. audiences, despite many rumours to the contrary. . . .

The question is, can Python's attack, which is highly visual, be translated well enough onto the disc and back up into our mind's eye? Fortunately the answer is yes. [On *The Album of the Soundtrack of the Trailer of the Film of "Monty Python and the Holy Grail"* they've] taken the most rib-tickling bits of their movies, thrown in some conceptual jokes, running commentary, and assorted oddities . . . and packaged them all very cleverly. Python devotees will not be disappointed with this record. Be, however, forewarned that this album, like most spoken-word recordings, does not wear well with age—it's not an album you'll get more from in repeated listening. On the other hand, unlike most comedy records, this is good the first time you hear it.

> Jon Tiven, "The Column: 'The Album of the Soundtrack of the Etc.'," in Audio (© 1975, CBS Publications, The Consumer Publishing Division of CBS Inc.), Vol. 59, No. 12, December, 1975, p. 89.

GEORGE ARTHUR

Unlike the media recreations of [Lenny] Bruce, Monty Python doesn't care about being loveable. If Monty was, say, a traveler on a train, he would be someone to avoid. Python is as cheerfully mindless, cruel, vulgar and gross as any cross-sampling of midwest auto dealers. They create grotesqueries of monumental distastefulness (on [*Monty Python Matching Tie & Handkerchief*], an unlikely British mum skinning and deep-frying a dog while a media-modulated doctor's voice compares the human brain to a fish), but they make you laugh. They turn the most threadbare—and for Americans, obscure—of comic conventions (Australians as hard-drinking blockheads, actors as idiots) into some of their best routines.

The force that makes this kind of inanity work is their vision of a conventional world gone mad—a sophisticate's slapstick landscape, laughed at from a cynic's remove. Priceless routines which first surfaced on their two largely unnoticed . . . releases, *Another Monty Python Record* and *Monty Python's Previous Record*, developed visually in the television shows and recapitulated on *T&H*, offer an absurdist congruity to their work which enables the audience . . . to laugh at a world where all food is inedible, all daily activities are as mad as [Lewis] Carroll's exemplary Hatter, and nobody knows when to expect the Spanish Inquisition. . . .

Nearly everybody gets cuffed about on the album, but there's a nasty edge of class snobbery to a good deal of it. If it represents a chance taken . . . , it must be counted a failure of transcendence. . . . Snobbery knows no class lines, but the Oxford-Cambridge background of the Pythonians makes any kind of democratic raffishness a little strained. That great leveler, the tube, takes away a lot of potential sting, making it hard to say who the joke's on.

> George Arthur, "Another Monty Python Review," in Crawdaddy (copyright © 1975 by Crawdaddy Publishing Co., Inc.; all rights reserved; reprinted by permission), December, 1975, p. 70.

CLIVE BARNES

Pure, unadulterated madness has invaded the City Center 55th Street Theater. A bunch of lunatics calling themselves Monty Python have taken over the theater and are forcing unsuspecting people to laugh. Almost at gunpoint. They are vulgar, sophomoric, self-satisfied, literate, illiterate, charmless, crass, subtle, and absolutely terrific. They are the funniest thing ever to come out of a television box. . . .

How is one to describe Monty Python? A candid consensus of critics who might be called Charlie Cobra, could easily have written in the East Ham Gazette, describing them: "As coming from the streets of Bergamo—like the commedia dell'arte and pizza. Raw and earthy, they combine the wry savagery of Tom Lehrer and the poetic anarchy of 'Hel'zapoppin.' Were we to accept the Bergsonian concept of humor—which not for a moment we do—we would suggest that their depiction of the polarization and the alienation of modern man, the almost touching juxtaposition, as it were, of foot with banana skin, is a symbolic metaphor of an industrial society totally enraged. Monty Python truly is the snake in the Garden of modern Eden—a child of our time, a reptile of truly significant immediacy."

Devotees, aficionados, fans and other idiots, will recognize the provenance of many of the sketches that the Python people perpetrate—for they are lifted, screaming but intact, from the television shows, which for some time have made nonsense out of family hour viewing. From the rousing opening chorus of "There is nothing quite as wonderful as money" to the indescribably disgusting expletive at the end, apparently intended to clear the theater, the fun is moderately fast and downright furious. . . .

This anthology of Pythonomania seems intent on leaving nothing out. Here are the people declaiming **"How Sweet to Be an Idiot"** or that innovative television quiz game **"Blackmail."** . . .

In **"Blackmail,"** a hidden camera catches some innocent in some not-so-innocent activity, and the victim (or player as he is usually regarded) has to bargain with the master of ceremonies on the telephone to have the show stopped—the longer the film runs the higher the price the player has to pay. As a game show it has everything—suspense, money, greed. . . .

The humor is occasionally raunchy, but for sheer irreverence, impertinence and spaced-out zaniness there has been nothing to beat it since Genghis Khan.

> *Clive Barnes, "Stage: Screaming and Intact, 'Monty Python Live!'" in* The New York Times *(© 1976 by The New York Times Company; reprinted by permission), April 16, 1976, p. 11.*

THOMAS MEEHAN

[The Pythons] have a singular genius for making nonsensical fun of all who are pompous, pretentious, humorless, or boring, or who take themselves too seriously. In short, people like me. . . . Since having watched Monty Python's TV election returns, I haven't been able to watch American TV election returns . . . without having to suppress a slight case of the giggles. They do that to you, the Pythons—so hilariously lampoon something like TV election returns that the real thing forever after seems strangely ludicrous.

Unlike almost all other comedians these days, on TV or elsewhere, the Pythons are shamelessly willing to go in for absolute nonsense—to dress up in women's clothes, to talk in non sequiturs, and to be not only utterly silly but also often in outrageously bad taste. . . . "Undergraduate humor," scornfully say the Pythons' critics, but there is such off-the-wall originality and intelligence in most of what they do that it might better be called "overgraduate humor."

To watch a typical half-hour of Monty Python's Flying Circus is a bit like making a dizzying journey through a surreal fun house. Mixing filmed sketches that rarely last longer than a minute or two with bizarre pieces of animation, the program leaps wildly about in time and place. . . . Nothing is sacred to the Pythons, certainly not the church, the British Government, the Royal Family or even the wines of Australia, and there is something in their programs to offend virtually everyone. Also, with talk of bums, bottoms, private parts and a variety of bodily functions, often punctuated by what are euphemistically called rude noises, the Pythons are frequently almost schoolboyishly vulgar. Yet part of their infinite charm is that they're willing to try almost anything and to lampoon just about anyone.

To their further credit, the Pythons have neatly solved an artistic problem that has been plaguing the writers of comic sketches ever since the form was invented—i.e., how to find an ending to a sketch that will top it with a bigger laugh than all that has gone before. And their solution to the problem is simplicity itself—they don't end a sketch but instead stop it in midsentence whenever it appears to have worn out its comic welcome. (pp. 34-5)

A considerable number of the sketches are parodies of TV programs, especially of news, panel, interview and audience-participation shows. As an example there is **"Interesting People,"** on which an egregiously smarmy host . . . introduces such "interesting people" as Ali Kazan, "an Egyptian who is stark raving mad," Ken Duff, "the most interesting man in Dorking," whose hobby is shouting and a man who, by coughing directly into their faces, "can give influenza to cats." . . . In the best tradition of the Pythons, **"Interesting People"** is utter nonsense, and yet, like so many of their sketches, it is also a devastatingly accurate parody—in this case, of the sort

of TV audience-participation shows that have been putting bricks to sleep in Britain and the United States ever since television came along. (p. 35)

Why, I've been asked, do you think the Pythons are funny? Well, if comedy is surprise, the sudden intrusion of the incongruous and totally inappropriate, then the Pythons are unquestionably funny, for everything that they do and say is unexpected, incongruous and often outrageously inappropriate. Of course, I'd have to concede that they're not always funny—when one of the sketches is bad, in fact, it's godawful, although even at their worst they can never be accused of being trite or unoriginal. I realize, too, that there are people around who don't find anything in the least funny about the Pythons. But most of those who don't like the Pythons, I've observed, tend to be rather stuffy types—certified public accountants, corporation lawyers, Wall Street lawyers and others of the humorless sort. . . . In short, they are exactly the kind of pompous Americans whose British counterparts are made fun of by the Pythons, and who thus perhaps feel threatened by the Pythons. On the other hand, even someone with a fairly lively sense of humor has to have a high tolerance for nonsense in order to find the Pythons funny and maybe also has to be something of an Anglophile. For there is a tradition in England of nonsense—from Lewis Carroll to "The Goon Show" to Peter Cook and Dudley Moore—that pretty much doesn't exist in this country outside of the Marx Brothers' movies and the writings of Robert Benchley or, to a degree, S. J. Perelman and Woody Allen.

But now perhaps, [the American public] is at last ready to embrace nonsense. (p. 36)

> *Thomas Meehan, "And Now for Something Completely Different," in* The New York Times Magazine *(© 1976 by The New York Times Company; reprinted by permission), April 18, 1976, pp. 34-6.*

PETER REILLY

That motley crew, Monty Python's Flying Circus, is up to their squalid, sordid little tricks in another hilariously funny album [*Monty Python: Live! At City Center*]. . . . While some of the best lines are overlapped by audience laughter, there is enough classic Pythonomania intact to make it required listening. My all-time favorite is included: *The Death of Mary Queen of Scots,* a pseudo-BBC radio drama introduced by one of those appallingly jaunty, Britannic airs. . . . It opens with an inquiry as to whether the lady is indeed Mary, Queen of Scots, and, when the reply is in a heavily burred affirmative, the next minute or so is spent on the noisiest sound effects heard since World War II to indicate Mary's dispatch. After a brief silence one of her assaulters comments, "She must be dead." "Oh no, I'm not!" is her game retort, and the noises continue into fadeout. This is Episode Two of the serial, and to me represents the specially endearing looniness of the Python style: the mere thought of a supposed audience sitting down week after week in front of the "wireless" to hear Mary being pursued around her castle by what sounds like half of the English army, exchanging wise nods with each other as sound effect piles upon sound effect, is to me what makes Python as incisive about mocking the English character as anyone since [George Bernard] Shaw. (pp. 110-11)

> *Peter Reilly, "Recording of Special Merit: 'Monty Python: Live! At City Center'," in* Stereo Review

(copyright © 1976 by Ziff-Davis Publishing Company), Vol. 37, No. 4, October, 1976, pp. 110-11.

ARTHUR ASA BERGER

The Flying Circus's ''thing'' obviously is absurdity and whackyness: famous people are caricatured, clichés are ridiculed, and the madness of English society is mirrored in a mad show. But the problem with *Monty Python's Flying Circus* is that it is too studied and, at the same time, poorly done. . . .

What *The Flying Circus* fails to realize is that the *humor must do more than reflect the madness of a given society. That is the fallacy of imitative form. The function of the artist—and comic artists are included here—is to point out the madness and absurdity in a society by assuming some kind of a stance.* *The Circus* is full of crazies whose pose makes them forfeit all claim to seriousness. They do focus attention on some of the more absurd aspects of society, but they do not carry their criticism far enough. (p. 172)

The show [I saw] had no logic or structure to it, though it did have a certain amount of continuity. In fact, it was the element of continuity in the script that made me look for some kind of organization and for some kind of a satisfactory closure. The show, instead, seems to be open-ended, which is perfectly acceptable as long as the program makes no intimations of coherence. Probably the best word for *The Flying Circus* is *sophomoric.* It is a collection of gags, most rather banal, that don't add up to anything, and seems very much like the kind of thing students do in amateur theatricals in America, or camp counselors do when the staff has a variety show to put on. (p. 173)

Arthur Asa Berger, ''Humor on the 'Telly', or What Makes Englishmen Laugh?'' in his The TV-Guided American *(copyright © 1976 by Arthur Asa Berger; used with permission from the author), Walker and Company, 1976, pp. 164-75.**

JAMES STOURTON

Few books of films are as complete as that of *Monty Python and the Holy Grail* with the entire dialogue including corrections and crossings out and a bit of related material such as accountant's statements which show an almost antiquarian interest. Apart from a few moments of marvellous bathos I didn't think the film was successful, as the essence of Monty Python is the very imaginative editing of skits and cartoons which really are ''completely different''. I doubt if many, except the most avid Monty Python fans, will want to plod through this very thick, type-written book. (pp. 674-75)

James Stourton, ''The Good Loo Books,'' in Punch *(© 1977 by Punch Publications Ltd.; may not be reprinted without permission), Vol. 273, October 12, 1977, pp. 674-75.**

BARRY TOOK

As you would expect from the Python team [*Monty Python's Life Of Brian* is] as dangerous as a sweating stick of nitroglycerine in the hands of a man suffering from palsy. . . .

You'll have to take my word that nowhere does the film denigrate Jesus nor, if my memory serves me, is He depicted or even mentioned. . . .

True religion, being un-mockable, is not mocked, but bogus, catchpenny and lunatic fringe religion *is,* and who would have it otherwise? That said, I will be very surprised if every religious bigot in the world doesn't use *Monty Python's Life Of Brian* as an excuse for airing their neuroses. Not that the film is all that concerned with religion. Like the sets which are a marvellous mixture of ancient Tunisian and modern lathe and plaster, the story is an ingenious blend of the 2000-year-old and now. Not that there are any anachronisms—no jokes about ''What's the time?'' ''X past IV''—but the past seen in terms of the present.

A puzzled and anxious proletariat, incompetent rulers, ineffective revolutionary committees, property developers, snobbism and bigotry, a mass of minorities jockeying for their own petty advantage. In short, civilisation as we know it today. The same chaos of irreconcilable views, wilful misunderstanding and downright stupidity we know all too well in 1978, there then, as it must have been (all right *might* have been) in AD minus 1.

All this and funny too. All in all a film to be cherished, the more so as the Monty Python team come together only rarely these days. . . . The delightful prospect of seeing them all together again is sharpened by the fact that they've also matured. *Monty Python's Life Of Brian* is a sharp, astringent reminder of what the talented sextet gave us on TV in the early Seventies, except that it's bigger and, I should guess, better.

Barry Took, ''Python Preview,'' in Punch *(© 1978 by Punch Publications Ltd.; all rights reserved; may not be reprinted without permission), Vol. 275, November 29, 1978, p. 970.*

RICHARD SCHICKEL

[*Monty Python's Life of Brian*] is a send-up biblical epic recounting the biography of a chap born in the manger down the alley from the one people sing about each Christmas. Brian . . . is just a regular guy. . . . He does his best to mind his business peaceably (his only message to would-be followers is a perfectly sensible ''You'll have to work things out for yourselves''), but ends up being crucified anyway. To make matters worse, one of his fellow sufferers on Golgotha is one of those awful people who grow only more cheerful as the situation becomes grimmer. He insists on leading the condemned in choruses of a Broadway-style tune, *The Bright Side of Life,* as they hang from their crosses.

This is an excellent example of the movie's contempt for both taste and religion. *Life of Brian* is even now being protested by spokesmen for various pious groups. They are quite right to do so, for this is no gentle spoof, no good-natured satire of cherished beliefs. The Pythons' assault on religion is as intense as their attack on romantic chivalry in *Monty Python and the Holy Grail.* . . . They are funny lads, but detest all formal systems of belief, all institutions,: the political left and right, popular culture, motherhood, womanhood, homosexuality, conformity and nonconformity.

The movie is occasionally undone by the Pythons' resistance to comic coherence. But such is the group's inventiveness and cheek that the audience is always confident, even when things are running a bit thin, that good stuff will be along shortly. Adolescents are flocking to *Brian,* as if it were another *Animal House.* But it is a richer, funnier, more daring film—too good to be left solely to the kids. Maybe all the earnest protests will attract those who need it most: adults who have not had their basic premises offended, and therefore have not examined them, in too long.

> Richard Schickel, "Bright Side: 'Monty Python's Life of Brian'," in Time (reprinted by permission from Time, The Weekly Newsmagazine; copyright Time Inc. 1979), Vol. 114, No. 12, September 17, 1979, p. 101.

THE NEW YORK TIMES BOOK REVIEW

Most books published as tie-ins to newly-released movies are unnecessary things, worth only a quick flip through after an evening at the cinema. A notable exception is a two-sided, double-named large format paperback [the latest from the Monty Python group]. Open it from one side and it's **"Monty Python's The Life of Brian,"** the profusely illustrated shooting script of [the] film. . . . Turn the book upside down and around and it becomes **"Montypythonscrapbook,"** a hodgepodge of photographs, diary entries, letters, cartoon strips, half-developed ideas and trash accumulated by the six men who call themselves "Monty Python" during the years the film was being created. Study it, if you like, as an execrable example of what currently passes as humor or read it for a good laugh in the spirit of the late 1970's. In either case, the book has a raison d'être of its own.

> "Schizophrenic," in The New York Times Book Review (© 1979 by The New York Times Company; reprinted by permission), September 30, 1979, p. 43.

WILLIAM F. BUCKLEY, JR.

[Monty Python's TV episodes are] most easily described as a National Lampoon romp through history. The rule, in this sort of thing, is that nothing, nobody, should be taken seriously. Much humor is based on simple iconoclasm. . . . Which crawls over at the morbid end of the spectrum to gallows humor. . . .

It is inevitable that performers will cross the line. It is inevitable that people will tell jokes about the suffering of others, or jokes that make fun of whole races or religions. It is not inevitable that mature critics will encourage that sort of thing.

The Monty Python people now come out with a movie [*Life of Brian*] in which the life of Christ is burlesqued. When Christ said that the meek would inherit the earth, the Monty Python people got this as "the Greek" shall inherit the earth, because they couldn't hear the words exactly. Blessed are the peacemakers is heard by Monty Python at the edge of the crowd as blessed are the cheesemakers. Easy stuff for a professional scriptwriter trained in inversion. . . .

But Monty Python will not be stopped until he reaches Golgotha and is crucified. This scene becomes a great comic orgy. . . .

Mr. Richard Schickel, the principal movie reviewer for *Time* magazine, has the strangest comments of the season on this grotesquerie [see excerpt above]. "Adolescents are flocking to [Monty Python] as if it were another *Animal House*. But it is a richer, funnier, more daring film—too good to be left solely to the kids. Maybe all the earnest protests"—Mr. Schickel is referring to the Catholics, Protestants, and Jews who have issued a solemn denunciation of this venture in blasphemy— "will attract those who need it most: adults who have not had

their basic premises offended, and therefore have not examined them, in too long." . . .

We are told that all our basic premises need occasionally to be "offended." Well, one of our basic premises is that people ought not to be persecuted on account of their race or religion. Is Mr. Schickel saying that we should have an occasional holocaust? Or is he saying that if we go for a stretch of time without a holocaust, at least we ought to engage the Monty Python players to do a comedy based on Auschwitz? With the characters marching into the gas chamber dancing, say the mamba? Led by Anne Frank?

A basic premise of our society is tenderness toward, for instance, aging parents. We are enjoined by Mr. Schickel, if we read him right, to toss them out into the street from time to time; or if that is not feasible, either because we lack the courage or are lazy about it, Monty Python might do a comedy based on the frailties of the elderly. . . .

The First Commandment, which enjoins us not to take in vain the name of the Lord, is unrelated to a carefree expletive when you stub your toe, or lose money in the stock market, or lose three straight sets at tennis. It is commandingly august as an injunction against an inversion of those few qualities that distinguish us from the beasts, and there is no period, not even the *Fasching* in Munich or the Carnival in Rio, or Monty Python, when we are relieved of the obligation to experience sorrow at man's inhumanity to man, let alone man's inhumanity to God.

> William F. Buckley, Jr., "Didja Hear the One About . . .," in National Review (© National Review, Inc., 1979; 150 East 35th St., New York, NY 10016), Vol. XXXI, No. 43, October 26, 1979, p. 1387.

LAWRENCE CHRISTON

The Monty Python octet, rooted in British university and music hall humor, likes to go after some of the fundamental ideas and institutions of Western civilization, beginning with Christianity and taking circuitous Lewis Carroll routes through politics and schizoid social behavior in which taut propriety masks an underlying lunacy.

The Python group is welcome here because it has a perspective that is generally denied American comedians, who tend to operate out of a sense of individual helplessness. With Monty Python we see the healthy comic alternative that has offshoots in Edward Lear and Gilbert and Sullivan and is part of a tradition of wit and literacy that prizes its critical remove while seeing its social object clearly. . . .

Lenny Bruce once noted how it was the familiar that was as heartwarming to people as any sense of complicity between comic and audience. But for the uninitiated, this Python concert [at the Hollywood Bowl] seems precious and ingrown. A number of their situations have glorious beginnings, but don't develop. To have Karl Marx, Che Guevara and Mao Tse-tung on a quiz panel in which the winner gets a living-room set is a cunning idea—the real test of revolutionary idealism isn't theory but comfort. . . .

[The show gives us the] sense of a group in a bind, richly talented personnel who have been rewarded so well by sporadic effort that they feel no incentive to work up sustained, suitable forms for their comic impulses. Perhaps they're coasting and giving their audience some familiar licks before moving on to something else. Perhaps not. The adulation is there just the same. In the world of entertainment it isn't only power that corrupts.

Lawrence Christon, ''Monty Python Octet at Hollywood Bowl'' (copyright, 1980, Lawrence Christon; reprinted by permission of the author), in Los Angeles Times, *September 29, 1980.*

STEVE SIMELS

The Pythons . . . have come up with a new album, [**"Monty Python's Contractual Obligation Album"**, which is] every bit as tasteless and funny as its predecessors. The emphasis this time is on songs, and a couple here are absolute classics, especially a 19-second John Denver parody and a rousing, Nelson Eddy-ish Mountie number that expresses the sublime sentiment *Sit on My Face*. But a couple of the nonmusical skits are pretty snappy too. *Rock Notes* does to the gossip column of *Rolling Stone* what should have been done years ago, and *Book Shop* rivals the Pythons' famous dead-parrot routine for sustained lunacy. By way of a finale, there's a children's choir singing the inspirational hymn *All Things Dull and Ugly,* which should be required listening for all card-carrying members of the Moral Majority. So, come to think of it, should the entire album. This is wonderfully sick stuff, and I heartily recommend it. (pp. 96-7)

Steve Simels, ''Recording of Special Merit: 'Monty Python's Contractual Obligation Album','' in Stereo Review *(copyright © 1981 by Ziff-Davis Publishing Company), Vol. 46, No. 1, January, 1981, pp. 96-7.*

Van Morrison

1945-

Irish songwriter, singer, and musician.

Morrison's best lyrics take emotion as their subject. His most compelling visions are mystical and unusually poetic. There is an authenticity to Morrison's images and projections that can only be attributed to his having deeply experienced the emotions they describe. Although many critics have found his lyrics at times strained and ambiguous, most believe that they convey true feeling. Morrison's statement, "you don't create, you go into," is the basis for his songwriting, and this ability accounts for Morrison's acclaim.

Morrison began singing when he was twelve and by the age of thirteen was learning to play guitar, saxophone, and harmonica. At sixteen he dropped out of high school to tour Europe with a rock group called the Monarchs. At nineteen he returned to his native Belfast and formed the band Them. With Morrison as lead singer, the group developed a strong following. Them had several hit singles in England, and Morrison's own "Gloria" was a commercial success in the United States in 1965 and 1966. Although Them disbanded in 1967, Morrison's "Brown-Eyed Girl" was successfully introduced in the same year. In 1968 Morrision signed a contract with Warner Brothers and moved to the United States.

His first album for that company, *Astral Weeks*, was a radical departure lyrically and stylistically from the work Morrison had done with Them. A moving document of one man's spiritual anguish, *Astral Weeks* introduced the kind of "mystic visions" Morrison has pursued on many of his subsequent albums. *Astral Weeks* was a tremendous critical success and resulted in a cult following for Morrison. His next album, the lyrical and intense *Moondance*, was successful commercially and critically, as was the later *His Band and Street Choir*. *Tupelo Honey* outsold all previous albums and seemed to climax favorable critical opinion of Morrison's work. This album presents a note of optimism and hopefulness sometimes evident but never dominant in his earlier work. It also reveals an emotionally confident Morrison, a man who has recognized redeeming graces in his love for a woman and in human relationships generally. Following the release of *Hard Nose the Highway*, *It's Too Late to Stop Now*, and the controversial *Veedon Fleece* in 1974, Morrison disappeared from public view until the release of *A Period of Transition* in 1977. Although many critics loyal to Morrison felt that the album was significant in its indications of things to come, others dismissed it as a groping after the lost beauty of *Astral Weeks* and the earlier albums. The albums that followed, *Wavelength, Into the Music*, and *Common One*, were generally well received, although few critics seemed to feel that Morrison was writing with the grace and power he had once exhibited.

It is often acknowledged that Morrison's best work strips down and examines the most painful human emotions. Thus the serenity of his later work is felt to have somewhat diluted the impact of his lyrics. Morrison remains, however, an acclaimed and respected artist for the introspective nature of his lyrics and his independence from popular trends.

HAPPY TRAUM

Van Morrison is one of the most important singer song-writers working today. His songs and vocal style are intense, dramatic, and written with rare depth and perception. [*Astral Weeks*] could never be classified as "easy listening." In fact, to get into it takes much more hard work than most records, but it will be well worth the effort. The songs are long and introspective, and it takes time to sort the words out from his thick Belfast accent—but when you do you will hear stunningly poetic lines and songs about things people don't usually write about. His voice, intense and emotion-charged, is powerful and chilling—as in **"Madame George,"** the story of an aging "queen," playing dominoes in drag, running from the cops, the "one and only Madame George." . . . Van Morrison is original, unusual and an important voice—listen to him.

Happy Traum, "Record Reviews: 'Astral Weeks'," in Sing Out! (© 1970 Sing Out! Magazine, Inc.; 505-8th Ave., NY, NY 10018; excerpted with permission), Vol. 19, No. 5, March-April, 1970, p. 46.

JON LANDAU

Van Morrison's road has been rocky, and it has not left him unscarred, but it is now obvious that he has not only made it through his personal bad times, but that he has come upon a period of great personal creativity. Beginning with *Astral Weeks,* he has released three albums of extraordinary quality in the last two years.

Moondance is, in my mind, one of the great albums of 1970. In it Van presented his fully developed musical style. . . . The lyrics were simple, personal and intense. . . .

If *Moondance* had a flaw it was in its perfection. Sometimes things fell into place so perfectly I wished there was more room to breathe. Every song was a polished gem, and yet too much brilliance at the same time and in the same place can be blinding. The album would have benefitted by some changes in mood and pace along the way. One or two light and playful cuts would have done the job.

On *His Band and the Street Choir* he seems to have realized that and has tried for a freer, more relaxed sound. Knowing he could not come up with another ten songs as perfectly honed as those on *Moondance,* he has chosen to show another side of what goes on around his house.

"Give Me A Kiss," "Blue Money," "Sweet Jannie," and **"Call Me Up In Dreamland"** are all examples of Van's new rollicking, good-timey style. . . .

As **"Domino"** opens the album with a show of strength, **"Street Choir"** closes it with a burst of both musical and poetic energy which is not only better than anything else on the album but may well be one of Van's two or three finest songs. . . . Van's lyrics take over to complete the album's statement. . . .

His Band and the Street Choir is a free album. It . . . was obviously intended to show the other side of *Moondance.* And if it has a flaw it is that, like *Moondance,* it is too much what it set out to be. A few more numbers with a gravity of **"Street Choir"** would have made this album as close to perfect as anyone could have stood.

But notwithstanding its limitations, *His Band and the Street Choir* is another beautiful phase in the continuing development of one of the few originals left in rock. In his own mysterious way, Van Morrison continues to shake his head, strum his guitar and to sing his songs. He knows it's too late to stop now and he quit trying to a long, long time ago. Meanwhile, the song he is singing keeps getting better and better.

Van Morrison: Rock on.

> *Jon Landau, "Van Morrison," in* Rolling Stone *(by Straight Arrow Publishers, Inc. © 1971; all rights reserved; reprinted by permission), Issue 75, February 4, 1971, p. 54.*

RICHARD WILLIAMS

Thank heavens. I was beginning to wonder after **"His Band And The Street Choir,"** whether perhaps Van's mercurial talent was on the wane.

Although that album improved a lot with repeated playings, it still sounds perhaps a little too comfortable, with more inconsequential throw-aways than any other Morrison album.

"Tupelo Honey" sweeps away all fears because, although it doesn't represent a return to the anguish of **"Astral Weeks"** or the sensual tautness of **"Moondance,"** it consolidates **"Street Choir's"** sense of happiness, and makes something worthwhile of it. Whereas with **"Street Choir"** he was simply saying,

"I'm here, and I'm happy," now he's telling us why he's at peace, and what makes him feel good. . . .

"Old, Old Woodstock," for instance, is a masterful song of rest and tranquility, on the same theme as [Bob] Dylan's "Time Passes Slowly," and its air of total self-conscious contentment aptly characterizes a very powerful album. Van Morrison can rock a bit, you know.

> *Richard Williams, "Follow the Van," in* Melody Maker *(© IPC Business Press Ltd.), November 20, 1971, p. 10.*

JON LANDAU

[*Tupelo Honey*], like all of Van Morrison's albums, is both a synthesis of what has preceded it and a statement of something new. It has the musical compactness of *Moondance* and some of the spirited looseness of *Van Morrison His Band and The Street Choir.* It is also the best sounding recording he has done so far. . . .

Thematically, Van's songs of dedication and devotion to women are elevated and transformed into an opus. *Tupelo Honey* is Morrison's "domestic" album and as surely as his earlier work often expressed frustration and despair over his mistreatment by others, *Tupelo Honey* revels in the happiness and appreciation he feels towards those people who now give him love and strength. It differs from other thematically related albums in its absence of any sense of complacency, smugness, or condescension to those who do not feel the same way. And, conversely, it is dominated by an air of intensity that tells us Van feels his current needs with no less passion than he felt past ones, even as the texture of the album sometimes passes into a bubbly lightness, uniquely reflecting Van's very personal sense of joy.

On the first few plays, *Tupelo Honey* might strike the casual listener as merely a superior collection of pop tunes but every repeated play reveals its deeper level of meaning. For nine songs Van consistently and consciously develops the theme of "starting a new life" through the growth of his own strength and confidence. . . . The cuts on the album are then arranged and structured like cuts in a movie: moods are built, lessened, and rebuilt until the album reaches an almost inexorable climax in **"Moonshine Whiskey."** . . .

Van's humor often takes a concrete form on this album as he makes two good natured references to Dylan's *New Morning* during **"Moonshine Whiskey."** . . .

"Wild, Wild Night," is a statement of the past, a song done almost from memory, encompassing the style and form of some of Van's earliest music. It is a remembrance of a different kind of need and the ultimate loneliness that always followed from it. . . .

"Straight to Your Heart" transmutes the expression of generalized need for excitement and fulfillment on **"Wild, Wild Night"** into an expression of desire for a single person. By the time we get to **"Woodstock"** he is no longer flying down an endless street but being "blown by a cool night's breeze" down a country road towards a home and a family waiting for him. Thus in the space of three songs, Van has moved from a statement of almost desperate isolation to one of need and acceptance of personal stability.

"Starting a New Life," seen in this context, is both the simplest and lyrically the most significant cut on the album as Van spells out with perfect clarity the statement of *Tupelo Honey:* it expresses his need to take stock of himself, to see how far he has come, to record the support of those who have helped him get there, and together with them to "start a new life." It is fitting that **"You're My Woman"** is literally about starting a new life. The song is about woman giving birth to child. In it Van not only expresses his love for the woman but his happiness over his newly found place in the order of things. . . . Not only does he accept his own need for love but he accepts the need of others for his. Only when he is sure of the mutuality of the need, which is externalized through the birth of the child, can he say "that it's really real." Having said that, he can take the song home with the line "You're my woman" and we can share it with him because only after hearing the whole body of the song do we know the full implications of the line. And the song ends once again with the affirmation that "it's really, really real."

"Tupelo Honey" is Van, now hitting his stride, certain, confident, and protective of his feelings. It is a song of pure devotion, a song of dedication, and through its incredible repetitions of the chorus, a song of rededication. **"I Wanna Roo You"** is a playful courting song, as old-fashioned in mood as it is lyrically. **"Want You to Be Around"** (". . . to keep my both feet on the ground") continues in the same vein with a pure good-timey song of mutual need and desire.

The album culminates in a song of celebration which is the reversal of **"Wild, Wild Night."** For while the opening cut is a sort of last tribute to the life of the loner "looking for a love," **"Moonshine Whiskey"** is a joyful statement about the existence and continuation of love and the stability it offers.

Thus the album's themes revolve around Van's conflicting statements of needs, resolved in the end only by the stability he has achieved through relationships and the strength it gives him to renew himself in every way. If the development of this vision is related to us in sequence, with the songs providing the lyrical jumps and changes in mood, the music paints a broader picture and ultimately provides us with the context. It never merely enhances the meaning, it always defines it. (p. 56)

Tupelo Honey is in one sense but another example of the artist making increased use of the album as the unit of communication as opposed to merely the song or the cut. Everything on it is perfectly integrated. . . . While the best cuts on the album, **"Wild, Wild Night," "Old, Old Woodstock," "You're My Woman," "Tupelo Honey,"** and **"Moonshine Whiskey"** are clearly a cut above the others in their conception, the performance and devotion to the craft are evident on every cut on the album. For *Tupelo Honey* is not only an album of beautiful themes, dazzling musical motifs, and exquisite performances. It is an album that was conceived and delivered by a very proud man. A man proud enough and happy enough ". . . to put on his hot pants and promenade down Funky Broadway until the cows come home . . ."

The next time he does I would be proud to be promenading right next to him. (pp. 56-7)

Jon Landau, "Van Morrison: Promenading Down Funky Broadway," in Rolling Stone (by Straight Arrow Publishers, Inc. © 1971; all rights reserved; reprinted by permission), Issue 96, November 25, 1971, pp. 56-7.

DEBORAH LANDAU

Finally we have Van Morrison's long-awaited LP [*Tupelo Honey*]. Weeks before the album was available, the two singles, *Tupelo Honey* and *Wild Night,* were already smash hits, and with good reason. The title song is one of the most joyous love melodies to have come around in a long time. . . . With that kind of preview, it was surely an album to look forward to. But now that it's here, it seems anticipation outstripped fulfillment.

This album, like Morrison himself, should appeal mostly to very young listeners. Not that his work is immature—there is no denying Morrison is a strong singer with a well-developed style—but it's rather his orientation. He's playing it safe, not taking any chances. We would have been ready for this album years ago. Aside from its lack of originality, there's nothing wrong with it, really, and though his songs don't say much . . . they're pleasant to listen to and highly melodic. Morrison's distinctive, emotion-packed voice is at least as expressive as "heavy" lyrics might be—a gentle joy in life, in love itself. But this is one area where consistency isn't a virtue. Every artist has to evolve and grow, but Morrison doesn't seem to be going anywhere, at least in light of his previous work. Van Morrison could make much better use of his unique voice than he does here.

Deborah Landau, "Entertainment: 'Tupelo Honey'," in Stereo Review (copyright © 1972 by Ziff-Davis Publishing Company), Vol. 28, No. 1, January, 1972, p. 110.

DAVE MARSH

After *Tupelo Honey* Van Morrison must have been faced with a choice. He could continue with his domestic tranquility myth, which was as artistically false as it might have been literally true, or he could head for new turf. He has chosen the latter course (wisely I think). If the result is more curious than classic, perhaps that is the price of adventure.

There are strands of nearly every kind of music Van Morrison has ever made in [*St. Dominic's Preview*]. It is short on the darkness and fire of Them, but the lilting r'n'b of **"Domino"** and **"Blue Money,"** the exotic improvisation and searching of *Astral Weeks* and the mystic yearnings of *Moondance* are finally full-fledged. For the most part, *St. Dominic's* is old concerns seen in new lights, and a smattering of new ones, and the music follows suit.

If this record had followed *Astral Weeks* directly, it might have been both confusing and frustrating. At a distance of three years, *St. Dominic's Preview* somehow seems newly seminal, as though Van were finally capable of a conception that might transcend (though never drawf) the brilliance of *Astral Weeks.* I think Morrison has made a transitional album in a different way than *Tupelo Honey* was. The latter sounded like a summation: *Preview* might be just what it claims. . . .

[For] a few numbers Van Morrison defines himself on terms as difficult and brilliant as any. "I shall search my very soul" comes from him not as the nebbish promise of the limpid balladeer, but as the committment of someone as strong as The Rock itself.

Morrison has a way of making spiritual statements, that would sound either false or trite from almost anyone else, valid and refreshing. He has always, I think, dealt with a certain kind of spiritual regeneration, a type of self-discovery that is continually essential and essentially continuous. (p. 54)

In a way, it is fitting that [**"Independence Day"**] ends the record, for more than anything else here **"Independence Day"** is the kind of song, both musically and lyrically, Van Morrison might be doing more of in the future. It is an intricate, detailed, painstaking search for an America Van sees with love, at a time when almost everyone else views it with fear and loathing.

This is not without its contradictions: **"St. Dominic's Preview"** is occasionally almost an indictment of America, not for any part in the Irish Wars, but merely for its attitudes in general. . . .

Maybe I am overdrawing things, but it seems important to me that Van chose to make his comment on the struggle in Ireland by contrasting it with life in San Francisco. Perhaps, too, I am overextending myself by thinking that "they're trying hard to make this whole thing blend" is how an immigrant must look at politics in the U.S. . . .

[The recently released] *Them, Featuring Van Morrison* is a classic, two-record testament of middle '60's rock, wavering between the punky earth music of the British Invasion and the artistically outreaching eclecticism which characterized late '66 and '67.

All the music Van has ever made has its roots here, from the gutter-snipe hymn **"Gloria,"** to the breathlessly beautiful "It's All Over Now Baby Blue," which might cut even Dylan's masterful performance. Almost all of it is primordial, earth-shaking, phenomenal, a landmark in rock history. It is quite possible that Them's will be the longest lasting music of the middle '60's; even now, it sounds contemporary. . . .

They were an Irish band, from Belfast, and those street-fightin', belligerent Celtic roots showed through. Every cut here, no matter how tender the intent, is tough as nails. . . .

Them Featuring Van Morrison is probably the most worthy reissue since UA's Legendary Master's Series last year; one would hope that London would continue to delve into its archives for some of the other excellent material it has around.

In any event, this reissue is a complete success. There is nothing left to ask, for the Van Morrison fan, at least not at the moment: the re-release of his blindingly brilliant old stuff and a stiffening of the spine on his new material. It's a delight. (p. 55)

Dave Marsh, "Listen to the Lion," in Creem *(© copyright 1972 by Creem Magazine, Inc.), Vol. 4, No. 5, October, 1972, pp. 54-5.*

STEPHEN HOLDEN

Hard Nose the Highway is psychologically complex, musically somewhat uneven and lyrically excellent. Its surface pleasures are a little less than those of *St. Dominic's Preview* and a great deal less than those of *Tupelo Honey,* while its lyric depths are richer and more accessible than those of either predecessor. The major theme of *Hard Nose* is nostalgia, briefly but firmly counter-pointed by disillusion. The latter sentiment Van spews out in the album's one ugly, self-indulgent song, **"The Great Deception,"** a vicious indictment of hip urban culture and rock affluence. . . .

The cut-by-cut schematization of *Hard Nose* is fairly loose. Side one comprises five songs, beginning with **"Snow in San Anselmo"** and closing with **"The Great Deception."** "Snow" is alternately contemplative and rapturous in its recollection of a near-miraculous occurrence. . . .

[**"Warm Love"**] embodies in all its details a sensuous appreciation of life and music. . . .

"Wild Children," which delves deeply into Van's personal mythology from childhood through adolescence, is the album's most historically resonant song. Against early memories of returning soldiers, Van identifies his growing-up with the figures of Tennessee Williams, Rod Steiger, Marlon Brando and James Dean. . . .

As was the case in *St. Dominic's Preview,* the second side of the album turns out to be better than the first. The ten-minute **"Autumn Song"** demonstrates anew Van's gift at creating extended meditations that accumulate emotional power as they unfold in modified, impressionistic streams of consciousness. . . . [Morrison evokes,] as few contemporary composers have, the ineffable joys of daily life in attunement to a pleasant environment.

Stephen Holden, "Van Morrison: Nostalgia & the Mystic," in Rolling Stone *(by Straight Arrow Publishers, Inc. © 1973; all rights reserved; reprinted by permission), Issue 144, September 27, 1973, p. 100.*

LESTER BANGS

[*Hard Nose the Highway*] is an object lesson in Giving the People What They Deserve any way you look at it. If you think they deserve a ration of anguish to keep their molars bright, you can find it here if you read between the ferns. If you dream at night of infinite Gitcheegumee lapping panaceas to salve us all through the Seventies, *Hard Nose* will soft-on in seconds flat. If, even, you kinda feel that this prevalent public (and critical, yup yup) attitude of blanket *acquiescence* for the existential excreta of all these droll mulling popeye geniuses deserves finally to be rubbed in the used Kleenex of its own passivity by the overbearingly downy stroke of just one gross and sustained insult to your intelligent sensibilities—you got it right cheer.

But look where he's been of late, it's making him lazy. Last year Van parlayed a somewhat bluff hand with *St. Dominic's Preview,* where amongst warmtoast expectables he retrenched a bit by throwing his nets across both the mosaics of *Astral Weeks* prosody and what burgeoned in our confusion as a potential whole new dreamscape of mysterious, starrily extensible musical and verbal possibility: **"Listen to the Lion"** and **"Almost Independence Day."**

Nobody knows what those songs "mean," because they don't mean. They stand shimmering in the endless radiance of their opaque associations. Just maybe all that mystification was ultime profundity, and just as maybe it was hollow shuck of the diurn. They *were* standing, no "Baby Please Don't Go" rushes or pumpkin punting moondances no more. This was Zen, Jack, and you could take it or slumber. But you had your doubts like crickets in the gut.

All things must pass, and V.M. may be passing fair but he's possibly passing soon, and *Hard Nose* poses pretty passing itself off with perfect supine awkwardness. . . .

Van has no shame, maybe because nobody's told him yet what a spectacle he is really beginning to make of himself, so he takes this twilight buggy to the end of the limb. The entire second side of the new Van Morrison album is taken up with a sort of suite on the subject of falling leaves. . . . **"Autumn Song"** [is] idiotically convivial in its crayola catalog of falltime nature snacks ("leaves of brown"::"pitter patter rain";:"glamour sun"::roasting chestnuts).

The first side is better, though maybe that's just because the songs are shorter. **"Snow in San Anselmo"** is the best thing on the album, in spite of shots of deer crossing the road right out of those slick picture magazines put out by the Chamber of Commerce. . . . Later on he gets a little topical with a line about how the local speedfreaks sit up all night in the International House of Pancakes, and tries to cop himself a smidge of Bogart *High Sierra* macho with some insistence about "My waitress my waitress my waitress." It's all a lot of crap, but the musical bones of the song are fraught with sufficient lamentation to bring you back. . . .

After that the wooze begins to overtake the ooze. **"Warm Love"** the single has dumb lyrics on a par with **"Autumn Song,"** but it's shorter and catchier. . . .

The title cut is one of the few goodies here, a bit of cuff doodling that works, but much more interesting is **"The Great Deception,"** where Van, with monumental pettiness and petulance clodhops drunkenly on his soapbox and delivers a 5 minute lecture to all the crass unappreciative creeps who didn't wise up when John Lennon told them that genius was pain. . . . Before this speil's over he'll castigate a fork-tongueing power-to-the people rockstar (who is obviously Sly Stone) as well as the poor herd of stereotypic hippies, but the real payoff comes when he juxtaposes that stuff about the Caddyvroomin star with: "Have you ever heard about the great Rembrandt/. . .how he could paint/And he didn't have enough money for his brushes. . .''

Aw, gee! There is no justice on this bitch of an earth. Oh well, childishly reactionary as it is, it's at least a temperamental (if not a musical) improvement over all that rustic cud-chewing. Maybe by this time next year Van Morrison'll be de-mellowed to the point of cutting a whole album of ridiculous bile. He could call it something like *Mo Ostin is a Lousy Bastard,* or even *Only the Trees Appreciate Me.*

> Lester Bangs, "Hard Nose: Soft On," in Creem (© copyright 1973 by Creem Magazine, Inc.), Vol. 5, No. 6, November, 1973, p. 67.

MELODY MAKER

[In compiling **"Them, Featuring Van Morrison Lead Singer"**, Nick] Tauber has had a relatively easy task in selecting essentially from the two albums that Van made with Them—he's got all the accepted classics like **"Gloria,"** **"Here Comes The Night"** and **"Mystic Eyes"**—but he's also come up with a number called **"Hey Girl,"** totally new to me, whose pastoral lyricism is quite unlike the rawness of the rest of the material and seems to presage **"Astral Weeks"** in its introspection. Generally, though, what's fascinating about this early stuff is how favourably it compares to what Morrison has since done on his own. . . . But Morrison's own potential is so obvious—and not just vocally—that it's difficult to see why interest didn't truly focus on him until **"Madame George"** at the end of '68. Why is it that the Animals, whose sound was roughly comparable, were more accepted, both by public and critics? Conversely, of course, Eric Burdon now finds it hard to whip up enthusiasm, while Morrison mythologises himself with each new album. This compilation makes me think that a book of history and analysis is about due on him.

> M. W., "Pop Albums: 'Them'," in Melody Maker (© IPC Business Press Ltd.), November 3, 1973, p. 32.

BOB SARLIN

[*TB Sheets*] is, substantially, a rerelease of Morrison's 1967 solo album . . . , *Blowin' Your Mind,* the album that produced **"Brown Eyed Girl."** . . .

For Morrison fans this album is a necessary addition to the collection. For those who've never heard the [earlier] releases except for the ubiquitous **"Brown Eyed Girl,"** it should be an exciting listening experience, defining some of the unfilled corners of this man's development as an artist. (p. 69)

The title tune, **"T. B. Sheets"** is a nightmare set to music. The liner notes explain that Van broke down in tears after recording this memory of life with a girl dying of tuberculosis. Whether or not this girl lived in Van's flat or his imagination, this song to her remains an amazing document. Here he tries to reconcile the emotions summoned up when someone is dying young: the bitterness, the sorrow, the disgust and the anger. A painful track and worth crying over. You can, indeed, almost smell Julie's T. B. sheets and it's not a pleasant experience— but it's a claustrophobic killer of a song.

"Ro Ro Rosey" is a throwaway rock number, sister to **"Brown Eyed Girl,"** which follows and caps the album. But even here, in throwaway land, Van's lyrical qualities have a way of peeking out from behind the crass. . . . [A] bit of Irish folk song slips into even this mindless little number.

The same Irish poetry dominates **"Brown Eyed Girl,"** a fabulous and innovative single when it first appeared and still a delightful song. . . . Here, replete with falsetto choir, clearly structured music and charming, wild poetic lyrics is the essence of the early, the middle, the late, the eternal Van Morrison. (p. 70)

> Bob Sarlin, "Records: 'T. B. Sheets'," in Crawdaddy (copyright © 1974 by Crawdaddy Publishing Co., Inc.; all rights reserved; reprinted by permission), April, 1974, pp. 69-70.

KEN EMERSON

Like the white middle class it entertains, rock music exhibits a certain rootlessness, a lack of a living history. This is rock's greatest asset—it is spontaneous and free, contemporary and temporary—but it can also be a liability. The ever-recurrent rock revivals and our fondness for golden oldies express the absence of a past, the very word "revival" indicating that the past is dead. Many artists are exploring that past, but the then and the now are so disjunct that more often than not such efforts are camp, lifeless, effete and irrelevant, or crudely exploitative.

Van Morrison, one of the few . . . for whom the American musical tradition is passionate and alive, loves this tradition with the insight and fervor of a foreigner. There's no more zealous flag-waver than a citizen by adoption. . . . Morrison's ardor doesn't require him to imitate the past; his music is so suffused with it, that everything he writes and sings expresses and interprets the past in light of the present, and the present in light of the past.

Because Morrison's music continues an ongoing tradition, it is never diverted by faddish ephemera and never becomes dated. . . . *It's Too Late to Stop Now,* his 11th album including two he did with Them, celebrates the entirety of Morrison's career. And unlike Bob Dylan's recent tour, for example, these recordings are not a mere remembrance of things past. Even the album's title impels us forward and all of the material, from **"Gloria"** to **"St. Dominic's Preview"** is very much alive.

The oldies and his own songs [reveal Morrison to be] . . . at once a great traditionalist and an original talent: traditionalist because of his roots, original because he never stops growing—*It's Too Late to Stop Now.*

Yet Morrison has never enjoyed the mass popularity he deserves. This is partly because he stands quite deliberately outside the pop/rock mainstream, but more importantly because of his relative indifference to lyrics.

On *Astral Weeks,* he tried to write purposefully but ended up with poetastery and parodies. Recently he again tried to write purposefully, but with only intermittent success, most notably **"Saint Dominic's Preview."** Words seldom interest Morrison except as sounds, and without this in mind you'll be confused when he babbles "sodomysodomysodomy." He's just messing around with the words "inside of me." Having nothing to say, with only emotions to express, his songs must be felt, not thought about. What matter are the stops and starts, the twists and turns, the splutters, the scats and the yowls. Morrison battles with words, distending them, gutting them, forsaking them altogether, as if they blocked the pure sound and the pure feeling toward which he strains. Not even Mick Jagger, one of Morrison's early models, imitates him. . . .

Through three sides of the album Morrison's energy never flags, not even during the long and arduous **"Saint Dominic's Preview"** and **"Listen to the Lion."** Only on the fourth side does the intensity dissipate as he overindulges in protracted fooling around. But more than an hour's music is crammed into the preceeding sides, and it would be churlish to demand more. The man has given so much.

> *Ken Emerson, "Van Makes a Present of the Past," in* Rolling Stone *(by Straight Arrow Publishers, Inc. © 1974; all rights reserved; reprinted by permission), Issue 159, April 25, 1974, p. 61.*

JIM MILLER

Van Morrison is an enigmatic figure. Although he practices the art of a flamboyant soul trouper, he maintains an oddly detached, awkward stage presence. His vision is hermetic, his energy implosive; yet his vocation is public.

These are curious contradictions for a performer to sustain, but they help lend Morrison's art its resonance. His distinction lies in his fusion of a visceral intensity with an introspective lyric style—a potentially powerful amalgam owing as much to Bobby Bland as Bob Dylan. Although his lyrics have often been ludicrous, and his bands merely competent, Morrison's singing animates his material. . . .

[His] lyrics, at best carrying the conviction of spontaneous creation, can become belabored, intentionally arty. Morrison in fact walks a thin line between pretense and passion.

[*Veedon Fleece*] illustrates the pitfalls, in Morrison's approach. With its splintered lyrics reiterated over swells of sound, the record's first side returns to the style of *Astral Weeks.* While this approach can be hypnotic, its recycling on *Veedon Fleece* flounders in Morrison's own cliches. . . .

[**"You Don't Pull No Punches but You Don't Push the River"**] is pompous tripe. Van Morrison doesn't need it, and neither

do we. How do you breathe soul into a phrase like "contemplatin' William Blake and the Eternals"? . . .

Coming from anyone else, *Veedon Fleece* would merely be an embarrassment. Coming from Van Morrison, it seems more like another aberration in a fitfully inspired career.

> *Jim Miller, "Van: Fleece Brutality," in* Rolling Stone *(by Straight Arrow Publishers, Inc. © 1975; all rights reserved; reprinted by permission), Issue 177, January 2, 1975, p. 62.*

CHARLES NICHOLAUS

Van Morrison, I've been thinking lately, is the intellectual's Grateful Dead. They offer an amplified nirvana, fueled by chemicals; he offers the dark night, fueled by despair, self-pity, ennui. In either case it is easy to listen, but I'm beginning to wonder why anyone should want to.

I would like to find something nice to say about *Hard Nose the Highway,* . . . but that would be silly. It was a bad record. [*Veedon Fleece*] is not. It is a boring one, and in a way, I think bad records are preferable. They at least require outrageous response. With records like this, one must be careful. A little too much, on one side or the other, and the album begins to sound interesting. That would be misleading.

Van Morrison found his blues early, stepping out into the unknown with *TB Sheets* and *Astral-Weeks.* . . . [But,] like other prodigies (Bob Dylan comes to mind, and if you think this album is dissipated and banal, wait till you hear *Blood on the Tracks),* Morrison's early achievements have not been sustained. **"Wild Night"** was the last song he wrote which I can still get worked up about, though **"Listen to the Lion"** and **"St. Dominic's Preview"** have hints of something grand.

But Morrison's problem is that, since *St. Dominic's Preview,* he's just kept hinting. He listens to his heart, and responds by delivering that unnamed growl, but I think that his function, as an artist, might be simply to name those terrors of the heart. Or at least get closer than we mere pedestrian moralists and listeners are able. As it is, he bugs me, man. It's as though Thor Heyerdahl had made it within ten miles of Tahiti, and dropped anchor. The pleasant moments on this record, which are several, cannot make up for the brilliant ones which might await us if Morrison had only had the nerve to continue. (pp. 66-7)

> *Charles Nicholaus, "Van Morrison Slugs It Out with Himself: 'Veedon Fleece'," in* Creem *(© copyright 1975 by Creem Magazine, Inc.), Vol. 6, No. 9, February, 1975, pp. 66-7.*

JONATHAN COTT

Sometimes, in moments of bewilderment or happiness, you may catch yourself singing or whistling a song whose words, on reflection, explain how things really are with you—"Good Day Sunshine" when it's raining, "Rain" when it's sunny, "Hello Goodbye" when you don't know whether to stay or go. In all kinds of weather and situations, the song interprets you. . . .

To the sound of the slow-motion footfall of acoustic guitar and bass, Van Morrison's radiant and archetypal vision of a woman on her horse of snow has recently brought back to me perhaps the most extraordinary of these mysterious songs, **"Slim Slow**

Slider,'' the three-minute blues reverie that concludes the timeless *Astral Weeks* album recorded in 1968.

Coming as it does after **"Madame George"** and **"Ballerina"**—with their almost Blakean commitment to the themes of sexual organization, childlike vision and angelology—**"Slim Slow Slider"** can certainly be taken simply as the last of the album's three mythopoeic images: the transvestite, the dancer, the rider on her horse. . . .

I used to think that Morrison should have ended **"Slim Slow Slider"** after [the] first stanza, whose image-making power, as [William Butler] Yeats knew, not only wakes analogies but also penetrates to the Great Memory. The horse-as-symbol is, of course, both a complex and ubiquitous phenomenon in mythology and dream interpretation, representing, at various times and places, the instincts, the unconscious, clairvoyant powers and even the cosmos itself.

Interestingly, in German and Celtic mythology, to dream of a white horse was once thought to be an omen of death. And in an astonishing if unconscious way, Van Morrison draws on this ancient symbolic meaning and, in four additional telegraphed stanzas, uses this wondrous hovering image—Yeats's "transparent lamp about a spiritual flame"—in order to convey two simultaneous ideas: the dissociation and alienation from Pure Being and the loss and death of Love. . . . From a horse white as snow to a Cadillac: the beloved rides away—out of reach, won't be back, dying—the world falls from grace. . . .

There are plenty of songs to dance to; there are so few songs for dreaming, inviting you to recompose and re-create them, extending the dream onwards.

> *Jonathan Cott, "A Song for Dreaming," in* Rolling Stone *(by Straight Arrow Publishers, Inc. © 1976; all rights reserved; reprinted by permission), Issue 216, July 1, 1976, p. 20.*

MICHAEL WATTS

It's paradoxical that **"Astral Weeks"**, Van Morrison's best and most enduring album, should be unrepresentative of his general body of music; as is in fact that his reputation was not truly established until his second album for Warner Brothers, **"Moondance"**, which set the course for a succession of records, generally excellent and sometimes more, in an R&B-cum-jazz mode that was markedly different from **"Astral Weeks"**.

Of all subsequent albums, only his last, the almost forgotten but immensely underrated **"Veedon Fleece"** comes close to capturing the quietly obsessive quality of the first, its songs each like tender, curling snapshots. . . .

Both [**"Astral Weeks"** and **"Moondance"**] were also notably inspired by Morrison's nostalgia for Ireland; there are echoes of **"Cypress Avenue"** and **"Madame George"** throughout **"Veedon Fleece,"** which was written after Morrison returned to Ireland in 1973 after many years' absence. These albums, suffering and poetic, are pronouncedly Irish, with something of the sensibility of Liam O'Flaherty, and less "American" than the others in the sense of the geography of those lyrics. . . .

There is also a paradox concerning Morrison's new album, **"A Period Of Transition,"** which centres upon the question implicit in its title: if it's intended to be a bridge between **"Veedon Fleece"** and some other, unknown shore, why does its content

recall the music made between **"Moondance"** and **"Hard Nose The Highway,"** only a good deal inferior?

After my laudatory preamble, this is admittedly a brutal judgement; yet this lousily-titled record violates all the expectations aroused by listening again to **"Veedon Fleece,"** just as it forces another question: what has happened to Morrison in the past three years?. . .

The musicianship and musical construction are unexciting, but so, largely, are the songs. Since all are seemingly held together by the choruses (frequently the title itself), whose repetition they are dependent upon not just for their effect but also for their actual length, Morrison would appear to have been lacking inspiration these past three years. To single out one song, **"Heavy Connection"** has not only been padded, but its lyric also hinges upon the particularly trite phrase "a real heavy connection," a handicap from which it never recovers. . . . **"It Fills You Up,"** a song which seems to be in praise of music itself, is lyrically impoverished, but it rides along on its riffy instrumental and insistent vocal . . . . **"The Eternal Kansas City"** is a fine, if unspectacular, celebration of that city's esteemed place in jazz history, which it quirkily invokes with the repeated line "excuse me, do you know the way to Kansas City?" Of the songs on side two, the slow, moody **"Cold Wind In August,"** which ends the album on a downbeat note, has a melancholy power and one good phrase, "I was putzin' through September in the rain"; but **"Joyous Sound"** and **"Flamingos Fly,"** both uptempo, are not nearly as uplifting as their titles. . . .

[Has Van Morrison ducked out], really for the first time in his career, by reacting against the reception for **"Veedon Fleece"** with a record as different again, on which he's tried drastically (in both senses) to simplify his music? **"A Period Of Transition"** merely keeps inviting questions. Like the blue-toned photography of Morrison, reminiscent of old bubblegum cards, that occupies the back sleeve, the final impression it leaves is oddly self-conscious. The answers, of course, are all with Morrison; but, as always, he's not talking.

> *Michael Watts, "Morrison: A Bad Crossing," in* Melody Maker *(© IPC Business Press Ltd.), April 23, 1977, p. 22.*

PETER KNOBLER

People had started talking about Van Morrison in the past tense. In the three years since his last album release [*Veedon Fleece*] his presence had grown to become some vaguely attainable level of excellence it seemed no one, not even Morrison himself, could ever truly achieve, or *had* ever truly achieved. Bruce Springsteen acknowledged him and Graham Parker took his rough edges as a persona. His albums, grown familiar after so many years of constant play, were beginning to be referred to as classics and, as happens with the greats of the ages, were more discussed for impact than actually listened to for pleasure. Van the Man became an Influence—like Beethoven, Chuck Berry or Lenny Bruce—not on the scene and increasingly hard to conjure as a real human being. . . .

A Period of Transition is Van Morrison's comeback album and with it he steps from influential absentia directly back to the top. It is far and away the best album of the year. It is better than any record released last year. Quite simply, it shows everybody how this sort of thing is supposed to be done.

Transition is a throwback to Morrison's classics, *Moondance* and *His Band and Street Choir.* After some years fooling around, experimenting with combinations of cosmic lyrics and strings, Morrison has apparently decided to return to basics. . . . The transition . . . is back to the land of the living.

Morrison has generally appeared to be a morose, diffident figure, not easy with his intimacies. On *A Period of Transition,* though, he's pouring it all. The first thing that hits you about the album is its tone; from open to close it is confident, polished, accessible—fun! The agonies of Morrison's earlier works are submerged—not obliterated, mind you, or denied, but not crowding out the obvious pleasure that carries the album forward. . . .

Throughout the album Morrison's writing is sparse; he doesn't throw around many cute phrases or catchy concepts. The very simplicity demands attention, makes one stop and listen to the sentiments, which are similarly uncluttered. . . .

So, Van Morrison has returned with a flourish. He is still very much a mystery, but at least these days he seems a happy mystery and somehow that is very uplifting.

> Peter Knobler, "The Van Who Would Be King," in
> Crawdaddy *(copyright © 1977 by Crawdaddy Publishing Co., Inc.; all rights reserved; reprinted by permission), June, 1977, p. 82.*

LESTER BANGS

Who has not been waiting for the next great Van Morrison LP? Whether you thought his last masterpiece was *Veedon Fleece* or *Tupelo Honey* or even (what I think) *Moondance,* you certainly were never prepared to write him off. Nobody's going to write him off because of *Wavelength* either, but it's obviously not the album he is still destined to make.

Something comes clear here. Ever since *Moondance,* Van Morrison has staked his claim to the rare title "poet," mostly on the basis of what amounts to a bunch of autumn leaves. Look at those records lying there—*Tupelo Honey, Hard Nose the Highway*—the best as good as the worst, and all of 'em slowly turning brown. You wanta kick 'em just like a pile of crumbly leaves? Well, go ahead and do it. And kick Van Morrison too. Because he's a saint. Yeah, that's exactly why he needs the boot.

Morrison's got a beautiful obsession with something he can't quite state, and we've got a beautiful obsession with Morrison. Which is fine for *him,* but what are we to do? (pp. 77-8)

[We're] supposed to notice the lyric sheet [of *Wavelength*]— the only other Morrison LP that had one was *Hard Nose the Highway,* itself a rather pointed statement regarding leaves and such. "Such": that's what Van Morrison's interested in—roamin' in the gloamin' and divers other top-hat autumnal falderal. Linden Arden stole the highlights, but where did he take them? Way back home, that's where. Leaving us with another album of furry-nosed nuzzlings in the fleece. But about this time, one begins to wonder: nowadays does this artist ever come bearing anything other than said fleece? Naught.

Wavelength is a very nice record. . . . It probably would . . . be really groovy for somebody's idea of a wine-and-joints, Renaissance-fair garden party. It makes a lovely sound, breaks no rules and keeps its grimy snout (or, rather, that of its maker) out of the dark places that mainstreams step correctly over. Rigid. . . .

[It's] obvious that Morrison ain't playing out no dramas here. Nor has he been for some long while now. Perhaps he is more interested in apprehending the exact configuration of an ace of sunlight and presenting it to us. A lost or stolen moment in time, when meaning went rollin' by like the trains on the tracks, like the breeze through a door. But the question is: DO WE CARE? Obviously the man is possessed, obviously he is driven to seek some definition in the most mundane curbstone air, certainly he is a mystic whose light shines for he and thee and all of us, but he flat-out refuses to say anything but the patently obvious and then calls that poetry—which it is.

So maybe we should knight Van Morrison poet-errant of the New Drowse. Meaning, don't ever ask him what his beautiful obsession is actually about. Because if you do, he'll come out with embarrassing sludge. . . . Still, though, it do confound how such a monumental talent can mire himself in such twaddle, fine as some of it may be.

There is a kind of resolute silliness about a lot of the stuff Van Morrison's been doing for the last few years: he wants to make records for cookouts, we keep probing for his bardic soul, and the whole mess is ridiculous because he was actually only specific for one very tight stretch there, enclosing **"T.B. Sheets"** and *Astral Weeks.* . . . (But what kind of perverted universe reigns—and what kind of bray-orbed, Fellini-trite monstrolas might issue forth—when filigree *becomes* the body?) What, finally, are his beloved, infinitely extensive out-choruses *but* filigree? The last half of **"Madame George"** may be the all-time tightrope act, but, on *Wavelength,* he really gets down to it and dubs the endless out-choruses of **"Santa Fe"** a whole new *song.*

So I guess he has finally achieved what he maybe set out to do in the first place: make the edge the center. The result, unfortunately, is a perfect bubble of smoked cheese. It'll do for the party, but it leaves certain sorta primal questions so far from resolved that—well, no, we never quite give up, do we? It is damn well roundabout known that Van Morrison records about four times as much music as he releases. Some of these great, edgy, eternity-shale, sax-bitten pieces leak out occasionally, and that's just fine. We're gonna deserve something beautiful to listen to in our old age. (p. 78)

> Lester Bangs, "Van Morrison's Beautiful Obsession," in Rolling Stone *(by Straight Arrow Publishers, Inc. © 1978; all rights reserved; reprinted by permission), Issue 278, November 16, 1978, pp. 77-8.*

DAVE SCHULPS

Roy Wood and Van Morrison can be called two of rock's true eccentric geniuses, the success of whose careers have never quite matched the brilliance they displayed when properly motivated. . . .

The titles of their respective new albums, however, suggest a renewed enthusiasm on the part of both Wood and Morrison, who have both experienced qualitative, if not quantitative, flops during the past few years. . . . In both cases, there are flashes of greatness exhibited, but neither of these albums sustains them long enough to qualify as an all-around success.

Of the two, Morrison's [*Into the Music*], surprisingly, is the stronger, probably his best studio LP of the last five years in terms of coherence and enthusiasm. Morrison seems to have entered a period of intense love, and this LP seems a paean to that love—which on the strength of the lyrics would seem to point to not only emotional and physical fulfillment, but spiritual as well. . . . [If] Morrison's songs were a bit stronger, if the tendency toward plodding repetition were curbed, if the emotion that goes into a six-minute song were to be compressed into three minutes, *Into the Music* would indeed have been a stunner. Instead, it's about half a great album, which, I suppose, is better than none.

Dave Schulps, "Records: 'Into the Music'," in Trouser Press *(copyright © 1979 by Trans-Oceanic Trouser Press, Inc.), Vol. 6, No. 10, November, 1979, p. 36.*

TOM CARSON

Van Morrison has an extraordinary knack for inventing brick walls to butt his head against, whereas anybody else would just walk right through. If an explanation were asked for, Morrison, resting between blows, would most likely answer: "Because it's there." This artist has staked his whole career on a wrestle with the unnamable. And unless you're sympathetic to such obsessions from the start, he can be a closed book—seemingly obscure, willful, often portentous, humorlessly full of himself. Morrison's argument is intractable by definition: he can change lives, but only if they chance to rhyme with his.

Lately, though, Morrison has been trying to change himself—inwardly, by way of an evermore-overt turn toward Christianity, and outwardly, via a revitalization of his recording career. On *Common One,* there's almost none of the knotty darkness and cryptically private imagery that have made him so difficult to many in the past. Instead, as befits the next step in his recent groping for serenity that began with the deck-clearing of *Wavelength* (1978) and continued on last year's *Into the Music,* the current mood seems calm and soothing.

Yet, in other ways, *Common One* draws the line more starkly between those who take Morrison the only way he can be taken (on faith), and those who don't take him at all. . . . [If] the lyrics—for the most part, bald homilies about living in the country and being happy—are simple enough on the surface, much of their significance is still locked inside Morrison's head. In **"Summertime in England,"** one of the fifteen-minute epics, the singer's penchant for the blandly pastoral is blended with a name-dropping guided tour of British poetry that initially sounds close to self-parody.

Since Van Morrison has always seen life as a mystic experience, his acceptance of orthodox Christianity can't help but reduce him in scale. Religion regularizes his cosmology and solves the mysteries he's forever chasing by offering the answers secondhand. In an everyday context, a line like "And the sufferin' so fine" is striking. Put inside the box of Christian theology, however, it comes out not merely trite but distasteful.

What saves Morrison—and makes *Common One,* despite its narrowness, boring stretches and large and small retreats, impossible to dismiss—is his unwilling, embattled awareness that inner peace is every bit as demanding as emotional warfare. Time and again, he finds that nothing is more difficult than becoming simple, and this makes him seem, paradoxically, more hermitically alone than ever. Morrison is attempting to explain his discoveries to an old audience (or a former self) from which he now feels isolated, but he's also unable to join the new flock. What at first sounds like the work of a complacent man turns out, comically and affectingly, to be that of a man who desperately wishes he could be complacent.

All this emerges almost by accident. The LP's overt theme is flat and unconvincing, while the real action is on the periphery. (pp. 51-2)

Morrison's singing sometimes contradicts his central message. He'll often hone in on lines or images that look like throwaways on the lyric sheet. In **"Summertime in England,"** his physical, uncontainable delight at the words "You'll be happy dancin'" (and surprise, too, as if he'd forgotten about the dancing and was glad it was there) communicates the specific rapture he's been reaching for far better than all the ponderous fluff about "your red robe dangling" and being "high in the art of sufferin'." As a framing reference, that list of poets in **"Summertime in England"** is nowhere near as apt or fresh as *Moondance*'s "Ray Charles was shot down but he got up." . . . Instead, it's more like a lout's idea of one-upmanship. . . . But it succeeds anyway, because it's funny—especially when the singer starts running through the names distractedly, snapping his fingers like a man checking a grocery list. Which is, of course, exactly what he's doing: shopping for usable myths.

Only in **"Satisfied,"** though, does the simplicity that Morrison is striving for arrive as something natural and effortless, as a gift of grace. Again, the best line comes out of left field. The artist's boast, "I got my karma from here right to New York," scores not because it makes sense (it doesn't) but because it's such a wonderfully absurd bit of blues bragging in a tradition that goes all the way back to Robert Johnson. . . .

If **"Satisfied"** is *Common One*'s sole masterpiece, the record's most revelatory moment is located elsewhere. Because language is Morrison's passion, lyrics are a battle and a torture for him, and throughout the LP, he equates serenity with silence. In the opening composition, he's grateful for "the words we do not need to speak," and ends side one by asking, "Can you feel the silence?" But in the middle of **"When Heart Is Open,"** the album's rather overblown and meandering finale, the singer suddenly veers off into a wordless half-groan/half-wail, distorted to hyena pitch by a harmonica. All at once, this naked, ragged noise of animal terror brings everything the record has been trying to avoid up to the surface like a drowned corpse who, despite what he thought his convictions were, can't rest peacefully. It's a moment of tremendous emotional and musical daring, and Morrison hurries past it: when he hums the same notes at the fade, they're simply the sound of a workingman glad that his job is done.

But the memory lingers, and that moment is the key to *Common One:* the lone admission that, even in a new life, heaven is kept alive only by the possibility of hell. Thankfully, this is something that Van Morrison, no matter how hard he tries, can't ever forget. (p. 52)

Tom Carson, "Van Morrison Tries for Heaven but Can't Forget Hell," in Rolling Stone *(by Straight Arrow Publishers, Inc. © 1980; all rights reserved; reprinted by permission), Issue 329, October 30, 1980, pp. 51-2.*

BARRY ALFONSO

"Rock poet" has become almost a dirty word in critical parlance, invoking Moody Blues florid gush or worse. Matching verse to music is still a valid activity, however, provided the words aren't intended primarily for the printed page and the resulting song is strong on record.

At his best, Van Morrison achieves this synthesis. Though barely coherent on paper, his lyrics take on a brooding power when sung, seeming like great wisdom even if they border on nonsense. On *Astral Weeks,* Morrison set gloriously elusive images to a baroque jazz blend, proving himself a true rock poet—a versifier who was also a skilled musician.

Common One, to be up-front, isn't *Astral Weeks;* the spark of melancholic abandoned genius which graced the earlier record is only present sporadically. Morrison's latest is a mannered, thoroughly professional effort, slick even when the singer attempts to cut loose and dive headlong into the mystic. In this respect the LP resembles 1974's *Veedon Fleece* in its collection of vaguely evocative but still polished tunes. After 16-plus years in pop music, Morrison has too many artistic tics and trademarks to go as wild as he did on *Astral Weeks.* Still, nobody can do quite what Morrison does, even when he's a bit stiff at it. . . .

Morrison's words are best absorbed as part of the overall mix. Rather than making linear sense, the verse functions best as incantations, taking on a certain glow when chanted and whispered. Intellectually, the album has little to offer. There's an ode to the relics of England (**"Haunts of Ancient Peace"**), a toast to a lady-love (**"Wild Honey"**) and a funkified Buddhist rap (**"Satisfied"**). When Morrison works himself into a near-trance, toying with and reworking a number to fit a flash of emotion, ordinary concerns about meanings aren't important anymore. The very sound of his voice communicates everything.

"When Heart Is Open" is Morrison's most successful extended song-poem since **"Almost Independence Day."** Simmering with the fire of a dark Scottish ballad, the cut's droning qualities lace the singer in bold relief. The imagery is almost cosmically weary . . . , ineffably sad yet tranquil and content. . . .

Where does *Common One* fit in the Van Morrison catalogue? Near the top, I'd say, though rankings of any kind are probably unfair. This work is meant to be appreciated on its own merits as a spiritual testimonial, a mature pop exercise—and, yes, an example of musical poetry.

Barry Alfonso, ''Records: 'Common One','' in Trouser Press *(copyright © 1980 by Trans-Oceanic Trouser Press, Inc.), Vol. 7, No. 11, December, 1980, p. 50.*

Agnes Eckhardt Nixon

1927-

American television writer and producer.

Nixon is perhaps best known as the creator and head writer for the serials *One Life to Live* **and** *All My Children*. *All My Children* **focuses on young love, and many young adults identify with the characters and their problems. The show has a strong following among college students and has been studied in several college courses.**

The plots of both of these shows are realistic, based on Nixon's own experiences. Nixon's work on these serials is also indicative of her originality in both concept and production. Her inventiveness is particularly evident in *All My Children*. **While daytime television programs are usually produced at considerably lower expense than nighttime television, nighttime production quality was introduced on this series when Tom and Erica's honeymoon was filmed on location in St. Croix.**

Nixon began her career as a writer for Irna Phillips, whose traditional soap opera formula dominated the airwaves for more than thirty years. Nixon has updated this formula to include relevant social issues and, as she says, "compelling, believable characters the audience can identify with." She believes "that the way to entertain women is to make them think," and she often takes an instructive approach in her stories. She wrote a segment for *The Guiding Light* **which dealt with the Pap test, informing women about uterine cancer. Nixon was also one of the first writers to provide continuing roles for black characters in her scripts.**

Nixon has shown consistent determination to upgrade the standards of daytime drama. The quality of her work and the popularity of her shows has earned her the title "queen of the soaps." Her influence is noticeable throughout daytime television as an increasing number of writers adopt more realistic formats for their shows.

Courtesy of Agnes Nixon

AGNES ECKHARDT NIXON

Time after tedious time, when critics suffer an aridity of fresh, inventive phrases with which to denigrate a film, play or book, they fall back on "soap opera"; it has become the classic cliché of derogation. . . .

[The] syndrome persists that soap opera is a Never-Never Land where hack writers and inferior producers, directors and actors serve melodramatic pap to a lunatic fringe of female children who grow older but never grow up. . . .

What is the appeal of the soap operas? What causes them to have millions upon millions of faithful viewers, or, if you will, "addicts"?

For a serial to be successful it must have a compelling story. That story, in turn, must concern interesting, believable characters. And the fact that it is a continuous story, allowing the development of these characters in episode after episode, permits the audience to become deeply involved with what is happening to them.

Our detractors say this becomes a vicarious experience bordering on sickness, but ask the lady who watches one and

VARIETY

"Search for Tomorrow," which is a low-budgeted soaper, nevertheless should do a good job for its bankroller, Proctor & Gamble. Agnes Eckhardt, who is scripting the series, appears able to endow it with some fairly mature dramatic values. . . .

On the [premiere] the episode eschewed the usual soap opera technique of presenting the entire dramatis personae. Instead it was played with only four of the central characters in three tight scenes. It started with an argument between Victor Barron, a domineering executive, and his son Victor, who prefers photography to his dad's contracting business and bridles under his father's domination. This was sensitively handled with the antagonists' views stated sharply and with validity.

"Television: 'Search for Tomorrow'," in Variety *(copyright 1951, by Variety, Inc.), September 5, 1951, p. 41.*

you'll find it is the very normal empathetic response that a good tale, well told, has held from time immemorial. . . . This is what the soap opera gives us. There is always tomorrow. A tomorrow fraught with problems, tragedies and traumas, to be sure, with hate mixed with love and sorrow with joy. But how does that differ from life itself? There are more of humanity's horrors to be found in any issue of the daily newspaper than abound in all of Sudsville.

Perhaps it is not mere coincidence that Charles Dickens, one of the greatest creators of immortal literary characters, started his career as a writer of serialized stories. He knew, and demonstrated with genius, that for a public to stay with a story they had to care about the characters in it. . . .

Though no soap writer suffers the grandiose delusion of being a Charles Dickens, certainly we learned from him, perhaps by osmosis rather than scholarly scrutiny, that the development of characters in depth, the audience's ability to follow their lives, to love them and hate them, is an intrinsic part of the serial's appeal to its audience. Certainly it is by this very hold that the soap opera has been able to do stories which have performed a public service to the national community in a way which no other kind of television entertainment could achieve.

As an example, the axiom and the battle cry of the American Cancer Society is that this disease can be prevented if caught in time. Yet how many people turn off the Society's program or throw away its pamphlets unread because the name strikes terror into their hearts.

It was for this reason that several years ago **"The Guiding Light"** undertook a campaign to reach the "ostriches" among women viewers, with the message of the Pap Smear test for the prevention of uterine cancer. This story was preceded by painstaking research and detailed planning so that the message would be gotten across by integration into a gripping long-term story with many dramatic elements and no "preaching." . . .

The women who would never have watched or heeded a Cancer Society program with its obvious public service appeal, were, in effect, a captive audience for our message because Bert Bauer was to them like a sister or a very old and dear friend. . . .

No fan of **"As The World Turns"** will ever forget when Ellen, an unwed mother, had her baby and gave it out for adoption. But quite aside from the compelling story, the sequence was researched with meticulous care and the writer worked at great length with the Children's Aid Society to present to the public—and to the thousands of young women who, statistics tell us, yearly find themselves in this situation and do not know where to turn—information on how one can seek help and thus insure that one's baby will find a loving home and parents. . . .

The young are frequently exposed to articles, books and movies about LSD, some that are good and some that are bad. But no viewer, young or old, who has watched the travails of Lee Randolph on **"Another World"** can any longer doubt the potential horrors of this chemical mind-expander and the long range destruction it is capable of effecting, not only on the person who has taken it but on future generations. . . .

[It] would be fatuously dishonest to pretend that daytime soap operas have, in the past, done as much toward providing jobs for Negro actors as they should. The serial must stand accused along with the rest of the industry, and the American business establishment in general, in this regard. Nor is a possible ex-

planation—as one person sees it—in any sense a valid excuse. Apathy can at times be more insidious than prejudice because it is less tangible a foe. . . .

All this is changing rapidly now, although belatedly. A sequence has been running on **"Another World"** which closely involved a Negro couple, the wife being a legal secretary and the husband a somewhat unsympathetic police detective. . . .

And on [**"One Life to Live"**], two leading characters will be Negroes with deep, long-lasting story involvement, and as the various plots unfold, there will be other important roles for Negro talent. . . .

And so that's how it is in Never-Never Land, folks. . . .

We are doing a job we like, getting a satisfying response from the audience we are trying to entertain and even have the feeling, at times, of accomplishing something truly worthwhile along the way. So if the critics wish to cite us as a paradigm of puerility we really don't mind. But we do think that these erudite ladies and gentlemen of the press, before they next invoke our names for the purpose of scorn, should be warned that they may actually be paying their target a compliment.

Agnes Eckhardt Nixon, "They're Happy to Be Hooked," in The New York Times, *Section II (© 1968 by The New York Times Company; reprinted by permission), July 7, 1968, p. 13.*

HARRY F. WATERS

Escapism, voyeurism, masochism, catharsis by comparison with others worse off—these are . . . what the soaps are selling. And if the daily bath of bathos packs a bit more tingle these days, so much the better. It may even provide an educational experience. Agnes Nixon, a refreshingly thoughtful writer who has been manufacturing soaps for fourteen years, likes to point out that episodes concerning alcoholism, adoption and breast cancer have drawn many grateful letters from those with similar problems. It may even be argued that soaps serve as a sort of television "Dear Abby" for the psychologically afflicted, or that they dispense their own brand of hope. "On soap operas there is always tomorrow," says Mrs. Nixon. "A tomorrow fraught with problems, tragedies and traumas, to be sure, but how does this differ from life itself?"

The difference, of course, is that life also has a light side. . . . (p. 104)

Harry F. Waters, "New Sins in Soapland," in Newsweek *(copyright 1968, by Newsweek, Inc.; all rights reserved; reprinted by permission), Vol. LXXII, No. 24, December 9, 1968, pp. 100, 103-04.**

STEPHANIE HARRINGTON

A report in The Times heralding ABC-TV's new soap opera, **"All My Children,"** was headlined: "Social Activism Grips Soap Opera; Heroine of Serial on ABC to Be a Mother for Peace."

Well, the show has been on the road for well over a month now, and the grip is still rather tentative.

The heroine, Amy Tyler—described in an ABC press release as "a liberal political activist dedicated to the peace movement, who married into a conservative family with considerable wealth and stature in the community"—has so far stuffed approximately one and a half envelopes. And the only other indications of her dedication to the peace movement have been her political arguments with her conservative in-laws . . . and the solicitous observations of Amy's own family, friends and doctor that all that exhausting peace work seems to be getting her on edge and that maybe she ought to take it easy for a while.

Well, we may not yet have seen very much of Amy's peace work (following the classical rules of Greek tragedy, all those unspeakable things, like gouging out one's eyes or working for peace, are accomplished offstage). But we do know what is really wearing her out. And it isn't the Moratorium. For, while she is for peace, and she is a mother, no one, not even her husband or the child himself, knows she is a mother—except for her sister and brother-in-law who adopted her illegitimate son when he was two weeks old.

Phillip, the son-nephew, is a high school senior of draft age, and he, his mother-aunt, father-uncle and aunt-mother are all very concerned about the war and his possibly having to fight in it. But his going into the Army is presented . . . as a ramification of his family problems rather than vice versa. (p. 21)

Everyone is, of course, horrified at the idea of his enlisting—particularly Aunt Amy, who has nightmares about it. Nightmares are one of the repetitive gimmicks that pass the time on soap operas and thereby enable them to drag on over the days, months and years. **"All My Children"** is big on repetitive, melodramatic, pseudo-psychoanalytic nightmare scenes which usually have Amy on a battlefield somewhere trying to help Phillip or up against an unrelenting wall of her stony-faced, steely-eyed relatives who are accusing her of something or other. In the end she struggles her way up through the layers of her unconscious, represented on the home screen by what looks like a blob of olive oil in a bowl of water.

Because Phillip is considering getting out from under his family problems by enlisting, and because of Amy's off-camera peace work, just about everyone talks about the war, but the talk is always peripheral to the ongoing central obsession with personal and/or family problems.

However, the soap suds theory of social service, as explained [by Agnes Nixon] is that important social issues are gotten across to viewers, not by direct preaching, which would turn them off, but by integrating the message "into a gripping long-term story with many dramatic elements and no preaching" and by developing characters with whom the viewers come to feel personally involved. (pp. 21-2)

Mrs. Nixon has a point. And in **"All My Children"** she has a sympathetic character, Amy Tyler, involved in the peace movement. And Amy is played by Rosemary Prinz, a soap-opera superstar with whom millions of women previously identified when she played Penny Baker, the heroine of "As the World Turns." Thus Mrs. Nixon is probably opening the minds of a good number of "my-country-right-or-wrong" ladies—who are also Rosemary Prinz-right-or-wrong ladies—to the legitimacy, even respectability, of peace activism.

But Amy's peace activities have so far been presented (or rather alluded to) so gingerly, so obliquely, that one wonders if, without meaning to, Mrs. Nixon is underestimating her audience, whose maturity and intelligence she has defended in print. In real life, of course, for people who do not have a son, brother or father fighting in the war or threatened by the draft, the war is a constantly hovering concern, but not one that

drowns out personal matters. And in that sense, the tangential approach to the war in **"All My Children"** is plausible.

But for women who are as active in peace work as Amy is supposed to be, the war is much more consuming, in terms of time, energy, concentration and discussion. And, so far, Amy has not been to one meeting and has participated in exactly one (off-camera, of course) demonstration, of which her mother-in-law disapproved. But, as TV critic Marvin Kitman wrote in Newsday recently, "It takes a week to close the door in daytime serials." And if Amy does too much in the first few weeks, there may be nothing left for her to do next October. So her activism may really be activated in time. But slowly. (p. 22)

Stephanie Harrington, "Will Amy Work for Peace? Will Phillip Enlist? Will . . . ," in The New York Times *(© 1970 by The New York Times Company; reprinted by permission), February 22, 1970, pp. 21-2.*

BEATRICE BERG

Out there in Middle America, where the rate of addiction to soap opera is high, viewers of ABC's **"One Life to Live"** . . . have been getting regular five-minute doses of unrehearsed, spontaneous confrontations between real-life former dope addicts and the actress who plays Cathy Craig, **"One Life"**'s troubled teen-ager. . . .

When Amy Levitt, who acts Cathy, began to interact with the ex-addicts the cameras turned, the resulting talk was much gutsier than the written dialogue usually heard on daytime TV. . . .

Mrs. Agnes Nixon, writer of **"One Life"** . . . , claims that this is the first time a soap has blended fact with fiction. Since the start of the Odyssey House episodes, heart-rending letters have been pouring into ABC by the hundreds. . . .

As a result of such responses, Mrs. Nixon is now planning to have a mockup of an Odyssey House storefront rehabilitation center built in the **"One Life"** studio. Instead of ending the dope episodes this month, as originally intended, she will have Cathy continue her improvisational group therapy sessions with real Odyssey House inmates for an indefinite time. . . .

So O.K., be snobby about soap operas. But the producers of the show believe this is a way of reaching people "who don't read The New York Times and won't look at documentaries about the drug problem because they don't want to be preached to." Maybe—just maybe—**"One Life"** will help some of those kids, and some of their parents.

Beatrice Berg, "Real Life Comes to 'One Life to Live'," in The New York Times *(© 1970 by The New York Times Company; reprinted by permission), August 2, 1970, p. D13.*

TERRY ANN KNOPF

For those of us who watch the soap operas, once the citadel of escapism, it is clear that we are living in an age in which even such places as Oakdale, Pine Valley, Henderson, Bay City and Somerset—all soap opera locales—can no longer remain completely aloof from the forces at work in our society. . . . But the question is: Just how far have we come?

Unfortunately, a closer look at the situation reveals that, despite some creeping social relevance, the soaps have yet to come to grips with reality in any meaningful way; that for too long they have been the perpetuators of outworn beliefs and values, reflecting a generally conservative bias; and that the networks presenting these shows still live in another world in which they have yet to fully appreciate their responsibilities.

All too often, attempts made in the general direction of relevance have been half-hearted and not very effective. The brief, sad history of the character called Amy Tyler on **"All My Children"** illustrates the point. When the show had its premiere about two years ago it was announced as a bold experiment. . . .

Nevertheless, once the show got under way, Amy's peace activities seemed rather obscure. . . . After the show had been on for well over a month, Amy had participated in exactly one demonstration, and that was off-camera. Several months later, when it was discovered that she had an illegitimate child, Phillip, her marriage was dissolved and Amy abruptly left the show "to travel around the world," presumably in the cause of peace. Presumably, she's still traveling. Asked if social relevance had been dropped from the show, an ABC spokesman told me: "Oh no, Phillip is now into ecology." . . .

Taboos remain another problem. While it is true that some of the more ridiculous ones have fallen by the wayside, others are still very much with us. Both the networks and sponsors exercise a measure of control over all shows regarding subject matter, references and story content. . . . The exact nature of control depends upon who owns the soap—Procter and Gamble, say, or the network. . . .

What is immediately clear . . . is that some control, occasionally in the form of outright censorship, does exist and is a fact of soap life.

The result is that terms like "venereal disease" and "slept with" are not used, while more controversial issues such as homosexuality are not likely to be treated for some time. The subject of drugs has recently been introduced—but is being handled with excessive caution. . . .

The use of the word "abortion" is interesting. Thanks largely to the passage of New York's abortion law, the word can now be uttered on these shows. However, the stigma formally attached to the term apparently still bothers some officials in soap land. Therefore, the tendency is for "good" women on the soaps to "have their pregnancies terminated," while the "bad" ones go out and "get an abortion." Accordingly, sweet, virtuous Meredith Wolek on ABC's **"One Life to Live"** had her pregnancy terminated due to a blood condition, while Erica Kane Martin on **"All My Children"**—a spoiled, selfish, manipulative woman who didn't want her child—had an abortion. (The same principle helps explain why the "good" women on soaps drink sherry, while the "baddies" lean toward the hard stuff like Scotch or vodka).

Terry Ann Knopf, "The 'Good' Women Still Drink Sherry," in The New York Times (© 1972 by The New York Times Company; reprinted by permission), *May 7, 1972, p. D17.*

AGNES NIXON

As the creator-writer of both **"One Life To Live"** and **"All My Children,"** two soap operas of which Terry Ann Knopf was particularly critical in her . . . article, "The 'Good' Women Still Drink Sherry"—in which she hurled the indictment that

"the soaps have yet to come to grips with reality in any meaningful way" [see excerpt above]—I am impelled to a counter-indictment. Ms. Knopf has either failed in a reporter's primary function of thoroughly researching her subject (in regard to the above mentioned programs) or she has deliberately ignored some basic facts about them in order to write a slanted story.

She first accused **"All My Children"** of not presenting the character of Amy Tyler in the role of a peace activist, as she had been described in an ABC press release. Ms. Knopf added that, "after the show had been on for well over a month, Amy had participated in exactly one demonstration, and that was off-camera."

Since the program is live on tape within the four walls of a studio—with a tight cast budget—showing a peace demonstration *on* camera would of necessity have made for a very poor turnout of activist sympathizers. However, Amy's work for peace, her fight for an end to the war in Vietnam, included not only off-camera demonstrations—many more than one—but membership in other groups working for the same goal as she, among them "Mothers Work For Peace." And these groups, and Amy's participation in them, were talked about—and fought about—day after day.

Yes, Amy was written out of **"All My Children"** after six months because Rosemary Prinz, who played the part, had prior commitments. . . . But after Amy's departure we spent weeks dramatizing the return of an escaped prisoner of war and his reunion with his family. The character, Paul, talked freely of the horrors of that war, of the men still in POW camps and the families suffering by their absence. After that, the character of Philip was drafted, much against his wishes, and is now serving with a MEDIVAC unit in Vietnam from where he writes letters describing the suffering he is seeing daily. Was it to this that Ms. Knopf was referring when she said "All too often, attempts made in the general direction of relevance have been half-hearted and not very effective"? . . .

Did Ms. Knopf also fail to read The New York Times of Sunday, Aug. 2, 1970, when almost the entire television page was given to Beatrice Berg's article "Real Life Comes To 'One Life To Live'" in which she detailed our on-location shooting of unwritten and unrehearsed group therapy sessions with eight real-life teen-age ex-drug addicts at New York's Odyssey House Rehabilitation Center? The piece [see excerpt above] went on to explain that segments of these sessions were inserted into shows over the entire summer with the sole hope of getting across to the youth of America, and their elders, a message about drugs from other youths who had been there and knew what it was like. Ms. Berg's main point was that what these young people said about themselves and their own lives was very *real* and meaningful!

Yet Ms. Knopf dismisses our efforts and Ms. Berg's opinion with the deprecating, "The subject of drugs has recently been introduced—but is being handled with excessive caution." One wonders, just what would one have to do to win Ms. Knopf's approbation? . . .

Ms. Knopf also states that "the tendency is for 'good' women on the soaps to 'have their pregnancies terminated,' while the 'bad' ones go out and 'get an abortion.' Accordingly, sweet, virtuous Meredith Lord [Wolek] on ABC's 'One Life To Live' had her pregnancy terminated due to a blood condition while Erica Kane Martin on 'All My Children'—a spoiled, selfish, manipulative woman who didn't want her child—had an abortion. (The same principle helps explain why the 'good' women on soaps drink sherry while the 'baddies' lean toward the hard stuff like Scotch or vodka.)''

My next question is, what was Ms. Knopf drinking while watching those programs? Meredith Lord did *not* have a termination, abortion, miscarriage, dilation and curettage or anything else one wants to call it; she had a full nine-month pregnancy. And while Erica Martin *did* have an abortion, the term was used interchangeably with termination and a very strong point was made by the doctors on the show that abortions are legal, easy to obtain, and often advisable.

When Ms. Knopf addresses herself to the matter of censorship of soap operas, concluding, ''the result is that terms like 'venereal disease' and 'slept with' are not used,'' I begin to feel like a cross between Kafka's Joseph K and Alice at the Mad Hatter's tea party.

For over *eight months* on **"One Life,"** we have had discussions among three doctors, a black Congressman, a newspaper publisher, his editor and writers and housewives and other cast members on the endemic proportions of venereal disease and all its ramifications, with never a euphemism employed. We then went on to have a young reporter on the program supposedly write an article for the local newspaper which was discussed at length and then, about eight weeks ago, this ''article'' was offered to the public free of charge by simply writing in for it. The title embodies the very term Ms. Knopf says is taboo: ''Venereal Disease: A Fact We Must Face and Fight.'' . . .

[Unquestionably] Ms. Knopf has an inalienable right to her own low opinions of our programs and an equal right to express them, but to present those opinions as fact and to withhold— either out of ignorance or by design—documented information on the credit side of the ledger is a shocking, flagrant abuse of the reportorial standards maintained by a newspaper of The New York Times's stature.

> *Agnes Nixon, "What Do the Soaps Have to Do to Win Your Approval?" in* The New York Times *(© 1972 by The New York Times Company; reprinted by permission), May 28, 1972, p. D3.*

TERRY ANN KNOPF

Given Ms. Nixon's involvement in the more creative aspects of television, I am especially dismayed by her remarks insofar as they reveal qualities all too commonly found among network officials—defensiveness and a lack of critical perspective. Despite her vigorous defense of Amy's peace activities on **"All My Children,"** the show's attempt at social activism in this area was, at best, superficial. One also wonders why—given Ms. Nixon's and ABC's presumed commitment to presenting the peace issue—another actress wasn't found to replace Rosemary Prinz. Replacements for departing actors and actresses are a common practice on soaps. . . .

The . . . point I made concerning the stigma attached to abortion on the soaps still tends to hold true. On ''As The World Turns,'' Lisa is a scheming, tormented, unhappy woman. As befits her character, on May 11 a doctor on the show initially diagnosed her illness as a ''butchered abortion.'' The very same day—in fact a half-hour later on ''Love Is a Many Splendored Thing''—a friend of Iris Garrison (a fine, upstanding woman who is in the midst of a complicated pregnancy) wondered aloud ''if the pregnancy is going to be terminated.''

I could go on in this vein, trading quips with Ms. Nixon's quibbles. But to do so would, I think, detract from the more disturbing aspects of her letter. For despite the impression given by Ms. Nixon, my piece was not specifically about her two shows, but about the state of the soaps *in general* as regards social relevance. Her failure to examine my piece in terms of the basic issues raised represents a lamentable narrowness of view as well as an abdication of her responsibilities as a prominent figure in the television industry.

Are you, Ms. Nixon, satisfied by the manner in which blacks and other minority groups are portrayed on the soaps generally? How do you feel about the way women are presented? Aren't you bothered by the lack of strong male figures and the extent to which men have been emasculated by so many soap women? And finally, as a writer yourself, how do you feel about the amount of censorship with which you must contend? These are the kinds of issues I attempted to deal with in my piece.

> *Terry Ann Knopf, "What Do the Soaps Have to Do to Win Your Approval?" in* The New York Times *(© 1972 by The New York Times Company; reprinted by permission), May 28, 1972, p. D3.*

BETH GUTCHEON

[Soap] operas have come a long way. . . . Soap writers are increasingly using the serial form—as Charles Dickens once did—to educate audiences or lead them to question their insular attitudes in ways that little else in their lives may do. (p. 42)

"Search for Tomorrow" evolved a long romantic plot line featuring a mysterious character who was deaf and unable to speak. . . . When the suds settled, viewers had learned a good deal of sign language; they were also exposed in considerable depth to the ways in which families, schools, communities, and society at large discriminate against the handicapped. . . .

"Search for Tomorrow," still doing business with the same old characters at the same old stand for 23 years, has somehow become the most forthrightly feminist soap on the air. . . .

When I asked Agnes Nixon, queen of the soap writers, how she—and others—got off the nonstop, pro-marriage, baby-boom go-round popular for so long, she took the novel view that the best way to entertain people is to make them think. . . .

Nixon likes to beef up the suds with high-protein filler. Soap operas are considered audio entertainment; it is assumed that the viewer is looking at the enzyme presoak most of the time and not at the screen. So whatever the actors are doing, it's up to the writer to keep the dialogue continuous, which explains all that homey chitchat about meat loaf and slipcovers. Agnes Nixon, however, drops in one-liners about pollution or zero population growth. As long as the ratings are up and the sponsors happy, she can even elevate a public service conversation to a subplot. (p. 43)

[When Cathy Craig on **"One Life To Live"**] was found to be ''experimenting with drugs,'' Nixon arranged with drug therapist Dr. Judianne Densen-Gerber to have ''Cathy'' participate in a group therapy program at New York's Odyssey House. Taped segments of the real thing were integrated into the soap. ABC and Odyssey House were swamped with calls from people who don't watch documentaries, or read the New York *Times,* and perhaps could not have been reached any other way.

Nixon respects her audience to a certain extent; enough, for example, not to offer to them a staged drug-rehabilitation therapy group when she could get them the real thing. (pp. 43, 79)

Murders, marriages, organized crime, diseases, and psychoses are soap staples, as they are on prime time. Race and class issues are rarely met head-on—a fairly suspicious circumstance since demographics indicate that a sizable proportion of the audience is blue collar or black, or both. . . . Only **"One Life To Live"** has ever evolved a major plot line focusing on (rather than pointedly ignoring) race. . . . Agnes Nixon created a black woman who passed for white because as a light-skinned black she had been rejected by both white and black communities. The point was to examine the motivations and consequences of denying race and heritage: the woman, established as white, fell in love with a black man. Throughout the romance only the writers knew she was going to turn out to be black, and the moment the couple first kissed, every TV set below the Mason-Dixon line went blank. (p. 79)

I'm not suggesting that soaps are great art; just that they are often good television, and that there are legitimate uses (as well as abuses) of television. Soaps, regardless of their plots, consistently deal with aspects of women's physical and emotional health that one certainly finds nowhere else on television. . . . (p. 80)

I like soaps because they are about women and because they occasionally have ideas in them; further, I prefer the serial form to the episodic because I am interested in the details of life as well as the climaxes. **"All My Children"** may be sentimental, but currently it's unfolding a plot about the causes and consequences of child abuse. As a daughter and a mother I'm interested in the ways parents damage children—so when it's my turn to wash the dishes I'll probably do them at one o'clock while I listen—maybe I'll find out why I sometimes feel like slugging my son. Maybe I'll find out why my mother slugged me. . . .

Soaps may be melodramatic and predictable, but they are never as devoid of intellectual content as "Cannon" or "Mannix" or the Daddy-figure prime-time doctor/lawyer things. Soaps are better than those and watching them hasn't made me any more ridiculous than I was before. . . . I'm tired of seeing soaps treated as a joke—partly because the writers and actors honestly deserve better, and partly because the joke is really aimed at me. (p. 81)

Beth Gutcheon, "There Isn't Anything Wishy-Washy about Soaps," in Ms. *(© 1974 Ms. Magazine Corp.), Vol. III, No. 2, August, 1974, pp. 42-3, 79-81.**

FERGUS M. BORDEWICH

Although soap opera aficionados would seem to be a minority among college students, there are nonetheless thousands of young people around the country who daily put aside their Sartre, Machiavelli and Freud—not to mention such obsolete writers as Fanon and Debray—to watch the moiling passions of middle-class America as portrayed on daytime TV. What is it about these slow-moving melodramas with their elasticized emotions that today's college students find so engrossing? . . .

[In] recent years the subject matter of daytime TV has changed and become much more relevant to the interests of young viewers. Into the world of frazzled passions and leaden drama, which could grip chiefly the bored housewife . . . , contemporary issues have been injected. The "generation gap," abor-

tion, obscenity, narcotics and political protest are now commonly discussed and dealt with on the soap operas of TV.

From its inception in January, 1970, **"All My Children"** has consistently employed topical material. "It was a kind of 'first,'" explains Lewis Antine, an American history graduate student at New York's City University. "It was a sense of your *stuff* being on TV for the first time, like 'Hey, they're talking about us on Mom's show! How will they handle it?'" . . .

Some students claim they watch the soaps for a dose of "realism," others for a taste of "unreality"; some say they find them thrilling and exotic, while still others see in the soap opera an emotional blueprint of their own home life. . . .

[At] best, perhaps, the soaps manage to portray life in all its true banality rather than attempting to squeeze art from what is inherently a pretty bland affair.

Fergus M. Bordewich, "Why Are College Kids in a Lather over TV Soap Operas?" in The New York Times, *Section II (©1974 by The New York Times Company; reprinted by permission), October 20, 1974, p. 31.*

ANTHONY ASTRACHAN

The contrast between [the realism of **"One Life to Live"** and the classical canon of daytime television drama embodied in **"As the World Turns"**] shows that what James Thurber once called "Soapland," like American society as a whole, is torn between the need to keep up with changing realities and the desire to stick to tried-and-true formulas that have never expressed reality—to tell it like it isn't. The search for relevance has led daytime drama to deal with social issues like drugs, venereal disease and the Vietnam war, to take feminist positions on questions like abortion and women working, and to bring blacks and ethnics into the WASP population of Soapland. . . .

Change and constancy, realism and fantasy all testify that soap operas make up one of the main currents of American culture. So does their appeal to some of the feminists who have done so much to start society on the road to change. Some like the new ideas in daytime drama and don't like to see anything that appeals to millions of women treated as a joke. Further testimony can be found in the soaps' appeal to college students, professors and psychiatrists, and in the employment and training that the soaps give to scores of actors who also do "serious" films and theater. (p. 12)

[Paul Rauch], now producer of "Another World" at NBC, refuses to admit that classical soap opera is fantasy, however. . . . [He] insists that his program "truly reflects middle-class, Middle-West culture. Its characters are realistic, believable, do things that a lot of the viewing public do."

In the reflection of reality on "Another World," only four of the 14 women characters have jobs, only one of them because she needs the money she earns. Sex is frequent enough but seldom talked about, and social issues are seldom mentioned. The real Midwest has other dimensions. . . . [In Peoria, the stereotype of Middle America and a real town about the same size as the program's fictional Bay City, women] have set up an abortion clinic despite determined opposition and have created an atmosphere in which an elementary schoolteacher can appear on television to talk about her abortion and her husband's vasectomy.

Even the liberated characters on socially conscious soap operas don't go that far. Two have had legal abortions in order to pursue their careers—the kind of development that has become a symbol of the new relevance in Soapland. Erica Kane, the bitch-character of ABC's "**All My Children**," had television's first legal abortion in May, 1971, so that her pregnancy would not interfere with her plans to work as a model. The writers presumed that Middle America would be shocked, and Erica was duly punished by getting septicemia from the abortion. . . .

"**One Life to Live**," which seems the most consistently innovative soap opera, has a recurring feminist story line in the adventures of Cathy Craig. (p. 54)

Sex has even begun to be seen on screen as well as mentioned in the new kind of daytime drama. . . . [These] changes add up to the fact that people are managing to have unmarried sex with minimal consequences on at least four soaps, a dozen years after the start of the sexual revolution in real life.

Racial attitudes are also changing, a dozen years after the peak of the civil-rights movement. Many programs have one or two black characters. . . . "**One Life to Live**" has gone one step further by making its black characters really important in the story line. . . . Usually, daytime drama shows only two or three blacks in an all-white world, and their problems tend to be classified as human rather than racial. The amount of realism remains a matter of dispute.

"**One Life to Live**" also tries for a greater degree of realism in having an important set of characters who are both blue-collar and ethnic, whereas most soap operas merely drop in an occasional Italian or Jewish name to add what is thought to be a desirable touch of the exotic. "**One Life**" also had a Jewish-Christian marriage (until the Jewish husband "died") with one-liners about Christmas and Hanukkah.

The blue-collar couple on this program also provide something else that is a rarity in the old-fashioned kind of soap opera humor. It tends toward slapstick, as in a scene in which they test a water bed when they set out to buy furniture for their new home. But even the middle-class WASP's in "**One Life**" are capable of wit by Soapland standards. . . . (pp. 54, 56)

"**One Life to Live**" and "**All My Children**" were both created by a woman who cheerfully takes credit for much of daytime drama's new willingness to face social issues—Agnes Eckhardt Nixon. . . .

Mrs. Nixon likes to introduce into her soaps not only . . . relevant issues but scenes and people from real life. (p. 56)

Mrs. Nixon put the ultimate contemporary reality into "**All My Children**" with three sequences related to Vietnam. When the program went on the air five years ago, it generated publicity about a character called Amy who belonged to the peace movement. Some viewers thought the sequence was a cop-out because tight budgets prevented the dramatizing of antiwar demonstrations, and there was little more than talk about Amy's activities. . . . Mrs. Nixon bristles at the charge of cop-out. She followed Amy's departure with a sequence about the return of a Vietnam P.O.W., and she drafted Phillip Brent against his wishes and sent him to Vietnam. Last year, "**Children**" reconstructed a Vietnamese village on the banks of the Connecticut River for a story line involving Phillip and two Vietnamese, a woman who cared for him and a man who had lost his legs in a bombing. Both Vietnamese characters were played by Vietnamese.

"**All My Children**" and the other socially conscious soaps remain dramatic entertainment, of course, full of the romantic fantasy that keeps the audience coming back for more. (p. 58)

Soapland is full of female villains. The nastiest and most celebrated in recent years has been Rachel Davis Matthews Clark Frame of "**Another World**." . . . Rachel is no longer merely a girl who turned bitchy because she grew up poor and fatherless. She is now visibly capable of real affection and love, and her marriage to a wealthy older man has impelled her to acquire tastes for Mozart, Matisse and Chateau Margaux. She will undoubtedly get nasty again the next time she is deprived of love. (pp. 58, 61)

"**All My Children**" has apparently become the favorite soap opera of college students—despite its realism, rather than because of it. George Forgie taught a seminar on the history of pop culture at Princeton a year ago. At the start, he asked the students what they thought about the syllabus. They told him he had devoted too much of it to "kid culture" and suggested that he include a soap opera because of its mass audience. They voted overwhelmingly for "**Children**." Forgie says their motivation turned out to be the appeal of gossip, the desire to get involved with the lives and emotions of people close to their own age and outlook—without having responsibility for them. (p. 62)

Forgie says that the students expressed a dislike of the social issues on the program, except for women students concerned with women's issues. Yet most were activists concerned with social issues in real life, not victims of the passivity and privatism reportedly widespread on today's campuses. Similar reactions to "**Children**" have been reported from as far afield as North Illinois University and U.C.L.A.

University interest, in any case, is part of the evidence that soap opera has achieved a secure place in American culture. (p. 64)

> *Anthony Astrachan, "There's a Schism in the World of the Grand Old Soap Opera: Life Can Be Beautiful/ Relevant," in* The New York Times Magazine *(© 1975 by The New York Times Company; reprinted by permission), March 23, 1975, pp. 12-13, 54-64.**

ROD TOWNLEY

Partly because of her concern for three-dimensional characters, Agnes Nixon's shows are among the most popular on daytime TV. (p. 13)

More than anyone else, Agnes Nixon has let reality into the claustrophobic sound studios of soap operas. Not too much reality, of course. Certain subjects, such as homosexuality, never come up in soap-opera conversation. Family anguish and romantic misalliances still dominate the plots. Yet, over the past couple of years, viewers have been exposed to information on VD, drug-rehabilitation centers, child abuse, Pap tests and racial discrimination. These subjects had all been treated on television before they surfaced on Mrs. Nixon's soaps, but in most cases she was the first to bring them to daytime drama.

Other soap writers have begun to realize, through Mrs. Nixon's example, that social issues can have a leavening effect on ratings. . . . There are the makings of a trend here.

Mrs. Nixon has also tried to dress up her shows, incorporating sequences of impressionistic recall, subliminal flashes, fantasies and dreams. . . . (pp. 13-14)

Agnes Nixon was recently very much concerned with the highly sensitive subject of child abuse. After consultations with experts, she began introducing the subject on *All My Children*. "It's always done in an affirmative way, not a punitive way," says Mrs. Nixon. "If you're punitive, the people you're trying to reach will just turn off the set."

All this makes Agnes Nixon sound like an evangelist for social change. She isn't, and doesn't pretend to be. "Our primary mandate is to entertain," she says, adding, "but I do think people are entertained by being made to think." For television, many would consider this an original, almost radical thought. . . .

Perhaps appropriately, *All My Children* is currently a rage on campuses, where students find a temporary escape from their education in the "educational" soap operas of Agnes Nixon. . . .

In a mobile society, where children split off early from parents and grandparents, the soap opera can be a little like an extended family. . . .

Agnes Nixon succeeds because she has something for everyone: romantic escape for housewives, a home for the homeless, even an occasional bracing dose of reality for those who find thinking a form of entertainment in itself. (p. 16)

> Rod Townley, "She Introduced a Stranger to the World of Soaps," in TV Guide® Magazine (copyright © 1975 by Tringle Publications, Inc., Radnor, Pennsylvania; reprinted by permission), Vol. 23, No. 3, May 3, 1975, pp. 13-14, 16.

R. E. JOHNSON, JR.

A structuralist study of [*All My Children*] might begin by trying to reconstruct and describe one feature or phase of the relationship between the writer and the audience. Such a relationship we can call a model or paradigm. The analysis can then go on to describe various transformations of this model into other aspects of the writer's relationship to the reader. For example, let us say that the "principal" relationship obtaining between writer and audience is an exchange whereby the writer preserves his identity and/or his job by manipulating the viewer's sense of time. A transformation of this might be the familiar technique of granting the character total and exact recall of a scene that may have occurred days or months before.

The example I have used may suggest that there is a mechanical or cause and effect connection existing between the model and its various transformations. But such is not the case; or, at least, I make no claim that this is the case. The transformations are, in this sense, unmotivated. They are similar in structure to one another as, say, the possible positions nouns may fill in various sentences are similar in structure, but this is their only similarity. Therefore, the designation "model" is not intended to be honorific. It results from an arbitrary choice and in no sense is to be equated with the concept of a "center." Any of the transformations is as much a model as the one which, in order to begin, we might call "primary." We could as easily start with the technique of total recall and consider it the generative relationship.

This point perhaps becomes more clear when we remember that the model is a relationship, not a specific content. . . . There is no inherent meaning in any of the things which are related in and by the various transformations of the model, meaning only comes in the act of association. . . . *All My Children*'s Dr. Tyler is a manikin until he is set down in the

context of his wife, Phoebe; whereupon, he begins to generate meaning or acquire value.

Such meaning, however, is quite different from that generated by his placement within the ambience of his daughter, Anne, or his secretary, Mona. This is true despite the fact that he has certain constant characteristics. These characteristics only begin to emerge, to matter, when he is given an environment in which they are challenged. . . . Dr. Tyler's "meaning" is ultimately his possible relationships with other characters.

Character relationships are not the only configurations which transformations of the model may take. In fact, it seems more useful to subsume plot and character relationships and so forth into four categories of transformations which assimilate, but operate independently of, traditional categories of literary analysis. The four categories I employ are: repetition, juxtaposition, interruption, and location.

All My Children develops from a hypothetical middle which is always rippling outward. It "began" in the middle about seven years ago and, for all practical purposes, it is still in the middle. There is not, and there must not be, any end in sight. Such non-movement is achieved by reducing everything to dialogue: the characters are interchangeable in several senses; the sets—epitomized by the "car" which belongs to all the cast, which has been wrecked, been the scene of proposals as well as criminal propositions—are almost comically irrelevant. What action there is serves chiefly to give people something to talk about. Moreover, there is no outside world. Supposed contacts with it—references to contemporary events, for example—are as transparently phony as the lights and noise which are supposed to establish that the car is in motion. Even the ostensible echoes of the "real" world are not in fact echoes of that world at all but echoes of the way a book, movie, newspaper or even television defines or interprets this part of the world. Thus, when Linc initiates Kitty into the "mystery of wine" his speeches appear to have been lifted, intact, out of a wine-appreciation book. . . . Even Caroline's description of how she felt on losing her husband in Viet Nam is similarly generalized as are all of the programs, invocations of popular romance, popular religion, popular sexology, popular psychology and sociology.

What remains, dialogue, is an attempt to reconcile time with infinity. Hence the *infinite* repetition of a structure which implies *progress*: coming and going, the beginning and ending of a conversation. The ostensible subject of this conversation, the reason for the coming and going, is always the same: a new event. However, the real subject, the faithful presentation of desire, is the coming and going itself.

The mythic world of this soap opera, then, emerges through and is characterized by, a dialogue between novelty and repetition: the reopening—always to the first page—of the elaborately bound volume, entitled *All My Children,* which begins every episode, the return to the beginning which precedes and follows every movement toward an end. Perhaps the most prominent feature of this world is total recall. Such a repetition creates a very serviceable eternal Now, that not only reinforces whatever needs to be reinforced, but also provides a dramatic irony capable of driving its point home on even the most unperceptive. The inclusion of such a feature, however, makes it obvious that the world *All My Children* presents is a deformed version of an interpreted, rather than a "real," world. The soap apparently is realistic enough to know the naivete inherent in the concept of simple realism.

The world deformed is a patently linguistic world, largely a world of formulas. There is, for example, the Baby Litany: 1.

Every woman wants a baby more than anything else. 2. A baby will make everything "all right" between _____ and _____. 3. A baby takes precedence over everything else in determining who belongs to whom. (pp. 561-63)

There are also only entirely predictable responses to "tragic events" (or, in fact, any event): "Why Mary? Why did this have to happen to Mary?" Ruth asks. "It's this insane world we live in," replied Joe, "all the evil in it. We wouldn't be human if we didn't want to see justice done." The pattern becomes hilarious when the repetitions start multiplying: the machine appears to have gotten out of control. (p. 563)

Similarly, the explanations for human behaviour are entirely formulaic: "If you go to Phil, he may never want to have a baby by you, and then where would you be?" "When something like this happens, it makes you stop and take stock of your own life, doesn't it?" "I was just using Margo to try to forget Ann." . . . There are clichéd ways of describing relationships: "The bond of love that ties them together;" "the love we shared;" "the need they have for each other;" "She was pregnant with my child." . . .

Moreover, there are repeated patterns or laws which generate much, if not all, of the program's action. The characters group themselves into seven constellations. . . . Group one is composed of doctors and lawyers. Generally, it is a group of people to whom others turn when in trouble and so on. In this category are Dr. Joe Martin, Dr. Tyler, Lincoln Tyler and Paul Martin. Nick, Hal and Phil, the occupants of slot two, are sexually attractive, restless, generally self-interested—though capable, on occasion, of sincere unselfish action—not always principled or orthodox. By contrast, the members of the third category are the nice guys: Chuck, Jeff and Frank—all of whom will grow up to be in category one. (p. 564)

Ruth and Kate belong in constellation four. They are the complements to Joe et al., but they are less obtrusive and less important in either reacting to, or determining, the action. Following them is a group even more gentle and passive, a group of women who "lead with the heart," yet who are "an inspiration to others:" Mary, Kitty, and Mona. However inspirational, no member of the last two groups is half as catalytic as the female villains, who are generally selfish, egocentric and unscrupulous in achieving their own designs. This sixth category includes Claudette, Margo, Erica and Phoebe Tyler. The seventh classification is filled by Anne and Tara, two women who are basically good . . . like their soul-sisters in groups four and five, yet they are not as passive as Mary-Mona nor as asexual as Ruth-Kate. Their emotions are more developed and they are subject to dilemmas created by the conflict between those emotions and their sense of what's right. (pp. 564-65)

The most productive of the events which unfold through the working of these laws are those which provide for repetition of earlier episodes. One such type of pattern is the event which evokes another by their similarity: Lincoln and Kitty's wedding which brings flashbacks to a number of the characters. Another is the event—Mary's death, for example—which forces a rethinking of one's life and, therefore, inevitably, a remembering of the past.

Other conditions which connote forward movement but whose overall effect is repetition are achieved with the juxtaposition/superimposition transformation. We frequently have a happy scene—Chuck and Tara discussing "their" son—set alongside one that undermines it one way or another—Phil asking Ruth

if this same child is actually his. Or we have someone unknowingly on the edge of catastrophe, but only the audience gets the resonance because of what we've just seen.

Some scenes merely reinforce each other by being examples of the same idea—how one family member can make life miserable for the rest, for example. We have Phoebe's return from Europe, with her consequent demands on Charles, Anne and Linc, immediately juxtaposed with Claudette's blackmail of her mother and the consequent advent of dissention between Margo and Paul. Other juxtapositions clarify or merely reinforce certain important, or even unimportant details.

Still other juxtapositions, however, don't so much increase the tension between repetition and progress as they do reveal it. Such are the contradictions which exist largely as a consequence of the nature of the form itself. (p. 565)

The soap can never be rounded out as life . . . or the book. The writer must hope that the soap will never end; how can he, then, see everything from the perspective of that end? Therefore, there will always be certain exigencies that arise which cannot have been anticipated six months or six weeks before and a character or an event in the past is changed and the viewer is required to forget or to alter his memory of the past.

Thus, we have changes of character in two senses: physical (depending on the fortune of the actors) and psychological (depending on the present intention of the writers). Phil may go to Viet Nam with one face and come back with another, Anne may be a 5′7″ blonde one day, a 5′2″ brunette the next day and, two weeks later, be a 5′7″ blonde again. . . . Or events can be changed. If it is useful for us now to see Margo as a manipulator, we are "reminded" that Margo arranged her daughter's marriage to Spencer Montgomery III. However, . . . Margo, at the time, was happy about the event, did everything possible to prevent any interference with it, but did not arrange it.

An interesting variation on this is the yoking together of figures who would seem to be extremely dissimilar but who come to be somewhat redefined by their juxtaposition. At one point Charles Tyler says essentially the same thing Nick has just said in another scene. Charles, of course, is the epitome of paternal devotion to others and thus we are forced to recognize that beneath Nick's tough exterior there is unlimited concern for at least those persons he is close to—Anne, Mona, and Phil. Such concern enables him to cease to pursue Anne when his pursuit has become unbearably redundant. (p. 566)

The characters live within the illusion that they are free, that they can determine their own destiny. When someone, Tara, for example, talking about little Phillip's accident, does express a belief in a kind of fatedness, this is the exception rather than the rule. On one level the viewer accords the character this freedom. On another he sees their past, present and future as entirely arbitrary. Such arbitrariness again forcefully points up the essential emptiness of the character until he is given a temporary value in the interchange between the writers and the audience, a value he possesses not by virtue of any similarity to something in another world but purely by virtue of his location.

The most emotionally disjunctive juxtapositions are those that are heavily laden with irony, especially those which involve some violent interruption from the outside world. (Any such penetration of the membrane that protects and sustains this limited cosmos is inevitably violent, no matter what the source.) (pp. 566-67)

Such actions not only cause endless reevaluation but they activate the blame game which, in turn, permits much more circling. . . . The blame game like the moral complexity game—i.e., what am I to believe, both sides have a seemingly valid point—is chiefly useful in allowing the viewer to see through, and thus symbolically exorcise, the problem of guilt or the cloud of greyness. . . .

The prototypical interruption, however, is the arrival/departure. These actions, are, of course, transitions as well as interruptions. And the fact that they, like the show's other transitions, are almost always constructed on a question and/or accompanied by news, alcohol or tea (or all three) testifies to its dual nature. The interruption is awkward and must be mediated by news or alcohol; the transition is mechanically smooth and must be mediated by some disruptive tension. (p. 567)

[There] are arrivals which are genuine interruptions and which strain the tension between progress and regress to the fullest. Such scenes dramatize the structural concept of repetition as a rearticulation which duplicates but is never the same, of change without advance. They thus also illustrate the degree to which all movement is internal rather than external, in the middle, rather than proceeding from one point in time to another. . . .

Mrs. Tyler, Erica, and Claudette are the principal servants of the writers in the double relationship whereby they dash the hopes of their viewers for a happy outcome while they build their concern about what's to come. Claudette is the most interesting, in this respect, because she is pure disruption; she has no independent life of her own: her status is, appropriately, divorced. However, we have never seen her married and there seems to be no attempt to create an interest in her private life—her drug addiction and sexual looseness only serve to symbolize her lack of any ground. The only reason for her existence is to be a thorn in the side of others—Margo, Hal, Mrs. Tyler, Erica, Kitty . . . She is constantly on the go from place to place talking, and thereby "making trouble," for others. Her characteristic action is the leering smile after she has just dropped a bombshell on someone and he is trying hard to disguise its effect. In a bit of stage direction, the writers themselves call her "narcissistic." Her identity is the contemplation of her own empty image; she is all voice.

But if there is disruption there must be something to disrupt, if not progress, then the illusion of progress. What is continually disrupted is the attempt to locate LOVE, the word that invokes the wonderful kind of happiness which is always eluding the character, yet which is his constant goal. Anne speaks for most of the others when she says: "I've got to give myself a chance to find some kind of peace and contentment—some kind of happiness. . . ." (p. 568)

The viewer is left trying to locate *his* happiness in the character's to the degree to which he repeats their design, internalizes their desire. This is the way Love could or should be. . . .

Love is an absence which the viewer is supposed to fill, continually, while the program empties it. . . . [The] idea of Love is what keeps the show going and, as such, it is crucial that it be contentless. Thus it can be the rationale for any irrationality, the dustbin into which can be swept any failures of plot or character to cohere, in short, an ever-available *deus ex machina.* (p. 569)

R. E. Johnson, Jr., "The Dialogue of Novelty and Repetition: Structure in 'All My Children'," in Journal of Popular Culture (copyright © 1976 by Ray B. Browne), Vol. 51, No. 3, Winter, 1976, pp. 560-70.

TIME

[Agnes Nixon has welded Irna] Phillips' home truths to such trendy themes as cervical cancer, racial prejudice and drug addiction. Nixon has at one time or another written almost every soap and created two: *One Life to Live* and *All My Children,* the thinking man's soap that has a 30% male audience. She is the soaps' crusader: *All My Children* went to Viet Nam and is now into women's liberation. After considerable tension, a young black couple have agreed to live in different cities for five days a week so they can pursue their different careers as doctor and social worker. Nixon's most memorable creation, however, was a traditional type, Rachel, the Circe of *Another World.* In 1966, when Nixon arrived at *World,* the show was in trouble. Within a year she had introduced Rachel as the bewitching homewrecker and one of the soaps' durably popular villainesses. (pp. 48, 51)

"Sex and Suffering in the Afternoon," in Time *(reprinted by permission from* Time, The Weekly Newsmagazine; *copyright Time Inc. 1976), Vol. 107, No. 2, January 12, 1976, pp. 46-8, 51-3.**

DAN WAKEFIELD

The **"All My Children"** phenomenon is part of a confluence of different forces that are making soap opera respectable. . . .

I am not about to stake a theoretical claim that soap is the latest "art form of the future," destined to bury the novel, the feature film, the stage, the nighttime TV detective programs, . . . or in fact any other form of dramatic entertainment. But I do believe the television soap opera is a valid and important and, God knows, popular part of the spectrum of contemporary entertainment, and is worthy of discussion and appreciation as such, with all its built-in restrictions of time and production. The originality and excellence of **"All My Children"** make it not only a marvelous kind of entertainment, but also, like all good storytelling, a reflection of the way we live now, and the way we wish we lived. (p. 18)

In the absence of "real" homes and families, and often in big cities a lack of "neighbors" whom you know and speak to, the daytime television serial can provide at least a fictional substitute. In a mobile and constantly shifting society, often without roots or ties, a serial like **"All My Children"** is something to hold on to, to depend on, and I think that is one of its appeals to collegians. . . . (p. 159)

I think the viewers also find appeal in the sense of values they find in Pine Valley, values that are generally felt to be too old-fashioned or square or irrelevant to be discussed in contemporary movies or "serious" fiction. I mean, for instance, how residents of Pine Valley, even the young ones, talk about family loyalty and the importance of "roots." When young *Phil Brent* is laid off his job with the Environmental Protection Agency in Pine Valley and then is offered a position in their Dallas, Texas, office he can't imagine leaving Pine Valley. The principal reasons of course are that he is still in love with *Tara* and he wants to be near his natural son and hers, *Little Phillip,* but even aside from those factors he explains to his mother he can't conceive of leaving Pine Valley, because "my *roots* are here." (pp. 159-60)

In between the traumas and trials of contemporary life, which are portrayed with emotional and social credibility in Pine Valley, there are also respites, . . . and in Pine Valley these occasions usually emphasize the sense of family, of home, of roots, and how those elements are sources of nourishment. (p. 160)

[These] scenes are worked in naturally, as part of the fabric of the place, along with the sophistication and the traumas of modern life, but it is important to know that these touches are done gracefully, and are not only nostalgic but fictionally credible. I think it's important to emphasize that Pine Valley is not one of those corn-ball, cracker-barrel, pseudo-folksy pipe-dream places such as we have seen presented in nighttime viewing, most obnoxiously (to me anyway) in "Apple's Way," with George Apple, supposedly a contemporary man who is seeking his roots by going back to Iowa and living in a converted mill with his wife and kids and good old Grandpa, all of them aw-gee-in' and shucks-in' along like a bunch of castoffs from the down-home commercial where Euell Gibbons slurps his Grape-Nuts.

Only in nighttime television, supposedly for "adult" viewing, can they get away with that pap. I seriously doubt that a daytime audience would swallow it. They are accustomed to contemporary patterns of speech and thought, and the spectacle of a bunch of grown-ups gee-whizzing and golly-sakes-alive-ing around an old converted mill while they sought the good life and anguished over whether to risk their life savings in hopes of rescuing the town paper because they feel a community needs a locally owned paper, is part of what a community is all about, part of the values the rosy-cheeked Apples were trying to find when they moved back here to the land—well, shucks-a-Friday, you can get a better and more believable story than that by tuning in to any daytime serial. . . . (p. 161)

The people of Pine Valley are up-to-date, if not on the latest headlines, on the general customs and attitudes and concerns of contemporary life. Almost everyone has cocktails before dinner, and some imbibe a fine wine at one of the local gourmet restaurants. There are abortions and divorces, mental hospitals and shock treatment, drugs and betrayal, wars and unemployment, just like in our "real" world. But there is also the feeling that somehow behind all that, propping up and providing a floor for the people of Pine Valley, are these big solid pillars of tradition, and behind them, protected by them, a huge vat of Grandma *Kate's* vegetable soup that will ease all sorrows, cure all ills. And that is one of the deep appeals of the place. (p. 162)

[This is Agnes Nixon's] gift, to bring us here and make us believe it, make us feel we belong and share in it, even if only through her imagination and then our own.

Home. (p. 182)

> *Dan Wakefield, in his* All Her Children *(copyright ©1976 by Dan Wakefield; reprinted by permission of Doubleday & Company, Inc.), Doubleday, 1976, 182 p.*

MANUELA SOARES

All My Children is a light-hearted soap—perhaps the only light-hearted soap on the air. It may also be characterized as a home-and-family soap, in the doctor-lawyer formula. (p. 33)

In its home-and-family orientation, *All My Children* very much resembles traditional soaps. But there are differences in tone. *All My Children* seldom succumbs to dark feelings of loneliness or instability (as does *As the World Turns*) or to sexual despair (as does *Days of Our Lives*). On *All My Children,* there is little serious evil. Bad characters like Phoebe, Erica, Mrs. Lum, or Benny Sago, tend to be fun, or funny. They do not ask much of us. For example, when Phoebe Tyler is left drinking alone on Christmas Eve, she gives a sarcastic, rather maudlin toast. If she pities herself, we don't. . . . [There] is remarkably little real suffering on *All My Children,* compared to other soaps— little at least that we must take seriously. Many viewers seem to identify with the writers—speculating on what development will take place next—instead of sympathizing with the troubled characters.

If there is a message to the show, it is that people with all their destructive emotions are "only human"; and that happiness is best found in the sharing of experience with a loved one, within the context of an extended family. Characters tell one another that they can find happiness if they do not demand too much of themselves or others.

The show is, in other words, optimistic. Dialogue is shot through with references to hope and faith. "You have to have faith that things will work out" is said in many forms, and very often. . . . Men spend a lot of time encouraging younger women, who are fatalistic, guilt-ridden, irrational, and sometimes right.

It is said that as much as 30% of the audience for *All My Children* is male. Well, there really are an awful lot of very admirable men on this show (Dr. Charles, Dr. Chuck, Dr. Frank Grant, Lincoln Tyler, Danny Kennicott, Paul Martin, etc., etc.). Except for Phil Brent, who has been troubled, male characters are generally rational or reliable. The only bad guys are people who don't belong in Pine Valley and who do not stay (for example, Hal Short, Benny, and Tyrone the Pimp).

Most of the dramatic interest comes from women. Villains are delightfully overdrawn. Phoebe and Erica are so bad as to be funny, and so good as to set all kinds of improbable plots in motion. The story, however, tends to revolve around sensitive, vulnerable types like Tara, Kitty, Anne, Ruth, and Donna. Here there is an effective mixture of real-life and fantasy-based material. Ruth's marital breakdown was an adult situation, sensitively played (at least until the end). This was, typically, off-balanced by a fantasy of the innocent prostitute (Donna), and the search for the long-lost mother (Kitty). *All My Children* treats difficult life problems, such as the maintenance of marriage and career. But fortunately there are always a few fun-and-far-out storylines going at the same time. Most fun (and more heavily drawn here than elsewhere) are confrontations between black and white, right- and wrong-headed characters (Mona vs. Erica; the good black doctor vs. the bad black pimp).

Although *All My Children* is a modern-looking show, with a young following, it is respectful of old soap conventions. The show features an eternal triangle, complete with a child who does not know his own father (the Phil/Tara/Chuck triangle). . . . There are also the usual troubled pregnancies and well-timed illnesses. . . . True, there are some social issues: a speech against war; some rumbling about drugs and women's lib; a not-very-well-integrated sequence on child abuse. But this is essentially a fun romantic drama. We listen to the women's lib rhetoric, and feel good about it, but what we really want to know is whether *she* will stay married to *him*. (p. 34)

[*One Life to Live*] was at one time thought to be one of the young trendy shows. The Jenny and Tim romance was compared to that of Phil and Tara (*All My Children*). Issues were "relevant." Cathy Craig was known to be a feminist. There were a few ethnics and even a Jewish family (the Siegels). In short, storylines were such as to interest college-aged viewers.

Recently, however, *One Life to Live* has begun to sound more like a traditional soap. Adultery, mysterious parentage, kidnapping of babies, etc., is what is happening now—good storylines in the old mold. There have been frequent changes in storyline direction, and inexplicable (though highly interesting) changes in character, particularly among the evil set. Characters are becoming less realistic, more melodramatic. For the present, "relevant" storylines seem to have disappeared. (pp. 38-9)

Manuela Soares, "A Viewer's Guide to the Soaps," in her The Soap Opera Book (copyright © 1978 by Latham Publishing; used by permission of Harmony Books), Harmony Books, 1978, pp. 28-44.*

RUTH WARRICK with DON PRESTON

[Nixon's] inventive mind spins out a constant skein of exciting and relevant plots that have made *All My Children* the leading show in the daytime lineup. (p. 129)

And where do those ideas and themes come from? From life, from the world around us, as perceived by a writer highly attuned to the problems and passions that move us all. This, without doubt, is Agnes Nixon's most valuable asset and greatest talent, this finely tuned sensibility both to the moods of the time and to its stresses. If her invention sometimes seems boundless, it is nevertheless highly disciplined. Truth is the criterion against which she measures her fiction—the changing truths of our time and society, the eternal truths of our hearts.

The basic human motives—love, hate, greed, jealousy—have always been with us and have always been grist for the writer's mill, but each moment of history tends to concentrate on certain social and personal problems it considers immediate and urgent. Divorce, for example, once taboo on daytime television, is now virtually epidemic in the serials, as it is in real life. Even more timely is the subject of abortion. . . . [The split] between those who regard abortion as murder of an unborn human and those who regard a woman's right to control her own biological destiny as sacred is reflected in the soaps. When Erica, who was clearly too neurotically immature for motherhood, opted for abortion, all the arguments—pro and con—were given careful and balanced presentation. (Many disagreed vehemently with her decision, but most would have to admit that the question was treated with scrupulous fairness and good taste.) Devon, on the other hand, decided to keep her child, even though her pregnancy had resulted from an immature attempt to get even with one boy by sleeping with another. Devon's choice, aided by Wally's devotion and her mother's loving support, was indeed an affirmation of life, though she (and viewers, one hopes) now sees how self-destructive her immature sexual behavior really was. Perhaps some of the show's young fans will get the message and avoid becoming one of the million-plus teenage mothers produced by this sexually permissive society every year.

Agnes Nixon has often said that she hopes to "open people's minds a little bit" by showing that many of life's situations are not so black and white as they may at first appear. When Donna Beck, the sweet-faced and earnest young runaway who had been coerced into teenage prostitution, became Mrs. Chuck Tyler, many fans condemned Phoebe for her refusal to accept the girl into the family. After all, Donna was trying so hard to straighten out her life and be a good wife. How could Phoebe not welcome her with open arms and a forgiving heart? (pp. 129-30)

[A] woman was very hard on Phoebe at one of our mall show appearances [Warrick created the role of Phoebe Tyler], demanding that I "leave that poor girl alone." Phoebe stared her down and asked her to answer one question with complete honesty: "If *your* grandson came to you and said the girl he was planning to marry was an ex-hooker, a woman who had had sex with hundreds of men for money, how would you *really* feel?"

The woman was clearly torn by mixed emotions. Obviously she would not approve of such a thing in real life, yet she had sympathy for the guileless girl she'd come to know and love on *All My Children*. (Even poor Donna's obsessive attempts to better herself are seen as admirable, though her gaffes must leave viewers with a mixture of amusement and pain. . . .) (p. 130)

We may laugh at Billy Clyde and Benny, too, and sometimes even at Phoebe's somewhat boozy imperiousness, but we feel for them all. And that is the secret of a successful serial: characters. Real people, with real problems and pains you can share, living out their lives as we all must, by trial and error, through tragedy and triumph. They are us, the people of Pine Valley, and their world is a surrogate for ours. The problems we share with them are our problems too, and as we watch them cope we can learn from their mistakes as well as their successes. In fact, in this mobile, often isolated world we now inhabit, where the loving support of extended family and life-long neighbors is often unavailable, Pine Valley may well be a substitute for those things we have lost. In the Martin and Tyler families we see how people interact, how they blunder and hurt one another but remain close, how they work their problems through within the framework of their world. That is why for many—if not most—of *All My Children*'s millions of fans, Pine Valley actually is, in one sense, more real than their own neighborhood. They have unique access to those fictional lives and emotions, and can learn from them. (p. 131)

The question of whether the soaps actually reflect the real world has always been hotly debated, though the attacks seem often to come from those who have never actually watched the shows they castigate. "How could anyone have all those problems, one after another and one on top of another, in real life?" We hear that sort of question all the time, and the best answer I can give is: *One* couldn't, perhaps . . . , but *All My Children* has at least thirty-nine continuing characters, plus dozens that have been written out, killed off, or left in some limbo from which they may or may not return. Altogether there have been close to a hundred major characters—and uncounted minor ones—on the show during its first decade; and with that many people interacting over that span of time, even real life would have come up with a respectable list of marriages, divorces, deaths, and personal conflicts both petty and tragic. (p. 134)

The three-act play, like the nighttime dramatic show or the movie or the novel, distills experience into a single series of circumstances leading to a climax that will, one way or another, resolve the conflict. The soap opera, since it consists of many plot strands and since those many story lines will continue next week and next month, cannot achieve that cathartic resolution. What it *can* offer, however, is a *series* of catharses, with one story reaching a resolution (often temporary) while another one builds toward its own crisis. (p. 135)

Ironically, those who argue that the soaps are not realistic seem determined to disregard the obvious: The two-hour movie, the three-act play, or the one-hour episode of a nighttime dramatic show or situation comedy simplifies and isolates one set of characters and one chain of circumstances in a way that real life never does. The soaps, with their large casts and broad tapestry of stories, actually mirror at least one important aspect of reality in a far more direct fashion than any play ever could. But the soaps, too, are selective, since we are no more likely to relish dull trivia in a continuing story than we are to applaud if Macbeth spends the evening polishing his armor. But such selectivity is not unreal. It is simply a recognition of what we consider important enough to occupy our time and thought.

Yes, it may be true that the citizens of Pine Valley seem to have more problems than your family and neighbors confront, and they may seem to live at an emotional pitch few of us could endure for long. But look around you: How many salesmen do you know who suffer like [Arthur Miller's Willy Loman in *Death of a Salesman*], and how many cops face the perils of Kojak? For that matter, how many fathers have the problems that plagued [Shakespeare's] King Lear? Life contains conflict, and drama is a distillation of life, a prism that refracts the moving and important while omitting the insignificant.

The soaps, undeniably, mirror a very large number of ordinary life's manifold problems. . . . Such controversial subjects as interracial romance, interreligious marriage, and even antiwar activism have figured in the story, as they do in everyday life. . . . Times change, and the serials change with them. "We are first an entertaining medium," Agnes Nixon says, "but we are also a teaching medium. We don't set the tone, but we reflect the times and we encourage viewers to reflect on them."

Thus, *All My Children* is a teaching medium that neither preaches nor lectures. Rather, it permits viewers to *experience* problems vicariously and to measure their own beliefs against the decisions and actions of the characters. Perhaps this helps to explain why soaps are no longer solely the province of "bored housewives," if indeed they ever were. (pp. 135-6)

All My Children has proven any original doubters wrong and Agnes Nixon, as usual, right. The show was originally criticized for being too family oriented, too old-fashioned in its treatment of complicated relationships among people of several generations, committed to one another by bonds of blood and love. But Agnes Nixon believed in those things, and she made believers of the networks, the sponsors, and ten million loyal fans. The Martins and Tylers and the others of Pine Valley may have problems and even deep conflicts, but they are held together by those ties of family and community that are uniquely American. (p. 138)

For millions of Americans, Pine Valley is *their* hometown . . . , and from it they can draw guidance and comfort and reassurance that a common tie binds us all. (p. 139)

[One of the most poignant and thought-provoking sequences ever shown on daytime television was] the sadistic, unprovoked rape of Ruth Martin by Ray Gardner. The act itself was of course not explicitly shown, but, more to the point, its pathological motivations and appalling personal and legal consequences—all carefully researched by Agnes—were explored in depth. Society has too often failed to understand the essential nature of rape: a hate-filled crime that has nothing to do with normal sexuality. Agnes has done many admirable things, but her tasteful, yet unflinchingly candid treatment of this repellent social problem must be one of her finest achievements. (p. 177)

If it is true that America is turning back to romance in its popular entertainments, I'd have to say that *All My Children* has been there all along. Tara and Phil, Jeff and Mary, Cliff and Nina—at no time have we been without at least one story line dealing with idealized young love. There are conflicts, problems, even tragedies, to be sure, but through it all the emotions of the young lovers run pure, intense, and full of yearning. Agnes Nixon may have a sharp eye for timely issues, but she also has a heart that understands the simple things that always move us most. (p. 180)

There is something of Erica in all of us—and something of Mona and Chuck and Benny and Brooke and every other inhabitant of Pine Valley. It was Agnes Nixon's genius to isolate and identify those somethings, to clothe them with imagined personalities and to turn them into vivid, believable characters. (p. 214)

Ruth Warrick with Don Preston, in their The Confessions of Phoebe Tyler *(copyright © 1980 by Ruth Warrick; reprinted by permission of Prentice-Hall, Inc., Englewood Cliffs, New Jersey), Prentice-Hall, 1980, 227 p.*

(Mary) Flannery O'Connor

1925-1964

American short story writer, novelist, and essayist.

O'Connor was by birth and by faith a Roman Catholic who lived much of her life in the heart of the Southern Protestant Fundamentalist Bible Belt. Most of her fiction is set in the small towns and backwoods areas of that region. It is not, however, "southern" in its concerns. Rather, her work is gounded in the theology of orthodox Christianity, and its major concerns are spiritual and religious.

O'Connor was disturbed by what she saw as the contemporary Christian's loss of spiritual consciousness. She attributed this loss mainly to increased materialism and to an unqualified acceptance of modern rationalist thought. In theology, rationalism's doctrines state that human reason, without the assistance of divine revelation, is capable of discerning religious truths. In practice, rationalists believe that reason alone can determine correct behavior. In O'Connor's orthodox Christian view, modern rationalism diluted dogma and negated the need for faith and redemption. Material concerns, she felt, took precedence over spiritual ones.

In her fiction, O'Connor uses scenes and characters from her native environment to comment on the issue of modern spirituality. In the intense and often violent religiosity of Protestant Fundamentalists, she sees spiritual life, however bizarre and extreme its manifestations, struggling to exist in a nonspiritual world. Hazel Motes in *Wise Blood* and Francis Marion Tarwater in *The Violent Bear It Away* are involved in such a struggle. However much they try to believe otherwise, the devil and God are real to them. They are examples of what have come to be known as O'Connor's "Christ-haunted" protagonists: souls torn between their vision of God and the devil and the temptation to deny the reality of that vision. Because of their spiritual struggle they are isolated, and in their frustration and isolation they commit violent acts. They are grotesque in personality and behavior. Nonetheless, O'Connor's sympathies lie more with these characters than with the smug and confident Christians of their society. In her view, spiritual consciousness is, regardless of its distortions, battling for life in a world that has become spiritually numb.

Most critics believe that O'Connor's vision is unique and compelling even to readers who may not share her religious beliefs. Ironically, some of the severest criticism that has been written about her fiction has come from Catholic critics. Interpretations vary in detail, but critics consistently acclaim her as a brilliant spokesperson for a complicated theology, and many consider her untimely death a great loss to American literature. (See also *CLC*, Vols. 1, 2, 3, 6, 10, 13, 15, and *Contemporary Authors*, Vols. 1-4, rev. ed.; *Contemporary Authors New Revision Series*, Vol. 3.)

FLANNERY O'CONNOR

In the greatest fiction, the writer's moral sense coincides with his dramatic sense, and I see no way for it to do this unless his moral judgment is part of the very act of seeing, and he is free to use it. I have heard it said that belief in Christian dogma

Joe McTyre

is a hindrance to the writer, but I myself have found nothing further from the truth. Actually, it frees the storyteller to observe. It is not a set of rules which fixes what he sees in the world. It affects his writing primarily by guaranteeing his respect for mystery. (p. 161)

It may well be asked . . . why so much of our literature is apparently lacking in a sense of spiritual purpose and in the joy of life, and if stories lacking such are actually credible. The only conscience I have to examine in this matter is my own, and when I look at stories I have written I find that they are, for the most part, about people who are poor, who are afflicted in both mind and body, who have little—or at best a distorted—sense of spiritual purpose, and whose actions do not apparently give the reader a great assurance of the joy of life.

Yet how is this? For I am no disbeliever in spiritual purpose and no vague believer. I see from the standpoint of Christian orthodoxy. This means that for me the meaning of life is centered in our Redemption by Christ and that what I see in the world I see in its relation to that. I don't think that this is a position that can be taken halfway or one that is particularly easy in these times to make transparent in fiction. (pp. 161-62)

[Writers] who see by the light of their Christian faith will have, in these times, the sharpest eyes for the grotesque, for the perverse, and for the unacceptable. In some cases, these writers may be unconsciously infected with the Manichaean spirit of the times and suffer the much discussed disjunction between sensibility and belief, but I think that more often the reason for this attention to the perverse is the difference between their beliefs and the beliefs of their audience. Redemption is meaningless unless there is cause for it in the actual life we live, and for the last few centuries there has been operating in our culture the secular belief that there is no such cause.

The novelist with Christian concerns will find in modern life distortions which are repugnant to him, and his problem will be to make these appear as distortions to an audience which is used to seeing them as natural; and he may well be forced to take ever more violent means to get his vision across to this hostile audience. When you can assume that your audience holds the same beliefs you do, you can relax a little and use more normal ways of talking to it; when you have to assume that it does not, then you have to make your vision apparent by shock—to the hard of hearing you shout, and for the almost blind you draw large and startling figures. (pp. 162-63)

> *Flannery O'Connor, "The Fiction Writer and His Country," in* The Living Novel: A Symposium, *edited by Granville Hicks (reprinted with permission of Macmillan Publishing Co., Inc.; © 1957 by Macmillan Publishing Co., Inc.), Macmillan, 1957, pp. 157-64.**

WILLIAM ESTY

There is the Paul Bowles—Flannery O'Connor cult of the Gratuitous Grotesque. . . . Flannery O'Connor tells us that she writes out of a "deep Christian concern." The story of hers which, in Allen Tate's view, best exemplifies this concern is the tale of an embittered, virginal Southern bluestocking with a wooden leg who accompanies a young Bible salesman into a barn to seduce him ["**Good Country People**"]. Her "victim" produces, out of a dummy Bible, whiskey, contraceptives and dirty playing cards. In the end he runs off with her wooden leg in his suitcase. All of these overingenious horrifics are presumably meant to speak to us of the Essential Nature of Our Time, but when the very real and cruel grotesquerie of our world is converted into clever gimmicks for *Partisan Review,* we may be forgiven for reacting with the self-same disgust as the little old lady from Dubuque. (p. 588)

> *William Esty, "In America, Intellectual Bomb Shelters," in* Commonweal *(copyright © 1958 Commonweal Publishing Co., Inc.; reprinted by permission of Commonweal Publishing Co., Inc.), Vol. LXVII, No. 23, March 7, 1958, pp. 586-88.**

CAROLINE GORDON

Miss O'Connor's work . . . has a characteristic which does not occur in the work of any of her contemporaries. Its presence in everything she writes, coupled with her extraordinary talent, makes her, I suspect, one of the most important writers of our age. (p. 3)

Miss O'Connor writes lean, stripped, at times almost too flat-footed a prose, and her characters . . . move always in the harsh glare of every day. But they, too, are warped and misshapen by life—in short, freaks. The difference between her

work and that of her gifted contemporaries lies in the nature and the causes of their freakishness. (p. 5)

The affair between Haze Motes and Sabbath Lily Hawks [in *Wise Blood*] proceeds to a logical and . . . terrifying conclusion. . . . She will go to almost any lengths to get her man and to even greater length to fulfil another womanly function, maternity. Haze yields to her blandishments partly as a way of proving his faith in the Church of Christ Without Christ. They set up housekeeping in a rented room. Haze's friend— or enemy—Enoch Emery, obeying a compulsive impulse, or, as he would put it, his "wise blood," steals a mummy from a city museum. He hears Haze preaching his gospel: "The Church Without Christ don't have a Jesus but it needs one! It needs a new jesus"—and he rushes home, wraps the mummy up and deposits it at Haze's door. Haze is lying on the bed, a bandage over his eyes. Sabbath receives the bundle, unwraps it and after a few moments, during which her face has "an empty look, as if she didn't know what she thought about him or didn't think anything," cradles him in her arms and begins to croon to him. The unholy family is now complete.

Miss O'Connor does not stop there but piles horror on horror. (pp. 5-6)

Miss O'Connor's talent, occurring in such a milieu, is as startling, as disconcerting as a blast from a furnace which one had thought stone-cold but which is still red-hot.

Haze Motes, Miss O'Connor's hero, is illiterate and of lowly origins, but he is spiritually kin to more highly placed Americans. His whole life is given over to a speculation on the nature of Christ, the union of the divine with the human. . . . Haze, a man of action and, it seems to me, a tragic hero, dies in a ditch, self-blinded as the penalty of his disbelief. (pp. 6-7)

In Miss O'Connor's vision of modern man—a vision not limited to Southern rural humanity—all her characters are "displaced persons," not merely the people in the story of that name. They are "off center," out of place, because they are victims of a rejection of the Scheme of Redemption. They are lost in that abyss which opens for man when he sets up as God. This theological framework is never explicit in Miss O'Connor's fiction. It is so much a part of her direct gaze at human conduct that she seems herself to be scarcely aware of it. I believe that this accounts to a great extent for her power. It is a Blakean vision, not through symbol as such but through the actuality of human behavior; and it has [William] Blake's explosive honesty. . . . (pp. 9-10)

> *Caroline Gordon, "Flannery O'Connor's 'Wise Blood'," in* Critique: Studies in Modern Fiction *(copyright © by* Critique, *1958), Vol. II, No. 2, 1958, pp. 3-10.*

ROBERT McCOWN, S.J.

Flannery O'Connor's phenomenal power of giving life to her characters is due to a complete mastery of her art which renders with rapid precision their psychological makeup. What Mr. [William] Esty mistakes for the gratuitous grotesque [see excerpt above] is, much of the time, none other than this realism in picturing living, breathing, sweating humanity. . . . Flannery O'Connor, a Catholic by conviction as well as by birth, writes from a deep Christian concern for the spiritual. Her stories, the characters that live in them, the excellencies of her style, are not ends in themselves but rigorously subordinated means of showing us reality, the quality of goodness and the subtle malice of sin, either of which have power to determine our destiny.

One of the first things which strike us in these stories [in *A Good Man Is Hard to Find*] is the peculiar rigor with which the author limits her canvas to things of her own direct and intimate knowledge—people with whom she has grown up, against the countryside of her own native Georgia. . . . Yet, within these self-imposed limits, she has created characters of extraordinary depth, originality, and color; with all the strength of mind, prejudices, fears—fears of shame, of poverty, of the foreigner—which go to make a Southerner.

Miss O'Connor is admittedly influenced by the writers of the Catholic revival of France and England, notably Bloy, [François] Mauriac, and Greene. Like them she is deeply concerned with the palpable reality of sin, of the blight it can bring to human existence, and of its mysterious communication from one generation to another. Her stories often show that God-fearing, humble parents, no matter how ignorant and shiftless, will generally produce psychologically and morally sound children; whereas the children of the proud and contemptuous, whatever natural gifts they may otherwise have, are likely to turn out warped in some way. (pp. 286-87)

[A] penetrating study of children is **"A Circle in the Fire."** . . . In the swelling psychological conflict which . . . moves steadily toward disaster there is such perfection of balance and restraint in the narrative that the reader finds it hard to take sides either with the self-righteous woman as she strives to maintain her dignity and the semblance of benevolence in the face of [the boys's] encroachment, or with the delinquent boys whose insolence soon grows to lawlessness. Implicitly the root causes of social strife are laid bare as the envy and violence of the *have-nots* contend with the pharisaical pride and avarice of the *haves*. We find here a fully developed tragedy of character and circumstance, written with an astonishing command of details, in barely seventeen pages.

"The River" is the best example of Flannery O'Connor's remarkable talent for creating children characters, and of molding them, as it were, from the inside out, exploring with tenderness, but without a trace of sentimentality, the mysterious processes of their thought and motivation. (p. 287)

The extraordinary quality of Miss O'Connor's humor and the ease with which she puts it into a compressed yet lucid prose come from a thorough knowledge of the people of whom she writes, of the bits of wisdom, truths and half-truths—and down-right prejudices—which make up their mental equipment. **"The Artificial Nigger"** will one day be considered a classic of American humor. . . .

Miss O'Connor's genius for catching the psychological attitude of her characters in brief, penetrating descriptions and bits of dialogue is seen in **"The Life You Save May Be Your Own,"** a sort of tragedy in miniature. (p. 288)

The quality of the tragic element of this story is even higher than that of **"A Circle in the Fire."** The picture of helpless innocence being ground to death among the conflicting forces of pride, hatred, and prejudice, is one of the most important spiritual elements in Flannery O'Connor's writing. We see it first in the title story, **"A Good Man Is Hard to Find,"** but it receives its most complete development in **"The Displaced Person."**

In **"A Good Man Is Hard to Find"** the blood-curdling realism describing the treatment of the helpless family by The Misfit, an escaped convict, following directly upon the light and humorous atmosphere of the first part of the story, might prove a bit too much for the unsuspecting reader. Also, since this story is placed first in the collection, and titles it, it has given rise to much of the adverse criticism of the whole volume. Of course, this fierce contrast of black against white—or very light gray—has its purposes, and there is no denying the mastery of description in the simple strokes which draw the sinister visitant. In two or three pages we see the horror of a soul blasted by the sin of despair, a soul which, we feel, had at one time had a glimpse of the light and of a way of peace, but had rejected it. . . .

Although the structure of **"The Displaced Person"** is somewhat looser and, in a few places, its punch weaker, it is undoubtedly the *pièce de résistance* of the volume. Here are stated explicitly many of the ideas only hinted at in the other stories. (p. 289)

[In] the figure of the awkward, inarticulate foreigner, Mr. Guizak, mistrusted and despised by everyone, is seen the suffering Body of Christ. The scene of his murder is perhaps the most powerfully moving of the whole book.

There are few modern writers whose wit is more unexpected and brilliant, or whose satire is more scathing than Flannery O'Connor's—a sample of her when she *really* wants to be mean is her satire on the South and its nostalgia for the days of glory long-past-but-not-forgotten, in **"A Late Encounter With the Enemy"**—yet her greatest strength lies in another quality which is at a premium among satirists: compassion for those whom she satirizes. The current of irony runs deep throughout her stories, but rarely does it run as deep as her compassion. It is in **"Good Country People"** that is found the richest blend of these two qualities. (p. 290)

Because of her genuine horror of sentimentality, at just the point where many writers would soften, Flannery O'Connor's wit appears to become more wry and her satire more scathing, the result being a quality of humor remarkably akin to that of Chaucer in which the author tells with apparent ease and gusto side-splitting stories, which, nonetheless, contain implicitly matter for some very sobering thought.

In **"Good Country People,"** particularly, we must look beyond the bluff and the sparkling wit to the heart of the matter, to the girl's loss of faith in God's providence resulting from her bitter affliction, to the loneliness, to the wasted talent, to the lack of understanding or sympathy in those who surround her, which have driven her so far into the wasteland of self that she can only be brought back to reality by the scourge of self-knowledge and humiliation. It was against this story in particular that Mr. Esty leveled the charge of "gratuitous grotesque." I think, to the contrary, that it contains a delicately balanced, Christian humanism. . . . (pp. 290-91)

In her first novel, *Wise Blood* . . . , Flannery O'Connor showed an extraordinary writing ability; in *A Good Man Is Hard to Find* she proved herself a storyteller of genius. In not a few respects one might offer her to aspirant young writers as a model to be imitated: in her dedication to her art, in the clear understanding she shows of the limitations of fiction and of the fiction writer, in her many varieties of humor, in her aversion to the apologetic approach. But more than all these there is a certain quality which gives the reader of her stories the immediate impression of being confronted with something real and living, something of one piece with his own experience.

Who would not recognize the dusty clay hills of Georgia covered with granite pines, the speckled old women, the tow-headed children with silver-rimmed spectacles before pale, vacant eyes, their strange wisdom and unpredictable energy, the middle-aged widows with their invincible prejudices. Flannery O'Connor has great talent indeed, but it is, above all, her fidelity to truth which gives her stories their quality of realism; it is a fearless trust in reality itself as something eminently worth knowing, and, when known, more satisfying than all its substitutes. (p. 291)

> Robert McCown, S.J., ''Flannery O'Connor and the Reality of Sin,'' in Catholic World (copyright 1959 by The Missionary Society of St. Paul the Apostle in the State of New York), Vol. 188, No. 1126, January, 1959, pp. 285-91.

SUMNER J. FERRIS

Flannery O'Connor's [*The Violent Bear It Away*] has a number of immediately striking resemblances, in its religious theme, its Southern setting, its frequently violent or macabre action, and its spiritually tortured characters, both to her short stories, especially those collected in *A Good Man Is Hard to Find* (1955), and to her first and only other novel, *Wise Blood* (1952). (p. 11)

Disregarding both the more and less obvious matters for the time being, there are several parallels between [*The Violent Bear It Away*] and some of Miss O'Connor's other works. Haze Motes in *Wise Blood*, like Tarwater here, was obsessed first with denying and then with accepting Christ. Harry Bevel in "The River" was drowned in "the water of life," as is Bishop. The relation between the boy and his great-uncle, especially in the flashback recounting a visit by the two to the city, reminds one of "The Artificial Nigger." The fires Tarwater lights are like the one in "Circle in the Fire," in both provocation and significance. Rayber as a rationalist is like Asbury in "The Enduring Chill." Miss O'Connor still uses half-whimsical symbolic names: "Bishop" and "Tarwater," the latter with its implications of dirt and of a panacea, fit neatly into a novel about baptism. Humor is less obtrusive here than in some of her other works (especially *Wise Blood* and Haze's unforgettable and triumphant "What do I need with Jesus? I got Leora Watts") but this novel has its moments, too; and as usual with Miss O'Connor, comic incongruities rather add to than detract from her seriousness: the great-uncle's monomania for kidnapping and baptizing his infant male relatives is particularly funny. And lastly, some of Miss O'Connor's favorite symbols, sometimes laid on a little thick in other works, reappear here too, and as before they tend to carry two or more opposing meanings simultaneously. Thus, water brings life and death; fire destroys and purifies; eyes reveal and impose purpose; and a physical infirmity (Rayber is deaf) mirrors a spiritual one.

By and large, then, Miss O'Connor's writings are strikingly alike in topic, theme, and technique. Consequently, her admirers as well as her detractors must realize that she has restricted herself to a particular locale, a particular society, and a particular kind of theme; and it is unlikely that she will surprise her readers in any of these respects for some time. It follows that it is just as unlikely that her popularity will grow, that her increasing mastery of both the craft and the art of

fiction will be much noticed, that her greater and greater spiritual vision will be taken for anything but a preoccupation with the same subjects, and, in short, that she will be considered anything but a Southern woman novelist. (pp. 12-13)

But such observations do not give the novel itself the attention and the praise it deserves. For, first of all, *The Violent Bear It Away* is an excellently constructed novel. Although *Wise Blood* had a beginning, a middle, and an end, the connections of its parts with one another were often obscure. But the three parts of this novel are both distinct from and dependent on one another, and the individual chapters (except the sometimes awkward flashback of Chapter II, a price paid for the immediacy of Chapter I) are not merely episodes in themselves, such as a short-story writer might be expected to produce, but cumulative and effective insofar as they are parts of the whole novel.

All writers of imaginative literature are between two horns: either underlining their meaning through repetition and recurring symbolism or trusting that their slightest hint will be—or ought to be—picked up by the hawk-eyed reader. But Miss O'Connor, as a writer on a religious subject with a religious theme . . . , escapes the dilemma neatly: references to Habbakuk, Jonas, and Elias and Elisha; profanity that, in context, takes on an air of blasphemy (Rayber never says "God damn" or "Jesus Christ" but the reader feels its significance); and the very subject matter of the book not only are dramatically appropriate to her story but also underline her meaning and serve as leitmotifs to unify it.

But another, and for some readers perhaps a better, kind of unity and emphasis is provided by the structure of the novel itself. At the end of the first chapter, Tarwater, after burning the cabin, has hitched a ride with a traveling salesman:

> "Look," Tarwater said suddenly, sitting forward, his face close to the windshield, "we're headed in the wrong direction. We're going back where we came from. There's the fire again. There's the fire we left!"
>
> Ahead of them in the sky there was a faint glow, steady, and not made by lightning. "That's the same fire we came from!" the boy said in a high voice.
>
> "Boy, you must be nuts," the salesman said. "That's the glow from the city lights. I reckon this is your first trip anywhere."
>
> "You're turned around," the child said; "it's the same fire." . . .

In the last chapter, Tarwater, after hearing his call to prophecy, walks away from Powderhead:

> The moon, riding low above the field beside him, appeared and disappeared, diamond-bright, between patches of darkness. Intermittently the boy's jagged shadow slanted across the road ahead of him as if it cleared a rough path towards his goal. His singed eyes, black in their deep sockets, seemed already to envision the fate that awakened him but he moved steadily on, his face set toward the dark city, where the children of God lay sleeping. . . .

And if only these two passages were offered in evidence, Miss O'Connor's prose style could be called brilliant. The uniformly staccato rhythms of *Wise Blood* have been developed into smoother and more flexible ones. Consider just the pauses and the emphases of "a faint glow, steady, and not made by lightning" or the subtle but certainly intentional effect produced by the omission of the comma in the last sentence of the second long passage, where the lack of the anticipated rhetorical pause signals also how Tarwater's destiny is now beyond his control. Or the dialogue, all the more horrible for being matter-of-fact and blatantly colloquial. Or the way in which description is merged with narration and both are charged with symbolic meaning. Or the compassionate moving-in of the first passage, from "Tarwater" to "the boy" to "the child"; matched and contrasted beautifully in the second by a moving-away, from "the boy's" to "the children of God"—of whom, we realize, Tarwater is not one any more. Or the unobtrusive way—any teacher of writing knows it can't be taught—that the author's description alternates and merges insensibly with Tarwater's observations in the second passage. But to talk of Miss O'Connor's style in general would be gratuitous. It is never idiosyncratic; and, like that of all artists, it bears and rewards the closest attention.

The theme of *The Violent Bear It Away* is announced by means of an epigraph on the title pages: "From the days of John the Baptist until now, the kingdom of heaven suffereth violence, and the violent bear it away." . . . This passage is taken by various Catholic exegetes . . . to have two different meanings: either that, with Christ's ministry begun, the faithful may at last attain the kingdom of heaven or . . . that the Pharisees, despite John's prophecy and Christ's ministry, still remain unbelievers and try to deny the faithful their reward. Much of the power of this novel comes from Miss O'Connor's rendering in her characters of the two attitudes represented by these two interpretations, that of the believer and that of the unbeliever, the violent and the passive, the saved and the damned.

This novel has already been praised for its "psychological realism." The comment was misdirected; for insofar as these characters are significant and interesting, it is not because of their personalities but because of their souls. Rayber, for example, seems at first to be the merest pasteboard figure: his school's expert on psychological testing, who sheltered his uncle—Tarwater's great-uncle—for four months only to observe him and, in an article in a "schoolteachers' magazine," describe him as a "nearly extinct type," that is, the religious fanatic. Rayber was shot in the ear with buckshot many years before when he tried to retrieve Tarwater from the old man; and the hearing aid he now wears, and can turn on and off at will, is an obvious, if amusing, device to characterize him as a modern rationalist who has ears to hear and hears not. "Do you think in the box," Tarwater asks him about the hearing aid, "or do you think in your head?"

But Rayber has not simply had a symbolic role thrust on him by the author. His condition, the condition of the Pharisee, is the result of an act of will; for he had, at Tarwater's age (the age of apprenticeship and of confirmation), willingly chosen the way of rationalism and thereafter avoided the extremes of religion, which, he tells Tarwater, "are for violent people." (pp. 14-15)

Tarwater's rejection of God is more violent and less pharisaical than Rayber's. But Tarwater has an important task to perform. "Himself baptized by his great-uncle into the death of Christ," he must in turn bring spiritual life through baptism to his cousin Bishop: "Precious in the sight of the Lord even an idiot," his great-uncle has told him. But he goes to the city not to do this

but to see whether what he had been taught about the history of the world was true; that is, for knowledge rather than grace. But grace pursues him. Rayber can not only teach him nothing but even keeps impressing, although unintentionally, his mission on him; and Bishop, whom he wants to ignore or hate, is drawn to Tarwater almost as though he knew why he had come.

Yet the long middle section of the novel, which treats the period between Tarwater's coming to the city and Bishop's death, does not often investigate the workings of Tarwater's mind; for it would be a mistake to suppose, as Rayber does, that the boy is simply responding to his great-uncle's psychological indoctrination. Rather, for all the old man's fanaticism, it is clear that for Miss O'Connor the baptism of Bishop is the most important action Tarwater could perform; and that he is being forced to do it by a concatenation of circumstances beyond his control and different from the merely psychological—which, to the Christian, is another way of saying by Providence. Twice in the novel Bishop tries to jump into a fountain; the second time he is illuminated by a sudden bright shaft of sunlight as by a nimbus. And even when Tarwater has decided, as a final act of rejection, to drown his cousin (for, he thinks, "In dealing with the dead [that is, his great-uncle] you have to act. There's no mere word sufficient to say NO"), Bishop himself stands up in the boat, climbs onto Tarwater's back like the Christ child onto St. Christopher's and falls into the water with him. That is, Bishop, having been refused salvation through baptism by his own father, forces Tarwater to give it to him, although it is the moment of Tarwater's most violent rejection of God and although it is at the cost of his own physical death.

Both Rayber and Tarwater, then, are described in different ways by the title. Rayber's passivity has done violence to Bishop's soul; Tarwater's violence, though it involved Bishop's death, has at least thrust him into the kingdom of heaven. And although a certain pathos undoubtedly attaches to Rayber, Tarwater's action must be, in the world Miss O'Connor depicts, for the greater glory of God.

This is not to say, however, that Tarwater himself is saved; for he may be an instrument of God's providence without being of His company. (One reason, it seems, why Rayber could not drown Bishop was that he could not baptize him at the same time.) Early in the novel, after the old man has died, a "stranger," whom Tarwater soon comes to think of as just his "friend," begins to talk to the boy in his mind, to sow doubts in his mind about the religious teaching he has received, and to urge him not to give the corpse Christian burial (and thus, in orthodox theology, the hope of resurrection at the Last Judgment). Tarwater, of course, follows the stranger's suggestions, recoiling from his uncle's vision of the final reward of the just, "The Lord Jesus Himself, the bread of life":

> The boy would have a hideous vision of himself, sitting forever with his great-uncle on a green bank, full and sick, staring at a broken fish and a multiplied loaf. . . .

This image is not picked up immediately, but it becomes crucial to the interpretation of Tarwater's end. In the city the boy becomes dissatisfied with the unfamiliar food his uncle gives him; and, when they reach the resort together, he finds himself increasingly unable to eat. In the last section of the novel, after Tarwater has assisted in his cousin's drowning, and he himself has come to identify his physical hunger with a spiritual hunger, he is unable to eat the half of a chicken sandwich a truckdriver has given him and is refused a bottle of pop by a store-owner who has heard of his intended desecration of his great-uncle's corpse. It is hardly extreme to equate the sandwich and the pop with the sacramental bread and wine, which in turn become the body and blood of Christ and nourish the faithful; and so Tarwater's proud rejection of God has excommunicated him from the society of the faithful. The brutal assault he suffers is therefore an image of what he has done to himself, an awful reflection of the perverted love of man without God; for he has refused the bread of life.

The call that Tarwater hears and obeys at the end of the novel, after he discovers that his great-uncle had after all been buried, is thus a specious one, a capitulation to circumstances rather than to God; for although he has fulfilled God's will, he has rejected God's ways. It is with the passion of fanaticism and despair, not of religion, that, hellfire behind him and darkness before him, he begins to walk back to the city.

Miss O'Connor's world is a violent one, but the violence is ultimately spiritual, inflicted by the characters on themselves. Her theology is, furthermore, Catholic. . . . God neither saves nor damns any of the characters who have free will; although He provides that the helpless Bishop he baptized and thus saved, He does no more than give Rayber and Tarwater the opportunity to work out their own salvation or damnation. And it is this characteristic that makes *The Violent Bear It Away* not only a subtle and profound and disturbing study of spiritual states but a great religious novel. Miss O'Connor has shown that a Christian tragedy can be written; for in her novel fate and doom do not conspire against man. Either struggling against grace or opening his arms to accept it, his choice is his own. (pp. 16-19)

> Sumner J. Ferris, "The Outside and the Inside: Flannery O'Connor's 'The Violent Bear It Away'," in Critique: Studies in Modern Fiction *(copyright © by* Critique, *1960), Vol. III, No. 2, 1960, pp. 11-19.*

ROBERT O. BOWEN

The promotion of *The Violent Bear It Away,* Flannery O'Connor's second novel, plus the recent promotion of her career indicate that she is being groomed as A Current Great Writer. . . . Where she has succeeded and how raise several questions in both literature and public relations. (p. 147)

At an increasing rate since World War II judgment has dwindled in literary criticism, academic and non-academic, and prestige in letters has come proportionately to rest on personality. As with Hollywood figures, we now learn about the writer, and by inference his writing, through his public image. (p. 147)

Must we acknowledge that she is writing literature *simply* because her stories are negative—along with Nabokov's and Bellow's and [Jack] Kerouac's? Should we—as indeed we have with Truman Capote and James Jones—accept the avowal of her serious intention as adequate justification for her work? Must we accept her work as "Catholic" because she is "Catholic"? Shall we do as others do: tally her Guggenheims and Ford grants and reach an actuarial measure of her success? Lastly, is it not time that we questioned the work and some of these clichés? Must not the critic insist that a work pretending toward literature demonstrate some pertinence to life? Must he not somehow get at the organizing principle in the work?

The factor most commonly assigned Flannery O'Connor is religious profundity. Caroline Gordon has described her vision as "Blakean" and sees in it "Blake's explosive honesty" [see excerpt above]. The tag requires a decision as to what sort of Gothic we have in O'Connor's grotesqueries. If the figures are delineated by the pure, organic vitality of Blake's "bounding line," well and good. If the narratives are Gothic in the convention of [Horace Walpole's] *The Castle of Otranto,* we have a different matter and can hardly liken it to Blake.

In Miss O'Connor's earlier work the Blakean vision was lacking. The minor images of her first novel, *Wise Blood,* far from expressing minor analogies to support the major analogy of the book's dramatic form—as the mediaeval Gothic does—were quirkish and often bungled. . . . [In *Wise Blood*], as well as in many of Miss O'Connor's stories, we find a language that draws attention to itself rather than to its subject.

The prose of the first novel was that of a professional but not an artist, of Truman Capote but certainly not William Blake. From time to time a passage did break through to serve a more literary purpose, as in the terrible conclusion of *Wise Blood,* in which Hazel Motes is beaten to death in a ditch, the universal end, as it were, in this world. In that passage the starkness of language matches a proper callosity of tone. The passage, however, does not represent the entire work.

The Violent Bear It Away, on the other hand, contains little irresponsible imagery. Odd as it may appear that a writer should establish in a novel and a book of short stories a distinct style and then establish in a second novel a different style, that appears to be the case here. Perhaps it is not so odd at that since Miss O'Connor's scope is so narrow that this novel may be said to be no more than a redaction of her earlier work. (pp. 147-48)

Often the prose in [*The Violent Bear It Away*] demonstrates a boldness, a disdain for what is occasionally an affected clinical accuracy in a Naturalistic novelist. For example, when Tarwater drowns the idiot, nothing suggests that the death be taken as a matter of criminal law. The narrative does not concern itself with law, and thus Miss O'Connor intrudes the gimmickry of Dragnet no more than [Edgar Allen] Poe does in "The Fall of the House of Usher."

The narrative is simple. A fourteen-year-old boy, Tarwater, lives in an isolated Southern clearing with his very old prophet great-uncle. The old man has raised Tarwater to be a prophet, leaving him two commands: that Tarwater bury the old man properly beneath a cross, and that Tarwater begin his own prophetic career by baptizing the idiot son of his one other blood kinsman, a would-be-atheistic schoolteacher named Rayber. The story opens with the old man's death and Tarwater's refusal to bury the corpse. The bulk of the book deals with Tarwater's attempt not to baptize the idiot and Rayber's attempt to cure Tarwater of his religious delusion. The essential difference between these two is in Tarwater's faith that he has the ability to act. This ability, he believes, makes him capable not only of willing but of creating significance in life through intentional action.

The thought which the book carries through Tarwater and his uncle is hardly profound in the main. . . . The idea that the old man, Tarwater's great-uncle, prophesizes because "wanting a call, he called himself" is elaborated through the schoolteacher. The dramatic movement of scenes is often powerful in its grotesqueness, but the thought seldom rises above the level offered here.

The particular kind of natural law that governs the world of this novel is stark, dark, and distinctly deterministic. . . . In spite of himself, Tarwater does baptize the idiot and so *is driven* to his prophetic task. He does not choose. He is also forced to acknowledge that in meaningful actions his will does not function to serve his ends, being negated either by a failure of intellect—acting on the wrong object—or an inability to control his actions at the critical moment of applying the intention he wished. Probably the most telling single event is that in which he drowns the idiot only to hear the words of baptism "coming out of himself" without his volition. Clearly his will is not his own. His consciousness serves only to provide awareness of suffering. Nor is the suffering a Russian Orthodox, Dostoevsky-like purgation which will lead eventually to a higher state.

The narrative offers a world of near total desolation and anguish. Instead of a *rejection,* we see the *acceptance* of a physical world . . . , but we are also asked to accept an "Other World" equally terrible. The prophet is not saved to redemption; he is saved to damnation. The terms, of course, negate each other. Tarwater, we are told, "knew, with a certainty sunk in despair, that he was. . . called to be a prophet." And as a prophet he sees "himself trudging into the distance in the bleeding stinking shadow of Jesus, until at last he received his award, a broken fish, a multiplied loaf. The Lord out of dust had created him, had made him blood and nerve and mind, had made him to bleed and weep and think, and set him in a world of loss and fire . . ."

The foregoing citation is not set in any Jamesean irony to indicate a tragicomic misreading of Tarwater's fate on his part. In the world of *The Violent Bear It Away* this vision is a true one. A question of taste intrudes here in that the misreading of the loaves and fishes detracts from what must be intended as high seriousness. However, the alternative to the vision is more significant. Rayber, the evangelical atheist, offers as an alternative a "world where there's no saviour but yourself. . . The great dignity of man," [Rayber] said, "is his ability to say: I am born once and no more. What I can and do for myself and my fellowman in this life is all of my portion and I'm content with it. It's enough to be a man." Barren or not, such rationalism is dignified, and if it allows no Other World, man is free to enjoy this one.

However, the novel makes clear through various prophecies by Tarwater and other prophets that Rayber's rational alternative is no more than a silly delusion. In the world of this novel the characters move in an absolutely relentless deterministic pattern. Although at moments peculiar dramatic devices intrude to raise vague issues, nothing seems to relieve the underlying determinism of the narrative. (pp. 149-50)

After even a casual perusal of *The Violent Bear It Away,* the only reason one might refer to Flannery O'Connor as a "Catholic" author is a personal one. Since this novel has been widely spoken of as "Catholic," it seems imperative that one point out that like so much current negative writing, this book is not Catholic at all in any doctrinal sense. Neither its content nor its significance is Catholic. Beyond not being Catholic, the novel is distinctly anti-Catholic in being a thorough, point-by-point dramatic argument against Free Will, Redemption, and Divine Justice, among other aspects of Catholic thought.

Though the novel assumes a dramatic structure by pursuing the development of Tarwater's fate, a good deal of the stage paraphernalia is Southern Gothic. That is, to some degree the book makes sense, but the total negativism of its statement

added to its Gothic stage mechanisms qualifies it as perhaps High or Academic Gothic as distinguished from the Gothic as found in *The Castle of Otranto* or James Purdy's *The Color of Darkness.* Telepathy is fairly common in the novel, and we have a Hell-fire, prophetic, crippled, little girl preacher with a voice "like a glass bell." There is a homosexual debauchment, a corpse sitting at a breakfast table; a sex delinquent's child is born in an auto wreck. . . . Much of the violence, such as the drowning of the idiot, tends toward the Gothic in being staged without regard for the mundane details of police procedure or other trivia so that the reader is overcome by terror. If this were the only such detail, since it is structurally unified, we might say that its handling showed a Classical starkness akin to that of [Franz] Kafka or Poe. But though we may justify the drowning so, we cannot defend every scene of violence with an organic unity argument.

The most thoroughgoing Southern Gothic detail falls late in the book. Tarwater is drugged and assaulted by a "pale, lean, old-looking young man with deep hollows under his cheekbones." The rape is vague, as is common in the Southern Gothic, and about all that it does contribute is more anguish as if to suggest that one should suffer every violation even to being raped by a homosexual. The assault is not enriched any by the fact that it is stuck into the text rather anticlimactically and is perpetrated by a total stranger who picks up Tarwater as the latter is hitch-hiking. A question of taste rises here, as often in the novel. Apparently the homosexual is a divine agent sent to impose a sign on Tarwater. At almost any turn in the narrative a slight probing will produce similar questions and implied intentions. Yet if the book as a whole is intended as religious, one wonders how deeply this intention goes.

Beyond the religious question, a book as negative as this raises a question about its insight into current American culture. Such books appear to be praised for two reasons: first, because they feed some partisan need in certain would-be critics who wish to see any positive faith attacked; second, they are merely a new form of the Gothic novel, which is to say that they sell well on the popular market. They are thriller books for intellectuals. . . . Thus we see the link between the Southern Gothic with its homosexuality and the Northern aberrational tale such as Nabokov's *Lolita;* both are negative, both thrilling, and both are said to be compassionate and profound, no doubt because of their passion-charged trappings and confusion.

It is impossible to avoid pointing out that The New Critical concern for method has so removed intent or principle from "critical" concern that books of almost no significance as literature are now analyzed calmly and thoroughly as serious literary efforts. . . . Apparently Flannery O'Connor is [but a sample]. Whether or not she is pulling her own leg is not the place of a reviewer to say, but it is certain that she has tried to pull the legs of many others and with frequent success. (pp. 150-51)

The basic element lacking in the kind of novel that *The Violent Bear It Away* represents is redemption. Always we find in these horrors that there is no hope because the people in the books are already damned and in torment. There can be neither compassion nor virtue in such a world because either depends by definition on redemption. Beyond the sentimentality of such books, though, and beyond their questionable taste, as novels they are subversive of literature itself; for, by its nature, literature is a statement of faith and of hope. When despair becomes its statement, the art has ended. Perhaps even more than that has ended, for where hope cannot exist in art, it has already failed in life. Ultimately, if we weigh *The Violent Bear It Away* seriously, we are forced to conclude that its truth is that there is no hope in this world or in the next. I offer, then, as a considered statement, that Flannery O'Connor in this novel is an enemy of literature and of life, for the book is a pointless bit of comic book sentimentality. (p. 152)

Robert O. Bowen, "Hope vs. Despair in the New Gothic Novel," in Renascence *(© copyright, 1961, Marquette University Press), Vol. XIII, No. 3, Spring, 1961, pp. 147-52.*

MAURICE BASSAN

In the light of a disturbing abdication of responsibility among major critics with respect to the continuing importance of reading our modern writers, the recent critical neglect of Flannery O'Connor should not be surprising. . . .

Since the appearance of her first novel, *Wise Blood,* over ten years ago, Miss O'Connor has not exactly overwhelmed either critics or readers with her gifts. There has not been merely neglect, however, but hostility as well. . . . Even her professed friends have often damned her with the faint praise of continuing the great modern tradition of "Southern Gothic." One barrier to her acceptance has surely been that, rather like the farmers in her region who are paid not to overproduce, her production has been severely limited in quantity. She has written only two novels and a baker's dozen of short stories. Her small "quota" is a function, I think, not only of her exquisite sense of perfection, but of the narrow range of theme and subject-matter she has allowed herself to explore. Yet within this self-imposed boundary, and setting aside the question of whether one need embrace her values, Flannery O'Connor is one of the best writers of fiction we have. If she were never to write another line, her position as a distinguished minor American writer would be as secure as that of Sarah Orne Jewett or Elinor Wylie. (p. 195)

One key . . . to Miss O'Connor's flamboyant technique is that she seeks deliberately to shock and startle an audience which is basically a *Christian* audience. The surface hardness and apparent cynicism of her stories can be very deceptive indeed, and lead the naively cynical reader to assume that in these "Gothic" visions of terror seen in the blaze of a Georgia noon Miss O'Connor is merely reproducing, perhaps even with approval, the blasted moral sensibility of her times. Nothing could be further from the truth. It is worth noting in this connection that in the technique of the completely removed author, and especially in her cold hard phrases, Miss O'Connor very much resembles Stephen Crane and Hemingway, rather than any Southern writer I know. Yet she would have little sympathy for the real cynicism of the former, or the romantic, essentially autobiographical projections of the latter. A final problem that the reader of her work faces is related both to the matter of her *donnée* and to the question of her aesthetic and moral distance from the characters she creates. Although a fervent Catholic, Miss O'Connor does not go out of her way to flatter her Catholic characters, either the doddering old priest in **"The Displaced Person,"** for example, or the "big nun" in **"A Temple of the Holy Ghost"** who lovingly mashes the side of a girl's face into the crucifix hitched onto her belt. There are few Catholics in her fiction; she writes of the red clay roads, the old farms, the loves and prejudices, and the (to her) backward Protestantism of the South, and there are not many Catholics there. But the image of Grace as conceived by a beau-tifully disciplined Catholic mind hovers always just behind the scenes. (pp. 196-97)

["**A Temple of the Holy Ghost**"] seems a slight tale, yet it is very rich indeed in its perception, and it has been thus far either ignored or . . . misunderstood. **"A Temple of the Holy Ghost"** is a study of the flowering of a religious sensibility in an environment alien to and contemptuous of such a sensibility; of its flowering within a child whose shattering honesty enables her to pierce the ludicrous shams surrounding her. This basic theme—the terrible disparity between the divine potentialities of human beings and their depraved acts, conditioned by their secular environment—can be turned to tragic purposes in such heightened shockers as the novel *Wise Blood* or the recent long story **"The Lame Shall Enter First"**; but the theme yields also to comic treatment, as in the story before us, or to a combination of modes, as in her best work, *The Violent Bear It Away.* Indeed, more and more Miss O'Connor has chosen to concentrate upon the evil secular character of her hero's environment, as the polarity which impedes his receptiveness to the Word of God; there is an angriness about *The Violent Bear It Away* and **"The Lame Shall Enter First"** which we do not find in **"A Temple of the Holy Ghost,"** whose heroine is not tempted by the positivist devil. Unlike the children in **"The River"** and **"The Lame Shall Enter First,"** she does not have to resist her parents or flee her home in order to be saved; and unlike young Tarwater in *The Violent,* she does not disavow the movement of grace within her soul. The unnamed child of this story is a proto-saint, who, like several of Miss O'Connor's genuinely heroic figures, is not intellectually aware of the operations of grace within her. In **"A Temple,"** the materials are treated gently, as it were, with comic descriptive touches, deliberately broad satire, some burlesque, and a continual tone of merriment and hilarity which stems from both the child's quaint imagination and the depth of her ironic penetration of reality.

Although Miss O'Connor's tale is brief, its scenes are carefully focused upon the development of the sense of grace within the child, and its contrasts with her deplorable environment. (p. 197)

The imagination that creates the story is capable of using symbols originally and sometimes shockingly. **"A Temple of the Holy Ghost"** is a symbolic story tracing the progress of the martyr-saint through a world of brutality and outrage and denial of salvation to "the red clay road," the road of this world, which inevitably leads to God. The visible signs of salvation are real, undeniable: the sense of moral honesty and humility in the child; the humble acceptance of God's judgment by the freak within an obscene and exploitative framework; the elevation of the Host. These are linked in Miss O'Connor's story by their being manifestations of the Word; all three characters—childs, freak, priest—are in their own ways temples of the Holy Ghost. There is a glorious sense of cosmic optimism in her comic fable, as she makes the essentially Catholic assertion that in the imagination of a child, the mind of a freak, the sanctified actions of a priest, Grace is still operative in a universe basically hostile to it. (pp. 199, 211)

Maurice Bassan, "Flannery O'Connor's Way: Shock, with Moral Intent," in Renascence *(© copyright, 1963, Marquette University Press), Vol. XV, No. 4, Summer, 1963, pp.195-99, 211.*

BRAINARD CHENEY

The shock of Flannery O'Connor's death came not in its unexpectedness but in the startling realization that her work is done. . . .

There must be recognition that the two novels, less than twenty short stories, and fewer essays are the work complete of the fiction writer, in my opinion, most significant in our time. But is her work done, indeed? (p. 555)

She began with the Woe, *Woe to you who are filled, for you shall hunger,* as theme, given embodiment in her novel *Wise Blood,* in 1952. It was satire; it was bitter parody on the atheistic Existentialism then pervading the literary and philosophical scene. But it was more. Haze Motes, with his self-mutilated sightless eyes and other penitential mortifications, and his landlady and fascinated pursuer, at the *dénouement,* foretold a hunger now apparent. (p. 556)

[In] addition to being a brilliant satirist, she was a true humorist and possessed an unusual gift for the grotesque. But she resorted to something far more remarkable to reflect her Christian vision to a secular world. She invented a new form of humor. At least I have encountered it nowhere else in literature. This invention consists in her introducing her story with familiar surfaces in an action that seems secular, and in a secular tone of satire or humor. Before you know it, the naturalistic situation has become metaphysical and the action appropriate to it comes with a surprise, an unaccountability that is humorous, however shocking. The *means* is *violent,* but the end is Christian. And obviously, it works.

It occurs to me here that she accomplished what she set out to do to an astonishing degree. She got attention. She got reaction. And I believe that she got across her Christian vision to a significant public. This last is evident in the sympathetic critical emphasis her work now receives in the Catholic and in much of the Protestant press. As a measure of hostile attention and reaction, I would cite her front-rank appearance in "the structure of the American Literary Establishment," as this putative *entente* was presented in *Esquire* magazine, in July, 1963. Her prominence in this company is the more notable, since the prevailing vision of the Establishment is secular and atheistic.

But, *complete?*

Miss O'Connor said in her revealing essay ["**The Fiction Writer and His Country**"] that the writer's country "is inside as well as outside him" and that "to know oneself, is above all, to know what one lacks." Is this not a clue?

I have said that her theme changed but little, yet I think there was a progress. Without trying to step it off we may note that, in her short masterpiece, "**The Displaced Person,**" its successive protagonists, Mrs. Shortley and Mrs. McIntyre, come to a tragic realization of the secular delusion; and, in her second novel, *The Violent Bear it Away,* little Bishop, as he is being drowned, is baptized. In her last story yet published, "**Revelation,**" the world is no less secular, nor is the Christian revelation any less devastating to one corrupted by the world. Yet her heroine, Mrs. Turpin, finds the need and the humility . . . to measure herself "against Truth."

Do we not have here the *blessed* corollary of the Woe with which we began?

It is much too early to attempt any ultimate assessment of Flannery O'Connor's work. There is as yet but limited understanding of this original, powerful, and prophetic writer. But the prophet is not expected to wait on the fulfilment of his prophecy. In her own words, "The creative action of the Christian's life is to prepare his death in Christ." And this, I feel sure, she did. (pp. 557-58)

Brainard Cheney, "Flannery O'Connor's Campaign for Her Country," in The Sewanee Review *(reprinted by permission of the editor; © 1964 by The University of the South), Vol. LXXII, No. 4, October-December, 1964, pp. 555-58.*

WARREN COFFEY

We now have all the work by which Flannery O'Connor will be remembered in the world. Of her last stories, collected in *Everything That Rises Must Converge,* it is certainly the just praise, and maybe the highest after all, that they are up to her first ones. She wrote best in the short story and has left a handful of them at least that are likely to last as long as literacy. When she died at thirty-nine last year, it was with her work done, I think, and work of an imaginative order and brilliance rare in the world at most times, perhaps always in American writing. . . . [*A Good Man Is Hard to Find* and] *Everything That Rises Must Converge,* . . . contain some of the surest and most original comic writing ever done by an American.

Her novels are another matter. They suffer, I think, from an excessive violence of conception. They are the children of a rape or, better, of a five-months birth, on their way to being something perhaps very fine, but not there yet. *Wise Blood* . . . seems more the work of somebody who has a Master's degree in creative writing from the University of Iowa in pocket—as she had—than a book that has seen its way to saying something. Though the early train scenes have some wildly comic writing, the book as a whole seems as much a product of the determination to write a full-length novel as of anything more august. (pp. 93-4)

Flannery O'Connor's other novel, *The Violent Bear It Away,* has passages of great and strange beauty—the scenes toward the end, for example, leading up to young Tarwater's walk back to the city—but it makes a mistake that the stories never make: the vehicle plainly does not fit the tenor. The whole novel is based on the idea that young Tarwater has inherited a compulsion to baptize from his mad preacher uncle. At the level of metaphor, the idea is entirely sound: large numbers of people do wish to convert us to their beliefs, i.e., to *baptize* us. But concretely and physically, where metaphor should have its base, it ceases entirely to work, for nobody inherits, I think, and very few acquire, the compulsion to push other persons under water. And it is on a physical drowning, a literal baptizing, that all of *The Violent Bear It Away* centers. I honor the Flannery O'Connor novels. They are mistakes of a promise that nobody else could have managed, and they have passages of great brilliance. But her strength was at the epiphany . . . , the leading of the reader up to a dazzling revelation in a moment of time or away from that moment on the waves of its resonance. "**Good Country People**" is an example of the one and "**Revelation**" of the other. For the longer stretches of time and the wider range required of the novel, she did not have the gift. (p. 94)

Faulkner's *As I Lay Dying* was apparently one of a few books [O'Connor] pressed on friends. And her debt to Faulkner is plain, mainly I should say in her refusal to deal with life in abstractions and in her power with regional detail—clay roads, stands of pine, barns, and so forth—and the gritty concreteness of language that are the badge in narrative and in style of that refusal. Her "major" at the Woman's College of Georgia had been the social sciences, and yet in her books to speak the bright language of those studies is infallibly the sign of the fool and generally of the knave as well. In this way, Flannery

O'Connor was, I suppose, a Southern writer. The South gave her her terrain and the people she wrote about first and last. And William Faulkner gave her a start at a way of treating them. But her way of seeing them was her own and would have been the same, I think, if she had lived in North Dakota or Nova Zembla. Her writing is so different from that of the other Faulknerians—so different from that of Capote, for example, or the even more girlish [Tennessee] Williams—that one is taken even less far than usual by labels like "Southern" or "Faulknerian" when talking about her books.

She owed almost as much, I should say, to Ring Lardner and Nathanael West as to Faulkner. To Ring Lardner, the satirist's trick of catching cliché as it falls and freezes the banality of a life or mind. . . . [It] tells us something of her independence that she should have started with somebody as much out of fashion as Ring Lardner—Flannery O'Connor went on to make merry with the pretensions of social workers and intellectuals and anxious mothers and wives of Dixie hog-farmers. With an ear as fine as Lardner's own for dialect and for the way of a man with a cliché, Flannery O'Connor had what is even rarer, a conscious and austere control of the art of the story. She avoids the wandering and the sprawl that are the inherent dangers of Lardner's method—however racily the ball-player talks, he often becomes tedious in his brainlessness and illiteracy—by always telling her stories in her own person and thus staying on top of her matter.

Nathanael West's *Miss Lonelyhearts* was another of the books . . . that Flannery O'Connor used to press on her friends. And her debt here, though not plain, is again extensive. To extreme and painful situations she brought, as West did, a great deal of mocking ironic poise. If she has no girls without noses, she has them with artificial legs and with acne-blued faces. She has one-armed men and men covered with tattoos, and she is fond of thrusting this grotesque part of humanity into confrontations with characters more comfortably housed in the flesh. Her purpose in all this, and West's, is not, I think, that of the Fat Boy in [Charles Dickens's *David Copperfield*]: "I wants to make your flesh creep." Rather, these violent confrontations and the violent action that grows out of them show her willingness to take a chance on the assertion that behind the grotesquerie and violence a God presides. West, using the same surreal methods, questioned that assertion. Miss O'Connor's success in making hers stick in a literary way varies a good deal, from stories like **"A Temple of the Holy Ghost,"** which strikes me as rather pat and wan, up through such later brilliant successes as **"The Enduring Chill"** and **"Revelation."** . . . Nathanael West has greater range and greater knowledge of the world, but he does not, I think, cut [as deep as she does in **"Revelation"**]. Flannery O'Connor had from him the daring to face big questions and part of the technical dash to get them stated in fiction, but her way of resolving them was her own.

She was—that rare thing among Catholic writers in this century—a Catholic born. The Catholicism never gets stated in her stories, but it is always assumed, and it always glimmers in the distance as a kind of unwritten and implied *Paradiso* for the dark comic goings-on in the stories themselves. As an American Catholic, Flannery O'Connor was, of course, a Jansenist. . . . I think that Jansenism, more than anything else, explains both her very considerable power at the short story and her limitations. The pride of intellect, the corruption of the heart, the horror of sex—all these appear again and again in her books, and against them, the desperate assertion of faith.

Out of these themes grows the paradigm story, for Flannery O'Connor, like most authors, had a paradigm story which she wrote again and again, in her case a kind of morality play in which Pride of Intellect (usually Irreligion) has a shattering encounter with the Corrupt Human Heart (the Criminal, the Insane, sometimes the Sexually Demonic) and either sees the light or dies, sometimes both. **"The Lame Shall Enter First,"** which is perhaps a better paradigm than story anyway, will illustrate. We meet a social worker named Sheppard—*shepherd,* I suppose, though the author once wrote to a professor of English who had asked about the symbol-value of one of her characters' names, "As for Mrs. May, I must have named her that because I knew some English teacher would write and ask me why." Sheppard, who disbelieves in God and the devil, has undertaken to rehabilitate the thieving club-footed Rufus Johnson by taking the boy into his own household, buying a new shoe for the bad foot, and providing access to the *Encyclopaedia Britannica.* Johnson, who at fourteen boasts of his possession by Satan, is the corrupt human heart that Flannery O'Connor saw as beyond the reach of any therapy but the grace of God. He steals, peeps into windows, lies, smashes up houses, dances in Sheppard's dead wife's girdle, and—just at the point where Sheppard admits the failure of therapy—drives his would-be benefactor's son to suicide and goes off insisting to the police that Sheppard had made sexual advances to him.

That is the paradigm, and though not all the stories are written to it, not even all the best ones, a good many are and the point, I think, is that God gets asserted out of the abyss of the human heart. **"The Lame Shall Enter First"** is itself a reworking of *The Violent Bear It Away,* where the paradigm may also be seen. Variations of it appear in **"Revelation"** and **"The Enduring Chill,"** where Irreligion appears as mere Conventional Religiousness—low-on-the-hog Protestantism in the one and high-tea Catholicism in the other. The Corrupt Heart can become a pathological killer—the Misfit in **"A Good Man Is Hard to Find,"** or a shifty Bible salesman in **"Good Country People"** or a whore in **"The Comforts of Home."** In a somewhat lower key, the redneck grandfather in **"The Artificial Nigger"** is appalled to discover himself capable of telling a lie denying kinship with his own grandson.

Though I have dwelt at some length on the horror of sex as an element in American Jansenism and in Flannery O'Connor's books, I do not wish to overstate this, because it seems to me that her record in the whole matter is better than that of almost any Catholic writer of the century. **"Good Country People"** is a story a man would give his right arm to have written. . . . Sex here is both terrible and wildly funny. Yet **"Good Country People"** alone among the Flannery O'Connor stories explodes out of the kind of encounter between a man and a woman that [Anton] Chekhov thought of as the most basic of human and fictional situations. . . . Outside of **"Good Country People,"** even in it for that matter, sex generally has something of the demonic about it for Flannery O'Connor—the homosexual attack on young Tarwater in *The Violent Bear It Away,* for example, or the club-footed boy leering in at windows in **"The Lame Shall Enter First."** (pp. 95-8)

More than anything else, . . . horror of sex has robbed Catholic writing of the range, the sanity, and the shrewd and generous humanity that it had when Geoffrey Chaucer rang for the last time the great Catholic bell and rang it in plague-time too.

Some years ago, and before he went on to higher things, Conor Cruise O'Brien wrote an acute book of literary criticism, *Maria Cross,* in which he dealt with recurring "imaginative patterns" in eight Catholic writers—[François Mauriac, Georges Bernanos, Graham Greene, Evelyn Waugh], and others, all of them worlds removed from Flannery O'Connor. Her writing in general owes almost nothing to theirs, though Manley Pointer has something perhaps of Waugh's Basil Seal about him. So it is the more remarkable to find behind Miss O'Connor's writing the exact pattern that O'Brien has found behind that of her European fellow Catholics and near contemporaries: a pattern of intense and incommunicable pain arising from sex and transformed by religion into art. . . . The pain and the acceptance of pain are behind [O'Connor's] art, which is where they surely belong, not in it. This it is that enables Waugh to take the long view, to write with immense comic assurance of the most painful kinds of human experience—death itself, for example, or cannibalism for that matter. In the same way, Flannery O'Connor fits into a comic view of the world such things as manic killers, deformed bodies, intense hatreds, and violent deaths. With all of this, her comic art, like Waugh's, is able to live as merry as cup and can. The one thing that both of them find too terrible in the world to contemplate is ordinary sexual experience, love as anything other than a crucifixion—though it must be granted that both writers are admirably open when put against a Mauriac or a Graham Greene. (pp. 98-9)

Catholic writing has often had in this century great austerity and control, as it has again in the stories of Flannery O'Connor. It can never make peace with the world, but I think at last it is going to have to make its peace with Henry Miller. The cost of not doing so is the loss of range and humanity and the retreat to an ever more waspish perfection in ever smaller literary forms. That is the direction in which Flannery O'Connor's writing sometimes fails. **"The Comforts of Home,"** for example, does **"Good Country People"** over in reverse gear, which is more ingenious than efficient. And *Everything That Rises Must Converge,* which has excellent and varied stories, has none as raucously funny as **"The Artificial Nigger"** or **"The Life You Save May Be Your Own"** in her earlier collection. She would not go wider than her ground, and nobody could have gone deeper there.

She had done her work, I think, when she died and done it very well. It is all native stone of her own quarry. She found the human heart a pretty dark place, as most writers have done who have cared to look very long. But she was not a hater, and she never trafficked in despair. She did much of her writing with death more or less in the next room but went on until she had sent into the world the tough and brilliant comic stories of which all readers now become, in an old formula, the heirs and assigns forever. "Nothing is here for tears . . . nothing but well and fair."(p. 99)

Warren Coffey, "Flannery O'Connor," in Commentary *(reprinted by permission; all rights reserved), Vol. 40, No. 5, November, 1965, pp. 93-9.*

BOB DOWELL

A perusal of Miss O'Connor's fiction will reveal that Christ-haunted figures furnish the author her principal subject matter. Through the conflicts, often violent ones, of these protagonists who oscillate between belief and unbelief, between self-will and submission, the author presents her view of reality. This grotesque drama that she presents takes place in a discernible theological framework in which there is an implicit acceptance of the concept of a created universe, "with all that implies of

human limitations and human obligations to an all-powerful Creator." . . . Such a view heightens man's every action, for his every action is seen "under the aspect of eternity." . . . Thus, Miss O'Connor's fiction is primarily concerned with man's life-and-death spiritual struggle. The protagonist, rebelling against belief, forces a crisis that reveals to him his haughty and willful misconception of reality, at which time he experiences what Miss O'Connor has called his "moment of grace." Without exception this moment comes at great price. . . .

In the O'Connor world whether one commits himself to evil deeds or good deeds makes little difference ultimately, for without Christ one's actions only lead to evil. (p. 236)

I suspect the comic technique employed in most of [O'Connor's] stories to be, for the most part, a necessary vehicle for carrying her unpopular theme. Humor is always an accessible mask for saying what one actually believes, for somehow humor proves an accepted convention for voicing what would otherwise be resented.

Though willing to exploit his unwilling antics, Miss O'Connor never loses sight of man as a created being whose soul is precious to his Creator. Despite his ignorance, his rebelliousness, and his tendency toward evil, man still realizes his fullest potential by participating in a supernatural relation with his Creator. This depends upon his recognition of the existence of evil, of his own tendency toward evil, and his ability to triumph over evil through grace, a supernatural gift from God which comes only with man's full realization of his lost condition and his dependence on Christ. With this realization, which constitutes his moment of grace, man's salvation is begun; he can then begin to fulfill the purpose of his existence, which is to reflect the goodness of his Creator and to share the happiness of heaven with Him. This is Miss O'Connor's view of ultimate reality. (pp. 237-38)

Miss O'Connor sought to give new life to what she believed to be significant religious truths that were once a living reality but which the modern mind has tended to either distort or reject. Her stories, which are in a sense grotesque parables, dramatize the existence of evil. Satan's greatest triumph, her works seem to suggest, lies in the fact that he-has convinced the world that he does not exist. But for Miss O'Connor he does exist. The backwoods fanatics who either believe he exists or at least are preoccupied with the possibility of his existence may seem ludicrously grotesque to most readers. Yet Miss O'Connor gives serious treatment to these grotesques because their concerns are her concerns. In their defense, she has publicly stated that "their fanaticism is a reproach, not simply an eccentricity. Those who, like Amos or Jeremiah, embrace a neglected truth will be seen to be the most grotesque of all." . . . The conflict between grace and evil in the lives of her characters reflects for the author the most significant drama in the realm of human experience. (p. 239)

Bob Dowell, "The Moment of Grace in the Fiction of Flannery O'Connor," in College English *(copyright © 1965 by the National Council of Teachers of English; reprinted by permission of the publisher and the author), Vol. 27, No. 3, December, 1965, pp. 235-39.*

ROBERT DRAKE

The fiction of the late Flannery O'Connor . . . poses a unique problem. Unlike some contemporary Christian writers, she makes no concessions to the non-Christian world: on the whole, she refuses to make her ideology palatable to non-Christian readers by suggesting any philosophical frame of reference other than that of Christian orthodoxy. And today this is an extremely big risk to take: such a theme and such methods inevitably deny the Christian writer many readers. Significantly, many of those same readers find Dante and [John] Milton as rewarding as ever. But one suspects that they may be reading *Paradise Lost* and the *Divine Comedy* simply as "poetry" and discounting what they believe to be the theological residuum as "history"—interesting but no longer relevant in these enlightened times.

This approach, however, is almost impossible with Miss O'Connor. For one thing, she is only recently dead: in a sense, she has not yet passed into history. The settings of her novels and stories are thoroughly contemporary; and, more significantly, her overriding strategy is always to shock, embarrass, even outrage rationalist readers—and perhaps most especially those like the sort mentioned above who think Dante and Milton are great poets as long as one does not have to take their theology seriously. Such readers, significantly, are very quick to defend the King James Bible against the encroachments of modern translations—not on any theological grounds but rather as a literary masterpiece in danger of competition from cheap imitations. T. S. Eliot has pointed out that such a defense assumes of course that the theological content is dead: it is just the literature they are interested in.

But Miss O'Connor really seems to believe all that stuff, and she cannot be written off for a long time as "history." The theology is simply there—as such—and must be reckoned with. In her case the theology is perhaps even more obtrusive than it is in a writer like Eliot, many of whose poems seem "patient of" a Christian interpretation but not exclusively so. Furthermore, she often seems to regard her function as prophetic or evangelistic and makes no bones about it: she has, in a sense, come to call the wicked to repentance—and none more so than the modern intellectuals who have no use for Christianity, the Church, or its traditional doctrines. And this may be what does limit her audience: she makes a crucial problem of belief. And the fact that she is writing in what has been called the post-Christian world (as Dante or even Milton were not) may force her to adopt a kind of shock tactics.

But by no means is this to say that Miss O'Connor was writing programmatic or propagandistic fiction: if she had been, she would not have written nearly so well. She was not writing just tracts for the times; though, in the broadest sense, her fiction is that too. It is to say, however, that her vision of man in this world was uncompromisingly Christian: she saw all of life in Christian terms; she thought the Gospels were really true; and she accepted the historic teachings of the Church. And this intellectual and philosophical position informed everything she wrote. She was not trying to "sell" Christianity; she was—as indeed any writer is—trying to "sell" her particular perception of life in this world as valid.

Though born and bred a Roman Catholic, Miss O'Connor rarely wrote about her fellow communicants, largely, one suspects, for geographical and historical reasons. As an almost lifelong resident of rural Georgia, she inevitably knew more—and perhaps more about—Protestants, particularly those in the fundamentalist and pentecostal sects. But there was nothing narrow or sectarian in her theology: she was Catholic in the oldest and widest sense of the term. Indeed, one suspects that Miss O'Connor's hot-gospelers and the Church of Rome have much more

in common than not, though of course many of her fictional characters do look on the Pope as the Whore of Babylon.

Certainly, it does not seem true, as has been once or twice suggested, that she was a sophisticated Roman making sport with the eccentricities and grotesqueries of her good Southern Baptist brethren. Such a charge is wide of the mark. If anything, Miss O'Connor seems to take a grim, ironic pleasure in siding with the Southern fundamentalists against the modern, willful intellectuals or the genteel, self-sufficient schemers who are her greatest villains. The Southern Baptists or the Holy Rollers may be violent or grotesque or at times even ridiculous; but, she implies, they are a whole lot nearer the truth than the more "enlightened" but godless intellectuals or even the respectable do-gooders and church-goers who look on the Church as some sort of glorified social service institution while preferring to ignore its pricklier doctrines.

In the light of these observations, then, Miss O'Connor's major theme should come as no surprise to us. It is that the Christian religion is a very shocking, indeed a scandalous business . . . and that its Savior is an offense and a stumbling block, even a "bleeding stinking mad" grotesque to many. He "upsets the balance around here"; He "puts the bottom rail on top"; He makes the first last and the last first. In short, He revolutionizes the whole Creation and turns the whole world upside down, to the scandal of those who believe that two plus two always equals four (and, with craft, possibly five) or those who believe that they do not need any outside help (a savior) because they are doing all right by themselves. And this Christ comes not lamb-like and meek, as a rule, but comes in terrifying glory, riding the whirlwind: He is more like Eliot's "Christ the tiger" than gentle Jesus meek and mild. There is nothing sweet or sentimental about Him, and He terrifies before He can bless.

This theme, along with several related sub-themes, constitutes the principal burden of Miss O'Connor's work; and, even when it is not obvious, it is usually lurking in the background (like her Christ), ready to spring out to confront her rationalists and do-gooders (and the reader) with its grisly imperative: "Choose you this day whom ye will serve." And it is impossible, implies Miss O'Connor, to blink the issue: there is no place for Laodiceans in her world. For this reason her fiction, though carefully ordered, even sedate and regular in its narrative progressions, has often the urgent intensity, the ordered ferocity of a dramatic but sober evangelistic sermon. And one feels that, in her continuing insistence on the immediacy and importance of the four last things, she recaptures (as indeed the fundamentalist sects try to do) something of the atmosphere of the Primitive Church.

Indeed, the world of Miss O'Connor's fiction seems to wait hourly for Judgment Day—or some new revelation or perhaps a transfiguration, in any case, some sign that the Almighty is still "in charge here." Exactly *what* the event will be is not so important as that her world is subject to the continuous supervision of the Management, who makes itself known sometimes quietly and sedately but, more often here, in a "purifying terror." (pp. 183-85)

Though [O'Connor] seems to have wanted to write more novels, her real *forte* was the short story—and for reasons which are perhaps not difficult to ascertain. The violent but fiercely controlled intensity with which she wrote is extremely difficult to sustain for the length of a novel, and the ironic reversals on which so many of her plots turn seem to demand the shorter form. Her prose style is lean and spare, her narrative method swift and sinewy—perfectly adapted to her highly compressed story form. Full-scale portraiture and character development have little place in such fiction, and indeed what seems to be the principal flaw in her novels is that they are just too spare: too much of the canvas remains empty after the bold outline has been violently brushed on.

Wise Blood, her first novel, is perhaps the least successful of Miss O'Connor's more ambitious works. And the reason may be that her shattering perceptions about fallen man have not sufficiently coalesced into a strong thematic design. Her familiar themes, her trade-mark characters are here aplenty; and the whole fabric of the novel pulsates with frenzied energy. But it might be that Miss O'Connor was trying too hard to say too much too soon. (pp. 185-86)

Though *Wise Blood* is uneven and sometimes not sufficiently "rendered" or even coherent, Miss O'Connor's major themes are already emerging. Man cannot justify himself; he cannot find salvation in any of the modern saviors, whether sex or technology or consumer goods; and Christ, when accepted, is sometimes a terrible Savior indeed—scandalous to the "enlightened" but stern and all-demanding to the converted. Attempts to escape Him or deny Him make man at once warped and ridiculous. Yet it is often those whom the upright and wholesome regard as grotesque and morbid who become chosen vessels indeed. And this is the scandal of the Gospels: the real grotesques are the self-justified; the apparent grotesques may be the blessed.

It should never be forgotten, of course, that always in Miss O'Connor's fiction behind the grotesque lies the ultimate concept of straightness or "oughtness," without which the grotesque is meaningless: we cannot know that anything is crooked unless we know that something else is straight. It is certainly this fundamental assumption that distinguishes Miss O'Connor's grotesquerie from that of many members of the Southern Gothic School.

A Good Man Is Hard to Find, Miss O'Connor's second volume and first collection of stories, contains much of her most characteristic work. Indeed, it may be her best single volume and the one by which she is longest remembered. The ten stories here are prefixed with an epigraph from St. Cyril of Jerusalem: "The dragon is by the side road, watching those who pass. Beware lest he devour you. We go to the father of souls, but it is necessary to pass by the dragon." Exactly who or what the dragon is here may be a little hard to determine. Is it the Devil, who has many protean forms, some horrible, some seductive? Or is it perhaps even Christ the tiger, Who, in a sense, does devour us when we fail *His* sphinx-riddle: "What think ye of Jesus?"

In any case, the ten stories here do, in one way or another, put this question to the reader in a variety of ways. (Miss O'Connor herself once described them as "stories about original sin.") And some of them are very shocking indeed. Perhaps the most typical is the title story. It concerns a family of husband, wife, three children, and the husband's mother, all of whom meet violent death at the hands of a pathological killer who calls himself "the Misfit" and his henchmen. The husband and wife and the two older children (the third is an infant) are obnoxious, and the grandmother is little better. She fancies that gentility and refinement can save her soul, until the Misfit, who is something like the Anti-Christ Hazel Motes, puts the question to her in the imperative Gospel mode:

> "Jesus was the only One that ever raised the dead . . . and he shouldn't have done it. He

thown everything off balance. If He did what He said, then it's nothing for you to do but throw away everything and follow Him, and if He didn't, then it's nothing for you to do but enjoy the few minutes you got left the best way you can—by killing somebody or burning down his house or doing some other meanness to him. No pleasure but meanness. . . .''

When the grandmother begs him to pray to Jesus for help, the Misfit replies, "I don't want no hep. I'm doing all right by myself." He has met the issue head-on, though; unlike many people and unlike many of Miss O'Connor's villains, he refuses to pretend the issue—and the choice—do not exist. And therefore, ironically, he wins from us a grudging admiration that the murdered family does not command. (pp. 187-88)

He remains a rather grand Satan—and perhaps nobler than Milton's—to the very end.

Another shocker among these stories is **"Good Country People."** . . . Again, it is the sort of Anti-Christ figure of the Bible salesman who wins something of our admiration: he may be a devil but he is not a fool, as Hulga is. (p. 189)

Miss O'Connor takes a dim view of modern man's "advancement": again and again she demonstrates a profound distrust in "progress" and "enlightenment," which are won at the expense of the sacramental, whole view of life. And one feels that Tarwater, the teenage prophet of *The Violent Bear It Away,* may be speaking for her when he scorns flying as another form of justification by technology: "I wouldn't give you nothing for no airplane. A buzzard can fly."

The role of women in Miss O'Connor's fiction is particularly interesting. There is certainly little enough conventional romantic interest attributed to them there, and sex as such is a negligible theme. Significantly, there is not even much warm domestic life in Miss O'Connor's works. Such ties as do exist—and not always for the best either—are more often found here between grandparents and grandchildren rather than between parents and children. And on more than one occasion it is Christ Himself Who causes family dissensions—true to the Gospel promise. Often Miss O'Connor's women constitute some of her most villainous characters, almost as though she believed in some sort of spiritual double standard. Such women are usually widows or divorcées who are apparently as independent of God as they are of sex and marital involvement: it is almost as though they regard men as an imperfection or a scandal (like Christ?) that the universe would be better off without. Usually these women live alone or with one or two children on a Georgia farm which they are determined to make pay off. The cows *are* going to produce the required amount of milk, and the Negro hands are *not* going to get by with slacking. In short, these women seem to think that by taking sufficient thought for the morrow they can beat the racket. But such independence of spirit, though commendable in many ways, becomes evil when it verges close to the Satanic pride of the Misfit's "I'm doing all right by myself." (pp. 189-90)

[In one of her finest stories, **"The Displaced Person"** in *A Good Man Is Hard to Find,* Miss O'Connor is grinding no ax], either Roman or ecumenical. She *is* dramatizing the predicament of the willfully blind who see the whole truth only in judgment. (*Vision*, it should be noted, is a recurring motif in her work, with physical sight often used symbolically to suggest inner, spiritual knowledge.) When Mrs. Shortley dies, apparently of a stroke and with her eyes twisted askew in death, her family "didn't know that she had had a great experience or ever been displaced in the world from all that belonged to her." And her eyes then "seemed to contemplate for the first time the tremendous frontiers of her true country."

Almost the same dramatic device is used to indicate the vision of judgment (and damnation) that comes to Mrs. May in **"Greenleaf,"** a story which has not the obvious Christian implications of **"The Displaced Person."** As the proud and willful Mrs. May lies dead, impaled on the horns of a bull, "she had the look of a person whose sight has been suddenly restored but who finds the light unbearable."

Mrs. May, like many of the O'Connor widow-divorcées, has really thought to justify herself by works. ("Before any kind of judgment seat, she would be able to say: I've worked, I have not wallowed.") And certainly as things in this world go, she seems far superior to the shiftless poor-white Greenleaf family who work on her farm, especially Mrs. Greenleaf, who indulges in a particularly repulsive kind of "prayer healing." ("'I'm afraid your wife has let religion warp her,' she said once tactfully to Mr. Greenleaf. 'Everything in moderation, you know.'") But, Miss O'Connor implies, religion is not for "moderates"; it does warp one—away from the ways of this world. The final irony remains that it is really the hard-working but prideful Mrs. May who is really warped. And it is such *hubris* which appears the cardinal sin in Miss O'Connor's works. (pp. 190-91)

Closely allied to pride of will in Miss O'Connor's work is pride of intellect, a relationship which reminds one of [Nathaniel] Hawthorne, as does also Miss O'Connor's obvious allegorical bent. Of no group is she more scornful than the modern intellectuals, particularly those who look on Christianity as merely the paraphernalia of outmoded superstition. This is particularly evident in the posthumous volume in a story like **"The Enduring Chill."** Here Asbury Fox, a Southern intellectual, has come home from New York to die (he thinks). And mainly to annoy his Methodist mother, who does have something of the McIntyre-May air about her, he asks to see a Jesuit priest. . . . Asbury expects of course to find in the Jesuit a charming, sophisticated man of the world with whom he can at last, even in Georgia, hold an intellectual conversation. Instead he gets old Father Finn, deaf in one ear and blind in one eye, who cares not a whit for the intellect as such but wants to know whether Asbury knows his catechism and says his prayers regularly. (pp. 192-93)

[One] by one, all Asbury's attempts at self-justification are revealed as stale, flat, and unprofitable. Ironically, he is not even going to die!. . . . [At] the end of the story, with all his illusions about life and himself stripped away, Asbury lies awaiting the coming of some new life to supplant the old, now exhausted. "The last film of illusion was torn as if by a whirlwind from his eyes," and he sees that for the rest of his life he will live in the face of a "purifying terror." Asbury vainly struggles; "but the Holy Ghost, emblazoned in ice instead of fire, continued, implacable, to descend." (p. 193)

There is no salvation in works, whatever form they may take, or in self, Miss O'Connor implies again and again: only in that Name which is above every name in earth and heaven—Christ the lamb, Christ the tiger, Christ the Lord.

This then is the substance of the scandalous gospel, the harrowing evangel Miss O'Connor proclaims, which is not peace but a sword. A few words may be in order here about the form in which her unsettling visions are embodied. It has already

been suggested that her strength lies in the short story rather than in the novel: she does seem to lose some depth of density of texture in the longer form. Her prose style itself is often almost plain and graceless—certainly sober and direct, as are her themes. Occasionally, it seems downright ugly, as if to emphasize her healthy respect for all that is not light, bright, and secular. And occasionally this deliberate awkwardness and cacophony of style remind one of [John] Donne or [Gerard Manley] Hopkins—a stylistic comparison which may suggest a further thematic resemblance to these two poets of the warped and the skew. They, also, knew something of the terrible speed of mercy.

But despite her respect for the ugly, she is not insensitive to the beauty of nature or perhaps even the beauty of right actions. . . . In **"A Temple of the Holy Ghost,"** in the first volume of stories, her sacramental view of the world is made explicit. Here all the horrors that warped body and soul are heir to seem to prevail, but they have not here the last word: "The sun was a huge red ball like an elevated Host drenched in blood and when it sank out of sight, it left a line in the sky like a red clay road hanging over the trees." And this is but one of many instances. Miss O'Connor's world is, like Hopkins', bent and brown, with its pasture and encircling lines of trees— what Robert Fitzgerald has called her signature—suggesting some fierce spiritual arena where her characters wrestle now with the Devil, now with God. But always over the fallen Creation there broods the Holy Ghost, with His warm breast and bright wings, blessing and sanctifying our smudged world and lightening our darkness, whether in rest and quietness or in the blinding revelation of the Damascus Road.

Miss O'Connor's themes and her presentation of them, though unique in contemporary American fiction, would seem inevitably to deny her the widest audience, even among the most genuinely sophisticated readers. Often, with the best will in the world, such readers will simply not be able to accept her uncompromising theological frame of reference: some tension in that quarter seems unavoidable. Nevertheless, whether or not they can accept her particular interpretation, many readers would agree that Miss O'Connor's diagnosis of the human condition is pretty accurate. For all its darkness and terror, her Georgia is no foreign country; and we are none of us strangers there. (pp. 195-96)

Robert Drake, "'The Bleeding Stinking Mad Shadow of Jesus' in the Fiction of Flannery O'Connor," in Comparative Literature Studies *(© 1966 by The Board of Trustees of the University of Illinois), Vol. 3, No. 2, 1966, pp. 183-96.*

V. S. PRITCHETT

All the characters in the very powerful stories of Flannery O'Connor are abnormal: that is to say they are normal human beings in whom the writer has discovered a relationship with the lasting myths and the violent passions of human life. It would be fashionable in America to call [*Everything That Rises Must Converge*] Gothic: it certainly has the curious inner strain of fable—replacing the social interest—which is a distinguishing quality of the American novel. . . . The Southern writers have sometimes tended to pure freakishness or have concentrated on the eccentricities of a decaying social life; but this rotting and tragic order has thrown up strong, if theatrical themes. Flannery O'Connor was born too late to be affected by the romantic and nostalgic legend of the tragic South; the grotesque, for its own sake, means nothing to her. In the story called **'Parker's Back'**, an absurd truck-driver has indulged a life-long mania for getting tattooed and in a desperate attempt to reawaken the interest of his wife, who had once been captivated by this walking art gallery, he has one final huge tattoo done on his naked back which up till then had been a blank wall. He pays for the most expensive tattoo there is: a Byzantine Christ. She throws him out because on this great deal he has wrecked a tractor. The point of this story is not that it is bizarre; it is that, perhaps because of the confused symbols that haunt the minds of the Bible Belt people, an inarticulate man wishes to convey to her that he has some claim to an inner life. He wishes to show that he is someone. The act is an agonised primitive appeal. It is also an act of defiance and hatred.

The passions are just beneath the humdrum surface in Flannery O'Connor's stories. She was an old Catholic, not a convert, in the South of the poor whites, of the Bible Belt, and this gave her a critical starting-point and skirmishing power, the formative element in American society being Protestant. But the symbolism of religion, rather than the acrimonies of sectarian dispute, fed her violent imagination—the violence is itself rather Protestant, as if she had got something out of the burning, Bible-fed imagery in the minds of her own characters. The symbols are always ominous: at sunset a wood may be idyllic, but also look blood-sodden. They usually precede an act of violence which will introduce the character at the end of the story 'into the world of guilt and sorrow'. This is her ground as a fabulist or moralist. We are left with an illusion shattered, with the chilly task of facing ourselves. . . . The essence of this artist is that she sees terror as a purification—unwanted, of course: it is never the sado-masochist's intended indulgence. The moment of purification may actually destroy; it will certainly show someone changed.

Symbolism has been fatal to many writers: it offers a quick return of unearned meaning. . . . [With very few exceptions,] whenever one detects a symbol, one is impressed by Flannery O'Connor's use of it: it is concrete and native to the text. (p. 469)

Many of the stories are variations on the theme of the widowed mother who has emasculated her son; or the widower who is tragically unaware of what he is doing to his child. In one instance, a widower destroys his grandchild. These stories are not arguments about the kind of family troubles which seem to be obsessional in American life: they are not case-histories or indignation meetings. They are selected for the violence which will purify but destroy. The characters are engaged in a struggle for power which they usually misunderstand. A mature and sensible young historian living with his mother is maddened by her naive and reckless do-gooding behaviour. She rescues an amoral girl who calls herself a 'nimpermaniac' and has her to stay. The girl instantly makes a set at the historian who shows her that he hates her. There is a revolver in the house. Who will be killed? A probation officer—a widower—in another rescue story, takes into his house a young boy crook who introduces his son to fatal Bible Belt fantasies about Heaven—again, who will be killed? This story, particularly, is an attack on practical ethics as a substitute for religion; in another, Art is shown to be inadequate as a substitute.

If these stories are anti-rationalist propaganda, one does not notice it until afterwards. Like all the Gothic writers, Flannery O'Connor has a deep sense of the Devil or rather of the multiplicity of devils, though not in any conventional religious sense. To the poor-white Gospellers, Satan has become literature. For her the devils are forces which appear in living shape:

the stray bull which kills the old farming widow whose sons let her down; the criminal child who is proud of being an irredeemable destroyer because he has been called a child of Satan. He looks forward, eagerly—it is his right—to an eternity in the flames of hell, which he takes to be literal fire; the delinquent girl who has been taught by psychiatrists to regard her vice as an illness sees this as an emancipating distinction. The author is not playing the easy game of paradox which is the tiresome element in the novels of Catholic converts: for her, the role of the diabolical is to destroy pride in a misconceived virtue.

A short story ought to be faultless without being mechanical. The wrong word, a misplaced paragraph, an inadequate phrase or a convenient explanation, start fatal leaks in this kind of writing, which is formally very close to poetry. It must be totally sustained. There are no faults of craftsmanship in Flannery O'Connor's stories. She writes a plain style: she has a remarkable ear for the talk of the poor whites, for the clichés and received ideas of the educated; and she creates emotion and the essence of people by brilliant images. We see all the threatening sullen life of a poor farmer in this sentence: 'His plate was full but his fists sat motionless like two dark quartz stones on either side of it.' . . . Flannery O'Connor is at pains to make us know intimately the lives of these poor whites and struggling small-town people. They are there as they live, not in the interest of their rather ignorant normality, but in the interest of their exposure to forces in themselves that they do not yet understand. Satan, they will discover, is not just a word. He has legs—and those legs are their own. (pp. 469, 472)

V. S. Pritchett, "Satan Comes to Georgia," in New Statesman *(© 1966 The Statesman & Nation Publishing Co. Ltd.), Vol. 71, No. 1829, April 1, 1966, pp. 469, 472.*

WALTER SULLIVAN

At her death in 1964, Flannery O'Connor left two novels and nineteen short stories and on these her literary reputation finally must rest. The novels, however, are not finished works of art. Both are structurally imperfect, but, of more importance, the very devices and perceptions that are the hallmarks of Flannery O'Connor's skill as a short story writer wear thin and brittle in the larger ambiance of a book-length work. The incisive dialogue loses some of its sharpness: detail and gesture become stylized: even violence, seen in the broader context, fails to shock. This is not to say that the novels are bad novels. But they are not as good as the short stories, and in any effort to delineate the achievement of Flannery O'Connor they must assume a supportive role.

Add to the novels a few short stories that are, by O'Connor standards, distinctly inferior. In my opinion, there are at least four of these and I shall be foolhardy enough to name them: **"A Stroke of Good Fortune," "A Temple of the Holy Ghost," "A Late Encounter with the Enemy,"** and **"Judgement Day."** If these stories, along with the novels, are relegated to a position of secondary importance in the O'Connor corpus, then the level of her accomplishment must be established principally by fifteen stories—a slight exhibit from a quantitative point of view.

But large reputations have been built on as little or less. Stephen Crane comes to mind, and properly so. His fame rests principally on one slim novel and one short story: and in spite of the obvious differences between them, his work has much in common with that of Flannery O'Connor. Like hers, his essential style was inflexible: he wrote everything the same way. . . . He was the master of the existential crisis, of the pure confrontation between man and his mortal destiny: his sense of cosmic irony was impeccably accurate, and his notion of what happened to men under the stress of absolute danger was, as he continued throughout his life to reconfirm for himself, absolutely right. What this seems to me to mean is that Crane's talent, vast as it was, was good for only one human posture, one metaphysical relationship. And when he abandoned this relationship, he failed.

The same was true of Flannery O'Connor. For instance, **"A Late Encounter with the Enemy"** is a bad story, not because the material is faulty or because the writing, *per se,* is inferior to the prose in her other stories. The dialogue is not drab, the images are not unimaginative or non-functional. But the style and the material fail to jibe. Without much exaggeration, one might say that in this story O'Connor was working Crane's territory, writing of the old Civil War soldier who thought he was never going to die, but who finally did. Crane could have done the old man with extraordinary insight: he was always good with soldiers, because more acutely than most people, perhaps, soldiers are aware of the inevitable meeting between themselves and what Crane called "the great death." For O'Connor, death was of no enduring significance. This may be one of the reasons that her work is so bloody: to die is simply to take the next step forward within the Christian order, to move on toward purgatory or hell or heaven and Judgement Day. But to say merely that her theme is Christian is not to be specific enough.

In speaking of herself, Flannery O'Connor referred frequently to her Catholicism and to her Southernness and it was her view that her work flowed from the amalgamation of these two somewhat disparate traditions. In the Roman Church, she found the complete theology which alone gives meaning to the human condition, and which had so sadly deteriorated in Southern protestant hands. Yet, in the Bible-reading South she found the sense of narrative and of image that the Church, concerned with its abstractions, often fails to achieve. So she took the Southern feel for story and the Southern attachment to the individual and the Southern ability to deal, often creatively, with the grotesque; and she undergirded these with her absolute knowledge, drawn from the Church, of good and evil, of truth and falsehood, of the inviolable prospositions of the Faith. Her vision was of a race of people suffering their wilful separation from God, and her basic fictional situation, comparable to Crane's posture of man facing destruction, is that of the gnostic, believing in himself and asserting the myth of his own independence.

Her intellectuals are her most obvious examples. (pp. 304-05)

But there are variations on the fundamental posture: intellectual pride is not confined to those whose minds have been specially trained. The mother in **"The Comforts of Home"** sets out to redeem Sara Ham, the prostitute, with no qualifications for the job except a tender heart. Mrs. May in **"Greenleaf"** feels secure in knowing how her farm ought to be run, but her grown sons have abandoned her to her knowledge. Julien in **"Everything That Rises"** attempts to reform his mother from the center of his superior perceptions, but ends by recognizing his own guilt.

Even those who claim for themselves a place among the Christian faithful are subject nonetheless to a manifestation of the gnostic sin. . . .

In **"The Displaced Person,"** the gnostic theme receives its fullest and most complex development in terms of the conflict between the major influences that shaped Flannery O'Connor's work. Mrs. McIntyre, the Shortleys, the two Negro hands are all part of the stable society of South Georgia. They are certain of their identities; they know where they belong; they are aware of their relationship to each other. Or so they think. But their traditional culture is dissipated by the decay of faith. (p. 306)

On the McIntyre farm, the loss of God and the accompanying belief in the efficacy of human effort and human understanding have destroyed all sense of vocation, tainted personal relationships and dulled aesthetic perceptions. . . . Since no one is working for God, everyone is working for himself, trying to get or get away with as much as he can, and as a consequence, people can no longer trust each other. The old stability is upset. No one will perform his tasks properly, and the tenant families come and go, one after another. The peacocks, ancient symbols of Christ, and of value only for their beauty are being allowed to die off and neither Mrs. McIntyre nor Mrs. Shortley can understand why the priest admires them.

Into this decay come the Guizacs, the Polish family made homeless by the displacements of World War II. They are foreign, speaking another language, practicing another religion, one according to Mrs. Shortley, not as advanced as her own. "There was no telling what all they believed since none of the foolishness had been reformed out of it." But it is not only their foreignness that distresses Mrs. Shortley: she cannot come to terms with the agony they have suffered. . . . For Mrs. Shortley, the Guizacs are continual reminders of a terrible truth: man is sinful and therefore capable of the most shocking depravity. And no matter how intelligent he may become or what skills he may develop, he cannot redeem himself.

In ignorance of local mores, Mr. Guizac proposes to have his cousin marry one of the Negroes that she may be released from a displaced persons' camp. When Mrs. McIntyre learns this, she is convinced that Guizac must go, but before she can gather her strength to discharge him, he is run over by a tractor while she and Shortley and Sulk stand silently by. At the death of the immigrant, all roles are reversed: he is no longer the wanderer, the man displaced. Mrs. McIntyre watches as the priest administers last rites. When Father Flynn stands up straight, having put the Host in the dying man's mouth, Mrs. McIntyre "only stared at him for she was too shocked by her experience to be quite herself. Her mind was not taking hold of all that was happening. She felt she was in some foreign country where the people bent over the body were natives, and she watched like a stranger while the dead man was carried away in the ambulance."

Much is achieved in this final irony. Death, that bugaboo of modern man, is pushed back into its proper perspective. Mundane struggles are shown for what they are. And behind this extraordinary development of theme, this exposure of the plight of man who has cast himself upon the mercy of his own devices, there is a remarkable technical achievement. It is an ordinary method of fiction writers to allow the physical predicament to stand for the spiritual state: Flannery O'Connor often took this approach as in the case of Hulga's leg or Mr. Shiftlet's arm or Rayber's deafness. In **"The Displaced Person,"** a dramatic climax is wrought in just the opposite way. The sharp reversal shows the mundane state to have been misleading. Things are not what they appear and much of the joy of really good fiction comes from our being led to discover this.

Also present here is Flannery O'Connor's subtle exploitation of symbolism. The priest, seeing the peacock raise its tail, says, "Christ will come like that." And later, "The Transfiguration." But Mrs. McIntyre says only, "Another mouth to feed." As the story nears its conclusion, the conversation between Father Flynn and Mrs. McIntyre develops the sort of off-center ambiguity that Flannery O'Connor employed so frequently. He speaks of Christ: she speaks of Mr. Guizac. The priest would have her be charitable to Mr. Guizac for the sake of Her Savior; she lumps Christ and the D. P. together: they are both "extra": there is no place for them. In this sort of narrative development there is no one to one symbolic relationship. Neither the peacock nor Mr. Guizac is Christ. But in many ways, both allegorical and actual, they are closer to Christ than Mrs. McIntyre or the Shortleys.

It seems to me that the essential qualities of Flannery O'Connor's genius are as fully displayed in **"The Displaced Person"** as in anything else she ever wrote. That her achievement was considerable is obvious, but exactly how considerable, it is perhaps too early to say. This much, however, appears to be certain. In her amalgamation of the two traditions—the Christian and the agrarian—she developed the only truly original voice among all her Southern contemporaries. And she is the only Southern writer of any generation who has yet made the old images viable for our immediate time. (pp. 307-09)

> *Walter Sullivan, "The Achievement of Flannery O'Connor," in* The Southern Humanities Review *(copyright 1968 by Auburn University), Vol. II, No. 3, Summer, 1968, pp. 303-09.*

ABIGAIL ANN HAMBLEN

Flannery O'Connor's stories, though varied as to setting and characters, give even the casual reader a single impression. They all seem to say that she does not have a very great regard for her fellowmen. . . .

Going deeper, the reader discovers that, disturbingly, more than contempt for the human race is involved. Running through the stories is one dominating theme: that of innocence versus evil, innocence victimized by evil.

A good illustration of this may be found in the story **"A Good Man Is Hard To Find."** Here, plainly underscored, we see the vivid allegory of unabashed Innocence destroyed by unabashed Evil. And here also the allegory is given depth and color by a companion revelation, an idea not often included in stories of the Light against the Darkness, namely, that often the Innocent and the Evil share a single set of values.

The impact of **"A Good Man Is Hard to Find"** depends almost entirely upon the significance of the allegory and its attendant message, as well as upon the richness of irony which pervades the whole. The plot is childishly simple. . . .

Here Innocence is plainly represented by the travelling family, no member of which may be called very intelligent. (p. 295)

As a representation of full-flowered Innocence [the grandmother] can hardly be surpassed in all American fiction. Sprightly, talkative, importunate, and excessively annoying, her intentions are always of the best. . . .

When, finally, the whole group is cornered by the criminals, she tries to "reform" the character, The Misfit. . . .

Her efforts at reformation are fruitless. For if she and her family represent Innocence, the murderers embody pure Evil. "'No pleasure but Meanness,'" The Misfit says with a snarl. Deliberately he orders the mother, father, and children led into the woods and shot in cold blood. Deliberately he shoots the desperate, pleading grandmother himself.

Note, however, that as Innocence is, Evil here is mindless. The Misfit knows he has been in jail for a crime, but he has no recollection of what crime he committed. Unmixed Evil, as the author presents it, is weak after a fashion, and far from intelligent. . . . (p. 296)

This curious encounter of vulnerable Innocence and triumphant Evil is not quite so simple as it first appears. In it the sensitive reader sees something fundamental to the whole social order called in question. Jesus, proclaims The Misfit, "'was the only One that ever raised the dead.'" And Jesus was wrong, for by so doing "'He thrown everything off balance. If he did what He said, then it's nothing for you to do but throw away everything and follow Him, and if He didn't, then it's nothing for you to do but enjoy the few minutes you got left the best way you can—by killing somebody or burning down his house or doing some other meanness to him.'"

In other words, if one accepts the Christian teachings, one must give up everything else. If one repudiates it, one may revel in sin. The Misfit's remark is perhaps the supreme ironical point in a story that glows with almost sinister irony. (pp. 296-97)

The view of life presented by **"A Good Man Is Hard to Find"** is unmistakable—and interesting. Briefly it is that reason does not guide events, that victimizers and victims alike are shuffled unwittingly into strange patterns as broken and casual as those of a kaleidoscope. Further, though Evil is stronger than Innocence, it is no less foolish, and no more artful. The Misfit and his fellow convicts kill in a leisurely fashion, as if the mere killing were an idle pastime, hardly worth planning. The grandmother, on the other hand, is in a childlike way cunning: she conceals the cat, because she knows her son would not want to take it along. She falsely tells the children the mansion she remembers has a secret panel, thus rendering them riotous in their demands to see the house.

And finally, we contemplate the picture of senseless Evil and artful Innocence, we see them joined in a bizarre and terrible way. The Misfit has remarked that if the Jesus story were not true, nothing else matters—the evil in any man may triumph without let or hindrance. Would not the grandmother (and Bailey, and the young mother in slacks) believe this, too? If they were capable of analyzing their situation, would they not see it to be a confrontation of the Christian with the nonbeliever? That is, they are constrained to be "good" because they believe Jesus's words, and The Misfit, a doubter, is free to be bad.

Foolish Innocence and senseless Evil, Flannery O'Connor is saying, are doomed to wander the earth, suffering, and inflicting pain. And, paradoxically, they are linked by a single set of values. As The Misfit observes, because He raised the dead, Jesus "'thrown everything off balance.'" (p. 297)

> *Abigail Ann Hamblen, "Flannery O'Connor's Study of Innocence and Evil" (copyright 1968 The Curators of the University of Missouri; reprinted by permission of the author), in* University Review, *Vol. XXXIV, No. 4, Summer, 1968, pp. 295-97.*

MICHAEL D. TRUE

[Flannery O'Connor] brought a vision as accurate and piercing as any Old Testament prophet; and her work, like the prophets', was aimed at quickening the conscience and calling an estranged people to the tragic glory of God's chosen. . . . In the fiction of Flannery O'Connor one finds a . . . preoccupation with the woes and evils of a decaying civilization—a civilization in which the law and fervor and even fanaticism of the backwoods prophets test the metal of the prophets of the secular city, the mouth-wash liberals and Northern do-gooders, and warns them, in the words of Isaiah . . . : "Woe to you that are wise in your own eyes, and prudent in your own conceits . . . for they have cast away the law of the Lord of hosts, and have blasphemed the world of the Holy One of Israel" (5:24). A dominant theme in her fiction strongly resembles the lament of the Prophet: "The city of thy sanctuary is become a desert, Sion is made a desert, Jerusalem is desolate. The house of our holiness, and of our glory, where our fathers praised thee, is burnt with fire, and all our lovely things are turned into ruins" (64:10-11).

Unlike many of the writers of the past century who confronted essentially religious questions, sometimes even consciously exploiting traditional Christian symbolism (T.S. Eliot and Graham Greene, for example), Flannery O'Connor spoke openly—never defensively—about her religious mission as a fiction writer. Like any great writer, she understood extraordinarily well her own limitations and assumed the responsibilities of her craft within these limits. She knew that she spoke to an audience that did not share her preoccupations, her feeling that "the meaning of life is centered in our Redemption by Christ . . . and that what I see in the world I see in its relation to that." So she had to find a way of conveying the fact of Redemption to an audience, readers of fiction in the 1950's, who dismissed any Christian principle or, worse, did not care enough even to deny Salvation. The not caring about Redemption was to her a distortion—a more serious distortion than the physical disabilities or the mental deficiencies of her characters, both heroes and villains. Asked once why her people were so grotesque, she answered that she would be willing to argue whether her characters were really more grotesque than the man in the gray flannel suit; whether a man was truly grotesque or not depended upon your angle of vision and the strength of your perception. In order to "make these appear as distortions to an audience which is used to seeing them as 'natural,'" she had to make her vision apparent "by shock—to the hard of hearing you shout, and for the almost blind you draw large and startling figures."

Whether or not Flannery O'Connor conveyed this vision will depend upon the reader to some extent, I suppose; obviously, in some of her stories this vision is not conveyed as effectively as it is in others. The meaning, "the integrity of the completed form" (in Northrop Frye's phrase), is less clear; the vision is delivered in an injured state, without unity; occasionally the story is a mixed bag of humorous episodes, peculiar characters, and violent events. But even in these failures she manages to escape the doom, once described by Chad Walsh as the unlucky fate of the Christian writer who manages to be only "an esoteric, coterie figure, speaking only to those who share his pair of eyes."

She manages to escape this trap by the use of comic irony which, in her work, helps the reader see the world consistently and see it whole, aware—but never self-consciously aware—of the intelligent narrator who takes him through the Inferno,

never passing up a chance to remind him that he is, after all, in hell. Some of the characters are evil . . . , some ripe for redemption (Obadiah Elihue Parker in **"Parker's Back,"** Mrs. McIntyre in **"The Displaced Person"**); and others merely gross and shiftless, like Mrs. May's hired man in **"Greenleaf."** . . . But all the types inhabit the same universe, and often one is as likely as the other to be the recipient of God's grace. In this chaotic world, the just and the unjust await redemption, and like stupid Mr. Greenleaf, they may become the instrument of salvation, that "strange discovery" Mrs. May makes through Mr. Greenleaf just as she dies.

Now this irony would not be so powerful if, as in the work of other modern writers (Katherine Anne Porter, Eudora Welty, and sometimes Faulkner), there was not such a strong basis for the standard of behavior applied here. In the best stories, in **"Revelation"** or *Wise Blood,* for example, the irony is never detached; it is not merely the play of a sensibility about surfaces. In a brief preface to the second edition of *Wise Blood,* Miss O'Connor called the book "a comic novel . . . and as such, very serious, for all comic novels that are any good must be about matters of life and death." The statement reminds one of the tradition within which she writes, and it explains also why, like many comic writers, from Aristophanes to Evelyn Waugh, she combines a radically conservative religious position with a great distrust of detached intellectualism and shuns such "easy" terms as compassion and tolerance. If she often, in her fiction, defends the indefensible, a woman prejudiced toward Negroes or a man who is a religious fanatic, it is because she insists upon recognizing the strengths of these people—their family loyalty and bumbling generosity—and particularly their capacity for grace and redemption. If her stories indicate an anguish, she once said (she satirized in her fiction and at times in conversation the popularized *Time*-magazine-style existential *angst*), it is that the South "is not alienated enough," that the region is being forced out "not only of our many sins but of our few virtues. This may be unholy anguish but it is anguish nevertheless." For her, the Southern narrative tradition and the Christhaunted environment were virtues not to be lost to "them cold interleckchuls" up North. (pp. 212-15)

I mention the region here because, in defining and understanding the nature of her heroes, the backwoods prophets, one must understand the importance of region in the formation of the religious temperament. She never pretends that the region (the backwoods) is all good, just as she never claims that the South is necessarily Christ-centered. . . . But, for the religious vision of both those who preach the Church *With* Christ . . . or those who preach the Church *Without* Christ . . . , the backwoods origin is a source of their strength. Jesus lives in the woodland country; and those who lose Him temporarily in the city (such as little Bevel in **"The River,"** and the idiot child in *The Violent Bear It Away*) find "the Kingdom of Christ in the river" or in the primitive surroundings of a Southern revival. (pp. 215-16)

In the city, the Christian message degenerates into a social, life-adjustment message; the blood of the lamb becomes the milk of human kindness; the salt loses its savor. Miss O'Connor is never confident that, without an iron faith and a kind of fanatic zeal, the Christian message will survive in the midst of the corrupting, "civilized" urban intelligence that threatens to reason us out of our reason. She is careful, however, not to make her indictment against the modern city too generalized, and she seems often at pains not to confuse and to mistake secularization and dechristianization, while at the same time insisting upon the necessary distinction between the secular and the sacred. As with all prophets, however, she never doubts that there is a difference. Her suspicions are those of the traditionalist that ''all who seek to interpret revelation by reason alone inevitably reduce it to a secular truth and eliminate mystery.'' (pp. 216-17)

Her stories explore again and again that area of man's experience which ''remains sacred and never becomes secular,'' where God is present to men and faith is never ''mastered by human intelligence.'' As a writer of fiction, however, Miss O'Connor could not enjoy the luxury of merely figurative language. Like the prophets, she might have tried to ''convey by analogie a remote idea of the reality of which they speak.'' But unlike the prophets, she had to convey the idea in flesh and blood fact, as well. As readers we participate in her narrative, her ritual, through our response to rhythm and pattern. For the modern reader, the word must be made flesh first, before it can move beyond immediate reality to total significance and symbolic meaning. In the stories . . . , the Word becomes flesh particularly and paradoxically through the demonic characters. The reader experiences it viscerally, as she intended, shocked into the recognition that for these anti-Christs, the matters they are concerned with *count*.

The peculiar nature of her demonic ''heroes,'' the backwoods anti-prophets, is best illustrated by characters in three stories, the Misfit in **''A Good Man Is Hard To Find,''** Rufus Johnson in **''The Lame Shall Enter First,''** and Manley Pointer, the Bible salesman in **''Good Country People.''** . . . In these prophetic tales, the ''villain'' is often treated very sympathetically; he becomes, in these thinly disguised romances (Good and Evil jousting for the highest stakes), a hero of a religious quest. (pp. 217-18)

The paradox of keeping Christ alive by making heroes of His most formidable antagonists lies in the center of Miss O'Connor's fiction, best illustrated by a remarkable story in the posthumously published volume called **''The Lame Shall Enter First.''** The central character, a fourteen-year-old boy named Rufus Johnson, brings the message of Christ, salvation, and agonizing love to a man named Sheppard and his son, by taking the devil's part. Rufus recognizes that Sheppard, for all his condescending tolerance, is an atheist; having failed to continue the religious education of his son after the death of his wife, Sheppard prides himself on his intelligence and his no-nonsense, anti-Biblical humanism. He has destroyed any remnants of his son's religious faith, and he tries his pseudopsychology on Rufus, in an effort to ''save'' him from his ridiculous beliefs in the resurrection and the prophets. But Sheppard is completely unsuccessful with his scheme; in fact, Rufus wins Sheppard's son, Norton, to his side by telling the boy stories from the Bible. Eventually, Norton, in an effort to ''rejoin'' his mother in the sky, commits suicide.

Rufus is the son of a backwoods prophet, a descendant of a man with the terrible vision of the religious fanatic. When Norton asks Rufus once where his father has gone, Rufus tells him, ''He's gone with a remnant of the hills . . . Him and some others. They're going to bury some Bibles in a cave and take two of different kinds of animals and all like that. Like Noah. Only this time it's going to be fire, not flood.'' The glory of Rufus is that he believes in it, too; that is the reason he chooses the devil's part, submitting to Satan's power, as he says, with a kind of joy. . . . For Rufus, Satan's friend, there is only one Jesus Christ. For him, as for Flannery O'Connor, one of the major sins is for anyone else to behave as if

he were Christ, without the proper respect for His Book, and for His enemy, the devil.

The trouble with Sheppard is that, with all his education, his dogooder philosophy, he never knows evil when he sees it and, consequently, is easily victimized by a really evil person like Rufus Johnson. His stupidity is shared by many of the educated people in Flannery O'Connor's fiction: by Rayber, the nephew of a backwoods prophet in *The Violent Bear It Away,* . . . by Asbury, the maudlin undergraduate who comes home to die in **''The Enduring Chill''** . . . by Mary Grace, the fat, ugly Wellesley girl (her face ''blue with acne'') who sits and scowls over a book entitled *Human Development,* in **''Revelation.''**

But the stupidity of all these characters is outdone by the central character in another of the early stories, **''Good Country People.''** Hulga (née Joy) Hopewell is a woman with a Ph.D. in philosophy, an artificial leg, and no common sense. Hulga feels superior to her mother and her friends because of her formal education—she's read the existentialists and the logical positivists (or at least has picked up a few clichés about them) and decided, like any other ''thinking modern,'' that the world is blind chaos. One day an itinerant Bible salesman named Pointer, describing himself as a simple country boy making a living by spreading the word of God, comes to her house and wins her mother's affection by exchanging clichés, much in the manner of the Grandmother and Sammy Butts in **''A Good Man is Hard to Find.''** He indicates an interest in Hulga. . . . When the Bible salesman makes advances, she agrees to meet him in the barn loft. As it turns out, however, he is more interested in seeing how her artificial leg hooks on and off than in making love to her, especially since she's ''too intelligent'' to say she loves him with much feeling. (pp. 219-21)

The Bible salesman, like the Misfit and Rufus, are obviously heroes for Miss O'Connor. If the secularist pseudo-Christians (the social workers, psychologists, sociologists, existentialist philosophers) find no antagonists in the true believer among the faithful, they should find a real antagonist in the devil, in the Satanic characters who give witness to Christ by wilfully defying Him. In the stories described here, the weak in spirit, the vulgar in speech, the superficial and even insipid in moral and religious values, the demonic characters often stand out clearly as the ones to be preferred. Better the honesty and directness of the latter than the vapid, pseudoethic of the ubiquitous, condescending mouth-wash liberal, Miss O'Connor seems to say; in a chaotic world, plagued by casual violence and meaningless pursuits, she finds much to admire in those valiant foes who take the devil's part knowingly and enthusiastically, bent on the annihilation of a world without meaning. . . .

In **''A Good Man Is Hard to Find,'' ''The Lame Shall Enter First,''** and **''Good Country People,''** the myth of the triumph of the powers of darkness is recounted with great vividness; and at the end of each story the personification of evil, having banished the pretenders to reason and good sense, triumphs. Evil, one discovers, has through the creative power of language, been given a kind of magnificent, if destructive form. Whether the world harbors forces of light sufficiently strong to triumph over the powers of darkness is not entirely clear in the body of Flannery O'Connor's fiction. (p. 222)

What Flannery O'Connor does in her fiction is to confront the crisis of divinity in the modern world without hesitancy and at times without hope. As in the Biblical prophets, whenever she found God, He brought not peace, but a sword. Divinity lived for her, not as for the woman in [Wallace] Stevens'

"Sunday Morning," "within herself," but in the fiery furnace of violent death or severe judgment.

She finds God in the backwoods prophet, in the misfit, in sin, in deformity, in guilt, in perversion—as if it were necessary "to traffic with insanity," as Michael Harrington said of Thomas Mann, in order to make sense out of a mad world. God lives more surely, she seems to say, among those who boldly deny Him or cannot find Him; He seems most absent from those who pretend to call His name. In her stories, however joyful the sweet music of salvation, the prophet's news that God is not dead, after all, strikes man's untrained ears with the harshness of a sonic boom. He receives the prophecy of his redemption, "with the look of a person whose sight has been suddenly restored but who finds the light unbearable."

Maybe, to conclude on a somewhat more positive note, through a character like the young Francis Marion Tarwater, in *The Violent Bear It Away,* the work of the Redemption will be continued. At the end of the novel, the young inventor of the Law succeeds in fulfilling the mission imposed upon him by his uncle. He baptizes Rayber's idiot child (though drowning him in the process), and receives the prophet's command, heralded by a red-gold tree of fire: "He knew that this was the fire that had encircled Daniel, that had raised Elijah from the earth, that had spoken to Moses and would in the instant speak to him. He threw himself to the ground and with his face against the dirt of the grave, he heard the command, GO WARN THE CHILDREN OF GOD OF THE TERRIBLE SPEED OF MERCY." The vessel of honor, like the power of darkness, brings a rather terrifying fate. Although the difference between the Misfit, the antiprophet, and young Tarwater, the true prophet, is obvious on one level, on another level, it is rather slight. Tarwater moves into "the dark city," "where the children of God lay sleeping," with much the same fierceness as the Misfit does, doing meanness: "His singed eyes, black in their deep sockets, seemed already to envision the fate that awaited him." Both are children of the backwoods with a mission in the modern city—one to destroy and another to warn. But as religious heroes, reminiscent in their awful strength of the paradoxical relationship between the great sinner and the great saint, they both move with "a terrible speed" and with a singlemindedness that the reader is forced to admire. (pp. 222-23)

Michael D. True, "Flannery O'Connor: Backwoods Prophet in the Secular City," in Papers on Language and Literature *(copyright © 1969 by the Board of Trustees, Southern Illinois University at Edwardsville), Vol. V, No. 1, Winter, 1969, pp. 209-23.*

ROBERT DRAKE

To even the casual reader it would appear that Miss O'Connor really had only one story to tell and really only one main character. This principal character is, of course, Jesus Christ; and her one story is man's absolutely crucial encounter with Him—an encounter so crucial that it is literally a matter, quite often, of life-or-death, Heaven-or-Hell. There is, furthermore, very little about her Savior that seems comfortable and even less that is sweet, in the invidious sense of that word. He is certainly not the sentimental, effeminate Christ too often depicted in funeral-home or Forest Lawn iconography: He is hairy and sweaty, in many ways a quite literal holy terror, Who often terrifies before He can bless. And Miss O'Connor's arch-villains, who are significantly often villainesses, regard him as an offense and a scandal to their modern, rationalistic intellects

or, if they are professing Christians, are considerably discomfited by this harrower not of Hell but of the very Zion in which they have become all too much at ease. This, with only slight modifications from time to time, is the story that constitutes the burden of her four published books, whether in her stories or in her novels. (p. 434)

Now what was Miss O'Connor's true country, where was she most at home, even unavoidably there? It was right back with that one story, played out, for the most part, against the red clay earth, the woods-encircled and often sinister green pastures of deepest, darkest Georgia. And her characters are the natives of the place, even when they make so bold to go as far away as Atlanta or even New York. Whether it was her own Baldwin County, her own Milledgeville that she kept writing about, whether she drew her "material" (how any writer hates that word!) from real, live folks is an altogether and literally impertinent question. But this was the one place she knew, the one place she could speak about with authority—and not as those scribes mentioned in the Gospels, a tribe who are perhaps the blood brothers of those determined men [Percy Bysshe] Shelley asserted could never *will* themselves into writing poetry.

And it was this authority, this absolute and fundamental heart and head knowledge of time and place that gave Miss O'Connor her Ancient Mariner's glittering eye. And it is this authority, at once both a gift and an obligation, which any writer, true to himself and to his craft, can never repudiate with any integrity. (pp. 436-37)

And it was Miss O'Connor's great strength that she was never false to this true country. She never betrayed what she took to be her calling, whether to report the news from Georgia or to heap up the local horrors, sexual, racial, or otherwise, and give us a sociological study of the facts of life as lived therein. As the late Professor Randall Stewart once observed of William Faulkner, she was not reporting on conditions but rather on the human condition. . . . (p. 437)

Now literally rural Georgia was Miss O'Connor's true country, man's encounter with Jesus Christ her true story. But there is more to the phrase than all this might seem to imply. More than once Miss O'Connor intimated, sometimes even stated directly, whether in fiction or in criticism, that she believed man's true country was not to be found in this world but only in his life—and death—in Christ. And we come back to our original intention—to explore more widely Miss O'Connor's "true country," its terrain, its *flora* and *fauna.*

And we sense at the outset some of her difficulties. What was she to do, concerned, even obsessed as she was with this theme (and I hope by now I've made clear, at least by implication, my conviction that Miss O'Connor had not a *message* but a *theme*) in a world that, when it wasn't just, like the Levite, passing by on the other side, simply was not there to hear? (And even the Ancient Mariner's power would be limited if the Wedding Guest failed to turn up!) How was she to write, what strategy was she to adopt, to speak, to prophesy (and in a sense she did conceive her function as somewhat *vatic,* which is not to say programmatic) to a world both blind and deaf to such concerns? It is significant here that she hardly ever referred to herself as a "Christian writer": I suspect that she would probably have found such a label as ludicrous and misleading as the terms "Democratic writer" and "Republican writer." She usually described herself as a writer with "Christian convictions" or "Christian concerns." And her solution to the problem of finding and holding an audience was direct and forthright, even violent: "you have to make your vision apparent by shock—to the hard of hearing you shout, and for the almost blind you draw large and startling figures."

And this is precisely what she proceeded to do in story after story. To some extent, it explains her preoccupation with the grotesque, that element in her fiction most often misunderstood. Nothing could be further from the truth than the observation of more than one critic that her *grotesquerie* is gratuitous and therefore ultimately meaningless. Such may be the case with some of the less able members of the so-called Southern Gothic School. . . . (pp. 438-39)

Miss O'Connor's use of the grotesque can . . . be regarded as an instance of shock tactics resorted to when nothing else will do for those who have eyes to see and see not, ears to hear and hear not. More than this, however, Miss O'Connor's *grotesquerie* represents . . . an outward and visible sign of an inward and spiritual dis-grace. And as such the grotesque is absolutely functional in her overall dramatic design. It can be both horrible and at the same time absurd, as the term itself implies, just as man himself can be when he forgets his only source of energy, his only Author and Begetter, and tries to set up shop on his own. . . . Such a man is at once a perversion of what his Creator intended him to be, a distortion often reflected in that very temple of the Holy Ghost, his body; he is also a fairly ludicrous parody of what he was meant by that same Creator to be. And more than one writer, more than one theologian has suggested that the Devil is finally an ass. (pp. 439-40)

Miss O'Connor's Christian concerns did ultimately lose her some part of her potential audience: there is no denying this. She did, unlike Eliot or even the Metaphysical Poets, make an *issue* of Christian belief. But to make the issue, to dramatize man's, as she saw it, inevitable and inescapable choice between God and the Devil—or whatever other name he may for the moment bear, *was* her principal concern, her major theme, and finally her only real story. And I myself can see no way around the limitation it imposes on her readership. . . .

I suggest now that her fidelity, her complete commitment to her vocation and her one story might well be taken as a paradigm and a model for emulation by the beginning or the aspiring writer today. (p. 441)

Make no mistake about what I'm suggesting: I'm not trying to turn Miss O'Connor into a major writer. I sincerely believe that, like [John] Donne or [Gerard Manley] Hopkins, whom she resembles in so many ways, both thematically and technically, she remains a major minor figure. She is a better short-story writer than a novelist. And she has not significantly changed the shape of American fiction as, for example, [Nathaniel] Hawthorne or [Herman] Melville or Hemingway or Faulkner has done. She has perhaps opened up new avenues for subsequent writers to explore: she has helped to revitalize older themes almost defunct in our literature and suggested the possibility of considering overtly once more—and with no concessions to the opposition—man as a God-created being living at once and for always ever in his great Taskmaster's eye and in a world that is, in every sense, the Lord's and all that therein lies. And this is no inconsiderable achievement.

What she has shown—and what we should never forget—is what a writer can achieve who seeks only to tell the truth about his true country, no matter how limited it may appear to be, whether geographically, ideologically, or otherwise. Her com-

mitment to her true country was not therefore a weakness or ultimately a limitation; it was at once her strength and the source of her authority. And, verily, she has had her reward: she has made us believe that her Georgia is, in a sense, finally the emblem of the whole wide world.

In this sense she is "wide"; in another, of course, she is "narrow." There are many areas—I'm almost tempted to call them vast ones—in human experience that she leaves almost totally out of account. And concerned (there's the word again) as she was with a theme almost totally discounted by the contemporary world, she obviously decided that, for her, the best defense was an offense, in every sense of that word. And she had to pay the inevitable price for such a strategy. But when all this is conceded, her work abides because she told the truth, as she saw it, about human beings and the world they live in. Even those readers who cannot accept her theology must grant this much: her true country, her world is real and true for many of them, too, though they sometimes have difficulty with her explicitly Christian frame of reference. But in the narrow, constricted world of her one story she goes down just about as deep as one can go. . . . (pp. 441-42)

> Robert Drake, "The Paradigm of Flannery O'Connor's True Country," in Studies in Short Fiction (copyright 1969 by Newberry College), Vol. VI, No. 4, Summer, 1969, pp. 433-42.

JOSEPHINE GATTUSO HENDIN

The great strength of O'Connor's fiction seems to me to spring from the silent and remote rage that erupts from the quiet surface of her stories and that so unexpectedly explodes. It appears, for example, when the Misfit with great politeness has the family exterminated, or when he answers the grandmother's "niceness" with a gunshot and thereby suggests that neither Christian charity nor Southern politeness can contain all the darker human impulses. It appears again in the punishment of the vain, self-satisfied Mrs. Turpin who gets a book thrown at her. Perhaps it has a quieter voice in those sweetly nasty comments Mrs. Turpin's Negroes make as they talk among themselves to comfort her: "You the sweetest lady I know." "She pretty too." "And stout." And perhaps it is there in the impulses of all those resentful sons and daughters in the pages of Flannery O'Connor's fiction, who are frozen in an extended, rebellious adolescence where, in a perpetual dependency because of illness or fear, the price they ought to pay for being cared for is silence, acquiescence to an exasperatingly polite and very controlling mother.

Perhaps there is something of this rage even in O'Connor's love for peacocks. Did she admire the ease with which they gobbled up all the flowers in sight, destroying her mother's flower beds and turning the lawn white with droppings? Were those majestic birds that broke all the rules what Flannery O'Connor wanted to be? The curse on the bird is its yowl—the ugly voice that makes it most beautiful when silent. But to Flannery O'Connor, that voice sounded like "cheers for an invisible parade." Was that parade the procession of Misfits, prophets, and lonely and murderous children who unleash their violence so freely in the fiction of Flannery O'Connor?

Flannery O'Connor never yowled in public. She never gave voice to whatever her mute scowl expressed. But she would render it in pictures as powerful as the tableau of the grandmother and the Misfit, bound to each other through a ritual of politeness. The Misfit can find no words to speak his rage at his would-be mother. Fury explodes from his gun in three eloquent shots. And one of the revelations in **"Revelation"** is Mary Grace's peculiar wrath. As her mother criticizes her with Mrs. Turpin, Mary Grace accepts her mother's remarks politely, but grows enraged at Mrs. Turpin. She gets so angry she throws a book at her. She attacks her mother's "double" while leaving her own mother alone, much in the way the Misfit claims there was "no finer" woman than his mother, but goes on to murder a woman who suggests all the forces of tradition and family and who claims he is "one of her babies."

O'Connor's murderous children are always "ladies" and "gentlemen." They always say the right thing or nothing at all; they behave properly to their parents. But they are always furious at the parents who have made them so polite, or who try to destroy their pride in being misfits. Some have a secret, inner world where they never obey. And in quiet acts of violence, others give voice to their mute fury.

O'Connor wrote about what she knew best: what it means to be a living contradiction. For her it meant an eternal cheeriness and suffering; graciousness and fear of human contact; acquiescence and enduring fury. Whether through some great effort of the will, or through some more mysterious and unconscious force, she created from that strife a powerful art, an art that was both a release and a vindication for her life. If she set out to make morals, to praise the old values, she ended by engulfing all of them in an icy violence. If she began by mocking or damning her murderous heroes, she ended by exalting them. Flannery O'Connor became more and more the pure poet of the Misfit, the oppressed, the psychic cripple, the freak—of all of those who are martyred by silent fury and redeemed through violence. (p. 41)

> *Josephine Gattuso Hendin, "In Search of Flannery O'Connor," in* Columbia Forum *(copyright © 1970 by the Trustees of Columbia University), Vol. XIII, No. 1, Spring, 1970, pp. 38-41.*

PRESTON M. BROWNING, JR.

Flannery O'Connor's preoccupation with the spiritual condition of modern man . . . led her to write fiction of a peculiar cast, but her religious concerns fortified rather than weakened the artistic integrity of her creations. (pp. 9-10)

Her fiction abounds in grotesque situations and many of her most memorable characters are driven, "possessed" individuals. Freaks, fanatics, and psychopaths stalk the unfriendly streets and desolate clay roads of her fictional world, which often appears designed to simulate as nearly as possible a chamber of horrors. Thus can one explain the confused and sometimes hostile reaction of those who, in the early and middle 1950s, saw in Flannery O'Connor a disciple of the nihilistic-deterministic writers spawned by the Depression and the Second World War and the spiritual and cultural stagnation which followed them.

Yet Flannery O'Connor's own estimate of her vocation could not be more seriously religious: "I don't think you should write something as long as a novel around anything that is not of the gravest concern to you and everybody else and for me this is always the conflict between an attraction for the Holy and the disbelief in it that we breathe in with the air of the times." It is almost certainly this rare coincidence of apparently opposing forces and motifs in her life and work which has often made Flannery O'Connor a puzzling figure. . . . [It] is my

conviction that out of this tension grew Flannery O'Connor's extraordinary creative power and unique vision. (p. 11)

The crime and violence and the apparent nihilism of some of Miss O'Connor's characters combine with a recurring "Hound of Heaven" motif to suggest an imagination in many respects similar to that of Dostoevsky. (p. 12)

In my assessment, [Miss O'Connor's artistic] vision is constructed of an extremely delicate blending of what seems to be totally incompatible ways of apprehending reality. On the one hand there is the espoused, orthodox Christian understanding of man. Alongside it one finds a traditional though qualified Southern view of human nature manifest in her satiric attacks upon the materialism, secularism, and liberal optimism of contemporary life. On the other hand there appears to be an attraction for the extreme, the perverse, the violent, and for the grotesque for its own sake and not merely as a fictional technique, which calls to mind Thomas Mann's comment (he was thinking of Dostoevsky and Nietzsche) that "certain attainments of the soul and the intellect are impossible without disease, without insanity, without spiritual crime." Spiritual crime: here is a concept paradoxical enough to illuminate some of Flannery O'Connor's most puzzling stories. (p. 13)

[My] conclusions are that Flannery O'Connor's work may be conceived as an effort to recover the idea of the Holy in an age in which both the meaning and the reality of this concept have been obscured; that she perceived that loss of the Holy involved for contemporary man a concomitant loss of "depth" and a subsequent diminution of being; and that she further understood that in reclaiming depth and being . . . , contemporary man might very well become involved in a journey through the radically profane, embracing evil in order to rediscover good, pursuing the demonic in order finally to arrive at the Holy. The journey upon which she set many of her most unforgettable characters entails, in short, "spiritual crime"— crime whose ultimate motive is a desperate desire to affirm a basis for human existence which transcends the waywardness and willfulness of the individual human self.

But the quest for being or the Holy is only one side of Flannery O'Connor's creative enterprise. The other is her portrayal of the world of unbelief within which that quest occurs. When she spoke of "the disbelief in [the Holy] which we breathe in with the air of the times," "the times" clearly embraced for her a good deal more than mid-twentieth-century America. Yet, in a special sense, it was the ethos of the 1950s against which Miss O'Connor's stories were directed. I use "against" deliberately, for Miss O'Connor was a satirist of extraordinary vigor, and, in a decade when "positive thinking" was as much a part of the American way of life as cookouts and rock-and-roll, Flannery O'Connor produced a magnificent assortment of stories, many of which might well have been entitled "The Power of Negative Thinking."

Gifted with an imagination delicately attuned to the nuances of manners and folkways, Flannery O'Connor detected in the manners of the 1950s such smugness, optimism, and self-righteousness that only the harshest attack could hope to move them. She also perceived, at the root of this shallow complacency, what she felt to be a fatuous belief in the omnipotence of a highly rationalized, technological society whose manipulation of human beings is calculated to turn out, as an end product, persons like a character in **Wise Blood** who is said to be "so well-adjusted that she didn't have to think anymore." The attitudes which Flannery O'Connor satirizes are those of an age in which the intellectuals are positivists and the nonintel- lectuals are "positive thinkers." And, whether found in an inveterate rationalist such as the social worker Sheppard or in a self-righteous snob such as Ruby Turpin ("**Revelation**"), these attitudes signified to Flannery O'Connor a deathly in- capacity for existence in depth which she considered the be- setting affliction of the contemporary world.

Time and again in her stories, the spokesmen for a self-satisfied secularism run afoul of representatives of . . . the twisted, the guilt-ridden, the satan-possessed, and the God-haunted pro- tagonists who might best be designated "criminal-compul- sive." It is in the encounter of these representatives of opposing views of reality that Miss O'Connor characteristically drama- tizes the "conflict between an attraction for the Holy and the disbelief in it" which is the gravitational center of her moral and artistic vision. And though it was the "criminal-compul- sives" who earned her the reputation for gratuitous grotesquerie and violence, they play an indispensable role in this paradig- matic conflict: it is they who act as spiritual catalysts, admin- istering the shock which awakens the positivists and the pos- itive thinkers from their dream of a world made secure by superficial rationality or conventional goodness.

Because of the prominence of the three character-types, I fre- quently refer to them and to the conflicts generated among them, as exemplifying the typical O'Connor story. It will be self-evident, however, to readers at all familiar with her work that no such classification can be inclusive and, furthermore, that characters who seem to lend themselves to identification by type often prove far more complex than they initially ap- peared. Also, while there is a good deal of repetition of situ- ation in O'Connor's fiction—especially in the short stories, where the widowed or divorced mother and the disaffected son or daughter are common features of the landscape—there is no single "O'Connor story" other than the drama of the fall of man which furnishes the background for everything she wrote. (pp. 13-16)

In *Wise Blood* the self-satisfaction of positive thinking threatens the very bases of human life itself and finds its most eloquent spokesman in the landlady, Mrs. Flood, who is incapable of distinguishing between "being a saint" and "walling up cats." The fraudulent blind preacher, Asa Hawks, exemplifies some of the traits of the criminal-compulsive and plays a major role in bringing Hazel Motes to his moment of truth, while the latter character combines elements of the criminal-compulsive and the positivist (the philosophy which Haze at one point expounds can scarcely be mistaken as a parody of logical positivism). It is only in the second novel, however, that Miss O'Connor fully adapted the types to her longer fiction: Rayber . . . is a pos- itivist *par excellence,* although the conflicting forces within his soul make inappropriate a simple, unqualified identifica- tion; and young Tarwater possesses a certain likeness to such criminal-compulsives as The Misfit and Rufus Johnson, though here also the designation would be misleading if not properly qualified.

The stories in *Everything That Rises Must Converge* exemplify a somewhat different configuration of characters. There are, to be sure, still positivists (most notably Sheppard of "**The Lame Shall Enter First**"), just as there are positive thinkers (e.g., Mrs. May of "**Greenleaf**" and Ruby Turpin of "**Rev- elation**"). The mentally disturbed college student of the latter tale and the promiscuous, feline Sarah Ham of "**The Comforts of Home**" are not unlike some of the neurotic, criminal types of the earlier stories. And Rufus Johnson ("**The Lame Shall

Enter First**"), is, of course, the prototypical O'Connor spokes- man for spiritual crime, haunted by the devil while at the same time convinced of the truth of the Gospel. Yet in some of the finest of these tales—"**A View of the Woods**," "**Parker's Back**," "**Everything That Rises Must Converge**"—the conflicting views which in earlier stories had usually been expressed by different characters, are now lodged in the same individual. Hence, though in each of these stories there is a conflict between individuals, and the epiphany or "moment of grace" comes about as a consequence of that conflict, the antagonists are no longer criminals who appear without warning to destroy the bubble of self-sufficiency and smugness in which the protag- onists are encased. They are instead persons close to the pro- tagonist—a mother, a wife, a granddaughter—who embody one aspect of the protagonist's personality or who reflect a character trait so deeply repressed as to be almost atrophied. In "**A View of the Woods**," for example, there is a conflict within the protagonist, so subtle and so threatening to his ideal- ized self-image that he can acknowledge it only as annoying disobedience in his granddaughter. When he attempts to punish her, however, he discovers an "enemy within" which destroys him even as he (inadvertently) kills its embodiment in the child. The stories in *Everything That Rises Must Converge* are char- acterized by such complexity of human relations; and it is, I believe, Flannery O'Connor's growing perspicacity as a com- mentator upon human psychology, perhaps more than anything else, which her final collection bears witness to. (pp. 16-18)

[The] art of Flannery O'Connor is religious in two senses, and a criticism which attempts to interpret this art from an exclu- sively "non-religious" standpoint will inevitably distort it while failing to comprehend its deepest significance. In the most obvious sense of the word, Flannery O'Connor's art is religious because many of her characters consciously face the choice of Jesus or the devil, belief or nonbelief, faith or apostasy. And even in stories where this appears not to be the case, e.g., "**Everything That Rises Must Converge**," "**The Life You Save May Be Your Own**," and "**Greenleaf**," symbol, allusion, and mythological motif coalesce to infuse them with a distinctly religious aura. In another and more basic sense Flannery O'Connor's art is religious, in that it endeavors to trace the figuration of that modern sensibility which permeates the lit- erature of the West from Goethe and Carlyle through Dos- toevsky and Baudelaire to Kafka and Camus and about which it is now a cliché to assert that it is a sensibility whose timbre ensues from the erosion of faith in the seventeenth and eigh- teenth centuries and the "death of God" in the nineteenth and twentieth centuries. Fundamentally, then, Flannery O'Connor is a religious writer not because the subject matter of her stories is "religious"—though explicitly or implicitly it almost always is—but because she has been occupied in all of her major fiction with the primary spiritual question of our era. (p. 21)

Preston M. Browning, Jr., in his Flannery O'Connor *(copyright © 1974 by Southern Illinois University Press; reprinted by permission of Southern Illinois University Press), Southern Illinois University Press, 1974, 143 p.*

DIANE TOLOMEO

[The] shocking or violent incidents in [Flannery O'Connor's] stories strike chords that reverberate loudly and lengthily re- gardless of a reader's own bias.

In most of O'Connor's major stories, these moments of vio- lence or death occur on or near the last page: the Misfit shoots the Grandmother, Sheppard discovers Norton's body, Julian's mother dies on the pavement, Mr. Guizac is run over by a tractor, Hazel Motes is found in a ditch. But not all of O'Connor's violent endings require a death to render them shocking. In fact, some of her best shocks are created by an assault on the psyche. This is what happens to Asbury, who comes home to die, but doesn't; to Mrs. Cope, who can't, as she watches her woods burn; or to Joy-Hulga as Manley Pointer, the phony Bible salesman, runs off with both her artificial leg and her intellectual naivete. Such endings are never intended merely to create revulsion or shock as ends in themselves. Rather, they announce moments of recognition for a character and perhaps more importantly for the reader. (p. 335)

O'Connor's assumption in most of her writing seems to have been that her audience did not in fact hold the same Christian beliefs that she did, and she could not, therefore, relax her writing to a "more normal means of talking."

But in her last three stories, written during her final illness, there is a remarkable shift in her use of shock tactics to create an awareness in her audience. **"Revelation," "Parker's Back,"** and **"Judgement Day"** were her last works to be published, the latter two posthumously in 1965. While none of these three stories is so radically different that O'Connor's pen is not easily recognizable, still each illustrates a definite transition away from the pattern of a plot ending in a physical or psychic assault on a character. While in these later stories such assaults do occur, they do so at a much earlier stage in the narrative. This makes a considerable difference in the effect they have on the movement of the story. Instead of ending with a character's confrontation of death or his moment of recognition and insight, such events are moved to an earlier stage in the story. Once the climax has been reached, the remainder of the story can then be concerned with the implications such an awareness holds for the character. A major part of the guesswork is thereby removed, as any major changes in the character can be explicitly portrayed and not just implied.

In terms of the reader, there is a similar effect: he, too, is no longer left with a final devastating image which stuns him momentarily before he closes the book and either contemplates its meaning or turns to something else. Instead, because the climactic incident is moved forward, after it occurs the reader cannot just wipe it from his mind, for when he turns the page he is confronted with the implications of what he has just encountered. (p. 336)

But this would also assume that the reader belonged to an audience which held the same beliefs and knowledge of scripture that O'Connor did, and that she was even perhaps preaching to those who were already saved. It is apparent from her own essays and talks about the problems facing the Christian writer that this could not have been her assurance, or even her faintest hope. . . .(p. 338)

To end Parker's episode at that point where his awareness begins to grow, O'Connor would have had to implant more indicators earlier in the story to make the conclusion that he is being prepared for inevitable. Such inevitability is difficult to convey when it must go further than the end of a story. When, for example, Sheppard realizes too late that he has betrayed his own son and substituted humanism for genuine love, we do not know that he has learned something which will enable him henceforth to lead a new life. The final shock of his son's death makes him "reel back like a man on the edge of a pit," and while we may assume that his future after

such a vision will be one of growth out of himself, we are not shown the process by which this becomes a fact.

In the last three stories O'Connor seems especially concerned that we do see the results such visions have on the characters and know for a certainty that they are of a religious nature. Mrs. Turpin goes home to wrestle with the problem of God's justice in the world. Her theodicy is resolved in the pig parlour when she is humbled and sees all things transfigured, and we are explicitly told that, while her vision faded, "she remained where she was, immobile." Obadiah Elihue Parker escapes death and races off to have a picture of God tattooed on his back. Using a brilliant allegorical device, O'Connor lists the faces of God that Parker rejects: "The Good Shepherd, Forbid Them Not, The Smiling Jesus, Jesus the Physician's Friend." He must reject these "up-to-date pictures" in favor of those which are "less reassuring," for the experience he has had has introduced him to an all-demanding God of power and might. When he finally selects the "haloed head of a flat stern Byzantine Christ," his choice reflects the nature of the profound change he has undergone. He prefers not the friendly eyes of the modern pictures but the sterner eyes which make him feel transparent. They seem to urge him to "Go Back," yet his response is not on an intellectual level but on an intuitive or instinctive plane. His sense of urgency to have the tattoo completed complements his need to return to the sharp-tongued Sarah Ruth, yet even she seems to him soft and gentle in comparison with the Byzantine image of Christ.

That the eyes tell him to "Go Back" is of course tied to the pun in the title, for the story is not only about Parker's back, but is also a statement that Parker is back, or at least is on his way back, to his true nature as a child of God. Thus the story ends with he "who called himself Obadiah Elihue—leaning against the tree, crying like a baby." He has not yet attained a spiritually adult understanding of the events that have summoned him to a higher awareness, but that he has somehow encountered God is indisputable. His wife's cold accusation that the tattoo is idolatrous offers a contrast to Parker's childlike belief that God's likeness can be drawn. Yet he understands something that Sarah Ruth does not, that an encounter with God does not produce a series of dogmatic assertions but yields a new intensity in everyday life.

Thus the real kernel of the story lies not in Parker's miraculous near-miss of death but in the dramatic response it creates within him. As in the previous story, the unwinding of the implications the climax suggests explains much more about the protagonist's resolution of inner conflict than mere hypothesis would ever allow. O'Connor's insistence that we understand fully contains an urgency that is not entirely present in the earlier stories, which by comparison seem to present her vision through a glass darkly.

Her final story, **"Judgement Day,"** is a reworking of the first story of her master's thesis, **"The Geranium."** It seems entirely appropriate that she should end where she began, thereby making her alpha and omega points one. Of the two stories, however, it is only the later version which fits the pattern here being described. A first consideration of this story may seem to contradict that pattern of moving the moment of violence forward so that its results may be effectively worked out, for **"Judgement Day"** does in fact end with the death of Tanner. But his death is not the most violent event in the story. The worst moment for Tanner must certainly be the confrontation with the young Negro actor, or "preacher," as Tanner insists on calling him. What the Negro does not understand is that

Tanner genuinely desires to befriend him, to make him a substitute for the Negro, Coleman, who had both annoyed and befriended Tanner for thirty years. But this Negro actor is a Northern counterpart not to Coleman but to Dr. Foley, the Southern half-Negro who had bought up the land Tanner's shack was on. Both belong to the class of Negroes who had risen in the world to a level where they could be their own bosses instead of working under a white man. Thus when Tanner treats his neighbour as if he too were an exile from the South, the Negro responds with vehement anger. He slams Tanner against the wall, and the force of his shove makes Tanner's tongue swell up and render him unable to "talk or walk or think straight" for days. Whether this action precipitates or even hastens Tanner's death is never made clear. His death is instead connected more explicitly to his insatiable yearning to return "home" to Corinth, Georgia. For it is while Tanner begins his painstakingly slow journey that he suffers his fatal stroke.

In fact he gets no further than the landing at the top of the stairs, but as far as he is concerned he is already "on his way." When his legs give out from under him and he swoons forward, he is already nearly home. He initially mistakes the Negro bending over him for Coleman, but then in disappointment realizes who it really is. Yet he is already living his long-awaited dream of waking up to the Judgement Day, and his final words—"Hep me up, Preacher. I'm on my way home!"—are buoyant ones uttered without any trace of doubt that he is in fact finally going home. The story adds a brief epilogue to Tanner's death which informs us that his body is eventually shipped back to Corinth, his geographical home, even as we have seen his spirit looking towards his heavenly home.

Each of these three stories, then, ends with a character's going back, back to his true home as well as to a new vision of life. Mrs. Turpin turns from her vision of the heavenbound souls to "[make] her slow way on the darkening path to the house." As she returns home she carries with her the new eyes which have seen into "the very heart of mystery": the once repulsive pigs now "pant with a secret life," and the chorus of crickets becomes for her the "voices of the souls climbing upward into the starry field and shouting hallelujah."

Parker goes back to his home where Sarah Ruth waits with her broom to thrash him. But he is not allowed to physically re-enter his house until he is able to enunciate his Christian name. To return home for him means to accept his true nature, and only when he calls himself by his name does he experience what he had been seeking all along: "'Obadiah,' he whispered and all at once he felt the light pouring through him, turning his spider web soul into a perfect arabesque of colors, a garden of trees and birds and beasts." It is not his tattooed body which has become that "arabesque of colors" but his restored soul which is born when Parker is back.

And, finally, while Tanner dies an exile from his home, he also believes that he is on his way back. He is an alien in New York City, where he sees people living not in proper homes but in "pigeon-hutches." "It was no place for a sane man," he thinks, and directs all his energies to getting away. He has a fundamental faith, and believes in the Four Last Things: Death, Judgement, Heaven and Hell. In O'Connor's frame of reference, then, his journey home does not represent the returning of a lost sheep home to the fold but rather the going home of a man in exile from his true country. (pp. 338-41)

Diane Tolomeo, *"Home to Her True Country: The Final Trilogy of Flannery O'Connor,"* in Studies in

Short Fiction *(copyright 1980 by Newberry College), Vol. 17, No. 3, Summer, 1980, pp. 335-41.*

HAROLD BEAVER

Flannery O'Connor is often billed as a Southern writer, or as a Catholic writer. But, however helpful, these are confining terms. For she was an artist of the most exacting and universal perception. . . .

Almost a dozen books and innumerable articles have been published since 1964 on her small but intense *oeuvre*. . . . But far the longest and most important posthumous publication is that of her letters, a collection of more than 600 pages spanning the years 1948-64. For wealth of anecdote and intellectual variety and emotional depth, *The Habit of Being* too will prove an incomparable American work.

Its keynote is joy. Confined to hospital in 1950, with what was then diagnosed as "acute rheumatoid arthritis", she wrote: "I have been reading [T. S. Eliot's] *Murder in the Cathedral* and the nurses thus conclude I am a mystery fan." But the nurses were right. She was a "mystery fan"; and she confronted life's mystery with an extraordinary aptitude for laughter. . . .

There is nothing in the least coy about her. She intensely disliked the work of Carson McCullers. The key characters in her life, as in her fiction, are all ordinary, plain folk like those nurses or her mother who so devotedly helped her, or her mother's farmhands. Of one such farmhand, who was actually taking a correspondence course in Catholicism, she reported: "He is not going to be a Catholic or anything—he just likes to get things free in the mail." But she bred peachicks and surrounded herself with peacocks, since "you can't have a peacock anywhere" (as she wrote of **"The Displaced Person"**) "without having a map of the universe".

No wonder commentators are obsessed with her symbolism, chasing and explicating those images through her texts. For she saw the world transfigured. Even her turkeys with the sorehead, for which the cure was liquid black shoe polish, ran about in blackface "like domesticated vultures". Her comedy is divine; yet no one could say of her, as one Jesuit visitor said of a Sister who wrote poetry: "Boy, I bet she's crucified." Flannery O'Connor was not "crucified" in that vulgar sense. For it was she, of course, who quoted the remark. It was precisely a feeling for the vulgar that was her natural talent. . . .

The stories might be hard, but they were never brutal or sarcastic. They were hard because there was nothing harder or less sentimental than what she called "Christian realism". . . .

The most abiding childhood influence on her, she admits, was a volume "called *The Humerous Tales of E. A. Poe*". Was she some latterday Poe, then, converted to Catholicism? In her own experience, everything funny she had written was more terrible than it was funny, or only funny because it was terrible, or only terrible because it was funny. Simone Weil's life she considered the most comical life she had ever read about and the most truly tragic and terrible. For that juncture of comedy and terror for her was naturally located in the Incarnation. . . . Catholic orthodoxy was essential to her. "I feel that if I were not a Catholic", she insists, "I would have no reason to write, no reason to see, no reason ever to feel horrified or even to enjoy anything. I am a born Catholic, went to Catholic schools in my early years, and have never left or wanted to leave the

Church. I have never had the sense that being a Catholic is a limit to the freedom of the writer, but just the reverse.''

All this puts her on the extreme edge of the American tradition. No wonder, then, claims are made to view her symbol-laden, frustrated, forced entries into the Kingdom of Heaven as maverick Protestant texts. She herself had a saner perspective. In her opinion, the only thing that kept her from being a regional writer was being a Catholic and the only thing that kept her from being a Catholic writer, in the narrow sense, was being a Southerner. As one correspondent astutely pointed out, the best of her work sounds like the Old Testament would sound if written today, since her characters' relations are more directly with God than with other people. . . .

[She] was impatient not only with academic but all high-flown intellectuals. Some time in the early 1950s she was taken by Robert Lowell and Elizabeth Hardwick to have dinner with Mary McCarthy (then Mrs Broadwater):

> We went at eight and at one, I hadn't opened my mouth once, there being nothing for me in such company to say. . . . Having me there was like having a dog present who had been trained to say a few words but overcome with inadequacy had forgotten them. Well toward morning the conversation turned on the Eucharist, which I, being the Catholic, was obviously supposed to defend. Mrs Broadwater said when she was a child and received the Host, she thought of it as the Holy Ghost, He being the "most portable" person of the Trinity; now she

thought of it as a symbol and implied that it was a pretty good one. I then said, in a very shaky voice, "Well, if it's a symbol, to hell with it". That was all the defense I was capable of but I realize now that this is all I will ever be able to say about it, outside of a story, except that it is the center of existence for me; all the rest of life is expendable.

It is in this light that one must read her definition of fiction as "the concrete expression of mystery—mystery that is lived". It was almost impossible for her to write about supernatural grace in fiction. She had to approach it negatively. In the words of Matthew, taken for the title of her second novel: "Since the time of John the Baptist until now, the kingdom of heaven suffereth violence, and the violent bear it away." Or, as she wittily put it years later: "In the gospels it was the devils who first recognized Christ and the evangelists didn't censor this information." For her violence revealed those human qualities least dispensable to a man's personality, "those qualities which are all he will have to take into eternity with him"; and since all her characters are on the verge of eternity, all are evading, or half glimpsing, or intruding on various states of grace, most urgently revealed in that final trio of stories (**"Revelation"**, **"Judgement Day"** and **"Parker's Back"**) written in the last year of her life.

Harold Beaver, "On the Verge of Eternity," in The Times Literary Supplement *(© Times Newspapers Ltd. (London) 1980; reproduced from* The Times Literary Supplement *by permission), No. 4051, November 21, 1980, p. 1336.**

(Ann) Philippa Pearce

1920-

British novelist for young adults and younger children and short story writer.

Pearce is among the most highly respected writers of books for young people. Although not prolific, she is considered among the foremost of the British writers who emerged at the end of the 1950s, such as William Mayne, L. M. Boston, and Rosemary Sutcliff. Her books probe the realities of childhood on many different levels. She uses elements of fantasy and the supernatural to complement the realism of her stories, and often demonstrates how heightened experience or a strong need can cause a supernatural event. Other themes concern the past and its influence on the present and future, social differences caused by class structures, and the loneliness and isolation that can exist within the family unit. Adults play important roles in Pearce's works, rather than being absent or ineffectual as in some other books for this audience. She uses the Cambridgeshire countryside of her childhood as the setting for most of her books, and her precise descriptions and vivid sense of place are often noted.

It is unanimously agreed that Pearce's greatest achievement is *Tom's Midnight Garden,* in which a lonely summer spent with his aunt and uncle leads Tom to discover a garden and a girl from the past. Essentially, this is the story of a desire for companionship so strong that it breaks through the barriers of time; Pearce firmly links fantasy with reality to suggest the effectiveness of imagination in overcoming limitations. She was praised for the originality of her theory of time and the consistency and logic of her approach. Some critics have called this work the most perfect book ever to have been written for children. *A Dog So Small* deals with fantasy in a different manner as it describes Ben's escape from reality in the form of an imaginary puppy. Triggered by his intense longing for a pet and the loneliness he feels as an excluded child, Ben learns through experience to distinguish possibility from impossibility. The unfolding of his thoughts and emotions is characteristic of Pearce's style, and is represented in several of her other titles.

Pearce's collections of short stories are often felt to be as successful as her novels. In *What the Neighbors Did and Other Stories,* she concentrates on everyday actions and events, and conveys their deeper essence as well. In *The Shadow-Cage and Other Tales of the Supernatural,* Pearce writes a series of ghost stories in the classic tradition, but with her own distinctive approach. In *The Squirrel Wife* she emphasizes human emotions and values, thus giving an uncommon immediacy to the fairy tale genre. As a collaborator, Pearce provided a novelistic structure for Brian Fairfax-Lucy's autobiographical reminiscences of his Edwardian youth, *The Children of the House;* directed to young readers, the work was praised for its unusual viewpoint and for the beauty of its sad though unsentimental ending. Ironically, the book was criticized for its unclear explanation of the passage of time, a feature felt to be handled successfully in *Tom's Midnight Garden.*

Several of Pearce's later works are considered minor by critics, some of whom have stated that she has yet to regain success

on the scale of *Tom's Midnight Garden.* However, it is generally agreed that her combination of reality and fantasy is unique, and that her writing style has been exceptional throughout her career. Young people attracted to her works have found believable characters and situations with which to identify, while discovering a writer of imagination, depth, and quality. Pearce won the Carnegie Medal in 1958 for *Tom's Midnight Garden,* which was also given the Lewis Carroll Shelf Award in 1963, as was *The Minnow on the Say* in 1958. *The Battle of Bubble and Squeak* was given the Whitbread Award in 1971. (See also *Contemporary Authors,* Vols. 5-8, rev. ed., and *Something About the Author,* Vol. 1.)

THE JUNIOR BOOKSHELF

[*Minnow on the Say*] is captivating from the beginning. . . . There is a neat balance of hopes and disappointments, and the reader's concern for Adam and his aunt causes him to share their feelings for the shabby old house whose future is threatened with their own, and heightens the suspense. At the same time the aunt's outburst when Adam uproots a prize rose in his mania [to find an Elizabethan treasure] is a welcome reminder that some things matter more than treasures, and the same sense of proportion is maintained elsewhere. The boys are a well matched, likable pair, and their conversation rings true, while the adults, who might easily have been only "character" parts, *have* character instead. Many children will recognise something of their own fathers in David's. . . . And what a relief to meet a bus-driver who is a person instead of a conscientious exponent of lower-middle class virtues! The other characters are just as clearly seen, the humour is quiet but constant, and there is that ingredient of consciousness of the past working in the present—the past of individuals, families, and the town—which always adds a special dimension. The interest of clue-detection during a first reading is replaced in later readings by an appreciation of the clues themselves and by increased pleasure in the people encountered on the search. The final scenes are all that could be desired. . . . (pp. 234-35)

> *"The New Books: 'Minnow on the Say',"* in The Junior Bookshelf, *Vol. 19, No. 4, October, 1955, pp. 234-35.*

MARGARET SHERWOOD LIBBY

We can think of no other [story] which has such an unusual combination of plot, characterization and vivid sense of place [as does **"The Minnow Leads to Treasure"** (published in Britain as **"Minnow on the Say"**)]. There is a cleverly detailed challenging puzzle. The alert reader is in constant suspense and eager to unravel the clues with the boys. The study of the two heroes, their families and minor characters is perceptive, and dominating the whole book is the wonderful feeling for the river, with all its twists and turns.

> *Margaret Sherwood Libby, "Books for Boys and Girls: 'The Minnow Leads to Treasure',"* in New York Herald Tribune Book Review (© *I.H.T. Corporation; reprinted by permission), March 9, 1958, p. 13.*

ETHNA SHEEHAN

For all its search and puzzle, [**"The Minnow Leads to Treasure"** (published in Britain as **"Minnow on the Say"**)] is no one-dimensional mystery yarn. Here are real people. . . . There is a villain, but his villainy stems from obtuseness rather than cold-blooded wickedness. And the other grown-ups are all rounded characters, each of whom has an essential function in the dénouement. There are drama and old, remembered heartache in the story, but it is as if it had happened "all on a golden afternoon, full leisurely***." . . . [One] sees and almost smells the garden and fields and shares the joys of exploration and discovery.

> *Ethna Sheehan, "Search on the River Say," in* The New York Times Book Review (© *1958 by The New York Times Company; reprinted by permission), May 4, 1958, p. 32.*

THE JUNIOR BOOKSHELF

The second novels of brilliant beginners are so often disappointing. Miss Pearce's successor to **Minnow** has now appeared after three years, and her most enthusiastic admirer need have no fear. Here is no second and inferior **Minnow,** but a book entirely different in every respect except excellence. (p. 333)

[**Tom's Midnight Garden**] is an original treatment of a "time" theme, with a brilliant surprise ending—at least it took one reader completely by surprise.

Miss Pearce's magic comes from several sources, from her deep understanding of her characters young and old, from a sense of time, most of all from a mastery of words. Her prose is a miracle of simplicity. Using no tricks, she evokes the atmosphere of the lost garden so vividly that the reader shares Tom's experiences in it and sees with him its ghostly inhabitants. This is a very clever book, but its greatest cleverness is that only on reflection does the reader realise how brilliant the writing is, how sound the observation, with what minute care every detail of the story is fitted into the mosaic. Most children will see none of this, but will surrender readily to its charm and interest and come under the influence of its beauty and wisdom. Don't let us say: "Better (or less good) than **Minnow.**" Merely: "Thank you, Miss Pearce, for a book of rare quality!" (p. 334)

> *"The New Books: 'Tom's Midnight Garden',"* in The Junior Bookshelf, *Vol. 22, No. 6, December, 1958, pp. 333-34.*

MARGERY FISHER

Personal experience, transmuted by imagination and fine writing—these are found . . . in Philippa Pearce's ***Tom's Midnight Garden.*** In this story, time loses its limits. (p. 122)

Although time stands still in Tom's world while he is in the past, it does not stand still for Hatty [Tom's playmate in the garden]. She is growing up even as Tom plays with her, and the magic, the wonder of the garden, the transcending of time must come to an end with the ending of her childhood. This familiar ending to time fantasies is beautifully handled, with great sympathy for the boy who suddenly sees his companion as a young woman. And there is a bold twist to the ending which sends the whole book back on itself, sends the reader rethinking the whole. For Tom, on the very day he is due to go home, meets the owner of the house, old Mrs Bartholomew, who lives in seclusion upstairs. He climbs to her flat, opens the door—and finds that she is Hatty. So, did he go back in the past, or did she create the past with her dreams as she lay in bed, an old woman?

The subtlety of this circumstance is something children may pay more attention to if they reread the book in their late teens. As a child's story it is magnificent. It is at once philosophical, swift and gay. The conversations of Hatty and Tom are natural, the incidents probable and presented with beautiful clarity. The style is impeccable—loose-jointed and flexible, colloquial when the occasion demands, at other times rhythmical and poetic. The fantasy will be real to children because it is real to the author; she has carried out C. S. Lewis's advice that 'the matter of our story should be part of the habitual furniture of our minds.' (pp. 122-23)

[**Minnow on the Say**] is one of the best children's books of recent years. . . . This exquisite story has innumerable threads in its rich canvas—the pervasive presence of the river, every ripple exactly described; the treasure hunt, with its intricate and unexpected ending; the sure handling of a child's joy in living. . . . But one of the most interesting threads is the sensible, subtle treatment of class difference; the contrasting, by implication, of the Moss household, with its safe, small prosperity, and the old house where Miss Codling fights to preserve her standards. (pp. 287-88)

Margery Fisher, in her Intent Upon Reading: A Critical Appraisal of Modern Fiction for Children *(copyright © 1961 by Margery Fisher), Hodder & Stoughton Children's Books (formerly Brockhampton Press), 1961 (and reprinted by Franklin Watts, Inc., 1962), 331 p.**

THE TIMES LITERARY SUPPLEMENT

[*A Dog So Small* is] most moving. . . .

Philippa Pearce's book is full of truth and truths for all sensitive readers to pick up if they will. She never writes "between the lines" for a grown-up audience. Everything is outspoken. Ben feels deeply, but his emotions are all those that children will recognize. This is not the best of this distinguished writer's books, but it has a fine finish, and like the work of a craftsman seems carefully made to satisfy, firstly, her exacting self.

"Animal Challenge: Opportunities for Heroism," in The Times Literary Supplement *(© Times Newspapers Ltd. (London) 1962; reproduced from* The Times Literary Supplement *by permission), No. 3144, June 1, 1962, p. 397.**

THE JUNIOR BOOKSHELF

A Dog So Small is [excellent and unusual], and more. . . .

Miss Pearce, in addition to her command of words, characterisation and setting, is a master in the invention of complex, unexpected and convincing plots. . . .

Much of the action goes on in Ben's head, which is difficult enough for many children; and the relationships between Ben and his mother and Ben and his grandfather, which are fundamental to the story, depend for their understanding on hairline subtleties. *A Dog So Small* in fact is likely to be a "minority" book but one which, with its wisdom and sympathy, its profound understanding of human behaviour, its fresh and lively portrayal of town and country society, is likely to be for a few children a rung in the ladder by which they mount to adult life.

"The New Books: 'A Dog So Small'," in The Junior Bookshelf, *Vol. 26, No. 3, July, 1962, p. 139.*

MARGERY FISHER

The Hattons of Stanford Hall [in *The Children of the House*] belong to the privileged classes but life for the children is one of scant food and strict discipline. . . . [The] Hattons led a strangely tribal life, ceremonial, ingenious and tolerably happy.

This life is pieced together in one episode after another. A lucid prose style in which every word counts makes these episodes unsensationally vivid. . . .

Lucky the child who acquires a sense of period from reading such books as this, books which do not set out to teach but, by the wealth and choice of detail and by the behaviour of their characters, do pass on the flavour of a particular world. . . . Brian Fairfax-Lucy writes of a world he knows from inside, Philippa Pearce with intuition about just such periods and estates.

The three interlocking yet separate groups at Stanford are kept precisely clear. We perceive the children's innocently sharp view of servants and parents; the servants are seen on both sides of the baize door; the worried contrivances and remote affection of the parents are demonstrated as they talk to each other, to the servants, to the children. We see how the four children, while accepting rules and influences, remain triumphantly themselves.

This has been a most successful collaboration. There is no visible join or jarring of mood in the book. Humour and grace decorate a confident picture of inheritance and environment.

Margery Fisher, "Special Review: 'The Children of the House'," in her Growing Point, *Vol. 7, No. 1, May, 1968, p. 1121.*

MRS. E. D. MOSS

"The Children of the House" is an elegant piece of writing, sad but at times wryly humorous. . . . The four children are alive and individual; their exploits, under Tom the heir, those of imaginative, country-loving children. Philippa Pearce has given this chronicle, which is a tragedy in muted tones, shape, form, and meaning. Her sense of period is exact, enhanced by an extraordinary flair for dialogue; her love of fun is much in evidence in this [story].

Mrs. E. D. Moss, "Historical Fiction: 'The Children of the House'," in Children's Book News *(copyright © 1968 by Baker Book Services Ltd.), Vol. 3, No. 4, July-August, 1968, p. 205.*

THE JUNIOR BOOKSHELF

[*The Children of the House*] is a most interesting and unusual experiment in authorship. It is collaboration of a sort but not joint authorship in the normally accepted sense. The foreword informs us that Brian Fairfax-Lucy wrote a story for adults and that what we now have is a re-writing of this story by Philippa Pearce for juniors—a case of ghost-writing in which it is not a matter of "as told to" but "from a story by". From Miss Pearce's pen we expect a book to be readable and she has not failed us. She has succeeded in a most interesting way in her presentation of the events in Mr. Fairfax-Lucy's story of another age. . . .

In an age when servants were kept in their place, the wish of the children to be friendly with them is nicely told. The drawback to the story is the lack of a sense of the passage of time. It is difficult to get a feeling of the ages of the children from one chapter to another, and too abruptly they pass from childhood to a kind of semi-adulthood—at one moment a boyish escapade and the next a commissioned officer. Apart from this, it has a great deal to commend it.

"The New Books: 'The Children of the House'," in The Junior Bookshelf, *Vol. 32, No. 4, August, 1968, p. 237.*

JEAN C. THOMSON

[*The Children of the House* is a] book designed to leave its readers downcast. . . . [It is] a juvenile book reduction of the Sitwells' dilemma. The fantasy play that [E. Nesbit's] characters indulged in under similar circumstances is absent here. . . . [The children] never have any real adventures. An epilogue reveals the children's fates: Tom and Hugh killed in World War I; Laura dead from a disease caught while nursing soldiers; Margaret, the sole survivor, living abroad alone. Though the theme and tone are more appropriate to an adult short story . . . , this slim, well-written novel may have a certain melancholy charm for pre-teen readers. Presenting an emphatically gloomy statement about a side of aristocratic life seldom well and truly exposed elsewhere in juvenile books, this can also be read as a social document—an interesting, if weird, experience for young readers. (pp. 84-5)

> *Jean C. Thomson, "Grades 3-6: 'The Children of the House',"* in School Library Journal, *an appendix to* Library Journal *(reprinted from the November, 1968 issue of* School Library Journal, *published by R. R. Bowker Co./A Xerox Corporation; copyright © 1968),* Vol. 93, No. 20, November, 1968, pp. 84-5.

BARBARA WERSBA

Every so often, one finds a book that speaks for its generation—and **"The Children of the House"** is such a book. . . .

These are the memories of Brian Fairfax-Lucy's childhood—and, as told by Philippa Pearce, they are eloquent. The simplicity, truth, and lack of emphasis in this story are virtually Chekhovian, and it is a stouthearted reader who will not weep.

> *Barbara Wersba, " 'The Children of the House',"* in The New York Times Book Review, Part II *(© 1968 by The New York Times Company; reprinted by permission),* November 3, 1968, p. 38.

CONSTANTINE GEORGIOU

Unlike traditional fairy tales, this beautifully written fantasy [*Tom's Midnight Garden*] does not depend on supernatural performance to turn the trick. Rather, it is the magic of the characters' personalities and of the mysterious movement in time that lifts this story beyond the usual time and dream fantasies in children's literature. (p. 270)

Philippa Pearce's particular contribution to this fantastic adventure in time is in the way she makes her characters come alive with natural dialogue, colloquial at times, but breezy and clear-cut. Tinged with poetry, the beautiful narrative is firmly rooted in reality and presented in probable terms. (p. 271)

> *Constantine Georgiou, "Fantasy in Children's Literature,"* in his Children and Their Literature *(© 1969 by Prentice-Hall, Inc.; reprinted by permission of Prentice-Hall, Inc., Englewood Cliffs, New Jersey),* Prentice-Hall, 1969, pp. 241-302.*

RUTH HILL VIGUERS

In Philippa Pearce's **Tom's Midnight Garden** . . . the idea that time has no barriers was embodied in nearly perfect literary form. No loose ends, no inconsistencies mar the book. Miss Pearce can explain with few words but great conviction such supernatural events as Tom's passing through a closed door or the actual process of a room's transformation from its unfamiliar past appearance to its familiar present. Tom's acceptance of the fact that he can enjoy a garden that had existed long before his birth and friendship with a girl who had played in the garden more than half a century before is wholly believable. The book is a model of what can be done with an intricate

theme by a writer endowed with literary style, understanding of children, and a clear insight into her own vision. (p. 477)

> *Ruth Hill Viguers, "Worlds without Boundaries: Literary Fairy Tales and Fantasy,"* in A Critical History of Children's Literature, *by Cornelia Meigs, Anne Thaxter Eaton, Elizabeth Nesbitt, and Ruth Hill Viguers, edited by Cornelia Meigs (copyright © 1953, 1969 by Macmillan Publishing Co., Inc.), revised edition, Macmillan, 1969, pp. 446-83.*

ELEANOR CAMERON

[In **Minnow on the Say**] one finds the same devouring awareness of the natural world, the same complexity and maturity of thought . . . , the same artistry of phrasing, and the same unwillingness to compromise in any of these areas [as in the books of Lucy Boston] because she is writing for children that we find in Lucy Boston's and William Mayne's work. Therefore in her time fantasy [**Tom's Midnight Garden**] one is not in the least surprised to discover, woven into the firmly plotted movement of the story, certain philosophic overtones in her handling of Time as it relates to Tom's gradual understanding of what he has been experiencing in the garden. In this work, too, as in Lucy Boston's, is found what I can only describe as an atmosphere of poetic dimension, tenderness without sentimentality, though expressed quite differently: not so much in paragraphs one can read aloud as examples as in the effect of the book as a whole, in Tom's relationship to the child Hatty and in his almost visceral love for and need of the garden. Here . . . is passionate attachment to place and person. (pp. 118-19)

In a book such as this . . . , one sees the fertile and perceiving mind of the writer joyously at work, unafraid of convolutions (so unexpectedly playing Hatty's time against Tom's Relative Time), ready to explore to the end every possibility opened up by each new pattern of circumstance. Such writers never cease searching for all that any particular pattern will yield. Yet, whatever fresh and original perceptions are arrived at, the results as far as story is concerned will be clear and firm and satisfying to both the analytical and the aesthetically sensitive adult, as well as to the less consciously critical child. The reader, whoever he may be, will sense a fine proportion, a plausible economy of effect. (pp. 121-22)

> *Eleanor Cameron, "The Green and Burning Tree: A Study of Time Fantasy" (a revision of a talk presented at University of California, Irvine, October 26, 1967),* in her The Green and Burning Tree: On the Writing and Enjoyment of Children's Books *(copyright © 1969 by Eleanor Cameron; reprinted by permission of Little, Brown and Company in association with The Atlantic Monthly Press),* Atlantic-Little, Brown, 1969, pp. 71-134.*

BRIAN JACKSON

[Philippa Pearce's] achievement, wonderful enough in itself, is representative of how (without forsaking the adult note) a truly gifted writer can now write directly for the child, and for the ordinary child, in a way seldom achieved before. . . .

[**Minnow on the Say**] has the hypnotic craftsmanship of a first class detective story. And as the story winds its fascinating course, the book engages the reader even more deeply in the lovely recreation of a boy's life in a small East Anglian village. In doing so, it brings back many childhoods. . . . It spills over with a child's geography, places that only a child would know. . . . (p. 196)

It is, if you like, a very conservative book. Children are expected to be polite to adults, to make things—scraping and varnishing their canoe—not to destroy. There are all the tiny ceremonies of inviting friends to tea, or calling on strangers. Pocket money is earned and carefully counted, and very neatly you pick up the nuances of children and adults observing the codes. . . .

Of course, the boys—being boys—are sometimes rude and destructive, thoughtlessly or at moments of stress. There is the moment when Adam, obsessed by the treasure, suspects treasure under the lovely pinky-yellow rose bush that stands by itself in the garden. . . . (p. 197)

Without being in the slightest moralistic, the book has the rare capacity to create goodness, to make the decencies of life ring true.

Her effects come through her art; her negatives—'a deep, raw hole, empty now of any rose-tree roots'—imply her positives.

And yet there is more; already at least a pre-echo of the Philippa Pearce music, that note of controlled poignancy that is to make *Tom's Midnight Garden* a classic of its literature. (p. 198)

Again the tale has the same breathless, detective pull. . . .

Who, once having read them, can forget the chapters when boy and young woman skate up the river to Ely?

For it is in these final sections that the art transcends itself. Through scenes of haunting and sometimes painful beauty, Tom perceives that the old woman in the upstairs flat was once a child like Hatty, and that age and life will make Hatty an old woman like her. . . . It is, if you like, one of the ordinary insights of life; but one, perhaps, we most easily slur over. . . . Philippa Pearce makes you find it, feel it—and for her child audience it is maybe the first uncovering. . . .

[*A Dog So Small* again] has the clean narrative pull, the delicious quiet humour, an essential inwardness. . . . (p. 200)

It is a very fine book, and yet—coming where it does in her work—it is something of a pendant, a detour. So much is there, but not the music. The theme of obsession (which of course informed the treasure hunt in *Minnow on the Say*) now dominates and fills the gap. There is something of the psychological study about it, and—ever so slightly—the eye slips off the child audience. Characteristically, she no longer relies wholly on her art to do its own work, but—again, ever so slightly—tops up the insights with glimpses of *sententiae*. . . .

It seemed at that stage that either *Tom's Midnight Garden* had exhausted the more elusive and precious vein, or that having hit such brilliant moments the writer was reluctant to make the even more demanding commitment to her talents that was perhaps required.

In the event, she felt her way out of the situation with cautious instinct. . . . [*The Children of the House*] was originally drafted by Brian Fairfax-Lucy, as a tale for adults. Philippa Pearce worked on the existing draft and, as the introductory note says: 'made it one that can be enjoyed and understood by children'. She did a good deal more than that. She made it a classic. The setting could be that of one of the Victorian or Edwardian writers. (p. 201)

What takes it out of the standard Victorian mould (as it does E. Nesbit) is a refusal to identify with the assumptions and aspirations of the upper class home—the sense of the house through the servants' eyes, of the eldest daughter denied a useful education, of the old men combing the bins, or the ironic stonebreaker on the roadside. . . . (p. 202)

Compared to her previous books—and perhaps because of the curious joint authorship—it takes some chapters before the vision becomes as freed from its setting as this. And it nowhere has the potent narrative thread.

But it has the music. The beautiful, piercing sense of childhood swept along—and overswept—in the stream of time. The art is superb. The ordinary incidents of childhood—boiling a moorhen's egg, a forbidden hair-clipping, finding a half-crown—lap quietly in the reader's mind: months and years imperceptibly vanish at each chapter's end.

So apt and unforced is the second half, that you may not realise how it is all building up inside you until the marvellous final section, the *adieu*. There is something almost Tchekov-like in those last dozen pages. For one splendid stretch she again meets and tops the great Victorians in their own arbour.

I do not think any age previous to ours could have so brought out Philippa Pearce's talent. Her clean, plain prose opens up her books to any child who reads at all easily. I fear that isn't at all true of many revered classics of the past. Her work brims with life, and with life decent, positive, ongoing. Again one wonders if a critical look at some of our Edwardian inheritance might find that this was precisely what some of them lacked. She writes—mostly—to and for the child: not through the child to other adults. (p. 203)

Brian Jackson, "Philippa Pearce in the Golden Age of Children's Literature," in The Use of English *(© Granada Publishing Limited 1970), Vol. 21, No. 3, Spring, 1970, pp. 195-203, 207.*

LESLEY AERS

There is the most explicit attempt in *Tom's Midnight Garden* to understand the nature of time, one's attitude to it, its relation to one's own existence. Many aspects come over powerfully: the child growing up and changing; the destruction of the garden and its transformation into a housing estate; and a mean little yard mirroring a whole changed pattern of society. But I think that Philippa Pearce's resistance to the new polluted environment loses its impact because it becomes identified with the feelings towards the loss of childhood, which is an inevitable process, whereas the pollution of the environment *need* not be. . . .

Tom is only really aware of time in relation to his own immediate living, and to the things he wants to do. . . . (p. 79)

This refers only to a week in Tom's life, but it reflects the larger truth of time as the creator and the destroyer. Thus we have in this book the sense of Tom's own holiday and the larger sense of Hatty's whole life, and even the background—the objects—changing and being destroyed. The sense of loss, as shown by the central image of the tree falling, is stronger than the sense of creation and growth. This is what the novel emphasizes. Yet these are essential truths about time, in which we are bound to have our achievement and our termination. And it is the truth of *Tom's Midnight Garden* that conflicts with the magical aspect—why the thirteenth hour? Is it not enough to accept that Tom and Hatty are dreaming the same dreams? Is not a dream a valid experience? Given this, one can understand the way that Tom's brother Peter enters one of the dreams—but the way in which Abel sees Tom is not so reconcilable. When the whole movement of the book is to contradict the idea of Time No Longer—for time is continual change—how can this living in the past be anywhere but in dream and memory, which is the only place, as Mrs. Bartholomew says, where things stand still? There are other difficulties of course; the skates which were left in the house for Tom years before his birth—so did Hatty meet him in her actual past? There are two movements of time in the book. One is inexorable and uncompromising, but one is fluid.

The beauty and poignancy of course remain. It is a celebration of childhood—but with the apprehension that children suffer keenly. The fact that the weather is always fine—except in the beauty of the frost—shows, as Tom recognizes, the way in which Mrs. Bartholomew's mind selects its own images of childhood, ones that suggest her regret. Everything, it seems, should be teaching Tom what he himself will lose and what he will feel. (p. 80)

Tom and Mrs. Bartholomew know what they have shared together, and the closeness between the boy and the old woman is finely and delicately described. But *Tom's Midnight Garden* is in many ways hardly a children's book at all; it is a cry from an adult awareness. (p. 81)

> Lesley Aers, "The Treatment of Time in Four Children's Books," in Children's literature in education (© 1970, Agathon Press, Inc.; reprinted by permission of the publisher), No. 2 (July), 1970, pp. 69-81.*

DAVID REES

Minnow on the Say employs a familiar formula for a children's book—the successful search for a long-buried treasure, with its usual attendant props, the false clues, villain racing to beat the children in their quest, etc. If the book were no more than this it would scarcely be worth writing about but it is however an unusual book in many respects; and it is worth noting that none of the subsequent novels employs such a well-tried device. The main characters—Adam, David and Miss Codling—are drawn with a convincing detail that immediately places the book on a higher level than its plot suggests. Adam has many of the characteristics of the heroes of *Tom's Midnight Garden* and *A Dog so Small*, particularly their passionate obsession to achieve their hearts' desires. Adam is irrational, often bad-tempered, often depressed; he swings mercurially from one extreme emotion to another. . . . He is much the most interesting character in the book, and altogether a surprising person to find in a quiet and leisurely English children's novel.

David, in contrast, is practical and down-to-earth, much the sort of son we would expect of Bob Moss, who drives the country buses and grows prize roses. Yet Bob Moss was once known as Bad Bobby Moss, Terror of both the Barleys; and David too, experiences the longing, the unfulfilled desire that torments all Philippa Pearce's heroes. . . . (pp. 40-1)

[Mr Smith] is one of the book's failures. He is observed at such a distance and so unsympathetically as to be scarcely credible. The author is not really interested; Mr Smith is no more than a necessary piece of the plot—the one scene in his house, curtains drawn and weak disembodied voice, is unnecessarily melodramatic, and his relationship with his daughter,

Elizabeth, is like that of Mr Rochester and his wife in [Charlotte Brontë's] *Jane Eyre,* and no more convincing. Elizabeth never succeeds in being credible either; and the recognition scene between her and Adam is particularly weak. Melodrama in fact is the book's main weakness; particularly in the last part of the book, one larger-than-life scene succeeds another. . . . The last part of the book deteriorates in quality; the pace slackens, too many interviews take place behind closed doors and have to be reported, the denouement is slow and an anti-climax. But it must be said that all the succeeding books are totally free of these particular faults.

The book seems to go wrong at the point where the Smiths enter the story, and perhaps the deterioration is because the author clearly dislikes Mr Smith. . . . Philippa Pearce's least successful creations seem to be people she dislikes—Mrs Melbourne, Sir Robert Hatton—though these are not as unconvincing as Mr Smith. (pp. 41-2)

For all its faults, *Minnow on the Say* is an impressive first novel. It could never be mistaken for a book by anybody else, despite its well-worn storyline, for the virtues that delight us in the succeeding books are already there. Ultimately it is not the treasure-hunt, or the Smiths that we remember so much as Miss Codling's anxieties and dignity, the unusualness of Adam, the quiet pastoral background of the Barleys, the boys' and the author's sensuous delight in the river—absent from hardly any page of the book—the warmth and naturalness of David's home and family.

The voice we associate with the later books is already there—the rendering of the sensuous physical world, linking it so often with a past that is only just under the surface, in sentences in which the rhythms and cadences express exactly the right pleasure or sadness that the words mean.

Tom's Midnight Garden is the novel more than any other on which Philippa Pearce's reputation rests. It is not without its faults, however, and striking though the imaginative conception of the story is, I am not sure that the two subsequent novels are not better done. The opening chapters seem laboriously written, the characters a little wooden, and measles is certainly not a good enough reason for packing Tom off to his Aunt Gwen's. However when Tom enters the garden, all is well; the writing loses its uncertainty, and seems to change into a triumphantly major key; it is as if the author, having eventually got her central character into the situation she is most interested in, is relieved at being able, at least, to say what she wants to say. . . . (pp. 42-3)

Like Adam Codling, Tom Long is obsessed by one fixed idea. This is to explain to himself the mystery of the garden, and ultimately to stay in it for ever. Other children in the book, Tom's brother Peter and Hatty Melbourne, are as single-minded and passionately concerned with their own longings as Tom is: Peter with joining Tom in the garden (some of the most moving writing in the book expresses Peter's frustration at being left out of things), and Hatty with finding her own satisfactory modus vivendi in the unsympathetic Melbourne family. . . . [Her] happiness as an adult seems to reinforce a feeling that pervades the whole book, that children of Tom's age experience joy and disappointment with an intensity that adults hardly ever realize: it is the force with which this intensity is expressed that is one of the book's main strengths. . . . (p. 43)

As well as this intensity, the characters share other characteristics, impulsiveness, unreasonableness, even rudeness; adults as well as children. . . .

In contrast with this feverishness of emotion in almost all the characters, the landscape has a cool, unchanging certainty about it; this was the function of landscape, particularly the river, in *Minnow on the Say* and Tom's garden, though its seasons may alter, or lightning on one occasion strike down a tree, is always there, inviting, full of promise. . . .

The 'magic' of the garden is that it is a Garden of Eden, a symbol of Tom's and Hatty's innocence; they have to leave it as they grow up—Tom's appearances become rarer as Hatty grows older; he grows so thin that she can see through him. It is no coincidence that when Tom finds himself excluded finally it is Hatty's wedding day. Hatty is in love with Barty, so she has no more need of her imaginary friend; Tom is banished simply because she doesn't think of him any more. The relationship between Tom and Hatty is like an innocent love affair in this Garden of Eden; and other parallels with the Book of Genesis can be seen—Adam and his descendants were gardeners, according to tradition; Adam's sons were Cain and Abel; our gardener is called Abel. Our Abel, however, is in his simplicity and religious devotion, inside Eden with Tom and Hatty, not outside like the Abel of Genesis. However, just as Eden was destroyed so is this garden; sold off by James for building land. (p. 44)

Many people reading the book for the first time, who have not noticed that Mrs Bartholomew and Hatty are one and the same person, speak of the almost unbearable tension as the book proceeds into what is a seemingly inescapable tragedy, and their sense of relief when this is averted, and their delight that the ending is so credible. The fact that the ending is not just a happy coda stuck on so that the reader won't be upset, is because Hatty *is* Mrs Bartholomew, and always was, since before the beginning of the book. In other words, the author knows precisely what she is about. The clues are all there for us, early on. The first appearance of Mrs Bartholomew is when she comes downstairs to wind up the clock, a sort of Father Time figure. A page is spent on showing this seemingly irrelevant character carrying out a seemingly insignificant action, but as the clock is the great link between time past and time present, and Mrs Bartholomew is shown as its keeper or guardian now (just as the angel on the dial is its keeper in time past), it seems clear that the purpose of the scene is to suggest that she has a much more significant connection with the past than Tom, at the moment, realizes. And at the end of the chapter, when Tom enters the garden for the first time, the game is virtually given away by a further apparently irrelevant comment. Mrs Bartholomew 'was lying tranquilly in bed; her false teeth, in a glass of water by the bedside, grinned unpleasantly in the moonlight, but her indrawn mouth was curved in a smile of easy sweet-dreaming sleep. She was dreaming of the scenes of her childhood.' (pp. 45-6)

Another reason why the ending seems so effective is because the author herself seems to be growing up as a writer in the process of writing this book. There is a great difference in the quality of the last chapters compared with the first; not only is there simply more certainty and maturity in the way the language of the sentences is put together with their increasing poetry, subtlety of rhythm and cadence, but the insights and sympathies deepen all the time; we feel that the author has a more profound knowledge of Tom and Hatty at the end than she had at the beginning. The same is true of Tom's relationship with the Kitsons, it is developing all the time in sympathy, and in humour. Nevertheless it must be said that the problems of that relationship remain unsolved; Alan and Gwen are no nearer understanding Tom than they were at the beginning, and the debt of gratitude Tom should owe them is scarcely commented on. The speculation about the nature of time grows more thoughtful as the book continues; Tom's ideas on the subject become more complex and adult, and his imaginative leaps seem to hold more truth than Uncle Alan's scientific explanations. (p. 46)

The certainty with which these things are done shows a great advance on *Minnow on the Say* and if that book can be said to be an unusually interesting first novel, *Tom's Midnight Garden* is nearly a masterpiece.

I can think of only one blemish in her next book, *A Dog so Small*, and that is the somewhat irrelevant story of what happened to the picture after Ben lost it, which seems to show the old unfortunate taste for melodrama. But in Ben Blewitt we have the most interesting of Philippa Pearce's heroes. Though she tells us more than once that Ben is a perfectly ordinary boy, we can scarcely believe her; Ben is surely the oddest person she has ever written about. No other character in her novels departs so far from reality into his private obsession as Ben does; Tom Long's fantasy world was confined to night time but Ben's operates during the day as well as in his dreams. . . . Ben's problems with his family do not come solely from the fact that he is the odd one out in age; he is also the only one with any real sensitivity or imagination. . . . Ben has an additional problem that none of the heroes of the other novels has to face; there is no possible outlet for his frustrations, no person sufficiently unpleasant for him to dislike, or blame. *A Dog so Small* has no villain. The Blewitt family are remarkable for their niceness, so Ben's troubles turn in on himself. . . . This withdrawal from reality the author suggests is sad and reprehensible. . . . The answer is that the Blewitt parents should have given Ben a dog in the first place; had they known what damage the absence of a dog was causing him they would almost certainly have done so. But they never know, and this points to another sadness in this book—that even in the nicest of families real communication between its members can be impossible.

The construction of *A Dog so Small* is interesting; its opening pages and its conclusion contain the most memorable moments. Like *Tom's Midnight Garden* it opens with the hero's world crashing about his ears; Ben's discovery that he has not been given a dog for his birthday would be so easy to sentimentalize, but in fact the author is quite merciless, showing no let-up in the portrayal of Ben's disappointment, every humorous and uncomprehending remark from his family making the situation worse and worse. Ben is not allowed any escape from the moral dilemma; it would be so easy if he could just quietly hate his grandparents but Grandpa Fitch has written 'TRULY SORY ABOUT DOG' and for Ben there is no way out of that. So Ben's feelings as elsewhere, turn inwards. The last chapter, too, could so easily be a sentimental happy ending. Instead we have something that is psychologically far more truthful; as Granny Fitch says, 'People get their heart's desire, and then they have to begin to learn how to live with it'; Ben makes the miserable discovery that a real dog, given to him at last, is no adequate substitute for the chihuahua of his imagination. It would be a cruelly tragic ending if Ben were to leave Brown on the Heath in the growing dusk; right up to the last page it looks as if he will. But he does not, fortunately. By this I don't mean I necessarily want the book to end happily . . . but the reasons and feelings Ben has for keeping the dog are consistent with the development of his character in the last third of the book. Since the accident he has begun to grow up, to accept, however slowly, the fact that he has to live in the real world. . . . This book, more than the others, charts the changes and growth of its hero's personality. . . . (pp. 47-9)

[The] unusualness of *A Dog so Small* lies in its ability to suggest the sheer pleasure humans can derive from the animal world, and the intensity some people feel for animals, when there is an emotional gap left by the deficiencies of other human beings. (p. 49)

[Though *The Children of the House*] is the saddest of all the books, there is nevertheless an emphasis on the companionship and pleasures of friendship between the brothers and sisters, in direct contrast with the family in *A Dog so Small* which splits into a pair of brothers and a pair of sisters, leaving Ben, number three of five, a solitary. Margaret in *The Children of the House* we are told 'wished above all for the companionship of the other three'—the very thing that ultimately is denied her; she only wishes to exist as a member of a group, an adjunct of the other three, and this over-riding desire . . . gives the writing a poignancy and total sense of loss when she is separated from [Hugh and Laura], a feeling not only of loneliness, but of existence being without any further meaning. . . .

However, much of the book concerns the adventures the children share together. . . . The others grow up, Tom and Laura are impatient to leave, only Margaret wants to play 'Do you remember?' Laura cannot leave quickly enough, we are told more than once that she is a girl of spirit, that she has her father's high temper and determination. Tom also wants to leave, to be a soldier; he is pathetically unaware of what we, with the hindsight of history, know is waiting for him. (p. 50)

Hugh is more in the tradition of Philippa Pearce's previous heroes—Adam, Tom Long, Ben. He has the same passion (an example is his furious disgust with Tom, when Tom wonders whether the stone breaker deserves to be given a shilling) and shrinks from situations of possible violence that his brother Tom might relish. . . .

This sharp distinction of character is necessary in a book in which four people are sharing the same activities. It is worth noting that *The Children of the House* is the only novel of Philippa Pearce's in which girls play a central role, in which we look at the world through the eyes of the girls as well as the boys. There is, of course, Hatty in *Tom's Midnight Garden*, but we rarely observe Tom from her point of view; it is usually the other way round. Less successful creations in *The Children of the House* are the parents, Sir Robert and Lady Hatton, particularly Sir Robert. While it is true that the author is trying to emphasize in this novel that life fifty or sixty years ago is not the pleasant magic world lost beyond recall of *Tom's Midnight Garden* that one aspect of life that was less satisfactory was the relationship between parents and children. Sir Robert Hatton does not come off as a credible Victorian-Edwardian father, conscious of status, chilling and distant to his children; he seems inhumane, improbable, devoid of any parental feelings at all. . . . (p. 51)

No matter what part of the authorship of the novel belongs to Philippa Pearce, it is as if *The Children of the House* was a deliberate corrective to a view of the past suggested in *Tom's Midnight Garden*. (p. 52)

The Children of the House differs from the other three novels in that there is almost no narrative. The plot consists of a series of incidents—punting, the walk to Honeford, the attempt to

see Victor—which are connected only by their being shared by the same four characters; there is no story as *Minnow on the Say* has a story. . . . But we never feel that the book is aimlessly episodic; the style of the writing is its great unifier. In no other novel of Philippa Pearce is this more evident or more successful. It reads like one long prose-poem from its melancholic opening sentence 'No children live at Stanford Hall now' to its last dying echo, the name 'Elsie—Elsie—Elsie' reverberating through the empty rooms. . . .

Like the work of most great artists, her work is an expression of her own needs and feelings and values, and it is this that gives to it its peculiar strength and appeal. (p. 53)

David Rees, "The Novels of Philippa Pearce," in Children's literature in education (© 1971, Agathon Press, Inc.; reprinted by permission of the publisher), No. 4 (March), 1971, pp. 40-53.

MARGERY FISHER

In this grave and beautiful piece of writing in traditional storyteller's style [*The Squirrel Wife*], magic rises naturally from the impulses of generous or unkind temperaments, with love and loyalty given full value in the working out of the fortunes of two brothers. Philippa Pearce shows no trace of uneasiness in following the patterns, in rhythm and vocabulary, of the fairy-tale tradition which she is not imitating so much as continuing with complete confidence. Like Hans Andersen, she has put human emotion and human values in the forefront of a tale that has its own strong magic.

Margery Fisher, "Legend and Fairy Tale: 'The Squirrel Wife'," in her Growing Point, Vol. 10, No. 6, December, 1971, p. 1852.

FRANK EYRE

[*Tom's Midnight Garden* is] the perfect fantasy of our time. . . . This deeply moving, beautifully written and completely convincing time-fantasy is one of the most perfectly conceived and executed children's books of the past twenty years. (p. 128)

The author makes beautifully subtle and complex use of [the] time-shift. . . .

Such a story in other hands could be mawkish and unconvincing, just another time fantasy. In Philippa Pearce's it becomes almost unbearably moving. A wonderful book. . . . (p. 130)

Although it is typical of the author's highly individual outlook that the social problem [in *Minnow on the Say*] should be turned upside down and it is the bus driver's family that leads the happy, secure and well-fed life, while the upper class family is in difficulties, this is not a 'social consciousness' novel. It is a straightforward adventure story, with a long-sustained search for buried treasure by the river; a moderately nasty villain, an old mill, lovable (and unlovable) country characters, and even a happy ending. But the author's style and manner transmute these ordinary ingredients into pure gold and this is a fine book which, although not a fantasy, is unmistakably by the author who was shortly to produce *Tom's Midnight Garden*. To have been runner-up for the Carnegie Medal with one's first book and win it with one's second must be a rare feat, but Philippa Pearce achieved it, and deserved to. (p. 131)

[*The Children of the House*] is, as might be expected, well done, but it is a surprising thing for so original and creative a writer to have done. It will be interesting to see what she does next. Whatever it is, it will be original, imaginative, and written with truth and sincerity, for she creates a real world that is far removed from the imaginary worlds in which so many children's books are set. (p. 132)

> Frank Eyre, "Fiction for Children," in his British Children's Books in the Twentieth Century *(copyright © 1971 by Frank Eyre; reprinted by permission of the publishers, E. P. Dutton & Co., Inc.; in Canada by Penguin Books Ltd.),* Longman Books, 1971, Dutton, 1973, pp. 76-156.*

PHILIPPA PEARCE

As a child, I intended to be a writer—a novelist, of course. It's a common dream. The nearest I seemed likely to get, as an adult, was in the job of scriptwriter-producer for the School Broadcasting Department of the BBC. This experience, over thirteen years, must have helped as much as any to make me into a writer of children's books. I wrote for the same public, changing only the medium. (p. 169)

In 1951, while I was working for school broadcasting, I contracted tuberculosis. I went into hospital in Cambridge for most of that summer, a particularly fine one. I didn't feel ill at all, and it seemed almost unbearable to be lying in bed missing all of the summer on the river, only five miles away, in Great Shelford, where I had been born and brought up. . . . Imprisoned in hospital, I went there in my imagination as I had never done before—as I had never needed to do, of course. I knew, by heart, literally the *feel* of the river and the canoe on it. It became hallucinatory, like vividly-imagined fiction.

At last I went back to work; but now began to dawn on me the idea that I could do it too—write a children's story. One needed a good, reliable plot, of course: a search for treasure; a family home on its last legs; and so on. As for the setting, I had that already; and that was what really interested me.

I wrote **Minnow on the Say** mostly with pleasure. I was just about to let the heroes find their treasure (at a point half way through what is now the finished story) when I realized that the whole thing would be on the short side. So, with a dislocating wrench, I changed the plot: the treasure wasn't there, after all, and the characters had to plod on through renewed complications. (pp. 169-70)

I began to think out **Tom.** At first, in reaction against the first book, this one was to have had a minimum of plot; but, of course, it changed and grew. At least it has more of a theme than a plot. I still think it the best of the books I have written: I think it's the best done, and it's the closest, dearest.

I used to think—and to say in print—that authors of children's books usually wrote out of childhood experience: that I myself certainly did. Now I'm not sure; almost, I'm sure not. That is, I think I write out of present experience; but present experience includes—sometimes painfully—the past. (p. 170)

> Philippa Pearce, in her essay in A Sense of Story: Essays on Contemporary Writers for Children *by John Rowe Townsend (copyright © 1971 by John Rowe Townsend; reprinted by permission of J. B. Lippincott, Publishers),* Lippincott, 1971, pp. 163-71.

VIRGINIA HAVILAND

[*The Squirrel Wife*] is constructed of fairy-tale components: a protagonist, Jack, an overworked young swineherd; a species of fairymen—the green people; and the motif of kindness rewarded by magic. Paralleling the seal-wife or fox-wife of folklore is Jack's brown-haired, brown-eyed squirrel-wife. . . . Jack's older brother, jealous of Jack's well-being, caused him to be jailed and lose his squirrel-wife. But a perfectly wrought solution sweetens the tale. . . . Relayed with the directness of a long-known tale, but with more shadings and tenderness, the narrative is as totally pleasing as any long-lived story. The creation of the little wife is charming. . . .

> Virginia Haviland, "Spring Booklist: 'The Squirrel Wife'," in The Horn Book Magazine *(copyright © 1972 by The Horn Book, Inc., Boston),* Vol. XLVIII, No. 3, June, 1972, p. 265.

MARGERY FISHER

To use Edward Blishen's invaluable phrase, [the stories in **What the Neighbours Did and Other Stories**] have "a child's eye at the centre" but they do not reflect an exclusively child-centred world.

It is the world of the Barleys, Great and Little, the Cambridgeshire world of Ben Blewitt's grandparents, the scene of the river adventure of **Minnow** and of Hattie Bartholomew's childhood. . . . In a sense the story [**Still Jim and Silent Jim**] celebrates—as they all do—that pace and closeness in village life of which one aspect is that crabbed age and youth can and do live together.

Let nobody suppose, though, that these are not stories for children to read. They describe with memory and with verbal skill the doings of childhood. . . . The impeccable art in the stories, the prose that never obtrudes but is always active, pointed, lucid—these are for adults to enjoy consciously and for the young to absorb without having to indulge in any comprehension exercise. Such books form taste, through delight. (pp. 2051-52)

> Margery Fisher, "Special Review: 'What the Neighbours Did and Other Stories'," in her Growing Point, *Vol. 11, No. 6, December, 1972, pp. 2051-52.*

THE TIMES LITERARY SUPPLEMENT

Philippa Pearce's book of short stories, **What the Neighbours Did,** confirms her, if confirmation were needed, as the most important writer for children at the present. It is exceptionally finely written and conceived—indeed it is hard to think of another children's book this year that could be considered in the same class. Such high claims must be insisted on partly because the book seems to make none for itself. It is a collection of stories written over a dozen years or so, in consistently understated and low-keyed tones, describing the quiet lives of country children. Yet its impact is the greater because Philippa Pearce has deliberately dispensed with all the usual props of children's fiction—whimsy, fantasy, magic, talking toys or animals, the looking-glass world of the past. Instead she has limited herself to the severest realism. The unlikeliest event in the volume is Still Jim's return from Little Barley in his bathchair. . . . It is probably significant that this particular story, **"Still Jim and Silent Jim"** was the earliest of these tales to be written. The later pieces reject even this degree of delicate farce in favour of simpler, more ordinary activities—getting up in the middle of the night, picking blackberries, retrieving an old tin box from a pond.

Yet everywhere the commonplace surface of life is parted to reveal the deeper mysteries of existence. Like Sausage, the short-sighted hero of **"Return to Air"**, we are invited to peer into the dark and unknown depths beneath the familiar pond. Like Dan, fascinated by the freshwater mussel that burrows into the sand so rapidly, we too are fascinated by the contrary urges that emerge and disappear again in the different characters of the tales. The most poignant and moving of them all, **"Lucky Boy"**, is an exploration of frustration and disappointment, a day wasted, a paradise lost. It is easy enough for the critic to recognize traditional themes and patterns handled in these stories, but their lively presentation of familiar experience also gives them a very immediate appeal to children. . . .

What the Neighbours Did has those classical qualities of seriousness and profundity which make most writing look tawdry by comparison.

"Quiet Country Lives," in The Times Literary Supplement *(© Times Newspapers Ltd. (London) 1972; reproduced from* The Times Literary Supplement *by permission), No. 3692, December 8, 1972, p. 1490.*

MARCUS CROUCH

Tom's Midnight Garden . . . is one of those rare, miraculously individual books which belong to no category and demand absolute acceptance from the reader. Philippa Pearce wrote here a kind of ghost story, except that the ghost was still alive, and a kind of historical novel, its period carefully concealed from the reader. (p. 198)

The concluding passages have a perfection unmatched in children's literature.

Part of the wonder of *Tom's Midnight Garden* lies in purely literary qualities. Philippa Pearce is a master of style. Unlike William Mayne, a greater virtuoso performer who is often carried away by the enchantment of his own skill, she is always in control. She uses words as if she had just discovered them. With them she discloses the mystery of the garden and explores in depth the complex personalities of Tom and Hatty. No one, not even E. Nesbit in the 'Arden' books, has managed better the transition from present to past. . . .

Minnow on the Say . . . is an enchanting story of a treasure-hunt . . . , as fresh and fragile as a spring day. It is structurally disastrous. In three years Miss Pearce learnt all about her craft. The construction of *Tom's Midnight Garden,* its firm development, the subtle variation from episode to episode, is beyond criticism. (p. 199)

Marcus Crouch, "Self and Society," in his The Nesbit Tradition: The Children's Novel in England 1945-1970 *(© Marcus Crouch 1972), Ernest Benn, 1972, pp. 196-229.*

PAUL HEINS

[Philippa Pearce] writes with a hushed expectancy that does not necessarily end in solemnity, but—on many occasions—spills over into humor or into plain realism. . . . [All the stories in *What the Neighbors Did and Other Stories*] capture the environmental experiences and the domestic adventures of children living in a present-day English village. . . . As in the stories of Sara Orne Jewett, the effect of the narratives depends upon the author's powers of observation and sympathy; and

the exquisite simplicity of her style is never precious. (pp. 592-93)

Paul Heins, "Stories for the Middle Readers: 'What the Neighbors Did and Other Stories'," in The Horn Book Magazine *(copyright © 1973 by The Horn Book, Inc., Boston), Vol. XLIX, No. 6, December, 1973, pp. 592-93.*

PENELOPE FARMER

"In the Middle of the Night," the best story here in Philippa Pearce's [**"What the Neighbours Did and Other Stories,"**] is very funny. . . . [It] is as finely structured as music; at the last note, sighing pleasurably, you wish for nothing more: a distinct achievement. On the other hand, some of these stories are often oddly unsatisfactory. The tone varies, of course. Two are first person, some slangy, others formal or detached or both. But all have Miss Pearce's strong sense of place, her wit and slyness of observation (adding, incidentally, to her special gallery of obstinate old men). Some may not be children's stories at all. The title one, for instance, shows a small, awful, adult wasteland. The best are too good to be confined to children anyway.

A few, inevitably, work less well—**"Lucky Boy"** perhaps or **"The Great Blackberry Pick"**—though the human observations are as good as ever. I find in some respects, the most interesting story **"Fresh,"** the most introspective, reminding me of the strangeness and intensity of the best of Philippa Pearce's earlier work. . . .

[It's] sad that a writer of this quality appears to have turned so resolutely from certain facets of her talent; and not just her talent for fantasy; her realism was often as powerful. Then I think of the end of her **"The Squirrel Wife"**—significant not so much for the hero's acceptance of the loss of his wife's forest powers, as for his lack of apparent regret. Maybe so. I regret it all the same. But I also know Philippa Pearce must go her own way. And since this collection would be beyond the powers of most of us, it seems churlish not to welcome and enjoy them as they are.

Penelope Farmer, "What the Neighbors Did," in The New York Times Book Review *(© 1974 by The New York Times Company; reprinted by permission), January 20, 1974, p. 8.*

JOHN ROWE TOWNSEND

Miss Pearce has . . . the storyteller's gift, . . . the novelist's power to create memorable people and the almost-architectural ability to complete a properly balanced and proportioned work. *Tom's Midnight Garden* (1958) is as near as any book I know to being perfect in its construction and writing, while satisfying also as fantasy and as a story about people. Only Philippa Pearce could have written it. (p. 246)

The book has a profound, mysterious sense of time; it has the beauty of a theorem but it is not abstract; it is sensuously as well as intellectually satisfying. The garden is so real that you have the scent of it in your nostrils. . . .

If I were asked to name a single masterpiece of English children's literature since the last war—and one masterpiece in thirty years is a fair ration—it would be this outstandingly beautiful and absorbing book. (p. 247)

John Rowe Townsend, "Not So Flimsy," in his Written for Children: An Outline of English-Language

Children's Literature *(copyright © 1965, 1974 by John Rowe Townsend; courtesy of J. B. Lippincott, Publishers; in Canada by Kestrel Books), revised edition, Lippincott, 1974, pp. 235-47.**

MARGERY FISHER

Just as M. R. James lures his readers, word by word and paragraph by paragraph, till they feel the un-ordinariness of the curtains, the sheets on the bed, the dusty old book, so Philippa Pearce leads us—cunningly, with a disarmingly conversational reporting of people's talk and actions—to a state of acceptance [in *The Shadow Cage and Other Tales of the Supernatural*]. (p. 3113)

In many of the stories the supernatural element is skilfully projected from the recognisably ordinary behaviour of ordinary people, part of the fabric of themselves.

This novelistic element makes Philippa Pearce's stories subtly different from those of M. R. James, while inviting comparison for certain qualities of elegance and concentration in the writing. There are other tales in her book whose supernatural apparitions are extra-human in every sense. . . . The shiver, the shock of surprise, always come slowly, after an everyday setting has been firmly established—a village school, a mill on the river, a bungalow "in the middle of nowhere in particular". Such clichés of "ghost stories" as attics or isolated, shrub-shrouded mansions, come up as good as new with Philippa Pearce's polishing.

People, their sad or wicked memories, their present alarms and astonishments, are the activators of the stories, but places supply their inspiration and their poetic force. Perhaps the most tightly wrought of all, *The Running-Companion,* shows this fusion of person and place at its most remarkable. (pp. 3113-14)

The plain, measured, disarmingly simple voice of the storyteller quickens and deepens towards the foreseen yet shocking climax. Philippa Pearce works her illusions with the greatest skill, now stating, now surmising, now dropping the lightest of hints, always mindful of the fact that the supernatural belongs to the natural. (p. 3114)

Margery Fisher, "Special Review: 'The Shadow Cage and Other Tales of the Supernatural'," in her Growing Point, Vol. 16, No. 1, May, 1977, pp. 3113-14.

THE JUNIOR BOOKSHELF

[The short stories in *The Shadow Cage and Other Tales of the Supernatural*] are not 'ghost' stories in the usual sense of the word, but something much more spine-chilling and evocative of atmosphere. The author has used ordinary things and places as a springboard for her imagination . . . and created with them a feeling of the supernatural and a sense of foreboding that makes the reader almost afraid to turn the page. Each story is unexpected in its ending. . . . The reader is never insulted and deflated by explanations which reduce the happening to the commonplace. Here too is the perceptive observation of character and the felicitous and effective use of words, which the reader has come to expect and appreciate from this author. . . .

A collection which will join the connoisseur's shelf of stories of the supernatural world of which we know so little.

"The New Books: 'The Shadow-Cage and Other Tales of the Supernatural'," in The Junior Bookshelf, Vol. 41, No. 3, June, 1977, p. 182.

JULIA BRIGGS

The power of imagination and memory to transfigure everyday life, to create a subtle haunting, has always distinguished Philippa Pearce's writing—when Tom entered his midnight garden, he and Hatty experienced each other almost as spirits, traditional ghostly playfellows. So the title of her latest book, *The Shadow-Cage and Other Tales of the Supernatural,* sounds particularly promising. Her previous and much underrated *What the Neighbours Did* recreated ordinary events with the intensity of vision of the child—or the artist. It seemed as if the new book might play [Samuel Taylor] Coleridge to the [William] Wordsworth of the earlier collection, the charm of novelty imparted to "things of everyday" giving place to those shadows of the imagination that set out to procure for themselves a "willing suspension of disbelief". . . .

Philippa Pearce has tried to soften the uncompromising terrors of the ghost story, preferring to end, where possible, with the evil exorcised. . . . Two stories deal with the misery gathered around the object of a childhood trauma, although this is probably a subject that requires an adult perspective to gain its full force. . . .

Two pieces make no concessions to nervous readers, and both, in their different ways, are notable contributions to this kind of writing. I disliked the first as much as I liked the second: **"The Dear Little Man with his Hands in his Pockets"** is a horror story. . . . The repulsive physical detail of Betsy touching the dark sticky liquid at the bottom of the head, although appropriate to this type of story, is unhappily out of key with the rest of the volume. On the other hand, **"The Shadow-Cage"** is a most successful example of the classical ghost story. . . . Using simple and familiar elements, an old bottle, a curious local place-name, and the climbing-frame in the school playground, Philippa Pearce here creates a model of economical storytelling that fully exploits elements of suspense and terror, while keeping them under perfect control. The explanation comes with a neatness and inevitability that will make this story a favourite with anthologizers.

Most of the pieces in this rather uneven . . . collection are obviously experimental. Only one, **"At the River-Gates"**, recalls the author's earlier achievements—it is an old man's memories of his childhood passed on a millstream with a much-loved elder brother, killed in the Great War. Here the ghost is really incidental and the story has a spontaneity and freedom of imagination which, for all their liveliness and modernity, the other stories rather lack.

Julia Briggs, "Evil Exorcised," in The Times Literary Supplement (© Times Newspapers Ltd. (London) 1977; reproduced from The Times Literary Supplement by permission), No. 3931, July 15, 1977, p. 864.

DOROTHY NIMMO

[*The Shadow Cage and Other Tales of the Supernatural*] is not a collection of ghost stories intended to appeal to children of a certain age who, as is well known, like spooky stories. It isn't a way of keeping children quiet for an hour, or a way of persuading them to exercise new-found skills in reading. It isn't designed to make them more understanding, more sensitive or more aware of the world around them. It is not, in short, an educational device. It is literature.

Most children must know the feeling that some places and things are frightening for no obvious reason. Philippa Pearce knows about them: the dark place at the back of the cupboard, the space behind the window of the empty house, the inexplicable nastiness of the old biscuit barrel. She expresses this sense of mystery and menace without in any way explaining it away.

> Dorothy Nimmo, "Seven to Eleven: 'The Shadow Cage and Other Tales of the Supernatural'," in The School Librarian, *Vol. 25, No. 3, September, 1977, p. 245.*

ROGER ALMA

One of the few . . . books for children which uses an adult and modern open-ended form is the very fine novel by Philippa Pearce and Brian Fairfax-Lucy, *The Children of the House.* . . . In this story, the reader shares in the tragic damage caused in the lives of four children by unloving parents, external events—in particular the First World War—and time. The tragic note is sounded in the first sentence of the Epilogue: "No children live in Stanford Hall now." In the last two pages of the novel, the full extent of the loss is suggested, and the process is seen as an inevitable one. Only echoes remain in the old house. It seems to me that such books are necessary if the younger reader is to make the transition from the comfortable, closed world of children's fiction to the more challenging and uncomfortable world of the adult novel. (pp. 20-1)

> Roger Alma, "The Novels of Molly Holden" (copyright © 1978 Roger Alma; reprinted by permission of the author and The Thimble Press, Lockwood Station Road, South Woodchester, Glos. GL55EQ, England), in Signal, *No. 25, January, 1978, pp. 16-24.**

ROSEMARY STONES

So many superlatives have been applied to Philippa Pearce's work that a new book from the Pearce stable is in danger of being treated with undue deference by reviewers.

With *The Battle of Bubble and Squeak,* however, superlatives are definitely in order. Philippa Pearce returns to the theme of a child's intense longing for a pet (first treated in *A Dog So Small*) and the repercussions that this yearning has within a family. . . .

The theme sounds rather tortured but Philippa Pearce writes with a dry humour and lucidity that capture for the young reader the complexity of people, especially adults, and makes them comprehensible, even sympathetic. Indeed the book treats family interaction so subtly and with such acute observation that it will be read and reread.

> Rosemary Stones, "Life Savers," in The Times Literary Supplement (© Times Newspapers Ltd. (London) 1978; reproduced from The Times Literary Supplement by permission), *No. 3979, July 7, 1978, p. 771.*

MARGERY FISHER

The successive stages in Sid's attitude to the animals [in *The Battle of Bubble and Squeak*]—enthusiasm, indifference, a fury of protectiveness, desperate misery—accompany and give point to each chapter of this small, significant domestic drama. There is enough colour and movement in the narrative, enough precise detail of sound, venue and personality, to hold the reader's attention. There is, though, much more. Alice Sparrow's reaction to the gerbils, a necessary guiding line for the plot, is also part of a silent, secret, continuing battle between this house-proud, inhibited woman and her warm-hearted second husband, who once kept white mice and whose sympathy with the children involves him in divided loyalties. This is no deep marital probe but a suggestion of family tensions as quiet and inexorable as the definition of parental roles in that memorable short story, "In the Middle of the Night". Philippa Pearce has always written expandable books, direct and open in style, simple in plot, but with so much in them of wisdom and humour that they offer new insights at every reading. Her new story could be understood and greatly enjoyed by children as young as seven or eight, as the tale of a pair of gerbils and their disruption of the family life of the Parkers and Sparrows. But when one has said that, one has only just begun. (p. 3415)

> Margery Fisher, "Points of Intersection," in her Growing Point, *Vol. 17, No. 4, November, 1978, pp. 3414-19.**

THE JUNIOR BOOKSHELF

[A writer of Philippa Pearce's] unmatched integrity can do nothing trivial, and even her slightest book has the Pearce fingerprints all over it. In [*The Battle of Bubble and Squeak,* a] nice little tale of how two gerbils capture a family's affections and in so doing transform the life of each member, she demonstrates the famous use of language. Each word is weighed, measured and then fitted into place with a craftsman's precision; nothing could be farther from the clichés and the second-best of much present-day writing, for children as for their elders. There is no cliché either of character or situation. The story works itself out in terms of people and their reactions to crisis and to one another.

This however is only the machinery. What matters is what it produces. The story of how the Parkers came to terms with their pets has warmth and tenderness and a little heartbreak. Above all it is the story of Mrs. Parker . . . , not at all the conventional mother, who finds it hardest of all to love the gerbils and plays a key part in their salvation. Here in a little book is a big study.

> "The New Books: 'The Battle of Bubble and Squeak'," in The Junior Bookshelf, *Vol. 42, No. 6, December, 1978, p. 302.*

MARGERY FISHER

Elm Street in North London, bounded by the stump of a tree at the Park end and by Woodside School (and gimlet-eyed George Crackenthorpe) at the other, to the outward eye a row of terrace houses like any other, is a territory to the children who live there, their cohesion proved by the fact that at school they are known to their peers from other streets as "the Elm Street lot". The six stories that chronicle their adventures [in *The Elm Street Lot*] were written ten years ago . . . but at least the passage of time has showed the dateless character of Philippa Pearce's writing. Progress has not yet put an end to the self-contained, village atmosphere of many London streets which is reflected in this book. . . .

Elm Street's individuality is supported by the device of "populousness", the method by which an author, defining only a handful of characters, creates the illusion of a far larger cast. . . . The illusion of populousness is simply and elegantly sustained. . . . (p. 3538)

The quiet humour that illuminates all Philippa Pearce's books rises naturally out of situations in these tales. A bath too big to go through the door, a lost kite, a broken window, a leaking roof, a hamster escaped, a cat run over—each circumstance engages the attention of the neighbourhood in varying ways, and while the energetic improvisations of nine-year-olds sets the tone, there are plenty of hints of more mature confrontations and relationships going on. The simplicity of the book is a matter of selection, not of omission. The style is concrete and precisely phrased; the stories run easily like reminiscences to be listened to but they are complex enough in content for the slower scrutiny of private reading. . . . The artistry of the Elm Street stories, different in scale but not in kind from that of Philippa Pearce's longer books, confirms me in my conviction that there is nobody to equal her in her chosen sphere. (p. 3539)

> *Margery Fisher, "An Old Favourite: 'The Elm Street Lot'," in her* Growing Point, *Vol. 18, No. 2, July, 1979, pp. 3538-39.*

JUDITH ARMSTRONG

Ghost stories, especially those which concentrate on the relationship between a single person and his ghost, as in the work of Philippa Pearce, are anti-fatalist. The person and the event are singular and positive, but they are shadowed by their negatives, which are many—all the people we might have become, and did not; all the things we might have done, and did not. The richness of our lives and being is in the depth of their shading. This perception lies behind the title story of *The Shadow Cage*, Philippa Pearce's collection of ghost stories.

The making of identity is a continuous process which involves selection of one course and rejection of all others. Ghost stories show us how to escape from the finality of this choice, and from a fatalism which makes us suspect that there was actually no choice in the first place, so that the way we went was the only way we could ever have gone. They allow us to keep alive parallel possibilities forever, enriching the way that was chosen by making us experience other ways, and confirming through this expansion our current sense of ourselves. The present unity of the me-now points in the ghost story to the plurality of all those not-mes, not-now.

For example, in Philippa Pearce's "Guess," in *The Shadow Cage*, Netty is connected with Jess, a ghost-girl released by the fall of a tree in a gale. Jess is clearly a part of Netty, both alien and intimate ("there was something familiar about her"), but not a part Netty wishes to acknowledge. . . . The ghost forces Netty to see herself—not as usual, from the inside looking out, as though our bodies were hollow trees and the eyes peepholes for the spirit—but from the outside looking in, as though, like the tree-ghost, she were temporarily homeless. She is made to rehearse a detachment from the single self she normally assumes herself to be, so that she can acknowledge other selves both currently within and potentially without. (pp. 119-20)

To learn to acknowledge and accept the otherness within, the selves we might have been and are not, the ones we may become, which are all but unrecognisable to our present selves, is a necessity which comes upon us at adolescence: it is part of growing up. Netty is eleven. The detachment of a dawning objectivity about one's self has to be balanced with the maintenance of the subjectivity of childhood: this is what the story is about. Its expression in the form of a ghost story makes it possible to dramatise an abstract concept, the ghost standing for the unrealised parts of the living girl. It is meeting the ghost that makes it possible for Netty to conceive of herself as potentially different from the person she has always assumed herself to be. It is a statement both that we normally express and acknowledge only a small part of ourselves as we are now, and that our future selves are equally various. The ghost Jess, who cannot really be named apart from Netty—she might have said "Guess" not "Jess"—points to an unrealised part of the eleven-year-old girl; the much older ghost, "an untidy young woman" who bears a "striking resemblance" to her younger counterpart, also released by the fall of the tree, points to the now-unknowable but always potential Netty-growing-up. The departure of Jess Oakes to Epping Forest, her own appropriate place, restores Netty to hers, at home under her mother's sharp eye, but with a new independence won through her experience. (p. 120)

The spook element in the ghost—the threat and the fear—are integral to its nature, because ghosts are essentially uncontrollable. They are independent and self-willed . . . unpredictably dramatising relationships, either between different people or between different parts of a single personality. They are insubstantial and temporary—the time being only so long as the story lasts—because they represent intensities which are palpable only at their peak. Stories like **"Guess"** make out a strong case for a conceptual model of the personality as an interaction between various parts of the self, recognised and unrecognised, now and not-now, realised and unrealised, active and passive. There is no fixed and static "real" self hidden at some notional core normally disguised by appearances, but a fluid and even bizarre association of a limitless number of selves.

Recognition and surprise are simultaneous conditions for the sense of mystery inherent in all ghost stories. For a relationship to exist, it must be potentially recognisable, and for it to be worth the making, the two elements must be disparate enough to occasion surprise. The movement towards recognition which is going in the opposite direction from the perception of separateness creates the tension in the story, which is also the mystery, which thus defines itself as paradoxical. Philippa Pearce's use of language often reflects this. (pp. 120-21)

Ghost stories take what is out of bounds and put it temporarily within bounds, where it is recognisable, but not at home. Ghosts are modified aliens, like enough to real people to be of use, but unlike in their exaggeration and powerfulness, which, paradoxically, makes them insubstantial. For substance is in thrall to the checks and balances of the real world; ghosts act out of a brief authority which is undeniable while it lasts, untrammelled by substance, but therefore not familiar, not at home. This characteristic—nebulousness conjoined with power—is emphasised in another of Philippa Pearce's stories, **"Beckoned,"** where a living boy, Peter, is lured by a ghost, Mrs. Fawcett, to the bed of her husband, so that he will himself be taken for a ghost, thus freeing the old man from an obstinate oath concerning his long-dead son. A living boy unwittingly acting as a ghost at the behest of a real ghost again shows the complexity of which the form is capable. The ''home'' is any fictional set—theme, characters, and plot—which defines the bounds into which the ghost seems to leap from the outside (surprise), but is soon acknowledged to have been bred from within (recognition). (p. 121)

Ghost stories end with the disappearance of the ghost. This is so integral to the convention that it is worth examining why the disappearance of the ghost should be a reconciling, satisfying experience, rather than an empty one. For ghosts are rhetorical scene-stealers: they do not go unnoticed. Therefore, their disappearance might be expected to be experienced as an impoverishment. Again, characters do not generally go in search of a ghost; the ghost comes unwilled and takes them over. So how is this intrusive, negative experience of being haunted changed into something positive? If possession by a ghost is undesirable because unwilled, is dispossession freedom or emptiness? Philippa Pearce is clear that although being haunted may not be a pleasant experience, it is a rewarding one. The strange illness of Mr. Arthur Cook, in the story of that name, is caused because he attempts to ignore the ghost of Mr. Baxter. When Mr. Cook acknowledges the ghost by carrying out his orders, he is cured, and learns a new skill into the bargain. (p. 122)

Judith Armstrong, ''Ghost Stories: Exploiting the Convention,'' in Children's literature in education *(© 1980, Agathon Press, Inc.; reprinted by permission of the publisher), Vol. 11, No. 3 (Autumn), 1980, pp. 117-23.**

AIDAN CHAMBERS

Beneath [the top tune of the plot of *The Battle of Bubble and Squeak*] are played variations on the themes of family relationships, developing independence in children, the learning of social give-and-take, and the urgency of emotional desires and compulsions.

It's not hard to see resemblances between this story and the author's earlier novel *A Dog So Small*. . . . A boy's desire for a pet, his distress at not being allowed one, a family living on an ordinary housing estate, an act of emotional and psychological withdrawal, and a happy resolution with everyone's honor satisfied—these are common elements in both books. But there is nothing tired or repetitive in the treatment. On the contrary, *Bubble and Squeak* feels fresh, vigorous, and contemporary and places its emphasis differently—on social interactions rather than on one character's point of view and interior life. The book is primarily about living together.

What one enjoys at once, as with anything she writes, is Philippa Pearce's pellucid style. (p. 229)

Another of the qualities that impresses me about this short book is the way the author opens up an adult's interior life for . . . young readers. . . . Mrs. Sparrow is very nearly a central character, along with Sid—it's as much her story as his. She has remarried after the death of her first husband, who was the father of all the children.

Thus, another thread is added to the tale, giving it a richer texture. The delicate position that Bill Sparrow, the new husband, finds himself in as a kind of buffer between his wife and Sid; the way his sympathies are all on Sid's side, while his loyalties lie on his wife's; not to mention the danger of his intruding unasked and ham-fistedly into the battle between

mother and son—are all beautifully suggested and handled. And because Bill is not the natural father and must behave circumspectly, Mrs. Sparrow feels all the more keenly her tussle with her family.

Philippa Pearce shows the strength of Mrs. Sparrow's aversion to animals, her hesitancy, her worry, and the inner struggle caused by a mother's instinct to please her children at odds with her natural temperament and fastidiousness. It would have been easier and more sensational—and the line most children's writers would have taken—to let Mrs. Sparrow be seen only in externals, an adult behaving selfishly against her children's entirely reasonable desire to keep pets.

The harder, more worthwhile, and truthful thing is to show why the adult behaves as she does and to gain sympathy and understanding for her without losing any of the young reader's preference for the child hero. The author does this with apparent ease and absorbs it all so completely into the story that at first one doesn't notice what she has achieved. (p. 230)

[We are] persuaded that in this story everyone matters, not just the hero or the other children. Adults have rights and three dimensions, too, and more in them than meets the eye. Most children's novels remind me of the father who told Paul Hazard, ''the time will come when men will be oppressed by the children.'' But not this one. (pp. 231-32)

It is the contemplation of the narrative, the *why* of life, that this story is really about—not the *what*. Bravo to that. (p. 232)

No one [creates carefully arranged variations on basic English orchestrated for tunefulness and elegance of line] better than Philippa Pearce, and she produces writing of precisely the kind she told me she is always striving for. What she wants, she said, is that the reader feel her writing is like an open window through which he can reach and touch what lies on the other side.

She carries that intention through into her plotting and structure. Each chapter is patterned so that we get another satisfying stage in the story and are led on in our understanding of the characters, and through story and characters, to a deepening appreciation of the thematic underlays. Elegant is indeed the modish critical word that comes at once to mind. If you wanted a handbook demonstration of how to arrange and handle narrative material in this dominant traditional manner, you couldn't find a better one than this.

The disadvantages are obvious. Life gets to seem all too neat and sequential. The characters are a mite too trim and explainable. The resolution is overly pat. There's plenty to think about, but the reader is given little room for maneuver within the text. And although the themes are subtly handled, they are finespun, their presence easily ignored. You can read this book without ever breaking through the surface—as no more than an amusing story about a kid who wins his fight to keep a couple of pets—something you cannot do with the story of *Tom's Midnight Garden*. . . . There the top tune leads you below the surface; otherwise you might soon find the book unsatisfying, which is why most of us would call it a more difficult and challenging novel. (pp. 232-33)

The Battle of Bubble and Squeak is exactly what it set out to be and is a fine example of that order of novel which begins by accepting children as they are—their likes and dislikes, their superficial preferences, and their predictable tastes—and then takes them on in literary terms by shifting the gears of their reading to match the participation demanded by a multifaceted story.

That's putting it far too pedagogically, and Philippa Pearce won't thank me, I think, for doing so. She doesn't set out to be a writer providing literary training courses for children. And, indeed, what I mainly want to do here is give straightforward expression to the pleasure I take in knowing that she and her books are there for all of us to enjoy. (p. 233)

Aidan Chambers, "Letter from England: Reaching through a Window," in The Horn Book Magazine *(copyright © 1981 by Aidan Chambers; reprinted by permission), Vol. LVII, No. 2, April, 1981, pp. 229-33.*

Richard Peck

1934-

American novelist for young adults and adults.

While he has written thrillers, ghost stories, and romances, Peck is best known for his works portraying young people caught up in personal problems. His subjects include teenage pregnancy, rape, divorce, suicide, and other topics which have been avoided until recently in young adult novels. To keep his topics relevant, Peck travels widely, meeting young people to hear their opinions and concerns first hand. This respect for his audience has helped to make him one of the most popular contemporary young adult writers.

Peck's first novel, *Don't Look and It Won't Hurt*, illustrates his commitment to realism. Its title is the advice the protagonist gives to her older sister, who is unmarried, pregnant, and afraid of giving her child up for adoption. The book was generally felt to be poignant and compassionate, although it was criticized for its lack of depth, a comment which has been applied to several of Peck's later titles. *Are You in the House Alone?* is perhaps his most controversial work, depicting the trauma of a young girl who is pursued and eventually raped by a disturbed classmate. Several critics applauded Peck's restraint in the handling of this subject and his indictment of the American social stigma and legal treatment of rape and rape victims.

Critics have usually found Peck to be an honest and perceptive writer whose books project an uncommon authenticity. He writes from the perspective that growing up today is more difficult than ever before and that literature directed to young people should reflect and explore this fact honestly. His popularity among young adults suggests that his own books successfully meet this criterion. Peck was awarded the National Council for the Advancement of Education Award in 1971, and won the Edgar Allan Poe Award from Mystery Writers of America in 1976 for *Are You in the House Alone?* (See also *Contemporary Authors*, Vols. 85-88, and *Something About the Author*, Vol. 18.)

KIRKUS REVIEWS

Don't look and it won't hurt—Carol's advice to Ellen who's wondering how she can bear to give her baby up for adoption—is neither true nor very comforting [in *Don't Look and It Won't Hurt*], but [the] teenage characters bend themselves to cheerfully hard-boiled sarcasm—particularly tough Mitsy Decker . . . and the precociously poised minister's daughter Shirley Gage. It won't hurt if you read it for the humor, but don't look for any hidden profundity.

"Older Fiction: 'Don't Look and It Won't Hurt'," in Kirkus Reviews (copyright © 1972 The Kirkus Service, Inc.), Vol. XL, No. 16, August 15, 1972, p. 949.

LETTY COTTIN POGREBIN

There are no absolutes [in **"Don't Look and It Won't Hurt"**]: abject poverty is tempered by humor; a ne'er-do-well father is allowed an unlikely streak of compassion; and the pregnant sister gives her baby up for adoption only after the subtleties of her predicament are seen and felt.

Rather than arousing judgemental passions, **"Don't Look and It Won't Hurt"** leaves the reader empathic and terribly moved. (pp. 8, 10)

Letty Cottin Pogrebin, "Dreams for Children, Nightmares for Teen-agers," in The New York Times Book Review (© 1972 by The New York Times Company; reprinted by permission), November 12, 1972, pp. 8, 10, 14.*

PEGGY SULLIVAN

[The advice in the title of *Don't Look and It Won't Hurt*] typifies the bitter wisdom of this family of losers. . . . [The story] is well written but concludes with few solutions and only sketchy plot development. Nevertheless, as a slice of none-too-enjoyable life, Peck's first novel will interest many readers.

Peggy Sullivan, "Junior High-Up: 'Don't Look and It Won't Hurt'," in School Library Journal, an appendix to Library Journal (reprinted from the De-

cember 15, 1972 issue of School Library Journal, *published by R. R. Bowker Co./A Xerox Corporation; copyright © 1972), Vol. 97, No. 22, December 15, 1972, p. 68.*

KIRKUS REVIEWS

Not once, but three different times, Brian Bishop finds himself staring into the "Awful Face of Death" [in *Dreamland Lake*]. Brian's stunned reactions to the suddenness of death and the ultimate incomprehensibility of a corpse are in stark counterpoint to his other memories of his thirteenth summer. He and his friend Flip subsist largely on sly adolescent wit. . . . After the two boys find the body of an old tramp in the woods Flip, who lives up to his name and has a cruel streak besides, encourages Brian in another illusion: perhaps the pathetic fat boy Elvan, who has been trying to interest them in his collection of Nazi souvenirs, knows something more about the tramp's death? Their efforts to build their discovery into a full-scale mystery eventually leads to a real tragedy—a startlingly convincing freak accident which sets the seal to Brian's chronicle of innocence remembered and lost. Less convincing, however, is the implication that Flip is actually responsible for what happens to Elvan. This assignment of guilt by hindsight adds an unsettling dimension to an otherwise finely tuned shocker. Though the fraternal naivete of boarding school life in another generation has been replaced with a kind of wry public school prescience, this ambiguous mixture of nostalgia and guilt is invariably reminiscent of [John Knowles's] *A Separate Peace.* The message is somewhat less than meets the eye, but for boys at a certain stage of growing up, *Dreamland Lake* projects a firm reality.

"Young Adult Fiction: 'Dreamland Lake'," in Kirkus Reviews *(copyright © 1973 The Kirkus Service, Inc.), Vol. XLI, No. 12, June 15, 1973, p. 648.*

ALICE H. YUCHT

Beautifully told, [*Dreamland Lake*] has just enough foreshadowing to heighten the sense of impending doom. Everything rings true—the dialogue, the minor characters as well as Flip and Brian, small scenes of English class and of the boys' newspaper route, and, most of all, Brian's painful coming of age. Even slower readers will grab this book, captivated first by the mystery, and then by its deeper levels of meaning.

Alice H. Yucht, "Grades 3-6: 'Dreamland Lake'," in School Library Journal, *an appendix to* Library Journal *(reprinted from the November 15, 1973 issue of* School Library Journal, *published by R. R. Bowker Co./A Xerox Corporation; copyright © 1973), Vol. 20, No. 3, November 15, 1973, p. 53.*

KIRKUS REVIEWS

In [*Through a Brief Darkness*] Peck wisely relinquishes any pretense to relevance or depth and comes out with a tightly drawn romantic melodrama about sixteen-year-old Karen, protected daughter of a big time crook, who is suddenly pulled out of boarding school and hustled off to "relatives" in England, there to discover gradually that she has actually been kidnapped by ruthless members of a rival syndicate. The unconvincing presence of a handsome young Etonian . . . who comes to Karen's rescue makes it impossible to take the adventure seriously, but Karen's gradual admission of the ille-

gality of her father's activities gives it what little ballast is needed, and—most important—the shocks and terrors of Karen's captivity and flight and the unexpected reversals when "nice" people turn out villains and vice versa are handled by a calculating mastermind who knows just how to maximize suspense.

"Young Adult Fiction: 'Through a Brief Darkness'," in Kirkus Reviews *(copyright © 1973 The Kirkus Service, Inc.), Vol. XVI, No. 23, December 1, 1973, p. 1314.*

ZENA SUTHERLAND

[*Dreamland Lake* is a] subtle and provocative novel. . . . There is some humor in the rather caustic depiction of classroom scenes, but the story is serious; it is not grim, however, despite the fact that it begins and ends with death, because the skilful construction, the sound characterization and dialogue, and the realistic fluctuation and conflict in the relationships outweigh the fact that the boys are reacting to death. (pp. 83-4)

Zena Sutherland, "New Titles for Children and Young People: 'Dreamland Lake'," in Bulletin of the Center for Children's Books *(reprinted by permission of The University of Chicago Press; © 1974 by the University of Chicago), Vol. 27, No. 5, January, 1974, pp. 83-4.*

THE NEW YORK TIMES BOOK REVIEW

Ending with a sudden and shattering tragedy, ["**Dreamland Lake**"] is more somber perhaps than the usual teenage mystery. Yet the author has a light, controlled touch, and an emotional depth to his narrative that turns it into an unusually strong and subtle novel of early adolescence.

"For Ages 4, 5 . . . 15: 'Dreamland Lake'," in The New York Times Book Review *(© 1974 by The New York Times Company; reprinted by permission), January 13, 1974, p. 10.*

ZENA SUTHERLAND

Peck's writing [in *Representing Super Doll*] is admirable. It has vitality and flow, vivid characterization and dialogue, a fresh viewpoint that makes the story convincingly that of an intelligent adolescent, and a deeper treatment of a theme than most beauty contest books achieve.

Zena Sutherland, "New Titles for Children and Young People: 'Representing Super Doll'," in Bulletin of the Center for Children's Books *(reprinted by permission of The University of Chicago Press; © 1974 by the University of Chicago), Vol. 28, No. 3, November, 1974, p. 51.*

JEAN ALEXANDER

[Older characters in *Representing Super Doll*,] for the most part, are stereotype adults: the teasing father, the devoted mother, the English teacher who wears straight skirts and gives assignments on "Your hopes, your dreams."

Verna is a midwestern farm girl attending a small-town high school after her earlier years in a country school. . . . She becomes friends with three town girls, one of whom is the beautiful but stupid Darlene Hoffmeister.

Mrs. Hoffmeister, a divorcee living on alimony, enters her daughter in several beauty contests, one of which is Miss Teen Super Doll. When Darlene wins the regional contest she gets to travel to New York City and compete in the national event, and Verna is given the chance to go along with her as a chaperone.

In New York the two of them meet up with more stereotypes and Darlene bungles her chances in the big contest by her vague confused answers to all questions. Bernice begins to learn that she herself is attractive and, unlike Darlene, is able to answer questions. When the chance comes on a television quiz show to guess who is the real Miss Super Doll, Verna is asked to participate because one of the contestants fails to appear. Guess who everyone thinks is the Miss Super Doll?

The author fails to make his point. The beautiful Darlene is really the heroine of this novel although Mr. Peck maybe didn't intend it that way. She makes her own choices. She will not be the beauty queen that her mother insists she be. Perhaps in her own fumbling, inarticulate way she found the only way out of her mother's plans. Unfortunately we see this person, an early teenage Marilyn Monroe, through the eyes of smug Verna whose only goal was to become what Darlene chose not to be.

> Jean Alexander, "Girls Growing Up," in Book World—The Washington Post (© 1974, The Washington Post), November 10, 1974, p. 8.*

KIRKUS REVIEWS

"There are several opinions that people hold regarding ghosts, and not one of them would clinch an argument." So Richard Peck, betraying a twinge of embarrassment, sort of backs in to the ghost story genre [with *The Ghost Belonged to Me*]. But once under way he has a great time, calling up a classic spook, little Inez Dumaine. . . . This haunting is slapstick most of the way, and anyone who worries about the tender feelings of Inez . . . might find it all impossibly silly. But Peck throws in enough scary moments to prove that he'd be a winner in any campfire storytelling session, and in that spirit he will keep his audience giggling and just a little frightened at the same time.

> "Younger Fiction: 'The Ghost Belonged to Me'," in Kirkus Reviews (copyright © 1975 The Kirkus Service, Inc.), Vol. XLIII, No. 8, April 15, 1975, p. 456.

JOAN GOLDMAN LEVINE

At the turn of the century, in a barn loft in Bluff City, Middle America, the ghost of the drowned Inez Dumaine—a benign and pitiable apparition—appears to young Alex Armsworth [in *The Ghost Belonged to Me*] and makes a cryptic request: "To be among my own people . . . above the ground, but at rest." She tells Alex to find other "true believers" to assist him. And he does.

The journey is humorous and Peck is reminiscent of [Mark] Twain; but for the most part, the droll intimations of a Twain are in Alex's perceptive glimpses of family and friends. For example, Alex on his mother's social aspirations: "We have given up being Baptists in favor of being Episcopalians, which is one step up socially but a step down when it comes to hymn singing." . . .

Such sophisticated humor could easily come from Uncle Miles, the gadfly, but coming from Alex it exemplifies the problem with this book. Alex is supposedly an adult looking back to his 13th year. . . . But the voice is unsteady, rarely evoking the feelings of a child. The voice of a child is distinctly missing except, ironically, in the encounters with the soggy spirit of the dead child, Inez Dumaine.

> Joan Goldman Levine, "The Spirits Are Willing: 'The Ghost Belonged to Me'," in The New York Times Book Review (© 1975 by The New York Times Company; reprinted by permission), July 27, 1975, p. 8.

BRUCE CLEMENTS

All ghost stories turn on the question of whether the ghost is real or not. . . . If she's real, the writer has to be very good to keep the story from becoming melodramatic claptrap.

[In *The Ghost Belonged to Me*] Peck is very good. His ghost is believable and affecting, and so is his hero. Alexander is direct, he knows what he wants, he's not too embarrassed by his faults, he's observant, he's honest. And he has an elegant style, at once down-to-earth and courtly.

Alexander's most impressive quality is his sense of justice, the care he takes to report honestly what he saw and felt and to give everyone, with the unfortunate exception of his family, a fair hearing. He talks eagerly about his adventures with Inez but in a style that reflects his reluctance to believe in her. The evidence of her reality accumulates slowly; avenues of scientific or medical explanation are shut off gently, carefully, clearly, one by one. As a result, the reader believes in the ghost before Alexander does and inwardly urges him to accept her. We become evangelists in her behalf.

Peck does a few things that are unpleasant and don't work. For comic purposes, and to add a little of the mandatory sex, he gives Alexander a silly older sister and allows her more freedom by far than her class or her parents would ever have permitted her. Her big scene, a coming-out party destroyed by a drunken suitor, is believable but it's not important and it's not funny. A second comic female also bombs. She's the kitchen-maid, Gladys, and every time she comes on the scene it's like watching a rerun of *The Brady Bunch*.

In place of a mother and father we get cartoons: flat, predictable, failed people, one hysterical and the other given to sardonic one-liners. They would be easier to accept if Alexander weren't telling the story, if we were listening to someone less intelligent and fair.

After Inez has found rest, Alexander loses his gift. He knows, he says, that there will be "no place for being receptive to the Spirit World in my future." So the notion that childhood is a time of revelation is given another ride, probably for the usual purpose, to permit us to praise openness without feeling that we ought to try to imitate it.

Why should Peck, having written such a neat story, feel the need to reassure young readers that they will soon be grown-up, happy, and narrow? It's an odd, unnecessary and unpleasant way to end a well-told story. (pp. 11, 75)

> Bruce Clements, "Believable Ghosts and Heroes," in Psychology Today (copyright © 1975 Ziff-Davis Publishing Company), Vol. 9, No. 4, September, 1975, pp. 11, 75.

MARGERY FISHER

It is hardly surprising to find kidnapping a favourite theme for writers who want to keep up with the times. In *Through a brief darkness* Richard Peck has allied this fashionable subject with an equally fashionable boy-girl situation. In the course of a lonely life Karen Beatty has come to realise that the work that surrounds her with luxury but keeps her father away is distinctly shady and dangerous. By the time she is sixteen she has achieved a certain wry philosophy though, surprisingly, not enough common sense to look twice at the way she is persuaded to take a flight from New York to London at short notice. In effect, she is kidnapped. . . . In fact, Karen is remarkably slow to realise anything, and this gives the author a pretext for the entrance of the hero. . . . The glimpses of Eton are as oddly off-key as the escape to a supposedly empty Devonshire mansion. . . . Undeniably topical, forcefully narrated, the story has a slick and artificial air that should not go unnoticed by perceptive young readers.

> *Margery Fisher, "Fashion in Adventure," in her* Growing Point, *Vol. 14, No. 9, April, 1976, pp. 2844-48.**

KIRKUS REVIEWS

[In *Are You in the House Alone?*,] Gail Osborn's ordeal begins with an obscene note pinned to her school locker, builds until she is raped and beaten by her best friend's disturbed steady, and is intensified throughout by her isolation. . . . The rough stuff is discreetly elided from both the notes and the attack itself. But Peck's view of affluent Connecticut, and of Gail's snobbish, self-centered parents in particular, is harsh enough. Distortingly harsh, and insofar as Peck presents this as an accurate profile of rape and its aftermath, readers might conclude that it's futile for any victim to seek protection or justice. As we expect this to be read as a chiller rather than a case study, we'll rate it medium cool—fast-paced and frighteningly accurate but without the quality of inevitability that keeps one awake after lights out.

> *"Young Adult Fiction: 'Are You in the House Alone?'"* in Kirkus Reviews *(copyright © 1976 The Kirkus Service, Inc.), Vol. XLIV, No. 17, September 1, 1976, p. 982.*

JUNIOR BOOKSHELF

Kidnapping, like hi-jacking, is very much the thing. . . . [In *Through a Brief Darkness*] Mr. Peck at least manages a flourish of novelty in having Rachel kidnapped in a very elaborate way en route, as it were, between New York and London. . . . The yarn certainly moves rapidly—in terms of locale as well; Mr. Peck seems to make use of places he once knew. It is a pity that a slight taint of cynicism seems to colour the whole. It is such a good novel that one feels like reading it all over again once one has reached the end.

> *"'Through a Brief Darkness',"* in The Junior Bookshelf, *Vol. 40, No. 5, October, 1976, p. 283.*

ALIX NELSON

[In **"Are You in the House Alone?"**] the author's purpose is to show how rape victims are further victimized by society and the law. As a feminist, as the mother of two daughters, and as one who was sexually assaulted at the age of 11, I think all children should be warned and wary; however, I'm not sure it serves a function to do so in melodramatic terms. . . .

Mr. Peck has chosen just such a format, building up a sense of mystery and terror preceding the attack by the use of menacing, obscene phone calls and anonymous threatening notes, and by having the rapist be a psychopath who stalks the girl as she baby-sits alone at night. Although he knocks her unconscious prior to the actual rape—so the event itself is neither experienced directly by the victim or the reader—I wouldn't want my 12-year-old to read this book: The fear that foreshadows the encounter seems far worse than its realization (fear of the dark, of being alone, of being watched at every turn). Nonetheless, my 15-year-old read it, empathized, wept, became incensed at the legal inequities, appreciated the complexity of the issue and its social and medical aftermath, didn't object to the way the deck was stacked to serve the thesis . . . and found the victim's plight and courage subsequent to the attack edifying and convincing. As for the Hitchcock kind of hysteria that comes before it, she thought that made it more interesting and gave one a reason for turning the page.

My reservation, therefore, should be viewed merely as my own bias, and Mr. Peck ought to be congratulated for connecting with, and raising the consciousness of, his target audience (14 and up) on a subject most people shun.

> *Alix Nelson, "Ah, Not to Be Sixteen Again," in* The New York Times Book Review *(© 1976 by The New York Times Company; reprinted by permission), November 14, 1976, p. 29.**

JANET LEONBERGER

[*Are You in the House Alone?* is] a sensitive, tasteful *and* realistic novel for young adults on rape. Gail Osborne is a true-to-life teenager. . . . In the end, no one ends up with the same old friends; loyalties—if they ever really existed—change and Gail emerges knowing herself and the real world a lot more thoroughly. The reader emerges with helpless yet outraged questions about what can be done to handle rape. . . . Highly recommended for purchase by all young adult collections and for inclusion in the Best Books for YA's List. (pp. 89-90)

> *Janet Leonberger, "Reviews: 'Are You in the House Alone?'"* in Young Adult Cooperative Book Review Group of Massachusetts, *Vol. 13, No. 3, February, 1977, pp. 89-90.*

ZENA SUTHERLAND

Peck brings [*Are You in the House Alone?*] to a logical, tragic conclusion . . . but it isn't *what* happens that gives the story impact, although that is handled with conviction, and although the style, dialogue, and characters are equally impressive—it is the honest and perceptive way that the author treats the problem of rape. For Peck sees clearly both the society's problem and the victim's: the range of attitudes, the awful indignity, the ramifications of fear and shame. (p. 112)

> *Zena Sutherland, "New Titles for Children and Young People: 'Are You in the House Alone?'"* in Bulletin of the Center for Children's Books *(reprinted by permission of The University of Chicago Press; © 1977 by the University of Chicago), Vol. 30, No. 7, March, 1977, pp. 111-12.*

PAMELA D. POLLACK

Peck treats rape as a serious issue [in **Are You in the House Alone?**], effectively dramatizing it in the style of a Hitchcock thriller, with the heroine hounded by obscene notes and heavy-breather phone calls. The book is a page-turner at the same time that it is a rallying cry against antiquarian, antiwomen rape laws; but, most importantly, Peck creates a character with the grit and determination not to be permanently scarred by her scarifying experience. (p. 199)

> *Pamela D. Pollack, "Sex in Children's Fiction: Freedom to Frighten?" in* SIECUS Report *(copyright © 1977 by The Sex Information and Education Council of the U.S., Inc.; reprinted by permission), Vol. V, No. 5, May, 1977 (and reprinted in* Young Adult Literature: Background and Criticism, *edited by Millicent Lenz and Ramona M. Mahood, American Library Association, 1980, pp. 198-203).*

THE JUNIOR BOOKSHELF

[The] characters and setting [of **The Ghost Belonged to Me**] establish themselves very firmly, and the sense of period . . . is finely conveyed. There is a ring of authenticity in the local gossip, with all its gruesome detail. . . . Blossom Culp [is] a splendid creation. . . . [At] first she seems merely brazen, but the depth of her feelings emerges as quietly she involves herself in Alexander's and Miles' efforts to lay the bones of the ghost . . . with her ancestors in New Orleans. . . . The rescue [of Alexander's sister from a stupid affair] is exciting, as is the dig for the skeleton, and the book is full of really funny scenes, like Lucille's disastrous coming-out garden party. The beautifully-handled variety of interests holds the reader's attention. (pp. 182-83)

> *"The New Books: 'The Ghost Belonged to Me'," in* The Junior Bookshelf, *Vol. 41, No. 3, June, 1977, pp. 182-83.*

KIRKUS REVIEWS

So closely does [**Ghosts I Have Been**] follow **The Ghost Belonged to Me** . . . that at times Peck's sequel on Second Sight verges on *déja vu*. Once again there's a child-ghost in trouble and once again an eccentric oldster steps in to take Alexander and Blossom on exotic travels. But no matter. This is still a blithe and spirited occult comedy with fewer genuine spooky moments but plenty of out-and-out belly laughs. Plucky Blossom Culp, Bluff City social outcast, in 1914, starts out as a mystic manqué tricking gullible classmates, but then suddenly she starts having honest-to-goodness visions: first of a car accident, then strange flashforwards (even one of the moon landing), and finally a trip back twenty months in time to relive the watery demise of a British boy who sank on the *Titanic*. For Blossom—and readers— it's a night to remember. . . . Never one for false modesty (on page one Blossom bills herself as "the most famous girl in two countries"), Peck's heroine proves to be such a redoubtable "Seeress" that despite the extravagant self-promotion, she just about manages to live up to the hype.

> *"Younger Fiction: 'Ghosts I Have Been'," in* Kirkus Reviews *(copyright © 1977 The Kirkus Service, Inc.), Vol. XLV, No. 18, September 15, 1977, p. 991.*

JOYCE MILTON

It isn't easy to pull off a sequel to a burlesque, but Richard Peck manages it [in **"Ghosts I Have Been"**] with humor that's as flyaway as ectoplasm, and the enormously entertaining strategy of spinning ghost stories and spoofing them at the same time.

> *Joyce Milton, "Children's Books: 'Ghosts I Have Been'," in* The New York Times Book Review *(© 1977 by The New York Times Company; reprinted by permission), October 30, 1977, p. 34.*

ZENA SUTHERLAND

Blossom Culp . . . tells her own story [in **Ghosts I Have Been**], and she's completely convincing. . . . She gets involved in strange dramatic situations, becomes famous when her prescience is proven accurate, and takes it all in her stride. Somehow, in this melange of eccentric characters and dramatic, fantastic events, Peck instills in Blossom and her story a sturdy, lively believability.

> *Zena Sutherland, "New Titles for Children and Young People: 'Ghosts I Have Been'," in* Bulletin of the Center for Children's Books *(reprinted by permission of The University of Chicago Press; © 1978 by the University of Chicago), Vol. 31, No. 7, March, 1978, p. 117.*

PUBLISHERS WEEKLY

Count Peck's new novel [**"Father Figure"**] as the best of many that have won him honors, and assuredly one of the best for all ages in many a moon. . . . Callowness and vanity make Jim mess up somewhat but he learns some poignant truths. Peck makes everyone so human and interesting that readers believe in and care about one and all.

> *"Fiction: 'Father Figure'," in* Publishers Weekly *(reprinted from the July 17, 1978, issue of* Publishers Weekly *by permission, published by R. R. Bowker Company, a Xerox company; copyright © 1978 by Xerox Corporation), Vol. 214, No. 3, July 17, 1978, p. 168.*

WINIFRED ROSEN

James Atwater, a sensitive 17-year-old stranded on the shoals of adolescence, narrates the latest addition to Richard Peck's notable list of titles for young adults. As he tells it, **Father Figure** is more a situation than a story, since its pivotal dramatic events take place outside the narrator's range of vision. But it is a situation dramatic enough in itself to seize and hold our attention. And, in the end, we admire the restraint with which it is described.

Although told in the vernacular of today, the novel's stark setting and strangled emotional atmosphere give the tale a Victorian quality. . . . James, already an overanxious father figure, . . . finds himself more responsible than ever for his poetic younger brother, Byron [after the death of his mother, who had raised the boys after their father's disappearance eight years before]. . . .

What happens is predictable enough. . . . What is remarkable is that the book does not rely on the usual cliché dramatic episode to induce artificially a reversal in the characters' relationships. There are no sudden storms at sea, fires in the condominium or sharks sighted offshore. Only time—the simple, often tediously slow passing of the days—eventually wears down James' resistance, and it is this reliance on time rather than chance which gives the novel's resolution its ring of truth.

On the other hand, it should be noted that the author's restraint, while sometimes an asset, can also be a liability. His narrator's concerns are too cleaned-up to be truly contemporary and seem instead to reflect the concerns of the author's own adolescence. Although Peck never exploits his situation, he never quite gets inside of it either—never really penetrates his characters' skins to connect with their deeper, more private selves. One sometimes suspects that it is the author's reticence which makes it so hard for his characters to get past their own restraints and into a deeper intimacy with each other.

> Winifred Rosen, "Pick a Peck of Pickled Pinkwater," in Book World—The Washington Post (© 1978, The Washington Post), November 12, 1978, p. E4.*

JANE B. JACKSON

The narrative [of *Ghosts I Have Been*] gets a bit heavy-handed when Blossom foresees World War I and moralizes on the futility of war, but in general the story is an engrossing adventure and Blossom an engaging narrator. A blurb on the jacket accurately compares Peck's style to Mark Twain's; as in some of Twain's books, the wit and insight of the narrator will be missed by most of the audience the book is intended for. But the story alone should make it popular with YA readers. (p. 12)

> Jane B. Jackson, "Fiction: 'Ghosts I Have Been'," in Kliatt Young Adult Paperback Book Guide (copyright © by Kliatt Paperback Book Guide), Vol. XIII, No. 6, Fall, 1979, pp. 10, 12.

JENNIFER BROWN

Would you believe a group of runaway children living in the department store of your local shopping mall? No, neither would I, but I'm willing to wager that . . . students will be lining up to read [*Secrets of the Shopping Mall*]. One of the elements that makes this basically fantastic story fun to read is the characterizations of Teresa and Barnie. . . . There is both humor and pathos in their personalities, as they use their streetwise ways to deal with the suburban runaways living in the department store and the "Mouth Breathers," who threaten them from the outside. I may not believe it, but I certainly enjoyed it!

> Jennifer Brown, "'Secrets of the Shopping Mall'," in Children's Book Review Service (copyright © 1979 Children's Book Review Service Inc.), Vol. 8, No. 2, October, 1979, p. 19.

KIRKUS REVIEWS

One problem with this broad, ham-handed satire [*Secrets of the Shopping Mall*] is that Peck has no sharp sight on his targets: a mall with Gucci labels and a K mart is hard to place; an outmoded junior miss department buyer promoting the Dale Evans western look is *too* far out even to be a credible figure of fun; and Peck's stereotyped, commodity-oriented runaways are more recognizable as prevailing clichés than as the plastic people he intends to mock. Worse, Teresa and Barnie have no

personalities either and their thoughts and conversations no vitality.

> "Older Fiction: 'Secrets of the Shopping Mall'," in Kirkus Reviews (copyright © 1979 The Kirkus Service, Inc.), Vol. XLVII, No. 20, October 15, 1979, p. 1213.

JACK FORMAN

[In "**Secrets of the Shopping Mall**"] Mr. Peck endows his two heroes with too many "smarts" to be entirely believable, but it doesn't really matter. He pokes fun, exposes hypocrisy and treats with refreshing humor subjects too often talked to death. It's not a pretty place Mr. Peck shows us, but he makes us laugh at ourselves and wonder what is going on in the marketplaces of our society. (p. 41)

> Jack Forman, "Children's Books: 'Secrets of the Shopping Mall'," in The New York Times Book Review (© 1979 by The New York Times Company; reprinted by permission), December 2, 1979, pp. 40-1.

KIRKUS REVIEWS

[In *Amanda/Miranda*] Peck has unearthed one of the hoariest of chimney-corner romantic devices—the wobbly course of love and intrigue when two young things of diverse origins and temperament look exactly alike and cross destinies; and he displays it here in late-Edwardian satin, with agile prose and a straight face. . . . Throughout, there are subplot and character diversions aplenty: a dark ghostly matter involving the Whitwell's "dead" son; the bright pan-banging gossip of servants; the mayfly nuptial dance of a straggly housemaid. And the proceedings are always accompanied by parades of viands and sumptuous living. All in all, a gorgeously romantic, implausible affair comfy as eiderdown.

> "Fiction: 'Amanda/Miranda'," in Kirkus Reviews (copyright © 1980 The Kirkus Service, Inc.), Vol. XLVIII, No. 1, January 1, 1980, p. 32.

PUBLISHERS WEEKLY

A wry, though accurate, portrait of Edwardian social manners, ["**Amanda/Miranda**"] is something more: a penetrating study of two unusual women, written with a subtlety and vigor of style that are a continual delight.

> "Fiction: 'Amanda/Miranda'," in Publishers Weekly (reprinted from the January 18, 1980, issue of Publishers Weekly by permission, published by R. R. Bowker Company, a Xerox company; copyright © 1980 by Xerox Corporation), Vol. 217, No. 2, January 18, 1980, p. 130.

ZENA SUTHERLAND

[In *Secrets of the Shopping Mall* Barnie and Teresa] take refuge in a department store and soon learn that there is a whole group of young people there, living secretly in the store and rigidly organized into a tight, defensive society, with Duty Personnel, a Chairperson, guards, Night Patrol, etc. The organization and its members lampoon their real life grey flannel equivalents, so there's intrinsic wry humor to the writing, but this isn't a humorous story; although it presents an intriguing concept, it is not quite believable as realism and not quite fanciful enough to be fantasy. . . . Dialogue and writing style are up to Peck's usual standards, in sum, while the story line is not.

Zena Sutherland, "New Titles for Children and Young People: 'Secrets of the Shopping Mall'," in Bulletin of the Center for Children's Books (reprinted by permission of The University of Chicago Press; © 1980 by the University of Chicago), Vol. 33, No. 6, February, 1980, p. 115.

JANE LANGTON

Good news for would-be writers! You too can create a costume romance about the British aristocracy, a profitable novel selected by book clubs, auctioned off to competing paperback publishers and optioned by film producers. . . . That is to say, anybody who has put in a lot of television watching time on *Upstairs, Downstairs* and *The Duchess of Duke Street* and all the rest of those imports, is ready to go. Just scramble them together and out will pop your novel. Of course you must try to think up a plot as brisk as [that of Richard Peck's *Amanda/Miranda*], in which two brunette beauties—an innocent lady's maid and her nasty mistress—are miraculously identical. Oh, what confusion in dark hallways when the brutish chauffeur lays his rough hands on the wrong girl! Oh, what excitement when maid and mistress sail for America in 1912 on a certain "unsinkable" liner of the White Star line (just like Lady Margery, remember?)! . . .

Missing [from this novel] is that valuable quality, authenticity, with its small surprises. . . .

Richard Peck could probably write a good novel about his birthplace in Illinois, or about army bases in Germany, or even about the university in England where he was a student for a while. But his Whitwell Hall, with its columned portico, its balustraded terraces, its marble floors, paneled walls, canopied beds, Grecian temple and circular drive, is a confectionary stereotype, a palace made of sugar.

Authenticity creeps into the book only once, in a skillful description of the sinking of the *Titanic*. One suspects that the author was writing at last from experience, the eyewitness accounts of survivors. It is a welcome relief in this jumbled hand-me-down from Mishmashterpiece Theatre.

Jane Langton, "Build Yourself a Best Seller," in Book World—The Washington Post (© 1980, The Washington Post), March 23, 1980, p. 12.

RISE BILL

In his first adult novel [*Amanda/Miranda*], Richard Peck whets our appetite for suspense. He includes all the classic elements of intrigue, from sumptuous passions to a voyage on the ill-starred Titanic. The implausibility of the story, however, while it might indeed charm a teenager into several flashlight-under-the-bedcovers sessions, is hardly food for the serious older reader. While *Amanda/Miranda* carries sophistication in its style and vocabulary, the characters cry out for a little intellectual substance. Nor do any of them vibrate with sincere emotion; they slide among an astonishing number of events with sheer gymnastic ability. Yet I recommend this novel to those interested in an imaginative story line and a glimpse of England's haut monde.

Rise Bill, "Fiction: 'Amanda/Miranda'," in Best Sellers (copyright © 1980 Helen Dwight Reid Educational Foundation), Vol. 40, No. 2, May, 1980, p. 50.

RICHARD PECK

If we "YA" authors hang on and hang in, one of these days we'll find ourselves writing for the Second Generation—for the offspring of parents who grew up reading Judy Blume and Paul Zindel and S. E. Hinton. (p. 440)

The themes that last will surely be rephrased in future volumes. I can only assume that the enduring ones will have nothing to do with the sexual revolution, the drug culture, and racial politics. The young now and in the future are not going to be able to solve these problems. It's a sickness from the '60s that we ever expected them to. They're going to continue to draw back from such problems in search of smaller, safer worlds. Possibly the writers' challenge will be to write adventurous books on "safe" subjects.

Books that explore friendship, which is a more potent preoccupation than sex to the young, and easier to contemplate. Books that continue to examine the family structure rather than celebrating collectivist alternatives. Books set in suburbs that still purvey a liberating hint of larger, more stimulating worlds.

A second generation of such books might do well to include a dimension now missing. We might continue plumbing the coming-of-age theme and then follow our young characters into adult life. That way we could depict not only actions, but their ultimate consequences. And I'm not talking about cautionary tales that warn young unwed mothers and fathers that they've blighted their entire lives. Such a message might not even be true.

But it would be pleasantly expansive to indicate to the young that all of life need not be as cruelly conformist and conservative as adolescence—unless you want it to be. That the most truly successful men and women were not high-school hotshots, beauty queens, super jocks, or manipulative gang leaders.

But maybe that's expecting too much. I imagine that the most acceptable new titles of the 1990s will be books about the sorrows of friendship and the painful necessity of growing up in a world new to no one but yourself. Books that include a little cautious nudge of optimism to offset what is blaring from a TV without an off knob. Books that invite the young to think for themselves instead of for each other. (p. 441)

Richard Peck, "The People behind the Books: Richard Peck," in Literature for Today's Young Adults by Kenneth L. Donelson and Aileen Pace Nilsen (copyright © 1980 Scott, Foresman and Company; reprinted by permission), Scott, Foresman, 1980, pp. 440-41.

Lou Reed

1944-

(Born Louis Firbank) American songwriter, singer, musician, and actor.

Reed is known as an unconventional, sometimes bizarre, songwriter and performer. He began his career writing summer-love/surf's-up songs for a major recording company in the early 1960s, then formed the Velvet Underground in order to play the kind of songs he really wanted to write. The music Reed wrote, along with John Cale, was unlike any other at the time. His lyrics were some of the first to mention such topics as drug use, death, and sexual perversion. He was attacked for the despairing decadence revealed in his early works, yet these songs are now often called brilliant. As a part of Andy Warhol's mixed-media show, "The Exploding Plastic Inevitable," in the late 1960s, the Velvet Underground concentrated on wild visual effects in their live performances. Although the group did not gain widespread recognition before disbanding in the early 1970s, their music and concerts generated a new style of rock and roll, influencing the new wave and glitter-rock movements represented by David Bowie, Roxy Music, and Talking Heads.

Reed's second solo album, *Transformer*, gained him a wide following in the United States and Europe. The lyrics are not substantially different from those of the Velvet Underground era, but the album's popularity among young people reflects the changing attitudes of society toward previously taboo subjects. *Transformer* deals mainly with homosexuality, but instead of the revelations that might be expected from a professed homosexual, critics found the imagery mostly timid and stereotyped. One song, however, appealed to fans and critics alike. "Walk on the Wild Side" became a national top-ten hit for Reed, and some critics consider it an example of his ability to write powerful rock and roll.

Berlin was received with conflicting reactions. Thematically it recounts the story of Reed's disastrous first marriage, and while certain reviewers have termed the album a failure, others consider it a brilliant concept album. A basically simple story, it includes all of Reed's major themes—emasculation, sadism, misogyny, drug abuse, and emotional deterioration. The depressing tone, most often cited as the album's biggest flaw, is relieved only occasionally by Reed's sardonic humor. Reed followed this album with several unremarkable works, including *Metal Machine Music*, two records with exactly 16.1 minutes on each side, consisting of the sound of a blank tape running and some scratching noises. Such works as these, and Reed's alienating behavior in public, drastically lowered his credibility with critics and all but his most loyal fans.

Reed redeemed himself somewhat with *Street Hassle*, which critics generally thought exhibited the mastery first displayed in his work with the Velvet Underground. On *Street Hassle* he attempts to explain why most of his work has failed to live up to the promise of the Velvet Underground albums. Reed's characteristic mix of horror and humanity amid stylistic oddities is present, but the personalized emotionalism of the lyrics distinguishes the album from his former releases. *Growing Up in Public* is also highly autobiographical. Here Reed explores

Photo by Lynn Goldsmith/LGI©1981

some of the forces that shaped him, and also loosely outlines the events leading to his second marriage. Reviewers tend to agree that despite the strongly literary lyrics, the music is pedestrian and keeps *Growing Up in Public* from being Reed's finest work.

The poetic quality of Reed's lyrics and the life-is-tough message that he expounds in all his work probably accounts for his consistent appeal to young adults. Critics, however, continue to disagree on his status as a songwriter. Some are still waiting for him to match the quality of his work with the Velvet Underground, while others feel that he has done so repeatedly and recognize Reed as one of the most important personalities in contemporary rock and roll.

SANDY PEARLMAN

With the Velvet Underground the pussyfooting has stopped. They do songs like "Venus in Furs" . . . , "Heroin," "The Black Angel's Death Song." That shows us what their world view is like. When the Stones did their first nihilist album (*December's Children*) you could have missed it without the album cover's help. You might have thought it merely beautiful. But the world system of the Velvets—rooted in sex, violence, disorder, perversion and stuff like that—is far too obvious. These guys are so serious that they have a coherent position. (p. 23)

Sandy Pearlman, "Saucer Lands in Virginia," in Crawdaddy (copyright © 1967 by Crawdaddy Publishing Co., Inc.; all rights reserved; reprinted by permission), October, 1967, pp. 20-4.*

RICHARD WILLIAMS

The Velvet Underground have made just three albums. . . . But that trio of albums constitutes a body of work which is easily as impressive as any in rock.

If you doubt that statement, then it's unlikely that you've listened hard to the albums, because they yield up their treasure only to a listener who is prepared to treat them with respect and intelligence. . . .

It was immediately obvious that they were very different from the hundreds of other groups springing up during the American Rock Renaissance.

Their music was hard, ugly, and based in a kind of sadomasochistic world which few dared enter. The first album [was] called **"The Velvet Underground And Nico,"** . . . and a scary document it is. . . .

"Femme Fatale" takes a standard pop-song form and turns it into something tantalising and frightening, while **"All Tomorrow's Parties"** is a grim view of the life of a Lower East Side good-time girl.

"Parties" and another track, **"Venus In Furs,"** share the group's best trademark: a kind of heavy, almost martial beat, very hypnotic and quite unrelated to any other music you can think of. . . .

By the time their second album, **"White Light/White Heat"** . . . , came round . . . they had got further into some of the McLuhanistic tricks hinted at in the first album. . . .

The songs [on **"The Velvet Underground"**] were, in the main, quieter and more restrained, but the old cruelty was still there, manifesting itself in the overall mood and many of the words— if anybody bothered to listen to them.

For a start, nobody realised that the whole album was a continuous suite, although not billed as such. It traced the progress of a girl, Candy, from permissiveness through a realisation of evil, and back to decadence.

The tracks are linked so inextricably that it's difficult to talk about them separately, but **"I'm Set Free"** is probably the best tune they've written. . . .

Typically, the key track—**"Murder Mystery"**—has been distorted so that the words can't be heard, but it serves, as the group intended to make the listener think hard. This suite is so subtle and sophisticated that it's on a par with [The Who's] "Tommy" and so far ahead of "Sgt Pepper" that it makes that album sound like a series of nursery rhymes.

It's beginning to look as if the Velvet Underground will never make it, commercially. Nevertheless, groups like them do the spadework which enables less-talented musicians to progress. It's just a shame that nobody listens.

Richard Williams, "It's a Shame that Nobody Listens," in Melody Maker (© IPC Business Press Ltd.), October 25, 1969, p. 19.

LENNY KAYE

Lou Reed has always steadfastly maintained that the Velvet Underground were just another Long Island rock 'n' roll band, but in the past, he really couldn't be blamed much if people didn't care to take him seriously. With a reputation based around such non-American Bandstand masterpieces as **"Heroin"** and **"Sister Ray,"** not to mention a large avant-garde following which tended to downplay the Velvets' more Top-40 roots, the group certainly didn't come off as your usual rock'em-sock'em Action House combination.

Well, it now turns out that Reed was right all along, and the most surprising thing about the change in the group is that there has been no real change at all. *Loaded* is merely a refinement of the Velvet Underground's music as it has grown through the course of their past three albums, and if by this time around they seem like a tight version of your local neighborhood rockers, you only have to go back to their first release and listen to things like **"I'm Waiting For The Man"** and the **"Hitch-Hike"**-influenced **"There She Goes Again"** for any answers.

And yet, though the Velvet Underground on *Loaded* are more loose and straightforward than we've yet seen them, there is an undercurrent to the album that makes it more than any mere collection of good-time cuts. Lou Reed's music has always concerned itself with the problem of salvation, whether it be through drugs and decadence (*The Velvet Underground and Nico*), or pseudo-religious symbolism (**"Jesus," "I'm Beginning To See The Light"**). Now, however, it's as if he's decided to come on back where he most belongs. . . .

And once stated, the Velvets return to their theme again and again, clearly delighted with the freedom such a declaration gives them. Each cut on the album, regardless of its other merits, is first and foremost a celebration of the spirit of rock 'n' roll, all pounded home as straight and true as an arrow. . . .

Loaded also shows off some of the incredible finesse that Lou Reed has developed over the years as a songwriter, especially in terms of lyrics. . . . Reed constructs a series of little stories, filling them with a cast of characters that came from somewhere down everybody's block, each put together with a kind of inexorable logic that takes you from beginning to end with an ease that almost speaks of no movement at all.

In **"New Age,"** for instance, he opens with what must be one of the strangest lines that have ever graced a rock 'n' roll song . . . and from there, mingles cliche . . . with poignant little details about marble showers and Robert Mitchum, all combined into one of the most beautiful "love" songs to be heard in a while. . . .

"Sweet Jane" [is] possibly the Velvets' finest song since the cataclysmic **"Sister Ray."** . . . You can talk all you want about your rock poets, but I can't think of many who could come close to matching [the lyrics of **"Sweet Jane"**].

In fact, there's so much variety on the album that you could go through any number of the cuts and pick out much the same things, those extra little touches that make each one special and able to stand up in its own right. . . .

Yet as good as *Loaded* is (and as far as I'm concerned, it's easily one of the best albums to show up this or any year), there are some minor problems which tend to take away from its overall achievement. . . .

None of which can detract from any of the power and beauty contained in *Loaded*.

Lenny Kaye, "'Loaded'," in Rolling Stone *(by Straight Arrow Publishers, Inc. © 1970; all rights reserved; reprinted by permission), Issue 73, December 24, 1970, p. 51.*

RICHARD WILLIAMS

As far as I'm concerned, ["**Lou Reed**" is] the album we need most of all right now—the one which takes us above and beyond all the superstar crap and back into music. Or forward into music, because I don't want to say that this is a "back to the roots" album. It's just that listening to it gives me the kind of charge I haven't had in God knows how long.

Velvet freaks (and there are more than you think) will recognise in [the lyrics of "**Wild Child**"] the characteristic quality of Lou's best writing: what Geoffrey Cannon has pinned down as Reed's journalistic approach. . . . [His] reportage [is] as evocative as any newsreel.

Thus, for example, he approaches Lorraine, the Wild Child, through other people, and what he talks to them about. Directly, he says almost nothing about Lorraine herself—but by the time the song's over, she's become the most intriguing lady since Nico. . . .

My personal favourite track is "**Berlin**." Lou's never been there, but uses his knowledge of Nico as a filter for his feelings about the city. The verses have a candlelit night-clubby atmosphere, . . . while the chorus rocks a little harder and is totally memorable. . . .

The ballads are, in fact, every bit as remarkable as the rockers. "**Lisa Says**" is as beautifully constructed as "**Berlin**" (and even more enigmatic). . . .

The piece-de-resistance, the big production of the album, is "**Ocean**," which is the album's equivalent of "**European Son (To Delmore Schwarz)**" (from the Velvets' first LP) in that it tries hardest to take you furthest. It's an insane trip, glimpses of suicide from a Big Sur cliff. . . .

This, then, is the new Lou Reed, and it could well do for him what "Every Picture" did for Rod Stewart. No kidding—it's great rock 'n' roll, any old way you choose it.

Richard Williams, "Lou Reed: Then and Now," in Melody Maker *(© IPC Business Press Ltd.), May 13, 1972, p. 17.*

STEPHEN HOLDEN

Hail hail rock and roll! And hail Lou Reed for getting right back to the essence of what it's all about. . . .

This almost perfect album [*Lou Reed*] has ten cuts—all of them containing some of the grittiest rock sounds being laid down today. It is skeletal rock—sexy, pimply, crude and sophisticated, all at the same time. . . .

Just as arresting as Reed's voice are his lyrics, which combine a New York street punk sensibility and rock song cliches with a powerful poetic gift. On "**Lisa Says**," Reed sings, "Lisa says hey baby if you stick your tongue in my ear / Then the

scene around here will become very clear." That says as much about raw sex as any two lines I can think of in rock literature. On "**Wild Child**," my favorite cut on the album, [the lyrics are an example] of Reed's brilliantly offhand incisiveness. . . .

Reed's tunes, which are based on the cliche phrases of Fifties teen laments, are inconsequential but endearing as sung in his lost adolescent's cracked voice. His artistic self-awareness, however, is so secure that he invariably turns less into more. For he not only awakens nostalgia for Fifties rock, he shows that it is still a vital resource for today's musicians. . . . The overall impression is that of a knowing primitivism, as serious as it is playful, and never less than refreshing. Listening to Reed is not only a pleasure, it is a lesson in how to make first-rate rock and roll music. By keeping close to the roots he is keeping the faith.

Stephen Holden, "Records: 'Lou Reed'," in Rolling Stone *(by Straight Arrow Publishers, Inc. © 1972; all rights reserved; reprinted by permission), Issue 109, May 25, 1972, p. 68.*

HENRY EDWARDS

[Reed] was the first rock composer to open the Pandora's Box of unsavoriness. His hard-driving rock anthems, "**Run, Run, Run**," "**White Heat/White Light**" and "**I'm Waiting for the Man**," are still revived by hard rock bands in the process of paying their dues.

Reed is also still paying his dues. The public has never discovered him and, unfortunately, "**Transformer**" will not help his cause. Here, the Phantom seems to have been given a Mickey Finn and the result is a flaccid piece of work.

The composer offers up an obligatory cut about polymorphous sexuality, "**Walk on the Wild Side**," which seems to be a nostalgia item for those few who wish to return to the Warhol heyday. His "**Vicious**" is not as vicious as it pretends to be. Ballads like "**Perfect Day**" alternate with primitive rockers ("**Hangin' Round**") and show tunes ("**I'm So Free**") and novelty items ("**Goodnight Ladies**"). There is no over all point of view, no projection of the current Reed persona, and one's attention drifts. (pp. 34-5)

Henry Edwards, "Freak Rock Takes Over?" in The New York Times *(© 1972 by The New York Times Company; reprinted by permission), December 17, 1972, pp. 34-5.**

NICK TOSCHES

Lou Reed is probably a genius. During his days . . . with the Velvet Underground, he was responsible for some of the most amazing stuff ever to be etched in vinyl; all those great, grinding, abrasive songs about ambivalence, bonecrushers, Asthmador, toxic psychosis and getting dicked, . . . and those wonderful cottonmouth lullabies. . . . His first solo album, *Lou Reed*, was a bit of a disappointment in light of his work with the Velvets. . . .

[Homosexuality] was always an inherent aspect of the Velvet Underground's ominous and smutsome music, but it was always a pushy, amoral and aggressive kind of sexuality. God knows rock & roll could use, along with a few other things, some good faggot energy, but, with some notable exceptions, the sexuality that Reed proffers on *Transformer* is timid and flaccid.

"**Make Up**," a tune about putting on make-up and coming "out of the closets / out on the street," is as corny and innocuous as "I Feel Pretty" from *West Side Story*. There's no energy, no assertion. It isn't decadent, it isn't perverse, it isn't rock & roll, it's just a stereotypical image of the faggot-assissy traipsing around and lisping about effeminacy.

"**Goodnight Ladies**" is another cliche about the lonely Saturday nights, the perfumed decadence and the wistful sipping of mixed drinks at closing time.

"**New York Telephone Conversation**" is a cutesy poke at New York pop-sphere gossip and small talk, as if anyone possibly gave two shits about it in the first place.

Perhaps the worst of the batch, "**Perfect Day**" is a soft lilter about spending a wonderful day drinking Sangria in the park with his girlfriend, about how it made him feel so normal, so good. Wunnerful, wunnerful, wunnerful.

And then there's the good stuff. Real good stuff. "**Vicious**" is *almost* abrasive enough and the lyrics are great. . . . It's the best song he's done since the days of the Velvet Underground, the kind of song he can do best. . . .

"**Walk on the Wild Side**" is another winner, a laid-back, seedy pullulator in the tradition of "**Pale Blue Eyes**," the song is about various New York notables and their ramiform homo adventures, punctuated eerily by the phrases "walk on the wild side" and "and the colored girls go 'toot-ta-doo, too-ta-doo.'" Great images of hustling, defensive blowjobs and someone shaving his legs while hitchhiking 1500 miles from Miami to New York. . . .

"**Hangin' 'Round**" and "**Satellite of Love**" are the two remaining quality cuts, songs where the sexuality is protopathic rather than superficial.

Reed himself says he thinks the album's great. I don't think it's nearly as good as he's capable of doing. He seems to have the abilities to come up with some really dangerous, powerful music, stuff that people like [Mick] Jagger and [David] Bowie have only rubbed knees with. He should forget this artsy-fartsy kind of homo stuff and just go in there with a bad hangover and start blaring out his visions of lunar assfuck. That'd be really nice.

> *Nick Tosches, "'Transformer'," in* Rolling Stone *(by Straight Arrow Publishers, Inc. © 1973; all rights reserved; reprinted by permission), January 4, 1973, p. 61.*

ROBOT A. HULL

[*Transformer*] is further proof even that Lou Reed has turned into something sicker than a homicidal-rapist-mass murderer-porno editor. Far gone is that prevailing commercial bubblegum flair so evident on the first album (e.g.—"**I Love You**," "**Lisa Says**," "**Love Makes You Feel**," etc.). Instead, it's more like what the third Velvet Underground album would have sounded like if David Bowie had been in charge of production back then. There's a couple of cute ditties on here that perhaps belong on [The Mothers of Invention's] *We're Only In It For The Money* . . . , but other than that this album proclaims itself as most masterpieces proclaim themselves: IT GROWS ON YA!!

Primarily this is because of the lyrics. There are so many good lines thrown at ya at once that, in fact, you could even make a scrapbook. Prime examples are for instance like on "**Vicious**," a chunky rocker. . . .

Then there's "**Wagon Wheel**" which is even more frantic than "**Vicious**" except that it features a prayer by Lou wherein he confesses all of his sins. Yeah, it's got good lines. . . . (p. 65)

But none of em, absolutely none of em, can top "**Walk on the Wild Side**" which is most certainly the best thing Lou Reed has come out with since "**Rock & Roll**." The song is one of those impromptu "**Wild Child**" ramble-epics which feature exclusively Lou's magnificent sense of sneeze-phrasing. . . . But it's the words that curdle your oily lubricants. . . .

Yup, he's a full-fledged social degenerate now, and I really don't see how he could get any lower. Not even *Candid Press* would have the guts to touch him these days.

Nevertheless, other than the fact that this album is great, there's something especially fine about it which sets it apart from all the other crappy platters being released lately. I mean, hell, at least it ain't anal retentive. (p. 66)

> *Robot A. Hull, "Records: 'Transformer'," in* Creem *(© copyright 1973 by Creem Magazine, Inc.), Vol. 4, No. 9, February, 1973, pp. 65-6.*

STEVE SIMELS

["**Transformer**"] is a major disappointment after [Reed's] brilliant first effort. Who would have thought that the man who wrote *Sister Ray* could turn out—and so soon—to be just another pretty face?

Well, of course, that's not really fair. Reed, you'll recall, was the creative force behind the Velvet Underground, that strange and still misunderstood aggregation that sang about heroin and Jesus before either was pop-fashionable. In 1966, in fact, Lou and the Velvets were about as avant-garde as could be—which consequently obscured the fact that they were a classic hard-rock band cut from the same cloth as the original Byrds or the early Rolling Stones . . . and that Lou was an exquisitely acute songwriter. . . .

That's all *still* true, but you'd be hard put to prove it with anything from Reed's new "**Transformer**." There are a few cuts that suggest the Reed of old, and predictably they're the rockers—the cosmic punk-stupidity of *Vicious* and *Hangin' Round*, for instance—but even there the effort is sabotaged by limp production values. . . . I could probably abide this (after all, a similar problem flawed the last album) if so many of the songs weren't obvious throwaways. *Good Night Ladies*, for example, is a music-hall monologue that is perhaps wryly amusing the first time through, but to say that it lacks staying power is something of an understatement.

I won't dwell on the sexual posturing of the rest of the material; Lou's gayness interests me even less than Bowie's; if anything, it comes off here simply as a commercial ploy. On that level, at least, I wish him luck; if some of the Bowie magic rubs off on him, fine, but artistically it's a dead end. What Lou should do—and fast—is to get himself back to New York City where he belongs, and find a powerhouse band that understands him.

> *Steve Simels, "Bowie and Hoople and Reed," in* Stereo Review *(copyright © 1973 by Ziff-Davis Publishing Company), Vol. 30, No. 2, February, 1973, p. 92.**

LARRY SLOMAN

Lou had always been a master narrator, a short story writer at heart, who always lacked a producer who could transform his literary sensibilities into vinyl dramas. In fact, Lou's entire output with the Velvet Underground can be seen as a four-record passion play dealing with depravity, perversion and, ultimately, redemption. . . .

[*Berlin* is] an incredibly powerful story full of depravity, emasculation, violence, suicide, detachment and anomie. . . . It's not an overstatement to say that *Berlin* will be the *Sgt. Pepper* of the Seventies.

> Larry Sloman, "Lou Reed's New Deco-Disk: Sledgehammer Blow to Glitterbugs," in Rolling Stone (by Straight Arrow Publishers, Inc. © 1973; all rights reserved; reprinted by permission), Issue 144, September 27, 1973, p. 18.

MICHAEL WATTS

[Though Reed's two solo albums] each have had notable tracks, it's doubtful if many discerning souls, if any, would prefer them to the Velvets' records—a comparison that I daresay he's become heartily bored with. Nevertheless, his malleability is even more exposed on "**Berlin.**" . . . [Bob Ezrin's] production establishes a sense of nihilism that's underlined by Reed's old, squeezed husk of a voice—a tone of aridity that's well-suited to the downer nature of this album with a "story": two speed-freaks in exile, on the moral and physical decline. A very simple story, in fact; the girl is separated from her kids for not being a fit mother, and her lover then describes how she slashes her wrists.

Now only Lou could have come up with a concept like that, but in the past he would never have treated it as he has here. Instead of observing a detached, almost journalistic viewpoint, as was done in the story of Waldo and Marsha, he has indulged his emotions to the point of self-pity. . . . What some see as harrowing I see merely as maudlin and fake. In fact, it's infinitely more camp and grotesque than anything that Alice [Cooper] has ever done. Somehow, Lou Reed has gone soft; he's turned himself inside out. Boo hoo! If this album is a masterpiece of pathos, it still has to be allowed that Lou's insights into the "drug experience" are acute. "**How Do You Think It Feels**" is a very good song, with its personalised account of a speed-freak's reactions to his surroundings. . . . But his obsession with that aspect has become a little wearing. Without reversing his whole aesthetic one would have expected him to enlarge his preoccupations. It's not enough that all that "decadent" bullshit is trotted out again, especially when it's given the cabaret-styled heading of "**Berlin.**" Then again, maybe he does have to spell himself out once more for his new audience. But oh! for that old terse style.

> Michael Watts, "Broken Reed," in Melody Maker (© IPC Business Press Ltd.), October 13, 1973, p. 35.

LESTER BANGS

[*Berlin*] is the most disgustingly brilliant record of the year. There has always been a literary instinct behind Lou's best writing—classics like "**Sweet Jane**" were four minute short stories with recognizable characters acting out their roles, manipulated for Lou's amusement in a way he certainly considers Warholian. In *Berlin*, his first feature length presentation, the silhouettes have been filled in till they're living, breathing monsters.

A concept album with no hit singles, but shy of the "rock opera" kiss of death, Lou refers to it as a film. So I guess it's his attempt . . . at Warhol *Trash*. . . .

What it really reminds me of, though, is the bastard progeny of a drunken flaccid tumble between Tennessee Williams and Hubert (*Last Exit From Brooklyn*) Selby, Jr. It brings all of Lou's perennial themes—emasculation, sadistic misogyny, drug erosion, twisted emotionalism of numb detachment from "normal" emotions—to pinnacle.

It is also very funny—there's at least one laugh in every song—but as in *Transformer* you have to doubt if the humor's intentional. *Transformer* was a masterpiece at least partially by the way it proved that even perverts can be total saps—whining about being hit with flowers, etc.—and this album has almost as many risible *non sequiturs* as that did. . . . (p. 58)

It may be the grandest dreariness you ever heard. . . .

Side one tends to drag a bit as Lou is constrained to try and express affection, although "**Men of Good Fortune**" establishes the protagonist's hostile passivity. . . .

Side two is all welts and bruises and antipathy so total it becomes a sort of whimsy. . . .

Has anyone in all of rock ever had such a vision of love? Well, yeah, all those old "My Boyfriend's Back" goingsteady whines were brimfull of cheap malice. But this is plain gutted. The real amorality all those other preening simps keep dancing around. . . . It all mounts to that snowcap climax, precisely as cinematic as his conceit wills it, leaving you drained and befuddled.

I told you this album was a charmer. Interviewed recently, Lou said: "I haven't been excited in years, but I'm excited about this." If *this* is what gets him excited, he really is one of the most loveable kooks of our time. Because Lou tops himself with each album, exactly proportionate to the degree that he gets more wasted-sounding and resonates with bigger, more dunced-out *non sequiturs* as the absurdity of his vision of evil becomes more apparent. Just like Caroline said, it's a bum trip, but it's the most interesting bum trip on the boards.

My only reservation is that where *Transformer* brimmed with variety, the unrelieved gloom and dirgelike tempos of *Berlin* may be too much for even us most enthusiastic sickie partisans of Lou's work to take. It's depresso beyond depresso, and if that's a kind of triumph, it's also a real limitation. Any vision of unrelieved squalor—even one as brilliant as, say, Tennessee Williams'—has gotta become self-parody after awhile. If Lou is as close to Williams as any writer in rock, we still gotta question where he can take it from here, and if he's not ballooning into an ever more epically grotesque joke. In the meantime, get *Berlin* and treat yourself to the real goat's head soup—this quagmire is *le sleze de la sleze*. (p. 59)

> Lester Bangs, "Brilliance You'd Hate to Get Trapped With," in Creem (© copyright 1973 by Creem Magazine, Inc.), Vol. 5, No. 7, December, 1973, pp. 58-9.

JOHN ROCKWELL

Strikingly and unexpectedly, Lou Reed's "**Berlin**" . . . is one of the strongest, most original rock records in years. . . .

His last two albums had their virtues, but left him open to the charge of being burned out. Now, with **"Berlin,"** he has proven conclusively that he must be counted as one of the most important figures in contemporary rock. . . .

Reed is really a poetic artist who creates unified statements through the medium of the rock record. The backings are clothed in rock dress, but the form is more operatic and cinematic than strictly musical in the traditional pop sense, and the sentiments are entirely personal.

Where others prance and play at evoking an aura of drugs and sexual aberrance, Reed is coldly real. **"Berlin"** is a typically dreamlike saga of a sado-masochistic love affair in contemporary Berlin. But the contemporaneity is enriched by a subtle acknowledgment of [Bertolt] Brecht and [Kurt] Weill, and the potential sensationalism of the subject is calmly defused by a sort of hopeless matter-of-factness.

Reed doesn't revel in his characters' promiscuity and indifference and quick descent into violence and tragedy. He just tells his story, and lets the music, through a steady accumulation of strings and other "classical" effects, lift it up to the level of a moral allegory. There is a touch of soap-opera sentimentality on the second side, but it is hardly enough to spoil the record's over-all effect.

Through it all, Reed's poetic and melodic inspiration are at their compulsive, insistent best.

> *John Rockwell, "Pop: The Glitter Is Gold," in* The New York Times *(© 1973 by The New York Times Company; reprinted by permission), December 9, 1973, p. 34.*

STEPHEN DAVIS

Lou Reed's *Berlin* is a disaster, taking the listener into a distorted and degenerate demimonde of paranoia, schizophrenia, degradation, pill-induced violence and suicide. There are certain records that are so patently offensive that one wishes to take some kind of physical vengeance on the artists that perpetrate them. Reed's only excuse for this kind of performance . . . can only be that this was his last shot at a once-promising career. Goodbye, Lou.

> *Stephen Davis, "'Berlin'," in* Rolling Stone *(by Straight Arrow Publishers, Inc. © 1973; all rights reserved; reprinted by permission), Issue 150, December 20, 1973, p. 84.*

JEFF WARD

It seemed we had to wait until **"Berlin"** for a Reed album with full musical and lyrical conviction. Now, this live album, [**"Rock 'n' Roll Animal,"**] complements it. Together they make a good set.

One track, **"Lady Day,"** is indeed from **"Berlin"** but the other four date back to the Velvet Underground: **"Sweet Jane," "Heroin," "White Light White Heat"** and **"Rock 'n' Roll."** Thus in one way we get the best of both worlds, old numbers in fresh, retrospective style. . . .

It makes sense to choose these numbers from the live act because to take current songs would probably be mere duplication. However, on side two **"Lady Day"** overwhelms its neighbouring tracks, its potent structure coming over more powerfully than on **"Berlin."** A certain venom—not evident on the studio

cut—in Reed's voice underlines the desolate cityscape of the lyrics. . . .

The new sound of this dark classic [**"Heroin"**] is at once dreamy and phantasmagoric. One begins to see the relevance of the album title and how Reed, like a modern day [Edgar Allan] Poe, blends chilling description with the signal force of his imagination. One could call it dramatic sense or a compensating factor in his mentality. For the listener, Reed's strange alchemy of personality shackles him ever to a sense of reality plunged in the depths of nightmare and delusion. Once the diapason has struck in songs of this virulence and intensity, especially in the heat of live performance, it haunts the mind long after.

> *Jeff Ward, "Reed: Live and Well," in* Melody Maker *(© IPC Business Press Ltd.), March 16, 1974, p. 31.*

STEVE LAKE

[If Andy] Warhol's paintings and films were merely reflecting the commercial day to day existence of Twentieth Century America then the Velvets' achievements were more specific still. They were holding up an auditory mirror of middle-Sixties New York with its suicides and addictions, its downer trips, loneliness and utter joylessness.

And like any well-conceived horror film, the Velvet Underground had a sick attraction all their own—that gory magnetism that draws passers-by to the sites of road accidents.

Of course, as part of his Disaster series of paintings, Warhol had exhibited grim blow-ups of horrific car crash photos. In their own way, the Velvets did the same thing, exploiting the sordid side of human nature. . . .

[Following] the release of **"The Velvet Underground And Nico,"** the great record buying public became fascinated by songs like **"Waiting For The Man"** and **"Heroin."**

The issue that caught the attention was the ambiguity of the lyrics. . . . [Was] **"Heroin"** a warning to stay away from the deadly stuff, or was it some kind of junkies' torch song? . . .

"Lady Godiva's Operation," [a] horrific tale (it's about a hysterectomy), broke new ground for the liberation of the rock lyric. Indeed, it's only the clinical associations of the subject that prevent the piece from being straight pornography. . . .

After the release of **"White Light,"** the Velvets soldiered on, getting ever less serious about their music. . . .

And so the old structures—like **"The Black Angel's Death Song"** which promised so much—were never developed. . . .

A kind of song cycle relating to a young lady named Candy and her moral progress (rather like [John] Bunyan's Pilgrim's Progress in reverse), [**"The Velvet Underground"**] superficially appeared much prettier, far more casual than the first two. . . .

But, lyrically, it was as journalistically sharp and cruel as any of Reed's stuff. Best of all, though it's genuinely difficult to say, was **"What Goes On,"** certainly the most interesting song in construction. . . .

"Murder Mystery" is the key track as far as words are concerned, with two voices saying different things simultaneously. The idea being that if one person's saying something funny and the other saying something sad, the listener might laugh and cry at the same time.

It's an interesting idea, but not quite as innovative as Reed probably imagined. . . .

[The] Velvet's new identity became that of a half-wrecked, half-competent, bar band, playing for half-wrecked, half-interested dancers.

A fourth album, **"Loaded,"** which probably contains the finest songs that Lou Reed has ever written, was recorded. But, before its release, Lou quit the group. . . .

For though the Velvets never achieved the success that Lou has since put under his belt, the old legend continues to haunt the hell out of [John Cale, Nico, and Reed]. . . .

Reed is in the strangest position of all. . . .

For the sad truth is that he's never composed anything else as memorable or as powerful as the earlier material, and no single song as devastating as **"Heroin,"** which he wrote when he was fifteen.

But the Velvet Underground's influence has pervaded, and created, a whole new area in rock music. First off, they were one of the very first heavy metal prototypes. . . .

It's in image that they've probably been most influential. That dark, brooding, Satanic menace that was to be mirrored by almost the entire German rock music scene, for a start. . . .

Whereas most American music from Chuck Berry to the Beach Boys to Moby Grape was traditionally "up" and bouncing, the Velvets were doomy and leaden. . . .

But however much one generalises and talks of detecting the Velvets' influences, one must inevitably come to the conclusion that just like Warhol, they were an "ideas" band. . . .

The Velvets opened the musical doors of perception that little bit wider, but they never had the musicianship to be the revelation that they ought to have been.

> Steve Lake, *"Velvet Underground: Opening Doors of Perception,"* in Melody Maker (© IPC Business Press Ltd.), May 25, 1974, p. 27.

PATTI SMITH

Lou Reed didnt seem hung up. Not on [*1969 Live*]. The cross dont seem his true shape. The boy on this record was riding a wave—seeming in a state of suspended joy. Longing checked in some roadhouse like Steve McQueen in *Baby the Rain Must Fall*. Not Mick Jagger no muscular sailor just ONE caught in a warp in some lost town and rising. The Velvets winding up the Sixties laying one long clean rhythmic fart across the West called Live in Texas; with Lou Reed winking right in the eye of that fart. I mean these boys may been outa tune but they were solid IN TIME. . . .

And who beyond the performer is the most hungry for poetry in any form but the children the new masses and Lou Reed KNEW it—never played down back then—cause he knew that youth can eat the truth. . . . I see my friends they say man I gotta simmer down its too much pain but jesus let me rock back like peter pan I'd rather die than not take it out on the line one more time another risk is bliss.

That's why I love this record so much. It goes beyond risk and hovers over like an electric moth. Theres no question no apol-

ogising there is just a trust a bond with time and god their relentlessly relaxed method of getting it on and over the land of strain. Like [poet Arthur] Rimbaud we rebel baptism but you know man needs water he needs to get clean keep washing over like a Moslem. Well this drowning is eternal and you dont have to track it lambkin you just lay back and let it pour over you. Dig it submit put your hands down your pants and play side C. **"Ocean"** is on and the head cracks like intellectual egg spewing liquid gold (jewel juice) and Lou is so elegantly restrained. It nearly drives me crazy. The cymbal is so light and the way they stroll into **"Pale Blue Eyes"** not unlike Tim Hardin's "Misty Roses" the way it comes on like a Genet love song. . . .

[This] set stands in time like a Cartier gem. . . . L.R. + V.U.69 are a kool creem oozing soothing mesmerising like hypnos scooping wind down pain mountain. This double set is completely worth it not a bad cut always with it. It will relax you help it all to make sense the Sixties ended in a sea of warm puke delicate enough to be called art. . . . And if Lou dont remember how it felt to shell it out you will not soon forget how it feels to hear. When the musics over and you turn out the light its like . . . coming down from a dream.

> Patti Smith, *"Records: '1969 Live',"* in Creem (© copyright 1974 by Creem Magazine, Inc.), Vol. 6, No. 2, July, 1974, p. 64.

STEVE SIMELS

Much as Lou would probably prefer it, the Underground just won't go away. And frankly, if you feel (as I do) that Lou has been generally making an ass out of himself since their demise, and that **"Animal"** was just too slick a presentation of songs that walk a thin line between being moronic and sublimely terrifying, then you're going to dig the hell out of [**"1969 Velvet Underground Live"**]. I certainly do. . . .

So what do we get? Most of the band's best numbers, some previously unrecorded gems featuring Lou at his most corny and charming (*Over You*) and some early thoughts on tunes later resurrected on the solo albums. The results are by and large incandescent. . . .

The lesson of all this is that Lou Reed is (was?) one of the great rock singer/songwriters, and that in the Velvet Underground he found the perfect musical means to express his not inconsiderable ideas. This new set is a gas, one of the best live rock albums of this or any other year, and if it's not quite as good as **"Loaded"** (the band's penultimate studio statement, where their raunch was even more completely distilled) it's damn close, and that's saying something. If your only exposure to Lou has been his increasingly disappointing post-Velvet work, then **"1969 Velvet Underground Live"** will come as a remarkable surprise. If you're already a fan, I don't have to tell you. For both factions, as well as those who just like first-rate rock-and-roll, the bottom line is *get it*. (p. 74)

> Steve Simels, *"Throwing Some Light on the Velvet Underground,"* in Stereo Review (copyright © 1974 by Ziff-Davis Publishing Company), Vol. 33, No. 2, August, 1974, pp. 73-4.

ALLAN JONES

In a way I hope that [**"Sally Can't Dance"**] is the last album that Lou Reed ever makes. There's no longer any way of avoiding the fact that since the demise of the Velvet Underground, Reed's been balancing precariously on the edge of total artistic disintegration.

Discounting **"Rock and Roll Animal"** . . . Reed's produced four solo albums, including the one under consideration here.

On those four albums there are maybe half a dozen cuts—and that's an optimistic assessment—that could just possibly be compared to his work with the Velvets. And that's sad, because at his peak Reed was years ahead of almost everyone in terms of intelligence, vision and the exploration of themes which the rest of rock has still to catch up with. This album isn't quite the ultimate disaster I'd anticipated, but it's close enough for me to wish that Lou would take a long cool look around and move into the shadows. It's too late, I fear, for him to skin off all the Skull City death duets with which he's become inextricably involved. This album amounts to little more than obsessive self parody, and if Reed can't see that then he's past all danger and already way out beyond the recall point. The first side is totally dismissable. It sounds as if he's gone through his old notebooks taking a line here and there to compile a series of songs that echo facets of his style—ya know, that cold, detached, penetrating, reportage—and come up with songs so jaded and lifeless they could have been recorded at a mortuary in the Bronx on a Sunday night when the entire population of New York was too bored to die and too wiped out to live. I don't think Reed does care anymore. It's as simple as that. He's content to slide through his usual territory with both eyes closed existing purely in a state of half life. What's happened to the reality, man? . . . If you really want an excursion into mental therapy that'll jive you out of your head get hold of a copy of [Sylvia Plath's] ''The Bell Jar'' or even [Ken Kesey's] ''One Flew Over The Cuckoo's Nest.'' Reed's version [**"Kill Your Sons"**] is comic book stuff. The title track is virtually the only commendable song on the entire album, and does contain some decent lines. But for the rest . . . Well, the most that one can recommend is that you turn out your Velvets albums. They'll at least confirm that Reed did have it once. I just wish he'd find out where he lost it. Wrap your troubles in dreams, and watch them drift away, Lou.

Allan Jones, "Give Up, Lou," in Melody Maker *(© IPC Business Press Ltd.), October 5, 1974, p. 45.*

JAMES ISAACS

Nathaniel West once wrote about Hollywood, "Few things are sadder than the truly monstrous." In the case of Lou Reed's [*Sally Can't Dance*], that line might be amended to read, "Few things are more depressing than limp attempts by an aging rock 'n roller to titillate a mass audience." So far has Reed's musical/sensibility stock plummeted.

There was a time when, beneath the facades of kinkiness, paranoia and demimonde weariness, Reed's songs were compassionate, even tender. Short stories on messy people and situations. Reed's material at its zenith qualified as near poetic expressions of desperation. . . .

[The] difference between the Reed style of, say, **"Some Kinda Love,"** with its subtly stalking melody, exemplary phrasing and beautifully turned lines . . . , and any of his current output is rather like comparing the works of [the Marquis] DeSade with a peep show. Any likenesses between the two are purely incidental.

Whereas a Reed lyric was once bitter and empathetic, and almost uniformly incisive, the present Reed *oeuvre* is marked by sloganeering tendencies. Can it be that he has determined that his audience is comprised of callow, post-pubescents who will "get off" to his merely listing various instances of Jesus-I'm-bored deviance in different songs? With *Sally Can't Dance,* "decadence," always a hollow, albeit occasionally interesting state, has foundered to new levels of vacuity. (p. 65)

Gallows humor of the forced variety abounds throughout **"Animal Language,"** and it would appear that Reed has conquered new worlds of corn with **"Kill Your Sons"**; but this is perhaps because the latter song was his reaction to psychoanalysis, the draft, the war and, from what I can ascertain from the lyric, his sister wedding a corpulent, self-satisfied Long Island commuter. In any case, **"Sons"** plods along dolefully. . . .

Finally (and at long last) we have **"Billy,"** a character study about a long-term friendship between two men with contrasting personalities. Billy was a straight arrow who scored touchdowns, got all A's and went to Med. school. Lou was a lout who got D's, played a lot of pool and dropped out of college. Truly an odd couple, no? Billy is drafted, goes to war and comes back shattered. Lou channeled his doltishness into being in a rock 'n roll band and building a mystique on his putative self-destructiveness—a mystique, incidentally, which he seems to be intent on debunking on this record. One would imagine that Lou sought to capture the bittersweet feeling inherent in any such situation in which two friends since childhood face the attendant problems of ought, in the philosophical sense. Instead, the song's denouement is a cop-out.

"No one could figure which one of us was the fool," Lou intones wearily. I'll leave that one up to you. (p. 66)

James Isaacs, "Records: 'Sally Can't Dance'," in Creem *(© copyright 1974 by Creem Magazine, Inc.), Vol. 6, No. 7, December, 1974, pp. 65-6.*

JIM CUSIMANO

After the frustrations and relative failure of *Berlin,* his *magnum opus,* you'd think that Reed would sing of something people and critics could identify with, like the surging cost of toilet paper. Instead, *Sally Can't Dance* continues Lou's fascination with death and decay in the civilized underground of his youth, primarily through what sound like *Berlin* outtakes. If *Sally* is a commercial success, Lou will have orchestrated the greatest irony of his irony-loving life. (p. 79)

Sally is not simply an anthology of outtakes, however, and not all the numbers with the feel of refurbished oldies recall *Berlin.* With its bestial *menage a trois,* **"Animal Language,"** shorn of its funk, is reminiscent of **"I Can't Stand It"** from the first solo album. And **"Billy"** . . . belongs to another time entirely. Apparently, Lou never throws anything away. . . .

For the first time in years Lou has made an album without the help of some obvious talents like Bowie, Ezrin or [guitarist Steve] Hunter. The result is so safe, tidy and danceable that this tarnished genius might find a place once more in the Top 40. The possibility that, say, **"Baby Face,"** a tune which documents the sleazy meanness of a perverse affair's finish, might be engraved on the minds of this country's youth by millions of radios to sell Big Macs and Clearasil, almost boggles my mind. (p. 80)

Jim Cusimano, "Records: 'Sally Can't Dance'," in Crawdaddy *(copyright © 1975 by Crawdaddy Pub-*

lishing Co., Inc.; all rights reserved; reprinted by permission), January, 1975, pp. 79-80.

LESTER BANGS

Why is this guy surviving, who has made a career out of terminal twitches ever since the Velvet Underground surfaced dead on arrival in 1966? Well, for one thing, the Velvets emerged from under one of the many entrepreneurial wings of Andy Warhol, who has managed to accomplish more in this culture while acting (in public at least) like a total autistic null-node than almost any other figure of the 60s. Lou learned a lot from Andy, mainly about becoming a successful public personality by selling your own private quirks to an audience greedy for more and more geeks. The prime lesson he learned was that to succeed as this kind of mass-consumed nonentity you must expertly erect walls upon walls to reinforce the walls that your own quirky vulnerability has already put there.

In other words, Lou Reed is a completely depraved pervert and pathetic death dwarf and everything else you want to think he is. On top of that he's a liar, a wasted talent, an artist continually in flux, and a huckster selling pounds of his own flesh. A panderer living off the dumbbell nihilism of a 70s generation that doesn't have the energy to commit suicide. Lou Reed is the guy that gave dignity and poetry and rock 'n' roll to smack, speed, homosexuality, sadomasochism, murder, misogyny, stumblebum passivity, and suicide, and then proceeded to belie all his achievements and return to the mire by turning the whole thing into a monumental bad joke with himself as the woozily insistent Henny Youngman in the center ring, mumbling punch lines that kept losing their punch. Lou Reed is a coward and a sissy by any standard of his forebears such as Tennessee Williams and William Burroughs.

Lou Reed's enjoyed a solo career renaissance primarily by passing himself off as the most burnt-out reprobate around, and it wasn't all show by a long shot. People kept expecting him to die, so perversely he came back not to haunt them, as he perhaps would like to think (although I think he'd rather have another hit record if he had to sing about it never raining in California to get it), but to clean up. In the sense of the marketplace. (p. 38)

Lou Reed is my hero principally because he stands for all the most fucked up things that I could ever possibly conceive of. Which probably only shows the limits of my imagination.

The central heroic myth of the Sixties was the burnout. Live fast, be bad, get messy, die young. More than just "hope I die before I get old," it was a whole cool stalk we had down or tried to get. Partially it has to do with the absolute nonexistence of real, objective, straight-arrow, head-held-high, noble, achieving heroes. Myself, I always wanted to emulate the most fucked up bastard I could see, at least vicariously. As long as he did it with some sense of style. Thus Lou Reed. Getting off vicariously on various forms of deviant experience compensated somehow for the emptiness of our own drearily "normal" lives. It's like you never want to see the reality; it's too clammy watching someone shoot up junk and turn blue. It ain't like listening to the records.

That's why Lou Reed was necessary. And what may be even more important is that he had the good sense (or maybe just brain-rot, hard to tell) to realize that the whole concept of sleaze, "decadence," degeneracy was a joke, and turned himself into a clown, the Pit into a puddle. Any numbskull can

be a degenerate, but not everybody realizes that even now; like Jim Morrison, Lou realized the implicit absurdity of the rock 'n' roll *bette noir* badass pose, and parodied, deglamorized it. Though that may be giving him too much credit. Most probably he had no idea what he was doing, which was half the mystique. Anyway, he made a great bozo. . . . The persistent conceit of Lou's recent press releases—that he's the "street poet of rock 'n' roll"—just may be true in an unintended way. The street, after all, is not the most intellectual place in the world. In fact, it's littered with dopey jerkoffs and putzes of every stripe. Dunceville. Rubbery befuddlement. And Lou is the king of 'em all, y'all. (pp. 38-9)

Lester Bangs, "Let Us Now Praise Famous Death Dwarves or, How I Slugged It Out with Lou Reed & Stayed Awake," in Creem (© copyright 1975 by Creem Magazine, Inc.), Vol. 6, No. 10, March, 1975, pp. 38-9.

CREEM

Lou Reed reminds me of Jack Kerouac near the end, dozing in an arm-chair with a beer, a flask of bourbon and a script for Obetrols, mumbling the same old stories at anyone within range. "Hey, ya wanna hear me make up a complete Shakespearean sonnet right outta my head?"

Like Kerouac, Reed was mostly responsible for a movement that he didn't want much to do with. Kerouac in his Catholic guilt didn't want to be aligned with a whole generation of screwed-up young Americans. He claimed he wanted to write like Thomas Wolfe. Likewise Reed shied away from, and virtually spit on, the whole gay-flash-rock 'n' roll-decadence scene; "Hey, why don't they listen to the ballads?" You can tell the guy would have really liked to be a poet, but the Sixties beat him to it.

"Records: 'Lou Reed Live'," in Creem (© copyright 1975 by Creem Magazine, Inc.), Vol. 7, No. 1, June, 1975, p. 63.

PAUL NELSON

Perhaps the fact that Lou Reed's curious career continues is more important than what he does with it at this particular stage. Had he accomplished nothing else, his work with the Velvet Underground in the late Sixties would assure him a place in anyone's rock & roll pantheon; those remarkable songs still serve as an articulate aural nightmare of men and women caught in the beauty and terror of sexual, street and drug paranoia, unwilling or unable to move. The message is that urban life is tough stuff—it will kill you; Reed, the poet of destruction, knows it but never looks away and somehow finds holiness as well as perversity in both his sinners and his quest. . . .

The man's accomplishments may be few of late, but he is still one of a handful of American artists capable of the spiritual home run. Should he put it all together again, watch out.

Paul Nelson, "Records: 'Lou Reed Live'," in Rolling Stone (by Straight Arrow Publishers, Inc. © 1975; all rights reserved; reprinted by permission), Issue 188, June 5, 1975, p. 60.

PETER LAUGHNER

[*Coney Island Baby*] made me so morose and depressed when I got the advance copy that I stayed drunk for three days. . . .

Now, when I was younger, the Velvet Underground meant to me what the Stones, Dylan, etc. meant to thousands of other midwestern teen mutants. I was declared exempt from the literary curriculum of my upper class suburban high school simply because I showed the English department a list of books I'd glanced through while obsessively blasting **White Light/White Heat** on the headphones of my parents' stereo. All my papers were manic droolings about the parallels between Lou Reed's lyrics and whatever academia we were supposed to be analyzing in preparation for our passage into the halls of higher learning. **"Sweet Jane"** I compared with Alexander Pope, **"Some Kinda Love"** lined right up with T. S. Eliot's "Hollow Men" . . . plus I had a rock band and we played all these songs, fueled pharmaceutically by our bassist who worked as a delivery boy for a drugstore and ripped off an entire gallon jar full of Xmas trees and brown & clears. In this way I cleverly avoided all intellectual and creative responsibilities at the cleavage of the decades (I did read all the Delmore Schwartz I could steal from local libraries, because of that oblique reference on the 1st Velvets LP). After all, a person with an electric guitar and access to obscurities like "I saw my head laughing, rolling on the ground" had no need of creative credentials. . . . Who needed the promise of college and career? Lou Reed was my Woody Guthrie, and with enough amphetamine I would be the new Lou Reed!

I left home. I wandered to the wrong coast. (Can you imagine what it was like trying to get people in Berkeley, California to listen to **Loaded** in 1971? . . .) When Lou's first solo album came out, I drove hundreds of miles to play it for ex-friends sequestered at small exclusive midwest colleges listening to the Dead and Miles Davis. Everyone from my high school band had gone on to sterling careers as psych majors, botanical or law students, or selling and drinking for IBM. . . . All the girls I used to wow into bed with drugs and song married guys who were just like their brothers and moved to Florida or Chicago, leaving their copies of [Bob Dylan's] *Blonde on Blonde* and **White Light** in some closet along with the reams of amphetamine driven poetry I'd forced on them over the years. By the time **Metal Machine Music** came out, I'd lost all contact. . . .

So all those people will probably never pay any attention to **Coney Island Baby**, and even if they did it wouldn't do much for what's left of their synapses. The damn thing starts out exactly like an Eagles record! And with the exception of **"Charlie's Girl"** which is mercifully short and to the point, it's a downhill slide. **"My Best Friend"** is a six year old Velvets out-take which used to sound fun when it was fast. . . . Here it dirges along at the same pace as **"Lisa Says"** but without the sexiness. You could sit and puzzle over the voiceovers on **"Kicks"** but you won't find much. . . .

Side two starts off with the WORST thing Reed has ever done, this limp drone self-scam where he goes on about being "a gift to the women of this world" (in fact this whole LP reminds me of the junk you hear on the jukeboxes at those two-dollar a beer stewardess pickup bars. . . .) There's one pick up point, **"Oo-ee Baby"** with the only good line on the record "your old man was the best B&E man down on the street," then this Ric Von Schmidt rip-off which doesn't do anything at all.

Finally there's **"Coney Island Baby."** Just maudlin, dumb, self pity: "Can you believe I wann'd t'play football for th' coach" . . . Sure, Lou, when I was all uptight about being a fag in high school, I did too. Then it builds slightly . . . into STILL MORE self pity about how it's tough in the city and

the glory of Love will see you through. Maybe. Dragged out for six minutes.

Here I sit, sober and perhaps even lucid, on the sort of winter's day that makes you realize a New Year is just around the corner and you've got very little to show for it, but if you are going to get anything done on this planet, you better pick it up with both hands and DO IT YOURSELF. But I got the nerve to say to my old hero, hey Lou, if you really mean that last line of **"Coney Island Baby":** "You know I'd give the whole thing up for you," then maybe you ought to do just that.

> *Peter Laughner, "If You Choose, Choose to Go,"*
> in Creem *(© copyright 1976 by Creem Magazine,*
> *Inc.), Vol. 7, No. 10, March, 1976, p. 63.*

PAUL NELSON

To capture the correct mood—exactly what has been missing from most of his RCA records—for *Coney Island Baby,* the artist has forsaken his recent daze for the days of *1969* and *Loaded* to reclaim the warmth of some of the songs (**"Pale Blue Eyes,"** particularly) he loved to sing. Such a move does *not* imply that Reed was then or is now a moony sentimental fool—*1969, Loaded* and *Coney Island Baby* are all extremely tough LPs. But it does infer that since he left the Underground (in more ways than one), too much of his work has been a cheap, sensationalized self parody of the more freakish side of his persona. Those who admire the contrived outrageousness of the simple, speed-crazed Monster may be more than a little nonplused by the ambiguity and extra dimension—call it ironic, friendly reality—its creator has added to almost every song on the new album. *Coney Island Baby* in no way whitewashes the warp and woof of the quintessential Reed, but a balance has been restored and one can *understand* the new "monster," once again take him seriously. . . .

The songs themselves—as structured and melodic as any Reed has written—are timeless, terrific rock & roll. . . .

[Much] of this record is about integrity, with the singer setting down coherent moral confrontations—"Hey, man, what's your style? / How do you get your kicks for living?"—from the outlaw code that provides him with his own brand of respect. Lou Reed seems more than willing to put his unorthodox lifestyle on the line any time anyone wants to call him on it, but there is no malice in his challenges, . . . and often considerable regret. . . .

The three longer songs, all of which build in a manner highly reminiscent of the Velvet Underground (Reed uses repetition so well), tackle the major themes of friendship, intimidation and taking stock of one's life and doing something about it. . . . **"Coney Island Baby"** is the album's masterpiece, an anthem about courage, loss and the high price an outsider pays for his way of living. When Lou Reed talks about "want[ing] to play football for the coach" and "giv[ing] the whole thing up for you," he is expressing the profound dream of the damned—and his loss is given greater intensity because both he and we know that such wishes were impossible from the very beginning. So we reaccept it. And it hurts all over again.

You can play on my team any day, Lou. (p. 54)

> *Paul Nelson, "Lou Reed's Forward Pass: It's How*
> *You Play the Game,"* in Rolling Stone *(by Straight*
> *Arrow Publishers, Inc. © 1976; all rights reserved;*
> *reprinted by permission), Issue 209, March 25, 1976,*
> *pp. 52, 54.*

PETER REILLY

I've always had the feeling that there is considerably less to Lou Reed's work than meets the ear. Members of the "thinking" pop press—often down in the depths of the ninetieth floor, at least in regard to their own social consciences after one lavish publicity lunch too many—immediately took to Reed from his earliest days with the Velvet Underground, and they seemed to fall all over each other in proclaiming him some new kind of 33-rpm François Villon, alternating their tsk-tsks with a goggle-eared attention to his every new grunt. This must have been because his songs often dealt with drugs or homosexuality or the bitterly desperate street life of teen-age burnt-out cases. That the songs often had what seemed to be autobiographical tidbits strewn through them served only to add to the titillation, and consequently Reed has been the reigning in-house decadent for some time now.

Well, I'm here, fresh from the haunt of the coot and the tern, to tell you that ["Coney Island Baby"] strikes me as an extremely patchy effort, intermittently entertaining, and about as dissolute as a waffle bake over at Mary Hartman's. The songs, considerably more upbeat this time out, include two that are very good—*Coney Island Baby*, a song about the search for personal values, and the charmingly bad-ass *Charley's Girl*. . . .

His admirers seem to find him a significant mixture of William Burroughs, Jean Genêt, and Bob Dylan. To me he seems more like a gifted actor who is never comfortable for too long in one role (thus the radical changes from album to album) and whose roots are in the stylish low life of [Josef] Von Sternberg, the chic drugging of [Jean] Cocteau, and the performing style of one of the better Brechtian character actors from the Berliner Ensemble.

> Peter Reilly, "Popular Discs and Tapes: 'Coney Island Baby'," in Stereo Review (copyright © 1976 by Ziff-Davis Publishing Company), Vol. 36, No. 4, April, 1976, p. 90.

BRUCE MALAMUT

I love [Lou Reed]. Like his ex-brethren from the Underground, he's got guts. No compromises. *Berlin* was the most naked exorcism of manic/depression ever to be committed to vinyl. His technique is to alienate the listener so bad that the listener perceives himself as some sorta in-squad just to say he digs Lou Reed: this is hip. Lou Reed has last laugh; voila *Metal Machine Music*. Other praise: pushing free sexuality come-out. Problem is, he's come out so far he's fallen in. (p. 72)

> Bruce Malamut, "Lou Reed Is Not Jimmy Reed," in Crawdaddy (copyright © 1976 by Crawdaddy Publishing Co., Inc.; all rights reserved; reprinted by permission), May, 1976, pp. 71-2.*

ALLAN JONES

The notion may seem rather fanciful, but it strikes me that Lou Reed is becoming increasingly like an old lover whom you might occasionally meet by chance. Sometimes, the original infatuation is revived and the relationship consummated. On other occasions there is no romantic revival, and you might even question the original attraction.

Right now, faced with Reed's ["Rock And Roll Heart,"] I'm reminded of my admiration for his achievements, but I'm wondering whether that is quite enough to provoke more than a passing enthusiasm for this record. In other words, "**Rock And Roll Heart,**" despite its manifest flaws, could persuade me to get involved in some heavy petting but I don't think I'd go, as they say, all the way.

The record will no doubt disappoint those admirers of Reed who were encouraged by the signs of artistic rehabilitation on his . . . "**Coney Island Baby,**" and supply with fresh ammunition those critics who are convinced of his decline.

Of its predecessors, "**Rock And Roll Heart**" most closely resembles "**Transformer.**" It is characterised by the same irritating blandness and features some songs as equally facile as those which afflicted the earlier record.

"**I Believe In Love,**" which opens this album, is, for instance, perplexingly like the kind of inane mush Marc Bolan might have recorded had he come from New York (though it's not nearly so vapid as the two tracks that follow, "**Banging On My Drum**" and "**Follow The Leader**").

Even so, only Lou Reed could appear with a line like "I believe in the Iron Cross," and there is something seductive in the mischievous humour of the song. . . .

If I sound a little unenthusiastic thus far about "**Rock And Roll Heart,**" it is only because one expects so much from Lou Reed, and there are at least five tracks here that bear some reasonable comparison with past and recent glories. . . .

Lyrically, [the title track is] one of Reed's sharpest songs in a while. . . .

Even better is "**Ladies Pay,**" a curious composition which I would tentatively describe as a lament for the wives of servicemen overseas, who are themselves hopelessly lost. . . .

This track, and the weary, evocative "**You Wear It So Well**" . . . , would not have been out of place on the violently underrated "**Berlin,**" as they are both distinguished by their entrancing, cold mystery.

There is humour in this collection, too: "**Vicious Circle**" . . . is an absolute sidesplitter. . . .

"**A Sheltered Life**" . . . is a more elaborate and obvious joke— it has Reed denying any hedonistic activities and features the laughable assertion that he's never been into narcotics. . . .

"**Temporary Thing,**" which closes the album, proves that there is still fire in Reed's music. . . .

And there you have it. "**Rock And Roll Heart**" is, on most fronts, entertaining. It also features moments that revive one's faith in Reed as a composer. If it was by anyone else, I'd maybe hesitate before recommending its immediate introduction to your record collection.

But it is Lou Reed we're talking about. And he's still one of the most compulsively fascinating performers rock and roll ever invented. There, I've talked myself into a one-night stand. At the very least.

> Allan Jones, "Entertaining Mr. Reed," in Melody Maker (© IPC Business Press Ltd.), November 6, 1976, p. 20.

FRANK ROSE

Lou Reed has been making a lot of noise about rock & roll lately, but his new album is less a collection of rock & roll songs than a series of meditations which comprise the philosophy of Lou Reed. This is not to say the music isn't rock & roll. But the spirit is not rock & roll. Rock & roll is aggressive; *Rock and Roll Heart* is reflective. . . .

Rock and Roll Heart is a replay of every snarl he ever put onto wax. On its 12 songs he contemplates a variety of typical Lou Reed subjects—love, hate, good times, bad times, fame, hipness—in a manner that's deceptively perfunctory. He seems to have reduced his work to a series of skeletal phrases which he fleshes out with music that's lean and raw. The key phrases are all refrains. . . . He has scooped out their depth and given us nothing but surface. (p. 94)

Reed obviously expects us to accept these compositions as songs. You could certainly take the cynical view: at this point in his career, Lou has only to sing a line with "vicious" in it eight times and throw in a couple of other lines (as he does in "**Vicious Circle**") and his fans will fill in the rest. Of course, this kind of lyrical shorthand is a lot easier to pull off when you have a voice that sounds like it was created for words like "vicious," but then some people just have a gift.

Yet, as any TMer knows, meditation can lead to higher truths; surface effect can also conceal deeper intent. After a few listenings, the images Reed pounds into our heads begin to coalesce. Connections form and re-form under layers of irony. When he follows "**Banging on My Drum**" with "**Follow the Leader**," he contrasts masturbation as a source of solitary pleasure with the New York hustle as a source of harried irritation. . . .

It's in the five songs that follow "**Chooser and the Chosen**" that Reed recalls his role as chronicler of the idle hip—four songs, actually, and another that sounds like a joke. That one is "**A Sheltered Life**," and in it he facetiously paints himself as a rube who's going to have to lose his "hometown ways." It's a jive rap, not unlike some of Tom Waits'. . . .

In equally vivid contrast to the narcotizing catalog of recycled theme songs that comprises the bulk of the album are its two obvious focal points: "**I Believe in Love**" and the title cut. Both are about rock & roll. . . .

[There] are few outward similarities between *Rock and Roll Heart* and *Coney Island Baby*, Reed's last album for RCA. The RCA record was one of Reed's greatest; this one is not. *Coney Island Baby* was an album of musical experimentation and real songs, characterized by unusual honesty and depth. *Rock and Roll Heart* is an album of familiar music and familiar posturings. But they're posturings with a difference. They're not blatantly exploitative, as they were in *Sally Can't Dance;* this time they're pensive, sour and almost nostalgic. *Coney Island Baby* was also nostalgic; it was the album in which Reed returned to the scenes of his youth. *Rock and Roll Heart* is the album in which he surveys his career. . . .

It's like a rock & roll exorcism; Reed has finally lapsed into a glossolalia of the gutter. What emerges is an unexpected moralism, a skewed philosophy (by bourgeois standards) that values good times and indolence above ambition and competitiveness. This moralism has always been implicit in Reed, in the way he dishes the people he immortalizes; but it takes the idea of "good-times rock & roll" to throw it into relief. This album is about innocence and corruption and the beauty of simplistic illusion versus the ugly complexity of reality—because in the world Reed sings about, innocence is as illusory as love. This preoccupation with lost innocence is Reed's real link with the current rock & roll revival. (p. 96)

Frank Rose, "Lou Reed Remembers," in Rolling Stone *(by Straight Arrow Publishers, Inc. © 1976; all rights reserved; reprinted by permission), Issue 227, December 2, 1976, pp. 94, 96.*

STEPHEN DEMOREST

I liked Lou's last album, *Coney Island Baby,* for its integrity, combativeness, and character, but *Rock and Roll Heart* flashes none of these qualities. Lou promised this would be a rock 'n' roll album, but I call it stuff 'n' nonsense. For the most part, these tracks are merely notations for songs, unfinished sketches of ideas that are pretty stale anyway. Unlike *Coney Island Baby,* this collection sounds almost completely insincere; how suddenly he forfeited that self-assured conviction. It's the record of an artist out of touch with his core, so he clowns around instead—anything to entertain, eh? . . .

"**Banging On My Drum**" sounds like a warmup for [the New York Dolls's] "Personality Crisis," and the words make [the Ramones's] "Now I Wanna Sniff Some Glue" seem deep by comparison. "**You Wear It So Well**," drenched in the sarcastic ooze of *Berlin,* rings truest to Lou's conflicted persona, but he dodges developing any storyline or character. "**Ladies Pay**" is a decent dockside soap opera rocker that challenges the emotional depth of [Alice Cooper's] "Only Women Bleed." . . .

Somewhere in the "creative" stage, Lou abandoned this LP. Lyrically, there's no exploration of any topical stuff like, say, illicit love nests of the Yankee bat boys, or a gay look at the New York police riots, or Lou's highs from snorting the ashes of burned legal contracts.

Sure, this may be yet another perverse joke he's pulling to goof on anyone's expectations. Some people, who consider Lou Reed's career a comic spectator sport anyway, think this album is hilarious. Yeah, it's so funny I forgot to laugh.

Stephen Demorest, "Records: 'Rock and Roll Heart'," in Creem *(© copyright 1977 by Creem Magazine, Inc.), Vol. 8, No. 8, January, 1977, p. 58.*

JOEL VANCE

Lou Reed is touted in some quarters as a serious artist, but there is nothing on ["**Rock and Roll Heart**"] to support such a fantasy. He seems deliberately mediocre and dull. He is an anti-musician, much as his mentor and former employer Andy Warhol (from their Velvet Underground band association) was an anti-artist and anti-film director. . . . Reed's monotone vocals and non-songs are considered deceptively simple statements with deep underlying meanings.

The truth is that Reed and Warhol are, consciously or unconsciously, con men. Like all con men, they hold their victims in contempt and their pleasure comes in seeing just how gullible their audience can be. . . .

Since he *is* an anti-musician, it is impossible to judge Reed on the basis of music. Sample: on three of the selections here, the titles of the tunes are the only lyrics, and they are repeated over and over to the accompaniment of a not more than competent band. It would be comforting to dismiss him as a rascal, but that cannot be done. Even as a con man he has no flair, and his contempt for his audience is ugly.

Joel Vance, "Popular Discs and Tapes: 'Rock and Roll Heart'," in Stereo Review *(copyright © 1977 by Ziff-Davis Publishing Company), Vol. 38, No. 2, February, 1977, p. 101.*

JIM TROMBETTA

[If] you can hear [Lou Reed's best songs] at all, it's through bone conduction, like your own voice. Not even the Velvets' unique pulsating beat and highly danceable rhythms could make such intimacy into mass entertainment. The ordinary rock star stances of dominance and doper cool are easy enough to swallow, but Lou based his self-assertion on the hidden undersides of those attitudes: passivity, melancholia and the dubious ecstasies of self-destruction. . . . Nobody wants to identify with that kind of bad news. . . .

Shock was never the only resource in the Reed repertoire: There's a great street voice, poetic complexities in simple lines, enchanting melodies and screaming energy, and terse guitar electronics which perfectly express the tension in real human fingers. . . .

Lou's solo emergence under the wing of Dave Bowie relied more on personality than his music, evoking an explicit gay posture and animalistic bad taste. . . . [*Walk on the Wild Side: The Best of Lou Reed* is] a mixed trick-or-treat bag of melting Baby Ruths, jawbreakers with soft centers and a few fishhooks for laughs. . . .

The soft, sensitive tunes are the most successful here. "**Satellite of Love**," that uncanny romance, is the album's only undeniable classic; its only hit, "**Walk on the Wild Side**," is a justifiable fave; and the three-hanky "**Coney Island Baby**"— "wanna play football for the coach"—is a touching, tuneful delight which sums up Reed's favorite obsession.

Lou is always wanting to play football for the coach in the lost past; or else he's waiting for the man, all tomorrow's parties or the train to come 'round the bend in the future. Lou evokes the desire whose satisfaction can never be grasped in any present moment, only in vanished yesterday or longed-for later-on. It's the iron commitment to deferred gratification that the lamest junkie shares with the most compulsive overachiever. Lou's most characteristic music climbs to an ecstatic rush ("**Sister Ray**") which is itself fragmentary, leaving Lou waiting "until tomorrow, but that's just another time." . . .

[Much] of this decent *Best of* music just moves air molecules around in the usual way.

> *Jim Trombetta, "Reed Out," in* Crawdaddy *(copyright © 1977 by Crawdaddy Publishing Co., Inc.; all rights reserved; reprinted by permission), July, 1977, p. 64.*

DAVID DALTON and LENNY KAYE

The Velvet Underground cauterized their time, searing the bloodstream of hedonism and frustration. Theirs was a demimonde, offering salvation in place of morality, ends justified by means. To be real, they vowed, pitting the absurd against the vulgar. The black angel would peal its death song, sufferance and understanding as final reward, while terror and certainty fused in scenes of rumbling destruction, buildings toppling, cities left smoldering in ruins.

They stood alone, regarded as a curiosity or a "bum trip," their darkling visions no match for the optimism engloving America. It was only later, when they'd at last broken under

the pressure of hindsight, that their truth would become known: beauty in evil, evil in beauty, taking the strange twists of the human soul and glorifying them in a play of passions, "**All Tomorrow's Parties**." Even their name . . . seemed to hint at unknown depravities better whispered in private. The Velvet Underground, as early as 1966, was the first band of the seventies, twisting violence and catharsis into a haze of articulate noise, prophetic and provoking. (pp. 198-99)

[The] Velvets exposed a new wound of festering consciousness. Their style was set by drugs and urban dishevelment. . . . (p. 199)

[The] Velvets' first album, simply titled *The Velvet Underground & Nico*, . . . outlined their subculture with diffracted accuracy, turning each song on the next to question and subvert meaning, culminating in the broken glass and subterranean distortions of "**European Son**." . . . Multi-phrenic, Reed wrote introspectively for Nico, melodic ballads that placed her as a mirror, a "**Femme Fatale**." With himself, he plummeted brain-first into debauchery, overpowering his senses from without, seeking escape and unassayed relief. "**Venus In Furs**," "**Run Run Run**," "**Heroin**"—each became a mannered recitation of sin, a confessional neither idealized nor exorcised by the pain of its telling. (p. 200)

The music [on *White Light/White Heat*] was harsh, blurred and indistinct. . . . There was a feeling of hurriedness to it, an urgency which intensified each cut, an element of paranoia that began "**I Heard Her Call My Name**" abruptly, in mid-phrase, almost as if it were afraid the side would start without it. . . . The album's masterpiece, "**Sister Ray**," mixed a throbbing single chord in a Genet-like altar of sailors and ding-dongs. . . . Reed spit his images into the wind of a drone played at top volume, words sharding into separate syllables and then individual letters, an aural nightmare of blind, naked stasis.

They had stepped over the edge; there was only return left. (pp. 200, 202)

The turnabout was even-handed. When the Velvets returned to the studio with Reed in control, the result was almost ascetic in comparison. "**Candy Says**" genteelly mentioned that which "others so discreetly talk about." . . . Velvet Underground's religious symbolism and forebearance were made official in the following year's *Loaded*, where Reed stipulated just what he meant by the salvation of one's soul. Relinquishing Jack his corset and Jane her vest, he told the story of Ginny from Long Island, playing with the dials of a radio. "You know her life was saved by rock and roll. . . ." . . .

A real good time was had by all. (p. 202)

> *David Dalton and Lenny Kaye, "Outer Limits," in their* Rock 100 *(copyright © 1977 by David Dalton and Lenny Kaye; used by permission of Grosset & Dunlap, Inc.), Grosset & Dunlap, 1977, pp. 193-206.**

ALLAN JONES

Like so much of Reed's recent work ["**Street Hassle**" is] an inconsistent, constantly frustrating outing with the brilliance of [the title cut]—an ambitious and largely successful work— french kissing in terminal intimacy rather lacklustre performances like "**Shooting Star**"—which deals, with no surfeit of musical or lyrical inspiration, with the transience of stardom. . . .

The album's tour-de-force (which elsewhere will probably be slagged into a coma), is **"Street Hassle,"** an extraordinary narrative about a love affair (whether hetero/homo/transexual is not yet clear), that traces its disintegration and, finally the death of one of the lovers. An OD, naturally. At least it shows that Dick Stewart just which one's the champ in evoking underworld romance. The musical setting is as incisive and as unusual as the language. . . .

I'll suspend final judgment on this album until I've had a chance to listen to it more closely. . . .

Allan Jones, "Lou Slips Away," in Melody Maker *(© IPC Business Press Ltd.), March 4, 1978, p. 20.*

SUSIN SHAPIRO

A funny thing happened to [John] Milton on the way to Paradise. He discovered the devils to be more fascinating than the angels, and that gave him hell. Lou Reed has also been prey to such problems. His new album, *Street Hassle,* is up to its neck in devils. But at last Reed has introduced them to his angels. "Gimme gimme gimme some good times/gimme gimme gimme some pain," the opening chant of [*Street Hassle*] . . . carries the same jolt. Like [poet Rainer Maria] Rilke, who felt that if his demons were exorcised by psychoanalysis his angels would also split, Reed has juggled the heroes and villains. He hasn't offed his demons, but he's in control of them now; he's severed the excesses and self-indulgences that made him look foolish in the past.

For me, Lou Reed becomes a hero with *Street Hassle*. Heroes are validated only by their acts, while villains reek of personality. . . . Reed has sacrificed his gangsterism to his aspirations. He's too film noir to ever be Randolph Scott, but I admire his trying. He's too East of Eden also, but it's getting very populous there. If the people accept him, the rebel will go respectable, he'll be a Zapata, a Fidel. Maybe Reed wants to be a superstar; maybe he's getting softer, less cynical. He's in no need of restraint any longer, or sympathy. . . .

The devil unclothed, turns out to be just another babe in the bulrushes, finally, after nine solo LP's, fighting a heroic battle.

Susin Shapiro, "Lou Reed Reads Runes" (reprinted by permission of The Village Voice *and the author; copyright © The Village Voice, Inc., 1978), in* The Village Voice, *Vol. XXIII, No. 12, March 20, 1978, p. 51.*

TOM CARSON

Near the beginning of this brilliant new album [*Street Hassle*], Lou Reed sings: "It's been a long time since I've spoken to you." The line has a resonance far beyond its literal meaning. In the years following the breakup of the Velvet Underground, Reed's bizarre and half-baked semistardom became a travesty of his art, as one of the most magical raw nerves of our time coarsened into a crude, death-trip clown.

Whereas Reed with the Velvets had once broken our hearts with a compelling vision of sin and redemption, he now broke them by turning his post-Underground LPs into floating freak shows. While much of Reed's solo work was far from bad, one has to remember that his admirers expected him to surpass Bob Dylan, and the Velvets' LPs had promised nothing less. So each comeback failed—not so much as rock & roll but as

myth—and the repeated failures only compounded the problem. [In **"Street Hassle"** he explains what went wrong]. (p. 53)

While a less vulnerable artist might have been able to resolve [the] contradictions, the salvation-obsessed Reed wasn't even a very adept or convincing sellout. Because he was so sensitive, his posturing as the Rock & Roll Animal was too painfully cruel to be valid even on its own slumming terms. It's possible total dishonesty could have made Reed a commercial success, but the partial and intermittent dishonesty he practiced marred even his good records almost beyond repair. Still, we waited. If he couldn't produce the expected masterpiece, he could at least give us a dignified admission of failure.

Street Hassle, oddly enough, is both: a confession of failure that becomes a stunning, incandescent triumph—the best solo album Lou Reed has ever done. Side one begins with an electrifying, Promethean challenge. As the hauntingly familiar chords of **"Sweet Jane"** lurch into focus, they are abruptly slapped down by Reed's sneering commentary. . . . **"Sweet Jane,"** that incalculably beautiful hymn to human endurance, has become the emblem of Reed's decay, a sleazy, crowd-pleasing rocker. By trashing the song so completely at the outset of this record, Reed deliberately raises both the stakes and our expectations almost impossibly high. (pp. 53, 55)

Street Hassle does not celebrate a resurrection. Its premise is to accept being damned as an irrevocable condition, and then speak as truthfully as possible about what that might mean. . . . When Reed quotes the Texas singer Bobby Fuller ("I fought the law, and the law won"), he is acknowledging the odds and underlining his determination finally to tell the story right, no matter what it takes. . . .

In his trashiest LP, *Sally Can't Dance,* Lou Reed turned his own poetry into graffiti; on *Street Hassle,* he turns street graffiti into poetry, with all the telephone numbers left in. Now when he revisits the Rock & Roll Animal persona, its ugliness and obscenity seem almost justified. . . .

The recognition of his own self-destruction has been made integral to *Street Hassle*'s concept, and the effect is double-edged: as we respond to the album's excellence, we are never allowed to forget just how much it cost.

The title cut is a real tour de force. . . . Reed delivers three brief narratives—no more than fragments, really—with little overt connection except their common themes of loneliness, sexual anguish and death. Here, the erotic images, cynicism and beautiful moments . . . are all made equal and lifted to the level of tragedy by the terrible transience of the **"Street Hassle"** motif. . . .

Unlike the more sentimental, nostalgic material on *Coney Island Baby* (much of which seems, in retrospect, like a preliminary draft of *Street Hassle*), the self-referential concept at the center of the new album broadens Reed's vision instead of limiting it. . . .

Street Hassle closes with a supremely graceful kiss-off, a throwaway masterpiece. . . . Placed immediately after the tortured nihilism of **"Leave Me Alone,"** **"Wait"** at first seems like cheap irony. But the song, like the whole of *Street Hassle,* transcends that, and doggerel is again raised to grandeur. Lou Reed is shrugging off everything that's gone by as temporary and inconsequential, yet reminding us just how much those temporary, inconsequential moments have come to matter.

After all this time, he still cares. How strangely moving that is. (p. 55)

Tom Carson, "Lou Reed Fights the Law and Wins," in Rolling Stone *(by Straight Arrow Publishers, Inc. ©1978; all rights reserved; reprinted by permission), Issue 262, April 6, 1978, pp. 53, 55.*

JAY COCKS

Danger is what Lou Reed's music has always been about. And that makes it classic, vital rock 'n' roll.

Beginning with Reed's tenure in the Velvet Underground more than a decade ago, he has been fashioning some of the strongest music you can hear anywhere. . . . *Street Hassle* is one of his very best, bitterest and most adventurous records, prime rock unconditionally guaranteed to give you the night sweats. . . .

Reed constantly recalls old rock songs, phrases lifted from ancient hit parades, but his images evoke Céline masquerading as an all-night FM deejay. . . .

In the mid-'60s, [Reed] became the generative force behind the Velvet Underground, a band notable in the era of peace, posies and good vibes, for laying down rock music that virtually throttled the listener. Some of the Velvet's music is still among Reed's finest work, including a lengthy threnody called *Heroin* that is as devastating a drug song . . . as anyone has ever written.

There has never been anything polite about Reed's music, then or now; not a laid-back note or a smug lie. . . .

[Tunes] in the album include a denunciation of a former associate called *Dirt* and, best of all, *Street Hassle,* the album's centerpiece, an eleven-minute kaleidoscope of destruction compressed into three separate dramatic vignettes and linked by a single musical phrase. Tough stuff, often outright scary. . . .

What keeps these excursions along the wild side from being slumming expeditions is Reed's own rapt sympathy for the grifters, freaks and crooks who populate much of his music. Many of his songs are shot through with the kind of dead-end romanticism that would stir Bruce Springsteen. . . . If Lou Reed gives no quarter in his music, neither does he yield to sensationalism or condescension. . . .

[Listen] to his nightshade music enough, and if distinctions do not actually start to disintegrate and boundaries blur, you will at least know there is one mean street where such things happen. And you will have a taste of what it is like to live there.

Jay Cocks, "Lou Reed's Nightshade Carnival," in Time *(reprinted by permission from* Time, The Weekly Newsmagazine; copyright Time Inc. 1978), Vol. 111, No. 17, April 24, 1978, p. 79.*

SCOTT ISLER

Frightening. Moving. Repellent. Fascinating. And, ultimately, touching. That's *Street Hassle.*

Lou Reed rides the all-night shuttle between humorously perceptive observation and terminal mental burn-out. Along the way he accumulates artistic maturity. *Street Hassle* finds him rebounding from the joviality of *Rock and Roll Heart.* Instead (for the most part) here's the metallic android we love to hate. But unlike earlier incarnations (when we could ignore Reed's trivial tastelessness) the songwriting on this record is as chill-

ingly effective as the Velvet Underground nightmares that brought Lou to prominence. A cruel mix of humanity with horror whets *Street Hassle*'s razor's edge. . . .

The album's obvious showpiece is the title cut. . . . The contrast between the repetitious (and therefore mundane) music, the emotionless vocal and the charged words makes "**Street Hassle**" one of Reed's crowning achievements.

Not everything on the lp is so resonant. "**Dirt**" and "**Shooting Star**" are both typical Reed put-downs . . . for the faithful. . . .

["**I Wanna Be Black**"] is a dubiously ironic/sarcastic tribute to blacks, self-loathing whites or both; Reed conceives of racial envy in mostly sexual terms. . . .

[Music] and words share an intensity that makes this undoubtedly the most powerful Lou Reed solo album.

Scott Isler, "Lonely Street," in Crawdaddy *(copyright © 1978 by Crawdaddy Publishing Co., Inc.; all rights reserved; reprinted by permission), May, 1978, p. 69.*

MIKAL GILMORE

[*Take No Prisoners*'s] real bounty is its formidable last side, featuring petrifying versions of "**Coney Island Baby**" and "**Street Hassle**"—the definitive accounts of Reed's classic pariah angel in search of glut and redemption. "**Street Hassle,**" in particular, is the apotheosis of Lou's callous brand of rock & roll. The original recording . . . was Reed's most disturbing song since "**Heroin.**" The new, live version of "**Street Hassle**" is an even more credible descent into the dark musings of a malignant psychology, littered with mercenary sex and heroin casualties, and narrated by a jaded junkie who undergoes a catharsis at the end. . . .

Reed has created a body of music that comes as close to disclosing the parameters of human loss and recovery as we're likely to find. That qualifies him, in my opinion, as one of the few real heroes rock & roll has raised. (p. 12)

Mikal Gilmore, "Lou Reed's Heart of Darkness," in Rolling Stone *(by Straight Arrow Publishers, Inc. ©1979; all rights reserved; reprinted by permission), Issue 287, March 22, 1979, pp. 8, 12-16, 18.*

JON SAVAGE

What do you buy when you buy Lou Reed, and do you still need to buy him? It's now almost a decade since he described over four albums with the Velvet Underground, a perennial cycle—perversity to desperation to (illusory) redemption to the salve of hothouse pop—that most fail to complete during a lifetime. Is it fair for us to expect any more from him, and for him to expect us to buy this, his product?

A qualified yes. In his chosen career, Reed can hope to make money and satisfy his art more than grow old gracefully. "**The Bells**" correspondingly features a representation of familiar Reed themes, in a more consistent form than of late, with a decisive twist in the title track. . . .

Set free to find a new illusion, Reed opts for a new vulnerability. Here, you buy a series of conversations and anecdotes (personal and general), leavened by a certain humour and a brutal, Manhattan attitude. Often tasteless, more often razor-sharp, rarely dull, Reed has the knack of telling a story well and making the explicitly personal general. . . .

From all indications, however, Reed's personal inspiration is drying up on both lyrics and music; his choice of collaborators (always another talent), is impeccable. . . . The only cut that Reed writes all by himself, **"Looking For Love,"** is the weakest on the album. Throughout, there are few audible memorable lines; agreeable and witty, yes, but a disappointment from one of the most quotable, epigrammatic writers in the idiom.

There are successes: **"I Want To Boogie With You"** is a straight funk song, personal and real; **"Disco Mystic"** is amusing, moronic and stylish enough to be both highly commercial and parodic. . . . **"Families"** sets Reed back in the suburbs, feeling the gulf widen, wondering why he keeps returning home: personal-to-general, highly compassionate. The title track, superficially suffocating in its stagey, opaque mystery, at length emerges as a tour de force, [with its] . . . sustained, theatrical yet powerful sense of foreboding. . . .

Finally, there's a lack of especial silliness on **"The Bells"**; such silliness was, however, always one part of Reed's approach, complemented by astonishing perception and a kind of truth: from the numb unpleasantness of **"You're Dirt"** to the pathos and compassion of **"Street Hassle."** There are no such highs or lows here: **"The Bells"** is a more consistent work throughout, yet at present lacks anything so memorable or cutting as **"Street Hassle."** . . .

Take **"The Bells"** on its own terms. . . . The aim then, is to sell records; if you can make something stick at the same time, all well and good.

"The Bells" is expected to be very successful on these terms. If well promoted, **"Disco Mystic"** has every chance of being a single hit, while the album contains enough stellar musicianship and "artistic progression" to satisfy the criterion of Commerciality With Honour.

You won't mind if I say that I find this ultimately depressing, will you? Will you?

> *Jon Savage, "A Ringing in Your Ears," in* Melody Maker *(© IPC Business Press Ltd.), May 5, 1979, p. 32.*

LESTER BANGS

Lou Reed is a prick and a jerkoff who regularly commits the ultimate sin of treating his audience with contempt. He's also a person with deep compassion for a great many other people about whom almost nobody else gives a shit. I won't say who they are, because I don't want to get schmaltzy, except to emphasize that there's always been more to this than drugs and fashionable kinks, and to point out that suffering, loneliness and psychic/spiritual exile are great levelers.

The Bells isn't merely Lou Reed's best solo LP, it's great art. Everybody made a fuss over *Street Hassle,* but too many reviewers overlooked the fact that it was basically a *sound* album. . . . Most of the songs were old, and not very good, with a lot of the same old cheap shots.

The first indication that we've got something very different here is the no-bullshit cover art; the second, a cursory listening to the lyrics. Immediately, one notes the absence of mirror shades, needles and S&M. Lou Reed is walking naked for once, in a way that invites comparison with people like Charles

Mingus, the Van Morrison of "T.B. Sheets" and *Astral Weeks,* and the Rolling Stones of *Exile on Main Street. The Bells* is by turns exhilarating . . . , almost unbearably poignant (all of the lyrics) and as vertiginous as a slow, dark whirlpool (the title opus). (pp. 93-4)

As for the lyrics—well, people tend to forget that in numbers like **"Candy Says," "Sunday Morning"** and **"Oh! Sweet Nothing,"** Lou Reed wrote some of the most compassionate songs ever recorded. Though Reed's given folks reason to forget, every lyric on *The Bells* offers cause for recollection. This album is about love and dread—and redemption through a strange commingling of the two. To have come close to spiritual or physical death is ample reason to testify, but it's love that brings both fathers and children, artist and audience, back from that cliff, and back from the gulf that can sometimes, in states of extreme pain, be mistaken for the blue empyrean ever. In **"Stupid Man,"** someone who's been self-exiled too long . . . rushes home to his family, desperate not to have lost the affection of his little daughter. Like all of Reed's people on this record, he's looking for love. A tune with that same title emphasizes how jet-set stars, hustlers and kept professionals (and middle-American boys and girls) may be united by a common longing. It's a nation of rock & roll hearts. **"City Lights"** . . . isn't only about Charlie Chaplin but about a lost America, the implication being that, in these late modern times, all the lights in the world might not be enough to bring us together.

On side two, everything coalesces in unmistakably personal terms. . . .

"Families" is most personal of all. A friend described this and certain other parts of *The Bells* as "the gay outsider's occasional yearning for the straight life and its conventions," but that's inaccurate. **"Perfect Day"** was Reed's maudlin streak, yet sexual preference really has nothing to do with the anguish behind [**"Families."**] . . . What Reed may not realize is that, through this very song, some reconciliation is effected, because he's fulfilled a promise that very few of us are ever able to keep by finally being able to forgive and love in spite of all the tragedies that go down in every family. . . .

With **"The Bells,"** more than in **"Street Hassle,"** perhaps even more than in his work with Velvet Underground, Lou Reed achieves his oft-stated ambition—to become a great writer, in the literary sense. More than that I cannot say, except: Lou, as you were courageous enough to be our mirror, so in turn we'll be your family. . . . You gave us reason to think there might still be meaning to be found in this world beyond all the nihilism, and thereby spawned and kept alive a whole generation whose original parents may or may not have been worthy of them. (p. 94)

> *Lester Bangs, "Lou Reed's Act of Love," in* Rolling Stone *(by Straight Arrow Publishers, Inc. © 1979; all rights reserved; reprinted by permission), Issue 293, June 14, 1979, pp. 93-4.*

ELLEN WILLIS

The Velvets were the first important rock-and-roll artists who had no real chance of attracting a mass audience. This was paradoxical. Rock and roll was a mass art, whose direct, immediate appeal to basic emotions subverted class and educational distinctions and whose formal canons all embodied the perception that mass art was not only possible but satisfying in new and liberating ways. Insofar as it incorporates the elite, formalist values of the avant garde, the very idea of rock-and-roll art rests on a contradiction. Its greatest exponents—the Beatles, the Stones, and (especially) the Who—undercut the contradiction by making the surface of their music deceptively casual, then demolished it by reaching millions of kids. But the Velvets' music was too overtly intellectual, stylized, and distanced to be commercial. Like pop art, which was very much a part of the Velvets' world, it was anti-art made by anti-elite elitists. Lou Reed's aesthete-punk persona, which had its obvious precedent in the avant-garde tradition of artist-as-criminal-as-outlaw, was also paradoxical in the context of rock and roll. The prototypical rock-and-roll punk was the (usually white) working-class kid hanging out on the corner with his (it was usually his) pals; by middle-class and/or adult standards he might be a fuckoff, a hell-raiser, even a delinquent, but he was not really sinister or criminal. Reed's punk was closer to that bohemian (and usually black) hero, the hipster: he wore shades, took hard drugs, engaged in various forms of polymorphous perversity; he didn't just hang out on the corner, he lived out on the street, and he was a loner.

As white exploitation of black music, rock and roll has always had its built-in ironies, and as the music went further from its origins the ironies got more acute. Where, say, Mick Jagger's irony was about a white middle-class English bohemian's (and later a rich rock star's) identification with and distance from his music's black American roots, his working-class image and his teenage audience, Lou Reed's irony made a further leap. It was not only about a white middle-class Jewish bohemian's identification with and distance from black hipsters (an ambiguity neatly defined when Reed-as-junkie, waiting for his man on a Harlem street corner, is challenged, "Hey white boy! Whatchou doin' uptown?") but about his use of a mass art form to express his aesthetic and social alienation from just about everyone. And one of the forms that alienation took pointed to yet another irony. While the original, primal impulse of rock and roll was to celebrate the body, which meant affirming sexual and material pleasure, Reed's temperament was not only cerebral but ascetic. There was nothing resembling lustiness in the Velvets' music, let alone any hippie notions about the joys of sexual liberation. Reed did not celebrate the sadomasochism of "Venus in Furs" any more than he celebrated heroin; he only acknowledged the attraction of what he saw as flowers of evil. . . . Like Andy Warhol and the other pop artists, he responded to the aesthetic potency of mass cultural styles; like Warhol, he was fascinated by decadence—that is, style without meaning or moral content; but he was unmoved by that aspect of the pop mentality, and of rock and roll, that got off on the American dream. In a sense, the self-conscious formalism of his music—the quality that made the Velvets uncommercial—was an attempt to purify rock and roll, to purge it of all those associations with material goodies and erotic good times.

Though it's probable that only the anything-goes atmosphere of the sixties could have inspired a group like the Velvets, their music was prophetic of a leaner, meaner time. . . . For all Lou Reed's admiration of Bob Dylan, he had none of Dylan's faith in the liberating possibilities of the edge—what he had taken from *Highway 61 Revisited* and *Blonde on Blonde* was the sound of the edge fraying. Like his punk inheritors he saw the world as a hostile place and did not expect it to change. In rejecting the optimistic consensus of the sixties, he prefigured the punks' attack on the smug consensus of the seventies; his thoroughgoing iconoclasm anticipated the punks' contempt

for all authority—including the aesthetic and moral authority of rock and roll itself. (p. 76)

In reducing rock and roll to its harshest essentials, the new wave took Lou Reed's aesthete-punk conceit to a place he never intended. For the Velvets the aesthete-punk stance was a way of surviving in a world that was out to kill you; the point was not to glorify the punk, or even to say fuck you to the world, but to be honest about the strategies people adopt in a desperate situation. The Velvets were not nihilists but moralists. In their universe nihilism regularly appears as a vivid but unholy temptation, love and its attendant vulnerability as scary and poignant imperatives. Though Lou Reed rejected optimism, he was enough of his time to crave transcendence. And finally—as **"Rock & Roll"** makes explicit—the Velvets' use of a mass art form was a metaphor for transcendence, for connection, for resistance to solipsism and despair. Which is also what it is for the punks; whether they admit it or not, that is what *their* irony is about. (pp. 77-8)

If the Velvets suggested continuity between art and violence, order and chaos, they posed a radical split between body and spirit. (p. 78)

[For] Reed awareness and the lack—or refusal—of it have an intrinsically moral dimension. While he is not averse to using the metaphors of illusion and enlightenment—sometimes to brilliant effect, as in **"Beginning to See the Light"** and **"I'll Be Your Mirror"**—they are less central to his theology than the concepts of sin and grace, damnation and salvation. Some of his songs (**"Heroin," "Jesus," "Pale Blue Eyes"**) explicitly invoke that Judeo-Christian language; many more imply it.

But "theology" too is an unfairly pretentious word. The Velvets do not deal in abstractions but in states of mind. Their songs are about the feelings the vocabulary of religion was invented to describe—profound and unspeakable feelings of despair, disgust, isolation, confusion, guilt, longing, relief, peace, clarity, freedom, love—and about the ways we (and they) habitually bury those feelings, deny them, sentimentalize them, mock them, inspect them from a safe, sophisticated distance in order to get along in the hostile, corrupt world. For the Velvets the roots of sin are in this ingrained resistance to facing our deepest, most painful, and most sacred emotions; the essence of grace is the comprehension that our sophistication is a sham, that our deepest, most painful, most sacred desire is to recover a childlike innocence we have never, in our heart of hearts, really lost. And the essence of love is sharing that redemptive truth. . . . (p. 79)

For a sophisticated rock-and-roll band with a sophisticated audience, this vision is, to say the least, risky. The idea of childlike innocence is such an invitation to bathos that making it credible seems scarcely less difficult than getting the camel of the gospels through the needle's eye. And the Velvets' alienation is also problematic: it's one thing for working-class English kids to decide life is shit, but how bad can things be for Lou Reed? Yet the Velvets bring it off—make us believe/admit that the psychic wounds we inflict on each other are real and terrible, that to scoff at innocence is to indulge in a desperate lie—because they never succumb to self-pity. Life may be a brutal struggle, sin inevitable, innocence elusive and transient, grace a gift, not a reward . . . ; nevertheless we are responsible for who and what we become. Reed does not attempt to resolve this familiar spiritual paradox, nor does he regard it as unfair. His basic religious assumption (like [poet Charles] Baudelaire's) is that like it or not we inhabit a moral universe, that we have free will, that we must choose between good and evil, and that our choices matter absolutely; if we are rarely strong enough to make the right choices, if we can never count on the moments of illumination that make them possible, still it is spiritual death to give up the effort.

That the Velvets are hardly innocents, that they maintain their aesthetic and emotional distance even when describing—and evoking—utter spiritual nakedness, does not undercut what they are saying; if anything it does the opposite. The Velvets compel belief in part because, given its context, what they are saying is so bold: not only do they implicitly criticize their own aesthetic stance—they risk undermining it altogether, ending up with sincere but embarrassingly banal home truths. The risk is real because the Velvets do not use irony as a net, a way of evading responsibility by keeping everyone guessing about what they really mean. On the contrary, their irony functions as a metaphor for the spiritual paradox, affirming that the need to face one's nakedness and the impulse to cover it up are equally real, equally human. If the Velvets' distancing is self-protective (hence in their terms damning) it is also revelatory (hence redeeming); it makes clear that the feelings being protected are so unbearably intense that if not controlled and contained they would overwhelm both the Velvets and their audience. The Velvets' real song is how hard it is to admit, even to themselves.

That song in its many variations is the substance of *Velvet Underground*. This album can be conceived of—non-linearly; the cuts are not at all in the right order—as the aesthete-punk's *Pilgrim's Progress*, in four movements. (pp. 79-80)

"Sunday Morning," a song about vague and ominous anxiety, sums up the emotional tone of this movement: "Watch out, the world's behind you." **"Here She Comes Now"** and **"Femme Fatale,"** two songs about beautiful but unfeeling women (in the unlovable tradition of pop—not to mention religious—misogyny, Lou Reed's women are usually demonic or angelic icons, not people), sum up its philosophy: "Aah, it looks so good / Aah, but she's made out of wood." These songs underscore the point by juxtaposing simple, sweet, catchy melodies with bitter lyrics. . . . **"White Light/White Heat,"** a song about shooting speed, starts out by coming as close as any Velvets song does to expressing the euphoria of sheer physical energy; by the end of the trip the music has turned into bludgeoning, deadening noise, the words into a semi-articulate mumble. (p. 81)

"Heroin" is the Velvets' masterpiece—seven minutes of excruciating spiritual extremity. No work of art I know about has ever made the junkie's experience so powerful, so horrible, so appealing; listening to **"Heroin"** I feel simultaneously impelled to somehow save this man and to reach for the needle. The song is built around the tension between the rush and the nod—expressed musically by an accelerating beat giving way to slow, solemn chords that sound like a bell tolling; metaphorically by the addict's vision of smack as a path to transcendence and freedom, alternating with his stark recognition that what it really offers is the numbness of death, that his embrace of the drug . . . is a total, willful rejection of the corrupt world, other people, feeling. In the beginning he likens shooting up to a spiritual journey: he's gonna try for the Kingdom; when he's rushing on his run he feels like Jesus' son. At the end, with a blasphemous defiance that belies his words, he avows, "Thank your God that I'm not aware / And thank God that I just don't care!" The whole song seems to rush outward and then close in on itself, on the moment of truth

when the junkie knowingly and deliberately chooses death over life—chooses damnation. It is the clarity of his consciousness that gives the sin its enormity. Yet that clarity also offers a glimmer of redemption. In the very act of choosing numbness the singer admits the depths of his pain and bitterness, his longing for something better; he is aware of every nuance of his rejection of awareness; he sings a magnificently heartfelt song about how he doesn't care. . . . Reed ends each verse with the refrain, "And I guess that I just don't know." His fate is not settled yet. (pp. 81-2)

"Beginning to See the Light" is the mirror held up to **"Heroin."** . . . In **"Beginning to See the Light,"** enlightenment (or salvation) is getting out from under the burden of self-seriousness, of egotism, of imagining that one's sufferings fill the universe; childlike innocence means being able to play. There is no lovelier moment in rock and roll than when Lou Reed laughs and sings, with amazement, joy, gratitude, "I just wanta tell you, *everything* is all right!"

But **"Beginning to See the Light"** is also wickedly ironic. Toward the end, carried away by euphoria, Reed cries, "There are problems in these times / But ooh, none of them are mine!" Suddenly we are through the mirror, back to the manifesto of **"Heroin":** "I just don't care!" Enlightenment has begotten spiritual pride, a sin that like its inverted form, nihilism, cuts the sinner off from the rest of the human race. Especially from those people who, you know, work very hard but never get it right. Finally we are left with yet another version of the spiritual paradox: to experience grace is to be conscious of it; to be conscious of it is to lose it.

Like all geniuses, Lou Reed is unpredictable. In **"Street Hassle"** he does as good a job as anyone of showing what was always missing in his and the Velvets' vision. As the song begins, a woman (or transvestite?) in a bar is buying a night with a sexy young boy. This sort of encounter is supposed to be squalid; it turns out to be transcendent. Reed's account of the odd couple's lovemaking is as tender as it is erotic: "And then sha la la la la he entered her slowly and showed her where he was coming from / And then sha la la la la he made love to her gently, it was like she'd never ever come." Of course, in part two he almost takes it all back by linking sex with death. Still.

What it comes down to for me—as a Velvets fan, a lover of rock and roll, a New Yorker, an aesthete, a punk, a sinner, a sometime seeker of enlightenment (and love) (and sex)—is this: I believe that we are all, openly or secretly, struggling against one or another kind of nihilism. I believe that body and spirit are not really separate, though it often seems that way. I believe that redemption is never impossible and always equivocal. But I guess that I just don't know. (pp. 82-3)

Ellen Willis, "Velvet Underground," in Stranded: Rock and Roll for a Desert Island, *edited by Greil Marcus (copyright © 1979 by Alfred A. Knopf, Inc.; reprinted by permission of Alfred A. Knopf, Inc.),* Knopf, 1979, pp. 72-83.

DON SHEWEY

Lou Reed is the master of halfisms. The songs on **"Growing Up in Public"** are half-joking, half-serious, half-spoken, half-sung, half-finished, and half-raw, but somehow he ties it all together to give the album a tone of both self-mockery and personal bravery. . . .

The punk and the comic intertwine on **"Growing Up in Public."** In one case, he describes "a weak simpering father" who is cruel to "a harridan mother," who in turn counsels her children against smiling. In another he naively reflects on heterosexual love. It's unclear just how much of this is autobiographical—though Reed, polymorphously perverse and proud of it, was recently married. Nonetheless, songs such as *How Do You Speak to An Angel, My Old Man,* and *Smiles* have the endearing awkwardness of public confession.

There are plenty of flaws to the record. . . . But when all his best attributes line up in the same groove—as on *So Alone,* an emotional roller-coaster ride in which he attempts to console a woman jilted by another man—**"Growing Up in Public"** becomes as powerful and as personal as a rock record can be.

Don Shewey, "Records: 'Growing Up in Public'," in High Fidelity (copyright © by ABC Leisure Magazine, Inc.; all rights reserved; excerpted by permission), Vol. 30, No. 7, July, 1980, p. 97.

SCOTT ISLER

The Lou Reed dialectic continues. In the past, this artist's work has zigzagged between extremes of light and darkness with pendular regularity. The felicitously titled *Growing Up in Public* at first seems to have dug out of the emotional depths plumbed by *Street Hassle* (and, to a lesser extent, *The Bells*). . . . *Public*'s material is medium-to-up-tempo songs, thoroughly composed from start to finish. The lyrics are the thing here, emphasized by being printed on the inner sleeve—a rare departure from the Reedian norm.

Those lyrics give the lie to the album's boppy music. . . . It would be too ingenuous to take the words at face value—this is a Lou Reed album, remember—but the temptation sure is strong. Reed casually tosses around the first person singular . . . , and refers to parents on four of the album's 11 cuts. **"Families"** (on *The Bells*) was merely an appetizer in this respect; Reed's house is rocking with domestic problems. **"My Old Man"** is a sordid confessional about outgrowing blind father-worship . . . , **"Standing on Ceremony"** presents familial relationships from that father's viewpoint. . . .

In contrast, *Growing Up in Public*'s other major theme is romance. Again, Reed's own recent marriage encourages a personal reading. . . . The album even follows a loose structure: boy meets girl (**"How Do You Speak to an Angel"**), confesses his past (**"My Old Man"**), ends his current relationship (**"Keep Away"**), scores (**"So Alone"**), pops the question (**"Think It Over"**). The viewpoint is unabashedly heterosexual; one wonders if the closing track, **"Teach the Gifted Children,"** refers to the union's inevitable progeny. (pp. 30-1)

It's hard to recall when Reed has been this—*likable* (there, it's said). *Growing Up in Public* bubbles over with words like an amiable drunk (which persona Reed assumes on **"The Power of Positive Drinking"**). He writes sensitively (**"Think It Over"**), frankly (**"Smiles"**—an attack on insincerity—and the family songs), and on **"So Alone"** dissects the pick-up game like a leather-jacketed Woody Allen. The imbalance of perfunctory music to literary brilliance alone keeps this album out of the highest echelon of Lou Reed LPs. Perhaps Reed should go back to writing his own tunes, not that he isn't free from an occasional mixed metaphor or archaism himself. (p. 31)

Scott Isler, "Album Reviews: 'Growing Up in Public'," in Trouser Press (copyright © by Trans-Oceanic

Trouser Press, Inc.), Vol. 7, No. 6, July, 1980, pp. 30-1.

MIKAL GILMORE

With *The Bells,* Lou Reed fulfilled—maybe even laid to rest—a longstanding ethos: one of grim choices and unsparing accountability. A song like **"Families"** sounded as if it used up the whole of Reed's emotional being. It didn't seem possible that either his art or his life could ever be the same again. They can't. *Growing Up in Public* tells us why, and then tells us something more. . . .

Growing Up in Public is an album about summoning high-test courage: the courage to love, and along with it, the will to forgive everybody who—and everything that—ever cut short your chances in the first place. As Reed himself has noted, there's always been a powerful personal quality to his work that, on the one hand, implied an "agreement of mores" between the artist and his audience, while, on the other, suggested that the singer and the first-person characters in his songs were more than likely identical. This led certain listeners—especially those reared on **"Heroin"** or *Berlin* (the latter an embittered dramatization of Reed's brief first marriage)—to applaud Lou Reed as a jaded proponent of decadence and nihilism. Conversely, most critics championed him as a compassionate commentator on sin and salvation in an urban mythos.

On *Growing Up in Public,* Lou Reed's material bridges the difficult chasm between moral narrative and unadulterated autobiography. In part, the new compositions are about Reed's decision to marry again—a decision that flabbergasted many of the people who'd pegged him as a middle-aged, intractable gay—but they're also seared recollections of the prime forces that shaped and almost fated him. . . .

Much of this record is like the family scrapbook that nobody wants to share with polite company: sharp recountings of the ways in which parents thrust their disillusions upon their children. . . .

He shatters the claustrophobic web of hatred and self-defeat—easily the most frightening he's ever constructed, because it's also the most universal—by choosing to run the same risk at which his parents failed: the risk of the heart. . . .

[The words of **"Think It Over"**] might be the bravest lines Reed has ever sung. Why? Because the faith they advertise runs against the grain of his past and maybe his chances. More important, because he's placed his faith in somebody else's heart—and that's never a small risk. They're also brave because they could anger a cultist crowd that prefers Lou Reed as some sort of pariah-poet of bleakness. It was Reed, after all, who helped spawn a burgeoning rock & roll movement that feels more at home singing songs of alienation, hostility and nothingness than of romance, marriage or even sex.

But Lou Reed has never advocated despair. He called it *choice,* even when it entailed self-negation. His choice now is to believe in the indispensability of love. Reed's love is like the love that Pete Townshend sings about on his into-the-fray solo disc, *Empty Glass:* unflinching and lucidly compassionate—love in spite of dread. In other words, even if the world is imploding and love can't save it, come out for love anyway. It's the ultimate act of defiance. . . .

[On **"Teach the Gifted Children"**] Reed doesn't offer the children blithe promises but realistic certainties and a prayer that the world might show them a little more mercy than it ever showed him. **"Teach the Gifted Children"** is a tune about redemption in the truest sense, since it reaches beyond a concern for one's own fate toward a concern for the whole of humanity. . . .

Reed's entire career—more accurately, his entire life—has been leading up to *Growing Up in Public.* It may or may not be his finest album, but it's surely his hardest-fought victory: a record of the long road back from *Berlin.* There were foreshadowings of it in last year's **"All through the Night"** ("With a daytime of sin and a nighttime of hell / Everybody's going to look for a bell to ring"). Now that Lou Reed has found his bell, it tolls for you and me, loud and clear, pealing a clarion call of hope that the glory of love—despite our daytimes of sin and nighttimes of hell—might see us all through yet. (p. 54)

> *Mikal Gilmore, "'Growing Up in Public'," in* Rolling Stone *(by Straight Arrow Publishers, Inc. © 1980; all rights reserved; reprinted by permission), Issue 321, July 10, 1980, pp. 53-4.*

JEFF NESIN

For more than three weeks I've struggled dutifully with this record. As with all of Lou Reed's music I was looking forward to it, but the longer it took me to reach an accommodation with *Growing Up In Public* the more disturbed and distracted I became. A dilemma: On the one horn Lou has only rarely wasted his time (or mine) over the last 15 years. On the other horn, taking Lou too seriously can lead to the dreaded [Lester] Bangs Syndrome, which turns normally clear headed critics desperately grim and feverishly apocalyptic, causing them to grapple to the finish with Lou in a two out of three fall steel cage feature. . . .

However, as much of the writing in our critical journals regularly indicates, one can do a lot worse than Bangs Syndrome, especially since Lou Reed is the smartest person regularly recording rock 'n' roll. Taking him as seriously as I dare, I have finally concluded that *Growing Up In Public* is a difficult and unsatisfying album for several related reasons. . . .

The music on *Growing Up* does not have palpable strength and character of its own, nor is it inextricably wedded to the content—it's often as clever as the lyrics, but it's rarely essential. . . . [The] songs, extremely—sometimes excruciatingly—personal, don't fall very far from the vest and the music is unable to enhance their universality and suggestibility as the best rock 'n' roll should. With the exception of a few codas where the spirit is finally unleashed (**"How Do You Speak To An Angel"**), the music is completely subordinate to the lyrical content—always an unproductive balance of rock 'n' roll trade. . . .

Lou's relentless investigation of psycho-sexual mores and behavior has turned inward with . . . decidedly mixed results. I have witnessed Lou Reed in many strange incarnations over the years, but never could I have imagined him as a prattling, self-absorbed Central Park West analysand. He's still as smart as ever, but that's colder than usual comfort in this context. Even more disturbing is that many of the songs sound oddly distanced and less moving than the more formally abstracted work (e.g. **"I Want To Boogie With You"** and **"Families"**) on last year's album. Perhaps all this marks significant psychoanalytic progress, but it sounds like a major rock 'n' roll setback to me. A track by track comparison with previous work

leaves little to get excited about. The problems I've enumerated are evident in different degrees in all the songs on the album—no song is utterly without redeeming virtue, but all of them could stand considerable work. As a follow up to *The Bells,* Reed's best recorded work since *Coney Island Baby, Growing Up in Public* is truly depressing, and I wish Lou would get off the couch and back into the streets.

> *Jeff Nesin, "Records: 'Growing Up in Public'," in* Creem *(© copyright 1980 by Creem Magazine, Inc.), Vol. 12, No. 3, August, 1980, p. 55.*

ROY TRAKIN

[The Velvet Underground] made four harrowing albums that exposed the seamy underbelly of the late '60s counterculture's acid-soaked dreams of peace and love. Songs like *Heroin, Venus in Furs, Femme Fatale, I'm Waiting for the Man* and *White Light/White Heat,* all of which left little to the imagination in their lurid detail, but still managed to seek redemption for man even in his squalor and pain. . . .

Rock 'n' Roll Diary takes you from *Waiting for the Man* through *Street Hassle,* with a healthy mixture of tunes from each of Reed's many stylistic periods. If you don't have any of this (some quite rare) stuff, by all means, go out and turn on to one of the most literate songwriters in rock, a middle-class Jewish boy . . . whose neuroses and hang-ups mirrored his generation's now seemingly aimless search for values.

Still this otherwise honorable project warrants a few complaints. . . . [There] is a not-surprising bias toward Lou's Arista period, reflected in the unfortunate inclusion of three tracks from last year's *Growing Up In Public,* not one of Reed's strongest works. Still, all in all, this is a long-overdue retrospective for the hard-edged NYC street poet who never feared letting it all hang out in public, often with a uniquely touching vulnerability.

> *Roy Trakin, "Record Reviews: 'Rock 'n' Roll Diary'," in* Hit Parader *(© copyright 1981 Charlton Publications, Inc.), Vol. 40, No. 202, June, 1981, p. 23.*

ROBERT A. HULL

The history of the Velvet Underground is so incidental that it almost doesn't matter. That is the first clue to the band's immortality, the very idea that their story is so offhand that it cannot eclipse the total impact of their music. The second clue is this: the very inadvertency of their actions is the best definition of the band's meaning. It's as if the Velvets' lack of foresight had, in some way, to be compensated for by an abundance of critical hindsight.

There is no tribute to the Velvet Underground that hasn't already been written, no praise that has not already been sung. Yet, as with the Beatles and Elvis Presley, the Velvets approach so close to the borders of myth that their story remains amorphous, adrift on the time of retelling. To write about the Velvets is to discover the frustration of [Jorge Luis] Borges' *Book of Sand,* a nightmarish text that never ends.

Many feel that the Velvets introduced (to steal the band's phrase) a New Age to rock and that with them modern rock truly began. . . . However, the real gift of the Velvets was out-and-out cultism, the beginning of an era when private obsession and solipsism would be the rule of thumb. . . .

Even if their history seems accidental, the Velvets did intentionally cater to the idea of becoming a curio of cultism (why else name a rock group after an obscure paperback about sexual depravity?), and as a result, they became the first example of a seminal cult band in rock history. The question is not why the Velvet Underground remained a cult band during their brief existence (1965-1970)—that was obviously what they wanted and perhaps secretly what their fans wanted, too; the question is, what essentially prevented the Velvets from becoming just another case of terminal rock cultism . . .? (p. 22)

By and large, the Velvets belonged to the garage band tradition. (p. 23)

But the Velvets were not merely an artistic version of the Seeds or the Sonics, for the band refused to be confined by the restrictions of a genre, the necessary transcendence that separates the immortals from the morons. If they were an extension of garage music, they were also an antidote to punk's by-product, psychedelia. While truth was being sought through love, peace, and flowers . . . , the Velvets were finding harder truths by not even seeking them—through images of death, the sounds of the city, and flowers of evil.

The Velvets' first album seemed almost designed for the Museum of Modern Art. There were Andy's peelable banana, critical accolades where liner notes should have been, and color photos of the Exploding Plastic Inevitable light show exploding cartoonishly all over the band. Judging by its surface, the work appears garish and pretentious, a mere period piece.

Warhol envisioned the Velvets as something more than that, of course. He picked them up off the street, so to speak, and planted them as a prop beside his films. Around that idea evolved the concept of mixed media—slides, amoebaeic lighting, strobes, and dancing whips competing in a chichi arena that predated other multimedia events. This was all pure form, somehow cold and deliberate like Warhol's art.

To many, the addition of the German chanteuse Nico was the final proof that the Velvets were simply Warhol's band—distanced, humorless, and removed from the land of the living. (p. 25)

Nico is the key to understanding why the Velvets remained obscure and misinterpreted. She was an integral part of Warhol's scheme, an actress in his films and a glamourous graduate from *La Dolce Vita.* But in the Velvets, she was an outcast among outcasts. . . . The split between Nico and the Velvets was assuredly mutual but at some cost. For as long as Nico was around, the Velvets were easily identifiable, even marketable. They were still involved in a scene, Warhol's camp. Yet without her, there was no point of reference.

But there never really was a point of reference. It is time that the word so frequently bandied about in discussions of the Velvets—*decadence*—finally be put to rest. The Velvet Underground was a band of contradictions and juxtapositions. They have been labeled both "folk-rock" and "art-rock," but they were neither—their music cannot be hyphenated. The Velvets embodied both Lou Reed's street-sense and John Cale's classical background; as a result, the band has come to represent dualism, dialogue, and the process of exchange. Their music deals with body/soul, heart/mind, white blank hate/dark religious compassion. In practically every song, the Velvets alternate between concealment and revelation, as it is to say that their choice is not to choose. . . .

The final irony is that the Velvets created more art in less than five years than Andy Warhol, the man who stamped his approval on their beginnings, has accomplished in a lifetime. To call that art decadent is to demean its impact. . . .

The rhythms were repetitive. . . . [Their] "implied" beat was the Velvets' secret invocation: it suggested ancient rituals, sanctification, religious passion at its most febrile. It is what would become regarded as the band's trademark—the perpetual drone. . . . And after you've heard it enough . . . you become sentient to the idea that the Velvets, contrary to popular wisdom, were not bent upon self-destruction or devoted to the brutal and the ugly but were, in fact, obsessed with mysticism and the deeper concerns of the heart. Their drone is mantra; their implied beat, the unknown god they're trying to reach.

It's not hard to see the Velvets, then, as a religious band in search of a moral center. Considered under the light of this holy glow, their music seems more focused than confused. Their third album (*The Velvet Underground*), for example, is often viewed as an anomaly, a fading whisper, a blink amidst the band's harrowed chaos. But "Candy Says," "Some Kinda Love," "Pale Blue Eyes," "I'm Set Free," and "Jesus" are nothing less than spiritual illuminations; they are the epiphanies of the soul toward which the Velvets had been striving all along. From beneath the weight of shadows, these songs richly convey the romantic desire for transcendental experience on the profound levels of [Van Morrison's] *Astral Weeks* and [Bob Dylan's] *John Wesley Harding.* (p. 58)

From the perspective of the rock audience in the late 60's, however, the Velvets were about as close to the realm of religion as the antichrist. . . . This was the unfortunate misunderstanding, the reason the band was doomed to the clutches of cultists. For most people, the Velvet's world was only one of dark perversions, of utter despair, of drug paranoia, of black depravity . . . of total breakdown. These were the pathways to the band's music, and to follow them was to become a member of a scene. Yet the Velvets' music was never so much *about* a lifestyle as it was an evocation of it in sound. **"Heroin"** only works, within its seven minutes of spiritual torture, because the sound of the whole song becomes a metaphor for the drug rush. Through manifestation—through the transformation of a public scene—the Velvets could attain a certain distance from their environment, and thus obtain a sense of salvation. On **"Heroin,"** the singer can *claim* he feels like Jesus' son, but that would only seem artificial if the song itself did not sound like it was headed toward a blissful state of transcendence.

Unfortunately, the Velvets did not make their need for redemption apparent until nearly all the band's members had departed—by then, it was too late. The album, *Loaded,* was their last studio release; the song, **"Rock & Roll,"** going by its innumerable cover versions and the general attention it garnered, might just as well have been their first. In 1970, the world was suddenly ready for the Velvets' vision, but John Cale and Lou Reed had already called it quits. **"Rock & Roll"** was a felicitous summation of what the Velvets had always been saying, and it seemed to herald a second coming. A life saved by rock 'n' roll—it had been said before, of course, but never so concisely and never with so much eagerness and compassion. Even more surprising, on songs such as **"Sweet Jane," "Cool It Down,"** and **"Head Held High,"** the Velvets were claiming that life was blooming with affection and that all complications could eventually be surmounted. Many read this as a change within the Velvets, and so, embraced them wholeheartedly. The fact of the matter was that the band barely existed. . . . (pp. 58-9)

There's no irony, though, behind **"Rock & Roll"** being the Velvets' final yet most successful statement—it would appear that that was intentional (perhaps the band's most purposeful act). The Velvet Underground had unlimited opportunities to reveal their message of rock 'n' roll as salvation, and to have provided a conspicuous link with Little Richard and Jerry Lee Lewis would have been their saving grace, possibly negating their cult status. But the Velvets were fond of obfuscation—they saw it as a necessary part of their image, recognizing in it our desire for detection, our love of a good mystery. For them, therefore, revealing everything meant virtual suicide. **"Rock & Roll"** was Lou Reed's way of saying *not* that the Velvets' cover should be blown but there was no longer any point in maintaining that cover.

Hence, decoding the Velvets' music is a process not unlike reading runes—the band's cryptic code beckoning us like a good mystery novel. Significantly, the Velvets understood that, by cloaking their identity in mystery, a myth could be sustained. . . .

It is enough, the Velvets consistently suggest, to look, and though the clues may never fall into place, at least through observation some insight can be gained into the persistence of an eternal mystery. (p. 59)

THE CONSUMMATE CLUE. **"European Son"** is dedicated to Delmore Schwartz, an established poet and a mentor to Lou Reed when he was in school. Schwartz was also somewhat of an authority on T. S. Eliot, and this certainly must have influenced Reed's own thinking. Critic Richard Mortifoglio has pointed out that "Reed's unique combination of plain talk and elegant late-medieval imagery suggests T. S. Eliot as an influence." Mortifoglio argues that this fact proves there's a classical severity in Reed's makeup that should counteract the cries of decadence.

Further, Reed has expressed his astonishment that Eliot could write the brilliant, timeless "Love Song of J. Alfred Prufrock" at the vigorous age of 25. "That is not what I meant at all," says the voice of Eliot's poem again and again. We can hear that remorseful voice echoed in **"Heroin"** as Reed ends each verse with the still refrain, "And I guess that I just don't know."

We can also turn to the opening passage of Eliot's masterful poem and read: "Streets that follow like a tedious argument / Of insidious intent / To lead you to an overwhelming question . . . / Oh, do not ask, What is it?" What *is* the strange **"New Age"** really all about? What *is* the kind of compassion that **"Candy Says"** defines? What *is* the Velvets' essential quest? *Oh, do not ask, 'What is it?'*

And yet . . . over a decade after the Velvet Underground has ceased to exist, we are still searching through the ruins, tirelessly digging for a clue and settling instead for its shadow. (p. 60)

Robert A. Hull, "The Velvet Underground: White Light/Dark Shadows," in Creem *(© copyright 1981 by Creem Magazine, Inc.), Vol. 13, No. 2, July, 1981, pp. 22-3, 25, 58-60.*

Erich Maria Remarque

1898-1970

(Born Erich Paul Remark) German-born novelist, playwright, journalist, poet, and essayist.

Remarque is considered one of the most important war novelists in contemporary literature. At one time he wrote articles on sports, travel, and the "good life" for various magazines. Critics dismissed Remarque because of the frivolous nature of many of these pieces. He also wrote two early novels and a collection of poems and essays which were virtually ignored by critics and readers before the publication of his highly-acclaimed war novel *All Quiet on the Western Front*. In this novel and the ones that followed, however, Remarque seems to disregard technique in his concern with illustrating the physical and spiritual doom of the First World War generation in Germany. Remarque's strengths as a writer are cited as the simple, direct language of the war novels—in contrast to the often violent subject matter—and his ability to create moving, realistic characters and situations, but some critics feel that his writing occasionally suffers from an emphasis on content.

Remarque is best remembered for *All Quiet on the Western Front*. Although an introductory paragraph states that the novel is supposed to represent the feelings of a whole generation, it actually deals only with those soldiers who learn to hate the futility and destruction of war. Initially *All Quiet* was enthusiastically received by critics for its realistic presentation of the war and what it meant to the average soldier. Eventually, however, the book was attacked by certain political factions in Europe for its pacifist denunciation of the war. *All Quiet* was one of the books publicly burned by the Nazi regime in 1933. Generally, though, Remarque's illustration of the inhumanity of war through the words and reactions of a common foot soldier is highly praised.

Because of political conflicts, Remarque moved to Switzerland in 1938, renouncing his German citizenship, and later became an American citizen. He continued to write about the war, particularly its aftereffects, but none of his later books received the critical acclaim of *All Quiet*. *The Road Back*, a sequel to *All Quiet*, recounts the collapse of the German army and the efforts of returning soldiers to adjust to civilian life. *Arch of Triumph*, the story of World War II refugees struggling to survive in Paris, is generally viewed as Remarque's only important novel after *All Quiet*. *A Spark of Life*, set in a concentration camp, is noted for its grim, moving depiction of one man's attempt to measure the amount of pain one can tolerate.

Critics often deny that Remarque's works have literary merit, citing the author's uneven writing style and frequent use of sensationalism. Nevertheless, Remarque's novels are still extremely popular with readers. Most importantly, however, Remarque will be remembered as a humanitarian decrying the brutality of war. (See also *Contemporary Authors*, Vols. 77-80.)

RICHARD CHURCH

Surely everyone, again and again, has asked himself with misgiving and horror what is this conspiracy of silence maintained

Jerry Bauer

by the men who returned from the War? For it is true that, in spite of the many professional books written, no convincing revelation has been made of the heroism, the treachery, the foul intimacies, the brutality and coarseness, the gradual moral, social, and emotional decay, which made up, with a myriad other happier factors, the story of the soldier's life in the trenches. One timidly and somewhat shamefacedly asks questions of the individuals who were there, and the courteous and interested replies are always evasive and hopeless. It is as though the men despair of making one see the first elements of that world; as though they are trying to make one understand a race, a scenery, even a law of gravitation, peculiar to another planet, and so incapable of explanation in terrestrial terms to terrestrial senses.

One, therefore, comes upon [*All Quiet on the Western Front*], and trembles. This is no literary trope; it is true. I read a few pages, and stopped. I returned, read on for a little, found myself living at last in that world forbidden to the civilian, and again I had to stop, gropingly trying to orientate my mind, my nervous organism, to the overwhelming experience re-enacted by the genius of this German soldier. It is not an armchair experience, a vicarious life in the library. It is three-dimensional, nay, *four-dimensional* life, pulsing in one's arteries and loading one's brain with a weight of memories of things seen, heard, and suffered, so that one's life is no longer the same as it was; is older, more honest and disillusioned, stripped of false politeness and pruderies, and all the idle amenities of our normal social intercourse. (pp. 624-25)

[This novel makes] one realize that in four years of this hell which no nightmare could imitate, the culture and intricately beautiful civilization built up since the beginning of human history, was torn off by these men as a frivolous appendage, and trampled angrily into the crimson-streaked mud of the trenches. But you may ask, "What, then, held these people together: what was that which kept them sane, and prompted them to such magnificent endurance, and to such ferocity of effort when occasion demanded?" And the answer is simply "Comradeship." That is the soul of this book. It was the young soldier's one light. He had been too young to find anchorage in love, religion, or a profession. No memories of these things, no hope of return to them, were there to support him. Comradeship was his substitute for these forces, and by its strength he conquered death, and carried through to some sort of preservation. (p. 625)

> *Richard Church, "War," in* The Spectator *(© 1929 by* The Spectator; *reprinted by permission of* The Spectator), *No. 5260, April 20, 1929, pp. 624-25.*

FRANK ERNEST HILL

Erich Maria Remarque was a German soldier during the World War and has written a record of life in the trenches ["**All Quiet on the Western Front**"]. . . .

[As] the terse story marches forward we encounter the things that other war books have made known to us: the trench mud, the lice, the ineradicable rats, the tension, noise, fear, pain, hunger, horror. . . .

On this long pilgrimage, so often ghastly and ferocious, there is more than the routine of the trenches. . . . Perhaps most important there is the inner drama—the fever that rises and falls in the souls of the fighters as the war goes on. To this, indeed, the whole story is shaped—its sharply etched descriptions of suffering, endurance, grim humor and climactic event. . . .

"**All Quiet on the Western Front**" will give any sensitive reader a terrific impact. It is a book that strikes a succession of hard, inescapable blows. In this sense it is a work of art. For only because of its economy of design, its compactness of episode and its trenchancy of utterance has it managed to fuse the almost unmanageable minutiae of war material into a narrative that has the lean savagery of an Ibsen tragedy. It pays in loss of color and sense of greatness for this concentration of utterance, yet the price is perhaps not too big. . . .

One could quote much and poignantly from this record. There are the passages of vulgar humor, Germanic yet universal in character. . . .

Remarque says in a few sentences of foreword that he will "try to tell of a generation of men who, even though they have escaped its shells, were destroyed by war." This task is well performed. Never obtruding his feelings, he reveals them naturally and convincingly as they grow. . . .

> The generation that grew up before us, though it has passed these years with us here, already had a home and a calling, now it will return to

its old occupations, and the war will be forgotten—and the generation that has grown up after us will push us aside. We will be superfluous even to ourselves, we will grow older, a few will adapt themselves, some others will merely submit, and most of us will be bewildered—the years will pass by, and in the end we shall fall into ruin.

This philosophy, rounding out the compact record, is in its permeative quality German. So, perhaps, is the thorough devotion to duty which seems to leave the soldiers incurious as to their enemies, except in prison camps. Yet the book is surprisingly un-national; it might almost have been written by a Frenchman or an American, or an English common soldier of intelligence. . . . It remains a gaunt, dynamic thing, lacking, I feel, something important in literary texture, speaking with remarkable directness of life-in-death. (p. 2)

> *Frank Ernest Hill, "Destroyed by the War," in* New York Herald Tribune Books, *June 2, 1929, pp. 1-2.*

LOUIS KRONENBERGER

In ["**All Quiet on the Western Front**"] it is the war as, in all its physical horror, it passed before the eyes of a twenty-year-old German private, an intelligent but not unusual boy who, with no preparation, with no fixed principles, was sent away to fight. We are told in a foreword that it is not to be a confession, or an accusation, or an adventure he chronicles, but the tale of a "generation of men who, even though they may have escaped its shells, were destroyed by the war." They were destroyed because they were cut off from life before they had found a fixed scheme for living. . . .

[The] sense, less of being uprooted than of never possessing roots, is the governing motif of the book, the tragedy that Paul Bäumer and all his fellows instantly recognized and that has proved itself in the ten years since the war. Here are boys bewildered not only by war, but also by lacking standards to which they can revert in a psychological escape from war. . . .

One may see how badly the war upset these lives and yet realize that theirs was not the supreme torture. For this soldiery of whom Remarque, through Paul Bäumer, writes took the war more unflinchingly, more directly, in a certain sense more phlegmatically, than many other participants. Certainly they saw it in all its physical horror, and in "**All Quiet**" we have a picture of that physical horror unsurpassed for vividness, for reality, for convincingness, which lives and spreads and grows until every atom of us is at the Front, seeing, mingling, suffering. For us readers, indeed, the picture finally acquires a kind of fascination; it so rivets our senses that it no longer terrorizes our imaginations. Under such a spell we can take in everything and need run away, psychologically, from nothing.

It almost certainly had no such fascination for these soldiers; yet "**All Quiet**" remains, essentially, a document of men who—however else their lives were disrupted—could endure war simply as war. It is for that reason representative of the largest number of men who fought, an Everyman's pilgrimage through four years of fighting. For the same reason, it is about youngsters who were half-puzzled over what it all meant: who were not driven to mental torture because they could not endure what they knew or check their imaginations at what they saw. They sit around, half shrewd, half naïve, and speculate now and again. . . . But there is no sense of terrible knowledge, of moral responsibility. That is why, as pure revelation, **"All Quiet on the Western Front,"** though magnificent within its own limits, is yet definitely limited.

Louis Kronenberger, "War's Horror as a German Private Saw It," in The New York Times Book Review *(© 1929 by The New York Times Company; reprinted by permission), June 2, 1929, p. 5.*

JOSEPH WOOD KRUTCH

[In **"All Quiet on the Western Front"**] a German tells in three hundred simple and vivid pages that same "truth about the war" which his fellows on the other side have already told: War is an interminable, exhausting, and nightmarish business without alleviation or purpose. The soldier is prepared by the gratuitous brutality of the training camp for the necessary brutality of the trenches, and, once he has been launched in his trade, there is no variety except in the kinds of misery.

Remarque tells his plain tale with a sort of naivete which is the result, not of too little experience, but of too much. He has given up rhetoric because it is inadequate and given up analysis because he has gone through more than can ever be analyzed. He must be content to record with a simplicity which is terrible because it could never have been arrived at except through an experience so long as to make the unspeakable commonplace. . . .

"All Quiet on the Western Front" is the German equivalent of [Anders] Latzko, [Henri] Barbusse, and [John] Dos Passos. Inferior to none of the others in vividness or power it is, like them, not only impressive in itself but still more so when taken in conjunction with its fellows. Four men of different race, education, and temperament are thrown into the same great catastrophe. Each, victor and vanquished alike, returns to his own home and each reports, not only men and events, but moods and manners, so precisely similar that if a few words were obliterated it would be impossible to tell which was French and which was German, or Hungarian, or American. All agree in what they leave out—glory and patriotism; all agree in what they put in—suffering, and fear, and disgust. "Death is not an adventure to those who stand face to face with it," says Remarque, and each in his own way has said the same. Between them (and with the aid of numerous less-talented confreres) they have created a new image of war. In literature at least it can never be the same again. Brass-band versions of the old romanticism may serve the practical purposes of statesmen very well when the next occasion arises, but in art there is no pride, pomp, or circumstance left for Glorious War. Too many literate persons survived to tell their tale with a unanimity which leaves no room for doubt.

Joseph Wood Krutch, "Glorious War," in The Nation, *Vol. CXXIX, No. 3340, July 10, 1929, p. 43.*

THE NEW YORK TIMES BOOK REVIEW

The world has gained a great writer in Erich Maria Remarque. Of that there can be no longer any question. On the two themes which he has thus far chosen, Remarque has surpassed all his contemporaries. **"All Quiet on the Western Front"** justly won its place as the best picture of the common soldier in the war to be done in any language; now, in **"The Road Back,"** Remarque has given the most powerful handling it has had to the story of that soldier in the post-war years. **"The Road Back"** is a finer book than **"All Quiet,"** a book that drops like a plummet into the hearts of men. . . .

It is a finer book than **"All Quiet,"** first of all because it is a book with a wider vision, with a fuller range of life for its scope. And it is better written. It reveals Remarque as a craftsman of unquestionably first rank, a man who can bend language to his will. This is prose . . . which can be piercingly sweet or vibrantly dramatic, as the theme demands. Whether he writes of men or of inanimate nature, Remarque's touch is sensitive, firm and sure.

The form is again the loosely autobiographical one which was employed in **"All Quiet"**; the difficult readjustment to the world at home is seen through the eyes of a returned soldier. . . . The story opens on the eve of the armistice, in a temporary silence so strange, so unaccustomed, that Ernst and his comrades grow calm and "are almost glad to hear again the familiar, trusty noises of death." It ends on a note of peace and hope that the road back to life may be found. . . .

The period between had its terrors and disillusionment, its despair and its grasping at life no less sharp, no less keenly felt, than those of the war itself, and it is these which make the substance of **"The Road Back."** That for the youth of Germany these trials were heightened by poverty and disruption more acute than was suffered by any other nation, except Russia, does not destroy the universal basis on which this story rests. Just as in **"All Quiet,"** Remarque spoke for the youth of all the world, crushed beneath the heel of machine-made war, so in **"The Road Back"** he gives voice to the cry of youth the world over, returning and not finding what it had hoped to find. . . .

And for the sensitive youth like Ernst, thrown into the front line at the very moment when life was opening before him, yet still held its mysteries and its soft promises, there was the wrenching effort to recapture that bloom which the world once wore. . . .

Because Remarque's vision is clear and whole, he sees that for some of his comrades, less sensitive than he, the readjustment was not so difficult, just as others, without his resilience, are crushed in the effort to make it. His book, therefore, springing from the personal as every true book must, transcends it.

J. D. A., "Remarque's Farewell to Arms," in The New York Times Book Review *(© 1931 by The New York Times Company; reprinted by permission), May 10, 1931, p. 1.*

WILLIAM FAULKNER

There is a victory beyond defeat which the victorious know nothing of. A bourne, a shore of refuge beyond the lost battles, the bronze names and the lead tombs, guarded and indicated not by the triumphant and man-limbed goddess with palm and sword, but by some musing and motionless handmaiden of despair itself. . . .

It is the defeat which, serving him against his belief and his desire, turns him back upon that alone which can sustain him: his fellows, his racial homogeneity; himself; the earth, the implacable soil, monument and tomb of sweat.

This is beyond the talking, the hard words, the excuses and the reasons; beyond the despair. . . . Victory requires no explanation. It is in itself sufficient: the fine screen, the shield;

immediate and final: it will be contemplated only by history. While the whole contemporary world watches the defeat and the undefeated who, because of that fact, survived.

That's where the need to talk, to explain it, comes from. That's why [in *The Road Back*] Remarque puts into the mouths of characters speeches which they would have been incapable of making. It's not that the speeches were not true. If the characters had heard them spoken by another, they would have been the first to say, "That is so. This is what I think, what I would have said if I had just thought of it first." But they could not have said the speeches themselves. And this method is not justified, unless a man is writing propaganda. It is a writer's privilege to put into the mouths of his characters better speech than they would have been capable of, but only for the purpose of permitting and helping the character to justify himself or what he believes himself to be, taking down his spiritual pants. But when the character must express moral ideas applicable to a race, a situation, he is better kept in that untimed and unsexed background of the choruses of Greek senators.

But perhaps this is a minor point. Perhaps it is a racial fault of the author, as the outcome of the War was due in part to a German racial fault: a belief that a mathematical calculation would be superior to the despair of cornered rats. (p. 23)

[*The Road Back*] is a moving book. Because Remarque was moved by the writing of it. Granted that his intent is more than opportunism, it still remains to be seen if art can be made of authentic experience transferred to paper word for word, of a peculiar reaction to an actual condition, even though it be vicarious. . . . No matter how vivid it be, somewhere between the experience and the blank page and the pencil, it dies. Perhaps the words kill it.

Give Remarque the benefit of the doubt and call the book a reaction to despair. Victory has its despairs, too, since the victorious not only do not gain anything, but when the hurrah dies away at last, they do not even know what they were fighting for, what they hoped to gain, because what little percentage there was in the whole affair, the defeated got it. If Germany had been victorious, this book would not have been written. And if the United States had not got back its troops 50-percent intact, save for the casual cases of syphilis and high metropolitan life, it would not be bought (which I hope and trust that it will be) and read. (pp. 23-4)

[*The Road Back*] moves you, as watching a child making mud pies on the day of its mother's funeral moves you. Yet at the end there is still that sense of missing significance, the feeling that, like so much that emerges from a losing side in any contest, and particularly from Germany since 1918, it was created primarily for the Western trade, to sell among the heathen like colored glass. From beyond the sentimentality, the defeat and the talking, this fact at least has emerged: America has been conquered not by the German soldiers that died in French and Flemish trenches, but by the German soldiers that died in German books. (p. 24)

> *William Faulkner, "Beyond the Talking," in* The New Republic, *Vol. 67, No. 859, May 20, 1931, pp. 23-4.*

BERNARD DeVOTO

Remarque's range is limited, but within it he has no superior among living novelists. One skill he has conspicuously, an ability to make commonplaces evoke the profoundest emotion,

to focus immensities through the smallest and simplest details. . . . In "**Three Comrades**," his new novel about the Germany of 1928, a gang fight between two garage staffs over the possession of a wrecked automobile comes close to epitomizing ten years of human and social deterioration. When Lenz, one of the three comrades, is killed for no reason except the impulse of a storm-trooper, one of the "young bastards who were still in their cradles then," he is buried in his old uniform blouse with the blood-stains and shrapnel tears of an earlier wound. . . .

The shooting of Lenz is the only scene in which the theme of the disintegrating Germany is overt. Elsewhere it is neither phrased nor alluded to, but it is the ether in which all the events of the book, all the acts and feelings of the characters, necessarily and inexorably exist. (p. 3)

Remarque's method is simple and so stark that sometimes, especially in the last scenes, it suggests [Ernest] Hemingway; but the book moves on many more levels of meaning than ever got into a Hemingway novel. The last scenes, too, have a setting that recalls "The Magic Mountain," but are the very antithesis of [Thomas] Mann's metaphysical drama. Remarque is content to tell the immediate story of immediate individuals; he tells it with a compassion that brings the universe in their wake. He plumbs deep through a narrow aperture, sees far off by looking near at hand. "**Three Comrades**" is a memorable love story; it is also a memorable novel about the tortured spirit of man. It tells a story of four inconsiderable items in the back streets of Berlin, and how they lived from day to day in a small routine of hazard and panicky competition; so it contrives to tell, gravely and implacably, more about Germany in the vortex than has been told in any other novel. One reads it with an intensity so quiet that not till the end is it recognizable as desperation. This significance that comes upon you unaware, as a necessary consequence of an imaginary story of imagined lives which seem to be only themselves and to symbolize nothing more, is surely as fine a quality as fiction can have. "**Three Comrades**" is the art of fiction in its properest functioning, unmixed with anything extraneous, a novel to be remembered much longer than most, an achievement of the first order. (pp. 3-4)

> *Bernard DeVoto, "Germany in the Vortex," in* The Saturday Review of Literature *(copyright © 1937, copyright renewed © 1964, by Saturday Review; all rights reserved; reprinted by permission), Vol. XVI, No. 1, May 1, 1937, pp. 3-4.*

J. DONALD ADAMS

The qualities which distinguish Remarque as a writer are abundantly displayed in "**Three Comrades.**" Simplicity and strength, humor and tenderness, a poet's sensitive reactions both to the things that are tangible and to those that are not—all these have been united in his work from the beginning, but to them there is added now, I think, a growing power of characterization. The people of "**Three Comrades**" are more fully depicted than those of Remarque's two earlier books, and there is evident for the first time the power to build up the story of the unfolding of a human relationship—for "**Three Comrades**" has for its focus one of the most poignant love stories that have been told in our time.

The development of that story is definitely a new achievement for Remarque. Looking back on "**All Quiet**" and "**The Road Back**," it is the perfection of certain detached episodes that one best remembers; in **"Three Comrades"** the episodes are handled in as masterly a fashion, but there is a continuity that was lacking before, a progression in the tale that seemed essential to Remarque's full development as a novelist. . . .

[When] Pat Hollmann stepped into Robby's life the world slowly but perceptibly changed. They would not admit to themselves or to each other at first that it was so, but their steadily growing consciousness that this was not a casual relationship but the central fact in their lives, is what, in Remarque's delicate and sure delineation, gives the story of these two its quality and points the tragedy of its conclusion.

It is a story that brings inevitably to mind that of Lieutenant Henry and Catherine Barkley in Hemingway's "Farewell to Arms." **"Three Comrades"** ends with an identical scene, on an identical note, after Pat's death from tuberculosis in the sanatorium. It seems to me that Remarque's story is more than a little the better, good as Hemingway's is. And for the reason, I think, first of all, that the relationship in **"Three Comrades"** is more fully developed and the characters of Robby and Pat are more fully realized. And Remarque's is the greater compassion and the more completely stated understanding of love.

> J. Donald Adams, "Erich Remarque's New Novel: 'Three Comrades' Marks an Advance in His Creative Power," in The New York Times Book Review (© 1937 by The New York Times Company; reprinted by permission), May 2, 1937, p. 1.

GORONWY REES

Herr Remarque has the high merit of being very readable; yet [*Three Comrades*] is a failure. It has three themes, comradeship, love, and their contrast with the futility of life and the horror of the War that is over and yet continues; for Herr Remarque cannot forget the War. . . . [His] intense obsession with an important and universal subject gives Herr Remarque dignity, though the intellect will not accept his book; indeed, it is perhaps precisely the feeling that "the living seem more shadowy than they" which makes the ostensible subject of his book less real than the shadow which falls across it.

The girl herself is a shadow, an angel-shadow, the darling object of love, the subject of nothing; and comradeship here is inarticulate, and perhaps has to be so, for if Herr Remarque submitted it to the same bitter examination as life in general, it might not maintain its high place in his esteem. To these criticisms must be added that the novel suffers from what is perhaps a purely technical defect. It is narrated in the first person by Lohkampf; but Herr Remarque destroys the unity of effect which such a method might give by allowing the narrator soliloquies, outbursts, expostulations in which his character is not his but his author's; and this brutality and arbitrariness to his own creation antagonises the reader.

All this is unfortunate, because Herr Remarque by his experience is well fitted to be a chronicler of the times; and at moments he is a vivacious and sharp observer. But throughout a note of falseness breaks in, disturbing and difficult to identify although unmistakable. If one were asked the root of it, one might perhaps say that it grew out of an unfounded spirituality, which wholly abstracts certain elements, love and friendship, from the dirt of human life, and finds compensation for truths felt to be unbearable by concentrating on these abstractions an overwhelming sweetness; and by the trick, oddly like Hemingway's, of making his characters inarticulate, except when he takes their place, Herr Remarque tries to protect them from

too prying a scrutiny. This does not prevent him from assuring us that what they feel is of the highest quality, the more so for being invisible; this quality is indeed demonstrated in actions shining like good deeds in a naughty world, but the trouble is that the actions do not belong to the characters but are Herr Remarque's demonstrations. Herr Remarque has two admirable qualities, moral disgust and a lively sense of fiction; but they never coalesce into the integrity of an artist.

> Goronwy Rees, "The Shadow of a War," in The Spectator (© 1937 by The Spectator; reprinted by permission of The Spectator), Vol. 158, No. 5681, May 14, 1937, p. 916.

BEN RAY REDMAN

Remarque's subject [in **"Flotsam"**] is profoundly important and alive with tragedy: the fate of the exiles, the refugees, the many thousands who have been made homeless in recent years because of race or political sentiments. It is from Hitler's Germany that most of these unfortunates have been uprooted, and it is with Hitler's victims that **"Flotsam"** is chiefly concerned. . . .

Remarque has fully depicted or briefly illuminated almost every aspect of the exile's life, with the very different responses of very different characters to a common fate. He has painted an animated, changing gallery of haunting portraits. The episodes that he has selected for the elaboration of his theme range from the horrible, through the monotonous, to the ludicrous; and he makes every one of them, of whatever kind, effective. He has been content to let his story speak for itself—or, rather, his many stories: there is no personal intrusion of an author moved to fury by his outrageous subject. Fury is there, but it burns beneath the surface. Shall we say, as a novelist's fuel?

That Remarque is a skillful and powerful writer has been demonstrated often, and in **"Flotsam"** it is demonstrated again. Yet one reviewer cannot escape the conclusion that the parts of **"Flotsam,"** or some of them, are greater than the whole. The entire novel is less affecting than, for example, the single scene in which Steiner bids farewell to his wife after his escape from the concentration camp—yet the scene requires only four pages. The reason is that the novel does not build, does not gather power as it goes forward. It moves without rising. Each episode is effective, but the effectiveness is not cumulative. Remarque has, I think, created a fictional pattern that exhibits more artifice than art, and owes much to cinematic technique. Time and again he lights the path of Kern and Ruth with hope only to thrust them back, time and again, into the darkness. Repetition, approaching monotony, dulls the reader's sensitivity, diminishes the intensity of his response on successive occasions. There can be no quarrel with the happy ending that is finally provided for the young couple, for life itself often provides happy endings. And Steiner's end is as fine and moving as it is inevitable. But one may suggest that the love story which figures so largely in **"Flotsam"** would have been more convincing and more stirring if all fleshly elements had not been so zealously excluded from its telling. I admit to having had a sensation of bafflement, feeling that the Kern-Ruth story was being only half told.

However, all this adds up only to the judgment that **"Flotsam,"** as a whole, is not as great as its theme; and when one considers the greatness of the theme one need not wonder at any novelist's failing to realize its possibilities fully. Remarque's comparative success compels admiration.

Ben Ray Redman, "The Breaking of Men," in The Saturday Review of Literature, *Vol. XXIV, No. 1, April 26, 1941, p. 5.*

WILLIAM K. PFEILER

Neither in length, scope, nor importance can the work of Erich Maria Remarque, whose novel, *Im Westen nichts Neues* [*All Quiet on the Western Front*] (1928), became a world sensation, be compared to the epic achievement of [Arnold] Zweig. Its success will perhaps never be satisfactorily explained, but one fact seems certain: it cannot be due exclusively to extraordinary merit.

Remarque is an artist. By his impressionistic talent he knows how to draw characters and situations that engage attention and arouse deepest sympathy. His language is versatile and concise; his narrative is rich in contrast of situations and reflections, and his composition is done with a brilliant stage technique. Lyric and idyllic scenes alternate with the most lurid and coarsest sort of realism. The intricate problems of life and of the War are cleverly reduced to such plain propositions that even the poorest in spirit can grasp them. (p. 141)

But what are the facts and ideas of this book which claimed to tell of the fate of a whole generation?

A number of adolescents, college students, have been induced by their teacher to volunteer for war service. They and a few older men form a group somewhere at the Western Front. Their fate is the subject of the story, which was to be "neither an accusation nor a confession" but an attempt to give a report of "a generation that was destroyed by war, even though it might have escaped its shells." These pretensions of the author must be refuted. Ample evidence shows that the heroes of Remarque are not representative of a whole generation, but only of a certain type. This is not to criticize Remarque for military and other inconsistencies, but it is significant that in a book which claims to be a report of the front by a front soldier, of 288 pages of text only about 80 pages deal with situations at or right behind the front, and even they are heavily interspersed with reflections. Furthermore, it may be characteristic that the actual life at the front is described in general terms without ever a definite location given, while scenes behind the front, at hospitals, at home, in the barracks, etc., are given in a more clearly outlined realism. The implication is obvious; it leaves little doubt that many of his situations are fictitious.

What is more, the ethical character of the book provokes critical reflection. Through sordid detail and the description of gruesome and inhuman happenings, through reflection and innuendo, the condemnation of war amounts in the last analysis to a sweeping indictment of the older generation. It is as simple as that, and it would not evoke any criticism on our part, the guilt of the elders being a genuine problem, were it not for the superficial way in which Remarque goes about his task. Their teachers get the blame for the boys' being in a war which is of use "only to the Kaiser and the generals." With adolescent swagger, they call all culture "nonsense" [*Quatsch*] because they have to be out at the front, and when they have a chance they will pay their torturers back. . . . [In one scene,] Lieutenant Mittelstedt "gets even" with his former teacher, now a drafted private. This particular scene . . . , told with the malicious glee of an adolescent, is typical of the immature and sophomoric attitude of the heroes. So is the ever-recurring swagger and boastfulness of the young men who pose as old

warriors well versed in all the tricks of warfare, though there is not one description of a feat actually executed, such as we find so abundantly and realistically in many other war books.

Individual incidents are given typical significance, less by an abstract process than by the exclusiveness with which they are presented. Thus the reader gets the impression that all officers are brutes; all teachers are cowardly shirkers who let others do the bloody and dangerous job of fighting for Germany's glory while they stay safely at home; and all doctors are inhuman monsters. Against this world of brutality are set off in shining lights the simple but genuine virtues of the common soldiers. They are all good fellows, and it arouses our sympathy to see them fall prey to power-drunk, sadistic superiors.

Immaturity and partiality by omission detract from the ethical import of this work which must be admitted to have force and human appeal. That the writer projects his 1927 mentality into the life of young World War soldiers is perhaps not so great a defect as is his wilfully narrowed outlook. *Im Westen nichts Neues* is scarcely a serious ethical document. Rather it is symptomatic of an age that saw the final revelation of the war in the adolescent self-pity, resentment, and sentimentality the novel embodies. Really it is the story of an egocentric, immature youngster of whom one may well wonder how he would have developed without the war. There is, indeed, plenty of authority for holding that the war helped many to find themselves and prove their mettle, and that it also exposed the brittle human substance that might have been broken by life anyway, without ever having been exposed to the destructive shells of war. It goes without saying that this observation—contradicting point-blank Remarque's claim to speak for a whole generation—implies neither that the war did not destroy the best of human values, nor that war was justifiable because it developed character. (pp. 141-44)

William K. Pfeiler, "Remarque and Other Men of Feeling," in his War and the German Mind: The Testimony of Men of Fiction Who Fought at the Front, *Columbia University Press, 1941, pp. 140-52.**

ROBERT PICK

In our own time there have been few, if any, parallels to the instantaneous success of **"All Quiet on the Western Front"**— and as the author of that novel, Remarque has ever since 1929 enjoyed international fame. It was not easy to place him as a literary figure, or even to balance the literary merits of his triumphant first novel against the courage of its humanitarian appeal. Remarque's art had not broadened in his later efforts; the book preceding ["Arch of Triumph"] came close to being a failure. It is gratifying now to receive from his pen a volume—his fifth—which possesses many of the characteristics of a great novel. At any rate, it is one of those rare books which, fated for bestsellerdom, will at the same time interest, move, and satisfy the serious, adult reader. . . .

"Arch of Triumph" is above all the story of a great love. There have been pathetically few distinguished love stories these past years. This one, moreover, is free from any pseudopsychological theorizing. Sex is the natural basis, not the goal, of Ravic's and Joan's relationship. Many a subject is touched on in their long (perhaps overlong but never verbose) dialogues, but whatever they are talking about, they talk love. . . .

There is an occasionally bewildering wealth of episodes throughout this book. Most of them are astonishingly full-blooded. Madame Rolande, for instance, the petty bourgeois overseer of the brothel, seems to come directly out of a [Guy de] Maupassant story.

The author even tries his hand at a colorful picture of society life in the mid-summer Paris of '39. Perhaps "Paris on the brink of catastrophè" has been the subject, or background, of too many recent novels, which may be the reason why Remarque's otherwise so richly rewarding book is less impressive as a historical study.

To be sure, some of his figures—such as the disillusioned American heiress married to a titled good-for-nothing, or the Czarist ex-colonel and present nightclub doorman—have had their predecessors; and when all is said, Joan Madou is but another *femme fatale*, although less demonic and much more winning than any of her nineteenth-century sisters. But Ravic is a masterpiece of original characterization. He is the twentieth-century man who survives.

> Robert Pick, "Prelude to Disaster," in The Saturday Review of Literature *(copyright © 1946, copyright renewed © 1973, by* Saturday Review; *all rights reserved; reprinted by permission), Vol. XXIX, No. 3, January 19, 1946, p. 7.*

CHARLES POORE

["**Arch of Triumph**"] is a novel of Europeans between wars yet forced to be perpetually at war, a novel that is animated by a spirit of savage disillusionment toward this last war before it had even begun, foreseeing the war's caprices and disasters.

"**Arch of Triumph**" is a part of Erich Maria Remarque's somber, stylized panorama of modern Europe's broken and dispossessed, begun in "**All Quiet on the Western Front**," continued in "**The Road Back**," "**Three Comrades**" and "**Flotsam**," and now given a classic setting and told in the classic way, a story of exiles in a land of exiles. It makes absorbing reading, though it is sometimes overcontrived; it is briskly paced, though the lacquered writing lacks the simple spontaneity of "**All Quiet on the Western Front.**" And through its penetrating stories of human fortitude it should stir even those of us who have been telling ourselves that the people who helped us win our common victory are not really as badly off as some would say. . . .

What Remarque has to tell us is often unbearably true; the way he chooses to tell us is often unnecessarily theatrical. The taut lines of puppet strings guide Ravic, the brilliant, sardonic hero of the story. . . .

It may be that only by theatrical situations can we be stirred through the layers of protective complacencies we have built up. . . . [Some scenes] could be less theatrical, with advantages in credibility. But they are skillfully done, though Ravic himself sometimes notes that a scene is "like a melodramatic movie." Even then, the scene is saved by such a detail as an actor carefully dusting his knees after he has knelt before a woman he has just fatally shot. (p. 1)

No one since Eliot Paul has rendered the look and smell and substance of Paris more devotedly than Remarque, and probably no one at all has ever written so much about the Arch of Triumph in all seasons. The bistros and the boulevards are here, the quays and bridges, the endless courtyard of the Louvre, the Luxembourg gardens and the strange, small hotels, the parks and fountains and churches and cemeteries, the taxis and the light. The chicanery and skulduggery that go on in Paris are probably not too different, in the aggregate, from the chicanery and skulduggery that go on in any other city its size, but somehow authors take a special pleasure in searching out things like that in Paris and Remarque conscientiously follows that rule. (pp. 1, 22)

> Charles Poore, "Blackout before the Deluge: A Novel of Munich-Haunted Paris—'A Time between Two Catastrophes'," in The New York Times Book Review *(© 1946 by The New York Times Company; reprinted by permission), January 20, 1946, pp. 1, 22.*

ORVILLE PRESCOTT

Mr. Remarque in all his works has shown his fierce concern with the major issues of our time, war and collapsing social structures and the tragedy of exile. *Arch of Triumph* is a story of exiles in Paris in 1939, which illuminates with masterly skill all the despair and misery, the sense of impending doom, the folly, futility and fear of that lull before the storm. It is a sad and melancholy book, a tired and disillusioned one. But because it is steeped in a stoic atmosphere of fortitude in adversity, it is not without an affirmative faith of a grim and ironic sort.

Through the eyes of a refugee German surgeon Mr. Remarque shows us Paris as a city: its grimy night life, its desperate poor, its cynical and corrupt elements, its garish violence. The surgeon is in love with a worthless woman, and he is bent upon revenge if a certain Gestapo agent should ever cross his path. The love story and numerous flamboyantly theatrical scenes of surgery and vice are the weaker parts of *Arch of Triumph*. Its strength lies in its fine gallery of representative characters wonderfully revealed through expert dialogue, its narrative power, and its eloquent interpretation of human character in a time of catastrophe.

> Orville Prescott, "Outstanding Novels: 'Arch of Triumph'," in The Yale Review *(© 1946, copyright renewed © 1974, by Yale University; reprinted by permission of the editors), Vol. XXXV, No. 3, March, 1946, p. 573.*

QUENTIN REYNOLDS

"**Spark of Life**" is a grim, agonizing but terribly wonderful story of what happened to the political and religious nonconformists in Hitler's Germany. It concerns itself with the horrible reality of a concentration camp as it was in 1945, but the six years that have intervened are not strong enough to dilute the importance of his theme. Remarque is crying angrily, "Watch out or this may again come to pass. Be on guard against those who would curb your liberties, for this is the inevitable result."

"**Spark of Life**" is a book which is hard to read; it is a book that once begun is impossible to put down. Once you know the tragic remnants of humanity who, too weak to work, are segregated to die in what was known as The Small Camp (at Mellern), you find it impossible to desert them. . . .

His meticulous research (he spent five years on this book) was directed to finding the answer to the question, "What kept [the prisoners] alive?" He found the answer in that passage in Genesis which begins, "So God created man in his own image," and at first called his book "Gottes Ebenbild" ("God's Image"), a reflection perhaps of his own abiding Catholic faith and a reaffirmation of the doctrine that there is within man a divine spark. Remarque discovered, just as John Hersey had discovered before him, that the ones who had the courage to kindle this spark and keep it burning under conditions of utter despair, humiliation and starvation were the ones who survived. Those who had nothing but physical strength didn't last long; men like 509 who were able to draw upon the inexhaustible resources of the spirit stayed alive the longest.

Inevitably **"Spark of Life"** must recall "The Wall." [John] Hersey's monumental epic, however, concerned itself with one group—the Jews of the Warsaw ghetto and of how when all else had failed they drew strength from their ancient religion. The heterogeneous group in Barrack 22 had no such spiritual common denominator as a Jewish heritage; each man had to find his own particular well of strength on which to draw. (p. 1)

> Quentin Reynolds, "The Divine Light That Defies Darkness," in The New York Times Book Review (© 1952 by The New York Times Company; reprinted by permission), January 27, 1952, pp. 1, 23.

FREDERIC MORTON

"Only the unhappy man appreciates happiness. The happy man . . . displays it merely." These are words spoken in **"Three Comrades,"** the novel by Erich Maria Remarque which would seem farthest from his latest because it is set in peace and relates young men's revels. Yet they are words that would make an accurate epigraph to **"A Time to Love and a Time to Die,"** as well as to every other major work Remarque has written. As he returns, for the first time since **"All Quiet on the Western Front,"** to the stench and terror of bomb shelter and infantry trench, it becomes apparent that he has never really left them. All his stories are moral, if not physical, war novels; all his heroes soldiers that dream of peace. . . .

With **"A Time to Love and a Time to Die,"** . . . Remarque brings up to date a raw documentary of our century. He pictures an era in which crisis has become routine, catastrophe moves on ball bearings, death is efficiently administered and unsentimentally cleaned up, terror is commonplace and melodrama humdrum. Not only do individuals perish, but individuality collapses. For a while the malaise seemed to infect Remarque's own literary faculties. In recent books he expended them on events and conditions, not on beings and feelings. In **"Arch of Triumph"** and **"Spark of Life"** particularly he was concerned with the technical minutiae of suffering rather than the personal agony of the sufferer. . . .

Unpretentious as this story is, it encompasses all the panicked perversions of war, all the brave incorrigibility of peaceful hope, and the tragic paradox that both these things root deeply in the human heart.

It is a story refracted entirely through the nerves and thoughts of its protagonist [Private Graeber]. . . . It is a book that seizes on incidents that have become stale through other tellings and, by pinpointing details with tiny relentlessly zeroed-in spotlights, thrusts upon a familiar picture an almost unbearable fresh glare.

Most important of all, **"A Time to Love and a Time to Die"** is a book forged out of two searingly contemporary themes. The first involves Graeber's discovery of a moral will inside himself. . . . Storm Troop Commander Binding incarnates [a new challenge for Graeber]. One of the most effective characters in the book, Binding is a lackadaisical, jovial fellow,

sincerely generous with the loot he has accumulated from his victims. From him Graeber learns that to be lazy about evil, whether in spectacular fashion as in Binding's case, or only passively as in his own, is to become part of evil oneself. Graeber's schoolboy-like groping for what is good, and his adult manful commitment once the search is over, climax the narrative. He dies under the command of his conscience. Having made the first true choice in his life, he reconquers in death his identity.

This represents a broadening of Remarque's scope. His previous heroes were too busy toiling at sheer survival to have leisure for ideals. . . . Because of this added dimension, there is added humanity in **"A Time to Love and a Time to Die."**

The book's other theme has run through all of Remarque's work. Handled masterfully even in his weaker novels, it is the realization that the preciousness of existence may be distilled out of its very precariousness, that life is doubly sweet because, as Graeber says, "we are no longer dead and we are not yet dead." In every Remarque book there is at least one scene where its characters, staggering down the slope of destruction, grasp hands, halt, and celebrate the everlasting miracle of life.

In his earlier books this was accomplished by a single incident; in **"A Time to Love and a Time to Die"** it is conveyed by the relationship of Graeber and the girl Elizabeth, not limited to passages but throughout the book. (p. 14)

In **"A Time to Love and a Time to Die"** all motivations except blind obedience and fear have been crushed from military life. Griping and goldbricking, so characteristic among American soldiers as protest against the unnaturalness of military compulsion, are unhealthily absent. Only tired utilitarian exchanges remain about bread, frostbite, and the disposal of the dead. It isn't merely danger which saps these young men. They were calloused and animalized even before they entered the army.

Thus the naive infinite capacity for horror which made **"All Quiet on the Western Front"** so indelibly human a document has been extinguished. The new hero is no longer willing to be shocked. His fate appalls and deluges the reader moments before it touches him. Remarque has let his sensibilities harden along with those of his figures. I am not quite sure whether it is because of or despite this fact that **"A Time to Love and a Time to Die"** ranks with Theodor Plievier's "Stalingrad" as the most laceratingly powerful German novel to come out of World War II. While Plievier conjures up the inferno of divisions, Remarque recreates, more immediately and vulnerably, the hell of a single private.

Viewed against Remarque's career so far, the new novel shows that he still writes whereof he suffers. Like Hemingway, he was permanently damaged and therefore permanently inspired by war. Like Hemingway, he dramatizes a generation "hard . . . afraid of feelings, without trust in anything but the sky, trees, the earth, bread, tobacco that never played false to any man." (The quotation, taken from **"Three Comrades"** could easily be fitted into "The Sun Also Rises.") But whereas Hemingway, being American, had to nurture the vision of violence in foreign bull rings and transatlantic wars, Remarque, the German, saw it redescend upon his own country. Exile became *his passage d'armes.* He does not possess the genius for bare symbolic dramaturgy of his American counterpart, but, on the other hand, his figures are not encumbered with the heavyweight-contender-complex of some of Hemingway's hairy prima donnas. Remarque, for all his international celebrity, his familiarity with the villas of Lago Maggiore and the bistros of Beverly Hills, has not lost the sensitivity or eloquence of his old wounds. In **"A Time to Love and a Time to Die"** he has said something enduring with the truth of pain. (p. 15)

Frederic Morton, *"The Sweetness of Death," in* The Saturday Review, *New York (copyright © 1954 by Saturday Review; all rights reserved; reprinted by permission), Vol. XXXVII, No. 21, May 22, 1954, pp. 14-15.*

MAXWELL GEISMAR

A central "school" in modern fiction has been made up of writers who have considered themselves the outlaws and outcasts of modern society. . . . In the Forties and Fifties the tone of this literature had shifted from the tragic to the satirical: the comedy or farce of social desperation.

Erich Remarque's [**"The Black Obelisk"**] fits perfectly into this new category. The scene is the post-World-War-I Germany of economic inflation. . . .

Whether it is great literature, is difficult to know; but it is such good reading that I am suspicious of it. The first half of the novel, at least, is a brilliant tragi-comedy of these poor provincial souls who have become so desperate as to be both outrageous and hilarious. The effect of the narrative is rather like a cross between "The Three-Penny Opera" and "The Tropic of Capricorn," just as Remarque has something of both Berthold Brecht and Henry Miller in his own temperament. He is a brooding poet of despair, who takes refuge in outlandish farce. (p. 4)

The tombstone business is also in a bad way, since each sale is another step toward bankruptcy. But Ludwig Bodmer, the provincial hero, keeps it, or himself, solvent by unorthodox means. He is a war veteran, a frustrated writer (there are fine sections on the Poetry Society of Werdenbrück), a lover of women who is always disappointed, a seeker after truth. What is life?—and Remarque provides a series of bitter and witty aphorisms on this recurrent refrain. Ludwig is in love with Isabelle, the schizophrenic beauty of the local lunatic asylum, who perfectly represents the splintered universe that surrounds him. When she recovers her "sanity," she cannot remember her love.

Perhaps all the "characters" in the novel represent aspects of Remarque's own vision of life rather than complete human beings. In this work he is not so much a novelist as a poet of the social underworld—of the homeless, the dispossessed, the ruined little men and their unspeakable women. (But why, thinking over the novel, does one begin to laugh all over again?) I am sure there are altogether too many freaks, cranks and subhuman oddities in this weird German town of Werdenbrück. It is impossible—until one remembers that this scene also represented the last flowering of German individuality, macabre as it may seem, before the resurgent "patriotism" and "discipline" of the Nazi party. (pp. 4, 18)

Maxwell Geismar, *"Men and Women in a Lunatic Time," in* The New York Times Book Review *(© 1957 by The New York Times Company; reprinted by permission), April 7, 1957, pp. 4, 18.*

THE NEW YORKER

[*The Black Obelisk*] is set in a small city in Germany in 1923, when the effects of the First World War are still cruelly felt and the signs of the war to come are growing clear. Ludwig Bodmer, twenty-five years old and a war veteran, has taken up life again in his native city and is scraping a living as the advertising manager of a tombstone firm. . . . Bodmer, who tells his own story in the present tense, is a man of singularly attractive personality. His view of life is tough, romantic, sympathetic, and amused. He feels anger at the injustice and despair he observes all around him, but he refuses to allow his anger to spread into a habit of daily bitterness. It is doubtful whether he can ever be sour. He has the air of a man who can see his most treasured dreams break and not try to console himself by picking up the pieces; consolation is not a thing he expects to find in life. He is looking for a girl to have an affair with, and his attempts at courtship are as funny and awkward as they are direct. . . . Mr. Remarque is completely in command of his story and in the best of form, whether he is evoking the dreams and desires of youth or observing the wretched struggle of ordinary people in defeat or simply passing the time in a city that he remembers well and that he makes familiar from the first page. The story is tragic, on the whole, and alive with the everyday manifestations of human pain, but from beginning to end it is characterized and illuminated by an incorrigible and irresistible humor. (pp. 174-75)

"Briefly Noted: 'The Black Obelisk'," in The New Yorker *(© 1957 by The New Yorker Magazine, Inc.), Vol. XXXII, No. 8, April 13, 1957, pp. 174-75.*

MAXWELL GEISMAR

In some respects Erich Maria Remarque has had a curious career, but it is a great tribute to this aging literary veteran of World War I that now, at the age of 66, he has produced what may be his best novel. A famous European counterpart to Hemingway, Remarque has, through the years, almost converted a handsome minor talent into a major one; whereas Hemingway almost reduced his own large talent into a more limited one.

At least I think **"The Night in Lisbon"** is Remarque's most brooding and thoughtful novel; it is the novel most involved with the destiny of 20th-century man. It is the novel in which the artist most fully comes to grip with the meaning of his own life and his own historical period, and which he leaves to us as the testimony that art is always the final witness to history. . . .

In the forties, with such works as **"Arch of Triumph,"** he had settled, apparently, for a kind of charming entertainment and love romance, yet I remember that even as I read that novel with a sense of disappointment, I was still beguiled by it, for precisely like Hemingway, Remarque had an extraordinary sense of surface texture in his prose.

His Paris of bordellos, refugees, expatriates and social outcasts of a city and a culture on the brink of catastrophe is still vivid to me, even if the tormented and cynical love romances of that period of Remarque's work were both sentimental and theatrical. But what has not been sufficiently recognized, I think, is that in the middle and late fifties, in his late phase, Remarque has again been writing notable and serious fiction.

"The Black Obelisk" (1957) was a brilliantly satirical novel of German life at the outset of Hitler and his National Socialism—the chronicle of a diseased nation almost in the style of Brecht. . . . Remarque's new novel, while very different in technique and tone, is every bit as good. A desperate, depressing, horrifying, touching, beautiful and tragic tale of the German refugees under the Nazi terror, it may not quite be a great novel, but it is surely one of the most absorbing and eloquent narratives of our period.

In this novel Remarque reveals his extraordinary talent for entertainment and narrative suspense. He is a very gifted artist on the human level who can be playful, witty, nostalgic and tender in turn; like Charlie Chaplin he is both hilariously funny and a great tear-jerker. At the same time, **"The Night in Lisbon"** is a kind of modern inferno describing the disintegration of Western European culture.

It is almost a manual of underground refugee existence, depicting the life and "culture" of the hunted and dispossessed during these years. It is also an indispensable "introduction" to the 20th century, the age, as Remarque says, "of technological progress and cultural retrogression." The central story is a curious kind of romance—that of a desperate, cunning and obsessive German exile who returns to the Nazi bastion in order to find the German wife whom he had never really loved or understood.

This love affair, which Remarque describes so well and which becomes an absorbing human relationship in the novel, subsumes elements of all love affairs and all marriages. It also points the way to an understanding of the refugee heart, and this is the novel's central and brilliant achievement. The odd hero is "Mr. Schwarz," who is not really Mr. Schwarz at all, but who has taken the identification papers of a dead Mr. Schwarz (who was also not the real Mr. Schwarz). . . .

The story employs a difficult technique: that of a night-long monologue by the present Mr. Schwarz. He is telling his life story to another refugee to whom he has given his passport to America and to freedom. This is the "Night in Lisbon," and during this night we follow the whole course of refugee history and existence—the underground railway of the doomed souls of Western culture—from Germany and Austria and France to Switzerland, Italy, Spain and Portugal, the last gateway to life.

The novel's heroine, Helen, escapes from Germany along with Schwarz because she has not yet realized, as Remarque says wryly, that "bourgeois stagnation is a moral, not a geographical condition." And how brilliantly German culture, both before and during the Nazi period, is described here, with unfathomable depths of moral indignation, anger, hatred—and yet with a lingering, ironical belief in that God of justice and decency who, Schwarz believes, must still be searched for, even if never found.

Against the nihilism of this chilling, terrifying and desolate "modern World," which Remarque renders so intimately, so deeply, so personally, he still pits the vestigial, if now almost vanished, faith of a late 19th-century novelist of the human condition. This novel is in many sections an almost unbearable ordeal of human degradation, suffering and death, during an epoch whose true nature is still largely unknown to American readers. But that Remarque and his Mr. Schwarz can, despite all, retain even that bitter, hopeless vestige of love, faith, affection and humor, is what makes **"The Night in Lisbon"** such a memorable novel.

> *Maxwell Geismar, "Terror Marched with a Goose Step," in* The New York Times Book Review *(© 1964 by The New York Times Company; reprinted by permission), March 22, 1964, p. 1.*

MELVIN MADDOCKS

On its lacquered surface, *Shadows in Paradise* shows all the familiar Remarque gloss. There is the typically commercial title, second only to *Heaven Has No Favorites.* There is the often wordy dialogue—pretentiously sophisticated, as if spoken by an impostor duke. There is the slightly too chic setting: in this case, places like El Morocco, the fashion-and-art salons of New York and the swimming pools of Hollywood in 1944.

A young German wearing the new name of Robert Ross has just arrived in America, the victim of both French and German concentration camps. He is, as Remarque must put it, "an Orestes pursued by the distant cries of the Furies." How will this creature of survival be restored to the human race? Remarque knows but one way. He produces his interchangeable Remarque woman, in this instance an exotic model named Natasha, half Anna Karenina, half Playmate of the Month. . . .

As usual, love à la Remarque almost but not quite works, trailing away into a gentle melancholy, a secondary sort of exile and loss. And those subplots—amusing, a bit cynical, dotted with European jokes about America—constitute the best parts. By their very gaucherie they suggest appealingly the embarrassment of an author trying to bridge modern experience, from the sheer horror of war to the sheer banality of peace.

Remarque's curious polarization between holocaust and Hollywood may reflect less calculation than nasty skeptics have supposed. In retrospect, his tales seem the defense mechanisms of a romantic trapped in a bad time. Remarque needed illusions as large, as desperate, as his master disillusion with World War I. But he was not alone. So, for better and for worse, did his readers.

> *Melvin Maddocks, "Between Holocaust and Hollywood," in* Time *(reprinted by permission from* Time, *The Weekly Newsmagazine; copyright Time Inc. 1972), Vol. 99, No. 6, February 7, 1972, p. 84.*

ROBERT W. HANEY

Except for a few scenes set in Hollywood, Robert Ross, the principal character in [**"Shadows in Paradise"**], explores and uses the sights, sounds and people of Manhattan, as Remarque himself knew them in the closing years of the Second World War.

For readers of our own time, all-too-conscious of what has become of Gotham or, if you will, Mayor Lindsay's inadvertently ironic "Fun City," Remarque's title smacks of poignancy, if not sarcasm. . . .

But we soon discover that what the title suggests to us is not at all what the author intends. For Ross and his friends, New York is indeed a paradise; so, too, are whatever other portions of America that they know. They themselves are the shadows. . . .

[Ross's] affair with Natasha and his experiences as an assistant to an art dealer fill stage center of the novel. In the background we glimpse the lives and destinies of his immigrant friends. . . .

While studying two paintings by El Greco in the Metropolitan, Ross realizes that everything is "at once connected and unconnected" and that a conception of coherence is "nothing but a human crutch, half lie and half imponderable truth." This insight, which seems to be familiar to Remarque, provides a clue to understanding why this, the last of his novels before his death, is so annoyingly unsatisfying. . . .

Remarque has something to say that is worth pondering; what happens to his characters in 1944-45 is not so remote from what many people know at first hand today—albeit for somewhat different reasons. But the novel's central insight is never developed in any consistent way. Remarque's angle of vision seems blurred. Instead of pursuing his intention, he suddenly introduces, for no useful purpose, the language and preoccupations of the washroom. He gives more attention to the consumption of vodka than to the exploration of his theme.

The central relationship between Ross and Natasha lacks focus—no small fault in a novel written from the retrospective viewpoint of a first-person narrator. This very lack of focus arouses a suspicion about the book's true character. What we have here may be a book-for-a-script-for-a-Hollywood-film, the fate of so many of his other novels. This is a waste; Remarque's people deserve a better fate.

> Robert W. Haney, *"Unremarkable Remarque,"* in The Christian Science Monitor *(reprinted by permission from* The Christian Science Monitor; © *1972 The Christian Science Publishing Society; all rights reserved), March 9, 1972, p. 13.*

MICHAEL O'MALLEY

The way [Andrew] Wyeth paints: no thunder in his picture, just a modulation of blues to make you see the sky's a bit strange and, like a letter shoved under the door, the dog's white muzzle lifted to the far-off sound. Truth got at sideways to ease the pain in it. Quick storms of terror flash past in [*Shadows in Paradise*] and suddenly are gone, like eerie tableaux set into the wall of the subway. . . .

I think that Remarque, in this last of his novels . . . , was trying —with a noble disdain for pathos—to face what it was to be a thinking German in the time of his life. He comes through as a tough, brilliant, sophisticated realist: another of those who teach us that even though indictments do no good, they must be drawn and presented. Shame for his German people clings to him. Innocent himself, he and his protagonist wear their nationality as Philoctetes his rotting foot: the unearned badge of God's resentment. . . .

What I mean by "truth got at sideways" is that this quiet novel —with its meticulous description of refugee life in Manhattan during the final year of the Second World War, with its fierce refusal to encourage or even allow your pity—manages somehow to slip into your permanent consciousness the way Wyeth's dog does, and through its deceptive insouciance to make the banal sufferings and suicides of its homesick Jews and bewildered Viennese more terrible than any detailed catalog of horrors.

I think we are not used to this in America. We do not really love the men who paint with fine brushes in tempera, who are precise about shadings and textures, who do not agonize. We prefer the slashing, smashing scarlet trumpet flatulence that characterizes so much contemporary art. I think this book may be too finely drawn for most Americans. (p. 80)

The affair between Ross and Natasha—from the initial furious storming of her body so often required in taking sex from the speculative to the physical, to what Natasha says as she dresses and leaves Ross for the last time: "Don't look at me. I don't want you to look at me anymore,"—is in every word and detail one of the best descriptions you will ever read of what might be termed cool city sex: sex between equals; without vows, without loyalties, but also without deceptions on either side.

We have testaments in abundance about the 57 other varieties of love, but not a great deal has been written by good novelists about the rational, cynical, slightly sordid, and often tired affairs that are so much a part of city life. Remarque has it down, and at first we are disappointed. We tend to passion: we want empires to fall for love, drunks reformed, whores made holy, and all for love. When nothing much happens to the lovers, when their unhappiness and loneliness and uncertainty are not cured, not even lessened, but only relieved for moments at a time—small lights lit in their bodies, put out when bodies part—we shrug and complain that nothing much is happening. That, of course, is the point. Passion, in passion (as in art, science, insurance) is extremely rare. Ross knows this. When the novel, and Ross' affair with Natasha, are finished, we know it too. (pp. 81-2)

This novel is more about a life, and a way of life, in New York City than about the city itself. It is about eating and drinking and cursing fate: "coffee and sadness" with the shadowy refugees who cannot enjoy paradise because their souls are in Berlin and Vienna. It is about loneliness and suicide—by hanging, by shooting, by pills; Gräfenheim, who does it with sleeping pills, believes that "the possibility of suicide was one of God's greatest gifts to man, because it could put an end to hell, as Christians call the torment of the mind." It is about the consolations of art, even though (as Remarque puts it so well) "works of art are not nurses." And it is very much about the consolations of the flesh.

Most of the people in it are drawn with a master's skill and economy; only Natasha—with her barbaric, childish selfishness—never comes fully to life. . . .

I would say Remarque went out in style on this one. *Shadows in Paradise* is a fine novel. At the essence it's about frustration: about living. (p. 82)

> Michael O'Malley, *"Books: 'Shadows in Paradise',"* in The Critic (© The Critic 1972; reprinted with the permission of the Thomas More Association, Chicago, Illinois), Vol. XXX, No. 5, May-June, 1972, pp. 80-2.*

BRIAN A. ROWLEY

All Quiet on the Western Front (*Im Westen nichts Neues*) is one of the most surprising phenomena in the history of literature. Its commercial success was unparalleled. . . .

But the novel was not simply a best-seller. It also became a focus of intellectual and, indeed, of political life. Immediately upon its appearance, it provided a *casus belli* for the battle, in the Germany of 1929, between militarists and pacifists, right wing and left. (p. 101)

[The] reasons for the success of *All Quiet* are likely to be somewhat more complex than is commonly supposed.

On the one hand, timing is obviously of significance. The interval of ten years since the war was short enough for the memories of participants not to have faded, but long enough for the ex-servicemen to have recovered from their immediate post-war desire to forget. At the same time, the developing political situation at the end of the 1920s made modern war into a live issue. . . . By beginning the serial publication of the novel on the eve of the tenth anniversary of the Armistice—10 November 1928—the house of Ullstein was deliberately tying the novel in to this political controversy. In this sense, *All Quiet* is one of a group of novels whose reputations fed on their times: Ludwig Renn's *Krieg* (*War,* 1928) in Germany; Manning's *Her Privates We* (1929) in England; Hemingway's *A Farewell to Arms* (1929) in America.

But not all these were best-sellers; so Remarque's success was due also to the book's intrinsic qualities. Some of these, we may feel, are journalistic rather than strictly literary. The particular blend of suffering, sensuality and sentiment suggests that Remarque had gauged public taste. The horror and degradation of war is represented, but it is shown with irony, wit, and even humour. To a large extent, this is made possible by the choice of a group of characters who are close to the reader. And this again depends upon Remarque's command of a clear but lively, indeed pungent style. All these features owe something to journalism. Yet this is not to deny the book's very real literary merits. (pp. 102-03)

The fact that *All Quiet* was read for its indecencies was recognised from the start. . . . This was certainly a reason for the novel's success. Yet Remarque never lets indecency become obscene, still less pornographic. More important, he is able to show, because of the point of view of his narrative, that an emphasis on creature comforts is part of the soldier's psychology; less trivially realistic, that it is part of his defence against the otherwise unbearable brutality of war. This is illustrated, in the farcical mode, by the goose-roasting sequence in Chapter V after the horrors of the wire-laying fatigue in IV; and in the lyrical mode, by the love-scene in Chapter VII after the battle-scene of VI. And finally—as Paul's love-scene with his brunette suggests—it is a mode of experience through which the soldier's contact with the deepest springs of life, threatened as it is by war, can be renewed. (p. 104)

Nature, too, . . . restores the lost contact with life. The intimate connections between war and nature are reinforced by Remarque's use, from time to time, of a grammatical device—a kind of zeugma which links, without overt comment, experiences from the two spheres. . . . On the success of Remarque's rendering of the brutal reality of war there has been, from the beginning, more agreement than on most other issues. Some details, certainly, were challenged: notably the screaming of the wounded horses, in Chapter IV. . . . It was also, more widely, argued that war is not always so brutal and so ignominious as this novel depicts it; but that is to miss the point that trench warfare in Flanders in 1914-18 is not war in general, but a particularisation of the brutalising tendencies inherent in all warfare to a point of no return. And this sort of warfare *is* captured by Remarque's sober realism, more successfully than ever before. . . . (pp. 105-06)

[His] descriptions do not give the impression of deriving from literary models. It is rather that his experience as a journalist has taught him how to select facts and convey them in a style that heightens, rather than blurs, their impact; and that this journalistic skill is here put to literary use.

To say this, however, is to remind ourselves that truth is a matter of style as much as of content. The style of *All Quiet* has been more praised than analysed. A striking feature of the syntax is the prevalence of simple—one-verb—sentences, and of compound ones without coordinating conjunctions, or at most with 'and'. (p. 107)

The style of the book is not Remarque's style, and the opinions are not Remarque's opinions; at least, not in the first instance.

From the beginning of Chapter I until two paragraphs from the end of Chapter XII, the novel is narrated by the central figure, Paul Bäumer. This narrative stance provides Remarque with a realistic context for a naive and simple style, which is part of the novel's popular appeal; but also for a fragmented, uncoordinated syntax, and for the use of the present tense with its immediacy; these features thus become part of the famous 'frog's eye view' of the war. He is able to give the shortsighted comments on events of Paul Bäumer himself, and through him of the other characters, without the need to provide an omniscient narrative perspective—indeed, with a requirement *not* to do so. In short, style and point of view are matched, and both reflect the incomprehensibility of war.

The choice of a first-person narrator does however create one possible problem. The two concluding paragraphs have to stem from a new, apparently omniscient third-person narrator, whose intervention is needed after the first-person narrator's death. Strangely, however, the novel does not suffer from this change of viewpoint; nor from the absence of any explanation of the mechanics by which it came to be set down. . . . (p. 108)

Narrative viewpoint and the focus on the central character are also closely linked with structure. At one level, the work is divided into many small sections, separated by asterisks. . . . This again is a feature that makes for easy reading; but, combined with the predominance of the present tense, it also makes for a realistic effect—that of a journal entry or a brief conversation. A journalistic approach has been adopted for aesthetic effect. . . .

The novel operates structurally, in fact, on an alternation between the cruelty and despair of the battle-scenes, and a gradual return to life during periods in reserve. Chapters VI and VII are the major instance of this alternation; but, ironically, the fact that Paul and his friends escape from this battle is not a guarantee that they will escape from the war; the second half of the novel moves inexorably to their destruction. (p. 109)

The progression of the novel is thus one of increasing alienation from any world but that of war. This alienation is implicit, and indeed explicit, at the beginning, but the characters still behave as if they can escape, whatever they may say. Paul himself hopes for a miracle in the love-scene in Chapter VII, but it is hard to believe that he finds one, except for the existential moment. And the sterility of his leave: coming, as it does, after the big battle, it should celebrate his safety, but instead it confirms his despair. So the structure of the novel articulates its themes.

The most basic of these is the monstrous unacceptability of modern trench warfare—manifest especially in Chapter VI. A second theme is the moral bankruptcy of leaders who have encouraged young men to volunteer for this holocaust—expressed already in the discussion of their form-master Kantorek in Chapter I. Yet a third theme is the suggestion that, when the war is over, something must be done to change the world we live in—intimated, for example, in the Duval scene in Chapter IX. More important is the 'lost generation' theme, already sounded in the book's epigraph:

> This book is meant neither as an indictment nor
> as a confession. It is meant only to try to report
> on a generation that was destroyed by the War—
> even when it escaped the shells. . . . (p. 110)

The sense of comradeship which awareness of belonging to a 'lost generation' engenders is yet another theme. And finally, there is the existential theme of the assertion of self, in the face of the nothingness of war, through sensual experience and through contact with nature—a theme which gradually fades from the novel as alienation becomes more pervasive.

The narrative standpoint of *All Quiet* does not allow these themes to be fully reconciled with one another, or even to be fully articulated. It is also true, as many critics have observed, that Paul Bäumer and his friends are not, as he claims and the novel implies, representative of the effect on all soldiers of trench warfare and its horrors. And yet, it is wrong to demand, either, as Remarque's Nationalist critics did, that these victims should have been more heroic, or, as Marxist critics do, that they should have been more consciously revolutionary. What Remarque achieves is more true to life than either of these: a depiction of mean sensual man, crushed by circumstances and yet preserving his humanity in unexpected ways. It is this that, ultimately, captured his readers; and it is this, and the unobtrusive formal mastery with which he achieves it, that is at the heart of his literary value. Like all major writers, he shows us what is wrong with our world, not how to put it right. (pp. 110-11)

> *Brian A. Rowley, "Journalism into Fiction: 'Im Westen nichts Neues'," in* The First World War in Fiction: A Collection of Critical Essays, *edited by Holger Klein (copyright © 1976 by The Macmillan Press Ltd.; by permission of Barnes & Noble Books, a Division of Littlefield, Adams & Co., Inc.), Barnes & Noble, 1977, pp. 101-12.*

MODRIS EKSTEINS

Between 1928 and 1930 Germany and Great Britain especially, and France and America to a lesser extent, experienced a sudden and remarkable 'boom' in war books, plays, and films. For a decade after the end of the war, publishers, theatre directors, and film makers had treated war material gingerly, viewing it as a poor commercial proposition, on the assumption that the public wished, contrary to annual remembrance day exhortations, to forget the war. . . . What some felt to have been a 'conspiracy of silence' was shattered with a vengeance. (p. 345)

Interestingly, no one has . . . investigated the war boom. This article will do so, but from a particular vantage point; that of a novel which stood at the centre of the war boom, in popularity, in spirit, and as a source of controversy—Erich Maria Remarque's *All Quiet on the Western Front* (*Im Westen nichts Neues*). . . .

While a number of war books had appeared immediately before it, *All Quiet* clearly triggered the explosion of war material in 1929 and unleashed a bitter and acrimonious debate on the essence of the war experience.

Why had relatively little war material, apart from official histories and the odd memoir and novel, appeared in the previous decade? Was this the doing solely of commercial interests? Explanations usually revolve around the state of nervous exhaustion from which nations suffered after the war. . . . In general, the memory of the war was too painful; moreover, the task after the war, it was felt, was not to wallow in the tragedy but to build a better future. (p. 346)

Yet, underlying this natural desire to forget and to look to the future was also a sense of confusion, confusion as to the meaning of the war. Already during the war this confusion had become increasingly noticeable. The war had been presented on one side as a struggle for civilized values against tyranny and aggression; and on the other side it had been seen as a war for *Kultur* against enslavement by materialism. But the total dehumanization of the conflict, as it became a gruesome war of attrition, cast a pall of irony over all ideals and all values. . . . A decade after the armistice, however, Remarque helped to unearth the whole question and sparked off an intense debate.

Prior to the publication of *All Quiet* Remarque had led a moderately successful, though unsettled, life as a dilettante intellectual and aspiring author. (p. 347)

Two of his novels were published, *Die Traumbude* in 1920 and *Station am Horizont* in 1928, but he appears to have derived little satisfaction from them. Trite sentimentality relegated the first work to the rank of pulp fiction. Remarque was to say of *Die Traumbude* later:

> A truly terrible book. Two years after I had published it, I should have liked to have bought it up. Unfortunately I didn't have enough money for that. The Ullsteins did that for me later. If I had not written anything better later on, the book would have been reason for suicide.

In 1921 he sent a number of poems to Stefan Zweig for comment and attached a letter of near despair: 'remember that this is a matter of life and death for me!' An attempt to write a play left him in deep depression.

The leitmotiv of suicide here is, of course, striking. Together with the derivative romanticism and the itinerant existence it points to a deeply disconsolate man, searching for an explanation for his dissatisfaction. In this search Remarque eventually hit upon the *Kriegserleben*! The idea that the war experience was the source of all ills struck him, he admitted, suddenly. (pp. 348-49)

Remarque was . . . more interested in explaining away the emotional imbalance of a generation than in any kind of comprehensive or even accurate account of the experience and feelings of men in the trenches. (p. 349)

Having fixed upon the *Kriegserleben*, Remarque sat down in mid-1928 to write. . . . The suddenness of the inspiration, the speed of composition, and the simplicity of the theme, all indicate that Remarque's book was not the product of years of reflection and digestion but of impulse born of personal exasperation. (p. 350)

The simplicity and power of the theme—war as a demeaning and wholly destructive force—are reinforced effectively by a style which is basic and even brutal. Brief scenes and short crisp sentences, in the first person and in the present tense, evoke an inescapable and gripping immediacy. There is no delicacy. The language is frequently rough, the images often gruesome. The novel has a consistency of style and purpose which Remarque's earlier work had lacked and which little of his subsequent work would achieve again.

Very few contemporary reviewers noted, and even later critics have generally ignored, that *All Quiet* was not a book about the events of the war—it was not a memoir—but an angry postwar statement about the effects of the war on the young generation that lived through it. Scenes, incidents, and images were chosen with a purpose to illustrate how the war had destroyed the ties, psychological, moral, and real, between the front generation and society at home. . . . The war, said Remarque in 1928, had shattered the possibility of pursuing what society would consider a normal existence.

Hence, *All Quiet* is more a comment on the postwar mind, on the postwar view of the war, than an attempt to reconstruct the reality of the trench experience. (pp. 350-51)

All Quiet is in fact then a symptom, rather than an explanation, of the confusion and disorientation of the postwar world, particularly of the generation which reached maturity during the war. The novel was an emotive condemnation, an assertion of instinct, a *cri d'angoisse* from a malcontent, a man who could not find his niche in society or the professions. That the war contributed enormously to the shiftlessness of much of the postwar generation is undeniable; that the war was the root cause of this social derangement is debatable, but Remarque never took part in the debate directly. There are, moreover, sufficient indications . . . that his own *agonie ennuyeuse* had roots predating the war.

Despite the opening declaration by Remarque of impartiality—that his book was 'neither an accusation nor a confession'—it was in fact both. It was a confession of personal despair, but it was also an indignant denunciation of an insensate social and political order, inevitably of that order which had produced the horror and destruction of the war but particularly of the one which could not liquidate the war and deal with the aspirations of veterans. Through characters identifiable with the state—the schoolmaster with his unalterable fantasies about patriotism and valour, the former postman who functions in his new role as drill sergeant like an unfeeling robot, the hospital orderlies and doctors who do not deal with human suffering only bodies—Remarque accused. He accused a mechanistic civilization of destroying humane values, of negating charity, love, humour, beauty, and individuality. Yet Remarque offered no alternatives. The characters of his *generazione bruciata* do not act, they are merely victims. Of all the war books of the late twenties . . . Remarque's made its point, that his was a truly 'lost generation', most directly and emotionally, indeed even stridently, and this directness and passion lay at the heart of its popular appeal. (pp. 351-52)

Remarque's success came at what we now see to be a crossroads in the interwar era: the intersection of two moods, one of vague imploring hope and the other of coagulating fear; the Locarno 'honeymoon' and a fling with apparent prosperity intersecting with incipient economic crisis and mounting national introspection. (p. 357)

Remarque's book, written in the first person singular, personalized for everyone the fate of the 'unknown soldier'. Paul Bäumer became the individual everyman. In the tormented and degraded *Frontsoldat*—and he could just as easily be a tommy, *poilu,* or doughboy—the public saw its own shadow and sensed an evocation of its own anonymity and yearning for security. . . . *All Quiet* seemed to encapsulate, in popular form, the whole modern impulse: the amalgamation of prayer and desperation, dream and chaos, wish and desolation. (p. 358)

Remarque blamed the war for his personal disorientation; the German public, too, assumed that its suffering was a direct legacy of the war. Indeed, *All Quiet* actually raised the consciousness of Germans on the question of the war as the source of their difficulties. (p. 359)

The great discovery that foreign readers said they made through *All Quiet* was that the German soldier's experience of the war had been, in its essentials, no different from that of soldiers of other nations. The German soldier, it seemed, had not wanted to fight either, once the emotional decoration put on the war by the home front had been shattered. Remarque's novel did a great deal to undermine the view that Germans were 'peculiar' and not to be trusted. Furthermore, *All Quiet* promoted at a popular level what historical revisionism was achieving at an academic and political level: the erosion of the idea of a collective German war guilt. (p. 361)

Remarque's novel exuded a mood of dissatisfaction, confusion, and yearning. The events and the international temper of 1929 displayed a similar disorientation. The novel became enormously successful not because it was an accurate expression of the front-line soldier's war experience, but because it was a passionate evocation of current public feeling, not so much even about the war as about existence in general in 1929. It was a poignant cry of 'help' on behalf of a distraught generation. (p. 362)

Modris Eksteins, "'All Quiet on the Western Front' and the Fate of a War," in The *Journal of Contemporary History (copyright © 1980 The Institute of Contemporary History), Vol. 15, No. 2, April, 1980, pp. 345-65.*

Trina Robbins

1938-

American cartoonist and editor.

Robbins's cartoon stories express her positive feelings about the feminist movement. When she has used her work to vent her anger at a male-dominated society, her cartoons have been somewhat violent.

For years Robbins was a creator of strictly underground comics (those that, in her words, cannot get published anywhere else). Robbins's strips are finally appearing in such magazines as *Playboy, National Lampoon,* and *High Times.* Her cartoons are now being recognized by many critics as valid statements about today's culture. Robbins believes her work has suffered from the negative reputation of underground comics for violence, sexism, and sexual explicitness. She feels her work is just the opposite: her violence is clean and usually in the form of self-defense, her heroines are beautiful because beauty appeals to her artist's eye, and sex, as she depicts it, is loving and natural.

Some critics feel her cartoons display a negative attitude toward men, but Robbins charges these critics with reading too much into the actions depicted. She asserts that the sense of her work is exactly what she writes and draws, without all of the connotations present in so many underground publications. Robbins once said that she wanted to draw pictures that tell stories, and she has attempted through her comics to tell the story of woman's freedom from male oppression.

LES DANIELS

[Trina Robbins] has gained a reputation as the foremost female creator of underground comics. She had some success in *Gothic Blimp Works* with Panthea, a creature half lady and half lion who was transported from Africa with painful results. The somewhat submerged concern for feminist principles which this series suggested was to emerge in 1970, when Trina became the principal contributor to *It Ain't Me Babe,* the first comic book devoted exclusively to Women's Liberation. The cover, which featured renderings of Sheena, Wonder Woman, and Mary Marvel, suggested how much comic book fantasies have done to provide images suitable to a new view of women and her place in the world. (p. 176)

> Les Daniels, *"Underground Comics," in his* Comix: A History of Comic Books in America *(copyright © 1971 by Les Daniels and Mad Peck Studios; reprinted by permission of the publisher, E. P. Dutton, Inc.), Outerbridge & Dienstfrey, 1971, pp. 165-80.*

LYNNE BRONSTEIN

R. Crumb may have fantasies of voyages down sewer pipes and S. Clay Wilson may draw visions of lesbian pirate battles, but neither of them would have ever thought up the legend of Speed Queen. She is a creation of Trina Robbins, an underground comicperson who happens to be female. Like most of the women who draw freaky funnies, she's concerned with the problems of being female—and the result is the hip, 70's an-

Leialoha

swer to Wonder Woman—the adventures of an assortment of gutsy, tall and Trina-faced heroines who *don't take no shit* from any mere male! . . .

Subject matter in the women's comix ranges from sexuality problems like pregnancy and lesbianism to women trying to educate men in new lifestyles to the speculative fantasies of Trina, whose women (the astronaut Speed Queen, the black hooker Fox, Amazons, feminists and lesbians) are all tall, beautiful, articulate and heroic. They are the much-needed fantasy women who transcend their roles to achieve success.

> Lynne Bronstein, *"Female Underground Comix," in* The L.A. Star, *1972.*

NICK CHINN

I've always enjoyed Trina Robbins' artwork and style. It is a happy medium polished overground art and on the other side of the spectrum, those trashy, poorly-drawn comix I can't stand to look at. . . .

[*Scarlett Pilgrim* follows] Scarlett, a San Francisco "working girl," and an older, retired hooker named Dollface, who both get involved as pawns in some C.I.A. derring-do in a Middle-East-type foreign country, getting tangled in a political revolution. For entertainment, Scarlett finds herself in the bedsheets of every important governmental or guerrilla leader in the fictional country Bahraq.

The story line is both light-hearted while overdramatic, fast-moving, and poking fun at international politics and the C.I.A. It's a lot of fun reading.

The book climaxes with Scarlett and Dollface double-crossing the C.I.A., and ends with a letter telling Scarlett that her cousin is coming to stay with her for awhile . . . unfortunately the family doesn't know anything about Scarlett's occupation, a situation setting up the next Scarlett Pilgrim book. I can't wait.

> *Nick Chinn, "Reviews: 'Scarlett Pilgrim'," in The Heroine's Showcase (© 1978 The Comics Heroine's Fan Club), No. 14, Summer, 1978, p. 33.*

RONALD LEVITT LANYI

Trina Robbins [is] one of the most challenging writers and lyrical draftsmen now active in underground comics. . . . (p. 737)

Trina's stories often involve strong, independent and very attractive women who are set upon but ultimately victorious over viciously hostile men. In **"Speed Queen Among the Freudians,"** for instance, which appeared in the first issue of *Girl Fight,* a solitary woman space traveller, upon arriving on Freuda, a planet inhabited solely by white men who worship a giant black phallus, is instantly seized for landing her "phallic craft next to our monument to the Great Maleness" and thrown in a dungeon "for the heresy of penis envy." . . . At the last moment she breaks free of her captors, grabs a ray gun and shoots it out with them while taking cover behind the giant black phallus. This her adversaries inadvertently shoot down, which causes them to see her through eyes suddenly cleared and cry happily, "Mommy! Mommy!" The story concludes with Speed Queen back in her space craft, leaning back in her seat and dangling the white key to Freuda over her crossed knees, which are covered by exceptionally long black boots. (p. 739)

[Robbins: What] I always wanted to do was draw pictures that told stories, and that's comics. I think of it as the ideal method of communication. More than that, I think of it as what I want to do more than anything else, draw pictures that tell stories. I mean, it's heaven for me. (p. 740)

[Lanyi: To] succeed in the male-dominated underground comics medium, didn't you at first and don't you still have to conform in some ways, some rules of the game, such as that sex and violence should be presented in an open and undisciplined manner? (p. 741)

[R.: As] far as I'm concerned, the underground is still a place where I can print something I can't print anywhere else. But I don't want to stay underground. I think the underground is a drag. It doesn't pay enough, and it has a lousy reputation. It's got a reputation for sex and dope and violence, and my stories aren't really sex and dope and violence stories. And so here I am: Because I do underground comics, I share the reputation I don't really deserve.

As far as sex is concerned, I never show the act. I'm very proud of the fact that not on any of my books have I ever had to put "For Adults Only." Because there's nothing in those books that a kid can't see. The only time I've ever shown penetration is in **Wet Satin** because that's what it's for. That's a different trip. . . .

[L.: To] succeed in the field, didn't you and don't you still have to deal in explicit violence?

R: I've never shown that kind of violence; I've never shown graphic, hideous violence.

L: Fox's knifing of two men in her story in the first issue of *Girl Fight*?

R: Knifing isn't graphic, hideous violence. My knifing is always nice and clean. I never show guts. I never show dismemberment. No one's ever had a head chopped off or a limb chopped off or been disemboweled. When I say "violence," I mean the violence the men show. My stories are no more violent than a good Alfred Hitchcock movie. There's no yucky stuff. (p. 742)

L: Your work seems strongly indebted to those overground comic books of the '40s that featured heroines like Sheena, Queen of the Jungle, [Senorita Ria, Nyoka, Jann of the Jungle, Torchy Todd, Phantom Lady, and Rulah, Jungle Goddess]. (p. 743)

[L: What] I want to get at is this: Although the central message in your stories is unmistakably feminist, you invariably people those stories with cartoon cheesecake types similar to the ones just mentioned. Many feminists . . . consider such types a betrayal of or at least a hindrance to the movement. Why don't you?

R: Because I like beautiful people. I'm very visual. . . .

L: The beautiful women you draw are also very sexy. It's that which could be found offensive, that the image of woman is as man's plaything.

R: No, that's where you're wrong. That's a terrible misconception that people seem to have, that sexism goes with sex. They think it's sexist for a woman to be attractive. And that's not true. I'm an artist; I'm visual. Things feed my eyes. They actually make my eyes feel good. I like beauty, and there's nothing sexist about beauty. (p. 744)

L: Unlike the '40s works I mentioned a moment ago, your own tales of cartoon cheesecake are often structured on challenging ideas that have some currency among feminists and feminist sympathizers. **"Speed Queen Among the Freudians,"** for instance, seems to be based on the idea that phallic superiority and the covetousness of "castrated" females are notions that operate in male minds only, where they serve as fragile defenses against an ever-threatening awareness of female biological and spiritual superiority. (pp. 744-45)

[L: Although] there is this intellectual difference between your own works and most of the '40s overgrounds for girls and women, attitudinally there is considerable similarity. Would you agree that attitudinally much of your work says what, say, the cover of issue eight of *All Top Comics* [November] said: Rulah, her beautifully black and coiffured mane cascading down to her bare shoulders, is in her skimpy, two-piece giraffe skin and winking bewitchingly at the reader. Then one notices not only that she is straddling a cleanly severed log that is somehow floating in air but that in each hand she is holding a rope that extends just below the log; from the end of each rope swings a small, surly and securely-bound black man.

R: No. As I said, the Rulah comics were really the most twisted and violent and sick of that whole bunch. . . . I don't think that at all! It has nothing to do with what I say.

L: Remember, I'm not talking about the intellectual statement per se but the attitudes behind it. Here's another indication of that attitude as expressed by Gershon Legman in *Love and Death: A Study in Censorship:* "Reading and dreaming . . . [women] fiercely delight in tales of triumphant bitchery, in which the immemorial tables are reversed, in which woman is master, and man the slave; in which man, the murderer is murdered."

R: I don't completely disagree with that. I think that whenever the tables are turned, whenever there's a revolution and the oppressed group rises up from under, they have to go through a period of getting their revenge. (p. 745)

L: Then you're talking about an attitudinal similarity with the Rulah cover.

R: Well, no, there's the tables turned and then there's just plain—you know, that Rulah cover sounds real sick, phallic and violent. Two little black men dangling on ropes and everything. I mean, I'd never go that far.

L: Your **"Speed Queen Among the Freudians"** story, as I recall, concludes with something which is symbolically similar: Speed Queen is dangling the small, white, obviously phallic-shaped key to Freuda over her long black boots.

R: Oh no, I don't think of that key to Freuda as a phallic shape at all. Sorry to disappoint you. What I had to say in there was that with their own guns they destroyed their phallic image. They shot it down themselves. Shooting at her, they missed and shot it down. And then she leaves after they've presented her with the key to Freuda. She leaves and says, "Well, it's a nice place, but I wouldn't want to live there."

L: Of course "there" is an exclusively masculine society, and the key which she is dangling is a symbol of that masculinity.

R: I'm just really sorry, but I didn't think of it as phallic. My only phallic symbol was the obvious one, which they shot down. I was just trying to do a traditional key, really. I mean, what can I tell you?

L: Okay.

R: I mean, Speed Queen didn't want to castrate them; they wanted to clitoradectomize her. I've never had castrating women, never. They never do anything nasty to men. (pp. 745-46)

L: In **"Sacrifice in the Temple"** in the first issue of *Girl Fight* you seemed to be registering an at least subconscious awareness that displays of aggressiveness greater than women are supposed to make may be too challenging to the male ego: Two women archeologists discover a well-endowed, nearly naked young man in an ancient temple and revive him from his sleep of thousands of years. The leader, relinquishing her hold on his loincloth in order to take him by the hand, says, "Come on, handsome, . . . [we] have things to discuss in my tent!" But as soon as she gets him into the light of day, he disintegrates.

R: Oh no, it wasn't because of her aggressiveness. It was because of something about the air down there that had kept him so perfectly preserved until the sunlight hit him. I mean, that's an old rip. That's been done in so many science fiction and horror stories.

L: Sure, but what she was going to do is try to lay him. And so it seemed that that's what you were saying through the device of disintegration, that the male ego crumbles—

R: Oh no, I wasn't saying that. I was simply using the old rip of the sunlight making him crumble. That's what happens in *Lost Horizons:* When they leave the mountain, she turns into dust. So I just used that rip; that's all. See, you're reading far too much meaning into my work. Well, it's charming—you and Gershon Legman. He also read meaning into everything. But it's like Freud saying that sometimes a good cigar is just a good cigar, you know? (p. 747)

[L: You] indicated that as far as your own comics are concerned, there is nothing of a sexual nature in them, with a few exceptions, that a child should be prevented from seeing. But what about, say, the explicit lesbian lovemaking that sometimes appears in your work? According to current cultural standards, isn't that pornographic, deviant, and unsuitable for children?

R: I always show sex as a beautiful thing. I never show it along with violence and hostility toward the other person, except when Fox is being raped and she knifes the guy to protect herself. That's self-defense. . . . Explicit sex is never horrible and never bad. (pp. 747-48)

L: Let's go back to female homosexuality in your work. In an article entitled "Not for Lesbians Only," Charlotte Bunch spoke of lesbian-feminism as "a political critique of the institution and ideology of heterosexuality as a cornerstone of male supremacy." Would such a critique lie behind your depiction of "sister/lovers," as you call them in one of your stories? (p. 749)

[R: I'm] not putting down heterosexuality or saying that heterosexuality represents male dominance.

L: What about **"Fox,"** your story of a black heroine? . . . Her only satisfying sexual experience in the story is with a white woman; their scene occurs under a large poster bearing the women's liberation symbol.

R: Well, there I just felt that it would be nice and pleasant and revolutionary to have some lesbian scenes, that's all. Because nobody else was doing them; certainly the men weren't about to do them. The men were really horrified by lesbians and terribly threatened by them and at that point felt that all feminists were dykes. I thought it was a pleasant change from the sex scenes that men always show, basically. I thought it would be nice to have women making love to women, because I think that's very pretty. But I really haven't done that for a while either. That was a reaction. You know, a lot of things I've done have been reactions to what was going on around me. These days my comics are terribly heterosexual.

L: So you weren't at all considering your lesbian work as a reaction against "heterosexuality as a cornerstone of male supremacy?"

R: No, I think that lesbians may feel that way, but in my work I didn't feel that way. That wasn't my reaction. Back then, when I did those comics, I was still a new feminist, and most new feminists, women who become feminists and start exploring the world of feminism, get turned on to the fact that their sisters can be attractive. And some of them either become lesbians or flirt with the idea of lesbianism. And I was more like one of the ones who flirted with lesbianism. . . . What you do is explore all those facets of yourself that have never come out before. Because you've been only living by, as I said before, male standards. So one of the facets is love of other women, because we're all bisexual inside. So all these things come out, you know? You try them all out and think about them. And you get to what you really prefer. . . . My anger was another thing I tried out. My anger had never been allowed to come out before, so I tried it out. It was fun. If you don't try these things out, they stay inside. (pp. 749-50)

L: In panel three [of **"Visit with the Artist in Her Own Studio"**] you have your cartoon image to say to male readers: "I admit to a lot of genuine hostility! I'll start liking you better when you start liking women better!" In the lower right hand corner of that panel, the one preceeding it, and two succeeding it, you indicate your outside-the-picture daughter calling to take her to the bathroom, but instead of placing her call in conventional word balloons, you place it in something I've never seen before in comics. For those four panels the lines that should be coming together to form the lower right hand corner instead arch northwesterly and form a phallic shape that grows larger with each panel. You probably intended this inventive use of formal content to be an indicator of annoying insistence, but what it seems to indicate on a deeper symbolic level is that to some degree, either consciously or subconsciously, you associate problems of a non-male origin with maleness. Thus you imply that the hostility toward men you referred to in panel three and which has been a basis for a large amount of your work does not always proceed from a realistic base. (p. 750)

[R: You] see phallic shapes everywhere! What's happening is that that's reality intruding into my word balloon, pushing its way into the balloon, so that finally the fantasy balloon pops. And there I am in reality. . . .

[R:] The balloon is fantasy, and when she finally pops it, there I am in reality in patched jeans. I'm not wearing all those nifty outfits, and I don't have people handing me joints and champagne. It's all fantasy. The reality is that I'm a mother with a child who wants to go to the bathroom. It has nothing to do with phallic symbols. . . .

R: I mean, I hate to disappoint you, but none of these heavy meanings are in there. Really, it's just what's there. It's just what I say and just what's there and that's all. I can't believe what you're reading into this! . . .

L: I may be a riot, but my job is to explore facets, to find sense, right?

R: You're finding sense. The sense is in what I say! The sense is in exactly what I put there. (p. 752)

[R: I] have been in darkness, and I've had to fight my way out of it. I've had to fight against all the stereotypes that I truly believed in, all the things in a male-dominated culture that were told me that I accepted. The fact that I dislike authority so much now is because I used to accept authority so readily in the past. I accepted all those things that I was told and had to fight my way out of that. I had to fight my way into realities, into understanding myself and understanding my sisters: that we're people. And understanding men too: that you're people. None of us are cliches. We're all multitudes. We're all masses of contradictions. (p. 753)

Ronald Levitt Lanyi, "Trina, Queen of the Underground Cartoonists: An Interview," in Journal of Popular Culture *(copyright © 1979 by Ray B. Browne), Vol. XII, No. 4, Spring, 1979, pp. 737-54.*

BILL SHERMAN

It took me a couple of years after I first discovered her (San Francisco Comix Book #2, **"The Tiger's Revenge"**) to appreciate Trina Robbins's comix work. For a long time I ignored it. It wasn't the relative crudity of her artwork—at that time a lot of comix artists were crude—but something else: her working with comics material I thought at the time I'd outgrown. Trina's Golden Age tributes, comix consciousness meshed with comics style, seemed alien to me, too simultaneously close to childhood. . . .

There was the matter of her feminism, too. "If you're taking it personally it probably was meant for you," she wrote of her sex satires in *Girl Fight #2,* and for a time her evocations of Amazons and angry women did make this male comix reader uncomfortable. But while Trina got more sophisticated in her treatment of feminist topics, I got less defensive on more than one front: by '74, when she'd written the above, I was a fan of hers. . . .

[Trina Robbins] was in the underground from its earliest years, a time when women artists were even rarer than they were in the overground, and . . . has since become one of its best, most consistent artists. (p. 47)

Bill Sherman, "An Interview with Trina Robbins, The First Lady of Underground Comix," in The Comics Journal, *No. 53, Winter, 1980.*

Smokey Robinson

1940-

(Born William Robinson) Black American songwriter and singer.

Robinson has been critically and commercially successful for more than twenty years and is credited with having written some of the most moving songs of the 1960s. One of the first popular songwriters to receive serious critical attention, he has influenced many lyricists and is often described as a master of the romantic ballad. Robinson's lyrics express a humanistic philosophy and a faith in the power of love. He is renowned for his ability to create compelling metaphors and similes from simple language and is especially popular with critics and listeners who find his romanticism appealing in an era of increasingly unromantic, sexually-oriented popular songs. Some critics feel that Robinson has proven that it is possible to maintain high aesthetic standards and be commercially successful. He is one of the few artists whose songs of the 1960s have withstood the many changes in popular music and are expected to endure.

Robinson formed the Miracles in 1957 while its members were still in high school. Under the guidance of Motown founder Berry Gordy, he became one of the company's most prolific and successful writers. Early hit songs written by Robinson and performed by the Miracles helped to establish Motown as a strong force in the record industry. He also wrote "My Guy" for Mary Wells, "My Girl" for the Temptations, and other giant commercial successes early in his career. Robinson's work of the 1960s has received overwhelmingly favorable reviews. Of the songs written in that decade, "The Tracks of My Tears" and "The Tears of a Clown" have been the most popular and most acclaimed. Their themes are characteristic of many of Robinson's lyrics; the heartache, the fears, and uncertainties of love. "The Tears of a Clown" is perhaps the best example of his famous "pain behind the smile" motif. Critics consider both songs classics of popular music.

In 1972, Robinson left the Miracles to begin a solo career. Few of the songs he has written since have been as acclaimed as those he wrote in the 1960s but most have been well-received. Robinson has experimented with various musical forms but his themes remain fundamentally the same. As is true of his earlier work, albums like *Smokey, Warm Thoughts,* and *Love Breeze* take love as their basic subject. Although some critics feel that Robinson's work is marked by repetitiousness, most seem to see his recent songwriting as the mature reflections of a sensitive artist. His popular longevity is attributed to his ability to combine old and new musical forms with a growing lyrical perspective. It is generally believed that Robinson has made, and continues to make, significant contributions to popular music.

PAUL GAMBACCINI

On first listen ["**The Tears of a Clown**" is] a certain smash. . . .

A circus atmosphere is established by the opening phrase that works as effectively as (but ever-more-subtly-than) the intro to James Darren's "Goodbye Cruel World." This phrase reoc-

Jerome Addison

curs throughout, giving the song an air of levity that belies the misery-and-woe lyrics.

And what lyrics! Smokey Robinson may or may not be America's greatest living poet, but he is certainly its most erudite writer of soul songs. Not only would no other composer mention Pagliacci in his verses, few would understand the allusion.

It's worth noting that "**Tears of a Clown**" is structured precisely, more so than some of the recent stiffs that were freer in form. In this sense it is vintage Miracles and should enjoy the success of another 1967 release, "**I Second That Emotion.**" (p. 185)

Paul Gambaccini, "Singles: 'The Tears of a Clown',"
in Rolling Stone *(by Straight Arrow Publishers, Inc.*
© 1970; all rights reserved; reprinted by permission), No. 70, November 12, 1970 (and reprinted as
"Soul: 'The Tears of a Clown'," in The Rolling
Stone Record Review, *edited by the editors of* Rolling
Stone, *Pocket Books, 1971, pp. 184-85).*

VINCE ALETTI

Smokey Robinson's last album, *What Love Has Joined Together,* was a masterpiece of polished, high-gloss soul. In a departure from established album formula, Smokey and the Miracles devoted themselves to exploring at length six songs about love. [In *A Pocket Full of Miracles,*] the group returns to the standard six-songs-to-a-side album and while the results vary, Smokey again proves his mastery of sophisticated soul in small, concentrated doses.

The beauty of the Miracles comes not only from Smokey Robinson's unbelievably sweet lead singing but from the just-right balance of his production work and the brilliance of his songwriting as well. So creatively does Smokey use these talents that frequently a vocal flourish, a particularly fine turn of phrase or tastey piece of orchestration will redeem, even make irresistible, what would otherwise be an unremarkable song. . . .

Pocket Full is a fine album, not exceptional but enjoyable. If you can dig rhythm and blues without the roughness and funk, Smokey and the Miracles remain unsurpassed.

> Vince Aletti, "Records: 'A Pocket Full of Miracles'," in Rolling Stone (by Straight Arrow Publishers, Inc. © 1971; all rights reserved; reprinted by permission), Issue 75, February 4, 1971, p. 58.

RUSSELL GERSTEN

Like all Miracles albums of the past 12 years, [*One Dozen Roses* is] almost all sad love songs, some fast, some slow, with a dance song or two thrown in. Smokey hits the same themes as always—illusion and disillusion, the pain behind the smile—but with greater musical maturity than ever. . . .

What's great about **"When I'm Gone,"** and a lot of the earlier Miracles songs like **"The Tracks of My Tears"** is how out in the open all the pain and bitterness is. What's exciting about **"I Don't Blame You"** is the tension. He never comes out and says how hurt he is. You just sense it from the way he tells her not to "hang her head," and from the insistence of his denials. . . .

Smokey gets across his illusion-disillusion theme in a truly sublime fashion.

> Russell Gersten, "Records: 'One Dozen Roses'," in Rolling Stone (by Straight Arrow Publishers, Inc. © 1971; all rights reserved; reprinted by permission), Issue 96, November 25, 1971, p. 58.

RICHARD WILLIAMS

[Smokey] is still virtually a ghetto singer. For some reason, we can't seem to accept and come to terms with his greatness.

That's all the more extraordinary in view of the current success of his old contemporaries, Curtis Mayfield and Marvin Gaye. Eight years ago, the three of them were running parallel, the top male exponents of "New Wave R & B."

Following the comparatively lean years of the late sixties, Marvin and Curtis suddenly changed tack and earned a wide measure of popularity among white fans—specifically those who wouldn't normally bother to buy Soul records.

The way was led by Isaac Hayes, who developed a style which couched the music's essential funk inside swathes of rich strings, woodwinds, harp, voices, and percussion. He also adapted the "long form" to Soul, stretching his songs out to ten minutes and more. . . .

It worked like a charm, and became a revolution. Gaye and Mayfield quickly picked up on it, and produced their own albums in a similar style, but with a wider verbal vision. Both were still in the ghetto, but they were looking at the ghetto's problems. . . .

Robinson, I'm sure, could have done everything they've accomplished, and far more besides. He's easily the most talented of all of them. . . .

But he declined to enter the lists on their terms. . . .

No, he's just carried on doing what he always did best, writing those little three-minute songs which encompass the most startling variety of feelings. . . .

[It's] not that the feelings [Robinson] expresses are so unusual, it's his attitude to them, and the way he verbalises it. Smokey always was a big one for the metaphor and the simile . . . and no one in pop has been able to make such beautiful and unpredictable use of images which are superficially everyday and banal.

"The way you smile so bright, you know you could have been a candle; I'm holding you so tight, you know you could have been a handle" comes from the old **"The Way You Do The Things You Do,"** and in Smokey's hands it becomes the simplest, most natural expression of faith. Sometimes he can get really far out, as in the similes of **"Swept For You Baby:"** "You're like a broom, I'm like dust in the room / Aah but I'm swept for you baby."

When he's not being adoring, he's being hurt and trying to hide it. Everybody knows **"The Tracks Of My Tears,"** probably his greatest record, but even something as apparently trivial as **"I Don't Blame You At All"** . . . has that undercurrent of desperation: . . . The words themselves are flat and cliched. But when Smokey sings them in that high, ululating counter-tenor, he invests them with a tortured, feverish agony without equal in pop.

All the time, in songs like these, he seems to be on the point of throwing away the last vestiges of dignity. What saves him is his very defencelessness, and that's where his high voice comes in. We couldn't take that kind of sentiment from a rich baritone like Isaac [Hayes], or even a light, mournful baritone like Marvin Gaye. It would be too incongruous.

But Smokey sings with a woman's voice, so we can accept the sentiment without laughing at him. . . .

He has such lovely ideas for songs, too. . . . There's **"A Legend In Its Own Time,"** from the Miracles' **"Four in Blue,"** in which he says that he's not bothered about his love for his woman being remembered centuries later, like Anthony and Cleopatra or Dido and Aeneas. He wants it to be a legend in its own time. It's a beautiful thought, something that might genuinely occur to an ordinary kid. . . .

There are fewer throwaways than usual [on **"One Dozen Roses"**], and some really excellent songs. **"I Love You Dear"** is a restrained but emphatic ballad, in which Smokey plays the part of a man in love with a married woman. He begs her to leave her husband, pleads with her, and finally introduces the cruncher: "I know you wanna wait awhile, 'till your child is up and grown / But baby, it's worst on you and the child, to live where there's no love in the home." Smokey's a preacher, okay, but it's good, sound, practical counsel that he's giving, not the sly innuendo of a Joe Tex or the righteous screaming of James

Brown. Smokey's songs are real conversations put to music, not fantasies. . . .

I find it hard to stop trying to share with as many others as possible the genius of a man who can write this line: "Just like 'push' can turn to 'shove' 'like' can turn to 'love'—that's my philosophy." I'm an Isaac Hayes fan, but honestly you won't find something of that class in any of his songs . . . or anybody else's, come to that.

> Richard Williams, "The Way You Do the Things You Do," in Melody Maker (© IPC Business Press Ltd.), January 1, 1972, p. 15.

DAVID MORSE

Robinson's songs are immediately identifiable by their unusual structure, their unexpected rhythmic emphases, their slowly moving, terraced chords, . . . and their tortuous, suffocated melancholy. They focus almost obsessively on painful and contradictory feelings, on the discrepancy between dream and reality, between mask and face. Love is a guessing game (*Dog- gone Right*). There is a need to turn dream into reality (*Dreams, Dreams*) or to recognize an illusion for what it is (*The Love I Saw in You Was Just a Mirage*), to come to terms with the paradox that each hurt makes one's love stronger than before (*Ain't That Peculiar*). The victim is placed in an intolerable position of dependence (*You Neglect Me*), while in *The Tracks of My Tears* and *The Tears of a Clown* the conflict between keeping face and inner feelings of despair becomes unbearable. (p. 74)

[*The Tracks of My Tears* is the Miracles] masterpiece. It is composed of at least four musical elements; the gay, humming theme with which it opens is associated with the singer's self-confident public role, while the plangent refrain is linked with the painful feelings of his real self. The verse expresses, almost from the outside, the tension created by this discrepancy. The song moves towards a recognition of failure—the outside masquerading contrasted with the fading hope within—and the stress-pattern becomes more and more emphatic. The confessional character of the song is gradually intensified until it swells into an overwhelming incantation of masochistic self-humiliation. The singer begs his woman to look deeply into his face—and then to look again, even more closely. This is not simply a song but a powerful emotional statement.

The songs of Smokey Robinson are unusual in their integrity and their truth to experience. By comparison the work of, say, Irving Berlin, despite its distinctive musical thumbprint, is vapid and generalized; it has no conception of this kind of impersonal authenticity. With a touch of hyperbole Smokey Robinson could be described as the Petrarch of modern popular music, because he has taught artists, from Dylan to The Beatles, the relevance of the advice "Look in your heart and write." He, more than anyone, has made it possible for us to think of the popular song as a kind of poetry. (pp. 74, 77)

> David Morse, "Come and Get These Memories: Martha Reeves and Smokey Robinson," in his Motown and the Arrival of Black Music (reprinted with permission of Macmillan Publishing Co. Inc.; in Canada by David Morse; copyright © 1971 by November Books Limited), Macmillan/Collier Books, 1972, pp. 66-77.*

BOB EISNER

[Smokey Robinson is] possibly the most individualistic and recognizable R&B writer and performer in history. The songs this man has written are incredible. . . . (p. 69)

[He is] a rarity of the times, a popularly acclaimed and financially successful poet. (p. 70)

Smokey Robinson songs invariably bear his trademark, his unique ability for handling a simple melody, combined with his special gift for phrasing. His themes are never cryptic, his poetry is up front, his style unmistakable. (p. 72)

> Bob Eisner, "Smokey Robinson: The Artist as Corporate Man," in Crawdaddy (copyright © 1973 by Crawdaddy Publishing Co., Inc.; all rights reserved; reprinted by permission), March, 1973, pp. 69-74.

MARK VINING

A friend urged [*Smokey Robinson and the Miracles: 1957/1972*] on me with the recommendation that, though he was not a Miracles fan, it gave him chills. . . .

[The] music here is superb. . . . The tunes are the essential ones, the trivial and the classic, and they yield a concise and accurate picture of the legendary group. From the late fifties ballad **"Bad Girl"** . . . to '72's **"We've Come Too Far to End It Now,"** the style hasn't changed. It has matured intact, rising above the posturing so much soul music has engendered in its annexation to rock. . . .

The Miracles' spartan fidelity to the form and content of R & B is but the slightest reason for their greatness. There's also their willingness to give all there is, musically, lyrically, emotionally, the quality that has produced some of the finest records ever made. . . .

And yet, behind the gaiety, an unspoken sadness permeates the whole performance. It's there in Smokey's introductions, his banter, his giddy laugh as he fields the audience requests. The remarkable photo on the back sleeve gives us an awful picture of it, this feeling the album conveys, the one we long to suppress. It really *is* goodbye.

> Mark Vining, "Records: 'Smokey Robinson and the Miracles: 1957/1972'," in Creem (© copyright 1973 by Creem Magazine, Inc.), Vol. 4, No. 10, March, 1973, p. 63.

RICHARD WILLIAMS

No artist ever deserved the showcase of a solo album more than Smokey Robinson. . . .

Yet there's a temptation, on first listening to ["**Smokey**"] to murmur silently that the only thing it lacks is Messrs Moore, White, Rodgers, and Tamplin—in other words, the Miracles. . . . Prolonged familiarity, however, banishes such uneasiness, which was always falsely rooted. . . .

Of Smokey's new material, the most immediately appealing are **"Sweet Harmony"**, parting-is-such-sweet-sorrow benediction to his former colleagues, and **"A Silent Partner In A Three-Way Love Affair"**, based on a lyric concept worthy of his very best songs, maintaining the tension between the mask and the reality explored in earlier things like **"Tracks Of My Tears"** and **"The Tears Of A Clown"**. **"Holly"** is the story of a goodtime girl gone rotten, explained with tenderness and understanding, with a glorious tune to top it off. **"Just My Soul Responding"** is maybe the most unusual, based around a tribal chant. . . . **"Wanna Know My Mind"**, **"The Family Song"**, and **"Baby Come Close"** are at least up to the standard of the Miracles' old album material. . . .

Perhaps **"Smokey"** isn't the total mindblast his ability always promises, but neither is it the product of a busy Executive Vice-President's spare time. His many adherents will cherish it.

> Richard Williams, *"'Smokey': A Solo Set to Cherish,"* in Melody Maker *(© IPC Business Press Ltd.), July 28, 1973, p. 41.*

NOË GOLDWASSER

Smokey Robinson, whose crystalline falsetto has been synonymous with late-night party boogeying and backyard barbeque funkiness ever since way back when, shows with his solo, *Smokey,* just where all that energy comes from.

Smokey's album is just as personally crafted as [Stevie Wonder's *Innervisions*]. . . . Along with the expected (and solidly hit-bound) love-and/or-heartache ballads . . . , Smokey spills out some of his more recent personal experience. . . .

[The] most interesting and exciting cut on this lp is . . . the soul-documentary number, **"Just My Soul Responding."** It deals with the same themes as Wonder's "Living for the City"— even contains some parallel images. . . .

On the whole, *Smokey* . . . is a truly enjoyable album. Great to have you back, Smoke. (p. 68)

> Noë Goldwasser, *"Records: 'Smokey',"* in Crawdaddy *(copyright © 1973 by Crawdaddy Publishing Co., Inc.; all rights reserved; reprinted by permission), October, 1973, pp. 67-8.*

FRED DELLAR

There are certain rare occasions when I hear records that make my toes turn up and my body feel that it's in total levitation— everything becomes wonderfully unreal. And it happens whenever Smokey's around—it really does. If I play *I don't blame you at all* [on *Greatest Hits Vol. 2*] and hear Smokey soaring over those breaks, or move on to even the first few bars of the closing *We've come too far to end it all*, I know I shall head for astral planes again. . . .

> Fred Dellar, *"Miracles and Other Happenings"* (© Link House Publications Ltd, 1973; reprinted by permission of the author), in Hi-Fi News & Record Review, *Vol. 18, No. 10, October, 1973, p. 2029.**

VINCE ALETTI

I could hardly do anything less than swoon over [*Smokey,*] . . . Robinson's first solo album. . . . [**"Holly"**] is a melodramatic "Lucy in the Sky," and **"Just My Soul Responding,"** only more Motown current-affairs "relevance," but these are petty complaints. **"Holly"** glows in spite of its daytime TV story and **"Just My Soul Responding"** has the strength and conviction to overcome lines like, "Now I'm on a reservation livin' in a state of degradation." No one but Smokey can make a song based around astrological signs (**"The Family Song,"** about his own family) or yet another my-girl-and-my-best-friend song (**"Silent Partner in a Three-Way Love Affair"**) work so well. . . . [**"Wanna Know My Mind"**] is another Robinson gem, frothy but never flimsy. All this . . . and I am swooning.

> Vince Aletti, *"For the Record: 'Smokey',"* in Rolling Stone *(by Straight Arrow Publishers, Inc. © 1973; all rights reserved; reprinted by permission), Issue 147, November 8, 1973, p. 76.*

PETER REILLY

[*Smokey* consists of] good-natured, obliging performances by someone who lives up to his name. Smokey is the best possible description of Mr. Robinson's singing; it wafts. Exactly at the moment when you think he has come upon a musical idea or is about to really say something, vapor sets in. *Sweet Harmony* ought to be a good song, and perhaps it is, but Robinson shrouds it in spun sugar. I didn't mind a bit of it, as I listened, but then I didn't think very much about it afterward either.

> Peter Reilly, *"Popular Discs and Tapes: 'Smokey',"* in Stereo Review *(copyright © 1974 by Ziff-Davis Publishing Company), Vol. 32, No. 2, February, 1974, p. 96.*

KEN EMERSON

Although it falls short of the magic of the Miracles, [*Pure Smoke*] is an interesting album. . . . [Robinson] now deals with subjects that include a mother in her 30s whose turn it is to live, a divorced parent clinging to his visiting rights, and the father of a knocked-up teenager. Such songs plus two sweet ballads should boost Smokey's somewhat disappointing solo career. Unfortunately, a few tracks are trivial . . . and the album lacks a striking single.

> Ken Emerson, *"Records: 'Pure Smoke',"* in Rolling Stone *(by Straight Arrow Publishers, Inc. © 1974; all rights reserved; reprinted by permission), Issue 161, May 23, 1974, p. 79.*

GEOFF BROWN

It was, perhaps, a sad commentary on certain features of today's music scene that one could predict with almost complete accuracy the erroneous hatchet jobs which passed for "critiques" of **"Smokey,"** Robinson's first solo album since splitting with the Miracles.

That album had nine tracks. Two were not written by Smokey and thus not wholly his meat. Of the other seven **"Just My Soul Responding,"** **"Holly"** **"Sweet Harmony,"** **"A Silent Partner in A Three-Way Love Affair"** and **"Baby Come Close"** were as good as most of the stuff he recorded previously. That sort of success ratio doesn't make an album a stinker. **"Pure Smokey"** is Robinson's second solo shot and is a disappointment after the promise of **"Smokey."** The ballads aren't as strong as **"Holly"** or **"Baby Come Close"**; the refined rockers aren't as compelling as **"Just My Soul Responding."** The topics Robinson's newer songs deal with are contemporary and specific. They deal with sex in the "permissive" and "enlightened" age. . . . The lyrics lack Smokey's usual sharp imagery. . . . However, three tracks are up to his standard. **"Asleep On My Love"** and **"Fulfill Your Need"** are simple, warm love songs—one says realise I love you, the other says make use of my love. The last track on the album is the best.

It is called **"A Tattoo,"** was written by Robinson . . . and has the strength of metaphor we've come to expect in Smokey's writing. It doesn't erase the sense of disappointment fostered by **"Pure Smokey."**

Geoff Brown, "Smokey: Pure and Simple," in Melody Maker (© IPC Business Press Ltd.), June 22, 1974, p. 42.

ROBERT PALMER

[The] sensuality of its lyrics and the loose, improvisational feel of the backup suggest that [the title tune of *A Quiet Storm*] is going to be Robinson's *What's Going On* or *Innervisions*, a formula-defying statement of both personal and social import. But Robinson is moved neither by Marvin Gaye's macho sensibilities nor by Stevie Wonder's semimystical mental images. . . . [He] naturally passes over both self-celebration and prophecy in favor of love and happiness. And his instincts for the perfect hook, the well-placed quaver and the arresting turn of phrase mean that even his seven-minute songs (**"Storm," "Happy"**) retain the thematic compactness and lustrous patina of Motown singles. . . . **"Wedding Song"** is burdened by the sappiest words Robinson has written ("Oh what a beautiful day to take a vow on / Pray that the things we say will last from now on"). . . .

In fact, Robinson's much touted abilities as a poetic lyricist aren't very important here, the sexy directness of **"Storm"** and **"Backatcha"** notwithstanding. His production and singing carry the album. . . . [The album suggests evidence] that one of black music's brightest lights is still a dynamic creative force. We can look forward to many more delights from him; if success were going to spoil him, it would have done so long ago.

Robert Palmer, "Records: 'A Quiet Storm'," in Rolling Stone (by Straight Arrow Publishers, Inc. © 1975; all rights reserved; reprinted by permission), Issue 192, July 31, 1975, p. 58.

PETER REILLY

[*A Quiet Storm* is] a beautifully produced and recorded album by Smokey Robinson. He performs, with his usual pliant ease, another collection of his own songs, and there is some entertainment to be found in *Happy* and *Love Letters*. The main problem with Robinson's work is that he has a broad streak of marshmallow sentimentality which, while it may be genuine on his part, eventually seizes me in the kind of clammy embrace that means turn-off. (p. 80)

Peter Reilly, "Popular Discs and Tapes: 'A Quiet Storm'," in Stereo Review (copyright © 1975 by Ziff-Davis Publishing Company), Vol. 35, No. 2, August, 1975, p. 80.

SIMON FRITH

The Temptations had been around Motown in one form or another for a couple of years, but it wasn't until 1963 that they settled on the line-up of Eddie Kendricks and David Ruffin as lead voices. Their immediate importance was to provide a new medium for Smokey Robinson and a series of beautiful love songs—**"The Way You Do The Things You Do", "My Girl", "It's Growing", "Since I Lost My Baby",** and many more. . . . Partly Smokey was inspired by the Temptations' own abili-

ties—Eddie Kendricks, for example, whose falsetto was usually used as first lead, had a tougher voice than Smokey's own, without losing a whit of tenderness; partly, with [Motown staff composers Eddie Holland, Lamont Dozier, and Brian Holland] taking care of the rockin' business, Smokey could give his romanticism full flow—lyrically, these songs have never been matched. . . . [Take **"It's Growing"**]:

Like a snowball rolling down the side of a snow-
  covered hill
—it's growing,
Like the size of the fish that the man claims broke his
  reel
—it's growing,
Like a rose-bud growing in the warm of the summer
  sun
—it's growing,
Like a tale by the time it's been told by more than one
—it's growing.

These are typical Smokey lyrics—a series of comparisons that have charm from their unexpectedness (what's coming next?) and point from their contrasts, between the natural growth of a rose and snow-ball and the fake growth of human claims—perfect similes for the feelings of a man in love. And the chorus exactly captures the ambiguities. . . . Smokey Robinson—love, ecstasy and fragility. This was great music; add it to that of the Supremes, the Four Tops and all the others and no wonder that Motown, 1964-1967, is an era that many soul fans never wanted to leave. (pp. 50-1)

Having built its success in the sixties on a succession of sophisticated and elegant love songs, [Motown] found it difficult to adjust to the new demand for adult, personal, sensual raconteurs. In competition with the great egoists—Isaac Hayes, Barry White, Bill Withers, even Al Green—Smokey Robinson faltered. He left the Miracles but on his solo albums the necessary elaborations of arrangement and production have to struggle with his natural diffidence and the results are uneasy—he lacks seventies black virility and his place as Motown Lover has been wholly assumed by Marvin Gaye. . . . (p. 61)

Simon Frith, "You Can Make It if You Try: The Motown Story" (copyright © 1975 by Simon Frith), in The Soul Book by Ian Hoare, Clive Anderson, Tony Cummings, and Simon Frith, edited by Ian Hoare, Eyre Methuen Ltd., 1975 (and reprinted by Dell Publishing Co., Inc., 1976, pp. 39-73).*

IAN HOARE

The influence of sixties' rock on its black counterpart is more often overestimated than underestimated. With events occurring on the scale of the Watts riots, the murder of Martin Luther King and the rise of militant groups such as the Panthers, the nature of black Americans' social self-awareness was changing rapidly and profoundly. A new audience, in effect, was emerging that demanded an appropriate perspective in the songs provided for it by its musician-spokesmen. (p. 199)

In general, increased attention began to be paid by black songwriters to developing the kind of literary techniques that had previously tended to remain the province of white balladeers. Smokey Robinson was the master in this area—the artist most responsible for taking the root concerns of R&B and crystallizing the themes, particularly through the use of metaphor, into a full-fledged soul romanticism. In his early songs, some of the traditional preoccupations of black music are expressed in an unprecedently elegant manner. For the Temptations, he created **"The Way You Do The Things You Do"**, a song *about* style in which one of his own stylistic trade marks comes fully into play: the sustained list of comparisons between his girl and some rather unlikely objects—a candle, a handle, a broom, perfume. In **"Shop Around"** he used an extended metaphor to illuminate the finance-romance link. In Mary Wells' **"You Beat Me To The Punch"**, the language relates in the most direct way possible to the notion of the sex battle, but the tone is qualified by a delicate irony that suggests tenderness can perhaps conquer all in the end—the punch is love as well as rejection. In **"Two Lovers"**, also a hit for Mary Wells, he takes the key male stereotypes—the good man and the no-good man—and throws them together in one "split personality", teasing the listener with the initial hint that she's talking openly about an adulterous relationship.

One aspect of Smokey's genius as a lyricist is his ability to highlight the paradoxical nature of love in the kind of incisive, immediate language that's suited to his medium. He writes great *lines* using traditional poetic devices such as antithesis with deceptive facility:

I don't like you, but I love you.
                    (**"You've Really Got A Hold On Me"**)

I know that flowers grow from rain
But how can love grow from pain?
                    (**"Ain't That Peculiar?"**)

I got sunshine on a cloudy day
When it's cold outside, I got the month of May.
                    (**"My Girl"**)

The inversion of the pathetic fallacy in **"My Girl"** is a feature that leads directly into the songs of his most mature work, where a major preoccupation becomes the relationship in love between appearance and reality. In **"The Love I Saw In You Was Just A Mirage"** (1967) he focuses on the way a girl's soulful expression can be tragically misleading. **"The Tracks Of My Tears"** (1965), and the follow-up **"Tears Of A Clown"**, are confessions of how his own private experience contradicts the impression he gives other people. The effectiveness of **"Tracks"** is partly due to the fact that although he's contrasting his inner sadness with other people's image of him as the life of the party, he stresses that the truth of the matter is readily available in his *physical appearance*. . . . The song is the most eloquent expression on record of one of soul's favourite themes. (pp. 199-201)

Smokey's mid-sixties' lyrics are at the centre of a tradition of metaphorical language in soul which has thrived in the seventies, partly determined by the omnipresent censorship problem and partly by the more pronounced leaning towards literary culture. The "clowning" and "acting" images, for instance, which figure prominently in Smokey's work, have cropped up regularly in all the music's regional and historical variations, with the most common approach being an apparent effort to squeeze as many points of reference out of the basic metaphor as possible. (p. 201)

Ian Hoare, "Mighty, Mighty Spade and Whitey: Black Lyrics and Soul's Interaction with White Culture" (copyright © 1975 by Ian Hoare), in The Soul Book by Ian Hoare, Clive Anderson, Tony Cummings, and Simon Frith, edited by Ian Hoare, Eyre Methuen Ltd., 1975 (and reprinted by Dell Publishing Co., Inc., 1976, pp. 146-210).*

JOHN ROCKWELL

Smokey's Family Robinson is hardly a concept album in the more labored sense of the term. But it makes sense as a whole, the songs linked by musical style and thematic associations, flowing seamlessly together with thought paid to contrast and balance. . . .

Smokey's Family Robinson might seem to be plunging headlong into disco, except that Robinson, with his patented, light-footed control, never sacrifices his own individuality and ends the album with two ballads that count among the finest things he's ever done. . . .

Robinson's deepest gift has always lain in the sexually charged, achingly erotic love ballad. . . . Robinson's lyrics, in fast and slow songs alike, are almost invariably about love. Whether he is a "great poet" seems rather open to question, if poetry is the juxtaposition of words in a way that has interest in itself. Much of what Robinson writes mixes undeniable verbal freshness with an earnest yet somehow endearing awkwardness, replete with sincere homilies and labored metaphors. (p. 60)

Robinson's gift for quintessential make-out music is apparent throughout this album . . . but it blossoms in the last two songs, **"Like Nobody Can"** and **"Castles Made of Sand."** . . . [Both] are fine songs in themselves, with words that elevate clichés into verities and musical constructions that set his singing in an ideal context. (p. 62)

John Rockwell, "Smokey and Co. Second That Emotion," in Rolling Stone (by Straight Arrow Publishers, Inc. © 1976; all rights reserved; reprinted by permission), Issue 212, May 6, 1976, pp. 60, 62.

DAVID DALTON and LENNY KAYE

The early years of Tamla-Motown belonged to Smokey Robinson, whose Miracles not only established the company as a major force (with **"Shop Around"**) but musically set the succession of styles to be embellished in later administrations. [He was as] delicate a writer as he was a performer. . . . Between 1960 and the emergence of the Supremes four years later, he accounted for a majority of Motown's success, working with the Marvelettes, Marvin Gaye, Mary Wells and the Temptations, as well as boosting the Miracles to becoming one of the most visible and prolific attractions in the pop market.

Robinson wrote with intelligence and sophistication, underplaying his lyrical hand to separate the contradictions between fantasy and reality. He was at his best within the sad, sweetly-taken ballad, the milky quality of his voice flirting with heartache and devotion, reversing images one over the other: **"The Hunter Gets Captured By The Game," "What's So Good About Good-Bye," "My Girl,"** and **"The Love I Saw In You Was Just A Mirage."** When called on to write more uptempo material, he responded with a broad grin, **"Mickey's Monkey"** and **"Goin' To A Go Go,"** the Miracles stepping lithely around him. (p. 140)

David Dalton and Lenny Kaye, "Four on the Floor: The Motown Sound," in their Rock 100 (copyright © 1977 by David Dalton and Lenny Kaye; used by permission of Grosset & Dunlap, Inc.), Grosset & Dunlap, 1977, pp. 139-46.*

BOB GALLAGHER

I can find nothing to suggest that **"Love Breeze"** expands the Robinson legend.

To be blunter still, I'm damned if I can find more than one track that lodges in my memory.

The exception is **"Shoe Soul,"** a trickily constructed mid-tempo pop song carrying a lyric rich in mischievous metaphor and a lilting hook ideally suited to a falsetto voice. If the album is to yield a *bona fide* hit single, then I reckon that will be it. . . .

"Love So Fine" is perhaps the most interesting production of the eight. In a way, it's Smokey's "Sir Duke," pop/jazz that calls upon some blowsy horns, what seems to be an upright bass and a sprightly piano as assistance to a swinging vocal.

"Love Breeze" is neither a triumph nor a defeat, and Smokey's most loyal fans will no doubt accept it gratefully, but it's no more than that.

> *Bob Gallagher, "Smokey's Legend Falters," in* Melody Maker *(© IPC Business Press Ltd.), April 1, 1978, p. 23.*

MIKE FREEDBERG

The very first song on [*Love Breeze,*] Smokey Robinson's best album since his quitting the Miracles, makes you restless while you dance, blue when you kiss. Since Robinson's previous outings as a soloist have been at best incidental music to a public relations campaign for love, who was expecting him suddenly to serve up lyrics and music as eloquent as **"Tracks of My Tears"**? No PR here. . . . This is Al Green's map of love: something that makes you do right, do wrong.

Like Green on *The Belle Album,* Smokey on *Love Breeze* finds the search for love lonely and wearying. . . .

But where Green paces out the space between Saturday night and Sunday morning, Robinson measures an interpersonal distance. His lyrics fix on the place where fact and dissembling meet—*there's* the place for touching. . . .

Blues fans will hear Robert Johnson's troubles in Robinson's new songs—Smokey seeks answers and finds only deaf ears, seeks affection and gets the clash of wills. You can't listen to *Love Breeze* without worrying about Smokey's sanity. He rebels and then surrenders; he frustrates and disarms you, while the music pitter-patters as if it's running away. Almost instinctively, you dance or dream away from Robinson's struggles—*anything* to hide from the combat Smokey knows he must endure to reach another person.

> *Mike Freedberg, "Tears of His Tracks," in* Crawdaddy *(copyright © 1978 by Crawdaddy Publishing Co., Inc.; all rights reserved; reprinted by permission), May, 1978, p. 71.*

RICHARD WILLIAMS

Whatever Smokey Robinson's faults and failures, he's always sounded like no-one else, and on **"Where There's Smoke . . ."** at least he has the courage to pursue and renew his own clichés.

The album's centrepiece is, inevitably, his own bid for 1979 disco prominence, a remake of his old classic for the Temptations, **"Get Ready."** You might say that this extended, bass-propelled version exposes the creeping decadence of popular music, when juxtaposed with the miniaturist tautness of the 1966 original. . . .

Longtime Smokey fans will prefer the throwaway romance of **"Share It,"** with its . . . shiver-down-the-spine spoken asides, and—particularly—**"Cruisin',"** a vintage collaboration between Robinson and his steadfast guitarist Marvin Tamplin. **"Cruisin'"** successfully approximates the old heady, billowing, rapture of **"Swept For You Baby"** and **"You Must Be Love"**—although, of course, it lacks the vital innocence of those mid-Sixties beauties. . . .

[Get Robinson's album] only if you can't live without him. . . .

> *Richard Williams, "Chairmen of the Board," in* Melody Maker *(© IPC Business Press Ltd.), July 28, 1979, p. 20.**

PHYL GARLAND

Perhaps I was spoiled by **"Smokin'"** . . . , Smokey Robinson's last live album. It was a treasure trove of all the aged-in-soul songs that made him the dean of rhythm-and-blues writers back in the early Sixties when Motown was synonymous with the vibrant sound of an emerging urban generation. It would be difficult even for Smokey to produce another gem comparable to *Ooh, Baby Baby,* but if he could, it isn't on [**"Where There's Smoke"**]. Of course, these songs are new and haven't had a chance to imbed themselves in our minds to the point where the lyrics seem like old friends, but in their freshness and consistent quality they are nevertheless a pleasure to hear.

The range of the material is relatively broad, from *It's a Good Night,* an interesting disco play on the basic melody of the standard *It's a Good Day,* to *Share It,* which is almost old-fashioned in its directness and simplicity. Indeed, one of the elements of Robinson's staying power is the elegant leanness of his music. Where others employ electronic gimmickry and endless overdubbing, he relies steadfastly on the music to convey its own message. . . . Maybe this isn't a landmark album in Robinson's long and fertile career, but it is solid, ingratiating music that should wear well.

> *Phyl Garland, "Popular Discs and Tapes: 'Where There's Smoke'," in* Stereo Review *(copyright © 1979 by Ziff-Davis Publishing Company), Vol. 43, No. 4, October, 1979, p. 112.*

RICHARD WILLIAMS

[**"Let Me Be Your Clock"** is] closely tied to Smokey's Sixties idiom. Cast in the beseeching slow-drag mould of **"The Tracks Of My Tears"** and **"Swept For You Baby"**, it's firmly in the line of his metaphor songs: "Let me be the pendulum that strikes your chime / For the very first time" surely harks back to the era of "I'm holding you so tight / You know you could've been a handle" and "You're like a broom / I'm like dust in the room". . . .

The rest of [**"Warm Thoughts"**], his ninth solo album since leaving the Miracles in 1972, is typically spotty. There's a heavy-handed dance tune (**"Heavy On Pride"**) . . . ; there's a collaboration with Stevie Wonder (**"Melody Man"**) ruined by impossibly twee words; there's a slushy Vegasy torch song (**"What's In Your Life For Me"**); there's the feature for his wife, Claudette (**"Wine, Women & Song"**); there's filler (**"I Want To Be Your Love"**); and there's the disastrous **"Into Each Rain Some Life Must Fall"**, crippled by the cringe-inducing reversed metaphor of the title. . . .

[Smokey's] long since lost the concentration necessary to produce an album of sustained merit. By this current standard, even 1974's **"Pure Smokey"** (on which he addressed the concerns of maturity) now seems like a triumph. Ah, well; fans like me should simply be grateful that he's still around at all.

Richard Williams, "Ticking Over," in Melody Maker (©IPC Business Press Ltd.), March 29, 1980, p. 24.

STEPHEN HOLDEN

Robinson's **Warm Thoughts,** an album of reflective love ballads, is so far beyond anything he's done before that it makes me wonder if he's only been half-trying all these years.

With a talent like Robinson's, of course, half-trying has produced a lot of classic pop, most of it recorded in the '60s with the Miracles before he went solo. Of the six solo albums Robinson made prior to **Warm Thoughts,** only the diaphanous, moody *A Quiet Storm* (1975) worked as a whole. With disco then on the rise, however, *A Quiet Storm* didn't make the impact it should have. Now, with the post-disco ballad revival upon us, Robinson has seized his moment. . . .

For all of *A Quiet Storm*'s sumptuousness, its tunes had a sameness that's always plagued Robinson's songwriting. Aside from a dozen or so great songs, his music has tended to be static, with harmonies that shift endlessly between minor-sevenths and tonics. . . . The fitful magic of his records came mostly from the chemistry of his voice and lyrics. Robinson's falsetto personality, unlike that of his imitators, isn't the jive attitude of a man flattering the angel he desires, but an expression of gentleness and rare vulnerability. He portrays erotic love as an earthly paradise which once gained must be reverently attended in order to last. For Robinson, love isn't a conquest but a mutual surrender filled with uncertainty.

Warm Thoughts's best cuts offer unprecedentedly moving and mature visions of this paradise, in the kind of orchestral production they've always demanded but seldom received. The album's moment of truth—one of several songs in which Robinson decisively extends his melodic range is a lavish ballad, **"What's in Your Life for Me,"** co-written with Donny Soul. In it, Robinson poses the agonizing, unanswerable questions that all lovers ask, even at the best of times: "Will tomorrow bring me sorrow / 'Cause I confessed my love today? . . . There's no daily guarantee / I'll take the tears to know the joy / Of a chance to really see / What's in your life / What's in your life for me." . . . This is no adolescent plea for gratification but a mature man's expression of his continuing need for a complete emotional/sexual relationship. The only other pop singers who could communicate grown-up desire this directly have been Frank Sinatra, Billie Holiday, and Nina Simone. But where these three, at their most eloquent, all dwelt on disillusion, Robinson expresses a more passionate faith than ever in the reality and power of human love. . . .

On **"Wine, Women and Song,"** Robinson and his wife Claudette duet in a story about unhappily married husband-and-wife performers. Oddly, Robinson doesn't play the part of the husband who drinks and plays around, but of an ardent fan and would-be lover of the wife. Robinson characteristically doesn't tidy up the emotions of the situation. Much as she'd like to, the wife can't bring herself to stray, and life just goes on. The story is as inconclusive as it is believable, and it shows that, far from exhausting his ideas as a songwriter, Robinson may have discovered a whole new arena in domestic drama.

Robinson still deals with love convincingly because his best songs go so deep that the impulse to love becomes synonymous with the life force itself. "If I receive the love I need, then on your behalf I'll be whole," he vows in **"What's in Your Life for Me."** Robinson makes you believe that music and true love are the only things that matter. That's why *Warm Thoughts* is the first masterpiece of '80s soul.

Stephen Holden, "Smokey Robinson Finds Paradise" (reprinted by permission of The Village Voice and the author; copyright © News Group Publications, Inc., 1980), in The Village Voice, Vol. XXV, No. 16, April 21, 1980, p. 65.

PHYL GARLAND

Though he has been one of the anchormen of vocal soul music for over twenty years, William "Smokey" Robinson manages to sing with the warmth, sincerity, and emotional involvement of a very young man still anticipating life's greater and yet-untasted pleasures. There is no hint of flagging enthusiasm, no sign that he has lost any of his customary purity of sound or style. Many musical modes have come and gone in the two decades he has been before the public, but he continues to rely on the same effective cool-sweet approach, the essence of "laid back" long before that term came into popular over-use. (pp. 73-4)

"Warm Thoughts" contains eight selections that bear all the familiar characteristics of vintage Smokey even though they are brand new. This appealing blend of the old and the new is, in fact, probably the key to his remarkably evergreen popularity. There is a distinct echo of the early Sixties, for example, in the way he manages to *suggest* sensuality without flaunting it in the more modern style, and both melodies and lyrics flow over the mind with a delectable suggestion of the *déjà vu*. There are whole stretches of this new music so cleverly tuneful that it seems immediately familiar and hummable, lyrics that capture our attention at once with clever new twists on old clichés—such as the song *Into Each Rain Some Life Must Fall.*

Critical attention will probably focus on *Melody Man,* the most imaginative and rousing track here . . . , but I am more drawn to the understated brilliance of Smokey's own *Let Me Be the Clock* and *I Want to Be Your Love.* . . . [Smokey] has the gift of making the most personal of these musical dreams spring miraculously to life—warm thoughts indeed. (p. 74)

Phyl Garland, "Smokey Robinson's 'Warm Thoughts': Unflagging Enthusiasm, Understated Brilliance," in Stereo Review (copyright © 1980 by Ziff-Davis Publishing Company), Vol. 45, No. 1, July, 1980, pp. 73-4.

ROBERT PALMER

Smokey Robinson is one of those perennials whose creativity and staying power contradicts the notion that pop music, and especially the pop music of the rock-and-roll era, is necessarily ephemeral. . . .

Bob Dylan once called Mr. Robinson "America's greatest living poet," and the remark wasn't at all ludicrous. His work will surely endure. . . .

If Mr. Robinson's songs have one overriding concern, it is quiet but intense pain—the heartache behind the smile, the tears of the clown.

> Robert Palmer, "Pop: Smokey Robinson Moves with the Times," in The New York Times (© 1980 by The New York Times Company; reprinted by permission), July 27, 1980, p. 33.

ROBOT A. HULL

William "Smokey" Robinson was blessed at birth with an extraordinary poetic vision: God stepped down from His lofty perch and kissed the newborn's brow. Since then, Smokey . . . has made us swoon, massaging our hearts with a romantic lyricism that justly earned him the title of World's Greatest Living Poet. . . .

Warm Thoughts . . . is the Motown Symbolist's most vital effort at keeping the embers of love burning since *One Dozen Roses*, his '71 twilight masterpiece with the Miracles. His lyrics still rely upon the turned around phrase ("**Into Each Rain Some Life Must Fall**")—a sure sign of an intrinsic faith in language—but more than that, they reflect the poetic maturation of an artist no longer deceived by a mirage. . . .

To comprehend the adulthood of Smokey's rhyme scheme is to understand why the soul of his ballads belongs to a heaven light years away from the sleazy pit where Barry White and Teddy Pendergrass croon in June about spoons.

The album, of course, is not without flaws, but they are tactical errors, due primarily to the presence of intruders. . . .

Nevertheless, the erotically rhythmic moments of the album . . . offset any of its headaches. . . . *Warm Thoughts* (its revealed intimacies perhaps even designed for our own bedrooms) may become the make-out album of the year. So start smooching.

> Robot A. Hull, "Records: 'Warm Thoughts'," in Creem (© copyright 1980 by Creem Magazine, Inc.), Vol. 12, No. 3, August, 1980, p. 54.

JOE McEWEN and JIM MILLER

Most of Motown's roster consisted of Detroit acts unearthed at local talent shows; here as elsewhere, Smokey Robinson's Miracles set the pattern. When Robinson first approached Gordy late in 1957, most of the group was still in high school; three years later, when **"Shop Around"** hit, the Miracles' oldest member was barely 21.

During the next ten years, however, the Miracles became a seasoned troupe, while Robinson became one of the most prolific and popular producer/songwriters in the Motown stable. In person, the Miracles' performances were erratic, depending on the state of Smokey's fragile falsetto. . . . In the studio, on the other hand, Robinson knew few rivals, composing and producing . . . torchy soul/pop hits. . . .

Smokey was his own best interpreter, and the Miracles remained one of Motown's most consistent groups throughout the Sixties. At the outset, their chief asset was the anguished eroticism conveyed by Robinson's pristine falsetto (listen to **"You Can Depend on Me,"** from 1960). But by the mid-Sixties, Robinson had also blossomed as a composer and lyricist. . . . [Many] of his finest lyrics hinged on an apparent contradiction: "I'm a choosy beggar," "I've got sunshine on a cloudy day," "The love I saw in you was just a mirage." Despite a spate of uptempo hits, from **"Shop Around"** and **"Mickey's Monkey"** (1963) to **"Going to a Go-Go"** (1965), the Miracles' forte was ballads. Here Robinson—whether confessing his dependence, as on **"You've Really Got a Hold on Me"** (1962), or pleading for forgiveness, as on **"Ooo Baby Baby"** (1965)—could use his voice to transcendent effect. **"The Tracks of My Tears"** (1965) remains one of the most emotionally demanding Motown singles of the Sixties. (p. 240)

> Joe McEwen and Jim Miller, "Motown," in The Rolling Stone Illustrated History of Rock and Roll, edited by Jim Miller (copyright © 1980 by Rolling Stone Press; reprinted by permission of Random House, Inc. and Rolling Stone Press), revised edition, Rolling Stone Press, Random House, 1980, pp. 235-48.*

GEOFF BROWN

Smokey certainly isn't the consistently stunning writer he was in the Sixties. His bitter-sweet love songs have lost their sharpness but he's matured as a composer with considerable dignity and has occasionally responded to the challenge of writing interesting lyrics about home, family and more adult topics which superceded those in the older songs of teenage love.

Consequently, his recent albums have been professionally done affairs with one or two tracks retaining the grace and appeal of his best work.

Since splitting with the Miracles in 1972 I can think of only one Robinson solo album, **"Smokey's Family Robinson"** in 1976, that was a total disappointment. On the four albums since then . . . , there have been plenty of the composer's creamy rich melodies from the jaunty **"It's A Good Night"** to the romantic **"I Love The Nearness Of You"** . . . , from the hipness of **"Cruisin'"** to the conscious cuteness of **"Shoe Soul"**.

And last year's **"Warm Thoughts"** set kicked off with two excellent tunes, **"Let Me Be The Clock"** and **"Heavy On Pride"**. . . .

[The] four songs [on **"Being with You"**] which Robinson wrote himself are the best.

The title track . . . is a typically simply realised mid-tempo ballad. . . . Never can holding on to the affections of a potentially troublesome lover under the disapproving gaze of family and friends have been made to sound so attractive.

"Food For Thought" . . . has a doomwatch lyric wagging a "concerned" finger at cigarette manufacturers, industrialists who're polluting the oceans, rampant male fornicators and inattentive wives.

Stringent warnings definitely aren't Smokey's strong point. His melodies are too gentle, his voice too soft and warm.

"If You Wanna Make Love (Come Round Here)" is a plainly done ballad with a gorgeous chorus and attractive Piccirillo guitar riff while **"You Are Forever"** is another subtly worked meditation on true love, setting up the premise of eternal devotion being stronger than monarchies and Mother Nature in the first verse and sort of *musing* thereon for the rest of the track. . . .

So, two good, Seventies-style Smokey songs in **"Being With You"** and **"If You Wanna Make Love"**, plus one quite good, one barely so-so.

Geoff Brown, "Lifetime of Devotion," in Melody Maker *(© IPC Business Press Ltd.), March 14, 1981, p. 20.*

STEPHEN HOLDEN

Smokey Robinson is that rare pop singer whose rhapsodic lyricism hasn't diminished with approaching middle age. Indeed, time has added a metaphysical depth to his art. The postadolescent Romeo who created **"The Tracks of My Tears"** and **"Ooh, Baby Baby"** exudes the same sweetness today he did fifteen years ago. . . . Smokey Robinson's faith in the redemptive power of erotic love continues unabated. In Robinson's musical world, sexual happiness isn't the product of spiritual equilibrium but its source. . . .

[Again] and again on *Being with You,* Smokey Robinson performs unassuming aesthetic miracles. In contrast to last year's *Warm Thoughts* (which, with *A Quiet Storm* is the pinnacle of Robinson's solo career), the tunes . . . on the new album are smaller-scaled. There aren't any grand ballads to compare with **"What's in Your Life for Me,"** no lavish production numbers like **"Melody Man."** Instead, the heart of *Being with You* consists of simple midtempo songs, produced with a light touch in the spirit of the artist's mellow Sixties hits. . . .

Three of the record's four Robinson originals look back to more innocent days. **"Food for Thought,"** a reggae-calypso hybrid that warns against everything from pollution to adultery, is the exception, and Smokey Robinson sounds uncomfortable singing it. In **"Being with You,"** . . . Robinson takes the same guileless tone that characterized his earliest love songs and begs a lover not to leave him. **"If You Wanna Make Love (Come 'round Here)"** echoes the easygoing sinuousness of **"You Really Got a Hold on Me,"** while **"You Are Forever"** extends a promise of eternal love so beautifully and directly that you practically forget how shopworn the sentiment is. (p. 93)

Following the sophisticated *Warm Thoughts, Being with You* seems almost resolutely old-fashioned. But underneath its gloss, *Warm Thoughts* was just as traditional, since it too expressed Robinson's awesome commitment to romantic love. In a time when pop music grows more and more sexually explicit, pure exaltation is increasingly difficult to evoke with much conviction. After all, instant sex has rendered many of the conventions of classical courtship obsolete. Don't think, however, that Robinson's songs aren't filled with sex. They are. But in this man's art, sex isn't a fast roll in the hay, it's sweet manna shared during a leisurely stroll into paradise. . . . While his is a world in which tears are copious, the tears are as natural—and desirable—as rain. And the sun, when it shines, is dazzling. (p. 95)

Stephen Holden, "Smokey Robinson's Awesome Romanticism," in Rolling Stone *(by Straight Arrow Publishers, Inc. © 1981; all rights reserved; reprinted by permission), Issue 341, April 16, 1981, pp. 93, 95.*

JOHN PICCARELLA

A more rhythmic vocalist can bump in sexy syncopation off a complement of polyrhythms, but Smokey is all melodic caress; his cool, aching lyricism must float free and uncomplicated. *Being with You,* by all means a pop triumph, allows him that simplicity and generates more potential hitpower than any of his previous solo outings. In fact, the title cut sounds better on the radio (and spends more time there) than any post-Miracles tune in his catalogue. . . .

Less viable is the reggae imitation **"Food for Thought,"** not because the steel drum riff doesn't generate the Caribbean breeze it's supposed to, but because it has nothing to do with the protest-for-the-hell-of-it of Robinson's lyric, which attacks first cigarette manufacturers, then industrial pollution, then stud machismo, and then wives' lack of interest in their husbands. Though the chorus and instrumentation are catchy, Smokey's vocal charm is considerably diminished by the uncomfortable way he negotiates both the affected lyrics and the affected rhythm. . . .

Throughout his solo career his writing has lacked the concision and wit of his classic Miracles tunes. Yet he's created a graceful persona, with occasional interesting quirks, like the ridiculous sexual metaphors scattered through *Warm Thoughts. Being with You* not only offers continuing proof of Smokey Robinson's lyrical gift, but reaffirms his powers as a pop seducer. When it comes to sweet nothings, Smokey talks in tongues.

John Piccarella, "Smokey Robinson's Sweet Nothings" (reprinted by permission of The Village Voice *and the author; copyright © News Group Publications, Inc., 1981), in* The Village Voice, *Vol. XXVI, No. 17, April 22-28, 1981, p. 59.*

MITCHELL COHEN

Being With You is marked with the rapturous possibilities and elegance of expression that characterized the finest 60's work of the Miracles. Three of the four Robinson originals—the title song, **"You Are Forever,"** and **"If You Wanna Make Love (Come 'Round Here)"**—are temperamentally and lyrically akin to such indestructible songs as **"I'll Try Something New,"** **"More Love,"** and **"If You Can Want."** . . .

[In the past] Smokey Robinson's songs were built on clever metaphorical conceits. . . .

What they're up to now is an extension. Even when they're saying almost the same thing, the difference is in the approach. . . .

Robinson produced only one song on *Being With You* . . . and wrote but half of the eight (one, a cautionary calypso, **"Food For Thought,"** is negligible). **"Who's Sad,"** composed in emulation of the Smokey school of smiles-masking-heartbreak (and lifting its opening line straight from Bacharach and David's **"Walk On By"**), is the best of the ringers; **"I Hear The Children Singing,"** pious pap about finding the child inside the man, is the worst.

Being With You is something of a slip-up after 1980's semi-miraculous *Warm Thoughts* (in a barren year, I gratefully accepted Smokey's resurgence as a personal gift). . . .

For two-thirds of my life, I've believed in the gospel according to Smokey. It hasn't worked all the time, but I still figure it's worth a shot.

Mitchell Cohen, "Records: 'Being with You'," in Creem *(© copyright 1981 by Creem Magazine, Inc.), Vol. 13, No. 1, June, 1981, p. 52.*

Jerome Siegel

1914-

Joe Shuster

1914-

DOES SUPERMAN HAVE THE
POWER TO SAVE HIS CREATORS?

Siegel—American comic strip and comic book writer.

Shuster—Canadian-born American comic strip and comic book illustrator.

Siegel and Shuster are the creators of Superman, perhaps the most well-known and popular comic book character. Superman is an archetypal hero, combining the strength of Hercules with the nobility of Galahad; an alien, he uses highly developed attributes such as strength, hearing, invulnerability, flight, and x-ray vision to protect the American people from war, crime, and injustice. In order to maintain his privacy, Superman poses as timid newspaper reporter Clark Kent, reassuming his true identity when his rescuing talents are needed. The problems in maintaining this dual identity are complicated by Superman's relationship with Lois Lane, another reporter who adores Superman but dislikes Clark. This situation is felt to be both the crux of the Superman story and the element that has kept it interesting for over forty years.

Young people have been Superman's most enthusiastic fans; it has been noted that the story typifies adolescent daydreams of imaginary triumphs. Superman's creators were teenagers themselves when they developed the character, forming their partnership as high school students with a mutual interest in science fiction. They began publishing fan magazines on the subject filled with artwork and book reviews; one of the issues contained a review of Philip Wylie's novel *Gladiator,* on which Siegel and Shuster based the character of Superman. The strip was peddled unsuccessfully to newspaper syndicates and comic book publishers for five years. In 1936 the team began working for New Fun Comics Inc., which later became National Periodicals, doing cops and robbers and adventure strips. In June, 1938, the first Superman episode appeared in *Action Comics.*

Superman comics were immediately successful. The story of how the infant Superman came to earth, sent by his father in a rocket ship before their planet Krypton was destroyed, has achieved the status of a myth or legend for Superman fans. Initially Siegel and Shuster concentrated their strips on Superman's amazing physical attributes as he fought local criminals. World War II provided a wide range of villains: Superman became a symbol of courage and patriotism as he battled the Nazis and Japanese. Later, Superman reflected scientific and technological advancements as his own capabilities and those of his adversaries increased. Throughout his development, Superman's moral outlook has been consistent: Siegel developed a clear division between good and evil that is still the basis for superhero comics; he also gave Superman a strong social consciousness and a sense of humor which has been described as his most appealing feature. The writers who succeeded Siegel have been criticized for deemphasizing Superman's essential simplicity in favor of more sophisticated characters and plots. Siegel and Shuster were themselves censured for the smugness of their comic's righteous attitude and for creating prejudice in their young readers against the ethnic and political villains depicted in the strips. Some educators and psychologists in the 1940s and 1950s felt that reading *Superman* led young people to negative, even criminal, behavior; now, however, these comics are felt to be acceptable influences due to Superman's high ideals of justice and morality. As concepts of masculinity, patriotism, and heroism changed, Superman's popularity became less universal. The comics have had a steady following, however, and the character of Superman attracted a new audience when the first of a planned series of Superman films was released in 1978.

After Siegel and Shuster left National, they split up their team to freelance. Siegel created cartoons such as *Funnyman* and *Reggie Van Twerp*, but none of them achieved the long-term success of *Superman*. Shuster went to Hollywood to work on animated films, but his output dwindled as his vision failed. Both men, however, are recognized as being among the most important contributors to the comic book genre. Superman has gone beyond the confines of the comic strip into international acceptance and has become an integral part of popular culture.

SLATER BROWN

It was only two years ago that Superman was first revealed to the youth of this country. . . . But the response which greeted his appearance was so enthusiastic and so immediate that already Superman has surpassed such long established classics as Little Orphan Annie, Dick Tracy and Popeye. . . .

[It is not], to those versed in primitive myth or to students of the blacker arts of modern demagogy, difficult to understand why this new comic should have become so generally and so fantastically popular. For Superman, handsome as Apollo, strong as Hercules, chivalrous as Launcelot, swift as Hermes, embodies all the traditional attributes of a Hero God. He is, moreover, a protective deity whose role, according to the authors, is the "savior of the helpless and oppressed." In other words, the comic strip, besides affording entertainment for the romantic young, seems also to fill some symptomatic desire for a primitive religion. And though one cannot help wondering if [philosopher Friedrich] Nietzsche, sourly contemplating Time's Ruins, would consider this popular vulgarization of his romantic concept with equanimity, even as [Jonathan] Swift may shudder over the final and ironic destiny of his Gulliver, I, at least, cannot share whatever disapprobation he may feel. For in Nietzsche's own native land and in the neighboring

country where he lived, it is not the children who have embraced a vulgarized myth of Superman so enthusiastically; it has been their elders.

Slater Brown, "The Coming of Superman," in The New Republic, *Vol. 103, No. 10, September 2, 1940, p. 301.*

JOHN KOBLER

[The] Man of Steel, with his super-hearing, super-sight and super-vitality, has become all things to all boys. He has shaken the pedestal of many a classic boyhood idol: Tarzan, whom he can outleap and outfight; Nick Carter, whom he can outsleuth; Galahad, whose purity is as tarnished brass compared to his. More than this Superman accomplishes with casual ease feats that are common to every boy's daydreams. . . . And to top it all, his motivating traits are "super-courage, super-goodness and super-justice"; his mission in life "to go to the rescue of persecuted people and deserving persons."

Perhaps the greatest of all Superman's achievements is that he is a miracle man in fact as well as in fancy. No other cartoon character ever has been such an all-around success at the age of three. No other cartoon character ever has carried his creators to such an accomplishment as Siegel and Shuster enjoy at the age of twenty-six. (p. 14)

The young creators of the Man of Steel would have been hailed by [Sigmund] Freud as perfect clinical illustrations of psychological compensation. For here are two small, shy, nervous, myopic lads, who can barely cope with ordinary body-building contraptions, let alone tear the wings off a stratoliner in midair. As the puniest kids in school, picked on and bullied by their huskier classmates, they continually moped off into what Doctor Freud termed "infantile phantasies," wherein they became colossi of brute strength, capable of flattening whole regiments of class bullies by a flick of their pinkies. . . .

[There] were years of struggle and discouragement. The partners brewed many a strong potion—Doctor Occult, a sort of astral Nick Carter who kept tangling with zombis, werewolves and such; Henri Duval, a doughty musketeer in the image of D'Artagnan—but no editor hastened to press riches on them. What few continuities they did place were bought by Major Malcolm Wheeler-Nicholson, a grand-mannered, bespatted ex-Army officer, who in February of 1935 had published New Fun Comics, [the] first original comic magazine. . . . But the major couldn't see Superman for two pins. . . .

[As Siegel related,] "I am lying in bed counting sheep when all of a sudden it hits me. I conceive a character like Samson, Hercules and all the strong men I ever heard tell of rolled into one. Only more so. I hop right out of bed and write this down, and then I go back and think some more for about two hours and get up again and write that down. This goes on all night at two-hour intervals, until in the morning I have a complete script." . . .

The story [Siegel and Shuster told in their first twelve strips of how Superman was sent to Metropolis, U.S.A., as a baby] is now as familiar to the average American boy as George Washington and the cherry tree. (p. 70)

We next see him grown to supermanhood, a broad-shouldered, Greek-profiled titan. In the process he has acquired a dual personality. Part of the time the world knows him as Clark Kent, a distinctly prissy reporter for the Daily Planet, who tends to shy away from unpleasantness. But let evil show its fangs and he ducks into privacy, shucks his college-cut clothes and stands forth, bold as truth, in the gaudy working clothes of Superman. This Doctor-Jekyll-and-Mr.-Hyde arrangement enables Clark Kent to hand his paper some extraordinary scoops on Superman's latest coups.

Most of them are brought off in behalf of Lois Lane, the Planet's toothsome girl reporter, whose nose for news is constantly landing her in dire straits. (p. 73)

Besides being the greatest soliloquizer since Hamlet, Superman is also a humorist full of whimsey and light banter. No matter how rough the action or how grim the crisis, he is always ready to toss off some blithe gaiety. "May I get in on this?" he inquires with elaborate mock courtesy, as he slams himself through brick and glass into [Lex] Luthor's hide-out. . . .

With millions of parents ready to ban Superman from the house should ever his high moral sense falter, the company takes its civic responsibilities seriously.

Superman is never allowed, for example, to destroy property belonging to anybody except the villain, and then only when absolutely unavoidable. He will readily project himself through a building, rendering it utterly uninhabitable, but only when Lois Lane's predicament inside is so desperate that to use the conventional entrance might mean a fatal delay. Superman never kills anybody and never uses a weapon other than his bare fists. He knocks evildoers silly at the drop of a hat, tosses them clear into the stratosphere and generally scares the daylights out of them. But those who get killed are always hoist by their own petards, as when a gangster whams Superman on the skull with a crowbar, only to have the crowbar rebound and shatter his own noggin.

Rarely by so much as a word or a glance is the tender passion suggested between Superman and Lois Lane. For one thing, Superman himself has shyly confessed that he would never embrace a girl, lest he inadvertently crack her ribs. It is a curious evidence of children's precocity that most of them sense how Superman and Lois feel about each other anyway. (p. 74)

John Kobler, "Up, Up and Awa-a-y! The Rise of Superman, Inc.," in The Saturday Evening Post *(reprinted with permission from The Saturday Evening Post Company © 1941), Vol. 213, No. 51, June 21, 1941, pp. 14-15, 70, 73-4, 76, 78.*

MARTIN SHERIDAN

[Superman's] popular appeal is due to the fact that America is a land of hero worshippers. Superman is the ultimate in heroes. He outdoes everybody in everything, even to bursting through steel doors and catching bullets between his teeth.

Superman is for the right and against the wrong. With two-thirds of the world at war people take delight in following the adventures of a fictional being who can dictate to dictators and make tyrants say "uncle." He's a comforting fellow to have around—even if he is an imaginary character—for the stimulus to our morale. (pp. 235-36)

Martin Sheridan, "Superman," in his Comics and Their Creators: Life Stories of American Cartoonists *(copyright © 1944, copyright renewed © 1972, by Martin Sheridan; reprinted by permission of the author), revised edition, R. T. Hale & Company, 1944 (and reprinted by Hyperion Press, Inc., 1977), pp. 233-36.*

COULTON WAUGH

[Superman] is a national figure, perhaps the most worshiped and adored of our time. (p. 256)

The simple and marvelously effective idea back of "**Superman**" was to take one of the interplanetary heroes who . . . had added supernormal powers to their sex-bursting physique, and allow him to whip through the setting of our place and time. . . .

We have always worshiped heroes, and Superman is only a modern cousin to Paul Bunyan, who once took an annoying tornado by the dark, fast-twisting, deadly tail, and cooped it up in a homemade cage. . . . (p. 257)

There is, of course, a deeper reason for Superman's present, enormous popularity. The world, life itself, has come to be fearfully difficult for millions of people. When one considers that millions of people of Jewish ancestry were despotically and deliberately destroyed by Hitler, it is obvious that tyrannical forces have been in operation which make Caspar Milquetoasts out of such mild little tyrants as Hannibal, Genghis Khan or Napoleon. The body of the great public is highly disturbed; it would like to do something about it, but it doesn't know what to do. The individuals who make it up feel their own smallness, their soft brains and bellies—then along comes Superman. A vast, nation-wide sigh of relief and delight. . . . (p. 258)

The odd, pathetic thing about it is, that people have such a respect for anything that gets into print that they actually believe the enemies of democracy or the law are being tumbled over backwards by these ballpointed heroes. However, the activities of Superman are by no means all in the world of make-believe. The owners and creators of this strip have very wisely turned the big guy's enormous influence into a number of socially useful channels; he has taught young people to keep clean and healthy, and he has held up our national ideals in a very definite manner. . . . (p. 259)

Coulton Waugh, "The Star-Startled Manner," in his The Comics *(reprinted with permission of Macmillan Publishing Co., Inc.; © 1947 by Coulton Waugh; copyright renewed © 1974 by Odin Waugh), Macmillan, 1947 (and reprinted by Luna Press, 1974), pp. 247-63.**

GEOFFREY WAGNER

I do not personally believe that the hollow, self-gratulatory note of the Superman comic means that the USA has a bad conscience; rather I think it may suggest that the publishers of the stuff cannot help but be a little queasy in their consciences at the dilapidation of taste they are so systematically perpetrating. War-mongering? I wouldn't know. But I have found in the Superman ethic undeniable signs of that philosophy I best describe to myself as *Jim Crow While U Wait*. (p. 86)

Geoffrey Wagner, ''Comics: The Curse of the Kids,'' in his Parade of Pleasure: A Study of Popular Iconography in the USA, *Derek Verschoyle, 1954, pp. 71-114.**

FREDRIC WERTHAM

Superman (with the big S on his uniform—we should, I suppose, be thankful that it is not an S.S.) needs an endless stream of ever new submen, criminals and ''foreign-looking'' people not only to justify his existence but even to make it possible. It is this feature that engenders in children either one or the other of two attitudes: either they fantasy themselves as supermen, with the attendant prejudices against the submen, or it makes them submissive and receptive to the blandishments of strong men who will solve all their social problems for them—by force.

Superman not only defies the laws of gravity, which his great strength makes conceivable; in addition he gives children a completely wrong idea of other basic physical laws. Not even Superman, for example, should be able to lift up a building while not standing on the ground, or to stop an airplane in mid-air while flying himself. (p. 34)

There are also super-children, like Superboy. Superboy can slice a tree like a cake, can melt glass by looking at it. . . . Superboy rewrites American history, too. In one story he helps George Washington's campaign and saves his life by hitting a Hessian with a snowball. (pp. 35-6)

One third of a page of this book is a picture of Washington crossing the Delaware—with Superboy guiding the boat through the ice floes. It is really Superboy who is crossing the Delaware, with George Washington in the boat. All this travesty is endorsed by the impressive board of experts in psychiatry, education and English literature [who approve the suitability of comic books for young readers]. (p. 36)

If I were asked to express in a single sentence what has happened mentally to many American children during the last decade I would know no better formula than to say that they were conquered by Superman. And if I were further asked what is the real moral of the Superman story, I would know no better answer than the fate of the creator of Superman himself. . . .

[We] have often seen troubled children, children in trouble and children crushed by society's punishments, with Superman and Superboy comic books sticking out of their pockets.

How did the Superman formula work for his creator? The success formula he developed did not work for him. Superman flies high in comic books and on TV; but his creator has long since been left behind. (p. 265)

Fredric Wertham, ''You Always Have to Slug 'Em'' and ''The Upas Tree,'' in his Seduction of the Innocent *(copyright 1953, 1954 by Fredric Wertham; reprinted by permission of Holt, Rinehart and Winston, Publishers),* Holt, 1954 (and reprinted by Kennikat Press, 1972), pp. 17-44, 251-72.**

STEPHEN BECKER

[By 1942, the critics were in action, pro and con, regarding Superman.] Superman was the ideal outlet for youth's unruly instincts; Superman was in the tradition of the American hero; Superman was a force for good in a world of evil. Or: Superman expressed an irresponsible social philosophy in which the average citizen abjured his own duties and let the marvel fulfill them; Superman was a glorification of the physical; Superman represented absolute power, which is ultimately corrupting. While the battle raged, kids bought the comic books, listened to the radio programs, heeded Superman's preferences in literature, clothing, bubble gum and toys.

He seems a little easier to explain now, twenty years later. The thirties were a period of trial, and many of us had lost our old faith in the traditional virtues. The gangster was an American institution, a salient figure in fact and fiction. War was imminent in Europe; Hitler seemed the personification of absolute evil with unlimited power. Superman may have been partly a wish fulfillment: hesitant to accept battle with the evil loose in the world, parents quietly approved the presence of this fictional strong man who would have been such a comfort had he existed. And then there were legitimate elements of suspense and melodrama. Superman's origins (he was a native of the planet Krypton) were mysterious and other-worldly. Set down on earth, he had become an American, which is properly patriotic. When war broke out, the country went through the necessary psychological preparations for battle, which included the process of persuading men that they were heroes. Irresponsible social philosophy or not, Superman was the sensation of the early forties. . . . He has persisted successfully into the fifties, as both a comics hero and a television hero. With trick photography now a fine art, his deeds are potentially as spectacular as they ever were, and his popularity seems as high. (pp. 240-41)

Stephen Becker, ''More Big Business,'' in his Comic Art in America: A Social History of the Funnies, the Political Cartoons, Magazine Humor, Sporting Cartoons and Animated Cartoons *(copyright © 1959 by Stephen Becker; reprinted by permission of the author),* Simon & Schuster, 1959, pp. 237-45.**

HEINZ POLITZER

[Superman] has hardly more than his name in common with [Friedrich] Nietzsche's blasphemous and iconoclastic phantasm; in fact one suspects that he originally owed his ''super'' to the ''super-duper,'' the ''*ne plus ultra* and then some'' of advertising usage. This Superman is a Li'l Abner without Mammy Yokum and without popular background, a hillbilly without the fertile background of folklore or remnants of creed. He is a Goliath rather than a David, but a Goliath who has joined the side of the conventionally right. The most serious objection to him I have heard from the mouth of a child: that he is immortal, and therefore the amazing things he does are not miracles.

The emblem of his supermanhood is inscribed on his chest, not on his forehead. He is as guileless as Li'l Abner, but he lacks the primitiveness of the country boy; the old magic that flows from the contrast between city and country is missing. Li'l Abner is at home in Dogpatch, Superman in the universe—that is, nowhere. Superman is on the side of the right as well as of hygiene. He uses violence against violence. His eyes penetrate granite walls and steel plates, but he does not see what Mickey Mouse always sees: reality. Plants serve him and the elements lie at his feet, but in the main his accomplishments are limited to smoking out a small gang of criminals or outsmarting some master mind. The mountain labors and—with the help of modern technology—brings forth a stunt.

An example of the irony unintentionally provided by Superman is the sequence in which he magnanimously carries away a glacier in order to help a village with its drainage problem. His work done, he has to bring a new glacier from the North Pole, because nature . . . plays a trick on the winged lord of creation and floods the village. Superman has about him something of [Johann von] Goethe's Sorcerer's Apprentice, of Dr. Faust, of Hercules, and of Atlas. To be sure, Jules Verne and H. G. Wells also make their contribution to his costume and trappings, but essentially he owes his effect to the vanishing remnants of ancient mythology, that collective memory of mankind which has here been combined with utopian anticipation. He does not *embody* all this, for Superman has never achieved such density of personality as Li'l Abner, for example, but he does draw constantly from a plentiful, if shallow, reservoir of watered-down myths and pipedreams of the future.

Superman is a product of the last war, the shadowy but legitimate son of the Hitlerian age and the atom bomb. Although, as we have stressed, he comes in the wake of a long tradition, it is upon the miracle of technology that he finally calls in situations that can no longer be met with the implements of reality. The *deus ex machina* has become the *machine* god. Superman is the boy's dream in pictures, but through the dehumanization of the miracle and the substitution of technical for poetic fantasy, his face has acquired a terrifyingly unhuman, aggressive, and hard profile, foreshadowing a world in process of formation, a world that is certainly new but far less brave than it thinks and claims to be. Seen politically, Superman is the promise that each and every world problem will be solved by the technical trick. He is the Man of Tomorrow; so he says himself. (pp. 50-1)

Myths crumble, heroic figures can be watered down, but symbols and names cannot be used with impunity. And even though this bashful, amiable Superman is to the petty *Ubermensch* who unleashed the Second World War as Robin Hood to a storm trooper, they have one thing in common: they both blur the transition from the technically possible to the miraculous-irrational, their efficacy rests on the vague hybridism of heroism and Utopia, of technology and the miracle.

Superman announces himself the ally of right, the people, and democracy. Prankster is his enemy, Lynch is a thorn in his side; he issues forth to vanquish the *tyrannosaurus rex*, as Siegfried did to slay his dragon. But his credo, like the "balloon" in which he expresses it, is loosely attached and interchangeable. It is not the natural expression of himself, like Li'l Abner's far more modest self-avowals. He has merely put on

his credo like his winged cloak. He lacks human reality; is it not precisely his mission to abolish reality?

Superman, in fact, is a figure of dual identity. He slips from the civilian clothes of his everyday life into the ceremonial garb of his miraculous deeds and back again; he is a quick-change artist, and even more amazing than the ease of his metamorphoses are his trifling reasons for undertaking them. But the dual identity motif is the schema of Dr. Jekyll and Mr. Hyde—a pattern bordering on that of the pathological swindler and criminal. For a popular figure, it is not without its dangers. The double face and the split personality are symptoms of a disease that has attacked our civilization. And, more often than not, it is also an attribute of modern dictators, perhaps of the tyrants of all epochs.

Superman has become anchored in those sections of the population that are most naive, most capable of enthusiasms, and most susceptible to revolutionary impulses. By the technique—general in the comics—of breaking off the text just before the climax, by creating new climaxes almost from day to day, it creates an excitement close to enchantment and frenzy. A toy, a puppet, Superman is a monstrous carnival figure combined of wishful dreams and present anxieties, of sensationalism and abused enthusiasm. Accustomed to change his identity, Superman has it in him to become a political figure. To play with him is to play with the dynamite of our times. (pp. 52-3)

> *Heinz Politzer, "From Little Nemo to Li'l Abner," in* The Funnies: An American Idiom, *edited by David Manning White and Robert H. Abel (excerpted with permission of Macmillan Publishing Co., Inc.; copyright © 1963 by The Free Press of Glencoe, a Division of Macmillan Publishing Co., Inc.), The Free Press, 1963, pp. 39-54.**

JULES FEIFFER

The particular brilliance of Superman lay not only in the fact that he was the first of the super-heroes, but in the concept of his alter ego. What made Superman different from the legion of imitators to follow was not that when he took off his clothes he could beat up everybody—they all did that. What made Superman extraordinary was his point of origin: Clark Kent.

Remember, Kent was not Superman's true identity as Bruce Wayne was the Batman's or (on radio) Lamont Cranston the Shadow's. Just the opposite. Clark Kent was the fiction. (p. 18)

Superman had only to wake up in the morning to be Superman. In his case, Clark Kent was the put-on. The fellow with the eyeglasses and the acne and the walk girls laughed at wasn't real, didn't exist, was a sacrificial disguise, an act of discreet martyrdom. *Had they but known!*

And for what purpose? Did Superman become Clark Kent in order to lead a normal life, have friends, be known as a nice guy, meet girls? Hardly. There's too much of the hair shirt in the role, too much devotion to the imprimatur of impotence—an insight, perhaps, into the fantasy life of the Man of Steel. Superman as a secret masochist? . . . For if it was otherwise, if the point, the only point, was to lead a "normal life," why not a more typical identity? How can one be a cowardly star reporter, subject to fainting spells in time of crisis, and not expect to raise serious questions?

The truth may be that Kent existed not for the purposes of the story but for the reader. He is Superman's opinion of the rest of us, a pointed caricature of what we, the noncriminal element, were really like. His fake identity was our real one. That's why we loved him so. (p. 19)

What matter that the stories quickly lost interest; that once you've made a man super you've plotted him out of believable conflicts; that even super-villains, super-mad scientists and, yes, super-orientals were dull and lifeless next to the overwhelming image of that which Clark Kent became when he took off his clothes. So what if the stories were boring, the villains blah? This was the Superman Show—a touring road company backing up a great star. Everything was a stage wait until he came on. Then it was all worth-while.

Besides, for the alert reader there were other fields of interest. It seems that among Lois Lane, Clark Kent, and Superman there existed a schizoid and chaste *ménage à trois*. Clark Kent loved but felt abashed with Lois Lane; Superman saved Lois Lane when she was in trouble, found her a pest the rest of the time. Since Superman and Clark Kent were the same person this behavior demands explanation. It can't be that Kent wanted Lois to respect him for himself, since himself was Superman. Then, it appears, he wanted Lois to respect him for his fake self, to love him when he acted the coward, to be there when he pretended he needed her. She never was—so, of course, he loved her. A typical American romance. Superman never needed her, never needed anybody—in any event, Lois chased *him*—so, of course, he didn't love her. He had contempt for her. Another typical American romance.

Love is really the pursuit of a desired object, not pursuit by it. Once you've caught the object there is no longer any reason to love it, to have it hanging around. There must be other desirable objects out there, somewhere. So Clark Kent acted as the control for Superman. What Kent wanted was just that which Superman didn't want to be bothered with. Kent wanted Lois, Superman didn't—thus marking the difference between a sissy and a man. A sissy wanted girls who scorned him; a man scorned girls who wanted him. Our cultural opposite of the man who didn't make out with women has never been the man who did—but rather the man who could if he wanted to, but still didn't. The ideal of masculine strength, whether Gary Cooper's, Lil Abner's, or Superman's, was for one to be so virile and handsome, to be in such a position of strength, that he need never go near girls. Except to help them. And then get the hell out. Real rapport was not for women. It was for villains. That's why they got hit so hard. (pp. 20-1)

Jules Feiffer, in his introduction to The Great Comic Book Heroes, *edited by Jules Feiffer (copyright ©️ 1965 by The Dial Press; reprinted by permission of The Dial Press), Dial, 1965, pp. 11-55.**

part of our folklore already, one might argue. And the most engaging feature of the Superman stories was surely not the fellow's prowess at bending bridges into pretzels or dispatching felons with a flick of his cuticle—for, by definition, he was invincible, so what suspense could there be over the outcome?—but the fruitless romance between Lois and Superman-Kent.

First, any good logician would have to question the assumption, perpetuated by the comic strip itself, that Superman was real and Clark Kent was the put-on. It is important to recall the famous episode . . . describing how Superman got here from the doomed planet Krypton: "A scientist placed his infant son within an experimental rocket-ship, launching it toward earth!" A nice rumpled couple discover the baby who is shipped to an orphan asylum till that nice couple decides to adopt the tiny strongman. No indication, mind you, of any documents on the rocket ship identifying the child (and had there been any, they surely would not have identified him as "Superman"—you wouldn't call a baby that, even on Krypton). No, the Superman part had to be invented, for that nice couple was named Kent, and their little hulk grew to supermanhood as a member of the family. When his adoptive parents died, "Clark decided he must turn his titanic strength into channels that would benefit mankind. And so was created—SUPERMAN, champion of the oppressed," etc. So no one's going to tell me Clark Kent slept with that costume on under his pajamas.

But why did he maintain the two identities? . . . Surely Superman could have performed his constabulary function quite as well without retaining the Kent alter ego. Why all that skulking around in closets and men's rooms and on window ledges shucking his baggy Clark Kent suit? I'll tell you why. . . . [Because] Superman wanted *love*. He looked like a man, talked like a man, indeed *was* a man, albeit a peculiarly endowed one. Why assume he had no libido? Is it not more logical to assume he had a *super* libido? He could, of course, ravage any woman on earth (not excluding Wonder Woman, I daresay)—may well have, in fact. But that is not love. Nor, understandably, did he want to be loved for his supermanhood. After all, anyone can love a Superman. What he wanted was to be loved as a mortal, as a regular guy; *ergo*, the Clark Kent identity. He was *testing* Lois Lane. But she, the dumb bitch, never got the picture; she was unworthy of him. Yet—yet I think he loved her; why else did he keep saving *her* and not a million other skirts? Beyond this, there is a tantalizing if somewhat clinical and highly speculative theory about why Superman never bedded down with Lois, never really let himself get hotted up over her; Superman, remember, was the Man of Steel. Consider the consequences of supercoitus and the pursuit of The Perfect Orgasm at the highest level. So Supe, a nice guy, had to sublimate. . . . [It] is a sign not of strength that Superman never goes near girls but, rather, of his critical flaw. (pp. 111-12)

Richard Kluger, "Sex and the Superman" (reprinted by permission of the author and Georges Borchardt, Inc.; copyright ©️ 1966 by Partisan Review, Inc.), in Partisan Review, *Vol. XXXIII, No. 1, Winter, 1966, pp. 111-15.**

RICHARD KLUGER

Superman is the most fabulous of the comic book heroes—

RODERICK NORDELL

What saddens me is that the Man of Steel seems to be going

the way of that mighty hero of the past, Hercules. Perhaps humanity can stand the superhuman only so long without laughing. At any rate, it appears that after all his Herculean labors, Hercules became for the ancients a figure of fun, brought on stage for comic relief. . . .

[In] those early days—"It's a bird! It's a plane! No, it's . . . !"— the Man of Steel stood on his own two feet. Superman was the star. He was enough.

But at some point Superman's drawing power must have faltered, as I used to think none of his other powers could. Like the bygone strong men in the current film *Hercules, Samson and Ulysses,* he was teamed with another comic-book hero, Batman. The Man of Steel and the Cowled Crusader joined forces to arrest any mutual decline in popularity.

Also in the shadow of Superman's cape came Superboy and Supergirl and even Krypto, the Dog of Steel. (p. 104)

And now the men behind Superman have gone so far as to make him a grandfather. Can *Superman Meets Donald Duck* be far behind? Think of the Man of Steel as a second banana!

Such thoughts reduced my gravity as I read **The Three Generations of Superman**. The children had told me the Man of Steel had a grandson of steel, but I couldn't believe it.

Yet there it was, in red and blue and yellow, tempered only by the disclaimer that this was an "*imaginary tale,* which *could* happen in the future, but *may not.*"

There was the graybeard pointing with his cane to a picture of one of his former triumphs: "Heh, heh . . . If I say so myself, son, you've never topped *my* fame . . . though you've equaled it!"

And the middle- or working-generation Superman says: "It's too bad that repeated encounters for many years with *green Kryptonite* so *weakened* your superpowers that you had to retire. I know I can't replace you, but I try!"

And the third generation—Superbaby, as the children say— plies his grandfather with questions about the old days before crime was stamped out.

I could not help enjoying the victory of Supergrandpa and Supergrandson over robots controlled by outer-space "alien plotters," who conclude: "We'll never try again to invade that world! What chance would we have, when our mightiest machines were defeated by an *old man and a child?*"

But surely in that direction lie comic books that can hardly be taken seriously. Pop art may have made museum pieces of the comics. Camp taste may have found sophisticated entertainment in them. But when Supermen become grandpas and grandchildren, they cannot be far from supporting roles on the *Dick Van Dyke Show.* (pp. 104-05)

Roderick Nordell, "Superman Revisited," in The Atlantic Monthly *(copyright © 1965, by The Atlantic Monthly Company, Boston, Mass.; reprinted with*

permission), Vol. 217, No. 1, January, 1966, pp. 104-05.

TED WHITE

It was 1938, and the country was shuddering its way out from the crippling blow to its economy in 1929. The air was full of talk of war in Europe, and of the mad clown named Hitler. . . . It was a time of idealism and of shattered ideals. We were down but not out. Our world had crumbled, but we knew we could build a better one.

We hadn't grown up yet.

Enter Superman. (p. 28)

For a man who was setting out to "help those in need," Superman had a remarkably pedestrian mind. For the most part he did not occupy himself with sweeping social change; instead he battled crooks and racketeers, uncovering corruption in low places. (p. 29)

It's fortunate for Superman that neither Siegel nor Shuster had absorbed much from their high-school science classes, or, for that matter, from the science fiction of that time. Had the laws of inertia been in force while Superman was standing steadfast before a speeding car, the outcome might often have been quite different. And if Superman had actually had sufficient internal mass to stop a speeding car, I hate to think of the holes he would have kicked in the sidewalks with each of his aerial leaps.

But those were simpler times. And if the comic book had not originally been aimed at a specific age group, it had certainly found one: the kids. How many kids knew the science that would debunk Superman? *How many kids,* knowing it, *would have cared?*

Superman was a myth-figure: he was our dreams personified, even as he must have been Siegel and Shuster's. Superman was, almost literally, the perfect Boy Scout. We still believed in Boy Scouts then.

Most of the Superman myth was established within the first year of Superman's publication. (pp. 29-30)

Most of those early stories dwelled, with what I can only describe as a magnificent sense of wonder, upon Superman's physical attributes. . . . The pages in which Superman did little but outrace trains or cars, leap buildings, or toss crooks around . . . probably outnumbered those in which the plot (if there was one) was materially advanced.

But war was coming. Everyone could see it. In several 1939 and 1940 stories Superman found himself in mythical European countries fighting off invasions of one sort or another. (p. 30)

Then came 1941.

Suddenly, we *were* at war. It must have thrown Superman's publishers into a tizzy. Here was this marvelous man, this superman, who had already demonstrated his ability to handle almost any size war—what were we going to do with him? If he went to war against Hitler, how could we explain the fact that America had not instantly won?

The solution was ingenious. As Clark Kent, Superman went down to his local draft board to enlist. But in his nervous desire to get into the Army, he accidentally employed his x-ray vision during the eye test. Instead of reading the chart before him, he read the one in the room beyond! He was flunked out as a 4-F. The shame—!

Why this should keep Superman *as Superman* out of the war they never explained, but it at least solved the real-life problem. While Captain America, Sub-Mariner, and a host of other superheroes or quasi-super-heroes in the comics went off to war, Superman stayed home to deal with fifth-column saboteurs and war profiteers, and to continue helping little old ladies safely across the streets.

As time went on, Superman lost his early fragility. Rays, gasses, and even bursting shells no longer bothered him. Although he continued to leap into the air in his peculiarly characteristic way, resembling a leap-frog in motion, somehow he had found the power of sustained flight. His relationship with Lois Lane mellowed somewhat, and indeed led briefly to marriage. (pp. 30-1)

[By the mid-forties] he revolutionized the comics industry as a whole. (p. 31)

If Superman was such a hit, surely spin-offs of Superman would do equally well, or so the publishers reasoned. Thus *Superboy—the Adventures of Superman when he was a Boy*. . . .

Early "Superboy" stories tried to be faithful in their fashion. The young Clark Kent wore a miniature Superman costume, but he was concerned with boyish pursuits. One cover showed him shooting marbles with his awed pals; a story in another issue of *Adventure* concerned soap-box racers—a plot closer at heart to those in the boys' books than to comic book superheroes. . . .

By the mid-fifties, Superboy seemed to live in the present (the cars were all modern, and clothes and plots equally so—every home had television), coexisting with his older self.

By the late fifties, he had time-travel completely under control, and was spending most of his time in the future with that Legion of Super Heroes . . . and had established a high-school enmity with the youthful [Lex] Luthor. . . . (p. 32)

Of course, by then Superman himself was hardly recognizable. He was, we were told, totally invulnerable to *anything* except Kryptonite and—get this!—*magic*.

Kryptonite was introduced in the mid-forties (on his radio program, I believe) because Superman was, even then, becoming too powerful to be easily dealt with by his writers and artists. There was no excitement in a story about a man capable of doing anything required (including travelling in time) to right whatever was wrong within the first two pages of any story. It was decided, therefore, that if gas, rays, or automobiles no longer affected him, perhaps bits of radioactive material from the core of his exploded home planet, Krypton, might diminish his strength. (pp. 32-3)

In the late fifties Kryptonite mutated into a whole spectrum of materials: Red Kryptonite, Gold Kryptonite, etc., each with its own special powers over Superman. The authors of Superman stories have since gained a good deal of mileage from these convenient new forms.

In addition, they have given us Supergirl (another survivor of Krypton), Superdog, Supercat, and even Superhorse. . . .The mythos has become cluttered.

Indeed, if one wants to write a Superman story today, he will find little if anything of the original Siegel-Shuster Superman has survived. His story must fit within the ever more constrictive net woven by the interlocking mythos of Superman, Superboy, Supergirl, the stories in *Superman's Girl-Friend, Lois Lane,* and the stories in *Superman's Pal, Jimmy Olsen,* to say nothing of the shared Superman-Batman adventures in *World's Finest Comics*.

It is not altogether surprising that the best stories published in the last six to eight years have been the *Imaginary Stories*. In these stories the author can depart from the mythos. He can pretend Superman *has* married Lois Lane, and go on from there to see what might happen next. (pp. 33-4)

But, what nonsense, really! The proprietors of Superman have virtually painted themselves into a corner with their overwhelming mythos of sub-characters and sub-plot situations. Detail has been piled upon detail until the character and quality of Superman which so endeared him to us have been totally submerged. (p. 34)

> Ted White, "The Spawn of M. C. Gaines," in All
> in Color for a Dime, *edited by Dick Lupoff and Don*
> *Thompson (copyright © 1970 by Richard A. Lupoff*
> *and Don Thompson), Arlington House, 1970, pp. 20-*
> *43.**

LES DANIELS

Superman, the ultimate expression of human aspirations to power and pure freedom, was an instant triumph, a concept so intense and so instantly identifiable that he became perhaps the most widely known figure ever created in American fiction. Almost immediately it became apparent that he was too super to ever lose his war against crime. Once it was known who he was, it was known what would happen to him—for all intents and purposes, nothing. Consequently, it might have been possible that his very invulnerability would have been the source of his defeat, in the public eye if not in his adventures. Some devices, like the introduction of Kryptonite, the alien element with a deleterious effect on the Man of Steel, were to prove reasonably useful in keeping up interest. What really made the series a success, however, was already built into the story.

The most fascinating feature of **Superman** . . . is the tension existing between Superman and his alter ego, Clark Kent, especially as it reflects itself in the problems both have with their "love interest," girl reporter Lois Lane. As has often been noted, Superman is unique among the vast number of heroes with secret identities in that it is not the heroic role which he adopts, but rather the average, Clark Kent, and not that fantastic flying figure, is the phony. Some practical reasons have been offered for this impersonation. It frees the hero from constant harassment and frees his friends from potential peril. It also has a certain value in increasing sales, since the frail half of the dual character makes an immediate reader identification with the hero more feasible. Yet this factor, operating as it does outside the framework of the tales, does not provide the internal logic which can be sensed lurking below the surface of Superman. Since Superman, loved by Lois, maintains the guise of Kent, whom Lois despises, [it has been] suggested that he may be somewhat masochistic. In fact, however, his amusement with this eternal triangle suggests that the element at work here is less a capacity for neurotic suffering than for entertaining himself. What makes the apparent contradictions work cohesively is Superman's sense of humor, which was to be emphasized more and more as his career progressed. (pp. 11-12)

Les Daniels, "The Birth of the Comic Book," in his Comix: A History of Comic Books in America *(copyright ©1971 by Les Daniels and Mad Peck Studios; reprinted by permission of the publisher, E. P. Dutton, Inc.), Outerbridge & Dienstfrey, 1971, pp. 9-17.*

ARTHUR ASA BERGER

In recent years Superman has been changing. . . . When we discarded our old legacy of rugged individualism and self-sufficiency, we also abandoned the view that a heroic super-powerful individual might solve all our problems with some magnificent gesture.

But what is important about Superman is not that he is changing. . . . It is what Superman represents, as a symbol, *before* he started changing that I am most interested in; and it is his symbolic significance that is most important, I feel, for our purposes.

Though he may have been a relatively simple-minded hero in the old days before he became socially conscious, *as a symbolic figure he presents many difficulties*. This is because his symbolic significance has many different dimensions. For example, the notion of a superman, a strong, heroic figure who transcends ordinary man, has obvious Oedipal interpretations. The desire of young boys to rid themselves of their fathers coupled with their need for the knowledge and protection of their fathers is very closely realized in the role Superman plays in his adventures.

Superman also is a superego figure, a symbol of conscience. He is pledged to be a champion of the oppressed and to help people in need. In the course of his activities he often must fight with evil, and his triumphs can be seen, from a Freudian perspective, as representing the dominance of a highly developed superego. . . . Superman's fantastic powers make the superego's dominance most apparent. (pp. 147-49)

[Superman] may also be analyzed from a sociological and political standpoint. After all, there is something strange about a democratic, equalitarian society having a hero who represents values that are antithetical to our basic beliefs, and which have been associated with Nazi Germany, in particular, and European elitist culture in general.

There is a fairly close relationship, generally, between a society and its heroes; if a hero does not espouse values that are meaningful to his readers, there seems little likelihood that he will be popular. The term "super" means over, above, higher in quantity, quality, or degree, all of which conflict with the American equalitarian ethos. I believe the answer to this dilemma lies in Superman's qualities and character. He is, despite his awesome powers, rather ordinary—so much so that he poses as a spectacled nonentity of a reporter in order to avoid publicity and maintain some kind of privacy.

His superiority lies in his powers, and though he possesses great physical attributes and abilities, they are always at the service of his fellow man. He is not, by any means, an aristocrat who values "breeding" and has a sense of superiority. What [Ralph Waldo] Emerson said about Napoleon, an everyman with superhuman capacities, can also be said of Superman; he is "the idol of the common men because he had in transcendent

degree the qualities and powers of common men" ("Napoleon, Man of the World").

Thus a difference in degree (of power) has not led to a difference in kind (sense of superiority). It might even be said that Superman is rather shy and quite bland. In a society which will not tolerate pretensions, which has no hereditary aristocracy, even Superman is forced to present himself as a supreme democrat. He is an ordinary person who just happens to be the strongest man in the world. (pp. 151-52)

The problem that Superman faces is that, as a superior man in a society which is stridently equalitarian, he must disguise himself, lest people be envious and cause difficulties. In the tale of his origin this is made evident. A scientist from the doomed planet Krypton sends his infant child to earth, where it is discovered by an elderly couple, the Kents. (p. 152)

As he grows older, his powers develop. After his fosterparents die, we find the following:

> Clark decided he must turn his titanic strength
> into channels that would benefit mankind. And
> so was created—Superman, champion of the
> oppressed, the physical marvel who had sworn
> to devote his existence to helping those in need.

The language almost has a Biblical ring, with the use of the passive tense in "and so was created." This suggests that his origin has a mythical dimension, and perhaps a sacred one. The Biblical parallel is furthered by the similarity between the way Moses and Superman were found. (p. 153)

The matter of *identity* is one of the central problems of Superman. Underneath the mask, the persona of an incompetent reporter, is a Superman. There is some kind of schizoid split in having one person with two separate beings. As Kent, Superman is often fooled by Lois Lane; it is quite inconceivable that Superman would fall for her tricks, yet Superman and Clark Kent are the same person. It is almost as if there were two separate beings with complete dominance with their particular sphere of operations. When Superman is pretending to be Clark Kent, he actually is Clark Kent and when Superman is Superman, he bears no relation to Clark Kent, though they are one and the same being. Superman seems to be a "divided self," to use R.D. Laing's term from *The Divided Self*, except that Superman/Clark Kent does not seem to be psychotic.

There is a great deal of confusion in *Superman*. Clark Kent likes Lois Lane, who spurns him, while Lois Lane likes Superman, who in turn spurns her. We find ourselves in a situation in which a woman likes and dislikes the same man or, rather, his different identities. The only way we can explain such matters is to postulate two separate identities in the same person which are autonomous in their own particular realm.

In this respect the costumes Superman and all superheroes wear are significant. When he has his usual work suit on, and his glasses, Superman is not really Superman, so to speak. He is timid, somewhat incompetent, and terribly boring. It is only when he strips off his veneer and his suit, and emerges resplendent in his cape and leotards, that he acts like Superman. The Superclothes make the Superman; no doubt about that. (pp. 153-54)

It is the costume that counts, and Superman's costume is probably a version of the old costume of the swordsman and nobleman, brought up to date for pseudo science fiction.

Superman's lack of interest in Lois Lane correlates closely with symptoms found in schizophrenics. . . . The narcissist takes himself as an object of love, though it must be pointed out that self-love cannot be equated with self-interest; indeed, the two are often opposed to one another. The point is that a withdrawal of the libido and an element of self-love might possibly explain Superman's lack of interest in Lois Lane. As a Superman he has learned, so Nietzsche explains, to forgo fleeting pleasures—one of which may be romantic involvement with Lois Lane, members of the opposite sex in general, and perhaps everyone. After all, a Superman "deserves" a Superwoman.

In a number of ways Superman's divided self and history are significant (and perhaps even paradigmatic) for American society and culture in general. Superman has left a destructive—in this case self-destructive—place of origin for a new world where his powers make him the strongest man on earth. His history is similar to that of the Puritans, who left a corrupt old world for a blissful new one, where their spiritual powers might flower. And like Superman the Puritans labored heroically for goodness and justice, as they interpreted both.

Just as Kryptonite weakens Superman, so does contact with the corrupting old world weaken innocent Americans and destroy their moral integrity. . . . [The] notion of America as innocent and Europe as corrupt is part of the conventional wisdom and mythology of the American mind. Superman, like the American, thus must avoid contact with the past in order to maintain his powers. With the American this has led to an antihistorical attitude, a belief in the future and repudiation of the past. (pp. 155-56)

The schizoid split within Superman symbolizes a basic split within the American psyche. Americans are split like Superman, alienated from their selves and bitter about the disparity between their dreams and their achievements, between the theory that they are in control of their own lives and the reality of their powerlessness and weakness.

Superman's identity problem is very similar to ours. The American's obsession with identity is a well-known phenomenon. It is because we have no sense of the past that we have no sense of who we are. Like Superman we perform superheroic tasks, one after the other, but they do not seem to give us any sense of being. Just as Superman keeps his identity hidden, so do we hide ours by repudiating the past. (pp. 157-58)

> *Arthur Asa Berger, "Dissociation in a Hero: Superman and the Divided Self," in his* The Comic-Stripped American: What Dick Tracy, Blondie, Daddy Warbucks, and Charlie Brown Tell Us about Ourselves *(copyright © 1973 by Arthur Asa Berger; used with permission from the author), Walker and Company, 1973 (and reprinted by Penguin Books Inc., 1974), pp. 146-59.*

MORDECAI RICHLER

[The] real Superman controversy has always centred on his assumed identity of Clark Kent, a decidedly faint-hearted reporter. Kent adores Lois Lane, who has no time for him. Lois is nutty for Superman, who in true 'aw shucks' tradition has no time for any woman. . . . [The significant factor in this is] the Canadian psyche.

Yes. Superman was conceived by Toronto-born Joe Shuster and originally worked not for the *Daily Planet* but for a newspaper called *The Star*, modelled on the Toronto *Star*. This

makes his assumed identity of bland Clark Kent not merely understandable, but artistically inevitable. Kent is the archetypal middle-class Canadian WASP, superficially nice, self-effacing, but within whom there burns a hate-ball, a would-be avenger with superhuman powers, a smasher of bridges, a breaker of skyscrapers, a potential ravager of wonder women. (pp. 302-03)

> *Mordecai Richler, "The Great Comic Book Heroes" (1974; reprinted by permission of the author), in* The Cool Web: The Pattern of Children's Reading, *edited by Margaret Meek, Aidan Warlow and Griselda Barton, The Bodley Head, 1977, pp. 299-308.**

LESLIE A. FIEDLER

[It was the late 1930's before comic books] were accepted as fit for children in whose innocence parents were still pretending to believe. Moreover, the children themselves demanded more than parody of the daily scripts in which sex was absent and violence trivialized; they yearned for a new mythology neither explicitly erotic, overtly terrifying nor frankly supernatural, yet essentially phallic, horrific and magical. Such a mythology was waiting to be released in pulp science fiction, a genre recreated in the United States in 1926 by Hugo Gernsback, who published the first magazine devoted entirely to the genre. He did not invent the name, however, until 1929, just one year before a pair of 16-year-olds, Jerry Siegel and Joe Shuster, reviewed Philip Wylie's *Gladiator* in one of the earliest s.f. fanzines. . . . (p. 339)

Out of that novel, at any rate, emerged the first and most long-lived of all comic book characters, Superman. . . .

[It] required the imminence of World War II before the super-goy dreamed up by a pair of Jewish teenagers from Cleveland in the Great Depression could reach an audience of hundreds of millions starved for wonder but too ill at ease with Gutenberg forms to respond even to science fiction. Only then did the paranoia that is their stock in trade become endemic—the special paranoia of men in cities anticipating in their shared nightmares the saturation bombing that lay just ahead and the consequent end of law and order, perhaps of man himself. The suffering city, Metropolis, which under various names remains the setting for all subsequent Superheroes, is helpless before its external enemies because it is sapped by corruption and fear at its very heart.

But the old American promise of an end to paranoia is there, too, the equivocal dream that had already created the Ku Klux Klan and the vigilantes and the lynch mob, as well as the cowboy hero and the private eye—the dream of a savior in some sense human still, but able to know, as the rest of us cannot, who the enemy really is and to destroy him as we no longer can—not with technology, which is in itself equivocal, but with his bare hands. (p. 340)

I found pathos as well in the double identity of the hero, that Siegel and Shuster invention, product of God knows what very Jewish irony undercutting what it seemed to celebrate. He was a man of steel in one guise, but in the other a short-sighted reporter, a crippled newsboy, an epicene playboy flirting with a teen-age male companion. Phallic but impotent, supermale but a eunuch, incapable of consummating love or begetting a successor; and, therefore, he was a *last hero*, doomed to lonely immortality and banned by an ultimately inexplicable taboo from revealing the secret that would make it possible at least to join the two halves of his sundered self and thus end his comic plight of being forever his own rival for the affection of his best beloved. Ultimately, therefore, the Siegel and Shuster Superman turns out to be not a hero who seems a shlemiel, but a hero who *is* a shlemiel. If this is not essentially funny . . . , it is because the joke was on all of us and there was no one left to laugh—not even when the war was over and it had become clear that what it had achieved was the end of heroism rather than of paranoia. (p. 341)

> *Leslie A. Fiedler, "Up, Up and Away: The Rise and Fall of Comic Books," in* The New York Times Book Review *(© 1976 by The New York Times Company; reprinted by permission), September 5, 1976 (and reprinted in* Young Adult Literature in the Seventies: A Selection of Readings, *edited by Jana Varlejs, The Scarecrow Press, Inc., 1978, pp. 338-44).**

ALVIN SCHWARTZ

Before the scientific hypothesis came along with its dependence on stored data and libraries and a written language, we structured the truths of our world in both physical and psychological terms by means of myths, legends, and fairy tales. The transmission of these fictional forms from one generation to the next was by word of mouth. . . . But when we examine the collected and printed forms of our oral tradition, we note how much of it, fairy tales in particular, has been relegated to the role of children's literature. . . . The fact is, of course, that fairy tales were never originally intended for children. But with universal literacy, children are the only ones left among whom the oral transmission of culture is still active for the simple reason that reading is not an innate capacity. Nor should we ignore the fact that fairy tales, owing to the kind of archetypal characters that people them, lend themselves particularly to the kind of acting out developmentally associated with childhood. (pp. 119-20)

[It] occurred to me that Superman too was not originally written for children, yet somehow it had been taken over by them for the same reason that they had adopted fairy tales. I was to discover, bit by bit, that Superman was as much an archetype as many of his legendary predecessors and shared with them both a certain healing magic and a certain autonomy.

The Superman strip first emerged out of the world of pulp fiction at a time when that world was being transposed from the purely printed word into the graphic form of the comic strip. . . . Unlike many comic strips that have had a long history marked by a moderately ascending curve of popularity, Superman achieved a meteoric rise in a relatively brief period. But it peaked out within a period of about a decade, a meagre span compared to the longevity of appeal of many of our leading North American comic strips. At the same time, Superman spawned a host of secondary elaborations, "union suit" characters which in one modality or another tended to duplicate various extrinsic features of the Man of Steel without quite achieving his archetypal verisimilitude. (p. 120)

Superman may be ignored or forgotten . . . , but where he appears, he tends to retain his intrinsic character. And while Superman, like any other folkloric image, may become a subject and even a target for humor, within the strip itself, he can never become, as did Batman, a parody of himself. The differences between Superman and his "union suit" derivatives go deeper than that, however, as the following exegetical treatment of Superman's "secret" identity suggests.

> Clark Kent, mild-mannered reporter for the Daily Planet, is walking along when, suddenly, his super-hearing picks up the sounds of a robbery in progress. He steps into a nearby phone-booth. An instant later and the Man of Steel streaks toward the scene of the crime. . . .

In the spate of recent books and articles on comics, I've not noted anywhere a sense of the significance of this familiar transformation scene. In switching from Clark to Superman, the comic strip hero is not donning a disguise but, in fact, stepping out of one. This is because Superman is the reality; Clark Kent is the disguise. To take this a step further, Superman is a hidden reality; his visible aspect, with the aid of his costume, is a highly colorful one, pointing precisely to his hiddenness.

Hiddenness in this special sense is a symbolic property since a symbol is one of the habiliments of value, and value is one of those ineffabilities that can only be made visible by its clothing. To put this seemingly paradoxical concept another way, there is that which we call "value" and which has no value unless it rests finally and absolutely in itself. That is, there is no "value" without a highest value and all other values derive from it hierarchically. This is a basic tenet of contemporary axiology, the science of value. (p. 121)

In his dormant or non-active, invisible, or "mild-mannered" phase, Superman is Clark Kent. In his active, otherworldly, or, if you like, avatar phase, he is made visible or *incarnate* by his colorful costume. Apart from that costume, he is largely colorless, pure essence rather than personality—and this is the case even apart from his role as Clark Kent, which is, at best, a simulacrum of colorlessness. It plays a part in the story, if you will, but it is not the essential colorlessness I refer to here. This notion will become clearer as we proceed with a more detailed analysis of Superman's Clark Kent persona.

Clark Kent, as we have already seen, is one of the aspects of Superman. As a reporter, standing at the center of the newspaper world of information and facts (how appropriately the newspaper is called The Daily Planet!), he symbolizes only a single higher function of Superman—the rational mind. In that role, he is the conforming, self-conscious mass man, completely anonymous, the split-off rational portion of that manifestation of wholeness which appears only at moments of crisis, embracing not only the mind but the imagination by its capacity for flight, by its otherworldliness, its irresistible power, its avatar role as it responds to threatening and extreme situations. Like the archetypal hero of many a myth, Superman broke into a particular segment of history, his moment of *kairos*, like an irrigation, a vivifying force arising out of what Carl Jung has described for us as the collective unconscious. And in the same way that Jung has treated the mythic tale as a "healing fiction," so too the adventures of Superman provide this type of "fiction par excellence"—a representation of reality from beyond the surface of the everyday; the Hidden, colorfully made manifest. But it is precisely by means of the "fiction," that is, the plot or story, that healing takes place.

To those of us with a secure share in the literate world of technology and information, who possess, in consequence, a variety of life options, there is no crisis and no healing irruption of the sort that Superman is capable of providing. But there are those who like children were much closer to the oral tradition when Superman first appeared. It was, it may be recalled, the height of the Great Depression. There were blacks, Chicanos, Puerto Ricans and, around the world, masses of semi-literate ghetto inhabitants, minorities, persons displaced by the devastating urbanization of rural cultures, who, in one way or another, were excluded; who, like children, had not attained that level of differentiated functioning that separated them from the oral tradition. And then too there were even those of us who maintained a firm grip on the rational until consciousness and rationality were shattered by World War II. This produced, to my mind, one of the most persuasive pieces of evidence that Superman had a certain healing quality for those who had no external choices. For during the war, fifty percent of the circulation of Superman went to the armed forces. . . . At the end of hostilities, when the conscript armies disbanded, Superman's circulation dropped severely. As ethnocentrism developed a new pride and new options among blacks, Chicanos, Puerto Ricans, and other ghetto minorities during the fifties and sixties, Superman's circulation dropped further still.

What remains is now largely a children's market, not enough to sustain Superman at his previous meteoric level, but sufficient to keep him around for a while longer at a fairly steady rate. Children, of necessity, cannot escape from the kind of story-awareness that belongs to the oral mode. It is, in fact, one of the requirements of healthy psychic growth. (pp. 122-24)

If, as I have proposed here, Superman represented an archetypal intrusion from the unconscious, then for that reason alone there was a need for a separation of the realms. The promiscuous mixing of conscious and unconscious contents makes for psychological chaos and the character would have lost much of his numinous power and remarkable influence since he would then have been completely lacking in what E. F. Edinger has predicated of any genuine symbol—"a subjective dynamism which exerts a powerful attraction and fascination on the individual." So, in a sense, the character himself determined the conditions under which he was to operate, not the authors and editors.

It might also be worth noting that Superman, taken by himself, was like many heroes of his type, dull. Far more interesting were the Superman villains who, it should be remembered, had many things in common with Jung's description of the Shadow archetype. I refer particularly to such characters as the Prankster, the Toyman, Luthor, and certainly that fifth dimensional imp, Mr. Mxyztplk. . . . (p. 125)

The question as to why a hero such as Superman should be dull raises a similar question often posed in connection with [John] Milton's *Paradise Lost,* in which many have insisted that Satan rather than God is the real hero, since he is so much more fully realized as a character. The late C. S. Lewis has suggested that this is merely because we are incapable of fully realizing someone so much more perfect than ourselves. I don't think this is quite the case. Without the villains, there is no story, no plot, no "healing fiction." The problem of the separation and the need to reunify the opposites, the drama of the differentiated functions, imagination and rationality, consciousness and unconsciousness, struggling toward equilibrium, toward a self-regulating balance, is the important thing. Drama is never about wholeness. Wholeness is another state of being. It is unmanifest, withdrawn into itself. *The cosmic dance goes on in costume.*

Consider too that the Superman villains, like those in Batman and other comic strips of this type, are *un*wholesome precisely because they are specialists—not whole men. And it is out of their very lack of wholeness, that is to say, out of the conflict engendered by their fragmented or split-off personalities, that the drama develops and realization of sorts arises. (pp. 125-26)

[With] the Superman villains, their unwholesomeness depotentiated into a kind of dramatic humor by the healing magic of story. I introduced these comments on what we call "union suit" characters by suggesting that I was in thrall to an archetype. In fact, we all of us are. But not all of us have become conscious of it. There were several of us who wrote and edited and worked on the various Superman comic books, daily and Sunday newspaper continuities, and none of us, at the time, were in any way aware of what might be called the logic of the unconscious that compelled us to set up certain conditions for Superman's way of operating which, instead, we explained by means of the rationalizations I have described above. But in spite of our illusion of conscious control, Superman functioned with an autonomy real enough to have made his way into folklore. (p. 126)

Alvin Schwartz, "The Real Secret of Superman's Identity," in Children's Literature: Annual of The Modern Language Association Seminar on Children's Literature and The Children's Literature Association, *Vol. 5, edited by Francelia Butler (© 1976 by Francelia Butler; reprinted by permission of The Children's Literature Foundation, Box 370, Windham Center, CT 06280), Temple University Press, 1976, pp. 117-29.*

PHILIP DEMUTH

The saga of Superman takes on an entirely different cast if we regard it psychologically. . . . In this light, the character of Superman becomes simply the elaborate fantasy wish-fulfillment of mild-mannered Clark Kent.

Imagine Clark, a frail child, raised in the claustrophobic atmosphere of Smallville. He is an only child, introverted by nature; his parents are straight, old and remote. Although little is known of his early childhood, somewhere along the way Clark seizes upon the idea that he is "special." Many children entertain the idea that they might secretly be adopted, but for Clark this holds a peculiar fascination. He turns it over in his mind. Could it be that his real parents were great scientists from another planet?

By the time Clark reaches high school, his style is set. Unable to cope with the social demands of adolescence, he retreats more and more into his fantasy world. At school, he is bullied by the boys, who regard him as a weakling; the girls don't regard him at all. He doesn't participate in sports, doesn't date and promptly returns home after school every day to work in Pa Kent's general store or look at his rock collection.

Perhaps Clark's most remarkable feature is his attenuated moralistic outlook, his seeing in all events a clear-cut conflict between the forces of good and the forces of evil. Whenever the external situation becomes anxiety provoking, he withdraws into fantasy. As Superboy, the most popular girl in his class, Lana Lang, loves him, while it is he who can afford to be standoffish. His parents respect him, and he becomes the envy of his peers. He gets to go out on exciting adventures every day instead of sweeping up the store or staring at his rocks. His inferiority complex has given rise to a compensatory delusional system.

In adulthood, the pattern continues unabated. He seeks out an employer who chews him out regularly. The sole woman in his life, Lois Lane, thinks of him as a spineless jellyfish. His only friend seems to be Jimmy Olsen, who is kind of an inadequate personality himself. But really he has no friends. Whenever situations make him tense, he flees into his Walter Mitty fantasy life where he is worshiped by Perry [White, his employer], Lois, the police and indeed the whole world. He sedulously guards the existence of his secret identity, however, because somehow he knows that if he were to reveal it, it would cease to exist (a phenomenon psychotherapists often observe in such borderline cases). Apart from his fantasy solutions, Clark's main means of dealing with problems is through avoidance. In fact, he frequently needs to escape into a telephone booth (a return to the womb). Can we detect in his desire to dress up in leotards and tights some repressed homosexual tendency, as well?

Even as Superman, however, he is not omnipotent. Naturally, there are various underworld (read *unconscious*) forces out to get him at all times, so he has to keep alert. His nemesis is green kryptonite, fragments of his exploded planet that have become radioactively toxic to him. An exposure instantly saps his powers. This is because it symbolizes the breakup of his fantasy world. A psychoanalyst might detect certain scatological elements in green kryptonite as well.

The question of the proper psychiatric diagnosis is a tricky one. Technically, Clark Kent is not a multiple personality, because he is really the same person playing two roles. The dual identity is only a ruse to fool outsiders. Similarly, he is not quite psychotic or schizophrenic, because he shows an adequate grasp on reality—holding down a job, thinking and writing clearly and so on. He doesn't really believe he is Superman, he just enjoys the fantasy.

In fact, Clark displays the characteristic anomalies of the *schizoid personality:* shyness, inability to show anger and daydreaming his problems away. (pp. 64-5)

[The] revival of Superman represents more than a nostalgic longing to return to the bliss of bygone decades. If this were all, it would be little more than a socially sanctioned form of regression—a retreat from the anxieties of the present into a magical fantasy world, much like Clark's own form of escapism. . . .

Humanistic psychology affirms that we are more than the sum total of our external repertoire of roles and achievements, more than we ourselves even know, and yet such inner promptings and intuitions find no articulation or credible counterpart in our crass and competitive culture. This alienation we share with Clark Kent. Superman has the freedom physically that we all desire psychologically. In this sense, the superman myth becomes, in a secular, technologically complex society, the bearer of our hopes for self-actualization. (p. 65)

Philip Demuth, "The Secret Life of Superman," in Human Behavior *(copyright © 1978 Human Behavior* Magazine; reprinted by permission), Vol. 8, No. 1, January, 1979, pp. 63-5.*

John Steinbeck

1902-1968

American novelist, short story writer, playwright, nonfiction writer, journalist, and screenwriter.

Steinbeck's novels of the common people and the troubles that beset them have earned him the reputation as one of America's greatest writers. He has employed various forms, from short story to allegory to morality play, yet his approach is consistently realistic. Critics often feel that the realism is marred by his sentimentality, but Steinbeck's clear, forceful writing and his sensitive treatment of his characters are considered his strengths.

Steinbeck often used religious motifs to universalize his work. The Eden theme and the Cain and Abel story are predominant in *East of Eden*. *The Grapes of Wrath* relies on a combination of Old and New Testament symbols for its emotional impact. Steinbeck's work also reveals a preoccupation with biological relationships and patterns, an interest promoted by his friendship with the marine biologist Edward Ricketts. Steinbeck discerned parallels between animal and human life that he believed could produce a better understanding of human behavior. An accurate observation of the land and its inhabitants resulted from Steinbeck's interest in science.

Steinbeck was impressed with the Arthurian legends and contended that *Tortilla Flat* was written as a modern-day example of the Knights of the Round Table. However, some critics have difficulty finding the Arthurian theme in the book. Steinbeck later began translating Sir Thomas Malory's *Morte d'Arthur* into more accessible, contemporary language. The incomplete work was published posthumously as *The Acts of King Arthur and His Noble Knights*. It was received with great enthusiasm; critics praised Steinbeck's use of language in this book as the best of his career.

The social outcast is a prevalent character in Steinbeck's work. In *Cannery Row* Steinbeck infuses a group of these characters with a dignity and nobility that makes it possible for the reader to like them in spite of their irresponsible ways. The working class is also represented in Steinbeck's novels, especially in *In Dubious Battle*. Here Steinbeck attempts to present an objective view of illegal strikes and shows genuine concern for the workers not only as employees, but also as people.

The Grapes of Wrath, an accurate and moving account of the mass migration during the American Depression, is probably Steinbeck's best-known novel. Here again he attacks social injustice, but there are several other essential themes. Along with traditional religious beliefs, Steinbeck explores the implications of the transcendentalist belief that each person is a part of the over-soul and that individual actions cannot be interpreted as right or wrong. The family as a source of strength to its members and the community as a whole is another important theme of the book. The Joad family is a universal symbol for the need for group effort and support to accomplish the greater good for the greater number of people.

Steinbeck is remembered primarily as a writer who was unafraid to denounce the faults of individuals and society as he saw them. His sympathetic portrayal of the proletariat endears

Steinbeck to readers of every generation, and the skill with which he wrote has earned him a place among America's most important writers. Steinbeck was the recipient of numerous awards, including the Nobel Prize for Literature in 1962 and the Pulitzer Prize in 1940 for *The Grapes of Wrath*. (See also *CLC*, Vols. 1, 5, 9, 13, *Contemporary Authors*, Vols. 1-4, rev. ed.; *Contemporary Authors New Revision Series*, Vol. 1; obituary, Vols. 25-28, rev. ed., and *Something About the Author*, Vol. 9.)

LOUIS PAUL

The weeds and the willows and the tall waving grain of California's sweet valleys, rabbits and mice and a woman's soft hair, the hot slanting sun and the hungry desire of a pair of floaters to own a handful of dirt are the materials out of which this lovely new novel by John Steinbeck is evoked. Purling water is purling water here, without overtones; a gracious sky is as beautiful as in any lyric poetry. The men are lads sent down to the ranch from Murray and Ready's in San Francisco: Lennie, like Nature itself, whose powerful fingers killed little animals before he knew it, and George, struggling to become human. **"Of Mice and Men"** is another of John Steinbeck's parables of earth, and no writer I know shapes the soil into truer patterns for us to understand.

In **"Pastures of Heaven"** this dream had its first fruition. A tapestry whose threads were woven from the design the lives of the men and women of a fertile valley created in the author's imagination, these stories are unforgettable. A prose that seemed made of wind and weather and growing acres came alive in them. **"To a God Unknown"** continued Steinbeck's inner examination of earth, when a tree and a mossy rock and the silent fury of a drought murdered the fragile human figures. And then, because Nature is anything but monotonous, this versatile novelist went down into Monterey, bought himself a "balloon" of claret, made the acquaintance of Danny and his paisano pals, and decided to recount the adventures and achievements of Pilon, Pablo, Big Joe and Company in **"Tortilla Flat."** Again when the fun of living with the childlike was done, the writer presented for our information, in **"In Dubious Battle,"** what is unquestionably the most important study of strike technique to find its way on paper in this nation.

These works have been called dissimilar. Versatile, perhaps; in a day when success has the tendency to standardize, versatility in a novelist or any one else is thought of with some astonishment. The threads that run continuously through these stories by John Steinbeck are, under examination, more than perceptible. . . . Here . . . is an intelligence as explicit as any research scientist's, an intelligence directed toward the understanding of the relationship between men and earth. In each successive book this desire to explore the complex affinity is more apparent, until, with the publication of **"Of Mice and Men,"** it achieves such cumulative impact as to be undeniable.

"Of Mice and Men" is made of a theme which some lesser novelist might have called too insignificant to expound—two indigent members of the strange tribe of casual workers destroyed by the simple mystery of loyalty. But before they are destroyed there burns brilliantly between the covers of this little book the image of the fire inside the flesh of two human beings, whom fate has crushed before birth, human beings whose lives mean no more to Nature than robins caught up by hawks.

The story seems simple when accomplished by a superb craftsman: the desire and struggle of those who till the soil for others to own a tiny plot of the earth for themselves; against this primitive hunger, like the rising tide of a destructive river, is played the forces which make a naive aspiration impossible of attainment. . . .

[The] poet who immortalizes the fleeting tragedy of two such men as George and Lennie is his own social force. That Lennie was an idiot, no less, and victim of a pathological disease, is entirely beyond the point. John Steinbeck does not know what makes men idiots and victims of disease; such knowledge comes slowly and painfully, as does the cure for cancer. We sting the flesh of our economic body with patent medicines, wondering, let us say, if Lennie's tragedy might not be avoided if the government in Washington gave every crop floater and bindle stiff and lettuce picker and wheat sacker a little farm in Salinas Valley. Such nonsense invalidates the very spirit in which the author of such a work as **"Of Mice and Men"** is creating.

The verities we can live with are those thoughts born out of dreams which, in the end, distinguish us from the robins and the waving grain. Of such verities does John Steinbeck write, out of a warm and a rich knowledge. With the genuine artist's

respect for his materials and love of his craft he puts away cheap prejudice, the distortion which comes from anger; his thought is to tell the little truths he had discovered with his eyes and calloused hands and intelligence and if these truths do not touch your social conscience nothing can. In **"Of Mice and Men"** the truth is made into a moving and profoundly beautiful book full of singing prose and enchantment. If, standing upon some pinnacle of dry logic, we suspect that his creations of these ignorant American laborers are idealizations, that without the magic of his poetry they must remain sweat-soaked beasts of the fields, we but doubly assure ourselves of his essential humanity and pay his artistry the highest compliment we know.

Louis Paul, "Prose Made of Wind and Soil and Weather," in New York Herald Tribune Books *(© I.H.T. Corporation; copyright renewed © 1965; reprinted by permission), February 28, 1937, p. 5.*

CARLOS BAKER

"The Wayward Bus" may confidently be taken as a twentieth-century parable on the state of man. Although Steinbeck is not quite so insistent on his moral as Jonathan Swift, the underlying conception in what he has to say was succinctly summarized by the King of Brobdingnag in **"Gulliver's Travels"**: "I cannot but conclude the bulk of your natives to be the most pernicious race of little odious vermin that nature ever suffered to crawl upon the surface of the earth." Steinbeck's moral is therefore hardly new, and it has been occasionally exploited in our own day by such artists as John O'Hara and such polemicists as Philip Wylie. But in recent years the subject has rarely received so searching a treatment as Steinbeck gives it. Both because of the richness of its texture and the solidity of its structure, this new novel, unlike many parables, makes good reading. And it might even be good for one's soul.

The wayward bus is an ancient, aluminum-colored conveyance which serves the public as connecting link between two great arterial highways in central California. But its chief importance is that it serves Steinbeck as a vehicle of thought and action. He assembles in it eight members of his cast, carefully graded as to age and sex, and sends them talking and fighting across the forty-nine miles of rain-sodden and flood-swept country which lies between Juan Chicoy's lunchroom-filling station at a crossroads named (perhaps significantly) Rebel Corners and a point within eye-shot of the lights of a town called (perhaps significantly) San Juan de la Cruz. . . .

Steinbeck makes the bus ride an excuse for a long look at the internal substance of his characters. What he finds beneath the skin will not cause [readers] to jump out of theirs, but it may well cause them to squirm in their chairs at the partial but painful truth of Steinbeck's implied conclusions.

The passengers in the bus are none of the pleasantest, possibly because Steinbeck examines their respective constitutions with such meticulous care and clinical exhaustiveness that one gets to know them from the inside out. . . . The one reasonably self-possessed individual of the lot is the half-Irish, half-Mexican owner-driver of the bus, Juan Chicoy. To underline the introduction of Juan as a measuring stick or touchstone character, Steinbeck permits himself one of the rare asides in the book. Juan, he says, is a man. "There aren't very many of them in the world, as everyone finds out sooner or later." About Juan's lonely, selfish, puzzled, cynical, childish, sour-souled and Godless passengers one is not long in discovering the rough truth of the aside. They are all creatures of their bodily chemistry, torn and ravaged by subliminal sexual drives, misdirected loves and irrational hatreds. If the reader sniffs closely between the lines he may catch from time to time a gamy odor which will recall that of the Yahoos in the last book of ''Gulliver's Travels.''

What prevents Steinbeck from swinging completely over into a savage indignation like Swift's is, however, a saving sense of humor and a deep strain of pity. . . .

Yet readers will do well to handle this parable with care. It is loaded—with the powder of longing and the lead of vice. (p. 1)

The long build-up to the bus ride begins before dawn at the lunchroom, and the darkness of evening settles over the bus as it nears its destination. Those harrowing tensions which develop in the course of the ride are established during the breakfast hour, heightened at mid-day by the dangers of the flood-racked bridge, and brought to climactic explosion in mid-afternoon when Juan skids the bus into a ditch and vanishes up the road. But in the end, with their passions spent and Juan as their conductor, the passengers arrive. The novel has as subtle and neat horizontal structure as Steinbeck has ever evolved.

Of equal interest, though less for formal than for philosophical reasons, is what may be called the vertical structure. The route of the bus is through a clean and rain-washed countryside, and Steinbeck often, though quietly, draws the reader's eyes outward to the rich, calm beauties of the springtime land. Across the scene chugs the vehicle with its mundane human freight, while above its dashboard, like an unheeded and enigmatic guardian angel, hangs Juan's ''connection with eternity,'' a small metal Virgin of Guadalupe painted in brilliant colors of gold and blue. The vertical structure of God, man and nature is not the less powerfully effective for being underplayed.

Among the hints by which Steinbeck enlightens his audience, readers may observe the bumpers of the wayward bus, where its modern name, Sweetheart, is boldly painted. Still dimly visible beneath the newer lettering is an older and far more serious inscription: El Gran Poder de Jesus—the great power of Jesus. This modern version of a medieval palimpsest will provide, for the thoughtful, one more handle to Steinbeck's parable of Everyman. (p. 31)

Carlos Baker, ''Mr. Steinbeck's Cross-Section,'' in The New York Times Book Review (© 1947 by The New York Times Company; reprinted by permission), February 16, 1947, pp. 1, 31.

MARK SCHORER

Probably the best of John Steinbeck's novels, **''East of Eden,''** is long but not ''big,'' and anyone who, deceived by its spread in space and time (c.1860-1920), says that it is ''epical in its sweep,'' is merely in the usual grip of cliché. Its dramatic center is a narrow story of social horror that rests quite disarmingly on the proposition that ''there are monsters born in the world to human parents.'' But through the exercise of a really rather remarkable freedom of his rights as a novelist, Mr. Steinbeck weaves in, and more particularly around, this story of prostitution a fantasia of history and of myth that results in a strange and original work of art.

''East of Eden'' is different from any of the earlier Steinbeck novels. It is, in a sense, more amorphous, less intent on singleness of theme and effect. . . .

Mr. Steinbeck's tightly constructed short novels, in fact, and even such longer work as **''The Grapes of Wrath,''** have given us no preparation for this amplitude of treatment that enables him now to develop, within this single work, not only a number of currents of story, but a number of different modes of tracing them. . . .

[The] novelist reconstructs the history of his maternal grandfather, Samuel Hamilton, who came to the Salinas Valley in about 1870 with his wife, and there produced a brood of children. From the history of Samuel Hamilton, which, although it is a story of economic failure is also a sunny and exhilarating account of a rich and various family life set against the rigorous background of a recalcitrant land, we move into the dark and violent story of Adam Trask.

In about 1900, Trask arrives in Salinas with a strange and very pretty wife. His own home was a Connecticut farm which he could not share with his brother, Charles, the Cain to Adam's Abel, and when he finds the girl, Cathy, beaten nearly to death on his doorstep, he nurses her back to health, marries her, and takes her to the West. . . . It is her story that seems most to concern the novelist.

These stories in themselves are less interesting than the whole that they compose, and more especially, than the various ways in which the novelist creates that whole. There is, to begin, the speculative voice of Mr. Steinbeck himself, a kind of democratic chorus that broods on implications of the action but is itself, in this role, entirely separate from the action. . . . Then there is the narrator when he sinks into the narrative, involved in his own ancestral history and even, fleetingly, in his boyhood. (p. 1)

Then there is that family history, particularly of Samuel Hamilton, through whom we are taken into the social history of Salinas County. Hamilton, an eloquent Irishman, and his friend, Lee, an eloquent Chinese servant, are the most moving characterizations in the novel, and both are ancillary to the story.

As we come into that story, we observe further varieties of method: the rapid, impersonal narration of which Mr. Steinbeck is a positive master, a method that has not found much room in the contemporary novel with its Jamesian emphasis on the dramatic unit; then the narrative method constantly erupting into the jagged intensities of the dramatic, or rather, the melodramatic method. . . .

With Adam Trask, we move . . . into the core story, the incredible story of his wife, the ''monster'' Cathy Ames, most vicious female in literature, whose story, if we accept it at all, we accept at the level of folklore, the abstract fiction of the Social Threat, of a Witch beyond women.

This account may suggest a kind of eclectic irresolution of view which is, in fact, not at all the quality of the book. I have hoped to suggest, instead, a wide-ranging, imaginative freedom that might save the life of many an American novelist.

There are defects in Mr. Steinbeck's imagination, certainly. He has always been fascinated by depravities that he seems helpless to account for; hence the melodrama. Inversely, he has always accepted certain noble abstractions about human nature that his melodrama is hardly designed to demonstrate; hence the gap between speculative statement and novelistic presentation, or sentimentalism. These qualities cause familiar discontinuities in **''East of Eden,''** yet the tone of this book, the bold ease with which the ''I'' takes over at the outset and appears and disappears and reappears throughout, both holds it together and gives it its originality, the relaxations of its freedom. (pp. 1, 22)

I am trying to praise the audaciousness with which this novelist asserts his temperament through his material, and the temperamental means by which he defines that material for us. (p. 22)

Mark Schorer, "A Dark and Violent Steinbeck Novel," in The New York Times Book Review *(© 1952 by The New York Times Company; reprinted by permission), September 21, 1952, pp. 1, 22.*

MARTIN SHOCKLEY

I propose an interpretation of *The Grapes of Wrath* in which [Jim] Casy represents a contemporary adaptation of the Christ image, and in which the meaning of the book is revealed through a sequence of Christian symbols.

Before and after *The Grapes of Wrath* Steinbeck has used symbolism and allegory; throughout his work he has considered a wide range of Christian or neo-Christian ideas; in relation to the context of his fiction as a whole, Christian symbolism is common. His use of Biblical names, for instance, is an inviting topic yet to be investigated. *The Pearl* is an obvious allegory on the evil of worldly treasure. The Pirate in *Tortilla Flat* exemplifies a Steinbeck character type, pure in heart, simple in mind, rejected of men, clearly of the kingdom of heaven. More pertinent perhaps, the title of *The Grapes of Wrath* is itself a direct Christian allusion, suggesting the glory of the coming of the Lord, revealing that the story exists in Christian context, indicating that we should expect to find some Christian meaning. . . .

Consider . . . the language of the novel. Major characters speak a language that has been associated with debased Piedmont culture. It is, I suggest, easy to find in vocabulary, rhythm, imagery, and tone pronounced similarities to the language of the King James Bible. These similarities, to be seen in qualities of simplicity, purity, strength, vigor, earnestness, are easy to illustrate. The novel contains passages of moving tenderness and prophetic power, not alone in dialogue, but even in descriptive and expository passages.

Like the Israelites, the Joads are a homeless and persecuted people. They too flee from oppression, wander through a wilderness of hardships, seeking their own Promised Land. Unlike the Israelites, however, the Joads never find it.

More specifically, let us examine the Christ-Casy relationship. Jesus began his mission after a period of withdrawal into the wilderness for meditation and consecration; Preacher Casy comes into the book after a similar retreat. (p. 87)

Jim Casy is by the same initials identified with Jesus Christ. Like Jesus, Jim has rejected an old religion and is in process of replacing it with a new gospel. In the introductory scene with Tom Joad, Tom and Jim recall the old days when Casy preached the old religion, expounded the old concept of sin and guilt. Now, however, Casy explains his rejection of a religion through which he saw himself as wicked and depraved because of the satisfaction of natural human desires. The old Adam of the fall is about to be exorcised through the new dispensation.

It should not be necessary to point out that Jim Casy's religion is innocent of Paulism, of Catholicism, of Puritanism. He is identified simply and directly with Christ. . . . (pp. 87-8)

Yet Casy's doctrine, "all that lives is holy," comes close to the doctrine of one of the most distinguished Christian theologians of our time, Albert Schweitzer, whose famous and familiar phrasing of the same concept is known to us as "reverence for life."

The third article of Casy's faith is a related one: "'Maybe,' I figgered, 'Maybe it's all men and women we love; maybe that's the Holy Sperit—the human sperit—the whole shebang. Maybe all men got one big soul ever'body's a part of.' Now I sat there thinking it, an' all of a sudden—I knew it. I knew it so deep down that it was true and I still know it." Casy's knowledge of the oversoul is derived from . . . within himself, or if you prefer, from God speaking within him. (p. 88)

I should like to go on from this formulation of a creed to the expression of doctrine through deeds, to the unfolding of the incidents of the plot in which Jim Casy reveals himself through significant, symbolic acts.

First, he feels a compulsion to minister, to serve, to offer himself. . . . When Tom is about to be arrested, Casy tells the police that he is the guilty one. . . . Jim Casy had taken upon himself the sins of others.

Casy's death symbolically occurs in the middle of a stream to represent the "crossing over Jordan" Christian motif. Particularly significant, however, are Casy's last words directed to the man who murders him, "Listen," he said, "You fellas don' know what you're doin'." . . . Jesus said, as they crucified Him, "Father forgive them; they know not what they do."

One of the major emotional climaxes of the novel is the scene in which Tom tells Ma goodbye and explains why he must leave. He has told Ma about Casy, who "Spouted out some Scripture once, an' it didn' soun' like no hellfire Scripture." He goes on to repeat what Casy told him about two being better than one. . . . At this point Tom becomes Casy's disciple. He has learned from his master, and now he takes up his master's work. Two of Jesus' disciples were named Thomas. Most of those chosen by Him to found the religion we profess were called from among people like the Joads. (pp. 88-9)

I find in the novel what seems to me to be adequate evidence to establish the author's intention of creating in Jim Casy a character who would be understood in terms of the Christ symbol.

Beyond this personal identification, I find further use of Christian symbols. The conclusion of *The Grapes of Wrath* has been said to be extreme, sensational, overwrought. The Joads have reached at last a condition of utter desolation. Rosasharn, her baby born dead, is rain-drenched, weak, her breasts heavy with milk. In the barn they come upon a boy and a starving old man, too weak to eat the bread his son had stolen for him. Ma knows what must be done, but the decision is Rosasharn's: "Ma's eyes passed Rose of Sharon's eyes, and then came back to them. And the two women looked deep into each other. The girl's breath came short and gasping.

"She said, 'Yes.'"

In this, her Gethsemane, Rosasharn says, in effect: "Not my will, but Thine be done."

The meaning of this incident, Steinbeck's final paragraph, is clear in terms of Christian symbolism. And this is the supreme symbol of the Christian religion, commemorated by Protestants in the Communion, by Catholics in the Mass. Rosasharn gives what Christ gave, what we receive in memory of Him. The ultimate mystery of the Christian religion is realized as Rosasharn ''Looked up and across the barn, and her lips came together and smiled mysteriously.'' She smiles mysteriously because what has been mystery is now knowledge. *This is my body,* says Rosasharn, and becomes the Resurrection and the Life. Rose of Sharon, the life-giver, symbolizes the resurrective aspect of Christ, common in Christian tradition and literature, used by Mr. Eliot in his ''multifoliate rose'' image. In her, death and life are one, and through her, life triumphs over death.

Cited incidents occur at points of major importance in plot and action, accompany major emotional crises, and relate to the major and most familiar examples of Christian symbolism. Other less obvious examples might be brought in. . . . (p. 89)

It is not within the scope of this paper to explore these labyrinthine shadows. Suffice it to say that we recognize in Christianity elements of older religions. Further, it is easy to identify elements of Steinbeck's ideology with other religions. For example, the principle of reverence for life, or ''all that lives is holy,'' has been believed and practiced for centuries by Buddhists.

Such, however, I regard as incidental. In *The Grapes of Wrath* the major intended meaning is neither Buddhist nor Freudian nor Marxist; it is, I believe, essentially and thoroughly Christian. In my interpretation, Jim Casy unmistakably and significantly is equated with Jesus Christ. (p. 90)

> Martin Shockley, "Christian Symbolism in 'The Grapes of Wrath'," in College English (copyright © 1956 by the National Council of Teachers of English; reprinted by permission of the publisher), Vol. 18, No. 2, November, 1956, pp. 87-90.

ELIZABETH JANEWAY

[This ''fabrication,'' **''The Short Reign of Pippin IV,''**] is a froth of a book which must have been great fun to write. In addition, it is one of the purest expressions of true, simple, American affection for the French that has ever been written— compounded with our equally simple conviction that they are also, after all, a funny race.

Mr. Steinbeck's hero is Pippin Arnulf Héristal, a middle-aged amateur astronomer. . . .

The unfolding of M. Héristal's story is directed not by anything he has done, but by something that he is: in his veins flows the blood of Charlemagne. . . . Thus, when sometime in the near future a French government expires into slightly more than normal anarchy, and every other party has talked itself hoarse, the patient monarchists are able to make themselves heard. . . . [An] ancient descendant of the Merovingian nobility is able to propose that the line of Charlemagne be revived, and that a certain M. Héristal, Numero 1, Avenue de Marigny, be crowned at Rheims. And, reluctantly he is.

Reluctantly, M. Héristal, now suddenly Pippin the Fourth, is quite as aware as Hamlet that the times are out of joint, but for fifty-four years he has had no inkling that he was born to set them right. Here the moral of Mr. Steinbeck's fabrication— and he is a highly moral writer—begins to show through the joke. For Pippin is both *l'homme moyen sensuel,* and the ordinary citizen, who is suddenly confronted with responsibility. What is he to do? Lend himself to the shabby face-saving that has set him up as a figure-head, or try to be what a king should be? (p. 6)

This, however, is not poor Pippin's only dilemma. Does he want to rule? Should he? . . . Pippin is thus confronted not only with the practical problem, on the material level, of whether he *can* be king. He is also involved in the moral problem of whether it is right for him to try to be king.

I'm afraid it's too much weight for the book to carry. Pippin's allies, with whom he discusses the alternatives he faces, come from the borders of the realm of farce. (pp. 6, 18)

[Sister Hyacinthe and Pippin's uncle, Charles Martel], at any rate, are amusing conceptions, but if we are to accept them at all, it can only be as figures of farce. When we whizz by them at ninety miles an hour, they are very funny indeed. . . . But when we sit down to discuss moral dilemmas with them, this soufflé of a book threatens to collapse into a sodden crust.

To insist on taking Mr. Steinbeck's fun too seriously is to be a spoilsport. Let us pass over in silence, as Cicero liked so inaccurately to say, that Puritan structure of morality which our author can never quite ignore, and enjoy the fabrication he has draped about it. (p. 18)

> Elizabeth Janeway, "A Star-Gazing King," in The New York Times Book Review (© 1957 by The New York Times Company; reprinted by permission), April 14, 1957, pp. 6, 18.

DAN VOGEL

More than a mere allegory, **"Flight"** reveals characteristics of myth and tragedy. A myth is a story that tries to explain some practice, belief, institution, or natural phenomenon, and is especially associated with religious rites and beliefs. The natural phenomenon, for Steinbeck, is not the facts of nature, with which historical myths deal; rather, it is . . . the development of innocent childhood into disillusioned manhood. The myth that Steinbeck wrought also contains another quality of myth, the rite. The plot of **"Flight"** narrates symbolically the ritual: the escape from the Mother, the divestiture of the Father, and the death and burial of Childhood. To discern these mythic symbols, it is necessary to review the narrative facts.

At the beginning of the story, Pepé, though 19 years of age, has all the innocence of the ''toy-baby'' his mother calls him. . . .

When his rather domineering mother—who constantly taunts him with his inability to be ''a man''—asks him to go to Monterey, ''a revolution took place in the relaxed figure of Pepé.'' . . . He is asked, surprisingly, to go alone; he is permitted to wear his father's hat and his father's hatband and to ride in his father's saddle. (p. 225)

When Pepé returns, he has killed a man with his father's knife, left behind him at the scene of the crime. The look of innocence is gone; he has been shocked by a fact of life, an extreme independent act. His mother quickly understands and helps him outfit himself for the flight into the mountains. She gives him especially his father's black coat and rifle. Weighted down by the accoutrements of his father, Pepé separates himself from his mother. She recognizes the change. She tells the little boy, ''Pepé is a man now. He has a man's thing to do.'' . . . Logically, however, this is not necessarily so. A man might possibly have been expected to give himself up and pay for his crime. It seems to me, then, that Pepé's mother perceived that her son is entering manhood and must stand alone. This he must do.

The ordeal of transformation from innocence to experience, from purity to defilement begins. There is the physical pain of the ordeal, symbolized by a cut hand that soon becomes gangrenous. There is the psychological pain—the recognition of a strangeness in this life that is omnipresent, silent, watchful and dark—the sense of Evil, or Tragedy, or Retribution. This realization is symbolized by the narratively gratuitous, unrealistic presence of the black figures, the "dark watchers" who are seen for a moment on the tops of ridges and then disappear. . . . These are the silent inscrutable watchers from above, the universal Nemesis, the recognition of which signals a further step into manhood. (pp. 225-26)

Only [when] having been separated from his mother and having cleansed himself of all the accoutrements and artifacts of his father, can the youth stand alone. But to Steinbeck this is far from a joyous or victorious occasion. It is sad and painful and tragic. Pepé rises to his feet, "black against the morning sky," . . . astride a ridge. He is a perfect target and the narrative ends with the man against the sky shot down. The body rolls down the hillside, creating a little avalanche, which follows him in his descent and covers up his head. Thus innocence is killed and buried in the moment that Man stands alone.

Thus the myth ends, as so many myths do, with violence and melodrama. What the myth described is the natural miracle of entering manhood. When serenity of childhood is lost, there is pain and misery. Yet there is nevertheless a sense of gain and heroism which are more interesting and dramatic. It is a story that has fascinated many from [William] Wordsworth to [Ernest] Hemingway, and what Steinbeck has written is a myth that describes in symbols what has happened to each of us. (p. 226)

> *Dan Vogel, "Steinbeck's 'Flight': The Myth of Manhood," in* College English *(copyright © 1961 by the National Council of Teachers of English; reprinted by permission of the publisher and the author), Vol. 23, No. 3, December, 1961, pp. 225-26.*

ERIC F. GOLDMAN

Shortly after Labor Day, 1960, Steinbeck left his Long Island home for a swing around the United States.

Three months and 10,000 miles later the 58-year-old novelist was back, physically and emotionally exhausted. But it was all decidedly worth the effort. The resulting book ["**Travels with Charley**"] is pure delight, a pungent potpourri of places and people interspersed with bittersweet essays on everything from the emotional difficulties of growing old to the reasons why giant Sequoias arouse such awe. . . .

He traveled accompanied only by his aged French poodle, Charley. The poodle is wonderful. Charley takes over a good deal of the book, the *ambassadeur extraordinaire* between mere human beings, always the companion and judge of the man who indulged himself in the whimsy that he was his master. . . .

Once past Chicago, Steinbeck's prose takes on a new lift. This was his kind of country, and the Pacific, his Pacific, was nearing. By the time he reached Montana, he was engaged in an unabashed love affair with nature. The calm of the mountains and grasslands, he was sure, had seeped into the inhab-

itants. Out here even the casual conversation, in Steinbeck's glowing reportage, has an earthy sagacity. . . .

On to Seattle and then down into northern California. Naturally the clash between old and new produced the sharpest twinges in the area of Steinbeck's boyhood and of his novels. . . .

Texas undid Steinbeck. He was determined not to go along with the usually easy denunciations of the state, and in this chapter he leans backward so far that at times he tumbles into saccharinity and even near incomprehensibility. But no one can doubt his meaning as he reached New Orleans and "Cheerleaders" scream at a tiny Negro girl making her terrified way into a desegregated school. Here is the most powerful writing in the book, stinging with the cold lash of outraged decency.

The trip really ended in Louisiana. Tired and homesick, Steinbeck soon had his foot far down on the accelerator, and Charley, who was no dog to fight inevitabilities, settled into soulful snoring. All kinds of thoughts went through Steinbeck's head as he hurried home—yet, apparently, the most obvious one did not. He had traveled thousands of miles to learn what America was really like nowadays, but he had avoided its new heartland. The cities, he raced through; the suburbs, he ignored. This is a book about Steinbeck's America and, for all the fascination of the volume, that America is hardly coincident with the United States of the Sixties. . . .

Increasingly in his travels Steinbeck caught himself when he wanted to lash out at the most fundamental result of that drive, the rampant industrialization. "It is the nature of man as he grows older to protest against change. . . . The sad ones are those who waste their energy in trying to hold it back, for they can only feel bitterness in loss and no joy in gain."

For such talk Charley had no comment at all. A wise dog does not try to top wisdom.

> *Eric F. Goldman, "Steinbeck's America, Twenty Years After," in* The New York Times Book Review *(© 1962 by The New York Times Company; reprinted by permission), July 29, 1962, p. 5.*

HARRY MORRIS

[Nothing] more clearly indicates the allegorical nature of [*The Pearl*] as it developed in Steinbeck's mind from the beginning [as the various titles attached to the work—*The Pearl of the World* and *The Pearl of La Paz*]. Although the city of La Paz may be named appropriately in the title since the setting for the action is in and around that place, the Spanish word provides a neat additional bit of symbolism, if in some aspects ironic. In its working title, the novel tells the story of The Pearl of Peace. When this title was changed to *The Pearl of the World* for magazine publication, although the irony was partially lost, the allegorical implications were still present. But Steinbeck had apparently no fears that the nature of the tale would be mistaken when he reduced the title to merely *The Pearl*. . . . (pp. 487-88)

Steinbeck knew that the modern fabulist could write neither a medieval *Pearl* nor a classical Aesopian Fox and Grapes story. It was essential to overlay his primary media of parable and folklore with a coat of realism, and this was one of his chief problems. Realism as a technique requires two basic elements: credible people and situations on the one hand and recognizable evocation of the world of nature and of things on the other. Steinbeck succeeds brilliantly in the second of these tasks but perhaps does not come off quite so well in the first. In supplying realistic detail, he is a master, trained by his long and productive journeyman days at work on the proletarian novels of the thirties and the war pieces of the early forties. His description of the natural world is so handled as to do double and treble duty in enrichment of both symbolism and allegory. Many critics have observed Steinbeck's use of animal imagery that pervades this novel with the realistic detail that is also one of its strengths. . . . (p. 489)

Kino is identified symbolically with low animal orders: he must rise early and he must root in the earth for sustenance; but the simple, pastoral life has the beauty of the stars, the dawn, and the singing, happy birds. Yet provided also is a realistic description of village life on the fringe of La Paz. Finally, we should observe that the allegory too has begun. The first sentence—"Kino awakened in the near dark"—is a statement of multiple allegorical significance. Kino is what modern sociologists are fond of calling a primitive. As such, he comes from a society that is in its infancy; or, to paraphrase Steinbeck, it is in the dark or the near-dark intellectually, politically, theologically, and sociologically. But the third sentence tells us that the roosters have been crowing for some time, and we are to understand that Kino has heard the cock of progress crow. He will begin to question the institutions that have kept him primitive: medicine, the church, the pearl industry, the government. The allegory operates then locally, dealing at first with one person, Kino, and then with his people, the Mexican peasants of Lower California. But the allegory works also universally, and Kino is Everyman. The darkness in which he awakes is one of the spirit. The cock crow is one of warning that the spirit must awake to its own dangers. The allegorical journey has often been called the way into the dark night of the soul, in which the darkness stands for despair or hopelessness. We cannot describe Kino or his people as in despair, for they have never known any life other than the one they lead; neither are they in hopelessness, for they are not aware that there is anything for which to hope. In a social parable, then, the darkness is injustice and helplessness in the face of it; in the allegory of the spirit, darkness concerns the opacity of the moral substance in man.

The social element is developed rapidly through the episode of Coyotito's scorpion bite and the doctor's refusal to treat a child whose father cannot pay a substantial fee. Kino's helplessness is conveyed by the fist he crushes into a split and bleeding mass against the doctor's gate. This theme of helplessness reaches its peak in the pearl-selling attempt. When Kino says to his incredulous brother, Juan Thomás, that perhaps all three buyers set a price amongst themselves before Kino's arrival, Juan Thomás answers, "If that is so, then all of us have been cheated all of our lives." And of course they have been.

Kino is, then, in the near dark; and, as his misfortunes develop, he descends deeper and deeper into the dark night of the soul. The journey that the soul makes as well as the journey that the living Kino makes—in terms of the good and evil that invest the one and the oppression and freedom that come to the other— provides the allegorical statement of the novel.

In the attempt to achieve believable situations, create three-dimensional characters, Steinbeck met greater difficulties that he did not entirely overcome. The germ-anecdote out of which he constructed his story gave him little more than the bare elements of myth. . . . (p. 490)

[In] Steinbeck's source [are] all the major elements of his expanded version: the Mexican peasant, the discovered pearl, the belief that the pearl will make the finder free, the corrupt brokers, the attacks, the flight, the return, and the disposal of the pearl. But there are also additions and alterations. The episodes of the doctor and the priest are added; the motives for retaining the pearl are changed. While the additions add perhaps some realism at the same time that they increase the impact of the allegory, the alterations tend to diminish the realistic aspects of the hero. (p. 491)

In these alterations, employed perhaps to add reality to a fable, Steinbeck has diminished realism. Narrative detail alone supplies this element. The opening of chapter three, like the beginning paragraph of the book, is descriptive. . . . Symbol, allegory, and realistic detail are again woven satisfactorily together. The large fish and the hawks symbolize the doctor, the priest, the brokers, and the man behind the brokers, in fact all enemies of the village people from time prehistoric. Allegorically these predatory animals are all the snares that beset the journeying soul and the hungering body. Realistically these scenes can be observed in any coastal town where water, foul, and animal ecology provide these specific denizens.

Somewhere in every chapter Steinbeck adds a similar touch. . . . All these passages operate symbolically as well as realistically, and some of them work even allegorically. (p. 492)

Kino's flight may be seen as a double journey, with a third still to be made. The journey is one half spiritual—the route to salvation of the soul—and one half physical—the way to freedom from bodily want. The second half is obvious; it is the theme of most of the early Steinbeck works; it is delineated in the list of things Kino will buy with the pearl. The first half may not be obvious, since for a long time now critics have been calling Steinbeck's writing non-teleological, by which they mean it does not concern itself with end-products, with what might be, what should be, or what could be, but only with what is. Especially is he unconcerned with eschatology. This view has long seemed to me mistaken. An allegorist with no teleology, no eschatology is almost a contradiction in terms. How this view of Steinbeck came into being is easy to see. His early novels such as *In Dubious Battle* and *The Grapes of Wrath* are a-Christian. No set of characters ever swore by Christ's name or cried out their disbelief in the church more often than those in *In Dubious Battle*. . . . But these are early works. In Steinbeck's latest novel, *The Winter of Our Discontent* (1961), the central character, Ethan Allen Hawley, is a regular member of the Episcopal Church; his problems are oriented about morality in a Christian framework, and much of the incidental symbolism is sacramental. Perhaps we have witnessed in Steinbeck himself an orthodox conversion, which, once witnessed, gives us cause to look for signs of it in previous writings. *The Pearl* is one of the first in which I detect a change; Juan Chicoy's bargains with the Virgin of Guadalupe in *The Wayward Bus* may be reluctant religion, but they represent at least a willingness to sit at the arbitration table with what used to be the enemy. *East of Eden,* in my view, among other things is an allegory of redemption through grace.

One of Kino's journeys then is the search for salvation. (pp. 493-94)

The Indian boy of the germ-story had quite falsely identified his hold on the pearl with a firm grasp on salvation, a salvation absolutely assured while he still went about enveloped in flesh and mortality: "he could in advance purchase masses sufficient to pop him out of Purgatory like a squeezed watermelon seed.'' Kino also holds the pearl in his hand and equates it with freedom from want and then, mystically, also with freedom from damnation: ''If I give it up I shall lose my soul.'' But he too has mistaken the pearl. The chances are very much more likely that with freedom from want his soul will be all the more in danger from sin. The Indian boy becomes free only when he throws the pearl away, only when he is ''again with his soul in danger and his food and shelter insecure.'' The full significance of Kino's throwing the pearl back into the sea now becomes clear: the act represents his willingness to accept the third journey, the journey still to be made, the journey that Dante had still to make even after rising out of Hell to Purgatory and Paradise, the journey that any fictional character has still to make after his dream-vision allegory is over. Kino, Dante, Everyman have been given nothing more than instruction. They must apply their new knowledge and win their way to eternal salvation, which can come only with their actual deaths. (p. 494)

Kino is not defeated. He has in a sense triumphed over his enemy, over the chief of the pearl buyers, who neither gets the pearl nor kills Kino to keep him from talking. Kino has rid himself of his pursuers; he has a clear road to the cities of the north, to the capital, where indeed he may be cheated again, but where he has infinitely more opportunity to escape his destiny as a hut-dwelling peasant on the edge of La Paz. He has proved that he cannot be cheated nor destroyed. But his real triumph, his real gain, the heights to which he has risen rather than the depths to which he has slipped back is the immense knowledge that he has gained about good and evil. This knowledge is the tool that he needs to help him on the final journey, the inescapable journey that everyman must take.

A final note should be added concerning some parallels between Steinbeck's novel and the anonymous fourteenth century *Pearl*. (pp. 494-95)

The importance of the medieval *Pearl* for a reading of Steinbeck's novel is centered in the role of the children in each. Coyotito can, in several ways, be identified with Kino's ''pearl of great value.'' The pearl from the sea is only a means by which Coyotito will be given an education. For the doctor, who at first refused to treat Coyotito, the child becomes his means to the pearl, i.e. the child is the pearl to him. But more important than these tenuous relationships is the fact that with the death of Coyotito the pearl no longer has any significance. The moment the pursuer with the rifle fires, Kino kills him. Kino then kills the two trackers who led the assassin to him and who were unshakable. This act gives Kino and his family unhindered passage to the cities of the north, where either the pearl might be sold or a new life begun. But the chance shot has killed Coyotito, and though Kino and Juana are now free, they return to the village near La Paz and throw the pearl back into the sea. Thus the sole act that has altered Kino's determination to keep the pearl which has become his soul is the death of his child; and, as I read the allegory, Kino and Juana turn from the waterside with new spiritual strength, regenerated even as the father in the medieval *Pearl*. (p. 495)

However, I do not think that anything overmuch should be made of [the] similarities. Possibly the mere title of Steinbeck's allegory brought memories to his mind of the fourteenth century poem. He may have gone back to look at it again, but he may have satisfied himself with distant evocations only. For myself, whatever likenesses I find between the two works serve only to emphasize the continuing tradition of true allegory and the modern writer's strong links with the past. (p. 505)

Harry Morris, '''The Pearl': Realism and Allegory,'' in English Journal *(copyright © 1963 by the National Council of Teachers of English; reprinted by permission of the publisher and the author), Vol. LII, No. 7, October, 1963, pp. 487-95, 505.*

JOSEPH FONTENROSE

In the fall of 1937, while returning from New York and Pennsylvania, where he had worked on the stage version of *Of Mice and Men,* Steinbeck drove through Oklahoma, joined migrants who were going west, and worked with them in the fields after they reached California. *The Grapes of Wrath* is thus a product of his own experience and direct observation; its realism is genuine. (p. 68)

[The] story ends *in medias res.* Some readers have objected to the closing scene, in which the young mother who lost her child suckles a grown man. The episode not only has folkloristic and literary antecedents . . . , but for Steinbeck it is an oracular image, forecasting in a moment of defeat and despair the final triumph of the people—a contingent forecast, for only if the people nourish and sustain one another will they achieve their ends. More than that, the episode represents the novel's most comprehensive thesis, that all life is one and holy, and that every man, in Casy's words, ''jus' got a little piece of a great big soul.'' The Joads' intense feelings of family loyalty have been transcended; they have expanded to embrace all men. Another image could have symbolized this universality, but, for Steinbeck, perhaps no other could have done it so effectively.

The novel has thirty chapters, fourteen of which carry the Joad story. The other sixteen chapters (called interchapters even though the first chapter is one of them) take little more than one sixth of the book and are either expository essays or sketches of typical situations in the great migration. They present the social, economic, and historical background, telling the story of all the migrants. With two exceptions the general experiences described in an interchapter are illustrated by the Joads' experiences in the following narrative chapter. Some of these interchapters are masterpieces in themselves. (p. 69)

Steinbeck uses a variety of prose styles in these interchapters. In these short sketches he could experiment, endeavoring in each to evoke both a vivid picture of something that happened and a feeling tone. He employs paratactic Biblical language, go-getter talk, conversational narrative in Okie speech, the sound track of documentary films. Some interchapters are literally poetic. (p. 70)

The Grapes of Wrath has little plot in the ordinary sense; there is no complex involvement of character with character, no mesh of events. The story of the Joads could be the true story of a real family. But there is character development, as Tom Joad, ''jus' puttin' one foot in front a the other'' at first, gradually reaches an understanding of Casy's message and takes up Casy's mission. And the Joads as a whole progress from an exclusive concern for family interests to a broader vision of cooperation with all oppressed people. . . . As the Joad family's fortunes decline, the family morale declines, too: the family loses members and is threatened with dissolution. But as the family grows weaker, the communal unit of united workers, which came to birth in the roadside camps on the westward trek, grows stronger, and this upward movement is accompanied by the growth of Casy and Tom Joad in understanding of the forces at work. We can put the process another way:

the family unit, no longer viable, fades into the communal unit, which receives from it the family's strength and values.

Collective persons are important characters in this novel too, since the plot movement must be expressed in group terms. It can be read as a story of conflicts and interactions among several group organisms. . . . The Joad family is a democratic, cooperative organism; it is a cohesive group, and yet no member loses his individual character in the group. When the Joads act as a family, they act as a unit. . . . The Oklahoma land company is another sort of organism entirely. It is one of the monsters of Chapter Five which "don't breathe air, don't eat side-meat." . . . As Doc Burton said in *In Dubious Battle,* a group's ends may be entirely different from the ends of its individual members. The monster is the sort of organism that absorbs its members, drains them of their individualities, and makes them into organization men. (pp. 70-1)

The monster is in fact Leviathan. . . . [I allude] to the relation of the group organism to Thomas Hobbes's symbol for the state as collective person, "that great LEVIATHAN, or rather, to speak more reverently, . . . that *mortal god,* to which we owe under the *immortal God,* our peace and defence." Steinbeck's monster is as despotic as Hobbes's Leviathan, but hardly as beneficial to man. He is rather the original Leviathan of Isaiah 27 and Psalm 74, enemy of the Lord. . . .

The Joad family fled the Oklahoma Leviathan, only to run into his brother, the California Leviathan—the Farmers' Association and its typical member, the Hooper ranch, a veritable prison with its barbed-wire fences and armed guards—much the same sort of creature, but even meaner. (p. 72)

The conflict of organisms is necessarily an ecological struggle, a disturbance of an ecological cycle. . . . The agricultural corporations and big growers need pickers in great numbers to harvest their manifold crops. In the thirties they advertised everywhere for pickers with the object of bringing in more job-seekers than they needed; with too many men on hand they could lower wages and increase profits. When one crop was picked, the workers had to hurry on to another crop, if they were to make a bare subsistence. They never stayed long enough in one county to qualify for relief, and so the growers were saved higher taxes. When the time for the next harvest approached, the growers advertised again for pickers, sending handbills everywhere to bring workers back in great numbers. But there were flies in this ointment too: labor leaders, radical agitators, socialists, made the pickers dissatisfied with wages and working conditions, organized them in unions, promoted strikes, and were cordially hated by the growers.

Critics, of course, have noticed the biological features of *The Grapes of Wrath,* but without realizing how literally the monster, the family unit, and the workers' commune are meant to be real organisms. In fact, the biological and organismic side of the novel has been slighted, if not ignored. The mythical side, however, has been much more fortunate, in marked contrast to the neglect of mythical themes and structure in earlier novels. (pp. 74-5)

On the road west the Joads met men who were going back to Oklahoma from California. These men reported that although California was a lovely and rich country the residents were hostile to the migrant workers, treated them badly, and paid them so poorly that many migrants starved to death in slack periods. In Numbers 13, scouts whom Moses sent ahead into Canaan came back with the report that "surely it floweth with milk and honey"; nevertheless they made "an evil report of

the land which they had searched unto the children of Israel, saying, The land . . . is a land that eateth up the inhabitants thereof"; and the natives were giants who looked upon the Hebrews as locusts. Yet the Joads, like Joshua and Caleb, were determined to enter the land. The meanness of California officers at the border, the efforts to turn back indigent migrants, the refusal of cities and towns to let migrant workers enter, except when their labor was needed—in all this we may see the efforts of the Edomites, Moabites, and Amorites to keep the Israelites from entering their countries.

In spite of the Canaanites' hostility the Israelites persisted and took over the promised land. The Book of Joshua ends with victory and conquest. But *The Grapes of Wrath* ends at a low point in the fortunes of the Joads. . . . The migrant Okies met defeat because they had not learned to give up selfish desires for money and possessions: still too many wanted to undercut the pay of fellow-workers and had no feeling of a common cause. But they would accomplish nothing if they did not stand together. The issue is left there, and a happy ending depends on an "if": if the migrants should realize their strength in union. Casy, Tom, and Pa Joad predict a change that is coming, a better time for the people, when they will take matters into their own hands and set them right. And the author foresees doom for the oppressors: "Every little means, every violence, every raid on a Hooverville, every deputy swaggering through a ragged camp put off the day a little and cemented the inevitability of the day." Only future events will tell us how the story ends: it had not ended in 1939.

Perhaps the most striking episodic parallel to Exodus occurs near the end of the novel. When Tom killed the vigilante who struck Casy down and left the region when it looked as if he would be found out, he acted as Moses had done. For "when Moses was grown" he saw an Egyptian beating a Hebrew laborer, and he killed the Egyptian and hid his body in the sand. . . . In the Pentateuch this happened in Egypt before the Exodus; in *The Grapes of Wrath* it happened in California after the migration. . . . The "house of bondage" is in the new land; in the old land the people had lived in patriarchal contentment until they were forced to leave. It was more like Israel's earlier migration from Palestine to Egypt. Just after reaching California, Tom said to Casy, ". . . this ain't no lan' of milk an' honey like the preachers say. They's a mean thing here." So Moses' task of delivering his people from bondage is just beginning, not ending; it is now that he strikes the first blow. The migrants have gained nothing by merely exchanging one land for another; they must deal with the "mean thing."

Hence a stillborn child is set adrift upon a stream at the end of the story, rather than a living child at the beginning. It was a "blue shriveled little mummy." This time the first-born of the oppressed had died; yet it was a sign to the oppressors. John Joad said, "Go down an' tell 'em. Go down in the street an' rot an' tell 'em that way. That's the way you can talk." What message? It is given in Chapter Twenty-Five: oranges, corn, potatoes, pigs, are destroyed to keep prices up, though millions of people need them. "And children dying of pellagra must die because a profit cannot be taken from an orange."

Tom Joad becomes the new Moses who will lead the oppressed people, succeeding Jim Casy, who had found One Big Soul in the hills, as Moses had found the Lord on Mount Horeb. (pp. 76-8)

In colloquial language Casy and Tom express the book's doctrine: that not only is each social unit—family, corporation, union, state—a single organism, but so is mankind as a whole, embracing all the rest. (p. 80)

In no Steinbeck novel do the biological and mythical strands fit so neatly together as in *The Grapes of Wrath*. The Oklahoma land company is at once monster, Leviathan, and Pharaoh oppressing the tenant farmers, who are equally monster's prey and Israelites. The California land companies are Canaanites, Pharisees, Roman government, and the dominant organism of an ecological community. The family organisms are forced to join together into a larger collective organism; the Hebrews' migration and sufferings weld them into a united nation; the poor and oppressed receive a Messiah who teaches them unity in the Oversoul. The Joads are equally a family unit, the twelve tribes of Israel, and the twelve disciples. Casy and Tom are both Moses and Jesus as leaders of the people and guiding organs in the new collective organism. Each theme—organismic, ecological, mythical; and each phase of the mythical: Exodus, Messiah, Leviathan, ritual sequence—builds up to a single conclusion: the unity of all mankind.

To liken the Okies to the Israelites—this too may seem incongruous. Yet the parallel is really close. The oppressed laborers in Egypt were as much despised by their masters as the migrant workers in California. Moses was certainly a labor agitator, and Jesus appealed to the poor and lowly and called rude fishermen and tax-gatherers to his company. Again the mythical structure imparts a cosmic meaning to the tale. These contemporary events, says Steinbeck, are as portentous for the future as was the Hebrews' migration from Egypt, and for the same reasons. (pp. 82-3)

Steinbeck left the conclusion of his story to events. How did it turn out? On September 1, 1939, fewer than five months after *The Grapes of Wrath* was published, Hitler invaded Poland and began the war which interrupted the course of events that Steinbeck foresaw. In 1940 America began to prepare for war and was in it before the end of 1941. This meant an end of unemployment. The Okies and Arkies came to work in the shipyards of San Francisco and San Pedro bays; they replaced enlisted men in industries and businesses everywhere; and many, of course, were enlisted, too. They found houses to live in, settled down, and remained employed when the war was over. Mexicans and Orientals once more harvested California's crops, and "wetbacks" became a problem. So did *The Grapes of Wrath* never find a conclusion, cut off by the turn of events? Had the owners learned their lesson and improved conditions? Disquieting reports have been coming from the fields: more Americans are now employed in migratory farm labor than a few years ago, pay is low, and conditions are bad. Perhaps the story has not ended yet. (p. 83)

The central narrative throughout [*East of Eden*] is the fictional biography of Adam Trask from his birth in the second year of the Civil War until his death in the last year of World War I. Five short chapters (three of these are introductions to the Parts) present the historical and moral contexts of the Trask and Hamilton stories in fulfillment of the author's promise to write the story of his family and country. The design and magnitude of *East of Eden*, and Steinbeck's own remarks about it, indicate that it was meant to be a climactic work, his greatest achievement, for which every earlier book was practice. But few Steinbeck readers will place it higher than *The Grapes of Wrath*, the majority may see it as a second peak in his career, but not nearly so high as the first.

Although morality has now nearly eclipsed biology as a formative principle in Steinbeck's fiction, his biological knowledge

still makes an occasional appearance and remains an important source of metaphor and simile. For example, the vicious Cathy Ames was a psychic monster, produced by "a twisted gene or a malformed egg." But the group organism, prominent in earlier novels, has almost disappeared from view. It is employed in only a few instances. The army is depicted as a group that tolerates no individual differences in its members, absorbing them completely into itself. Lee, the Trasks' sage Chinese servant, used as a spokesman by the author, says that a family is something hard to root out, once it has dug into the earth and scratched out a home. Towns like Salinas are described as having an occasional "mild eructation of morality," which results in raids on gambling joints. That is about all—statements that another novelist might have made, and which would require no notice here had not Steinbeck established the organismic theme in earlier novels. In fact, in one moralizing section, the concept of the group, because it is hostile to "the free, exploring mind of the individual," is rejected in favor of "the individual mind and spirit of a man," which is the only "creative instrument"; the group never creates anything. Leviathan is cast into outer darkness. *East of Eden* does not deal with groups, aside from families—and not even the Hamilton family looks like a single organism.

The mythical vehicle of Steinbeck's moral message is the story of Cain and Abel, as the title indicates. And in this novel Steinbeck is not content with a subtle suggestion of the myth, but must make sure that his readers will not miss it. (pp. 119-20)

Steinbeck, of course, puts more into the story than can be found in Genesis 4, which says nothing about either brother's attitude towards Adam. The irony of the fathers' partiality in *East of Eden* is that neither Adam nor Aron loved his father, whereas Charles loved Cyrus and Cal loved Adam, and each tried hard to please his father. Again, Steinbeck introduces rivalry over a woman into both generations of brothers, more obscurely in the first, since Charles disliked Cathy; but he did admit her to his bed and left her half of his fortune when he died. In the next generation Abra, Aron's boyhood sweetheart, transferred her love to Cal after Aron's enlistment. Steinbeck read a good deal about Genesis while writing *East of Eden* and probably came upon a later Jewish legend (current before 300 A.D.) which elaborates the brief and bare scriptural narrative: both Cain and Abel had a twin sister, each intended to become her twin's wife and so ensure the survival of mankind. Abel's twin sister was so beautiful that Cain wanted her; therefore he picked a quarrel with Abel, killed him, and married Abel's twin, that mysterious wife of Cain who bore his son Enoch in the land of Nod (Genesis 4:17).

Furthermore, Steinbeck had to fuse Adam and Jehovah in one person, Cyrus Trask in the first generation, Adam Trask in the second. Cathy is a fusion of Eve, the Eden serpent, and Cain's wife—the beating which the whoremaster gave her had left a scar on her forehead. Steinbeck emphasizes her serpent nature by giving her a heart-shaped face, an abnormally small mouth, a little pointed tongue that sometimes flicked around her lips, small sharp teeth with the canine teeth longer and more pointed than the others, tiny ears without lobes and pressed close to her head, unblinking eyes, narrow hips. She liked the dark and shunned light. When Sam Hamilton delivered her twins, she snarled at him with lips drawn up from her teeth and bit his hand severely. Since Steinbeck accepts the Christian identification of the Eden snake with Satan, he also represents Cathy as a devil: "There was a time when a girl like Cathy would have been called possessed by the devil." (p. 122)

The story of Cain and Abel, Lee said to Adam and Sam, "is the symbol story of the human soul," "the best-known story in the world because it is everybody's story." The three men found the story perplexing when they first discussed it. Ten years later, when they had gathered for the last time, Lee had cleared up the difficulties with the help of four aged Chinese sages, who had studied Hebrew for just this purpose. They solved the problem of Genesis 4:7, as given in the King James version, "And unto thee shall be his desire, and thou shalt rule over him," by translating the verb form *timshol* (not *timshel* as Steinbeck has it) "thou mayest rule" instead of "thou shalt rule"; and they took "sin" as antecedent of the masculine pronouns. This, Lee said in triumph, "was the gold from our mining": the translation "thou shalt rule" implies predestination; "do thou rule," as in the American Standard version, orders a man to master sin; but "thou mayest rule" gives a man a choice: he can master sin if he wants to. "Thou mayest," Lee said, "might be the most important word in the world," for "that makes a man great, . . . for in his weakness and his filth and his murder of his brother he has still the great choice." (p. 123)

The reader is never clear about the relation of good to evil in this novel, for it is presented in four inconsistent ways. (1) Good is opposed to evil. . . . Charles, Cathy, and Cal have bad traits opposed to the good traits of Adam and Aron. In the "thou mayest" doctrine, evil can be rejected and good chosen. (2) Good and evil are complementary. Lee thought that they might be so balanced that if a man went too far either way an automatic slide restored the balance. Good and evil are symbolized by the church and the whorehouse, which "arrived in the Far West simultaneously," and each "intended to accomplish the same thing: . . . [to take] a man out of his bleakness for a time." (3) Evil is the source of good and may even be necessary to good. The evil Cathy, quite without intending it, "set off the glory in Adam." The wealth which Cyrus Trask acquired dishonestly was inherited by Adam Trask, an honest man who used the money to rear and educate his sons. The wicked Cathy-Kate was mother of the good Aron and left her ill-gotten money to him. . . . (4) Good and evil are relative terms. Lee said to Adam . . . , "What your wife is doing is neither good nor bad," although she was operating the most perverted and depraved brothel in California. This seems to hark back to Casy's doctrine: Kate's activities were simply not nice.

Good is identified both with admirable individual qualities (philanthropy, kindness, generosity, self-respect, courage, creativity) and with conventional moral goodness (sexual purity, abstinence from carnal pleasures of any kind). Evil is identified with ignoble individual qualities (meanness, cruelty, violent temper, avarice, hatefulness, selfishness), with criminal acts (murder, arson, theft, embezzlement), and with carnal pleasures, particularly sex acts; and not only with prostitution and perversions, but with sexual satisfaction in general. That is, the author appears to accept Cal's label of "bad" for his adolescent desires and impulses, and of "good" for Aron's self-indulgent purity and abstinence, and to accept Abra's use of "good" and "bad" when she says that Aron is too good for her, that she herself is not good, and that she loves Cal because he isn't good. Of course, this is the way that young people talk. But Cal and Abra are never allowed to reach a more enlightened view of "good" and "bad"; Steinbeck is using them to illustrate his thesis: that there is good and bad in everyone, and that some bad is necessary (that is, it is good to be bad); and he is understanding good and bad in their terms.

We should notice that in contrast to Steinbeck's treatment of sex in earlier novels, there is no good or healthy or lusty sexual intercourse in *East of Eden*. It is always sordid, joyless, depraved, or mercenary. The good married couples produce children, but they have no love life so far as this novel is concerned. There is a hint of passion between Cal and Abra in Chapter 54, but the curtain comes down abruptly and discreetly on the scene. In one passage Steinbeck decries human sexuality: what freedom men could have without it—only, he adds, they would no longer be human. This is not at all like the old Steinbeck who celebrated sexuality. It turns out that Steinbeck's view of good and evil is that of his mythical source: it is the Mosaic view, which is to say a legal view; particular acts are good or bad, regardless of circumstances. The earlier Steinbeck saw acts in context and evaluated them accordingly, if he evaluated them at all, dismissing the religious conception of "sin" entirely. For a novel on good and evil, *East of Eden* strangely lacks ethical insight. It is true, as I have pointed out, that its author evaluates qualities as well as acts, but they remain abstract. Adam is honest and kind, we are told; but these are negative virtues in him. In truth, virtue seems to be a function of lack of energy: pernicious anemia may account for George Hamilton's sinless life, and Adam Trask was passive, inert, non-resistant. The positive behavior of the "good" characters is at best unpleasant. Aron is selfish, inconsiderate, unloving. Adam neglects his boys for twelve years, never loves anybody except Cathy, and loves her blindly. His rejection of Cal's gift was brutal, unfeeling, and this after he had begun a cordial relationship with his son. Did Steinbeck, perhaps, intend to show that these "good" persons were not what others thought them to be? Hardly. Lee, his spokesman, said about Adam, "I think in him kindness and conscience are so large that they are almost faults. They trip him up and hinder him." Like Aron, he is too good; a man needs a little "bad" in him; you can be good if you don't have to be perfect, said Lee. We come back to moral confusion, since "good," "bad," and "perfect" are given conventional definitions, never questioned. If Steinbeck had delved into a father's ambivalent feelings for his sons, his awareness of favoring one son over the other, his fairness or unfairness to either son, and the moral and spiritual problems arising from his relation to his sons, then *East of Eden* might have been a great novel. As it is, we do not understand Adam's actions; in this novel we cannot resort to saying that they just happened.

We are indeed told that Adam could not help doing what he did. Lee said to Cal, "That's his nature. It was the only way he knew. He didn't have any choice." Why doesn't "thou mayest" apply to Adam as to other men? On his deathbed he did exercise choice by forgiving Cal with the blessing *Timshol*. Lee also said to Cal, "But you have. . . . You have a choice." And Cal then chose to get revenge on Aron. The final meaning of *timshol* for Cal is that his wicked deeds will not prevent his choosing to do od in the future. (pp. 124-26)

A reader can enjoy *East of Eden* for its many fine passages of description and many pages of skillful narrative; but the myth invoked does not adequately interpret the narrated events. (pp. 126-27)

The pleasantest part of this study has been to share Steinbeck's joy in myth and legend. He has relied principally on the Arthur cycle and Biblical tales, especially the Holy Grail and Fisher King, Garden of Eden, Cain and Abel, the Joseph story, Exodus, Leviathan, the Passion and Resurrection, the revolt of the angels. They are by no means his only myths: cosmogonic myths, dying god, Faust, Troy and Helen, Virgin Whore, legends of city-founding—all these and more have had their poetic use in Steinbeck's fiction. It is myth that attaches his work most closely to the great tradition of the European and American novel.

At one time Steinbeck said that all his work was meant to help people understand one another. He has wanted to enlist our sympathy for men of all degrees, for the wise and feebleminded, for beggars and kings alike. His most persistent theme has been the superiority of simple human virtues and pleasures to the accumulation of riches and property, of kindness and justice to meanness and greed, of life-asserting action to life-denying. In several ways he has asserted that all life is holy, every creature valuable. Herein lies his sentimentality, but also his strength. His great novels, like *The Grapes of Wrath,* will endure for their narrative power and strength of vision. (p. 141)

> *Joseph Fontenrose, in his* John Steinbeck: An Introduction and Interpretation *(© copyright, 1963 by Barnes & Noble, Inc.; by permission of Barnes & Noble Books, a Division of Littlefield, Adams & Co., Inc.), Barnes & Noble, 1963, 150 p.*

BRUCE K. MARTIN

Two very basic questions about ["**The Leader of the People**"] upon which its critics have been unable to agree are the identity of the main character and the nature of the change or development, if any, which he undergoes. (p. 423)

There is, of course, much to be said for Grandfather's importance in the story. His arrival at the ranch precipitates at least indirectly all of the important subsequent action. Also, the nature of each of the other characters is in large part determined by his response to Grandfather, since the old man is the common object of interest for Jody, his parents, and Billy. Nor can there be any question but that Grandfather's remarks to Jody after overhearing Carl's outburst—the old man's longest and most formal statement in the entire story—constitute a climax to what precedes them. Grandfather's revelation of what the frontier meant to him and of his loneliness in the frontierless present represents an emotionally compelling end to a chain of action that began with his arrival at the ranch. Clearly the story, as Steinbeck has fashioned it, does not permit the reader to ignore Grandfather.

However, to regard his presence or what he experiences as the central concern of the story is to raise some serious problems. Certainly his moving confession suggests a change of mood in the old man, yet when his speech is set against his earlier behavior, the basis of his despair seems something less than the total realization which some readers would attribute to him. What he tells Jody is that the era of leadership he once knew is gone and that what he has been doing is merely telling stories about that era. . . . As his confession indicates, he has been interested in the telling, in the affective value of the stories, not in the tales themselves as reality. And because Grandfather is established prior to the climax of the story as anything but a speedy reasoner, that he should grasp so quickly the rather sophisticated insight contained in his confession hardly seems probable. All that has happened since he was in what Steinbeck terms his "narrative groove" . . . is that he has overheard Carl's disparaging remarks about the stories and concluded that no one wants to hear them. While he certainly regrets the passing of an era in which he was the leader of the people, he has conceived of his role in the present as that of a skilled storyteller, and at this point he regrets most of all his failure in that role. His sorrow for an irrecoverable past began long before the opening of the story. Here he bemoans primarily his inability even to create moving tales from his adventures.

This view of Grandfather's discovery, while closer to his actual experience in the story than the more profound realization sometimes claimed for him, hardly distinguishes him as a main character. His learning that he has lost his audience, or that he never had one, seems insignificant in light of the more epic issues raised in his dramatic outburst to Jody, since the questions of the frontier, of leadership, of communication, and of aging clearly appear in "**The Leader of the People**." Beside such questions his discovery pales.

Nor can his presence really explain or justify certain sections of the story, especially the relatively lengthy opening section before he arrives at the ranch or the final paragraphs, after his confession, when Jody goes inside to make lemonade. The beginning and the ending of the story—frequently of crucial importance in determining what a work of short fiction is principally about—are, of course, more readily related to the experience of Jody himself. And, like the beginning and the end, the middle of the story, when Grandfather is present, is narrated from the boy's point of view, with occasional accounts of sometimes appreciable length regarding Jody's thoughts away from his grandfather. In terms of the content of the story, then, Jody might appear a more plausible main character.

But to say that Jody seems more important or that certain parts of the story appear unrelated to Grandfather is not, of course, to demonstrate the boy's predominance in the story. To do that, it is necessary to establish precisely what Grandfather means to Jody, what exactly happens to Jody and what part Grandfather, obviously an important element in "**The Leader of the People**," plays in moving the story to its conclusion. If it is difficult to see Grandfather undergoing the type of change demanded by the story's ideology, it is nevertheless necessary to show that Jody himself develops in a way worthy of the substantial concerns of the story.

One possibility is that Jody undergoes a basic change of character, moving away from an initial state of immaturity toward perceivably greater moral awareness. (pp. 424-26)

A careful look at Steinbeck's narrative focusing . . . undercuts the idea of basic moral change in Jody. . . . Jody's compassionate behavior at the beginning of the story marks his character as good. For example, in the first exchange between Jody and his grandfather, the narrator notes Jody's primary concern with gratifying the old man. . . . This same desire to appease the old man by whatever means necessary, which continues throughout the story, goes unrecognized by Jody's parents, as when Mrs. Tiflin miscalculates Jody's motives for including his grandfather in the promised mouse hunt by accusing him simply of desiring an accomplice in misbehavior. Perhaps the most striking indication of Jody's sympathetic nature comes in the showdown scene between Carl and Grandfather, when, while Carl is apologizing, the narrator describes Jody's sharp surveillance of the situation and his empathetic awareness of Carl's agony. . . . This keen feeling for the overly proud Carl precedes the climactic outburst of Grandfather to Jody and largely rules out the supposition that Jody lacks sympathy prior to the climax. Instead of pointing to a change of character in the boy, the lemonade incident at the end only further confirms the strong capacity for feeling that he exhibits earlier toward his antagonist. And, rather than signalling such a change, his mother's surprise at his wanting lemonade not for himself but for Grandfather only points up her belated recognition of the qualities in her son already abundantly evident to the reader.

If it is difficult to see Jody changing morally, it is equally difficult to ascribe certain other kinds of learning to him. Perhaps the simplest solution to the persisting problem of Grandfather's dramatic outburst and the response it produces in the boy is to say that at this point Jody learns from his mentor the disillusioning truth about the frontier. We have seen that the old man does not, or cannot, realize this himself in the short course covered by the story, but perhaps the boy—mentally sharper, less experienced and more curious—does. This hypothesis appears weak, however, in view of what Jody knows long before the climax. Early in the story, when the Tiflin family discuss Grandfather's impending visit, Carl observes the old man's obsession with a single topic of conversation, to which Jody answers excitedly, "Indians . . . Indians and crossing the plains." . . . But that the boy cannot confuse the frontier with present reality, that he knows that Grandfather's stories are only stories about a dead past, is suggested by his overhearing, immediately after this scene, his mother tell Carl to tolerate her father's monomania because the object of his life is past. . . . (pp. 426-28)

But if he knows that the great age is gone, why, then, does he evidently share the old man's enthusiasm for "Indians and crossing the plains"? The explanation for his excitement lies, of course, in his situation, as Steinbeck describes it in the first section of the story. Initially Jody appears scuffling his shoes "in a way he had been told was destructive to good shoe-leather" . . . and idly throwing stones: making gestures of uselessness and boredom. He views the prospect of hunting mice with relish: "They had grown smug in their security, over-bearing and fat. Now the time of disaster had come; they would not survive another day." . . . As the narrator's paraphrase of the boy's state of mind suggests, he regards the mouse-hunt as an epic mission, a means to excitement and chance to assert leadership. His thinking about mice points up not the ridiculousness of Jody's vision, but the constraint of the situation forcing him into such a vision. All he can do is hunt mice and curse; ranch life surrounds him with an unvarying and undemanding routine.

With this in mind—and Steinbeck's ordering of materials in this early part of his story suggests his intention for the reader to have this in mind—the significance of Grandfather to the boy becomes clear. To Jody the frontier stories represent a welcome source of temporary escape from a dull existence. He values Grandfather as a producer of diversion through his entertaining stories. And the boy can be entertained by them because, unlike his parents, he has very little else to entertain him.

However, this is not to say that Jody's behavior toward Grandfather is motivated solely by a self-interested desire to avoid painful reality. Having learned from his mother the need for encouraging the old man, Jody first approaches his grandfather with dignity, in contrast with his "unseemly running" immediately before. In their dialogue about the mouse-hunt, he speaks of it as "just play" and readily admits the greater significance of hunting Indians. This deference turns to a careful defense of the old man's feelings once they arrive at the house. When Jody sees Grandfather repeating himself to Billy Buck, to confirm Carl's earlier accusation, the boy conceives of himself partly as a mediator between conflicting positions, but mostly as a protector of Grandfather. At the supper table

Jody studies the responses of Grandfather and his parents very anxiously: Carl's moth-killing attempt to quiet the old man, his mother's anger at this, threatened lapses in the story-telling and Carl's remarking that he had heard the story before. At this point Jody "[rises] to heroism" . . . by asking Grandfather to tell about the Indians, a request dictated by his increasing identification with the old man as victim of his father's tyranny. Noting the others' inattention to the tale which follows, and himself anticipating the words of the story, Jody nevertheless works to preserve what he considers to be the old man's unawareness of the reality to which Carl would tactlessly expose him. Jody thus comes to regard the story-telling not so much as a way of solving his own problems but as a means of sheltering Grandfather, whom he loves and pities, from similar problems. His movement from self-concern to a concern with keeping up the old man's supposed illusions stems from the proneness to sympathy which he has exhibited initially, and represents not a basic change of character but only a shift of emphasis between two concerns which he has had from the beginning of the story. (pp. 428-30)

Jody's entire plan of protection has been based on the assumption that Grandfather lives in the past, that, unlike himself, Grandfather regards his stories as something more than tales of a dead frontier. He feels that by encouraging Grandfather to tell the stories, he can delude the old man into viewing the frontier as alive and real. What Jody thus learns from Grandfather's climactic outburst is that Grandfather already has realized that the past is dead and that his usefulness as a leader is gone. Jody now recognizes that he has not been promoting illusion in Grandfather, who has been fully aware of the facts. Like Jody, he has not confused fact with fiction. Jody learns that Grandfather too is trapped in present reality and that his plan to shelter Grandfather from painful truth was inherently futile. To the extent that Jody has patronized Grandfather initially, he might be said to suffer the moral discovery of his and Grandfather's "equality" as victims of reality. However, Steinbeck's characterization of the boy suggests nothing besides the desire to make happy someone whom he loves. In arguing with Grandfather that he (Jody) might lead the people in the future or that the frontier does not depend upon the mainland, Jody is attempting, futilely, to revive the old man's dream. The finality of Grandfather's reply—"It is finished"— causes Jody to recognize fully that Grandfather has lost this dream long ago, and that indeed Grandfather has discovered in his painful exchange with Jody's father not that the frontier is dead—this he's known for some time—but that no one cares to hear about it. In a sense, too, Jody suffers disappointment because he, a small boy, cannot please Grandfather in the way that adult attention might. Having turned from the "heroism" of the mouse-hunt to the greater challenge of instilling hope in his grandfather, Jody realizes more than before the constraint that his youth and status place upon him. Since he cannot shelter Grandfather from painful reality, all he can do is dull the pain slightly by offering lemonade. And, significantly, Steinbeck indicates the sort of "levelling" that life has imposed on Grandfather and Jody—the inescapable pressure of reality on all men—by reversing the relationship that the well-meaning Jody has envisioned earlier, for Grandfather ironically accepts the lemonade not to ease his own suffering but only to please the boy.

This reëxamination of **"The Leader of the People"** suggests, then, that what holds the story together is Jody Tiflin and his saddening discovery of how much his grandfather's plight parallels his own. Such a view certainly does not deny the significance of Grandfather; for though Jody appears the more important character, the education that he undergoes is wholly contingent upon the old man's equally painful discovery during the story. Steinbeck carefully develops Grandfather's responses as a subplot, and a highly necessary one, to the final reactions of Jody. Nor does this reading question the centrality of what many critics have seen as the major "themes" of the story—the frontier, aging, communication, and leadership—for Jody in the moment when he seizes upon the totality of his grand-father's misery is confronted at once with the tremendous pain attending the assumption of leadership, the losing of power, and the passing of time, all of which make it impossible for Grandfather to sustain the illusions Jody mistakenly attributes to him. And though, as I have suggested, it is difficult to see Jody undergoing any drastic moral change—rather than be-coming better ethically, he becomes more aware of the dilemma of adulthood—there is no question but that his earlier good intentions reflected somewhat naïve theorizing and that what he learns of Grandfather here will permit him in the future to apply his moral principles with more success. We have, then, Jody becoming better equipped, in terms of practical aware-ness, to serve as a "leader of the people" in his own age.

In the foregoing discussion I have attempted to answer two basic questions about the materials and order within the story. Lest a concern with identifying the main character and his experience seem pedestrian in light of what many perhaps would see as more important concerns, certain advantages of such an approach should be noted. For one thing, because the "themes" listed above apply to both Grandfather and Jody, a precise determination of which character's experience unifies the story permits one to speak more closely and accurately about econ-omy and subtlety in Steinbeck's narrative. For example, when one sees that Jody is the main character, Jody's initial behavior takes on a dimension of importance beyond mere "prepara-tion" for Grandfather. Second, because such "themes" relate to all of the **Red Pony** stories, this type of reading suggests more precisely the distinctive qualities of **"The Leader of the People."** And, conversely, it helps demonstrate the tightness of design in **The Red Pony,** for in all four stories we see Jody suffering often painful, but always valuable lessons in his quest for manhood. This is not to say that the approach employed here is the best or only approach, or that a more thematic approach does not yield equally meaningful insights, but simply that the question that I have considered here must be asked and must be answered for a total awareness of the artistry of **"The Leader of the People."** (pp. 430-32)

Bruce K. Martin, "'The Leader of the People' Reëx-amined," in Studies in Short Fiction *(copyright 1971 by Newberry College), Vol. VIII, No. 3, Summer, 1971, pp. 423-32.*

WILLIAM GOLDHURST

Of Mice and Men is a short novel in six scenes presented in description-dialogue-action form that approximates stage drama in its effect. . . . The time scheme runs from Thursday evening through Sunday evening—exactly three days in sequence, a matter of some importance, as we shall see presently. The setting is the Salinas Valley in California, and most of the characters are unskilled migratory workers who drift about the villages and ranches of that area picking up odd jobs or doing short-term field work and then moving on to the next place of employment. Steinbeck focuses on two such laborers who dream of one day saving up enough money to buy a small farm of their own. (p. 124)

The title of the story has a two-fold application and signifi-cance. First it refers to naturalistic details within the texture of the novella: Lennie likes to catch mice and stroke their fur with his fingers. This is a particularly important point for two reasons: it establishes Lennie's fatal weakness for stroking soft things and, since he invariably kills the mice he is petting, it foreshadows his deadly encounter with Curley's wife. Sec-ondly, the title is of course a fragment from the poem by Robert Burns ["The best laid schemes o' mice an' men/Gang aft a-gley."], which gives emphasis to the idea of the futility of human endeavor or the vanity of human wishes. . . . This notion is obviously of major importance in the novella, and it may be said to be Steinbeck's main theme on the surface level of action and development of character. (p. 125)

Viewed in the light of its mythic and allegorical implications, *Of Mice and Men* is a story about the nature of man's fate in a fallen world, with particular emphasis upon the question: is man destined to live alone, a solitary wanderer on the face of the earth, or is it the fate of man to care for man, to go his way in companionship with another? This is the same theme that occurs in the Old Testament, as early as Chapter Four of Genesis, immediately following the Creation and Expulsion. In effect, the question Steinbeck poses is the same question Cain poses to the Lord: "Am I my brother's keeper?" From its position in the Scriptural version of human history we may assume with the compilers of the early books of the Bible that it is the primary *question concerning man as he is,* after he has lost the innocence and non-being of Eden. It is the same question that Steinbeck chose as the theme of his later book *East of Eden* (1952), in which novel the Cain and Abel story is re-enacted in a contemporary setting and where, for em-phasis, Steinbeck has his main characters read the Biblical story aloud and comment upon it, climaxing the discussion with the statement made by Lee: "I think this is the best-known story in the world because it is everybody's story. I think it is the symbol story of the human soul." *Of Mice and Men* is an early Steinbeck variation on this symbol story of the human soul. The implications of the Cain-and-Abel drama are everywhere apparent in the fable of George and Lennie and provide its mythic vehicle. (pp. 126-27)

For his crime of homicide the Lord banished Cain from His company and from the company of his parents and set upon him a particular curse, the essence of which was that Cain was to become homeless, a wanderer, and an agricultural worker who would never possess or enjoy the fruits of his labor. Cain was afraid that other men would hear of his crime and try to kill him, but the Lord marked him in a certain way so as to preserve him from the wrath of others. Thus Cain left home and went to the land of Nod, which the story tells us lies east of Eden.

The drama of Cain finds its most relevant application in *Of Mice and Men* in the relationship between Lennie and George, and in the other characters' reactions to their associations. In the first of his six scenes Steinbeck establishes the two ideas that will be developed throughout. The first of these is the affectionate symbiosis of the two protagonists, their brotherly mutual concern and faithful companionship. Steinbeck stresses the beauty, joy, security, and comfort these two derive from the relationship. . . . (p. 127)

The second idea, which is given equal emphasis, is the fact that this sort of camaraderie is rare, different, almost unique in the world George and Lennie inhabit; other men, in contrast to these two, are solitary souls without friends or companions. . . . The alternative to the George-Lennie companionship is Aloneness, made more dreadful by the addition of an economic futility that Steinbeck augments and reinforces in later sections. The migratory ranch worker, in other words, is the fulfillment of the Lord's curse on Cain: "When thou tillest the ground, it shall not henceforth yield unto thee her strength; a fugitive and vagabond shalt thou be in the earth." Steinbeck's treatment of the theme is entirely free from a sense of contrivance; all the details in *Of Mice and Men* seem natural in the context and organically related to the whole; but note that in addition to presenting Lennie and George as men who till the ground and derive no benefits from their labor, he also manages to have them "on the run" when they are introduced in the first scene—this no doubt to have his main characters correspond as closely as possible to the Biblical passage: "a fugitive and a vagabond shalt thou be. . . ."

To the calamity of homelessness and economic futility Steinbeck later adds the psychological soul-corruption that is the consequence of solitary existence. (pp. 127-28)

If in Scene One Lennie and George affirm their fraternity openly and without embarrassment, in Scene Two George is more hesitant. "He's my . . . cousin," he tells the ranch boss. "I told his old lady I'd take care of him." This is no betrayal on George's part, but a cover-up required by the circumstances. For the boss is highly suspicious of the Lennie-George fellowship. "You takin' his pay away from him?" he asks George. "I never seen one guy take so much trouble for another guy." A short time later Curley also sounds the note of suspicion, extending it by a particularly nasty innuendo: when George says "We travel together," Curley replies, "Oh, so it's that way." Steinbeck is implying here the general response of most men towards seeing two individuals who buddy around together in a friendless world where isolation is the order of the day: there must be exploitation involved, either financial or sexual! At the same time Steinbeck is developing the allegorical level of his story by suggesting that the attitude of Cain ("I know not: Am I my brother's keeper?") has become universal. Even the sympathetic and understanding Slim expresses some wonder at the Lennie-George fraternity. "Ain't many guys travel around together," Slim says in Scene Two. "I don't know why. Maybe ever'body in the whole damned world is scared of each other." This too, as Steinbeck interprets the Biblical story, is a part of Cain's curse: distrust. Later on, in order to give the theme of Aloneness another dimension, Steinbeck stresses the solitude of Crooks and Curley's wife, both of whom express a craving for company and "someone to talk to." (p. 129)

Actually Steinbeck's novella advances and develops, ebbs and flows, around the basic image of the Lennie-George relationship. Almost all the characters react to it in one way or another as the successive scenes unfold. In Scenes One, Two, and Three, despite the discouraging opinions of outsiders, the companionship remains intact and unthreatened. Midway into Scene Three the partnership undergoes augmentation when Candy is admitted into the scheme to buy the little farm. Late in Scene Four Crooks offers himself as another candidate for the fellowship of soul-brothers and dreamers. This is the high point of optimism as regards the main theme of the story; this is the moment when a possible reversal of the curse of Cain seems most likely, as Steinbeck suggests that the answer to the Lord's question might be: Yes, I am my brother's keeper. If we arrive

at this point with any comprehension of the author's purposes, we find ourselves brought up short by the idea: what if this George-Lennie-Candy-Crooks fraternity were to become universal!

But later in the same scene, the entrance of Curley's wife signals the turning point as the prospects for the idea of brotherhood-as-a-reality begin to fade and darken. As throughout the story she represents a force that destroys men and at the same time invites men to destroy her, as she will finally in Scene Five offer herself as a temptation which Lennie cannot resist, so in Scene Four Curley's wife sows the seeds that eventually disrupt the fellowship. Entering into the discussion in Crooks' room in the stable, she insults Crooks, Candy, and Lennie, laughs at their dream farm, and threatens to invent the kind of accusation that will get Crooks lynched. Crooks, reminded of his position of impotence in a white man's society, immediately withdraws his offer to participate in the George-Lennie-Candy farming enterprise. But Crooks' withdrawal, while extremely effective as social criticism, is much more. It represents an answer to the question Steinbeck is considering all along: is man meant to make his way alone or accompanied? Obviously this is one occasion, among many others in the story, when Steinbeck suggests the answer. Crooks' hope for fraternal living is short-lived. At the conclusion of the scene he sinks back into his Aloneness.

From this point on, even though the dream of fellowship on the farm remains active, the real prospects for its fulfillment decline drastically. . . . Actually the plan was doomed to failure from the beginning; for fraternal living cannot long survive in a world dominated by the Aloneness, homelessness, and economic futility which Steinbeck presents as the modern counterpart of Cain's curse. Immediately following his discovery of Curley's wife's body, George delivers a speech that dwells on the worst possible aftermath of Lennie's misdeed; and this is not the wrath of Curley or the immolation of Lennie or the loss of the farm, but the prospect of George's becoming a Man Alone, homeless, like all the others and a victim as well of economic futility:

> I'll work my month an' I'll take my fifty bucks
> and I'll stay all night in some lousy cat house.
> Or I'll set in some poolroom til ever'body goes
> home. An' then I'll come back an' work an-
> other month an' I'll have fifty bucks more.

This speech represents the true climax of the novella, for it answers the question which is Steinbeck's main interest throughout. Now we know the outcome of the Lennie-George experiment in fellowship, as we know the Aloneness of man's essential nature. In subtle ways, of course, Steinbeck has been hinting at this conclusion all along. . . . (pp. 130-31)

But there are still other suggested meanings inherent in the dream-farm and the failure of the dream. The plan is doomed not only because human fellowship cannot survive in the post-Cain world, but also because the image of the farm, as conceived by George and Lennie and Candy, is overly idealized, the probability being that life, even if they obtained the farm, would not consist of the comfort, plenty, and interpersonal harmony they envision. . . . George and Lennie, who were to some extent inspired by questions growing out of the story of Cain in Chapter Four of Genesis, want to retreat to Chapter Two and live in Eden! Of all ambitions in a fallen world, this is possibly the most unattainable; for paradise is lost, as the name of Steinbeck's hero, George Milton, suggests. And though there will always be men like Candy, who represents sweet hope, the view of Crooks, who represents black despair, is probably a more accurate appraisal of the human condition: "Nobody never gets to heaven, and nobody gets no land. It's just in their head. They're all the time talkin' about it, but it's jus' in their head." Obviously in this context Crooks' comment about nobody ever getting land refers not to literal ownership, but to the dream of contentment entertained by the simple workmen who come and go on the ranch.

To pursue the [John] Milton parallel a step further, we perceive immediately that Steinbeck has no intention of justifying the ways of God to man [as Milton did in writing *Paradise Lost*]. On the contrary, if anything *Of Mice and Men* implies a critique of Hebrew-Christian morality, particularly in the area of the concept of punishment for sin. This opens up still another dimension of meaning in our interpretation of Steinbeck's novella. If George and Lennie fail to attain their dream farm (for reasons already explored), and the dream farm is a metaphor or image for heaven (as suggested by Crooks' speech in Scene Four) then the failure to achieve the dream farm is most likely associated with the question of man's failure to attain heaven. Steinbeck's consideration of this last-named theme is not far to seek. Along this particular line of thought, Lennie represents one essential aspect of man—the animal appetites, the craving to touch and feel, the impulse toward immediate gratification of sensual desires. George is the element of Reason which tries to control the appetites or, better still, to elevate them to a higher and more sublime level. . . . Steinbeck suggests throughout that the appetites and Reason coexist to compose the nature of man. ("Me an' him travels together.") He goes on to suggest that the effort to refine man into something rare, saintly, and inhuman is another unattainable ambition. Even when Reason (George) manages to communicate to the appetites (Lennie) its urgent message ("You crazy son-of-a-bitch. You keep me in hot water all the time . . . I never get no peace.") the appetites are incapable of satisfying Reason's demands. . . . The animal appetites, even though well attended and well intentioned, cannot be completely suppressed or controlled. Thus, the best man can hope for is a kind of insecure balance of power between these two elements—which is in fact what most of the ranch hands accomplish, indulging their craving for sensual pleasure in a legal and commonplace manner each payday. Failing this, man must suppress absolutely the appetites which refuse to be controlled, as George does in the symbolic killing of Lennie at the conclusion of the novella. Possibly this is a veiled reference to the drastic mutilation of man's nature required by the Hebrew-Christian ethic. At the same time the theological implications of *Of Mice and Men* project the very highest regard for the noble experiment in fraternal living practiced by George and Lennie; and possibly the time-scheme of their stay on the ranch—from Friday to Sunday—is a veiled reference to the sacrifice of Christ. He too tried to reverse the irreversible tide of Cain's curse by serving as the ultimate example of human brotherhood. (pp. 131-34)

William Goldhurst, "'Of Mice and Men': John Steinbeck's Parable of the Curse of Cain," in Western American Literature *(copyright, 1971, by the Western Literature Association), Vol. VI, No. 2, Summer, 1971, pp. 123-35.*

PETER LISCA

In one of the little essays Steinbeck did for the *Saturday Review* in 1955, **"Some thoughts on Juvenile Delinquency,"** he writes

as follows concerning the relationship of the individual to the society in which he lives: ". . . I believe that man is a double thing—a group animal and at the same time an individual. And it occurs to me that he cannot successfully be the second until he has fulfilled the first." The nice organic relationship which Steinbeck here postulates near the end of his writing career is seldom to be met in his fiction. Much more frequently we are presented with characters who choose one of two extremes— either to reject society's demands and escape into individualism, or to reject individualism and commit themselves to goals and values which can be realized only in terms of society.

In Steinbeck's very first novel, *Cup of Gold* (1929), in the figure of Merlin, is found not only an extreme example of escapism, but one of its most eloquent philosophers. As a young man, a greatly talented bard, he had taken up a hermit's life in a stone tower on a lonely mountain top. There he has grown old with his harp and his books of history and mythology, a legendary figure in his own lifetime. It is suggested that the cause of this self-imposed isolation may have been his losing a bardic contest through political influence. The consequent disillusionment is reflected in his remarks to the young Henry Morgan, who has come to consult him before going off into the world to make his fortune: "'I think I understand,' he said softly. 'You are a little boy. You want the moon to drink from as a golden cup; and so, it is very likely that you will become a great man—if only you remain a little child. All the world's great have been little boys who wanted the moon; running and climbing, they sometimes caught a firefly. But if one grows to a man's mind, that mind must see that it cannot have the moon and would not want it if it could—and so it catches no fireflies.'" Merlin goes a step further, and adds as a compensation for this loss of worldly ambition the attainment of community with mankind ("He has the whole world with him . . . a bridge of contact with his own people. . . ."), whereas the worldly successful and therefore immature man "is doubly alone; he only can realize his true failure, can realize his meanness and fears and evasions."

The fascination which this general intellectual posture had for the early Steinbeck is evident from another character in the same novel. James Flower is from an aristocratic, well-educated English family who in despair at his harebrained impracticality buy him a plantation in the Barbadoes, where he cannot embarrass them. "And so he had grown wistfully old, on the island. His library was the finest in the Indies, and, as far as information went, he was the most learned man anywhere about. But his learning formed no design of the whole. . . ." . . . In Steinbeck's first novel, then, we have two variations on the theme of escape; and although neither is the main character, Henry Morgan's life ultimately suggests that they were both wiser.

In Steinbeck's next book, *The Pastures of Heaven,* three years later, we find James Flower's same impracticality and indiscriminate bookishness in the character of Junius Maltby, who is treated at greater length and with more obvious sympathy. Again he is a man of "cultured family and good education." Also, his way into an escape from a worldly existence is an enforced one, a threat to his health, but is clearly congenial to him. Through his abstraction and impracticality the little farm which comes to him by marriage becomes unproductive; his wife's two children by former marriage die of influenza because they are undernourished while Maltby helplessly reads aloud *Treasure Island* and *Travels With a Donkey*. Finally his wife dies in childbirth, leaving him a son whom he names Robert

Louis. Maltby makes an attempt at practicality by hiring an old German to work the farm, but within a week the two men become boon companions and spend their days sitting around together "discussing things which interested and puzzled them. . . ." The three of them manage to survive, barefoot, ragged, ill-fed, but happy in their discussions of the battle of Trafalgar, the frieze on the Parthenon, the Spartan virtues, Carthaginian warfare, and other erudite topics. (pp. 75-7)

Surprisingly, the boy Robbie thrives in this environment and becomes a natural leader at school, fascinating fellow pupils and teachers alike with his poise and exotic knowledge. The school board, however, is more interested in Robbie's ragged clothes. . . . [The] story ends with Maltby and his son on their way to San Francisco and a return to a clerkship in order to provide the material benefits of society. . . . (p. 77)

Clearly, then, in his first two books of fiction Steinbeck demonstrates a serious interest and sympathy for what in today's slang might be called the "drop-out." A case might be made for discussing here his next novel, *To a God Unknown*, published just a year after *The Pastures of Heaven*, for in that novel too we have a character who in a secluded valley pursues a way of life unsanctioned by his society, in this case a dedication to mysticism and fertility rituals. In that novel, too, we find a hermit who, again in modern parlance, "does his own thing" with no Society For the Prevention of Cruelty to Animals nearby. But these similarities are peripheral, and not central to the theme of escape versus commitment. A more direct relationship can be established with the novel that followed in two years— *Tortilla Flat*.

This novel introduces two important changes in Steinbeck's treatment of the "drop-out" (which is a better term than "escapee"). First, whereas the earlier characters of this type had deliberately rejected the clear advantages available to them, in the form of family and education, these Mexican-American *paisanos* find themselves initially in a poor position to compete in modern society. Second, and more important, the "drop-out" is no longer a shy, retiring, solitary, but an active, gregarious member of a whole community of "drop-outs." They have in common with their prototypes in earlier novels, however, a disinclination toward industrious labor and a disrespect for material property, for through the loss of possessions comes sorrow—"It is much better never to have had them." They also share a love of the contemplative life. True, sometimes pure contemplation arrives at the practical result of procuring a jug of wine or a chicken in a highly imaginative manner, but the process is enjoyed as much as the result, and sometimes consoles them for material lack or loss. (p. 78)

In his fiction up to 1935, then, stretching over six years of the Great Depression, beginning with minor characters and culminating in *Tortilla Flat* with a whole community of "drop-outs," Steinbeck demonstrates a serious and sympathetic interest in the theme of escape from society. And only in one short story published in 1934 does he recognize even the existence of contemporary social issues. Instead, he set his fiction in the seventeenth, late nineteenth, and early twentieth centuries, thus in a sense performing as author the same escape as his characters.

All of this changes in 1936 with the publication of *In Dubious Battle*, which remains the best strike novel in the English language. Here Steinbeck demonstrates not only his detailed, quite professional knowledge of communist labor organization tactics in the field, but also presents us with central characters who are totally committed to bringing about substantial changes in American society. Prior to the strike novel, only **"The Raid"** had suggested this involvement by Steinbeck and had projected such commitment in the characters. In light of the importance which Judeo-Christian symbols and reference have in *The Grapes of Wrath*, it is interesting that this first treatment of proletarian subject matter should also find such references necessary. There is the master-apostle relationship of the two organizers, the portrait of their anonymous precursor who inspires them by his example, their own sense of sacrifice for mankind, and certain allusions in the dialogue. (pp. 80-1)

This commitment and self-sacrifice is even more extreme in Jim Nolan of *In Dubious Battle*, and in them he finds his personal fulfillment. . . . This commitment is accompanied by an even wider Christian reference. Whereas the neophyte in the short story had been merely *willing* to be used as "an example of injustice," Jim Nolan of the strike novel is so anxious as to have a martyr complex. Over and over he tells Mac, his mentor, "I want to get into it" and "I want you to use me." Only after he has gotten into it and has been wounded is he happy and sure of how strongly he is committed. . . . When he is killed, Jim does not have a chance to say "You don't know what you're doing"; he and Mac are ambushed and his face is blown off by a shotgun at close range, so that Mac finds him in a still kneeling posture and exclaims simply, "Oh, Christ!" Beginning with the book's title, epigraph, and numerous details taken from *Paradise Lost*, to the crowing of cocks and several allusions to the Holy Family (two of them pointed out by the characters themselves), clearly the committed hero is presented as an imitation of Christ.

Steinbeck's next published novel, *Of Mice and Men* (1937) offers a serious temptation and several pitfalls to anyone dealing with these two themes of escape and commitment. It could be used to illustrate the escape theme by pointing out the persistent dream of George and Lennie to get a place of their own; and even the mercy killing of Lennie by George could be seen as providing Lennie with permanent escape from a world with which he cannot cope, into the dream of the little house and a couple of acres, and rabbits. Or, by concentrating on George, and reading Lennie as a symbol of proletarian man, great in strength but helpless without leadership, the theme of commitment could be seen in George's sacrifices and devotion to Lennie. Or, by bringing out both of these patterns, the novelette could be made to illustrate the nice *balancing* of these two themes. But the escape theme in *Of Mice and Men* is essentially different from the "drop-out" kind of rebellion against society which concerns us here, and is clearly an illusion besides. The commitment is also questionable in its nature and intention. On one level, Lennie is necessary to George as an excuse for his own failure. Admitting *Of Mice and Men* to the present discussion would open the door for numerous other pieces, such as almost all the chapters of *The Pastures of Heaven* and some stories of *The Long Valley*, such as **"Flight,"** most obviously.

But in 1939, with *The Grapes of Wrath*, Steinbeck clearly returns to his theme of social commitment, utilizing, even more extensively than before, pertinent Judeo-Christian analogues and references. It is more than personal friendship that causes Jim Casy to give himself up to the deputies in place of Tom Joad and Floyd. It is an action consequent upon his turning from an individualistic, sin and hell-fire, Bible-belt evangelism to a revelation of the Holy Spirit, which he comes to identify with "all men and all women," the "human sperit—the whole shebang. Maybe all men got one big soul ever'body's a part of.'' And it occurs to him then that his commitment is not to Jesus but to the people. . . . (pp. 81-3)

The movement from escape to commitment is even clearer in Tom Joad. He enters the novel determined to avoid all involvement: "I'm laying my dogs down one at a time" and "I climb fences when I got fences to climb." But through the experiences of the migration and through Casy's words and deeds he becomes converted and committed to a vision of social justice beyond hope of his personal experience. Even more than Jim of *In Dubious Battle,* he knows that although he may be killed, "I'll be ever'where—wherever you look." . . . Beyond this mystic identification, no commitment can go. It is a commitment which gains strength and approval not only by means of its sacrificial Christ figures, but by a wealth of Judeo-Christian references extending from Exodus, Deuteronomy, Canticles and Prophets through John the Baptist, Gospels, and Revelation. *The Grapes of Wrath* is the high point in Steinbeck's theme of commitment. Two years later, in *The Forgotten Village,* a documentary film about Mexican village life, he still stresses commitment by having the young boy, Juan Diego, disobey his parents in bringing his little sister for an inoculation. At the end of the film he leaves home altogether, not to escape, but to go to the city and be trained to better serve and enlighten his people. (pp. 83-4)

In December of 1944, shortly after returning from a tour of duty as European war correspondent, Steinbeck published *Cannery Row.* With this novel Steinbeck turns once more to the theme of escape as treated in the last novel before his brief proletarian excursion—escape on the level of an entire community of "drop-outs." However, whereas the author of *Tortilla Flat* had accepted its inhabitants with an amused, slightly tongue-in-cheek air, the author of *Cannery Row* several times steps stage-front to proselytize his readers. . . . (p. 84)

The transfer of Christian reference from the committed characters of his proletarian fiction to these "drop-outs" is significant. In another passage, he calls Mack and the boys "Saints and angels and martyrs and holy men." The ground for these judgments had been indicated three years earlier in *Sea of Cortez* [cowritten with Edward F. Ricketts]: ". . . of the good we think always of wisdom, tolerance, kindliness, generosity, humility; and the qualities of cruelty, greed, self-interest, graspingness, and rapacity are universally considered undesirable. And yet in our structure of society, the so-called and considered good qualities are invariably concomitants of failure, while the bad ones are the cornerstone of success." It was probably disagreement with this premise that caused one well-known reviewer to say that *Cannery Row* is "a sentimental glorification of weakness of mind and degeneration of character." And so in a sense it is, if one accepts a Kiwanis, Rotary Club, Chamber of Commerce definition of noble character. Perhaps Steinbeck's original suspicions of such a definition were intensified by his experiences in the last years of the Depression and the war which was necessary to end it.

Whatever the reasons, this mood was strong enough to carry over into a variation on the theme in *The Pearl,* originally published in the same year. Strictly speaking, perhaps, this novelette, like *Of Mice and Men* and *The Moon Is Down,* enters only peripherally in this discussion. The pearl diver Kino does seek to physically escape an economically and socially repressive society, but only so that he may return to that same society at a higher level. He can be seen, in his struggle to escape, as what the author of *Cannery Row* called a "tiger with

ulcers." And he arrives within reach of his goal with much worse than "a blown prostate and bifocals." He arrives with his house burned down, his wife physically beaten, his only son killed, and the lives of three men on his soul. And then Kino and his wife make their true "escape." They return to their village, throw the Pearl of Great Price back into the sea, and return to the edge of unconsciousness, an unthinking existence governed by the rhythms of sun and tide.

In its interesting variation on the theme of escape, *The Pearl* looks forward to Steinbeck's next novel, published two years later (1947). With this novel Steinbeck finally comes to a resolution of his two themes. Society as pictured in Steinbeck's previous novels is essentially an institutional entity from whose evils a character might decide to escape, or to whose improvement he might dedicate himself. In either case, the monolithic magnitude of the antagonist, society, lent dignity and possible tragedy to his course of action. In *The Wayward Bus,* however, we get very little notion of society as institution; we see it instead as an aggregation of human characters, from the hypocritical businessman, Elliot Pritchard, to Camille Oaks, the honest stripper. Juan Chicoy's decision to escape, therefore, is made in terms of disentanglement from certain people—his neurotic wife and his querulous bus passengers. This, of course, leaves him with no simple distinct notion of direction such as motivated the "drop-outs" and committed characters of Steinbeck's previous fiction. Thus, immediately after abandoning his allegorical bus and its passengers, Juan Chicoy (whose initials are J. C.) becomes merely confused by his escape. "It didn't seem as good or as pleasant or as free" as he had imagined it would. . . . So he returns to the bus, as Kino in *The Pearl* returns to his village; but not with a sense of escape or commitment, rather with a sense of involvement without either acceptance or resignation.

Although Steinbeck published five novels after *The Wayward Bus,* the two themes which concern us here play little part in them. *Sweet Thursday* would seem, superficially, a return to the spirit of *Cannery Row* and its glorification of escape, but that escape is so compromised with bourgeois values and genteel spice and color as to become quite respectable. The wonderful whorehouse of *Cannery Row* becomes a school for brides. Doc gets married and accepts a fat research grant at Cal Tech. More interesting is *The Short Reign of Pippin IV.* Pippin is a middle-class Frenchman whose escape is to study the stars rather than society. Then he is discovered to be heir to the throne of a re-established monarchy. In one short speech he presents a seven-point plan of such obvious good sense and modest reasonableness as to antagonize everybody and get himself threatened with the guillotine. He escapes and returns to his simple home and his telescope (somewhat as Kino returns to his pearl-diving) a contented citizen in a society of corrupt characters. Steinbeck's last novel, *The Winter of Our Discontent,* also touches only peripherally on our topic. The main character, Ethan Hawley, blaming his lack of success in society on his own virtue (as Steinbeck had discussed this relationship in the quotation from *Sea of Cortez*), embarks with deliberate irony upon a course of deviousness which quickly brings him fortune and esteem. In a state of moral shock at his own ability, and that of his children, to adjust so easily to a corrupt society, he attempts a kind of escape through suicide, but allows a contrived excuse to dissuade him. The other two novels of this period, *Burning Bright* and *East of Eden,* do not seem to enter into our topic in any significant way.

What we have, then, in Steinbeck's last novels is neither the individual or communal escapes of his early work and the immediate post-war novels, nor the inspired, Christ-like, sacrificial commitment of his proletarian fiction. Instead, we have a further development of the adjustment made by Juan Chicoy in *The Wayward Bus.* Society continues to be corrupt, although the blame is not so easy to fix; but there is no need for escape or commitment to reform. Steinbeck finally seems to completely accept the observation he had made on marine ecology, in *Sea of Cortez:* "There would seem to be only one commandment for living things: Survive!" This is qualified in *East of Eden* only by a faith in every man's ability to choose between good and evil. This is an old man's wisdom. We continue to read Steinbeck for the folly of his youth. (pp. 85-8)

> Peter Lisca, *"Escape and Commitment: Two Poles of the Steinbeck Hero"* (reprinted by permission of the author), *in* Steinbeck: The Man and His Work, *edited by Richard Astro and Tetsumaro Hayashi, Oregon State University Press, 1971, pp. 75-88.*

LEO GURKO

Of the great religions, Manicheism generates the most suspense. In it, the contending principles of good and evil, God and Satan, light and darkness, soul and body are so evenly matched that for long periods darkness is actually triumphant over light. In Christianity, the rebellious angels rise up but are easily defeated in battle and contemptuously cast down into hell. One never gets the impression that Satan is a serious threat to God or that he has any real chance of prevailing. In Manicheism, he is not only a serious threat but for a time he actually does prevail. When God sends his agent, Primal Man, to put down darkness, Primal Man is defeated in battle and taken prisoner. Particles of light are captured by the nether forces and the realm of light itself driven back. (p. 11)

For self-evident reasons, Manicheism was branded as a heresy by other religions. But for a thousand years, from the third through the thirteenth centuries, it spread westward from Persia and exercised a pervasive and profound influence on Europe. Augustine himself was a Manichean for nine years before turning Christian. The emphasis of Manicheism on the power of fertility of darkness seemed closer to the facts of human experience than the more cheerful, perhaps even complacent mythology of other creeds. This may be one reason why it did not finally survive: its cosmology was too tragic and dangerous, its sexual demands too severe. But while not ultimately satisfactory, or satisfying, as religion, Manicheism is marvelously suited to drama. Nothing is more dramatic than a contest between two combatants of perfectly balanced strength, especially if the cosmos itself is divided between them. And it is on the dramatic side that Manicheism has made its appeal to modern literature. (p. 12)

The Manichean element . . . is visible in Steinbeck's work from the start, but it is not until *Of Mice and Men,* written when Steinbeck was at the height of his powers, that it becomes paramount. This celebrated little novel, wedged between *In Dubious Battle* and *The Grapes of Wrath,* wonderfully reveals Steinbeck in his Manichean aspect.

The antagonists appear at once, and embody the warring Manichean principles of mind and body. They are of course George and Lennie, locked together in the same life process but ultimately irreconcilable, with one compelled to slay the other. . . . They are ranch hands, working the earth. They are also itinerants, involved not with a particular plot of ground but with everywhere. Even their dream of owning their own place has

this omnipresent quality: it starts out as something in the sky, the pure product of their eager imaginations, then comes down to a specific section of ground with a previous owner and a price tag. The dream is both ideal and real—it extends over all the available ground. This element of universality, at once abstract and concrete, is one of the story's special qualities.

While George and Lennie are thus deeply joined, they are also profoundly separated. . . . George has a small body and a big brain, Lennie has a huge physique and a tiny brain. These deliberate polarities strain our belief in them as individual figures, but are absolutely necessary to establish them as reigning forces in the Manichean struggle for the world. The paradox of their existence is that they are at once partners and enemies. They strive for the same goal while destined by their natures to split apart. It is a paradox that lies both at the heart of the novel and Steinbeck's vision of the cosmos.

Sex, embodied in Curley's wife, is associated with what she calls "the big guy," i.e. Lennie. George seems apart from it, and even when he speaks of going to a brothel, he has as little interest in it as getting drunk. George is sober, chaste, almost monastic in his habits. Lennie, in contrast, is uncontrollably sensuous. His whole being seems concentrated in his hands. He doesn't *see* anything very clearly, being a creature of darkness; touch is the focus of his energies. . . . But his touch is deadly, and in the end he kills everything he touches. He doesn't mean to; his actions derive not from any centre of moral or psychological individuality but from his existence as a mindless, overwhelming force. As a force, he draws no distinction between life and death. He extracts as much pleasure in stroking a dead mouse as a live one.

Despite their radical dissimilarity, George feels obligated to "save" Lennie. In this he has a sense of almost religious mission. He grumbles about it throughout the novel. He is forever ragging Lennie about what a nuisance he is and how much happier he, George, would be if he could somehow be rid of him. But all this is on the surface. George feels deeply compelled to control Lennie. . . . And George has his hands full throughout. Lennie is his charge but also an immense counterweight pulling him constantly toward destruction. . . . Life with Lennie is complicated and dangerous; it can all blow up at any moment, and it is not just their jobs and their livelihood that are at stake, but their lives. The novel, in its immediate as well as larger implications, is literally a matter of life and death.

The cosmological element is further highlighted by the fact that both George and Lennie are killers. They assume the right to impose death as though they were gods, and this raises them beyond the mortal. George is conscious and calculating, so he shoots Lennie consciously and calculatingly. Lennie is spontaneous and irrational, so he kills mice, puppies, rabbits, and Curley's wife unintentionally and irrationally. These awesome acts are the same for each; they flow naturally and quite unimpededly from the center of their beings. Steinbeck's approach to them, persistent throughout his work, is to establish their surface authenticity, pass over and indeed deliberately ignore their psychological insides, and settle finally upon their role as forces in nature. Readers who demand attention to the psychological contours of the individual self, who regard the characterization developed so magnificently in the nineteenth-century novel as the norm of fiction, will inevitably find *Of Mice and Men* sentimental and pretentious: sentimental because it arouses emotions and emotional responses too large for the simply drawn characters to sustain; pretentious because it imposes upon a pair of ragged, marginal itinerant laborers, one of whom is a virtual idiot, the tragic struggle of nothing less than the universe itself.

If, however, Steinbeck's source is not the modern novel but the ancient parable—or the early epic, which is a kind of large-framed, fleshed-out parable—*Of Mice and Men* can be read as a peculiarly contemporary example of the genre. It is Steinbeck's Manichean parable, as *The Grapes of Wrath,* following it immediately in order of composition, is his Christian one. But the parable, while it eschews psychological embroidery and complexity of characterization, depends very much on surface credibility, on the authentic rendering of appearance, gesture, and word. And here even his harshest critics must concede Steinbeck's mastery. His ranch hands, whether communing in the bunkhouse or sweating in the field, look, sound, feel, even smell like what they are supposed to be. Their dialogue, credible enough in terms of grammatical construction, elision, monosyllabic diction, and colloquial nuance, is entirely free of any trace of abstraction, of that tendency to abandon the physical for the metaphysical that has tainted so much "uneducated" speech and dialect from Wordsworth to [William] Saroyan.

Even the refrain—the most formal device in evidence here—suggests the epic. At Lennie's urging, George recites the tale of their Promised Land: the little farm they will own some day. . . . Like an ancient scop or medieval troubadour, George relates this beautiful dream as though it were a chant or an orision. . . . He has a rapt audience of one, Lennie, sometimes two, Lennie and Candy. Like a congregation caught up in ritual prayer, Lennie breaks in at set intervals with his own aria. . . . The effect of all this—the chant, the dream, the repetitious rhythm, the enraptured teller and his spellbound audience lifted ecstatically out of themselves—is to blur the individual moment and universalize the event. The impression conveyed is that this sort of thing has been going on, in no very different terms, since the beginning of time. Even *Of Mice and Men*'s original title, **"Something That Happened,"** strengthens this impression by its deliberately toneless and impersonal anonymity.

The movement from the particular to the general is accelerated by Steinbeck's well-advertised intention of constructing his story like a play. Description is condensed. The cast of characters is stripped to its minimal impulses. Elaboration of any kind is foregone. The six separate chapters are treated as though they were acts on stage: related to one another, to be sure, in terms of advancing movement, but deliberately fashioned as autonomous, self-contained units with an existence of their own as distinct from their existence in the novel as a whole. They are divided neatly into three locales: chapters one and six take place by the river, two and three in the bunkhouse, four and five in the barn. This 1 2-2 3-3 1 arrangement is designed for concentration—each locale appears twice—and for climax: the return at the end to the scene of the beginning. In its simplicity, leanness, and brevity, it seeks to reduce everything to essentials, even to quintessentials. There is no room for commentary or nuance, none for the intricate machinery of the modern novel. Steinbeck's instinct has always been for a return to early forms of literature: the drama, the epic, and the parable. *Of Mice and Men* is his supreme combination of all these.

The lighting scheme of the novel supports its dramatic intentions. The prevailing atmosphere is a half-light shading toward darkness, precisely suited to the Manichean setting where the agents of God are always descending to do battle with the dark forces. (pp. 14-18)

Chapter five takes place during the afternoon in the main section of the barn. "The afternoon sun sliced in through the cracks of the barn walls and lay in bright lines on the hay." Lennie has left George, left Crooks, and is now alone with the animals in the subhuman world of the stable. Here, with the light and darkness splintered into alternating strips, the murder of Curley's wife triggers the sombre tragedy of the final chapter. Her unpremeditated death leads to the premeditated death of Lennie, back in the outer air by the river. The refrain motif of the story reaches its chromatic climax with the falling afternoon light on the last scene, on its way to completing the circle that began at the same point with the falling light on the opening pages. It is the interpenetration of light and dark, with each given an exactly similar weight and place with the other, that powerfully reinforces the Manichean idea that these contending cosmic forces are, until all but the very end of their struggle, of equal strength. (pp. 18-19)

[The] supporting characters in *Of Mice and Men* are a grab bag of the ordinary human world, the world which is in Mani's terms the final scene of the cosmological conflict. The elements in each are deliberately mixed. Curley's wife is the Manichean Eve, the purely sexual temptress who brings nothing but trouble to the surrounding males. But she is humanized by her unhappiness. . . . Curley himself seems wholly a creature of darkness, a vicious stunted figure seeking to compensate for his lack of sexual potency by training himself as a boxer and beating up helpless men bigger than himself. Yet he, too, is emotionally vulnerable, humanized in turn by his abnormal capacity to feel pain, by his feverishly hypersensitive reaction to those around him.

Each of the others bears within himself some splinter of light. . . . There is one figure who approaches an ideal standard: Slim, the expert muleskinner, the supremely skilful workingman, invested with superhuman qualities. Yet if he is a god, he is a curiously ineffectual one, commenting on events but unable to control or channel them. He is a sympathetic judge of George's dilemma. "You hadda, George. I swear you hadda," he comforts him at the end, but he is quite unable to prevent anyone from doing what his nature compels him to.

The moral equations are similarly mixed. In the novel, virtue nearly always leads to disaster. Lennie loves puppies and mice, but succeeds only in killing them. Candy's faithful attachment to his old dog leaves him in a state of shock and grief at its death. George's feelings for Lennie, an intricate amalgam of brother, father, and keeper, force him to slay his friend. There is an impersonality, an inevitability about these poignant events that reflects the character of the larger world in which they occur. That larger world joins light and darkness at their points of maximum interfusion. On the human level, the novel joins the redeeming emotion and the tragic action at exactly the same point, the moment when they meld into one another with maximum force.

Perhaps the most suggestive dualism of the novel is its contrast between men who travel together and those who travel alone. There are many more of the second than the first. Those who travel together are indeed so rare that they arouse comment. (pp. 19-21)

All the loners are drawn to the pair that are together. . . . This theme of human beings who are linked and those who are atomized, like the other themes of the novel, subtly underlines its Manichean character. The dark, psychologically disturbed figures—Curley, Curley's wife, Crooks—are drawn into Lennie's orbit. The one man drawn to George is Slim, endowed throughout with godlike attributes. . . . (p. 21)

Underlying the novel, and controlling it, is Steinbeck's vision of the universe as the scene of a decisive and unpredictable encounter of immense forces. It is this vision that gives *Of Mice and Men* its quality as a parable, makes it seem larger than the life it describes, and frees the characters from the sentimentality into which they would obviously sink if taken on their own literal, limitedly human terms. And the vision is essentially Manichean. Lennie and George are fated by their very natures to be joined in extraordinary intimacy and irreconcilable hostility. Moreover, the darkness represented by Lennie is just as "creative" and potent as George's light. George may be the executor of the dream, but it is Lennie who conceives it. It is George's incantatory voice that gives it verbal shape, but it is Lennie whom it lifts to ecstatic heights. And the dependence of one upon the other is total in both human and cosmic terms. Lennie and George are indispensable to one another as Manichean darkness and light are, and in exactly the same way.

It is true of Steinbeck . . . that Manichean psychology and drama are separated from its ethics and theology. The good-bad sides of God and Satan, the ultimate triumph of one over the other, an apocalyptic event accompanied by the dissolution of human history, are of little interest to [him. He concentrates] instead on what is visible and verifiable: The contending forces govern and shape our destinies. Both are equally potent and powerful sources of life. They are indispensable to one another while remaining irreconcilable, and the outcome of their perpetual combat is beyond prediction.

Of these ideas and visions, *Of Mice and Men*—lean, small-boned, delicately framed—is a supple and effective embodiment. (pp. 21-2)

Leo Gurko, "'Of Mice and Men': Steinbeck as Manichean," in The University of Windsor Review, *Vol. VIII, No. 2, Spring, 1973, pp. 11-23.*

MARK SPILKA

A minor classic of proletarian conflict, *Of Mice and Men* was written in 1937, first as a novel, then as a play. . . .

The sycamore grove by the Salinas River, so lovingly described in the opening lines, is more than scene-setting: it is an attempt to evoke the sense of freedom in nature which, for a moment only, the protagonists will enjoy. By a path worn hard by boys and hobos two migrant laborers appear. The first man is mouse-like. . . . He is the planner from the poem by Robert Burns: as with other mice and men, his best arrangements will often go astray. (p. 170)

The nearest town is Soledad, which means "lonely place" in Spanish; the town where they last worked, digging a cesspool, was Weed. Their friendship is thus quickly placed as a creative defense against rank loneliness; it will be reinforced, thematically, by the hostility and guardedness of bunkhouse life, and by the apparent advance of their dream toward realization. But the secluded grove, the site of natural freedom, provides the only substantiation their dream will ever receive; and when our mouse-like planner tells his friend to return there in case of trouble, we sense that the dream will end where it essentially begins, in this substantiating site.

The second man to appear is "opposite" to the first. . . . This bear-like man becomes equine when they reach the grove: flinging himself down, he drinks from the pool there, "snorting into the water like a horse." (pp. 170-71)

These animal actions and his childish speech place him for us quickly as an idiot. What the first man plans for, the second already has. Like other Steinbeck idiots—Tularecito in *The Pastures of Heaven* (1932), Johnny Bear in *The Long Valley* (1938)—he participates in natural life freely, has access to its powers, and his attraction for Steinbeck is his freedom to use those powers without blame or censure. (p. 171)

In his pocket the idiot carries an actual mouse, dead from too much handling. Later he kills a puppy with playful buffeting. A child fondling "lesser" creatures, he is Steinbeck's example of senseless killing in nature. He is also part of an ascending hierarchy of power. His name is Lennie *Small,* by which Steinbeck means subhuman, animal, childlike, without power to judge or master social fate. His friend's name, George Milton, puts him by literary allusion near the godhead, above subhuman creatures, able to judge whether they should live or die. . . . [In] a later set-up scene . . . old Candy, the lowly bunkhouse sweeper, says that he should have shot his own decrepit dog—should not have let a stranger do it for him. George too will decide that he must shoot Lennie, like a mad rather than a decrepit dog, for the unplanned murder of another man's wife; that he cannot allow strangers to destroy him.

Both shootings have been sanctioned by the jerkline skinner, Slim, "prince of the ranch," who moves "with a majesty achieved only by royalty" and looks with "calm, God-like eyes" upon his bunkhouse world. Since his word is "law" for the migrant farmhands, and since Milton, a rational farmhand, can recognize and accept such godlike laws, he must choose to shoot his friend. By *East of Eden* Steinbeck would conclude that it is choice which separates men from animals, a belief which supports one critic's view of George's decision as "mature." But it is not his "ordinariness" which George will accept, in destroying Lennie and the comforting dream they share, as this critic holds: it is his *humanness,* his responsibility for actions which the animal Lennie, for all his vital strength, cannot comprehend.

And yet George will be diminished—made "ordinary"—by his choice. As many critics insist, he uses Lennie selfishly, draws from him a sense of power, of superiority, which he sorely needs. If he is sensitive to Lennie's feelings—cares for and about him in demonstrable ways—he also "lords" it over him almost vengefully. . . . [Lennie] will always feed this satisfaction, will always do, in effect, what George desires—which means that George himself invites the troubles ahead, makes things go astray, uses Lennie to provoke and settle his own quarrel with a hostile world. (pp. 171-72)

This is to move from social into psychological conflict: but Steinbeck, in taking a boss's son and his wife as sources of privileged pressure on migrant farmhands, has moved there before us. He has chosen aggressive sexuality as the force, in migrant life, which undermines the friendship dream. This variation on the Garden of Eden theme is, to say the least, peculiar. (p. 172)

In *Of Mice and Men* Lennie first pets Curley's wife, then breaks her neck, without any awareness that she provokes both reactions. His conscious desires are simple: to stroke something furry, and to stop the furry thing from yelling so George won't be mad at him. But George has predicted this episode, has called Curley's wife a rat-trap, a bitch, a piece of jail-bait; and he has roundly expressed disgust at Curley's glove full of vaseline, which softens the hand that strokes his wife's genitals. Lennie has obligingly crushed that hand for George, and now he obligingly breaks the rat-trap for him, that snare for mice and men which catches both in its furry toils. (p. 173)

[A] frightening capacity for violence is what Lennie brings into the unsuspecting bunkhouse world: he carries within him, intact from childhood, that low threshold between rage and pleasure which we all carry within us into adulthood. But by adulthood we have all learned to take precautions which an idiot never learns to take. The force and readiness of our feelings continues: but through diversions and disguises, through civilized controls, we raise the threshold of reaction. This is the only real difference, emotionally, between Lennie and ourselves.

A great deal of Steinbeck's power as a writer comes, then, from his ability to bring into ordinary scenes of social conflict the psychological forcefulness of infantile reactions: his creation of Lennie in *Of Mice and Men* is a brilliant instance of that ability—so brilliant, in fact, that the social conflict in this compact tale tends to dissolve into the dramatic urgencies of Lennie's "fate." In his next novel, *The Grapes of Wrath* (1939), Steinbeck would find a situation commensurate with his own low threshold for idiot rage. . . . With Lennie's pathetic fate in mind, the meaning of Rose of Sharon's mysterious smile as she breastfeeds a starving middleaged man is not hard to fathom: she has found in the adult world what Lennie has never been able to find—an adequate way to satisfy inchoate longings, a way to nurture helpless creatures, perform useful tasks, indulge innocent pleasures, without arousing self-destructive anger. Steinbeck has called *Of Mice and Men* "a study of the dreams and pleasures of everyone in the world" and has said that Lennie especially represents "the inarticulate and powerful yearning of all men," their "earth longings" for land of their own, for innocent-pleasure farms. In a profoundly psychological way he was right about the pleasures, though strangely neglectful of the rages which, in his world at least, accompany them. Tom Joad's confident smile, his flaunting of homicide to a truckdriver as *The Grapes of Wrath* begins, and Rose of Sharon's mysterious satisfaction as it closes, suggest that fuller accommodation of universal urges which gives his greatest novel much of its extraordinary power.

Of Mice and Men helped him to release that power by making murder seem as natural and innocent as love. . . . There are natural killings too in *The Red Pony,* where the little boy, Jody, cuts up the bird he has stoned and hides the pieces out of deference to adults: "He didn't care about the bird, or its life, but he knew what older people would say if they had seen him kill it; he was ashamed because of their potential opinion." Jody is too small to push these primitive sentiments very far; but Lennie, a more sizeable child, is better able to amplify their meaning. After killing Curley's wife he flees to the grove near the Salinas River, as George has told him to. Back in his own element, he moves "as silently as a creeping bear," drinks like a wary animal, and thinks of living in caves if George doesn't want him any more. Then out of his head come two figures: his aunt Clara and (seven years before Mary Chase's *Harvey*) a giant rabbit. These figments of adult opinion bring all of George's petty righteousness to bear against him, shame him unmercifully, and threaten him with the only thing that matters: the loss of his beloved bunnies. Then out of the brush, like a third figment of Miltonic pettiness, comes George himself, as if to punish him once more for "being bad." But for

Lennie as for Jody, badness is a matter of opinions and taboos, not of consequences and responsibilities. He doesn't care about Curley's wife, who exists for him now only as another lifeless animal. Nor does Steinbeck care about her except as she arrives at natural innocence; but he does care about that, and through Lennie, who possesses it in abundance, he is able to affirm his belief in the causeless, blameless animality of murder. Of course, he also believes in the responsibility of those who grasp the consequences of animal passion, and it is one of several paradoxes on which this novel ends that George comes humbly now to accept responsibility for such passions, comes not to punish Lennie, then, but to put him mercifully away, to let him die in full enjoyment of their common dream. (pp. 176-77)

What makes this ending scary and painful and perplexing is the weight given to all that Lennie represents: if contradictory values are affirmed—blameless animality, responsible humanity; innocent longing, grim awareness—it is Lennie's peculiar mixture of human dreams and animal passions which matters most. George's newfound maturity is paradoxically an empty triumph: without Lennie he seems more like a horseless rider than a responsible adult. "The two together were one glorious individual," says Steinbeck of the boy Jody and his imagined pony, Black Demon, the best roping team at the Rodeo. Without such demonic vitality, by which any kind of meaningful life proceeds, George is indeed friendless and alone. With it, needless to say, he is prone to destructive rages. On the horns of that adolescent dilemma—that inability to take us beyond the perplexities of sexual rage—Steinbeck hangs his readers. Impales them, rather, since the rich tensions of this poignant perplex, however unresolved, are honestly and powerfully presented. (p. 178)

In *Tortilla Flat,* an otherwise comic novel, [Steinbeck shows] . . . how Danny tires of the chivalric life and reverts to the "sweet violence" of outlawry. "Sweet violence" means something more here than the joys of boyish rebellion: it means delight in pulling the house down on one's own and other people's heads, which is what Danny does when the friendship dream proves insubstantial, and he pays with his life—and later, with his friends' help, with his house—for the pleasure of destroying it. Lennie too pays with his life for the pleasure of destructive rages; but he serves in this respect as an extension of his friend's desires: he is George Milton's idiot Samson, his blind avenger for the distastefulness of aggressive sexuality. Which may be why their friendship seems impossible from the first, why the pathos of their dream, and of its inevitable defeat, seems less important than the turbulence it rouses. Once more "sweet violence" is the force which moves these characters, and which moves us to contemplate their puzzling fate.

By *East of Eden* Steinbeck would learn that rages generally follow from rejected love, that parental coldness or aloofness breeds violence in youthful hearts; and he would come also to accept sexuality as a vulnerable condition, a blind helplessness by which men and women may be "tricked and trapped and enslaved and tortured," but without which they would not be human. . . . But by accepting sex now as a human need, he would redeem his Lennie's and Danny's from outlawry and animality, and he would finally repair the ravages of sweet violence. *Of Mice and Men* remains his most compelling tribute to the force behind those ravages, "the most disturbing impulse humans have," as it moves a selfish master and his dancing bear to idiot rages. And once more it must be said to move us too. For however contradictory it seems, our sympathy for these characters, indeed their love for each other, is founded more deeply in the humanness of that impulse than in its humanitarian disguises. (pp. 178-79)

Mark Spilka, "Of George and Lennie and Curley's Wife: Sweet Violence in Steinbeck's Eden," in Modern Fiction Studies *(© copyright 1974 by Purdue Research Foundation, West Lafayette, Indiana), Vol. 20, No. 2, Summer, 1974, pp. 169-79.*

JOHN GARDNER

When John Steinbeck was at work on his **"The Acts of King Arthur and His Noble Knights"** in the middle and late 1950's, he hoped it would be "the best work of my life and the most satisfying." Even in its original form, the project was enormous—translation of the complete "Morte d'Arthur" of Sir Thomas Malory; and the project soon became still more difficult, not translation but a complete retelling—rethinking— of the myth. Steinbeck finished only some 293 uncorrected, unedited pages, perhaps one-tenth of the original. Even so, the book Steinbeck's friend and editor Chase Horton has put together is large and important. It is in fact two books, Steinbeck's mythic fiction on King Arthur's court, and a fat, rich collection of letters exchanged between Steinbeck, Horton and Elizabeth Otis, Steinbeck's agent. The first is an incomplete but impressive work of art; the second, the complete story of a literary tragedy—how Steinbeck found his way, step by step, from the idea of doing a "translation" for boys to the idea of writing fabulist fiction, in the mid-1950's, when realism was still king. (p. 31)

Steinbeck's Arthurian fiction is indeed, "strange and different," as he put it. The fact that he lacked the heart to finish the book, or even put what he did complete into one style and tone, is exactly the kind of petty modern tragedy he hated. The idea was magnificent—so is much of the writing—though we see both the idea and the writing changing as they go. In the early pages he follows Malory fairly closely, merely simplifying and here and there adding explanation for the modern young reader.

As he warms to his work, Steinbeck uses Malory more freely, cutting deeply, expanding generously. In the passage on Merlin's defeat by Nyneve he writes like a man retelling a story from his childhood, interpreting as he pleases and echoing hardly a line. . . .

[There] are still Malorian elements—sentences beginning with "Then" and "And," formulaic repetitions, archaic diction— but all the rest is modern. For instance, it is novelistic, not mythic, to speak of Merlin's "panting," "pleading and whimpering," or of "the inborn craft of maidens" and "the inborn helplessness of men." . . . By the time Steinbeck reached **"The Noble Tale of Sir Lancelot of the Lake,"** he had his method in full control. He makes authorial comments of a sort only a novelist would risk, cuts pages by the fistful, and at the same time embellishes Malory's spare legend with a richness of detail that transforms the vision, makes it no one but Steinbeck's. [There is a passage on Lancelot] with no real source in the original. . . . (p. 34)

What we have here is myth newly imagined, revitalized, charged with contemporary meaning, the kind of thing we expect of the best so-called post-modernists, writers like John Barth. Steinbeck creates a lifelike Lancelot, a veteran soldier who knows his business (how to grab sleep when you can and so on); shows, in quick realistic strokes, how the soldier wakes up, wrings his muscles against cold and cramp; and how magic starts to happen to this cool, middle-aged realist. The falsity of the magic is emphatic—"as frankly invented as [the designs] in an illuminated book." . . .

Steinbeck's whole purpose at this stage—a purpose close to Malory's yet utterly transformed—[is] to show in the manner of a fabulator how plain reality is transformed by magic, by the lure of visions that ennoble though they ultimately betray. It's a theme we've encountered before in Steinbeck, but a theme that has here the simplicity and power of myth.

"The Acts of King Arthur and His Noble Knights" is unfortunately not Steinbeck's greatest book, but as Steinbeck knew, until doubt overcame him, it was getting there. (p. 36)

John Gardner, "'The Acts of King Arthur and His Noble Knights'," in The New York Times Book Review *(© 1976 by The New York Times Company; reprinted by permission), October 24, 1976, pp. 31-2, 34, 36.*

ROBERT MURRAY DAVIS

Steinbeck critics have either ignored **"The Murder,"** refusing it even the attention of condemnation, or treated it very gingerly because on the surface it is an enormously disturbing story with a theme and action seemingly allied to the John Wayne mystique that only a dominated woman and a dominant man will be happy together.

Quite short, the story can be summarized still more briefly. After the death of his parents, Jim Moore marries and brings to his California valley ranch Jelka Sepic, repudiating her immigrant father's advice to beat her regularly in order to make her a proper wife. . . . One evening as he is going to town he meets a neighbor coming to inform him about the butchering of one of his calves. Jim investigates and returns home unobserved to find Jelka in bed with her male cousin. After a curious pair of meditations at the water trough, Jim shoots the cousin and departs without speaking to Jelka. He returns at dawn with the deputy sheriff and the coroner, who remove the body, exonerate Jim, and caution him not to be too severe with his wife. Jim beats her severely with "a nine-foot, loaded bullwhip," and she then fixes his breakfast. The implication, strongly reinforced by the closing paragraph which shows her smiling and him stroking her head and by an introductory view of the happy couple in the indeterminate future, is that both have learned their lessons and have reached a new understanding of each other.

Told thus baldly, the story seems to warrant the charges of racism and sexism which so far have been the only responses to it. Examined more thoroughly, with attention to overtones of statement and image and to Steinbeck's other work, it remains a disturbing story, but disturbing to conventional pieties and expectations in the same way as Steinbeck's best work of the 1930's. Seen in this way, the story focuses upon psychological rather than physical action and deals, not with Jelka's being pounded into a satisfactory wife but with Jim's becoming a satisfactory husband and a complete human being.

From the beginning of the story, Steinbeck takes care to show that Jim Moore lives in a limited world, in part inherited, in part elected. For instance, the first paragraph deals not with Moore but with the description of the Cañon del Castillo. . . . Just below the castle is a deserted ranch house, where Jim Moore grew up and to which he brought Jelka, with which he was intimately familiar and which now he cannot destroy because he has come to see that it represents ''a great and important piece of his life.'' Still further away from the dead end of the canyon and closer to the outside world in which the union of Jim and Jelka can reach the social level is the house which Jim builds for Jelka after the murder. If the castle represents among other things false ideals of chivalry, perhaps by contrasting the medieval reality with sentimental modern reconstructions, the ranch house represents Jim's false ideal of his childhood, including his parents, and the new house symbolizes the achieved marriage of Jim and Jelka on the basis not of received ideas and cultural patterns but of a realistic understanding of both partners' needs.

Before Jim can reach that stage, however, he must rid himself of false notions of maturity. He emerges into physical and social manhood in the familiar surroundings of the old house, but the limitations of his maturity are shown by his actions after the deaths of his parents: [he grows a beard, sells the pigs and buys a Guernsey bull]. . . . His dealings with the livestock are at first glance puzzling if not incomprehensible. However, Guernseys are a dairy breed, and the difference between a bull and pigs is that the one is used only for breeding—and milk producers rather than meat animals—while the only end of pigs is the slaughterhouse. By rejecting the one and choosing the other, Jim exhibits a delicacy which would divorce generation from death and thus deny and try to avoid part of the natural cycle.

Thus it is not surprising that he indignantly repudiates the counsel of Jelka's father that [he beat her regularly]. . . . Though Jim rejects the advice and the prediction, ''Sometime you see,'' he soon learns that Jelka is foreign, in fact almost animal-like. Only her dextrous hands seem human, and they are almost separate from her, ''wise hands'' that ''she seemed to regard with wonder and pride. . . .'' And though Jim desires to communicate with her on the level of language, he fails and thinks the barrier impassable. Sexually and physically they can communicate. . . . Fixed on the level of language and puzzled by his wife, Jim turns to the Three Star for ''the company of women, the chattery exchange of small talk, the shrill pleasant insults, the shame-sharpened vulgarity.'' To the stock question ''Where's your wife?'' he gives the stock answer ''Home in the barn.'' If Jelka has a traditional old-world idea of marriage, Jim seems to have no integrated, wholistic view at all.

This is the situation at the beginning of the central incident which occupies more than half the story. Although it begins in trivial domestic details of clearing the table and saddling a horse, Steinbeck soon indicates that the ensuing action will be far from ordinary. For one thing, setting sun and rising full moon, balanced on opposite horizons, give ''a mysterious new perspective to the hills'' and cast ''A huge, long-legged shadow of a horse and half a man. . . .'' If Jelka is not entirely animal because of her clever hands, this phrase shows that Jim is both partly animal and not fully human. However, he is oblivious to these implications as he rides past the castle, unknightly in a sordid quest. . . . (pp. 63-5)

Returning home, Jim discovers a strange horse in his barn. At this point the action slows and Steinbeck presents the first of five scenes with Jim at the water trough. In the first, Jim looks into it, sees nothing, and for the last time until he returns in daylight relies on language . . . as he plans his strategy for discovering the identity of his rival. Having done so, he returns to sit on the side of the trough. This time Steinbeck makes it clear that the trough is the image of Jim's mind and that in

looking all the way to the moonlit bottom he is drawing up material from his unconscious. At first, he represses the memory of what he has just seen and displaces it. . . . Then repressed material from the past surfaces as ''His thought turned to the way his mother used to hold a bucket to catch the throat blood when his father killed a pig. She stood as far away as possible and held the bucket at arms' length to keep her clothes from getting spattered.'' This memory, breaking through the block symbolized by Jim's sale of the pigs, shows him that his mother is, however reluctantly, involved in violence and that she is, in fact, fully human, not just the companion and conversationalist he expected a wife to be. Released by this memory from his false ideals of purity and chivalry, ''Jim dipped his hand into the trough and stirred the moon to broken, swirling streams of light. He wetted his forehead with his hands'' and, self-baptised into a new state, goes expressionlessly to kill his rival. Having done so, he returns to the trough, dips ''his head into the water'' to seal the change, and vomits. Then, leaving Jelka whimpering ''like a puppy,'' he mounts his horse and rides towards town. This time ''The squat black shadow traveled under him,'' for he has finally integrated in himself man and animal.

The next morning, returning with deputy sheriff and coroner, he immediately ''saunter[s] away towards the water-trough,'' now apparently for him a place of security. After the men leave, he approaches the barn and ''the high, puppy whimpering'' of his wife with the bull whip. Reemerging, he carries her to the trough and tends her wounds. After she fixes his breakfast, including ''thick slices of bacon,'' he announces that the two of them will go into town to order lumber for a new house. She agrees that ''That will be good'' and asks ''Will you whip me any more—for this?'' His reply—''No, not any more, for this''—pleases her and their new compact is sealed when she sits beside him and he strokes her hair and neck.

Fittingly, the story ends structurally in the daylight, just as it ends chronologically, in paragraph three, in the town. Even from the passages quoted earlier it is obvious that the sun-moon imagery provides a significant undertheme. From the point at which the two bodies appear on opposite horizons, both their positions and the changing quality of the light is emphasized well beyond the requirements of mere description. For instance, Jelka's infidelity is revealed by the moonlight, and after Jim beats her and is tending her wounds by the water trough, Steinbeck adds ''The sun shone hotly on the ground. A few blowflies buzzed about, looking for the blood.'' The night is clearly associated with the sensual and imaginative life: Jim can relate to Jelka only in the (obviously nocturnal) sexual act, and the moonlit trough reveals to him the underlying truth about his heritage and himself. The significance of the sun is less easy to determine, but it may signify the daylight world of conventional social reality. In the daytime, Jim plays and is forced by the coroner into the role of wronged husband. On the previous night, no such ideas—or any formulable propositions—enter his mind. However, the events of the night do lead to the emergence of Jim and Jelka into the daylight world of the town.

One might justly ask if this reading of the story takes us beyond Joseph Fontenrose's comment that ''in **'The Murder'** Jim Moore found an old-world Slavic order satisfactory for dealing with errant wives and their paramours.'' The answer is, I obviously think, yes on at least two counts. First, my reading shifts the focus from the result of the actions and from any racist or sexist ideas on which the process might be based and which disturb critics like Warren French and Robert Benton to the means by which Jim Moore responds on the deepest levels of his being to the particular situation. His alteration, not Jelka's subjection, is the focus of the story. Second, as French finally admits, the story's point "appears to be that people should be treated according to their own traditions even if we find them incomprehensible." One could go farther and invoke the system of "is" as opposed to "should" thinking most clearly articulated in *Sea of Cortez* but implicit in most of Steinbeck's work of the 1930's. By responding with a chivalric code, "should" thinking at its most rigid, Jim brings about a far greater evil than the advice of Jelka's father would produce and is forced to act in accordance with what the coroner thinks are ideas of honor and the bloody ways of maintaining it. (pp. 65-7)

Jim Moore is successful in preserving his home life by finally "getting in touch" with Jelka on the physical level and communicating with her on a level even more basic than the sexual. He achieves admiration on the social level because he has dared to exercise the "unwritten law" to preserve his home, but that is far less important than his accepting the past, integrating himself, and achieving self-respect. From the sentimental moralist's point of view, it is not a desirable end, still less desirable a means. But sentimental moralism, as represented by Jim's earlier attitude, is irrelevant to the reality, where slaughter— or sacrifice—as well as breeding, blood as well as milk, blows as well as touch are inevitable. Given his environment and his situation, both of which he is able to alter only after he has clearly understood and accepted them, Jim Moore is a successful man and even, in the local terms on which Steinbeck would insist, a good man. (pp. 67-8)

Robert Murray Davis, "Steinbeck's 'The Murder'," in Studies in Short Fiction *(copyright 1977 by Newberry College), Vol. 14, No. 1, Winter, 1977, pp. 63-8.*

PAUL McCARTHY

Like William Faulkner and Willa Cather, John Steinbeck wrote his best fiction about the region in which he grew up and the people he knew from boyhood. . . .

Far more extensive than Faulkner's county or Cather's homeland, the Steinbeck territory covers thousands of square miles in central California, particularly in the Long Valley, which extends south of Salinas, Steinbeck's hometown, for over one hundred miles and lies between the Gabilan Mountains on the east and the Santa Lucia Mountains along the Pacific coast. (p. 23)

In the territory appear Mexicans, Spanish, and Chinese, as well as German, Irish, and English; not only ranchers and farmers but also migrant workers, community leaders, assorted whores and bums, as well as fishermen, bartenders, schoolteachers, and radicals. The characters include the wealthy, poor, and economically in-between; the able, bigoted, mature, puritanic, psychotic, and happy. The vast territory is a factor also in shaping dominant themes in the fiction, including man's relationships with the land, the attractions of the simple life, the conflicts of the haves and have-nots, the failures or dangers of middle-class existence. (p. 24)

[*The Red Pony*] examines the relationship of man and the land. (p. 30)

Unlike the luckless Pepé in "**Flight**," Jody grows up on good, fertile land, benefits from a secure family life, and survives his encounters with death and unpredictable nature. Steinbeck's accounts of Jody's life and survival show a similarly graceful and detailed realism. We gain a firm impression of the outward boy, his playing with Doubletree Mutt, deference to his parents, and a close relationship with Buck. The sensitive language and point of view create a sense also of the inner Jody, of his daydreams about armies marching down the country road behind him, of the large colt next to Nellie. . . . Descriptions of farm activities, the countryside, and other people are inseparable from descriptions of a boy growing up. The descriptions, point of view, concentration on the farm scenes and activities and on Jody in particular unify the four parts of the novel. (pp. 31-2)

Learning from experience like Hemingway's young Nick Adams, but more soundly prepared by farm life and his elders, Jody Tiflin learns that dying is natural and living requires sacrifices. Like Nick he learns also that forces in nature can be unpredictable and dangerous. The closing scenes of *The Red Pony* dramatize Jody's maturing tolerance for others and indicate that eventually he will outgrow his teachers. (p. 32)

In portraying dreams, friendships, and grim necessities, Steinbeck wrote his best novel to date [*Of Mice and Men*]. A more sensitive and perceptive work than *Tortilla Flat* or *In Dubious Battle, Of Mice and Men* compares favorably with the best short novels of the decade. It is also the first and best of Steinbeck's experiments with the novel-play form, which combines qualities of each genre. . . . The individual chapters or scenes contain few descriptions of place, character, or action. The unities in *Of Mice and Men* are based on drastic limitations. Action is restricted usually to the bunkhouse. The restriction of time to three days—sunset Thursday to sunset Sunday— intensifies suspense and drama. With place and time compressed, the action is necessarily simple and dramatic; the superfluous and complex have been eliminated. There are no scenes of travel or of work and few of the past. Foreshadowing is obvious and suspenseful. Lennie's rough play with mice and the shooting of Candy's old dog foretell subsequent violence. Future action is more or less anticipated by what is said. And the characters themselves make for simplicity of action.

To create such effects, Steinbeck's craftsmanship was at its best. All aspects of the novel are finely done. A few techniques can be noted. A general technique, as the above would suggest, is a highly restricted focus. With the emphasis upon the scenic, a skillfully managed third-person point of view is also essential. To create a sense of the impersonal and objective, Steinbeck concentrates, with exceptions, on exteriors: a river bank, a bunkhouse, a character's appearance, card players at a table. The setting is not panoramic, as in the description of a valley scene in *In Dubious Battle;* it is, figuratively speaking, only as wide as a stage. The focus is also upon the present: what can be seen or heard. Thoughts, recollections, and fantasies are directly expressed by the characters involved, except in the case of Lennie's Aunt Clara and the giant rabbit in chapter 6. This interlude of fantasy may or may not violate the objectivity of the third-person narration. Generally, however, the point of view remains objective and exterior.

The prose style—particularly the rhythms and diction—possess greater sensitivity and naturalness than in *In Dubious Battle*. The language is generally more realistic and precise. Descriptions of the bunkhouse interior—walls, bunks, scanty possessions, stove and table, George's things—and of sights and sounds in Crooks's room and the barn, create a sense of the workaday world and its crudities. Hanging in the harness room, where Crooks stays, are "pieces of harness, a split collar with the horsehair stuffing sticking out, a broken hame, and a trace chain with its leather covering split." The precision is notable. Although there are no work scenes, references to bucking barley eleven hours daily, to workers who put in a month and leave, to evenings of card games and pulp magazines underline the weary monotony. The physical bareness of the bunkhouse, the mechanical neatness of bunks and wooden boxes, suggest a bareness of spirit as well. Yet, appearing throughout the novel, often in ironic contrast, are sensitive, sometimes poetic descriptions of the pleasant, secure, or beautiful: the pastoral scene at the beginning; the warm, sunlit scene in the barn on early Sunday afternoon; the late afternoon scene at the "green pool of the Salinas River" at the end.

The symbolism, which does not include the pervasive mythical materials of *In Dubious Battle,* is convincingly part of the talk, places, and incidents of the time. The river bank scene is at least suggestive of life-in-nature, a level Lennie is not too far above. The river bank is reassuringly peaceful until George fires the luger and destroys friend and dream. The ranch provides another kind of security and also a place for dreams, but for the Lennies and the Georges of the world it remains essentially unfulfilling.

The river bank and the ranch provide on one level the idyllic and real boundaries of their world. The centrally placed bunkhouse and barn, offering only physical security and a minimum of that, symbolize the essential emptiness and impersonality of that world. The fundamental symbol is the dream itself— "a little house and a couple of acres an' a cow and some pigs and . . ."—which keeps the two men together, stimulates hope for two others, and very likely expresses the hopes of still others. (The "little house" symbol reappears under more difficult circumstances in *The Grapes of Wrath.*) The action traced in *Of Mice and Men,* possessing a parable-like simplicity and theme, reminds one of journeys of other figures in American fiction, Wellingborough Redburn, Huck Finn, and Henry Fleming, who with others also search for ever-elusive goals.

Another mark of excellence appears in the variety and depth of characterization. . . . The superb dialogue gives life to all the characters.

In the last analysis, George and Lennie symbolize something of the enduring and hopeful as well as the meaningless. They manage—if only for a brief time—to rise above circumstances and to convince others as well as themselves that dreams are part of the territory, that all they have to do is keep working and hoping and some day they will have their own place. If they could only somehow control their own weaknesses and keep a little ahead of circumstances. But they cannot. These and other matters are examined by Steinbeck in more complex terms and with greater range and authority in *The Grapes of Wrath.* (pp. 60-4)

Appearing in a decade that saw the publication also of *As I Lay Dying* and *Absalom, Absalom!* by William Faulkner and the trilogy *USA* by John Dos Passos, *The Grapes of Wrath* is one of the period's brilliant, innovative works. It combines a long, eventful narrative and many passages of exposition, broadens the narrative level with several important structural patterns, and demonstrates, among other things, the writer's imaginative techniques and craftsmanship. (p. 67)

To create a work of such scope and depth, Steinbeck relied upon a number of techniques. The most general one pertains

to the language itself, which, in order to serve various functions, had to be supple and figurative, yet often plain. The novel has in fact several languages. . . . These various levels of language, both written and spoken, show affinities with the free verse of [Walt] Whitman and [Carl] Sandburg, the ironic simplicity of Hemingway, and the distinctive rhythm and phrasing of biblical passages. The most characteristic qualities of the written language are precision, natural and sometimes biblical rhythms, and imagery customarily based on elements of the land or daily life.

Craftsmanship in *The Grapes of Wrath* is generally excellent in other respects as well. While customarily narrated in the third-person voice, the novel's point of view varies dramatically in tone, purpose, and method, providing an elevated panoramic view, as in most intercalary chapters, or a close dramatic one, as in narrative chapters. The point of view within a chapter, moreover, may shift from the personal to the impersonal, from the objective to the ironic. (pp. 69-70)

The principal focus in early and later chapters . . . is not so much on the land as on the farmers themselves and their families. In a general sense *The Grapes of Wrath* is a book about families. These include the many anonymous families appearing throughout the novel, usually in intercalary chapters; the individual families, particularly the Joads and a few others; and, in a general or thematic sense, the family of men. (p. 72)

The views and feelings of dispossessed families are particularized in accounts of the Joads, Steinbeck's most significant family and as noteworthy in modern American fiction as Cather's Bergsons and Faulkner's Bundrens. (p. 73)

The Joads are impressively drawn: a down-to-earth farm family unexceptional in most respects but determined to survive and keep their identities intact. (p. 74)

The Grapes of Wrath can be read not only as fiction but as a social document of the time: a record of drought conditions, economic problems, the sharecropping life. Not separate from the fictional, this level or record is a vital aspect of it. The document clarifies the nature of family and small farm life and also of underlying concepts. One of the most important is the traditional agrarian idea of the simple rural life based on principles of natural rights. Those who live and work on the land, who pay for it with their blood, sweat, and toil, own the land. Muley Graves believes this, and up to a point so do the Joads. This way of life is seriously threatened by nature and, more ominously, by another tradition, a largely modern one that has reappeared in recent years: the combination of big farms and financial establishments. (p. 76)

The migration of hundreds of thousands of people westward was a major cultural phenomenon of the 1930s. Steinbeck's portrayal of that phenomenon is another example of *The Grapes of Wrath* as a form of social document. (p. 78)

The four novels appearing between 1947 and 1952 show the continued importance of western materials and a preoccupation with two familiar staples of his fiction, allegory and realism. Steinbeck's interest in allegory had appeared first in his boyhood love of *Morte d'Arthur,* a little later in characters and actions of a Stanford story, **"The Gifts of Iban,"** and then in *Cup of Gold* (1929) and *To a God Unknown* (1933). Characters and actions representing ideas or attitudes, archetypal patterns, and a strong ethical focus—all qualities of allegory, and particularly of parable—appeared most noticeably in *Tortilla Flat* (1935).

Although such qualities are less vital in the realistic Depression novels, portrayals of Joy and Jim and of the strike confrontations in *In Dubious Battle* (1936) include an allegorical level stressing ideas or qualities. That emphasis appears also in the two-dimensional figures and specialized situations and patterns of *The Grapes of Wrath* (1939). *Cannery Row* (1945) may be regarded as primarily a parable. . . . (p. 106)

Important though allegory and parable are in the postwar fiction, they are no more so than another longstanding Steinbeckian predilection, the realistic, which goes back almost as far as his interest in allegory, appearing, for example, in "**The Chrysanthemums**" and "**Flight**" in the 1930s and also in the Depression novels. In fact, as we shall see, novels of the late 1940s and early 1950s reveal a weakening of the allegorical emphasis and a strengthening of Steinbeck's disposition toward both realism and the romantic, a blending of which is evident also in his earlier works, including *The Grapes of Wrath*. (p. 107)

To regard *East of Eden* as a romance, or as significantly romantic, is to make the same kind of critical realignment that appears necessary for a reevaluation of *The Wayward Bus*. Both novels rely upon allegorical materials, with the important general difference that realism is the central shaping influence and mode in *The Wayward Bus* and romanticism provides that influence and mode in *East of Eden*. The romanticism of *East of Eden* differs from that of *Cannery Row* in being more complex, pervasive, and affirmative. In its confident treatment of many topics and various aspects of the national identity, and in its expansiveness and variety of remarkable characters and actions, *East of Eden* resembles [Herman Melville's] nineteenth-century romance *Moby-Dick*. (p. 118)

Although [inconsistencies in his treatment of the biblical motif] and other flaws provide ample evidence that Steinbeck's hopes for another major work were not to be realized, *East of Eden* remains impressive. It shows a largeness of vision and treatment evident previously only in *The Grapes of Wrath*. If the insights into good and evil reveal no unusual depths or subtlety, they do show a complexity seldom evident in Steinbeck's earlier works. The problem of evil—oversimplified in earlier works, sometimes avoided, or often expressed in largely political terms—is examined in the discussions between Sam, Lee, and Adam, and in the motivations and fates of several figures, principally Cathy-Kate, Charles, and Caleb Trask. Affirmations of the good are effectively dramatized through Sam and Lee, the former an inventive dreamer, and the latter a humanist who never loses faith in human dignity and reason; and through the persistence of Adam and Cal, who, despite odds, manage to illustrate that faith.

Although the novel's language lacks the vitality and richness of prose found in *The Grapes of Wrath*, it is usually equal to the demands the author places on it. *East of Eden*, despite failures, not only deals with a wealth of diverse materials but does so primarily through the elusive and challenging forms of romance. (pp. 123-24)

Literary historians may have difficulty in placing John Steinbeck and his work because neither belongs convincingly with a recognized trend or group. Developing as a writer about the same time as Fitzgerald, Dos Passos, Faulkner, and Hemingway—all born around the turn of the century—he appears separate from them in various ways. Unlike these writers, Steinbeck was not powerfully influenced by World War I; and unlike them and others he was not among the expatriates writing from Paris in the 1920s about the predicaments of Americans in Europe and at home.

Along with such writers as John Dos Passos and James T. Farrell, Steinbeck has been considered a social-protest writer of the 1930s. *In Dubious Battle, Of Mice and Men,* and *The Grapes of Wrath* strongly criticize economic injustices and particularly the plight of the have-nots. Yet the generic hallmarks of social-protest fiction—a revolutionary message, and characters and actions designed to express that message—rarely appear. The 1930s fiction and other works by Steinbeck have been described also as realistic or naturalistic, familiar terms for dominant literary trends or groups in those years. However, Steinbeck's fiction resists such categories, for in *The Grapes of Wrath* the realism is enriched by a poetic language and by concerns with the mystical aspects of the biological. The naturalistic emphases, which are sometimes as severe as those of Dos Passos, are moderated in that novel and in *Of Mice and Men* by down-to-earth humor and compassion. The man and his work may be regarded as western—possibly the most apt of these descriptions—until one thinks of various fictions and nonfictions that are not western and of others like *Tortilla Flat* and *Cannery Row* that appear to be western, but do not deal with such primary concerns as space, the land and nature, and man's place in them.

The nature and direction of Steinbeck's fiction may be understood more clearly if approached through characteristic symbols and themes, such as the tide-pool image. . . . The family is another important symbol, often at the center of the dramatic forces of a story or novel and illustrating human strengths and weaknesses. (pp. 139-40)

Territory and social protest are two other identifying marks of the fiction. Central California—most memorably Monterey and several valleys—and the area near Sallisaw, Oklahoma, may appear less familiar to readers than Frenchman's Bend, Jefferson, and the farms of Faulkner's Yoknapatawpha county, yet the Steinbeck treatment of land is nonetheless remarkable for its acute and graphic portrayal of environment and of the effects of nature on man. It is remarkable as well for an early and brilliant study of the predicaments of the small farmer and migrant worker confronted by the powerful alignment of big farmers and finance—a confrontation that persists into the 1970s. Social protest, a *sine qua non* in many of Steinbeck's novels, figures significantly in the satiric realism of *The Wayward Bus* and in a more subtle form in *The Winter of our Discontent,* as well as in the tougher-grained novels of the 1930s.

Instrumental in shaping such elements and the fictions themselves is Steinbeck's moral vision which has been variously described, interpreted, praised, and questioned through the years. Steinbeck's pervasive compassion for human beings appears most characteristically in portrayals of the most vulnerable: the naive, handicapped, and disenfranchised—the Maltbys, Danny and the paisanos, George and Lennie—who rarely find the promised land, at least not as they dream of it. Tolerance and sympathy are evident also in the complicated predicaments of Elisa, Doc of *Cannery Row,* Juan Chicoy, and Adam Trask. The fundamentally affirmative quality of the vision, however, tends on the one hand to minimize complexities and shadings of modern life, particularly in ethical values or choices, and on the other hand, to reveal more of group characteristics and ideas than of an individual's heart and mind. This is in keeping with the strong idealistic and intuitive elements in the vision. Major characters such as Danny, Jim Nolan, Tom Joad, and Sam Hamilton, whose feelings and motives are rarely probed in psychological depth, tend to lose concreteness as the novel's end approaches; they gradually become vague embodiments of social and economic views.

The literary craftsmanship and skill with which the themes, symbols, and moral vision are expressed would seem to identify most definitely Steinbeck's fiction and ensure his place with the best writers of his generation. With them he shared a ceaseless dedication to mastering the art of fiction. **"The Chrysanthemums," "Flight,"** and *Of Mice and Men* are distinguished for precision, clarity, and sensitivity of language and for economy and proportion of form. Characters in these and other works illustrate a versatility of execution from the minutely realistic Jody Tiflin, to a variety of allegorical figures in many of the fictions, to the symbolic realism of Ma Joad and Juan Chicoy, to the complicated and introspective narrator, Ethan Allen Hawley. No less effectively at times than Fitzgerald and Hemingway, Steinbeck experimented with nuances of dialogue and prose style and with varieties of point of view; and in diversity of works if not in richness he may have equalled Faulkner, creating not only stories and novels but also parables, plays, novel-plays, and nonfiction, among the latter being the superb *Sea of Cortez,* written with Ed Ricketts. (pp. 140-42)

Steinbeck's best works brilliantly expose mankind's "grievous faults and failures," alert us to social and economic dangers, and remind us of our forgotten commitments and dreams. Steinbeck's strongest convictions and passions appear in his fundamental belief in humanity, in his expectation that man will endure, and that the creative forces of the human spirit will prevail. (p. 143)

> *Paul McCarthy, in his* John Steinbeck *(copyright © 1980 by Frederick Ungar Publishing Co., Inc.), Ungar, 1980, 163 p.*

BARBARA B. REITT

John Steinbeck's *Travels with Charley* (1962), recounting his trip across the United States with his dog in a custom-made camper, was enormously popular. The book's many readers liked his anecdotal sentimentality. The dog with the crossed front teeth and bourgeois name made poodlehood forgivable, and the author avoided profound criticism of the country, lacing his account with vivid descriptions of the landscape and a variety of American characters. *Travels* is a collage that millions of Americans found to be pleasant, casual reading. . . .

Though *Travels* is one of [Steinbeck's] potboilers, ignoring it is a critical mistake, for both the circumstances surrounding its composition and its content and structure reveal much about Steinbeck as a writer. *Travels* was written during a transitional period in Steinbeck's later life when he was attempting not only to face the specter of decline but to accept his limitations as a writer. (p. 186)

Travels with Charley opens on a note of braggadocio that is most awkward: Steinbeck recounts his rescue of his boat during the height of a hurricane, when he moved it from its moorings close to shore to a point several hundred yards out where it could ride the winds in safety. Since "no skiff could possibly weather it for a minute," he says, he leaps into the water fully clothed and lets the fierce winds blow him back to shore. He claims to have suffered no more harm than a quick shot of whiskey could fix. The story is irrelevant, a strange way to begin the narrative of the trip that is soon to begin. Perhaps Steinbeck felt that he had to establish in his readers' minds the idea that he was still quite seaworthy, as it were, before he could confide his "secret reasons" for taking this unusual trip. He does not want to be one of those men, he says, who trade "their violence for the promise of a small increase of life

span." Fearful of packing his life in "cotton wool," of smothering his "impulses," of hooding his "passions," he asserts his determination to avoid what he calls the "sweet trap" of retiring from "manhood into a kind of spiritual and physical semi-invalidism." He elliptically refers to his illness as "one of those carefully named difficulties which are the whispers of approaching age"—here in the published narrative carefully *un*named. (pp. 191-92)

His determination to travel across the entire breadth of the American continent and back alone and anonymously was an obvious assertion of independence. And on one level he was indeed in full command. The plans he outlines in *Travels with Charley* are thorough. . . . He is certain that few people will recognize him as the novelist John Steinbeck and that few will even ask his name. And in fact, one of the themes of *Travels with Charley* is that Americans converse not only amiably but intimately under the protection of anonymity.

On another level, however, Steinbeck was not at all in command, and he knew it. (p. 192)

Steinbeck's confusion . . . , about both his trip and his artistic life, is obvious. He simultaneously asserts that command and control are what he needs and seeks, and that such control is not possible and seeking it is a sure way to be wrong. The ambivalence that grips him at the outset of the trip keeps a stranglehold on him until the very end. He affects the manner of the gypsy and wishes us to believe (and wishes he could believe) that the days of his journey will shape themselves, that he has the capacity to drift with events, to let what comes his way determine his course. In direct conflict with this intention is his tremendously strong determination to assert himself, to prove his ability to take the helm, to demonstrate that he need not yet relinquish control. This contradiction persists throughout both the public account and the letters he wrote home to his wife while he was on the road. The letters confirm what a close reading of *Travels* suggests: that Steinbeck could not resolve the difficulty. Would his personal and artistic problems resolve themselves of their own accord, or could he force a solution? (pp. 192-93)

The strongest theme in the narrative is Steinbeck's aversion to the juggernaut of progress, the urge among Americans to lay waste to their own country. He describes a people unwilling to discuss politics and confront the public issues squarely, a people in the grips of a compulsive restlessness and lack of roots (the mobile home becomes the symbol in his eyes for American homelessness), but most of all a people still utterly blind to the waste and decay they themselves have wrought.

The changes in Salinas and the Monterey Peninsula are like the changes he has seen everywhere. Steinbeck seems to be saying that whatever the eventual meaning of these changes might be, they have rolled over and past him, leaving him behind. It is the cry of someone who sees suddenly what getting old can mean. It is a cry of pain. (pp. 194-95)

Steinbeck's treatment of the South entirely in terms of the racial turmoil that was roiling to the surface in 1960 is understandable, for the mood of the South was brittle and anger was the dominant emotion of the time. He personifies that anger in the "Cheerladies" who gathered everyday in New Orleans to taunt the little black girl who was integrating a grammar school. This section . . . is one of the more powerful passages in *Travels with Charley.* But the unexpected note for anyone familiar with Steinbeck's fights for social reform is his reaction to the problem that grips the South. Although he foresees, if only dimly, the looming problems of urban decay, pollution, and waste of natural resources, he does not foresee the extent to which the racial problem would cease to be southern. Here in the South he feels like an outsider for the first time on the trip, and the feeling urges him home faster. Perhaps he feels like an outsider in other than strictly sectional terms; he is mistaken in believing that racism is a problem that only southerners can solve, but believing this may have been less painful than believing that generations of people not yet born will be the ones who establish racial justice. Every conversation with southerners in the *Travels* turns compulsively to the question of race, and Steinbeck's response, finally, is an exhausted one: the "dreadful uncertainty of the means" for solving the problem grips him. It may be that his "weary nausea," mentioned several times, is the consequence of his knowing that this is a battle in which he will not be a warrior. (pp. 195-96)

Travels with Charley ends on a sadly appropriate note: Steinbeck gets lost again, the last of many such incidents, in New York City, just a few miles from home. He pulls over to the side of the street; his hands are shaking with the "road jitters" and he is overcome with helpless, uncontrollable laughter. "And that's how the traveler came home again," concludes Steinbeck, echoing equivocally the theme from Thomas Wolfe he had used before.

It is odd that this travel diary of the black moods found so many readers who took pleasure in the book as light reading.

There are deft touches of humor, to be sure, but some of the jokes do not come off very well, and every once in a while sentimentality rather than depth of feeling grips the prose. The writing is quite uneven. Steinbeck wavers between praise and blame for his fellow Americans, and he is uncertain of his own role as observer.

Obviously the trip did not bring about artistic renewal and rebirth. Steinbeck planned his trip with restorative purposes in mind; he ended the trip overcome by weary nausea and helpless laughter, losing his way once again. The mood of the final pages cannot be seen as accidental unless we are to conclude that Steinbeck had utterly lost control of his writing. It is more reasonable to conclude that he had discovered some important truths on his journey, but ones quite contrary to his initial hopes. He could not go home again; more than that, if change is the master and if events will march relentlessly on, then he could not go back to any splits in the path to begin again. He had hoped to remake himself as an artist. The shape and manner of his narrative indicates that his hope had not been realized. (pp. 196-97)

Barbara B. Reitt, "'I Never Returned as I Went In':
Steinbeck's 'Travels with Charley'," in Southwest
Review (© *1981 by Southern Methodist University*
Press), Vol. 66, No. 2, Spring, 1981, pp. 186-202.

Noel Streatfeild

1897-

British author of fiction and nonfiction for young adults, younger children, and adults.

Streatfeild is a pioneer of the modern children's novel. She was one of the first authors for young adults to speak to her audience directly and without affectation. Her early fiction, for which she is best known, lacks the patronizing tone and unrealistic view of life typical of much of the fiction published for young people in the 1930s and 1940s. Her work is straightforward, informative, and often humorous.

Experts believe that the beginnings of the "career" novel can be traced to Streatfeild's first book for young adults, *Ballet Shoes* (1936). Thoroughly researched, this book realistically describes the physical and emotional challenges met by the young adult who hopes to dance professionally. Streatfeild used the same format and writing techniques for her *Circus Shoes*, which won Britain's Carnegie Medal in 1938. These books set the standard for all of her career stories. Her protagonists are generally ambitious, talented, and dedicated, and her female characters are allowed many of the same choices available to her male characters.

Streatfeild's writing is often noted for its warmth, perhaps because her childhood memories are the source for her work. She was a rebellious child whose family did not share her interest in the arts. In her fiction, Streatfeild often portrays individualistic young adults trying to assert themselves within their families. These families are generally of the British middle class—very proper and highly structured. But while Streatfeild is clearly an advocate of the child and the child's right to individualism, she is just as clearly a defender of the sanctity of the family unit. Love, loyalty, and family security are her major concerns.

The type of family conflict that Streatfeild presents in her fiction is very different from that found in the fiction of the last two decades. Her work reflects the mores of her generation and upbringing; she resolves family conflicts in such a way that the importance of the group is realized and reinforced, its unity preserved, and the integrity of its individuals maintained. Streatfeild has not addressed subjects like divorce, drugs, and sex, and her stories always end happily. This places her in a markedly different school than currently prominent writers for young adults, and some critics believe that her work is dated. But others repeatedly praise her willingness to uphold standards no longer emphasized in literature for young adults. (See also *Contemporary Authors*, Vol. 81-84, and *Something About the Author*, Vol. 20.)

PHYLLIS BENTLEY

Too much of *Parson's Nine* reads like E. M. Delafield's *Diary of a Provincial Lady* with the wit left out. The Reverend David Thurston's wife struggles to bring up her nine children decently on a parson's income, the while they prattle as never children did on sea or land. Then comes the war, the sensitive Baruch's tragedy and his twin's grief. The earnest sincerity of this novel

Courtesy of William Collins Sons & Co., Ltd.

makes one loth to condemn; but the 180 pages of childish reminiscence are really too many for an adult mind.

Phyllis Bentley, *"New Novels: 'Parson's Nine',"* in The New Statesman & Nation (© 1932 The Statesman & Nation Publishing Co. Ltd.), Vol. 3, No. 68, June 11, 1932, p. 778.

THE TIMES LITERARY SUPPLEMENT

At the beginning of ["**Parson's Nine**"] one has fears that its subject will be the dismal life of a parson's wife, worn out with childbearing and work in the house and parish. But Miss Streatfeild disappoints us most agreeably. . . . The vicarage family are an engaging and amusing set. . . . The governess, with her enthusiasms and her devotion to the family, is a delightful figure, and throughout the book we are conscious of Catherine, with her loving, yet sardonic view of husband and children. Miss Streatfeild has developed in more than one way since the publication of her first novel, **"The Whicharts."**

"Fiction: 'Parson's Nine'," in The Times Literary Supplement (© *Times Newspapers Ltd. (London)*

1932; reproduced from The Times Literary Supplement *by permission), No. 1588, July 7, 1932, p. 500.*

THE CHRISTIAN SCIENCE MONITOR

Simple in plot and construction, [**"The Parson's Nine"**] is, nevertheless, delightfully readable. The author possesses to a remarkable degree John Galsworthy's ability for character delineation. Each child is a distinct personality who becomes more fascinating as he matures. There is a particularly fine study of the twins Baruch and Susannah. . . .

"Wife to an Idealist," in The Christian Science Monitor *(reprinted by permission from* The Christian Science Monitor; © 1933 The Christian Science Publishing Society; all rights reserved), January 21, 1933, p. 5.*

THE TIMES LITERARY SUPPLEMENT

Nobody knows the stage child better than Miss Streatfeild; and [in *Tops and Bottoms*] her picture of Bobbie drafting his father's *Era* advertisements at the age of twelve and of Doris, the child prodigy, is deliciously amusing. But throughout the story runs Beaty's tragic destiny, which hangs like a cloud over the jollity and sardonic humour of the Timpson family's story—a story of the decline of the Variety Theatre and its people. Miss Streatfeild spares us nothing of sordidness in her picture of slum life in the beginning of the century, but the gaiety of the later chapters removes any implication of gloom from the book: even the final tragedy is so inevitable, so artistically shown, as to leave the reader with a feeling of satisfaction, while each character—even if, like Wee Weelum, it only strays into the pages for a few moments—is a complete and human creation.

"'Tops and Bottoms'," in The Times Literary Supplement *(© Times Newspapers Ltd. (London) 1933; reproduced from* The Times Literary Supplement *by permission), No. 1638, June 22, 1933, p. 426.*

THE NEW YORK TIMES BOOK REVIEW

Not the least interesting incidents and episodes [in **"Tops and Bottoms"**] are those dealing with [Beaty's gradual transformation from slum girl to proper lady under the guidance of the spinster Felicity]. . . .

The relations of the gentle Felicity with her strong-minded friend Agatha, her rival in the art of flower gardening, are described with delicious subtlety of humor. . . . Miss Streatfeild's gift of delicate satire is here displayed at its best.

Felicity's younger sister Mabel had married a social inferior, a hard-working professional juggler known in music-hall circles as Tiny Timpson. When Mabel died in an accident, Felicity conceived it her duty to go on tour with Tiny as unpaid governess for his children. Sadly she arranged to rent her beloved cottage, Little Thole, and, taking Beaty along, joined the bereaved family. How Beaty tried to adapt herself to vaudeville life while yearning for the lost joys of Little Thole is described with all fairness to contrasting ideals. . . .

As in **"The Whicharts,"** published about two years ago, Miss Streatfeild provides a vivid picture of back-stage life. In this part of the tale Tiny's mother, Marie, figures as the dominant personality. . . . Despite Marie's gushing emotionalism and the outrageous way in which she spoils her youngest grandchild, Doris (an angelically beautiful but insufferable little brat), the author deftly conveys the fact of her fundamental common sense and acuteness. . . . As a characterization Marie is unquestionably the more brilliant, but the delineation of Beaty as revealed in the account of her spiritual frustration, and her tragic romance with Bobby Timpson provided the chief emotional interest. . . .

That Miss Streatfeild should have succeeded so well in depicting three such diverse types of English life as slum, stage and country gentry is not the least notable of her achievements in the writing of this tender little story.

"London Music Halls," in The New York Times Book Review *(© 1933 by The New York Times Company; reprinted by permission), September 17, 1933, p. 15.*

E.B.C. JONES

Sarah, the would-be governess, when we first meet her [in *Shepherdess of Sheep*] is a chattering girl of nineteen, common, commonsensical, and far from engaging. She carries a certain conviction. But she never develops through all the years of our acquaintance. The plot of *Shepherdess of Sheep* requires that we should become aware of a great power of devotion in her, that we should believe in the love she felt for her charges, especially the neurotic Jane, for their mother, and for the young doctor whom she sacrifices to duty; but to convey feeling is one of the things of which, it appears, Miss Streatfeild is incapable. I have seldom read a book with less feeling in it, and this makes all that occurs a sort of busy but empty charade. Perhaps Miss Streatfeild was misled by injudicious praise of her earlier books into taking on a far too ambitious theme. Her talent, judging by *Shepherdess of Sheep* only, is for light, slight caricature. Her prose, never distinguished, is often bad; this would be less noticeable in a frivolous book.

E.B.C. Jones, "New Novels: 'Shepherdess of Sheep'," in The New Statesman & Nation *(© 1935 The Statesman & Nation Publishing Co. Ltd.), Vol. IX, No. 202, January 5, 1935, p. 20.*

MARGARET CHENEY DAWSON

It might seem on the face of it that a book describing faithfully and affectionately the life of a large English household, and especially the days and ways of its four children and their devoted governess, would have an appeal for all domestically minded persons. But [**"Shepherdess of Sheep"**] cannot be recommended quite so generally. To enjoy it without a number of reservations one should be not only a woman (men, definitely, lay off) but a very, very womanly woman; should, moreover, be a woman who admires self-sacrifice, no matter how futile, for its own sake; and should further be one who thinks that modern ideas of therapy for abnormal children are all tosh—that, for instance, the treatment for a budding pyromaniac should have nothing to do with doctors and sanitaria but should be confined to an increasing dosage of love, love, love.

Any one unable to subscribe to these beliefs is likely to find the story of Sarah Bertha Onion and her devotion to the Lane family a bit hard to swallow, rather like a large meal (for this is not a short book) made up entirely of vanilla junket. However, one woman's junket may well be another's raspberries and cream.

Margaret Cheney Dawson, "Some Recent Leading Fiction: 'Shepherdess of Sheep'," in New York Herald Tribune Books *(© I.H.T. Corporation; copyright renewed © 1963; reprinted by permission), March 10, 1935, p. 14.*

LOUISE MAUNSELL FIELD

No person at all familiar with English novels is in the least likely to envy the lot of the English governess. The difficulties and hardships of her life have been dwelt upon often, and in many different ways. Nevertheless, [in **"Shepherdess of Sheep,"**] Noel Streatfeild has found a comparatively fresh angle from which to view the fortunes of her heroine. . . .

Noel Streatfeild has that not too common ability, the power of making ordinary, everyday things interesting. Her people are human beings, her children real flesh and blood little mortals, neither imps nor angels. Mrs. Lane, the mother, is an invalid, and the effect upon her of her illness is well done. . . . But real as these other people become to us, it is Sarah whom we love best. . . .

An English novel, the book of course deals with conditions and relationships different from those existing in the United States. Charles Lane's attitude toward Bronson the butler, and Mrs. Leggitt, the housekeeper, for instance, as well as theirs toward him, are somewhat unlike those which usually exist in this country, and for that very reason the novel has a value for American readers different from that which it possesses for those belonging to its own people. Its realism, however, is uncompromising; few novelists would have resisted the temptation to close the book with wedding bells, avoiding the truthful ending Miss Streatfeild has given it.

Entirely a home-keeping book, concerned only with the events occurring in a single household and that one of no very particular importance, **"Shepherdess of Sheep"** is, within its obvious limitations, a fine, honest and interesting novel, blessed with an unusually agreeable if rather too self-sacrificing heroine.

Louise Maunsell Field, "An English Household," in The New York Times Book Review *(© 1935 by The New York Times Company; reprinted by permission), March 17, 1935, p. 7.*

THE TIMES LITERARY SUPPLEMENT

"Ballet Shoes" is a children's novel of the theatre written by somebody who knows all about stage training and little girls, apart from a delightful gift for inventing and telling a story that children will find absorbing, and their elders too most likely. . . . [Pauline, Petrova, and Posy] are nice, natural children, with a sensible nurse and a kind aunt-guardian; and every step of their progress is pleasant, amusing and very interesting, dealing as it does with facts that should prove very helpful to [aspirants] for life behind the footlights.

"Shoes and Ships," in The Times Literary Supplement *(© Times Newspapers Ltd. (London) 1936; reproduced from* The Times Literary Supplement *by permission), No. 1816, November 21, 1936, p. 971.**

JOAN MacWILLIE

Pauline, Petrova and Posy Fossil are three little foundlings who laugh and work their way through the Academy of Dancing and Stage Training [in **"Ballet Shoes"**]. . . .

It is greatly to Mrs. Streatfeild's credit that these talented children never become the precocious little prigs they might in clumsier hands. . . .

The author has made real a section of life too often distorted by fiction. By pointing out some of the things which make up stage magic, she has done a real service to the theater for its young audience.

Joan MacWillie, "Books for Young People: 'Ballet Shoes'," in New York Herald Tribune Books *(© I.H.T. Corporation; copyright renewed © 1965; reprinted by permission), July 4, 1937, p. 7.*

ELLEN LEWIS BUELL

[**"Ballet Shoes"**] gradually shapes itself into an interpretation of the nature of a dramatic artist's talents as well as a detailed description of her training. . . . [Most] interesting of all is the account of the flowering of Posy's unself-conscious genius.

The children's efforts to help tide the household through lean days is a gallant and touching story, but the mass of detail in the latter half of the book disappointingly obscures the original and humorous mood in which the tale was conceived, and reduces the proper development of the girls' personalities into sketchy outlines. The story will, however, be read with interest . . . for its graphic portrayal of the children's stage world in London.

Ellen Lewis Buell, "The New Books for Boys and Girls: 'Ballet Shoes'," in The New York Times Book Review *(© 1937 by The New York Times Company; reprinted by permission), August 15, 1937, p. 10.*

JANE SPENCE SOUTHRON

In spite of the similarity of some of the subject-matter, **"Caroline England"** is in every way far ahead of Miss Streatfeild's previous novel, **"Shepherdess of Sheep"**; and, by reason of its ambitiousness, is in a different category from her earlier works of fiction. To start with, she has taken in hand the question of her English. There is no resemblance between the loose discursiveness and, often, wearisome meandering that spoiled so much of the narrative of the other book and the tight, balanced prose of this. Miss Streatfeild's dialogue was good before. Now it is excellent.

It is a well integrated, smoothly planned novel. If one could have approached it without reference to its predecessor, it would have been regarded solely as yet another in the long line of fictional obituaries of the England that began, presumably, somewhere in the Eighteen Seventies and passed away, lingeringly, with King George V. Like the rest of its class, it is concerned with three generations, its central figure, Caroline, a member of England's county aristocracy, being born in 1870 and dying, a well-attested grandmother, early in 1936. As a matriarch she is outshone by many of her literary rivals who at 65 or so were just beginning to step out; but she outdoes most of them in sheer, natural intricacy of character. Miss Streatfeild's strength lies in an almost microscopic observation of the nuances of behavior, in delicate manipulation and in a ruthless refusal to rationalize conduct to suit fictional ends. Not only Caroline but the score and more of others whose lives impinge on hers are entirely human in their consistent inconsistencies and in the resulting surprises they are able to spring not only on the rest of their world but on themselves.

Unfortunately much of the excellence of **"Caroline England"** is staled by previous usage in **"Shepherdess of Sheep."** It is done very much better here in the long section devoted to Caroline's girlhood. . . . Miss Streatfeild's intuitional understanding of children has rarely been surpassed and her child portraits are second to none. But once was enough, unless the children had been completely different and the viewpoint widely divergent.

Aside from this and in itself the book presents a very charming pageant of a period that owes much of its glamour to nostalgia. The writer's ability to portray her own time is evidenced as the story moves, in easy gradations, to 1936. . . . You slip, almost without realizing it, from decade to decade, never out of date. Only Caroline retains the flavor of the Nineties in which she was a young woman.

Miss Streatfeild likes her that way. She shows her coping with present-day difficulties; and winning out . . . by simple force of temperament and character. . . .

The author is both nostalgic and realistic; and she ends by convincing us that the Victorians—as exemplified, at least, in her invincible Victorian, Caroline—were, beyond everything, realists. . . .

[Caroline] is the embodiment of the philosophy, shown here as peculiarly Victorian, of contentment with less than the ideally perfect.

Jane Spence Southron, "An English Matriarch," in The New York Times Book Review *(© 1938 by The New York Times Company; reprinted by permission), March 13, 1938, p. 34.*

GEORGE DANGERFIELD

Readers of fiction are now pretty familiar with the theme of the decay of an English upper middle class family. It is a pleasure to report that Miss Streatfeild's **"Caroline England"** is a variation which almost, if not quite, restores to this theme something of its original freshness.

There is little in the structure of this book which is original. Even that august and banal intruder, the royal funeral . . . , trails its sable across her closing pages. How often English novelists have used the obsequies of Victoria, Edward, and George to punctuate or pronounce the decline of some family! But even this tired device seems permissible here; for Miss Streatfeild has restraint, delicacy, integrity.

Her novel falls into two parts; and, if these two parts could have been reconciled, there would have been no denying its distinction. The first part tells of Caroline's Victorian childhood. It has all that homesick quality which English novelists can bring to the description of a past just beyond the reach of their personal memory. It is at once a lament and a fairy tale, half mournful, half enchanted. But Caroline the young rebel is completely distinct from Caroline the conventional wife of John England. Miss Streatfeild might have been writing of two different characters.

The novel's back is thus broken beyond repair. But Miss Streatfeild succeeds in carrying over into its second part some of the atmosphere which pervades the first. The tale is at once quiet and vivid; the characters spring from the author's brain and not, as is so often the case, from her theme. The theme is scarcely more than this—that women of Caroline England's type are passing from the English scene, just as surely as their

family possessions are passing into other hands. It is this reviewer's conviction that, until other aspects of English life are more fully explored, this particular theme cannot hope to recover whatever vitality it may once have had; but Miss Streatfeild comes as near to shaking this conviction as any novelist he has ever read.

George Dangerfield, "Family History with Variations," in The Saturday Review of Literature *(copyright © 1938, copyright renewed © 1963, by Saturday Review; all rights reserved; reprinted by permission), Vol. XVII, No. 22, March 26, 1938, p. 16.*

MAY LAMBERTON BECKER

I do like a book that takes me into a family—one that I like—in the first chapter. Before it is over in [**"Tennis Shoes"**] I not only knew, but had determined to keep on knowing, this family in the suburb of Tulse Hill. . . .

The children were variously gifted. . . . The twins, Jim and Susan, at nine were already showing signs of amazing good tennis. Nobody in the doctor's family had much money, and tennis—as you are to discover if you did not know it before—runs into money if you take it seriously. So their grandfather sets up a bank like a house, into which every member of the family puts every spare coin, so the twins can belong to a club. The ways in which money goes in and out of this bank are delightful. The children keep on steadily learning, not only about tennis—the book is equal to a course of personal lessons—but about the right way to grow up in the right kind of family. You chuckle constantly over the unexpectedness of what the children do and the rightness with which they are handled. . . .

When an English writer of adult fiction writes for children he is likely to lose the condescension too often displayed by the English who write only for them, and give young folks stories that measure up, in technique and in interest, to anything offered their elders in the same field. A tennis fan of any age plunges through this story; like **"Ballet Shoes"** last year it will be read by any one in the family who gets a good look at the first page.

May Lamberton Becker, "Books for Young People: 'Tennis Shoes'," in New York Herald Tribune Books, *July 10, 1938, p. 6.*

ELLEN LEWIS BUELL

The 10 to 14 year-olds who learned about the training of London stage children in Noel Streatfeild's original and entertaining **"Ballet Shoes"** will be equally diverted with its successor [**"Tennis Shoes"**]. They may not notice, offhand, that this account of the making of a junior tennis champion is a better-built narrative than its predecessor, but it is a considerably smoother performance. Gratuitous whimsy is happily lacking and the characterization is quite as amusing.

Indeed, Miss Streatfeild's first claim to distinction lies in her witty and astute observance of human foibles as evinced in the young, and if the four Heath children were all red haired and all talented tennis players, it is easy enough to tell them apart, for each one is an individual in his or her own right. The Heath family, all told, is well worth knowing. . . .

Susan and Jim played [tennis] as they did everything else, seriously, dutifully, and more than capably. The account of their prowess is interesting and amusing when set off against their very English dread of being noticed, but it is Nicky, cheeky and arrogant, who really holds one's attention. . . .

[The] account of the children's training, the strict discipline in manners and character as well as technique, will hold the attention of any youngster who ever swung a racquet and for those less sportily inclined the clashes of temperament in the Heath household will furnish ample entertainment. Miss Streatfeild writes in a deceptively simple style which is as forthright as a schoolgirl's theme and as effective as a good fast serve.

> *Ellen Lewis Buell, "New Books for Younger Readers: 'Tennis Shoes'," in* The New York Times Book Review *(© 1938 by The New York Times Company; reprinted by permission), July 10, 1938, p. 10.*

ELLEN LEWIS BUELL

Noel Streatfeild has the faculty of taking her readers backstage with an ease which gives them the feeling of first-hand experience whether it be in a dramatic school or the world of amateur tennis, and she adds the advantage of letting them see it through the eyes of children who are distinct personalities. In ["**Circus Shoes**,"] she gives a special fillip of interest through the inexperience of two young protagonists. . . .

The gradual development of their characters is as amusing and interesting as is this account of that world compounded of glitter, hard work and loyalty which the author describes with a knowledge and understanding gained on tour with a real circus—a Summer well spent indeed, as a vivid and entertaining book testifies.

> *Ellen Lewis Buell, "The New Books for Younger Readers: 'Circus Shoes'," in* The New York Times Book Review *(© 1939 by The New York Times Company; reprinted by permission), July 30, 1939, p. 10.*

MAY LAMBERTON BECKER

["**Circus Shoes**"] will entertain the family. Noel Streatfeild began as a writer of fiction for adults; the success of her first story for children, "**Ballet Shoes**," was in some measure due to her use of the same adult technique, while keeping inside the range of ten-year-old interests and experience. "**Circus Shoes**" is a thumping good circus story; it follows a real, easily identifiable circus through its complete routine winter and summer. . . . I did not wonder that the book received in England the medal corresponding to the Newbery Award [the Carnegie Medal]. . . .

[The] book shows [the two children's] education by trial and error and transformation from potential snobs to honest workers, from butter-fingered amateurs to solid professionals. Not professional circus people; just the kind of people they would have been if they had had, at home, the chance that honest life of Cob's Circus gave.

So you have a two-fold appeal; circus charm and the working-out, under the eyes of the reader, of a change many a child badly needs to undergo.

> *May Lamberton Becker, "Books for Young People: 'Circus Shoes'," in* New York Herald Tribune Books, *September 24, 1939, p. 6.*

IRENE SMITH

Among children's books there has always been extra space for the literature of the circus, so [*Circus Shoes*] takes its natural place with a welcome from all sides. It is a charming book, wise, humorous, and authentic. . . . This story from the inside of a top class circus satisfies every meaning that the word holds to normal children, including human and animal performers.

> *Irene Smith, "'Circus Shoes'," in* Library Journal, *Vol. 64, No. 17, October 1, 1939, p. 762.*

ELLEN LEWIS BUELL

The ten to fourteen year old readers who enjoyed "**Circus Shoes**" and Noel Streatfeild's earlier books are due for a shock with ["**The Secret of the Lodge**"]—but it will not be one of disappointment, and Miss Streatfeild's audience will undoubtedly be enlarged by a considerable number of boys, since it pushes deeper into the fields of their interests than any of the others. Indeed, this tale of a mystery which four children unravel in a remote mansion on the coast of Cornwall is every child's dream of triumph over villainous adults made as convincing as a billboard advertisement.

The Chandler brothers and sisters were not pleased to be shipped off to spend the Summer with their Uncle Murdock, known to them only by hearsay as an extremely unpopular member of the family. Nor was Uncle Murdock, secretary to the deposed dictator of Livia, any happier to see them. . . . In less than a day the children realized that they were practically prisoners, cut off entirely from the outside world. . . . This annoyed but did not trouble them until they heard from a gardener's lodge, strictly quarantined for typhoid fever, the unhappy crying of a child. They decided it was time for a secret investigation, and what they found there called for action of the speediest sort, action which will keep any reader galloping from page to page with suspense mixed with admiration for the courage and ingenuity which they exhibited in their various ways.

Like all Miss Streatfeild's characters, these are real boys and girls, terse-spoken, given to family wranglings, but fiercely loyal, and much of the interest depends upon their individual reactions to crisis. . . . This is an intelligent and timely mystery-adventure story, which avoids the cheaply sensational in an entirely plausible manner.

> *Ellen Lewis Buell, "On Cornwall's Coast," in* The New York Times Book Review *(© 1940 by The New York Times Company; reprinted by permission), August 4, 1940, p. 9.*

MAY LAMBERTON BECKER

The English author who rolled up an American public by lively stories of young folks working and playing in ballet shoes, tennis shoes and circus shoes, widens that audience by a genuine thriller such as ten-year-olds love. . . .

["**The Secret of the Lodge**"] pleases children by the reliance it places on children's quick wits and bravery, but it does not overestimate either: children really are quick and brave. Ten-year-old excitement in such English and such humor is worth noting.

> *May Lamberton Becker, "Four Kinds of Mystery," in* New York Herald Tribune Books, *November 10, 1940, p. 30.**

MAY LAMBERTON BECKER

The preceding **"Shoes"** stories lifted Miss Streatfeild into the first rank of contemporary children's authors. **"Theater Shoes,"** the best, lifts a book for children into general literature. We have novels for grown-ups about distinguished theatrical families and the working out of hereditary instinct in ways various and unexpected. Now for the first time we have a book for and about children, interesting them from the first and entertaining them till the last, which presents such a family, three generations at once on the stage, and holds the attention of any older reader interested in theatrical psychology.

> *May Lamberton Becker, "Stage Folk: 'Theater Shoes'," in* New York Herald Tribune Weekly Book Review, *November 11, 1945, p. 28.*

DOROTHA DAWSON

[*Theater Shoes* is another] spirited and charming story that compares well in style [with the popular *Ballet Shoes*]. . . . Vivid and interesting details of stage training and life and the natural attitudes and conversation of the children create an atmosphere which should appeal widely to young people twelve and older.

> *Dorotha Dawson, "Older Boys and Girls: 'Theater Shoes'," in* Library Journal, *Vol. 71, No. 1, January 1, 1946, p. 59.*

MAY LAMBERTON BECKER

Any one who has sent, perhaps at some personal sacrifice, a parcel of new wearing apparel to some one in England during the war, and then suddenly realized that the recipient must pay heavy duty, will take a personal interest in this latest, and I think best, of the famous "shoe" stories. For with constant humor and truth in every detail, [**"Party Shoes"**] shows what came of such a risk and how well it came out.

> *May Lamberton Becker, "Stories about Boys and Girls," in* New York Herald Tribune Weekly Book Review, *May 11, 1947, p. 16.**

JOSEPHINE E. LYNCH

[*Party Shoes*] describes in detail the preparations for and many characters involved in giving a pageant. Details may become boring to many readers, although Streatfeild fans will undoubtedly enjoy it. The children are natural; with a more extended plot the story would have been an interesting one of postwar Britain.

> *Josephine E. Lynch, "'Party Shoes'," in* Library Journal, *Vol. 72, No. 10, May 15, 1947, p. 818.*

ELLEN LEWIS BUELL

More tightly knit than most of Miss Streatfeild's stories, [**"Party Shoes"**] has also the sense of theatre glamour and family activity which has made her **"Shoes"** series so popular. . . . And she presents here a whole new gallery of those amusing characters, young and old, which always lend such color and conviction to her books.

> *Ellen Lewis Buell, "For Younger Readers: 'Party Shoes'," in* The New York Times Book Review (© 1947 by The New York Times Company; reprinted by permission), *June 1, 1947, p. 23.*

ELLEN LEWIS BUELL

One of the most engaging qualities about the children in Noel Streatfeild's stories is that they have their normal quota of human frailty. It is a debatable point if Jane, the central figure of [**"Movie Shoes"**], hasn't rather more than her share but who wouldn't sympathize with a plain middle child, whose older sister and younger brother are extremely talented? Yet when the English Winters family went to California to visit, it was Jane's very contrariness, plus her love for animals, which won her a chance to play Mary in a film version of "The Secret Garden." No sudden miracles are worked; Jane doesn't become all sweetness overnight, nor does she achieve an easy success. Therein lies the veracity of this story. Miss Streatfeild is as understanding of the nature of an "ordinary" child as she is of gifted youngsters. . . .

One of Miss Streatfeild's best stories, this will please children . . . and their parents by its restrained handling of the movie background.

> *Ellen Lewis Buell, "Plain Jane," in* The New York Times Book Review (© 1949 by The New York Times Company; reprinted by permission), *April 10, 1949, p. 26.*

LOUISE S. BECHTEL

From many angles [**"Movie Shoes"**] is the best of the popular "shoes" books for "middle age" young American readers. Here the very, very English point of view takes a big, honest bump on the shores of this country. The author does not minimize the shock to her English family, and the many little differences; the way she shows them, through the eyes of this gay and intelligent family, is excellent. Also, one cannot commend too highly her Hollywood portrait, chiefly of the lives of child movie actors. . . .

Jane, who does not wear any shoes except her normal ones, is one of the most continuously horrid heroines ever invented. . . . Children will believe in poor Jane, be glad that her sufferings do not reform her too much, and welcome her one saving grace—her ambition to be an animal trainer. They will enjoy all the adult characters too. . . .

In spite of the fantastic luck which attends the varied talents of the Winter Family, the underlying point of "earn it yourself" is shown to be what drives them on: that, plus such determined dreams as most youngsters have, but seldom carry through the hard road of practice. A jolly book.

> *Louise S. Bechtel, "Books for Young People: 'Movie Shoes'," in* New York Herald Tribune Weekly Book Review, *April 17, 1949, p. 8.*

NAOMI LEWIS

With its Cinderella-in-the-film-studios motif [*The Painted Garden*, British title of *Movie Shoes*] should be wildly popular, and cause considerable juvenile discontent. . . . The story is competently told, and the children, with all their dudgeons and vanities, are real enough. But a Presbyterian parent may hesitate before fostering, with this glossy tale, the universal California dream.

Naomi Lewis, "The Swineherd and the Turtle," in The New Statesman & Nation (© 1949 The Statesman & Nation Publishing Co. Ltd.), Vol. XXXVIII, No. 978, December 3, 1949, p. 660.

THE TIMES LITERARY SUPPLEMENT

Like not a few novels of its kind, *Mothering Sunday* deals with present day matters without always conveying the sense that the author is, in fact, thinking in present-day terms. Anna Caldwell, a septuagenarian lady, unexpectedly insists on living in seclusion. A day comes when she is visited by the various members of her grown-up family, with their children. In the course of this visit the personal histories of the characters are unfolded; and finally a dramatic climax takes place. Miss Noel Streatfeild is at pains to explain the natures of all these persons in her book; but we are not always convinced by her psychology. . . . The author seems to accept so much that is improbable that the accumulation results in the air of unreality which permeates the book. The heart-burnings of Carol, the American wife, seem, also, anything but American.

'Family Fortunes,'' in The Times Literary Supplement (© Times Newspapers Ltd. (London) 1950; reproduced from The Times Literary Supplement by permission), No. 2501, January 6, 1950, p. 5.*

PETER J. McDONNELL

["**Mothering Sunday**"] is told with a deft and economical hand. Precisely chosen conversational tidbits and natural actions are used in place of descriptive passages to build tremendous suspense for the family meeting. Where simple descriptions are used they are terse and pungent. . . .

The beauty of this fine tale lies in the fact that the reader is allowed to know the members of the family intimately before the meeting and is thus prepared for and anxious to see their reactions to each other. The book is a feast of characterization.

Peter J. McDonnell, "Mother Knows Best," in The New York Times Book Review (© 1950 by The New York Times Company; reprinted by permission), February 26, 1950, p. 34.

MARJORY STONEMAN DOUGLAS

[The Caldwell children in "**Mothering Sunday**"] had neglected their mother and would have gone on neglecting her if someone had not reported that she was behaving strangely. The discovery of her secret, its revelation through the chapters in which each member of the family is presented separately, has the suspense, almost, of a superior English detective story. Its working out resolves, almost too patly, all the other individual problems. But through the detailed method the people grow real. Their characters are soundly and clearly built. You believe in them. The story becomes the story of a real family.

It is curious that there is a quality here which suggests that rare and beautiful book of Virginia Woolf, "The Waves." If only the two could have been combined so that this one might have the spare, haunting beauty of Virginia Woolf's! And if "The Waves" could have something of the clarity and integrity of this book's character drawing, even a suggestion of its very real story, what a fine novel they would have made! To bracket the two in this sort of paragraph is at least a tribute to the fact that, in spite of its apparent faults—its wordiness, its long,

monotonous paragraphs, its vocabulary compounded half of English and half of American—"**Mothering Sunday**" has an impact, a value, which is worth remembering.

Marjory Stoneman Douglas, "Fiction Notes: 'Mothering Sunday'," in The Saturday Review of Literature (copyright © 1950, copyright renewed © 1978, by Saturday Review; all rights reserved, reprinted by permission), Vol. XXXIII, No. 10, March 11, 1950, p. 34.

THE JUNIOR BOOKSHELF

The sad thing about [*White Boots*] is that it does not ring true, and that is disappointing from the writer who made that strange story of the Fossils (in *Ballet Shoes*) so completely credible and satisfying. It is about two just ten-year olds: Lalla, rich but an orphan, cared for by an ambitious Aunt and a Nanny who has far less body to her than that delightful woman who looked after the Fossils—and Harriet whose family has come down in the world and now lives (parents and four children) in a shop that, by this account, would hardly have kept six hungry cats alive, let alone six humans. Harriet is given the run of a skating rink, *free* (as you are told rather often) because her doctor knew the owner. . . . Lalla, child of a famous skater, is to be a great ice champion and goes to the same rink regularly for coaching and practise. The girls meet. The limelight hovers now on Lalla, now Harriet; but instead of showing them more strongly, the effect is weakening and one feels that the author was never quite certain what she meant to do with them. The characters are not consistent and I felt the basic realities were unreliable. (pp. 226-27)

"For Children from Ten to Fourteen: 'White Boots'," in The Junior Bookshelf, Vol. 15, No. 5, November, 1951, pp. 226-27.

LOUISE S. BECHTEL

The "shoes" [in "**Skating Shoes**," the American title of "**White Boots**"] are those of young professional skaters. Lalla, the rich little orphan, meets Harriet, at a rink. Their friendship changes both their lives. . . . The outcome for both girls, in regard to their skating, as well as their characters, is very clever.

English family home life, with Harriet's amusing family living over their strange shop, is well pictured, and girls will like the three very different brothers. Lalla's aunt, with her snobbism and ambition, may be overdrawn, but someone like her must be behind every child star.

Miss Streatfeild writes so well that we welcome, for girls of about eleven to thirteen, whatever "shoes" she takes up. Her books are full of interesting characters, both young and old, of both quiet bits and emotional bits, which all add up to life in the round.

The talk here about professional skating is just enough to lure any girl who loves to skate, and to hint at the real drudgery that must be endured to be a star.

Louise S. Bechtel, "American Families, Then and Now," in New York Herald Tribune Book Review, November 11, 1951, p. 10.*

NANCIE MATTHEWS

[In "**The Picture Story of Britain,**" an] excellent and sensible book, Noel Streatfeild never talks down. She serves up hard facts about the United Kingdom from 55 B.C. to the present with a dressing of fascinating psychological data that makes the story easy to digest. Side by side with information concerning tradition, education, religion, the "most peculiar" money, government and industry are amusing tidbits. . . .

It will be a learned parent (as well as child) who cannot glean from this slim but meaty volume some rich pickings not found in ordinary history or guide books.

> *Nancie Matthews, "Albion," in* The New York Times Book Review *(© 1951 by The New York Times Company; reprinted by permission), November 25, 1951, p. 52.*

LOUISE S. BECHTEL

[In "**The Picture Story of Britain**"], a famous author does a good job for a prospective traveler of about twelve to fifteen. . . . [The text covers] a great deal of interesting information. Miss Streatfeild writes as one knowing children of both [Britain and the United States], and adds many imaginative touches. . . .

> *Louise S. Bechtel, "Books for Boys and Girls: 'The Picture Story of Britain'," in* New York Herald Tribune Book Review, *January 27, 1952, p. 12.*

THE JUNIOR BOOKSHELF

The idea of taking children through the door of history and introducing them to the past is by no means new, but Miss Streatfeild's manner of performing this miracle [in *The Fearless Treasure*] is unusual. . . . The sights, sounds and smells of the past are brought vividly to life, and in each historical 'picture' one of the children recognizes his or her ancestor. . . . Miss Streatfeild has evidently written this book with the idea of inspiring the new "young Elizabethans" with an ideal to live for, through an understanding of their past. I think she has succeeded in presenting the past very clearly and in giving children a sense of the continuity and importance of their heritage, and their need of sympathy and tolerance in the making of a new generation.

> *"For Children from Ten to Fourteen: 'The Fearless Treasure'," in* The Junior Bookshelf, *Vol. 17, No. 5, November, 1953, p. 243.*

CLAIRE HUCHET BISHOP

["**The First Book of the Ballet**"] is for girls and their parents who are fortunate enough to live not too far from a good teacher. It is the story of a ten-year-old girl who goes to the theatre, sees a ballet for the first time, and, like many other children under the same circumstances, thinks that she wants to become a ballerina. Only, she is in dead earnest, and we follow her through her first interview with the teacher, the beginning of her training, the development of her technique. The difficulties inherent to an artistic career, ballet especially, are not minimized by the author, who knows what she is talking about. . . .

[We] are surprised to find no mention of Isadora Duncan. . . .

Except for this one omission we find this first book on the ballet absorbing and distinguished in its simplicity. A must for all young devotees of the ballet.

> *Claire Huchet Bishop, "Resting from Holidays: 'The First Book of the Ballet'," in* The Saturday Review, New York *(copyright © 1954 by Saturday Review; all rights reserved; reprinted by permission), Vol. XXXVII, No. 6, February 6, 1954, p. 43.*

THE JUNIOR BOOKSHELF

Miss Streatfeild's story of the vicissitudes of the Bell family in their Rectory in South-East London [*The Bell Family*] is based on a radio serial which has held its place in Children's Hour for four years. While the rather picaresque plot certainly provides a happy mixture of grave and gay and a mirror in which many ordinary families may see themselves, there is no doubt that it does suffer more than slightly from its origin as a script for dramatic presentation. There is no faltering in incident or climax but here and there the grafting in of character to replace the effect of voice and intonation is apparent and may detract from the book's value for a perceptive child. But no amount of patching can destroy the essential lovableness of Ginnie, the adolescent perplexity of Paul, the mildness of Jane, the matter-of-factness of Angus and the timeless loyalty of Mrs. Gage.

> *"For Children from Ten to Fourteen: 'The Bell Family'," in* The Junior Bookshelf, *Vol. 18, No. 4, October, 1954, p. 202.*

NAOMI LEWIS

The rarest good books are about ordinary life today; one must admire, therefore, the expert hand behind *The Bell Family*—a particularly pleasant reminder of the narrative potentialities of rather poor (professional) families in rather large houses. . . . Readers have a choice of four nicely discriminated children, gifted or misunderstood, with which to identify themselves. . . . Our own choice would be the solid Virginia, who notes dispassionately that the games' captain and the head girl are not happily cast in the school play as the porcelain shepherd and shepherdess; and who did her good deed of minding the verger's baby with reluctance, because it had "a sneering face."

> *Naomi Lewis, "The Young Supernaturalist," in* The New Statesman & Nation *(© 1954 The Statesman & Nation Publishing Co. Ltd.), Vol. XLVIII, No. 1230, October 2, 1954, p. 404.**

MARY WELSH

From the very first page [of "**Family Shoes**," American title of "**The Bell Family**"] we are immediately in [the Bells' house, sharing their] tribulations. . . . There are wisdom and humor here and a delightfully sane family feeling. In her other "**Shoes**" books the author introduced us to real boys and girls; now she has created a highly diverting family, each member a definite personality.

> *Mary Welsh, "Vicar of London," in* The New York Times Book Review, *Part II (© 1954 by The New York Times Company; reprinted by permission), November 14, 1954, p. 32.*

THE JUNIOR BOOKSHELF

[*The Circus Is Coming* (British title of **"Circus Shoes"**) contains] rapid, lively pictures of the life of the circus. The men, the circus children and the animals all come to life under Miss Streatfeild's witty pen. The grown-up characters are a grand group of people, moving and speaking with completely convincing personalities, and even the animals appear as separate individuals as distinct as we are ourselves in their tastes, and prejudices and whims.

I cannot but admire wholeheartedly the shrewd and generous powers of observation, the wit and understanding which Miss Streatfeild has brought to this story.

> *"Coming of Age: 'The Circus Is Coming',"* in The Junior Bookshelf, Vol. 21, No. 5, November, 1957, p. 245.

THE JUNIOR BOOKSHELF

[In *Wintle's Wonders*] Miss Streatfeild has given us another gay and lively work peopled by a centre group of vivid personalities, while her intense interest in her subject gives detail and depth to the whole scene. Mrs. Wintle has a dancing school whose "Wonders" feed the choruses of popular shows and pantomimes. . . . Some of the characters are shadowy, some are caricatures by their exaggerated unpleasantness, but upon Rachel and Hilary, Uncle Tom, Mrs. Storm the governess, and Mrs. Purser the wardrobe mistress, Miss Streatfeild has lavished an intense sympathy and deep understanding so that the reader gains a real experience and something of the author's own insight into and perception of human nature. Miss Streatfeild seems here, however, to have patience with only her more likable characters. The villains of the piece are nearly always quite black and they are harsh and vague and less real because of that. The writing is excellent and the story spills out easily in an unhampered gay and chattering stream.

> *"For Children from Ten to Fourteen: 'Wintle's Wonders',"* in The Junior Bookshelf, Vol. 21, No. 6, December, 1957, p. 323.

VIRGINIA KIRKUS' SERVICE

I'm afraid the pattern is growing thin [in *Dancing Shoes*, U.S. title of *Wintle's Wonders*] after *Ballet Shoes, Movie Shoes, Theatre Shoes,* etc. . . . Despite the sentient portrayals of Aunt Cora and her partner, the plot thread somehow fails to cohere.

> *"Eight to Eleven: 'Dancing Shoes',"* in Virginia Kirkus' Service, Vol. XXVI, No. 3, February 1, 1958, p. 78.

MARGARET SHERWOOD LIBBY

The **"Shoes"** series, of which [**"Dancing Shoes"**] is the sixth, is greatly enjoyed by girls of eleven or so, and **"Dancing Shoes"** will be no exception. It has many popular ingredients, orphan sisters in an unsympathetic home, details of the life of stage children being prepared to do chorus work in musical comedy or television, the exciting rivalry for possible solo parts in pantomimes, plays or movies and the pleasure of seeing the "good" rewarded and the "bad" discomfited. . . .

To an adult this story, although it is as well written . . . and organized as the others, seems the weakest in the series not only because of the triteness of the Cinderella plot (complete

even to the embarrassment of the hard-hearted mother and sister) but because the career described seems unappealing. The reader cannot help feeling with Rachel that it is a mild ambition indeed to become a "Little Wonder."

> Margaret Sherwood Libby, *"Enterprising Orphans, a Western and Three Horse Stories,"* in New York Herald Tribune Book Review (© *I.H.T. Corporation; reprinted by permission), May 11, 1958, p. 24.**

MARGARET SHERWOOD LIBBY

[**"Queen Victoria"**] will hold young people's interest from beginning to end. It not only gives the outward facts of Victoria's life, without fictionalizing, but attempts to suggest the elements in her character and upbringing which influenced her as a queen, and by brief comments on her relations with Melbourne, Disraeli and Gladstone to make readers aware, if only in an elementary way, of the part played by the Crown in British government. Particularly valuable are the quotations from the magazines of the day, from the Queen's own diary and reminiscences, and from her letters and those of her Uncle Leopold. Girls old enough to remember seeing on television or in the movies the ceremonies of the coronation of Elizabeth II will be especially interested in the curiously lifeless account Victoria gives of hers. This is a book one might suggest to girls who have enjoyed the simpler, more romantic biography of Molly Costain Haycraft, to give a more rounded picture.

> Margaret Sherwood Libby, *"An Artist, a Naturalist, a Poet and a Queen,"* in New York Herald Tribune Book Review (© *I.H.T. Corporation; reprinted by permission), November 2, 1958, p. 28.**

VIRGINIA KIRKUS' SERVICE

To any adult who recalls with delight Noel Streatfeild's *Parson's Nine*, many years ago, this juvenile story of a clergyman's family in contemporary London [*New Shoes*] will have special appeal. The four Bell children take a sombre view of their father's decision to move to a city parish. . . . How these four inventive new Londoners integrate with their new surroundings and help their new neighbors cohere into a functioning group makes a lively, cozy story of a household one third mischief, one third ingenuity, and one third love. American children are a devoted claque for Miss Streatfeild's *Ballet Shoes, Movie Shoes,* etc. This affords a new angle.

> *"Eight to Eleven: 'New Shoes',"* in Virginia Kirkus' Service, Vol. XXVIII, No. 3, February 1, 1960, p. 90.

THE JUNIOR BOOKSHELF

Miss Streatfeild can write a masterly, sentimental tear-jerker of a story better than anyone, but *New Town* [British title of *New Shoes*] is by the doyenne of modern children's writers, not the magician who gave us, fresh and sweet with the dew on it, that exquisite story of the Fossil family so many years ago.

New Town is a story about the Bell family. It began as a Children's Hour serial, and bears the marks of its origin. The instalments are terribly tidy; the dialogue has that relentless brightness so characteristic of radio. It is very competent, exactly calculated, made to measure; uncommonly readable, too. It should be enormously popular. But how much better Miss

Streatfeild can do! The hallmark of her best work is its accuracy, the first hand authenticity of the background detail. *New Town* is sketchy in the extreme. What an odd new town it is, in setting and in administration! It may be argued that without this oddness the story falls down; Miss Streatfeild, however, knows better than anyone that the good writer does not make his setting fit his plot.

A disconcerting feature of this book is the unconventional syntax and punctuation. Miss Streatfeild may feel that she can afford to write as she likes. Her readers however are of an age to learn to write themselves; they may well choose her as their stylistic model, and the style of *New Town* is not the key to success . . . !

> *"For Children from Ten to Fourteen: 'New Town',"*
> *in* The Junior Bookshelf, *Vol. 24, No. 3, July, 1960,*
> *p. 165.*

MARGERY FISHER

By far the most successful theatre stories for children are those which, with children as their subjects, can show rivalries and ambitions unaffected, as yet, by the awkward, sordid, bewildering adult world. Here Noel Streatfeild is outstanding. Her young actors, skaters and ballet pupils are infatuated by the theatre. They are ambitious, self-centred, as deeply obsessed by technique as any young aspirant for a jumping rosette. She even succeeds, sometimes, in conveying that intangible but unmistakable thing, star quality—in Posy, for instance, youngest of the three girls in *Ballet Shoes,* who, when the brilliant teacher falls ill, inquires at once what is to happen to her own career; or in Rachel in *Wintle's Wonders,* whose talents are discovered almost by accident, but whom you recognize at once as a dedicated dancer. (pp. 187-88)

[Noel Streatfeild] has an insatiable curiosity about people, and especially about theatrical children, with their peculiar, hardworking, rigidly organized life; and she is curious, too, about the effects of publicity and performance on young people. Her books, for all the detail and skill of their backgrounds, are primarily studies in character. Mrs. Wintle's dancing-school is the battlefield for her daughter Dulcie, a conceited little girl who wants the best parts in all the shows, and the two children, Rachel and Hilary, who are taken into the family and threaten to steal some of Dulcie's thunder. The same theme, of the poor and modest child coming to the fore, is brilliantly used in *White Boots.* . . . In all Noel Streatfeild's books we have portraits of the professional child, set off by the occasional brave souls who resist the dazzle of the footlights, like Petrova in *Ballet Shoes,* whose heart is in motor-engineering, or Hilary, in *Wintle's Wonders,* whose attitude is entirely refreshing, when she is offered a star part. . . . The intrusion of . . . a robust point of view into the somewhat rarefied air of the theatre saves these stories, full of technical detail as they are, from becoming too specialized for the general reader. Noel Streatfeild has her feet firmly on the ground, and children who reread her books when they are older will bless her for this. (pp. 188-89)

> *Margery Fisher, "Fossils and Formulas," in her*
> Intent Upon Reading: A Critical Appraisal of Modern
> Fiction for Children *(copyright © 1961 by Margery*
> *Fisher), Hodder & Stoughton Children's Books (formerly Brockhampton Press), 1961 (and reprinted by*
> *Franklin Watts, Inc., 1962), pp. 170-96.**

THE JUNIOR BOOKSHELF

A new book by Noel Streatfeild is always something to which we look forward. Since the days of *Ballet Shoes* she has concerned herself with families where the children have marked talents for dancing, music, skating or acting, and where the parents take a prominent part in the working out of the story. The circus and the world of films have also been used as backgrounds, and the ordinary schoolchild with little or no talent in any of these directions, may well be fascinated for a time with the details of training for these professions. [*Apple Bough*] is no exception; David and Polly (the father and mother of the children) are musical and artistic; Sebastian, Wolfgang and Ethel are respectively highly talented as violinist, film star and ballerina—only Myra, the eldest, seems to have been left out when the fairies distributed their gifts. She, however, discovers that her grandfather's judgment of her character is correct—her talent is for "wisdom, and being a good sister," and it is through Myra that the family become united in the end. . . . (pp. 269-70)

The only drawback to Miss Streatfeild's stories, I find, is that they are beginning to get a little old-fashioned. We are still in the world where there are servants and governesses, and a cosy atmosphere pervades the relationship with grandparents (one set is called "Mumsdad" and "Mumsmum"). I suppose this cannot be helped if one is writing about the kind of family Miss Streatfeild obviously knows so well but it must be a closed world to many children of today. If the television authorities are looking for modern children's books to serialise, this author's books should prove fruitful ground; they have been popular on sound radio. Why not give them new life by introducing them to a wider world? (p. 270)

> *"For Children from Ten to Fourteen: 'Apple Bough',"*
> *in* The Junior Bookshelf, *Vol. 26, No. 5, November,*
> *1962, pp. 269-70.*

ZENA SUTHERLAND

The atmosphere of the artistic and musical world [in *Traveling Shoes,* U.S. title of *Apple Bough*] is vivid, the children are sophisticated but completely convincing; characterization and motivation are perceptively described. To adult readers, the whole milieu is reminiscent of the unconventional musical family of *The Constant Nymph.*

> *Zena Sutherland, "New Titles for Children and Young*
> *People: 'Traveling Shoes'," in* Bulletin of the Center
> for Children's Books *(reprinted by permission of The*
> *University of Chicago Press; copyright 1962 by the*
> *University of Chicago), Vol. 16, No. 4, December,*
> *1962, p. 66.*

MARCUS CROUCH

The most skilful, sincere and honest writer of [career-books]—and she was much more besides—was Noel Streatfeild. . . . *Ballet Shoes* [1936] established her immediately as a major writer for children. . . . [It] showed a profound understanding of child behaviour and a rare concern for accuracy in the factual background. What gave the book its enduring quality was its warm, strong tenderness. The three Fossils were characters who exist in their own right. Noel Streatfeild was too wise and industrious to adopt the soft option of a sequel, but she could not prevent the Fossils creeping back into later stories. The recurrent theme of Noel Streatfeild's writing is the virtue and the necessity of hard work; it was implicit in *Ballet Shoes* and was the very heart of *The Circus is Coming*. . . . Nothing ever came easy to her heroes and heroines. She showed in precise detail the stages of progress towards success and the rewards, in terms of self-respect, of success. Hers were, almost in Victorian terms, 'moral' and 'success' stories, but the moral was not imposed on a story but came from the heart of the writer. (p. 79)

> *Marcus Crouch, "Renaissance," in his* Treasure Seekers and Borrowers: Children's Books in Britain 1900-1960 *(© Marcus Crouch, 1962), The Library Association, 1962, pp. 55-86.**

NORA E. TAYLOR

["A Vicarage Family"] is an autobiography written as a story. Mostly it comes off very well, though every once in a while the impersonality becomes too self-conscious as, for instance, in the recurrence of the expressions "the children's father," or "the children's mother," where "father" and "mother" would have been natural.

But this is a small quibble about a story that evokes matter-of-factly the hardships and rewards of English clerical life in the early years of this century. Miss Streatfeild sees herself, the Vicky of her book, with the remarkably clear vision not only of hindsight but also of a warm and understanding maturity.

Perhaps she tends to excuse the inexcusable a bit too much. Vicky's "difficult" label, it quickly becomes clear, was due to adult misunderstanding, and to what seems to be deliberate obtuseness of parents and teachers to her needs. . . .

Aside from the record of hurdles cleared by Vicky, the story is a brilliant evocation of the period just prior to World War I, when Britain still lingered in the glow of the Victorian and Edwardian eras, class distinctions were a stable part of existence, and the seasons in nursery and parlor came and went in tranquillity.

In these mellow chapters Miss Streatfeild has carved a monument to her young days that is as unsentimental as a front-page news account—and as warming as a woodfire on a winter's night.

> *Nora E. Taylor, "Vicar's Vicky," in* The Christian Science Monitor *(reprinted by permission from* The Christian Science Monitor; *© 1963 The Christian Science Publishing Society; all rights reserved), November 14, 1963, p. 11.*

THE TIMES LITERARY SUPPLEMENT

Miss Streatfeild's account of a childhood spent in an Edwardian vicarage [*A Vicarage Family*] has the genuine flavour of a period piece. She writes easily and pleasantly within certain definite limits; she is often very funny and sometimes really moving.

> *"Private Lives," in* The Times Literary Supplement *(© Times Newspapers Ltd. (London) 1963; reproduced from* The Times Literary Supplement *by permission), No. 3220, November 14, 1963, p. 923.*

RUTH HILL VIGUERS

The common denominator of [Streatfeild's books for children] and the quality that lifts even the lesser ones out of the realm of the ordinary is the sense of family. And it is not merely a sense of family unity, though that is strong, but of people drawing strengths and weaknesses and individuality from different members of the family, from certain positions in the family, and from traditions, customs, activities, joys, and sorrows of the family group. [*A Vicarage Family*] is like an original painting: it has richness that even the most delightful copy cannot give. The book's substance is the fountainhead of all Miss Streatfeild's children's books.

Told as a story, this is nevertheless autobiography, as unselfconscious as any I have ever read. The Strangeways are the Streatfeilds, and Victoria, the middle girl, is Noel. . . . There is a definite plot; for Victoria, certain that she is the homely daughter and the one least cared for, in anger against the discrimination she finds because she so determinedly looks for it, creates a problem that her saintly father, her very human mother, and her completely normal siblings either cannot understand or refuse to take seriously. Every member of the family, every servant and friend is real. Here is a glimpse of England and of a rural vicar's family during four years just before the First World War, and here are new friends that cannot be contained merely between the covers of a book. For those adults who enjoy autobiography . . . ; for older girls who like stories of families and of girls growing up; and for all who loved *Dancing Shoes, Theater Shoes,* and the rest. . . . (pp. 611-12)

> *Ruth Hill Viguers, "Christmas Booklist: 'A Vicarage Family'," in* The Horn Book Magazine *(copyright © 1963, by The Horn Book, Inc., Boston), Vol. XXXIX, No. 6, December, 1963, pp. 611-12.*

THE TIMES LITERARY SUPPLEMENT

Possibly no one but Miss Noel Streatfeild could have carried off the outrageous plot of *The Children on the Top Floor* with such an air of insouciant plausibility. A winsome bachelor "television personality", delivering his Christmas message, rashly suggests that listeners with families of children are to be envied. Oh! to wake in the morning "to the squeal of delighted children opening their stockings!" Squeals the next morning there are: four assorted infants are lying on his step. Four Coram-like orphans, without the hint of a parent—a dashing fictional gesture . . . . . . Four talents and temperaments in Streatfeild country! A daydream to end all daydreams.

> *"Everybody's Children, For and Against Families," in* The Times Literary Supplement *(© Times Newspaper Ltd. (London) 1964; reproduced from* The Times Literary Supplement *by permission), No. 3274, November 26, 1964, p. 1062.*

BARBARA KER WILSON

All Noel Streatfeild's stories for children reflect something of her vivid memory of her own childhood, her consciousness of the way of life in which she was brought up, and her particular interests. (p. 11)

Although there were pleasant times, on the whole she describes her childhood as unhappy. She was the family misfit, a nonconformist in a constant state of rebellion. (p. 13)

In later life, the adult who was not a happy child can perhaps remember more acutely childhood feelings, can recall more vividly the barriers that exist between children and adults. . . . Such acute memory is shown again and again in Noel Streatfeild's stories. (p. 18)

A professional knowledge of the stage forms the main interest of *Ballet Shoes, Curtain Up* [British title of *Theater Shoes*], *The Painted Garden,* and *Wintle's Wonders,* and is used to advantage in several other stories—in describing the pageant preparations in *Party Frock,* for example. (p. 21)

Ballet Shoes contains the two chief elements for which, combined with her very individual style of writing, Noel Streatfeild has achieved distinction and popularity as a children's writer. First, the story involves the reader in the hopes, disappointments, and achievements of a *family.* Then, alongside the family interest, the reader is given a detailed picture of the professional training of children, in this case for the stage. (p. 23)

Apart from the fact that *Ballet Shoes* is an outstanding children's book, well written, entertaining, with an original theme, which well deserved its success, certain contributory factors played their part in [the book's] success. The book was published at a time when the concept of literature for children was beginning to change, after a long period of neglect. A few authors were producing notable stories for children. . . . But overall there was a dearth of books that would really interest and entertain young readers. (p. 24)

When she began writing *Ballet Shoes,* Noel Streatfeild herself was not aware of this state of affairs; she had been asked to write a children's story, and she simply carried out the task to the best of her ability as a writer, giving it the same care as she would an adult novel. She had no idea that this was rather an extraordinary thing to do at that time, when the average children's writer wrote with a patronising, or falsely simple, approach. It was no wonder that hosts of children seized upon *Ballet Shoes,* eagerly appreciative of the fresh attitude they found in it towards themselves as readers: that of equality with the author. (pp. 24-5)

In the world of children's books, Noel Streatfeild has established a tradition of her own, and is acknowledged as one of our outstanding children's writers both by the children who read her books and also by those who are connected with maintaining high standards in literature for young readers. (p. 29)

Noel Streatfeild's outstanding characteristic as a storyteller is the *rapport* she creates between her readers and herself. The children who read her books know that she cares about the story every bit as much as they do themselves; they have complete confidence in her ability to guide the fate of the characters they have got to know so well. She engenders in her writing a warmth and friendliness that extends both to her characters and her readers. This warmth, or 'heart' as Noel Streatfeild herself expresses it, springs partly from the immense care she takes in creating her characters, and also from her uninhibited approach to the child reader. She speaks to him directly, without preamble, treating him as an equal and assuming that he has the wit to understand exactly what she means to say. 'Of course,' she says to him in effect, 'you as a person of commonsense will realise that a given set of circumstances lead to a certain result.' (p. 30)

[All] too often the children's writer mistakenly adopts a patronising approach; he writes down to his reader. True simplicity is the hall-mark of the best children's authors. It extends

to every feature of a story: narrative style, plot, characterisation . . . and it underlies all Noel Streatfeild's writing for children.

The narrative style in her children's books is unfussy, the train of thought practical. She is never vague; her narrative is filled with facts. For instance, she always tells her reader the exact ages of the children in the stories, what they look like, and where they live, and there is a careful time sequence throughout each story. From the start the reader knows where he is. . . . (p. 31)

Descriptive passages of a picturesque nature are infrequent and brief. Noel Streatfeild writes in short, logical sentences which make a very definite impression on the reader's mind; an impression which leaves no doubt that she is *telling* the story, actually talking to her reader. And this is the essence of Noel Streatfeild's manner of writing: it is verbal. The natural result of this is that children are aware of the storyteller's personality as they listen to her narrative, and so a particular feeling of affinity between author and reader is formed. Noel Streatfeild's dramatic training, her professional awareness of spoken tones and inflections, is surely responsible to a large extent for this verbal approach to writing narrative.

As part of her strict professional attitude towards writing, Noel Streatfeild is meticulous in the research which underlies her stories. This not only involves finding out all the relevant facts about a subject, but also—which is more difficult—absorbing the atmosphere, the climate, surrounding it. (pp. 32-3)

The result of this detailed research was that in *The Circus is Coming* she created a completely convincing circus atmosphere, as well as including in her narrative all sorts of fascinating and interesting information. (p. 34)

The extreme trouble Noel Streatfeild takes over the research for her children's books is an integral part of her character as a storyteller. Those of her stories which are concerned with professional training for a particular career are documentary in their accuracy. (p. 36)

Such conscientious research and passion for accuracy could result in dullness on the part of an inexperienced or a lesser writer. But 'dull' is the last adjective to apply to Noel Streatfeild's writing. A lively sense of comedy and gaiety runs throughout her children's stories. The most fun is derived from her keen sense of the ridiculous; in humour of situation. . . . But when any of her important or 'serious' characters venture into ludicrous situations, Noel Streatfeild is careful not to detract from the reader's sympathy with them. In the tragi-comedy of the cat-swallowed goldfish in *The Bell Family* the reader feels a genuine sympathy with Andrew's distress and Ginny's anxiety, even while he laughs at the absurd situation.

In dialogue, the youngest members of the families often provide amusement by their use of difficult words, and in original mannerisms of speech, while 'below stairs' characters have some picturesque turns of phrase. A sort of light sarcasm often plays a part in the narrative. . . . (p. 37)

Apart from the actual comedy in the stories, the whole of Noel Streatfeild's writing for children is imbued with an intrinsic good humour, which reassures the reader that all will be well in the end. There are serious and sad moments, but these are resolved and pass away. Tragedy may be mentioned, but it is never explored; the overall atmosphere is light-hearted. In *Curtain Up,* for example, the Forbes children are faced with the tragic news that their father is missing at sea, and they may therefore be orphans. This event, however plays its part only as a starting-off point of the story. It is not a dramatic peak in the narrative. The information is given and digested, and other happenings absorb the main attention of the characters and the reader. Again, if the overall atmosphere of **Ballet Shoes** were not light-hearted, the three Fossil children—and the reader— might well be led to spare much more than a passing thought for their parents. But as it is, we are skilfully led away from speculation on that score. The girls are orphans, this is an essential condition of the story, and once it has been swiftly established, it is merely taken for granted throughout the rest of the narrative.

Noel Streatfeild the storyteller emerges from behind her narrative as a benevolent personality whose aim is primarily to entertain her readers, and who knows that worthwhile and successful entertainment demands the utmost attention to detail. (pp. 38-9)

Two main interests form the content of Noel Streatfeild's stories for children: family life, and the professional training of children for careers. . . . [Here] we may consider briefly the different aspects of professional training which she introduces into her stories.

First, there is the emphasis on dedication and hard work which distinguishes the professional from the amateur. (p. 40)

To the great majority of her readers, the single-minded attitude of the professional child towards work must appear as something unusual and novel. Noel Streatfeild portrays and explains this attitude without sounding in the least priggish; it is all merged into her overall desire to entertain, to tell a good story.

Recognition of outstanding talent and of the ability to get to the top is another aspect of this subject of professional training. (p. 41)

Problems of professional training, particularly those arising from the difficult temperament which often belongs to a talented child, are dealt with knowledgeably. (p. 42)

Not all the talented children in the stories are likeable characters. Talent is shown as a variable quality. (p. 43)

When a particular professional interest forms a vital part of a story, it is always introduced indirectly. It is fortuitous that the Fossil girls embark on their stage training in **Ballet Shoes,** for if Theo Dane had not become a boarder in their home, they would have never heard of Madame Fidolia's Academy. In **The Circus is Coming,** Peter and Santa are only introduced to Cob's Circus through the unexpected circumstance of their aunt's death. When the Winter family set off to stay in California in **The Painted Garden,** Jane's meeting with the Hollywood producer is sheer luck, and springs from her characteristic love of dogs. In **White Boots,** Harriet Johnson takes up skating haphazardly, as a means of strengthening her 'cottonwoolish' legs after she has been ill.

The events and plots of Noel Streatfeild's stories depend initially on a given set of circumstances, and are developed by the characters they affect. For instance, the story of **New Town** depends on the fact that Alex Bell is made Vicar of Crestal New Town and has to move from London; given this initial circumstance, the story is developed by his family's reaction to it. No time is wasted in putting the reader in the picture so far as the initial circumstances of a story are concerned. The most intricate situations are explained with the minimum of fuss. (pp. 44-5)

Noel Streatfeild is never afraid of introducing bold strokes of fate in order to implement a story. A striking example of this occurs at the beginning of **The Painted Garden,** when Miss Bean, or Peaseblossom, as the family call her, receives news of a thousand pound legacy by the very same post as Aunt Cora's invitation to California.

While Noel Streatfeild is adept at introducing incidents which relieve or lighten the main theme of a story, she is careful not to confuse the issue by bringing in too many sub-plots, or by exploiting more than one or two main characters very fully. (p. 46)

Noel Streatfeild lives with her characters for at least a year before she begins to write the story in which they are to appear; she is convinced that characters can come alive only when their author is in a position to know far more about them in his mind than he will ever write down on paper. As a result, the reader is aware that her characters did not suddenly spring into being with the first word of a book, and that their existence does not end with the last sentence: the story tells of selected incidents in their continuing lives. (pp. 46-7)

Another feature of Noel Streatfeild's characterisation is the constant physical movement of her characters. Time and again she draws the reader's attention to someone in particular by the equivalent of a stage direction in a play. And, like an apt stage direction, the character's movement tells the reader something about his feelings at that moment. (p. 49)

'My aim in a children's book is simplicity,' says Noel Streatfeild. 'I try, however large the canvas, to draw clearly the few important characters while at the same time attempting to get the feel of a school, or whatever it is, full of people dashing about doing different things but all the time remaining in the background as a noises-off effect. I do not think it is a good thing in a children's book to have too many characters.'

There is never a risk of confusion between any of the characters in her children's stories: major or minor, each one stands on his or her own feet, and has a distinct personality. Each has his own particular interests, his own way of talking, his own mannerisms, and is instantly recognisable. (pp. 50-1)

The minor characters in the stories are as a rule drawn with bolder strokes, and some are frankly exaggerated: more so than they would be in an adult novel. (p. 51)

Of all Noel Streatfeild's children's stories, perhaps **The Circus is Coming** gives one the strongest impression of a lively and varied background. While following the adventures of the chief characters, one is constantly aware of being in the midst of Cob's Circus, surrounded by lots of other people, all the animals, a whirl of noise and bustle.

Noel Streatfeild is fond of the characters in her children's stories: many of them have very human failings, some are selfish or petty, but none—save in **The House in Cornwall** [British title of **The Secret of the Lodge**]—are downright villainous. She guides their fortunes with a benign hand; however black the prospect may look at times, we know a satisfactory outcome will be reached.

A particular feature of her characterisation is the part grownups play in the stories. Many children's authors cannot tolerate adults in their books at any price; but Noel Streatfeild introduces the grown-ups naturally and as a matter of course, always referring to them by their Christian names—a habit which helpd considerably in lowering the barrier between them and the children. She gives the reader an insight into the grown-ups' minds in so far as it is relevant to the story. (pp. 51-2)

A genuine interest in one's fellow human beings is the basic requirement for successful characterisation. Without this, no author can hope to make any character appear convincing. Noel Streatfeild is intensely interested in her fellow human beings, observing them with a shrewd and often amused eye, and the result of her observation forms the basis of the characterisation in her stories. . . .

Rare indeed are writers who are able to judge their work dispassionately. And only when one regards their work as a whole is the most important feature of all apparent. This is the balance which an author achieves between one aspect and another: the successful blending of subjects, plots, atmosphere, characterisation, narrative style . . . all the ingredients which *together* make up a story. Noel Streatfeild's stories are never off-balance, because her talent as an author is of even quality throughout every aspect of her work. (p. 53)

All Noel Streatfeild's story-book families share certain characteristics. The most important and basic of these is the atmosphere of family unity that comes across to the reader. Noel Streatfeild believes strongly that children's stories should be built on secure foundations so far as family relationships between parents, parents and children, and brothers and sisters, are concerned. The children in her stories never doubt their parents' love for each other or themselves; however much the children may quarrel on occasion, at heart their loyalty to one another—to the family—is unshakeable. (p. 54)

Of course, not all the family units in the stories are families in the strict sense of the word; the Fossil 'sisters' are orphans looked after by a guardian, the Forbes children in *Curtain Up* are motherless, and during the story their father is a P.O.W. in Japan—but nevertheless the characteristic atmosphere of family solidarity is present. How is this achieved? Partly by the recurrence of family customs throughout a story, and by the use of special family words. (pp. 54-5)

The underlying feeling of family permanence and solidarity is certainly not built on a basis of material security in any of the stories; on the contrary, 'saving the penny and walking' is a common feature in all of them. There is always anxious thought about whether new clothes, holidays, and any extras can be afforded. But although money is scarce, the children are brought up to certain accepted standards of living and behaviour. The families are respectable socially, the one possible exception to this statement being the Johnsons in *White Boots*, who run a somewhat unorthodox and unbusinesslike greengrocer's shop. However, it is made clear that 'there had been a time when the Johnson family were rich'; it is only the improvidence of the previous generation that has reduced them to small shop-keeping. (pp. 55-6)

The other families are mostly professional middle-class. . . . (p. 56)

Good manners and certain criteria of well-brought-upness are always assumed. . . . Church-going too is an accepted habit in every family—not over-stressed, but mentioned casually as the normal thing.

Another shared feature of some, but not all, the families is the faithful helper, devoted to the children and their parents and usually referred to affectionately by a nickname. (pp. 56-7)

The families always run to at least three children, which affords good scope for the interplay of personalities—and also helps in achieving the impression of permanence. Although the mixture of girls and boys is on the whole about equal, the interest in the stories is focused mainly on the girls. The boys (save for some very engaging youngsters) tend to be drawn in a more reserved and less detailed manner than their sisters.

With a clear memory of her own childhood in a large family, Noel Streatfeild shows sympathetic understanding of the different viewpoints of the older, middle, and younger children. (p. 57)

It is the middle children of Noel Streatfeild's fiction families who are the most interesting, and who are generally singled out as the characters of chief interest in a story—and one remembers that Noel Streatfeild was herself a middle child. Moreover she was a child with the difficult temperament that belongs to a number of the middle children in her stories—to Nicky Heath, Phoebe Andrews, Jane Winter, and Ginny Bell. These children are all extremely independent and distinctly bossy; in their respective family circles they maintain a 'cat-that-walked-by-itself' attitude. They often say outrageous things to their brothers and sisters and even their parents, and are very apt to embark on wild-cat schemes in which they show an amazing faculty of self-delusion. They are proud of their reputations, and find it really hard to show unaccustomed feelings such as gratitude or contrition. Their 'uppishness' makes the rest of their families despair. They are filled with a determination which would be wholly admirable if it were not turned so often into the wrong channels. But, in spite of everything, these middle children are endearing to the reader, because they are presented in such an understanding and sympathetic manner—and besides, they are frequently so amusing, and always interesting in their unpredictable behaviour. (pp. 58-9)

Readers of Noel Streatfeild's stories are left with the impression that it would be pleasant to meet her fiction families, always supposing that for some reason they did not incur the disfavour of one of the middle children. They are nice people, with plenty to say for themselves, lots of initiative—and, of course, there are the specially talented amongst them. (pp. 60-1)

Barbara Ker Wilson, in her Noel Streatfeild (© *The Bodley Head Ltd 1961*), *Henry Z. Walck, Incorporated, 1964, 64 p.*

CAROLYN HEILBRUN

Twenty-seven years ago when there was no television but only books and the loneliness of long afternoons, I read **"Ballet Shoes"** by Noel Streatfeild. The memory of that book has persisted into afternoons that are not lonely enough, and into an age where, when we have mastered all our inventions, television may be the single one we continue to regret. Miss Streatfeild's new book, **"The Children on the Top Floor,"** is about two boys and two girls connected tangentially with television. The giant tube, whatever ills we may ascribe to it, has diminished neither the wonder of Miss Streatfeild's knowledge nor her story-telling gifts. . . .

"The Children on the Top Floor" is not about "the world of television." This novel, like **"Ballet Shoes,"** demonstrates, without platitudes or sanctimony, that to have a talent is to be blessed; that to love is to choose to give; that, as is evident to any child with proper parents, to be born is less satisfying than to be found on a doorstep and welcomed, on somewhat equal terms, into a world of adults more kith than kin.

Perhaps the incidents crowd in a bit toward the end of this tale, as life for children has lately become more eventful. But the 27 years which have changed me from a middle-aged child to a middle-aged woman have not, as this book makes clear, wearied Miss Streatfeild at all.

> Carolyn Heilbrun, "Books for Young Readers: 'The Children on the Top Floor'," in The New York Times Book Review (© 1965 by The New York Times Company; reprinted by permission), March 21, 1965, p. 26.

THE CHRISTIAN SCIENCE MONITOR

Miss Streatfeild brings to **"The Children on the Top Floor"** the good characterization and inside knowhow about children's careers that made her **"Shoes"** series so popular. But while she has updated the career side . . . the atmosphere remains prewar. Even if 10-14's swallow the quite-fantastic beginning, it is doubtful that they will have much sympathy with children who leave all the decisions to Nanny and the governess.

> "Children's Books in Review: 'The Children on the Top Floor'," in The Christian Science Monitor (reprinted by permission from The Christian Science Monitor; © 1965 The Christian Science Publishing Society; all rights reserved), May 4, 1965, p. 7.

THE TIMES LITERARY SUPPLEMENT

[**Away from the Vicarage**, the continuation of Noel Streatfeild's autobiography,] describes her attempt to break away from the restriction of her vicarage home and her saintly father's attempt to preserve there, if not in the parish, a vanished way of life. She is good at describing that disproportionate indignation which provides the rebellious child's necessary motive power, and good at the nostalgic recalling of details of daily life and relationships in 1918. We could have done with more such detail. The blurb claims "startling candour" for her treatment of her wild days as a R.A.D.A. student and actress. This is not apparent; it would have been better if she had either hinted more or revealed more. As it is she treats her young self with a rather grating grandmotherly tolerance and indulgence and the "frank" note is a little embarrassing.

> "Books Received: 'Away from the Vicarage'," in The Times Literary Supplement (© Times Newspapers Ltd. (London) 1965; reproduced from The Times Literary Supplement by permission), No. 3325, November 18, 1965, p. 1029.

RUTH HILL VIGUERS

Vicky's adventures and attitudes [in **On Tour**] represent what many considered typical of young women of the period. The novel is the author's own story, as **Vicarage Family** was, and it is told with the same directness and detachment. The poignance is never put into words, but it is felt. The fascinating, often amusing, background makes the book nostalgically appealing to adults who remember the twenties. It should give much pleasure to young people also, for Victoria, under her rebelliousness and brash independence, remains the sensitive, intensely loyal person she was as a child of the vicarage.

> Ruth Hill Viguers, "Stories for the Older Boys and Girls: 'On Tour'," in The Horn Book Magazine (copyright © 1965, by The Horn Book, Inc., Boston), Vol. XLI, No. 6, December, 1965, p. 638.

ZENA SUTHERLAND

[**On Tour** is] just as enjoyable as the author's description of her childhood; here the account of the Strangeways family is picked up at the end of World War I. Isobel is an artist, Louise is getting married, and Victoria (the author) is prepared to battle at the vicarage on behalf of her desire to be an actress. Surprisingly, no battle. The autobiography goes on, with a sort of wry relish, to describe Victoria Strangeways' theatrical career: her flapper days in London while studying, the local tour, and the tours in Africa and Australia. A vivid picture of the nineteen-twenties, of theatrical life, and of the Strangeways family. (pp. 170-71)

> Zena Sutherland, "New Titles for Children and Young People: 'On Tour'," in Bulletin of the Center for Children's Books (reprinted by permission of The University of Chicago Press; copyright 1966 by The University of Chicago), Vol. 19, No. 10, June, 1966, pp. 170-71.

THE JUNIOR BOOKSHELF

Miss Streatfeild, with her good background knowledge of ballet and theatre, makes an excellent guide to the young opera-goer. Unfortunately, [**Enjoying Opera**] is so condensed that she has no chance to give more than the briefest information. To anyone of about 12 who is just beginning to be interested, this is a useful introduction, giving notes on the history and production of opera, brief biographies of composers and performers, and short accounts of some of the best-known stories. It was a happy thought to include modern operas which appeal to children, such as "The little sweep" and "Amahl and the night visitors."

> "For Children from Ten to Fourteen: 'Enjoying Opera'," in The Junior Bookshelf, Vol. 30, No. 5, October, 1966, p. 319.

THE TIMES LITERARY SUPPLEMENT

The Growing Summer, which inverts the idea that children really want a ruleless, clockless, back-to-the-primitive life, shows Miss Streatfeild in excellent form. Father's only relative (his parents having been killed by a bomb) is legendary Great-Aunt Dymphna, who lives in Ireland. Mother's family is in the antipodes. So, when father is stricken by illness in the Far East, and mother is summoned to join him, it is to Aunt Dymphna's that the four . . . are hastily dispatched. . . .

To know this towering character is an education: she should be remembered long. Not so the spoilt young film-star runaway boy. . . . This dreary cardboard intruder should never have found his way into the book; he should be quickly forgotten.

> "The Lighter Side," in The Times Literary Supplement (© Times Newspapers Ltd. (London) 1966; reproduced from The Times Literary Supplement by permission), No. 3378, November 24, 1966, p. 1074.*

THE TIMES LITERARY SUPPLEMENT

The very young reader to whom Noel Streatfeild addresses her **Enjoying Opera** is not likely to be lured to the opera house by the potted history of opera forming the central chapters of this book, especially when towards the end it degenerates into little more than a list of names and dates. Now and again (as in the case of [Christoph] Gluck's and [Richard] Wagner's reforms) Miss Streatfeild's simple exposition hardly suggests specialist knowledge behind it. The author is happier in telling the stories of some favourite operas towards the end, and in her chattier chapters such as those on the function of the producer and designer.

"Men of Music," in The Times Literary Supplement *(© Times Newspapers Ltd. (London) 1966; reproduced from* The Times Literary Supplement *by permission), No. 3378, November 24, 1966, p. 1095.*

THE JUNIOR BOOKSHELF

Dr. Gareth goes to the East for a year leaving his wife and family behind. They are the traditional suburban family of "literature"; the odd thing is one never really meets a family like this. [In **The Growing Summer**] we are told it is unusual for the children to clear the table and wash up, and when they are left to their own devices in Ireland . . . , they put up a very poor show. What twelve year-old girl to-day is incapable of cooking anything beyond a boiled egg? The children are stereotyped, as is the "mad" great aunt with whom they are sent to stay. The story concerns this enforced visit and various adventures that befall them, but there is nothing new in the plot, we have had similar stories many times before. Today, at thirteen, many children are responsible young adults. Having lost their "nannies" they have had to learn to stand on their own feet at a much earlier age.

[It] is a book for the "lazy" reader, no demands are made on his imagination. Books for this age group should be interesting, lively and stimulating, none of these adjectives can be applied to the novel in question.

"For Children from Ten to Fourteen: 'The Growing Summer'," in The Junior Bookshelf, Vol. 31, No. 1, February, 1967, p. 61.

BARBARA WERSBA

["**The Magic Summer**," American title of "**The Growing Summer**"] is a charming book, and also an empty one. Something has gone very wrong.

What has gone wrong with "**The Magic Summer**" is its magic. The components are promising: a manor house in Ireland, a mad old aunt and four nieces and nephews who are bundled off to her for the summer. So far, so good. . . . A runaway boy appears and takes up secret residence in the house, giving us hope of suspense. Here the plot falters, and we are burdened with so many pages of the children's attempts to cook and clean, iron and launder, that we begin to think that the author is more interested in home economics than fiction. This, of course, is unfair. She is trying to contrast the youngsters' cautious practicality with Aunt Dymphna's unfettered love of life, and show how each child receives "a touch of the poet" by the end of summer. A worthy theme, but one—alas—which is drowned in dishwater.

Barbara Wersba, "Books for Young Readers: 'The Magic Summer'," in The New York Times Book Review (© 1967 by The New York Times Company; reprinted by permission, May 14, 1967, p. 30.

THE JUNIOR BOOKSHELF

Tim, the central character [of **Caldicott Place**], is one of Miss Streatfeild's most attractive: he does the opposite to what the adults suggest, with excellent results. Though her old loves of stage and ballet reappear here, the author's chief theme is the adjusting to serious tragedy which can disrupt any family suddenly. Here father's car crash results in a head injury which temporarily makes him withdraw from life. . . . The involuntary bad behaviour of the family under the stress of moving first into a cramped flat without treasured possessions and then into the vast unfamiliar mansion is sympathetically drawn. . . . Tim's faith brings about his father's cure in unorthodox manner. There are some delightful smaller characters like "Edup-when-pressed", so called through her mother's belief in her reluctance to work. The book is marred, however, by the scarcely veiled patronage towards suburbia at the beginning. (pp. 53-4)

"For Children from Ten to Fourteen: 'Caldicott Place'," in The Junior Bookshelf, Vol. 32, No. 1, February, 1968, pp. 53-4.

MARGERY FISHER

Noel Streatfeild's characters are built on a simple principle, one dominant trait for each. The central figure of **Caldicott Place** . . . has a certain bounce and independence which come to the fore when unexpectedly he is left a huge neglected mansion. . . . [The] idea of a holiday home for homeless children somehow grows and comes to fruition. So we get the familiar Streatfeild situation, a group of ill-assorted children— rich, spoilt Athene, timid Freddie who is heir to a great estate, the problem child Sophie; and from the assortment come the storms and calms of a highly skilled but somehow rather cold story. Readable though it is, up to the minute in social *mores*, I found myself thinking back wistfully to **White Boots** and **Ballet Shoes** and other stories from that early period when the Streatfeild boys and girls, still with one trait apiece, really came to life. (pp. 1091-92)

Margery Fisher, "Friends and Enemies," in her Growing Point, Vol. 6, No. 9, April, 1968, pp. 1089-92.*

ZENA SUTHERLAND

[**The Family at Caldicott Place,** American title of **Caldicott Place**] has a few contrivances and a pat ending; it also has several situations of great appeal: the integration of the foster-children, the move to the country and the solving of accompanying financial problems, and the return of father. The most appealing aspect of the book is, however, the easy, practiced writing of Mrs. Streatfeild: her attractive and varied (some just ever-so-slightly typed comic-rural) characters, the natural flow of the writing, and the conversations that show a keen ear for dialogue.

Zena Sutherland, "New Titles for Children and Young People: 'The Family at Caldicott Place'," in Bulletin of the Center for Children's Books (reprinted by permission of The University of Chicago Press; copy-

right 1969 by the University of Chicago), Vol. 22, No. 7, March, 1969, p. 119.

MARGERY FISHER

Noel Streatfeild has written few stories more pertinent than this study of young Harriet and her career as a champion ice-skater [*White Boots*]. The fierce pressure of competitions, the jealousies and contrivances, are related with quiet humour and with sympathy for children who suffer from parental ambition.

> *Margery Fisher, "A Pair of Ice Skates," in her* Growing Point, *Vol. 8, No. 6, December, 1969, p. 1452.**

THE TIMES LITERARY SUPPLEMENT

Noel Streatfeild's position in the children's book world is unique. She has had all the accolades. . . . Her first children's book, which has withstood the passage of time extraordinarily well, was published in 1936, the very year when the Carnegie Medal, that symbol of a new attitude towards literature for children, was first awarded. Miss Streatfeild herself has had a good deal to do with the changing attitude, and if, over this long span of time, her books have shown talent rather than genius, this does not trouble her child readers. It is we, the adults, who nowadays prefer fiction for children to be stronger and less predictable.

And Miss Streatfeild's subject-matter is easily despised. Her children belong mostly to the educated if impoverished middle classes and "the careers she writes about have tended rather to be the glamorous, wish-fulfilling kind", as John Rowe Townsend once observed rather chillingly. Even children have been known to express their preference for *The Growing Summer,* not because of splendidly eccentric Great-Aunt Dymphna but because no one in the family dances or plays the violin or even acts. (The cardboard boy film star is soon forgotten.)

At worst Noel Streatfeild can write very lazily indeed. . . . But mostly she is endlessly inventive, full of verve and real understanding of the surfaces of childhood. The stories are rich in documentary interest and entertainment, escapism of a most satisfying sort. She has managed, like her characters, to keep real feeling, deep emotion, at arm's length. Reading her attractive autobiography, *A Vicarage Family,* one begins to realize why. . . .

[*Thursday's Child*] is farther away from reality than ever, in spite of the details of life on the canals and in a stock company. Set at the turn of the century, when she was herself a child, it has all the ingredients of a romantic fantasy. The foundling girl, who turns out to be a natural actress, and the orphans, who turn out to be the grandchildren of a marquess, run away together from an orphanage ruled over by a villainous matron. The characters are thinner than usual but the plot is excellently worked and it is really only when one compares the orphanage with Joan Aiken's in *The Wolves of Willoughby Chase* that one realizes what a pale shadow of the possibility this book is.

> *"Pennies from Heaven," in* The Times Literary Supplement *(© Times Newspapers Ltd. (London) 1970; reproduced from* The Times Literary Supplement *by permission), No. 3583, October 30, 1970, p. 1263.**

THE JUNIOR BOOKSHELF

[Margaret Thursday] is a forthright, determined extrovert with a life of her own apart from the story [of *Thursday's Child*]. Her words and actions are a constant surprise and delight, and Miss Streatfeild never makes the mistake of solving her identity, though her resounding success on the boards at the end as Little Lord Fauntleroy may be intended as a clue. The rest of the story is less successful. No doubt orphanage matrons were greedy and villainous, but the enormities come not as social revelations but as piling on the agony. No doubt countesses occasionally noticed their understaff with kindness, but the story of Margaret's friend Lavinia and her two little brothers at the orphanage, whose noble descent is revealed by the Earl and Countess, is unashamed novelette, unworthy of that splendid creation Margaret Thursday.

> *"The New Books: 'Thursday's Child'," in* The Junior Bookshelf, *Vol. 35, No. 1, February, 1971, p. 72.*

MURIEL HUTTON

[*Thursday's Child* is a] substantial book of absorbing fiction, among so many puffed up with secondary virtues. 'After Dickens' in its wealth of incident and mosaic of chapters; focusing with varying intensity on each of four central orphans and many subsidiary characters, it has power to play upon our sentiments and on our credulity.

> *Muriel Hutton, "Book Reviews: 'Thursday's Child'," in* The School Librarian, *Vol. 19, No. 1, March, 1971, p. 73.*

MARY M. BURNS

Although the setting and situations [of *Thursday's Child*] are in the turn-of-the-century tradition of "orphan stories," the heroine is a remarkably contemporary character whose final decision to remain independent of her would-be benefactors is logical and consistent with a fully realized personality. A fresh and sprightly addition to a perennially popular genre.

> *Mary M. Burns, "Spring Booklist: 'Thursday's Child'," in* The Horn Book Magazine *(copyright © 1971 by The Horn Book, Inc., Boston), Vol. XLVII, No. 3, June, 1971, p. 294.*

SANDRA PAXFORD

[All Streatfeild's characters] have one thing in common—security. This security need not come from your own parents or relatives, but from someone who is with you all the time and cares about you. Indeed, they may be downright eccentric like Aunt Dymphna in *The Growing Summer* or matter-of-fact like the barge woman, Mrs. Smith, in *Thursday's Child*, sensible, practical and loving like Sylvia Brown, the children's guardian, in *Ballet Shoes*, or rather strait-laced, but thoroughly loyal, warm-hearted and trustworthy like Hannah, the housekeeper, in *Curtain Up*, but they always exist. Somewhere throughout the story, these people remain steadfast to provide the children with a measure of security, without which no healthy child can grow up satisfactorily.

I like the idea of the Johnstone family in *Caldicott Place* wanting to provide a home and a family background for "every child who wants somewhere to go during the holidays, but always the same place and the same people''. Certainly, they did not decide to do this until the end of the story, but if they had been inclined this way at the beginning of the book, they might well have been what I should term "sickening do-gooders"; it is only after they have come through certain difficulties and met other less fortunate children that they make this decision. In *Thursday's Child*, Margaret, the heroine, knows that she will always have a few friends available who care about her all the time and encourage her to be a person in her own right. In *The Growing Summer*, the Gareth children on holiday in Ireland cope with strange, unfamiliar surroundings and conditions— but they cope, as a family, quite admirably.

In Miss Streatfeild's earlier books for children, such as *Curtain Up, Party Frock* [British title of *Party Shoes*], and *The Children of Primrose Lane*, written during the Second World War, this same spirit of security runs through them all. One feels that "everything will come right in the end, if we can make it so, by keeping on trying". After many setbacks, everything does come right. I especially like the idea of the Andrews children producing a pageant in a small country village at the end of the war, and different people from different backgrounds coming to help with it. . . . (pp. 290-91)

However, two of my favourite books by Miss Streatfeild are *The Bell Family* and *The Fearless Treasure*, written in the 1950's. These books may sound dissimilar—but are they? Alex and Cathy Bell run their family in London, and later on in a new town with the minimum of money and the maximum of good family life. The parishioners of Canon Bell's London church, St. Mark's, ably assist him, but in Crestal, his own family have to rally round to make his new parishioners realise that he regards his church as a "family house". *The Fearless Treasure* is a book that stands in a class of its own (I did not manage to read it until I was 21, and I've never read anything like it before or since!) where six different English children are shown their individual patterns in history in most unusual, yet not unlikely, ways. At the end of the book, they go home to their different family backgrounds, as they know they will, but each means to follow his pattern and embroider it in the future. Each boy and girl has learned something to his or her advantage. . . .

"Thursday's child has far to go", and all her children are Thursday's children. Good luck to them. (p. 292)

Sandra Paxford, "Children Who Have Far to Go," in The Junior Bookshelf, Vol. 35, No. 5, October, 1971, pp. 290-92.*

THE TIMES LITERARY SUPPLEMENT

Beyond the Vicarage is the last volume of Noel Streatfeild's autobiographical trilogy. It is also probably the most significant, since it deals with her life as a writer. . . .

Miss Streatfeild is a person to be respected. She is remarkably clear-sighted about her own shortcomings; she considers herself and her friends to have been in their youth trivial and irresponsible compared with the young people of today. She knows she is a product of her class and generations, the last generation to have maids and to be waited on. She knows too that she does not write particularly well, in the academic sense; there are sentences in this book so clumsily put together that they have to be read two or three times to get the sense. She is realistic, too, about her strong points, such as, in the literary sphere, her ear for dialogue, which she puts down to her acting

experience. There are countless examples of this authentic gift in *Beyond the Vicarage*. . . . Her books will continue to give pleasure, especially (though she may not thank one for saying so) her books for children.

"Amusement and After," in The Times Literary Supplement (© Times Newspapers Ltd. (London) 1971; reproduced from The Times Literary Supplement by permission), No. 3633, October 15, 1971, p. 1252.

ISABEL QUIGLY

[In 1936 came *Ballet Shoes*,] a children's book still loved nearly two generations later, in which [Streatfeild's] gift for immediacy and solidity was used to the full. . . . There was an exactly reproduced copy in it of the form needed by a twelve-year-old going on the stage, filled in for the eldest of its three heroines. There was talk about money and the exact cost of clothes for auditions, about the impossibility of paying school fees . . . , rooms were let to make ends meet, Nanny took a cut in wages. It was admitted that looks were a thing that counted, even at twelve. This was stark realism in the children's book world of those days, steeped in its [Arthur] Ransome, always on holiday and horseback. . . .

[Streatfeild] simply wrote, without theories, because she had children's stories to tell, a publisher who guessed this and urged her to write them, and a child audience starved for the 'real' world and loving the exoticism of 'professional' middleclass children whose interests were at last made more adult and more responsible than those of the current toughies (those sheltered, boyish little girls!) with their contrived adventures. *Tennis Shoes*, the next book, was about young professionals in sport, dedicated prodigies with the tenacity to make champions. It was miles from the middleclass amateurism of those days, it took children out of the nursery into a harsher world of competition and high standards, removing some at least of the guards and screens and shutters and Nannies, and suggesting a wider field of adventure than tree-climbing, sailing and midnight feasts. If light now pours blindingly into the once discreet world of children's books, some of the credit for letting it in must go to [Noel Streatfeild]. . . . (p. 555)

Isabel Quigly, "Beyond the Vicarage," in The Spectator (© 1971 by The Spectator; reprinted by permission of The Spectator), Vol. 227, No. 7477, October 16, 1971, pp. 554-55.

THE JUNIOR BOOKSHELF

[*Beyond the Vicarage*] is written with objectivity, using the device of writing in the third person. It is an honest book which, while it answers many of the questions readers would like to ask their favourite authors, does not pander to idle curiosity nor add personal details for effect.

The most impressive section of the book deals with the author's experiences in the war in Deptford. It is not only a vivid and moving account of what happened, but one cannot read it without realising the unassuming courage of the writer and her compassion for those who suffered so greatly. Even in these tragic situations, her wry humour and sense of the ridiculous lights up what could have been unbearable occasions.

Noel Streatfeild's contribution to children's and adult literature has been a distinguished and popular one and she is always eminently readable. Her modest account of her life will give pleasure to old and young. It is entertaining, evocative and very human.

> *"The New Books: 'Beyond the Vicarage',"* in The Junior Bookshelf, *Vol. 36, No. 2, April, 1972, p. 122.*

LOIS E. SAVAGE

"Beyond the Vicarage" deals with surface details of a life that should be exciting and stimulating. The book is neither. Too many words are used to record incidental information about house furnishings, habits of pets, and problems with house-keepers employed for the author's mother. Such minutiae could be of interest only to neighborhood gossips, not the general public and certainly not to teenage readers.

Sections of the book which cover Miss Streatfeild's welfare work in the slums of London and her wartime experiences as a canteen worker during air raids show warmth and humor. Characterization of others is well done; description of her own career as a successful author is painfully self-conscious. (pp. 151-52)

> *Lois E. Savage, "'Beyond the Vicarage'," in* Best Sellers *(copyright 1972, by the University of Scranton), Vol. 32, No. 6, June 15, 1972, pp. 151-52.*

MAY HILL ARBUTHNOT and ZENA SUTHERLAND

Noel Streatfeild's *Shoes* books are all vocational in their themes, but they manage to avoid the heavy earnestness that generally pervades such books. The two best are *Ballet Shoes* and *Circus Shoes.* . . .

How [*Ballet Shoes*] manages to be as gay as it is rests entirely with Streatfeild's ability to make everyday events somehow amusing. . . .

For the child with a special interest in ballet or any sort of theatrical life, these books are valuable. They take a serious attitude toward professions and amplify the difficulties without minimizing the satisfactions. (p. 438)

> *May Hill Arbuthnot and Zena Sutherland, "Modern Fiction," in their* Children and Books *(copyright © 1947, 1957, 1964, 1972 by Scott, Foresman and Company; reprinted by permission), fourth edition, Scott, Foresman, 1972, pp. 420-93.**

VALERIE ALDERSON

[In *When the Siren Wailed*] Noel Streatfeild has written about evacuees from London. . . . In the end, of course, everything works out all right, but there is a theatricality about the whole plot which has little to do with the real events of the period. A somewhat over-romanticised story which has none of the authenticity of books like K. Barnes's *Visitors from London* or Miss Streatfeild's own *Children of Primrose Lane* which were written at the time.

> *Valerie Alderson, "Reviews: 'When the Siren Wailed'," in* Children's Book Review *(© 1975 by Five Owls Press Ltd.; all rights reserved), Vol. V, No. 1, Spring, 1975, p. 38.*

THE JUNIOR BOOKSHELF

Times remembered are often only real to those with whom we remember them, and it is not easy to bring them to life for others. The children in [*When the Sirens Wailed*] have a sadly dated quality without the dignity of historical imagery; they seem to hover in a no-man's land between past and present.

> *"The New Books: 'When the Sirens Wailed',"* in The Junior Bookshelf, *Vol. 39, No. 2, April, 1975, p. 136.*

B. J. MARTIN

However young the reader of [*A Young Person's Guide to Ballet*], the interest can always be accompanied by awareness. I wish, therefore, that Noel Streatfeild had included more about appreciation in her otherwise excellent story of a boy and a girl learning to dance, for there are at least seven companies of varying quality regularly touring the provinces now. Her earnest desire to give, perhaps too much, purely factual information has led in several places to stilted and unnatural dialogue. Also it is difficult to believe that the children's parents (a doctor and a vet) would be hard-pressed to find the price of a theatre seat.

But these things aside, the book is sure to delight the many ballet enthusiasts among the children of today. . . . It sensibly does not make light of the difficulties, hard work and disappointments which face the child bent on a dancing career, and by the end you really do care what happens to the children in the story.

> *B. J. Martin, "Arts and Crafts: 'A Young Person's Guide to Ballet'," in* The School Librarian, *Vol. 23, No. 3, September, 1975, p. 259.*

THE JUNIOR BOOKSHELF

[*A Young Person's Guide to Ballet*] has been written with the ordinary child in mind, the one who wants to learn to dance, with the result that some ballet steps are described, so is the way lessons are run and the history of ballet, together with synopses of some ballets and histories of dancers and choreographers. There is much here to absorb and interest children, so it seems a shame that it should all have been written from such a height. It is not a fictional story, in the proper sense of the word, so one does not expect to become absorbed in the story line or the characters, but it would have made easier, more pleasant reading if one had not been aware of the writer pulling the strings from first to last. In addition, in spite of the fact that the author has loved and watched ballet for years, the way she passes on the information makes it all seem very third hand, as if it were researched information rather than knowledge she had accumulated over the years. Balletomanes will enjoy the book regardless of the way in which it is written; those not so dedicated might not press on, thus losing much valuable information and knowledge on the subject.

> *"The New Books: 'A Young Person's Guide to Ballet'," in* The Junior Bookshelf, *Vol. 39, No. 5, October, 1975, p. 342.*

HEIDI von OBENAUER

I wish when I were around nine or ten, someone had given me this book to read. Like all other children who dream of dancing,

I was ripe for a book which viewed the ballet with wide-eyed wonder and common sense, one that could teach me about the art and make me see more clearly the work and problem sides of where my dreams would lead me.

"A Young Person's Guide To Ballet" is a down-to-earth introduction to what happens in a ballet class. . . . The attitude toward technique inherent in the text is an unusually sound one. And because the treatment of the male ballet student is so realistic (not overly encouraged by anyone but his teacher), this is an excellent book for a boy.

The historical material is reliable. . . .

This book's great virtue is its attitude toward studying and pursuing a career in ballet, which is portrayed as both genuine and realistic. (These children do not become prodigies of The Royal at the book's finish.) There are, however, problems with some of the other attitudes of the text. This is a British book. And it is most definitely a ballet book. The comments on Isadora Duncan, Martha Graham (who is likened in approach to Isadora) and the view of modern dance are subtly pejorative. . . .

As to the state of our ballet, the intimation in the text is that America is not quite classical, and our ballet is relegated to a nebish area the author calls "American dancing." No American ballet dancers are shown or discussed. Ironically, though the author states that the old ballets such as "Spectre de la Rose," "Petrouchka" and "The Dying Swan" are no longer seen, these works are currently in the repertoires of American dancers and American companies.

These biases should be pointed out to the young reader, and labeled as another possible viewpoint on the dance scene. But they are gentle enough that they need not deter you from buying and giving the book. It's charming nevertheless. I still wish I could have read it back when I was nine.

> *Heidi von Obenauer, "Books: 'A Young Person's Guide to Ballet'," in* Dance Magazine *(copyright 1975 by Danad Publishing Company, Inc.), Vol. 49, No. 12, December, 1975, p. 94.*

MARY CADOGAN

[In *Far to Go*] Noel Streatfeild skilfully conveys the stringent professionalism of the serious theatrical child: she communicates the total involvement behind the scenes and on stage that can transform even the performances of "tawdry, seedy, bad actors" into something which compels belief. She is slightly less successful, however, in sustaining a sense of period atmosphere, despite her colourful evocations of fog-swathed streets and horse-drawn cabs.

The story is slight but well structured, and lively enough to ensure a wide appeal. Its brisk pace quickens to the excitement of chase and melodrama when Margaret is abducted by the now insane ex-matron of her old orphanage. . . . Satisfyingly Margaret displays more fighting spirit than many authentic Victorian story-book heroines might have done in similar circumstances. Throughout *Far To Go* the robustness of Margaret Thursday has a modern rather than a Victorian flavour.

> *Mary Cadogan, "Victorian Melodrama," in* The Times Literary Supplement *(© Times Newspapers Ltd. (London) 1976; reproduced from* The Times Literary Supplement *by permission), No. 3900, December 10, 1976, p. 1552.**

MARY CADOGAN and PATRICIA CRAIG

The well-chaperoned child star of impeccable propriety had been a feature of American film studios as far back as the early 1900s; but it was not until the 1920s in England that the middle-class images of model child and child actress or ballet dancer began to coalesce. Noel Streatfeild was the first children's author to express the theatre's increasing social respectability . . . in a book which is respectable also from a literary point of view; and *Ballet Shoes*, which came out in 1936, remains the best example of the type of fiction which began with it— the family story with a theatrical bias.

It is appropriate that this book should use conventions of the media which provide its subject matter. It is stagey in the obvious sense of being about the preparation for careers on the stage, and also in the sense of being contrived; but the contrivance is that of a fairy tale, which is appropriate both for a children's book and for the theatre. The limitations imposed by a theatrical form are made to work here as a valid part of the author's whole disciplined approach. In the theatre, for example, every line must be relevant, and it is from the strict relevance of Noel Streatfeild's expression that much of her humour derives, since the most direct conclusions (particularly when reached by a child) usually are also the wittiest. (pp. 286-87)

The title *Ballet Shoes* perhaps is not the most apt one for this book, since only one child—Posy—has ambitions to be a dancer; but it is to Posy's ambitions that everything in the end is subordinated, including the artistic integrity of the oldest child [Pauline]. In Posy, the economy of the author's method of presentation is seen at its most stringent. Posy not only has no characteristic which does not relate to her dancing, she has no existence outside of a ballet-school context. She is simply the most basic idea of a ballet dancer embodied, and for this reason the author cuts out the "sensitive", soul-searching, self-realizing processes which so weakened the presentation of other theatrical or musical children. . . . Posy is ruthless, exhibitionist, and these qualities are suggested to be an effect of her startling ability. She remains, however, a charming fairy-tale figure. Noel Streatfeild often introduces a clichéd image or character trait only to give it an enlivening twist: here, the Russian child, Petrova, is the one who is *not* a dancer; "Madame" is there, imperial Russian to the soles of her dancer's feet, but she does not speak in the dreadful broken English common to most children's-book foreigners; Gum reappears in the last chapter, but is not in time to keep the family from splitting up, nor to prevent the sale of their orderly and sedate house in the Cromwell Road. . . . (pp. 287-88)

Not the least feature of the book's skilful construction is the character of Petrova Fossil; she is of a mechanical turn of mind, which provides a balance for the stage enthusiasm of the other two, without in the least upsetting the theatrical bias of the book as a whole. . . .

Petrova's obsession with cars and aeroplanes is an offshoot of the short-lived adulation which, in the '20s and '30s, was accorded to women who made their mark as aviators, explorers, engineers: the glamour of these as professions for women was related to their apparent unsuitability, to the potent attractiveness of the exception which is held to prove the rule. . . . The idea of women as mechanics or electricians lost much of its singularity during the war, when it became a commonplace; and in the post-war rash of propaganda designed to promote the return of all those working women to the home, occupations involving a high degree of technical skill became unfashionable.

With the three Fossils, however, Noel Streatfeild has managed to indicate a whole range of occupational possibilities open to girls; she even suggests that Petrova's ambition may be the most worthwhile. . . . (p. 288)

What *was* important, to Noel Streatfeild and her readers, was an image of child stars . . . which [fascinated] the author. . . . Speculation about the origin and lives of the glittery, sequined little performers . . . provided the germ for many of her books; her own experience of drama school and as a repertory actress . . . ensured a background authenticity which imposes order even on the least realistic of her plots. *Ballet Shoes* consciously avoids realism in its treatment of character; *Tennis Shoes* (1937), which followed it, contains as its star the first of her series of difficult, self-opinionated, prickly children who *are* real, in the sense that even in outline they are recognizable. (She was to perfect this type in Jane Winter in *The Painted Garden*, 1949.) Nicky Heath trains to be a tennis champion in secret; she cannot bear it to be known that she requires training. . . . (p. 289)

Noel Streatfeild took something of a risk with Nicky Heath: readers at the time were not used to heroines who behaved in a way which was consistently opposed to the principles of team spirit, self-effacement, thoughtfulness for others, and so on. None of the other characters is strong enough to shift attention away from perverse Nicky. She is surrounded with siblings who are superficially more attractive; but these too are less than understanding in their treatment of their sister. . . . The important point that *Tennis Shoes* makes is untypical: it is that ''team spirit'' is not conducive to individual achievement. Nicky comes out on top because of her perky, unsuppressible egotism; she has a self-assured disregard for conformist pressures which exasperates her sister. . . . This was written at a time when girls were being inundated with fiction which urged the suppression of one's own objectives and the promotion of everyone else's. The mythology of the best house in the school, the best team in the neighbourhood, the best school in the country, implied above all a concerted effort in which every girl was expected to do her bit, but in which no one personality was conceded to be of more ultimate importance than any other. As a corollary, other people's achievements could be applauded, but it was ''bad form'' to relish one's own. Nicky's ''unsporting'' behaviour culminates in an incident which takes place when she is playing in a county junior championship match: she serves a double fault, flings down her tennis racket, and stamps her foot. Her family is outraged. . . . (pp. 289-91)

The whole book, in fact, is an argument for the special treatment of special people—in spite of the explicit denial of this which occurs on the last page. . . . (p. 291)

Tennis Shoes was followed by *The Circus is Coming* (1938). Again, the background is meticulously observed; again, the two children who are its chief characters are treated fairly—so fairly, in fact, that they are not endowed with any special capabilities. . . . In the end, they are fitted out with training schemes: Peter prepares to be a groom, Santa a gymnast—but only because in that environment there is no place for anyone who does not work.

That principle can be shown to apply with equal force in a wider social context: almost all Noel Streatfeild's books are concerned with children who make the most of their abilities,

in order to earn money or simply as a means of self-expression. (Her performing children may be of either sex, though usually they are girls; no distinction is made between girls' ambitions and boys', and unlike most other ''career'' stories, there is no reference in Noel Streatfeild to the matrimonial advantages of any profession. Even pretty girls of sixteen or so never consider that they may be other than self-supporting, and certainly no ambitious child sets an artificial limit to the duration of her chosen career.) Two exceptions are *The House in Cornwall* [British title of *The Secret of the Lodge*] (1940) an unmemorable adventure story involving a kidnapped prince, and the more successful wartime *Children of Primrose Lane* [British title of *Stranger in Primrose Lane*] (1941), in which a group of resourceful working-class London children capture a spy: the actual capture is effected by two girls who wrap him up in a rug and sit on him. If spies have to be caught this obviously is the way to do it: with panache, exuberance, and a dogged British determination. . . . This type of thumbs-up, Dad's Army phraseology was used widely as part of the national effort to keep up morale. The mood in this country in 1941 was very much one of doing one's bit, the blunter aspects of which are bound to be conveyed in a lighthearted children's book. . . . However, patriotism here is as muted as possible; only once is the business of spy-catching acknowledged to be more than an exhilarating romp. . . . (pp. 291-92)

The character of Millie Evans, the child horror in [*Children of Primrose Lane*] is adjusted precisely to the requisite social level. Where the middle-class children of the other books are self-assertive and contrary, Millie is pert, self-satisfied, curled and frilled by the kind of mother who likes a good cry at the pictures. ''Our Millie'' whines if anyone speaks crossly to her . . . but the other five children, who conform more or less to an ideal of childhood unpretentiousness, will not put up with any kind of showing off. . . . (pp. 292-93)

It is an index of Noel Streatfeild's skill that she can create awful children and proceed to make them likeable, without altering their characters in any radical way. (Incidentally the qualities which *make* Millie awful are precisely those which tend to be imposed on pretty little girls by adults who subscribe to the most conservative theory of femininity: coyness, sugary sweetness, flirtatiousness, an ability to simper and a habit of trading on their good looks. Millie can be as sensible as anyone, but because she *is* clever she has found out that in certain circumstances it pays off to appear silly.) Nicky, Millie and the others come off not simply because they are amusing or true-to-type; they are acceptable almost on their own terms. (The qualification is necessary because their own terms *are* inflated: this is part of their awfulness.) Technically, this is achieved because their positive qualities are shown in action, not merely stated; on a realistic level because often they *do* have something to be conceited about; and morally, because the origins of their ill-adjustment are suggested. Jane Winter (*The Painted Garden*, 1949) suffers from acute resentment of the fact that her brother and sister are more obviously talented than she is. . . . When she is chosen to play the part of Mary in a film version of *The Secret Garden* she makes herself insufferable by lording it over everyone, on the set and off. She is not treated with the respect which she considers her due. . . . (p. 293)

Jane does not blossom into an accomplished actress. She has been considered suitable for this part only because of her natural resemblance to spoilt, cantankerous Mary at the beginning of Frances Hodgson Burnett's story; she can convey Mary's sulky aggressiveness with a minimum of acting. The transformation which is effected in Mary's nature is not repeated in Jane; the book's moral implications are more subtle than that. . . . It is, of course, the satisfaction which Jane gets from having done something well which makes her nicer; there is no suggestion that the niceness will remain. What she really craves is appreciation; this is a common, but not a "nice" trait. At its most tangible, vulgar and extravagant level, appreciation takes the form of orchids—"'Hundreds of them! Real, film star flowers.'" It is at the point when these are presented to Jane— incidentally, the end of the book—that her isolated acting success and her sense of personal worth can crystallize, to become something that is safely over, but which has had its effect. Jane's original ambition has been to train dogs; even here, there is no pandering to the readers' expectations of easy fulfilment. The boy who plays Dickon in the film, one of the few people whom Jane likes, presents her with a reed pipe like the one which he uses to tame wild animals. However, "To play pipes needs patience and a certain natural ability. Jane had neither." She makes no progress with her pipe playing, and obviously is in for a disillusionment when she tries it out on real animals.

The setting for *The Painted Garden* is California; two minor characters in the book are Pauline and Posy Fossil, who have grown up without any of the fuss, mawkishness or annoying unrealism which has attended the ageing of innumerable other children's-book characters. They remain fantasy figures, self-sufficient and unbothered by emotional troubles. Again, if people in children's books must grow up, this is one of the two ways in which it can be done: complete artificiality is necessary, or complete realism. . . . It is the in-between course which tends to result in over-blown sentimentality, hesitancy, or falseness of tone.

After *The Painted Garden* there is a slight but perceptible falling off in Noel Streatfeild's style. (Perhaps this was inevitable; *The Painted Garden* provided a standard which could not easily be maintained.) *White Boots* (1951) is a lightweight but competent tale of two young ice skaters: one has been brought up to be a champion . . . ; the other builds herself up steadily by unostentatious hard work. The author's admirable restraint is still in evidence: there is no spectacular success for Harriet, merely one or two indications that she *may* do well. *White Boots* is less successful than some of the earlier books chiefly because its subject matter to a certain extent has had an influence on its treatment; the kind of light, superficial glamour which adheres to ice skating, ballroom dancing, circus or music-hall performances, certain types of water sports such as surfing, has crept into the writing of this book. The author's detachment has receded by several degrees, which makes for a lessening in the sharpness of outline. Even the name Lalla Moore is almost too authentic in this context for an ice-skating child: it is neither outrageously idiosyncratic, like Posy Fossil, nor determinedly unpretentious, like Jane Winter. It imparts to the book its own philistine connotations.

The encroaching vulgarity in Noel Streatfeild's books culminates in the sleeveless black plastic mini-dresses which are worn by Gemma (another unfortunate name, this time because it was unfashionable at the time when the character was conceived) Bow, an ex-film star, and her two cousins, during performances of the sub-pop group into which they have formed themselves. In the four Gemma books there is hardly a memorable episode: there is the usual near-fatal accident (near-fatal this time in terms of career, not life); the usual end-of-term

play in which actress Gemma shines; the usual singing and ballet-dancing children; and a boring small boy whose only enthusiasm is for "swirling" tunes (perhaps it is because this word is *un*usual that it seems to be spattered all over the text). The Gemma books are propped up by their many references to contemporary facts of life: Headstone Comprehensive; kidney machines; television advertising; the children even speak occasionally in a diluted pop-world jargon: "'I don't need a room for my thing and Lydia does'". For this reason they may acquire a sociological interest. *Ballet Shoes* and certain other of Noel Streatfeild's better books, however, were not at any time considered out-of-date.

This is not to minimize the effect of their historical evocations, but simply to suggest that these are not detachable from the themes of the books. The victory atmosphere of *Party Frock*, the mood conjured up by the idea of a circus at Carlisle on a wet Saturday afternoon in the 1930s, have a mysteriously compelling cohering function. Perhaps the flashy, grease-paint ambience of a stage training academy needed to be balanced by a way of life as highly regulated as the Fossil sisters'. This, in its turn, is part of a wider orderliness which has all but disappeared, and this makes a similar theme more difficult to treat effectively in the 1960s, without a great deal of literary adjustment. (pp. 293-96)

Mary Cadogan and Patricia Craig, "New Vistas,"
in their You're A Brick, Angela!: A New Look at
Girls' Fiction from 1839 to 1975 *(© Mary Cadogan*
and Patricia Craig 1976), Victor Gollancz Ltd, 1976,
*pp. 286-308.**

DENISE M. WILMS

The happy ending Streatfeild fashions [in *When the Sirens Wailed*, U.S. title of *When the Siren Wailed*] could be called contrived, but it's satisfying—enough within the realm of possibility to be believed and certainly fitting Streatfeild's well-developed sense of the storytelling craft. (pp. 1095-96)

Denise M. Wilms, "Children's Books: 'When the
Sirens Wailed'," in Booklist *(reprinted by permis-*
sion of the American Library Association; copyright
© 1977 by the American Library Association), Vol.
73, No. 14, March 15, 1977, pp. 1095-96.

ZENA SUTHERLAND

Some of the terminology [in *When the Sirens Wailed*] will be unfamiliar to readers (the wartime trains "is something chronic," a woman complains) but can usually be understood because of the context. Streatfeild's style is lively and her descriptions colorful; the characters are well-drawn and the dialogue is excellent. While the problems and fortunes of the children should engage readers, it is the atmosphere of wartime England—both in London and in the country—that gives the book its strength.

Zena Sutherland, "New Titles for Children and Young
People: 'When the Sirens Wailed'," in Bulletin of
the Center for Children's Books *(reprinted by per-*
mission of The University of Chicago Press; © 1977
by the University of Chicago), Vol. 30, No. 8, April,
1977, p. 133.

THE JUNIOR BOOKSHELF

After forty years in the field Noel Streatfeild, incredibly, can still tell a story with the same glow and the same sturdy common-sense beneath the sparkle. *Far To Go* is a sequel to *Thursday's Child*. Margaret Thursday, the orphan with the mysterious antecedents, is as cocky as ever and as talented. . . .

The story is, appropriately enough, pure melodrama. This matters little, for Miss Streatfeild has always been able to turn dross into gold. The splendid heroine dominates the action and the well-drawn group of eccentrics who surround her. Surely a winner with children, both in its book form and in the television version which must surely follow.

> "'Far to Go'," in The Junior Bookshelf, *Vol. 41,
> No. 2, April, 1977, p. 121.*

MARGERY FISHER

A Vicarage Family [is] the first of three fictionalised autobiographies . . . which give Noel Streatfeild's many readers, young as well as adult, an insight into the source of her material and her humour. It is risky to claim this first tale of life in an urban vicarage at the turn of the century as a source of style as well, for it is not clear whether the unmistakeable Streatfeild dialogue, the chatter for instance of the three Fossils in *Ballet Shoes,* was based on a genuine family mode of speech such as appears in the ''story'' of the vicarage which was in fact written after the early children's stories. Anyhow it is evident that Vicky, the middle sister of three, always in and out of trouble, is not only an amused but not altogether partial portrait of the author but also the origin of many of the bright, cheeky, determined, self-conscious little girls who process through the story-books, while there are many instances of behaviour in artistic Isabel and beautiful, spoilt Louise which are reflected in other characters—even, suitably exaggerated, in nasty little exhibitionists like Dulcie Wintle. The third-person narrative seems far more suitable than a straight autobiographical approach since it is clear that Noel Streatfeild is not analysing her own character so much as presenting it, with humour and a certain novelist's detachment, within a family and social context. This is, in fact, the account of a way of life—of the contrivances and triumphs of a family chronically hard-up, of the obligations of being a vicarage child, and of the unsquashable nature of intelligent high spirits. (pp. 3136-37)

> Margery Fisher, "Life Styles," in her Growing Point,
> *Vol. 16, No. 2, July, 1977, pp. 3134-40.**

BOB DIXON

Since girls in general are so severely conditioned and repressed and so turned in upon themselves, they fall victims to fantasies in consequence. In Noel Streatfeild's *Ballet Shoes,* the aptly-named Fossils (all orphans) are brought up in a family of the three-servant-poor category (the book was first published in 1936) and go to the Children's Academy of Dancing and Stage Training. It's run by 'Madame' Fidolia who's presented as gracious, talented and immediately inspiring respect. Obviously, however, she's a person sickeningly obsessed with her own self-importance. Petrova Fossil is the tomboy. She's interested in cars and other 'masculine' pursuits. In the book, there's a never-ending concentration on dress and a preoccupation, as in other Streatfeild books, with knickers. It's very important that all clothes should be respectable and just right for the occasion. . . . *Ballet Shoes* also gives a good example

of a feature very important in girls' fiction—we get the development of an in-group with its own special language and practices. Here, of course, the in-group is centred on ballet and there's an argument, lasting about two pages, between the girls about whether a certain dance sequence was a 'pas de chat' or a 'capriole'. Really, it's the ending that gives the game away. It's the dreams and fantasies this writer is after, as we leave the Fossils headed for a glamorous future. Pauline's a success in films and accepts a Hollywood contract, Posy's to study ballet under a great 'maître' and Petrova's going in for flying and cars. At least, she's allowed to do this, which is a good thing but her object is to get the Fossil name into the history books and make it famous and in this she's clearly aligned with the others.

The Circus is Coming, by the same writer, begins with the sentence 'Peter and Santa were orphans.' In the last sentence of the first chapter, we are told that their guardian dies. . . . [The children run away to their Uncle Gus, who works in a circus]. Gus is by no means a stereotype. He can sew, darn, cook and look after himself in all respects. No doubt this, and many other positive features in Streatfeild's books, are due to the fact that she went to great trouble to get her details right. Her stories are always well-researched. . . . It's a pity that Streatfeild settled for the dreams. In this book, the children join the circus at the end.

Curtain Up [published in the United States as *Theater Shoes*] is almost a sequel to *Ballet Shoes* but with the addition of a boy. Also, the family is in the two-servant-poor category (the book was first published in 1944). Their poverty is constantly stressed. In this story, the emphasis is on theatre so the reader is involved in the stage-training side of the 'Madame's' Academy. Of course, the glamour of the theatre is stressed and there's a seemingly endless preoccupation with clothes again. Petrova is now a ferry pilot and in correspondence with Mark, the boy in this book, who isn't happy at the Academy. Before going off to a boarding school as a step towards his ambition of joining the navy, he gives a revealing view: 'I think the Academy is all right for girls, it isn't all right for boys at all.'

In *Thursday's Child,* Streatfeild settles very firmly on some 'feminine' themes but doesn't seem to be so much at home until she turns to the glamour of the entertainment world towards the end. This change in focus, I think, is why the structure of the story—normally a strong point with this writer—has so many flaws. At several points, it's simply difficult to believe what you're being told. The themes are like the ones in girls' comics, only not so crude. Margaret Thursday is a foundling fostered in a family of the one-servant-poor category. (The book was first published in 1970.) In the first paragraph, the reader learns that Margaret sometimes forgets that skipping is 'a crime'. When, one year, her mysterious annuity fails to arrive, she has to be sent off to an orphanage where her first meal consists of stale bread, margarine, one ounce of cheese and a bottle of water. The Matron has the very best of food, we learn later, and rewards tell-tales with extra food. She sells the clothes the children bring with them and dresses her charges in dingy rags. This doesn't go down well with Margaret, who is no ordinary orphan, as she keeps on reminding us: 'I was found on a Thursday on the steps of the church with three of everything of the very best quality.' 'Everything', you must understand, means clothes. In this sub-Dickensian setting the agony is piled on. The Matron says of Margaret, 'She has a proud air, she must be humbled' and later, when Margaret has committed some small misdemeanour, Matron adds, 'It will take time before she is moulded to our shape' whereupon Margaret gets 'ten strokes' on each hand. Margaret cannot bear the thought of the fine clothes she's brought with her being sold, so when she decides to run away, she has to find them and take them with her, including the 'drawers edged with lace'. . . . At the end, Margaret decides she'll become a famous actress. Again, the book has good points, not least the character of Margaret herself but it's a pity that this resourceful and determined girl can only escape from convention into dream. (pp. 13-16)

> Bob Dixon, "Sexism: Birds in Gilded Cages," in his Catching Them Young, Vol. 1: Sex, Race and Class in Children's Fiction (copyright © Pluto Press 1977), Pluto Press, 1977, pp. 1-41.*

CHRISTINE McDONNELL

[As a child,] *Ballet Shoes* enveloped me. I entered the world of the three Fossils completely, sharing their classes, performances, and everyday routines. (p. 191)

The world the Fossils inhabit is very tidy and scheduled, governed by strict ideas of what is proper. . . . Despite its financial precariousness, their world is secure. Everyday life is the focus of the story, and we enter their world through details. . . . Detail is the key—clear, precise, essential. It helps create the enjoyable combination of the incredible—three orphans collected by an old eccentric and left with his young niece in a big old house—with the concrete.

Just as the daily routine is fully described, the characters are thoroughly portrayed. In many ways *Ballet Shoes* is a celebration of individuality. Each of the three Fossils is distinct, with her own talents, tastes, and personality. In the course of the story, each one develops differently and discovers what gives her happiness. . . . The contributions and responsibilities of the children are taken seriously, and the money they earn is essential. But they remain children. Each has a temper and a sense of humor; each has her share of bad days, tantrums, stubborn streaks.

It is interesting to note that a book written forty years ago, presenting a tightly regimented world in which proper upbringing and a strong work ethic is stressed, seems so contemporary in the roles it depicts and encourages for women. Not only are the three girls all active and spunky, but with the exception of Mr. Simpson and the missing Gum, all the important adults in the story are women who work, who have responsibilities and skills, who make decisions, solve problems, and live independent lives. Furthermore, at the end of the book each of the three Fossils chooses a career. . . . Self-sufficiency is shown as essential, and independence taken for granted.

Although twenty years have passed since I first read *Ballet Shoes,* the Fossils do not seem to show their age. The author's clean, concise style is lively, and her characters are still believable. Individuality and independence are not out of fashion; indeed, in female characters they are much in demand. *Ballet Shoes* reminds me that such strong characters are not a recent invention. But unlike so many self-conscious, two-dimensional female protagonists, created to be positive models or images, the Fossils and the adults in their lives are natural, spontaneous, and very much alive. It is not their function to make a political statement; their job is to entertain and engage the reader. The *Ballet Shoes* performance is a four-star success. Where it has not been a long-running hit, a revival should be scheduled. (pp. 191-93)

> Christine McDonnell, "A Second Look: 'Ballet Shoes'," in The Horn Book Magazine (copyright © 1978 by The Horn Book, Inc., Boston), Vol. LIV, No. 2, April, 1978, pp. 191-93.

BENNY GREEN

Meanwhile, back in [Nesbitshire], nothing has changed. The parson still lives at the Rectory, whose boards are still trodden by our old pals of the Edwardian Repertory Players, the cook, the house parlour-maid, the kitchen maid and the nannie. Mummy, being an embarrassment to the plot, is shipped off to foreign parts with the obligatory dose of tuberculosis, clearing the way for the arrival of the mysterious new governess. Is she a fraud or isn't she? If so, is she a nice fraud or a nasty one? Read on and find out what happens to those five lovable juveniles the Maitlands. In *Meet the Maitlands* . . . Noel Streatfeild pulls out all the period stops; grandfathers take the waters at Baden Baden, cooks decamp and ladies make 'Accordian [sic]-pleated dresses'. All in all, preposterous and antiquated, but mysteriously readable and affecting from first page to last. (pp. 23-4)

> Benny Green, "Analogies," in The Spectator (© 1978 by The Spectator; reprinted by permission of The Spectator), Vol. 241, No. 7850, December 16, 1978, pp. 23-4.*

Mildred D(elois) Taylor

Black American writer for young adults.

Taylor's *Song of the Trees* and its sequel *Roll of Thunder, Hear My Cry* are felt to depict the oppression that has been a part of the black tradition with power and dignity. Taylor credits much of the inspiration for both books to stories told to her by her father about their ancestors and their struggles to establish themselves as landowners after the abolition of slavery. Taylor noticed the difference between this oral history and the history she was taught in school; while her father's stories emphasized the fact that her ancestors retained their pride despite their defeats and sorrows, she discovered that history books portrayed black Americans as weak and vulnerable. Taylor wrote her books to refute this image by telling the truth about her people, thus passing on the spiritual legacy of her ancestors.

Set in Mississippi during the 1930s, both of Taylor's works concern the Logan family; these books stress the family's independence and strength as they fight to maintain their land in the face of violence and the hatred of their white neighbors. These titles, part of a proposed four-volume series, drew an almost unanimously positive response. Critics have praised her ability to present emotional issues in an unsentimental, controlled style without losing the impact of her story. She has also been praised for the poetic quality of her prose, for her characterizations, and for the fact that her books are not social or political tracts disguised as fiction. Taylor's works have also been favorably compared to Alex Haley's saga, *Roots*. They appeal to a wide range of young adults, which suggests Taylor's successful interpretation of the universality of the black experience. *Song of the Trees* received an award from the Council on Interracial Books for Children and was named Outstanding Book of the Year by *The New York Times* in 1973. *Roll of Thunder, Hear My Cry* won the 1977 Newbery Medal. (See also *Something About the Author*, Vol. 15.)

JEAN FRITZ

First are the trees behind the house. . . . [They] are the joy of young Cassie's life—trunks to hug, leaves that sing, branches that protect. With such a forest, a girl can feel rich even though this is the Depression and money is scarce, particularly in Mississippi for black people. Cassie's father has to go clear to Louisiana to find work, and sometimes when he sends money home it is taken from the envelope before the family gets it. Still, no matter what happens, the trees sing their song, and that is a comfort.

But then come the white crosses on the trees, and the white men come. . . .

["**Song of the Trees**"] is a slender book and so moving, the temptation is to tell the whole story. But the important thing is that Cassie's father, David, comes home and that we, the readers, meet him. We are not likely to forget him. He is a man who knows the full measure of his manhood.

"A black man's always gotta be ready to die," he says. "And it don't make me any difference if I die today or tomorrow. Just as long as I die right."

So at the end the white men go away (at least for a time), and part of the forest is saved. Still, the sounds of those axes ring on long after the last page of this triumphant book. And well they may, for this is a true story and truly told. A story to linger over.

> Jean Fritz, "Children's Books Spring 1975: 'Song of the Trees'," in The New York Times Book Review (© by The New York Times Company; reprinted by permission), May 4, 1975, p. 39.

ANITA SILVEY

The dedication of [*Song of the Trees*]—thirteen lines which end "To my grandparents . . . who bridged the generations between slavery and freedom; and To the Family, who fought and survived"—immediately sets the tone of black pride that permeates every page. . . . [The] book is almost written to formula: Blacks encounter evil whites who attempt to rob them of their possessions and dignity, but a strong, black man counteracts with force. But what could have been a banal, trite book has been saved by its description of a child's feeling for nature which elevates the story from the socio-political realm. . . . The simple story has been written with great conviction and strength, and Cassie's descriptions of the trees add a poetic touch.

> *Anita Silvey, "Stories for the Middle Readers: 'Song of the Trees'," in* The Horn Book Magazine *(copyright © 1975 by the Horn Book, Inc., Boston), Vol. LI, No. 4, August, 1975, p. 384.*

ZENA SUTHERLAND

In a depression-era story based on an incident in the author's family history [*Song of the Trees*], a confrontation between a mercenary white man and a black man guarding his property is taut with drama. . . . The writing style is fairly brisk, verging on the poetic whenever Cassie speaks of her beloved trees; the characterization of the children is minimal, while that of the adults is stronger; the plot is nicely constructed for the length of the story.

> *Zena Sutherland, "New Titles for Children and Young People: 'Song of the Trees'," in* Bulletin of the Center for Children's Books *(reprinted by permission of The University of Chicago Press; © 1975 by the University of Chicago), Vol. 29, No. 2, October, 1975, p. 35.*

JOYCE E. ARKHURST

The confrontation [between the Logan family and the white work crew in *Song of the Trees*] symbolizes much of the history of Black struggle—economic defenselessness, the Black man's dramatic bravery in the face of white power, a child forced to assume adult responsibility and the children's fears in threatening situations. . . .

[This] story will be enjoyed by young readers.

> *Joyce E. Arkhurst, "The Bookshelf: 'Song of the Trees'," in* Interracial Books for Children Bulletin *(reprinted by permission of Interracial Books for Children Bulletin, 1841 Broadway, New York, N.Y. 10023), Vol. 6, Nos. 3-4, 1975, p. 8.*

SUSAN COOPER

[*Roll of Thunder, Hear My Cry* is] a good straightforward novel about racial prejudice, fierce without being bitter, wholly absorbing. . . . The author brings a controlled power from her own family background to electrify her calm prose toward a wonderfully shaped climax.

> *Susan Cooper, "Newbery Medalist Susan Cooper Reviews New Novels," in* The Christian Science Monitor *(reprinted by permission from* The Christian Science Monitor; © 1976 The Christian Science Publishing Society; all rights reserved), November 3, 1976, p. 20.*

SALLY HOLMES HOLTZE

[*Roll of Thunder, Hear My Cry*] presents injustice and several ways of dealing with it. . . . There is little relief from the tension of frightening events, and the reader is able to identify with Cassie's frustration and anger as she experiences great

unfairness and witnesses crimes against Black people. The events and settings of the powerful novel are presented with such verisimilitude and the characters are so carefully drawn that one might assume the book to be autobiographical, if the author were not so young.

> *Sally Holmes Holtze, "Stories for Intermediate Readers: 'Roll of Thunder, Hear My Cry'," in* The Horn Book Magazine *(copyright © 1976 by the Horn Book, Inc., Boston), Vol. LII, No. 6, December, 1976, p. 627.*

EMILY R. MOORE

[*Roll of Thunder, Hear My Cry*] describes a year during which Cassie Logan learns to handle the indignities inflicted upon herself, her family and neighbors. She also learns the importance of her family's struggle to keep their land and their economic independence. . . .

Throughout the book, the reader is moved to tears by Ms. Taylor's vibrant, exquisite and simple style. The dialogue is lightly seasoned with Southern colloquialisms.

After reading Cassie's last lines—"And I cried for those things which had happened in the night and would not pass. I cried for T.J. For T.J. and the land"—you want to turn back and start all over again.

Roll of Thunder, Hear My Cry deserves to become a classic in children's literature.

> *Emily R. Moore, "The Bookshelf: 'Roll of Thunder, Hear My Cry'," in* Interracial Books for Children Bulletin *(reprinted by permission of Interracial Books for Children Bulletin, 1841 Broadway, New York, N.Y. 10023), Vol. 7, No. 7, 1976, p. 18.*

RUBY MARTIN

Song of the Trees is so beautifully told, the prose rings poetry. . . .

The children are charming, disarming, personal, and not too private in their love and appreciation for the "sharp-needled pines," the "shaggy-bark hickories," and the "sweet alligator gum trees" which tower helplessly on "Big Ma's" land. They forebodingly await their devastation with their song quieted in an implied anticipation of their destruction.

The story builds smoothly and culminates in a clash of willfulness . . . and of the aesthetic forest which captures the reader with its tender personality.

The book has much to recommend it. Mildred Taylor handles her characters with a fine sensitivity. It is a story not only of trees but of children, and an interplay of their personalities is carefully woven into the text. (p. 434)

> *Ruby Martin, "Books for Young People" (copyright 1977 by the International Reading Association, Inc.; reprinted with permission of the International Reading Association and Ruby Martin), in* Journal of Reading, *Vol. 20, No. 5, February, 1977, pp. 432-35.*

MILDRED D. TAYLOR

I was blessed with a special father, a man who had unyielding faith in himself and his abilities, and who, knowing himself to be inferior to no one, tempered my learning with his wisdom. In the foreword to *Roll of Thunder, Hear My Cry* I described my father as a master storyteller; he was much more than that. A highly principled, complex man who did not have an excellent education or a white-collar job, he had instead strong moral fiber and a great wealth of what he always said was simply plain common sense. Throughout my childhood he impressed upon my sister and me that we were somebody, that we were important and could do or be anything we set our minds to do or be. (p. 402)

Through him my growing awareness of a discriminatory society was accompanied by a wisdom that taught me that anger in itself was futile, that to fight discrimination I needed a stronger weapon. (pp. 402-03)

The effects of those teachings upon me are evident to anyone reading *Roll of Thunder, Hear My Cry*. Also evident are the strong family ties. Through David Logan have come the words of my father, and through the Logan family the love of my own family. If people are touched by the warmth of the Logans, it is because I had the warmth of my own youthful years from which to draw. If the Logans seem real, it is because I had my own family upon which to base characterizations. And if people believe the book to be biographical, it is because I have tried to distill the essence of Black life, so familiar to most Black families, to make the Logans an embodiment of that spiritual heritage; for, contrary to what the media relate to us, all Black families are not fatherless or disintegrating. Certainly my family was not. (p. 403)

[At the many gatherings we had when I was a child] there was always time for talk, and when we children had finished all the games we could think to play, we would join the adults, soon becoming enraptured by their talk, for it would often turn to a history which we heard only at home, a history of Black people told through stories.

Those stories about the small and often dangerous triumphs of Black people, those stories about human pride and survival in a cruelly racist society were like nothing I read in the history books or the books I devoured at the local library. There were no Black heroes or heroines in those books; no beautiful Black ladies, no handsome Black men; no people filled with pride, strength, or endurance. . . . There was obviously a terrible contradiction between what the books said and what I had learned from my family, and at no time did I feel the contradiction more than when I had to sit in a class which, without me, would have been all white, and relive that prideless history year after year.

As I grew, and the writers of books and their publishers grew, I noticed a brave attempt to portray Black people with a white sense of dignity and pride. But even those books disturbed me, for the Black people shown were still subservient. Most often the Black characters were housekeepers and, though a source of love and strength to the white child whose story it was, they remained one-dimensional because the view of them was a white one. Books about Black families by white writers also left me feeling empty, not because a white person had attempted to write about a Black family, but because the writer had not, in my opinion, captured the warmth or love of the Black world and had failed to understand the principles upon which Black parents brought up their children and taught them survival. It was not that these writers intentionally omitted such essential elements; it was simply that not having lived the Black experience, they did not know it.

But I did know it. And by the time I entered high school, I had a driving compulsion to paint a truer picture of Black people. I wanted to show the endurance of the Black world, with strong fathers and concerned mothers; I wanted to show happy, loved children about whom other children, both Black and white, could say: "Hey, I really like them! I feel what they feel." I wanted to show a Black family united in love and pride, of which the reader would like to be a part.

I never doubted that one day I would grasp that bright spark of life in words for others to see, for hadn't my father always said I could do anything I set my mind to do? But as the years passed and what I wrote continued to lack the vitality of the world I knew, there began to grow within a very youthful me an overwhelming impatience, and the question: *when?*

Well, the *when* was not to come until almost four years ago, after I had seen much of the world, returned to school for graduate study, and become a Black student activist. It was then that on a well-remembered day in late September a little girl named Cassie Logan suddenly appeared in my life. Cassie was a spunky eight-year-old, innocent, untouched by discrimination, full of pride, and greatly loved, and through her I discovered I now could tell one of the stories I had heard so often as a child. From that meeting came *Song of the Trees*.

If you have met Cassie and her brothers—Stacey, the staunch, thoughtful leader; Christopher-John, the happy, sensitive mediator; and Little Man, the shiny clean, prideful, manly six-year-old—then perhaps you can understand why, when I sent that final manuscript off . . . , I did not want to give them up. Those four children make me laugh; they also make me cry, and I had to find a way of keeping them from fading into oblivion. In August, 1974, came the answer: I would write another book about the Logans, one in which I could detail the teachings of my own childhood as well as incorporate many of the stories I had heard about my family and others. Through artistic prerogative I could weave into those stories factual incidents about which I had read or heard, as well as my own childhood feelings to produce a significant tapestry which would portray rural Black southern life in the 1930s. I would write *Roll of Thunder, Hear My Cry*.

Writing is a very lonely business. It is also a very terrifying one emotionally if a writer knows and cares about the people of her novel as well as I know and care about the Logans. Cassie's fears were my fears and what she feared from the night men, so did I. More than once my dreams were fraught with burnings and destruction, with faceless men coming in the night, with a boy being beaten, with a boy about to die. (pp. 404-06)

[In the first draft of my book] I had attempted to make Cassie play too big a part in the climax. I had wanted her to be with David when his leg was broken, to be with him when the fire started, to fight the fire. After all, it was she who had to tell the story and how could she if she wasn't there? But the character of David Logan wouldn't let me put her into the center of the action. I thought of my own father and what he would have done. He, like David, would never have taken his young daughter on such dangerous missions. It was clear to me now. All I had to do was allow my characters to remain true to themselves; that was the key.

I believe that that key served me well in the writing of *Roll of Thunder, Hear My Cry*, and I hope that it will continue to guide me through the next two books about the Logans, which will chronicle the growth of the Logan children into adolescence and adulthood. . . . I will continue the Logans' story with the same life guides that have always been mine, for it is my hope that these four books, one of the first chronicles to mirror a Black child's hopes and fears from childhood innocence to awareness to bitterness and disillusionment, will one day be instrumental in teaching children of all colors the tremendous influence that Cassie's generation—my father's generation— had in bringing about the great Civil Rights movement of the fifties and sixties. Without understanding that generation and what it and the generations before it endured, children of today and of the future cannot understand or cherish the precious rights of equality which they now possess, both in the North and in the South. If they can identify with the Logans, who are representative not only of my family but of the many Black families who faced adversity and survived, and understand the principles by which they lived, then perhaps they can better understand and respect themselves and others. (pp. 407-08)

> *Mildred D. Taylor, "Newbery Award Acceptance" (copyright © 1977 by Mildred D. Taylor; reprinted by permission of the author), a speech delivered at the meeting of the American Library Association in Detroit, Michigan on June 18, 1977, in* The Horn Book Magazine, *Vol. LII, No. 4, August, 1977, pp. 401-09.*

PHYLLIS J. FOGELMAN

"A natural writer" is an overused expression I don't particularly like, but in speaking of Mildred Taylor it seems absolutely appropriate. Mildred's words flow smoothly, effortlessly, it seems, and they abound in richness, harmony, and rhythm. Her stories unfold in a full, leisurely way, well suited to and evocative of her Southern settings. Her ability to bring her characters to life and to involve her readers is remarkable. In short, Mildred is one of the few people of whom I have felt: This woman was born to write. (pp. 410-11)

> *Phyllis J. Fogelman, "Mildred D. Taylor," in* The Horn Book Magazine *(copyright © 1977 by the Horn Book, Inc., Boston), Vol. LIII, No. 4, August, 1977, pp. 410-14.*

NAOMI MITCHISON

Roll of Thunder, Hear My Cry is an extremely moving story of life down on the Mississippi during the times of the depression—not so long ago. The memory is still fresh; if it were not Mildred Taylor could not have made it into such an outstandingly gripping narrative. . . . There is the hideous shadow of violence everywhere, steadily rising to a fearful climax, with the mean whites shoring up their power. Yet, behind it all, there is the possibility of justice slowly coming.

The people in the book are real, and so is the background, cotton and forest, mouth-watering food. Young people shouldn't find the southern American speech too difficult, though it would be best read aloud. It is particularly interesting that the black family, only three generations from slavery, are not poor sharecroppers, but landowners and industrious farmers, clearly with a higher standard both of living and of intelligence than most of their white neighbours, yet they remain unaccepted. . . . We readers begin to sympathize with Cassie and her brother from the first racial insult . . . , we can't help feeling with her all the way.

> *Naomi Mitchison, "In Black and White," in* The Times Educational Supplement *(© Times Newspapers Ltd. (London) 1977; reproduced from* The Times Educational Supplement *by permission), No. 3258, November 18, 1977, p. 33.**

MARGARET PAYNE

It will be a pity if the literary title, the jacket illustration and Newbery Medal caption brand [*Roll of Thunder, Hear My Cry*] as another well written but self-conscious tale of civil rights. It does for its period and place what Laura Ingalls Wilder did for the pioneers, and had the author used Mrs Wilder's third person narrative, the impact might have been greater. As in the 'Little House' books, there are many incidents of fun, family conversations and drama which would repay re-reading when the moral implications could be absorbed in a more subtle way. It deserves a wide audience. . . . (p. 47)

> *Margaret Payne, "Seven to Eleven: 'Roll of Thunder, Hear My Cry'," in* The School Librarian, *Vol. 26, No. 1, March, 1978, pp. 46-7.*

MARGERY FISHER

Burningly honest as [*Roll of Thunder, Hear My Cry*] undoubtedly is, it has the air of autobiography in its crowded details and assumptive descriptions, while the raw emotionalism needs to be disciplined and channelled if it is to make a proper impact as fiction. There is much talent in this extended chronicle of a negro family in Mississippi in the early 'thirties, and a very evident truth in episodes derived from the author's father which show up the bigotries and brutal social alignments of the time. But the strength of feeling in the book has been too much for the characters. They remain dim, stiff figures manipulated for the sake of certain key situations, and they are so far based on the author's own family history that they never achieve the independent identity essential to a novel. . . . [Much] of Mildred Taylor's material would have been better used in a family memoir than in the exacting, deliberate form of a novel. (pp. 3286-87)

> *Margery Fisher, "Significant Forms," in her* Growing Point, *Vol. 16, No. 9, April, 1978, pp. 3282-87.**

Andrew Lloyd Webber

1948-

Tim Rice

1944-

Webber (not shown)—British composer, author, and producer.

Rice (pictured at right)—British lyricist, author, and producer.

The works of Webber and Rice are musical interpretations of biblical and historical figures and events. They are studies of charismatic young men and women who command great power. Webber's music is a pastiche of such twentieth-century popular styles as vaudeville, rock, calypso, country, and soul, although his works are often structured in classical and operatic forms. Rice's lyrics are important for their authentic presentation of the team's subjects in contemporary language. Webber and Rice began writing pop songs together in 1966, but had little success until their single "Jesus Christ Superstar" became a hit and convinced them to build an entire work around it.

With *Jesus Christ Superstar* Webber and Rice present the story of Christ's last days on earth in a non-traditional form, the rock opera. The purpose of the drama is to show the reaction to Jesus during His own lifetime. The work was immediately controversial; it is considered radical because it ends with Christ's crucifixion rather than with His resurrection. Another controversy generated by *Superstar* is the composer's sympathetic portrayal of Judas, through whose eyes the story is told; most critics, however, believe this point of view to be truly innovative. The film version of *Superstar* is considered as blasphemous as the play. However, many church officials acknowledged it as a favorable means of relating the Bible to young people in a form and language which appeals to them.

Prior to *Superstar* Webber and Rice collaborated on a shorter piece, *Joseph and the Amazing Technicolour Dreamcoat*, which was first written as a private production for a boys's school and is also based on a biblical story. Some reviewers see it as superficial, but many think it more charming and less pretentious than *Superstar*. With *Evita*, Webber and Rice created a genuine opera about the career of Eva Perón, an opportunist who became the wife of Argentine dictator Juan Perón in the 1950s. *Evita* shares *Superstar's* theme of the effects of mass popularity and is told by radical leader Ché Guevara. However, it is generally considered inferior to its predecessor, and many critics have felt it is saved only by its brilliant staging.

Rice's lyrics have been criticized for their banality, and both authors have been attacked for their uncertain handling of their subject. Audiences, however, have been receptive to *Evita*, just as they have to all of Webber and Rice's works. According to John Coldstream, their success is "on a scale matched in this generation by Lennon and McCartney."

RICHARD WILLIAMS

Just as Handel composed "Messiah" and Bach wrote his "St Matthew Passion," so Andrew Lloyd Webber and Tim Rice have produced "Jesus Christ—Superstar."

An outrageous statement, some will say. How dare they? But the point is that Handel, Bach, Lloyd Webber, and Rice have all created music which tells the same story in the language of their day. . . .

I guess a lot of people will laugh at it. Had it been called "Buddah—Superstar," or "Meher Baba—Freak's Guru," the same people would have taken it very seriously indeed.

Having listened to the whole thing several times now, I'm sure that the pair have undertaken the venture in an honest way, and have come up with a considerable achievement, against all the odds. . . .

It's not, of course, without its faults, as it's virtually impossible to tell this story in its original context with all the paraphernalia of rock without having the odd hang-up somewhere. Personally, I feel that the odd word or phrase is slightly out of tone with the music. . . .

I don't want anybody to get the impression that "**Jesus Christ— Superstar**" is to be compared in terms of aesthetic success to Handel and Bach. Even if it were, it would take decades to realise it. What I do think is that it's an honest attempt at a very hard job, and the amount of artistic success which is already definitely apparent is surprising and pleasing. The work demands more serious listening than it'll probably get.

> *Richard Williams, "Thou Shalt Not Knock 'Jesus Christ—Superstar',"* in Melody Maker *(© IPC Business Press Ltd.), October 10, 1970, p. 8.*

WILLIAM BENDER

Superstar builds to considerable impact and evocativeness, in part because it manages to wear its underlying seriousness lightly. What Rice and Webber have created is a modern-day passion play that may enrage the devout but ought to intrigue and perhaps inspire the agnostic young. . . .

Together they have fashioned a clever, youthful blend of skepticism and romantic questioning. . . .

Judas has rarely been treated so sympathetically as he is by Webber and Rice. According to the Judas of *Superstar,* his friend Jesus is a charismatic mortal—much like an adored rock singer or the leader of a radical movement—who has begun to believe in his own press clippings. . . . The Crucifixion is seen as the result of bungling self-indulgence, and Jesus' faith in his divinity, and hope of Resurrection, as delusions.

To a large extent, Webber and Rice share Judas' doubts. . . . Shorn of the Resurrection, of course, the Passion and what preceded it are something less than "the greatest story ever told." Perhaps that is why Webber and Rice . . . have not worked too hard in *Superstar* to get the Christianity out of Christ. Despite Judas, both libretto and music are provocatively ambiguous about Christ's divinity. . . .

What Webber and Rice seem certain of is that Christ was a profoundly humanitarian radical thinker, not unlike Martin Luther King and Robert F. Kennedy. . . .

Whatever the reaction to *Superstar* may be, Webber and Rice have fused words and music into such a convincing narrative style that rock may never be quite the same again. . . .

Superstar occupies the same assimilative position in the pop world that Ginastera's *Don Rodrigo* does in serious opera. Webber and Rice do not outdo the Beatles or the Rolling Stones or the Edwin Hawkins Singers, Prokofiev, Orff, Stravinsky or any other musical influence found in their work. But they have welded these borrowings into a considerable work that is their own. [The Who's] *Tommy* . . . was the first, flawed suggestion that rock could deal with a major subject on a broad symphonic or operatic scale. *Superstar* offers the first real proof.

> *William Bender, "Rock Passion," in* Time *(reprinted by permission from* Time, The Weekly News-magazine; *copyright Time Inc. 1970), Vol. 96, No. 19, November 9, 1970, p. 47.*

JONATHAN COTT

Messrs. Rice and Webber are talented and clever young Englishmen who command smooth lyrical and dramatic gifts. . . .

But primarily the tone the music and words [of *Jesus Christ Superstar* creates] is one of forced hipness and sentimentality, that of an egregiously over-sweet rock-coated Broadway musical. There are the dramatic declamatory descending modulations when Jesus sings of understanding what power really is about, a steal from *Tommy*'s "How can he be saved / From the eternal grave."

When Jesus rails at the polluters of the temple, his wailing ways sound more like Jimi Hendrix calling on his foxy lady than someone expressing a fine sense of moral outrage. And this is followed by a wispy, reflective passage that would have been more appropriate as a moment of the adolescent-dumb gloom Johnny Mathis might have felt after losing his latest passion.

Then there are the lyrics [such as Mary Magdalene's] sweet half-groupie, half-teenaged ballad for Jesus, the man she doesn't know how to love. And all the while Italian night club imitation rock music adjoining strings and horns create an embarrassing but melodious scene. . . .

[The opera] does nothing to enrich, expand, uncover, or commit itself to any personal vision, in the sense that [Pier Paolo] Pasolini and [Roberto] Rossellini have transformed the Gospels in their films. Frankie Lymon and the Teenagers or Ray Davies [of The Kinks] would have had more to say or see about Jesus.

> *Jonathan Cott, "Jesus Christ Sings an Aria," in* Rolling Stone *(by Straight Arrow Publishers, Inc. ©1970; all rights reserved; reprinted by permission), Issue 72, December 2, 1970, p. 10.*

NICK TOSCHES

All in all, [*Joseph and the Amazing Technicolor Dreamcoat*] covers a good nine chapters of the Book of Genesis and proffers a highly moving—much of which, I must admit, is due to the groovy score the operetta sports—testimony of one man's unswerving fidelity to God. . . .

Although at times the music does seem a bit irreverent to what's being recounted, the LP's "now sound" is often quite effective. . . .

> *Nick Tosches, "Records: 'Joseph and the Amazing Technicolor Dreamcoat'," in* Rolling Stone *(by Straight Arrow Publishers, Inc. © 1971; all rights reserved; reprinted by permission), Issue 85, June 24, 1971, p. 43.*

CLIFFORD EDWARDS

[In *Superstar* the] Christ of faith gives way to the Jesus of history. Rice and Webber have acknowledged modern scholarship's discovery that the New Testament picture of Jesus is colored throughout with propagandistic interpretation more intent on convincing the reader that Jesus is the divine God-man than in giving an historically accurate picture of the flesh-and-blood man of Galilee. (p. 218)

Rice and Webber attempt to dramatize the life-style of the historical Jesus in the midst of the life-styles and forces at work around him.

Is there any value in bypassing ecclesiastical propaganda to seek out this life-style? To an emerging culture suspicious of the establishment's propaganda, it allows a new and honest attempt to stand where the first hearers did, feel for oneself the impact of the Galilean's style, and answer for oneself, "Who do you say that I am?" . . . *Superstar* attempts to dramatize Jesus' life-style in the midst of competing life-styles, and then leaves one with questions rather than with answers. . . . (pp. 218-19)

Although the "opera" has no single, obvious climax, musically and dramatically the climax seems to be Judas' disintegration and death at the beginning of record four. . . . Judas and his life-style are of special significance.

How is one to characterize this Judas? He can perhaps best be described as the "Uncle Tom" of the Jesus movement, the personification of a "failure of nerve" within the emerging life-style, a failure of nerve which turns back in fear and betrays the emerging culture to the existing power structure. . . .

[The] very strength of *Superstar* is its willingness to raise hard questions while refusing to supply simple answers. The complexity of personal motives and the tangled consequences of our actions in real history become evident in Judas. No only are we uncertain of Judas' real motives and culpability, but we become aware that Judas is uncertain of his own motives. He protests too much that he is not betraying Jesus for his "own reward." He sulks because Jesus does not give him his due as "right hand man." At the Last Supper he seeks to blame what he is about to do on the requirements of Jesus' own "ambition." Before he dies, Judas realizes that the consequences of his betrayal have been hastened along by forces beyond his own control. . . . [There] is the recognition that complex forces in society magnify the consequences of our actions, that demonic powers can be set in motion far beyond our intentions and cannot be called back. . . .

The important place given Judas in *Superstar* contributes a problematic or ambiguous quality to the "opera," for who knows how far one should trust the observations of a Judas. It is this ambiguity which leads the audience toward the realization that it must arrive at its own interpretation of the figure of the Historic Jesus.

Mary Magdalene suggests the life-style described in Timothy Leary's advice: "Turn on and drop out." Whether the instrument of her turning on is acid, pot, yoga, or zazen, the end result is a detached, euphoric quality. . . . Jesus accepts the Magdalene's ministrations and defends her against Judas' criticism, but her oceanic feeling that "everything's alright" is transcended by the passion of his own search for "truth" or "God," and by the dramatic forces already unleashed. However, as with Judas, the portrayal of the Magdalene has its complexities. In a second solo, **"I Don't Know How to Love Him,"** she sings of her consternation that Jesus should so disturb her "cool." . . . Apparently the oceanic feeling can be shattered by an encounter with Jesus. Lest one be tempted to make too much of the Magdalene's relationship to Jesus, it should be noted that Webber and Rice have Judas wail this same love song to Jesus. For both the Magdalene and Judas, and we suppose for their spiritual descendants today, an encounter with Superstar is pictured as engendering love, fear, and mystery. . . . (p. 219)

In stripping away "the myth from the man," Webber and Rice find no profound philosopher, enlightened reformer, or heroic leader. The great strength of their portrayal of Jesus is their recognition that apart from the myth we have only the whisper of a voice and the outskirts of the life-style of a man. The triumph of *Superstar* lies as much in what Webber and Rice have not done as in what they have done. They have refused to create a fictional character to fill the void. . . .

Where does the portrayal of Jesus focus? On Jesus as a flesh-and-blood human being. Even the outskirts of Jesus' life-style reveal his real humanity. Having his face cooled "feels nice, so nice," he joins the crowd in a happy "Hosanna, Heysanna," screams at the temple merchants, and admits "I'm sad and tired" and "scared." . . . A common reaction to *Superstar* is: "It was the first time I ever thought of Jesus as a real person." The phantom-like portrayals of an otherworldly Christ on decades of funeral-home calendars and Sunday School walls apparently makes the focus on Jesus as a real person a remarkable revelation to this generation. . . .

The words he speaks are drawn largely from the Gospel pronouncements, with very few original contributions by Tim Rice. He advocates living in the present, claims that he could give "plans and forecasts" unfathomable to those around him, and admits that earlier he was "inspired" but now is "sad and tired." He defends the Magdalene, cleanses the temple, and sings "Hosanna" with the crowd one moment while screaming at it to "Heal yourselves" at another. At critical moments Rice supplies Jesus with the lines "To conquer death you only have to die," and "I look for truth and find that I get damned." These along with a Gethsemane prayer, are the closest Rice comes to providing Jesus with a summary of his life and mission. In Gethsemane Jesus pleads: "I'd wanna know my God, . . . I'd wanna see my God," and this possibility encourages him to accept the death his God seems to require. It is suggested that his death might make all he has said and done "matter more," but its full meaning is not revealed. (p. 220)

After Judas' death, the events involving Jesus seem almost anticlimactic as he maintains a near-silence through the trials and speaks essentially the traditional words from the cross. As if to fill this vacuum, the voice of the dead Judas returns to raise the questions we might ask of Jesus. . . . (pp. 220-21)

Superstar concludes with two minutes of tranquil music ("John 19:41") suggesting the garden containing Jesus' tomb. The audience is left to decide for itself whether this is the quiet following an honest man's death or the peace of a new Eden prepared by a greater Adam for his descendants.

Superstar is a conservative attempt to express the counter-culture's interest in Jesus, and its very conservatism has prepared a solid foundation for more creative and imaginative works in the future. It has avoided cliches, sentimentality, and mere fictionalizing, presenting Jesus' real humanity forcefully while allowing the audience great latitude for personal interpretation. (p. 221)

Clifford Edwards, "'Jesus Christ Superstar': Electric Age Messiah," in Catholic World *(copyright 1971 by The Missionary Society of St. Paul the Apostle in the State of New York), Vol. CCXIII, No. 1277, August, 1971, pp. 217-21.*

DOUGLAS WATT

["**Jesus Christ Superstar**"] is so stunningly effective a theatrical experience that I am still finding it difficult to compose my thoughts about it. It is, in short, a triumph. . . .

["**Jesus Christ Superstar**"] considers the seven last days of Christ in contemporary pop terms and, it must be added, with complete reverence.

Andrew Lloyd Webber's score is vibrant, richly varied and always dramatically right and . . . much the same things can be said for Tim Rice's lyrics. . . .

The story in itself is, of course, almost unbearably moving, but the great accomplishment of Webber and Rice has been to make it so strikingly immediate.

> *Douglas Watt, "'Jesus Christ Superstar' Is Full of Life, Vibrant with Reverence," in* Daily News *(© 1971, New York News Inc.; reprinted by permission), October 13, 1971 (and reprinted in* New York Theatre Critics' Reviews, *Vol. XXXII, No. 15, October 11-18, 1971, p. 242).*

CLIVE BARNES

Nothing could convince me that any show that has sold two-and-one-half million copies of its album before the opening night is anything like all bad. But I must also confess to experiencing some disappointment [with] "**Jesus Christ Superstar.**". . .

It all rather resembled one's first sight of the Empire State Building. Not at all uninteresting, but somewhat unsurprising and of minimal artistic value. . . .

Mr. Rice's intention was clearly to place Christ's betrayal and death into a vernacular more immediate perhaps to our times. His record sales would presumably indicate his success in this aim, but he does not have a very happy ear for the English language. There is a certain air of dogged doggerel about his phrases that too often sounds as limp as a deflated priest.

It is surely unfortunate, even bathetic, to have Christ at his moment of death remark solemnly: "God forgive them! They don't know what they are doing." The sentiments are unassailable, but the language is unforgivably pedestrian. . . .

The music itself is extraordinarily eclectic. It runs so many gamuts it almost becomes a musical cartel. . . . [Mr. Lloyd Webber] has emerged with some engaging numbers.

The title song, "**Superstar,**" has a bounce and exaltation to it, an almost revivalist fervor that deserves its popularity. I also much admire the other hit of the show, "**I Don't Know How to Love Him.**" This also shows Mr. Rice at his best as a lyricist, although it is perhaps surprising to find this torch ballad sung by Mary Magdalene to Jesus Christ—even a Jesus Christ Superstar. There is a certain vulgarity here typical of an age that takes a peculiar delight in painting mustaches on the "Mona Lisa" and demonstrating that every great man was a regular guy at heart. . . .

[This] is not an important rock score in the manner of "Tommy" by The Who. It is, unhappily, neither innovative nor original. . . .

For me, the real disappointment came not in the music—which is better than run-of-the-mill Broadway and the best score for an English musical in years—but in the conception. There is a coyness in its contemporaneity, a sneaky pleasure in the boldness of its anachronisms, a special, undefined air of smugness in its daring. Christ is updated, but hardly, I felt, renewed.

> *Clive Barnes, "Theater: Christ's Passion Transported to the Stage in Guise of Serious Pop," in The* New York Times *(© 1971 by The New York Times Company; reprinted by permission), October 13, 1971, p. 40.*

MARTIN GOTTFRIED

"**Jesus Christ Superstar**" is an enormously successful record album, called a "rock opera" in one of pop music's pathetic and pointless efforts to gain respectability by imitating orthodox forms. It is also an awful album, overproduced and overorchestrated in vain compensation for underinspiration and a complete lack of the qualities that make for rock music—vitality, rhythm, state of mind, musicality. . . . [It] required no imagination to envision as a commercially viable stage production. . . .

[It] is, at its worst, a production that leaves you with a so-what feeling. For all its physical beauty, extravagance, enormity of orchestration and complexity of audio production, it provides no feeling—no sense of anything happening in a theatre. It is simply there, a superexpensive juke box playing the entire . . . score of the record album, note for note and lyric for miserable lyric. There is one brief musical addition, but otherwise, you could as well be listening to the record—if you could stand it all the way through.

> *Martin Gottfried, "'Jesus Christ Superstar' . . . Easter Show at the Music Hall," in* Women's Wear Daily *(copyright 1971, Fairchild Publications), October 14, 1971 (and reprinted in* New York Theatre Critics' Reviews, *Vol. XXII, No. 15, October 11-18, 1971, p. 240).*

MALCOLM BOYD

Can Jesus survive "**Jesus Christ Superstar**"? Sometimes it is "Love Story" in Jerusalem. Other times it is only "The Greening of the Box Office.". . . But is it a serious work of art? And how does it deal with the Passion of Christ? . . .

In a myriad of details gone wrong, the show bears little resemblance to the New Testament. Yet, what is most important, Jesus' mission got misplaced somewhere from drawing board to Star Chamber.

Is this the Jesus of a significant counter-culture? Not at all. For we see him reject the sick and distressed victims of society who come to him for help. We see a restless and tired "star" Jesus arrogantly send Judas away to do the work of betrayal. Fatigue and introspection could have legitimately been portrayed. But despair looms too centrally in Christ, conveying a sense of mission lost and purpose forgotten. (p. 1)

[There] is clearly the absence of a cross rooted in earth in "**Jesus Christ Superstar.**" Such lack of specificity leads to those quasi-religious fantasies which obliterate detailed truth. I am not one of those purists who decry the show's bypassing of the resurrection. After watching Jesus hang on a Daliesque golden triangle (an avant-garde symbol of the cross?) for a glamorous simulation of the crucifixion, I offer thanks to the pantheon of gods that we were indeed spared a resurrection. But in its failure to come to terms with the sacrifice of a Christ-figure, or the Passion of Christ, "**Jesus Christ Superstar**" also fails to become a seriously motivated and constructed rock opera.

It is several things: a Rockette operetta, a Barnumian put-on, a religioso-cum-showbiz pastiche, and a musicalized "Sweet

Sweetback's Baadasssss Judas Song.'' The Jews seem to be guilty, once again, of causing Jesus' death. . . . We are thrust against energy without exuberance, torture without tragedy, in this collage-in-motion. . . . (pp. 1, 7)

The sharp intrusion of sex—again and again and again—into the show can only focus attention on Jesus' own sexuality. Is he Gay? Bisexual? Straight? Asexual? . . .

The sexuality of Jesus will undoubtedly comprise the Exhibit A controversy about the show. He and Mary Magdalene fondle and kiss each other; I felt an implicit acceptance of the fact that they have enjoyed intercourse. The exposure of this side of Jesus' humanity drew cheers from the audience, perhaps in reaction against the celibate Jesus of churchianity who has been used traditionally as a major argument against sex outside of (and before) wedlock as well as against homosexuality.

Jesus as a human being (as well as the Son of God) with sexual feelings may be far overdue in our puritanical, sexually hypocritical society. Yet I feel that his sexuality was not handled sensitively or with taste in this gaudily inhuman parody. . . .

The show gives us a confused, tired but plucky Jesus who is going to the cross even if it kills him. Mary Magdalene is a cool, mod and sincere chick who digs Jesus but senses that he is very different from other men whom she has known. She sings a gentle ditty about the love for him that she feels. However, it is clearly not sufficiently deep a love to bind her to him through his torture and death. . . .

Judas' feelings about Jesus provide the real basis for the utterly fictional story line that links the musical numbers. Judas feels that he is trapped in a terrible role, one scripted by God and directed by Jesus. . . . Judas' acceptance of a predestination to damnation smacks unappetizingly of Calvinism with bitters. So Judas plays a role instead of being himself.

It is an absurd irony that a simplistic success . . . has come out of the ambiguity and violent paradox of Jesus' Passion, presented here with all dimension flattened. Even the controversy of Jesus, intellectually ignored in this show, is made marketable in a plastic-ware production. It doesn't have a soul. (p. 7)

> Malcolm Boyd, '''Jesus Christ Superstar'—Two Views: A Priest Says, "It Doesn't Have a Soul," in* The New York Times, *Section 2 (© 1971 by The New York Times Company; reprinted by permission), October 24, 1971, pp. 1, 7.*

WALTER KERR

Lyricist Tim Rice has found for ["**Jesus Christ Superstar**"] a personal, and I think persuasive, tone of voice. The tone of voice is not merely mod or pop or jauntily idiomatic in an opportunistic way. It sheathes an attitude. It speaks, over and over again, of the inadequate, though forgivable, responses ordinary men always do make when confronted by mystery. . . .

[Rice's] are blunt, rude, pointedly unlyrical lyrics, not meant to coat any period with a little literary flavoring but to catch hold of thought processes—venal, obtuse, human. Delivered in the jargon we more or less live by, they become woefully and ironically recognizable.

Andrew Lloyd Webber's score functions well, too, using rock as a frame rather than an obsession. The beat and blare establish an angle of hearing, telling us to cock our ears for the jumpy

directness of the lyrics. Inside the frame, though, are going to appear the genuine sweetness of Mary Magdalene's "**Everything's All Right**," the ragtime insult of Herod's clog-dance about his captive, the college-bowl exultation of "**Hosanna, Heysanna**" for Palm Sunday—that is to say, all, or nearly all, of the convenient sounds people reach for when they want to sorrow or celebrate. The music is unselfconscious in its borrowings from the melodious and the commonplace; it wants to say that the world was commonplace then, as it is now, in the presence of what it could not, cannot, fathom. If it is young work, and work for the young, it has the consistency of innocence, of stumbling upon familiar things with surprise and reacting instantly in slang. "**Jesus Christ Superstar**" is a pop opera about pop attitudes, and I think it works. (p. 1)

> Walter Kerr, '''Jesus Christ Superstar'—Two Views: A Critic Likes the Opera, Loathes the Production,'' in* The New York Times, *Section 2 (© 1971 by The New York Times Company; reprinted by permission), October 24, 1971, pp. 1, 7.*

JACK KROLL

It is a bit silly for religionists to argue over the theological points in the libretto of "**Superstar**." Rice has assembled his simple and familiar narrative line from all the Gospels, moving from the feast at Bethany through the entry into Jerusalem, the Last Supper, the agony in Gethsemane, Judas's betrayal, the Crucifixion. His choosing to pivot the "plot" around the question of Jesus' divinity is a natural decision as a child of his time. It is a perspective, even if a naive one, and the important thing is that he lets the drama move in a simple crescendo toward the white heat of that self-dissolving question. The lyrics, like those of most opera librettos (and "**Superstar**" formally is the most traditional kind of straight opera), often seem numb and dull, but sometimes are dulcetly melted or dramatically tempered in the flow of the music.

As Jesus enters the last seven days of his mortal life, Mary Magdalene comforts him, singing gently, "Everything's all right yes everything's fine." This, of course, is Jesus' own message of redemption and grace, which in this Passion week he has no occasion to utter. It is a good touch to have it unconsciously uttered in Mary's strictly human terms, and that defines a dialectical tension between the human and divine that is in the opera, if not by design then as a consequence of simple good faith toward their subject on the part of the authors.

But this simplicity and naivete is only part of the story. "**Jesus Christ Superstar**" is one of the most amazing and complicated media events of the media age. As it proliferates through the ganglia of a traumatized society . . . it becomes a perfect image of mass culture's wish to have its Christ and eat him too, its reach for the impossible dream: a happy marriage between comfortable vulgarity and the ache for excellence. (p. 243)

> Jack Kroll, ''Theater: 'Jesus Christ Superstar','' in* Newsweek *(copyright 1971, by Newsweek, Inc.; all rights reserved; reprinted by permission), October 25, 1971 (and reprinted in* New York Theatre Critics' Reviews, *Vol. XXXII, No. 15, October 11-18, 1971, pp. 243-44).*

DAN MORGENSTERN

Can a work so monstrously successful [as *Jesus Christ Superstar*] be all bad? The answer, sadly, is yes. The Gospel according to Tim, Tom [director Tom O'Horgan] and Andy is a far cry from Matthew, Mark, Luke and John. The music is banal, the lyrics infantile, the staging monumentally vulgar, the theological conception of the Passion of Christ a travesty. It is its success—and only that—which forces one to give it serious consideration. (p. 1)

It is difficult to determine what the intentions of Messrs. Webber and Rice really were.

Is *Superstar* a cynical attempt to cash in on the current "counterculture" trend toward religiosity? Is it a gigantic put-on, and will the authors come forward and confess after salting away their first five million? Is it a naive but honest work inspired by true religious feeling but hamstrung by lack of talent, taste and comprehension? Or is it merely a fluke—a shoddy piece of hackwork brought to prominence by a combination of timeless and clever, massive merchandizing?

The latter theory probably comes closest to the truth. . . .

Of course, *Superstar* may really be a revolutionary reinterpretation of the Passion, indeed of Jesus himself, which sees him as a petulant neurotic bent on self-destruction and carried away with his popularity, a firm believer in predestination who won't listen to Judas' good advice, a hollow superstar whose closest followers are silly fanheads.

But the treatment is too inconsistent to allow for such an interpretation. To be sure, Judas is the most interesting character in *Superstar*. . . . But his repentance and suicide . . . contradict his hero role, just as the cynical sentiments uttered by him after death . . . contradict the repentance.

No, it is unprofitable to look for clever conceits in this mess. The odd interpretations of the teachings of Jesus, the implications of seemingly original ideas are ordinary ignorance and nonsense. . . .

The real issue is not the sad meanspirited *kitsch* that is *Jesus Christ Superstar,* but the culture than can turn such a thing into a gigantic success while letting its honest artists go begging for handouts. . . .

Superstar is a work spawned by the generation that was going to build a new moral foundation for society. Is it representative of that generation? Is this bowdlerization of the Christian ethos its vaunted message of love and peace? . . .

It was once possible to hope that rock, as a cultural genre, had a viable and promising future, but even before the year JCS 1 grave doubts had arisen. If *Superstar* is an indication of where rock and the counterculture are taking us, it will not be toward a new dawn but into a long night. (p. 13)

> *Dan Morgenstern, " 'Superstar': Beyond Redemption!" in* down beat *(copyright 1971; reprinted with permission of* down beat*), Vol. 38, No. 21, December 9, 1971, pp. 1, 13.*

CLIVE BARNES

[The] rock legend of Joseph, fresher and brighter than **"Superstar,"** is an understandable knockout in [**"Joseph and the Amazing Technicolor Dreamcoat."**] It is totally unpretentious and, perhaps by the same token, totally charming.

> *Clive Barnes, "Stage: A New Troupe Performs at Edinburgh Fete," in* The New York Times *(© 1972 by The New York Times Company; reprinted by permission), September 5, 1972, p. 45.*

JAMES R. HUFFMAN

With *Jesus Christ Superstar,* the segment most often pincered for separate analysis is the younger generation—or sliced even thinner for microscopy, and for sensational copy, the counterculture and the Jesus Movements. Yet these ripples in American society are only peripherally related to the popularity of *Superstar.* . . . (p. 262)

The very first fact that the critic must deal with—rationally, not in righteous indignation—is the tremendous popularity of *Jesus Christ Superstar.* . . . Like the Beatles, though without apology, *Superstar* is probably more popular than Christ himself. (p. 263)

[The] immediate question is popular with whom? Certainly not with most critics, though a few have had the temerity to emphasize favorable aspects, and the usual number have hidden their judgments equivocally behind banter until they could see how Clive Barnes voted. The most common assumption is that the affluent young are making the work a superstar, and that the counterculture, "Jesus Freaks" and other Jesus movements are boosting it. But young people's reactions vary a great deal. . . . Perhaps the only common denominator is that most think it's worth listening to at least once. . . .

The Jesus Movements seem to have little to do with *Superstar* directly. . . . *Superstar* seems to have as many enemies as friends on the religious fringes.

And although the apostles ask "What's that in the bread? It's gone to my head," the counterculture is only marginally related to the work. . . . [The] counterculture can't afford to go to [the] extravaganza. . . . [To] see this Jesus as mainly "the passion of our counterculture," another rock star who buckles under the demands of his followers, makes the work a self-parody of the McLuhan message-medium and grossly distorts the effect of a Superstar Christ on most of the audience. To be sure, *Superstar* reflects current cultural preoccupations, but it neither arose directly from nor seems to be influencing either the Jesus Movements or the counterculture.

Nor is it a youthful New Testament for our time. Someone suggests that *Superstar* provides the beginnings of a substitute religion for the young. . . . But the market is already too crowded with ersatz religions to support another. Setting up a Superstar Christ as another opiate of the people—more poppycock?—fails to take into account its relation to the original opiate. . . . [It] preaches nothing, and neither Christ nor Judas are prophetic pop heroes. Yet some critics take it as an anticlimactic apex of all youth movements . . . and denounce it for not fulfilling what it never claimed to attempt.

But I have been trying to define the main audience of the work. As one observer noted before *Superstar* opened on Broadway, so far most of its following seems to be "Middle America." . . . They are neither "all the people," fooled this time, nor that portion of the people which can be fooled all the time, though critical conceptions of mass audiences tend to oscillate between these extremes. Rather, they are apparently a very *mixed* group. . . . (pp. 262-65)

The conception of mass audiences . . . , and consequently the nature of popular art, is very Protean. . . . People can shape what they like out of much popular art; indeed, malleability helps determine success. Whatever can be all things to all people—or the most things to the most people—will be the most successful. I don't mean to have titillated you to an anticlimax. It just seems to me that critics have failed to deal adequately with the greatest force in any mass culture: inertia. . . . Works like *Jesus Christ Superstar,* which "ask the right questions" but allow each individual to provide his own answers, will be appropriated by nearly all—the atheist, the agnostic, and the believer. Only the indifferent will remain unimpressed; only the devout and the aesthetically critical may be offended. Since *Superstar* is basically neutral, it can profit from nearly everyone's inertia.

With a great deal of religious controversy supposedly surrounding *Superstar,* it may seem paradoxical to call it a theological neutral. Certainly some specific aspects of it seem anything but orthodox: Judas is given star status at times; Mary Magdalene, by implication, may have also cooled the fires *between* Jesus' head and feet; and Jesus himself is so human in his doubts and frustrations that several have objected to his lack of divinity and assurance. But Tim Rice has been very careful to balance most unorthodoxies with opposing evidence, and most protesters have apparently been part of small minorities. Judas the betrayer is not a man anyone would trust implicitly, and he is terribly inconsistent and unsure of his motives. . . . After that early titillating suggestion that Magdalene is Christ's mistress, Rice clarifies his position: "Only a moron or a gorilla could say that Christ and Mary had an affair. . . . The last verse of Mary's song proves there was no affair." Furthermore, Christ may be either man or God in the piece: "We approach Christ as a man—the human angle—rather than as God. But we don't want to destroy anyone's belief. Christ as a God is there if you want it." (pp. 266-67)

Rice and Webber indicate that the work is primarily agnostic, but intentionally leaves room for both faith and atheism. . . . The opera does not take up the resurrection because of the difficulty of projecting a neutral interpretation of the event; it's either a hoax or a miracle. Similarly, Mary the mother of Jesus, a potential for high controversy between Protestants and Catholics, is left out entirely. (pp. 267-68)

This interpretation of *Superstar*'s popularity implies several things about popular art. . . . If inertia, or the adaptation of a piece to one's own beliefs and prejudices, is a major force in popular art, then art may never be a great reformer of masses. . . . Similarly, popular art is unlikely to convert many critics. The very ambiguity that provides a lowest common denominator for the broadest audience frustrates the critic demanding a consistent interpretation. And while ambiguity and ambivalence can be beautifully balanced in a work of art, and have made several classic works popular, they may also slide into simple inconsistency and incoherence. The critic's reaction is therefore likely to be frustrated rejection. (p. 269)

> *James R. Huffman, "'Jesus Christ Superstar'—Popular Art and Unpopular Criticism," in* Journal of Popular Culture *(copyright © 1972 by Ray B. Browne), Vol. 6, No. 2, Fall, 1972, pp. 259-69.*

ROY HOLLINGWORTH

I thought that **"Superstar,"** and now **"Joseph and the Amazing Technicolour Dreamcoat,"** were quite surely more decadent than Alice Cooper.

It's quite okay, and very lovable to have jolly portrayals of God—to all intents and purposes styled upon Santa Claus. It's a best-seller to have rock 'n' roll angels, tidy lyrics, neon tablets, and satire based upon The Bible.

But I sat there, and thought, "Herewith really makes a beginning of the end." Surely, I was laughing, for **"Joseph"** has incredibly funny moments. But . . . like, ya know, if yer a thinker, then you start to think about God in Neon. And then you start to think about dear George Orwell, and then "1984," and before you know it. . . . You know George was right. And that my friends, is exceedingly frightening.

Not that Mr. Rice or Mr. Lloyd-Webber meant to slander the remnants of society. Nay—they're writers, and writing extremely enjoyable things really. But, without knowing, we creep towards 1984. You see, once you present God in Neon, then there's little else to present.

It's not a case of reading things into things. **"Joseph"** might be called harmless. It's funny—[and] it'll become a world-favourite.

But will it make God a Superstar?

> *Roy Hollingworth, "Joseph: God in Neon," in* Melody Maker *(© IPC Business Press Ltd.), March 3, 1973, p. 45.*

VARIETY

["**Joseph and the Amazing Technicolor Dreamcoat**"] continues to impress with its charm, wit and inventive staging. It not only popularizes a portion of the Old Testament, but on another level operates as show business parody, kidding such personalities as Gene Autry and Elvis Presley. It's no knockout, but certainly a pleasing and buoyant entertainment. . . .

But because of its short length, **"Joseph"** appears doomed to be the victim of debilitating grafts. In this instance, the evening's first half yields an all-new and supposedly related work called **"Jacob's Journey,"** which is intended to foreshadow the **"Dreamcoat"** saga. It's not of the same quality, being essentially a mini-musical with vaude overtones. . . . Nor is the Webber-Rice score up to their standard. The piece, in short, has none of **"Joseph"**'s evident virtues and makes the double-bill a schizoid affair. . . .

Maybe **"Joseph"** should be left to its own devices, and booked on an exhibition circuit more suited to its scale.

> *"Shows Abroad: 'Joseph and the Amazing Technicolor Dreamcoat' & 'Jacob's Journey'," in* Variety *(copyright 1973, by Variety, Inc.), March 7, 1973, p. 72.*

LORAINE ALTERMAN

[I came to the film version of **"Jesus Christ Superstar"**] with virgin eyes and ears both of which were glazed after one hour and forty minutes of almost unmitigated boredom. At the risk of being sacrilegious, I couldn't wait until they nailed Jesus. . . .

[There's] the scene where Jesus is tossing the moneychangers out of the temple which is filled with postcard stands and hookers. In fact, in charging through the temple, Jesus breaks up a lot of mirrors and one can only conclude the curse of seven years bad luck was the reason Jesus died. The shallowness of most of the portrayals and simple-mindedness of a lot of the lyrics hardly make you feel there's any other reason. There is just nothing truly moving or inspiring about this film. . . .

The film **"Jesus Christ Superstar"** only underlines to me the dangers of trying to be too hip and groovy with a story that is one of the most important in history.

Loraine Alterman, "Holy Boredom: The Jesus Christ Superstar Film," in Melody Maker (© IPC Business Press Ltd.), June 16, 1973, p. 3.

JAMES M. WALL

Guided by a longtime prejudice against Broadway musicals and reinforced by a decade dedicated to fighting bathrobe-and-beard Bible films, I attended a preview screening, fully prepared to attack *Superstar* with all the snide sophistication I could muster. To my absolute amazement, I found the film to be compelling, moving and visually stunning. It is superb cinema, stimulating theology, and in no way anti-Semitic.

Superstar . . . accomplishes something I have never before seen in a biblical film: it portrays Jesus in a first century setting with a 20th century sensitivity. . . . [My] reaction, both cinematic and theological, is that *Superstar* is a fitting marriage of message and medium. This film works because the gospel story is meant to be told in poetry rather than prose. All previous Bible films . . . were hung up on narrative prose, with each episode presented in lurid and literal detail. *Superstar* sings its message in a contemporary idiom; the familiar characters have been deliberately cast in unexpected guises to reveal new insights into the Gospels. . . . (p. 693)

No dialogue intrudes to impose prose on the film. The emotional interchanges are sung to emphasize their larger-than-life significance. The film's hero is Judas; he is the character with whom the audience identifies. Some fear had been expressed that with a black performer . . . in the role, a "racist" implication might be drawn. On the contrary, Judas is presented as the only real friend Jesus has, struggling desperately to make him follow a reasonable course of action which will avoid bringing down the wrath of the establishment upon the whole lot of them. . . . Judas' relationship to Jesus is one of perplexed admiration, leading him to take steps that may or may not help to turn Jesus back toward the earlier path that once promised to lead to success. Far from being racist, this portrayal of Judas makes him the film's "everyman," the figure drawn to Jesus and yet unable to comprehend the strange demands he makes both on himself and on his followers. (pp. 693-94)

The charge of anti-Semitism plagued the original stage production, and there are indications that similar criticism has already been heard regarding the film version. The Pharisees, obviously villains in this opera, are far from being "Jewish" villains. They constitute the establishment, troubled by the admiration evoked by the reckless life style of Jesus. . . . [The] Pharisees represent the same kind of ominous power that Sergei Eisenstein gave his elaborately costumed and hooded German soldiers as they fought across the ice against Russian troops in his classic film *Alexander Nevsky*. . . .

Any charge of anti-Semitism leveled against this film will be based not on *Superstar* itself but on feelings generated by earlier portrayals of Jews as "Christ-killers." Such dated emotions are understandable, for there is an ugly history of anti-Semitism in our popular culture; the charge, however, is not appropriate for *Superstar*. . . .

[The young performers] have presented a vision of the man Jesus in their own musical style, and in the process have raised the same questions that have always been raised about him: Who is he and what is this strange power that drives him?

Jesus Christ Superstar is a film with its light moments . . . and its profound insights. . . . Above all, it is a work of cinematic art which just might strengthen the viewer's faith in its original story. (p. 694)

James M. Wall, "'Jesus Christ Superstar': A Surprising Film Success," in The Christian Century (copyright 1973 Christian Century Foundation: reprinted by permission from the June 27, 1973 issue of The Christian Century), Vol. XC, No. 25, June 27, 1973, pp. 693-94.

JON LANDAU

Jesus Christ Superstar [the film] is intellectually as vacuous as the Tim Rice and Andrew Lloyd Webber rock opera it so faithfully follows, . . . and religiously as authentic as Sunday morning services at the White House. . . .

[Almost everything in the film is played] for either laughs, irony or earnestness—not a shot in the film is corrupted by genuine emotion or sentiment. Jesus' character is so poorly drawn that we never understand either the appeal that he generates or the hostility he provokes. . . .

The sheer triviality of this film is ultimately unsettling. Its makers failed to take the subject seriously, refused to honor their story, and never committed themselves to the fundamentally tragic nature of this most potent of Western myths.

Jon Landau, "Jesus Christ, Star of Stage, Screen & 'Hullaballoo'," in Rolling Stone (by Straight Arrow Publishers, Inc. © 1973; all rights reserved; reprinted by permission), Issue 140, August 2, 1973, p. 54.

WILLIAM S. PECHTER

[It's] almost impossible to suggest the imaginative impoverishment, the sheer stupefying banality, of . . . [the] version of the last days of Christ [in the movie *Jesus Christ Superstar*]. . . . In another respect, however, I underestimated the work; I had expected the alleged anti-Semitism of the film to be no more than the random fallout of its pandering to the anti-establishment sentiments of its audience, to be, in that sense, unintentional. But though the villainy of the Jews "works," all right, so, too, would the villainy of the Romans, who, if anything, could have been a good deal more easily made stand-ins for cops or American imperialists than can the Jewish priesthood be equated with any of the usual *bêtes noires* of the counter-culture. Yet the Romans are so thoroughly exculpated by the film of any responsibility for Christ's crucifixion as to become virtual instruments of the Jewish priests, who bring Jesus to a reluctant Pilate with the demand "We need him crucified!" And though the Romans are hardly made attractive . . . Pilate is at least given an introductory speech in which, reflecting on a dream, he worries about his prospective involvement in Christ's death and how the future will judge him: "Then I saw thousands of millions / Crying for this man / And then I heard them mentioning my name / And leaving me the blame."

This speech, whatever it may lack in scriptural grounding, is at least consistent with the obsession that almost all the characters at one time or another manifest with respect to their standing with posterity, their image. . . . And even Jesus himself, foreseeing his death, inquires of God, "Will I be more noticed than I was before?" and, later, cries out on the cross, "My God, my God, why have you *forgotten* me?"—though possibly this last is less a case of meaningful textual emendation than of simple indifference to meaning, as is, presumably, Christ's elsewhere wanting to know that he won't "be *killed in vain.*"

In fact, I'd be tempted to say that this preoccupation with public relations is the *only* thing that gives any thematic consistency to the work. For the rest, though Judas starts by raising some pseudo-serious objections to Christ's billing ("You've begun to matter more than the things you say"), which, being in line with the work's title, were perhaps pursued in earlier versions, this is quickly seen to amount to nothing. (pp. 76-7)

But there is one thing more in which the film also maintains a stubborn consistency, and that is its anti-Semitism: having this film in general release is a bit like having a performance of a with-it version of the Oberammergau Passion Play down every block. Though it's hard to believe the work's portrayal of Jesus, cast in the effete plaster-saint mold of previous Hollywood Jesuses . . . , could fail to give offense to any Christian audience, I think one must distinguish here between trivialization or vulgarization and active animus. Not only is all culpability in Christ's death passed on to a malignant Jewish priesthood and blood-thirsty Jewish mob; the priests are also portrayed in a way that is clearly indebted to classically vilifying stereotypes. . . . Judas, who is depicted as the tool of Jewish interests, is played by a black actor, and images of his being menaced by tanks and jet fighters, though not out of keeping with the movie's other deliberate anachronisms, cannot fail to suggest the notion of Third World victimization by the warlike might of Israel. . . .

I'm quite willing to believe that *Jesus Christ Superstar* was created by people who sincerely believe themselves to be free of any animus toward the Jews; in some ways, this makes only more disturbing the fact that the film is shot through with anti-Semitic feeling. Doubtless conceived in a spirit of unalloyed commerce, the work, like most other books, records, plays, and movies, clearly has as its muse the jackass. But the jackal's mark is unmistakably on it. (p. 77)

> *William S. Pechter, "Politics on Film: 'Jesus Christ Superstar'" (copyright © 1973 by William S. Pechter; reprinted by permission of the author), in Commentary, Vol. 56, No. 3, September, 1973, pp. 76-7.*

JOHN SIMON

[The movie version of *Jesus Christ Superstar* is] in many ways odious and in all ways absurd. . . .

[The] entire story is presented without any original point of view, the only slightly significant departure being Christ's virtually provoking and coercing Judas into betraying him so as to fulfill the grand design. But I doubt if, at this late date, that is likely to give rise to a new heresy or serious schism.

No, the offense is of a different order. It is, first, in the text, which is faithfully that of Tim Rice for the "rock opera," and translates the sublime prose of the gospels into witless doggerel. "Listen, Jesus, I don't like what I see / All I ask is that you listen to me," Judas expostulates with his master. . . . Jesus himself gives out with things like "Then I was inspired, /

Now I'm sad and tired" and "My time is almost through, / Little left to do. . . . " As Judas puts it to Jesus, "But every word you say today / Gets twisted round some other way," which will also serve as a fair description of Tim Rice's lyric-writing.

But if the words are all bad—sounding like the unholy writ of Edgar Guest in collaboration with Norman Vincent Peale—the music by Andrew Lloyd Webber is not all deafening commonplaces. Though it is not exactly the kind of rock you can build a church on—sometimes, in fact, it sounds like recycled Massenet—it does have its tuneful or rousing moments. . . . [The] supreme failure is the director's own for trying to fill in the vacuity of the material with desperate stratagems of montage and camera trickery, and by feverishly latching on to bits of contemporary relevance that no other cat would have dragged in. (p. 44)

Some six decades ago, the distinguished German aesthetician Konrad Lange accused the then nascent world film production of being in the hands of "semi-educated, aesthetically feelingless, ethically indifferent, in short, spiritually inferior people," and as one watches this movie, it would be hard to disagree. It is extremely doubtful even whether one can forgive them because, as the King James version had it, they know not what they do, or, as the present text prosaicizes it, they don't know what they're doing. (p. 46)

> *John Simon, "Films: 'Jesus Christ Superstar'" (reprinted by permission of Wallace & Sheil Agency, Inc.; copyright © 1973 by John Simon), in Esquire, Vol. 80, No. 4, October, 1973, pp. 44, 46 (and to be reprinted in his Reverse Angle, Clarkson N. Potter Inc., 1981).*

CLIVE BARNES

Being wrong is never funny. When I saw **"Joseph and the Amazing Technicolor Dreamcoat"** in London a couple of years or so ago [see excerpt above], I thought it was pretty good. Modestly good. Not incredible, but viable. . . .

In many ways it is better than **"Jesus Christ, Superstar."** At least it is not quite so pretentious. But those many ways are not enough. In London it seemed acceptable. In Brooklyn, with, I think, a slightly jazzed-up staging, it seems a loud and pushy bore. . . .

Why are so many modern—or so-distant modern—musicals based on biblical themes? This **"Joseph"** makes so many of its points—those such as it makes—with a semi-mocking attitude to its subject. It takes Joseph, gives him a plaintive voice, surrounds him with the blue-jeaned cohorts and an abundance of disco, go-go dancing. Some years ago this seemed moderately smart—it certainly seemed better than the gargantuan excesses of **"Jesus Christ, Superstar."** Now it seems empty. The music beats on and on, the story is made into a candy-colored legend, and only the staging engages the attention. . . .

The show looks good, but it just doesn't sound good. One musical number after another plonks lifeless on the deck. And the story never for a moment sustains its characters. We cannot get even remotely involved with Joseph—whether with his coat or not.

The music is soft-rock, and nowadays seems a paraphrase of a pastiche. It has no originality—a few liturgical notes with a great deal of rock frenzy—and the lyrics are merely simplistic. It is not especially clever, in itself, to bring a biblical story into modern times. Even the wretched "Godspell" was able to do that. . . .

Perhaps it was a show that had a special time and a special place, and perhaps the time was two or three years ago and the place was London. Or perhaps I was simply wrong the first time around. But it honestly did seem more attractive then.

> Clive Barnes, "Stage: 'Technicolor Dreamcoat'," in The New York Times (© 1976 by The New York Times Company; reprinted by permission), December 31, 1976, p. C3.

ERIC SALZMAN

Composer Andrew Lloyd Webber and lyricist Tim Rice of, first, the pop-rock musical *Jesus Christ, Superstar* and, now, *Evita* are a couple of pop-art geniuses; what they lack is talent. . . .

[Eva Peron's life] is certainly the stuff of opera, and opera is just what our heroes have propsed: great sumptuous orchestrations played by the London Philharmonic, funny off-key recitatives, Menotti-modern-opera scenes, choral madrigals, frenzied chants, and Latin lamentations, as well as heavy-beat rock music, much of it with a greasy sort of Latin overlay.

But is all this panoply mere show without substance? So it seems; one looks in vain for content. In the case of *Superstar,* Webber and Rice had some familiar dramatic material to work with. Here they need to sort it out themselves, and they don't. Politics gets short shrift, and so they miss out on the great background story of how a populist, working-people's movement becomes a fascist dictatorship with a sex symbol to sugarcoat the pill. There's no more than the minimum social background. . . .

The attitude toward the characters is ambiguous. Peron is a stooge and has virtually nothing to sing. The real male lead is someone ominously named "Ché" who seems to be more interested in pushing the new insecticide he's developed than in helping tell Eva's story. Whatever the *intent*, this character bears no resemblance to Ché Guevara . . . and he has no relevance to the plot. He is not even an effective commentator but really just a device to get on with the story. Eva herself is hardly dramatized at all; she is a puppet and, strangely, not at all likable. Even her big emotional addresses to the people of Argentina, set over and over again to the same music, are like a prostitute's bag of faked emotional tricks. Dramatization requires characters, conflict, discoveries, mysteries, comedies, tragedies, surprises, knowns, unknowns, ironies, loves, hates, sympathies, deceits—all of which our authors forgot or didn't know how to supply. And an opera (or music theater or lyric theater or whatever) must develop these motifs musically, not only expressing ideas and emotions but also carrying events on its musical back.

Perhaps one should forget about all this—after all, *Evita* is just a recording at this point, not a dramatic presentation—and concentrate on words and music. Both are great lumpy concoctions of clichés, awkwardnesses, and ripped-off ideas (would you believe *Swan Lake* and *Both Sides Now*?) leavened with flashes of brilliance. Now and again parts congeal into bouncy, cynical, outrageous, campy Latin-rock or folk-rock numbers. The focus of the whole is Eva's speech to the crowd at Peron's inauguration. This song or aria, . . . actually moving in a counterfeit sort of way, is based entirely on a couple of dumb

emotional tunes that are repeated over and over again (before, during, and after) so that they burn their way into your brain.

Up to the end of Part I we are carried along on the impetus of Eva's rise to power, set as a series of strokes of high banality and low camp. But once she has arrived, there is nowhere to go, musically or dramatically. Everything grinds to a halt. Part II is full of draggy, bad modern-opera-isms and fake Caribbean tunes along with endless repetitions of music from Part I, some of it pasted up in mawkish, awkward collage. In the end, we cannot untangle the dramatic, verbal, and musical skeins, and, indeed, the authors' ambitions do not permit us to do so. When the dramatic form crumbles, the musical ebullience and the flashes of brilliance flicker out too.

> Eric Salzman, "Another Little Eva Altogether," in Stereo Review (copyright © 1977 by Ziff-Davis Publishing Company), Vol. 38, No. 4, April, 1977, p. 108.

CHARLES PERRY

Tim Rice and Andrew Lloyd Webber have chosen Eva Perón . . . as heroine of [*Evita*,] their followup to *Jesus Christ Superstar,* and it must be confessed that there is a certain logic to the choice. The one memorable song from *Jesus Christ Superstar*, "I Don't Know How to Love Him," belonged not to the hero but to the blameless whore Mary Magdalene. Here the blameless whore is the centerpiece and once again has the song, "Don't Cry for Me, Argentina."

Outside of that bit of cleaning up, the rest is *Superstar* recycled: mobs of foolish actors, prissy, narrow-minded aristocrats, cartoonish Powers That Be, a cynical narrator who gives the lowdown on the celebrity hero. Once again the characters are one and all inferior to us in the audience—even the cynic is portrayed as a fool and an asshole. He is known only as Che, but this Che is a clown. . . .

The logic is good. . . . But it remains to be seen whether Webber and Rice can make the switch from luring teenagers to Jesus via rock & roll to stirring kind thoughts toward Eva Perón among tango fans. God alone knows, and He's keeping a straight face.

> Charles Perry, "Records: 'Evita: An Opera Based on the Life Story of Eva Perón 1919-1952'," in Rolling Stone (by Straight Arrow Publishers, Inc. © 1977; all rights reserved; reprinted by permission), Issue 236, April 7, 1977, p. 76.

MARTIN GOTTFRIED

[The likes of *Evita*] have never been seen before; while it uses techniques developed in such Broadway shows as *Cabaret* and *Follies*, it rises to still higher theatrical purpose. . . .

Like their previous *Jesus Christ Superstar*, Rice and Webber's *Evita* was initially written for a record album and termed a "rock opera." It is hardly biographical in the usual sense. It is a creature utterly of the stage. Rice's lyrics—his "libretto"—merely provided an excuse for [director Harold] Prince's elevation of the entire project to a new dimension. . . . [Webber's music] has been fleshed out and deepened to become a new kind of theater music, and crashing dissonances underlining light melodies. . . .

The intellectual content of [the plot] takes second place to theatricality, and wisely so, but perhaps inevitably the final act is a letdown. The first act was almost impossible to top. The intermission may have given too much of a break. Certainly, the second act could use new material, for it is repetitious in all respects—music, event, staging. Yet, there is no question of the entire production's strength and uniqueness. Whether *Evita* is British or American doesn't matter. It has made musical theater international.

Martin Gottfried, "Two Shots in the Arm for the London Stage," in Saturday Review (copyright © 1978 by Saturday Review; all rights reserved; reprinted by permission), Vol. 5, No. 26, October 14, 1978, p. 57.*

CLIVE BARNES

Evita is a stunning, exhilarating theatrical experience, especially if you don't think about it too much. . . .

[It is] a virtually faultless piece of Broadway fantasy that has shadow exultantly victorious over substance, and form virtually laughing at content.

First let me stress that this pop-opera . . . is wonderfully entertaining in everything but the aftertaste of its pretensions. But don't cry for [Andrew Lloyd Webber and Tim Rice] anyone—this deserves to be a sizeable hit. . . .

This is a more vital attempt at pop-opera than was the author's previous *Jesus Christ Superstar*. Rice has constructed his libretto with coherence and his deliberately abrasive lyrics generally achieve just the right slogan-like simplicity. . . . [Lloyd Webber's score] has a bull-dozing charm and the memorability of the already half-remembered.

The fault of the whole construction is that it is hollow. We are expected to deplore Evita's morals but adore her circuses. We are asked to accept a serious person onstage, of a complexity Hammerstein would never have even murmured to Rodgers, and yet the treatment of that person is essentially superficial, almost trivial. The gloss of the surface is meant to be impenetrable—and it is.

But what a gloss! . . .

You must see *Evita*. For all the disappointments of its undelivered promises and eroded aspirations, it is a definite marker-point in the ongoing story of the Broadway musical.

Clive Barnes, "A Stunning 'Evita' Seduces with Its Gloss," in New York Post (reprinted by permission of the New York Post; © 1979, News Group Publications, Inc.), September 26, 1979 (and reprinted in New York Theatre Critics' Reviews, Vol. XXXX, No. 17, October 1-8, 1979, p. 154).

WALTER KERR

There's an eerily prophetic line close to the very opening of **"Evita,"** the Tim Rice-Andrew Lloyd Webber musical that chooses to sing about the brief, bizarre life of Eva Perón and her joint rule of Argentina with her dictator-husband, Juan. The evening opens with the announcement of her death at 33. . . .

The lady's coffin is not yet closed, though. That will be done by Che himself, slapping the great lid shut and sending clouds of dust flying into the bleak, steelwork sky. He then sings the couplet that is going to prove both accurate and, to the enter-

tainment, damaging: "As soon as the smoke from the funeral clears / We're all gonna see she did nothing for years."

That is precisely the problem confronting director Harold Prince and the onetime authors of **"Jesus Christ Superstar."** As they have charted out the enterprise, Evita is going to use a sleek-haired tango singer to make her way to the big city, she's going to dump him for a succession of more and more important lovers, she's going to snare the mighty man who's about to win Argentina's lethal game of musical chairs, she's going to pose as a friend of the poor while accumulating an impressive supply of furs and diamond-studded gowns, she's going to be called a whore before she's through, and her body's due to waste away as cancer strikes her early.

Yet we almost never see any of these things happen dramatically onstage. We hear about them at second-hand, mainly from the omnipresent Che. . . . Whenever Che is briefly silent, we are getting the news from lyrics or recitative sung by top-hatted aristocrats, breathless messengers, almost anyone at hand. It is rather like reading endless footnotes from which the text has disappeared, and it puts us into the kind of emotional limbo we inhabit when we're just back from the dentist but the no-vocaine hasn't worn off yet.

To be fair, there are at least two passages in which we are really present at a key confrontation. The first occurs when Evita strides peremptorily into Perón's bedroom to dispossess the schoolgirl mistress in residence. "I've just unemployed you," she snaps to the youngster as she snatches her suitcase from beneath the bed and swiftly packs it. It's probably *because* two people have settled something face-to-face that we are so taken with the melodic plaint that follows (**"Another Suitcase in Another Hall"**). . . .

And, near the second act's end, there is a genuine personal clash between Evita and Perón, both pacing from one bedroom to another, she determined on being named Vice President, he bluntly pointing out that her glitter is gone and what's left will soon be ashes. If we ever begin, however remotely, to feel something for this no-holds-barred opportunist, it is as she crumples to the floor still insisting that half the power is hers. The contest between approaching death and a stubborn will stirs a faint twinge in us, I think, because it's been acted out, fought harshly before our eyes.

Otherwise we are condemned to hearing what we want to know—*need* to know, if we're to offer any kind of response—relayed to us by a narrator. The use of Che Guevara for the purpose seems to me approximately as opportunist as Evita's own manipulations. Not because, factually, he wasn't there at the time, had nothing whatever to do with the Peróns. But because he is most often employed to make certain that we won't go developing a crush on Evita ourselves. . . .

In effect, this keeps us permanently outside the action, unable to decipher Evita's complexities for ourselves. We ask ourselves, in vain, how this dubious and remote heroine managed to get close enough to Perón to work her will on him, what it was she did to endear herself to a gullible population. Because vital scenes are simply absent, there are no conclusions, no judgments, we can arrive at on our own. They've all been handed down, hammered down, from the outset. We're not participants, we're recipients of postal cards (and photographs) from all over. Which is a chilly and left-handed way to write a character-musical. (p. 149)

[One goes] home wondering why the authors chose to write a musical about materials they were then going to develop so remotely, so thinly. (p. 150)

Walter Kerr, "'Evita', a Musical Perón," in The New York Times *(© 1979 by The New York Times Company; reprinted by permission), September 26, 1979 (and reprinted in* New York Theatre Critics' Reviews, *Vol. XXXX, No. 17, October 1-8, 1979, pp. 149-50).*

HOWARD KISSEL

Like **"Jesus Christ Superstar,"** Tim Rice and Andrew Lloyd-Webber's **"Evita"** . . . is history seen as a form of show business. Since Eva Peron was more directly related to show biz than Jesus, one would expect the Rice-Lloyd-Webber material to be more pointed than their earlier show. Alas, it is only more banal.

Rice's lyrics have the naive outrage of Sixties radical kids. . . . Occasionally Rice achieves an old-fashioned musical comedy cleverness. . . . More often they merely convey rhetoric with no sense of style, euphony or grace.

Lloyd-Webber's music frequently sounds like mis-hummed fragments of familiar tunes. . . . Most of the music is characterless, often singsong—perhaps it was kept deliberately simple to guarantee we would be able to grasp Rice's banal lyrics. (pp. 154-55)

There have been reports **"Evita"** has been modified since its London production, where there was concern the fascistic heroine was somehow being glorified. If she had been, it would at least have given **"Evita"** a perverse fascination—like the one that surrounds "Don Giovanni" or "Richard III." As it is, **"Evita"** is an astringent character, too much an object of satire and moralistic comment ever to come to life. . . .

From its very title, **"Evita"** promises to be outrageous. It is as if a musical about Eva Braun were titled "Fraulein" or "Little Eva." These days, however, we have outgrown outrage. The material takes us back to the Sixties, even while the stage craft propels us into the Eighties. (p. 155)

Howard Kissel, "'Evita'," in Women's Wear Daily *(copyright 1979, Fairchild Publications), September 26, 1979 (and reprinted in* New York Theatre Critics' Reviews, *Vol. XXXX, No. 17, October 1-8, 1979, pp. 154-55).*

JACK KROLL

Last year, at the World Cup soccer matches in Buenos Aires, the huge crowd roared, "We want the thieves back! We want the thieves!" Why do the people of a relatively advanced, sophisticated country yearn for the neo-Fascist paternalism and fake messianism of an Eva Perón? That is the true horror of her story, and **"Evita"** doesn't confront it. Why isn't there at least one song given to the descamisados, in which we learn about their attitude toward their idol? Even Che Guevara could have been used to better effect. Late in his career he made initiatives toward the exiled Perón (as did Fidel Castro himself); there's an opportunity for a number in which the "true revolutionary" expresses his own ambivalence toward the ambiguous figure of Eva. But **"Evita"** only sentimentalizes her. (p. 153)

Jack Kroll, "'Evita' in Soft Focus," in Newsweek *(copyright 1979, by Newsweek, Inc.; all rights reserved; reprinted by permission), October 8, 1979 (and reprinted in* New York Theatre Critics' Reviews, *Vol. XXXX, No. 17, October 1-8, 1979, pp. 152-53).*

Richard Wright

1908-1960

Black American novelist, short story writer, and essayist.

Wright is considered the most esteemed spokesman for the oppressed black American in the late 1930s and 1940s. His earliest fiction, *Uncle Tom's Children,* portrayed the violent mechanics of Southern racial bigotry with unprecedented realism. Two of the stories, "Fire and Cloud" and "Bright and Morning Star," contain Wright's first explicit use of communism as a subject of his fiction and, in this way, anticipate his next work, *Native Son.*

Native Son chronicles the effects of racism and bigotry on the mind and life of Bigger Thomas, a young Northern black man. It is at once, and with varying degrees of success, a thriller, a psychological novel, and a social and political indictment. The violence in *Native Son* is intense and explicit and presented as the inevitable outcome of the black experience in America. Such a presentation was extremely radical for its time and verified the fact that Wright did not want sympathy or, in his words, "banker's daughter's tears," from his mostly white audience. Because of the book's implication that society has created and is responsible for the tragedy of Bigger Thomas, *Native Son* was read with great emotion and quickly became one of the most controversial books of its time.

Although Wright's interest in communism was evident in his early fiction, these works were mainly recreations of the experiences of his childhood and young manhood in the South. Of these early works, *Black Boy* is considered Wright's masterpiece. Unlike the sometimes didactic *Native Son,* it is thought to be one of America's most eloquent and effective protest autobiographies.

Wright seemed to experience a creative crisis after his break with the Communist party in 1944 and his move to France in 1946. While in France, he published several works of fiction and nonfiction that were considered inferior to his earlier work. Many critics attribute Wright's literary decline to his attempt to incorporate existential and Freudian tenets into his fiction.

The Outsider was the first novel Wright wrote after *Native Son.* Using an existential framework, the novel is the story of a black man who becomes involved with a Marxist group, murders several of its members, and is then murdered himself. *The Outsider* met with lukewarm reception; critics called it ambitious but poorly executed. Wright's next novel, *Savage Holiday,* pointedly avoids racial issues. Its white protagonist is symbolic of alienated modern humanity, caught in a tangle of despair and neuroses. Few American critics reviewed the book, and those who did were not complimentary. In *The Long Dream,* the last novel Wright wrote before his death, he studies the relationship between a black man and his son and black/white relations in a small Mississippi town. *The Long Dream* received mixed reviews from white critics and generally unfavorable notices from black critics who felt that Wright had lost touch with the black American experience.

In spite of Wright's poor critical success in the 1950s, he has without question made an important contribution to American literature. Critics continue to debate the literary merits of

Ellen Wright

Native Son, but most concede that the book was a watershed in the evolution of black protest fiction. *Black Boy* is considered an American classic. Interest in Wright was revived in the militancy of the 1960s; Stokely Carmichael, Eldridge Cleaver, and H. Rap Brown, among others, claim Wright as an influence and an inspiration. (See also *CLC,* Vols. 1, 3, 4, 9, and 14.)

W. E. BURGHARDT Du BOIS

["Black Boy"] tells a harsh and forbidding story and makes one wonder just exactly what its relation to truth is. The [subtitle], "A Record of Childhood and Youth," makes one at first think that the story is autobiographical. It probably is, at least in part. But mainly it is probably intended to be fiction or fictionalized biography. At any rate the reader must regard it as creative writing rather than simply a record of life. . . .

Not only is there [a] misjudgment of black folk and the difficult repulsive characters among them that he is thrown with, but the same thing takes place with white folk. There is not a single broad-minded, open-hearted white person in his book. . . .

One rises from the reading of such a book with mixed thoughts. Richard Wright uses vigorous and straightforward English; often there is real beauty in his words even when they are mingled with sadism. . . .

Yet at the result one is baffled. Evidently if this is an actual record, bad as the world is, such concentrated meanness, filth and despair never completely filled it or any particular part of it. But if the book is meant to be a creative picture and a warning, even then, it misses its possible effectiveness because it is as a work of art so patently and terribly overdrawn.

Nothing that Richard Wright says is in itself unbelievable or impossible; it is the total picture that is not convincing.

> *W. E. Burghardt Du Bois, "Richard Wright Looks Back," in* New York Herald Tribune Weekly Book Review, *March 4, 1945, p. 2.*

R. L. DUFFUS

In this poignant and disturbing book ["**Black Boy: A Record of Childhood and Youth**"] one of the most gifted of America's younger writers turns from fiction to tell the story of his own life during the nineteen years he lived in the South. The book is poignant because Richard Wright as a child and adolescent was a highly sensitive individual subjected to a series of cruel and almost unbearable shocks. It is disturbing because one wonders how many similarly sensitive individuals have been crushed by the circumstances which did not crush Richard Wright. . . .

It is not easy for those who have had happier childhoods, with little restraint or fear in them, to face up to the truth of this childhood of Richard Wright. One doesn't like to think that the world in which he lived was an American world. How many Negroes saw that world in the same way, to what extent Richard Wright's experience was exceptional, one doesn't know. . . .

Mr. Wright does not idealize either his relatives or his race. The reader will come to understand that the family troubles and dissensions were intensified by the fact of race and racial discrimination, but Mr. Wright does not make a thesis of this point. They were what they were. . . . Mr. Wright does not even believe in the passionate quality sometimes attributed to Negroes in America, the depth of feeling behind the mask. He came to think that "what had been taken for our emotional strength was our negative confusions, our flights, our fears, our frenzy under pressure."

Mr. Wright does not, in fact, speak for all Southern Negroes. Some of them, intellectual, highly educated and of unimpaired dignity, have managed to survive in the Southern environment. But this Mr. Wright, conditioned as he was by the circumstances in which he found himself, could not do. He did not feel himself inferior, yet in order to survive he had to act the part of an inferior. A human sense of dignity—not a black or white sense—was born in him. . . .

Wright could have been a poet and possibly, in his realistic way, is one. The question as to what extent his grim childhood and youth developed his creative power, or to what extent it twisted it, must remain unanswered. Certainly it did not kill it, for the power remains. But what would Richard Wright have been in a more genial social climate? In France, perhaps?

The Negro has his real as well as his merely self-acclaimed friends in the South. There is a movement there, not against segregation but against privileges for one race that are denied to the other. There are Southerners who are not afraid to preach the human dignity of the Negro, knowing that the abasement of any individual degrades in some degree all others. To such Southerners Richard Wright's book will be a challenge and an occasion for searching of hearts.

> *R. L. Duffus, "Deep-South Memoir," in* The New York Times Book Review *(© 1945 by The New York Times Company; reprinted by permission), March 4, 1945, p. 3.*

RAYMOND KENNEDY

["**Black Boy**"] has tremendous power. Its intensity of feeling, sustained drama, and sheer eloquence make reading it an unforgettable experience. This is because it is the product of a remarkable combination: an author of superb talent, a life story of pathos and tragedy, and a human theme of monumental significance.

The story of Wright's own life in the South during his childhood and youth is a true document of race relations in America, for, although as autobiography it is highly personalized, the author's eyes and ears and emotions were vibrantly sensitive, so that he missed as little of what went on around him as what went on inside him. Man and *milieu*, as described by Wright, demonstrate certain truths about the South, and about Negroes in the South, which seldom strike the consciousness of the American public—certainly not with the impact of this book.

"**Black Boy**" has been criticised by some reviewers for painting an unrelieved picture of misery, terror, and degradation among the masses of Negroes in the Southern States. Yet this is, in my judgment, the reality, as anyone who has come to know the situation intimately can testify. (pp. 762-63)

Probably the most common criticism of this book by reviewers is that there are no half-tones in the author's picture of Negro life in the South, that the scene is sketched entirely in stark black and white. Here again, in my opinion, the accusation of overdrawing is little justified. This, with few exceptions, is precisely how race relations are in the Southern States: clean-cut black and white. The Negroes must either surrender and allow themselves to be spiritually stunted and deformed, or they must get out of the South. To a sensitive and high-spirited Negro like Wright, surrender was impossible. ("I was not made to be a resigned man. . . . I could submit and live the life of a genial slave, but that was impossible.")

And so Wright left the South. His book ends at the moment of flight, and in a magnificent passage he delivers his valedictory beginning with these lines: "I was not leaving the South to forget the South, but so that some day I might understand it, might come to know what its rigors had done to me, to its children." (p. 764)

> *Raymond Kennedy, "A Dramatic Autobiography," in* The Yale Review *(© 1945, copyright renewed © 1973, by Yale University; reprinted by permission of the editors), Vol. XXXIV, No. 4, June, 1945, pp. 762-64.*

GRANVILLE HICKS

["**Uncle Tom's Children**," "**Native Son**," and "**Black Boy**"] not only made it clear that Mr. Wright was the most eloquent spokesman for the Negro people in his generation; they suggested that his was one of the important literary talents of our time. How important it is, and how little limited to a particular group of people, is demonstrated by his fourth book and second novel "**The Outsider.**". . .

"**The Outsider,**" [like "**Native Son,**"] is concerned with the quest for meaning: not, however, in terms of racial discrimination nor in any sociological terms whatever, but in purely philosophical terms. The leading character is, to be sure, a Negro, but his principal problems have nothing to do with his race. They are pre-eminently the problems of the human being as such, for this is, so far as I can recall, one of the first consciously existentialist novels to be written by an American. . . .

[The] true climax of the novel is in the realm of ideas, not that of violent deeds. Questioned about his attitude toward communism by a party leader after the murders, Cross sets forth his philosophy of history in a long speech that is comparable, as an expression of Mr. Wright's thinking to Mr. Max's speech . . . in "**Native Son.**" (p. 1)

"**The Outsider**" is both melodrama and novel of ideas, attempting to render Mr. Wright's "sense of our contemporary living" in both emotional and intellectual terms. If the ideas are sometimes incoherent, that does not detract from the substance and power of the book. It is in the description of action, especially violent action, that Mr. Wright excels, not merely because he can make the reader see but because he compels him to participate. There is not a murder in the book that the reader, at the moment of reading about it, does not feel that he would have committed under the same circumstances. Nor is the sense of participation limited to the dramatic scenes: the expression of ideas, even in the long and more or less incoherent speeches, becomes a form of action in which one is swept along. And Mr. Wright achieves all this in spite of a persisting clumsiness of style.

He has always been a demonic writer, and in the earliest of his stories one felt that he was saying more than he knew, that he was, in a remarkable degree, an unconscious artist. He has grown in awareness since then, and in "**The Outsider**" he has made his most valiant and his most successful effort to come to terms with his feelings about the human condition. But there are still unrecognized compulsions and one suspects that they have a great deal to do with the power of the book. No one who has read "**Black Boy**" can be surprised that Mr. Wright is preoccupied with violence, but almost certainly the causes of this preoccupation lie even deeper than the experiences he has described. The preoccupation would be less significant if this were a less violent world.

It must be clear that "**The Outsider**"—like [Ralph Ellison's] "**The Invisible Man,**" which it resembles in several ways— is only incidentally a book about Negroes. Being a Negro helps Cross Damon to understand that he is an outsider, as it helps Ralph Ellison's hero to understand that he is an invisible man, but there are many invisible men and many outsiders. "**The Outsider**" is, as it was intended to be, a book about modern man, and, because of Mr. Wright's irresistible driving force, it challenges the modern mind as it has rarely been challenged in fiction. It is easy to disagree with, impossible to disregard. (p. 35)

Granville Hicks, "The Portrait of a Man Searching," in The New York Times Book Review *(© 1953 by The New York Times Company; reprinted by permission), March 22, 1953, pp. 1, 35.*

ROBERT HATCH

Richard Wright's new novel [*The Long Dream*] is not a book to be studied from a distance, to gain perspective on a work of art. It should be examined myopically, close to the page, as one reads the chart of a strange and dangerous passage. . . .

The structure of *The Long Dream* is the step-by-step progress of Fishbelly, a shy black boy, from the safe, warm world of the Negro ghetto into the lawless world between the races where a few Negroes, preying on black and white alike, have the arrogance to live by their wits. It opens up aspects of the South not covered by dictionary words like "segregation" or "miscegenation." Its key words are "rape" and "blood," "lynch" and "hide," "lie" and "scream." And above all, "run." (p. 297)

But structure is not what you should look at in this book. Richard Wright is a man of considerable literary ability, a man who has made a living for twenty years or more with his writing, but who nevertheless is not primarily a writer. Many literary men have fought crusades; Wright is a crusader who fights with words. It makes a difference and it accounts for the special quality of his fiction. *The Long Dream* is not a badly-made book, as you will discover if you try to pull it to pieces. It is very strong, but its workmanship is careful only where care is needed for Wright's purpose. Elsewhere the book is boldly hammered together—not as a work of art but as the scaffolding for an idea.

Thus, in a given scene, the characters are so vivid that the noise and smell of them come straight to your senses. But how they get from scene to scene, how they develop in understanding and experience from episode to episode, is another matter. The fact is that, having made a point, Wright packs his people up and carts them to where they are needed for the next demonstration. What will throw you off, if you approach *The Long Dream* with the usual instruments of critical measurement, is that the narrative is a palpable machine, but the people are real. You do not often find flesh and blood thus contending on a stage for puppets; it happens this way because Wright spends his talent, not for art, but for an idea.

I do not doubt that if he were a greater artist, he would carry his idea with still greater power. On the other hand, if he concerned himself more with art, he might well fail of the great rough-hammered platforms he erects.

And he does polish his work as the years pass. He writes now with much more control than he once showed, his ear is wonderfully acute and his judgment of emotional degree and balance is subtle, varied and exciting. Still more he grows in understanding of the problem to which he has devoted his life. Wright is an advocate, not a judge, he sees race from the viewpoint of the Negro, and one does not look to him for any withdrawn, balanced appraisal of issues. But he is not bemused, either, by the sufferings of his people. He does not think that suffering is ennobling or that the Negro is a pure creature in an evil land. Corruption is corruption and Wright exposes it. (pp. 297-98)

There is real sorrow in this and an approach to love. It is in the poignant vision of the two races locked in terrible, degrading embrace that Wright, a truly proud Negro, has isolated the essence of the tragedy. (p. 298)

Robert Hatch, "Either Weep or Laugh," in The Nation *(copyright 1958 The Nation magazine, The Na-*

tion Associates, Inc.), Vol. 187, No. 13, October 25, 1958, pp. 297-98.

WILLIAM DUNLEA

[*The Long Dream* is] a novel throbbing with the same racial traumas that have done much to compel for its author a large interracial audience ever since *Native Son,* the classic Negro novel of social protest. That book appeared in 1940, and, judging by his latest, Richard Wright is angrier than he was then.

The color motif dominates all of Mr. Wright's novels to the extent that the social-historical context outweighs the literary. It is not only because *The Long Dream* is a more uneven work than the poignant *Native Son* that it is so disappointing. Hot with the fumes of an incendiary counterracism, it could not have chosen a less propitious time to be "timely." Certainly it is the most racist of all of this author's anti-racist fiction.

Richard Wright's work has in general been more race-conscious than social-conscious; its crusading timbre has helped to placard him for some as *the* spokesman of the American Negro. For the last ten years he has been in Paris, yet the time of this novel, which is set in the Black Belt of a fictive Clintonville, Mississippi, is exactly this past decade of his absence.

Besides taking Jim Crow in their stride, the Negroes in this story incur virtually every indignity and injustice known to their kind in fact or literature. Yet Wright is not martyrizing them nor exposing their forbearance to easy sympathy; he is deprecating their compliant submission as equivalent to conspiring in their own abasement. As he proceeds to hammer out his thesis, his writing, measured against its earlier attainments, registers loss in narrative sweep, gain in psychological acumen, with these factors operating at cross purposes.

Through the boy "Fishbelly," six when the novel begins, eighteen when it ends, the psyche of the contemporary Deep South Negro is explored; he is the chief medium for the almost incessant editorializing, which all too often entails scrubby prose like: "The emotionally devastating experiences . . . hung suspended in his psychological digestion like stubborn, cold lumps." Mr Wright means to see that the niceties get home. There is even "aside" comment on dialogue directly following much of it, making it look staged; more is the pity because Wright is very strong on dialogue. Actually the pervading feeling is theatrical: Wright is always on top of his material, always at the top of his voice.

The onus does not wear well on the unfledged hero. Never in his speech and seldom in his behavior does Fishbelly substantiate the restive, questioning, introspective boy of the author's exposition. His "sensitivity" is not projected from himself, rather is imposed through the numerous abuses he suffers at white hands. In effect his white tormentors are the plot's activators, though they are seldom onstage and when so are no more than hypothetical actors. Thus the novel's focus is not the black-white conflict in itself but the divisions it creates within and among the blacks; and this is telescoped by the friction between the boy and his father.

Just as he is being brutally awakened to the ghetto reality in which the Negroes around him live, Fishbelly begins to see Tyree, his father, as he really is: a man desperately trying to buy a cynical respectability and independence from the white folks.

William Dunlea, "Wright's Continuing Protest," in Commonweal *(copyright © 1958 Commonweal Publishing Co., Inc.; reprinted by permission of Commonweal Publishing Co., Inc.), Vol. LXIX, No. 5, October 31, 1958, p. 131.*

IRVING HOWE

[Wright] told us the one thing even the most liberal and well-disposed whites preferred not to hear: that Negroes were far from patient or forgiving, that they were scarred by fear, that they hated every moment of their humiliation even when seeming most acquiescent, and that often enough they hated *us,* the decent and cultivated white men who, from complicity or neglect, shared in the responsibility for their plight. No Negro writer had ever quite said this before, certainly not with so much force or bluntness, and if such younger Negro novelists as James Baldwin and Ralph Ellison were to move beyond Wright's harsh naturalism and toward more subtle modes of fiction, that was possible only because Wright had been there first, courageous enough to release the full weight of his anger. . . .

The bitterness and rage that poured out of Wright's books form one of the great American testaments, a crushing necessity to our moral life, forever to remind us that moderate analyses of injustice are finally lies.

And now, after fourteen years of voluntary exile in Paris, chosen, as he once told me, because he could no longer bear to live in the United States and see his children suffer the blows of race hatred, Richard Wright is dead . . .

Eight Men, Wright's most recent and apparently last book, is a collection of stories written over the last 25 years. Though they fail to yield any clear line of chronological development, these stories do give evidence of Wright's literary restlessness, his wish to keep learning and experimenting, his often clumsy efforts to break out of the naturalism which was his first and, I think, necessary mode of expression. The unevenness of his writing is extremely disturbing: one finds it hard to understand how the same man, from paragraph to paragraph, can be at once so brilliant and inept—though the student of American literature soon learns to measure the price which the talented autodidact pays for getting his education too late. Time after time the narrative texture of the stories is broken by a passage of jargon borrowed from sociology or psychology: perhaps the later Wright read too much, tried too hard, failed to remain sufficiently loyal to the limits of his talent.

The best stories are marked by a strong feeling for the compactness of the story as a form, so that even when the language is scraggly or leaden there is a sharply articulated pattern of event. (p. 17)

The main literary problem that troubled Wright in recent years was that of rendering his naturalism a more supple and terse instrument. I think he went astray whenever he abandoned naturalism entirely; there are a few embarrassingly bad experiments with stories written entirely in dialogue or self-consciously employing Freudian symbolism. Wright needed the accumulated material of circumstance which naturalistic detail provided his fiction; it was as essential to his ultimate effect of shock and bruise as dialogue to [Ernest] Hemingway's ultimate effect of irony and loss. But Wright was correct in thinking that the problem of detail is the most vexing technical problem the naturalist writer must face, since the accumulation of detail that makes for depth and solidity can also create a pall of tedium. In **"The Man Who Lived Underground"** Wright came close to solving this problem, for here the naturalistic detail is put at the service of a radical projective image—a Negro trapped in a sewer—and despite some flaws, the story is satisfying both for its tense surface and its elasticity of suggestion. (pp. 17-18)

The reality pressing upon all of Wright's work is a nightmare of remembrance, and without the terror of that nightmare it would be impossible to render the truth of the reality—not the only, perhaps not even the deepest truth about American Negroes, but a primary and inescapable one. Both truth and terror depend upon a gross fact which Wright faced more courageously than any American writer: that for the Negro violence forms an inescapable part of his existence. . . .

The present moment is not a good one for attempting a judicious estimate of Wright's achievement as a novelist. It is hard to suppose that he will ever be regarded as a writer of the first rank, for his faults are grave and obvious. Together with [James T.] Farrell and [John] Dos Passos, he has suffered from the changes of literary taste which occurred during his lifetime: the naturalist novel is little read these days, though often mocked, and the very idea of a "protest novel" has become a target for graduate students to demolish. The dominant school of criticism has little interest in the kind of work Wright did, and it rejects him less from a particular examination than from a theoretic preconception—or to be more precise, from an inability to realize that the kind of linguistic scrutiny to which it submits lyric poetry has only a limited value in the criticism of fiction. . . .

But I believe that any view of 20th-Century American literature which surmounts critical sectarianism will have to give Wright an honored place, and that any estimate of his role in our cultural life will have to stress his importance as the pioneer Negro writer who in the fullness of his anger made it less possible for the American society to continue deceiving itself. . . .

Richard Wright died at 52, full of hopes and projects. Like many of us, he had somewhat lost his intellectual way during recent years, but he kept struggling toward a comprehension of the strange and unexpected world coming into birth. In the most fundamental sense, however, he had done his work: he had told his contemporaries a truth so bitter that they paid him the tribute of striving to forget it. (p.18)

> *Irving Howe, "Richard Wright: A Word of Farewell" (© 1961 by Irving Howe; reprinted by permission of the author), in The New Republic, Vol. 144, No. 7, February 13, 1961, pp. 17-18.*

JAMES BALDWIN

[The] fact that [Richard Wright] worked during a bewildering and demoralizing era in Western history makes a proper assessment of his work more difficult. In [his last book,] *Eight Men*, the earliest story, **"The Man Who Saw the Flood,"** takes place in the deep South and was first published in 1937. One of the two previously unpublished stories in the book, **"Man, God Ain't Like That,"** begins in Africa, achieves its hideous resolution in Paris, and brings us, with an ironical and fitting grimness, to the threshold of the 1960's. It is because of this story, which is remarkable, and **"Man of All Work,"** which is a masterpiece, that I cannot avoid feeling that Wright, as he

died, was acquiring a new tone, and a less uncertain esthetic distance, and a new depth.

Shortly after we learned of Richard Wright's death, a Negro woman who was re-reading *Native Son* told me that it meant more to her now than it had when she had first read it. This, she said, was because the specific social climate which had produced it, or with which it was identified, seemed archaic now, was fading from our memories. Now, there was only the book itself to deal with, for it could no longer be read, as it had been read in 1940, as a militant racial manifesto. Today's racial manifestoes were being written very differently, and in many different languages; what mattered about the book now was how accurately or deeply the life of Chicago's South Side had been conveyed.

I think that my friend may prove to be right. Certainly, the two oldest stories in [*Eight Men*], **"The Man Who Was Almost a Man,"** and **"The Man Who Saw the Flood,"** both Depression stories, both occurring in the South, and both, of course, about Negroes, do not seem dated. Perhaps it is odd, but they did not make me think of the 1930's, or even, particularly, of Negroes. They made me think of human loss and helplessness. (pp. 182-83)

It is strange to begin to suspect, now, that Richard Wright was never, really, the social and polemical writer he took himself to be. In my own relations with him, I was always exasperated by his notions of society, politics, and history, for they seemed to me utterly fanciful. I never believed that he had any real sense of how a society is put together. It had not occurred to me, and perhaps it had not occurred to him, that his major interests as well as his power lay elsewhere. . . . I always sensed in Richard Wright a Mississippi pickaninny, mischievous, cunning, and tough. This always seemed to be at the bottom of everything he said and did, like some fantastic jewel buried in high grass. And it was painful to feel that the people of his adopted country were no more capable of seeing this jewel than were the people of his native land, and were in their own way intimidated by it.

Even more painful was the suspicion that Wright did not want to know this. The meaning of Europe for an American Negro was one of the things about which Richard Wright and I disagreed most vehemently. He was fond of referring to Paris as the "city of refuge"—which it certainly was, God knows, for the likes of us. But it was not a city of refuge for the French, still less for anyone belonging to France; and it would not have been a city of refuge for us if we had not been armed with American passports. It did not seem worthwhile to me to have fled the native fantasy only to embrace a foreign one. (pp. 184-85)

But now that the storm of Wright's life is over, and politics is ended forever for him, along with the Negro problem and the fearful conundrum of Africa, it seems to have been the tough and intuitive, the genuine Richard Wright, who was being recorded all along. It now begins to seem, for example, that Wright's unrelentingly bleak landscape was not merely that of the Deep South, or of Chicago, but that of the world, of the human heart. The landscape does not change in any of these stories. Even the most good-natured performance this book contains, good-natured by comparison only, **"Big Black Good Man,"** takes place in Copenhagen in the winter, and in the vastly more chilling confines of a Danish hotel-keeper's fears.

In **"Man of All Work,"** a tight, raging, diamond-hard exercise in irony, a Negro male who cannot find a job dresses himself

CONTEMPORARY LITERARY CRITICISM, Vol. 21

up in his wife's clothes and hires himself out as a cook. ("Who," he demands of his horrified, bedridden wife, "ever looks at us colored folks anyhow?") He gets the job, and Wright uses this incredible situation to reveal, with beautiful spite and accuracy, the private lives of the master race. The story is told entirely in dialogue, which perfectly accomplishes what it sets out to do, racing along like a locomotive and suggesting far more than it states.

The story, without seeming to, goes very deeply into the demoralization of the Negro male and the resulting fragmentization of the Negro family which occurs when the female is forced to play the male role of breadwinner. It is also a maliciously funny indictment of the sexual terror and hostility of American whites: and the horror of the story is increased by its humor.

"Man, God Ain't Like That," is a fable of an African's discovery of God. It is a far more horrible story than **"Man of All Work,"** but it too manages its effects by a kind of Grand Guignol humor, and it too is an unsparing indictment of the frivolity, egotism, and wrong-headedness of white people—in this case, a French artist and his mistress. It too is told entirely in dialogue and recounts how a French artist traveling through Africa picks up an African servant, uses him as a model, and, in order to shock and titillate his jaded European friends, brings the African back to Paris with him.

Whether or not Wright's vision of the African sensibility will be recognized by Africans, I do not know. But certainly he has managed a frightening and truthful comment on the inexorably mysterious and dangerous relationships between ways of life, which are also ways of thought. This story and **"Man of All Work"** left me wondering how much richer our extremely poor theater might now be if Wright had chosen to work in it.

But **"The Man Who Killed a Shadow"** is something else again; it is Wright at the mercy of his subject. His great forte, it now seems to me, was an ability to convey inward states by means of externals: **"The Man Who Lived Underground,"** for example, conveys the spiritual horror of a man and a city by a relentless accumulation of details, and by a series of brief, sharply cut-off tableaus, seen through chinks and cracks and keyholes. The specifically sexual horror faced by a Negro cannot be dealt with in this way. **"The Man Who Killed a Shadow"** is a story of rape and murder, and neither the murderer nor his victim ever comes alive. The entire story seems to be occurring, somehow, beneath cotton. There are many reasons for this. In most of the novels written by Negroes until today . . . there is a great space where sex ought to be; and what usually fills this space is violence.

This violence, as in so much of Wright's work, is gratuitous and compulsive. It is one of the severest criticisms that can be leveled against his work. The violence is gratuitous and compulsive because the root of the violence is never examined. The root is rage. It is the rage, almost literally the howl, of a man who is being castrated. I do not think that I am the first person to notice this, but there is probably no greater (or more misleading) body of sexual myths in the world today than those which have proliferated around the figure of the American Negro. This means that he is penalized for the guilty imagination of the white people who invest him with their hates and longings, and is the principal target of their sexual paranoia. Thus, when in Wright's pages a Negro male is found hacking a white woman to death, the very gusto with which this is

done, and the great attention paid to the details of physical destruction reveal a terrible attempt to break out of the cage in which the American imagination has imprisoned him for so long.

In the meantime, the man I fought so hard and who meant so much to me, is gone. First America, then Europe, then Africa failed him. He lived long enough to find all of the terms on which he had been born become obsolete; presently, all of his attitudes seemed to be historical. But as his life ended, he seems to me to have been approaching a new beginning. He had survived, as it were, his own obsolescence, and his imagination was beginning to grapple with that darkest of all dark strangers for him, the African. The depth thus touched in him brought him a new power and a new tone. He had survived exile on three continents and lived long enough to begin to tell the tale. (pp. 185-89)

Not until the very end of his life, judging by some of the stories in his last book, *Eight Men,* did his imagination really begin to assess the century's new and terrible dark stranger. Well, he worked up until the end, died, as I hope to do, in the middle of a sentence, and his work is now an irreducible part of the history of our swift and terrible time. Whoever He may be, and wherever you may be, may God be with you, Richard, and may He help me not to fail that argument which you began in me. (p. 199)

*James Baldwin, "Alas, Poor Richard: 'Eight Men'"
(originally published as "The Survival of Richard
Wright," in* The Reporter, *March 16, 1961) and
"Alas, Poor Richard: 'The Exile'" (originally published in* Le Preuve, *February, 1961), in his* Nobody
Knows My Name *(copyright © 1961 by James Baldwin; reprinted by permission of The Dial Press),
Dial, 1961, pp. 181-89, 190-99.*

GLORIA BRAMWELL

Wounded as he was by southern birth and upbringing, Richard Wright fought back blindly with the nearest weapon at hand—in his case, anger. Anger mounting to rage rushes across the pages of his work; too often it overflows and drowns it before it can take shape. And it is the terrible anger of a man who accepts and can see no way out, for his rage is thrust in against himself. That is the greatest irony of all, that a man should be guilty in America by reason of his difference from the majority and acquiesce in his guilt. But Wright is involved in guilt, not irony.

There is a further irony in the fact that the shaping tools he used for his work were first Communism and later, after his self-exile in France, existentialism. Both philosophies had the ultimate effect of weakening his work. (p. 110)

The irony of this lies precisely in the fact that the Negro is an existentialist, living as it were in a perpetual limbo. The Negro is forever outside seeking entry, the intellectual existentialist is inside looking for an exit. Wright, an emotional writer, could paint a stunning picture of the Negro's plight but when he attempted to intellectualize it he embraced it from the wrong angle, from the inside out rather than in terms of his own characters. . . .

While Communism failed him and existentialism provided only a weak adjunct to his writings, he was sustained by an overwhelming sense of guilt, an earlier age would have called it sin. It became increasingly clear to him as he wrote and as we read his work that lying at the bottom of every Negro soul is crushing guilt. For him Negro life took on the proportions of expiation for crimes committed, known and unknown. (p. 111)

Guilt and fear like some crazy quilt pattern themselves through his work. In the story **"The Man Who Lived Underground"** . . . an innocent Negro escapes from the law into the sewers. Fear motivates his flight underground, fear that he may be found guilty of an unknown crime. His miniature odyssey assumes symbolic as well as literal proportions as he views the world from his shelter of invisibility and acquires an anonymous identity paralleling that of Negroes above ground. From his underground vantage point he is able to participate anonymously in a series of social and unsocial acts peculiar to our society. Gradually he moves from fear to self-accusation ending in surrender to the police and death. But even at his death we are no closer to knowing the sort of man he really was. Whether he had family, friends, sweetheart, convictions to sustain him, how he lived till then we have no clue. The protagonist is merely presented as an instrument for the author's ideas moving from a lesser to a greater madness. One does not feel the sharp intelligence, the planned anarchy of Ralph Ellison's *Invisible Man,* a theme of similar dimensions. Ellison's man goes from naivete to wide-eyed awareness and ends as a sniper against the society that made him. He adopts consciously the fate thrust upon him and lives by outsmarting the forces that would keep him down. Wright's man, on the other hand, performs the deeds of theft and murder as a child rebelling against an overstern parent, only to return "home" at the end for the punishment he feels he merits. This inverse paternalism constitutes a major weakness of Wright's as an artist, but at the time of his earlier work it undoubtedly helped his popularity. Today Americans are more sophisticated and more likely to approve Ellison's action as he strips society's pretentions bare, laughs at it and himself, and mocks its attempts to destroy him. Wright was never far enough removed to do more than suffer and articulate that suffering incompletely—for without objectivity it must be incomplete—but powerfully enough to touch us. And he is merciless in the presentation of that suffering. Never will all the platitudes uttered about the Negro had one imagined it to be quite like this. It fascinated, it horrified, it aroused, it even repelled, but its force was undeniable. It has the hypnotic force of the most brutal of nightmares from which we cannot wake voluntarily. On waking finally while we lie there sweating and telling ourselves it is only a dream, our heart beats madly as we keep remembering. He articulated as no other an American nightmare. That he could not waken out of it himself is our loss. (pp. 111-12)

Gloria Bramwell, "Articulated Nightmare," in Midstream *(copyright © 1961 by The Theodor Herzl Foundation, Inc.), Vol. VII, No. 2, Spring, 1961, pp. 110-12.*

RICHARD GILMAN

Richard Wright is dead now and I have no intention of belaboring his memory; but he was simply not a good writer, not even a competent one, and it might be useful to make a notation upon what the sources of his reputation were. I think it clear that he was one of those authors about whom circumstances gather to distill extraliterary excitement and interest, in his case of course the circumstance being the fact that he was Negro and the first of his race to write about what that meant, in full acceptance of its terrors, frustrations and imposed shame.

I haven't read *Native Son* in many years. But if I say that I remember fairly vividly how it jolted me, as it did so many others, it is also true that the jolt was of the sociological order, not the esthetic, impelling me into recognitions that were certainly important, perhaps more important than literary ones, but nevertheless entering a different order of experience and therefore subject to another kind of judgment.

Eight Men has not even the advantage that *Native Son* had. We are long past the stage of shock and recognition. . . .

[It] is a dismayingly stale and dated book. Its tales of Negroes struggling to survive in a white world or being defeated by it creak with mechanical ineptitude; its attempts at humor, at tragedy, at pathos all fail; its two experiments—stories written entirely in dialogue—are painful to read; and the sensibility at work in it is so self-conscious, so liable to lapses of taste, so unsubtly enamored of literary effects, that all the pain and the earnestness, all the angels that hover over the "right side" cannot rescue it. (p. 130)

Richard Gilman, "The Immediate Misfortunes of Widespread Literacy," in Commonweal *(copyright © 1961 Commonweal Publishing Co., Inc.; reprinted by permission of Commonweal Publishing Co., Inc.), Vol. LXXIV, No. 5, April 28, 1961, pp. 130-31.**

GRANVILLE HICKS

[*Lawd Today*] is less powerful than either *Native Son* or *Black Boy,* but it has its own kind of interest.

It is the story of one day in the life of Jake Jackson, a Negro post office clerk in Chicago. (p. 37)

The day is described in unsparing detail. More than two pages, for instance, are devoted to Jake's combing of his recalcitrant hair. . . . The bridge game, with three sample hands, runs to nine pages. A medicine man's spiel takes six. Wright gives a full account of the processes by which mail is sorted, together with pages of the aimless conversation with which the four friends accompany their work.

Growing up in Chicago, and starting out as a writer in the middle Thirties, Wright could scarcely have failed to be influenced by James T. Farrell, who was just beginning to have a strong effect on American fiction. As Farrell had learned something about documentation from Dreiser, so Wright had learned from Farrell. At this point he was clumsier than Farrell, but he had found a way of expressing his vision of life in the Chicago he knew.

What interests me is that, although Wright was a Communist sympathizer and very possibly a member of the Communist Party when he wrote the novel, he did not make it a piece of direct Communist propaganda. Jake is no Communist; on the contrary, he denounces and ridicules the only Communist who appears in the novel. Nor does Wright portray Jake simply as a victim of the capitalist system. He is a victim, to be sure; but of a great complex of forces. Whatever Wright's political opinions may have been, his vision as a creative artist went far beyond them.

If the novel would have been disturbing to most orthodox Communists in the Thirties, it would have been equally distressing to many Negroes. Far from setting an example to members of his race, Jake is a contemptible person. . . . Although hatred of white discrimination is bred in his bones, he has no sense of racial solidarity . . . and he regards as fools those Negroes who work for the betterment of their people.

I have used so many negatives that one might get the impression that Jake has no positive qualities, but this is not true. He has a capacity for the enjoyment of life, and even in the dreary day Wright describes there are moments of excitement and satisfaction. At the end, when he is reflecting ruefully on the loss of his hundred dollars, he thinks, "But when I was flying I was a flying fool."

Jake, on this Lincoln's Birthday, is a slave—of an unjust economic system, of racial prejudice, of faulty education—but he is not merely a slave, any more than he is merely a Negro. He is a man, erring but alive. (pp. 37-8)

Wright, as [James] Baldwin says, was not made to be a political thinker, and it was his misfortune that he lived in a time that cast him in that role. He outgrew his Communism, of course; but he continued to think of himself as a novelist of ideas, and in 1953, under the influence of Jean-Paul Sartre and Simone de Beauvoir, he attempted an existentialist novel, *The Outsider,* which was weak precisely where he wanted it to be strong. . . .

Lawd Today was an apprentice work, and Wright soon learned to handle externals more adroitly, but even here what Baldwin says is applicable. Clumsy as the massing of detail sometimes is, we do come to know not only the society in which Jake lives but also Jake himself, and, despicable as he is, we come to feel with and for him.

We often have occasion to wonder why this American writer or that was frustrated and failed to fulfill his promise. With Wright we can make a good guess. It was his misfortune that he became first a Communist and then a self-appointed spokesman for the Negro people of the world. What he was capable of as a writer is evident even in so imperfect a work as *Lawd Today.* (p. 38)

Granville Hicks, "Dreiser to Farrell to Wright," in Saturday Review *(copyright © 1963 by* Saturday Review; *all rights reserved; reprinted by permission), Vol. XLVI, No. 13, March 30, 1963, pp. 37-8.**

RALPH ELLISON

[Why] is it so often true that when critics confront the American as *Negro* they suddenly drop their advanced critical armament and revert with an air of confident superiority to quite primitive modes of analysis? Why is it that sociology-oriented critics seem to rate literature so far below politics and ideology that they would rather kill a novel than modify their presumptions concerning a given reality which it seeks in its own terms to project? Finally, why is it that so many of those who would tell us the meaning of Negro life never bother to learn how varied it really is?

These questions are aroused by "Black Boys and Native Sons," an essay by Irving Howe, the well-known critic and editor of *Dissent,* in the Autumn 1963 issue of that magazine [see *CLC,* Vol. 3]. . . . [In] addition to a hero, Richard Wright, [the essay] has *two* villains, James Baldwin and Ralph Ellison, who are seen as "black boys" masquerading as false, self-deceived "native sons." Wright himself is given a diversity of roles (all conceived by Howe): He is not only the archetypal and true-blue black boy—the "honesty" of his famous autobiography established this for Howe—but the spiritual father of Ellison, Baldwin and all other Negroes of literary bent to come. Further,

in the platonic sense he is his own father and the culture hero who freed Ellison and Baldwin to write more "modulated" prose.

Howe admires Wright's accomplishments, and is frankly annoyed by the more favorable evaluation currently placed upon the works of the younger men. His claims for *Native Son* are quite broad. . . .

There are also negative criticisms: that the book is "crude," "melodramatic" and marred by "claustrophobia" of vision, that its characters are "cartoons," etc. But these defects Howe forgives because of the book's "clenched militancy." One wishes he had stopped there. (p. 22)

In his loyalty to Richard Wright, Howe considers Ellison and Baldwin guilty of filial betrayal because, in their own work, they have rejected the path laid down by *Native Son*; phonies because, while actually "black boys," they pretend to be mere American writers trying to react to something of the pluralism of their predicament. . . .

Wright believed in the much abused idea that novels are "weapons"—the counterpart of the dreary notion, common among most minority groups, that novels are instruments of good public relations. But I believe that true novels, even when most pessimistic and bitter, arise out of an impulse to celebrate human life and therefore are ritualistic and ceremonial at their core. Thus they would preserve as they destroy, affirm as they reject.

In *Native Son* Wright began with the ideological proposition that what whites think of the Negro's reality is more important than what Negroes themselves know it to be. Hence Bigger Thomas was presented as a near-subhuman indictment of white oppression. He was designed to shock whites out of their apathy and end the circumstances out of which Wright insisted Bigger emerged. Here environment is all—and interestingly enough, environment conceived solely in terms of the physical, the nonconscious. Well, cut off my legs and call me Shorty! Kill my parents and throw me on the mercy of the court as an orphan! Wright could imagine Bigger, but Bigger could not possibly imagine Richard Wright. Wright saw to that.

But without arguing Wright's right to his personal vision, I would say that he was himself a better argument for my approach than Bigger was for his. And so, to be fair and as inclusive as Howe, is James Baldwin. Both are true Negro Americans, and both affirm the broad possibility of personal realization which I see as a saving aspect of American life. Surely, this much can be admitted without denying the injustice which all three of us have protested. (p. 24)

Howe seems to see segregation as an opaque steel jug with the Negroes inside waiting for some black messiah to come along and blow the cork. Wright is his hero and he sticks with him loyally. But if we are in a jug it is transparent, not opaque, and one is allowed not only to see outside but to read of what is going on out there; to make identifications as to values and human quality. . . . I was freed not by propagandists or by the example of Wright . . . but by composers, novelists and poets who spoke to me of more interesting and freer ways of life. . . .

No, Wright was no spiritual father of mine, certainly in no sense I recognize—nor did he pretend to be, since he felt that I had started writing too late. It was Baldwin's career, not mine, that Wright proudly advanced by helping him attain the Eugene Saxton Fellowship, and it was Baldwin who found Wright a lion in his path. Being older and familiar with quite different lions in quite different paths, I simply stepped around him. . . .

I felt no need to attack what I considered the limitations of [Wright's] vision because I was quite impressed by what he had achieved. . . . Still I would write my own books and they would be in themselves, implicitly, criticisms of Wright's; just as all novels of a given historical moment form an argument over the nature of reality and are, to an extent, criticisms each of the other.

While I rejected Bigger Thomas as any *final* image of Negro personality, I recognized *Native Son* as an achievement; as one man's essay in defining the human condition as seen from a specific Negro perspective at a given time in a given place. And I was proud to have known Wright and happy for the impact he had made upon our apathy. But Howe's ideas notwithstanding, history is history, cultural contacts ever mysterious, and taste exasperatingly personal. (p. 25)

Wright, for Howe, is the genuine article, the authentic Negro writer, and his tone the only authentic tone. But why strip Wright of his individuality in order to criticize other writers. He had his memories and I have mine. . . .

Must I be condemned because my sense of Negro life was quite different? Or because for me keeping faith would never allow me to even raise such a question about any segment of humanity? *Black Boy* is not a sociological case history but an autobiography, and therefore a work of art shaped by a writer bent upon making an ideological point. Doubtlessly, this was the beginning of Wright's exile, the making of a decision which was to shape his life and writing thereafter. And it is precisely at this point that Wright is being what I would call, in Howe's words, "literary to a fault." . . .

How awful that Wright found the facile answers of Marxism before he learned to use literature as a means for discovering the forms of American Negro humanity. I could not and cannot question their existence, I can only seek again and again to project that humanity as I see it and feel it. To me Wright as *writer* was less interesting than the enigma he personified; that he could so dissociate himself from the complexity of his background while trying so hard to improve the condition of black men everywhere; that he could be so wonderful an example of human possibility but could not for ideological reasons depict a Negro as intelligent, as creative or as dedicated as himself.

In his effort to resuscitate Wright, Irving Howe would designate the role which Negro writers are to play more rigidly than any Southern politician—and for the best of reasons. We must express "black" anger and "clenched militancy"; most of all we should not become too interested in the problems of the art of literature, even though it is through these that we seek our individual identities. And between writing well and being ideologically militant, we must choose militancy.

Well, it all sounds quite familiar and I fear the social order which it forecasts more than I do that of Mississippi. Ironically, during the 1940s it was one of the main sources of Wright's rage and frustration. (p. 26)

Ralph Ellison, "The World and the Jug," in The New Leader *(© 1963 by the American Labor Conference on International Affairs, Inc.), Vol. XLVI, No. 25, December 9, 1963, pp. 22-6.**

RONALD SANDERS

[In] *Native Son* Wright almost succeeds in achieving the imaginative liberation he sought by writing it. The book even-

tually runs aground in the author's own intellectuality, a quality which, for the novel's sake, he had succeeded in suppressing both too well and not well enough.

The first two-thirds of *Native Son* constitute one of the most exciting stretches of melodrama in American literature. (p. 33)

From [the moment of Mary Dalton's death] until Bigger's capture by the police on a snow-covered tenement rooftop some two hundred pages later the novel is pure movement, the kind of overwhelming narrative torrent that Wright had already made into a trademark in a story like "**Down By the Riverside.**" In *Native Son* this narrative flow serves the additional function of showing what has happened to Bigger's existence. Every one of his acts now, in contrast with the torpor that had prevailed in the descriptions of his life prior to the murder of Mary Dalton, is swift, vigorous and meaningful, another element in a headlong process of self-definition.

Wright spares no horror in this unfolding of the hidden meaning of his protagonist's existence; Bigger's ultimate and most completely unforgivable act of violent self-assertion is his murder of his mistress Bessie, with whom he has shared his secret and whose life has therefore become intolerable to him. According to Constance Webb, Wright wanted to include this episode in the novel so that there would be no mistaking Bigger's stark responsibility for his acts, no catering to the sensibilities of bankers' daughters. In retrospect, it seems also to be another of the novel's prophetic glimpses of the ghetto revolt of the sixties, ultimately turning against itself and burning down homes with black women and children inside. This, then, is the culminating act of Bigger's self-emancipating revolt, his one unequivocally wilful act of annihilation—performed upon a poor black working-girl. Did Wright mean for the irony to read this way? Is it an intended qualification to his vision of a black revolutionary apocalypse, or an inadvertent prophecy? Miss Webb does not tell us, but this much must be said: if this is ultimately the outcome of Bigger's revolt, then it is not so likely to disturb the sensibilities of bankers' daughters after all.

The last third of the novel, dealing with Bigger's imprisonment and trial, is Wright's final bout with the Communist worldview, and the narrative moves slowly and indecisively again. . . . He seems to want to give what he can back to the Communists after the heresy he has committed in the first two-thirds of the book; it is only they, for example, who show compassion and some understanding towards Bigger, and he is deeply appreciative of this despite his refusal to be categorized by them as a mere phenomenon of the oppressed part of mankind. . . . The old lawyer Max tries to defend Bigger from the death sentence in a long courtroom summation indicting society's injustices. Max is even able to see, beneath the blanket of Communist myth, the more unruly revolutionary force that Bigger represents. . . . But ultimately it is Max who comes forth, not only in the courtroom but within Wright's internal moral dialectic, as the last defender of the old vision of a coalition of the oppressed. . . . (pp. 34-5)

The spirit of Max, partly consumed in a European nostalgia shared by every American Jewish intellectual, was never completely exorcised by Wright. He had absorbed this nostalgia as part of his education, and his vision of black revolt was as blurred by it as his pursuit of the vision was spurred by a passion to shake it off. This is the meaning of Bigger's final but somehow inconclusive show of defiance before Max in his death cell, ending with "a faint, wry, bitter smile" through the bars as the lawyer walks down the corridor. Here is the way Wright's revolt ends, not with a bang but a smirk. . . .

In his search after a certain notion of the primitive, Wright had come dangerously close to creating a character who was a mere vehicle for ideas. Bigger still works despite the ambiguity, but Wright's growing preoccupation with the metaphysics of blackness turned many of the characters he subsequently created into hardly more than metaphors. . . . ["**The Man Who Lived Underground**"] is an interesting attempt to use blackness as a metaphor for the condition known in Jewish literature as that of "one who sees but is not seen"; but the idea—originally inspired by a reading of Dostoyevsky—is more appealing than the realization is successful. . . . (p. 36)

[*Black Boy*] is his masterpiece, and yet it would seem, from Miss Webb's narrative, that it was written almost inadvertently, after Wright's agent surprised him by suggesting that he try an autobiography. Persuaded to drop the mantle of a writer of fiction for a moment (although he uses the techniques of the novel here most effectively), Wright has recourse in this book to "telling it like it is" without drawing upon his arsenal of symbolism and melodramatic plot-making. A simple and powerful account of his boyhood and young manhood in the South, it is his one book-length narrative that does not border on solipsism but contains a whole array of real characterizations. Even the whites that appear, almost all of them as persecutors, are more real and hence human than such caricatures as Dalton or the private detective in *Native Son*. Focusing more resolutely on real experience than he had ever done before, Wright had lighted upon conventions that were, for the first time, entirely his own. Evoking, as Ellison says, "the paradoxical, almost surreal image of a black boy singing [the blues] lustily as he probes his own grievous wound," the book suggests possibilities for a whole genre of Negro writing, signs of which we are now beginning to see today.

But in Wright's own life and work, *Black Boy* proved to be the swan song of his struggle to achieve his own identity as a writer and a man in America. In the latter half of 1946 he visited France as the guest of its government, and in the summer of the following year he brought his wife and five-year-old daughter to Paris to settle there for good. . . . By merely trading in the lilt with which he once had sung the blues, Wright became eligible to put on the French-made mantle of Negritude, whose graceful and classic lines obscured the homely contours of Mississippi and Chicago. In other words, his color became in France what he had always sought to make it: a kind of metaphor.

This transmutation is reflected in Wright's next book, *The Outsider.* . . . It is a novel laden with language and concepts borrowed from French existentialism. . . . Cross Damon, a new variant of Bigger Thomas perceived through the French philosophical sensibility, commits a series of murders that read like ritual metaphors for the series of rejections Wright had made in his own life. . . . In the end it is not the law but the Communists who destroy him, shooting him down in the street.

The thrust of Wright's work had now brought him to a point of extreme alienation. His next novel, *Savage Holiday* . . . is a suspense thriller about a retired white insurance executive who, stepping out of the shower to pick up his newspaper in the hallway one Sunday morning, finds himself trapped there naked when his door accidentally slams shut. Caught naked in the hallway—this is what had become of Wright's creative metaphor, of his very inner identity!

During the next few years, Wright made strenuous efforts to recover roots for a theme that had now become, in literary terms, a mere abstraction. . . . [*Pagan Spain*] was a recapitulation of his old quest on for a primitive reality behind the mask of Communist myth. Pagan Spain, whose border with France marks "the termination of Europe and the beginning of Africa," was the dark truth that had reposed beneath the right-left conventions of the Spanish Civil War era. So also, at the Bandung Conference, did Wright perceive an underlying reality—formed out of race and religion—that was "beyond left and right." He was thus moving in the direction of what was in fact another left-wing myth—that of the Third World— which was being generated in France during this period. It was a possible outcome of the logic of his own development: in a sense, Bigger Thomas could be viewed retrospectively as a representative of Frantz Fanon's theories about the self-realization of the colonized through violent revolt. But this, in the end, would tend to make Bigger as much a creature of Jean-Paul Sartre's universe as the lawyer Max had wanted to make him of the universe of American Communism in the nineteen-thirties.

Wright did not seem content with this resolution, either; he had been very keenly aware, for example, of the gulf between himself and the black man of Africa during his trip there. The short time that now remained of his life was filled with what seems to have been a frantic struggle to recover his themes, as he thrashed about through possibilities both old and new. He tried writing again about the Negro in the American South, but the resulting novel, *The Long Dream,* published in 1958, was severely criticized for its manifest remoteness from reality; it was far more popular in France than in the United States. His short stories, mere fanciful creations, were better because they were able to bear up somehow under the weight of being intellectual constructs. A story published in 1957, "**Big Black Good Man,**" suggests the possibility that the course of Wright's sensibility was seeking to come full circle. . . . Does the similarity of name to those of Big Boy and Bigger suggest what Wright was trying to do? It is one of his few stories displaying some of the sunniness and humor for which he was apparently well known in person. Was he making his peace at last, and if so, where was it to take him? No one will ever know, for he was dead three years later, in the fall of 1960. (pp. 36-9)

Ronald Sanders, "Richard Wright and the Sixties" (reprinted by permission of Georges Borchardt, Inc.; copyright © 1968 Ronald Sanders), in Midstream, *Vol. XIV, No. 7, August/September, 1968, pp. 28-40.*

EDWARD MARGOLIES

Wright at his best was master of a taut psychological suspense narrative. Even more important, however, are the ways Wright wove his themes of human fear, alienation, guilt, and dread into the overall texture of his work. Some critics may still today stubbornly cling to the notion that Wright was nothing more than a proletarian writer, but it was to these themes that a postwar generation of French writers responded, and not to Wright's Communism—and it is to these themes that future critics must turn primarily if they wish to re-evaluate Wright's work. (p. 3)

Wright not only wrote well but also he paved the way for a new and vigorous generation of Negro authors to deal with subjects that had hitherto been regarded as taboo. [His] portraits of oppressed Negroes have made a deep impression on readers the world over. (p. 4)

Wright's existentialism as it was to be called by a later generation of French authors, was not an intellectually "learned" process (although he had been reading Dostoevsky and Kierkegaard in the thirties) but rather the lived experiences of his growing years. The alienation, the dread, the fear, and the view that one must construct oneself out of the chaos of existence—all elements of his fiction—were for him means of survival. There were, of course, externals he grasped for as well. (p. 6)

In general, Wright's nonfiction takes one of two directions. The first concerns itself with the devastating emotional impact of centuries of exploitation on its individual victims. The second is the overall cultural characteristics of oppressed peoples. The first is largely psychological; the second socio-anthropological. Obviously no such absolute division obtains since it is impossible to discuss one without making reference to the other, but for purposes of analysis it may be said that Wright lays greater or lesser stress on one or the other of these issues in each of his works of nonfiction. *Black Boy* (1945), Wright's autobiography of his Southern years, serves perhaps as the best point of reference from which to make an examination of his ideas, since, as we have seen, Wright generalizes from his own experiences certain conclusions about the problems of minorities everywhere. (p. 15)

Possibly the problems presented by *Black Boy* are insoluble since the environment in which *Black Boy* operates is so alien to the average reader that it is almost essential for Wright to hammer home in little digressive essays the mores of the caste system so that *Black Boy*'s psychology and behavior may be better understood. As a result, its authority as autobiography is reduced—Wright frequently appears to stand aside and analyze himself rather than allow the reader to make inferences about his character and emotions from his actions—and its strength as sociology seems somewhat adulterated by the incursions of the narrative. Yet, despite these failures—or possibly because of them—the impact of the book is considerable and this perhaps is Wright's artistic triumph. (p. 16)

Wright's theme is freedom and he skillfully arranges and selects his scenes in such a way that he is constantly made to appear the innocent victim of the tyranny of his family or the outrages of the white community. Nowhere in the book are Wright's actions and thoughts reprehensible. The characteristics he attributes to himself are in marked contrast to those of other characters in the book. He is "realistic," "creative," "passionate," "courageous," and maladjusted because he refuses to conform. Insofar as the reader identifies Wright's cause with the cause of Negro freedom, it is because Wright is a Negro—but a careful reading of the book indicates that Wright expressly divorces himself from other Negroes. Indeed rarely in the book does Wright reveal concern for Negroes as a group. Hence Wright traps the reader in a stereotyped response—the same stereotyped response that Wright is fighting throughout the book: that is, that all Negroes are alike and react alike. (p. 18)

[It] is in [*Uncle Tom's Children*] that the reader may find the theme, the structure, the plot, and the ideational content of all his later fictional work. Although Wright, when he wrote these stories, was a convinced Communist, it is revealing how related they are to the later phases of intellectual and political development. Here, for example, one finds Wright's incipient Negro nationalism as each of his protagonists rises to strike out vi-

olently at white oppressors who would deny him his humanity. More significantly his Negro characters imagine whites as "blurs," "bogs," "mountains," "fire," "ice," and "marble." In none of these stories do his heroes act out of a sense of consciously arrived at ideology (most of them, as a matter of fact, are ignorant of Marxism), but rather out of an innate, repressed longing for freedom—or sometimes merely as an instinctive means of self-survival. Often the act of violence carries along with it a sudden revelatory sense of self-awareness—an immediate knowledge that the world in which the protagonist dwells is chaotic, meaningless, purposeless, and that he, as a Negro, is "outside" this world and must therefore discover his own life by his lonely individual thoughts and acts. We find thus in these first short stories a kind of black nationalism wedded to what has been called Wright's existentialism—the principal characteristics of Wright's last phase of political and philosophical thinking.

Paradoxically, Wright's Marxism seldom intrudes in an explicit didactic sense. . . . To be sure, Communists are viewed in a kindly light in the last two of Wright's stories, but they are only remotely instrumental in effecting his heroes' discovery of themselves and their world. Oddly enough, in three of the stories ("**Down by the Riverside**," "**Fire and Cloud**," and "**Bright and Morning Star**"), Wright's simple Negro peasants arrive at their sense of self-realization by applying basic Christian principles to the situations in which they find themselves. In only one ("**Bright and Morning Star**"), does a character convert to Communism—and then only when she discovers Communism is the modern translation of the primitive Christian values she has always lived. There is a constant identification in these stories with the fleeing Hebrew children of the Old Testament and the persecuted Christ—and mood, atmosphere, and settings abound in Biblical nuances. Wright's characters die like martyrs, stoic and unyielding, in their new-found truth about themselves and their vision of a freer, fuller world for their posterity. . . . The spare, stark accounts of actions and their resolution are reminiscent in their simplicity and their cadences of Biblical narrations. The floods, the songs, the sermons, the hymns reinforce the Biblical analogies and serve, ironically, to highlight the uselessness and inadequacy of Christianity as a means of coping with the depression-ridden, racist South. Even the reverse imagery of white-evil, black-good is suggestive in its simple organization of the forces which divide the world in Old Testament accounts of the Hebrews' struggle for survival. (pp. 57-9)

There is a thematic progression in these stories, each of which deals with the Negro's struggle for survival and freedom. In the first story ["**Big Boy Leaves Home**"] flight is described—and here Wright is at his artistic best, fashioning his taut, spare prose to the movements and thoughts of the fugitive. (p. 61)

Although "**Big Boy**" is a relatively long story, the rhythm of events is swift, and the time consumed from beginning to end is less than twenty-four hours. The prose is correspondingly fashioned to meet the pace of the plot. The story is divided into five parts, each of which constitutes a critical episode in Big Boy's progress from idyll, through violence, to misery, terror, and escape. As the tension mounts, Wright employs more and more of a terse and taut declaratory prose, fraught with overtones and meanings unspoken—reminiscent vaguely of the early [Ernest] Hemingway. (pp. 62-3)

"**Down by the Riverside**," the next story in the collection, is not nearly so successful. If flight (as represented by "**Big Boy Leaves Home**") is one aspect of the Negro's struggle for survival in the South, Christian humility, forbearance, courage, and stoic endurance are the themes of Wright's second piece. But here the plot becomes too contrived; coincidence is piled upon coincidence, and the inevitability of his protagonist's doom does not ring quite true. (p. 63)

Yet, there is a certain epic quality to the piece—man steadily pursuing his course against a malevolent nature, only to be cut down later by the ingratitude of his fellow men—that is suggestive of [Mark] Twain or [William] Faulkner. And Mann's long-suffering perseverance and stubborn will to survive endow him with a rare mythic Biblical quality. Wright even structures his story like a Biblical chronicle, in five brief episodes, each displaying in its way Mann's humble courage against his fate. But if Mann's simple Christian virtues failed to save him, it was in part because the ground had not yet been laid on which these virtues might flourish. The recognition that the bourgeois ethic is incapable of providing men with the possibility of fulfilling themselves is an element of Wright's next story ["**Long Black Song**"]. (p. 65)

The success of the story, perhaps Wright's best, lies in the successful integration of plot, imagery, and character which echo the tragic theme of Silas's doomed awareness of himself and the inadequacy of the bourgeois values by which he has been attempting to live. Silas's recognition is his death knell, but he achieves a dignity in death that he had never known in life. (pp. 65-6)

It is Sarah, though, who is the most memorable portrayal in the story. The narrative unfolds from her point of view—and she becomes, at the end, a kind of deep mother earth character, registering her primal instincts and reactions to the violence and senselessness she sees all about her. But for all that, she remains beautifully human—her speech patterns and thoughts responding to an inner rhythm, somehow out of touch with the foolish strivings of men, yet caught up in her own melancholy memories and desires. . . . Wright conveys her mood and memories and vagaries of character in sensuous color imagery—while certain cadences suggest perhaps Gertrude Stein whom Wright regarded as one of his chief influences. (pp. 66-7)

Sarah is Wright's most lyrical achievement, and Silas, her husband, Wright's most convincing figure of redemption. (p. 67)

Wright's militant Negroes, despite their protestations to the contrary, often sound more like black nationalists than Communist internationalists. It was perhaps this facet of Wright's work, in addition to the obvious, extreme, and frequent isolated individualism of his heroes that [began] to disturb Communist Party officials. Yet regardless of whether Wright had been at heart a Communist, an outsider, or a nationalist when he wrote these pieces, there can be little doubt that they draw a good deal of their dramatic strength from the black and white world Wright saw. There is little the reader can do but sympathize with Wright's Negroes and loathe and despise the whites. There are no shadings, ambiguities, few psychological complexities. But there are of course the weaknesses of the stories as well.

How then account for their overall success? First of all, they *are* stories. Wright is a story teller and his plots are replete with conflict, incident, and suspense. Secondly, Wright is a stylist. He has an unerring "feel" for dialogue, his narrations are controlled in terse, tense rhythms, and he manages to communicate mood, atmosphere, and character in finely worked passages of lyric intensity. But above all they are stories whose

sweep and magnitude are suffused with their author's impassioned convictions about the dignity of man, and a profound pity for the degraded, the poor and oppressed who, in the face of casual brutality, cling obstinately to their humanity. (pp. 72-3)

Unlike the pieces in **Uncle Tom's Children,** [the stories in the posthumously published **Eight Men**] are not arranged along any progressively thematic lines; instead the order in which they are assembled indicates that Wright was more concerned with showing a variety of styles, settings and points of view. To be sure, they all deal in one way or another with Negro oppression, but they do not point, as Wright's previous collection of stories did, to any specific social conclusion. (p. 73)

The only significant work of fiction Wright produced in the decade of the forties was his long story, "**The Man Who Lived Underground.**" (p. 76)

Here Wright is at his storytelling best, dealing with subject matter he handles best—the terrified fugitive in flight from his pursuers. Like Wright's other fugitives, Fred Daniels exercises a kind of instinct for survival that he perhaps never knew he possessed. But what makes him different from the others is that he is not merely a victim of a racist society, but that he has become by the very nature of his experiences a symbol of all men in that society—the pursuers and the pursued. For what the underground man has learned in his sewer is that all men carry about in their hearts an underground man who determines their behavior and attitudes in the aboveground world. The underground man is the essential nature of all men—and is composed of dread, terror, and guilt. Here then lies the essential difference between Wright's Communist and post-Communist period. Heretofore dread, terror, and guilt had been the lot of the Negro in a world that had thrust upon him the role of a despised inferior. Now they are the attributes of all mankind. (pp. 78-9)

Fred Daniels is then Everyman, and his story is very nearly a perfect modern allegory. The Negro who lives in the underground of the city amidst its sewage and slime is not unlike the creature who dwells amidst the sewage of the human heart. And Fred Daniels knows that all of the ways men attempt to persuade themselves that their lives are meaningful and rational are delusions. . . . But paradoxically despite Fred's new found knowledge of the savagery of the human heart and the meaninglessness of the above-ground world, he recognizes its instinctive appeal as well, and he must absurdly rise to the surface once more. (pp. 79-80)

The dread, the terror, the guilt, the nausea had always been basic thematic elements in Wright's fiction—and now in "**The Man Who Lived Underground,**" they are made the explicit components of the human personality. Like Wright's heroes, the characters of existentialist authors move about in a world devoid of principles, God, and purpose—and suffer horror at their awesome godlike powers as they create their own personalities and values out of the chaos of existence. But in some respects Wright's heroes are different. They are alienated often enough not from any intellectually reasoned position (at this stage in Wright's career), but by chance happenings in their lives or an accident of birth—race, for example. (In Fred Daniels' case, for instance, he is a Negro who quite by chance happened to be near the scene of a crime.) They arrive then accidentally at their insights, and as a result of having discovered themselves outside the rules of conventional social behavior recognize that they are free to shape (and are therefore responsible for) their own lives. But this is not primarily why they suffer guilt. Wright seems to prefer a Freudian explanation; guilt is instinctively connected with the trauma of birth. Hence, for Wright, a man's freedom is circumscribed by his very humanity. In ways he cannot possibly control, his nature or "essence" precedes his existence. But however different the routes French existentialist authors and Wright may have taken, they meet on common ground in regard to their thrilled horror at man's rootlessness—at the heroism of his absurd striving.

"The Man Who Lived Underground" undoubtedly owes something in the way of plot and theme to [Victor Hugo's] *Les Miserables,* and to what Camus called the "Dostoevskian experience of the condemned man"—but, above all, Fred Daniels' adventures suggest something of Wright's own emotions after ten years in the Communist underground. The air of bitterness, the almost strident militancy are gone—momentarily at least—and in their place a compassion and despair—compassion for man trapped in his underground nature and despair that he will ever be able to set himself free. (pp. 80-1)

The fifties saw Wright experimenting with new subject matter and new forms. Problems of race remain the central issue, but are now dealt with from changing perspectives. For the first time there are two stories with non-American settings, and race neurosis is treated more as the white man's dilemma than as the black man's burden. This shift in emphasis from black to white is accompanied by corresponding shifts in social viewpoint. Racial antagonisms do not appear to be immediately—or for that matter remotely—traceable to compelling class interests. It is clear that Wright was trying to broaden the range and scope of his fiction—that he was trying to move away somewhat from the psyche of the oppressed Negro peasant or proletariat toward characters of varying social and ethnic backgrounds. The three novels Wright produced in this ten year period bear out this conclusion. In the first, *The Outsider* (1953), he wrote of his hero that though a Negro "he could have been of any race." *Savage Holiday,* written the following year, contains no Negro characters and deals with the misfortunes of a white, "respectable" middle-aged retired insurance executive. *The Long Dream* (1957) is written from the point of view of an adolescent, middle-class Negro boy. Wright was apparently reaching for a universality he felt he had not yet achieved—but his craft was not quite equal to the tasks he had set for himself. Too often, as before, his whites appear as stereotypes, and his Negroes are a bit too noble or innocent. In the 1930's Wright's social vision lent his stories an air of conviction, a momentum all their own; in the 1950's Wright's quieter catholicity, his wider intellectuality, perhaps removed his stories from this kind of cumulative dread tension, the sense of urgency, that made his earlier works so immediately gripping.

Nonetheless it cannot be said that Wright's new stories do not possess their own narrative qualities. . . . What these stories sorely lack are the charged, vibrant rhythms and vivid lyric imagery that so rounded out character and theme in his earlier works. Perhaps Wright wanted to pare his prose down to what he regarded as bare essentials—just as he may have fancied his idol, Gertrude Stein, had done. Whatever the reasons, the results are only occasionally successful. (pp. 82-3)

Native Son possesses many of the characteristic failings of proletarian literature. First, the novel is transparently propagandistic—arguing for a humane, socialist society where such crimes as Bigger committed could not conceivably take place. Secondly, Wright builds up rather extensive documentation to prove that Bigger's actions, behavior, values, attitudes, and fate have already been determined by his status and place in American life. Bigger's immediate Negro environment is depicted as being unrelentingly bleak and vacuous—while the white world that stands just beyond his reach remains cruelly indifferent or hostile to his needs. Thirdly, with the possible exception of Bigger, none of the characters is portrayed in any depth—and most of them are depicted as representative "types" of the social class to which they belong. Fourthly, despite his brutally conditioned psychology, there are moments in the novel when Bigger, like the heroes of other proletarian fiction, appears to be on the verge of responding to the stereotyped Communist version of black and white workers marching together in the sunlight of fraternal friendship. Finally, Wright succumbs too often to the occupational disease of proletarian authors by hammering home sociological points in didactic expository prose when they could just as clearly be understood in terms of the organic development of the novel.

Yet if *Native Son* may be said to illustrate some of the more flagrant conventions of proletarian fiction, there are aspects of this novel that reveal Wright exploring problems of character portrayal, prose style, and theme. . . . [There] is first of all the sympathetic presentation of perhaps one of the most disagreeable characters in fiction. That Wright had to a large degree achieved this may be attested to as much by the loud protests of his critics as by the plaudits of his admirers. Second, although *Native Son* makes its obvious sociological points, one should bear in mind that for well over two thirds of the novel Wright dwells on the peculiar states of mind of his protagonist, Bigger, which exist somehow outside the realm of social classes or racial issues. . . . Hence if categorizing terms are to be used, *Native Son* is as much a psychological novel as it is sociological, with Wright dwelling on various intensities of shame, fear, and hate. . . . To require of his readers that they identify themselves with the violent emotions and behavior of an illiterate Negro boy is no mean feat—but Wright's success goes beyond the shock of reader recognition with its subsequent implications of shared guilt and social responsibility. A rereading of Wright's novel some twenty-five odd years after its publication suggests that Wright was probing larger issues than racial injustice and social inequality. He was asking questions regarding the ultimate nature of man. What indeed are man's responsibilities in a world devoid of meaning and purpose? . . . The contradiction is never resolved, and it is precisely for this reason that the novel fails to fulfill itself. For the plot, the structure, even the portrayal of Bigger himself are often at odds with Wright's official determinism—but when on occasion the novel transcends its Marxist and proletarian limitations the reading becomes magnificent. (pp. 104-07)

The entire action described in Book I totals fewer than seventy-seven pages. Bigger's character and circumstances are related in a few quick almost impressionistic episodes—but the real plot movement does not actually commence until Bigger confronts the Daltons. Yet Wright has forecast Bigger's doom from the very start. Bigger knows deep in his heart that he is destined to bear endless days of dreary poverty, abject humiliation, and tormenting frustration, for this is what being a Negro means. Yet should he admit these things to himself, he may well commit an act of unconscionable violence. . . . Hence, Bigger's principal fear is self-knowledge—and this, of course, is the theme and title of Book I. The other kinds of fear that constitute Bigger's life are by-products of this basic error. (pp. 108-09)

[Bigger opts for] the identity of a murderer. In an absurd, hostile world that denies his humanity and dichotomizes his personality, Bigger has made a choice that has integrated his being; "never had he felt [such] a sense of wholeness." Ironically, Bigger has assumed the definition the white world has thrust upon the Negro in order to justify his oppression. If the Negro is a beast at heart who must be caged in order to protect the purity of the white race, Bigger will gladly accept the definition. It is at least an identity—preferable to that of someone obsequious, passive, and happily acquiescent to his exploitation. Bigger's choices are moral and metaphysical—not political or racial. He might have chosen love or submission, instead he has elected violence and death as a sign of his being, and by rebelling against established authority—despite the impossibility of success—he acquires a measure of freedom. None of the above is intended to deny that oppressive environmental factors do not limit the modes of Bigger's actions; nonetheless, environment by itself does not explain Bigger. (pp. 110-11)

The chief philosophical weakness of *Native Son* is not that Bigger does not surrender his freedom to Max's determinism, or that Bigger's Zarathustrian principles do not jibe with Max's socialist visions; it is that Wright himself does not seem to be able to make up his mind. There is an inconsistency of tone in the novel—particularly in Book III, **"Fate,"** where the reader feels that Wright, although intellectually committed to Max's views, is more emotionally akin to Bigger's. Somehow Bigger's impassioned hatred comes across more vividly than Max's eloquent reasoning. (p. 113)

The failures of *Native Son* do not then reside in the proletarian or naturalistic framework in which Wright chose to compose his novel. Any great artist can after all transcend the limitations of form—if he so wishes. In any event if Wright had stuck closer to an organic naturalistic development, his novel might have achieved more consistent artistic results. The basic problems of *Native Son* lie elsewhere. There is an inconsistency of ideologies, an irresolution of philosophical attitudes which prevent Bigger and the other characters from developing properly, which adulterate the structure of the novel, and which occasionally cloud up an otherwise lucid prose style. There are three kinds of revolutionism in *Native Son*—and none of them altogether engages the reader as representing Wright's point of view. Max's Communism is of course what Wright presumes his novel is expressing—yet this kind of revolutionism is, . . . more imposed from without than an integral element of Bigger's being. . . .

A second kind of revolutionism is of a Negro nationalist variety—and this is far more in keeping with Bigger's character. (p. 115)

But Bigger's nationalism, whatever its components, is nothing compared to what Camus has subsequently described as metaphysical revolution. "Human rebellion ends in metaphysical revolution," Camus writes in *The Rebel*—and it is in the role of the metaphysical revolutionary that Bigger looms most significantly for modern readers. The metaphysical revolutionary challenges the very conditions of being—the needless suffering, the absurd contrast between his inborn sense of justice and the amorality and injustice of the external world. He tries to bring the external world more in accord with his sense of justice, but if this fails he will attempt to match in himself the injustice or chaos of the external world. (p. 116)

Bigger's crimes then signify something beyond their therapeutic value. In a world without God, without rules, without order,

purpose, or meaning, each man becomes his own god and creates his own world in order to exist. Bigger acts violently in order to exist and it is perhaps this fact, rather than his continued undying hatred of whites, that so terrifies Max at the close of the novel. It is possible that Max senses that as a Communist he too has worked hard to dispense with the old social order—but the metaphysical vacuum that has been created does not necessarily lead men like Bigger to Communism, but may just as easily lead to the most murderous kind of nihilism. (pp. 116-17)

James Baldwin writing of *Native Son* says every Negro carries about within him a Bigger Thomas—but that the characterization by itself is unfair in that there are complexities, depths to the Negro psychology and life that Wright has left unexplored. To depict Bigger exclusively in terms of unsullied rage and hatred is to do the Negro a disservice. In Baldwin's view Bigger is a "monster." This, of course, is precisely the point Wright wishes to make—and herein lies its most terrible truth for the reader. Wright is obviously not describing the "representative" Negro—although he makes clear that what has happened to Bigger can more easily befall Negroes than whites. He is describing a person so alienated from traditional values, restraints, and civilized modes of behavior, that he feels free to construct his own ethics—that for him an act of murder is an act of creation. . . . But do such "monsters" as Baldwin calls them exist? Our tabloids could not exist without them. But even supposing they do not commit murder, their sense of isolation and alienation is growing in the face of an increasingly impersonal, industrialized mass society. And in mass, the isolated, the alienated, are capable of consent or indifference to nuclear holocaust or extermination camps. It is perhaps in this respect that *Native Son* is so much more disturbing a novel today than when it was first published. It is not that Bigger Thomas is so different from us; it is that he is so much like us. (pp. 119-20)

Edward Margolies, in his The Art of Richard Wright *(copyright © 1969 by Southern Illinois University Press; reprinted by permission of Southern Illinois University Press), Southern Illinois University Press, 1969, 180 p.*

WARREN FRENCH

One would like to think that the recent flurry of interest in Richard Wright (I write in the unquiet spring of 1969) is not just a by-product of the fashionable enthusiasm for "Black American Literature," but rather an effort to render at last his due to a man praised too soon for the wrong reasons and too soon dismissed for more wrong reasons. One doubts, however, that this man who so much longed to be recognized as an individual would be freshly honored except as a racial symbol. In death as in life, Wright has been forced to win as a Negro who happened to be a writer the recognition that he desired as a *writer* who happened to be a Negro.

Although much of Wright's best work was done during the 1930s, he was virtually unknown outside the cliquish ranks of the native Communists until 1940 when *Native Son* exploded over the literary landscape, first as a hauntingly controversial novel, then (under the aegis of Orson Welles—another abused genius) as a grimly powerful play. (p. 125)

Native Son was an extraordinary success not just because it was an exciting novel by a Negro writer, not just because its sensational episodes fed the public appetite for violence, not just because its flights of rhetoric wrung the hearts of the champions of the oppressed, but most of all because it was that rarest of coups—a work that was familiar in form but unfamiliar in content. Wright had managed to produce an innovation within the nearly exhausted framework of the twentieth-century liberal literary tradition. He had written the Negro equivalent of [Theodore] Dreiser's *An American Tragedy.*

Wright consolidated his triumph with his next major work, *Black Boy* (1945), an account of his childhood in Mississippi, which, even with some final chapters deleted, became an emblem of America's shame and a kind of universal history of the genius frustrated by discrimination.

What few noticed in the hubbub over Wright's powerful apologia is that: (1) a great many Negroes and members of other minority groups had suffered as he had without ever being able to find an adequate vehicle for the articulation of their personal grievances; (2) Wright's account had many similarities to other non-Negro portraits of the artist as a young man, including [James] Joyce's famous novel. While the torments that a white man with Wright's sensibility would have suffered would probably have been different—more subtle, more genteel—they would have been none-the-less mortifying because Wright was *doubly* different from his complacent countrymen. Actually his fellow Communists and fellow Negroes probably understood him only slightly better than his white oppressors and not nearly so well as the few of any color or persuasion who possessed his capacity to respond to life.

Wright seemed, nevertheless, firmly established as the most articulate literary spokesman for the oppressed Negro minority in the United States, the first Negro novelist of really major stature. Then about the same time that John Steinbeck left California for New York, Wright left America for France. This parallel is, I think, more than coincidental. Steinbeck is, in many ways, the fellow artist that Wright most nearly resembles. Wright was actually doing in his work for the American Negro what Steinbeck was doing for the little less despised and little more secure white rejects in our society—those who had been left behind in the shift from an agrarian to an urban society. (pp. 126-27)

Although some critics have labored to find merits in *The Outsider* and other fictional products of Wright's French period, there seems no reason to deny that his career as a serious creative artist ended with his departure from this country in 1946. Like Steinbeck, he can best be described during these later years as a provocative and increasingly querulous journalist. He became as firmly identified with the Negro struggle for political freedom and self-identification throughout the world as Steinbeck became associated with Adlai Stevenson's sophisticated folksiness as the basis for a democratic society. Steinbeck managed to remain at least a small force in American politics; whereas Wright was scorned by the *Time-Life* empire and other mass-media taste-makers for his tart-tongued pushiness. Both, however, were generally and justifiably considered to have ceased to have any artistic significance. (p. 128)

My theory is that Richard Wright (like John Steinbeck) produced his best imaginative work when he was in immediate, daily contact with the people whose behavior he tried to recreate in his writings—when he wrote about Chicago Negroes as he did in *Lawd Today* and the first two parts of *Native Son.* The further he drifted away from an intimate relationship with his subject, the more contrived and artificial his work became. The fiction that he wrote in France had no relationship to the world of his daily experience. He was able to avoid capitulating to Communism in Chicago and New York because his immediate experience made him aware of the shortcomings of a narrowly ideological response to life, and he sought to write of individual people and their agonies rather than intellectual constructs. In France, however, he succumbed to the enchantment of existentialism, because of his failure to establish the kind of rapport with his total environment that he had in the United States. (pp. 134-35)

Lawd Today shows that Wright had a talent for objective, critical fiction that he never had a chance to exhibit publicly during his lifetime. In view of the cool reception that greeted the books *Lawd Today* most nearly resembles (like Steinbeck's *In Dubious Battle,* which theoreticians complained misrepresented the programs prescribed for labor organizers), it is unlikely that Wright's novel could have been valued on its own terms. The people of the 30s did not want to see things as they were or to read a work about a Negro which was only in a very limited sense a "Negro novel" (because the principal character's problems would not have been basically different regardless of his race, color, or residence).

Wright did not make the mistake of treating violence and oppression in the "muted form" that [Edward] Margolies says he did in *Lawd Today* when he wrote the short stories collected under the title *Uncle Tom's Children* [see excerpt above]. Certainly no one would have suspected that the author of these harrowing stories was much interested in literary experimentation, for they were traditional in structure. . . . As opposed to the stories of [Anton] Chekhov and Joyce, which have been the most influential models in the twentieth century, "a good deal 'happens' in Wright's short stories." . . . Wright operated—possibly at the behest of his Communist mentors—in the mode acceptable to the popular magazines and the radical theorists of the day. Although the grim vividness of these stories has caused them to be hailed as outstanding examples of protest literature, they have rarely received attention as examples of the art of the short story.

Native Son was at the time of its publication and has remained such a powerful emotional shock that few people have been able to control their responses well enough to observe that it is a very uneven novel. (p. 136)

Again Margolies' comments make it apparent that Wright had an extraordinary talent for the reporting of events that allowed the reader to reconstruct them kinesthetically, but that the novelist had little ability to maintain stylistic consistency in his work when he began to present purely intellectual arguments. What Margolies does not point out is that one of Wright's main concerns—that Bigger's crime goes undiscovered as long as it does because as a Negro Bigger is literally "invisible"—is announced, but never effectively dramatized. Ralph Ellison, on the other hand, who is one of the few successful intellectual novelists in recent years, succeeds in communicating this same idea of "invisibility" allegorically in *Invisible Man.* It is an ironic evidence of the inadequacy of much recent criticism that Ellison's involved and intricate allegory is often dismissed as an episodic, picaresque tale, whereas Wright's engrossing picaresque that might have the most powerful impact if the long ideological dialogues were eliminated is regarded as a "novel of ideas."

The uncritical enthusiasm for *Native Son* probably did as much as anything else—except probably the move to France—to doom Wright as a creative artist. His activities during the next decade suggest, in fact, that either he had written himself out or he had no encouragement to produce further work in his most effective vein. He turned from fiction to autobiography and produced what is quite possibly his most valuable work, *Black Boy* . . . . *Black Boy* is an outstanding account of a particularly sensitive type of artistic personality striving for identity, but it is as erroneous to read it as an account of the representative Negro experience as it would be to read Winston Churchill's memoirs as an account of the representative British schoolboy's "making his way."

Black Boy probably did, however, have the effect of committing Wright after its publication to maintaining a public stance as a defender of the Negroes' aspirations rather than as an explorer of his own unique situation. Coupled with the move to France that put him out of touch with the physical realities of the Negro situation in America, this attitude meant that until very nearly the end of his life his new works drew upon only a small facet of his vast talent. (pp. 137-38)

In the original version at least. . . , **"The Man Who Lived Underground"** is not [contrary to the opinion of Margolies] an allegory at all, because allegory is an art form in which one thing (character or event) stands for another. The story, however, is an account in the spare style of the second section of *Native Son* of how a man who had been rejected by society might behave given the ideal opportunity to secrete himself from the world. The story is fantastic, but not allegorical, and what Wright succeeds in communicating to the reader is the exultant feeling of the singular individual who has made good his retreat. While Margolies seems more impressed with the second published version of the story—in which the "underground man" comes forth to lead others to his retreat and is shot by a suspicious policeman—than the first, I feel that the second ending is "thought" rather than "felt.". . . (p. 139)

Certainly the penchant for allegory overwhelmed Wright in the ill-conceived *Savage Holiday,* in which he attempted to write of a world with which he had no direct experience. Toward the end of his life he began to recover something of his original strength in *The Long Dream,* in which he returns to the still kinesthetically vivid memories of his childhood; but, as Margolies observes, in the last section of the novel, Wright's feeling for "social detail and concrete physical setting" seems "rather perfunctory." Clearly Wright had not deeply felt nor carefully meditated upon his Paris experiences; or else—once more like Steinbeck—he could not bring himself to discuss his adult experiences like marriage and parenthood with the kinesthetic precision he could his childhood and adult memories of deprivation.

The parallels with Steinbeck that I have several times emphasized deserve to be pressed, because some are remarkable. Wright got off to a later and slower start; there is nothing in his career to compare with the novels from *Cup of Gold* to *Of Mice and Men* that won Steinbeck a hearing and are still responsible for much of his reputation. Beginning with *In Dubious Battle* and *Lawd Today,* however, the parallels are strong. Both novels are remarkable for a cool objectivity in dealing with human tragedy that neither author was able again to achieve. *Uncle Tom's Children* and *The Long Valley,* too, contain analagous accounts of young persons' seeking to free themselves from a repressive environment. If Steinbeck is only rarely as sensational as Wright (and "Flight" and "Vigilante" do have the same kind of impact as Wright's stories), he did have the opportunity to develop into a far more accomplished artist, as he is in *The Grapes of Wrath,* which, like *Native Son,* deals

passionately with an oppressed minority, but which achieves largely through the impact of its carefully calculated form results that Wright could achieve only through the grim details of his narrative.

Both men turned to allegory at almost the same time with *The Moon is Down* and the second version of **"The Man Who Lived Underground,"** but Wright was to give us his last major artistic statement in the form of an ostensibly literal autobiography, *Black Boy,* rather than in the masked form of a cryptic but bitter fictional transformation of observed situations like Steinbeck's *Cannery Row.*

The ill-managed *The Wayward Bus* has parallels to the clumsily allegorical *The Outsider,* as the basically historical *East of Eden* has to the autobiographically inspired *The Long Dream;* but none of these works contributed to their authors' artistic reputations. Both writers also turned principally to journalism in the declining years of their careers. Both wandered about the world. Wright went to the Gold Coast (now Ghana), Spain, Indonesia. Steinbeck visited Russia and Italy and toured the United States with a poodle. Both showed genuine interest in penetrating the masks of the societies they visited and discovering something about the behavior of the common people; but by the time that Wright wrote his last non-fiction book, *The Color Curtain* (1956), and Steinbeck wrote *Travels with Charley,* both were failing to penetrate very deeply beneath the surfaces of things and were living in terms of their private visions rather than serving as hypersensitive media for the transmission of intense personal observations. (pp. 139-40)

Although his being a Negro made him deeply concerned with the plight of other Negroes, Wright never really understood the problems of a racial group as well as he understood his private reactions as an artist to immediate stimuli. Other Negroes like James Baldwin who have had reservations about Wright's techniques have not been entirely fair, because Wright told us more about what it meant to be an artist in an insensitive world than what it meant to be a Negro. The "rage" that Baldwin objected to in Wright is the outcry not of a racial apologist but of a distressed individual.

Since Wright was a Negro in a culture that denied the Negro individual dignity, he told us harrowing things about what it meant to be both Negro and artist—and thus doubly afflicted in a society that was predominantly white and Philistine; but when he tried to intellectualize his racial position and find personal comfort in moving away from the society with which he could establish a painful sensory rapport, he cut himself off from such a large part of the wide spectrum of stimuli to which he was sensitive that he could function only as a competent, outspoken journalist. . . . He rarely realized his potential; but, as I have emphasized in the parallel that I have kept pushing with another more honored artist, neither did John Steinbeck.

We can scarcely be surprised, therefore, that Wright accomplished no more of artistic merit than he did. We can only be surprised and happy that he achieved what he did and helped to advance as much as he did the dignity of the Negro at the expense ultimately of his own artistic self-realization. (p. 141)

Warren French, "The Lost Potential of Richard Wright," in The Black American Writer: Fiction, *Vol. 1, edited by C.W.E. Bigsby (copyright © C.W.E. Bigsby, 1969), Everett/Edwards, Inc., 1969 (and reprinted by Penguin Books, Inc., 1971, pp. 125-42.)*

DARWIN T. TURNER

Richard Wright's *The Outsider* . . . disappointed many critics who, for more than a decade, had waited for a second novel from the author of *Native Son*. . . . (p. 40)

The critics were partially correct. *The Outsider* fails to evoke the emotional intensity which stunned readers of *Native Son* in 1940 and which continues to affect many readers who discover the book for the first time in 1969. *The Outsider*'s frequent echoes of [Dostoyevsky's] *Crime and Punishment* and of the now familiar tenets of existentialism—these disclose the conscious craftsmanship of a well-read author. Thus, the book lacks the aura of uniqueness, originality, and artless spontaneity which characterizes Wright's first novel. *Native Son* seems to be a hoarse cry from the heart of the ghetto; *The Outsider* is an idea shaped by philosophical men who have conquered their emotions.

Nevertheless, *The Outsider* should not be judged merely as a failure by a competent naturalistic novelist who, succumbing to foreign influences, made the mistake of dabbling in existentialism. Actually, Wright leaned toward existentialism long before the philosophy earned its literary reputation in America and perhaps even before he fully realized the philosophical position which he was articulating. Whereas many readers of *Native Son* saw only the implacable forces of environment crushing a helpless black pawn, Bigger Thomas evolves from that pawn into a protagonist who instinctively, not consciously, rejects the standards of a world which is meaningless to him. As Edward Margolies has explained [see exerpt above], once Bigger has murdered, he becomes a metaphysical revolutionary challenging an absurd, hostile world and determined to bring that universe into accord with his sense of justice. . . . (pp. 40-1)

Considered in this respect, *The Outsider* is not Wright's first venture into existentialism. Instead, it can be viewed as an effort, after he had broken fully with Communism, to redefine the idea which he had failed to clarify in *Native Son*. Simultaneously, he attempted, consciously or unconsciously, to improve his work artistically by answering critics' objections to the characterization of his protagonist and to the development of his thesis. (p. 41)

Critics of [*Native Son*] raised an objection which may have troubled Wright. Some argued that Bigger seemed too sensitive to be considered typical. That is, insisting that Bigger be evaluated as a naturalistic representative of uneducated, working Negroes, they presumed that such Negroes not only would be incapable of articulating their feelings but would even be unaware of their hatreds and their fears. Furthermore, most critics evaluated the work merely as Wright's protest against the treatment of Negroes in America.

Wright attempted to redirect the thoughts of his critics. In **"How Bigger was Born,"** he explained that he had not intended to portray Bigger merely as a naturalistic pawn; he wanted to show an individual capable of making conscious choices about his life. Moreover, Wright continued, Bigger's story is not merely the story of an American Negro; it is the story of the oppressed peoples of the world. Whether or not Wright believed that he had persuaded his critics through his essay in [*The Outsider*] he retraced the pattern of *Native Son*. (pp. 43-4)

In general plot idea, *The Outsider* corresponds to *Native Son*. Like *Native Son*, it is located first in Chicago in winter. Structurally also it resembles *Native Son*. It is divided into five sections: Dread, Dream, Descent, Despair, and Decision. Section I—Dread—corresponds to Section I of *Native Son*—Fear. Section I in *The Outsider* begins with a scene of banter among Cross and three friends. Except for the differences in the ages of the characters, the scene closely resembles Chapter Two of *Native Son*, a chapter in which Bigger Thomas talks and jokes with three friends. Interestingly, Wright first proposed to begin *Native Son* with that chapter. In Section I of *The Outsider* as of *Native Son*, accidental death leads to a new life for the protagonist.

The most significant parallels are seen, however, in the background of Cross Damon and his relationship to other people.

For many readers, the resemblances between Cross Damon and Bigger Thomas are obscured by the differences resulting from Cross's superior educational background and his conscious interest in ideas. A former college student, Cross can find employment as a postal clerk rather than as a chauffeur. Although he is not wealthy, he lives on a standard which Bigger and his family identify with the successful white man. He owns a house and car—or, in the tradition of America, the finance company owns a house and car for which he is paying. Undoubtedly, Bigger would envy Cross's possessions and his opportunities. Considered in this way, Cross represents the middle-class Negro who aspires to the American dream. In contrast, Bigger is the lower-class individual who, glimpsing the dream only in romantic motion pictures, rejects it as an impossibility.

By creating a character on a different economic and social level, Wright emphasized the theme which some critics failed to discern in *Native Son*. He was concerned with the problem of existence itself, a frustrating enigma not merely for the poor and the black but for all who refuse to accept the roles in which they are cast.

Apparent differences between Cross and Bigger, however, are more superficial than actual. Education seems to have relieved Damon of some of the problems which vex Bigger; but, in reality, by creating new awareness and new aspirations, it has reproduced the same problems on a different level. For example, Bigger suffers from economic deprivation. He lives in one room with his family; he subsists on welfare. Cross Damon has a job, a house, a car, and an apartment. But these are minimal standards for his class. To pay for them, he must borrow money. Who then is freer economically—Bigger, who must borrow pennies from mother, or Cross, who borrows hundreds from the union?

In character, the two seem identical. Bigger bullies others to conceal his own fears; Cross plays practical jokes. Both rebel against their mothers, who typify an older generation which urged Negro children to live according to the ethics taught in Christian churches and prescribed for Negroes by a society dominated by white men. (pp. 44-5)

Neither Bigger nor Cross can realize satisfactory companionship with women because both subconsciously regard women essentially as instruments for the temporary relief of physical and emotional needs. However, because he has been taught that a man should protect a woman's honor, Cross feels guilt when he betrays that principle. Therefore, the relationships with women do not merely fail to bring him close to another human being, they also intensify his hatred of himself.

Alienated from others, both Cross Damon and Bigger Thomas hate themselves. (p. 46)

Both Bigger and Damon are reborn through accidental deaths of white people. Bigger finds meaning for his life in his efforts to benefit from his accidental murder as well as to escape its consequences. Damon experiences rebirth in a more obviously symbolic scene. Having plunged underground in a subway train, he finds himself trapped inside the overturned car. His legs are wedged to the wall by a train seat held in place by a white man's head. The only way he can free himself is to smash the dead man's head. Wright describes the action in words which echo the horror and tension of the moment at which Bigger discovered that he needed to hack off Mary Dalton's head in order to conceal her body in a furnace. Having freed himself from the pinned position behind the seat, Cross can escape from the train only by stepping on the body of a dead white woman.

As I have stated, the symbolism is obvious. In revising his idea, Wright took no chances that a reader's imagination might be limited to consideration of a Negro youth's lust for a drunkenly helpless white girl. By specifying the race of the individuals blocking Damon's path, Wright emphasized his belief that Negroes can find freedom and new life only after they have first crushed the male and female white forces that trap them in a separate and submerged world.

Once free, Cross, like Bigger, wants to share his new understanding with a woman. Cross confides in Jenny, a white prostitute, as Bigger confides in Bessie. Both protagonists subsequently berate themselves when they realize that the women are incapable of perceiving the emotional and spiritual significance of what has happened. In both works, Wright suggests that the male protagonist cannot discover the needed intellectual and spiritual companionship with women of a particular type. Bessie and Jennie can ease physical and mental tensions; they are opiates which one may use to escape from reality; but they lack the resources to share reality.

In *Native Son,* Wright's meaning is blurred somewhat because he used one figure—Bessie—to represent both the Sambo mentality which Bigger must destroy and the personality of the inadequate female. Consequently, readers may misinterpret Bigger's murder of Bessie as his need to destroy the inadequate female. Wright clarified his meaning in *The Outsider* by representing the concepts through two different individuals. Since Jenny merely represents the sensual companionship in human relationships, Damon does not need to destroy her; instead, he deserts her as previously he has alienated himself from his mother and from Negro women, both as wives and as lovers. He symbolically destroys his Negro personality by murdering Joe, a fellow postal clerk. In an obvious parallel to the murder of Bessie, he hits Joe on the head and drops him from a window to a roof, where his body lies for some time before it is discovered. (pp. 47-8)

Bigger fears Communists but learns from the Communist lawyer Max a way of articulating his new ideas. In 1940 Wright had not clarified his own dilemmas. Although he continued to work with the Communist Party and to respect its philosophy, he was disillusioned by the methods used by the Party. By 1953, however, his break was complete, and his ideas were clear. He had been forced to reject the Communist philosophy as one which could not be attained because of the limitations of the human beings who controlled the Communist Party. Cross Damon reflects Wright's new certainty. Able to judge Communists objectively, Damon rejects or destroys them as mercilessly as he rejects Fascists.

At this stage of *The Outsider,* therefore, Wright reached a philosophical position which he could not have attained through

uneducated, inarticulate Bigger Thomas. Cross Damon is an intellectual, a student of philosophy who read voraciously until he learned that books did not include the ideas he sought. Through Damon, Wright could ask, "What happens to an individual who finds no comfort in the traditional human relationships and institutions?" (pp. 48-9)

Perhaps the problem is more critical for a black man, but it seems to pose an irresolvable dilemma for any man. Family, marriage, church—all have failed him. His passion is ideas, but he finds no solution in the dominant ideas—democracy, capitalism, fascism, communism. What is the future for such a man?

Wright had no satisfactory answer. Bigger Thomas is executed by a capitalistic democracy. In *The Outsider,* the district attorney, a legal representative of the capitalistic democracy, admits that he cannot destroy Cross Damon, but Damon is murdered by Communists. In the revision, as in the original, Wright suggested that the sensitive, questioning individual, the existentialist, will be destroyed by the organized institutions which fear him because they do not understand him and fear his questions because they cannot answer them.

These parallels, I believe, suggest that Wright either consciously or unconsciously was trying to develop more effectively the theme which he explored in *Native Son.* Intellectually, he succeeded: the thought of *The Outsider* is more persuasive. But artistically he failed.

The fault lies partly in his conception of the protagonist. When he created Bigger Thomas, he planned an individual who would provoke shock rather than pity. Bigger does. Nevertheless, readers experience an indefinable feeling of compassion, emerging perhaps from the pathos of the realization that Bigger is not an absolutely self-determining individual but has been grotesquely distorted by a society in which he is inarticulate.

Compassion cannot be felt as easily for Cross Damon. Because he possesses the conventional attributes of the middle-class, his problem does not evoke the sentimentality which can be showered on those judged to be socially and economically inferior. His more intellectual, more abstract problem lacks an emotional analogue. That is, even if one cannot identify emotionally with Bigger's frustration as a Negro, he can relate emotionally to Bigger's efforts to elude the investigators and the police. There is no such emotional analogue in *The Outsider.* Strangely, however, Damon's problem might elicit more sympathetic response in 1969 than it did in 1953, for it suggests the current rebellion of affluent youth against a society which offers material comfort but no spiritual satisfaction. (pp. 49-50)

Darwin T. Turner, "'The Outsider': Revision of an Idea," in The Southern Humanities Review *(copyright 1970 by Auburn University), Vol. IV, No. 1, Winter, 1970, pp. 40-50.*

KENETH KINNAMON

For a useful gloss on Wright's apprentice novel [*Lawd Today*] with its theme of the brutalization of Black life in the urban North, one may turn to his important theoretical essay **"Blueprint for Negro Writing,"** published soon after he moved to New York. The essay seems a clear statement of the novel's intention if not its achievement. Rejecting the exotic bohemianism of the Harlem Renaissance, Wright urges the assimilation of Black folklore into a sophisticated sensibility steeped in modern literature and guided by a Marxist analysis of society. So equipped the Black writer can bring a sharpened class and social consciousness to the problems of his people, utilizing the rich folk tradition but at the same time attempting to transcend the Black nationalism, imposed by a segregated society, out of which this tradition grew. For a novel with such a purpose, *Lawd Today* contains remarkably little overt propagandizing; certainly this is the case when one compares it to other radical novels of the time, including Wright's own *Native Son*. For the most part, Wright was content in his first novel to let the implications of his protagonist's blighted and futile existence speak for themselves. . . .

The simple but neat structure of *Lawd Today* was implicit in Wright's choice of a subject—one sordid but typical day in the life of Jake Jackson, a Chicago postal clerk who hates his job, his wife, his race, and himself, from the time he awakes until he sinks into a drunken sleep some twenty hours later, bleeding from cuts suffered in a vicious brawl with his wife. (p. 16)

This day, the reader infers, is a typical one of Jake's life, but it is also a particular day—12 February 1937. *Lawd Today* not only presents the frustrations and misery of an individual Black man, but turns also to the larger forces which have shaped—or warped—his life and which he so thoroughly misunderstands. . . . [The] most successful device for achieving this dual focus is the recurrent use of snatches from a radio broadcast celebrating Lincoln's birthday and the Northern victory in the Civil War. Here the irony is more complex, for the point is not merely Jake's bored reaction to the broadcast and the contrast between the importance of the events it relates and the triviality of Jake's life, but also the tragic failure of America to fulfill the promise of the idealism of Lincoln and Garrison, a failure that made possible such a life as Jake's, so that the tones of the radio speaker are inevitably pompous and hollow.

Irony is indeed the pervasive mood of *Lawd Today,* but the method is an unsparing naturalism. The dreary monotony of work in the post office, for example, is recorded in minute detail. In classic naturalistic tradition moreover, individual lives are determined by biological as well as by socio-economic forces. The exigencies of food, drink, and sex, particularly the latter, influence Jake and his friends as much as racial and economic discrimination.

Jake's frustration is thus both social and personal. In the dream from which he is awakened by the Lincoln Day radio broadcast at the beginning of the novel, he is climbing an endless stairway, called on by the voice of his boss. This dream clearly represents the futile treadmill of his life, for as a Chicago Black in the Depression he can hardly hope to rise higher than his position as a postal clerk, but it also has a Freudian significance immediately reinforced by the erotic dream which follows it as he drowses before being fully awakened by the arrival of the milkman, whose innocent chat with Lil, Jake's wife, arouses his jealousy. Sexual frustration indeed, is a central theme of *Lawd Today*. (p. 17)

It must be conceded, however, that Wright is not successful in relating Jake's sexual frustration to the economic and social implications of his existence. The difficult rapprochement of [Sigmund] Freud and [Karl] Marx is not achieved in *Lawd Today*.

Nor does Wright manage to weave his interest in urban Black folklore closely enough into the fabric of his tale of Jake's day. Often the reader is uncomfortably aware of the abrupt shifts of emphasis from Jake to Black life in general, as in the de-

scriptions of the policy parlor, the street vendor of a bottled panacea, and the Black Nationalist parade. . . . It is not that the often tediously detailed descriptions of such matters are unrelated to the thematic concerns of *Lawd Today;* on the contrary, the circulars which Jake finds in his mailbox advertise policy diviners and patent medicines for sexual impotence and alcoholism, thus indicating that sex, drink, and gambling are the opiates of Black people, and the description of the obese street vendor is a satirical vignette of the American petit-bourgeois capitalist similar in spirit and detail to one of William Gropper's *New Masses* caricatures. . . . The point is rather that the sociological themes of the novel are not fully integrated into the story of Jake's ordeal, but often seem to be included for their intrinsic interest, which is great (who would wish to dispense with the magnificently obscene comedy of the bout at the dozens between Jake and Al?), or for their doctrinal import.

This failure in the fusion of the novel's materials accounts in part for the relaxed effect of the narrative, though of course this quality of aimlessness results also from the meaningless routine of Jake's life. What is most strikingly absent from *Lawd Today* when compared to the rest of Wright's early fiction is the extraordinary tension of the first two parts of *Native Son* and the concentrated intensity of the stories in *Uncle Tom's Children*.

Lawd Today is not a story of crises in the lives of the Black proletariat, however, but the story of an ordinary day in the life of Jake Jackson, a *Lumpen-Proletariat* with unfulfillable bourgeois illusions. Despite its moments of tedium, its failure to integrate its dual focus on Jake and on his environment and its weaknesses of proportion, *Lawd Today* offers much vivid writing, as in the physical description of Jake awakening or in the wildly sensual atmosphere of the brothel. Above all, the novel conveys an undeniably real impression of Black life in the Chicago of the thirties. . . . The cyclic nature of Jake's day—and his life—is clear enough. Characteristically, Wright presents in *Lawd Today* an emotionally crippled protagonist living a blighted life. Characteristically also, Wright does not permit the reader to evade his wrathful indictment of the society responsible for creating a Jake Jackson. In both its subject and its intended effect, *Lawd Today* is an apprentice novel which stakes out some of the major concerns and attitudes that its author was to develop further in his later fiction. (pp. 17-18)

> Keneth Kinnamon, "'Lawd Today': Richard Wright's Apprentice Novel," in Studies in Black Literature (copyright 1971 by Raman K. Singh), Vol. 2, No. 2, Summer, 1971, pp. 16-18.

JAMES R. GILES

[Only] two years after its publication, Wright dismissed *Uncle Tom's Children* as an overly sentimental, naive book. The evaluation seems to have remained unchallenged ever since. Yet it seems, *pace* the author, as shortsighted as the criticism that the book lacks unity.

[The thematic progression in both] *Uncle Tom's Children* and *Native Son* is the same—from a spontaneous, fear-motivated reaction by a black character against "the white mountain" of racial hatred to a realization of the necessity for concentrated Marxist organization of the poor. Also developed in both works are the ideas that sexual taboos between the races confuse and confound the black man's struggle for justice and that nature herself often seems to join with the white man to oppress the

Negro (Bigger, fleeing from the police through the hostile, unrelenting Chicago snowstorm) permeate both books. Similarly, such images as "the white mountain" or "the white fog" to refer to the crushing weight of white society on the individual black man appear in both *Uncle Tom's Children* and *Native Son*. It is contended here that *Uncle Tom's Children* not only possesses unity and makes an unsentimental artistic statement about the position of the black man in the South, but that it employs several of the central images and themes of *Native Son* in an aesthetically more sophisticated manner than does the later and more famous work.

The first edition of *Uncle Tom's Children* contained only the four stories, **"Big Boy Leaves Home," "Down by the Riverside," "Long Black Song,"** and **"Fire and Cloud."** Subsequent editions added the introductory essay, **"The Ethics of Living Jim Crow,"** and the concluding story, **"Bright and Morning Star."** Both these additions significantly contributed to the aesthetic integrity of the work. In fact, their absence in the first edition probably explains to a large degree that initial critical reaction to the book which so dismayed Wright; in fact, neither Wright nor his critics seem ever to have realized how much these two additions contributed, both to the aesthetic unity and to the thematic militancy of the volume. At any rate, they are invaluable additions in both regards. The essay, **"The Ethics of Living Jim Crow,"** is a much abbreviated version of the racial outrages described in Wright's autobiography, *Black Boy*. . . . The essay ends with Wright quoting a Memphis elevator operator he had known: "'Lawd, man! If it wuzn't fer them polices 'n' them o'lynch-mobs, there wouldn't be nothin' but uproar down here!'" **"Ethics"** is an aesthetically valid introduction to the stories which follow, both because of its concentrated description of the brutality endured by Wright himself in the South and because of the warning contained in this closing quotation. The five stories are all concerned with similar instances of degradation and the final message of the book is an answer to "them polices 'n' them ol' lynch mobs." As will be seen later, the addition of **"Bright and Morning Star"** brings this answer much more sharply into focus than it was initially.

One must note here that four of the five stories depict a brutal death suffered by a black man at the hands of white sadists and the other (**"Fire and Cloud"**) describes a flogging. However, beginning with the third and climactic story **"Long Black Song,"** there is a marked shift in the manner in which the black victims meet the white brutality. It is as if the viewpoint most dramatically stated in Claude McKay's famous 1919 poem, "If We Must Die" becomes the central theme of the last half of the book. In **"Long Black Song,"** the character, Silas, dramatically enacts McKay's message of courage and defiance. In contrast, the main characters in the first two stories, **"Big Boy Leaves Home"** and **"Down by the Riverside,"** react to white intimidation in a definitely non-militant way.

"Big Boy Leaves Home" describes the tragic events which occur after four young black boys decide to go swimming in a pond on the property of a notorious local white racist. While splashing about joyously in the nude, they are horrified when they look up and see a white woman standing by their clothes, transfixed in apparent horror (and fascination?) as she watches them. Big Boy, the "leader" of the gang, forces the inevitable tragedy to a swift culmination by climbing out of the pond, approaching the woman, and begging her to leave their clothes so that they can dress and go. The woman simply remains by the clothes and begins to scream. . . . Now terrified, the other three boys climb out of the pond and rush for their clothes. Instantly, a young white soldier (who is later revealed as the woman's fiance and the son of the notorious racist) rushes up with a rifle. The predictable results are that two of the black boys are shot, and Big Boy has to shoot the white soldier in order to save himself and his remaining friend Bobo. The woman stands terrified but unharmed throughout the scene— that she is a more fortunate forerunner of Mary Dalton, the white woman of *Native Son* who also causes tragedy by more or less unconsciously stumbling against the American racial-sexual taboo, is obvious.

After a brief respite at home, during which his mother gives him some corn bread, Big Boy goes to hide out in some deep kilns he and his friends had dug. The kilns are close to a highway, and a plan is laid for Big Boy and Bobo to wait in them overnight before catching a ride in a truck which a friend will drive to Chicago the next morning. As he is about to crawl into the first hole, Big Boy is met by a huge rattlesnake which he must kill. With the snake, Wright calls attention both to the sexual overtones of the beginning of the tragedy and to the theme, mentioned earlier, of a hostile nature.

Big Boy does spend the night hiding in a kiln—a night during which he sees his remaining friend, Bobo, caught and burned alive by a white mob just a few feet away from him. Also, just as it begins to rain, filling the kiln with freezing water, a bloodhound discovers Big Boy and the terrified youth has to grab the animal and choke it to death; again, the rain and the hound are elements of a nature which seems in league with white society to persecute the individual black man.

In the morning, the truck arrives on time and Big Boy does make his escape to Chicago:

> The truck swerved. He blinked his eyes. The blades of daylight had turned brightly golden. The sun had risen.
>
> The truck sped over the asphalt miles, sped northward, jolting him, shaking out of his bosom the crumbs of corn bread symbolic of the rejected South, making them dance with the splinters and sawdust in the golden blades of sunshine.
>
> He turned on his side and slept.

Despite the symbolic overtones of rebirth in this passage, the rest of the book and certainly all of *Native Son* assert that fleeing to Chicago is not the answer to the Southern black man's oppression. It is merely a form of sleeping. Big Boy is, in fact, a younger Bigger Thomas in several ways—like Bigger, he is the leader of a gang, which he dominates physically, and he stumbles inadvertently into violence because of a white woman and then seeks refuge in **"Flight"** (the title of part two of *Native Son*). Also, Big Boy's reflexes are every bit as controlled by **"Fear"** (part one of *Native Son*) as are Bigger's. The conclusion, then, that Chicago will prove to be no more of an answer for Big Boy than it is for Bigger Thomas seems inevitable. (pp. 256-59)

The next story in the book, **"Down by the Riverside,"** repeats the basic ingredients of **"Big Boy"**—a helpless black individual, Mann, is forced by white bigotry into an act of violence and is forced by white oppression to flee from the inevitable consequences. But unlike Big Boy, Mann is killed trying to escape. The symbolism of the main character's name is quite important here; Big Boy and Bobo are youths, but the adult

"Mann" dies pathetically while trying to flee. Thus, Wright reemphasizes the main point of the volume's first story: flight is no answer. **"Down by the Riverside"** also occurs during a flood, which represents a structural transition from Big Boy's water-filled ditch and reinforces the hostile nature theme. (p. 259)

The next story, **"Long Black Song,"** contains a significant change in mood. It is the character Silas who personifies this change. He dies, as [Claude McKay's poem "If We Must Die"] advocates, dealing the "one death-blow." But the reasons for his action lie as much within the character of his wife Sarah as within himself; and the story focuses on her at length. She is associated with all the forces—white oppression, the animosity of nature, and the violation of sexual taboos—which have destroyed Bobo and Mann and forced Big Boy to flee. Sarah, a primitive earth-mother figure, allows herself to be seduced by a young white traveling salesman of graphophones (a combination clock-gramophone) while Silas is away buying farm supplies. "I offer you time and music rolled into one," brags the salesman, unaware that Sarah has no use for time and is the soul of music. Sarah's contempt for such an abstract concept as time is emphasized at the beginning of the story when she gives her baby a clock to beat on. . . . (p. 260)

When he hears the full truth, Silas drives Sarah out of the house with their baby in her arms and awaits the return of the white salesman. The description of Sarah running away through the fields grasping the child and not really comprehending what she has done, emphasizes beautifully the earth mother motif. Like [William] Faulkner's Lena Grove, she is as incapable of controlling the animalistic side of her self as she is of comprehending an abstract concept like time.

In the morning, the salesman does return, and Silas shoots him. Knowing that a lynch mob is inevitably coming for him, Silas still refuses to flee, even after Sarah returns with the baby to beg him to do so. His speech to her is the turning point of *Uncle Tom's Children:*

> "The white folks ain never gimme a chance.
> They ain never give no black man a chance!
> There ain nothin in yo whole life yuh kin keep
> from 'em! They take yo lan! They take yo free-
> dom! They take yo women! N then they take
> yo life! . . . N then Ah gets stabbed in the back
> by mah own blood! When mah eyes is on the
> white folks to keep em from killin' me, mah
> own blood trips me up! . . . Ahm gonna be
> hard like they is! So hep me, Gawd. Ah'm
> gonna be *hard!* When they git me outta here
> theys gonna *know* Ahm gone! Ef Gawd lets me
> live Ahm gonna make em *feel* it!" . . .

Silas is true to his word. When the mob comes, he opens fire and kills several of them. The whites set fire to his house, hoping to drive Silas out; but they fail. Silas chooses to die in the fire fighting back as long as he can. (pp. 261-62)

It is interesting to note the parallels between Silas' death and that of Jean Toomer's Tom Burwell in *Cane*. Both men die in flames, without giving their white oppressors the pleasure of a single scream of pain, and both die defending the honor of a black woman, even though it has already been defiled by a white man. But as heroic as it is, Silas' death is not yet the complete answer. Since it is an individual act with no specific political overtones—the theme of Marxist unity has yet to be introduced. The remaining stories, **"Fire and Cloud"** and **"Bright and Morning Star,"** introduce that theme, while **"Long**

Black Song" serves as a transition story between the negative flight of the first two stories and the positive Marxist defiance of the last two. It is significant that the titles of the last two stories come from spirituals, but are not used ironically as in the case of **"Down by the Riverside."**

"Fire and Cloud" depicts Minister Taylor's initiation into real leadership of his people. Taylor has been a "black leader" in the past mainly because of the largesse of the town's white power structure. However, when a depression strikes his people and threatens them with starvation, Taylor rebels. At the instigation of two Communists (one white and one black—Wright's symbolic propaganda here is evident), Taylor encourages a protest march, but will not let his name be used in the leaflets promoting the demonstration. On the other hand, he also refuses to stop the planned march: to the mayor, the chief of police, and another white leader, he simply says over and over that his people are "jus plain hongry!" . . . Taylor is truly between two worlds: his religious orthodoxy and fear of the white establishment will not allow him to align himself openly with the Marxists, but his conscience will not allow him to stop the march. In contrast, there is his son Jimmy, a big boy with the courage of Silas, who wants to organize his band of black youths for open, pitched racial warfare.

Taylor's initiation into true leadership comes when his compromising only serves to bring out the bestiality of the white society. He is kidnapped and flogged, and a large number of his congregation are also brutally beaten. After the beating, Taylor has to struggle home through a white neighborhood, feeling that he is enclosed in a "white fog." Upon learning of his father's ordeal, Jimmy wants to rush out immediately and organize his band of black youths for revenge; but Taylor stops him. . . . (pp. 262-63)

Taylor has transcended even Silas and has learned, as it were, the lesson of McKay's "If We Must Die." He may not be ready to endorse Marxism in name—he still is a Christian minister—but he is ready to practice its doctrine (God is the people). Taylor does organize the march personally, and it is such a success that the starving poor whites join in, the combined forces bringing the white power structure to its knees. Taylor has become a real leader of his people, much in the way that Toomer suggests that Kabnis will do at the end of *Cane*.

The transition into **"Bright and Morning Star"** is one of the most aesthetically satisfying achievements of *Uncle Tom's Children*. This last story opens with the main character, an elderly black mother named Sue, remembering her conversion from Christianity to Communism because of the inspiration of her two Marxist sons. (Taylor, of course, has undergone a nearly identical transformation with similar inspiration.) The story also does a beautiful job of tying together all the ingredients of the preceding stories: it takes place during a driving rainstorm (again, hostile nature); at one point, Sue taunts a white sheriff into brutally beating her so that she can prove to herself that her faith in her new "religion" is as strong as was her belief in the old (this incident shows white oppression, of course, plus another example of the admirable, but finally futile, kind of courage earlier exemplified by Silas and Jimmy); Sue's hatred of white society is so intense that she is plagued by visions of "white mountains" and "white fog" (the latter, the most frequently used image in this book, as well as in *Native Son*); and, finally, there is a white girl, Reva, who is in love with Sue's son, Johnny-Boy (the racial-sexual motif again). In Reva, though, one sees the distance covered in this book between "**Big Boy**," "**Long Black Song**," and "**Bright and Morning Star**." Reva's love for Johnny-Boy is love, not just sexual fascination. Moreover, Reva exemplifies a sensitivity and sincerity which are infinitely superior to that possessed by Jan and Mary Dalton, the sympathetic white Communists of *Native Son*.

Sue herself personifies the final thematic element in the book. Just as Taylor's understanding of the need for group unity represents a thematic progression from Silas' individualistic heroism (which is itself an improvement over Big Boy's and Mann's attempts at flight), so Sue's belief in Marxism extends the characterization and depth of the kind of person Taylor is and Sue has been. Not only is she willing—unlike Taylor—to endorse Marxism openly and by name, but she accepts it with a religious fervor, much like Taylor's old feelings for the church, but with significant and promising social differences. Sue's faith in her new religion is in fact so strong that it nearly causes her to betray her party. (pp. 263-64)

[When her son is being tortured by a white mob, Sue tries to shoot him to relieve his suffering. Before she can], the gun is taken away from her. However, the sheriff simply takes the gun and shoots first Johnny-Boy and then Sue. Her death is still a triumph, however. . . . For the first time in the book, nature, as represented by a rain, is not a hostile force—Sue has, by fording the stream, conquered its treachery. Her death, by negating her unintended betrayal of the party and thus preserving Marxist unity, has prevented white oppression from destroying the potential power of the people (that God which Taylor in the preceding story had come to worship). In addition, Reva, a white woman who honestly loved a heroic black man, is safe in Sue's bed. Finally, the "white mountain" which has so intimidated all the black characters in the book has been obliterated in the killing of "the Judas" Booker.

"**Bright and Morning Star**" (the title comes from a spiritual describing Jesus, making the point that Sue and Johnny-Boy are the martyred saviors of the new "religion" of Marxism) effectively unites all the major elements of the book on a positive note. Certainly, then, the importance of the inclusion of this story after the first edition cannot be overstated. In fact, it adds so much to the overall work that its initial exclusion does undoubtedly explain the feeling of incompleteness on the part of the initial reviewers. That Wright himself sensed this incompleteness is proved by the beautiful transition between this and the preceding story; incomprehensibly, however, he apparently *never* grasped the degree to which "**Bright and Morning Star**" had improved his book. At any rate, the thematic progression of the book is now obvious—there is Big Boy the youth who runs, then Mann the adult who runs, then Silas who meets a heroic but lonely death, then Taylor the minister who will not openly endorse Marxism but who acts out its implications, and finally there is Sue who dies a martyred convert to Communism and thus triumphs over all the forces which have limited the characters in the first four stories.

Obviously, then, *Uncle Tom's Children* in its final form cannot be dismissed as a collection of unrelated stories, and Wright's own low opinion of his work represents an excess of self-criticism. The book makes the same progression in theme as *Native Son* (Bigger Thomas initially out of fear, runs, and finally comprehends the necessity of the unity of the masses) and achieves this progression symbolically, without a long editorial appendage to the reader by a Marxist lawyer. Moreover, such characters as Silas, Sarah, and Sue come much more vibrantly alive than does anyone in *Native Son*. Certainly

Reva is nowhere near so offensive, intentionally or otherwise, as Jan and Mary Dalton, the "good" white characters of Bigger's story. In fact, it seems much more likely that "bankers' daughters" would have "wept" over *Native Son* than over *Uncle Tom's Children*, an idea which the relative sales at least of the two books, at the time of their publication, would seem to confirm. (pp. 265-66)

James R. Giles, "Richard Wright's Successful Failure: A New Look at 'Uncle Tom's Children'," in PHYLON: The Atlanta University Review of Race and Culture, 4 *(copyright, 1973, by Atlanta University; reprinted by permission of* PHYLON*), Vol. XXXIV, No. 3, Third Quarter (September, 1973), pp. 256-66.*

ROBERT B. STEPTO

One of the curious things about Richard Wright is that while there is no question that his best works occupy a prominent place in the Afro-American canon, or that a survey of Afro-American literature would be incomplete without him, many, including myself, find it difficult to describe his place in the Afro-American literary tradition. . . . An author's place in a tradition depends on how he reveals that tradition. It is not simply a matter of when his works were published but also of how they illuminate—and in some cases honor—what has come before and anticipate what will follow. In Afro-American literature particularly, the idea of a tradition involves certain questions about the author's posture not only among his fellow writers but also within a larger artistic continuum which, in its exquisite commingling of materials spoken, played, and written, is not the exclusive property or domain of the writer alone. Richard Wright is a fine writer, perhaps a great one; he has influenced, in one way or another, almost every important black writer who has followed him. But Wright forces us to face a considerable problem: to what extent may we qualify his place in the artistic tradition and still submit that he is unquestionably a participant in it? I don't pretend to be able to solve this problem, but I can explore three of the questions involved: What was Wright's posture as an author, and how did it correspond with models provided by the tradition? How do his works illuminate or complement those Afro-American texts preceding them? And, what has been his effect on our contemporary literature and culture? In answering these we will be a little closer to understanding Wright's place—or lack of one—in the tradition.

Many passages in Wright's works illustrate the issues concerning his authorial posture, but the following one from "**I Tried to Be a Communist**" seems particularly appropriate, partly because it is autobiographical and partly because it raises all the familiar arguments regarding Wright's posture toward his audience. In the passage, Wright describes what happened when he spoke before a unit meeting of black Communists in Chicago. . . .

> The meeting started. About twenty Negroes were gathered. The time came for me to make my report and I took out my notes and told them how I had come to join the Party, what few stray items I had published, and what my duties were in the John Reed Club. I finished and waited for comment. There was silence. I looked about. Most of the comrades sat with bowed heads. Then I was surprised to catch a twitching smile on the lips of a Negro woman. Minutes

passed. The Negro woman lifted her head and looked at the organizer. The organizer smothered a smile. . . .

When the organizer finally breaks the silence, Wright recoils from his comments, significantly remarking, "His tone was more patronizing than that of a Southern white man. . . . I thought I knew these people, but evidently I did not." . . . Then Wright informs us:

> During the following days I learned . . . that I . . . had been classified as an *intellectual* . . . that the black Communists in my unit had commented upon my shined shoes, my clean shirt, and the tie I had worn. Above all, my manner of speech had seemed an alien thing to them. . . . 'He talks like a book,' one of the Negro comrades had said. And that was enough to condemn me forever as bourgeois. . . .

Wright's ambivalent attitude toward his race and its rituals is amply revealed here, and, while it is not a matter which should enter into our evaluations of his art, it does haunt and becloud our feelings concerning his place in the tradition. Aware of the vivid scenes in *Black Boy,* wherein racial bonds are shown to be either hypocritical or forms of submission, and recalling as well how he argues in **"Blueprint for Negro Literature"** . . . for Negro writers to transcend "the nationalist implications of their lives," . . . we are able to comprehend his behavior at the unit meeting but not necessarily approve of it. What brands him an intellectual in this instance is not, strictly speaking, his clean clothes or his articulateness. If this were the case, then most of the black preachers in America—whom Wright termed "sainted devils" . . .—would bear the same mark and be cast from church and pulpit. That Wright "talks like a book" is closer to the heart of the matter, for it is Wright's *mode* of articulation, and the related matter of how he did not (or could not) acknowledge kinship with his black brethren while articulating the Party line, which most troubled his black audience and, in turn, bothers us.

Wright's refusal to partake of the essential intra-racial rituals which the situation demanded suggest that he was either unaware of, or simply refused to participate in, those viable modes of speech represented in history by the preacher and orator and in letters by the articulate hero. The question of articulation does not rest exclusively with matters of verbal facility, but, on a higher plane, with the expression of a moral consciousness which is racially-based. And of course this involves a celebration of those honorable codes of conduct among one's kin.

Wright's dilemma reminds one of [W.E.B.] Du Bois' short story in *The Souls of Black Folk* entitled "Of the Coming of John," in which the "black" John, John Jones, comes home from college to teach school and "rescue" his black townspeople from their "backwardness." His chance to address neighbors and kin occurs at the black Baptist church, and despite his college-honed elocution he fails miserably in his purpose, partly, one imagines, because he attempts to assault those rituals of behavior which the humble building in which he speaks both represents and reinforces. (pp. 525-27)

In both the story of John Jones and Wright's **"I Tried to Be a Communist,"** the failure to articulate is at once a matter of the voice assumed and of how that voice relates to the audience at hand. While Jones did not speak to or of his audience, Wright compounded Jones's error by speaking beyond his immediate

audience to another, which in this case was Big Brother. (pp. 527-28)

The "unit meeting" passage hints at many complaints laid at Wright's door, but none loom larger than Ellison's lament . . . that Wright "could not for ideological reasons depict a Negro as intelligent, as creative or as dedicated as himself." . . . The charge pertains particularly to Bigger Thomas, but as we see in *Black Boy* and in **"I Tried to Be a Communist,"** Wright's limited depiction of the Negro extends occasionally to self-portraits as well. It is hard to believe that the bumbling black writer alienating black folk and performing a poor job of propagandizing for the Party is supposed to be Wright himself, but for reasons neither wholly self-effacing nor wholly aesthetic it is, alas, poor Richard.

The issue is really Wright's idea of the hero, although I believe none of his critics put the matter quite this way. If we assume, as I do, that the primary voice in the tradition, whether in prose or verse or music, is a personal, heroic voice delineating the dimensions of heroism by either aspiring to a heroic posture, as does the voice of [Frederick] Douglass and Du Bois, or expressing an awareness of that which they *ought* to be, as we see [James Weldon] Johnson's Ex-Coloured Man and [Ralph] Ellison's Invisible Man doing, then the mystery of what is unsettling about Wright's voice (and protagonists) begins to unfold. Bigger Thomas is hardly the only maimed or stunted or confused figure in Afro-American literature; this is not what makes him different. What *does* is his unawareness of what he *ought* to be, especially as it is defined not by the vague dictates of the American Dream but by the rather specific mandates of a racial heritage. (p. 528)

All in all, Wright's authorial posture is much like that of Booker T. Washington. Both men are, to use George Kent's phrase, "exaggerated Westerners," . . . especially with regard to the voice and posture each perfected in order to reach those whom they perceived to be their audience. . . . In the case of both men, the speech and thought they espoused led to a necessary denial, at least in print, of certain Afro-American traditions. Hence, they were, in their authorial posture, exaggerated individuals alienated from their race and, to some degree, themselves. Even when they are about the task of creating themselves in autobiographies, their vision is shaped and possibly warped by this state of "exaggeratedness." Thus, in *Up from Slavery,* Washington models himself as the ideal fund-raiser and public speaker and defers to the facile portraits of himself by journalists, while Wright, in *Black Boy,* suppresses his own extraordinary human spirit by rendering himself a black "biological fact." . . .

But as with most comparisons there are distinctions to be made. Beyond all questions of era and place rests the simple fact that Washington was in control of the implications of his authorial posture while Wright was not. . . . When Wright, . . . even in the writing of *Black Boy,* embraces the example of [Theodore] Dreiser, [Sinclair] Lewis, and [H. L.] Mencken far more than that of [Jean] Toomer, Johnson, [Langston] Hughes, or [Zora Neale] Hurston, we want to know [why]? In sum, Wright was more the victim of his posture than the master of it, and in this he is not alone in Afro-American letters. If he indeed occupies a prominent place in the tradition because of his views on author and audience, it is because the founders set aside a large space for confused men. (p. 529)

Despite Wright's apparent ignorance of Afro-American literature during his youth and rise to literary prominence, there are distinct links between certain preceding narrative types, the slave narrative and plantation tale in particular, and his own writings. But the question remains as to whether these links are mere repeated patterns or of the resilient stuff that establish author and text in an artistic continuum.

Native Son, for example, may be viewed as a plantation tale, not only because there are ties between it and the "revisionist" plantation tales of Charles W. Chesnutt, but also because certain features of setting, action, and character are recognizably those of a nineteenth-century American plantation society. The setting is roughly that of a plantation, with the slave quarters west of Cottage Grove Avenue, a respectful long block from the Big House of the Dalton's on Drexel Boulevard. Dalton may not be a slaveholding captain of early agri-business, but his immense profits do come from the land and from the hard toil of blacks in that, as president of the South Side Real Estate Company, he landlords over hundreds of over-priced rat-infested tenements, including that in which Bigger and his family lead their sorry lives. (p. 530)

Despite her flirtation with Communism, Mary Dalton is still the young, white, and (as her Christian name implies) virginal belle on the pedestal. She might at first sit alongside Bigger in the front seat of her father's car, but in the end, she removes to the rear with her boyfriend, Jan, only to reinforce the distance by reminding Bigger to cart her trunk to the station in the morning. And so the shuttle is set in motion, orders one moment, her drunken head on Bigger's shoulder the next. If Bigger is confused, the police and newspapers are not: Mary is the white beauty, Bigger the black brute.

These postures are, unfortunately in our world, timeless, and we would be wrong to suggest that they are in some way the exclusive property of the antebellum South. And because Mary and Bigger are in this sense conventional types, we must wonder whether the third major character, Attorney Max, is as well. Like Mary's boyfriend, Jan, Max resembles the sympathetic white found in the slave narratives who is somewhat removed from the system. But while Jan remains within the type—and is therefore as one-dimensional as are most of the novel's characters—Max's status is more problematic. While he never gains the intimacy with Bigger he so desperately seeks, Max does nevertheless, more than any other, spark Bigger's fleeting glimpse of the possibilities of life and of human communion. Moreover, as his courtroom speech implies, he sees, more than the rest, how America has made Bigger far more than Bigger has fashioned himself. Max's use of language is what allows him to break out of the plantation tale type. It contrasts not only with Bigger's verbal deficiencies and with the corruption of language by the State's Attorney and the press, but also, on a subtler scale, with Mary and Jan's insensitive verbal gropings across the racial chasm ("'Isn't there a song like that, a song your people sing?'") which only fill Bigger with "a dumb, cold, and inarticulate hate." . . .

Indeed, what most distinguishes *Native Son* from its antecedent plantation tale texts is not its bleak urban landscape but the fact that the traditional heroic modes of transcending travail in this world such as the gift of uncommon insight and speech have not been given to Bigger but apparently to Max instead. Thus, the issue of Bigger's sub-heroic posture is further confused by the question of whether Wright intends Max to be the novel's heroic voice and, by extension, Wright's voice as well. (p. 531)

If Max speaks for Wright, we must assume that he specifically does so in the courtroom episode where he is not only eloquent

but forthright and compassionate. Yet this poses a considerable problem, for in implicitly espousing the classic liberal notion that truth will invariably foster justice, Max blunts the raw revolutionary fervor which Bigger generated and which first seduced the Communists to come to his aid. In doing so, Max exchanges his credentials as a radical for a heroic posture which is very much in the American grain. Thus, while transcending the character type in the slave narratives which he first resembles, Max soon takes on the features of a familiar turn-of-the-century type, the "white moral voice." . . . Max is, then, a revolutionary manqué; a reformer possessing a grand but ineffectual idealism which leaves him horror-struck before the fact of Bigger's pending execution.

If Max is *not* Wright's voice, or at least not the heroic voice in the novel, then we would expect him to be sketched ironically, with the stress falling on what may be less than heroic in his words and character. But this is not the case. What we have instead is a confusion of political language and purpose, compounded by the troublesome fact that Wright seems to have bestowed the gift of eloquence on Max with no clearly discernible end in mind.

The problem with Max seems to be a fictive equivalent of Wright's own dilemma in **"I Tried to Be a Communist."** In each case, the speaker's articulateness does not meet the needs of the occasion and in that sense is a kind of illiteracy, especially of the sort that is enforced by America's rituals along the color line. If, in *Native Son*, Max is indeed Wright's voice, it is not because of the content of his speeches but rather because he shares with his author a misperception of audience, grounded in what we may term an extraordinary and almost myopic innocence. Thus, despite the novel's many and varied images of American slave society, the absence of an articulate hero whose posture and language tends to modulate the forces of a hostile environment renders *Native Son* a most problematic novel in Afro-American letters.

Black Boy, on the other hand, is more clearly conceived and is hence the better of Wright's two greatest published works. The dominant voice of the book seems to be finally that of its author precisely because it has a fair measure of human proportion. To be sure, we are almost overwhelmed by those relentless passages in *Black Boy* in which Wright fashions himself a black "biological fact." But countering these are the moments of marvelous self-assertion, the Whitmanesque catalogs of sensual remembrances, and overall, the presence of a questing human being seeking freedom and a voice. Here, a hostile environment *is* modulated by an emerging, extraordinary figure, and the resulting narrative establishes a place for itself in the continuum founded by the slave narrative.

One may list a number of motifs *Black Boy* shares with the slave narratives—the violence and gnawing hunger, the skeptical view of Christianity, the portrait of a black family valiantly attempting to maintain a degree of unity, the impregnable isolation, the longing and scheming to follow the North Star resolved by boarding the "freedom train"—but the most enduring link is the motif (and, one might argue, the narrative form) of the narrator's quest for literacy. . . . [It was] reading, as well as the writing of stories and even commencement addresses, which prompted young Richard to follow the North Star and, in a supreme act of self-assertion, free himself.

All in all, our comparison of *Black Boy* and *Native Son* provides us with a number of strong, revealing contrasts, but none presses with greater urgency and portent than that of the self-assertive, self-aware narrator of *Black Boy* seeking literacy and a voice appositioned against the image of Bigger and his inert cohorts assaulted by the mindlessness of B-grade Hollywood films and the rhetoric of propaganda emanating not only from the Communists but also from the Daltons, the government, and the press. Clearly, Wright could match his model of the writer described in **"Blueprint"** who is "something of a guide in [our] daily living," but it is remarkable that he did so only in the writing of his autobiography. (pp. 531-34)

As the Black Aesthetic critics and writers surfaced in the late sixties. . . , they embraced Richard Wright as a novelist and also as an aesthetician. In some instances, however, it was not so much Wright but Bigger Thomas who, strangely enough, was promoted as the black artist's model. . . . If indeed, as some are saying, the black art-as-sociology and Black Aesthetic theories of the 1960's are outmoded, it may be because the latter is but an extension and political radicalization of the former, and neither approach is fully in tune with the heartbeat of the artist and his art.

By and large, the chief limitation to most of the criticism of *Native Son* is that the critics have dwelled on what we may loosely call the novel's content. Whether *Native Son* actually shocked the proverbial banker's daughter (who might identify, one supposes, with Mary Dalton) as Wright hoped it would remains unclear. What *is* clear, however, is that Wright's critics have been preoccupied by those very features to the novel which are presumably distressing to proper young ladies. Generally, most of the criticism of *Native Son* falls into one of two categories: predictable, journeyman-like studies of imagery (light and dark; animal references) and symbolism (the soaring airplane, various timepieces, the Christian crosses); or, responses to those features which, as Baldwin has written, "whet the notorious national taste for the sensational." The problem, we discover, is that these approaches unduly isolate the text from the corpus of American and Afro-American literature and direct discussion of *Native Son* toward yet another ritualized, pseudo-scientific rehash of the Black Man's Plight.

As I have tried to indicate earlier in these pages, Wright's influence on the contemporary critic may lead to the pursuit of other types of questions. Our sense of an Afro-American literary tradition can be sharpened and enhanced, for example, by assaying Wright's departures from it. We need to develop what has already been ventured about Bigger and Wright's entanglement in the web of double-consciousness so that we may come to know them and the place of *Native Son* in the artistic continuum. We need to assess why, from the standpoint of artistic and even aesthetic considerations, Wright earnestly desired to become a jazz critic in the twilight of his career. Above all, we must not hesitate to discover the Americanness of Richard Wright. Such an activity is actually part of the legacy handed down by such pioneering Afro-American critics as William Stanley Braithwaite and Sterling A. Brown. Wright's departures from Afro-American traditions generally serve to confirm his place in the mainstream of American letters, and, for the moment, it seems like the knowledgeable Afro-Americanist critic is best suited to articulate Wright's stature in both literary worlds.

Turning to Wright's influence on the contemporary black writer, especially those writers first published during the last decade, we find a predictable array of responses ranging from celebrations of Bigger to what we can only deem more thoughtful considerations of Wright's work which frequently re-examine those rituals of black and white cultures of which we've already spoken. The celebrations of Bigger more often than not represent the exploitation of these cultural rituals, and seem to be generated by psychological needs surfacing as strategies for political power, or by unadulterated greed. Writers are often found in the former camp (Eldridge Cleaver, for example), while the would-be artists behind the spate of "blaxploitation" films may be designated to the latter. If indeed, as Kichung Kim writes, "For many Black Americans . . . Bigger is probably the one character they find most authentic in all of American literature . . . ;" we need not wonder why these writers and filmmakers have a considerable audience. None of this is Wright's doing or intention. The man who split the atom did not drop the bomb. However, like the scientist who foresaw the holocaust of Hiroshima, Wright, in his portraits of Bigger fantasizing at the movies and dreamily reading detective stories, seems to have prophesied what is a lamentable feature to our present cultural state. What he understandably could not foresee is that today not only is Bigger still in the audience, but his fantasized self is on the screen.

A far more honorable and direct response to Wright may be discovered in the recent fiction of black women authors. We have alluded to the effort to "humanize" Bigger but the attempts to revise and redeem Mrs. Thomas and both Bessies (the one in *Native Son* and the one in *Black Boy)*, launched mostly by black women writers, must be mentioned as well. There is little written discussion of this; but looking at the literature itself, we can find types of Mrs. Thomas and both Bessies leading richer lives and having more going for them than a false church, a whiskey bottle, and, as Wright says of the Bessie in *Black Boy*, a peasant mentality. (pp. 535-38)

All in all, the black women novelists of our age seem to be agreeing with Alice Walker that "black women are the most fascinating creations in the world." Thus, out of necessity, they are turning to Toomer, Hurston, [Gwendolyn] Brooks, and [Ann] Petry, and not to the majority of black male writers for their models and encouragement. In this light, the rise of a feminine and sometimes feminist voice in contemporary Afro-American fiction may be directly related to the narrow and confining portraits of black women in earlier modern fiction, including that of Wright. (p. 539)

In poems such as [Michael Harper's series "Heartblow"], Wright, I feel, is restored to his proper stature as a participant in Afro-American letters. Harper's mining of Wright's primary images and placement of them in the continuum, as well as his implied suggestion that Wright deserves a place in the pantheon where we find Du Bois, yields the kind of evidence which balances all we know of Wright's shortcomings. And it is this balanced view of Wright, as an author who could argue "Tradition is no longer a guide. . . . The world has grown huge and cold" while providing us with archetypes which generations of writers would in turn place *in* the tradition he rejected, that begins to define his stature in the Afro-American tradition. (p. 541)

Robert B. Stepto, "'I Thought I Knew These People': Richard Wright & the Afro-American Literary Tradition," in The Massachusetts Review *(reprinted from* The Massachusetts Review; © 1977 The Massachusetts Review, Inc.), *Vol. XVIII, No. 3, Autumn, 1977, pp. 525-41.*

MORRIS DICKSTEIN

Attacked, abandoned as a literary example by [James] Baldwin and [Ralph] Ellison, whose early work he had typically encouraged, [Richard Wright] became, after a long eclipse and after his death in 1960, the favored ancestor of a great many new black writers, who rejected his successors and felt more akin to his militant spirit. Parricide, after all, is one of the quicker methods of succession, and nothing can more conveniently legitimate the bloody deed than an appeal to the authority of the grandfather, himself the previous victim. (p. 159)

[It] would be superficial to think that Baldwin alone killed Richard Wright until the angry sixties came along to resurrect him. In some sense Wright's kind of novel was already dead or dying by the time he found it. (p. 160)

Nothing so clearly dates Baldwin's early essays, especially the attacks on Wright, as the assurance that the novel has intrinsically little to do with society but rather involves "something more than that, something resolutely indefinable, unpredictable. . . . The disquieting complexity of ourselves . . . this web of ambiguity, paradox, this hunger, danger, darkness. . . . This power of revelation which is the business of the novelist, this journey toward a more vast reality which must take precedence over all other claims." . . . [Writers] spoke of the novel that way all the time, as a mysterious inward quest toward some ineffable region of personality. . . . What chance had Richard Wright in that climate of critical "thinking"?

Native Son is an untidy novel, many novels. It looks backward to *An American Tragedy,* sideways to a lurid potboiler, forward, strikingly, to [Albert Camus's] *L'Etranger* and the ideas of [Jean-Paul] Sartre. Two-thirds of the way through it changes horses and devolves into a curious but inert ideological essay on a novel that has essentially ended, but that had until then been remarkably free of the clichés of proletarian fiction and the party line. This immensely long and disappointing coda has served to obscure the book and date it. The hidden strength of *Native Son*—hidden from formalist and Communist alike—is in essence Dostoevskian rather than Mike Goldian: a harrowing mastery of extreme situations, of the mind *in extremis,* a medium not so much naturalistic as hallucinatory, dreamlike, and poetic. The following lines describe the hunger of Bigger Thomas, in flight, trapped, hungry, cold: "He wanted to pull off his clothes and roll in the snow until something nourishing seeped into his body through the pores of his skin. He wanted to grip something in his hands so hard it would turn to food." Psychologically this is vivid, almost surreal, but it is also socially emblematic, a fierce heightening of the whole condition of the ghetto where he is trapped, within a police cordon that only makes more literal the color line that divides it from the rest of the city. (pp. 160-61)

It was just this dimension, which Dreiser and other American realists shared, that dropped out of serious American fiction toward the end of the forties. (p. 162)

[Where] Baldwin and even [Norman] Mailer—despite his fascination with power—must *reach out* to their public subjects (the Black Muslims, the march on the Pentagon) in order to make that distance, that ambivalence, their true subjects, Wright's *Black Boy,* though more purely autobiographical, sits in effortless mastery over *its* social theme, the condition of the black man in the South. Yet Wright's book is also more convincingly personal, even in incidents he may have invented. Neither Baldwin nor Mailer, immense egos both, have as yet written a true autobiography; their revelations are obsessive but selective. Genuine sons of the forties and fifties, they remain essentially private persons despite their fame. Wright, however, a disaffected son of the thirties, did write an autobiography at

age thirty-seven, but honed and sorted his memories into a coherent fable, aiming, like all great autobiographers, to fashion a myth—typically a myth of conversion or election—rather than to convey information about the past.

In scene after scene Wright presents his younger self as a rebellious misfit, incapable of adapting to the modes of deference that obtain in his coarse and brutal family and in Southern life as a whole. . . . [A] pattern of instinctive rebellion and savage counter-violence recurs repeatedly . . . throughout the book. When Wright goes out at last among whites, he makes an intense effort of self-restraint, but try as he will there is always a provocative hint of pride and self-respect, a touch of the uppity nigger about him. A latecomer to the white world, he is unable to quite master the shuffling, degraded, but apparently contented manner that will tell whites he not only knows his place but loves it. He is the perennial loser, always half-willingly skirting an abyss, awaiting the fatal misstep that might reveal his true feelings and get him killed.

The turning point of *Black Boy* comes in an incident that reverses this pattern and shows him (and us) the true nature of his situation. He goes to work for a benevolent Yankee but soon is typically hounded and threatened by two white co-workers. (pp. 163-64)

[Wright does not belabor the lesson, but to the reader it is clear enough: neither] the well-meaning Yankee, archetype of the ineffectual liberal paternalist, nor the defeated but unbroken black boy can buck the whole Southern way of life. Wright will break the mold by escaping to the North, becoming a writer and radical who will turn his rebelliousness from an ineluctable fatality to a fighting virtue. With word and deed he will try to change society rather than nest in the shelter of its exceptions. (p. 164)

[Wright's books] enunciate a fundamental pattern of black writing, that of the *Bildungsroman,* or "How I got my consciousness raised." The black writer is almost by definition someone who has made it, struggled out of the cave not only of oppression but illusion—a mental bondage that issues in impotence and self-hatred—and has come to deliver an account of his journey. Just as Wright in *Black Boy* develops from terrified deference to rebellion and flight, *Native Son* moves from a crime-and-punishment plot to an account of how Bigger Thomas, by accepting his crime, achieves a measure of freedom and awareness. But the theme and its material increasingly clash; the crime is finally *not* acceptable, nor is it reducible to symbolism. Pursuing the matter, Wright's own liberated consciousness becomes too heavy, too subtle for Bigger, yet remains too entangled in the remnants of the murder plot to evade moral confusion.

Ralph Ellison complains that "Bigger Thomas had none of the finer qualities of Richard Wright, none of the imagination, none of the sense of poetry, none of the gaiety," and in his own novel, *Invisible Man,* he transformed the *Bildungsroman* into a freewheeling, episodic, surreal mode in which the hero could contain and express the most diverse kinds of consciousness. In prose, black writers generally tend toward an urgent but impure mixture of fiction, autobiography, and discursiveness, and the most original thing about *Invisible Man* is its eclecticism and discontinuity, which foreshadows the style of the black humorists of the sixties, in whose work we have observed how technical, verbal, and structural inventiveness takes the place of realistic setting and psychology. Yet Ellison's book, which is finally too serious to be pinned down as black humor, essentially follows the pattern of *Black Boy* and *Native Son,* as do Malcolm X's autobiography, [Eldridge] Cleaver's *Soul on Ice,* and George Cain's impressive novel *Blueschild Baby*—whose hero is named George Cain, in which the distinction between fiction and autobiography has disappeared entirely. In this last book only the scene and subject change, not the basic pattern: for Cain the journey goes not from South to North but from heroin-addiction, prison, and self-hatred to self-respect, to writing, and above all, as with Cleaver, back to the arms of the black woman. (pp. 164-65)

For the angry young blacks of the sixties, who perhaps avoided the worst scars that Baldwin and Wright received so early, rage was their pride and their power, not a poison at the wellspring. Thus, paradoxically, while Baldwin rehashed and flattened what was once a richly complicated, ironic view of the race problem in America, partly out of a desperate attempt to keep abreast of the new mood, younger black writers regularly defined their own positions by attacking him, much as he once attacked Richard Wright. (p. 167)

> *Morris Dickstein, "Black Writing and Black Nationalism: Four Generations" (originally published in a different form as "Wright, Baldwin, Cleaver," in* New Letters, *Vol. 38, No. 2, Winter, 1971), in his* Gates of Eden: American Culture in the Sixties *(copyright © 1977 by Morris Dickstein; reprinted by permission of the author), Basic Books, Inc., 1977, pp. 154-82.**

OWEN BRADY

Lawd Today, written during the 1930's but unpublished until 1963, portrays the unrelieved frustration and consequent violence of black American life—themes Wright developed more strikingly in his next and greater novel, *Native Son. Lawd Today,* however, is not merely a preliminary sketch for the later novel. Unlike Bigger Thomas, Jake Jackson, *Lawd Today's* protagonist, develops no revolutionary consciousness of himself or his social condition because he aspires to a distorted version of the American dream and refuses personal responsibility for his actions.

As a postal clerk and recent arrival in Chicago from the South, Jake still belongs properly to the black masses; however, his steady employment in hard times, his attitudes toward the white society, and his aspirations to status based on material prosperity move him to the brink of the black middle class as described twenty years after the composition of *Lawd Today* by E. Franklin Frazier in his controversial study, *The Black Bourgeoisie.* Like Frazier, Wright exposes the degenerative influence of the illusory dream of bourgeois status on the black individual. But Wright brings the reader to an indictment of the dream and those who would cherish it primarily through art, not sociological data, by using structural ironies and satire.

The criticism of black bourgeois attitudes is achieved through the manipulation of the ideas of true dreams, coming from the character's feelings, and false dreams, coming to him from society and culture. By juxtaposing these kinds of dreams, Wright forces a recognition of the sterility of the bourgeois American dream for black people. The structure of the novel, which might be described as a little life rounded with a sleep, moves Jake from a true dream in the morning to an exhausted, dreamless sleep at night.

The novel opens with a true dream coming to Jake just before he wakes. The dream, the image of his repressed feelings,

brings a vision of Jake's hopeless, frustrating position in America. Despite mighty exertion and the goading of his boss's voice, Jake sees himself frustrated in his attempt to run up an interminable flight of stairs. In effect, Jake is frozen in his place, the very special place reserved by America for black men. The significance of the dream dawns on Jake before he is fully awake as he suddenly realizes that "I'm just wasting my time! Ain't moving a peg! There's a joke somewhere!" Ironically, Jake wakes to a Lincoln's Birthday radio broadcast chronicling the great 19th-century American struggle for emancipation, and quickly loses sight of his own dream's truth about his lack of freedom. Soon morning hunger and a sexual yearning overcome him. . . . The pattern of this opening dream episode, in which an intimate vision of truth is perceived, then lost in a welter of physical desires, structures Jake's experiences throughout the novel.

Having lost sight of the true feelings perceived in the dream, Jake persists in following the socially proposed American dream of personal fulfillment through materialistic pursuits; however, the severe social and psychological limits of racial oppression in 1930's America prohibit Jake from the same kind of fulfillment as white Americans might achieve. In rambling conversations with black friends and co-workers, Jake recognizes the social limits placed on the black man, lamenting that "When a black man gets a job in the Post Office he's done reached the top" . . . and then white people "don't even want us here." . . .

His response to the recognition is not a rejection of his condition and the racist capitalist society, but an accommodation—an acceptance of his place and an adjustment of the general American dream of material success. . . . Because he is powerless and willing to remain so, Jake can achieve fulfillment and status only through "fun"—sensual gratification and a pursuit of the illusion of wealth. . . . [In] pursuit of the false dream, Jake validates the insight of his true dream—he is frozen in place and the joke is on him.

Wright emphasizes the joke of espousing the wrong dream detailing Jake's subscription to the white world's standards of beauty in comically grotesque terms. . . . In an early scene, the pathetic and comic aspects of trying to look white emerge as Jake battles his kinky hair. Wright describes the scene satirically in mock epic terms with Jake as "a veteran field marshal" attacking and subduing "the fortifications and wire-entanglements of an alien army." . . . Wright's rejection of pursuing white standards of beauty is inherent in the comically grotesque image of Jake. . . . (pp. 167-69)

Wright's determinism goes beyond cultural conditioning. As in the case of his morning dream, Jake lets biological urges inhibit analysis of his feelings throughout the day. Sex and hunger conspire with a personal weakness of will to preclude action which might change Jake's condition or purge him of the source of his frustrations. Once, at work, feeling the monotony of his job and the humiliation of constant surveillance, Jake becomes aware that he is oppressed. Imagination molds his feelings into a vision of black revolution, the logical response to oppression. He fantasizes that he commands a black battleship which blows off the white head of the Statue of Liberty. . . . But revolutionary fervor and joy quickly abate as lunch-time is announced. (p. 170)

Wright refuses to place all the blame for Jake's foolishness and frustration on social conditioning, racial oppression, and biology. Jake's personal pride, a pride beyond reason, often keeps him in his place. . . . The mythos of the American dream and the status derived from associating with it feed Jake's pride. (p. 171)

The final section of *Lawd Today*, "**Rat's Alley**," exposes the foolish hope of chasing illusions by emphasizing Jake's impotence and self-destructive actions. The novel climaxes in a South Side bordello where "the lights were lowered just enough to give the room a dreamlike air." . . . During the visit Jake seems about to realize his dream to be a sporting man. Through freewheeling spending of his borrowed money and braggadocio, he woos Blanche, a light-skinned prostitute. In the end, however, Wright makes Jake the classic satiric gull. Jake achieves nothing and loses all: before he can make love to Blanche, he is set-up by her, pickpocketed by her friends, and, finally, beaten unconscious. Although recognizing that he has been done in by his own foolishness, Jake quickly turns defeat into a pathetic, self-aggrandizing, ironic joke. Beaten and bloody, Jake staggers to his feet, smiles and yells: "BUT WHEN I WAS FLYING I WAS A FLYING FOOL!" . . . Standards are clear; Wright provokes ironic laughter which rejects Jake's pride and blindness. But, despite our rejection of Jake's way of life, the laughter is also an affirmation, a grudging admiration of his human resilience.

Although Jake's proud joke, like his sense of humor throughout the novel, mitigates our judgment at this point, in the denouement, Wright turns laughter at a fool to repulsion by a grotesque beast. He completes the novel's dream structure, clearly exposing the futility and falsity of Jake's bourgeois dream. Returning home after his fiasco in the whorehouse, Jake unleashes his frustrations in a bloody battle with his wife. Ironically, the thin, sickly Lil overcomes the would-be All-American man. (pp. 171-72)

Jake has moved from the potentially useful truth of his morning dream to a hopeless, dreamless sleep. In pursuing the wrong dream, Jake's life, in Frazier's words, has lost "both content and significance." . . . He has become a cipher, a grotesque ghost, lost in darkness partly inflicted upon him by biology, but partly of his own creation. (p. 172)

> Owen Brady, "Wright's 'Lawd Today': The American Dream Festering in the Sun," in *CLA Journal* (copyright, 1978 by the College Language Association), Vol. XXII, No. 2, December, 1978, pp. 167-72.

STEVEN J. RUBIN

The early fiction of Richard Wright, comprised of short stories written in the thirties and culminating in *Native Son* (1940), is primarily an expression of personal outrage and frustration. Although Wright's literary heritage has been traced to the American Naturalists, recent readings of his works suggest that Wright was not as confined by that tradition as has generally been believed. Working within the framework of social protest, Wright probed other more metaphysical issues, which were later to become of even greater importance to him. In dramatizing the plight of each of his heroes, from Big Boy in "**Big Boy Leaves Home**," to Bigger Thomas in *Native Son*, Wright explored the motivating forces behind their actions. As their personal dramas unfolded, he developed such themes as the possibility of freedom, man's isolation and alienation, the inherent irrationality of modern American society, and the nature and form of personal rebellion within that society.

Native Son is, as Edward Margolies in *The Art of Richard Wright* [see excerpt above] points out, as much a psychological novel with clear existential implications, as it is sociological. Bigger Thomas is not only a Black man struggling against an oppressive white society, but also Wright's archetypal rebel, desperately seeking recognition and meaning within a world that has offered him none. Alienated from the mainstream of society and betrayed by his own environment, Bigger, like Wright's earlier heroes, searches for an effective means of vanquishing his personal sense of worthlessness. Ironically, like the protagonists of *Uncle Tom's Children*, Bigger's revolt is simultaneously victorious and self-destructive.

The literature of revolt is born from the recognition on the part of many modern writers that meaning and purpose are not an integral part of the universe in which man finds himself. *Native Son*, written at a time when Wright was preoccupied with social issues, also represents an examination of the nature of personal rebellion, a theme which dominated much of the thinking of such modern European writers as André Malraux, Jean-Paul Sartre, and especially Albert Camus.

In its most universal form, rebellion, according to Camus, involves a protest against the condition in which man finds himself. . . . Finding the world to be unjust, the rebel protests against being a part of that universe and attempts to reorder his world according to his own version of justice. The act of revolting, even when it involves a level of injustice to match that which is prevalent in society, results in apocalyptical moments of freedom and power. The result, according to Camus, is not only a new respect for one's self, but also a new sense of order and unity within the universe. This acceptance of a self imposed order is what ultimately moves both Camus's Meursault *(L'Etranger)*, and Wright's Bigger Thomas toward a peaceful reconciliation with their fates.

In Wright's first volume of short stories, *Uncle Tom's Children* (1938), physical rebellion becomes the dominant theme and the means by which his characters achieve freedom and identity. Wright's early heroes seek fulfillment of their personality and a purpose to their otherwise meaningless existence through violent action. In similar fashion, Bigger Thomas, confused and alone, can find no conventional way to bridge the gap between his aspirations and the reality of his condition. In "**How Bigger was Born**," Wright explained the need for rebellion: "In *Native Son* I tried to show that man, bereft of a culture and unanchored by property, can travel but one path if he reacts positively, but unthinkingly to the prizes and goals of civilization; and that path is emotionally blind rebellion."

As the novel opens, Bigger is seen as a man conditioned by hatred and a sense of racial exclusion. . . . Throughout Book I, "**Fear**," Bigger is portrayed as a man in conflict, not only with white society, but also with his surroundings, his family, his peers, and ultimately with himself. Bigger is not able to escape the sordidness of his condition through religion, as does his mother, or through alcohol, as does his mistress Bessie. For him there are no external evasions, and as his anxiety and frustration mount Bigger begins to feel a sense of impending disaster. . . . (pp. 12-13)

The murder [of Mary Dalton], although ostensibly a mistake, is an accident only in the narrowest sense, for Bigger has long dreamed of such an act. The full meaning of his crime does not become clear to him until after the murder, but he had long had a foreboding of such violence. . . . Bigger fantasizes about destruction, of dropping bombs on the white world, and in one rare moment of insight even admits to the possibility of murder as an antidote to his extreme anguish and despair. . . . (pp. 13-14)

Bigger's killing of Mary becomes the one meaningful act of his life, giving him a new sense of freedom and identity and a capacity for action on a grand scale. Up to this time Bigger has cowered in fear before the white world. Now, as he plots his next move, the many options that are opened give him a new sense of power and possibility. . . .

Out of apparent fear of betrayal, Bigger brutally slays his mistress Bessie. These two acts place him irrevocably outside the social order of all men, both white and black. Unlike his killing of Mary, the murder of Bessie is neither accidental nor truly necessary for his protection. It is simply proof of his new ability to act. Although Bigger is afraid he will be overwhelmed by a feeling of guilt, this second murder, like the first, gives him a sense of liberation and an even greater control over his destiny. . . .

In Camus's novel, *L'Etranger,* 1942 (*The Stranger,* 1946), Meursault's metaphysical rebellion originates because he finds himself adrift and isolated in a meaningless society. Bigger, like Meursault, is also alone in a world which has lost all metaphysical and moral foundation. Without God and without absolutes, he lacks an a priori basis for moral and ethical choice. (p. 14)

In 1940, the same year that *Native Son* was published, Camus first formulated his theory of the absurd and explained the irrationality of man's existence in terms very similar to those used by Wright. . . .

Although the motivating forces behind their actions differ, both [Bigger and Meursault] conform to a very similar pattern: alienation, a sense of frustration with conventional order and values, an accidental murder, a realization of the meaning of that murder in terms of their role in society, a separation (physical and emotional) from their world, and a final coming to terms with their individual fates. While in his cell, Meursault is moved to an awareness of his own mortality. He comes to accept the absurdity of the universe. . . . He learns that man cannot significantly change the course of his destiny, nor the brevity of his life. What is most important is how he relates and reacts to what he has been given. Meursault's final pronouncement indicates his ability to accept the conditions in which he lives. . . .

In the final pages of *Native Son,* Bigger Thomas, condemned to death, also attempts to understand the relationship between man and the absurdity of his environment. Rejecting the solace of religion, he is determined to die alone, as he has lived. In talking with Max, however, he realizes that other men have lived and felt as he has. He is finally able to send a belated gesture of fraternity to Jan, whose help Bigger has rejected throughout. . . .

As his death approaches, Bigger, like Meursault, is free of fear of life and death. He has finally made peace with himself by

realizing that his actions, although self-destructive, were the only possible responses to the series of injustices and irrationalities within his existence. As his execution nears, Bigger has no remorse; instead he is seen with "a faint, wry bitter smile." . . . (p. 15)

Although the reactions of these characters indicate a shared vision on the part of their authors, there is a basic difference in the pattern of revolt and its motivation between Wright's Bigger Thomas and Camus's Meursault. Meursault's actions are the result of his comprehending the chaotic nature of the universe. Bigger acts out of hatred, fear, and an innate longing to be free. Uneducated and inarticulate, he reacts unthinkingly to the underlying contradictions of an American society which proclaims the inherent worth of the individual and yet everywhere denies that worth to the Black man. Unlike Meursault, Bigger is not aware of the metaphysical implications of his protest. It is only after his action that he begins to experience a new knowledge of himself, his existence, and the nature of his surroundings. Directed immediately against the white majority, his rebellion eventually assumes a universal dimension and ultimately is, like that of Meursault and Ellison's invisible hero, a protest against the entire scheme of things.

Native Son is as much a study of an alienated and lonely individual struggling to understand his existence, as it is an examination of racial prejudice and its effects. Bigger is forced into an alien existence because of the irrational and unjust nature of the society in which he lives. For Bigger, the opposite poles of aspiration and satisfaction can only be briefly united through violence. Murder becomes, paradoxically, the one creative act of his life. . . . Like Cross Damon, Wright's Dostoevskian hero in *The Outsider* (1953), Bigger is able to kill without remorse, for good and evil have become meaningless to him. Killing has become part of Bigger's definition of himself; and although Wright does not attempt to justify or condone murder, he does strive to explain the necessity of Bigger's actions.

Although *The Outsider* has many obvious parallels to the works of Sartre, Camus, and the post World War II European writers, there is little to indicate that Wright was influenced by the French existentialists during the writing of *Native Son.* His vision of an absurd world emanated more from firsthand experience in America than from literary sources. Wright clearly perceived the inconsistencies of the American system and tried to show, through Bigger Thomas, a man struggling within that system. Living in a society that had placed him next to obscurity, Bigger turns to violence as the only meaningful action open to him. . . .

Written in 1940, [*Native Son*] gives an early indication of Wright's existential vision and the themes that were to preoccupy his thinking in the years to come. (p. 16)

Steven J. Rubin, "Richard Wright and Albert Camus: The Literature of Revolt," in The International Fiction Review (© copyright International Fiction Association), Vol. 8, No. 1, Winter, 1981, pp. 12-16.*

Roger Zelazny

1937-

American science fiction novelist, short story writer, and editor.

Zelazny's unique blend of fantasy, science fiction, and myth has earned him a prominent position among the writers of imaginative fiction. Zelazny was one of the first exponents, along with Harlan Ellison and Samuel R. Delany, of the new wave science fiction that arose during the mid-1960s in America. Supporters of the movement emphasized a shift in theme from the external world of hard sciences to the internal world examined through such disciplines as psychology, sociology, and linguistics. In the early 1960s Zelazny wrote prolifically for the magazines *Amazing Stories* and *Fantastic*, often using the pseudonym of Harrison Denmark. In 1965 he emerged as one of the most important contemporary writers of science fiction when he won Nebula awards for "He Who Shapes" (novella) and *The Doors of His Face, the Lamps of His Mouth* (novelette), and a Hugo Award for *And Call Me Conrad* (published in book form as *This Immortal*). Many critics believe Zelazny was at the peak of his creative ability during these years, when his works were characterized by refreshing originality, powerful scenes and language, and a double vision which used comedy to underline nobility. Zelazny's innovative techniques later gave way to what critics feel is a less impressive seriousness. Nevertheless, Zelazny is considered a superior writer of futuristic adventure stories.

Zelazny often incorporates myths and folklore in his plots to present a vision of the future, as in *Creatures of Light and Darkness* where he entwines elements of Christian, Greek, Egyptian, and Norse mythology. The books in Zelazny's "Amber" series are probably his best-known works. This series is Zelazny's version of the sword and sorcery motif, and was commended at the beginning for its freshness and zest. After five books, however, some critics feel the story is overworked and would be more effective if shortened to one volume. Among Zelazny's other works, *Isle of the Dead* and *Doorways in the Sand* are notable for their particularly successful character studies, a feat seldom accomplished in science fiction. Critics agree that with *Roadmarks* Zelazny approaches the brilliance of wit and imagination displayed in his early works; most critics, however, feel the overall effect of the book is diminished by an easy ending. Although critical acceptance of Zelazny has varied over the years, he has consistently appealed to young adults as an entertaining and imaginative science fiction writer. In addition to the awards already mentioned, he has received the Nebula and Hugo awards for "Home Is the Hangman" (1975), and the Hugo Award for *Lord of Light* (1967). (See also *Contemporary Authors*, Vols. 21-24, rev. ed.)

THE TIMES LITERARY SUPPLEMENT

Lord of Light is a weird allegorical fantasy which sets out to demonstrate how self-destructive is the human compulsion to create gods and demons. In a mistily realized future world, heaven and earth are ruled over by Hindu gods. . . . It sounds, and is, far-fetched. Much of the writing is reminiscent of those awful jokes, mercifully no longer fashionable, where scato-

logical content was meant to provide comic contrast with a mock biblical style. There are occasional "poetic" bits of description: "Morning's pink parasol opened above the tangled hair of the clouds . . ." and there is often a strong feeling that Mr. Zelazny must be parodying something—though one is never sure what.

"Other New Novels: 'Lord of Light'," *in* The Times Literary Supplement (© *Times Newspapers Ltd. (London) 1968; reproduced from* The Times Literary Supplement *by permission), No. 3444, February 29, 1968, p. 213.*

THE TIMES LITERARY SUPPLEMENT

Roger Zelazny has what most readers mean when they talk of style: an obtrusive style. *The Dream Master* is full of style— indeed, one hardly sees the wood for its multitudinous trees. Behind the trees stands an intelligent and basically simple story, concerning Render, a "neuroparticipant" who, operating through a machine, can enter his patients' minds and build from their contents complete illusions of reality, and a strong-willed blind woman who comes to him for help and education. . . .

It would work well as a modern myth, the myth of the man-on-the-couch turning on his psychiatrist. But Mr. Zelazny dilutes his effect by throwing in too many fragments of older legend—Daedalus, Tristan and Isolde, the Holy Grail, the Cabala, while his characters quote [Fyodor] Dostoevsky and [Walt] Whitman at each other. This takes up so much space that potentially interesting characters like Render's son and the blind woman's artificially mutated guide dog fulfil little function beyond decoration.

Given these reservations, Mr. Zelazny has his pleasures, his wit and his striking pictures, and a certain admirable throwaway sense of the future. . . . Roger Zelazny is young; one might hope for more substance and less filigree later were it not for his loyal fans, who tend to prefer exhibitionism to ratiocination.

> *"Do You Mind?," in* The Times Literary Supplement *(© Times Newspapers Ltd. (London) 1968; reproduced from* The Times Literary Supplement *by permission), No. 3448, March 28, 1968, p. 310.**

NORMAN CULPAN

Only a lover of fantasy who also had more than a passing acquaintance with the Buddhist religion could comment adequately on [*Lord of Light*]. But, without suggesting other common ground than fantasy itself, it might be hazarded that those who enjoy the work of J.R.R. Tolkien and Mervyn Peake will enjoy this book also. . . . The spell increases steadily as one reads on. I enjoyed it immensely. (pp. 199-200)

> *Norman Culpan, "Book Reviews: 'Lord of Light',"* in The School Librarian and School Library Review, *Vol. 16, No. 2, July, 1968, pp. 199-200.*

KIRKUS REVIEWS

Lo and on the "Thousandyear Eve," Anubis, Lord of the House of the Dead, gave his faithful servant the name of Wakim and sent him on a mission to the Midway worlds to search out and destroy "the Prince Who Was a Thousand" [in *Creatures of Light and Darkness*]. But Wakim was deceived for "the Prince Who Was a Thousand" was both his son and his father . . . ? It's psychedelic myth . . . chasing phantoms across eternal chasms . . . a very heady head trip . . . for probably very few passengers.

> *"Fiction: 'Creatures of Light and Darkness',"* in Kirkus Reviews *(copyright © 1969 The Kirkus Service, Inc.), Vol. XXXVII, No. 14, July 15, 1969, p. 745.*

KIRKUS REVIEWS

The "Alley" [in *Damnation Alley*] is the post-holocaust road from L.A. to Boston and one that has never been run alive until the last of the Hell's Angels is forced to try it. Boston is down with the plague and only L.A. has the antidote. Thus full speed through a country that rains rocks, has hordes of giant bats and gila monsters, butterflies and spiders and vicious human animals. Only a Hell's Angel could make it. Only a Hell's Angel could believe it.

> *"Fiction: 'Damnation Alley',"* in Kirkus Reviews *(copyright © 1969 The Kirkus Service, Inc.), Vol. XXXVII, No. 17, September 1, 1969, p. 956.*

PAULINE F. MICCICHE

[*Creatures of Light and Darkness*] is another of Zelazny's velvet fabrics with a warp of Christian, Greek, Egyptian and Norse myths spun into one thread and a weft of macabre fantasy about an order of existence which superposes and controls our own universe. The author manipulates the fantasy of the struggle for power between cruel and vindictive entities of the superposing existence around distortions of the various myths. He thus reveals the starkness of essential life and death. The creatures of this superposed world, the creatures of light and dark, have the quality of the shadows of Plato's cave seen indistinctly and constantly changing. In the end only the individuals in power have changed, not the power structure or the method of using power.

> *Pauline F. Micciche, "The Book Review: 'Creatures of Light and Darkness',"* in Library Journal *(reprinted from* Library Journal, *September 15, 1969; published by R. R. Bowker Co. (a Xerox company); copyright © 1969 by Xerox Corporation), Vol. 94, No. 16, September 15, 1969, p. 3086.*

TED PAULS

Roger Zelazny infuriates me. I am not speaking as a reader. As a science fiction reader for seventeen years, I am impressed almost to the point of reverence by Zelazny. Nor am I speaking in personal terms. I've met Roger, and he is at the very opposite end of the spectrum from infuriating. But in my capacity as a reviewer, I am infuriated by Roger Zelazny. He does things, magic things, with words, things that cannot be neatly marked, catalogued and described. He employs concepts and symbolism that shimmer like a mirage whenever I stare hard in an effort to make certain that I really comprehend. Whenever I am found perspiring under the heat of my desk lamp, staring at a piece of blank paper in the typewriter, and aimlessly twisting and untwisting a paper clip, chances are that Roger Zelazny is the culprit.

Take *Isle of the Dead*, for instance. You must read it, get inside of it, to appreciate all its dimensions; description is inadequate. The way in which the author uses words must be experienced. It is no good to cite examples, because pulled out of context the words lose their vitality and change into something else, like pieces of flesh torn out of a living body. . . . Roger must write like a poet, painstakingly searching always for just the right word with the precise shade of meaning. There is humour in *Isle of the Dead*—not funny passages that can be quoted in a review and sound amusing, but cumulative humour in the outlook of the central character, Francis Sandow, humour that depends upon the previous five or ten or fifty pages.

Roger has, deliberately I think, taken as the motive action event of the book one of the most banal and Ellery Queen-ish of ideas: the hero is receiving in the mail photographs of long-dead associates, and sets out to track down the sender, discover his motive (obviously some sort of revenge plot) and thwart his scheme. Upon that foundation Zelazny builds. (p. 208)

The story is narrated in the first person by Francis Sandow, and it is as a character study of this man that it succeeds most spectacularly. He is a man of immense wealth and god-like power, virtually immortal, who has lived through twelve centuries, yet he is completely human and comprehensible. This is a singular achievement for any author. Sandow's almost unchallengeable wealth and power, and his span of years, have given him a mildly cynical, mildly sardonic outlook on life which suffuses the narrative; the reader, observing the universe through his eyes, can feel the crinkling lines around his eyes during frequent wry smiles at man and his foibles. Sandow has fears, and weaknesses. He is in no sense the noble, unbending hero of tradition. Indeed, at the end, he is perfectly willing to buy off his mortal enemy so that both of them can go back to enjoying their lives (and the enemy is willing to be bought off—but the antithetical gods struggling through their human vehicles, being incorruptible, insist on a fight to the death). He is a likable and, in a way, a tragic figure.

Zelazny is versatile: action, dialogue, realistic background, philosophy, symbolism—each requires its own particular kind of ability, and he does them all well. Characterization is not confined only to Sandow: Marling, Sandow's Pei'an mentor, Gringrin, the original "villain," and even Mike Shandon, Sandow's mortal enemy, who does not really appear until near the end, are all portrayed with great skill and perception.

What else can one say? *Isle of the Dead* is a brilliant novel. Rush out and buy it if you haven't already. Read it. And savour it. (p. 209)

> Ted Pauls, "Book Reviews: 'Isle of the Dead'," in *Riverside Quarterly* (copyright 1970 by Leland Sapiro), Vol. 4, No. 3, June, 1970, pp. 208-09.

KIRKUS REVIEWS

Roger Zelazny is a genial writer who sometimes manages to give old themes new twists to accomplish something bordering on the extraordinary. He does this in four instances in this collection of fifteen stories [*The Doors of His Face, the Lamps of His Mouth*]—"Devil Car" in which the autos are self-mobile; "The Mortal Mountain" a long climb to the highest mountain in the near universe and well worth the struggle; "A Museum Piece" in which failed artists and cynical critics become living sculptures; and the best, "The Great Slow Kings," a truly funny piece that deals with dragons trying to discuss their contemporary problems over a span of centuries while the world moves on. Not all stars but O.K.

> "Fiction: 'The Doors of His Face, the Lamps of His Mouth and Other Stories'," in Kirkus Reviews (copyright © 1971 The Kirkus Service, Inc.), Vol. XXXIX, No. 8, April 15, 1971, p. 466.

JAMES BLISH

Nine Princes in Amber] is Zelazny's version of sword-and-sorcery, but it is not for addicts only. Zelazny has not borrowed the standard apparatus for this sort of thing, but has invented his own, and the result is an adventure story with real originality and zest.

True, the hero is suffering from amnesia after a blow on the head as the book opens, but this soap-opera ploy is milked so successfully for suspense that it is readily forgivable. As we find out, with the hero, more and more about his real situation, it becomes more and more evident that the smallest misstep will be fatal. Moreover, the author manages to create real doubt that he will win through, despite the almost insuperable handicap that he is telling his own story in the first person and therefore obviously did win through. . . .

In many respects, the story could have been set with no loss in an Italian court during the Borgia pontificate. The magic, however, is integral, not just pasted on. The language is the

mixture of poetry and slang characteristic of recent Zelazny, but it is not jarring here, since it makes a perfect fit with the hero's double life.

And the ending reveals, among other things, how the author managed to create that illusion of doubt—and leaves the door wide open for a sequel. I'll be looking for it.

> James Blish, "Books: 'Nine Princes in Amber'," in The Magazine of Fantasy and Science Fiction (© 1971 by Mercury Press, Inc.; reprinted from The Magazine of Fantasy and Science Fiction), Vol. 40, No. 5, May, 1971, p. 39.

NORMAN CULPAN

Just as able, as in his *Lord of Light,* to conjure a new mythology out of old religion, to mingle future science with a primitive past in a context of magic, to narrate the battles of gods on a cosmic scale and single combat on a heroic scale, [in *Creatures of Light and Darkness* Zelazny] takes the religion of ancient Egypt as his raw material. But whereas, in *Lord of Light,* we thought on the whole we could identify with Sam, a kind of Christ-Buddha, in this second novel we are often not sure where our sympathies lie. The awful grotesque is replaced by the comic grotesque; imaginative response is inflated only to be punctured; even comment seems parody of the earlier style: 'the motorcycle that is Time backfires as it races by.' Vigorous imagination, effective narration and powerful visual presentation are still there: but what are we to make of two rival soothsayers who quarrel bitchily over the omens to be read from the steaming entrails that one has just ripped out of the other with a knife? Whom is Zelazny parodying but himself? And yet I don't regret the time spent reading it! (pp. 143-44)

> Norman Culpan, "Literature: 'Creatures of Light and Darkness'," in The School Librarian, Vol. 19, No. 2, June, 1971, pp. 143-44.

JOHN IVES

[In *Damnation Alley*] Roger Zelazny takes the hoodlum hero of American pulp fiction, dresses him in the gear of the Hell's Angels and places him in a period several decades from now when the world has been devastated by atomic warfare. We are given a vivid and startling idea of what the future could be like after the nuclear holocaust as the hero makes a journey carrying plague serum between the two major surviving centers of civilization in North America, along the route known as Damnation Alley. However there is a dubious element of doublethink in the moral stance of the novel, for to achieve his mission of mercy the hero kills and maims steadily, and in wholesale quantities throughout the journey. This strong element of gratuitous violence operates at the mindless level of the American crime comic and leaves a nasty taste. This is a pity for Mr Zelazny has some lively ideas in the science fiction aspect of his novel.

> John Ives, "Book Reviews: 'Damnation Alley'," in The School Librarian, Vol. 20, No. 2, June, 1972, p. 172.

KIRKUS REVIEWS

Corwin, the most appealing superman since [Robert] Heinlein's Valentine Michael Smith, continues the family feud begun in *Nine Princes in Amber* (1970) [in *The Guns of Avalon*], battling in Shadow, which includes earth as well as Avalon, for the crown of the real world, Amber. Zelazny's dazzling blend of myth, science fantasy and (super) human nature suspends disbelief and raises the highest hopes for volume three.

> *"Fiction: 'The Guns of Avalon',"* in Kirkus Reviews *(copyright © 1972 The Kirkus Service, Inc.), Vol. XL, No. 16, August 15, 1972, p. 978.*

PSYCHOLOGY TODAY

The Guns of Avalon [is] a swashbuckling tale of parallel worlds. Corwin has his share of human vices, so even his struggle against the forces of darkness lacks the mythic clash of Tolkien's Ring novels. But this well-written, robust story teems with excitement, and one can enjoy it without knowing its predecessor. . . .

> *"Briefly: 'The Guns of Avalon',"* in Psychology Today *(copyright © 1973 Ziff-Davis Publishing Company), Vol. 6, No. 8, January, 1973, p. 20.*

THE TIMES LITERARY SUPPLEMENT

Roger Zelazny has become something of a cult figure among modern fantasy aficionados in the United States. [*Jack of Shadows*] is another of his extravagant fables set in a quasi-medieval landscape of revenge and paranoia. To many the whole paranormal affair might seem an extraordinary mish-mash of new and old literary ideas, couched in inferior Morcockian prose, with confusion absolute. But there are obviously some who like things that way.

> *"SF in Short: 'Jack of Shadows',"* in The Times Literary Supplement *(© Times Newspapers Ltd. (London) 1973; reproduced from* The Times Literary Supplement *by permission), No. 3715, May 18, 1973, p. 562.*

ROGER BAKER

I regard [*Jack of Shadows*] as something of a find for me. Mr Zelazny has written several well-received novels already, but I had never come across him before and I read *Jack of Shadows* with increasing delight and a sense of satisfaction. I doubt if Mr Zelazny can be, or would want to be, characterised as a particular sort of writer—but for the sake of argument I'll suggest he falls into the imaginative fiction category, somewhere between science fiction and fairy tales. In fact *Jack of Shadows* opens like a fairy story, with strange names and a sort of poetical prose. And, as with all good fairy stories, we are instantly caught, both by the actual narrative and the charm of the imagination that contrived the tale. . . .

The surface narrative is always fascinating, as Jack (who is a sympathetic character) meets, fights and evades his enemies. No incident is overwritten, but given due weight and power. . . .

Mr Zelazny has projected a world with two sides to it: one, the dayside is always bright and sunny with no night at all; the other, darkside is just that. Dayside is, in essence, the world of science and rational argument and not really a very agreeable place. . . . Darkside is the world of the supernatural, of spirits and superstition. In a central and crucial dialogue with Morningstar, Jack realises that there are different kinds of truth, and that the same phenomenon can be interpreted in more than one way, and that eternal truth is non-existent. . . .

Jack of Shadows is an assertion of a dark side, of its power and mystery. It has great charm and a nice sense of anachronism as, when among the primeval chaos he has created, Jack moans that he has crushed his last cigarette.

> *Roger Baker, "Fiction: 'Jack of Shadows'" (© copyright Roger Baker 1973; reprinted with permission), in* Books and Bookmen, *Vol. 18, No. 9, June, 1973, p. 103.*

DOUGLAS BARBOUR

If there's one thing Roger Zelazny has always had it's a sense of style. Often that's all he's had, but there's no doubt he made his mark early in the sixties . . . partly on the basis of it. *The Doors of His Face* is a collection of short stories from 1963 to 1968, but it's a strange collection to say the least.

Oh, a few of the big ones are here: the now famous title story and the equally famous **"A Rose for Ecclesiastes"** especially. . . . Other good stories include **"The Keys to December"** (a story that owes much to Cordwainer Smith), **"The Man Who Loved the Faioli,"** **"This Moment of the Storm,"** and possibly **"This Mortal Mountain"** (I must say Zelazny has a knack for good titles) all of which generate a real sense of involvement on the reader's part. The rest, however, is filler: short shorts, many of which just don't deserve re-publication.

Many of the short shorts, such as **"The Great Slow Kings,"** **"A Museum Piece"** (which proves to be an atrocious pun), and **"The Monster and the Maiden,"** for starters, could have been dropped without regret and replaced, say, by the early **"King Solomon's Ring"** . . . and **"For a Breath I Tarry,"** which I consider one of Zelazny's best ever. What kind of editorial policy kept these stories out?

If you're a true Zelazny fan this is a must, for it collects some of his better stories in hardcover, but if you're not, wait for the paperback—and hope he'll bring out a collection some day that will continually show him at his best. The man often *is* superficial (even **"For a Breath I Tarry"** could be considered all surface, but what a sparkling, moving, surface!) but he can write. In this collection, the longer, the true stories, reveal this to even the most sceptical reader; it's just that the shorter ones, the fluffy games, re-enforce that scepticism in all its force. Both Zelazny and his publisher should have known better. (p. 78)

> *Douglas Barbour, "New Asimov/Old Zelazny," in* Riverside Quarterly *(© 1973 by Leland Sapiro), Vol. 6, No. 1, August, 1973, pp. 77-8.*

PSYCHOLOGY TODAY

Roger Zelazny's *To Die in Italbar* . . . is an unusual work of science fiction that takes several disparate characters and gradually moves them together. While Zelazny is no feminist and makes it clear, a female god plays a major—and evil—role in his tale. There are enough elements in *Italbar* to make a dozen stories: intergalactic rivalry, telepathy, a world ruined by atomic war, a pathologist awaiting a cure for his own disease while existing for decades at the moment before death, a Typhoid Mary who can decimate whole planets with a variety of diseases, and the blue-skinned Deiban goddess Mar'i-ram. Only a master of science fiction could weave all these strands into his web, and Zelazny spins them in a deft and satisfying manner.

"Briefly: 'To Die in Italbar'," in Psychology Today *(copyright © 1973 Ziff-Davis Publishing Company), Vol. 7, No. 5, October, 1973, p. 138.*

SIDNEY COLEMAN

Maybe the Joe Blotz test will help.

The test is used by honest editors considering stories by famous writers: "What would I think of this if it were a story by somebody I had never heard of, by Joe Blotz?" I think I would give *To Die in Italbar* by Joe Blotz an ecstatic review. "Blotz writes well; he can describe fast action and strong emotions with equal skill; he has a fertile imagination and creates colorful characters. Joe Blotz is clearly one of the most promising new writers to appear in a long time. Perhaps he is too much influenced by Roger Zelazny, but . . ."

No, it doesn't help. There is no avoiding the shadow; it is impossible to write about late Roger Zelazny without comparing it to early Roger Zelazny.

In 1963 Roger Zelazny published **"A Rose for Ecclesiastes"**; in 1968 **Lord of Light** won the Hugo. These dates define Zelazny's prime; *sans peur et sans reproche*, he was the darling of science fiction. I remember asserting publicly in 1967 that there was more real science in a page of Zelazny than in the collected works of George O. Smith; at about the same time, Harlan Ellison wrote that Zelazny was the reincarnation of Geoffrey Chaucer. I quote these statements as evidence of the spirit of the age rather than of critical acumen; either of them could be translated as "Wow!" with negligible loss of content.

But we were wowing with good reason. In an important sense Zelazny really was without fear and without blame; he would try the most daring tricks, and bring them off. Zelazny's famous skill as a culture-magpie is an outstanding instance: He would cast a computer as both Faust and Adam, mix grail legend with electric psychotherapy, work a line from the *Cantos* into a story whose basic plot was the old pulp chestnut about the white hunter and Miss Richbitch. . . . Any fool could have tried these things, and, maddened by Zelazny's example, many did; for a time we had myths like some people have mice. But Zelazny was not his epigones; he made it work.

How did he do it? We can get a clue by looking at one of Zelazny's favorite devices, a rapid shift of viewpoint, or, better yet, shift of values. In the simplest case, this is a shift from a noble view of high heroism to a comic one. (pp. 51-2)

This is an old device. It is a form of internalized comic relief—not the porter in *Macbeth*, but Hamlet in *Hamlet*. . . . It is sometimes called irony, but this is not quite the right word, for the comic vision does not undercut the heroic one, but underlines it. Wit is a better word, if we remember that it is the root of both witty and witting. The double vision is richer than the sum of its parts, because each part illuminates the other.

This method of multiple vision, of playing one aspect of a thing against another, is characteristic of much of the best work of Zelazny's high period. . . . For example, any moderately well-trained English major could write pages on the way Frost is played against Faust in **"For a Breath I Tarry."** Parts of the story are direct parody; Frost makes Faust funny. This leads to an implicit comparison between Faust's sophistication and Frost's naivete; Faust makes Frost funny. The endings of the stories illuminate each other; Frost succeeds where Faust fails because it is better to seek humanity than divinity. Etc.

Another approach to the same statement: There are worlds in science fiction that stick in your mind; they are solid. Hal Clement's Mesklin, Frank Herbert's Dune, Ursula LeGuin's Winter are very different places in most respects, but they do have this in common. They extend beyond the books that contain them; one feels that there is more to be said. Typically, Zelazny's worlds are not like this. They have no physics, no ecology, no sociology. They are intricately patterned and brightly colored, but they are flat, stage-sets, cartoons. But they do not need to be solid; for Zelazny's purposes, a solid world would be as useless an object as a solid violin. The function of the thing is to resonate.

This is one great advantage of working with multiple visions, of being both witty and witting. It enables the writer to assimilate material that would be too thin, too inappropriate, or simply too silly to handle in any other way. Consider the problem of the Hero. . . . The problem is to keep the man who saves the world from being preposterous. One solution is to humanize him, show him as being sometimes afraid, confused, tired, and wrongheaded. (pp. 52-3)

Zelazny's solution was not to eliminate the preposterousness, but to exploit it. Conrad Nomikos is an immortal man who experiences high adventures and ends up owning Earth. You find this hard to take seriously? So did Zelazny. It's one of the things he plays against in **". . . And Call Me Conrad,"** and this play is not only interesting in itself, it makes the heroism more acceptable. Conrad the admirable real hero and Conrad the preposterous comic-book hero define two surfaces; in the space they enclose Zelazny creates his resonances.

(I except from most of this **"He Who Shapes"** (*The Dream Master*). This marvelous short novel is in many ways a direct contradiction of the main themes and method of Zelazny's early work. A sign: **"He Who Shapes"** is as full of myth as any Zelazny story of the period, but the myth is here explicitly identified with psychopathology. It occurs to me that this may be meta-wit: Zelazny playing against Zelazny.)

Of course, this is a paradigmatic Zelazny I have been describing, triple-distilled essence of Zelazny, Zelazny as Zelazny-hero, if you want. The real Zelazny was more complicated and requires a lengthier analysis with many more qualifying phrases. Nevertheless, I think I have the essential outlines right; this is how he did it, how he made it work. But this makes what happened in the late sixties very strange. For, about this time, Zelazny abandoned his method but retrained the material that made sense only when coupled with the method. *To Die in Italbar* has flat backgrounds: Italbar itself has the social and economic structure of an American town, for all that it is set on an alien planet and has a few pieces of futuristic machinery and a pet lizard or two stuck here and there in the foreground. It has gigantically larger-than-life protagonists: Two of the main characters have literally god-like powers, another is a highly-successful one-man commando army, fighting an interstellar state from his private fortress, another is a paranoid prostitute redeemed by love, another is a living dead man. You find this hard to take seriously? So do I, but Zelazny has no qualms: everything in *To Die in Italbar* is viewed straight on, with a single vision. . . . (pp. 54-5)

I do not know why Zelazny began this process of reverse alchemy five years ago, why he put away his magician's tricks and turned his gold into lead. Maybe he simply ran out of steam; it happens often enough in literary careers; being a genius is a profession for the young. Or it might have been the pressures of the market. Zelazny began free-lancing full time about five years ago, and the economics of sf writing are not such as to allow time for tinkering with the elaborate and delicate machineries of wit. I don't know why; all I know is that we once had something unique and wonderful, and it is gone, and what we have in its place is only a superior writer of preposterous adventures.

Still, I enjoy reading preposterous adventures as much as anyone, and I enjoyed reading *To Die in Italbar*, for it is a superior specimen of the type. It is well written; fast action and strong emotion are described with equal skill; the author has a fertile imagination and creates colorful characters. Pity it wasn't written by Joe Blotz. (p. 55)

> Sidney Coleman, "Books: 'To Die in Italbar'," in The Magazine of Fantasy and Science Fiction (© 1974 by Mercury Press, Inc.; reprinted from The Magazine of Fantasy and Science Fiction), Vol. 47, No. 2, August, 1974, pp. 51-5.

FREDERICK PATTEN

Action, tense personal conflict, realistic dialogue, vivid characters, and exotic locales have made [Zelazny's Amber series] hotly sought by SF fans. However, this third volume [*Sign of the Unicorn*] takes up the tale with no synopsis and plunges into action so fast that even readers of the first two books may want to check back to refresh their memories. Those unfamiliar with the prior volumes may be completely bewildered. And it all ends with the most dramatic cliff-hanger yet.

> Frederick Patten, "Book Reviews: 'Sign of the Unicorn'," in Library Journal (reprinted from Library Journal, February 15, 1975; published by R. R. Bowker Co. (a Xerox company); copyright © 1975 by Xerox Corporation), Vol. 100, No. 4, February 15, 1975, p. 412.

MARTIN SHERWOOD

Mystery gathers strength from having roots in reality. A shoot from soil we know is always more pleasing than the unoriented and monstrous growths that often pass for advanced science fiction. . . . [*Today We Choose Faces*] postulates strange habitats populated with weird people but, throughout, it remains in touch with what we know. It is a satisfying and successful novel which exercises the mind rather than befuddles it. (p. 404)

> Martin Sherwood, "'Today We Choose Faces'," in New Scientist (© IPC Magazines, 1975), Vol. 66, No. 949, May 15, 1975, pp. 404-05.

MICHAEL WOOD

The inhabitants of Roger Zelazny's *Sign of the Unicorn* are not human beings at all but a race of aristocrats who live in another dimension and who can slip in and out of Earth, which they call Shadow, when they feel like it. They are a squabbling crew of brothers and sisters, a sort of outsize Borgia family complete with daggers and swords and Renaissance castles, and the plot of the novel is closer to that of a thriller than to most science fiction plots. I mention the book, though, because it is good, because it solves the stylistic problem of science

fiction in an interesting way, and because it represents a sort of boundary of science fiction, the place where it ends.

To take the last point first, the members of the family can speak to each other by means of decks of playing cards, and can actually conjure each other up physically with them. This is a form of whimsical magic which has nothing to do with science, or science fiction. On the other hand, when on Earth the family can manipulate landscapes at will, so that trees, rocks, mountains, and weather compose themselves into whatever arrangement is required, and this, it seems to me, while remaining in the realm of magic and fantasy, has something of the conceptual interest of science fiction.

Witches and wizards in medieval romance can change scenery about, turn castles into hovels and so on, but we see it's been done, we don't see them doing it, and this is where Zelazny moves into that zone of ingenuity which is science fiction's domain. . . .

The writing of most science fiction, the movement of its style, is brisk and efficient but rather drab. Attempts at fine writing . . . don't seem to work, and the frequent solemnity of the genre . . . makes for worthiness rather than real persuasion. I know of only two more or less satisfactory solutions to the problem. One is John Brunner's (in *Stand on Zanzibar, The Sheep Look Up,* and more recently, *The Shockwave Rider*), and that is to write not badly but *anyhow,* because you're in a hurry and your interest is elsewhere. (p. 6)

And the other solution is Zelazny's, and that is to crash and collapse styles in much the same way as he conflates perspectives. His tone, when it is not simply deadpan, is jocular and in resolute bad taste. "Out of every life a little blood must spill," his hero hums after he has been stabbed. . . . The effect, as with Brunner, is to abolish the whole question of style, and this is in keeping with the brilliant pointlessness of Zelazny's novels. They simply can't be read for meaning, and I hope most of us have some sort of place for such fiction in our reading lives. (pp. 6-7)

[In mingling] triviality and intelligence Zelazny remains in the best tradition of that unnatural founding father, who created a synthetic life because he couldn't resist his own ingenuity, who stumbled so thoughtlessly on the contents of the sleep of reason. (p. 7)

> Michael Wood, "Coffee Break for Sisyphus," in The New York Review of Books (reprinted with permission from The New York Review of Books; copyright © 1975 Nyrev, Inc.), Vol. 22, No. 15, October 2, 1975, pp. 3-7.*

R. D. MULLEN

[Zelazny is perhaps as skillful as any other SF writer (with the obvious exception of Ursula Le Guin) and far more skillful than most.]

[Zelazny] would surely be a great success as a scriptwriter for soap operas, who found the theme best suited to his talents and inclinations in one of the stories in *Four For Tomorrow,* "**A Rose for Ecclesiastes,**" perhaps the best story ever on Mars as a dying world, but who went quite overboard in another, "**The Doors of His Face, the Lamps of His Mouth,**" perhaps the most turgid and cliché-ridden of all the retellings of [Herman Melville's] *Moby Dick.* The other two stories in the book, "**The Furies**" and "**The Graveyard Heart,**" are neither as effective as the former nor as mawkish as the latter.

Early on in *This Immortal* the centuries-old protagonist is addressed as follows: "I was curious as to the sort of sensibilities a human might cultivate, given so much time—especially in view of your position as a master of your world's history and art." But alas!, though we do have a quite original post-catastrophe Earth in this story, we learn very little about its history or art, and even less about the sensibilities of the narrator-protagonist, who turns out to be a great fighting man, and who describes his fights in great detail.

> *R. D. Mullen, "The Garland Library of Science Fiction: 'Four for Tomorrow'," in* Science-Fiction Studies *(copyright © 1975 by R. D. Mullen and Darko Suvin), Vol. 2, No. 7, November, 1975, p. 287.*

PETER ACKROYD

[*To Die in Italbar*] is classified as 'science fiction' and whenever I pick up a random sample of that genre, I am always struck by its banality. 'SF', as its fans like to call it, must be the most vacuous form of the novel, interesting only to fantasists and to those who prefer the shadow of the novel to its substance (which is why science fiction is always shown to best effect on the screen). This particular narrative opens somewhere near Italbar, "a thousand miles distant from the space port", where Heidel von Hymack is making his way through the shadowy rain forests of Cleech. . . . (p. 670)

As long as the novel stays at the level of simple, linear adventure, it has all the merits of a fast and furious plot. But science fiction has two weaknesses which are inherent to it and which always do their best to tear down the delicate tracery of the narrative. There is, first, the tenuous—not to say pallid—romanticism which lies at the heart of science fiction, and which takes it closer to the pre-Raphaelite nightmare than any other twentieth century form. In this novel, we are treated to H's visions, which go something like this: ". . . but the blue mists swirled about him and there were perfumes, breezes, a kind of quiet ecstasy. . .". And then there is the violence and the intergalactic warfare of the book; science fiction generally excises all interesting human motives, actions and reactions for the sake of a few tacky apocalypses—worlds are always being destroyed, races are always being exterminated. Everything is an end game. This, no doubt, has something to do with the fact that science fiction caters for our more obvious fantasies; as such it cannot help but fall into vulgarity and surrealism. Unfortunately, *To Die in Italbar* is only another example. (pp. 670-71)

> *Peter Ackroyd, "Vandals," in* The Spectator *(© 1975 by The Spectator; reprinted by permission of The Spectator), Vol. 235, No. 7691, November 22, 1975, pp. 670-71.**

T. A. SHIPPEY

[Roger Zelazny's *To Die in Italbar*] avoids central characters altogether, except in so far as a plague vector is central. We open with a series of apparently unconnected scenes whose characters share only a quality of bizarre invention: a telekinetic dream-sculptor, a frozen pathologist, a professional deicide, a man who is both disease-pool and universal panacea. As the book progresses these parallel figures are (as one of the characters remarks) "cramp'd into a *Planisphere*". But the sense of their separateness remains; Mr Zelazny relies heavily on his ability to suggest the presence in the background of whole

worlds and policies and technologies, all profoundly interesting but too large for comprehension. It is almost a pity that the convention of the novel forces a plot and an ending on him.

> *T. A. Shippey, "Obsequious in Space," in* The Times Literary Supplement *(© Times Newspapers Ltd. (London) 1976; reproduced from* The Times Literary Supplement *by permission), No. 3858, February 20, 1976, p. 187.**

DAN MILLER

[In *Doorways in the Sand*] Zelazny has succeeded in that most difficult creation in science fiction: a genuine three-dimensional character. He's Fred Cassidy, a 29-year-old perpetual student in an unnamed twenty-first-century university, with acrophilia which expresses itself in simian rooftop ramblings. . . . Zelazny uses his dry chuckle, superb writing, and a fascinating narrative to make the reader want to reach out and shake Cassidy's hand.

> *Dan Miller, "Science Fiction: 'Doorways in the Sand'," in* The Booklist *(reprinted by permission of the American Library Association; copyright © 1976 by the American Library Association), Vol. 72, No. 15, April 1, 1976, p. 1095.*

GERALD JONAS

In describing his own works of fiction, Graham Greene takes care to distinguish between two kinds of books: his serious novels, like "The Power and the Glory" and "The Heart of the Matter," and what he calls his entertainments, like "Stamboul Train" and "The Confidential Agent." By signaling his intentions so clearly, Greene has saved readers and critics a lot of trouble. Serious literature *may* be entertaining, but that is hardly its primary function; we may be abashed or uplifted by a book without being amused. When entertainment is the author's avowed purpose, however, different expectations are aroused and different standards of taste apply. . . .

[The] identification of science fiction with entertainment was so complete that if a book used a futuristic setting or scientific gadgetry but was unmistakably "serious"—like Aldous Huxley's "Brave New World" or George Orwell's "1984"—no one except a S.F. fanatic would have dreamed of calling it science fiction.

Things have gotten more complicated nowadays. People like Samuel Delany and Ursula LeGuin are writing books that are unmistakably science fiction but which, for better or worse, demand to be judged according to the standards of serious literature. And for the first time, it is possible to talk about a "science fiction entertainment" (in the Graham Greene sense) without being redundant. A good example is Roger Zelazny's **"Doorways in the Sand."** . . . The first-person narrator, Fred Cassidy, is a perpetual undergraduate who climbs up the outside walls of tall buildings for fun. He gets mixed up with some curious extraterrestrial aliens and some nasty terrestrial villains, all of whom are convinced that Fred knows more than he admits knowing about a missing alien artifact. Actually, Fred does know more than he says he knows, but for a long time he doesn't *know* that he knows. How he finds out is the story of the book.

Zelazny's style tends toward the telegraphic, but he is scrupulously fair to the reader, and once you accept his zany logic, the resolution is as reasonable as it is ingenious. Along the way, Fred is pleasant enough company—literate, cool-headed, with a good sense of humor. . . . Basically a loner, he is forced to accept allies in order to survive. Zelazny's theme—whoever said that entertainments can't have themes?—is that everyone gets the allies that he deserves.

> *Gerald Jonas, "Of Things to Come: 'Doorways in the Sand',"* in The New York Times Book Review *(© 1976 by The New York Times Company; reprinted by permission), May 23, 1976, p. 45.*

LEW WOLKOFF

Zelazny is writing a novel about Prince Corwin of Amber. But he's releasing each division as he finishes it, [*The Hand of Oberon*] being fourth in the series. It begins with the next paragraph after the end of *Sign of the Unicorn*, its predecessor, and concludes with a cliff-hanger that will be resolved in the next.

This creates some problems for the reader. Much dialog is background-as-conversation, never an easy trick, though Zelazny usually keeps one's interest. Even with a chapter-long flashback written to summarize past events, there is sometimes the feeling of having missed something important. Names are thrown at the reader, who may only learn some pages after the fact why the characters reacted as they did, the full explanation being in an earlier book.

Zelazny is inventive and knows how to use language. His description of Corwin's hellride from Amber to Earth is practically a cinematic montage. . . .

Corwin is a prince of Amber, the only true reality. All other worlds, including our own, are Shadows of Amber. Shadows that can be shifted or traveled between by Corwin and his family. Caught in the middle of a fratricidal struggle for Amber's throne and facing an invasion of demonic forces from without, Corwin struggles for answers in Amber, in Shadow, and in such realms between as a floating city visible only when the moon is seen in full.

Keep in mind my warning, but try this book. Better yet, read the series. It may be years before the work appears as a single volume, and it is too good to wait that long.

> *Lew Wolkoff, "Fiction: 'The Hand of Oberon',"* in Best Sellers *(copyright © 1976 Helen Dwight Reid Educational Foundation), Vol. 36, No. 6, September, 1976, p. 188.*

R. D. MULLEN

[*The Dream Master* and *Isle of the Dead* are two] very different novels even though similar in "style" (i.e. in diction and in making much use of myth). The first is a near future novel of psychological realism and tragic overreaching concerned with "neuroparticipant therapy" in which the psychiatrist participates in and shapes the dreams of the patient, and is in my opinion second only to [Thomas M. Disch's *334*]. . . . The second is a bang-bang interstellar adventure story, a puerile daydream, albeit one of the sixties rather than the twenties, and thus mixing Philip Marlowe with John Carter to produce a hero of a more "mature" type.

> *R. D. Mullen, "Books in Review: 'The Dream Master' and 'Isle of the Dead',"* in Science-Fiction Stud-

ies *(copyright © 1976 by R. D. Mullen and Darko Suvin), Vol. 3, No. 10, November, 1976, p. 303.*

ROBIN ADAMS

[*Doorways in the Sand*] is just great fun. Fred Cassidy, professional college student (thirteen years and no degree) is suddenly the target of everyone searching for a missing alien artifact. . . .

Classic space-mystery, this can not miss with the sci-fi crowd. And young adults might identify with someone who has spent nearly all his life in school.

> *Robin Adams, " 'Doorways in the Sand',"* in Young Adult Cooperative Book Review Group of Massachusetts, *Vol. 13, No. 2, December, 1976, p. 66.*

JAY DALY

The time [of *Deus Irae,* written by Zelazny and Philip K. Dick] is post-World War III; the place a wasteland America, peopled with mutant races and presided over by a God of Wrath, one Carleton Lufteufel, who had been instrumental in bringing about World War III in the first place. Tibor McMasters, an incomplete (born without arms or legs, fitted with bionic counterparts), is commissioned to seek out the God of Wrath and to paint his portrait. It is the search for Lufteufel, and its implications, which the book explores. Dick and Zelazny's names will draw hard-core science fiction freaks—the only ones who will stay with this philosophical, allusive tale.

> *Jay Daly, "Adult Books for Young Adults: 'Deus Irae',"* in School Library Journal *(reprinted from the March, 1977 issue of* School Library Journal, *published by R. R. Bowker Co./A Xerox Corporation; copyright © 1977), Vol. 23, No. 7, March, 1977, p. 154.*

ERIC KORN

Philip Dick and Roger Zelazny's co-production, *Deus Irae,* lavishly strews wheezes, rather than ideas. Post-atomic, fragmented, monster-laden world; sardonic religion, the Servants of Wrath, idolizes Carl Lufteuful, the man who pressed the ultimate button; limbless painter sent on pilgrimage on cow-powered cart to find the Holy Face; various encounters with weird philosophical beasts, machines, mutants and metaphysics. Much irony about the relativism of religion and morality, somewhat in the style of James Branch Cabell. Vigorous, jumpy, startling, unflaggingly inventive, and rather a bore.

> *Eric Korn, "So Many Notions tb the Page,"* in The Times Literary Supplement *(© Times Newspapers Ltd. (London) 1977; reproduced from* The Times Literary Supplement *by permission), No. 3930, July 8, 1977, p. 820.**

JEREMY WESTON

Roger Zelazny is one of my favourite authors. He writes well, with humour and quite astonishing invention and has earned several top SF awards. *Doorways in the Sand* is not one of his best but is still very enjoyable reading, with a mysterious alien artefact, galactic cops and robbers, lots of excitement and plenty of humour. Pure escapism—and I loved it!

Jeremy Weston, "Review: 'Doorways in the Sand'," in New Scientist (© IPC Magazines, 1978), Vol. 77, No. 1091, February 23, 1978, p. 520.

ALEX De JONGE

Whatever one's view of [J.R.R. Tolkien's] *The Lord of the Rings* there can be no doubt that it has done dreadful things to the young imagination. There are simply too many long, level-paced pseudo-epics, three-part sometimes, about these days, ranging from chivalric to post-cataclysmic settings. The will to epic has even affected the work of one of the most talented science fiction writers, Roger Zelazny, who used to do such wonderful things with myth. *The Hand of Oberon* . . . is as well written as ever, but it is part of his tiresome Amber epic, and much too much space is devoted to recapping or describing complicated intrigues which are simply not good to read about. This is largely a waste of his splendid imagination, and let's hope that Amber finishes soon.

Alex De Jonge, "Spring SF: 'The Hand of Oberon'," in The Spectator (© 1978 by The Spectator; reprinted by permission of The Spectator), Vol. 240, No. 2813, April 1, 1978, p. 24.

LEW WOLKOFF

There is no set "Roger Zelazny" story. He can take the reader on tour across a radiation-scarred America in one story and show him/her a wizards' duel in the next, swinging easily from hard science to dark fantasy. What his stories do have in common is a strong sense of background. He works as hard at making his settings three-dimensional as he does with his characters. (Or should I say "as he does with his *other* characters?") Setting, however, doesn't speak, and one can dwell only so long on descriptions of ruined towers and tattered robes. The rest has to be left to subtle hints and the reader's imagination.

Lew Wolkoff, "Science Fiction: 'The Illustrated Roger Zelazny'," in Best Sellers (copyright © 1978 Helen Dwight Reid Educational Foundation), Vol. 38, No. 3, June, 1978, p. 73.

KIRKUS REVIEWS

[*Courts of Chaos*] concludes a remarkably popular sword-and-sorcery chronicle about the children of Oberon, a swarm of rival royal siblings in a corner of space/time ("Amber") whose continued existence involves a sort of jiggery-pokery hopscotch court called "the Pattern." The madly shifting alliances of Corwin (the narrator), Brand, Fiona, Random, Deirdre, and the rest are sorted out in the final battle of Amber with its enemy and opposing principle, the Courts of Chaos. Often a clever and thoughtful writer, Zelazny here is an anything-goes artist who slaps together Yeatsian imagery and paradoxes of cause and identity with the aid of a perfunctorily realized fantasy-landscape and a style of jarring unpredictability. Admirers of the series profess to find in it all sorts of Jungian resonances and manipulation of witty incongruities. The rest of us will be rather relieved to see it end.

"Fiction: 'Courts of Chaos'," in Kirkus Reviews (copyright © 1978 The Kirkus Service, Inc.), Vol. XLVI, No. 16, August 15, 1978, p. 906.

LESTER Del REY

Recently, writers and publishers in the book field seem to be discovering the serial all over again. No, not the series of novels, in which each story has some kind of an ending. . . . I mean a serial—a single story published in several books. That's a matter of turning one into many, making each book only an installment of the whole.

That strikes me as being completely unfair to the reader, who purchases a book in the expectation that he's getting a story—only to find out that he must wait a year or two before he can discover what happens—and then may have to wait that long again. (p. 168)

The case in point is the five-part serial of Roger Zelazny that began back in 1970 with the publication of *The Nine Princes of Amber*. Now finally in 1978 the fifth and final (?) installment has just been issued—*The Courts of Chaos*. . . . In this series, an average of two years passed between installments. There were at least eighteen major characters to be remembered, most of them highly complex and interwoven even more complexly. (Nine princes, four princesses, five other major characters—one playing a dual role.) And there was nothing resembling a conclusion to any of the first four.

The basic situation and indicated plot were fascinating. (pp. 168-69)

As told in the first book, Corwin, the viewpoint hero, had been exiled and robbed of his memory long before. He had existed on our Earth for several centuries. Now, as a result of the power struggle going on, he is made aware of a few facts. (p. 169)

Back in Amber, Corwin walks a Pattern which seems to create or symbolize Amber, thus regaining his memory and powers. He gets caught up in the plot to overcome the efforts of brother Eric to take the throne, and all hell breaks loose.

Fine—who could ask for anything more in an original fantasy idea? Well, I could. I wanted some kind of an ending, and there was none. Corwin, having suffered because of one effort to defeat Eric, simply was about to try another, with none of the complexities untangled, none of the motivations straightened out, and even more confusion at the end than at the beginning. Aside from the lack of a resolution, however, it was a marvelous book.

By the time each of the next three volumes appeared, I'd lost a lot of the clues and threads and couldn't possibly remember the relationships of all the characters that interacted on each other. There were vague recaps planted on what had gone before, but they were quite inadequate. Characters that were supposedly dead in one book popped up in another. Characters that seemed to be major enough to remember just disappeared in the next book. And I didn't go back and reread the whole set each time; if I'd done so, I'd probably have grown tired of the first one by the fourth time I read it, anyhow. So the following books impressed me a lot less than the first, though each added a great deal to the complexity of the whole.

Well, the books have to be read from first to last. They form a single novel, not a series of novels. When the final one came, I went back to the beginning. And this time, volumes two, three and four stood up very well, on the whole, and everything tied together and kept the suspense going very well. The five volumes *must* be read as a whole.

The only real fault I found in going back continuously through the first four volumes was some repetitiveness that wouldn't have been there, probably, if the books had been written as one. How often can the hell-ride through the shadows seem fresh? Yet there it is in full detail, time after time.

Surprisingly, Zelazny kept his inventiveness and the rich feeling of the story fresh and vigorous from the first volume in 1970 to the fourth in 1976—and that's a long stretch for a writer to continue without flagging, particularly since he was writing other novels in between.

Finally, the fifth volume does tie up almost all of the threads and does complete the novel; however, it leaves all sorts of possibilities for further developments, since it offers a whole new pattern of shadowlands. The novel that was serialized over eight years is now complete—and if Zelazny has a sequel in mind, he hasn't said so yet.

Unfortunately, **The Courts of Chaos** seems to have lost something. Some of the inventiveness, potential, and freshness of the other books has been lost. Much of the book seems tired, somehow. There's a long trip to the Courts of Chaos, a strange region partly described in the third book, which seems flat. And the final scene at the Courts of Chaos doesn't come off effectively; Chaos was a region of strangeness and strange beings, but now the figures from it seem little different from any figures in any battle. The marvel of Oberon's fate came to its culmination in the fourth book, and Oberon now is just another tired old man, trying the best he can. What he does should have been emotionally stirring—but isn't. The body of the story is there, but some of the spirit is missing. (And the feeling while reading was quite strong, even though this was fresh and the story I enjoyed in the other books was familiar.)

This shouldn't be surprising, perhaps. It's difficult for a writer to hold the mood of a story year after year—and Zelazny did better than most could have done.

I wish Doubleday and Zelazny had shared the responsibility of treating this as the one book it is, with enough advance for Zelazny to write the whole as one effort and the chance to do it as one long story, complete in a single book. Had that been done, this could well have been a genuinely superb piece of fantasy. As it is, it's a good story—no more. (pp. 169-70)

> *Lester Del Rey, "Ex Uno Plurimum" (copyright © 1979 by The Conde Nast Publications Inc.; reprinted by permission of the author), in* Analog Science Fiction/Science Fact, *Vol. XCVIX, No. 2, February, 1979, pp. 168-75.**

ALEX De JONGE

Roger Zelazny is [a] favourite writer, when he is not writing about Amber. His latest, **My Name is Legion** . . . is not, as its title might suggest, another of his splendid re-workings of mythological material. The book consists of three ingenious stories about a kind of private detective who has achieved total anonymity by erasing his particulars from the Central Data Bank. The stories are highly imaginative, concerning such matters as possibly criminal dolphins and the interplay between artificial intelligence and artificial original sin. All good stuff.

> *Alex De Jonge, "July SF: 'My Name Is Legion',"* in The Spectator *(© 1979 by The Spectator; reprinted by permission of* The Spectator*), Vol. 243, No. 7877, July 7, 1979, p. 22.*

KIRKUS REVIEWS

Zelazny moves [in **Roadmarks**] from sword-and-sorcery to a literary time-travel/quest frolic that's only slightly less giddy than the hijinks of George Alex Effinger. . . . A confusing, meandering lightweight—but Zelazny's bright imagination and wry wit are in top working order; so readers who fancy erudite diversion may want to travel this road, even if it goes nowhere in particular.

> *"Fiction: 'Roadmarks'," in* Kirkus Reviews *(copyright © 1979 The Kirkus Service, Inc.), Vol. XLVII, No. 17, September 1, 1979, p. 1032.*

NORMAN CULPAN

Roger Zelazny is one of my favourite writers of light fiction, but though I have read some half a dozen of his books, [**My Name is Legion**] is the first to come my way which crosses the tenuous borderline between fantasy and SF. Here are three stories describing three missions by 'the nameless one', a big-scale, freelance, single-handed troubleshooter. All are narrated in the first person, and are rooted in a technology basically our own but advanced some few score years. The first concerns a man-made submarine volcano, the second dolphins, and the third a humanoid robot who seems to have run amok. Zelazny's action is nearly as fast as Harry Harrison's (and I know of none faster). The protagonist is untrammelled by [James] Bond-type sex diversions, and his superhuman ability and resource are cloaked by careful planning and training. Success is achieved with a minimum of suffering by others, whose deaths, when they come, are not usually at his hand. (pp. 410, 412)

> *Norman Culpan, "From Sixteen to Upper Sixth: 'My Name Is Legion'," in* The School Librarian, *Vol. 27, No. 4, December, 1979, pp. 410, 412.*

ORSON SCOTT CARD

Roger Zelazny is a frustrating writer. He is capable of startlingly original writing, powerful scenes and new ideas in a field where ideas tend to be a bit threadbare from overuse. And yet, about halfway through his latest novel, **Roadmarks** . . . , he seems to get bored and throws his book away. The ideas are potentially very good: a freeway through time, where new exits and new forks in the road are created whenever travelers make some change in history and where old roads fade away as they are left unused: the son of one of these time travelers, who searches up and down the road for the father who abandoned him in—of all places—Cleveland; a man who suspects he is immortal and keeps having fits of madness in which he dreams of earlier lives and earlier memories; a character obsessed with altering the past so that this time the Greeks win at Marathon. As he introduces these ideas and figures, Zelazny raises high expectations in the reader; this will be an intelligent novel, an emotional novel, a memorable experience. But then, once he has proved that he can actually juggle all these ideas in a rather complex form, he turns to an easy ending involving dragons, a few quick switches in the plot and finally a bad joke. I wish Zelazny had realized what a potential masterpiece he had with **Roadmarks**—in 500 pages he could have created something unforgettable.

> *Orson Scott Card, "Slantwise through Time," in* Book World—The Washington Post *(© 1979, The Washington Post), December 23, 1979, p. 7.*

MARSHALL B. TYMN, KENNETH J. ZAHORSKI, and ROBERT H. BOYER

[*Nine Princes in Amber*] is the first book in the Amber series, five closely related novels which, while of uneven quality (the middle three are the best), are on the whole excellent, both for their unusually original fantasy elements and for their literary qualities. Readers should be cautioned at the outset that the series must be read in the proper sequence to gain the full (or in some of the novels *any*) understanding of the world of Amber, one of the more ingeniously conceived secondary worlds in fantasy literature. . . . The series starts out like many standard sword and sinew works but develops rapidly in literary quality. Characterization improves; style becomes more polished; and philosophical complexities emerge. But even in the first book, such a secondary world as Amber is enough to draw the reader into the rest of the series. *Nine Princes in Amber* introduces readers to the princes and princesses of Amber. . . . Corwin is the narrator and central character throughout all the books. In this first one Corwin is living on our earth, his favorite Shadow Earth, as Carl Corey. . . . Corwin, with the help of Random, the playboy of the family, succeeds in returning to Amber and regaining his identity. . . . Despite Zelazny's inventiveness, *Nine Princes in Amber* is the weakest book of the series, and could turn readers away from the others. The book features quantities of gratuitous sex and countless unnecessary throat-cuttings and blood-spurtings. The style features a crude, supposedly swagger-style modern idiom that is jarring. It is not until the second book that readers who are stalwart enough to persevere will discover that these negative features have a literary function. (pp. 181-82)

Far superior to *Nine Princes in Amber*, *The Guns of Avalon* (Book II of the Amber series) makes clear the rich complexity of Zelazny's design, which will carry through the remaining books. At the outset Corwin, still under the influence of past habits, feels he must avenge himself on his brother Eric and take the throne for himself. He postpones his revenge, however, when he witnesses the effects of the curse he had uttered when Eric blinded and imprisoned him. . . . The change in Corwin, the principal focus of this book, is carefully developed and convincing. Two new characters of importance enter the series at this point: Ganelon (not the betrayer of Roland) becomes Corwin's companion in arms, and Dara becomes his companion in love. Zelazny employs an effective elliptical style in describing the creation of new Shadow Earths. (p. 182)

In [*Sign of the Unicorn*], the politics of Amber, with plots and counterplots, creates considerable interest and suspense. . . . One of the attractions of this third book is the most effective shadow-shifting episode in the series. Prince Random (he is well named because of his erratic behavior) turns up to save Corwin from some subhuman pursuers. While fleeing on a glider-kite, Random shifts the Shadow Lands, earth and sky, to confuse the attackers, creating a fascinating kaleidescopic sequence of scenes. (pp. 182-83)

Many readers will probably find Book IV, *The Hand of Oberon*, the best of the five novels in the Amber series. Zelazny shelves sex and bloodletting almost completely, in favor of the attractions of a dramatic, suspenseful plot and an array of magical happenings. . . . The theme of duty over personal gain emerges most clearly in this book. Random even marries and brings order to his life. Corwin forgets numerous personal wrongs committed against him, unifies the Royal Family, and attends to the good of Amber as a proper ruler ought. His change, begun late in Book I of the series, could easily end here. (p. 183)

The blurb on the jacket claims that "all your questions are answered" in this Book V, the conclusion of the Amber series. Actually, only one question is answered, but it is the most important one. Amber does triumph over the Courts of Chaos and over the mysterious apocalyptic storm that threatens to neutralize the victory. *Courts of Chaos* also makes explicit the theme of balance in the universe between chaos and order, a fruitful and dynamic relationship between creativity and discipline or matter and form or whatever similar pairings pertain. Another theme or lesson is the attainment of self-realization by striving even when success seems impossible. The opposite point of view is voiced by a bird named Hugi who perches on Corwin's shoulder and preaches surrender to the Absolute. *Courts of Chaos* also reminds the readers that Corwin, however noble he has become, has not become a Galahad. . . . Aside from letting the reader know who wins, making some thematic statements, and shading in a corner of Corwin's character, *Courts of Chaos* achieves little and requires considerable padding to reach novel length. Still, it serves the function of summarizing a long story and thereby extending the reader's enjoyment. If it rests on the laurels of its predecessors, it does so with considerable justification. It also leaves a few doors open in case Zelazny wants to resurrect the series. (pp. 183-84)

[*Jack of Shadows*] is a fast-paced and highly imaginative novel that has as its setting an Earth that no longer rotates—an Earth half in darkness, half in light. Magic rules the lives of the Darksiders, science the lives of the Lightsiders. The picaresque hero, a Darksider called Jack of Shadows (he magically derives power from shadows), has acquired a legendary reputation for his skill as a thief, but when he attempts to steal the Hellflame (a "fist-sized ruby") he is apprehended and summarily executed. All Darksiders, however, have more than one life, and after his ressurection Jack sets out to gain revenge on those responsible for the taking of his life. . . . Although a unique work, in some respects *Shadows* is similar to Jack Vance's *The Eyes of the Overworld*. Both novels feature a central character who is a thieving rogue with considerable magical powers, along with a large supporting cast of remarkably weird creatures (for example, the Borshin in *Shadows;* both novels are highly episodic; both are extraordinarily inventive and imaginative; both have exotic, vividly described settings (witness *Shadows'* Dung Pits of Glyve and High Dudgeon); and both are characterized by an abundance of Dunsanian names. Unlike *Overworld*, however, *Shadows* adds to the story line, or literal level, a distinctly allegorical level of meaning, and thus *Shadows* has a somewhat greater sophistication of plot and theme. The allegory in *Shadows* arises from its treatment of Jack's running battle with his "Soul"—Everyman's quest for spiritual meaning and fulfillment; and in its depiction of Man's dichotomous nature—the emotional/magical (dark) side versus the intellectual/scientific (light) side. Although *Shadows* has plenty of swashbuckling action, Zelazny avoids the heavy emphasis on blood and gore found in the first two books of the Amber series. (p. 184)

Marshall B. Tymn, Kenneth J. Zahorski, and Robert H. Boyer, "Core Collection: Novels and Short Story Collections," in their Fantasy Literature: A Core Collection and Reference Guide *(reprinted with permission of the R. R. Bowker Company; copyright © 1979 by Xerox Corporation), R. R. Bowker Company, 1979, pp. 181-84.*

MATT BERGER

To those familiar with science fiction, the recent work of Roger Zelazny must be considered something of a letdown. . . . Mr. Zelazny has not been especially popular these past few years. But with *Roadmarks,* his latest, there is reason to believe that his writing has regained the depth and fluency that have not been apparent for so long.

Roadmarks is written in the typical Zelazny style, which is often hard for an inexperienced science fiction reader to follow at first, but which reveals itself in later readings to be succinct and flowing. . . .

In terms of being a science fiction "mystery," *Roadmarks* is excellent, and it makes use of the "trick ending" method as well as any recent work. Readers concerned with hidden messages and allegories will find it loaded, and its appeal should cover both the "hard" and "soft" audiences of science fiction quite well.

> Matt Berger, "Fiction: 'Roadmarks'," in Best Sellers (copyright © 1980 Helen Dwight Reid Educational Foundation), Vol. 39, No. 10, January, 1980, p. 372.

DARRELL SCHWEITZER

[*Roadmarks*] is a throwaway novel, I'm sorry to report. It reminds me of a half a dozen Philip José Farmer books in which brilliant ideas are presented, then left underdeveloped, trivialized, or just cast aside in pursuit of an irrelevant plot. . . . In this case, the central premise is one of those outrageously literalized metaphors which only work in science fiction and fantasy. In mainstream they'd be gibberish. Consider a "road through time". Zelazny's Road, which may have been built by dragons, runs from the far past to the far future. . . . With discipline and imagination, there's no limit to what a first rate author like Zelazny could have done with it.

Unfortunately he does damn little. There are two narratives, the main one (chapters labelled "One") and a subsidiary, out-of-sequence one ("Two"). . . . Frequently a lot of attention is devoted to characters whose roles are quite trivial, and often they're interesting characters, e.g., the Chinese monk whose prior personality as a super-competent killer from the future is slowly returning. (There's a novel in him.) When the hero finally meets the guy who is causing all the trouble, the villain's motivations are glossed over before they make a bit of sense. When the son and father meet, little happens to justify the space devoted to this "subplot". There are several deus-ex-machinas all at once and one dragon-out-of-a-hat. The problems tend to solve themselves and most of the interesting questions are never resolved. As a result the best parts of the book tend to pull it apart. Something which looks interesting, develops a little ways then is abandoned, can only be distracting.

Roadmarks is, alas, second-rate Zelazny. It's failings are failings of storytelling and very serious ones. Now, I'm not one of those people who insist that Zelazny "lost it" ten years ago. After the work which established his reputation in the late 1960s, he shifted gears. He was writing in top form as recently as "Home is the Hangman" and *Doorways in the Sand,* even if it was a different form. But this new novel is just sloppy. It shows signs of haste and a lack of application. One hopes he will do a sequel in which he will make effective use of the marvellous potential inherent in the premise.

> Darrell Schweitzer, "The Vivisector: 'Roadmarks'," in Science Fiction Review (copyright © 1980 by Richard Geis; reprinted by permission of Richard Geis and Darrell Schweitzer), Vol. 9, No. 2, May, 1980, p. 20.

CARL B. YOKE

Renewal is an abiding concern of Roger Zelazny's writing, especially his early work. In fact, this theme is so deeply engrained in his thinking that most of his significant fiction uses it in one way or another. **"A Rose for Ecclesiastes"** treats the restoration of fertility to a barren Mars and the salvation of the natives from racial suicide. *This Immortal* treats the restoration of an irradiated Earth. *Lord of Light* treats the renewal of a society. The five **"Amber"** novels treat the restoration of the land and the salvation of the world of form from Chaos.

In Zelazny's writing, renewal comes in two distinct forms: renewal as a physical objective and renewal as a psychological objective. Most of the guises in which it appears are of the physical kind, such as the revival of a planetary ecology, the restoration of fertility, the restructuring of a culture, the remolding of a religion, and the salvation of a species. The most persistent form, however, is psychological. It manifests itself as a metamorphosis of personality, a general raising of consciousness.

Inevitably, Zelazny's protagonists must achieve what Carl Jung has called "individuation," that is, the psychological state created when a person has successfully integrated the opposing systems of his personality into a separate, individual unity—a whole. With this integration also comes complete knowledge of self. As Zelazny views it, however, the change it produces is so complete that enormous consequences are produced in the individual's life. (p. 106)

The key to these dramatic changes of personality is the accumulating experience of the character. That experience comes, in turn, through the adventures of the protagonist as he pursues his physical objective. Often the metamorphosis occurs within the story, but on some occasions, it has actually occurred prior to the start of the action. . . . In any case, however, the metamorphosis is integral to the playing out of the story. . . .

Despite the fact that most of Zelazny's heroes achieve metamorphosis, he is enough of a student of human nature to realize that this is not always the case, and in *The Dream Master,* he presents a failure. (p. 107)

Zelazny also recognizes other individual differences. He knows, for example, that people grow at their own rates and that it may take more experience to produce the same change in one person than it does in another. He also knows that the quality and intensity of an experience may alter the rate of psychological growth, and he recognizes that such growth is a process which will continue, in a healthy individual, as long as that individual is alive, even though there comes a point where the change is so marked that it can be identified as a metamorphosis.

There are many excellent examples of such a metamorphosis in Zelazny's work, but perhaps the best one is found in Carlton Davits, the protagonist of his Nebula-Award-winning novelette, **"The Doors of His Face, the Lamps of His Mouth."** In the pattern of his development, Davits mirrors the psychological evolution of many Zelazny protagonists. Prototypically, some negative element of personality becomes dominant in the character and blocks further *healthy* psychological growth. In the case of Davits and Gallinger, it is pride, but it can be any abnormally strong desire. Greed, power, or revenge, for example, are other frequently occurring personality faults in Zelazny's characters. The next stage of development for the evolving personality, however, is a personal failure or some other traumatic event which makes the character aware of his fallibility. This is followed by a period of readjustment. Finally, there is an integration of disparate elements which brings a broader and deeper awareness not only of self but also of humanity. The integration subsequently brings certain benefits, such as productivity, fertility, increased capability, or psychologically healthy love.

All of the elements of **"The Doors of His Face, the Lamps of His Mouth"** are geared to expanding and emphasizing Davits' individual metamorphosis, and many of them are adapted for the novelette from the Book of Job. In the character of Job, Zelazny found a broad model for Davits, though the baitman is not simply a recasting of the biblical sufferer in a science-fiction context. The first indication that there is a connection between the two works is found in the story's title **"The Doors of His Face, the Lamps of His Mouth."** It was constructed by placing the italicized words in line 18 of the following passage into parallel construction with line 14:

> Who can open *the doors of his face*?
> his teeth are terrible round about.
> His scales are his *pride*.
> shut together as with a close seal.
> Out *of his mouth* go burning *lamps*,
> and sparks of fire leap out
> > (41:14-19; emphasis mine)

The specific referent for the passage is the leviathan of Job, which in that book, as in Zelazny's novelette, symbolizes pride. Not only does this passage then generate Ikky, the beast of **"The Doors of His Face, the Lamps of His Mouth,"** it also provides the fault for Davits' characterization. Job stands in the same symbolic relationship to his leviathan as Davits does to Ikky, even though the dramatic context is vastly different.

The similarities between Davits and Job do not end here. The pattern of their character development is also very similar. Both have at one time held high status in their respective cultures, both fall from that state, both are tested, and both suffer physical damage as a result of their testing. Both finally resolve their problems and achieve a higher maturity. (pp. 107-08)

There is a significant difference in what wealth and status has brought each man, however, in terms of his personal relationships. Job has deep and meaningful relationships with family and friends, and at least as the Book of Job begins, he believes that his relationship with God is secure and that his affluence is a direct reflection of a long life of doing right. This view is quickly destroyed when randomness is inserted into that relationship, and this brings Job's subsequent confusion and eventual despair. Davits, on the other hand, has too much money and too little responsibility. He is very immature, and he has no real friendships because he does not understand that true friendship requires giving as well as taking. Wealth and position have brought him nothing of value in his personal relations. The difference between the two men is significant because in Zelazny's characterization of Davits, he is reflecting a prevalent view of our times—that money and influence are more desirable values than meaningful relationships.

A significant difference between the two can also be seen in the cause of their falls from high estate. Job falls because God permits Satan to test him. . . . There is no question that Job's fall has been generated outside of himself. By contrast, Davits' fall is self-generated. It is the result of overplaying his hand, of being too sure of himself. And this change of motive from Job to Davits is Zelazny's attempt to make Davits a character more identifiable to modern readers. Regardless of the stimuli, however, both Davits and Job fall for the same psychological reason—neither is mature enough to handle failure, whether real or imagined, because each is blocked from insight into his own unique circumstances by his pride.

Another example of Zelazny's attempt to make Davits more credible to his readers by psychologizing the character is found in the testing of the two figures. Job's trials are imposed on him by Satan, while Davits' are imposed on him by his own fear. And though the tests are different, the pattern of results is very much the same. Both men lose material wealth, suffer losses in personal relationships, and sustain physical injury. (pp. 108-09)

Ikky, the symbol of Davits' pride and the object of his fear, is also drawn from the Book of Job. (p. 109)

Zelazny's problem is to make the beast concrete. He accomplishes this primarily by delimiting the image and by giving it a definite referent. Specifically, he combines certain characteristics of the biblical monster with those of the plesiosaur, a thought-to-be-extinct marine reptile of the Mesozoic era. . . .

Making Ikky more identifiable to contemporary readers is important because the monster is a major symbol in the story, and the nature and extent of Carl's psychological problem is conveyed through it.

But the title of Zelazny's novelette, the paralleling of Davits with Job, and the general description of the sea-monster are not all that Zelazny has drawn from the biblical book. He has also taken his dominant field of imagery from it. Job is heavy with water images, particularly Chapters 9-14 and 38-42. The sea/rain/brook/tears/dew/ice cluster symbolizes the randomness of life, a fact Job comes to accept only after he has gained a new maturity. In its capacity to be either creative or destructive, water illustrates the final relationship between Job and God. (p. 110)

In the novelette, the water pattern not only forms the dominant submetaphor of the story but also stands in a much more complex relationship to it than the water pattern does in Job. So well is it integrated into the story, in fact, that it serves multiple purposes. First, it functions at the literal level as the medium through which Davits must travel in order to catch Ikky. Second, as rain it marks the purgation of his vanity and the beginning of his maturity. (As tears, it marks the same transition for Jean Luharich.) Third, as the sea, it functions both psychologically as an equivalent to Davits' mind and mythologically as an equivalent to Hell.

Tied closely to the water pattern is the voyage motif. During the course of the story, Carl makes both physical and mental journeys. At the physical level, he travels both across the seas of Venus and down into their depths. At the psychological (or mental) level, he travels deep into the recesses of his own mind to confront his fear, symbolized by Ikky. Also tied into the water pattern is the sea-serpent. Ikky is, at once, the physical object of his fishing trip and the symbolic manifestation of his fear. The variations of the water pattern are appropriate to the purpose of the story, which is Carl Davits' journey to maturity, because they help to reinforce, focus, and define it.

The water pattern is supported by a very important secondary pattern—sight-insight. Like so many elements of **"Doors and Lamps,"** this pattern also functions at multiple levels, in this case the physical one of sight, or lack of it, and the psychological level of insight, or, again, lack of it. (p. 111)

The sight-insight pattern in Zelazny's novelette is developed by many different devices and established almost at the outset of the story by a scene which mirrors Carl's psychological development. . . . In this brief scene, Zelazny sketches Carl's psychological journey for the reader. Before his first encounter with Ikky, his vision is opaque. In other words, his insight is blocked; he does not grow from his experience. Then, after being cast down by the sight of the monster, he goes through a period where most of what he sees is through an alcoholic stupor. Finally, at the beginning of the successful hunt for Ikky, the benefits of his physical and mental suffering begin to take effect, and the distortion resolves to clarity. Zelazny emphasizes the symbolic quality of the passage by the language he uses: "Cloud, illusion, resolve." Each word has a distinct conceptual relationship to the word *sight*. (pp. 111-12)

The most important supportive device of all, however, is the eyes symbol, especially as it relates to Jean. Before discussing how the symbol fits into the sight-insight pattern, it is necessary to define the relationship between Carl and Jean. Two key comments by Carl show that she is a psychological reflection of himself. . . .

That Jean is a reflection of Carl is borne out by the similarity of their personalities. When they first married, according to Carl, both were young, rich, strong, and spoiled. Evidence in the story indicates that both were also stubborn, highly competitive, and very athletic; in particular, both are excellent swimmers, each having saved the other from drowning. Moreover, both do most things well, disregard personal safety when facing a challenge, and have little respect for conventional rules. Most importantly, each felt at one time or another that he or she could do anything. . . . For each, the ultimate hunt is the Ikky. The difference is that Carl has tried and failed, thus realizing his human fallibility; but Jean has still to try.

Their vanity is clearly established. Job gives the first clue. Of the leviathan, it is written, ". . . he is a king over all / the children of pride" (41:34). Vanity is the keystone of Jean's personality. (p. 113)

If we accept the fact that Carl and Jean are psychological mirror images, certain important inferences can then be drawn. First, he is as vain as she. Second, their very brief, very rocky first marriage undoubtedly broke up because each was so busy loving himself or herself that he or she had neither time nor room to love someone else. Finally, Carl's drift into alcoholism after losing his catch was probably triggered by his inability to accept the fact that he had failed—pride had prevented him from dealing with his fallibility. There can be little doubt that Zelazny has once again drawn from Job and that Carl and Jean are meant to be the "children of pride" referred to in Job 41:34. Since that verse clearly stipulates that the leviathan is king over all the "children of pride," then it is obvious that neither Jean nor Carl will be able to catch Ikky until he or she has first conquered the beast within—vanity.

Besides serving as a psychological mirror, however, the character of Jean serves at least two other notable functions. She

is, of course, Carl's love object, but of equal importance is her role's third function—to serve as a guide for Carl's maturational development. Jean is not aware, of course, that she is performing this function in her own hunt for Ikky, and Carl, himself, has only a growing awareness of this fact until the time that Jean falters on the Inject. Then, he becomes fully cognizant that what is happening to her is exactly what has happened to him. With that realization, he makes her push the Inject and gives up the opportunity to catch Ikky himself. He knows that if she fails she will throw away her soul trying to find out about herself, and he prefers to have her psychologically whole.

How Jean functions as guide is best illustrated in the important scene in which she and Carl race under Tensquare. Even though Carl does not completely understand it at the time, he senses that Jean is, in fact, a fairly accurate reflection of himself as he existed a few years earlier, and in her actions he witnesses his own former attitudes. It is in this sense that she becomes his guide. And though these perceptions make him angry, Jean has begun to focus his insight. Equally important is the fact that through her actions during the race, she forces him from a passive to an active posture and from a negative to a positive attitude.

The action pattern in the story is a significant supportive metaphor to the sight-insight pattern. In the race under Tensquare, Carl learns an important truth about action through Jean—that there is an immense difference between reckless and right action. This observation is a sign of his developing maturity. (pp. 113-14)

Jean's actions, though reckless, are significant. The important aspect of the race scene is that she initiates it. . . . Throughout the race, she leads him. Sensing her role, he lets her. At various intervals, she steps up the pace, until about halfway under the raft she hits the compressed air jets. This is a reckless bit of action which is significant because it also forces him to take chances. A short time later, he must use his own rockets to prevent her from being torn up by the large windmill screws beneath the raft.

As a result of this experience, both Carl and Jean learn a lesson—that there is a correct time, a correct place, and a correct act for each situation. Moreover, they learn that there is a time to be passive and that judging the degree of force to apply in any situation is critical. Both, however, approach this principle from opposite ends of the active-passive continuum. Since his encounter with Ikky, Carl has become overly passive, and he must be driven from it. Jean's actions during the race accomplish this by making Carl examine his attitudes. The perceptions he has regarding his posture prepare him for actions that he will have to take later on in his quest for maturity. Specifically, he learns the lesson of judging how much force to apply and when to apply it. This preparedness is critical if he is to accomplish his two primary objectives: successful confrontation of Ikky and reconciliation with Jean, who is not only his love object but also the symbol of his love of self. Jean must, of course, learn the same lesson, and in the race scene she does this. Her close call with death brings a recognition of her own fallibility and prepares her for her own paralyzing confrontation with Ikky. These events start her toward a realistic perception of self and help her to understand what Carl has gone through. Eventually she makes the same maturational step that he does without suffering the prolonged period of self-doubt and passivity. (pp. 114-15)

Besides the action pattern, there is a second significant sub-metaphor for the sight-insight complex: the light-dark pattern. It is particularly appropriate because of the physical effect of light on sight and the subsequent figurative connection with insight. Even though Zelazny is limited to some degree in his use of the light metaphor by the physics of light, he maximizes its possibilities by the careful planning of scene and time.

In general, he has drawn Venus as a planet of mist and sea and cloud—a setting of minimal light. . . .

Moreover, many of the scenes are set at night and/or in storms. (p. 116)

Correlated with the storms, night, and the generally gray atmosphere are the descents into the sea. Here, as with the weather, Zelazny is somewhat limited by physical laws. In any body of water, light diminishes with depth. Nonetheless, by calling the reader's attention to the darkness and by emphasizing the degree, Zelazny is able to use the physical laws pertaining to light to support the sight-insight complex.

In order to understand how the subpattern works, it is first necessary to understand the meaning of two primary symbols in the story. At the psychological level, the sea represents Davits' mind and Ikky, his neurosis. In order for Carl to overcome his neurosis and return to a healthy mental state, it is imperative that he destroy his fear by destroying the leviathan that has come to represent it. Thus, the descents that he makes during the course of the story serve a psychological, as well as a physical, purpose.

There are three psychologically significant descents in the novelette. The first of these occurs with the race under Tensquare, which is important for two reasons. First, it establishes Jean as Carl's psychological guide. Second, it marks the beginning of a change in their present relationship. . . . [It] is important to note that Jean leads the race under the raft with Carl's permission. He periodically spots her with the beam of his torch, keeping her in sight, matching his stroke with her own. She looks back to be sure he is following. Eventually the failure of her jets causes Carl to challenge himself in order to save her. She has precipitated a sequence of events which renew his self-confidence, a necessary *psychological* step in his preparation. Moreover, the race marks a change in their relationship. Each of them is locked into a pattern of behavioral response toward the other which is expected by divorced parties. Only an event of significance can change that. Saving Jean's life accomplishes that purpose.

The "thirteenth day" descent is also psychologically significant. It too is preparatory. A very long cast forces Carl to descend much deeper than he has ever gone before (it is, incidentally, made by Jean, who continues to drive Carl towards his inevitable confrontation). Reacting to the great depth of his dive, Carl is gripped by fear. . . . Automatically, he retreats into the safety of darkness. "I didn't want to switch my torch on. But I had to. Bad! I still had a long way to go. I clenched my teeth and stuffed my imagination into a straight-jacket." . . . The psychological significance of these lines is that Carl is beginning to gain control of himself. He has become more aware of his problem. "I was near—too near—to where I never wanted to be," . . . he says. Yet, the point is that he is, in fact, there.

His new awareness is underscored by the light pattern. At first unwilling to turn on the torch, he finds out almost immediately that he is then equally unwilling to turn it off. . . . When he reaches the deck safely, he laughs in relief to himself at his newfound confidence. Nothing was there; his flight was ironic. His hands are steady, rather than shaking as they had been from his hemiplegia and fear. He yawns happily, and his shoulder feels as good as new. All of these positive signs mark the success of his probe into his fear. Most important of these, however, is his capacity to switch on and switch off the light at will. The descent is important from another aspect too. After the dive is completed, Jean apologizes to him for the overly long cast. She displays genuine concern for his safety. Her attitude toward him and her admission of fallibility are yet another step towards reconciliation.

The third descent, and most significant, occurs on "the day of the beast." Inevitably, it brings Carl face to face with both Ikky and his own fear. From a psychological point of view, only confrontation and then mastery will permit Carl to achieve mental health. Whether or not Carl will succeed depends, of course, upon his degree of readiness.

We get a clue to his state of mind in the paragraphs that precede the actual contact, and it is evident that his attitude is much different than it was on the "thirteenth day" descent. Unlike that occasion, Carl does not dwell on his fear. To the contrary, he is fairly confident. . . . Zelazny reinforces Carl's confident attitude by likening him to a bright comet. It is an appropriate comparison, for he means for the reader to accept the implicit connotation: a body locked on course, speeding towards its destiny. Clearly, Carl has been psychologically prepared.

As before, the light pattern underscores his mental journey and the intrinsic symbols of the story come into play. The sea represents mind, light is awareness (or insight), and dark is its opposite. (pp. 116-18)

The contact between diver and beast re-creates the psychological conditions that originally triggered Carl's neurosis. On the first occasion, he failed to act. His failure shattered his self-image, plunged him into doubt and bankruptcy, and caused the death of six men. Unlike that first time, however, this time his courage does *not* desert him. Even though overwhelmed by waves of death-fear, he performs the only act that will save him—he pulls the rest of the plugs on the squiggler. It immediately phosphoresces. Later he learns that Ikky took his artificial bait. The significance of Carl's deed cannot be overstated. This single act establishes the fact that he has finally gained control over himself. No longer is he the prisoner of his unconscious fear. No longer can he be pushed here and there by it. No longer will it control his destiny. (pp. 118-19)

Once Carl performs his act of self-survival, the symbolic value for the cluster of dark images shifts and the relationship between "light" and "dark" changes. These developments occur because, for the first time since his initial confrontation with Ikky, the conscious and subconscious elements of his mind have returned to a natural state of harmony. In accordance with Jungian psychodynamics, the period of Carl's neurosis is marked by the trapping of large quantities of psychic energy in the subconscious. The trapped energy feeds that element which Jung labels "the shadow" and which is also manifest in the story by Ikky. (The enormous size of the sea-beast is thus a reflection of the severity of Carl's neurosis.) However, when he pulls the rest of the plugs on the squiggler, Carl not only saves himself but also discharges the energy trapped by the shadow. That, in turn, alters the very nature of his subconscious. Whereas it was once a place filled with terror, it has now become a place of retreat, meditation, healing. It is, therefore, appropriate from a psychological as well as physical point of view that Davits "blacks out" after his panicked swim for the surface. The dark cluster has now come to signify a place of peace, and the relationship between "light" and "dark" is now one of peaceful coexistence. (p. 119)

[Because] he has brought himself into harmony with this psychic environment, Carl is quite literally a new man. He has metamorphosed.

Like him, Jean will also evolve to an inner state of harmony because Jung believes that the best friendships and marriages occur between persons who are fully individuated and who have achieved harmony within themselves rather than between persons who complement one another's weaknesses. Jean's metamorphosis is inevitable even though it occurs through a much shorter time frame than Carl's and avoids his deep-seated neurosis. Otherwise their development is parallel: both require recognition of their fallibility and the destruction of their vanity. Both must be tested. Jean's moment of truth comes in a scene near the end of the story which duplicates Carl's traumatic, initial confrontation with the sea-beast. The notable difference between encounters, however, is that Jean has Carl to urge her to action when she freezes at the sight of Ikky. His urging prevents her from repeating his mistake. In terms of its mental benefits, her act of pushing the "Inject" is psychologically synonymous with Carl's pulling of the plugs on the squiggler a short time earlier. And like him, when the act is completed, she "blacks out." This reinforces the idea that they are going through the same process.

It is only after both Carl and Jean have become fully individuated that they can enter into a mentally healthy relationship. For Zelazny, such a relationship is one which is in balance, which is creative, which preserves the integrity of each party while developing their union. The planet symbol in the last line of the story emphasizes this concept, ". . . but the rings of Saturn sing epithalamium the sea-beast's dower." . . . The image is perfect. The contrast of the glowing planet against the inky black of space visually suggests balance. It is a comment on the new relationship of Carl and Jean as well as reflecting the new relationship between the light and dark clusters of images in the story. No longer are the antithetical elements of the story at war; all have been brought into harmony. (pp. 119-20)

"Doors and Lamps" can be read at many levels. It is the story of a man's search for maturity. It is a story of mental health. It is a search for love. It is a comment on failure and success. It is an adventure about the ultimate hunt. And, it is a comment on man's ability to supersede himself. In the last analysis, of course, it is all of these and more, for as with all great literature it touches the core of experience that is common to all men. Whether its nature is conceptual, sensory, or emotional, it is integrated into that field which is labeled the individual personality. All of us share a core of basic experience, but we achieve our uniqueness because of the focus, intensity, or mix of that basic experience.

Because of this tendency of humans to integrate their individual thoughts, feelings, and emotions, it is nearly impossible to separate strictly one chain of experience from other chains of experience. For, at the core of being, all experience is fused together. The deeper into personality a story probes, therefore, the greater is its interconnectedness with other stories which also probe our basic human experience. **"Doors and Lamps"** is such a story. (pp. 120-21)

Carl B. Yoke, "Personality Metamorphosis in Roger Zelazny's 'The Doors of His Face, the Lamps of His Mouth'," in Extrapolation *(copyright 1980 by Thomas D. and Alice S. Clareson), Vol. 21, No. 2, Summer, 1980, pp. 106-21.*

ROLAND GREEN

[With *Changeling* the] prolific and popular Zelazny has produced a short but satisfactory fantasy novel on the "changeling" theme. A baby from a world of magic is brought to technological Earth, while an Earth child is carried off to the magic world. . . . The writing is clear, the characterization adequate, the background and system of magic intelligently worked out, [and] the pacing brisk. . . .

Roland Green, "Adult Fiction: 'Changeling'," in Booklist *(reprinted by permission of the American Library Association; copyright © 1980 by the American Library Association), Vol. 77, No. 1, September 1, 1980, p. 35.*

DARRELL SCHWEITZER

Someone recently made a very perceptive comment about Zelazny, which I'll repeat here: of his first two novels, *This Immortal* proved far more influential on his later work than did *The Dream Master,* and it might have been better the other way around. *Immortal* was jazzy, witty, and polished, but without much depth. *The Dream Master* was an elegant, substantial tragedy. The course he took later caused Judith Merril to ask, "Will Zelazny ever write the insides of his novels? *Can* he?"

He certainly didn't this time. *Changeling* is all around more satisfying than his previous one, *Roadmarks,* but still it has no insides. By way of improvement, it is a fairly *complete* story, which shows few signs of slapdash until the rather perfunctory end. It is not much ado about nothing, but the characters are sticks of wood.

Zelazny's powers of invention are working full force. The background is extremely good. . . .

The problem is that Zelazny has overlooked the potential for tragedy. Instead he has written a light romp, like a very literate prose comic book. Mark, the one from the scientific world raised in the magical one, starts out as a decent, sympathetic type who is warped by hatred and misunderstanding until he becomes destructive. Even his "twin" tries to work out a reconciliation with him, but he is driven to his end. This is powerful stuff, but most of it happens offstage and out of the book. Remaining are a set of one-dimensional figures, Hero and Villain, and when the latter conveniently falls off a ledge at the end, it hardly seems to matter. There are moments of wit, and wonder, and even beauty beforehand, but they don't add up to much. This is only an average quality novel after all. I'd rate it a C+.

Darrell Schweitzer, "Book Reviews: 'Changeling'," in Fantasy Newsletter *(© 1980 by Paul C. Allen), Vol. 3, No. 10, October, 1980, p. 6.*

PUBLISHERS WEEKLY

["**The Last Defender of Camelot**"] is a superlative collection by one of the genre's better authors. There are a number of early stories (including the author's first two), which are minor but vivid vignettes; and, at the heart of the book, several nov-elettes. . . . **"For a Breath I Tarry,"** which Zelazny indicates is his favorite, is a touching story of a machine, one of the guardians of a future Earth. Interested in the long-dead human race, the machine decides to become human, and so discovers, unexpectedly, fear and despair and love.

> *"Science Fiction: 'The Last Defender of Camelot',"* in Publishers Weekly *(reprinted from the October 17, 1980, issue of* Publishers Weekly *by permission, published by R. R. Bowker Company, a Xerox company; copyright © 1980 by Xerox Corporation), Vol. 218, No. 16, October 17, 1980, p. 64.*

ROSEMARY HERBERT

No large sf collection should be without Zelazny's latest an-thology [*The Last Defender of Camelot*], featuring the author's own choice of stories originally published over the last two decades. A brief but engaging introduction and the remarks prefacing each story explain the origin of each work, and oc-casionally leave the reader mildly amazed that, for instance, a cloud formation resembling a horse and rider could conjure up the compelling tale **"Horseman!"** Many of the stories are quite short, but all are effective.

> *Rosemary Herbert, "Fiction: 'The Last Defender of Camelot',"* in Library Journal *(reprinted from Li-brary Journal, November 15, 1980; published by R. R. Bowker Co. (a Xerox company); copyright © 1980 by Xerox Corporation), Vol. 105, No. 20, November 15, 1980, p. 2436.*

ALGIS BUDRYS

Roger Zelazny's **The Changeling** is 40,000 words of very pretty trade paperback, . . . and I rather wish there had been a few more words. Perhaps there were; there appear to be places where segments that ought to have occurred are simply missing, rather than skimped. . . .

But the author triumphs over the editing (?). . . . This is very good science fantasy, counterpointing the lives of two attractive male heroes who, as babies, were exchanged between a magical milieu and our mundane one. (p. 43)

[The] two young men do come into contention—partly because both of them are involved with a particular girl, partly because Mark is such a rockhead—and the old struggle between tech-nology and magic undergoes another climactic cycle.

As noted, this is not a perfectly told story, because of its discontinuities. But it's very good reading when there's some-thing there to read, and filling in your own blanks can be rewarding rather than annoying. There are some very attractive minor characters, one of whom is a dragon, and in general this is a very pleasant book. (pp. 43, 156)

> *Algis Budrys, "Books: 'The Changeling',"* in The Magazine of Fantasy and Science Fiction *(© 1981 by Mercury Press, Inc.; reprinted from* The Maga-zine of Fantasy and Science Fiction*), Vol. 60, No. 1, January, 1981, pp. 43, 156.*

PUBLISHERS WEEKLY

[In **The Changing Land**] Dilvish, of the Elvish race, bent on revenge against Jerelak, tries to gain access to the Castle and does so by being captured and thrown in the dungeon. Aided by other prisoners, he escapes, and eventually brings about the fall of Jerelak and Baran, the reorganization of the Castle by the Elder Gods and the re-creation of the universe outside it. Zelazny names one of his characters Hodgson in a nod to William Hope Hodgson's powerful "House on the Border-land." But unlike that novel, this book is at best a qualified success, a good idea given lackluster treatment.

> *"Science Fiction: 'The Changing Land',"* in Pub-lishers Weekly *(reprinted from the February 6, 1981, issue of* Publishers Weekly *by permission, published by R. R. Bowker Company, a Xerox company; copy-right © 1981 by Xerox Corporation), Vol. 219, No. 6, February 6, 1981, p. 371.*

SPIDER ROBINSON

The Last Defender of Camelot is subtitled simply, **"A Collection By Roger Zelazny."** The generally accepted definition of a "story" is a fiction in which one or more characters are faced with a problem and strive to solve it. By this definition, less than half of the 16 pieces in **TLDoC** are stories. Most are anecdotes, or situations, or conceits, which are economically sketched and left standing there. . . . Cute situations, but not stories. Nobody grows, no problem is solved or even attacked. Call them prose poems. If you agree that the situation is in-teresting or the conceit elegant—or if you simply enjoy the way Zelazny strings words together—you enjoy the piece.

I report that I enjoyed all 16, and I have a tendency to prefer story to non-story. My particular favorites were the original novella versions of **"He Who Shapes"** (Nebula winner) and **"Damnation Alley,"** both superior to the books they later be-came, **"For a Breath I Tarry,"** **"The Game of Blood and Dust,"** and the title story. . . . If you already own both **The Dream Master** and **Damnation Alley,** you own 54 percent of this book.

But if you don't own copies of *all five* favorites I cited, or **"Halfjack"** or **"The Engine at Heartspring's Center,"** you would be well advised to look this one up. (pp. 166-67)

> *Spider Robinson, "The Reference Library: 'The Last Defender of Camelot'" (copyright © 1981 by Davis Publications, Inc.; reprinted by permission of the author), in* Analog Science Fiction/Science Fact, *Vol. 101, No. 3, March 2, 1981, pp. 166-67.*

Appendix

THE EXCERPTS IN CLC, VOLUME 21, WERE REPRINTED FROM THE FOLLOWING PERIODICALS:

After Dark
America
American Anthropologist
American Political Science Review
Analog Science Fiction/Science Fact
Appraisal
The Atlantic Monthly
Audio
Best Sellers
Billboard
BMI: The Many Worlds of Music
Book Week—New York Herald Tribune
Book Week—The Sunday Herald Tribune
Book Window
Book World—Chicago Tribune
Book World—The Washington Post
Bookbird
Booklist
Books
Books and Bookmen
Bulletin of the Center for Children's Books
Canadian Children's Literature
Canadian Literature
Catholic Library World
Catholic World
Chicago Tribune
Children's Book News
Children's Book Review
Children's Book Review Service
Children's literature in education
Choice
The Christian Century
The Christian Science Monitor
Christopher Street
Cinéaste
CLA Journal
College English
Columbia Forum

The Comics Journal
Commentary
Commonweal
Comparative Literature Studies
Crawdaddy
Creem
The Critic
Critique: Studies in Modern Fiction
Daily News
Dance Magazine
Detroit Metro Times
down beat
Elementary English
English Journal
Esquire Magazine
Extrapolation
Fantasy Newsletter
Feature
Film Quarterly
Films and Filming
Films in Review
Gramophone
Growing Point
Harper's
The Heroine's Showcase
Hi-Fi News & Record Review
High Fidelity
Hit Parader
Holiday
Horizon
The Horn Book Magazine
Human Behavior
Human Organization
In Review
The International Fiction Review
Interracial Books for Children
JEMF Quarterly
Journal of American Culture

The Journal of Contemporary History
Journal of Popular Culture
Journal of Reading
The Junior Bookshelf
Kirkus Reviews
Kirkus Service
Kliatt Young Adult Paperback Book Guide
The L. A. Star
Language Arts
Library Journal
Life
The Lion and the Unicorn
The Listener
Lively Arts and Book Review
Los Angeles Times
Maclean's Magazine
The Magazine of Fantasy and Science Fiction
The Massachusetts Review
Melody Maker
Midstream
Modern Fiction Studies
Ms.
Music Journal
The Nation
National Review
Negro Digest
The New Leader
New Letters
The New Republic
New Scientist
New Statesman
New Statesman & Nation
New Times
New York Arts Journal
New York Herald Tribune
New York Herald Tribune Book Review
New York Herald Tribune Books

New York Herald Tribune Weekly Book
  Review
New York Journal-American
New York Magazine
New York Post
The New York Review of Books
New York Theater Critics' Reviews
The New York Times
The New York Times Book Review
The New York Times Magazine
The New Yorker
Newsweek
The Observer
Pacific Historical Review
Papers on Language and Literature
Partisan Review
PHYLON
Popular Music & Society
Psychology Today
Publishers Weekly
Punch
Quill and Quire
Ramparts
Records and Recording
Renascence

The Reporter
Riverside Quarterly
Rolling Stone
The Saturday Evening Post
Saturday Review
Saturday Review (New York)
Saturday Review of Literature
The School Librarian
The School Librarian and School Library
  Review
School Library Journal
Science Books
Science Books & Films
Science Fiction Review
Science-Fiction Studies
Scientific American
The Sewanee Review
SIECUS Report
Signal
Sing Out!
Sky and Telescope
The Social Studies
Society
The Soho Weekly News
The Southern Humanities Review

Southwest Review
The Spectator
SRRT Newsletter
Stereo Review
Studies in Black Literature
Studies in Short Fiction
Take One
Time
The Times Educational Supplement
The Times Literary Supplement
Trouser Press
TV Guide
Univeristy of Windsor Review
University Review
The Use of English
Variety
The Village Voice
Virginia Kirkus' Bookshop Service
Virginia Kirkus' Service
Western American Literature
Wilson Library Bulletin
Women's Wear Daily
The Yale Review
Young Adult Cooperative Book Review
  Group of Massachusetts

THE EXCERPTS IN CLC, VOLUME 21, WERE REPRINTED FROM THE FOLLOWING BOOKS:

Allen, Bob. Waylon & Willie: The Full Story in Words and Pictures of Waylon Jennings & Willie Nelson. *Quick Fox, 1979.*

Arbuthnot, May Hill. Children's Reading in the Home. *Scott, Foresman, 1969.*

Arbuthnot, May Hill, and Sutherland, Zena. Children and Books. *4th ed. Scott, Foresman, 1972.*

Astro, Richard, and Hayashi, Tetsumaro, eds. Steinbeck: The Man and His Work. *Oregon State University Press, 1971.*

Baldwin, James. Nobody Knows My Name. *Dial, 1961.*

Becker, Stephen. Comic Art in America: A Social History of the Funnies, the Political Cartoons, Magazine Humor, Sporting Cartoons and Animated Cartoons. *Simon & Schuster, 1959.*

Berger, Arthur Asa. The Comic-Stripped American: What Dick Tracy, Blondie, Daddy Warbucks, and Charlie Brown Tell Us about Ourselves. *Walker, 1973, Penguin Books, 1974.*

Berger, Arthur Asa. The TV-Guided American. *Walker, 1976.*

Bigsby, C.W.E., ed. The Black American Writer: Fiction, Vol. I. *Penguin Books, 1971.*

Blishen, Edward, ed. The Thorny Paradise: Writers on Writing for Children. *Kestrel Books, 1975.*

Browning, Preston M., Jr. Flannery O'Connor. *Southern Illinois University Press, 1974.*

Bruce, Lenny. How to Talk Dirty and Influence People. *Playboy Press, 1965.*

Butler, Francelia, ed. Children's Literature: Annual of The Modern Language Association Seminar on Children's Literature and The Children's Literature Association, Vol. 5. *Temple University Press, 1976.*

Cadogan, Mary, and Craig, Patricia. You're a Brick, Angela!: A New Look at Girl's Fiction from 1839 to 1975. *Gollancz, 1976.*

Cameron, Eleanor. The Green and Burning Tree: On the Writing and Enjoyment of Children's Books. *Atlantic-Little, Brown, 1969.*

Cohen, John, ed. The Essential Lenny Bruce. *Ballantine, 1967.*

Crouch, Marcus. Treasure Seekers and Borrowers: Children's Books in Britain 1900-1960. *The Library Association, 1962.*

Crouch, Marcus. The Nesbit Tradition: The Children's Novel in England 1945-1970. *Benn, 1972.*

Dalton, David, and Kaye, Lenny. Rock 100. *Grosset & Dunlap, 1977.*

Daniels, Les. Comix: A History of Comic Books in America. *Outerbridge & Dienstfrey, 1971.*

Davis, Stephen. Reggae Bloodlines: In Search of the Music and Culture of Jamaica. *Rev. ed. Anchor Press, 1979.*

Dickstein, Morris. Gates of Eden: American Culture in the Sixties. *Basic Books, 1977.*

Dixon, Bob. Catching Them Young, Vol. I: Sex, Race and Class in Children's Fiction. *Pluto Press, 1977.*

Donelson, Kenneth L., and Nilsen, Alleen Pace. Literature for Today's Young Adults. *Scott, Foresman, 1980.*

Egoff, Sheila. The Republic of Childhood: A Critical Guide to Canadian Children's Literature in English. *2nd ed. Oxford University Press, 1975.*

Eyre, Frank. British Children's Books in the Twentieth Century. *Longman, 1971, Dutton, 1973.*

Fawcett, Anthony. California Rock, California Sound: The Music of Los Angeles and Southern California. *Reed Books, 1978.*

Feiffer, Jules, ed. The Great Comic Book Heroes. *Dial, 1965.*

Fisher, Margery. Intent Upon Reading: A Critical Appraisal of Modern Fiction for Children. *Hodder & Stoughton, 1961, Watts, 1962.*

Fisher, Margery. Who's Who in Children's Books: A Treasury of the Familiar Characters of Childhood. *Holt, Rinehart and Winston, 1975.*

Fontenrose, Joseph. John Steinbeck: An Introduction and Interpretation. *Barnes & Noble, 1963.*

Georgiou, Constantine. Children and Their Literature. *Prentice-Hall, 1969.*

Goldman, Albert. Ladies and Gentlemen—Lenny Bruce!! *Random House, 1974.*

Guralnick, Peter. Lost Highway: Journeys & Arrivals of American Musicians. *Godine, 1979.*

Hicks, Granville, ed. The Living Novel: A Symposium. *Macmillan, 1957.*

Hoare, Ian; Anderson, Clive; Cummings, Tony; and Frith, Simon. The Soul Book. *Edited by Ian Hoare. Eyre Methuen, 1975.*

Hunter, Mollie. Talent Is Not Enough: Mollie Hunter on Writing for Children. *Harper & Row, 1976.*

Jan, Isabelle. On Children's Literature. *Edited by Catherine Storr. Schocken, 1974.*

Kael, Pauline. When the Lights Go Down. *Holt, Rinehart and Winston, 1980.*

Klein, Holger, ed. The First World War in Fiction: A Collection of Critical Essays. *Barnes & Noble, 1977.*

Kofsky, Frank. Lenny Bruce: The Comedian as Social Critic and Secular Moralist. *Monad Press, 1974.*

Lenz, Millicent, and Mahood, Ramona M., eds. Young Adult Literature: Background and Criticism. *American Library Association, 1980.*

Lukens, Rebecca J. A Critical Handbook of Children's Literature. *Scott, Foresman, 1976.*

Lupoff, Dick, and Thompson, Don, eds. All in Color for a Dime. *Arlington House, 1970.*

Lydon, Michael. Rock Folk: Portraits from the Rock 'n' Roll Pantheon. *Dial, 1971.*

Marcus, Greil, ed. Stranded: Rock and Roll for a Desert Island. *Knopf, 1979.*

Margolies, Edward. The Art of Richard Wright. *Southern Illinois University Press, 1969.*

McCarthy, Paul. John Steinbeck. *Ungar, 1980.*

Meek, Margaret; Warlow, Aidan; and Barton, Griselda, eds. The Cool Web: The Pattern of Children's Reading. *Bodley Head, 1977.*

Meigs, Cornelia; Eaton, Anne Thaxter; Nesbitt, Elizabeth; and Viguers, Ruth Hill. A Critical History of Children's Literature. *Edited by Cornelia Meigs. Rev. ed. Macmillan, 1969.*

Miller, Jim, ed. The Rolling Stone Illustrated History of Rock and Roll. *Rev. ed. Rolling Stone Press, Random House, 1980.*

Mitz, Rick. The Great TV Sitcom Book. *Marek, 1980.*

Morse, David. Motown and the Arrival of Black Music. *Collier, 1972.*

Newcomb, Horace. T.V.: The Most Popular Art. *Anchor Press, 1974.*

Pavletich, Aida. Rock-A-Bye, Baby. *Doubleday, 1980.*

Pfeiler, William K. War and the German Mind: The Testimony of Men of Fiction Who Fought at the Front. *Columbia University Press, 1941.*

The Rolling Stone Record Review. Pocket Books, 1971.

Sheridan, Martin. Comics and Their Creators: Life Stories of American Cartoonists. *Rev. ed. Hale, 1944, Hyperion Press, 1977.*

Soares, Manuela. The Soap Opera Book. *Harmony Books, 1978.*

Spirt, Diana L. Introducing More Books: A Guide for the Middle Grades. *Bowker, 1978.*

Townsend, John Rowe. A Sense of Story: Essays on Contemporary Writers for Children. *Lippincott, 1971.*

Townsend, John Rowe. Written for Children: An Outline of English-Language Children's Literature. *Rev. ed. Lippincott, 1974.*

Tymn, Marshall B.; Zahorski, Kenneth J.; and Boyer, Robert H. Fantasy Literature; A Core Collection and Reference Guide. *Bowker, 1979.*

Varlejs, Jana, ed. Young Adult Literature in the Seventies: A Selection of Readings. *Scarecrow Press, 1978.*

Vassal, Jacques. Electric Children: Roots and Branches of Modern Folkrock. *Translated by Paul Burnett. Taplinger, 1976.*

Wagner, Geoffrey. Parade of Pleasure: A Study of Popular Iconography in the USA. *Derek Verschoyle, 1954.*

Wakefield, Dan. All Her Children. *Doubleday, 1976.*

Warrick, Ruth, and Preston, Don. The Confessions of Phoebe Tyler. *Prentice-Hall, 1980.*

Waugh, Coulton. The Comics. *Macmillan, 1947, Luna Press, 1974.*

Wertham, Fredric. Seduction of the Innocent. *Holt, Rinehart and Winston, 1954, Kennikat Press, 1972.*

White, David Manning, and Abel, Robert H., eds. The Funnies: An American Idiom. *Free Press, 1963.*

Wilson, Barbara Ker. Noel Streatfeild. *Walck, 1964.*

ISBN 0-8103-0117-2